PETIDE AND PROTEIN HORMONES (continued)

Hormone	Abbreviation	Source	Major biological action
Motilin		Duodenum, pineal gland	Alters motility of GI tract
Secretin		Duodenum	Stimulates pancreatic acinar cells to release bicarbonate and water
Vasoactive intestinal polypeptide	VIP	GI tract, hypothalamus	Increases secretion of water and electrolytes from pancreas and gut; acts as neurotransmitter in autonomic nervous system
Peptide YY	PYY	GI tract	Regulation of energy balance/food intake

Heart

Hormone	Abbreviation	Source	Major biological action
Atrial naturetic factor	ANF	Atrial myocytes	Regulation of urinary sodium excretion

Hypothalamus

Hormone	Abbreviation	Source	Major biological action
Agouti-related protein	AgRP	Arcuate nuclei	Regulation of energy balance
Arg-vasotocin	AVT	Hypothalamus and pineal gland	Regulates reproductive organs
Corticotropin-releasing hormone	CRH	Paraventricular nuclei, anterior periventricular nuclei	Stimulates release of ACTH and β-endorphin from anterior pituitary
Gonadotropin-releasing hormone (Luteinizing hormone–releasing hormone)	GnRH (LHRH)	Preoptic area; anterior hypothalamus; suprachiasmatic nuclei; medial basal hypothalamus (rodents and primates); arcuate nuclei (primates)	Stimulates release of FSH and LH from anterior pituitary
Gonadotropin-inhibitory hormone	GnIH	Species-dependent loci	Inhibits release of LH (in birds)
Kisspeptin		Species-dependent loci	Enhances GnRH release
Somatostatin (Growth hormone–inhibiting hormone)		Anterior periventricular nuclei	Inhibits release of GH and TSH from anterior pituitary, inhibits release of insulin and glucagons from pancreas
Somatocrinin (Growth hormone–releasing hormone)	GHRH	Medial basal hypothalamus; arcuate nuclei	Stimulates release of GH from anterior pituitary
Melanotropin-release inhibitory factor (Dopamine)	MIF (DA)	Arcuate nuclei	Inhibits the release of MSH (no evidence of this peptide in humans)
Melanotropin-releasing hormone	MRH	Paraventricular nuclei	Stimulates the release of MSH from anterior pituitary (no evidence of this peptide in humans)
Melanin-concentrating hormone	MCH	Lateral hypothalamus	Increases food intake
Neuropeptide Y	NPY	Arcuate nuclei	Regulation of energy balance
Neurotensin		Hypothalamus; intestinal mucosa	May act as a neurohormone
Orexin A and B		Lateral hypothalamic area	Regulation of energy balance/food intake
Prolactin-inhibitory factor (Dopamine)	PIF (DA)	Arcuate nuclei	Inhibits PRL secretion
Prolactin-releasing hormone		Paraventricular nuclei	Stimulates release of PRL from anterior pituitary
Substance P	SP	Hypothalamus, CNS, intestine	Transmits pain; increases smooth muscle contractions of GI tract
Thyrotropin-releasing hormone	TRH	Paraventricular nuclei	Stimulates release of TSH and PRL from anterior pituitary
Urocortin		Lateral hypothalamus	CRH-related peptide
Cocaine and amphetamine-related transcript	CART	Hypothalamus; other brain regions	Involved in reward, food intake

(continued on inside back cover)

612.
405

NEL

An Introduction to
Behavioral Endocrinology
Fifth Edition

An Introduction to
Behavioral Endocrinology

Fifth Edition

Randy J. Nelson • The Ohio State University

Lance J. Kriegsfeld • University of California, Berkeley

Sinauer Associates, Inc. Publishers
Sunderland, Massachusetts

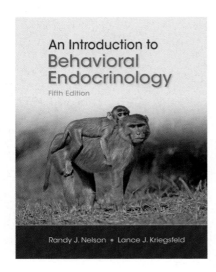

The Cover

Rhesus macaque, *Macaca mulatta*, female carrying young, Keoladeo Ghana National Park, India. © Bernard Castelein/ Nature Picture Library/Alamy Stock Photo.

An Introduction to Behavioral Endocrinology, Fifth Edition

For information, address
Sinauer Associates, Inc. P.O. Box 407, Sunderland, MA 01375 U.S.A.
Fax: 413-549-1118
E-mail: publish@sinauer.com
Internet: www.sinauer.com

Library of Congress Cataloging-in-Publication Data
Names: Nelson, Randy Joe, author. | Kriegsfeld, Lance J., author.
Title: An introduction to behavioral endocrinology / Randy J. Nelson, The
   Ohio State University, Lance J. Kriegsfeld, University of California,
   Berkeley.
Description: Fifth edition. | Sunderland, Massachusetts : Sinauer Associates,
   Inc. Publishers, [2017] | Includes bibliographical references and index.
Identifiers: LCCN 2016037315 (print) | LCCN 2016037902 (ebook) | ISBN
   9781605353203 (hardcover) | ISBN 9781605356464 (ebook)
Subjects: LCSH: Animal behavior--Endocrine aspects. | Human
   behavior--Endocrine aspects.
Classification: LCC QP356.45 .N45 2017 (print) | LCC QP356.45 (ebook) | DDC
   612.4/05--dc23
LC record available at https://lccn.loc.gov/2016037315

Printed in U.S.A.
6 5 4 3 2 1

For our family and friends…

Brief Contents

Contents

Chapter 5 *Male Reproductive Behavior 203*

Chapter 6 *Female Reproductive Behavior 275*

Preface

It is July 2016 as we submit the final pieces and parts of this book manuscript. The First Edition of this book was published over 20 years ago, and there have been many changes in the field and in this textbook over the past several editions. A co-author, Lance Kriegsfeld, has been added to this Fifth Edition of the book. Dr. Kriegsfeld joined Dr. Nelson's lab shortly after the First Edition was published, and has been deeply involved with subsequent editions. He is now a professor at UC Berkeley, occupying a faculty position in the same department in which Frank Beach, the founder of this field, spent much of his career. Dr. Kriegsfeld teaches the descendent of Dr. Beach's *Hormones and Behavior* course at Berkeley that enrolls over 250 students annually.

Behavioral endocrinology is a truly interdisciplinary field. It involves the study of phenomena ranging from genetic, molecular, and cellular levels of analysis to the study of individual and social behaviors. We had several goals when we began writing the Fifth Edition of this textbook, one of which was to continue to present information about the interactions between hormones and behavior from an interdisciplinary perspective. In an effort to provide students with information about the scientists who laid the foundation for modern studies of behavioral endocrinology, we presented current hypotheses and theories in the context of their historical origins. Naturally, after more than six years since the publication of the Fourth Edition, every chapter needed general updating to reflect recent developments, research, and studies in the field. Some areas, such as body mass regulation and circadian rhythm research, are moving forward with rapid advances announced weekly.

One criticism of the book received in the past, especially from our colleagues teaching in Psychology departments, is that there is too much comparative work in the text. This is a criticism that we continue to happily ignore. The comparative perspective is what gives behavioral endocrinology great strength, and has revealed some of the most fascinating discoveries in our field using nontraditional animal models. We present this broad comparative approach in this edition. It is our hope that presenting adaptive function along with molecular and physiological mechanisms will yield greater understanding than presenting either approach alone.

We both have taught this course out of Psychology departments and thus appreciate that many behavioral endocrinology students will be psychology majors. Thus, we have tried to keep the conceptual issues clear, and provide only sufficient details and examples that support the concepts. New to this edition are learning objectives and highlights of the main points for each chapter to help guide students through the text. We also added a marginal glossary so students can easily find definitions for key terms as they read. Based on our teaching experience with this course, we assume that psychology students will have taken a course in biopsychology or behavioral neuroscience by the time they encounter this textbook, but again, we have tried to keep discussions of endocrine physiology and biochemistry to a minimum level necessary to understand the hormone–behavior interactions being discussed. Because students are likely to be familiar with the behavior of common animals such as dogs and rabbits, we have continued to use them as examples to help explain many concepts in this text. This edition is supported by a student website that contains some wonderful videos and animations, which we hope help illustrate some of the behavioral and physiological concepts discussed in the text. We have continued to use and enhance color graphics that we hope will help clarify principles discussed.

Several topics had to be omitted or curtailed in the text. We assume that professors will use additional readings to make up for any deficiencies. Some topics covered in the text are controversial and will likely stimulate class discussions. At the end of each chapter are some questions for discussion that we hope will be potential starting points for such exchanges. An updated list of suggested readings is also provided at the end of each chapter where students can find reasonably current and more detailed information on the material in each chapter.

This is a very exciting time to be studying this field, either as a student or as a researcher in behavioral endocrinology. We hope that we have captured for the reader at least some fraction of the excitement of this field that we both have enjoyed.

Randy J. Nelson
Lance J. Kriegsfeld
July 2016

Acknowledgments

Completion of a textbook requires input from students, colleagues, editors, artists, production editors, photo editors, composers, and friends. There are so many people to thank who provided remarkable assistance to us as we worked on this edition. We remain profoundly grateful to the reviewers and colleagues who provided feedback and assistance that shaped all of the textbook editions. These individuals include: Elizabeth Adkins-Regan, Noah Ashley, Gregory Ball, Cydni Baker, Jacques Balthazart, Tim Bartness, Andy Bass, Tracy Bedosian, George Bentley, Dan Bernard, Staci Bilbo, Eric Bittman, Elliott Blass, Jeff Blaustein, Joan Blom, Jeremy Borniger, Robert Bridges, Sue Carter, Joe Casto, Frances Champagne, Silvana Chiavegatto, Yasmine Cisse, Nicky Clayton, Lique Coolen, Tara Craft, David Crews, James Dabbs, Greg Demas, Courtney DeVries, Don Dewsbury, Gary Dohanich, Debbie Drazen, Lori Flanagan-Cato, Alison Fleming, Laura Fonken, Nancy Forger, Karyn Frick, Stephen Gammie, Monica Gaudier-Diaz, Erica Glasper, Paul Gold, Bruce Goldman, Jim Goodman, Neta Gotlieb, Elizabeth Gould, David Gubernick, Achikam Haim, Tom Hahn, Joyce Hairston, Eric Herzog, Andrew Hotchkiss, Elaine Hull, Kim Huhman, Kim Jennings, Ellen Ketterson, Veronica Kim, Sabra Klein, Kelly Klump, Rosemary Knapp, Michael Leon, Al Lewy, Joe Lonstein, Vicky Luine, Robert Mason, Margaret McCarthy, Martha McClintock, Jim McGaugh, Lynn Martin, Chris Moffatt, Celia Moore, Ignacio Moore, Michael Moore, John Morris, Gretchen Neigh, Mai Nguyen, Karl Obrietan, Kathie Olsen, David Olton, Deb Olster, Vladimir Pravosudov, Brian Prendergast, Leah Pyter, Emilie Rissman, Mike Romero, Jay Rosenblatt, Ed Roy, Heather Rupp, Ben Sachs, Randall Sakai, Jen Sartor, Jill Schneider, Barbara Sherwin, David Shide, Rae Silver, Cheryl Sisk, Benjamin Smarr, Chuck Snowdon, Emilio Soto-Soto, Judith Stern, Brian Trainor, Anjali Trasy, Sari van Anders, George Wade, William Walker, James Walton, Gary Wenk, John Wingfield, Amy Wisniewski, Ruth Wood, Pauline Yahr, Kelly Young, Zachary Weil, and Irving Zucker.

We are especially grateful for assistance during the preparation of this Fifth Edition by many colleagues, who provided helpful, insightful, direct, critical, and immensely kind comments, including Elizabeth Adkins-Regan, Jill Becker, Laura Carruth, Ann Clark, Yvon Delville, Bryan Jones, Kimberly Kinzig, Benedetta Leuner, Farrah Madison, Luke Remage-Healey, Wendy Salzman, Beth Wee, and Susan Zup.

We attempted to incorporate virtually all of these reviewers' suggestions for changes into the various editions. Occasionally, because of stubbornness, laziness, or other negative traits on our part, we failed to address our friends' and colleagues' suggestions. Any and all remaining errors, sources of confusion, or other shortcomings in this new edition remain our responsibility.

We are especially grateful to our many colleagues who kindly provided reprint or preprint copies of their papers, as well as our colleagues and friends who generously provided permission to use their graphic or photographic material in the book or website.

We also thank the very hard-working folks at Sinauer Associates. Although only our names appear on the cover, this book is the result of enormously helpful and talented people. Dr. Nelson remains grateful for the friendship and guidance provided to him during the first two editions by Pete Farley, and during production of the Third Edition by Graig Donini. Graig started the Fourth Edition of this book, but it was completed by the remarkably kind and talented book editor, Sydney Carroll, who has gently nudged this Fifth Edition into existence.

We are grateful to Kathaleen Emerson and Alison Hornbeck, the production editors, whose attention for detail helped improve the book. Others who deserved special thanks at Sinauer include Chris Small, production manager; Janice Holabird, book designer and compositor; Elizabeth Morales, artist; David McIntyre, photo editor. We are grateful to Lou Doucette, our copy editor, who gently repaired our text. We also thank Jason Dirks, the media and supplements editor, for his help in designing, creating, and maintaining the website. This Fifth Edition of the textbook is much improved because of their unrelenting hard work and uncompromising standards.

Finally, we thank the hundreds of undergraduate students who have taken our courses in Behavioral Endocrinology over the past several decades. They have provided many helpful suggestions on improving the textbook. The study of the interactions among hormones, brain, and behavior is a fascinating field. If we were able to convey just a small part of the excitement in this discipline to students, then we'll both consider this book a success.

Media and Supplements

to accompany *An Introduction to Behavioral Endocrinology*, Fifth Edition

For the Student

Companion Website
sites.sinauer.com/be5e

The Companion Website provides a variety of resources to help students learn the material and to illustrate some of the behaviors and concepts discussed in the text. The site includes:

- **Animations**: Detailed animations explain selected complex concepts and processes
- **Videos**: Segments that illustrate interesting behaviors in a variety of organisms
- **Web Links**: Chapter-specific online resources, including articles, photographs, activities, and audio clips
- **Links** to journals, societies, and associations in the field of endocrinology
- A complete **Glossary**

For the Instructor

(Available to qualified adopters)
Instructor's Resource Library

The Instructor's Resource Library includes the following resources:

- **Textbook Figures & Tables**: Electronic versions of all the textbook's figures and tables (formatted and optimized for excellent legibility when projected) are provided in two formats: JPEGs and PowerPoint slides.
- **Test Bank**: Revised and expanded for the Fifth Edition, the Test Bank includes multiple-choice, short-answer, and essay questions for each chapter of the textbook. Prepared by the author, these questions are a helpful resource that can greatly speed the process of preparing exams and quizzes for the course.

Value Options

eBook

An Introduction to Behavioral Endocrinology, Fifth Edition is available as an eBook, in several different formats, including VitalSource, RedShelf, Yuzu, and BryteWave. The eBook can be purchased as either a 180-day rental or a permanent (non-expiring) subscription. All major mobile devices are supported. For details on the eBook platforms offered, please visit www.sinauer.com/ebooks.

The Study of Behavioral Endocrinology

1

Learning Objectives

The goal of this chapter is to introduce you to the rapidly growing field of behavioral endocrinology. By the end of this chapter you should be able to:

- define *behavioral endocrinology* and understand the historical roots of the field.
- define *hormones* and *behavior* and describe the general ways by which hormones and behavior interact.
- explain the various scientific techniques used to establish relationships among hormones, brain, and behavior.

Behavioral endocrinology is the scientific study of the interaction between hormones and behavior. This interaction is bidirectional: hormones can affect behavior, and behavior can influence hormones. **Hormones**, chemical messengers released from **endocrine glands**, travel through the blood system to influence the nervous system to regulate the physiology and behavior of an individual. Hormones change gene expression or the rate of cellular function, and they affect behavior generally by increasing the probability that a given behavior will occur in the presence of a specific stimulus. Hormones achieve this by affecting individuals' sensory systems, integrators, and/or effectors (output systems). Because certain chemicals in the environment can mimic natural hormones, these chemicals can profoundly affect the behavior of humans and other animals. Behavior is generally thought of as involving movement, but nearly any type of output, such as color change, can be considered behavior. A complete description of behavior is required before researchers can address questions of its causation. All behavioral biologists study a specific version of the general question "What causes individual A to emit behavior X?" Behavioral endocrinologists are interested

FIGURE 1.1 Lance Armstrong, seven-time Tour de France winner, was stripped of his titles and banned from cycling for life after not contesting charges leveled by the U.S. Anti-Doping Agency (USADA) that he used hormones, including anabolic steroids, to improve his performance.

behavioral endocrinology
The study of the interactions among hormones, brain, and behavior.

hormone   An organic chemical messenger released from endocrine cells that travels through the blood system to interact with cells at some distance away and causes a biological response.

endocrine glands   A ductless gland from which hormones are released into the blood system in response to specific physiological signals.

in the interactions between hormones and behaviors. Usually these hormones are internal, but sometimes, the effects of hormone treatments or environmental contamination by hormones can significantly affect behavior.

Lance Armstrong won the grueling Tour de France bicycle race a record seven times between 1999 and 2005. No other bicyclist had come close to this achievement during the long history of this race. In 2012, however, the International Cycling Union president, Pat McQuaid, announced the decision to strip Armstrong of his seven Tour de France wins and banned him from the tournament for life, based on a report by the U.S. Anti-Doping Agency (USADA 2012a,b). This USADA report documented the use of performance-enhancing drugs during Armstrong's remarkable record-setting years. The use of anabolic steroids (testosterone) and other performance-enhancing hormones such as erythropoieten (EPO), as well as corticosteroids, was widely documented. Armstrong denied the allegations many times over the years but finally admitted that he used performance-enhancing drugs. Purists of the sport were offended by this hormonal "cheating" (**FIGURE 1.1**).

Questions arise from Armstrong's bicycling: Is there a connection between anabolic steroids and athletic performance? If taking hormones increases athletic performance, then why don't all athletes simply inject themselves with anabolic steroids to "level the playing field"? In other words, what are the costs, if any, of anabolic steroids? Most athletes do not want to take anabolic steroids such as EPO or testosterone. EPO is used in so-called doping of athletes; typically, EPO is released from the kidneys and stimulates red blood cell production in the bone marrow. Injecting EPO increases circulating red blood cells that provide additional oxygen to muscles and other tissues, which obviously provides an unfair advantage at high elevations (World Anti-Doping Agency, 2012). Testosterone is a steroid hormone that builds muscle mass. However, it is a controlled substance, and obtaining testosterone without a medical prescription is illegal. In addition to illegality, a number of undesirable side effects, including increased heart size (the heart is also a muscle) that decreases pumping efficiency, damage to the kidneys and liver, and compromised immune function, are important costs of taking these hormones. Several psychological problems have also been associated with anabolic steroid abuse, including feelings of paranoia, aggressive ideation, depression, and violent rage.

Armstrong's reported orchestration of the drug use by his U.S. Postal Service team and his threats of retaliation against several individuals are consistent with anabolic steroid abuse. We will explore the nature of the association between anabolic steroids and violent behavior more fully in Chapter 8. Can hormones really "hijack" the nervous system to influence behavior? Many people informally know that hormones differ between males and females and that hormones change rapidly during puberty, while many hormone concentrations decrease slowly as folks age. Questions about the relationship between hormones and behavior arise in many circumstances. For example, is the sex drive of adolescents higher than the sex drive of adults? Is the sex drive of women higher or lower than the sex drive of men? Is sexual behavior of women influenced by menopause? Is homosexuality caused by hormone concentrations that are too low or too high? Why are men much more likely than women to commit violent crimes? How does exposure to acute or chronic stressors affect learning and memory? Can melatonin cure jet lag? Do seasonal cycles of depression occur in people? Does postpartum depression really exist? Can leptin or other hormones curb our food intake? You may have discussed these and other questions about hormones and behavior casually with your friends and family members. Researchers in the field of behavioral endocrinology attempt to address these kinds of questions in a formal, scientific manner. In contrast to popular beliefs, hormones do not cause behavioral changes per se; that is, hormones do not hijack the nervous system to influence behavior. Rather, hormones change the probability that a specific behavior will occur within the appropriate behavioral or social context. What constitutes an appropriate context is typically subject to social and cultural learning.

Historical Roots of Behavioral Endocrinology

The study of the interaction between hormones and behavior has been remarkably interdisciplinary since its inception; methods and techniques from one scientific discipline have been borrowed and refined by researchers in other fields. Psychologists, endocrinologists, neuroscientists, entomologists, zoologists, geneticists, molecular and cellular biologists, anatomists, physiologists, behavioral ecologists, psychiatrists, and other behavioral biologists have all made contributions to the understanding of hormone-behavior interactions. This exciting commingling of scientific interests and approaches, with its ongoing synthesis of knowledge, has led to the emergence of behavioral endocrinology as a distinct and important field of study (Beach, 1975b). The scientific journal *Hormones and Behavior* began publication in April 1967, and a scientific organization devoted to the study of hormones and behavior, the Society for Behavioral Neuroendocrinology, was founded in 1996. Both the journal and scientific society are growing.

Ebbinghaus (1908) stated that **psychology** has a short history but a long past, and the same can be said of behavioral endocrinology (Beach, 1974a). Although the modern era of the discipline is generally recognized to have emerged during the middle of the twentieth century with the publication of the classic book *Hormones and Behavior* (Beach, 1948), some of the relationships among the endocrine glands, their hormone products, and behavior have been implicitly recognized for centuries.

The male sex organs, or **testes**, produce and secrete a hormone called testosterone that influences sexual behavior, aggression, territoriality, hibernation, and migration, as well as many other behaviors that differentiate males from females. The testes of mammals are usually located outside the body cavity and can easily be damaged or removed. Thus, **castration**, the surgical removal of the testes, has historically been the most common manipulation of the endocrine system. For millennia, individuals of many species of domestic animals have been castrated to make them better to eat or easier to control, and the behavioral and physical effects of castration have been known since antiquity (**FIGURE 1.2**). Indeed, these effects were known to Aristotle, who described the effects of castration in roosters (and humans) with great detail and accuracy. For example, in *Historia Animalium*, written about 350 BCE, Aristotle reported:

> Birds have their testicles inside.... Birds are castrated at the rump at the part where the two sexes unite in copulation. If you burn this area twice or thrice with hot irons, then, if the bird be full-grown, his crest grows sallow, he ceases to crow, and foregoes sexual passion; but if you cauterize the bird when young, none of these male attributes or propensities will come to him as he grows up. The case is the same for men: if you mutilate them in boyhood, the later-growing hair never comes, and the voice never changes but remains high-pitched; if they be mutilated in early manhood, the late-growths of hair quit them except the growth on the groin, and that diminishes but does not entirely depart.

For centuries, royalty employed men castrated before puberty, called **eunuchs**, to guard women from other men. For example, the Old Testament reports that these emasculated males were used to guard the wom-

psychology   The scientific study of emotion, cognition, and behavior.

testes   The male gonads, which produce steroid hormones and sperm.

castration   The surgical removal of the gonads.

eunuch   A man who has been castrated (testes removed).

FIGURE 1.2   **St. Philip the Evangelist baptizing a eunuch** This biblical painting by Rembrandt (1606–1669) indicates that the relationship between the missing testes and behavior was understood for centuries.

FIGURE 1.3 Eunuch of the last imperial court of China, photographed by Henri Cartier-Bresson in 1949. Note the lack of facial hair and unusually long arms.

en's quarters of Hebrew kings and princes (Esther 1:10). Castration in humans often has little or no effect on physical appearance or future sexual behavior when performed after the unfortunate individual attains sexual maturation; however, if human males are castrated before puberty, they will develop a characteristic physical appearance marked by short stature and long arms (**FIGURE 1.3**), and sexual behaviors are unlikely to develop. The typical secondary male sex characteristics are also affected by prepubertal removal of the testes. For example, as noted by Aristotle, eunuchs never develop beards, and the pubertal change in voice does not occur. Normally during puberty, the vocal cords of males thicken in response to testosterone secreted by the testes. It is the thickened vocal cords that produce the deeper-pitched voice characteristic of males, just as the thick strings of a guitar produce deeper-pitched notes than the thin strings.

Castration was once a common practice in Europe and Asia. Young boys with exceptional singing voices were castrated to prevent the pubertal changes in pitch. These singers became known as castrati. Although castrati were prized by church choirs for centuries, their popularity reached a peak in Europe during the seventeenth and eighteenth centuries with the development of opera, which made castrati the first superstars of the entertainment world (Heriot, 1974). The first castrato opera star, Baldassare Ferri, died in 1680 at the age of 70 with a fortune that was worth the equivalent of $3 million today. In hopes of attaining this level of wealth and fame, young boys with musical aptitude were identified early, and poor families offered their sons outright to church leaders, singing teachers, and music academies. Thousands of boys lost their testes but never gained the celebrity or riches of the star castrati.

What did a castrato sound like? Essentially, castrati had the range of a soprano, but the greater development of the male lungs gave their singing remarkable power. An early critic remarked, "Their timbre is as clear and piercing as that of choirboys and much more powerful; they appear to sing an octave above the natural voice of women. Their voices…are brilliant, light, full of sparkle, very loud, and astound with a very wide range" (Heriot, 1974).

After 200 years, the tastes of the opera-loving public changed. The rise in popularity of the female soprano voice reduced the demand for castrati, and they soon became an oddity. In 1849, the last great castrato, Giovanni Velluti, retired from opera to his villa in Venice. The last known castrato, Alessandro Moreschi, who served as the Sistine Chapel Choir's director, as well as one of its soloists, died in 1922. Before his death, he made 17 recordings that, although of poor quality by today's standards, still provide a remarkable example of this art form. Samples of these recordings can be found on this book's Companion Website (sites.sinauer.com/nelson5E).

Berthold's Experiment

A useful starting point for understanding research in hormones and behavior is a classic nineteenth-century experiment that is now considered to be the first formal study of endocrinology. This remarkable experiment conclusively demonstrated that a substance produced by the testes could travel through the bloodstream and eventually affect behavior. Professor Arnold Adolph Berthold, a Swiss-German physician and professor of physiology at the University of Göttingen (**FIGURE 1.4**), demonstrated experimentally that a product of the testes was necessary for a cockerel (an immature male chicken) to develop into a normal adult rooster.

FIGURE 1.4 Arnold Adolph Berthold of the University of Göttingen, who in 1849 published what is now recognized as the first formal experiment in endocrinology.

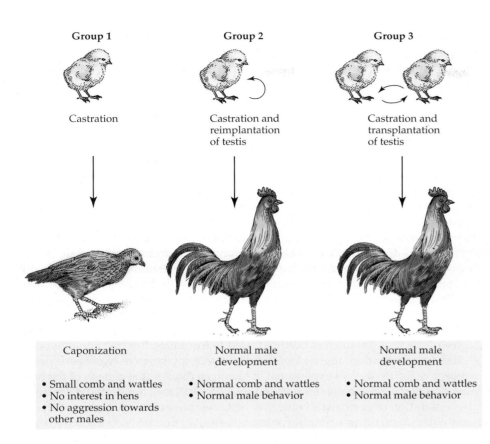

Group 1

Castration

Caponization

- Small comb and wattles
- No interest in hens
- No aggression towards other males

Group 2

Castration and reimplantation of testis

Normal male development

- Normal comb and wattles
- Normal male behavior

Group 3

Castration and transplantation of testis

Normal male development

- Normal comb and wattles
- Normal male behavior

FIGURE 1.5 Berthold's experiment
The birds in Group 1 were castrated, and when observed several months later, they were smaller than normal roosters and failed to engage in rooster-typical behaviors. The birds in Group 2 were also castrated, but one of each bird's own testis was reimplanted in its abdominal cavity. These birds looked and behaved like normal roosters when adults. The two birds in Group 3 were castrated, and one testis from each bird was transplanted into the abdomen of the other. Several months later, these birds also looked and behaved like normal roosters. Berthold found that the reimplanted and transplanted testes in Groups 2 and 3 developed vascular connections and generated sperm.

As you know, roosters display several characteristic behaviors that are not typically seen among hens or immature chicks of either sex. Roosters mate with hens, they fight with other roosters, and of course, roosters crow. Moreover, roosters are larger than hens and immature birds and have distinctive plumage. On the other hand, capons, male chickens that have been castrated prior to adulthood in order to make their meat more tender, do not show many of the behavioral and physical characteristics of roosters. They do not attempt to mate with hens and are not very aggressive toward other males. Indeed, they avoid aggressive encounters, and if conditions force them to fight, they do so in a halfhearted manner. Finally, capons do not crow like roosters.

The behavioral and physical differences among roosters, hens, capons, and immature chickens were undoubtedly familiar to Berthold (Berthold, 1849a,b) (**FIGURE 1.5**). He placed six cockerels in three experimental groups, each consisting of two birds. He removed both testes from each of the two cockerels in the first group, and as expected, these birds eventually developed as capons. They never fought with other males after castration, and they failed to crow; instead, Professor Berthold reported, they developed the "monotone voice of the capon." They avoided females and never exhibited mating behavior. Finally, these birds looked different from intact (noncastrated) adult males; their bodies and heads were small, and their combs and wattles were atrophied and pale in color.

The second pair of cockerels was also castrated, but Berthold reimplanted one testis from each bird in its abdominal cavity after ensuring that all of the original vascular and neural connections had been cut. Interestingly, both birds in this group developed normal rooster behavior. According to Berthold, they "crowed lustily, often engaged in battle with each other and with other cockerels, and showed the usual reactions to hens." Their physical appearance was indistinguishable from that of other young roosters; they grew normally and possessed highly developed combs and wattles that were bright red in color.

The remaining two birds were also castrated, but after the testes were removed, Berthold placed a single testis from each bird in the other's abdominal cavity. Like the cockerels in the second experimental group, these birds also developed the "voice, sexual urge, belligerence, and growth of combs and wattles" characteristic of intact males.

After observing all six birds for several months, Berthold dissected one of the cockerels from the second group and found that the implanted testis had attached itself to the intestines, developed a vascular supply, and nearly doubled in size. Eventually, he examined all the implanted testes under a microscope and noted the presence of sperm.

Based on the results of this experiment, Berthold drew three major conclusions: (1) the testes are transplantable organs; (2) transplanted testes can function and produce sperm (Berthold drew the analogy to a tree branch that produces its own fruit after having been grafted to another tree); and (3) because the testes functioned normally after all nerves were severed, there are no specific nerves directing testicular function. To account for these findings, Berthold proposed that a "secretory blood-borne product" of the transplanted testes (*productive Verhältniss der Hoden*) was responsible for the normal development of the birds in the second and third groups. It is worth noting that three of the four parameters Berthold used to formulate this hormonal hypothesis—mating, vocalization, aggression, and distinctive appearance—were behavioral.

In recent years, Berthold's experiment has been credited as the genesis of the field of endocrinology (and of behavioral endocrinology: **BOX 1.1**), but Berthold's intriguing demonstration of nonneural control of behavior was apparently not embraced with any enthusiasm by his scientific contemporaries; we find no citations to his paper for nearly 60 years after its publication. Berthold previously authored a well-known physiology textbook and had actively conducted research. His textbook makes it apparent that Berthold was a proponent of the pangenesis theory of inheritance. This theory, endorsed by many biologists prior to the discovery of how chromosomes and genes function, held that all body parts actively discharge bits and pieces of themselves into the blood system, where they are transported to the ovaries or testes and assembled into miniature offspring resembling the parents. Because of this theoretical stance, Berthold had two concepts at hand when evaluating the results of his testicular transplantation study: (1) various parts of the body release specific agents into the blood, and (2) these agents travel through the bloodstream to particular target organs. Why Berthold did not go any further with his interesting finding is not known; he died 12 years later in 1861 without following up on his now-famous study.

What Are Hormones?

Berthold took the first step in the study of behavioral endocrinology by demonstrating that the well-known effects of the testes were due to their production of a substance that circulated in the blood. Modern studies in behavioral endocrinology have documented the effects of substances from many different glands affecting an increasing number and range of behaviors.

We now know Berthold's "secretory blood-borne product" as a hormone, a term coined by Ernest Starling during a lecture in 1905. Previously, in 1902, Starling and fellow British physiologist William Bayliss identified a chemical messenger secreted by the duodenum that stimulated pancreatic secretions in dogs, a process previously considered to be regulated by the nervous system by Ivan Pavlov, a physiologist best known for his discovery of classical conditioning.

Hormones are released from these glands into the bloodstream (or the tissue fluid system in invertebrates), where they may then act on target organs (or tissues) at some distance from their origin. Hormones coordinate the physiology and

BOX 1.1 *Frank A. Beach and the Origins of the Modern Era of Behavioral Endocrinology*

For some time before behavioral endocrinology emerged as a recognized field, its foundations were being laid by researchers in other fields. The anatomists, physiologists, and zoologists who were doing the majority of the work on "internal secretions" prior to 1930 often used behavioral end points in their studies. Soon thereafter, psychologists began making important contributions in the study of hormones and behavior. In the early decades of the twentieth century, American psychology was undergoing a major change, both in ideology and methodology. Led by John B. Watson, students of the "science of the mind" were casting aside introspection as a method in favor of observation and experimentation. Watson argued that only overt behavior was observable, and psychologists began describing and quantifying all types of overt behavior.

Karl S. Lashley did his graduate work under Watson at the Johns Hopkins University and eventually joined the faculty at the University of Chicago. Lashley investigated the effects of removing parts of rats' brains to discover where in the brain various psychological processes were carried out; he was particularly interested in finding where memories were stored. Although he never published any reports on the interaction between hormones and behavior, Lashley was clearly interested in the subject (e.g., Lashley, 1938), and several of Lashley's students became important contributors to behavioral endocrinology, including Calvin P. Stone, Josephine Ball, and Frank A. Beach.

Beach, William C. Young (see Box 3.2), and Daniel Lehrman (see Box 7.1) were especially influential during the early studies of behavioral endocrinology. Beach's dissertation at Chicago, "The Neural Basis for Innate Behavior," examined the effects of cortical tissue destruction on the maternal behavior of first-time mother rats. In 1937, Beach began working as a curator in the Department of Experimental Biology at the American Museum of Natural History in New York and began contributing to the museum's tradition of comparative behavioral experimentation. One study completed at the museum, which was a logical extension of Beach's dissertation work, is of special note: he began investigating the effects of cortical lesions on the mating behavior of male rats. Some brain-damaged rats continued to mate, whereas others failed to do so. Beach was concerned that his lesions were interfering indirectly with the endocrine system, so he injected the nonmating brain-injured rats with

Frank A. Beach (1911–1988)

testosterone, the primary hormone secreted from the testes. The treatment evoked mating behavior in some of the lesioned rats, and this modification of behavior by hormones prompted Beach to learn more about endocrinology.

Beach audited a course in endocrinology at New York University but was distressed by the lack of information about the behavioral effects of hormones; the professor responded to Beach's complaint by allowing him to teach one session. While preparing for the lecture, Beach discovered that no comprehensive summary of hormone-behavior interactions existed, and he prepared such a review as a term paper for the endocrinology course. Several years later, Beach expanded his paper into an influential book, *Hormones and Behavior* (Beach, 1948). The publication of this book marked the beginning of the formal study of behavioral endocrinology. Beach is credited with the genesis of this scientific discipline, and he continued to provide intellectual leadership in shaping the field for the next 40 years.

behavior of an animal by regulating, integrating, and controlling its bodily function. For example, the same hormones that cause gametic (egg or sperm) maturation also promote mating behavior in many species. This dual hormonal function ensures that mating behavior occurs when animals have mature gametes available for fertilization. Another example of endocrine regulation of physiological and behavioral function is provided by the metabolic system. Several metabolic hormones work together to elevate blood glucose levels prior to awakening, in anticipation of

BOX 1.2 *Neural Transmission versus Hormonal Communication*

Although neural and hormonal communication both rely upon chemical signals, several prominent differences exist. Communication in the nervous system is analogous to traveling on a train. You can use the train in your travel plans as long as tracks exist between your proposed origin and destination. Likewise, neural messages can travel only to destinations along existing nerve tracts. Hormonal communication, on the other hand, is like traveling in a car. You can drive to many more destinations than train travel allows, because there are many more roads than railroad tracks. Likewise, hormonal messages can travel anywhere in the body via the circulatory system; any cell receiving blood is potentially able to receive a hormonal message.

Neural and hormonal communication differ in other ways as well. To envision them, consider the differences between digital and analog technologies. Neural messages are digital, all-or-none events that have rapid onset and offset: neural signals can take place in milliseconds. Accordingly, the nervous system mediates changes in the body that are relatively rapid. For example, the nervous system regulates immediate food intake and directs body movement. In contrast, hormonal messages are analog, graded events that may take seconds, minutes, or even hours to occur. Hormones can mediate long-term processes, such as growth, development, reproduction, and metabolism.

Hormonal and neural messages are both chemical in nature, and they are released and received by cells in a similar manner; however, there are important differences as well. As shown in the figure in (A), in response to the arrival of a neural impulse at a presynaptic terminal, there is an influx of calcium ions (Ca^{2+}) (1) that causes vesicles (2) containing neural chemical messages called neurotransmitters to move toward the presynaptic membrane. The vesicles fuse with the membrane (3) and release the neurotransmitter into the synaptic cleft (4). The neurotransmitters travel a distance of only 20–30 nanometers (30×10^{-9} m) to the membrane of the postsynaptic neuron, where they bind with receptors (5). As shown in the figure in (B), hormones manufactured in the Golgi apparatus of an endocrine cell (1) also move toward the cell membrane in vesicles (2) that fuse with the membrane, releasing the hormone (3). However, hormones then enter the circulatory system and may travel from 1 mm to 2 m (4) before arriving at a cell of a target tissue, where they bind with specific receptors (5).

Another distinction between neural and hormonal communication is the degree of voluntary control that can be exerted over their functioning. In general, there is more voluntary control of neural than of hormonal signals. It is virtually impossible to will a change in your thyroid hormone levels, for example, whereas moving your limbs on command is easy.

Although these are significant differences, the division between the nervous system and the endocrine system is becoming more blurred as we learn more about how the nervous system regulates hormonal communication. A better understanding of the interface between the endocrine system and the nervous system is likely to yield important advances in the future study of the interaction between hormones and behavior.

(A) Neural transmission

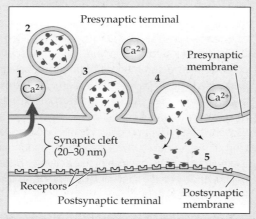

(B) Hormonal communication

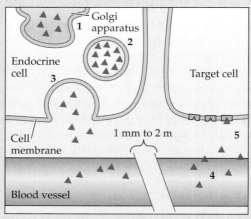

increased activity and energy demand. This "programmed" elevation of fuel availability coordinates the animal's physiology with its behavior.

Hormones are similar in function to **neurotransmitters**, the chemicals used by the nervous system in coordinating animals' activities. However, hormones can operate over a greater distance and over a much greater temporal range than neu-

neurotransmitters Chemical messengers that communicate between nerve cells (neurons).

rotransmitters (**BOX 1.2**). Hormones are also similar to **cytokines**, chemical signals produced by cells of the immune system, and may interact with cytokines to affect behavior, especially when individuals are ill or unduly stressed. Because of their structure, certain chemicals in the environment can mimic natural hormones and are generally referred to as endocrine disruptors. When such chemicals enter the food chain or water supply, they can affect the same hormone-behavior pathways as natural hormones. For example, about 16 million women in the United States use birth control pills. Much of the estrogen is secreted in their urine. According to the Freshwater Institute, part of Canada's Department of Fisheries and Oceans, the potent synthetic estrogens excreted by women taking hormone replacement therapy or birth control pills are not completely broken down during sewage treatment and are released into waterways (Kidd et al., 2007). Interestingly, the effects of these steroid hormones on reproductive development of wildlife and humans ingesting the water remain largely unspecified (Kidd et al., 2007). We will revisit the topic of endocrine disruptors' effects on behavior in subsequent chapters.

Importantly, not all cells are influenced by each and every hormone. Rather, any given hormone can directly influence only cells that have specific **receptors** for that particular hormone. Cells that have these specific receptors are called **target cells** for the hormone. The interaction of a hormone with its receptor begins a series of cellular events that eventually leads either to activation of enzymatic pathways or to effects on gene expression and protein synthesis. In the latter case, the newly synthesized proteins may activate or deactivate other genes, causing yet another cascade of cellular events. Recently, an additional mechanism has been reported; behavioral effects of hormones that are not caused by activation of the genetic machinery are called nongenomic effects of hormones on behavior and will be reviewed in Chapter 6.

Notably, sufficient numbers of appropriate hormone receptors must be available for a specific hormone to produce any effects. For example, if a capon had no receptors for testosterone, then implanting another testis (or giving testosterone hormone therapy) would not cause it to display testosterone-dependent traits. A common bias in behavioral endocrinology is the assumption that individual differences in the expression of a behavior reflect differences in hormone concentrations in the blood. In other words, it is assumed that roosters that fight frequently have higher blood testosterone concentrations than roosters that rarely fight. To a certain extent this assumption is correct. A minimal amount of hormone is required to activate sufficient receptors in neural networks to affect behavior; however, above that threshold, individual differences in hormone concentrations generally do not affect behavior. Individual differences in hormone-behavior interactions usually reflect complex influences of hormone concentrations, patterns of hormone release, numbers and locations of hormone receptors, and the efficiency of those receptors in triggering signal transduction pathways that ultimately affect gene transcription.

Hormones commonly alter the rate of normal cellular function. Another way that hormones can affect cells is to change their morphology or size. As mentioned, some athletes abuse anabolic steroids, which are synthetic hormones, because muscle cells grow larger after exposure to these substances. Hormones also may affect neuronal growth and development, as well as programmed cell death throughout the nervous system. Whereas the examples we have discussed so far have all demonstrated how the presence or absence of a hormone may affect behavior, it is important to appreciate that the interactive relationship between hormones and behavior is bidirectional: hormones obviously affect behavior, but, as we will see in subsequent chapters, behavior can also influence hormone concentrations and effects.

The Study of Behavior

Behavioral endocrinologists are interested in how the general physiological effects of hormones alter the development and expression of behavior and how behavior

cytokine A protein chemical messenger that evokes the proliferation of other cells, especially in the immune system.

receptor A chemical structure on the cell surface or inside the cell that has an affinity for a specific chemical configuration of a hormone, neurotransmitter, or other chemical compound.

target cells A cell that has specific receptors for, and is affected by, a particular chemical messenger.

FIGURE 1.6 Dark-eyed junco These small birds are common visitors to backyard bird feeders throughout much of North America. Juncos have been studied in the field to understand the role of testosterone in behavior and physiology.

may influence the effects of hormones. This book will describe, both phenomenologically and functionally, how hormones affect behavior.

What is behavior? Generally, we think of behavior as "output," and because muscles are the most common output organs, or **effectors**, we tend to consider behavior to be coordinated movement. Sometimes the lack of movement is an important behavior, especially when used in stalking prey or avoiding predators or during mating for females of many species. Importantly, excretion of scents and chemicals, changes in skin coloration, flashing lights of fireflies, and production of electrical signals by various species are also types of behavior, and many of these nonmuscular effector systems can be affected by hormones.

Problems of Behavioral Research

The goals of behavioral scientists are to determine what behaviors are relevant to the question being asked, to describe those behaviors, and to interpret their functions. These goals are not as simple to achieve as they may sound, and there are several pitfalls that behavioral investigators must avoid. We will examine several of these problems in the context of a simple example: the singing of a songbird, such as a dark-eyed junco (*Junco hyemalis*) (**FIGURE 1.6**). Although you may not have previously heard of this bird, you likely have heard it sing, as juncos are common visitors to backyard bird feeders throughout much of North America.

First, as soon as any observer begins to look at behavior, some degree of abstraction and bias is inevitable. When hens or roosters vocalize, we say that they "cluck" or "crow." However, the vocalizations of many birds are so melodious that we refer to their "singing." We may then explain the bird's singing as a result of its being happy, because we often sing when we are happy. This is obviously an anthropomorphic bias on our part. Behavioral scientists must take care not to attribute motives (e.g., hunger, fear, happiness) to animals based only on introspection and must make an effort to observe behavior as objectively as possible. For example, it is attractive to think that a junco is singing at the bird feeder because it is happy to have found food, but as you will see in Chapter 3, most birds sing to attract mates and defend territory.

Second, we must determine what other behaviors may be relevant to elucidating the behavior being examined. Even if an individual's behavior is videotaped continuously or observed directly for 24 hours a day, decisions must be made by the observer regarding which behaviors are meaningful and which are trivial in terms of answering the question at hand. In the case of the junco, for example, we must determine whether its presence at the bird feeder bears any relation to its singing.

Finally, to understand the causes (hormonal or otherwise) of any behavior, we must thoroughly describe that behavior (Tinbergen, 1951). When does the junco sing? What elicits its singing? Do all birds, or only some, engage in singing? As we saw in our discussion of Berthold's experiment, we must have a reasonably complete description of normal behavior before we can accurately assess the effects of any experimental manipulations on behavior.

The Simple System Approach

Even though we may ultimately be curious about the influence of hormones on human behavior, the unique and complex interactions of genes and environment make behavioral endocrinology studies of humans very difficult to interpret. For example, suppose that we observe that boys who undergo puberty before the age of 12 tend to be more socially aggressive than boys who undergo puberty after the age of 12. The cause of the difference in behavior may reflect differences in body

effectors The output system. In biology, usually refers to muscles.

size, which may result from differences in concentrations of hormones that regulate growth and development—bigger boys may be more aggressive. Alternatively, the differences in aggression may reflect differences in hormones that affect brain development and thus the development of confidence in social situations. There is also the chicken-and-egg problem to resolve; that is, do hormones affect behavior directly by affecting the brain or indirectly by affecting body size, which in turn affects brain and behavior, or does acting aggressive affect hormone concentrations, which in turn affect body development? Furthermore, humans are reared in a wide variety of environments, which complicates the assignment of causation to individual variation in behavior.

In order to untangle the contributions of various factors to hormone-behavior interactions, behavioral endocrinologists generally perform experiments on genetically identical animals in controlled environments. The development of behaviors and changes in hormone concentrations can be monitored throughout life under these conditions. Similar controlled experiments are difficult, but not impossible, to conduct on humans. Many clever scientists have conducted well-controlled studies on humans while keeping high ethical standards. Even though nonhuman animals represent "simple systems" relative to humans, it is important to appreciate that the behavioral repertoires of animals are extraordinarily varied and exquisitely adapted to specific historical biological niches.

Most research in behavioral endocrinology involves only a few types of simple behavior. This narrow focus on only a few behavioral measures is partially a response to the enormous variation inherent in observations of complex behaviors. There are advantages and disadvantages to this approach. The advantages of using simple behaviors include ease of replication and quantification. In this way, the simple system approach parallels the reductionist approach prevalent in physiological and biochemical analyses. On the other hand, the most apparent disadvantage to studying simple behaviors is the possibility that subtle, but important, interactions between hormones and behavior will be neglected and overlooked. Social and other environmental factors are often absent, or significantly reduced, in the laboratory but may also be important in attaining a complete understanding of hormone-behavior interactions. There are certainly cases in which investigators have endeavored to observe the hormonal correlates of complex behavior. But commonly, the behavioral end point studied is as simple as the presence or absence of birdsong or the occurrence of mounting behavior among male rodents.

Levels of Analysis

Once behaviors have been adequately described, we may proceed to ask about the causes of behavior (Alcock, 2013; Dewsbury, 1979; Tinbergen, 1951). For example, the zebra finch (*Taeniopygia guttata*) (**FIGURE 1.7**), a native Australian songbird, is one of the most frequently used species in studying birdsong. The circumstances in which zebra finches sing, the various notes that they produce, the parts of their brains that are used during song learning and song production, and even the specific muscles they use during singing have been extensively studied and described. Based on these extensive descriptions, many researchers are exploring the causes of singing in male zebra finches (as in most songbird species, females and immature zebra finches do not sing in nature) by developing hypotheses and testing them by means of observation and experimentation.

The generic question an animal behaviorist asks at this point in the research may be simply expressed as "What causes animal A to emit behavior X?" (Sherman, 1988), so many researchers have asked, in effect, "What causes zebra finches to sing?" You may be surprised to learn that there may be four

FIGURE 1.7 **Zebra finches** This small bird has been used extensively in the study of the hormonal and neural bases of birdsong. As with most songbird species, only the male zebra finch sings in nature. Courtesy of Atsuko Takahashi.

levels of analysis The set of overlapping and interacting questions about behavior that span different types of approaches, including immediate causation, development, evolution, and adaptive function.

immediate causation The physiological mechanism(s) underlying behavior.

development The role of experience in individual behavior.

evolutionary approaches The perspective(s) adopted by biologists who assume that evolutionary processes are central to issues in ecology, systematics, and behavior.

adaptive function The role of any structural, physiological, or behavioral process that increases an individual's fitness to survive and reproduce as compared with other conspecifics.

kinds of correct answers to this basic question, based on four different **levels of analysis**: immediate causation, development, evolution, and adaptive function (Tinbergen, 1951).

IMMEDIATE CAUSATION   The level of **immediate causation** encompasses the underlying physiological, or proximate, mechanisms responsible for a given behavior. Typically these mechanisms are mediated by the nervous and endocrine systems, which influence behavior on a moment-to-moment basis during the life of an individual. Various internal and environmental stimuli, as well as sensory and perceptual processes, are involved in the short-term regulation of behavior. Accordingly, experiments designed to address questions of immediate causation often use physiological methods such as alterations of hormone concentrations or direct manipulations of the brain. In the case of zebra finches, these kinds of experiments have revealed that elevated blood concentrations of estrogens and increased rates of neural activity in certain brain areas are immediate causes of singing, so one correct answer to the question posed above might be that zebra finches sing because blood estrogen concentrations are high. This class of explanation is the one most frequently used by behavioral endocrinologists, and it will be the primary focus of this book.

DEVELOPMENT   The behavioral responses and repertoires of animals change throughout their lives as a result of the interaction between genes and environmental factors. Questions of **development** concern the full range of the organism's lifetime from conception to death. For example, the behavior of newborns is initially quite rudimentary in many species but becomes more complex as they grow and interact with the environment. Hormonal events affecting the fetal and newborn animal can have pervasive influences later in life. Although the majority of research at the developmental level of analysis has focused on how events early in development influence animals later in life, the decay of behavioral patterns during aging is also of interest to behavioral biologists pursuing developmental questions. Possible answers to our question from the developmental perspective might be that zebra finches sing because they have undergone puberty or because they learned their songs from their fathers.

EVOLUTION   **Evolutionary approaches** involve many generations of animals and address the ways that specific behaviors change during the course of natural selection. Behavioral biologists study the evolutionary bases of behavior in order to learn why behavior varies between closely related species as well as to understand the specific behavioral changes that occur during the evolution of new species. Behaviors rarely leave interpretable traces in the fossil record, so the study of the evolution of behavior relies upon comparing existing species that vary in relatedness. An investigator working at the evolutionary level might say that zebra finches sing because they are finches, and that all finches sing because they have evolved from a common ancestral species that sang.

ADAPTIVE FUNCTION   Questions of **adaptive function** are synonymous with questions of adaptive significance; they are concerned with the role that behavior plays in the adaptation of animals to their environment and with the selective forces that currently maintain behavior. At this level of analysis, it might be argued that male zebra finches sing because this behavior increases the likelihood that they will reproduce by attracting females to their territories and/or dissuading competing males from interacting with their mates.

Thus, there are four different types of causal explanations for a particular behavior, and there may be many correct answers to the question "What causes male zebra finches to sing?" No one type of explanation is better or more complete than another, and in practice, the levels of questions and explanations overlap and interact in many situations. Nevertheless, it is important that researchers specify clearly the level of analysis within which they are working when hypotheses are being generated for testing. Care must be taken to avoid comparing noncompeting hypotheses at the different levels of analysis (Sherman, 1988).

For the sake of simplicity, these four levels of analysis can be grouped into sets of two, with questions of immediate causation and development grouped as "how questions" ("How does an animal engage in a behavior?") and questions of evolution and adaptive function as "why questions" ("Why does an animal engage in a particular behavior?") (Alcock, 2013). "How questions" have also been referred to as questions of *proximate causation*, and "why questions" as questions of *ultimate causation* (Wilson, 1975). To construct an exhaustive explanation of the causes of birdsong, then, we would want to study both how birds sing and why they sing (**FIGURE 1.8**). What developmental and physiological processes occur before and during singing? What is the evolutionary history of birdsong? When, phylogenetically (during evolutionary history), did singing appear among birds? What adaptive advantages do singers enjoy relative to nonsingers?

Researchers in different disciplines tend to favor particular types of questions and classes of explanations. For example, physiologists work almost exclusively at the level of immediate causation, whereas behavioral ecologists specialize in evolutionary and adaptive explanations of behavior. Behavioral endocrinologists who focus on physiology and neuroscience tend to work in laboratories, whereas behavioral endocrinologists who focus on behavioral ecology tend to work in the field. In general, laboratory data are more reliable (i.e., repeatable) than field data because the experimental conditions can be tightly controlled. However, field data tend to be more valid (i.e., more ecologically relevant) than laboratory data because the behavior and physiology of animals evolved in the field setting. The types of explanations that individual scientists pursue in conducting their research reflect their tastes and their training, but their combined efforts allow us to gain the most comprehensive understanding of animal behavior.

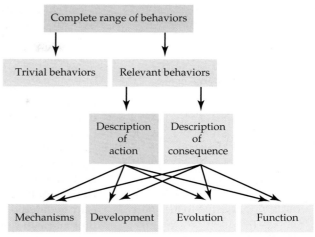

FIGURE 1.8   Stages of behavioral research From the complete range of an organism's behavior, the behavioral scientist must first determine which behaviors are relevant to the question under consideration, a process that is inherently prone to abstraction or bias. Descriptions of relevant behaviors may focus on the actions themselves ("description of action") or on their environmental effects ("description of consequence"). Examination of the causes of behaviors may proceed at any of four levels of analysis that address either proximate ("how") or ultimate ("why") questions.

How Might Hormones Affect Behavior?

In terms of their behavior, one can think of animals globally as being made up of three interacting components: (1) input systems (sensory systems), (2) integrators (the central nervous system), and (3) output systems, or effectors (e.g., muscles) (**FIGURE 1.9**). Again, hormones do not cause behavioral changes. Rather, hormones influence these three systems so that specific stimuli are more likely to elicit certain responses in the appropriate behavioral or

FIGURE 1.9   How hormones may affect behavior Behaving animals may be thought of as being made up of three interacting components: input systems (sensory systems), central processing systems (the central nervous system), and output systems (effectors, such as muscles). Hormones may affect any or all of these three components when influencing behavior. Note that there is a bidirectional causal relationship between hormones and behavior in that an animal's behavior (or the behavior of conspecifics or predators) may affect its endocrine state.

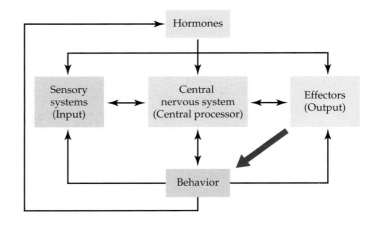

social context. In other words, as indicated previously, hormones change the probability that a particular behavior will be emitted in the appropriate situation. This is a critical distinction that can affect how we think of hormone-behavior relationships.

We can apply this three-component behavioral scheme by returning to our example of singing behavior in zebra finches. As noted above, only the male zebra finch sings in nature. If the testes of adult male finches are removed, then the birds reduce singing, but castrated finches resume singing if the testes are reimplanted or if the birds are provided with either testosterone or estradiol, a type of estrogen. Because some testosterone from the testes is converted to estrogens, the lack of estrogens likely accounts for the reduced singing. Singing behavior is most frequent when blood estrogen concentrations are high. It is apparent from these observations that estrogens are somehow involved in singing; now, how might the three-component framework just introduced help us to formulate hypotheses to explore estrogen's role in this behavior? By examining input systems, we could determine whether estrogens alter the birds' sensory capabilities, making the environmental cues that normally elicit singing more salient. If this were the case, females or competitors might be more easily seen or heard. Estrogens also could influence the central nervous system. Neuronal architecture or the speed of neural processing could change in the presence of estrogens. Higher neural processes (e.g., motivation, attention, or perception) also might be influenced. Finally, the effector organs, muscles in this case, could be affected by the presence of estrogens. Blood estrogen concentrations might somehow affect the muscles of a songbird's syrinx (the avian vocal organ). Estrogens, therefore, could affect birdsong by influencing the sensory capabilities, central nervous system, or effector organs of an individual bird. We do not understand completely how estrogen, often derived from testosterone (see Chapter 2), influences birdsong, but in most cases, hormones can be considered to affect behavior by influencing one, two, or all three of these components, and our three-part framework can aid in the design of hypotheses and experiments to explore these issues. This conceptual scheme of how hormones and behavior interact will provide the major organization for this book.

How Might Behavior Affect Hormones?

The birdsong example demonstrates how hormones can affect behavior, but, as noted previously, the reciprocal relation also occurs; that is, behavior can affect hormone concentrations. For example, the sight of a territorial intruder may elevate blood testosterone concentrations in the resident male and thereby stimulate singing or fighting behavior (Wingfield, 1988). Similarly, male mice (Ginsberg and Allee, 1942) and rhesus monkeys (Rose et al., 1971) that lose a fight show reduced circulating testosterone concentrations for several days or even weeks afterward. Similar results have also been reported in humans. Testosterone concentrations are affected not only in humans involved in physical combat but also in those involved in simulated battles. For example, testosterone concentrations were elevated in winners and reduced in losers of regional chess tournaments (Mazur et al., 1992). Perhaps not surprisingly, the relationship between competition and hormones is often complicated by social factors. For example, studies of rural Dominican adult and adolescent males during dice tournaments revealed that neither adult nor adolescent males increase testosterone concentrations when they defeat their friends, but testosterone increases when outsiders are defeated (Flinn et al., 2012).

People do not have to be directly involved in a contest to have their hormones affected by the outcome. For instance, fans of both the Spanish and Dutch soccer teams were recruited to provide saliva samples to be assayed for testosterone and cortisol before and during the final game of the 2010 FIFA World Cup soccer match. The experience of watching the game elevated testosterone and cortisol in male, but not female, fans compared with a control day (van der Meij et al., 2012)

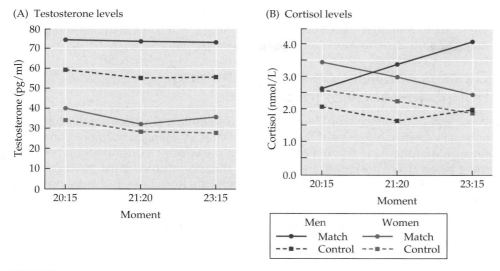

FIGURE 1.10 **Hormonal responses to viewing a soccer match** The experience of watching the game elevated testosterone and cortisol in male, but not female, fans compared with a day when they were not watching soccer. After van der Meij et al., 2012.

(**FIGURE 1.10**). Elevated cortisol secretion during the match was higher among fans that were younger. Also, elevated cortisol concentrations increased in association with the extent to which people identified themselves as strong fans of soccer. This match was extraordinarily important for citizens of the two nations. Over 90% of all television viewers in the Netherlands (~8.5 million people) and nearly 90% of all television viewers in Spain watched the match live on television (van der Meij et al., 2012), setting new television-viewing records in both countries.

Many other examples of how behavior (or even the anticipation of behavior) may influence hormone concentrations exist. For example, testosterone concentrations were measured in four heterosexual couples over a total of 22 evenings (Dabbs and Mohammed, 1992). There were two different types of evenings. On 11 evenings, the samples were obtained before and after sexual intercourse; on the remaining 11 evenings, two samples were obtained during the evening, but there was no sexual intercourse. To avoid the logistic complications of drawing blood samples, testosterone was measured in the saliva of the participants. Engaging in sexual intercourse caused testosterone concentrations to increase in both men and women. The early evening saliva samples revealed no difference between testosterone concentrations on evenings when sexual intercourse took place and concentrations on evenings when it did not. These results suggest that in humans, sexual behavior increases testosterone concentrations more than high testosterone concentrations cause sexual activity (Dabbs and Mohammed, 1992). Although this is certainly a reasonable conclusion, there are alternative explanations for the results of this study. For example, perhaps physical exercise alone increases testosterone concentrations. To rule out this possibility, additional studies are required in which the level of exercise is similar between experimental groups but differs in sexual content. Such studies have been conducted and will be reviewed in Chapters 5 and 6.

Testosterone concentrations also influence sexual behavior in women. In one recent study, the interaction between testosterone and sexual intercourse was compared with the interaction between testosterone and other activities (i.e., cuddling or exercise) in women (reviewed in van Anders, 2012). On three separate occasions, women provided a preactivity, postactivity, and next-morning saliva sample. After analysis, the women's testosterone was determined to be elevated prior to intercourse as compared with other times. Thus, an anticipatory relationship exists between sexual behavior and testosterone. Testosterone values were higher after intercourse compared with after exercise, hinting that engaging in sexual behavior may also influence hormone concentrations in women.

Classes of Evidence for Determining Hormone-Behavior Interactions

What sort of evidence would be sufficient to establish that a particular hormone affected a specific behavior or that a specific behavior changed hormone concentrations? Experiments to test hypotheses about the effects of hormones on behavior must be carefully designed, and generally three conditions must be satisfied by the experimental results for a causal link between hormones and behavior to be established (Silver, 1978):

1. A hormonally dependent behavior should disappear when the source of the hormone is removed or the actions of the hormone are blocked.
2. After the behavior stops, restoration of the missing hormonal source or its hormone should reinstate the absent behavior.
3. Finally, hormone concentrations and the behavior in question should be covariant; that is, the behavior should be observed only when hormone concentrations are relatively high and never or rarely when hormone concentrations are low.

The third class of evidence has proved difficult to obtain because hormones may have a long latency of action and because many hormones are released in a pulsatile manner. For example, if a pulse of hormone is released into the blood and then no more is released for an hour or so, a single blood sample will not provide an accurate picture of the endocrine status of the animal under study. We might come to completely different conclusions about the effect of a hormone on behavior if we measure hormone concentrations when they are at their peak rather than when they are at their nadir. This problem can be overcome by obtaining measures in several animals or by taking several sequential blood samples from the same animal and averaging across peaks and valleys. Another problem is that biologically effective amounts of hormones are vanishingly small and difficult to measure accurately. Effective concentrations of hormones are usually measured in micrograms (μg, 10^{-6} g), nanograms (ng, 10^{-9} g), or picograms (pg, 10^{-12} g); they are sometimes expressed as a mass percentage relative to 100 ml of blood plasma or serum (10 μg% = 10 μg/100 ml = 0.1 μg/ml). The development of techniques, such as the radioimmunoassay (see below), has increased the precision with which hormone concentrations can be measured, but because of the multiple difficulties associated with obtaining reliable covariant hormone-behavior measures, obtaining the first two classes of evidence usually has been considered sufficient to establish a causal link in hormone-behavior relations.

As we will see in subsequent chapters, the unique conditions of the laboratory environment may themselves cause changes in an animal's hormone concentrations and behavior that may confound the results of experiments; thus, it has become apparent that hormone-behavior relationships established in the laboratory should be verified in natural environments. The verification of hormone-behavior relationships in natural environments is becoming increasingly common, and it is critically important for differentiating laboratory artifacts from true biological phenomena.

Common Techniques in Behavioral Endocrinology

How do we gather the evidence needed to establish hormone-behavior relationships? Because we cannot directly observe the interactions between hormones and their receptors or their intracellular consequences, we must use various indirect tools to explore these phenomena. This section describes some of the primary methods and techniques used in behavioral endocrinology. Much of the recent progress in behavioral endocrinology has resulted from technical advances in the tools that allow us to detect, measure, and probe the functions of hormones and their receptors. Therefore, familiarity with these techniques will help you to understand and assess the research to be discussed in subsequent chapters. It should be useful to refer back to this section to recall the various techniques.

Ablation and Replacement

The **ablation** (removal or extirpation) of the suspected source of a hormone to determine its function is a classic technique in endocrinology. Recall that this was the method Berthold used to establish the role of the testes in the development of rooster behavior. There are four steps to this time-honored procedure: (1) a gland that is suspected to be the source of a hormone affecting a behavior is surgically removed; (2) the effects of removal are observed; (3) the hormone is replaced by reimplanting the removed gland, by injecting a homogenate or extract from the gland, or by injecting a purified hormone; and (4) a determination is made of whether the observed consequences of ablation have been reversed by the replacement therapy. This technique is commonly used in endocrine research today. A traditional complementary approach to the ablation-replacement technique is the observation of behavior in individuals with diseased or congenitally dysfunctional endocrine organs. When ablation occurs in the brain, the result is often called a **lesion**. Modern complementary approaches include administration of drugs to block hormone synthesis or hormone receptor activity. More recent technologies include manipulation of genes to block hormone production or hormone receptor function (see below).

The replacement component of this technique has been improved by technological advances, especially new recombinant DNA methods that have made highly purified hormones readily available. Access to this virtually pure material has allowed researchers to rule out "contaminants" as a cause of the physiological or behavioral effects of a particular hormone. Also, recent studies have emphasized the importance of replacing hormones in patterns and doses similar to those found in nature rather than using a single pharmacological dose. This has been made possible by the availability of implantable timed-release hormone capsules and minipumps that provide precisely timed infusions of purified hormones.

Immunoassays

Bioassays, which are assays that use living tissues or animals to test the effects of hormones or other chemical compounds, were useful historically because they measured a biological response to the hormone in question. In some cases, they allowed the determination of the presence or absence of a substance (as in the rabbit test for pregnancy), and in others they allowed quantitative measurement of specific hormones (as in the pigeon crop sac test for prolactin). However, bioassays usually required much time and labor, as well as the use of many animals for every assay conducted. The development of the **radioimmunoassay** (**RIA**) technique reduced these problems and increased the precision with which hormone concentrations could be measured. The ability to measure hormones precisely was such an important scientific advancement that one of the developers of this technique, Rosalyn Yalow, won the 1977 Nobel Prize in Physiology or Medicine. (Her close collaborator, Solomon A. Berson, died in 1972, and Nobel Prizes are not awarded posthumously.)

RIAs are based on the principle of competitive binding of an antibody to its antigen. An antibody produced in response to any antigen, in this case a hormone, has a binding site that is specific for that antigen. A given amount of antibody possesses

ablation   Removal, especially by cutting.

lesion   Damage to an area, such as a brain region, that is caused by accident, disease, or experimental procedure.

radioimmunoassay (RIA)   A technique used to measure hormones or other biological substances by using antibodies and purified radiolabeled ligands.

FIGURE 1.11   Radioimmunoassay

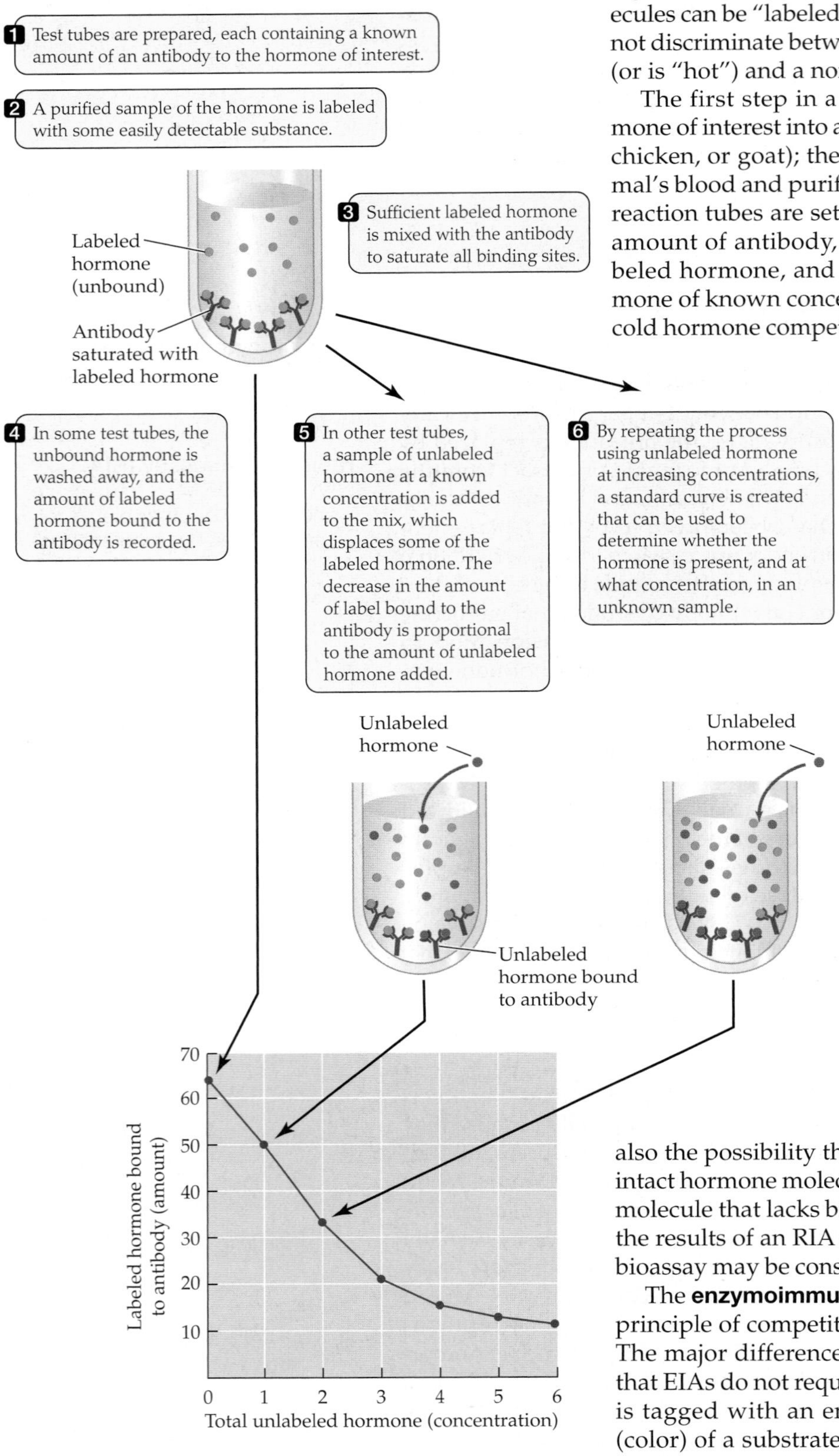

1 Test tubes are prepared, each containing a known amount of an antibody to the hormone of interest.

2 A purified sample of the hormone is labeled with some easily detectable substance.

Labeled hormone (unbound)

Antibody saturated with labeled hormone

3 Sufficient labeled hormone is mixed with the antibody to saturate all binding sites.

4 In some test tubes, the unbound hormone is washed away, and the amount of labeled hormone bound to the antibody is recorded.

5 In other test tubes, a sample of unlabeled hormone at a known concentration is added to the mix, which displaces some of the labeled hormone. The decrease in the amount of label bound to the antibody is proportional to the amount of unlabeled hormone added.

6 By repeating the process using unlabeled hormone at increasing concentrations, a standard curve is created that can be used to determine whether the hormone is present, and at what concentration, in an unknown sample.

Unlabeled hormone

Unlabeled hormone

Unlabeled hormone bound to antibody

[Graph: y-axis labeled "Labeled hormone bound to antibody (amount)" with values 10, 20, 30, 40, 50, 60, 70; x-axis labeled "Total unlabeled hormone (concentration)" with values 0, 1, 2, 3, 4, 5, 6]

a given number of binding sites for its antigen. Antigen molecules can be "labeled" with radioactivity, and an antibody cannot discriminate between an antigen that has been radiolabeled (or is "hot") and a normal, nonradiolabeled ("cold") antigen.

The first step in a radioimmunoassay is to inject the hormone of interest into an animal to raise antibody (often a rabbit, chicken, or goat); the antibody is then collected from the animal's blood and purified. To develop a standard curve, several reaction tubes are set up, each containing the same measured amount of antibody, the same measured amount of radiolabeled hormone, and different amounts of cold purified hormone of known concentration. The radiolabeled hormone and cold hormone compete for binding sites on the antibody, so the more cold hormone there is present in the tube, the less hot hormone will bind to the antibody. The quantity of hot hormone that binds can be determined by precipitating the antibody and measuring the associated radioactivity resulting from the radiolabeled hormone that remains bound. The concentration of hormone in a sample can then be determined by subjecting it to the same procedure and comparing the results with the standard curve (**FIGURE 1.11**).

As is the case with other techniques, there are limitations to the RIA method. First of all, a source of highly purified hormone is required so that a highly specific antibody against it can be prepared. There is the potential for contamination of the material used to immunize the rabbit to generate antibodies for an RIA. Also, because many hormones have similar chemical structures, RIAs must be tested for specificity to rule out the possibility that the antibody will recognize other antigens in addition to the one of interest. There is also the possibility that the antibody may bind not only to the intact hormone molecule but also to a fragment of the hormone molecule that lacks biological activity. For these reasons, when the results of an RIA do not agree with those of a bioassay, the bioassay may be considered more valid even if it is less precise.

The **enzymoimmunoassay** (**EIA**), like the RIA, works on the principle of competitive binding of an antibody to its antigen. The major difference between the RIA and EIA techniques is that EIAs do not require radioactive tags. Instead, the antibody is tagged with an enzyme that changes the optical density (color) of a substrate molecule. The home pregnancy test is a familiar example of an EIA (**FIGURE 1.12**). These tests, like the old-fashioned rabbit test for pregnancy, are designed to give a yes-or-no answer. However, most EIAs are developed to pro-

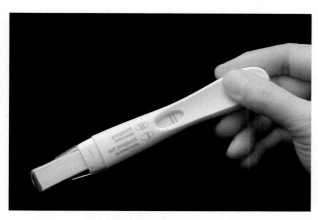

FIGURE 1.12 Home pregnancy tests use a form of EIA.

vide quantitative information. A standard curve is generated, as for RIAs, so that different known amounts of the hormone in question provide a gradient of color that can be read on a spectrometer. The unknown sample is then added, and the amount of hormone is interpolated by using the standard curves. This technique is also called an **enzyme-linked immunosorbent assay** (**ELISA**).

Attempts have been made to measure hormones in fluids or tissues other than blood in order to obtain samples without having to stress the individuals by restraint and blood draws. These so-called noninvasive methods have assayed hormones from saliva, feces, hair, or feathers with mixed success. Typically, the samples must be placed in a solvent to pull the steroids out (steroids are not very water-soluble, so they naturally migrate to a nonaqueous solvent layer of a mixture that can be removed and assayed with RIA or EIA). Obviously, the ability to assess hormones without disturbing individuals is an important priority in field or zoo studies.

Immunocytochemistry

Immunocytochemistry (**ICC**; when applied to cells) or **immunohistochemistry** (**IHC**; when applied to tissues) techniques use antibodies to determine the location of a hormone in the brain or elsewhere in the body. Antibodies linked to marker molecules, such as those of a fluorescent dye (see Polak and Van Noorden, 1997), are usually introduced into dissected tissue from an animal, where they bind with the hormone or neurochemical of interest. For example, if a thin slice of brain tissue is immersed in a solution of antibodies to a protein hormone linked to a fluorescent dye and the tissue is then examined under a fluorescent microscope, concentrated spots of fluorescence will appear, indicating where the protein hormone is located (**FIGURE 1.13**). Fluorescent dyes used for ICC include fluorescein and rhodamine or updated versions of these dyes. Other commonly used techniques include applying the enzyme horseradish peroxidase to catalyze reactions resulting in colored products, for bright-field or electron microscopy;

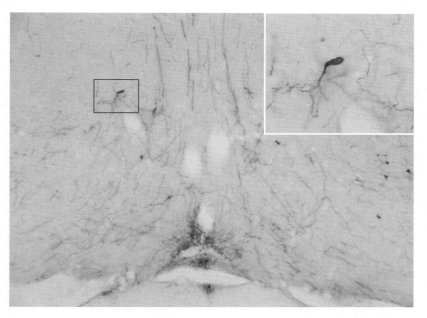

FIGURE 1.13 **Immunohistochemistry** Antibodies to a hormone can be linked to a dye and used to determine the location of a hormone in the body. If a slice of tissue is exposed to a solution of antibody linked to such a marker, the binding of the antibody will cause those parts of the tissue containing the hormone to selectively take up the dye, making them more visible under the microscope. This photomicrograph (×100) of a thin section of a rodent's brain shows a tangle of neuronal dendrites; immunocytochemically marked cell bodies that contain gonadotropin-releasing hormone (GnRH) are prominent. Courtesy of Lance Kriegsfeld.

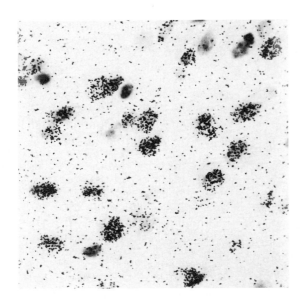

FIGURE 1.14 Autoradiography An animal is injected with a radiolabeled hormone, and adjacent tissue slices are either treated with stains to reveal cellular structures or exposed to film. Those parts of the tissue that bind with the radiolabeled hormone darken the film and, when combined with the stained section, show which cell structures have taken up the hormone in the largest amounts. In this autoradiograph, cell nuclei in a monkey brain that have accumulated radiolabeled estrogen are seen as darker than the background neurons. Courtesy of Bruce McEwen.

autoradiography A technique used to detect a radiolabeled substance, such as a hormone, in a cell or organism, by placing a thin slice of the material in contact with a photographic emulsion.

blot tests Techniques used to fractionate mixtures of proteins (Western), DNAs (Southern), or RNAs (Northern) so they can hybridize with markers that travel different distances in an electrophoretic gel based on their size.

electrophoresis A method that separates macromolecules (e.g., nucleic acids or proteins) on the basis of size, electrical charge, and other physical properties.

in situ hybridization A technique in which nucleic acid probes are used to locate specific nucleic acids (DNA in chromosomes and RNA in cells).

agonist A chemical substance that binds to receptors for a hormone or neurotransmitter and causes a biological response that is indistinguishable from the response elicited by the natural hormone or neurotransmitter.

antagonist A chemical substance that binds to receptors for a hormone or neurotransmitter, but does not cause a biological response.

the enzyme alkaline phosphatase, for biochemical detection; and the iron-containing protein ferritin, for electron microscopy.

A common alternative ICC technique involves raising a second antibody against the primary antibody that recognizes the substance to be measured, then coupling the second antibody to a marker. Sometimes the secondary antibody is linked to biotin, a water-soluble vitamin, which has a strong binding affinity to streptavidin, a bacterial protein. If streptavidin is coupled to a marker molecule, it can be used to detect bound antibody. A single biotin-antibody-antigen complex may link to multiple marker molecules, which essentially amplifies the signal indicating the presence of the antigen.

Autoradiography

Many older studies have demonstrated that hormone receptors are selectively concentrated in particular target tissues; estrogen receptors, for example, are concentrated in the uterus. **Autoradiography** is typically used to determine hormonal uptake and indicate receptor location. An animal can be injected with a radiolabeled hormone, or the study can be conducted entirely in vitro. Suspected target tissues are sliced into several very thin sections; adjacent sections are then subjected to different treatments. One section of the suspected target tissue is stained in the usual way to highlight various cellular structures. The next section is placed in contact with photographic film or emulsion for some period of time, and the emission of radiation from the radiolabeled hormone develops an image on the film. The areas of high radioactivity on the film can then be compared with the stained section to determine how the areas of highest hormone concentration correlate with cellular structures (**FIGURE 1.14**). This technique has been very useful in determining the sites of hormone action in nervous tissue and consequently has increased our understanding of hormone-behavior interactions.

Blot Tests

Other techniques allow the determination of whether or not a particular protein or nucleic acid is present in a specific tissue. In the so-called **blot tests**, the tissue of interest is homogenized and the cells are lysed with detergent. The resulting homogenate is run on a gel that is subjected to electrophoresis. **Electrophoresis** refers to the application of an electric current through a matrix or gel that results in a gradient of molecules separating out along the current on the basis of size (smaller molecules move farther than larger molecules during a set time period), which is then transferred to a membrane. The membrane is then incubated with a labeled substance that can act as a tracer for the protein or nucleic acid of interest: radiolabeled complementary deoxyribonucleic acid (cDNA) for a nucleic acid assay, or an antibody that has been radiolabeled or linked to an enzyme for a protein assay. If radiolabeling is used, the filter is then put over film to locate and measure radioactivity. In enzyme-linked protein assays, the filter is incubated with chromogenic chemicals, and standard curves reflecting different spectral densities are generated. The test used to assay DNA is called Southern blotting, after its inventor, E. M. Southern; the test used to assay RNA is called Northern blotting, and the test for proteins is called Western blotting (**FIGURE 1.15**).

In Situ Hybridization

An important tool used at the cellular level to examine gene expression is called **in situ hybridization**. This technique is used to identify cells or tissues in which messenger RNA (mRNA) molecules encoding a specific protein—for example, a hormone or neurotransmitter—are being produced. The tissue is fixed, sliced very thin, mounted on slides, and either dipped into emulsion or placed over film and developed with photographic chemicals. Typically, the tissue is also counterstained to identify specific cellular structures. A radiolabeled cDNA probe is introduced into the tissue. If the mRNA of interest is present in the tissue, the cDNA will form a tight association (i.e., hybridize) with it. The tightly bound cDNA, and hence the mRNA, will appear as dark spots (**FIGURE 1.16**). The techniques previously described, such as blot tests, can typically determine only whether or not a particular substance is present in a specific tissue, but in situ hybridization can be used to determine whether a particular substance is produced in a specific tissue. Recent advances in the technique allow for the quantification of the substance being produced. Also, blot test techniques cannot match the resolution or sensitivity of in situ hybridization.

Pharmacological Techniques

The identification of hormones and neurotransmitters, and the development for medical purposes of synthetic **agonists** (mimics) and **antagonists** (blockers) of these chemicals, has informed us about the functioning of the endocrine and neuroendocrine systems. Some specific chemical agents can act to stimulate or inhibit endocrine function by affecting hormonal release; these agents are called general agonists and antagonists, respectively. Other drugs act directly on hormone receptors, either enhancing or negating the effects of the hormone under study; these drugs are referred to as receptor agonists and antagonists, respec-

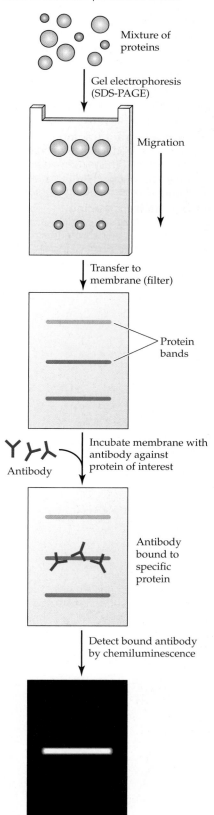

FIGURE 1.15 **Western blot** An assay used to measure proteins in tissue.

Mixture of proteins

Gel electrophoresis (SDS-PAGE)

Migration

Transfer to membrane (filter)

Protein bands

Antibody

Incubate membrane with antibody against protein of interest

Antibody bound to specific protein

Detect bound antibody by chemiluminescence

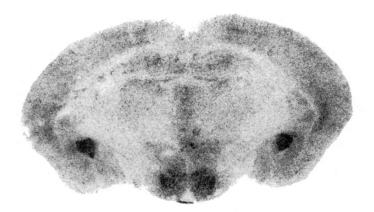

FIGURE 1.16 **In situ hybridization** The dark spots at the bottom of this slice of a rodent brain represent cells in the ventromedial hypothalamus (VMH) that contain mRNA for an oxytocin receptor. This tissue was treated with a specific cDNA that hybridized with the RNA that encodes the oxytocin receptor. Courtesy of Thomas Insel and Larry Young.

cannulation A technique in which hollow electrodes or fine tubes (cannulas) are inserted into specific brain regions or into specific blood vessels, so that substances can be introduced precisely into a particular place or a blood sample obtained from a specific location.

parabiosis The joining together of two circulatory systems.

anterograde tract tracing A method used to trace axonal projections from their termination (e.g., synapse) to their point of origin (the cell body or soma).

retrograde tract tracing A technique used to trace neural connections from their source to their point of termination (i.e., from cell body to synapse).

tively. For example, cyproterone acetate (CPA) is a powerful antiandrogen (e.g., antitestosterone) that has been used clinically as a treatment for male sex offenders (see Chapter 5). This antagonist binds to testosterone receptors but does not activate them, thereby blocking the effects of testosterone on behavior and physiology. Other examples of hormone agonists and antagonists will be presented throughout the book.

In the technique known as **cannulation**, hollow electrodes or fine tubes (cannulas) are inserted into specific areas of the brain and used to introduce substances into those sites. To find out where in the brain testosterone acts to affect sexual behavior, male rats were castrated, after which they stopped mating (Davidson 1966a). Testosterone was then introduced through cannulas into different areas of the brain in different rats; a control group of rats received cholesterol, the precursor of testosterone. Those animals that received testosterone in one specific location, the preoptic area of the hypothalamus, resumed sexual behavior; the rats that received cholesterol or received testosterone in other brain regions did not respond to the treatment.

Another type of cannulation involves inserting a small hollow tube into the jugular vein, carotid artery, or other blood vessel. In this way, specific hormones or pharmacological agents can later be injected directly into the animal without further disturbance, or blood samples can be obtained to correlate hormone levels with behavior. In a related technique, **parabiosis**, the blood systems of two animals are connected either directly or via cannulation tubing to see if the endocrine condition of one animal can cause a behavioral change in the other.

Anterograde and Retrograde Tract Tracing

Using the approaches above, one can determine which hormones regulate a behavior and where they act in the brain. However, most behaviors are not controlled by a single neural locus but, instead, by a more complex neural circuit. As described previously in this chapter, hormones can influence sensory systems, integration centers, and target effector systems. To uncover these more complete neural pathways, tract-tracing approaches that reveal neural circuitry can be used (**FIGURE 1.17**). To determine where in the brain a particular population of cells communicates, for example, axonal projections can be "mapped" from their source (cell bodies) to their point of termination by using **anterograde tract tracing**. To accomplish this task, lipophilic dyes or plant lectins (proteins that bind carbohydrates) are injected into a brain region of interest. These molecules are absorbed by cell bodies at the site of the injection and transported down the length of their axons. To allow visualization of these axonal projections, the brains can then be labeled immunohistochemically. Alternatively, to determine which cells communicate to a brain region that is involved in a behavior, **retrograde tract tracing** can be used. Performance of retrograde tracing is similar to that of anterograde tracing; in this case, molecules injected at the neural site of interest are absorbed by axonal terminals and transported to their source (cell bodies projecting to the region of interest). Again, these cell bodies can be visualized with immunohistochemistry.

There are two major limitations of this approach: First, brain mapping can only be accomplished one synapse at a time, making the discovery of complete circuits time-consuming, and second, all cells (anterograde) or axonal terminals (retrograde) absorb the tracers at the site of the injection, making specificity of the circuitry investigated difficult. To overcome the first obstacle, viral tracers can be employed that can cross synapses. The second shortcoming can be circumvented by using viral approaches (see below) that target specific cell types. Whatever approach is used, discovering the specific hormone-responsive circuits allows for a more complete picture of the hormonal control of complex behavior.

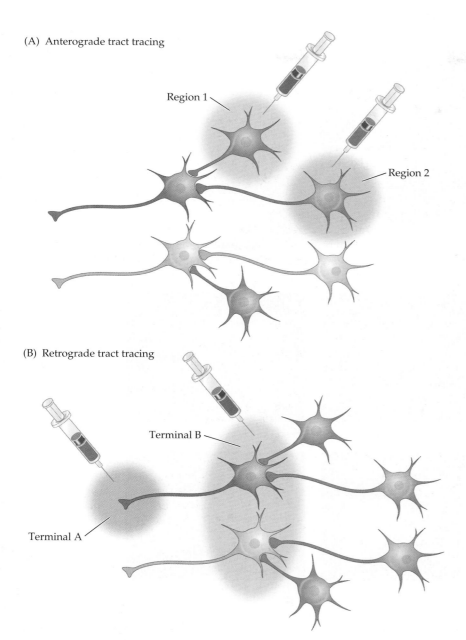

(A) Anterograde tract tracing

Region 1

Region 2

(B) Retrograde tract tracing

Terminal B

Terminal A

FIGURE 1.17 Tract tracing To map circuitry in the brain, non-transsynaptic tracers have traditionally been used. By conducting several experiments at different injection sites, neural circuits can be uncovered. For anterograde tracing (A), injections are made at the site of cell bodies of interest (regions 1 and 2) to explore their axonal projections. For retrograde tracing (B), injections are made at fiber terminals (terminals A and B) to examine cells projecting to those locations. Greater specificity is typically gained today through use of viral strategies that permit infection of specific cell types and the crossing of synapses.

Brain Imaging

There are several brain-scanning techniques used in behavioral endocrinology to determine brain structure and function (Rupp and Wallen, 2008; Van Bruggen and Roberts, 2002). For example, comparisons can be made between men and women or among individuals in different hormonal conditions. One important scanning technique used to determine regional brain activation is called **positron emission tomography** (**PET**). Unlike a simple X-ray or CT scan, which reveal only anatomical details, PET scanning permits detailed measurements of real-time functioning of specific brain regions of people who are conscious and alert. PET gives a dynamic representation of the brain at work. Prior to the availability of PET scanners, changes in neurotransmitter levels or hormonal activation of specific circuits could only be inferred on the basis of autopsy data.

Before the PET scan begins, a small amount of a radioactively tagged molecule that mimics glucose or a radioactive gas such as oxygen-15 is injected into the in-

positron emission tomography (PET) A technique for examining brain function by combining tomography with injections of radioactive substances used by the brain.

FIGURE 1.18 fMRI (A) A modern MRI scanner. (B, C) These images are the results of fMRI scans of groups of men's and women's brains that were superimposed on CT scans of the sagittal (left) and transverse (right) planes. Yellow areas represent the most active parts of the brain. Men and women were asked to navigate (via keyboard) through a spatial maze. (B) There was more activation in the right inferior parietal lobe of women compared with men. (C) There was more activation in the hippocampus of men compared with women when performing the maze. B,C from Grön et al., 2000.

(A)

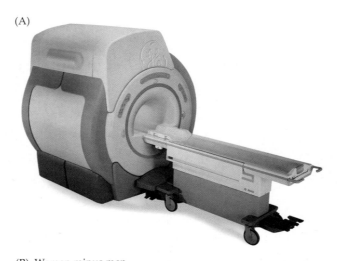

(B) Women minus men

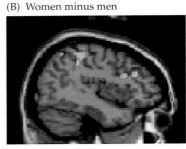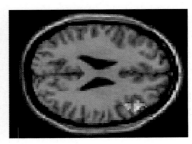

(C) Men minus women

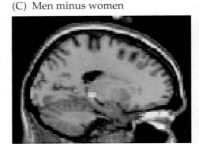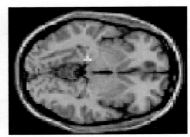

computerized tomography (CT)
Three-dimensional radiograph image of a body structure constructed by computer from a series of plane cross-sectional images made along an axis.

magnetic resonance imaging (MRI) An imaging technique that uses a magnetic field and radio waves to create detailed images of the organs and tissues within the body.

functional MRI (fMRI) A non-invasive procedure that can measure biological activity in the brain. fMRI relies on the magnetic properties of blood to visualize images of blood flow in the brain as a brain region (within 1 mm) is activated and while it is occurring (within 1 sec).

dividual. This radioactive material emits positrons and is taken up at high rates in the most active neurons. When a positron collides with an electron, the collision produces two gamma rays that leave the body in opposite directions and can be detected by the PET scanner. This information about where glucose is being metabolized or oxygen is being used is then converted into a complex picture of the person's functioning brain by a computer.

A **computerized tomography** (**CT**) scanner shoots fine beams of X-rays into the brain from several directions. The emitted information is fed into a computer that constructs a composite picture of the anatomical details within a "slice" through the brain of the person. **Magnetic resonance imaging** (**MRI**) does much the same thing but uses nonionizing radiation formed by the excitation of protons by radio-frequency energy in the presence of large magnetic fields (Van Bruggen and Roberts, 2002). MRI can be used in anatomical studies, and assessing anatomical irregularities is its main function when it is used as a medical diagnostic tool. **Functional MRI** (**fMRI**) uses a very high spatial (~1 mm) and temporal resolution to detect changes in brain activity during specific tasks or conditions. Most fMRI studies require the person to lie still in a narrow tunnel (**FIGURE 1.18A**), so only cognitive or affective changes can be monitored. As noted, when neurons become more active, they use more energy and require additional blood flow to deliver glucose and oxygen. The fMRI scanner detects this change in cerebral blood flow by detecting changes in the ratio of oxyhemoglobin and deoxyhemoglobin. Deoxyhemoglobin is paramagnetic (becomes magnetic in magnetic fields), whereas oxyhemoglobin is diamagnetic (does not become magnetic in magnetic fields). Thus, deoxyhemoglobin acts like little magnets in the large magnetic field of the MRI and dephases the signal. When brain regions increase activity, more oxygenated blood is present than before the activation. More oxyhemoglobin results in a net decrease in paramagnetic material (deoxyhemoglobin) that leads to a net increase in signal because of reduced dephasing of the signal. A complex computer program plots all of the phase changes of the signal and applies this picture on top of a structural picture of the brain, usually obtained with a CT scan (**FIGURE 1.18B,C**).

For very small animals, another type of imaging is often used. Researchers use expression of so-called immediate early genes (IEGs) to view brain regions associated with behavior or endocrine manipulation. In neurons, these immediate early genes are activated early during the signal transduction process whereby extracellular signals result in the expression of specific genes. The nature and function of the "activation" of IEGs remain controversial (Hull et al., 2002); nevertheless, the presence of their protein products is thought to indicate the initial activation of the genetic machinery of neurons. The protein products of IEGs, such as the *fos*, *jun*, and *egr-1* families, can be detected by immunocytochemical methods. Analysis of IEG protein products in neurons can help identify neuronal circuits involved in hormone-behavior interactions.

Genetic Manipulations

With new advances in molecular biology, it is possible to perform specific genetic manipulations. In behavioral endocrinology research, common genetic manipulations include **transgenic** or **knockout** genetic instructions encoding a hormone or the receptor for a hormone. The genetic instructions for each individual are contained in its DNA, located in the nucleus of nearly every cell. These instructions are encoded in the form of four nucleotides: adenine (A), thymine (T), cytosine (C), and guanine (G). The specific order of these four nucleotides along the "rails" of the twisted, double-helix DNA molecule forms the genetic instructions for all organisms, from those as simple as slime molds to those as complex as mice and humans. Each **gene** represents the complex instructions for the production of a specific protein in the cell. Thus, nucleotide "syntax" is critical in conveying the instructions encoded in the genes. To inactivate, or knock out, a gene, molecular biologists scramble the order of the nucleotides that make up the gene (Aguzzi et al., 1994; Soriano, 1995).

The genome of laboratory mice (*Mus musculus*) has been mapped, and mice are the most commonly used species in targeted gene deletion and gene overexpression studies among vertebrate animals. Knocking out a specific gene in a mouse was an arduous task that relied on several low-probability events that could take months. Since the mapping of the mouse genome, it has become increasingly faster and more reliable to delete or overexpress specific genes. After the gene of interest is identified, targeted, and marked precisely (**FIGURE 1.19**), a mutated form of the gene must be created (i.e., a piece of DNA that contains a marker gene or a genetically engineered, altered copy of the original gene; again, the altered order of the nucleotides renders the gene inactive). Mouse embryonic stem cells are harvested and cultured, and the mutant gene is introduced into the cultured cells by microinjection (Tonegawa, 1995). A very small number of the altered genes will be incorporated into the DNA of the stem cells through recombination (Sedivy and Sharp, 1989). The mutant embryonic stem cells will then be inserted into otherwise normal

transgenic   Relating to an animal in which a gene has been inserted, altered, or deleted.

knockout   An individual, usually a mouse, in which a specific gene has been inactivated.

gene   Discrete region of DNA within a chromosome that when expressed (transcribed), leads to the production of ribonucleic acid (RNA).

FIGURE 1.19 Production of mice in which a specific gene has been deactivated (knocked out) DNA that has been engineered to contain a mutant copy of the gene of interest is introduced into special embryonic stem cells (ES cells) that are growing in tissue culture. Cells with one mutant copy are introduced into an early embryo (blastocyst) that will incorporate these cells into the body of the developing mouse. Because these cells are equipotent, they may become incorporated into different parts of the body. Only if these ES cells are incorporated into the germ line (gametes) can they be used in generating a line of knockout mice (a low-probability event). Mice that are born from this manipulation (and contain one mutant copy in their germ cells) are called chimeras. The chimeric mice are mated to each other. By simple Mendelian genetics, one in four mice from this mating will contain two mutant copies of the gene. The entire process takes 6–12 months to produce a mouse missing both copies of the targeted gene.

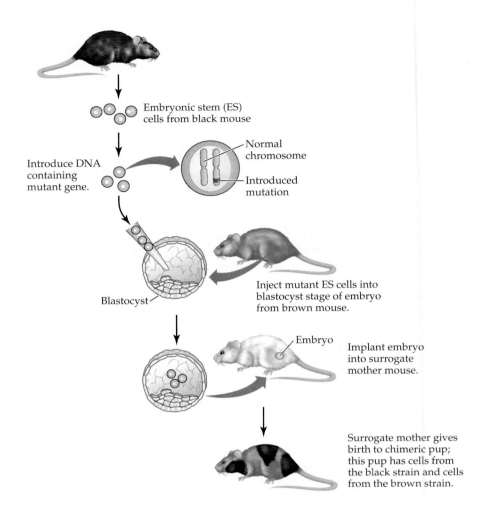

Embryonic stem (ES) cells from black mouse

Introduce DNA containing mutant gene.

Normal chromosome

Introduced mutation

Inject mutant ES cells into blastocyst stage of embryo from brown mouse.

Blastocyst

Embryo

Implant embryo into surrogate mother mouse.

Surrogate mother gives birth to chimeric pup; this pup has cells from the black strain and cells from the brown strain.

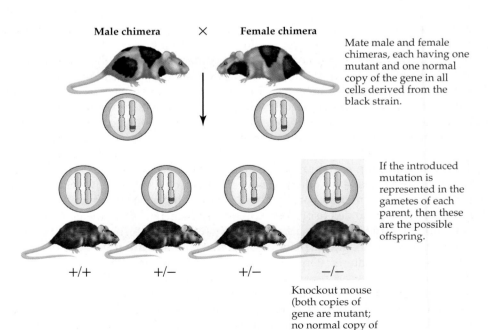

Male chimera ✕ **Female chimera**

Mate male and female chimeras, each having one mutant and one normal copy of the gene in all cells derived from the black strain.

If the introduced mutation is represented in the gametes of each parent, then these are the possible offspring.

+/+   +/–   +/–   –/–

Knockout mouse (both copies of gene are mutant; no normal copy of gene is present).

mouse embryos (blastocysts), which will then be implanted into surrogate mothers (Boggs, 1990; Le Mouellic et al., 1990; Steeghs et al., 1995). All of the cells descended from the mutant stem cells will have the altered gene; the descendants of the original blastocyst cells will have normal genes. Thus, the newborn mice will have some cells that possess a copy of the mutant gene and some cells that possess only the normal (wild-type) gene. This type of animal is called a **chimera**. If the mutant stem cells are incorporated into the germ line (the cells destined to become the sperm and ova), then some of the mouse's gametes will contain one heritable copy of the mutant gene. If the chimeric mice are bred with wild-type mice, then some of the offspring will be heterozygous for the mutation; that is, they will possess one copy of the mutant gene. If the heterozygous mice are interbred, then approximately one-fourth of their offspring will be homozygous for the mutation (i.e., have two copies of the mutation). These homozygous mice can then be interbred to produce pure lines of mice with the gene in question knocked out (Galli-Taliadoros et al., 1995). The product that the gene typically encodes will be missing from their progeny (Sedivy and Sharp, 1989). Behavioral performance can then be compared among wild-type (+/+), heterozygous (+/−), and homozygous (−/−) mice, in which the gene product is produced normally, produced at reduced levels, or completely missing, respectively. The comparison of +/+ and −/− littermates of an F_2 recombinant generation is probably the minimal acceptable control in determining behavioral effects in knockout mice (Morris and Nosten-Bertrand, 1996).

The use of new inducible knockouts, in which the timing and tissue-specific placement of the targeted gene disruption can be controlled, is an extremely important tool in current and future behavioral endocrinology research (Bouabe and Okkenhaug, 2013). Similarly, the use of transgenic animals, in which there is overexpression of specific genes, has become an increasingly common technique in behavioral endocrinology investigations.

GENE SILENCING RNA interference (RNAi) is an endogenous gene regulatory mechanism that inhibits gene expression by impeding either transcription of specific genes or translation of the gene product into a protein. Just 10 years ago, RNAi was of interest only to a small group of scientists working on the roundworm *Caenorhabditis elegans* (Fire et al., 1998). Soon thereafter, RNA silencing was established in mammalian cells (Elbashir et al., 2001). Currently, biomedical research and drug development interest is surging for RNAi, which is used to deplete protein products made in living cells. Common RNAi targets include RNA from viruses, developmental regulation, and genome maintenance. Small interfering RNAs (siRNAs) (aka short interfering RNAs or silencing RNAs) are key to the process of RNA interference. They comprise a class of double-stranded RNA molecules 20–25 nucleotides long. Specific RNAi pathway proteins are chaperoned by siRNA to the targeted mRNA where they break down the molecular target into increasingly small pieces that no longer can encode protein. A related type of RNA is transcribed from the genome itself and is called microRNA (miRNA). The siRNA can be harnessed for behavioral endocrinology research. For example, gene expression for hormone receptors can be temporarily blocked, or it can be blocked during specific epochs during development.

VIRAL AND PLASMID GENE TRANSFECTION Transfection is the process of adding DNA (and sometimes RNA) into cells with the goal of affecting protein expression of the transgene of interest (Alberts et al., 2007). There are two common ways to accomplish this goal: via viruses or plasmid (bacterial) mechanisms. Viruses have evolved mechanisms to transport their genomes and overtake their hosts' cellular replication machinery. Scientists have exploited this ability to deliver genes by creating safe, nontoxic viral vectors (vehicles). Protein-coding genes can be expressed using viral vectors, commonly to study the function of the particular protein. Viral vectors, especially retroviruses, stably expressing marker genes such as green fluo-

chimera An animal whose tissues are composed of two or more genetically distinct cell types; also called a *mosaic*.

rescent protein (GFP) are widely used to permanently label cells to track them and their progeny, for example in xenotransplantation experiments, when cells infected in vitro are implanted into a host animal. Gene insertion studies can be used to silence or overexpress specific genes.

With broad viral approaches, the virus is injected into the brain, and it nonspecifically infects, and alters gene expression in, cells near the site of the injection. If cells serving different functions are in the vicinity of the injection site, it is difficult to tease apart the specific cell populations underlying a particular behavior. To overcome this problem, it has become common to employ Cre recombinase (Cre) mouse driver lines in combination with the Cre-dependent expression of proteins using viral vectors. Cre is an enzyme that triggers the swapping, or recombination, of stretches of DNA in chromosomes and can be inserted into the mouse genome at target gene sites of interest. In this way, only cells expressing Cre can be targeted precisely with inhibitory or stimulatory viral strategies, allowing a determination of not only which genes, but also which cell populations, are involved in behavior.

To transfer genes by nonviral methods, plasmid DNA can be complexed by physicochemical techniques to provoke effective delivery into the cell's nucleus. Plasmids are small circular DNA molecules that naturally occur in bacteria and are used by the bacteria to transfer genetic information nongenomically (i.e., without adjusting the bacteria's own genome). Using gene transfer (aka genetic engineering) methods can change the types of proteins expressed in a cell. For example, behavioral endocrinologists may want to increase or decrease the number of hormone receptors in specific brain cells of interest.

Gene Arrays

gene array Solid support matrix upon which a collection of gene-specific nucleic acids have been placed at defined locations, either by spotting or direct synthesis.

probe A fragment of DNA or RNA of variable length (usually 100–1000 bases long), which is used in DNA or RNA samples to detect the presence of nucleotide sequences (the DNA target) that are complementary to the probe sequence.

target A cell that has specific receptors for, and is affected by, a particular chemical messenger.

Another technology that has become extremely useful in behavioral endocrinology is the DNA **gene array** (although RNA arrays are also used). The gene array technology is a marriage of genomics and computer microprocessor manufacturing. Essentially, a miniscule spot of nucleic acid of known sequence is attached to a glass slide (or occasionally a nylon matrix) in a precise location, often by high-speed robotics. This identified, attached nucleic acid is called the **probe** (Heise and Bier, 2005), whereas the sample nucleic acid is the **target**. The identity of the target is revealed by hybridization, the process by which the nucleotides link to their base pairs (i.e., A–T and G–C for DNA; A–U and G–C for RNA). Hybridization is the underlying principle of gene arrays.

In behavioral endocrinology, gene arrays might be used to determine relative gene expression during the onset of a behavior, or during a change in developmental state, or among individuals that vary in the frequency of a given behavior or hormonal state. For example, mRNA may be extracted from a brain region that is thought to regulate aggressive behavior. In a procedure to see whether specific gene expression differs in this region between intact and castrated rats, the mRNA extracted from the brain tissue would be labeled with fluorescent dyes and added to a cDNA microarray, where it would be available for hybridization to the attached cDNA probes. Because thousands of probe nucleic acids can be added to the array, an experiment with a single microarray can provide researchers information on thousands of genes simultaneously. This is obviously a dramatic increase in throughput as compared with the older molecular biology methods where only one or two genes could be assessed. Any differences in hybridization are indicated by changes in the color of the fluorescence readout. The relative amount of hybridization indicates the relative amount of gene expression in the tissue. Of course, the nucleic acid sequences of interest must be attached to the array to determine changes in gene expression. Also, because the gene array only provides relative information about gene expression, an additional method, such as semiquantitative polymerase chain reaction (PCR), must be conducted.

Electrical Recording, Stimulation, and Optogenetics

The electrical activity of single neurons can be monitored through the use of **single-unit recording**, which involves the placement of very small electrodes in or near individual neurons to record changes in their activity during and immediately after exposure to hormones. This technique can help to uncover the direct effects of various endocrine products on neural activity. Often, several neurons are recorded simultaneously and an average change in activity in multiple units is calculated.

By using **electrical stimulation** to "turn on" specific neurons in a dish or in specific brain centers in a live animal, we can discover the effects of various endocrine treatments on the central nervous system. With this technique, a fine electrode is precisely positioned in the brain, and a weak electric current is used to stimulate neurons. This technique has been used to study the releasing and inhibiting hormones of the hypothalamus (see Chapter 2), but this technique usually affects many neurons, so understanding the precise role of hormones on behavioral systems could be improved by finer resolution electrical stimulation. To date, behavioral neuroendocrinologists have been content with studying correlations between neural activity and behavior, and speculating on causality (i.e., what neural activity is necessary for the functioning of a circuit, how hormones affect this neural activity, and how this neural activity contributes to a behavioral output). The tools available for manipulating neural activity in vivo have been typically either nonspecific like electrical stimulation, which targets all types of neurons and both their anterograde and retrograde connections, or temporally imprecise like pharmacological manipulations, which span minutes or hours. However, a recent technique employing optogenetic methods now allows much better and precise control of neural activities and behavior.

In 1971, Walther Stoeckenius and Dieter Oesterhelt (Oesterhelt and Stoeckenius, 1971) discovered that *Halobacterium halobium* contains a purplish pigment (bacteriorhodopsin) that is chemically similar to rhodopsin and works as a light-driven proton pump. Channelrhodopsin (ChR2), which is homologous to bacteriorhodopsin, was discovered to play a role in phototaxis in green algae by having the characteristics of a light-gated channel selectively permeable for protons (Nagel et al., 2002). By causing ChR2 to be expressed in neurons, it was possible to drive the activity of these neurons by light with millisecond precision (Zhang et al., 2006) (**FIGURE 1.20**).

single-unit recording A technique that involves the placement of very small electrodes in or near one nerve cell to record changes in its neural activity before, during, and after some experimental treatment.

electrical stimulation Activation of nerve cells by electrical current.

FIGURE 1.20 Optogenetics This technique uses light to activate specific light-activated ion gates to activate or inhibit specific neuronal function in awake, freely moving animals. This technique is becoming more commonly used in conjunction with hormonal treatments to understand the precise regulation of hormone-behavior interactions.

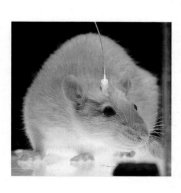
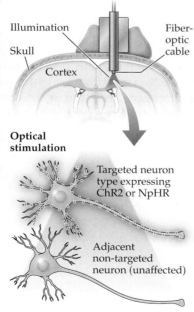
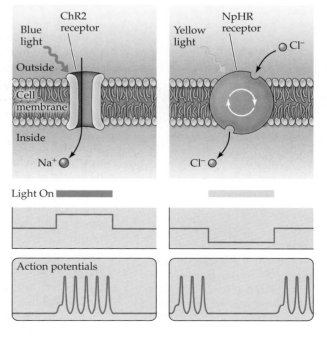

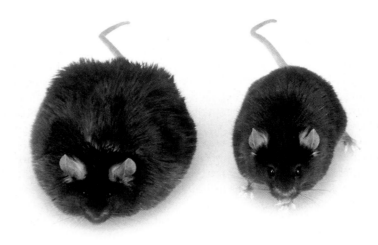

FIGURE 1.21   Effects of leptin on body mass in mice Both of these mice have defective *ob* genes. This mutation typically results in a large increase in food intake and subsequent obesity. The mouse on the right was treated daily with the protein encoded by the *ob* gene, called leptin. It weighs about 35 g. The untreated mouse weighs about 67 g. A mouse with a normal *ob* gene would weigh about 25 g at this age. Courtesy of John Sholtis.

It was soon reported that light-activated proton pumps could be used to inhibit neural activity by using other light-driven proton pumps such as halorhodopsin and archaerhodopsin (Arch) (Chow et al., 2010). With the use of the appropriate viruses and promoters, specific cell types with specific anatomical connections have be targeted in many different brain systems, revealing the functioning of many different neural circuits for the first time. Increasingly, the use of hormones in conjunction with optogenetics is revealing precise regulation of hormone-behavior interactions.

A Case Study: Effects of Leptin on Behavior

About a decade ago, a new hormone was discovered that is released from **adipose** (fat) cells. This hormone was named **leptin**, a term derived from the Greek word *leptos*, which means "thin." Studies of the behavioral effects of leptin will be used here to demonstrate how the various techniques described above are used to understand the biological functions of hormones.

For many years, specific mutations in mice have been recognized that cause extreme obesity in animals that are homozygous for the defective gene, known as *ob*. These animals may be considered natural knockouts for the *ob* gene. Two mutant strains that have been commonly used in studies of body mass regulation are the so-called *ob/ob* mice and *db/db* (diabetic) mice. The *ob/ob* mice have a pair of defective *ob* genes and are hyperphagic (they overeat), obese, and reproductively sterile (**FIGURE 1.21**). The normally functioning *ob* gene codes for the hormone leptin; leptin is released by adipose cells into the bloodstream, where it travels to specific protein receptors in the central nervous system and elsewhere to regulate feeding and energy balance. The *db* gene encodes a leptin receptor; mice that are homozygous for a mutation in this gene are diabetic. Since its identification in 1994 (Zhang et al., 1994), many of the techniques described in the previous sections have been used to understand the behavioral functions of leptin.

For years, the effects of the *ob/ob* mutation on the ability to maintain normal body mass in mice have been known. However, research into the mechanisms underlying this mutation began in earnest only with the identification and sequencing of the *ob* protein (i.e., leptin) (Zhang et al., 1994). Thus, researchers had available a so-called experiment of nature in which leptin was depleted (knocked out), and they could determine the behavioral effects that resulted from a lack of leptin. The leptin gene was cloned, and a copy of the gene was inserted into a bacterial system; purified leptin was thus made available to researchers. With this purified leptin, a "replacement study" was conducted in which leptin was provided to *ob/ob* mice to determine whether replacing their missing leptin would ameliorate their hyperphagia, energy impairments, and obesity. It did.

The availability of purified leptin also allowed researchers to produce specific antibodies to this substance that could be used in developing assays to determine blood

adipose   Connective tissue in which fat is stored.

leptin   A protein hormone secreted by fat cells that may communicate information to the brain about body fat content.

concentrations of leptin (e.g., Cohen et al., 1996). An RIA was developed to determine the blood plasma leptin concentrations of obese and diabetic humans to see whether leptin was implicated in human obesity or diabetes (McGregor et al., 1996); in this study, no connection was found. A leptin ELISA was developed for rats and mice, which was used to determine that fasting or exposure to low temperatures caused circulating leptin concentrations to fall (Hardie et al., 1996). Immunocytochemical localization techniques revealed that leptin was present in both white and brown adipose tissue (Cinti et al., 1997) as well as other peripheral tissues.

Injections of leptin into the third or lateral ventricles in the brains of mice were found to reduce food intake (Campfield et al., 1995). To determine the site of action of leptin in the brain, purified leptin was labeled with a radioactive tag and injected into mice. With the use of autoradiography, dense, specific binding of the tagged leptin was found in the choroid plexus, a brain structure located in the dorsal part of the third ventricle, as well as in the lateral ventricles (Lynn et al., 1996). This tissue was then used to clone a leptin receptor (Tartaglia et al., 1995). In situ hybridization showed that the mRNA for the leptin receptor was expressed in several brain regions, including the hypothalamus (Mercer et al., 1996; Zamorano et al., 1997).

In an effort to "cure" obesity, gene replacement therapy was attempted in mice and rats (Chen et al., 1996; Muzzin et al., 1996). The logic behind this effort was that mice deficient in the *ob* gene were obese because of a deficiency of leptin. If the leptin or the *ob* gene were replaced, then the individual should display normal food intake and body mass. When *ob/ob* mice were treated with a transgenic adenovirus expressing the mouse leptin gene, there was a dramatic reduction in both food intake and body mass (Muzzin et al., 1996). Similar findings were reported for rats (Chen et al., 1996). In addition to being obese, *ob/ob* mice are sterile; treatment of *ob/ob* mice with recombinant leptin reverses the sterility (Chehab et al., 1996; Mounzih et al., 1997).

These exciting findings suggested the possibility of treating obese humans with gene therapy. However, leptin appears to have significant weight-reducing properties only in rodents. Despite screening of thousands of obese humans, researchers have found only eight individuals in two families who display a mutation in the leptin gene (Montague et al., 1997; Strobel et al., 1998) (i.e., they are like the *ob/ob* mice) and three members of a single family who are homozygous for mutations in their leptin receptor gene (Clément et al., 1998) (i.e., they are like the *db/db* mice). Only moderate obesity is observed among people who are heterozygous (one normal and one mutant copy) for their leptin genes (Farooqi et al., 2001). The effects of leptin treatment on human obesity have been equivocal. One of the best outcomes resulted from treatment of a 3-year-old boy who was homozygous for a frameshift mutation in his leptin genes; he was given daily injections of recombinant leptin for 4 years. Leptin treatment reduced his body mass from 42 kg (92.6 pounds) to 32 kg (70.5 pounds) at age 7 (Farooqi and O'Rahilly, 2005) (**FIGURE 1.22A**). Leptin injections dramatically reduced the appetite and food intake of children with leptin deficiencies (**FIGURE 1.22B**). Because leptin is a novel protein for these individuals, their immune systems soon develop

(A)

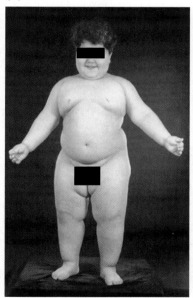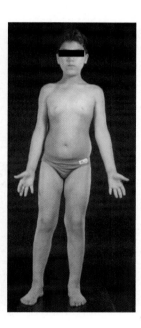

(B)

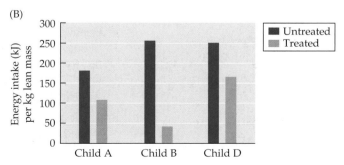

FIGURE 1.22 Effects of leptin on body mass and behavior in humans (A) A 3-year-old boy lacking leptin weighed 42 kg. After 4 years of leptin treatment, his weight was 32 kg. (B) The effects of leptin treatment on food intake among individuals who lacked the gene for leptin. From Farooqi and O'Rahilly, 2005.

antibodies against the hormone, and increased doses are necessary to overcome the immune responses. Treatment of obese individuals with normal leptin genes resulted in moderate body mass loss (−7.1 kg vs. −1.3 kg for the placebo group). Because obese people tend to have higher levels of leptin than lean people, it was proposed that obese individuals are "resistant" to leptin.

Leptin circulates in concentrations that are proportional to the total amount of fat in the body. When stored fat is being used for energy, the blood levels of leptin fall faster than the levels of fat being metabolized; this rapid reduction in circulating leptin suggests that this hormone is more likely a "starvation" signal that stimulates food intake when leptin levels fall, rather than a satiety hormone that curtails food intake when body fat levels and leptin levels increase (Flier, 1998). Consistent with the notion that leptin is an unlikely satiety protein, years of research show that leptin treatments are unsuccessful in reversing human obesity, except in the very rare cases of congenital leptin deficiency described previously (Dardeno et al., 2010). Although leptin has been identified for only about 15 years, much has been learned about this hormone. However, additional research is required to sort out the role of leptin in human and nonhuman energy balance. Also, it is important to discover whether nonmammals have leptin. Thus far, the search for a leptin gene in chickens, for example, has been unsuccessful (Sharp et al., 2008).

Taken together, all of these techniques are useful in elucidating hormone-behavior relationships; later in the book, other specific techniques will be introduced as we examine the details of specific hormone-behavior interactions. Many of the fruits of these techniques will be presented in Chapter 2, in the context of a general introduction to endocrine anatomy, chemistry, and physiology.

Summary

1. Behavioral endocrinology is the study of the interaction between hormones and behavior. This interaction is bidirectional: hormones can affect behavior, and behavior can influence hormone concentrations.

2. Hormones are chemical messengers released from endocrine glands. The endocrine system and the nervous system work together to regulate the physiology and behavior of individuals.

3. Hormones induce changes in the rate of cellular function and affect behavior by increasing the probability that a particular behavior will occur in the presence of a particular stimulus. Hormones can influence behavior by affecting an animal's sensory systems, integrators, and/or effectors. Peripheral structures can also be affected by hormones, and these effects can themselves influence behavior.

4. Behavior is generally thought of as involving movement, but nearly any type of output can be considered behavior. A complete description of behavior is required before researchers can address questions of its causation. All behavioral biologists study a specific version of the general question "What causes animal A to emit behavior X?"

5. The four interacting levels of analysis that can be used for exploring and explaining the causes of behavior are immediate causation, development, evolution, and adaptive function.

6. Three types of evidence are necessary to establish a causal link between hormones and behavior: (1) a behavior that depends on a particular hormone should diminish when the source of or actions of the hormone are removed; (2) the behavior should reappear when the hormone is reintroduced; and (3) hormone levels and the behavior in question should be covariant.

7. Several techniques have been useful in advancing research in behavioral endocrinology: ablation-replacement; bioassays; modern assays that utilize the concept of competitive binding of antibodies; autoradiography; immunocytochemistry; electrical stimulation and single-unit recording; pharmacological methods; methods that make use of cannulation, including gene arrays; and genetic manipulations.

Questions for Discussion

1. A researcher has found a new hormone that causes marked increases in learning ability when administered to rats. She is interested in determining where and how this hormone acts in the brain. How might she apply the techniques discussed in this chapter to uncover the neural loci and circuit on which the hormone acts? How might she then establish a cause-effect relationship between the hormone acting on this circuit and improvement in learning?

2. An experimenter is interested in the effect of a particular hormone on aggressive behavior in butterflies. It is hypothesized that butterflies fight because of high levels of this hormone. An alternative hypothesis is that the butterflies that fight to guard territories and potential mates produce more offspring in subsequent generations. If the results of an experiment rule out the hypothesis that the hormone is required for aggressive behavior, does that necessarily mean that the alternative hypothesis is true? Why or why not?

3. Hormones cause changes in the rates of cellular processes or in cellular morphology. Suggest some ways that these hormonally induced cellular changes might theoretically produce profound changes in behavior.

4. In recent years, investigations of hormone-behavior relationships have involved increasingly elaborate and precise methodology for identifying and locating hormones and their receptors. Discuss the proposition that comparable increases in sophistication, quantification, and so forth are needed on the side of behavior. Give examples of desirable and undesirable approaches.

5. In lesion studies or studies of animals with specific genes deleted, the behavioral tests study the effects of the missing brain region or the missing gene, respectively. Discuss how these conceptual shortcomings can be overcome in evaluating the results of studies using these types of procedures.

Suggested Readings

Adkins-Regan, E. 2005. *Hormones and Animal Social Behavior*. Princeton University Press, Princeton, NJ.

Beach, F. A. 1948. *Hormones and Behavior*. Paul B. Hoeber, New York.

Beach, F. A. 1975. Behavioral endocrinology: An emerging discipline. *Am. Sci.*, 63:178–187.

Fink, G., Pfaff, D. W., and Levine, J. (eds.). 2011. *Handbook of Neuroendocrinology*. Elsevier, New York.

Pfaff, D. W., and Joels, M. (eds.) 2017. *Hormones, Brain, and Behavior* (3rd ed.). Academic Press, New York.

Tinbergen, N. 1951. *The Study of Instinct*. Oxford University Press, Oxford.

Wilkinson, M., and Brown, R. E. 2015. *An Introduction to Neuroendocrinology*. Cambridge University Press, New York.

The Endocrine System

2

Learning Objectives

This chapter describes the major endocrine glands, as well as the major hormones produced by vertebrate animals. Hormone regulation and the mechanisms of hormonal action are also described. By the end of this chapter you will have read about the general aspects of the endocrine system, and you should be able to:

- identify the major endocrine glands and their hormones, and answer three general questions: Where do hormones come from, where do hormones go, and what do hormones do?

- describe negative and positive feedback effects of hormonal regulation.

- describe the different mechanisms of actions for the various types of hormones, including steroid, protein/peptide, monoaminergic, and lipid-based hormones.

- understand that the evolution of hormones reflects more of an evolution in uses rather than structures.

In order to understand the interaction between hormones and behavior, a basic understanding of the endocrine system is essential. A comprehensive review of endocrinology is both beyond the scope of this book and unnecessary to understand hormone-behavior interactions conceptually. But a basic working knowledge of the general principles of endocrinology, the hormones found in animals, and the organs that produce hormones will help you in reading the discussions that follow. The goals of this chapter are to provide a solid general background in endocrinology for students who are unfamiliar with this topic, to provide a basic review for students who have previously studied endocrinology, and to serve all readers as a general reference resource to aid in understanding the specific material in the following chapters. The major vertebrate endocrine organs involved in behavior and

Intracrine mediation

Intracrine substances regulate intracellular events.

Autocrine mediation

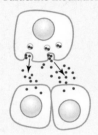

Autocrine substances feed back to influence the same cells that secreted them.

Paracrine mediation

Paracrine cells secrete chemicals that affect adjacent cells.

Endocrine mediation

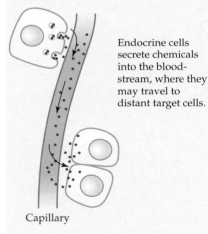

Endocrine cells secrete chemicals into the bloodstream, where they may travel to distant target cells.

Capillary

Ectocrine mediation

Ectocrine substances, such as pheromones, are released into the environment by individuals to communicate with others.

their various hormone products are described here, and this chapter is consequently rather densely packed with information. However, the individual hormones, their sources, and their physiological actions are also listed in tables in the inside covers of the book for easy reference and review. Hormones that have well-established effects on behavior and that will be featured prominently throughout the book include the steroid hormones (androgens, estrogens, progestins, mineralocorticoids, and glucocorticoids), the peptide hormones (e.g., prolactin), the gonadotropins (luteinizing hormone and follicle-stimulating hormone), oxytocin, vasopressin, and hypothalamic releasing hormones (gonadotropin-releasing hormone and corticotropin-releasing hormone).

The bulk of this chapter is devoted to providing specific answers to three questions, namely: Where do hormones come from, where do hormones go, and what do hormones do?" The general answers to these questions are straightforward: Hormones are produced by glands and secreted into the blood. They travel in the blood to target tissues containing specific receptors for the hormones. By interacting with their receptors, hormones initiate biochemical events that may directly or indirectly activate genes to induce certain biological responses. In some cases, hormone-receptor interactions result in nongenomic effects on cellular function by acting on receptors outside of the cell. Because they are relatively fast, the so-called nongenomic effects of hormones are being intensively studied in their role in mediating behavior, although *nongenomic* is likely a misnomer, as genes are certainly involved. In other cases, hormones bind to intracellular receptors to form complexes that alter gene transcription, so-called genomic actions. In the first section of this chapter, the general principles of endocrine and neuroendocrine physiology are reviewed. Next, a detailed description of the major endocrine and neuroendocrine glands and their locations, hormones, and physiological effects, are presented. This is followed by a discussion of the ways that hormones are regulated and their mechanisms of action. The final section discusses the evolution of hormones.

Chemical Communication

The endocrine system is only one example of chemical communication, a ubiquitous feature of life on Earth. All levels of biological organization make use of some form of chemical messages, ranging from those used to mediate intracellular processes to the substances used in communication between organs, individuals, and even populations. In all these cases, information is communicated by the release of chemical agents and their detection by receptor activation.

This chemical mediation within and between cells, as well as between individuals and populations, is conducted by several interacting physiological systems. A key component of these interacting systems is the endocrine system; however, there are other systems of chemical mediation (**FIGURE 2.1**). For example, chemical mediation of intracellular events is called **intracrine** mediation. Some intracrine mediators may have changed their function over the course of evolution and now serve as hormones or pheromones (Bern, 1990). **Autocrine** cells secrete products that may feed back to affect processes in the cells that originally produced them. For example, steroid hormone–producing cells possess receptors for their own secreted products (O'Malley, 1995). Chemical mediators released by one cell that induce a biological response in an adjacent cell are called **paracrine**

FIGURE 2.1   Systems of chemical mediation and communication Chemical mediation occurs at all levels of biological organization, ranging from the intracrine mediation of intracellular processes to ectocrine communication, which takes place between individual animals or populations of animals.

TABLE 2.1   *Chemical communication terminology*

Chemical messenger	Any substance that is produced by a cell that affects the function of another cell
Cytokine	A chemical messenger that evokes proliferation of other cells, especially in the immune system
Hormone	A chemical messenger that is released into the blood-stream or tissue fluid system that affects the function of target cells some distance from the source
Neurohormone	A hormone produced by a neuron
Neuromodulator	A hormone that changes (modulates) the response of a neuron to some other factors
Neuropeptide	A peptide hormone produced by a neuron
Neurosteroid	A steroid hormone produced by a neuron
Neurotransmitter	A chemical messenger that acts across the neural synapse

Source: After Hadley and Levine, 2006.

agents; neurons are well-known paracrine cells. Another example of paracrine processes is found during embryonic development, when cells may release chemicals that induce or influence tissue differentiation in neighboring cells. **Ectocrine** substances are released from an individual to the outside world and induce a biological response in another animal; pheromones are examples of ectocrine agents.

Many of these chemical communication systems have been studied independently by separate groups of scientific specialists (**TABLE 2.1**). For example, neuroscientists focus their studies on the chemical communication within the nervous system (i.e., neurotransmitters), endocrinologists study the chemical communication processes within the endocrine system (i.e., hormones), and immunologists focus their attention on the chemical communication within the immune system (i.e., cytokines). Although historically these three scientific disciplines have operated mostly independently of one another, it is becoming increasingly obvious that the chemical mediators from the nervous, endocrine, and immune systems interact significantly. For example, many immune system cells have receptors for neurotransmitters, hormones, and cytokines. Similarly, many neurons have receptors for hormones and cytokines, as well as neurotransmitters. Furthermore, the structural features of receptors and the cellular and molecular mechanisms involved in signal transduction, signal amplification, and gene transcription among the nervous, endocrine, and immune systems are very similar. In common with all scientific efforts, biologists tend to divide nature into small domains to help them manage and understand the complexities of interacting systems. However, biology is exceedingly complex and often defies these artificial boundaries. Thus, the hormone-behavior interactions that are the main focus of this book will also involve neuron-hormone-behavior interactions, as well as immune system–hormone-behavior interactions. The separate categories of neurotransmitters, hormones, and cytokines reflect divisions within the field of biology, but they all too often mask the integrative nature of various chemical messengers. In a few cases, the anatomical locations of their interactions have been identified; however, in most cases, the site(s) or mechanism(s) of integration among the nervous, endocrine, and immune systems remain to be specified.

General Features of the Endocrine System

The word *endocrine* is derived from the Greek root words *endon*, meaning "within," and *krinein*, meaning "to release," whereas the term *hormone* is based on the Greek

intracrine   Peptide hormones or growth factors that bind and act inside cells either after internalization by the cells or retention in their cells of synthesis.

autocrine   Pertaining to a signal secreted by a cell into the environment that affects the transmitting cell.

paracrine   A form of cellular communication in which a cell releases a product that induces changes in a nearby cell.

ectocrine   A parahormonal chemical substance that is secreted (usually by an invertebrate organism) into its immediate environment (air or water) which alters physiology or behavior of the recipient individual.

endocrinology The scientific study of the endocrine glands and their hormones.

neurohormone A hormone that is released into the blood from a neuron rather than from an endocrine gland.

neurosecretory cell A cell in the central nervous system that secretes its product beyond the synapse to affect function in other cells.

neuroendocrinology The scientific study of the interaction between the nervous system and the endocrine system.

endocrine gland A ductless gland from which hormones are released into the blood system in response to specific physiological signals.

exocrine gland A gland that has a duct through which its product is secreted into adjacent organs or the environment.

vesicle A secretory granule or sac within a cell in which hormone or neurotransmitter molecules are stored.

exocytosis The extrusion or secretion of substances from a cell by the fusion of a vesicle membrane with the cell membrane.

word *hormon*, meaning "to excite" or "to set into motion."[1] **Endocrinology** is the scientific study of the endocrine glands and their associated hormones. As we will see, in some cases, a special type of hormone, called a **neurohormone**, is released into the blood by a type of neuron called a **neurosecretory cell**, rather than by a gland. **Neuroendocrinology** is the scientific study of this transduction of a neural signal into a hormonal signal, as well as other types of relations between the nervous and endocrine systems, and will be discussed later in this chapter.

Although exceptions always exist, the endocrine system has several general features:

1. Endocrine glands are ductless.
2. Endocrine glands have a rich blood supply.
3. Hormones, the products of endocrine glands, are secreted into the bloodstream.
4. Hormones can travel in the blood to virtually every cell in the body and can thus potentially interact with any cell that has appropriate receptors.
5. Hormone receptors are specific binding sites, embedded in the cell membrane or located elsewhere in the cell, that interact with a particular hormone or class of hormones.

The products of **endocrine glands** are secreted directly into the blood (**FIGURE 2.2A**). Some glands in the body, known as **exocrine glands**, have ducts, or tubes into which their products are released into the internal or external environment. The salivary, sweat, and mammary glands are well-known examples of exocrine glands (**FIGURE 2.2B**). Some glands in the body have both endocrine and exocrine structures. The pancreas, for example, contains exocrine cells that secrete digestive juices into the intestines via ducts, whereas the endocrine compartment of the pancreas secretes hormones, such as insulin, directly into the bloodstream, where they travel throughout the body to regulate energy utilization and storage. Recently, the definition of an endocrine gland has had to be reconsidered. For example, adipose (fat) tissue produces the hormone leptin, and the stomach produces a hormone called ghrelin. Probably the most active endocrine organ, and the one that produces the most diverse types of hormones, is the brain.

Some endocrine glands, such as the thyroid gland, are among the most highly vascularized organs in the body. As noted above, hormones are released into the bloodstream, and in many instances, the agents that regulate the endocrine glands themselves are transported to the glands via the circulatory system. The large supply of blood speeds the transport of hormones to their target sites. Although many endocrine glands are devoid of direct neural connections, in some cases neural control of vascular flow rates can indirectly influence endocrine activity. In other cases (e.g., adrenaline and insulin), hormone secretion may be regulated by autonomic neural control.

Recall from Chapter 1 that hormones are organic chemical messengers produced and released by endocrine glands. Some hormones are water-soluble proteins or small peptides that are stored in the endocrine cells in secretory granules, or **vesicles**, each of which contains many hormone molecules suspended in a protein matrix. In response to a specific stimulus for secretion, each secretory vesicle fuses its membrane with the cellular membrane, an opening develops, and the hormones diffuse into the extracellular space. This process of extrusion is called **exocytosis**. The expelled hormones then enter the bloodstream from the extracellular space (see Figure 2.2A).

---

[1] This derivation should not be taken too literally, because as we will see, hormones may have inhibitory effects as well as stimulatory ones.

(A) Endocrine cells

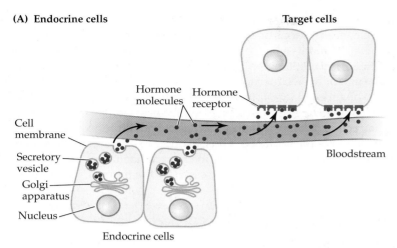

Target cells

Hormone molecules
Hormone receptor

Cell membrane

Secretory vesicle

Golgi apparatus

Nucleus

Endocrine cells

Bloodstream

(B) Exocrine cells

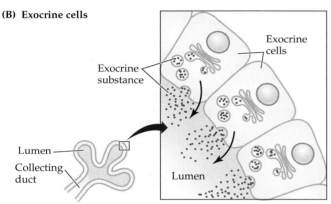

Exocrine cells

Exocrine substance

Lumen

Collecting duct

Lumen

FIGURE 2.2 A comparison of endocrine and exocrine cells (A) As noted in Chapter 1, hormones are secreted by endocrine cells into the bloodstream, where they may travel to distant target organs. (B) In contrast, exocrine cells, such as those found in the salivary, sweat, and mammary glands (and in parts of the pancreas), secrete their products into ducts that carry them to adjacent target organs or the external environment.

Other hormones, such as steroid hormones, are lipid-soluble (i.e., fat-soluble), and because they can move easily through the cell's phospholipid membrane, they are not stored in the endocrine cells. Instead, a signal to an endocrine cell to produce steroid hormones also serves as a signal to release them into the blood as soon as the cellular machinery produces them. It should be noted that the common precursor molecule of all steroids, cholesterol, can be stored in lipid droplets within cells.

All cells in the body, except those in the lenses of the eyes, have a direct blood supply. Thus, the circulatory system provides direct access to virtually every cell, and hormones can potentially interact with any cell that has appropriate receptors. Protein and peptide hormones are soluble in blood, an aqueous (watery) solution. In contrast, steroids are not very water-soluble and often form a reversible bond with a **carrier protein** while circulating in the blood. These carrier molecules have recently been discovered to serve important regulatory roles in the mediation of steroid hormone actions.

Hormone receptors, which are either embedded in the target cell membrane or located elsewhere within the cell, interact with particular hormones or classes of hormones. The receptor is analogous to a lock, and the hormone acts as a key to the lock. Receptor proteins bind to hormones with high affinity and generally high specificity. As a result of the high affinity of hormone receptors, hormones can be very potent in their effects, despite the fact that they are found in very dilute concentrations in the blood (some as low as one-millionth of a milligram [1 picogram] per milliliter of blood plasma). However, when the blood concentration of a hormone is high, binding with receptors that are specific for other, related hormones can occur in sufficient numbers to cause a biological response (i.e., cross-reaction).

carrier protein One of several different plasma proteins that bind to hormones of low solubility (primarily thyroid and steroid hormones), providing a transport system for them.

hypothalamus   A part of the diencephalon located just below the thalamus that is important in the regulation of autonomic and endocrine functions.

pituitary gland   An endocrine gland that sits below the hypothalamus and has two distinct anatomical components, the anterior pituitary and the posterior pituitary, each derived from different embryological origins and having different functional roles in the endocrine system.

When sufficient receptors are not available because of a clinical condition, or because previously high concentrations of a hormone have occupied all the receptors and new ones have yet to be made, a biological response may not be sustained. Such a reduction in the numbers of available receptors may lead to a so-called endocrine deficiency despite normal or even supernormal levels of circulating hormones. For example, a deficiency of androgen receptors can prevent the development of male traits despite normal circulating testosterone concentrations. Conversely, elevated receptor numbers may produce clinical manifestations of endocrine excess despite a normal blood concentration of the hormone. Thus, in order to understand hormone-behavior interactions, it is sometimes necessary to characterize target tissue sensitivity (i.e., the number and type of receptors possessed by the tissue in question) in addition to measuring hormone concentrations.

The Major Vertebrate Endocrine Glands and Their Hormones

The locations of the major endocrine organs in humans are depicted in **FIGURE 2.3**. Because the modern anatomical names for the endocrine glands typically originated from Greek or Latin terms that early anatomists used to describe the shape, location, or, occasionally, function of a structure, the derivations for many of these names are provided as an aid to remembering and understanding the terms.

The **hypothalamus** is located directly beneath the thalamus (*hypo*, "below") at the base of the brain. The **pituitary gland** is located at the base of the skull in a bony de-

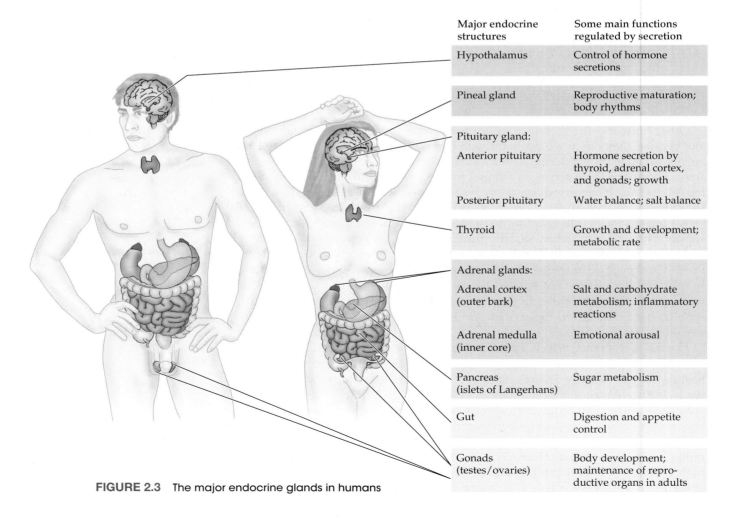

Major endocrine structures	Some main functions regulated by secretion
Hypothalamus	Control of hormone secretions
Pineal gland	Reproductive maturation; body rhythms
Pituitary gland:	
Anterior pituitary	Hormone secretion by thyroid, adrenal cortex, and gonads; growth
Posterior pituitary	Water balance; salt balance
Thyroid	Growth and development; metabolic rate
Adrenal glands:	
Adrenal cortex (outer bark)	Salt and carbohydrate metabolism; inflammatory reactions
Adrenal medulla (inner core)	Emotional arousal
Pancreas (islets of Langerhans)	Sugar metabolism
Gut	Digestion and appetite control
Gonads (testes/ovaries)	Body development; maintenance of reproductive organs in adults

FIGURE 2.3   The major endocrine glands in humans

pression called the sella tursica (*sella*, "saddle"; *tursica*, "Turkish") and is connected to the base of the hypothalamus near the median eminence by a funnel-shaped stalk called the infundibulum ("funnel") or pituitary stalk. The **thyroid gland** is an H-shaped organ located on the upper trachea. The **pancreas** resides within the curve of the duodenum (small intestine), behind the stomach and liver. The endocrine tissues of the gastrointestinal tract are somewhat primitively organized; small clumps of endocrine cells are scattered throughout the gut, rather than concentrated into a glandular organ. The **adrenal glands** are bilateral organs that are situated on top of the kidneys (*ad*, "toward"; *renes*, "kidneys"). The **pineal gland**, also called the epiphysis (*epi*, "over"; *physis*, "brain"), is located in the brain in mammals, between the telencephalon and diencephalon. The **gonads** are the reproductive organs. In sexually reproducing animals, there are two types of gonads: males have **testes**, often located in a sac outside the abdomen called the scrotum; females have **ovaries**, located in the abdomen. A temporary endocrine organ, the **placenta**, forms in the uterus of female mammals during pregnancy.

This section is organized with descriptions of each endocrine gland and their associated products arranged by the four classes of hormones: (1) protein and peptide hormones, (2) steroid hormones, (3) monoamines, and (4) lipid-based hormones. Generally, only one class of hormone is produced by a single endocrine gland, but there are some notable exceptions, as we will see later in this chapter. It is important and useful to discriminate among the four types of hormones because they differ in several important characteristics, including their mode of release, how they move through the blood, the location of their target cells' receptors, and the manner by which the interaction of the hormone with its receptor results in a biological response. Again, all of the hormones discussed here, as well as the glands from which they originate and their primary physiological function(s), are summarized in the tables printed on the inside covers of the book.

Protein and Peptide Hormones

Most vertebrate hormones are proteins. Protein hormones, in common with other protein molecules, are made up of individual amino acid building blocks. Protein hormones that are only a few amino acids in length are called **peptide hormones**, whereas larger ones are called **protein hormones** or polypeptide hormones (**FIGURE 2.4**). Protein and peptide hormones include insulin, the glucagons, the neurohormones of the hypothalamus, the tropic hormones of the anterior pituitary, inhibin, calcitonin, parathyroid hormone, the gastrointestinal hormones, ghrelin, leptin, adiponectin, and the posterior pituitary hormones.

Protein and peptide hormones can be stored in endocrine cells and are released into the circulatory system by means of exocytosis (see Figure 2.2A). They are soluble in blood and therefore do not require carrier proteins to travel to their target cells, as do steroid hor-

thyroid gland A double-lobed endocrine gland located on or near the trachea or esophagus in vertebrates that secretes several hormones important in metabolism, including triiodothyronine and thyroxine.

pancreas A composite vertebrate gland with both endocrine and exocrine functions.

adrenal glands Paired, dual-compartment endocrine glands in vertebrates consisting of a medulla and a cortex.

pineal gland An endocrine gland (also called the *epiphysis*), located in mammals between the telencephalon and diencephalon, that secretes melatonin, a hormone important in the regulation of daily and seasonal cycles.

gonad An endocrine organ that produces sex steroids and gametes; the ovaries and testes are gonads.

testes The male gonads, which produce steroid hormones and sperm.

ovaries The female gonads, which produce estrogen, progestin, and ova.

placenta A specialized organ produced by the mammalian embryo that is attached to the uterine wall and serves to provide nutrients, hormones, and energy to the fetus.

peptide hormones A class of hormones consisting of a relatively short chain of amino acids residues.

protein hormones A class of hormones consisting of a long chain of amino acid residues.

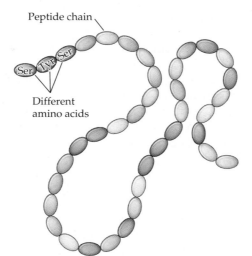

Peptide chain

Ser Tyr Ser

Different amino acids

FIGURE 2.4 Amino acids form chains that make up peptides and proteins Peptides are small chains of amino acids, whereas proteins are larger structures. Although no specific convention is agreed upon, generally chains greater than 50 amino acids are considered proteins.

FIGURE 2.5 **The hypothalamus** is located at the base of the brain (inset) and consists of several collections of neuronal cell bodies called nuclei. The hypothalamic nuclei integrate neural information from higher brain sites and coordinate numerous physiological processes by means of specialized neurosecretory cells that produce and secrete neurohormones into the pituitary gland. This schematic rendering of the hypothalamus is a composite based on anatomical studies of rodents and humans.

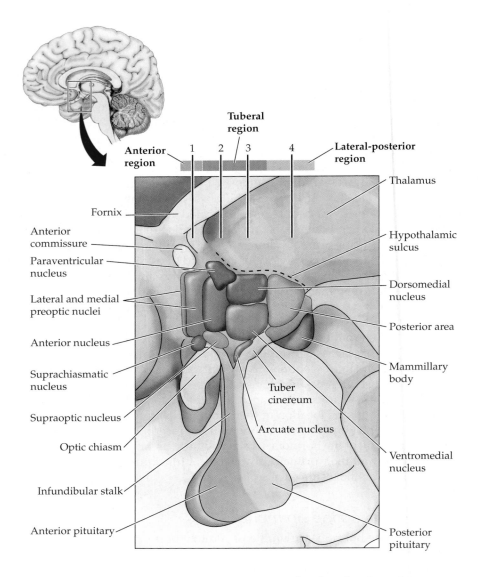

biological half-life The amount of time required to remove half of a hormone or other substance from the blood.

nuclei A collection of nerve cell bodies in the brain.

neurosecretory cells Cells in the central nervous system that secrete their products beyond the synapse to affect function in other cells.

mones. However, protein and peptide hormones may bind with other plasma proteins, which will slow their metabolism by peptidases (enzymes that break down peptides) in the blood. Hormones are removed from the blood via degradation or excretion. The metabolism of a hormone is reported in terms of its **biological half-life**, which is the amount of time required to remove half of the hormone from the blood (measured by radioactive tagging). Generally, larger protein hormones have longer half-lives than smaller peptide hormones (e.g., growth hormone has 200 amino acids and a biological half-life of 20–30 minutes, whereas thyrotropin-releasing hormone has 3 amino acids and a biological half-life of less than 5 minutes in humans) (Norris, 2007).

In several cases, a single hormone (especially peptides) can have autocrine, paracrine, and endocrine functions. For example, leptin is produced in adipose tissue, and when released into the blood, it functions as a hormone, by regulating energy balance at the level of the hypothalamus (endocrine). However, leptin is also produced in the anterior pituitary gland, where it diffuses locally to influence thyroid-stimulating hormone (TSH) secretion (paracrine). Finally, leptin stimulates expression of itself and its receptor (autocrine) (Chen et al., 2006). Many chemical messengers display similar diversity in function.

HYPOTHALAMIC HORMONES The hypothalamus comprises several collections of neuronal cell bodies, or **nuclei**, at the base of the brain (**FIGURE 2.5**). The hypothalamus is a part of the brain and receives information via axons that form tracts,

TRH

pGlu–His–Pro–NH$_2$

GnRH

1   10
pGlu–His–Trp–Ser–Tyr–Gly–Leu–Arg–Pro–Gly–NH$_2$

Somatostatin

1   14
Ala–Gly–Cys–Lys–Asn–Phe–Phe–Trp–Lys–Thr–Phe–Thr–Ser–Cys

CRH

1   10
Ser–Gln–Glu–Pro–Pro–Ile–Ser–Leu–Asp–Leu–Thr–Phe–His–Leu–Leu–Arg–Glu–Val–Leu–
20   30
Glu–Met–Thr–Lys–Ala–Asp–Gln–Leu–Ala–Gln–Gln–Ala–His–Ser–Asn–Arg–Lys–Leu–Leu–
    40 41
Asp–Ile–Ala–NH$_2$

GHRH

1   10   20
Tyr–Ala–Asp–Ala–Ile–Phe–Thr–Asn–Ser–Tyr–Arg–Lys–Val–Leu–Gly–Gln–Leu–Ser–Ala–Arg–
                                        30
Lys–Leu–Leu–Gln–Asp–Ile–Met–Ser–Arg–Gln–Gln–Gly–Glu–Ser–Asn–Gln–Glu–Arg–Gly–
40   44
Ala–Arg–Ala–Arg–Leu–NH$_2$

FIGURE 2.6 Known amino acid sequences for some releasing hormones The sequences of TRH, GnRH, somatostatin (GHIH), CRH, and GHRH have been characterized. Melanotropin inhibitory hormone (MIH) and prolactin inhibitory hormone (PIH) both appear to be dopamine. Pyroglutamyl is denoted by pGLU; NH$_2$ denotes amide of the C-terminal amino acid.

thyrotropin-releasing hormone (TRH) A tripeptide hormone secreted by the hypothalamus that stimulates the release of thyroid-stimulating hormone (TSH) (thyrotropin) from the anterior pituitary gland.

growth hormone–releasing hormone (GHRH) Also called *somatocrinin*. A polypeptide hormone that is released from the arcuate nucleus of the hypothalamus that provokes the secretion of growth hormone from the anterior pituitary gland.

gonadotropin-releasing hormone (GnRH) A decapeptide hormone from the hypothalamus that regulates FSH and LH release from the anterior pituitary.

melanotropin-releasing hormone (MRH) A hexapeptide that stimulates the secretion of melanotropin.

corticotropin-releasing hormone (CRH) A peptide hormone secreted by the hypothalamus that stimulates the release of ACTH (corticotropin) by the anterior pituitary gland.

somatostatin Also called *growth hormone–inhibiting hormone (GHIH)*. A peptide hormone secreted from the hypothalamus that reduces the secretion of growth hormone by the anterior pituitary gland.

gonadotropin inhibitory hormone (GnIH) A peptide hormone released from the hypothalamus that inhibits the secretion of hypothalamic GnRH and pituitary gonadotropins in a variety of species.

dopamine (DA) A neurotransmitter produced primarily in the forebrain and diencephalon that acts in the basal ganglia, olfactory system, and some parts of the cerebral cortex.

or *projections*, from various higher brain sites. This information is consolidated by several nuclei, which carry out many integrative processes, including the control of reproduction and metabolism (Griffin and Ojeda, 1988).

At the base of the hypothalamus, there are modified neurons specialized for the release of chemical messengers. Although these **neurosecretory cells** function primarily as endocrine glands, they are morphologically similar to conventional neurons, having dendrites, axons, Golgi bodies and neurotubules (for a review of basic features of the nervous system, see Breedlove and Watson, 2016). Their chemical messengers, called neurohormones, are released from the neuronal axon terminals in response to neuronal impulses in a manner analogous to the release of neurotransmitters, but rather than being released into a synaptic space, they are released into blood vessels in the pituitary gland. This chemical communication system between the hypothalamus and the pituitary is one of the areas where the boundaries between the endocrine and nervous systems are blurred.

Neurons in the hypothalamic median eminence secrete a number of releasing hormones and inhibiting hormones. These hypothalamic hormones are small peptides, ranging from 3 to 44 amino acid residues in length. The properties of releasing and inhibiting hormones are very similar to those of neurotransmitters. These hormones are best thought of as a special class of neurotransmitters that act on a variety of cells in the anterior pituitary. Indeed, several of these hypothalamic hormones act as neurotransmitters elsewhere in the central nervous system.

Six releasing hormones have been isolated and characterized: (1) **thyrotropin-releasing hormone** (**TRH**); (2) **growth hormone–releasing hormone** (**GHRH**) (also called somatocrinin); (3) **gonadotropin-releasing hormone** (**GnRH**); (4) **melanotropin-releasing hormone** (**MRH**); (5) **corticotropin-releasing hormone** (**CRH**); and (6) potentially kisspeptin. Two inhibiting hormones have also been characterized and isolated: **somatostatin** (also called *growth hormone–inhibiting hormone* [*GHIH*]), and a **gonadotropin inhibitory hormone** (**GnIH**) (**FIGURE 2.6**). **Dopamine** (**DA**), a well-characterized neurotransmitter and technically a monoamine, also serves as a neurohormone in the hypothalamus to inhibit the release of prolactin and melanotropin

	1	2	3	4	5	6	7	8	9	10
Mammal	pGlu–	His–	Trp–	Ser–	Tyr–	Gly–	Leu–	Arg–	Pro–	Gly–NH$_2$
Chicken I	pGlu–	His–	Trp–	Ser–	Tyr–	Gly–	Leu–	Gln–	Pro–	Gly–NH$_2$
Catfish	pGlu–	His–	Trp–	Ser–	His–	Gly–	Leu–	Asn–	Pro–	Gly–NH$_2$
Chicken II	pGlu–	His–	Trp–	Ser–	His–	Gly–	Trp–	Tyr–	Pro–	Gly–NH$_2$
Dogfish	pGlu–	His–	Trp–	Ser–	His–	Gly–	Trp–	Leu–	Pro–	Gly–NH$_2$
Salmon	pGlu–	His–	Trp–	Ser–	Tyr–	Gly–	Trp–	Leu–	Pro–	Gly–NH$_2$
Lamprey	pGlu–	His–	Tyr–	Ser–	Leu–	Glu–	Trp–	Lys–	Pro–	Gly–NH$_2$

FIGURE 2.7 Primary structures of species-specific forms of **GnRH** Amino acid residues that are different from the mammalian form of GnRH are enclosed in boxes. Presumably, point mutations have occurred during evolution to yield the current forms of GnRH in different types of animals.

prolactin inhibitory hormone (PIH) Dopamine; inhibits prolactin secretion from the anterior pituitary.

melanotropin inhibitory hormone (MIH) A peptide hormone that inhibits MSH secretion.

hypocretin Also called *orexin*. A polypeptide hormone that is mainly produced in the hypothalamus that inhibits the secretion of various other hormones, including somatotropin, glucagon, insulin, TSH, and gastrin.

from the anterior pituitary; in these contexts it is known, respectively, as **prolactin inhibitory hormone** (PIH) and **melanotropin inhibitory hormone** (MIH). A hormone called **hypocretin** (also called orexin) is found in cells located in the hypothalamus that project widely to the rest of the brain and spinal cord. This hormone is involved in sleep, metabolic balance, and possibly activation of the sympathetic nervous system.

Unlike steroid hormones discussed later in this chapter, which are structurally identical among all vertebrates, protein and peptide hormones can vary in their sequence of amino acids. Often, researchers isolate the mammalian version of a hormone first. Because the sequence of amino acids ultimately affects the shape of the molecule, protein hormones from one group of animals may not activate the receptors in another group of animals. Injection of the mammalian version of GnRH into a toad, for example, would probably not affect its reproductive function. After conducting such an experiment, it would not be prudent to conclude that GnRH is not involved in frog reproduction, although similar errors in logic have been made in endocrine investigations. Because species specificity is conveyed by the amino acid sequence of a hormone, it is important to identify the species-specific protein or peptide hormone before assigning a functional role to a hormone in a new species under investigation. Some variants of GnRH are shown in **FIGURE 2.7**. Small differences in amino acid sequences of protein hormones exist even between species of mammals. These small variations generally do not prevent a hormone taken from one mammal from having biological activity when injected into an individual of another mammalian species. If treatment with the foreign hormone continues for several weeks, however, the recipient may mount an immune response to the hormone. This is the primary reason that protein hormones extracted from the tissues of other animals are not used for clinical treatments in humans.

RFamide peptides Kisspeptin and gonadotropin inhibitory hormone (GnIH), both of which have been discovered and characterized relatively recently, belong to a large class of peptides called RFamide peptides. These neuropeptides are called RFamide peptides because they share a similar motif in their structure (arginine–phenylalanine-NH$_2$; *arginine* is abbreviated as *R*, whereas *phenylalanine* is

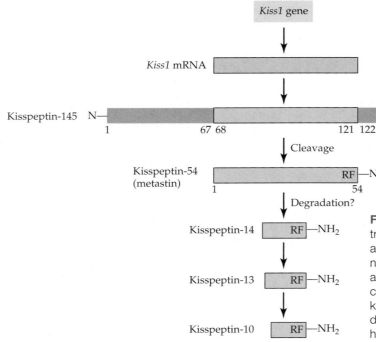

FIGURE 2.8 Kisspeptin is produced when the *Kiss1* gene is transcribed into a *Kiss1* mRNA, which is translated into a 145–amino acid peptide called kisspeptin-145. This peptide has no known biological activity. After processing, kisspeptin-54, a biologically active form of the peptide, is produced with the characteristic RFamide (NH$_2$) motif. Other kisspeptins, including kisspeptin-14, kisspeptin-13, and kisspeptin-10, may be produced; all of these RFamides are biologically active forms of the hormone. After Popa et al., 2008.

BOX 2.1 *The Discovery of Kisspeptin*

By the turn of the twenty-first century, it was generally assumed that neuroendocrinologists had discovered all major neuropeptides controlling reproductive function. As a result, it was quite extraordinary when, in 2003, two groups independently confirmed that mutations in an obscure cancer gene that encodes the receptor for kisspeptin (G protein-coupled receptor 54; the gene is *GPR54*) caused hypophysiotropic hypogonadism in humans and mice (de Roux et al., 2003; Seminara et al, 2003). Hypophysiotropic hypogonadism is characterized by a failure to reach sexual maturation, with low or absent luteinizing hormone in the bloodstream. Individuals with this condition respond to treatment with a GnRH agonist, indicating that the deficit is not at the level of the pituitary, but with the normal release of GnRH (**Figure A**).

Through the study of families in which several generations of individuals sought medical attention for this form of hypogonadism, genetic mutations localized to the *GPR54* gene were identified. At the time, the known ligand for GPR54 was a protein named metastin for its ability to suppress metastasis in breast and melanoma cancer cell lines (Lee and Welsh, 1997; Lee et al., 1996). The gene encoding metastin was named *Kiss1* because of its discovery in Hershey, Pennsylvania, home of equally famous Hershey's Kisses. The "ss" incorporated into the gene name stands for "suppressor sequence," reflecting the suppressive, antimetastatic properties of its protein product. Given that the function of the ligand for GPR54 extended beyond its role in cancer biology, the ligand is now referred to as kisspeptin.

To confirm the functional significance of GPR54 in reproductive function, male and female mice deficient in this receptor (*GPR54–/–*) were generated (Seminara et al., 2003). These animals fail to undergo sexual maturation and exhibit immature

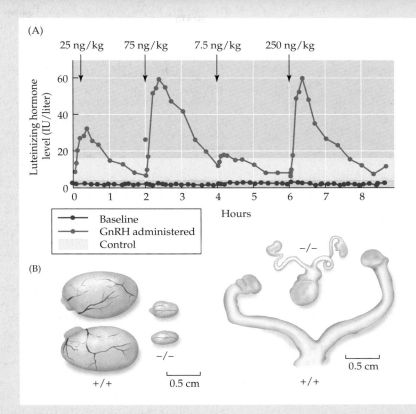

reproductive organs in adulthood (**Figure B**). *Gpr54–/–* mice have low circulating gonadotropin and sex steroid concentrations, and animals are infertile. Importantly, gonadotropin secretion can be elicited in these mice by injections of GnRH, mimicking the condition seen in humans.

The excitement over the discovery of such an important, positive regulator of reproductive function led to a revolution in the field, with hundreds of researchers actively focusing on the role of this neuropeptide in puberty, adult reproductive functioning, and seasonal changes in reproduction. In many cases, kisspeptin filled a gap in our understanding that could not have been accomplished without this breakthrough.

---

abbreviated as *F*). In rodents, kisspeptin-producing neurons are primarily located in the arcuate and anteroventral periventricular nuclei and project to the medial preoptic area, which contains many GnRH-producing neurons. Many neurons that produce kisspeptin also express steroid receptors in both female and male mice (Smith et al., 2005). Kisspeptin appears critical for normal puberty, probably by activating GnRH-producing neurons (de Roux et al., 2003; Kauffman et al., 2007; Seminara et al., 2003) (**BOX 2.1**). In common with ACTH, kisspeptin is made from a much larger molecule, referred to as kisspeptin-145, which has no known biological activity (**FIGURE 2.8**).

GnIH has the opposite effects of kisspeptin—it inhibits secretion of GnRH and the gonadotropins (Tsutsui et al., 2000, 2010). In common with neurons producing kisspeptin, GnIH-producing neurons also express sex steroid receptors and may mediate negative feedback regulation of reproductive function by steroids (Kriegsfeld et al., 2006). Among birds, the cell bodies of GnIH-producing neurons are located in the paraventricular nucleus of the hypothalamus, with projections to both the pituitary gland and GnRH neurons (Bentley et al., 2003). In rodents (including rats, mice, and hamsters), GnIH-producing neurons are located in the dorsomedial hypothalamus, with projections to the GnRH system and potentially the pituitary (Kriegsfeld, 2006). Injection of GnIH rapidly reduces luteinizing hormone levels across vertebrate species (Tsutsui et al., 2010). As will be seen throughout subsequent chapters, GnIH and kisspeptin have been shown to be important for sex differences in endocrine control (Chapter 4), adult reproductive function (see Chapters 5 and 6), and seasonal changes in reproduction (see Chapter 10).

anterior pituitary Front part of the endocrine gland that extends from the base of the brain and secretes a number of tropic hormones in response to hormonal signals from the hypothalamus.

posterior pituitary The rear part of the endocrine gland that extends from the base of the brain and stores and releases oxytocin and vasopressin, which are produced in the hypothalamus.

Anterior pituitary hormones The word *pituitary* is derived from the Latin word for "mucus"; early anatomists erroneously believed that this gland collected waste products from the brain and excreted them via the nose. The pituitary gland was once considered the "master gland" because it mediated so many physiological processes. Although it is true that the pituitary orchestrates many processes, we now know that the pituitary itself is one of the most regulated glands in the endocrine system.

The mammalian pituitary, also called the hypophysis (from the Greek *hypo*, "below"; *physis*, "brain"), is really two distinct glands fused into one (Kannan, 1987) (**FIGURE 2.9**). The two parts have very different embryological origins. The front part, the **anterior pituitary** (also called the pars anterior or adenohypophysis, from the Greek *aden*, "gland"), develops from an embryonic structure called Rathke's pouch, which pinches off from the roof of the mouth and migrates to the final location of the gland (**FIGURE 2.10A**). There the anterior pituitary joins the back part, or **posterior pituitary** (also called the pars nervosa or neurohypophysis), which is an outgrowth from the base of the brain (**FIGURE 2.10B**). Thus, the anterior pituitary is derived from the soft tissues of the upper palate, and the posterior pituitary has a neural origin in the base of the brain. The area where the two parts of the pituitary join has a distinct anatomical organization in mammals and is called the pars intermedia. Birds lack a distinct pars intermedia, and in some

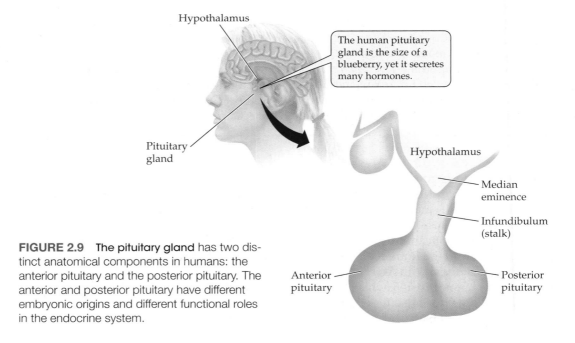

Hypothalamus

The human pituitary gland is the size of a blueberry, yet it secretes many hormones.

Pituitary gland

Hypothalamus

Median eminence

Infundibulum (stalk)

Anterior pituitary

Posterior pituitary

FIGURE 2.9 **The pituitary gland** has two distinct anatomical components in humans: the anterior pituitary and the posterior pituitary. The anterior and posterior pituitary have different embryonic origins and different functional roles in the endocrine system.

(A) Anterior pituitary

(B) Posterior pituitary

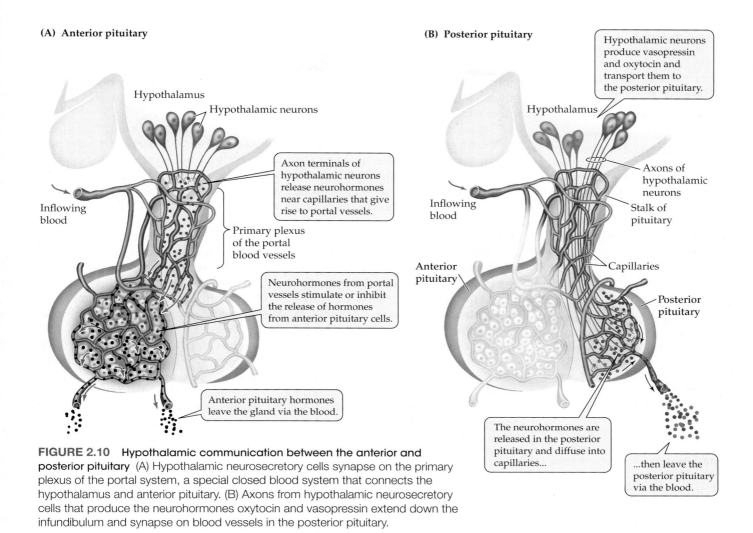

Hypothalamus

Hypothalamic neurons

Axon terminals of hypothalamic neurons release neurohormones near capillaries that give rise to portal vessels.

Inflowing blood

Primary plexus of the portal blood vessels

Neurohormones from portal vessels stimulate or inhibit the release of hormones from anterior pituitary cells.

Anterior pituitary hormones leave the gland via the blood.

Hypothalamic neurons produce vasopressin and oxytocin and transport them to the posterior pituitary.

Hypothalamus

Axons of hypothalamic neurons

Inflowing blood

Stalk of pituitary

Anterior pituitary

Capillaries

Posterior pituitary

The neurohormones are released in the posterior pituitary and diffuse into capillaries...

...then leave the posterior pituitary via the blood.

FIGURE 2.10 Hypothalamic communication between the anterior and posterior pituitary (A) Hypothalamic neurosecretory cells synapse on the primary plexus of the portal system, a special closed blood system that connects the hypothalamus and anterior pituitary. (B) Axons from hypothalamic neurosecretory cells that produce the neurohormones oxytocin and vasopressin extend down the infundibulum and synapse on blood vessels in the posterior pituitary.

primitive vertebrates (e.g., lampreys and hagfish), the two parts of the pituitary remain anatomically separate.

The hypothalamus communicates with the pituitary by two methods. Neurohormones from the hypothalamus reach the anterior pituitary via the **portal system**, a special closed blood circuit in which two beds of capillaries, one in the hypothalamus and one in the anterior pituitary, are connected by a vein (see Figure 2.10A). The portal system ensures that blood flows primarily in one direction (although there can be some backflow), from the hypothalamus to the anterior pituitary, and also ensures that hormonal signals from the hypothalamus will be received by the pituitary rather than diluted in the general blood circulation. These hypothalamic factors stimulate cells in the anterior pituitary to secrete hormones into the general circulation. Evidence for hypothalamic control of the pituitary via a portal system has been documented in all but the most primitive vertebrates.

The hypothalamic neurohormones secreted into the portal system are called by a variety of names, including releasing factors, releasing hormones, inhibitory factors, and inhibitory hormones. These small peptides act on the anterior pituitary to stimulate or inhibit the release of the anterior pituitary's own hormones. However, for the sake of simplicity, we will refer to these hormones as **releasing hormones**. When a stimulatory releasing hormone reaches the anterior pituitary via the portal system, the anterior pituitary releases appropriate hormones of its own. These pitu-

portal system A special closed blood circuit in which two beds of capillaries are connected by a vein; thus, the flow of blood is in one direction only.

releasing hormones One of several polypeptides released from the hypothalamus that increase or decrease the release of hormones from the anterior pituitary gland.

tropic hormones Hormones from the anterior pituitary that stimulate various physiological processes, either by acting directly on target tissues or by causing other endocrine glands to release hormones.

luteinizing hormone (LH) A gonadotropin from the anterior pituitary that promotes formation of the corpora lutea in females and testosterone production in males.

follicle-stimulating hormone (FSH) A gonadotropic hormone from the anterior pituitary that stimulates follicle development in females and sperm production in males.

thyroid-stimulating hormone (TSH) A glycoprotein hormone secreted by the anterior pituitary gland that stimulates and regulates activity of the thyroid gland.

glycoprotein An organic compound composed of both a protein and a carbohydrate joined together in a covalent chemical bond.

gonadotropin A hormone from the anterior pituitary (luteinizing hormone and follicle-stimulating hormone) or placenta (human chorionic hormone) that stimulates steroid production and gamete maturation in the gonads.

growth hormone (GH) A protein hormone that stimulates somatic (body) growth.

prolactin A protein hormone that is highly conserved throughout vertebrate evolution and has many physiological functions.

somatomedins Insulin-like polypeptides (growth factors) produced in the liver and in some fibroblasts and released into the blood when stimulated by GH.

itary hormones are also secreted into the portal system, but because of the one-way directional blood flow of the system, they join the general circulation rather than traveling to the hypothalamus. The anterior pituitary hormones are called **tropic hormones** (from the Greek *trophe*, "nourishment") because they stimulate various physiological processes, either by acting directly on target tissues or by causing other endocrine glands to release hormones.

The anterior pituitary contains three distinct types of cells, each of which produces a different group of tropic hormones. The hormones of the anterior pituitary are protein hormones that range in length from 15 to about 220 amino acids. If the anterior pituitary is removed from an animal, sliced very thin, mounted on a slide, colored with various stains to enhance visibility, and viewed through a microscope, then a characteristic pattern of cells can be observed. One type of cell in the anterior pituitary stains readily with acidic stains, another type takes up basic stains, and a third type does not readily take up either acidic or basic stains. These types of cells are called acidophils, basophils, and chromophobes, respectively. Through the use of modern techniques, particularly immunocytochemistry, we now know that specific types of hormones are made in these three cell types and that the acidophils and basophils can be further subdivided into more cell types, each producing a single hormone.

Luteinizing hormone (LH), **follicle-stimulating hormone (FSH)**, and **thyroid-stimulating hormone (TSH)** are secreted by the basophils. They consist of 200–220 amino acids. Approximately 10%–25% of the molecular structure of each of these three hormones is carbohydrate, and they are thus known collectively as **glycoproteins**. Each glycoprotein is composed of two subunits: α and β. These subunits have no biological activity separately; both subunits are necessary to produce a biological response. The α-subunits of LH, FSH, and TSH are identical. The β-subunit imparts the specific biological function of the molecule and also determines the species specificity. If the LH α-subunit and the TSH β-subunit are combined, the result is a biologically active TSH molecule. LH and FSH are also known as **gonadotropins** because, in response to GnRH, they stimulate steroidogenesis in the gonads as well as the development and maturation of gametes. In response to TRH from the hypothalamus, TSH is released from the anterior pituitary and stimulates the thyroid gland to release thyroid hormones.

Growth hormone (GH) and **prolactin** are secreted by the acidophils and are similar in structure; both are simple proteins consisting of 190–220 amino acids. Growth hormone is released from the anterior pituitary in response to GHRH from the hypothalamus. Growth hormone shows more species specificity in its biological activity among mammals as compared with most protein hormones. For example, rat GH has little or no biological activity in primates.[2]

Growth hormone stimulates somatic (body) growth. However, GH does not directly induce growth of the skeleton. Rather, it stimulates the production of growth-regulating substances called **somatomedins** by the liver, kidneys, and other tissues; the somatomedins cause bone to take up sulfates, leading to growth. GH and somatomedins also stimulate protein synthesis. GH promotes protein anabolism and acts as an anti-insulin. Other physiological effects of GH include fat mobilization, increased cell membrane permeability to increase the uptake of amino acids, changes in ion influxes, and increased blood sugar concentrations (hyperglycemia), as well as indirect effects on the thymus, an organ involved in immune function. Human GH also has inherent prolactin activity.

Human prolactin (PRL) has 198 amino acids and contains three disulfide bonds. The release of prolactin is stimulated by TRH from the hypothalamus. Prolactin is named for its well-known effect of promoting lactation in female mammals. How-

---

[2]Lowercase letters are used with the hormone abbreviation to indicate the animal from which a particular hormone is derived. Growth hormone from rats, sheep (ovine), cattle (bovine), pigs (porcine), and mice (murine) would be abbreviated rGH, oGH, bGH, pGH, and mGH, respectively.

ever, the first function discovered for prolactin was the promotion of corpus luteum function in the ovaries of rats; thus, it was originally named luteotropic hormone. Several years passed before prolactin and luteotropic hormone were discovered to be structurally identical. The term *luteotropic hormone* has faded from current use; however, it reminds us that prolactin has many functions other than promoting lactation in mammals.

Indeed, prolactin is a hormone that has been conserved throughout vertebrate evolution, and hundreds of different physiological functions of prolactin are known. These functions can be broken down into five basic classes of actions related to five different physiological processes: (1) reproduction, (2) growth and development, (3) water and electrolyte balance, (4) maintenance of integumentary structures, and (5) actions on steroid-dependent target tissues or synergisms with steroid hormones to affect target tissues. In terms of reproduction, prolactin stimulates the formation and maintenance of the corpora lutea in rats and mice, and it may do so in other mammals as well. An example of the importance of prolactin to growth and development is seen in certain salamanders called newts, which undergo a second metamorphosis from a terrestrial intermediate form to the aquatic sexually mature form; without prolactin, newts cannot undergo this metamorphosis. Prolactin has many osmoregulatory effects, especially in teleost (bony) fishes. Some species of minnows (e.g., *Fundulus heteroclitus*) are euryhaline—that is, they can migrate between seawater and freshwater. In the absence of prolactin, these minnows cannot adapt to freshwater (see Chapter 8). Prolactin is important in the development and maintenance of integumentary structures, which include the crop sac of pigeons and doves (see Figure 7.7) and the mammary glands in mammals. Finally, prolactin has synergistic actions on steroid-dependent target tissues. For example, prolactin is critical for maintaining LH receptors in the testes of some mammalian species.

Adrenocorticotropic hormone (**ACTH**) is made in the corticotrope cells, which are slightly basophilic cells. ACTH has 39 amino acids; however, only the first 23 amino acids of the ACTH molecule are required to maintain its full physiological activity. ACTH is released in response to CRH from the hypothalamus and stimulates the adrenal cortex to secrete corticoids (especially the glucocorticoids).

ACTH comes from a much larger parent protein called **pro-opiomelanocortin** (**POMC**) (**FIGURE 2.11**). This giant precursor molecule can be cleaved into a variety of biologically active substances. In some cases, the precise signal that determines the cleavage pattern is not known, but in most cases, tissue-specific enzymes are responsible for the different fates of the large precursor molecule. Some of the other products of POMC include the lipotropins

adrenocorticotropic hormone (ACTH) A polypeptide hormone that is secreted by the anterior pituitary gland that stimulates the adrenal cortex to secrete corticosteroids, such as cortisol and corticosterone.

pro-opiomelanocortin (POMC) A precursor protein that consists of 241 amino acid residues. It is synthesized in the anterior and intermediate pituitary gland.

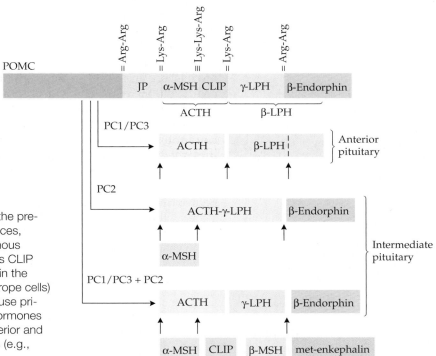

FIGURE 2.11 Pro-opiomelanocortin (POMC) is the precursor to a variety of biologically important substances, including ACTH, α-MSH, β-MSH, and the endogenous opioids β-endorphin and met-enkephalin, as well as CLIP (corticotropin-like intermediate lobe peptide). Cells in the anterior pituitary that secrete ACTH (called corticotrope cells) possess proteolytic enzymes (PC1/PC3), which cause primarily ACTH to be produced from POMC. Other hormones are produced from POMC in cells between the anterior and posterior pituitary, where other proteolytic enzymes (e.g., PC2) are located.

melanoctye-stimulating hormone (MSH) A peptide hormone secreted by the pituitary gland that regulates skin color in some vertebrates by stimulating melanin synthesis in melanocytes and melanin granule dispersal in melanophores.

β-endorphin An endogenous opioid produced in the anterior pituitary gland and hypothalamus in vertebrates; resembles opiates in its action as a "natural" painkiller.

met-enkephalin An endogenous opioid peptide with a short duration of action that has pain-reducing effects.

prohormone A molecule that can act as a hormone itself or can be converted into another hormone with different properties.

oxytocin A peptide hormone secreted by the posterior pituitary that induces uterine contractions during birth, triggers milk letdown in lactating females, and may be involved in other reproductive behaviors.

(which may mobilize fat); **melanoctye-stimulating hormone** (**MSH**), a pigmentation regulator; and the endogenous opioids **β-endorphin** and **met-enkephalin**.

Because the MSH molecule is produced by cleavage of the ACTH molecule, all ACTH includes inherent MSH activity; therefore, all ACTHs are also MSHs. MSH has little or no effect on the adrenal cortex but functions primarily to control pigmentation in nonmammalian and nonavian vertebrates. Melanocytes are pigment cells that contain melanin. MSH stimulates melanogenesis, the synthesis of melanin, thereby inducing a darker skin color. ACTH also results in melanocyte stimulation. Although the physiological function of MSH in mammals and birds is not well understood, this peptide does have some behavioral effects.

The opioids are endogenous (from within) "painkillers." They interact with opioid receptors throughout the central nervous system to ameliorate pain sensations. Exogenous opiates such as heroin and morphine interact with these same receptors. ACTH and β-endorphin are secreted simultaneously in response to CRH. These two hormones come from different parts of the POMC precursor molecule (Nakanishi et al., 1979), and both are believed to be part of the stress adaptation response. ACTH stimulates glucocorticoid secretion, which helps an animal adjust to stressful conditions. Stressful conditions may also trigger the release of β-endorphin to reduce pain. The behavioral effects of β-endorphin will be discussed in subsequent chapters. Secretion of ACTH and β-endorphin increases after adrenalectomy, suggesting that the glucocorticoids from the adrenal glands may normally feed back to control their own release.

POSTERIOR PITUITARY HORMONES A different set of hypothalamic neurosecretory cells directly innervates the posterior pituitary. Rather than being released into a portal system, neurohormones are secreted directly into this structure, where they enter blood vessels and the general circulation (see Figure 2.10B). The posterior pituitary serves as a sort of reservoir for two neurohormones, oxytocin and vasopressin, which are actually manufactured in the cell bodies of the magnocellular neurons of the supraoptic and paraventricular nuclei of the hypothalamus. Axons from these cells, which function both as typical neurons that conduct impulses and as endocrine cells, extend down the infundibulum and terminate in the posterior pituitary. Oxytocin and vasopressin made and packaged in the Golgi bodies of the neurosecretory cell bodies are transported down the axons and stored in vesicles at the axon terminals in the posterior pituitary, from which they are released in response to a neural impulse. When the cell membrane is depolarized by a neural impulse, the hormones are released from the terminals by exocytosis and enter the bloodstream. Thus, in contrast to the two-step process in the anterior pituitary, hormones can be released from the posterior pituitary as fast as a neural impulse is conducted.

These nonapeptides are produced from **prohormones** that also include a carrier protein, neurophysin (**FIGURE 2.12**). Thus, for each molecule of nonapeptide produced, one molecule of neurophysin is also produced. There are two types of neurophysin: the prohormone prooxyphysin is hydrolyzed to oxytocin and neurophysin I, and the prohormone propressophysin is hydrolyzed to vasopressin and neurophysin II plus a short glycopeptide (Norris, 2007). The relationship between the carrier protein and the nonapeptide is labile, and neurophysin increases the half-lives of vasopressin and oxytocin from 3 minutes to about 30 minutes in the blood when it is bound to them.

Oxytocin dramatically influences reproductive function in mammals. This hormone is important during birth, causing uterine contractions

(A) Vasopressin

$$Cys-Tyr-Phe-Gln-Asn-Cys-Pro-Arg-Gly-NH_2$$
$$1 \quad 2 \quad 3 \quad 4 \quad 5 \quad 6 \quad 7 \quad 8 \quad 9$$

(B) Oxytocin

$$Cys-Tyr-Ile-Gln-Asn-Cys-Pro-Leu-Gly-NH_2$$
$$1 \quad 2 \quad 3 \quad 4 \quad 5 \quad 6 \quad 7 \quad 8 \quad 9$$

FIGURE 2.12 Nonapeptide prohormones (A) Propressophysin (145 amino acids) is cleaved into vasopressin and neurophysin II plus an unnamed glycopeptide. (B) Prooxyphysin (104 amino acids) is cleaved into oxytocin and neurophysin I. The brackets indicate disulfide bonds that form in the mature molecules.

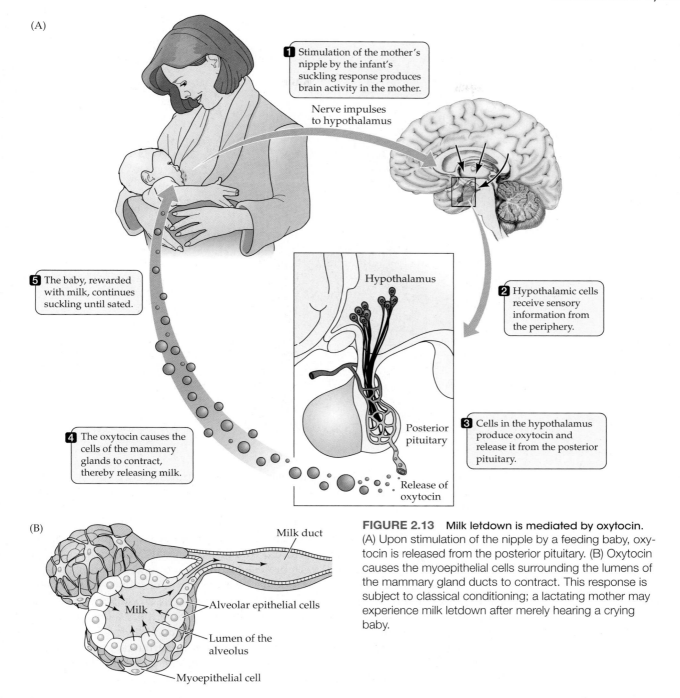

(A)

1 Stimulation of the mother's nipple by the infant's suckling response produces brain activity in the mother.

Nerve impulses to hypothalamus

5 The baby, rewarded with milk, continues suckling until sated.

Hypothalamus

2 Hypothalamic cells receive sensory information from the periphery.

Posterior pituitary

3 Cells in the hypothalamus produce oxytocin and release it from the posterior pituitary.

4 The oxytocin causes the cells of the mammary glands to contract, thereby releasing milk.

Release of oxytocin

(B)

Milk duct

Milk

Alveolar epithelial cells

Lumen of the alveolus

Myoepithelial cell

FIGURE 2.13 Milk letdown is mediated by oxytocin.
(A) Upon stimulation of the nipple by a feeding baby, oxytocin is released from the posterior pituitary. (B) Oxytocin causes the myoepithelial cells surrounding the lumens of the mammary gland ducts to contract. This response is subject to classical conditioning; a lactating mother may experience milk letdown after merely hearing a crying baby.

when the uterus is responsive to it. Oxytocin, or an artificial version of oxytocin, is often used medically to induce labor. Oxytocin cannot be used to induce abortions, however, because the uterus is responsive to it only when progesterone levels are low after an extended period of elevated estrogen concentrations that occur during pregnancy.

Oxytocin is also important in the suckling reflex. Oxytocin is released into the blood in response to sensory stimulation from the nipple and travels through the general circulation to the mammary glands (**FIGURE 2.13A**). The myoepithelial cells surrounding the milk-collecting lumens of the mammary glands contract upon exposure to oxytocin, causing milk letdown (**FIGURE 2.13B**). This suckling reflex can become associated with environmental stimuli such that oxytocin is released in an-

FIGURE 2.14 **The thyroid gland** is a highly vascularized, H-shaped organ that partially surrounds the upper trachea in humans (A). Embedded in the outer layer of the thyroid on each side are two lobes of the parathyroid gland (right, rear view). (B) The spherical, colloid-filled follicles of the thyroid synthesize, store, and secrete thyroid hormones.

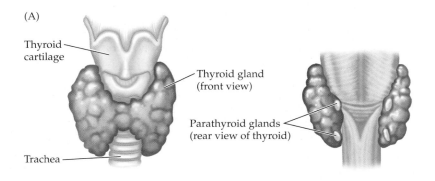

(A)

Thyroid cartilage

Thyroid gland (front view)

Parathyroid glands (rear view of thyroid)

Trachea

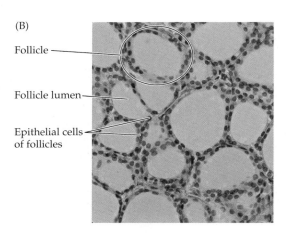

(B)

Follicle

Follicle lumen

Epithelial cells of follicles

ticipation of the sensory stimulation arising from the nipples. Hence, the sight of the milkmaid or the sound of the milking machine may evoke milk letdown in cows, and women may respond to the cry of a hungry baby in the same way, because of prior associations between these sights and sounds and nipple stimulation.

Vasopressin, also known as antidiuretic hormone (ADH) or arginine vasopressin (AVP), is another nonapeptide found in many mammals. ADH acts to retain water in tetrapod (four-footed) vertebrates. Alcohol is a potent inhibitor of ADH secretion, thereby increasing the frequency of urination after imbibing. ADH also has pressor (hypertensive) effects during serious blood loss; it causes constriction of blood vessels in response to severe hemorrhage, which helps to slow blood flow and presumably enhances the probability of survival. One of the possible serious consequences of ADH-induced pressor effects is that the arterioles of the kidney may be completely constricted, and the kidney may become permanently damaged during hemorrhage-induced shock.

THYROID AND PARATHYROID HORMONES The thyroid gland (**FIGURE 2.14A**) consists of many sphere-shaped, colloid-filled structures called **follicles** (*follicle*, "sac") (**FIGURE 2.14B**), which produce thyroid hormones in response to an anterior pituitary tropic hormone. The thyroid is unusual among vertebrate endocrine glands because it stores large quantities of these hormones; humans store sufficient thyroid hormone reserves for approximately 90 days. A functional explanation for this storage ability is that thyroid hormones contain iodine, which is uncommon in many human diets.

The thyroid hormones are derived from a single amino acid, tyrosine. Thus, they are technically not peptides but modified tyrosine molecules. However, the most common thyroid hormone, **thyroxine** (T_4), consists of two tyrosine residues and is thus considered a peptide hormone here.

vasopressin Also known as *antidiuretic hormone* (*ADH*). A nonapeptide released from the posterior pituitary gland that increases blood pressure during serious blood loss.

follicles An epithelial cell-lined sac or compartment of the thyroid gland, ovary, or other structure.

thyroxine (T_4) The primary hormone secreted from the thyroid gland; it acts to increase oxidation rates in tissues.

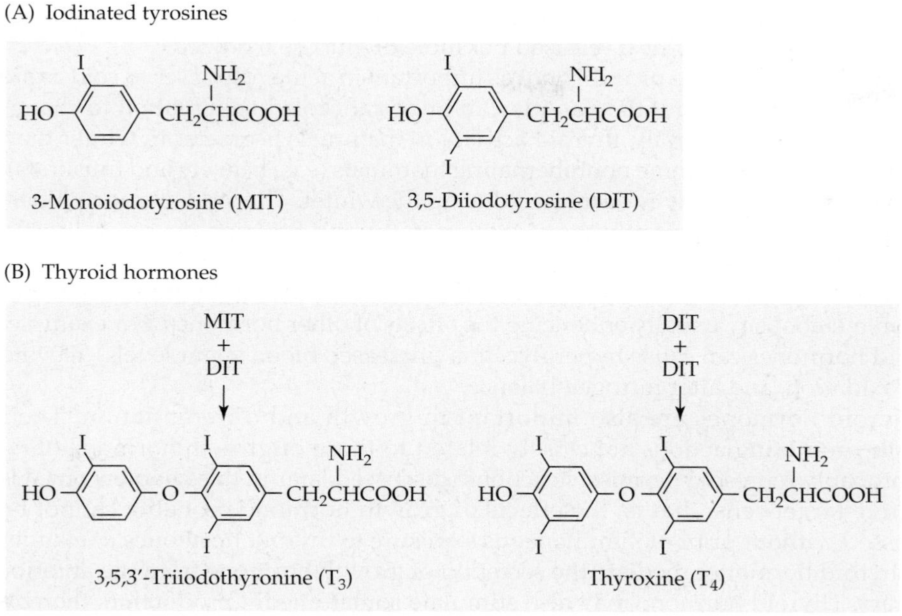

(A) Iodinated tyrosines

3-Monoiodotyrosine (MIT)   3,5-Diiodotyrosine (DIT)

(B) Thyroid hormones

3,5,3′-Triiodothyronine (T$_3$)   Thyroxine (T$_4$)

FIGURE 2.15 **Thyroid hormone synthesis** (A) The follicles of the thyroid produce a large glycoprotein molecule called thyroglobulin. Dietary iodine enters the bloodstream from the gut and is transported to the thyroid gland, where tyrosine components of the thyroglobulin molecule become iodinated and form 3-monoiodotyrosine (MIT) and 3,5-diiodotyrosine (DIT), the precursors of the two main thyroid hormones. (B) Triiodothyronine (T$_3$) results from the combination of MIT and DIT, and thyroxine (T$_4$) is formed by the combination of two DIT molecules.

The thyroid gland releases its hormones in response to TSH stimulation from the anterior pituitary. There are two biologically active thyroid hormones, both derived from a large, globular glycoprotein called thyroglobulin. The hormones are synthesized from iodinated tyrosine residues in the thyroglobulin molecule: essentially, inorganic dietary iodine reacts with water to form the "active" iodine that immediately binds to tyrosine residues in thyroglobulin. Binding of one active iodine atom to tyrosine at position 3 on the phenolic ring yields 3-monoiodotyrosine (MIT). A second iodine may attach at position 5, resulting in 3,5-diiodotyrosine (DIT) (**FIGURE 2.15**); the 3 position is always more readily iodinated than the 5 position. MIT and DIT are joined together through an ether linkage (–O–) between the phenolic rings to form the thyronine structure called **triiodothyronine (T$_3$)**, one of the secreted thyroid hormones. T$_4$, also known as tetraiodothyronine, is formed by the combination of two DIT molecules.

Both T$_3$ and T$_4$ are fat-soluble. Like steroid hormones, they diffuse rapidly across cell membranes, but they need the help of a carrier protein to travel through the blood. The thyroid hormones are easily removed from the blood by the kidneys and liver if not bound to a carrier protein. About 99% of circulating thyroid hormones are reversibly bound to serum proteins. In humans, about 75% of thyroid hormones are bound to α_2-globulins, 20%–30% are bound to albumin or prealbumin, and less than 1% are transported unattached in the blood; these proportions vary among species.

The thyroid hormones act to increase oxidation rates in tissue. They have three general effects in mammals: they affect metabolism, alter growth and differentiation, and influence reproduction. The thyroid is probably most commonly associated with its metabolic actions, especially its calorigenic, or heat-producing, effects. Thyroid hormones can increase the rate of glucose oxidation and thus increase the amount of metabolic heat produced in any given time. Also, it is thought that thyroid hormones can uncouple oxidative phosphorylation, which decreases the efficiency of adenosine triphosphate (ATP) synthesis, allowing the release of more heat. By analogy, if the motor of an electric fan heated up excessively when turning the fins, this would indicate that the motor was inefficient in converting electrical energy into movement. Because energy cannot be created or destroyed, excess ener-

triiodothyronine (T$_3$) A tyrosine-based hormone that is produced by the thyroid gland and acts to increase the basal metabolic rate, affect protein synthesis, and increase sensitivity to catecholamines.

gy is often released as heat. Likewise, a reduction in the efficiency of ATP synthesis increases the quantity of heat released per mole of glucose oxidized.

Thyroid hormones are probably not as important in acute responses to cold as are the adrenal corticoids, but they do play an important role in adaptation to changing temperatures. Generally, thyroid activity in mammals is greater in winter than during the summer. In some nonhibernating mammals (e.g., beavers and muskrats), however, thyroid activity is decreased during the winter. This is also true in hibernating species, but apparently the reduction in thyroid function does not directly cause hibernation.

Thyroid hormones also have specific effects related to carbohydrate, lipid, and protein metabolism, usually enhancing the effects of other hormones. For example, thyroid hormones can cause hyperglycemia (increased blood sugar levels), elevate lipid oxidation, and alter nitrogen balance.

Thyroid hormones are also important in growth and differentiation. Their growth-promoting actions are closely related to those of growth hormone (GH) and probably represent permissive actions (discussed later in this chapter) on GH-sensitive target cells; that is, the effects of growth hormone probably cannot be expressed without prior or simultaneous exposure to thyroid hormones. We know that thyroid hormones mediate the secretion of growth hormone from the anterior pituitary. Thyroid hormone may also stimulate somatomedin production, thereby augmenting the actions of GH.

Thyroid hormones have both direct and indirect effects on behavior. Hypothyroidism, the insufficient production of thyroid hormone, can have a number of detrimental effects. The primary tissue affected by low thyroid hormones is nervous system tissue. Hypothyroidism during development of the nervous system results in profound cognitive deficits, a syndrome called cretinism in humans; however, the addition of iodine to table salt has virtually eliminated this condition in industrialized countries.

Finally, the thyroid affects reproduction. Generally, sexual maturation is delayed in hypothyroid mammals. Spermatogenesis occurs in hypothyroid males, but blood testosterone concentrations are reduced; a reduction in serum testosterone levels can greatly affect many reproductive behaviors. Ovarian cycles are irregular in hypothyroid female rats.

PARATHYROID AND C-CELL HORMONES Embedded in the thyroid are other endocrine cells called **C cells**, which secrete a protein hormone called calcitonin that is involved in calcium metabolism. Also situated in the thyroid is the **parathyroid gland** (see Figure 2.14A, right), which usually has several parts; in humans, two lobes are present in the outer layer of the thyroid on each side. The hormones produced by the parathyroid gland and by the C cells of the thyroid are both protein hormones, and both are involved in calcium metabolism. **Parathyroid hormone (PTH)** is made up of 84 amino acids. In terrestrial vertebrates, PTH elevates blood levels of calcium (Ca^{2+}) by increasing resorption of Ca^{2+} from the bone and absorption of Ca^{2+} from the gut via its effects on vitamin D_3. PTH also inhibits phosphate resorption from the kidney, which reduces Ca^{2+} clearance.

Calcitonin (CT) is made up of 32 amino acids and has a single disulfide bond. CT is released from the C cells of the thyroid in land vertebrates or from the ultimobranchial organ in fishes. CT acts in opposition to PTH to lower blood levels of calcium by inhibiting the release of Ca^{2+} from bone. PTH and CT are both controlled directly by blood calcium levels; there are no pituitary tropic hormones involved in their regulation. The importance of CT in mammalian calcium regulation remains an open question, and the role of calcium regulation in behavior seems understudied.

PANCREATIC HORMONES The pancreas functions as both an endocrine and an exocrine gland (**FIGURE 2.16A**). Most of the pancreas consists of exocrine cells that

C cells Endocrine cells found in the interstitial spaces between the thyroid follicle spheres that secrete calcitonin.

parathyroid gland Separate endocrine tissue associated with the thyroid gland; produces hormones involved in calcium metabolism.

parathyroid hormone (PTH) A protein hormone that is secreted by the parathyroid gland that regulates calcium and phosphate metabolism.

calcitonin (CT) A polypeptide hormone secreted from the C cells associated with the thyroid gland that lowers blood calcium concentrations and affects blood phosphorus.

(A)

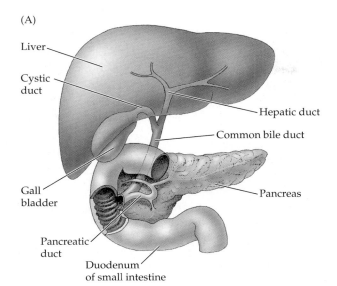

Liver

Cystic duct

Hepatic duct

Common bile duct

Gall bladder

Pancreas

Pancreatic duct

Duodenum of small intestine

FIGURE 2.16 **The pancreas** is located beneath the liver and rests in the curve of the duodenum of the small intestine (A). (B) While most of the pancreas consists of exocrine cells that secrete digestive fluids, islands of endocrine tissue called islets of Langerhans are also present. (C) The relative distribution of α-, β-, and δ-cells in a pancreatic islet; each cell type secretes a different protein hormone.

(B)

(C)

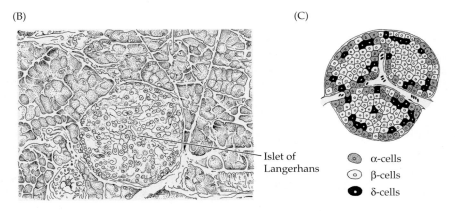

Islet of Langerhans

α-cells

β-cells

δ-cells

produce and secrete digestive juices into the intestines (Go et al., 1993), but nested throughout the exocrine tissue are islands of endocrine tissue called **islets of Langerhans** (**FIGURE 2.16B**). Within these endocrine islands are four cell types—α-cells, β-cells, δ-cells—and a few polypeptide-secreting cells, each of which secretes a different protein hormone (**FIGURE 2.16C**).

In many animals, the islets of Langerhans are innervated. In mammals, these cells are innervated by the vagus nerve, which stimulates insulin secretion when glucose concentrations in the blood increase, as they do after a meal. This mechanism allows an animal to anticipate the arrival of food in the intestines with a rapid secretion of insulin and thus promotes efficient movement of energy from the blood into the cells.

Four major peptide hormone products are secreted from the pancreas: insulin, glucagon, somatostatin, and pancreatic polypeptide. Insulin is composed of 51 amino acids and has three disulfide bonds in most vertebrates; it is made up of two short amino acid chains called the A-chain (21 amino acids) and B-chain (30 amino acids), linked together by two disulfide bonds. Proinsulin, the precursor of insulin, possesses a 33–amino acid C-peptide in addition to the A- and B-chains (**FIGURE 2.17**). The insulin molecule has not changed in structure during the evolution of animals and is evident in both vertebrates and invertebrates; in other words, insulin is a highly conserved molecule. Many hormones act to increase blood glucose levels, but insulin is the only known hormone in the animal kingdom that can lower blood sugar. Consequently, anything that disrupts insulin action has a profound effect on blood glucose regulation.

islets of Langerhans Islands of endocrine tissue nested throughout the exocrine tissue of the pancreas.

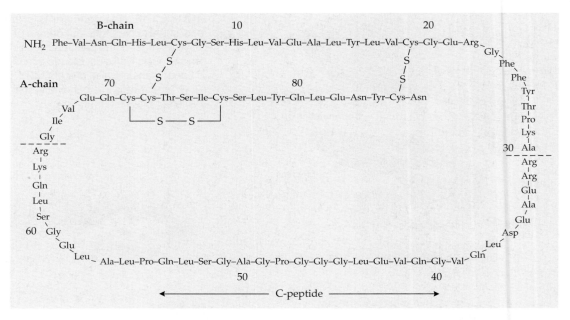

FIGURE 2.17 **Proinsulin,** the chemical precursor of insulin, consists of two short peptide chains called the A- and B-chains, which are bound together by two disulfide bonds (S—S), and a 33–amino acid C-peptide.

The first place insulin acts after its secretion by the β-cells of the pancreas is the liver, where it promotes energy storage in the form of glycogen. Except for central nervous system tissue, all cells have receptors for insulin. When a cell's insulin receptors are activated, blood glucose is taken up into the cell and used, or it is stored in muscle (as glycogen).

Glucagon is a simple peptide that is similar to those of the secretin family. Typically, glucagon has 29 amino acids. Once released from the α-cells of the pancreas, glucagon travels first to the liver, where it stimulates glycogenolysis, or the breakdown of stored glycogen. Glucagon thus acts in opposition to insulin and serves to increase blood levels of glucose.

Somatostatin is an inhibitory hormone released from the δ-cells of the pancreas. Somatostatin consists of 14 amino acids and inhibits the release of insulin and glucagons locally (paracrine) in the pancreas. Somatostatin is also released from the hypothalamus to regulate the release of growth hormone from the anterior pituitary.

Pancreatic polypeptide is released by the F cells (also called the pancreatic polypeptide [PP] cells) of the islets of Langerhans in the endocrine part of the pancreas. Pancreatic polypeptide consists of a 36–amino acid chain, and its secretion in humans is stimulated by protein consumption, fasting, exercise, and acute hypoglycemia. Somatostatin and glucose treatment inhibits its release. The precise biological role of pancreatic polypeptide in healthy individuals remains obscure, but it appears to regulate pancreatic enzyme secretion and gallbladder contractions. Importantly, treatment of healthy adults with pancreatic polypeptide suppresses appetite and reduces food intake (Batterham et al., 2003).

GASTROINTESTINAL HORMONES   As mentioned above, the endocrine cells of the gastrointestinal tract are scattered throughout the gut, in what is considered to be a primitive organization. Also, the gastrointestinal hormones regulate the cells and organs in which they are produced. Such intracrine or autocrine chemical mediation is usually considered a more primitive mechanism than endocrine mediation (O'Malley, 1989). Although more than two dozen hormones have been identified

glucagon   A protein hormone that is secreted by the α-cells of the islets of Langerhans in response to low blood glucose levels.

pancreatic polypeptide   A polypeptide hormone secreted by cells in the endocrine component of the pancreas gland.

BOX 2.2 *The Discovery of Secretin*

Despite Berthold's early work in 1849, the "official" beginning of the scientific study of endocrinology dates to the first 5 years of the twentieth century, when two British physiologists, William M. Bayliss and Ernest H. Starling, described the mode of action of the hormone secretin. Working in apparent ignorance of Berthold's earlier work, Bayliss and Starling convincingly demonstrated that chemical mediation of physiological processes could occur independently from the nervous system and that certain organs could release specific chemical agents that could travel through the blood and affect physiological processes at some distance from their sources.

Normally, the pancreas secretes digestive juices when food enters the intestine. Building upon the earlier work of physiologists such as Claude Bernard and Ivan Pavlov, Bayliss and Starling denervated a loop of jejunum (intestine) in dogs. When they perfused the jejunum with weak acid, they observed the pancreatic secretory response. This finding demonstrated that the pancreatic response does not involve the nervous system but must be stimulated by some substance that travels through the blood. However, when Bayliss and Starling injected the original stimulant, hydrochloric acid, directly into the blood, they did not observe a pancreatic secretory response. This result indicated the presence of a mediating factor. That mediating factor was found to be secretin, a hormone that is released from the cells of the duodenal mucosa in response to acidified food entering from the stomach. The hormone travels through the blood to the exocrine cells of the pancreas to stimulate the release of pancreatic digestive juices.

Bayliss and Starling published a series of elegant studies from 1902 through 1905. For example, they demonstrated the independence of secretin release and the pancreatic response from all neural influences by means of transplantation studies in which the intestinal loops containing the pancreas were moved to new locations without impairment of the secretin reaction. Their most convincing demonstration of the lack of

William M. Bayliss
(1860–1924)

Ernest H. Starling
(1866–1927)

neural involvement was obtained when the circulatory systems of two dogs were joined surgically. Introduction of acid into the duodenum of one dog stimulated secretion of pancreatic juices in both animals. For their work, they were nominated for the Nobel Prize in Medicine in 1913.

within the gastrointestinal tract, three major gastrointestinal hormones—secretin, cholecystokinin, and ghrelin—will be emphasized here. These hormones are released into the circulation and act to supplement the actions of the autonomic nervous system during the process of digestion. Many of these so-called gut hormones have also been found in the brain, and several behavioral effects have been attributed to them (see Chapters 8 and 11).

Secretin is a small peptide consisting of 27 amino acids. It and other members of the secretin "family," including vasoactive intestinal polypeptide (VIP), share many amino acid sequences in common. As noted in Chapter 1, the actions of secretin were first described by Starling and Bayliss in a series of papers that are generally considered to be the genesis of modern endocrinology (**BOX 2.2**). The release of secretin by the duodenal mucosa is stimulated by the passage of food into the duodenum (small intestine). Secretin stimulates the acinar cells of the pancreas

secretin A peptide hormone produced in the duodenum, in response to gastric acid secretion, to stimulate production of pancreatic secretions.

cholecystokinin (CCK) A hormone released by the lining of the small intestine that may be involved in satiation of food intake.

gastrin A peptide hormone that is secreted by the mucous lining of the stomach; induces the secretion of gastric secretions.

ghrelin A peptide hormone produced by stomach cells; it is thought to increase feelings of hunger.

adrenal medulla The inner portion of the endocrine organ that sits above the kidneys in vertebrates and secretes epinephrine and norepinephrine.

adrenal cortex The outer layer(s) of the endocrine organ that sits above the kidneys in vertebrates and secretes steroid hormones.

to produce water and bicarbonate (CHO_3^-), which aid in digestion. Other actions of secretin include the stimulation of hepatic (liver) bile flow and pepsin secretion, as well as the inhibition of gastrointestinal (GI) tract movement and gastric acid secretion. Secretin also influences insulin release, fat cell lipolysis, and renal (kidney) function.

Cholecystokinin (**CCK**), also called pancreozymin, is another member of the **gastrin** family of hormones. CCK consists of 33 amino acids and causes the exocrine pancreas to secrete digestive enzymes. CCK also causes the gallbladder to contract and release bile. There are several additional gastrointestinal hormones, including bombesin, substance P, motilin, galanin, neurotensin, peptide YY, and neuropeptide Y. Many of these hormones have also been identified in the brain, where they appear to function as neurotransmitters or neuromodulators. Bombesin, for example, is a 14–amino acid peptide hormone that was originally isolated from frog skin (genus *Bombina*) and subsequently identified in the mammalian brain and GI tract. A gastrin-releasing peptide (GRP), consisting of 27 amino acids, isolated from the GI tract of hogs has virtually the same amino acid sequence as bombesin at one end of the peptide. Both GRP and bombesin stimulate gastrin release in isolated rat stomachs. Bombesin or a bombesin-like substance in the brain may be involved in feeding behavior in mammals. Other gut hormones that have been found in the brain and implicated in mammalian feeding behavior include substance P, neuropeptide Y, and galanin. When such substances are secreted by neurons, they are considered neurohormones or neuropeptides and usually interact with receptors on adjacent neurons.

Though investigating drugs to stimulate GHRH, researchers discovered a hormone that stimulated GHRH release from the anterior pituitary. The hormone was named **ghrelin** (*ghre* is the Proto-Indo-European root for "grow," and *relin* indicates "release"). Ghrelin is a 28–amino acid peptide that is made in endocrine cells in the stomach (Casanueva and Dieguez, 2002). When ghrelin was administered to mice to see whether it would enhance GH secretion, their food intake and fat deposition increased. Human participants treated with ghrelin ate about 30% more food than individuals not given the hormone. Concentrations of ghrelin increased to peak levels prior to each meal (~80% increase) and fell dramatically after the meal. The potential of this hormone in clinical treatment of obesity is high, although obese individuals already have lower than average levels of ghrelin in their blood. A more immediate benefit of ghrelin is in the treatment of cachexia, the body-wasting syndrome associated with many cancers and AIDS. Additional discussion of this hormone and food intake is presented in Chapter 9.

There are several forms of the polypeptide gastrin, but the C-terminal tetrapeptide amide Trp–Met–Asp–Phe–NH_2 is common to all forms. Gastrin is produced by the gastrin (or G) cells in the antral glands of the stomach. Its release is promoted by acetylcholine or by vagus nerve stimulation. At low concentrations, gastrin stimulates the secretion of water and electrolytes by the stomach, pancreas, and liver, as well as enzymes by the stomach and pancreas. Hydrochloric acid in the stomach inhibits gastrin secretion via negative feedback. Gastrin also inhibits water and electrolyte absorption by the ileum. At high concentrations, gastrin stimulates the growth of gastric mucosa, release of insulin, and smooth muscle contractions of the gut, gallbladder, and uterus. Gastrin also inhibits gastric secretion at high concentrations.

ADRENAL HORMONES The adrenal glands are located on the top of the kidneys (**FIGURE 2.18A**). Like the pituitary gland, each adrenal gland is actually two distinct organs in mammals (James, 1992). An inner gland, the **adrenal medulla** (*medulla*, "marrow" or "innermost part") is surrounded by an outer gland, the **adrenal cortex** (*cortex*, "bark") (**FIGURE 2.18B**). In many nonmammalian species, these two parts of the adrenal gland are separate.

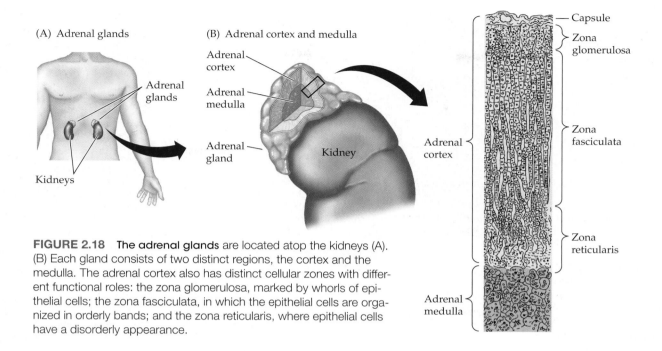

FIGURE 2.18 **The adrenal glands** are located atop the kidneys (A). (B) Each gland consists of two distinct regions, the cortex and the medulla. The adrenal cortex also has distinct cellular zones with different functional roles: the zona glomerulosa, marked by whorls of epithelial cells; the zona fasciculata, in which the epithelial cells are organized in orderly bands; and the zona reticularis, where epithelial cells have a disorderly appearance.

Adrenal medulla   The adrenal medulla is made up of **chromaffin cells**, so called because they have a high affinity for colored stains. During embryonic development these cells are derived from primitive neural tissue, specifically postganglionic sympathetic neurons, and after birth they function as part of the autonomic nervous system. In response to neural signals, the adrenal medulla releases three monoamine hormones—epinephrine, norepinephrine, and dopamine—into the general circulation. A class of protein hormones, the enkephalins, is also released from the adrenal medulla.

Enkephalins are released by the adrenal medulla in response to stress. A precursor protein consisting of 267 amino acids yields one leu- and six met-enkephalins. The individual enkephalins are released by the actions of trypsin-like enzymes on the proenkephalin precursor. As described above, enkephalins are also among the products derived from the POMC molecule. They are released by the anterior pituitary; however, the adrenal medullae are the major source of circulatory enkephalins. No definitive function has yet been assigned to adrenal medullary enkephalins, so their identification as hormones remains preliminary. Because these hormones are released in response to stress, it is reasonable to suggest that they are involved in adaptation to stress, but this remains to be determined.

Adrenal cortex   The adrenal cortex is composed of three distinct zones in mammals (Ganong, 2005) (see Figure 2.18B). The outer region, the **zona glomerulosa** (*glomeruli*, "small balls"), represents 10%–15% of the adrenal cortex and is characterized by whorls of epithelial cells. The middle zone, the **zona fasciculata**, is the largest zone of the adrenal cortex and makes up 75%–80% of this gland. The epithelial cells of the zona fasciculata are arranged as orderly bands (*fascicles*, "small bundles"). The **zona reticularis** is the innermost zone of the adrenal cortex. Here the epithelial cells are arranged in a somewhat disorderly fashion (*reticulum*, "net" or "network").

Human fetuses have very large adrenal glands that possess a fourth layer not found in adults. During fetal life, the zona glomerulosa, zona fasciculata, and zona reticularis account for only 20% of the adrenal cortex, while the other 80% of the

chromaffin cells   Cells that make and store epinephrine secretory vesicles.

zona glomerulosa   The outermost zone of the adrenal cortex, consisting of whorls of epithelial cells. Aldosterone is released from these cells as an indirect response to low blood sodium levels.

zona fasciculata   The middle (and largest) zone of the adrenal cortex, consisting of orderly bands of epithelial cells. Glucocorticoid hormones are released from these cells in response to ACTH stimulation from the anterior pituitary.

zona reticularis   The innermost zone of the adrenal cortex, consisting of a disorganized arrangement of epithelial cells. Sex steroid hormones are often released from this zone.

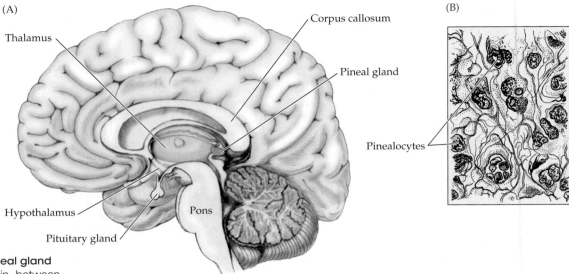

(A)

Thalamus

Corpus callosum

Pineal gland

Pinealocytes

Hypothalamus

Pons

Pituitary gland

(B)

FIGURE 2.19 **The pineal gland** is located within the brain, between the telencephalon and diencephalon (A). (B) The secretory cells of the mammalian pineal, known as pinealocytes, are nested in neural tissue; they produce both serotonin and melatonin and secrete melatonin. (C) Over the course of vertebrate evolution, the primary function of pineal cells has shifted from photoreception to neurosecretion.

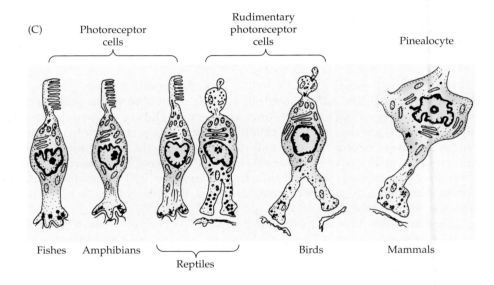

(C)   Photoreceptor cells

Rudimentary photoreceptor cells

Pinealocyte

Fishes   Amphibians

Reptiles

Birds   Mammals

cortex consists of the so-called fetal zone. The fetal zone undergoes rapid regression at birth, and its function remains unknown. There is no fetal zone per se in nonhuman animals, but an analogous layer of cortical cells appears perinatally in a number of laboratory mammals and has been named the X zone.

These anatomical divisions of the adrenal cortex represent functional divisions of hormone production. Although all three zones of the cortex produce steroid hormones, different types are produced in each zone. For example, aldosterone, which regulates sodium levels in the blood, is produced only in the zona glomerulosa. Furthermore, each zone differs in the way its steroid production is controlled. For instance, the secretion of aldosterone from the zona glomerulosa is regulated by blood concentrations of sodium and via a blood plasma α_2-globulin-derived hormone called angiotensin II, whereas the release of steroid hormones from the zona fasciculata and zona reticularis is regulated by tropic hormones from the anterior pituitary.

PINEAL HORMONES   The pineal gland (**FIGURE 2.19A**) is unique among endocrine organs in the extent of its evolution, both structurally and functionally, among the vertebrates (Reiter, 1982). In all mammals examined, individual pineal cells (**pinealocytes**) (**FIGURE 2.19B**) function exclusively as secretory structures (Hansen and

pinealocytes   The primary cells of the pineal gland that produce and secrete melatonin.

Karasek, 1982). In nonavian and nonmammalian vertebrates, the pineal gland functions primarily as a photoreceptor organ and is often referred to as the third eye (Eakin, 1973) (**FIGURE 2.19C**). The pineal also functions secondarily as a neurosecretory organ in these animals. In birds and some reptiles, the pineal cells possess rudimentary photoreceptive structures and also function as secretory cells. The avian pineal may also serve as an important biological clock.

The primary endocrine product of the pineal gland is melatonin. A number of small peptide hormones have also been found in the pineal, but thus far no functional role for these substances has been documented.

GONADAL HORMONES   The gonads have two functions, which are usually compartmentalized: (1) the production of gametes (sperm or eggs) and (2) the production of hormones (Neill, 2006). The hormones produced by the gonads, primarily steroid hormones, are required for gamete development and development of the secondary sex characteristics. These hormones also mediate the behaviors necessary to bring the sperm and eggs together. The functions of the gonads are regulated by tropic hormones from the anterior pituitary, known as gonadotropins.

Testes   The testes are bilateral glands, located in most mammals in an external sac called the **scrotum** and in most other vertebrates in the abdomen. Several cell types exist in the testes. When looking through a microscope at a thin cross section slice of a testis, you can identify the **seminiferous tubules**—long, convoluted tubes in which sperm cells undergo various stages of maturation, or spermatogenesis (**FIGURE 2.20A**). The heads of nearly mature sperm are embedded in specialized cells, called **Sertoli cells**, located along the basement membrane of the tubules; these cells provide nourishment to the developing sperm and also produce a peptide hormone, inhibin (discussed below) which is important in regulating one of the gonadotropins from the anterior pituitary. The primary hormone-producing cells in the testis are interspersed among the tubules and are called the **Leydig cells** or interstitial cells (*inter + stit* = "standing between") (**FIGURE 2.20B**). The Leydig cells produce steroid hormones under the influence of gonadotropins from the anterior pituitary gland. The androgens are the primary type of steroid hormones secreted by the testes.

scrotum   An external pouch of skin that contains the testes.

seminiferous tubules   The long, convoluted tubes in which spermatogenesis occurs.

Sertoli cells   Cells located along the basement membrane of the seminiferous tubules in which sperm cells are embedded while they mature.

Leydig cells   The interstitial cells between the seminiferous tubules in the testes that produce androgens in response to luteinizing hormone from the anterior pituitary.

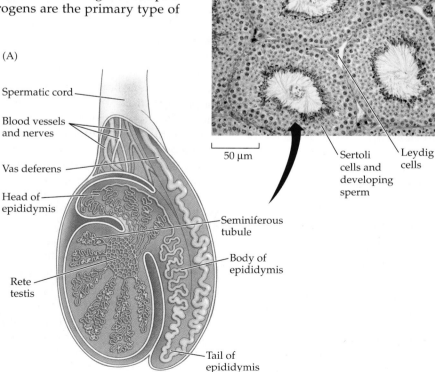

(A)

Spermatic cord

Blood vessels and nerves

Vas deferens

Head of epididymis

Rete testis

(B)

50 μm

Sertoli cells and developing sperm

Leydig cells

Seminiferous tubule

Body of epididymis

Tail of epididymis

FIGURE 2.20   The testes (A) A testis in cross section, showing the seminiferous tubules and vas deferens. (B) Seminiferous tubules in cross section, showing the heads of developing spermatozoa embedded in Sertoli cells and the steroid-secreting Leydig cells lying between the tubules.

FIGURE 2.21 **The ovaries** are almond-shaped, bilateral glands about 4–6 cm long in humans, located in the abdomen in the female (A). (B) A schematic diagram of one magnified mammalian ovary reveals several important anatomical features and the various stages of follicular and corpora luteal development. The mature follicle includes thecal cells and granulosa cells, which, prior to ovulation, collaborate to synthesize estrogens. After ovulation, the cells constituting the follicle enlarge and differentiate into luteal cells and combine with the theca interna cells to form the corpus luteum, which secretes progestins.

(A) Internal organs (frontal view)

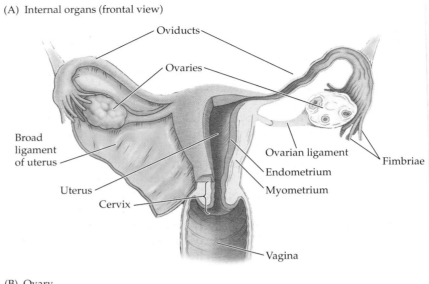

(B) Ovary

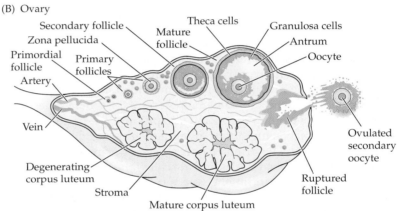

follicles   Epithelial cell-lined sacs of the ovaries.

ovum   A haploid female gamete.

corpora lutea   Endocrine structures that form from the remnants of the ovarian follicles after the egg is released. The corpora lutea secrete progestins, which support the uterine lining in preparation for blastocyst implantation.

stroma   The nonendocrine connective tissue of endocrine glands.

granulosa cells   The monolayer of flattened epithelial cells that surrounds the immature ova.

Ovaries   In mammals, the ovaries are paired glands located in the dorsal part of the abdominal cavity, normally below the kidneys (**FIGURE 2.21A**). Among many species of birds, only the left ovary is developed (Serra, 1983). Like the testes, the ovaries produce both gametes and hormones, and in the ovaries, as in the testes, the two functions are compartmentalized. However, active ovaries exhibit cyclic changes in both functions, whereas the testes are tonic, or constant, in their sperm-making and secretory activities during the breeding season.

The ovary has three functional subunits: **follicles**, which each contain a developing egg, or **ovum**; **corpora lutea**, structures that develop from follicles after the ovum is released; and supporting tissue, or **stroma** (**FIGURE 2.21B**). The functional potential of ovaries can be perceived microscopically early in their development. Within the fetal ovary are germinal epithelia that eventually develop into primordial follicles. The two ovaries of a human infant contain about 500,000 primary, or immature, follicles. No additional gametes are formed postnatally, and there is a continual degeneration of follicles throughout life through a process called atresia. Approximately 400 ova are ovulated by an average woman between puberty and menopause.

Each primary follicle consists of an oocyte (immature egg) surrounded by a monolayer of flattened epithelial cells called **granulosa cells**. The granulosa cells appear to be the source of two peptide hormones, inhibin and activin (discussed below), that are important in suppressing and enhancing, respectively, hormone secretion from the hypothalamus and pituitary gland. Under the influence of gonadotropins secreted by the anterior pituitary, a certain number of oocytes mature during each ovarian cycle. As an oocyte matures, the follicle tends to move deeper into the stroma, and the granulosa cells increase in number via mitotic division. Surrounding the granulosa cells, but separated from them by a basement membrane, are the theca interna and theca externa cells. The **thecal cells** secrete estrogens, the primary class of sex steroid hormones in females.

As the ovum continues to mature, its cell membrane becomes surrounded by an outer layer called the **zona pellucida**, and a multiple layer of epithelial cells surrounds the follicle. At this stage the maturing follicle is called a secondary follicle. A space develops between the ovum and surrounding epithelial cells. This space, called the antrum ("room"), fills with fluid prior to ovulation. As the antrum enlarges, the follicle is called a tertiary follicle. The antrum fluid is called the liquor folliculi (or follicular fluid) and is rich in steroid hormones. Just prior to ovulation, the follicle reaches its maximal size and is called a Graafian follicle. When the ovum is mature, it erupts from the Graafian follicle and travels to the mouth of the oviduct, through which it is transported to the uterus. In most mammals, fertilization normally occurs while the ovum is in the oviduct.

After the ovum is released, both the granulosa cells of the erupted follicle and the surrounding thecal cells undergo rapid mitosis, and capillaries generated from the thecal cells vascularize the granulosa cells. In this way the follicle transforms into the corpus luteum ("yellow body," so called because it appears orangish under a microscope). Although there is great species variation in the component tissues of the corpora lutea, in humans and many other mammals corpora lutea are derived from both granulosa cells and cells from the theca interna. The corpus luteum persists for some time on the surface of the ovary and produces another class of important sex steroid hormones, progestins. The corpus luteum eventually degenerates, leaving a scar called the corpus albicans ("white body"), which does not produce any hormones.

During the follicular phase (when the primary follicle is growing), the theca interna develops receptors for luteinizing hormone (LH) and produces androgens from cholesterol in response to LH stimulation of these receptors. The granulosa cells develop FSH receptors and, in response to FSH from the anterior pituitary, convert androgens into estrogens. LH receptors are also expressed in the granulosa cells near the time of ovulation in response to FSH and estrogenic stimulation. Stimulation of these receptors by LH causes the granulosa cells to produce progesterone.

Several peptide hormones are secreted by the gonads. Early during testicular development, the small peptide **Müllerian inhibitory hormone (MIH)** inhibits development of the Müllerian duct system, the embryonic duct system that gives rise to the female accessory sex organs (see Chapter 3). The Sertoli cells in the testes and the granulosa cells in the ovaries also secrete different forms of **inhibin**, a hormone that feeds back to block the secretion of FSH from the anterior pituitary. Inhibin also actively inhibits **aromatase**, an enzyme involved in the formation of estrogens from androgens, in the granulosa cells of the ovary. A closely related peptide, **activin**, has been discovered in both the testes and the ovaries. Its name comes from its stimulatory effects on FSH secretion. Its physiological function, if any, has yet to be determined in the testes, but activin directly stimulates aromatase activity in the ovarian granulosa cells. The activin-binding globulin, follistatin, is well characterized and antagonizes the effects of activin. Although additional research needs to be conducted on the inhibins and activins, these hormones certainly may have regulatory effects on hormone-behavior interactions.

Another peptide hormone found in the ovaries of mammals is called **relaxin**. Relaxin, first identified in 1932, is an insulin-related peptide hormone that is produced in the corpora lutea during pregnancy. It functions to soften estrogen-primed pelvic ligaments to allow them to stretch sufficiently to permit passage of the relatively large head of a mammalian fetus through the pelvis during birth. The role of these gonadal peptide hormones remains unspecified.

thecal cells Cells that form around the granulosa cells during follicular maturation. These cells participate in estrogen synthesis, but transform along with other cellular types into the corpus luteum after ovulation

zona pellucida The outer layer of cells surrounding the cell membranes of the maturing ovum.

Müllerian inhibitory hormone (MIH) A peptide hormone produced in the Sertoli cells in the developing testis that suppresses development of the Müllerian duct system.

inhibin A peptide hormone that is secreted by the ovarian follicular cells and the testicular Sertoli cells that acts to inhibit secretion of FSH from the anterior pituitary.

aromatase An enzyme that converts androgens into estrogens.

activin Peptide hormone synthesized in the anterior pituitary gland and gonads that stimulates the secretion of follicle-stimulating hormone.

relaxin A polypeptide hormone that is secreted by the corpus luteum during the last days of pregnancy; it relaxes the pelvic ligaments and prepares the uterus for labor.

PLACENTAL HORMONES   The placenta is a temporary endocrine organ that develops in the uterus during pregnancy in mammals. It forms from tissues derived from both the blastocyst and the maternal uterus. The placenta is important in maintaining nutritional, respiratory, and excretory functions for the fetus(es). It is also the source of several steroid and peptide hormones that affect both the mother and the offspring. In fact, the most common pregnancy tests measure human chorionic gonadotropin (hCG), a hormone produced by the rudimentary placenta that forms immediately after blastocyst implantation. This hormone maintains corpora luteal function (and progesterone secretion) during pregnancy and is part of the regulatory system that inhibits ovulation during pregnancy. The placenta is dislodged from the uterine wall during parturition (birth) and is expelled from the uterus at the end of pregnancy.

The placenta secretes a number of peptide hormones that can affect both the fetus and the mother. Some of these hormones are similar to hormones secreted elsewhere. For example, the placenta secretes prolactin and GnRH that are chemically similar to the versions released from the anterior pituitary gland and hypothalamus, respectively. Other peptide hormones are unique to the placenta but may augment the function of hormones from other sources. For example, chorionic gonadotropin(s) (CG), chorionic somatomammotropin (CS) (also called placental lactogen), chorionic corticotropin (CC), and chorionic thyrotropin (CT) act as "supplementary" tropic hormones to stimulate gonadal, mammary, adrenal, and thyroid functions. Recent evidence suggests that CS is important in initiating the onset of mammalian maternal behavior. Other hormones such as POMC, β-endorphin, and α-MSH are secreted by the placenta in vitro, and these hormones appear identical to the hypothalamic versions.

ADIPOKINE HORMONES   As noted in Chapter 1, leptin is a protein that is secreted from adipose (fat) cells. Leptin acts on receptors in the CNS and other sites to induce energy expenditure and inhibit food intake (Margetic et al., 2002). There is a relationship between body fat mass and blood leptin concentrations in some people. Leptin blood concentrations increase after a meal, in concert with insulin release. If leptin is a "satiety hormone," then it probably operates on the hypothalamus to reduce food intake, possibly by influencing the motivation to eat in some species, and by affecting the release of neuropeptides that regulate food intake (Cowley et al., 2001).

Adiponectin is a peptide that is released by fat cells (Saltiel and Kahn, 2001). Expression of adiponectin mRNA is decreased in obese mice and humans. Treatment with adiponectin lowers circulating glucose and free fatty acid levels in the blood, reduces insulin resistance, and decreases triglyceride storage in skeletal muscle in mice. Adiponectin receptors have been identified in the liver and skeletal muscles (Yamauchi et al., 2003). Mice that have been genetically engineered to lack the gene for adiponectin are insulin resistant and display diabetes. Additional research must be conducted to determine whether adiponectin is involved.

Many of the adipokine and gastrointestinal hormones operate on systems that are involved with energy balance (ingestive behaviors, activity, etc.) and also affect hypothalamic releasing hormones and tropic hormones from the anterior pituitary involved in reproductive regulation. The interaction between energy balance and reproduction will be considered in later chapters (see Chapters 9 and 10).

Steroid Hormones

The adrenal glands, the gonads, and the brain are the most common sources of steroid hormones in vertebrates. Vertebrate **steroid hormones** have a characteristic chemical structure that includes three six-carbon rings plus one conjugated five-carbon ring. In the nomenclature of steroid biochemistry, substances are identified by

steroid hormones   A class of structurally related fat-soluble chemicals that are derived from cholesterol and are characterized by three six-carbon rings plus one conjugated five-carbon ring.

the number of carbon atoms in their chemical structures (**FIGURE 2.22**). The precursor to all vertebrate steroid hormones is **cholesterol**. Although we mainly associate this waxy, artery-blocking substance with the bad cardiovascular consequences that can result from ingesting too much of it in our food, our bodies make substantial quantities of cholesterol from acetate in our livers. In addition to its role as a precursor to steroid hormones, cholesterol is important in many other biochemical reactions. The cholesterol molecule contains 27 carbon atoms. Thus, cholesterol is a C_{27} substance, although cholesterol itself is not a true steroid.

As noted above, steroid hormones are fat-soluble and move easily through cell membranes. Consequently, steroid hormones are never stored but leave the cells in which they were produced almost immediately. A signal to produce steroid hormones is also a signal to release them. The response can be a rather slow one: the delay between stimulus and response in biologically significant steroid production may be hours. Although ACTH stimulates corticoid secretion within a few minutes and LH acts quickly to affect progesterone production during the periovulatory surge, in most cases the signal to produce steroids is relatively slow.

Steroid hormones are not very soluble in water, and in the circulatory system they must generally bind to water-soluble carrier proteins that increase the solubility of the steroids and transport them through the blood to their target tissues. These carrier proteins also protect the steroid hormones from being degraded prematurely. The target tissues have cytoplasmic receptors for steroid hormones and accumulate steroids against a concentration gradient.

Upon arrival at the target tissues, steroid hormones dissociate from their carrier proteins and either interact with receptors embedded in the membrane or diffuse through the cell membrane into the cytoplasm or nucleus of the target cell, where they bind to cytoplasmic receptors. The amino acid sequence of steroid hormone receptors is highly conserved among vertebrates. Each steroid hormone receptor comprises three major domains; the steroid hormone binds to the C-terminal domain, the central domain is involved in DNA binding, and the N-terminal domain interacts with other DNA-binding proteins to affect transcriptional activation (Hadley and Levine, 2007). Steroid receptors are kept inactive by the presence of corepressors (consisting mainly of heat shock proteins [HSP]), which bind to the internal receptors and keep them inactive. It is the release of these HSPs after formation of the hormone-receptor complex that activates the steroid receptor, and if not there already, the activated steroid-receptor complex is transported into the cell nucleus, where it binds to DNA sequences called **hormone response elements** (**HREs**) and stimulates or inhibits the transcription of specific mRNAs. The precise mechanism by which the binding of a steroid-receptor complex to a specific HRE evokes activation or suppression of gene transcription remains unknown, but it appears certain that coactivator proteins are often necessary (Smith et al., 1997). The effects of environmental, social, or other extrinsic or intrinsic factors on the regulation of specific coactivators have not been studied enough and represent yet another process by which individual variation in hormone-behavior interactions may be mediated (Brosens et al., 2004). The mRNAs migrate to the cytoplasmic rough endoplasmic reticulum, where they are translated into specific structural proteins or enzymes that produce the physiological response (**FIGURE 2.23**). Changes in the types of proteins a cell makes (i.e., the gene products) can often be observed within 30 minutes of hormone stimulation.

The actions of steroids on target tissues, therefore, are based on three factors: (1) the steroid hormone concentrations in the blood, (2) the number of available receptors in the target tissue, and (3) the availability of appropriate coactivators. Blood concentrations of steroid hormones are themselves dependent on three factors: (1) the rate of steroid biosynthesis; (2) the rate of steroid inactivation by catabolism, which occurs mainly in the liver; and (3) the "tenacity" (affinity) with which the steroid hormone is bound to its plasma carrier protein. Recently, it has been deter-

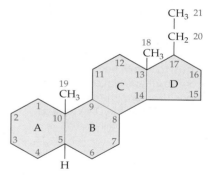

FIGURE 2.22 **Steroid chemical structure and nomenclature** All steroids have a chemical structure characterized by three six-carbon rings (A, B, C) plus one conjugated five-carbon ring (D). In the nomenclature of steroid biochemistry, each carbon atom is referred to by a number from 1 to 21.

cholesterol A white crystalline substance found in animal tissue, and an important part of cell membranes, cholesterol is a precursor to steroid hormones.

hormone response elements (HREs) The binding site for hormones on the DNA, where along with cofactor/transcriptional regulators, hormones regulate cellular function by either increasing or suppressing gene transcription.

FIGURE 2.23 **Steroid hormone receptors** are generally located in the cytosol or nucleus of a cell. The steroid hormone (S) binds to its receptor (R) to form a hormone-receptor complex (transcription factor), which binds to a hormone response element (HRE) on the DNA to begin transcription of mRNA.

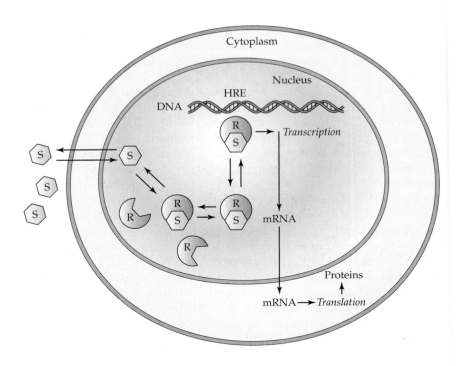

mined that different "types" of steroid receptors exist. For example, three versions of the estrogen receptor (α, β, and γ) are currently recognized (Hawkins et al., 2000). Multiple versions of steroid receptors represent another mechanism by which responsiveness to steroid hormones can be regulated. The regulation of receptors and coactivators is currently a very active research area in molecular endocrinology.

C_{21} STEROIDS: PROGESTINS AND CORTICOIDS   In response to various protein hormones from the anterior pituitary, cholesterol is converted into steroid hormones in the adrenals or gonads (**FIGURE 2.24**). The pituitary hormones induce an enzyme, called desmolase, that cleaves off the long chain of carbons from the top of the cholesterol molecule to yield **pregnenolone**, a C_{21} steroid. There are two general types of C_{21} hormones—**progestins** and **corticoids**. Pregnenolone is a progestin, and it is the obligatory precursor to all other steroid hormones. In other words, pregnenolone is a prohormone, a substance that can act as a hormone itself or can be converted into another hormone that has different endocrine properties. For example, pregnenolone can be converted to progesterone, another progestin. Progesterone is also a prohormone; it has several endocrine functions itself, and it is the major precursor for a variety of other C_{21} steroids, including the corticoids and another progestin called 17α-hydroxyprogesterone, which in turn is an important precursor of additional steroid hormone types.

Many progestins (e.g., pregnenolone and progesterone) are ubiquitous in vertebrates and are the obligatory precursors of all other steroid hormones (see Figure 2.24). Although named for their "progestational," or pregnancy-maintaining, effects in rodents, progestins are found in vertebrates wherever steroidogenesis occurs. In mammals, progesterone is important in maintaining pregnancy and also in the initiation and cessation of mating behavior.

In response to hormone signals from the anterior pituitary, pregnenolone is converted in the adrenal glands to progesterone and then to the various corticoids. Like all steroid hormones, the corticoids appear to be released as they are produced. These steroids have behavioral effects associated with the maintenance of bodily functions, such as mediating salt appetite.

pregnenolone   A C_{21} steroid prohormone that is the obligatory precursor for all other steroid hormones in vertebrates.

progestins   A class of C_{21} steroid hormones, so named for their "progestational," or pregnancy-maintaining, effects in mammals.

corticoids   A class of C_{21} steroid hormones secreted primarily from the adrenal cortices.

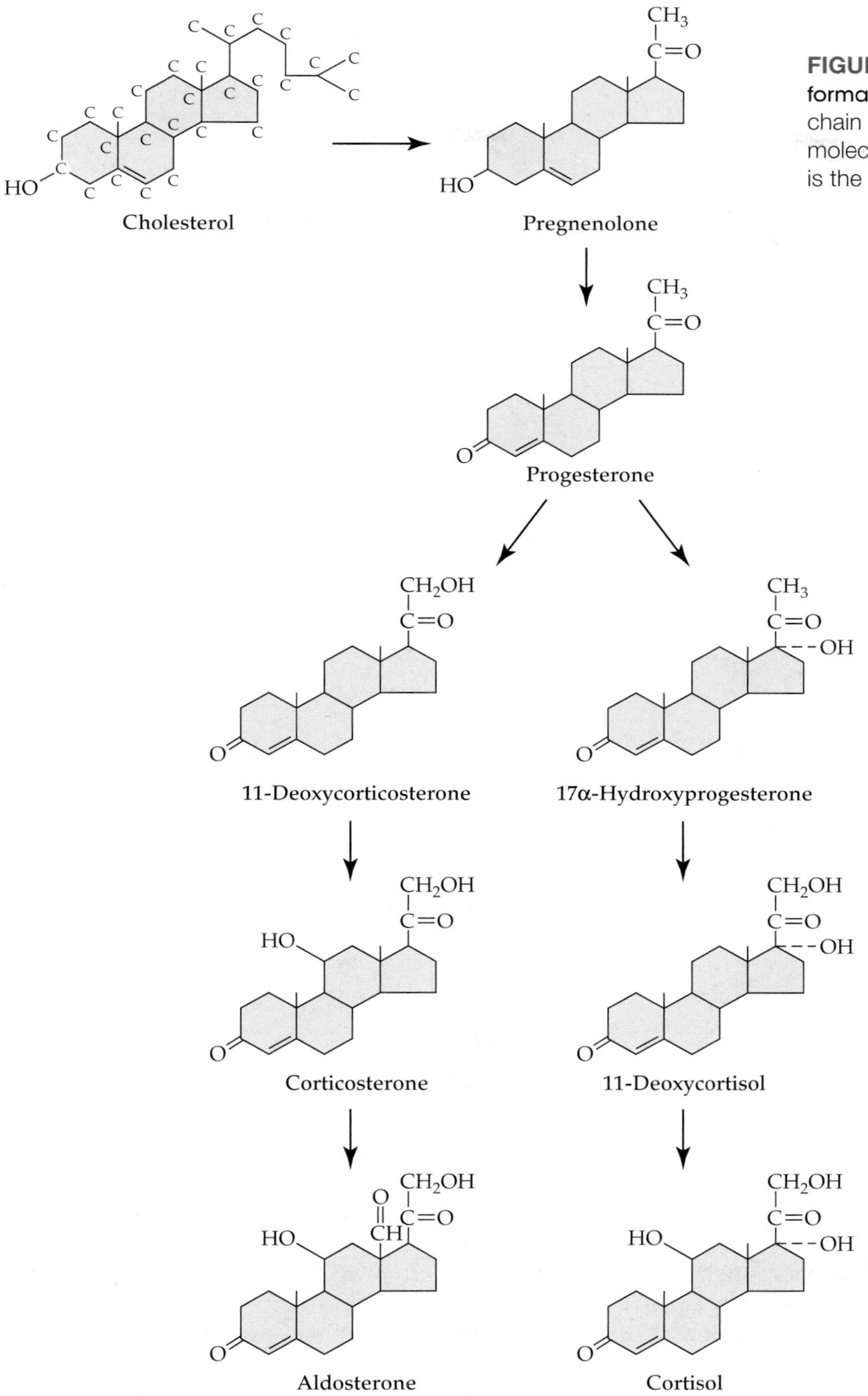

FIGURE 2.24 Biochemical pathways in steroid formation The enzyme desmolase cleaves the chain of carbons from the top of the cholesterol molecule to form pregnenolone, a C_{21} steroid that is the obligate precursor to all other steroids.

Cholesterol

Pregnenolone

Progesterone

11-Deoxycorticosterone

17α-Hydroxyprogesterone

Corticosterone

11-Deoxycortisol

Aldosterone

Cortisol

glucocorticoids One of the two types of corticoids secreted from the adrenal cortices; often released in response to stressful stimuli.

mineralocorticoids One of the two types of corticoids secreted from the adrenal cortices; important in ion exchange and water metabolism.

corticosterone Glucocorticoid produced in the adrenal cortices of most rodents and birds.

cortisol The principal glucocorticoid produced in the adrenal cortices of primates, including humans.

There are two types of corticoids: **glucocorticoids** and **mineralocorticoids**. Glucocorticoids are involved in carbohydrate metabolism and are often released in response to stressful stimuli; the two primary glucocorticoids are **corticosterone** (abbreviated *B*) and **cortisol** (*F*).[3] Most animals make either corticosterone or cortisol, and rarely are both glucocorticoids produced in large quantities, although Syr-

---

[3] The adrenal steroids were initially fractionated or isolated before their biological functions were known. Each fraction was designated by the name *compound A, compound B,* and so on. Later, when identified, they retained their original letter designations, but these are now becoming obsolete and are being replaced by abbreviations such as *CORT*.

FIGURE 2.25 Androgens, such as testosterone and androstenedione, are formed by an enzymatic cleavage of the ethyl group from a progestin precursor at C_{17}.

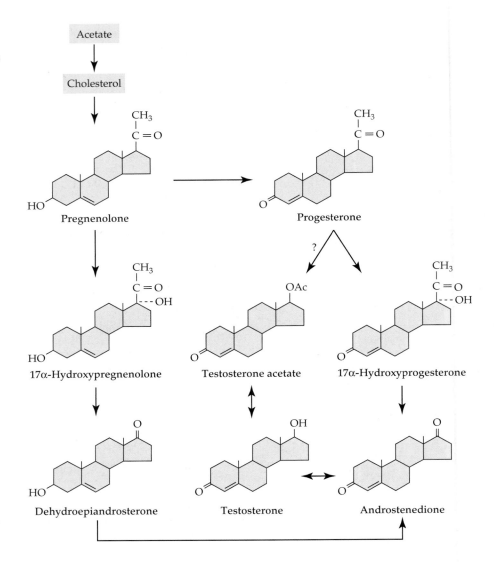

ian hamsters (*Mesocricetus auratus*) produce nearly equal amounts of both cortisol and corticosterone. All reptiles and birds secrete corticosterone from their adrenals. Some mammals also secrete corticosterone; rats and mice secrete corticosterone exclusively. The primary glucocorticoid secreted by teleost (bony) fishes and by humans and other primates, however, is cortisol.[4]

Of the mineralocorticoids, **aldosterone** is the most important, as it is secreted by all terrestrial vertebrates and is important in ion exchange and water metabolism. Aldosterone is primarily responsible for retaining sodium ions (Na^+) and excreting potassium ions (K^+).

C_{19} STEROIDS: ANDROGENS Just as a specific series of enzymes in the adrenals convert pregnenolone to the corticoids, specific enzymes found primarily in the gonads convert pregnenolone to several types of C_{19} steroid hormones, called **androgens** because of their *andros* ("male") producing effects (**FIGURE 2.25**). These

aldosterone A mineralocorticoid that causes the kidneys to retain sodium.

androgens The primary steroidal product secreted from the testes.

[4] It is important to be aware of this distinction between the two glucocorticoids. A physician-scientist recently argued that a procedure he was performing on mice was not stressful because "the levels of cortisol were very low." However, after he was persuaded to measure corticosterone, he discovered that his procedure indeed caused a substantial increase in this corticoid, which presumably reflected elevated stress.

C_{19} steroid hormones result from the enzymatic cleavage of the ethyl group from a progestin precursor at C_{17}. **Testosterone** and **androstenedione** are biologically important androgens, as are biochemically reduced versions of testosterone, **5α-** and **5β-dihydrotestosterone (DHT)**.[5] These androgens are produced in the well-vascularized Leydig cells of the testes; the Sertoli cells are the source of androgen-binding proteins that carry androgens from the Leydig cells to the nearby Sertoli cells to aid sperm maturation (see Figure 2.20). Sex hormone–binding globulin (SHBG), produced in the liver, acts as a carrier protein to move androgens through the general circulation. Testosterone is typically reduced to DHT or converted to an estrogen in order to have a biological effect.

The zona reticularis of the adrenal cortex also produces a relatively weak androgen called **dehydroepiandrosterone (DHEA)**. For the most part, the physiological functions of DHEA remain unknown, but blood concentrations of this hormone decline as individuals age. Replacement of DHEA at appropriate small doses appears to ameliorate certain effects of aging, including decreased muscle strength and weakened immune function (Yen et al., 1995). Based on these preliminary studies, alternative medical care providers have advocated DHEA supplementation as a treatment to reverse some of the effects of aging. However, long-term studies on the effects of DHEA therapy on human health are lacking, and it is probably prudent to await the results of such studies before indulging in self-administration of an active steroid hormone.

Androgens have many physiological and behavioral functions. These steroid hormones are necessary for spermatogenesis and the maintenance of the genital tract (e.g., the vas deferens). Androgens also maintain the accessory sex organs such as the prostate, seminal vesicles, and bulbourethral glands. The male secondary sex characters are also supported by androgens: well-known examples include the pattern and density of body hair in humans, comb size in roosters, and antler growth in deer. Some species show subtle morphological effects due to androgens; for example, in mice the salivary gland and kidney structures are affected by androgens. The liver, heart, and kidneys are generally larger in male mammals than in females with similar body masses. Of course, androgens have many effects on behavior, including courtship and copulatory behaviors, aggressive behaviors, and other social behaviors.

Androgens may also be synthesized in the adrenal cortex directly from corticoids if the appropriate enzymes are present. In certain congenital conditions in which excess converting enzymes are present, abnormally high levels of androgens may be produced by the adrenal glands, which can have masculinizing effects in females (see Chapter 3).

Metabolism is greatly affected by androgens. These hormones stimulate respiratory metabolism and are well known for their protein anabolic effects. The increase in muscle mass that results from treatment with anabolic androgens motivates many people to abuse these compounds. However, because many organs have androgen receptors, long-term problems in the liver, heart, and kidneys can result from chronic exposure to high androgen levels, as hypertrophy of these organs leads to a reduction in their functional efficiency. Reproductive problems are also common among people abusing anabolic androgens. Psychological problems have been reported for long-term androgen users as well. In many cases, however, a subjective sense of "invincibility" allows steroid abusers to dismiss warnings about the long-term health problems associated with androgen treatment (see Chapter 13).

C₁₈ STEROIDS: ESTROGENS Androgens are the obligatory precursors of all estrogens in the same way that progestins are the obligatory precursors of all androgens.

testosterone The primary androgen secreted by most vertebrate animals.

androstenedione The primary sex hormone secreted by the human adrenal cortex.

5α- and 5β–dihydrotestosterone (DHT) Potent androgens derived from testosterone that bind more strongly to androgen receptors than testosterone.

dehydroepiandrosterone (DHEA) A steroid hormone produced from cholesterol in the adrenal cortex, which is the primary precursor of natural estrogens, and is a weak androgen.

---

[5] The 5 in the name indicates that the reduction occurs with the addition of a hydrogen atom at carbon number 5; α and β refer to the orientation of the hydrogen molecule in space.

aromatization The process of converting an androgen molecule to an estrogen molecule via the enzyme aromatase.

Specific enzymes, primarily present in the ovaries, convert testosterone and androstenedione to estrogens by cleaving the carbon at position 19 from these androgen precursors (**FIGURE 2.26**). This process is called **aromatization** because the removal of the carbon leaves the estrogen with a phenolic A-ring, known as an aromatic compound. Biologically significant estrogens include 17β-estradiol, estrone, and estriol.

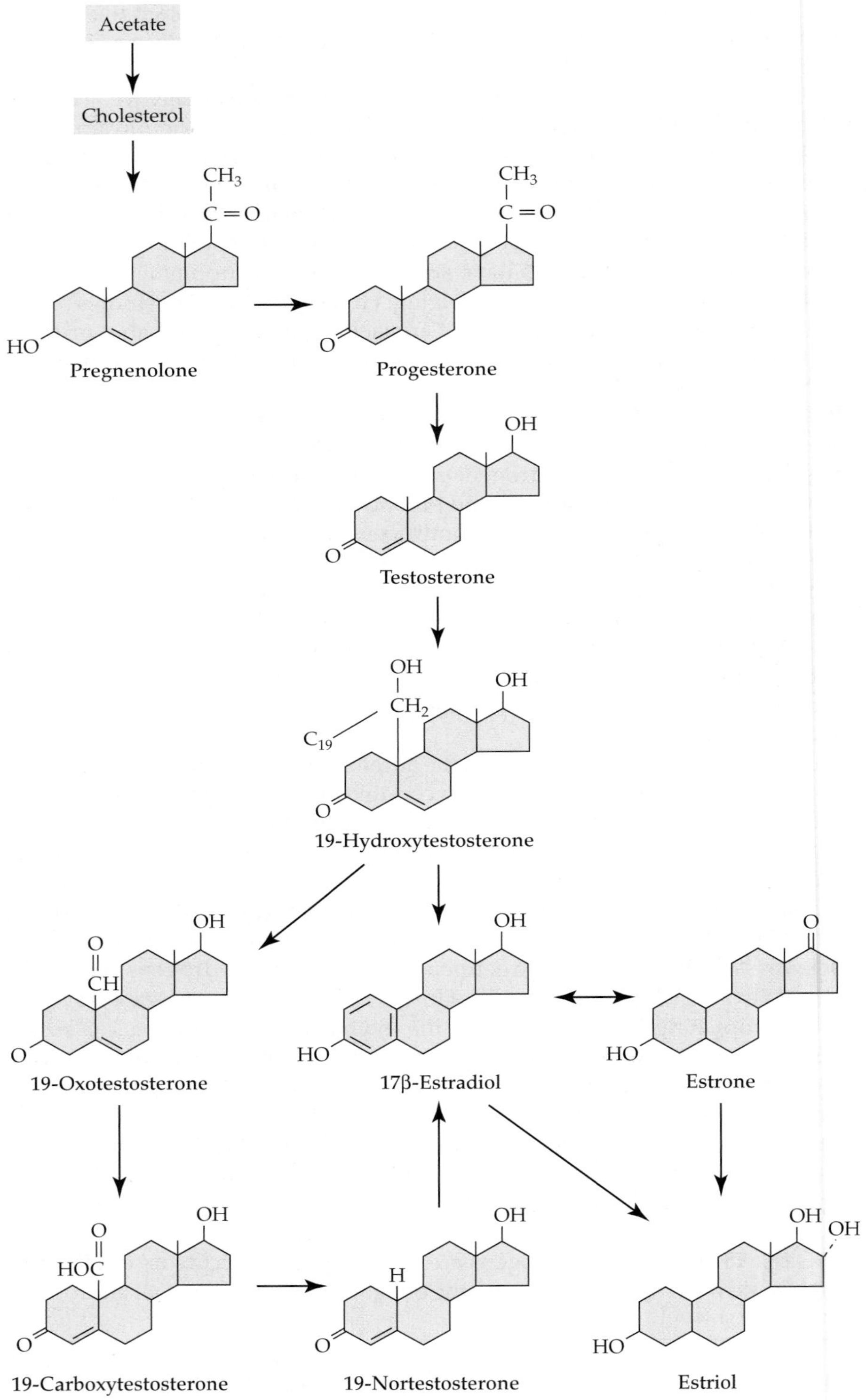

FIGURE 2.26 Estrogens, such as 17β-estradiol, estrone, and estriol, are formed when C_{19} is cleaved from an androgen precursor in a process called aromatization.

The interstitial tissues of the ovary (see Figure 2.21B) produce steroid hormones. The theca interna cells produce progestins, and enzymes in these cells act on those progestins to produce androgens. The blood flow in the ovary moves these androgens into the interstitial granulosa cells, where enzymes rapidly convert them into estrogens. The follicles of the ovary produce increased amounts of estrogens such as estradiol, estrone, and estriol as they mature. The corpora lutea produce progesterone in many vertebrate species but also release estrogens, androgens, and perhaps oxytocin, a peptide hormone.

Thus, ovaries produce substantial amounts of androgens, which are normally converted immediately to estrogens. However, in some cases, excess androgens are produced and enter the general circulation before they can be converted into estrogens, affecting female physiology and behavior. Also, if insufficient enzymes are present to convert androgens to estrogens in the ovaries, some androgens may be secreted into a female's blood circulation. On the other hand, if high levels of enzymes that convert androgens to estrogens are present in the testes, then estrogens will be secreted from the testes into the blood circulation of a male. Some androgens, such as DHT, cannot be aromatized and therefore cannot be converted to estrogens.

Estrogens have many functions. Estrogens initiate the formation of corpora lutea. They also affect the genital tract; for example, high levels of estrogens correlate with increased uterine mass. The secondary sex characters of female mammals are also influenced by estrogens. Estrogens have several metabolic functions as well, including effects on water metabolism. For instance, estrogens favor the retention of water in humans. Estrogens are important in calcium metabolism. More bone is made in the presence of high estrogen concentrations. During human menopause, estrogen production diminishes, and bone erodes away in a degenerative process called osteoporosis. Finally, estrogens are very important in sexual behavior and may also play a part in maternal aggression (see Chapter 7).

The placenta also produces steroid hormones. Both estrogens and progestins can be produced in significant amounts by the placenta; it also produces some androgens and corticoids. The contribution of these hormones from the placenta to the development of behavior is not well understood at this time. Unlike in most mammals, in many nonmammalian species of vertebrates there are no sex differences in the circulating concentrations of androgens and estrogens.

NEUROSTEROIDS   **Neurosteroids** are produced in both the central and peripheral nervous system, mainly in glial cells. They are synthesized de novo from cholesterol or from steroidal precursors produced elsewhere in the body. Common neurosteroids include 3β-hydroxy-δ5 compounds (e.g., pregnenolone and DHEA), their sulfated derivatives, and reduced steroidal metabolites (e.g., the tetrahydro derivative of progesterone, 3α-hydroxy-5α-pregnan-20-one [3α,5α-THPROG]). These compounds can function as allosteric modulators of neurotransmitter receptors, such as γ-aminobutyric acid A ($GABA_A$), N-methyl-D-aspartic acid (NMDA), and sigma receptors. Progesterone is also a neurosteroid, and a progesterone receptor has been identified in peripheral and central glial cells. Neurosteroid concentrations in different brain regions vary according to the environment and behavioral interactions. Behaviors associated with stress, memory, sexual behavior, and aggression have all been reported to be affected by neurosteroids. Neurosteroids may also be important regulators of affect (mood) and may modulate feelings of anxiety (Bitran et al., 2000; Dubrovsky, 2005).

A CAUTIONARY ASIDE   Although the androgens and estrogens are commonly referred to as sex hormones, it is important to emphasize that these hormones should not be considered "male" or "female." All male vertebrates produce some estrogens and progestins, and all female vertebrates produce androgens. The two sexes do differ in their relative concentrations of circulating androgens or estrogens, but this

neurosteroids   Steroids that are synthesized in the central nervous system (CNS) and the peripheral nervous systems (PNS), independently of the steroidogenic activity of the endocrine glands.

difference is due to the relative proportions of steroidogenic-specific enzymes in their gonads. Testes normally have more enzymes for making androgens and fewer aromatizing enzymes than do ovaries, but imbalances in the appropriate enzymes can lead to overt endocrine abnormalities. Androgens, with a few exceptions, are easily converted to estrogens. Importantly, testosterone can be considered a prohormone that is converted either to DHT or to an estrogen. Ovaries produce high concentrations of androgens, but high local concentrations of aromatizing enzymes rapidly convert those androgens to estrogens before they can enter the general circulation. Estrogens can theoretically be converted back to androgens, but this is an energetically expensive reaction and is rare in nature.

It is also important to emphasize that although sex steroid hormones are primarily formed in the gonads, they can also be produced in the adrenals, along with glucocorticoids and mineralocorticoids. The production of these various types of steroid hormones is zone-specific: the presence or absence of various enzymes in each of the three layers of the adrenal cortex determines the type of steroid hormone produced there. An aberrant gene coding for an incorrect enzyme can lead to an ovary or adrenal gland producing great quantities of androgens. The behavioral effects of such genetic anomalies will be discussed in Chapter 3.

Monoamine Hormones

Monoamines are hormones that are each derived from a single amino acid. There are two classes of monoamines that affect behavior: the **catecholamines** and the **indoleamines**. Recall that the thyroid hormones, too, are often classified as monoamines because they are derived from a single amino acid, tyrosine.

ADRENAL MEDULLARY MONOAMINE HORMONES The adrenal medulla is the main source of two catecholamines, **epinephrine** (adrenaline) and **norepinephrine** (noradrenaline); it also releases some dopamine (**FIGURE 2.27**). The catecholamines are derived from tyrosine and are called catecholamines because each is a catechol (i.e., a dihydroxyphenol) with an amine side group. In response to sympathetic neural signals, the adrenal medulla releases these hormones into the general circulation. Typical physiological stimuli that evoke catecholamine release include stress, exercise, low temperatures, anxiety, emotionality (fight or flight responses), and hemorrhage. In humans, norepinephrine and epinephrine are released at a ratio of 1:4 (James, 1992).

The catecholamines influence both the circulatory and metabolic systems. They have five general effects: (1) increased heart rate and cardiac output, (2) vasoconstriction of the deep and superficial arteries and veins, (3) dilation of skeletal and liver blood vessels, (4) increased glycolysis, and (5) increased blood glucagon concentrations and decreased insulin secretion. All of these effects serve to prepare the body for action. Epinephrine and norepinephrine have similar physiological effects but differ in several important respects. For instance, epinephrine elevates heart rate and affects metabolism more than norepinephrine. In contrast, norepinephrine is a more potent vasoconstrictor than epinephrine. The catecholamines affect their target cells via second messenger mechanisms.

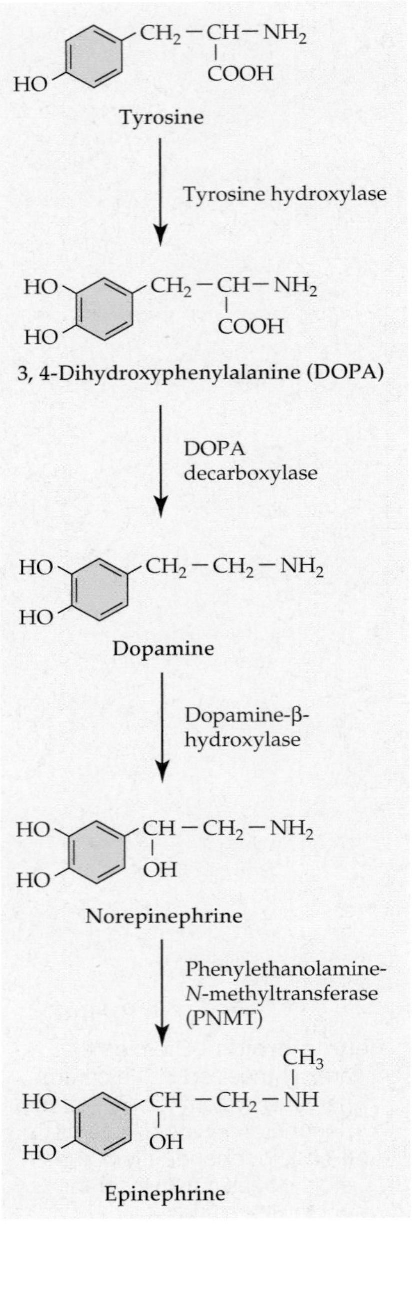

FIGURE 2.27 **Epinephrine, norepinephrine, and dopamine** are catecholamines, so called because each is a catechol with an amine side group. Of the three catecholamines, only epinephrine (adrenaline) acts primarily as a hormone; norepinephrine and dopamine are released from the adrenal glands and act as hormones, but they serve mainly as neurotransmitters. Catecholamines are all derived from the amino acid tyrosine, which is hydroxylated to form 3,4-dihydroxyphenylalanine (DOPA). DOPA may be decarboxylated in the cytoplasm to form dopamine, which in turn may be hydroxylated to form norepinephrine. Norepinephrine can be converted to epinephrine by the addition of a methyl group to the amine.

PINEAL GLAND HORMONES   Melatonin and serotonin are derived from the amino acid tryptophan. Melatonin is derived from serotonin in a two-step enzymatic reaction. These hormones are collectively called indole amines because the indole ring is common to both melatonin and serotonin (**FIGURE 2.28**).

Serotonin is the common name for 5-hydroxytryptamine (5-HT). Serotonin levels are high in the pineal gland during the light hours of the day but diminish during the dark hours as serotonin is converted into melatonin. The enzyme *N*-acetyltransferase converts serotonin to *N*-acetylserotonin, which is transformed into melatonin (5-methoxy-*N*-acetyltryptamine) by the transfer of a methyl group from *S*-adenosylmethionine (SAM) to the 5-hydroxyl of *N*-acetylserotonin by the actions of hydroxyindole-*O*-methyltransferase (HIOMT). Serotonin and *N*-acetylserotonin are probably not released from the pineal gland in appreciable quantities.

Melatonin is the major hormone secreted by the pineal gland. It is highly lipid-soluble and probably leaves the cell by diffusion in a manner similar to that of the steroids. Two melatonin receptors have recently been characterized; they code for 440–amino acid peptides that are found in the mammalian brain and amphibian skin (Bittman and Weaver, 1990; Dubocovich et al., 2003; Weaver et al., 1989). Many

monoamines   A hormone or neurotransmitter that contains one amine group.

catecholamines   Hormones that are derived from tyrosine and secreted primarily from the adrenal medulla.

indoleamines   Any of various indole derivatives, such as serotonin, containing a primary, secondary, or tertiary amine group.

epinephrine   A catecholamine produced in the adrenal medulla that increases cardiac tone and glucose levels.

norepinephrine   A substance that can act as either a hormone or neurotransmitter; secreted by the adrenal medulla and the nerve endings of the sympathetic nervous system.

serotonin   A neurotransmitter formed from tryptophan; the precursor to melatonin formation in the pineal gland.

melatonin   An indoleamine hormone released by the pineal gland.

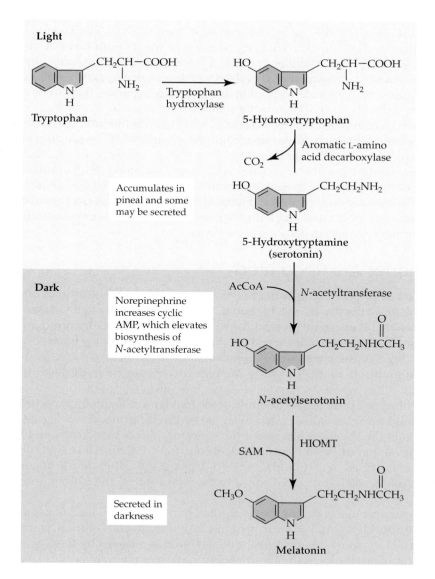

FIGURE 2.28   Serotonin and melatonin are formed from tryptophan. During the light hours of the day, tryptophan is converted in a two-step enzymatic reaction to serotonin. In darkness (shaded area), increased norepinephrine secretion causes an increase in *N*-acetyltransferase, the first of two enzymes that convert serotonin to melatonin. SAM = *S*-adenosylmethionine; HIOMT = hydroxyindole-*O*-methyltransferase.

prostaglandins A family of lipid-based hormones that possess a basic 20-carbon fatty acid skeleton; involved in several aspects of reproductive function.

lipid-based hormones Hormones derived from a fatty acid.

negative feedback A regulatory system that tends to stabilize a process when its effects are pronounced by reducing its rate or output.

mammals use the annual pattern of changes in day length as a cue to aid in the timing of various seasonal biological responses. Melatonin is an important hormone in the mammalian photoperiodic time measurement mechanism (Goldman, 2001). The effects of melatonin on the seasonal organization of breeding will be described more fully in Chapter 9.

Lipid-Based Hormones

Prostaglandins, a family of **lipid-based hormones**, were discovered in the 1930s. Their first known function was an ectocrine one: these compounds are found in seminal fluid and cause uterine contraction or relaxation in the recipient. Since their initial discovery, there have been reports of a vast array of biological actions produced by the prostaglandins. Prostaglandins affect several types of behavior in both vertebrates and invertebrates.

All prostaglandins possess a basic 20-carbon fatty acid skeleton, prostanoic acid, derived from essential fatty acids via cyclization and oxidation. The naturally occurring prostaglandins have been classified into four basic groups named E, F, A, and B. These groups are distinguished by differences in the cyclopentyl group of the fatty acid skeleton. Substitutions in the side chains and the extent of saturations provide a number of compounds within each group.

Prostaglandins in the E and F series are involved in reproduction. High concentrations of prostaglandins coincide with degradation of the corpora lutea of the ovary. In other systems, prostaglandins mediate a large array of actions, often opposing ones; for example, prostaglandins both stimulate and relax smooth muscle. Prostaglandins also affect cardiac functioning. In some circumstances they act as a pressor agent, whereas in other situations they have an antipressor effect.

Prostaglandins have also been implicated in influencing cyclic nucleotide formation. Prostaglandins inhibit cyclic adenosine monophosphate (cAMP) production in adipose cells, which can be stimulated by hormones such as epinephrine. In other cell types, prostaglandins can also stimulate cAMP formation and often modulate the second messenger response that mediates the actions of many peptide hormones. Prostaglandins are one type of the chemical messengers called eicosanoids. The prostacyclins, thromboxanes, and leukotrienes are closely related eicosanoids that may play important roles in behavioral processes.

How Hormones Are Regulated

There are two basic patterns of internal hormonal regulation: (1) hormones are regulated by the physiological by-products generated in response to their actions, and (2) hormones are regulated by the stimulatory or inhibitory effects of hormones. Within the second type of control system, there may be one, two, or three hormones in a regulatory chain, or there may be autoregulation via negative or positive feedback directly from the circulating levels of the regulated hormone itself (**FIGURE 2.29**).

Parathyroid hormone provides an example of the first type of regulatory mechanism. When blood levels of calcium decrease, parathyroid hormone is released. When the action of the hormone has raised the concentration of blood calcium to some optimal level, parathyroid hormone secretion stops. Calcium levels in the blood are thus maintained in an optimal range (**FIGURE 2.30A**). This simple **negative feedback** system works much the way a thermostat controls the temperature in your home.

GnRH is an example of a hormone that is regulated by a multiple chain of negative feedback controls (**FIGURE 2.30B**). In response to environmental stimuli, some internal pacemaker, or some other intrinsic event, GnRH is released by the hypothalamus and stimulates the release of the gonadotropins from the anterior pituitary

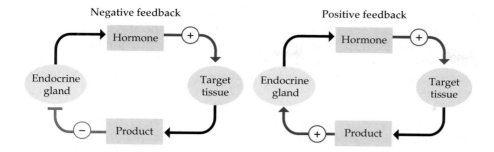

Negative feedback   Positive feedback

FIGURE 2.29 Models of negative and positive feedback In negative feedback, the production of a product by the target tissue feeds back on the source of the hormone to stop hormone production. During positive feedback, the production of a product stimulates additional hormone production. Negative feedback is much more common than positive feedback in endocrine regulation.

gland. The gonadotropins, in turn, stimulate steroid and gamete production in the gonads. The resulting steroid hormones feed back to turn off GnRH production in the hypothalamus, thereby shutting down gonadotropin secretion from the anterior pituitary. Peptide hormones from the gonads, such as activins and inhibins, may also be involved in the regulation of gonadotropins. The gonadotropins also feed back to shut down GnRH production, and GnRH also feeds back on the hypothalamus to regulate its own secretion (autoregulation). More detail regarding these multiple levels of control will be provided in Chapters 5 and 6.

In some cases, the feedback may drive hormone concentrations away from the preprogrammed setting. This sort of feedback loop is called **positive feedback**. Positive feedback is often involved when a relatively rapid endocrine response is

positive feedback   A regulatory process that tends to accelerate an ongoing process by increasing production in response to the end product.

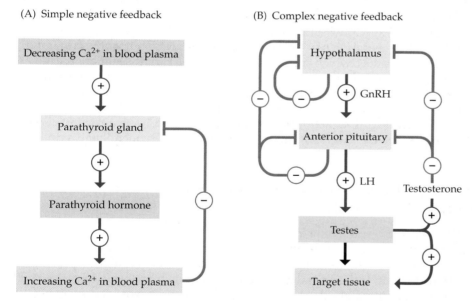

(A) Simple negative feedback

(B) Complex negative feedback

FIGURE 2.30 Negative feedback (A) The parathyroid gland is regulated by a simple negative feedback mechanism. When levels of calcium in the blood decline, the parathyroid gland is stimulated to release parathyroid hormone, which causes blood calcium levels to increase. These increased calcium levels feed back to the parathyroid and inhibit the release of further parathyroid hormone until calcium levels decrease again. (B) A more complex negative feedback relationship exists among the hypothalamus, anterior pituitary, and testes. In response to certain external or endogenous stimuli, the hypothalamus releases GnRH, which stimulates the anterior pituitary to release gonadotropins such as LH. In turn, the secreted LH stimulates steroid synthesis and secretion in the testes. In addition to acting on target tissues, the steroid hormones feed back to inhibit activity in both the anterior pituitary and hypothalamus. In parallel, increasing levels of gonadotropin slow down its secretion from the anterior pituitary and GnRH secretion from the hypothalamus. Likewise, as GnRH is secreted, the hypothalamus responds to increasing levels of the hormone by slowing down its secretion.

up-regulation   A process similar to positive feedback in which a hormone causes an increase in the production of receptors for that hormone.

down-regulation   A process that is similar to negative feedback in which the overproduction of a hormone causes occupation of virtually all available receptors so that subsequent high levels of hormones cannot have a biological effect.

pulsatile secretion   The episodic secretion of hormones in periodic bursts or spurts.

signal transduction pathway   The sequence of events that begins with a hormone binding to its receptor and ends with the response in a target cell.

necessary. Hormones associated with the stress response and with ovulation are regulated through a positive feedback system. Of course, positive feedback must be tightly controlled in short-term situations; otherwise, the equilibrium within the body will be seriously disrupted, with deleterious consequences for survival. Therefore, negative feedback is the most common type of regulatory mechanism in the endocrine system.

In addition to these two general types of internal controls, the secretion of many hormones is influenced by environmental factors. For example, rodents that breed only during the summer may inhibit pituitary LH and FSH secretion when exposed to short (winter-like) day lengths. In some species, this inhibitory effect of short days occurs even in castrated animals (i.e., even in the absence of internal negative feedback actions of the gonadal hormones).

Hormones often affect the levels of their own receptors. For example, an increase in blood concentrations of prolactin stimulates the production of more prolactin receptors; this process is called receptor **up-regulation** or homospecific priming. Similarly, high insulin concentrations reduce the number of insulin receptors in a process known as receptor **down-regulation**. Finally, hormones may regulate receptors for other hormones. Estrogens, for example, increase the number of uterine receptors for progestins. Such an effect, in which one hormone induces production of receptors for a second hormone or otherwise brings about the conditions necessary for the second hormone to be effective, is called heterospecific priming. Priming and other permissive effects are common in behavioral endocrinology.

Hormones are often released in spurts, a process called episodic or **pulsatile secretion**. For example, in male rhesus monkeys, GnRH is released in a pulsatile pattern. Approximately every 45 minutes or so, a quantity of GnRH is released into the hypothalamic-hypophyseal portal system. Shortly thereafter, a pulse of LH is released into the general circulation. Several minutes later, a burst of testosterone is released from the testes, which suppresses further GnRH release for another 45–90 minutes. This pulsatile pattern of hormonal release has functional implications. If one chronically infuses high levels of GnRH into an animal, all of the GnRH receptors are soon occupied, and no further biological action is possible. A hormone-free recovery period during which receptors are replenished is necessary to allow a physiological response. The many factors that affect pulse frequency and amplitude will be discussed later in this book in terms of their effects on behavior.

Cellular and Molecular Mechanisms of Hormone Action

Now that you know something about the major hormones produced and secreted by the endocrine glands, we will examine how hormones induce reactions at their target tissues. Hormonal messages, or signals, evoke intracellular responses via signal transduction: the chemical hormonal message is transformed into intracellular events that ultimately affect cell function. The sequence of events that begins with a hormone binding to its receptor and ends with the ultimate response in a target cell is called a **signal transduction pathway**. The initiation of these pathways in neurons is the most common mechanism by which hormones influence behavior.

Hormone Receptor Types

Many different kinds of molecules constantly bombard the outer surfaces of cells throughout the body. However, few molecules have a greater effect on cellular function than hormones. The ability of a target cell to recognize and respond to a given hormone is mediated by the presence of specific hormone receptors in that cell, but only a small fraction of the receptors needs to be activated to evoke the maximal

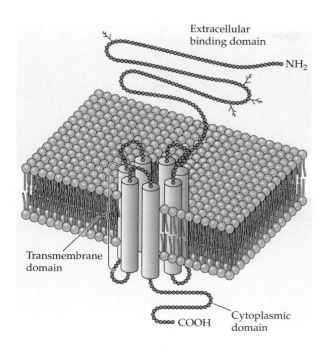

Extracellular
binding domain

NH₂

Transmembrane
domain

COOH

Cytoplasmic
domain

FIGURE 2.31   **Protein and peptide hormone receptors** are embedded in the phospholipid bilayer of the cell membrane. These receptors consist of three domains: an extracellular binding domain to which the peptide or protein hormone binds, a complex transmembrane domain that may traverse the membrane several times, and a cytoplasmic domain inside the cell.

cellular response. Steroid receptors differ in form and action from receptors for protein or peptide hormones, and we will now describe these differences in detail. Generally, hormones interact with receptors associated with neural cells to influence behavior.

STEROID RECEPTORS   Steroid and thyroid hormone receptors are located inside cells, either in the cytosol or in the nucleus. As mentioned earlier, steroids are lipid-soluble, so they can penetrate the cell membrane to bind with these intracellular receptors. When the receptors bind to a specific steroid or thyroid hormone, they migrate to the nucleus (if they are not already there) to regulate gene transcription. These receptors are part of a superfamily that also includes receptors for vitamin D and retinoic acid.

PROTEIN AND PEPTIDE HORMONE RECEPTORS   Protein and peptide hormone receptors are found embedded in the cell membrane and have at least three domains (a domain is a region of the receptor that has a specific recognized function), including (1) an extracellular domain that specifically binds to the hormone in question to form a hormone-receptor complex (in this context, the hormone is called a **ligand**— the name for any molecule that binds to a receptor), (2) a transmembrane domain, and (3) a cytoplasmic domain (**FIGURE 2.31**). These receptors are dynamic, changing in form and position in the membrane, and they turn over rapidly. Though all protein hormone receptors share a basic structure, they can be divided into two functional classes: (1) those with intrinsic enzymatic activity and (2) those that require an intracellular second messenger (see below) to exert their effects. Through a process called **enzyme amplification**, a single protein or peptide hormone molecule triggers synthesis of thousands of target molecules.

Receptors with intrinsic enzymatic activity have enzymes in the cytoplasmic domain that phosphorylate (add a phosphate to)—and thus activate—intracellular proteins. For instance, some of these receptors have a tyrosine kinase domain in the cytoplasm. Tyrosine kinase is an enzyme that catalyzes the transfer of a phosphate group from ATP to a protein kinase; in turn, the activated protein kinase phosphorylates various other enzymes that cause specific changes in cellular func-

ligand   A substance that binds to a receptor molecule.

enzyme amplification   A series of chemical reactions triggered by a hormone to produce not just one enzyme, but thousands.

FIGURE 2.32 Tyrosine kinase receptors are an important type of protein hormone receptor. When a peptide or protein hormone binds to its receptor, the cytoplasmic tyrosine kinase domain changes its shape. This conformational change allows the receptor to interact with an intracellular protein kinase and ATP. Phosphorylation activates the protein kinase, which can now activate other substrates within the cell. After enzymatic degradation of the bound hormone, the receptor releases its ligand and returns to its unoccupied state and conformation.

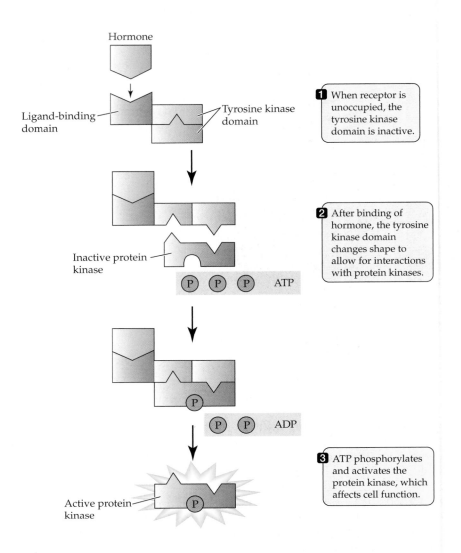

1 When receptor is unoccupied, the tyrosine kinase domain is inactive.

2 After binding of hormone, the tyrosine kinase domain changes shape to allow for interactions with protein kinases.

3 ATP phosphorylates and activates the protein kinase, which affects cell function.

second messenger A biological molecule released when a hormone binds to its receptor; the second messenger activates the cellular machinery of the target cell.

G proteins A class of proteins located adjacent to the intracellular part of a hormone or neurotransmitter receptor that are activated when an appropriate ligand binds to the receptor.

tion or membrane permeability (**FIGURE 2.32**). In addition to tyrosine kinase, this group of receptors includes some with guanylate cyclases that produce the second messenger cyclic guanosine monophosphate (cGMP) from GTP inside the cell (e.g., natriuretic peptide receptors), tyrosine phosphatases that dephosphorylate proteins, and serine/threonine kinases that specifically phosphorylate serine and threonine residues (e.g., receptors for activin) (Hadley and Levine, 2007).

The second class of protein and peptide hormone receptor requires a **second messenger**—a molecular middleman such as an enzyme or another protein—to transduce the hormonal signal. These receptors are coupled to **G proteins**, which can bind and hydrolyze GTP. There are several different types of G proteins, all of which have three different subunits, commonly labeled α, β, and γ (**FIGURE 2.33**). When a hormone binds to a G protein–coupled receptor, the hormone-receptor complex often activates an intracellular enzyme, adenylate cyclase, which in turn stimulates the formation of cAMP inside the cell. This cyclic nucleotide then activates specific protein kinases in the cell. When formed in response to binding of a hormone or other ligand, cAMP is referred to as a second messenger (the hormone is the first messenger).[6] In other cases, G proteins open ion channels, causing an

---

[6] Because G proteins often mediate between the hormonal signal (first messenger) and the cAMP or cGMP second messengers, students often ask why G proteins are not called second messengers and the cAMP and cGMP are not referred to as third messengers. Although this would be technically correct, the second messengers were discovered nearly two decades before the G proteins were, and the name has persisted.

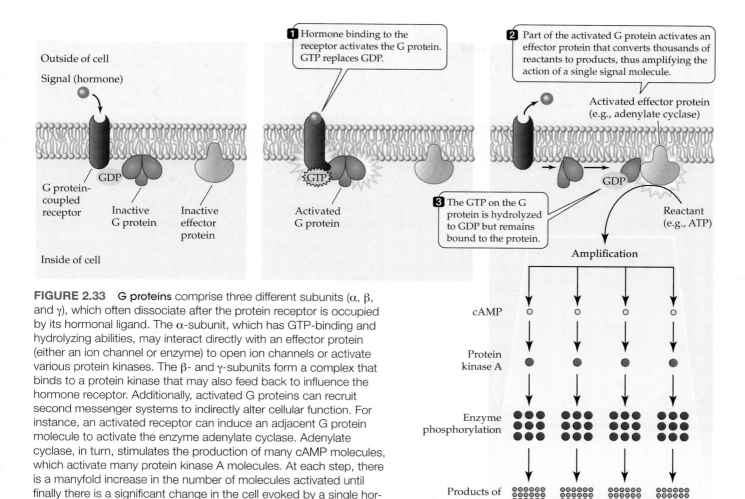

FIGURE 2.33 **G proteins** comprise three different subunits (α, β, and γ), which often dissociate after the protein receptor is occupied by its hormonal ligand. The α-subunit, which has GTP-binding and hydrolyzing abilities, may interact directly with an effector protein (either an ion channel or enzyme) to open ion channels or activate various protein kinases. The β- and γ-subunits form a complex that binds to a protein kinase that may also feed back to influence the hormone receptor. Additionally, activated G proteins can recruit second messenger systems to indirectly alter cellular function. For instance, an activated receptor can induce an adjacent G protein molecule to activate the enzyme adenylate cyclase. Adenylate cyclase, in turn, stimulates the production of many cAMP molecules, which activate many protein kinase A molecules. At each step, there is a manyfold increase in the number of molecules activated until finally there is a significant change in the cell evoked by a single hormone molecule binding to the G protein-coupled receptor.

increased intracellular influx of calcium that eventually stimulates cAMP (or cGMP) production, which then activates specific kinases. G protein-coupled receptors all have exactly seven transmembrane domains and are sometimes called serpentine receptors (see Figure 2.31). The G protein-coupled receptor family includes glucagon, oxytocin, and vasopressin receptors.

Different cell types have different specific cellular responses to cAMP. For example, when epinephrine binds to its adrenergic β-receptor, the ligand-receptor complex interacts with a stimulatory G protein called G_s, which in turn interacts with adenylate cyclase. Through signal amplification, adenylate cyclase generates many cAMP molecules (Norman and Litwack, 1987) (see Figure 2.33). Cell membranes also may contain another G protein, called G_i protein (i.e., inhibitory G protein); interaction with G_i protein inhibits the cAMP mechanism. We know that cAMP functions as the intracellular messenger for epinephrine because intracellular administration of cAMP duplicates all of the "hormonal" actions of epinephrine (Hadley and Levine, 2007). Once formed, cAMP can repeatedly combine with protein kinase A (PKA), an enzyme that phosphorylates (and thus activates) another enzyme called phosphorylase kinase in a variety of cells. In the liver, phosphorylase kinase then converts phosphorylase a into its active form, phosphorylase b which breaks down glycogen into glucose that can be released into the blood to provide energy for other cells (Norris, 2007). In fat cells, cAMP activates a hormone-dependent lipase that causes hydrolysis of stored fats for energy. In heart cells or neurons,

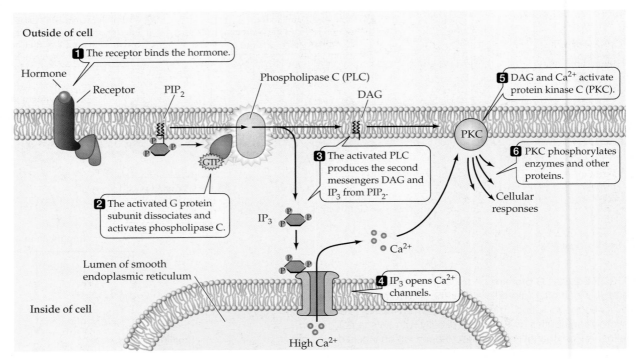

FIGURE 2.34 **Inositol triphosphate and diacylglycerol signal transduction** begins with the binding of a hormone to the extracellular domain of a G protein-coupled receptor. The α-subunit of the activated G protein activates phospholipase C (PLC), which evokes the hydrolysis of PIP_2 and subsequent formation of IP_3 and DAG. IP_3 mobilizes Ca^{2+} from stores in the endoplasmic reticulum (and possibly moves Ca^{2+} into the cell). The twin signals, the rises in intracellular DAG and Ca^{2+} concentrations, evoke PKC binding to the cell membrane and activation of Ca^{2+} channels.

Labels in figure:
- Outside of cell
- **1** The receptor binds the hormone.
- Hormone
- Receptor
- PIP_2
- Phospholipase C (PLC)
- DAG
- **5** DAG and Ca^{2+} activate protein kinase C (PKC).
- GTP
- PKC
- **3** The activated PLC produces the second messengers DAG and IP_3 from PIP_2.
- **6** PKC phosphorylates enzymes and other proteins.
- **2** The activated G protein subunit dissociates and activates phospholipase C.
- IP_3
- Cellular responses
- Ca^{2+}
- Lumen of smooth endoplasmic reticulum
- **4** IP_3 opens Ca^{2+} channels.
- Inside of cell
- High Ca^{2+}

transcription factor Substance that promotes or blocks the process whereby a single strand of complementary RNA nucleotides is produced from a single strand of DNA.

cAMP activates PKA and may also bind to Ca^{2+}-gated ion channels, which can depolarize the cell membrane. In addition to these cytosolic mechanisms of cAMP signal transduction, cAMP may migrate to the cell nucleus and bind to a cAMP responsive element binding protein (CREB). When bound to cAMP, CREB serves as a transcription factor that binds to DNA promoter regions in order to regulate gene transcription (see next page).

There are other signal transduction pathways that involve G proteins but do not rely on cAMP or cGMP. One important example is the inositol triphosphate (IP_3)/ diacylglycerol (DAG) pathway (**FIGURE 2.34**). As is the case with the G protein–coupled receptors we have discussed so far, the IP_3/DAG pathway begins with the binding of a hormone to the extracellular domain of a receptor and the activation of its associated G protein (see Figure 2.33). However, in this case, the dissociated α-subunit activates phospholipase C (PLC), resulting in the hydrolysis of phosphatidylinositol-4,5-biphosphate (PIP_2), which leads to the formation of IP_3 and DAG. IP_3 mobilizes Ca^{2+} from stores in the endoplasmic reticulum. These twin signals—that is, the rise in intracellular concentrations of both DAG and Ca^{2+}—evoke protein kinase C (PKC) binding to the cell membrane and activation of ion channels.

Transcription, Translation, and Posttranslational Events

The final common pathway through which hormones may affect behavior is by acting as **transcription factors**. The signal transduction pathways described above are diverse, and some, such as the cAMP/CREB pathway, ultimately affect gene transcription, the process by which the sequence of nucleotides in a single strand of DNA is transcribed into a single strand of complementary mRNA (**FIGURE 2.35**). Transcription factors bind to the beginning of the DNA sequence where the gene to be transcribed is located. This binding facilitates transcription of the gene.

In order to synthesize mRNA, the two tightly twisted strands of DNA must be unraveled by enzymes called helicases. A gene consists of a unique linear sequence of DNA. Among eukaryotic organisms, some of the nucleotide sequences within the gene are noncoding sequences, called introns, which alternate with coding se-

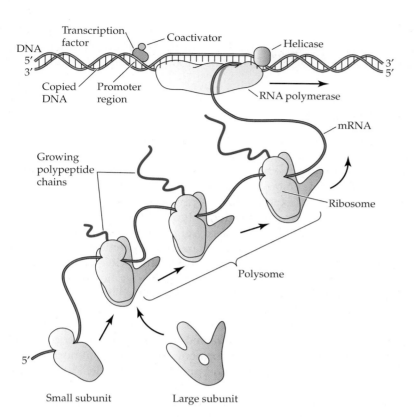

FIGURE 2.35 **Transcription and translation** During gene transcription, the strands of the double-helix DNA molecule must be chemically "pried apart" by helicases. Then, transcription factors bind to the promoter region of a gene; this allows an RNA polymerase to transcribe the DNA and produce mRNA. As soon as the message has been transcribed and processed, mRNA can leave the nucleus to be translated by the ribosomes. A complex of several ribosomes and mRNA is called a polysome.

quences, called exons. There are special marker sequences denoting the start and end points of each gene. A distinct sequence of nucleotides, called a promoter or facilitatory region, marks the start of the gene. The binding of a transcription factor to the promoter allows the enzyme RNA polymerase to attach to the promoter and begin the process of RNA synthesis. The sequence of RNA nucleotides, determined by the sequence of nucleotides along the DNA, eventually determines the sequence of amino acids in the protein product of the gene. After transcription, enzymes clip out the intron sequences; then other enzymes splice together the remaining segments (exons) to form messenger RNA (mRNA). The mRNA leaves the cell nucleus, travels to the rough endoplasmic reticulum (RER), and serves as the template for translation into a linear sequence of amino acids, which occurs on ribosomes.

When the protein being synthesized is itself a protein hormone, the first product of translation is called a **preprohormone** (**FIGURE 2.36**). At the N-terminal end of the preprohormone is a certain amino acid sequence called the signal peptide. This peptide is separated from the preprohormone during further processing of the protein, yielding a prohormone, which is then packaged into vesicles before being moved to the Golgi apparatus. Typically, additional posttranslational processing of the prohormone by special enzymes occurs within the rough endoplasmic reticulum, the Golgi apparatus, and the vesicles to yield the final version of the hormone

preprohormone A sequence of amino acids that contains a signal sequence, one or more copies of a peptide hormone, and other peptide sequences that may or may not possess biological activity.

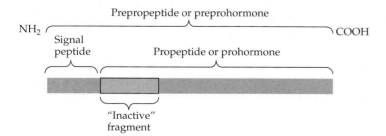

FIGURE 2.36 **The preprohormone** is the product of mRNA translation at the ribosome. The signal peptide is required for transport of the prohormone into the endoplasmic reticulum. Later, the prohormone is cleaved to produce the hormone and an "inactive" fragment, which are both usually released from the cell.

(or hormones) for secretion. In some cases (e.g., thyrotropin-releasing hormone), the prohormone is cleaved into several molecules of the hormone; in other cases (e.g., pro-opiomelanocortin), several different hormones can be produced from a single prohormone.

Evolution of Hormones

Behavioral endocrinologists are often interested in the phylogenetic relationships among hormones, endocrine gland anatomy, and behavior. Examination of these relationships provides insight into the function and evolution of hormone-behavior interactions. For example, to understand the evolution of hormonal effects on bird vocalization, it might be useful to examine the distribution of steroid hormone receptors throughout the nervous systems of different types of birds that vocalize. Because we can estimate when various bird species diverged from common ancestors, the evolution of various brain centers and their interactions with hormones can be discerned through the use of the comparative method to study diverse birds, such as roosters (see Figure 1.5), starlings, and parrots. We can learn whether analogous or homologous neural structures are necessary for vocalization in birds, whether these structures serve similar functions in reptiles or amphibians, and whether these structures have retained this function in mammals. Do hormones affect vocalization in all types of birds? If not, which birds are affected by hormones? Is reptilian or amphibian vocalization affected by the same hormones or by different hormones? What about mammals? The comparative method potentially provides insight into many fascinating questions.

In most cases, the evolution of hormones has been an evolution in the function of hormones. The chemical structures of steroid hormones are virtually identical among all vertebrate animals, but the functions of these hormones have changed many times across different species. Some protein hormones have also been conserved over evolutionary time and perform diverse functions. For instance, as noted above, insulin has been found virtually unchanged in species ranging from bacteria to humans (Norman and Litwack, 1987). Point mutations have occurred during the evolution of some other protein hormones, leading to species-specific versions of those hormones (e.g., GnRH; see Figure 2.7) or to new hormones. For example, growth hormone and prolactin have very similar molecular structures. Assuming that mutations occur at a constant rate, the sequence of amino acids of a peptide hormone can be compared between species to determine the evolutionary time when the proteins diverged. The amount of time, in millions of years, required for 1% of the amino acids in two proteins to differ can be quantified. By comparison of mammalian prolactin with mammalian growth hormone amino acid sequences, it was determined that these two hormones diverged in structure about 350 million years ago (Miller et al., 1983).

Substances that resemble vertebrate peptide hormones have been identified within tissues of flies, worms, protozoans, and even bacteria, but these substances probably function as tissue growth factors; that is, these chemical messengers may be released intracellularly to regulate cellular growth processes (Hadley and Levine, 2007; Norris, 2007). Cell-to-cell communication probably developed during the evolution of multicellular organisms so that processes could be synchronized among the various cells of an organism. Because mediation of the effects of hormones on target tissues requires receptors, there was probably simultaneous evolution of both hormones and receptors.

Studying the evolution of hormones, their receptor distributions, and behavior has provided behavioral endocrinologists with clues about how solutions to problems common to all species have evolved. During the process of natural selection, outcomes rather than specific mechanisms are selected. Consequently, vastly different mechanisms leading to similar outcomes have evolved among various species.

In the following chapters, many hormone-behavior interactions that have led to increased survival and reproductive success will be described.

Summary

1. Endocrinology is the study of the endocrine system. Endocrine glands are ductless glands that secrete their products, hormones, directly into the circulatory system. Tables listing the hormones and their primary physiological function are provided in the end papers.

2. There are four classes of hormones: (1) proteins and peptides, (2) steroids, (3) monoamines, and (4) lipid-based hormones. Peptide and protein hormones are made up of amino acid chains of various lengths. Protein hormone receptors are located on the cell surface and usually involve a second messenger to mediate the physiological response to the hormone. Steroid hormones are derived from cholesterol. These molecules are fat-soluble and thus travel through cell membranes easily; steroid receptors are typically found inside the cell.

3. Monoamine hormones are each derived from a single amino acid, whereas the lipid-based hormones are derived from lipids.

4. Hormones are often internally regulated by negative feedback mechanisms, either by their own concentrations or those of other hormones, or by regulatory physiological processes that involve the end products of target tissues. Many environmental stimuli also influence hormonal secretion.

5. The anatomical locations of the major endocrine glands in humans are depicted in Figure 2.3. The hypothalamus is located at the base of the brain. It integrates information from many higher brain sites into blood-borne signals, serving as one of the primary interfaces between the nervous system and the endocrine system. The hypothalamus secretes small peptide hormones that mediate anterior pituitary function. It communicates with the anterior pituitary through a portal blood vessel system, and with the posterior pituitary via nerve cell connections.

6. The pituitary gland is really two distinct organs with different embryological origins that are fused together in most vertebrate species. The anterior pituitary produces and releases a number of tropic hormones, which regulate the production and release of other hormones and additional physiological processes. Two nonapeptide hormones are typically released from the posterior pituitary. Oxytocin regulates smooth muscle contractions during milk letdown and birth; vasopressin participates in osmoregulatory functions.

7. The thyroid gland is located in the upper thorax in most vertebrate species and secretes two hormones in response to thyroid-stimulating hormone from the anterior pituitary. The thyroid hormones, triiodothyronine and thyroxine, elevate oxidation rates in tissues. Situated in or near the thyroid gland are two additional endocrine structures, the parathyroid gland and the C cells of the thyroid. These structures secrete protein hormones that regulate blood levels of calcium.

8. The pancreas is both an exocrine and an endocrine organ. The endocrine compartment of the pancreas consists of islands of hormone-secreting cells nested throughout the exocrine tissue. These islets of Langerhans contain three cell types that release three different protein hormones: insulin, glucagon, and somatostatin. Insulin is the only hormone that can lower blood glucose levels. Glucagon works in opposition to insulin to elevate blood sugar levels. Somatostatin is an inhibitory hormone.

9. The three major peptide gastrointestinal hormones—secretin, gastrin, and cholecystokinin—are secreted from specialized endocrine cells scattered throughout the gastrointestinal tract. Ghrelin is produced in the stomach. These and other gut hormones have also been discovered elsewhere in the body, particularly in the brain, where they may have behavioral effects. In the gut, these hormones mediate the digestion process.

10. Adipose (fat) cells also produce hormones, including leptin and adiponectin. Leptin acts on receptors in the CNS and at other sites to induce energy expenditure and inhibit food intake. Expression of adiponectin mRNA is decreased in obese mice and humans. Additional research is necessary to determine any behavioral effects of adiponectin.

11. The adrenal gland consists of two distinct organs. The outer part of the gland, the adrenal cortex, is arranged in three discrete bands of cell types, which secrete three distinct types of steroid hormones: mineralocorticoids, glucocorticoids, and sex steroid hormones. These steroids are primarily involved in mineral and carbohydrate metabolism. The adrenal medulla, or inner part of the gland, produces and releases two monoamine hormones, epinephrine and norepinephrine, which are important in the physiological response to stress.

12. The pineal gland functions as a photoreceptor in nonavian and nonmammalian species. The indole amine melatonin is its primary endocrine product in most vertebrates thus far examined. Melatonin has many effects on reproduction, especially in terms of the timing of puberty or seasonal breeding patterns.

13. The gonads are the reproductive organs, called testes in males and ovaries in females. The gonads have two major functions: production of gametes and production of sex steroid hormones. These two functions are compartmentalized in different cell types. In the testes, spermatogenesis occurs in the seminiferous tubules. The primary steroidal products of the testes are androgens. The ovaries produce ova (eggs), which develop in follicles in association with estrogen secretion. When an ovum is shed from an ovary during ovulation, the site of rupture develops into another steroid-producing structure called the corpus luteum. The primary steroidal products of corpora lutea are progestins.

14. The placenta is a temporary endocrine gland that forms in the uterus of pregnant mammals. The placenta secretes protein and peptide hormones that can affect both the mother and fetus(es).

Questions for Discussion

1. Hormones control many aspects of physiology and behavior. Discuss the proposition that hormones themselves are exquisitely controlled substances.

2. How do peptide and steroid hormones differ in production, secretion, and interaction with their receptors?

3. One should be cautious when taking steroid hormone supplements. Given what you've learned about the way steroid hormones are produced, why might taking a hormone naturally produced by your body be dangerous?

4. One focus of behavioral endocrinology has been on correlating the blood concentrations of hormones with behavior. Recently, this focus has shifted to target tissue sensitivity to hormones. Why are hormone receptor numbers important in understanding hormone-behavior interactions?

5. How are comparative studies useful in understanding hormone-behavior interactions? Are there any negative consequences of comparative analyses?

6. Describe the differences between the mechanisms controlling the release of LH and those controlling the release of oxytocin. Is the anatomy of the pituitary gland relevant to your answer?

Suggested Readings

Hadley, M., and Levine, J. E. 2007. *Endocrinology* (6th ed.). Benjamin Cummings, San Francisco.

Melmed, S., Polonsky, K. S., Larsen, P. R., and Kronenberg, H. M. 2016. *Williams Textbook of Endocrinology* (13th ed.). Saunders, Philadelphia.

Norman, A. W., and Henry, H. L. 2014. *Hormones* (3rd ed.). Academic Press, New York.

Norris, D. O., and Carr, J. C. 2013. *Vertebrate Endocrinology* (5th ed.). Elsevier Academic Press, San Diego.

Wilkinson, M., and Brown, R. E. 2015. *Introduction to Neuroendocrinology* (2nd ed.). Cambridge University Press, New York.

Sex Differences in Behavior

Sex Determination and Differentiation

3

Learning Objectives

The goal of this chapter is to describe the relationship between hormones and sex differences in brain and behavior. After reading this chapter, you should be able to:

- explain the difference between sex determination and sexual differentiation, as well as the difference between gender and sex.

- describe how hormones both organize (i.e., program) sex differences in the brain and later in life activate these sexually dimorphic circuits to yield behaviors.

Caitlyn Jenner, born Bruce Jenner, is a gold medal–winning track star who set a world record in the decathlon at the 1976 Summer Olympic Games in Montreal, Quebec, Canada, by scoring 8634 points (**FIGURE 3.1A**). After the Olympics, Jenner remained in the public eye through endorsements, speaking engagements, and TV appearances, representing the all-American man. Everyone old enough to remember the late 1970s can likely recall Jenner famously appearing on the Wheaties cereal box and being the spokesperson for the breakfast cereal for years thereafter. Jenner spent much of the late 1970s to the early 2000s starring in television and movies. As Bruce Jenner, he came into the public spotlight once again in 2007 with the premiere of the TV reality series *Keeping Up with the Kardashians*, in which he starred with his wife, Kris Jenner, children Kendall and Kylie Jenner, and stepchildren Kim, Kourtney, and Khloé Kardashian.

In early 2015, tabloid rumors began to spread that Jenner identified as transgender. In April of 2015, in an exclusive interview with Diane Sawyer on *20/20*, Jenner revealed that she identified as a woman and had begun hormone treatments. In June 2015, Jenner announced she is a woman on Twitter with the statement, "I'm so happy after such a long struggle to

FIGURE 3.1 Bruce and Caitlyn Jenner (A) Bruce Jenner at the 1976 Summer Olympic Games in Montreal, Quebec, Canada. (B) Caitlyn Jenner making her first public appearance at the ESPY awards in Los Angeles where she was awarded the Arthur Ashe Award for Courage.

(A)

(B)

be living my true self. Welcome to the world Caitlyn. Can't wait for you to get to know her/me." Caitlyn made her first public appearance when she walked on stage to a standing ovation at the ESPY awards in Los Angeles to accept the Arthur Ashe Award for Courage (**FIGURE 3.1B**). In the interview with Diane Sawyer before her transition, Jenner clearly declared a sexual attraction to women. As this book goes to press, Caitlyn, starring in the TV series *I Am Cait*, is uncertain whether she would ever date a man, and admits that she has only been with women.

Some people following the Caitlyn Jenner story were confused. Why would a man transition to being a woman if she is still attracted to women? In response to such confusion, Caitlyn states, "There's two different things here. Sexuality is who you personally are attracted to—who turns you on—but gender identity has to do with who you are as a person and your soul and who you identify with inside." When we consider sex and sex differences throughout this chapter, it will become clear that we cannot think of sex as a simple dichotomy. Sex is composed of multiple dimensions, including to whom one is sexually attracted, whether one identifies as male or female, one's chromosomal makeup, and the appearance of one's external genitalia. In many cases, there is concordance among characteristics defining sex. In others, some traits are male-like, some female-like, and some intermediary. Similarly, sex differences are equally as variable, whereby one individual might display "female" characteristics in one trait and "male" characteristics in another. The situation is further complicated by the fact that parental and cultural expectations often define what is considered male and female, making it difficult to definitively categorize behaviors under investigation.

The goal of this chapter is to examine **sexual differentiation**, the developmental process of becoming male or female. Because males and females differ in the ratio of androgenic to estrogenic steroid hormone concentrations, behavioral endocrinologists have been particularly interested in the extent to which behavioral sex differences are mediated by hormones. The primary step in sexual differentiation occurs at fertilization. In mammals, the ovum (which usually contains an X chromosome)

sexual differentiation The process by which individuals develop the characteristics associated with being male or female.

can be fertilized by a sperm bearing either a Y or an X chromosome; this process is called **sex determination**. The chromosomal sex of homogametic mammals (XX) is female; the chromosomal sex of heterogametic mammals (XY) is male. This chapter will discuss the steps that follow, from chromosomal sex to gonadal sex to hormonal sex to morphological sex and behavioral sex differences. The process of sexual differentiation is complicated, and the potential for atypical development is high. By studying individuals who do not neatly fall into the dichotomous boxes of female or male, behavioral endocrinologists glean hints about the process of typical sexual differentiation.

We will see that gonadal steroid hormones have organizing, or programming, effects upon brain and behavior and that an asymmetry exists in the effects of testes and ovaries on the organization of behavior in mammals. The organizing effects of steroid hormones are relatively constrained to the early stages of development, although sex steroid hormones can organize the brain and behavior as late as puberty. Hormone exposure early in life has organizational effects on subsequent rodent mating behavior; early steroid hormone treatment causes relatively irreversible and permanent masculinization of rodent copulatory behavior. These early hormone effects can be contrasted with the reversible behavioral influences of steroid hormones provided in adulthood, which are called activational effects. The activational effects of hormones on adult behavior are temporary and may wane soon after the hormone is metabolized.

After puberty, females display cycles of reproductive physiology and behavior that correspond to the cyclic release of eggs during the breeding season; males produce sperm at relatively constant rates throughout the breeding season and exhibit relatively constant reproductive behavior. The cyclic nature of female reproductive function compared with the relative steady state of male reproductive function will be discussed, but generally it represents differential exposure to androgens during development. Exposure to androgens early in development abolishes forever the potential to generate reproductive hormone surges. We will explore this phenomenon closely to understand several sex differences in brain and behavior.

Because in birds and reptiles sexual differentiation occurs in eggs and is separated from the mother's endocrine state, studies of these species provide insight into other ways that natural selection works in developing two distinct sexes with separate behavioral repertoires. Environmental factors such as temperature, intrauterine position, and exposure to chemicals that mimic hormones can influence sexual development. Because each individual is exposed to a unique set of environmental factors during development, determining the individual contribution of each biological and environmental factor to atypical sexual characteristics is complicated and challenging. For example, steroids move freely between tissues in the body, so in egg-laying creatures, such as birds and some reptiles, the mother's endocrine status is transferred to her eggs. If she has high levels of androgens or glucocorticoids at the time of egg production, then her eggs have high levels of those hormones. Therefore embryos develop in eggs with a range of steroid concentrations. This variation may reflect diverse maternal conditions, including social rank, food availability, and season of the year. The extent to which these maternal hormones affect the brain and behavior of the offspring remains somewhat unclear.

This chapter also examines the ultimate reasons for the evolution of sex. Individuals of asexual vertebrate species produce only one sex, females, which produce large gametes called eggs. Production of offspring by asexual reproduction is very efficient, but such species risk extinction if environmental conditions change drastically, because there is no genetic variation among the offspring. The recombination of genetic material during sexual reproduction, on the other hand, produces genetic variation. Sexual species produce two sexes: females and males. Thus, the ultimate cause of sex differences appears to reflect sexual selection, a subcategory of natural selection. Animals with polygynous mating systems display more sexual

sex determination   The point at which an individual begins to develop as either a male or a female.

dimorphic Having two different forms; usually refers to differences between the two sexes.

dimorphism than monogamous animals. Humans, who are mildly to moderately polygynous, display several sexual dimorphisms, as we will see.

Hens and roosters are different. Cows and bulls are different. Women and men are different. Girls and boys are different. Humans, like many animals, are sexually **dimorphic** (*di*, "two"; *morph*, "type") in the size and shape of their bodies, their physiology, and their behavior. The behavior of boys and girls differs in many ways. Girls generally excel in verbal abilities relative to boys; boys are nearly twice as likely as girls to suffer from dyslexia (reading difficulties) and stuttering and nearly four times more likely to suffer from autism. Boys are generally better than girls at tasks that require visuospatial abilities. Over 90% of all anorexia nervosa cases involve young women. Young men are twice as likely to suffer from schizophrenia as young women. Girls engage in nurturing behaviors more frequently than boys. Boys are much more aggressive and generally engage in more rough-and-tumble play than girls (Berenbaum et al., 2008; Hines, 2004). Many sex differences, such as the difference in aggressiveness, persist throughout adulthood. For example, there are many more men than women serving prison sentences for violent behavior. The hormonal differences between men and women may account for adult sex differences that develop during puberty, but what accounts for behavioral sex differences among children prior to puberty and activation of their gonads?

Behavioral endocrinologists, like most people, are interested in these and other behavioral sex differences. What are the proximate causes of behavioral sex differences? This question is one version of the enduring nature-versus-nurture question. Behavior, like any other phenotypic trait, is the result of the interaction of biological and environment factors. These environmental factors include learning and cultural influences (nurture), whereas biological factors include genes and their downstream physiological responses (nature). Researchers and students of behavioral endocrinology try to discover the extent to which behavioral differences between males and females are mediated by environmental influences, including social interactions, and the extent to which they are mediated by physiological factors, especially hormones. Trying to separate these influences can be difficult, if not impossible. Sex differences in some behaviors, such as snoring, are probably due exclusively to biological factors, whereas other behaviors, such as choosing a style of clothing or haircut, appear to reflect only cultural influences. Some human behavioral sex differences, such as pain responses and aggressive behavior, reflect a blend of biological and environmental factors that are tempered by societal expectations. Another example of this blend is reflected in the observation that college-aged women tend to perform less well, on average, in their math and physics courses than men. However, women can overcome this stereotype in experimental situations if they receive information about the test that reduces the stereotype threat (Spencer et al., 1999). For instance, telling the students that the test measures intelligence causes the female students to do less well, whereas informing them that there is no relationship between test performance and intelligence raises performance. Although researchers can remove the stereotypic threat in experimental conditions and equalize male and female performance, the question remains of how to remove these threats in real-world situations such as the classroom.

Even when behavioral sex differences appear early in development, there seems to be some question regarding the influences of societal expectations. One example is the pattern of human play behavior, during which males are more physical; this pattern is also seen in a number of other species, including nonhuman primates, rats, and dogs. Is the difference between boys and girls in the frequency of rough-and-tumble play due to biological factors associated with being male or female, or is it due to cultural expectations and learning? If there is a combination of biological and cultural influences mediating the difference, then what proportion of the variation between the sexes is due to biological factors, and what proportion is due to social influences? Importantly, is it appropriate to talk about "normal" sex dif-

(A)

(B)

FIGURE 3.2 Patterns of play behavior The play behavior of boys and girls is different from a very early age. (A) Boys tend to engage in rowdier rough-and-tumble play in large groups. (B) Girls tend to play games that involve dyads or triads and verbal cooperation. These patterns of play behavior probably reflect socialization and biological differences that may involve hormones.

ferences when these traits virtually always arrange themselves along a continuum rather than in discrete categories (see Chapter 4)?

It is easy to speculate on these questions based on our individual experiences. Visit any preschool and watch 3- or 4-year-old children at play. Even when gender-neutral toys are provided, boys tend to play aggressive, rowdy games in large groups, whereas girls tend to engage in play activities, often in dyads or triads, in which cooperation is valued (**FIGURE 3.2**). As important as the style of play is the choices of playmates. Most boys of this age choose to play with other boys, whereas most girls of this age target other girls for play. Again, are these differences mediated by biological influences, or are they due to cultural influences? Perhaps children learn sexually dimorphic modes of behavior from TV or from their friends at nursery school—boys play with guns and trucks, and girls play with dolls and tea sets. Boys who initially prefer dolls and tea sets will receive significant criticism from their peers and family members. Many boys are persuaded to give up these pursuits in communal play; a few are not. Of course, it is easy to produce examples of girls who enjoy rough-and-tumble play and of boys who enjoy playing nurturing roles. However, producing examples to support one's contentions is not the most effective way to determine the causes of a particular phenomenon. In order to ascertain the true causes underlying behavior, all biases must be eliminated from the data-gathering process. The most effective manner of obtaining information about an adequately described phenomenon is via the experimental method, primarily through the use of inductive reasoning (Platt, 1964) (**FIGURE 3.3**).

Behavioral endocrinologists are particularly interested in the extent to which hormones mediate human behavioral sex differences, because it is known that steroid hormone concentrations differ between males and females from almost the first trimester of gestation. However, it is extremely difficult to ascertain the proximate factors underlying sex differences in human behavior experimentally. Although the

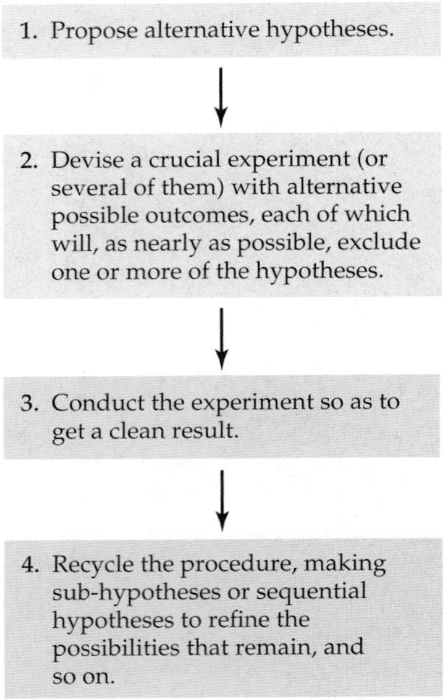

1. Propose alternative hypotheses.

2. Devise a crucial experiment (or several of them) with alternative possible outcomes, each of which will, as nearly as possible, exclude one or more of the hypotheses.

3. Conduct the experiment so as to get a clean result.

4. Recycle the procedure, making sub-hypotheses or sequential hypotheses to refine the possibilities that remain, and so on.

FIGURE 3.3 **Strong inference** is another term for inductive reasoning, associated with Francis Bacon. This method is an effective way to discover new relationships in the world. There are four steps in this process as depicted in the figure. Nothing is proved; science only advances by disproofs. Steps 1 and 2 require creative, intellectual inventions.

critical experiments can be designed as "thought experiments," they cannot ethically be performed on humans: Tracking hormone concentrations during sexual differentiation in utero might jeopardize the well-being of the fetus, although new technology allows for such assessments during routine amniocentesis procedures (Cohen-Bendahan et al., 2005) (see below). Assessing the role of hormones in rough-and-tumble play would require that children be castrated and receive hormone replacement therapy. Other children would have to be reared in social isolation to assess the contribution of social factors to aggressive play. Obviously, such studies are not possible. However, indirect evidence has been obtained from several converging sources that can help us to understand the behavioral differences between human males and females.

Four strategies that do not require experimentation on humans have been used to explore questions about the origin of human behavioral sex differences. First, animal models have been used to study sexual differentiation, which occurs before or immediately after birth or hatching. The study of nonhuman mammals has established that hormone concentrations during sexual differentiation guide the development of many physiological, morphological, and behavioral characteristics that are displayed later in life (**FIGURE 3.4**). The second strategy has involved studies of people or nonhuman animals that have undergone anomalous sexual differentiation. For example, studying the behavior of girls who were exposed to a male-typical hormonal milieu in utero helps to separate the contribution of rearing conditions from the hormonal factors that may underlie behavioral sex differences. Third, fluid samples can be obtained during routine amniocentesis testing, and the hormone concentrations in utero can be correlated with future behavioral patterns.

FIGURE 3.4 **Rough-and-tumble play in nonhuman primates** Although it is often difficult to account for behavioral sex differences in humans, studies of nonhuman animals can often provide insights. For example, strong sex differences in rough-and-tumble play are observed in nonhuman primates, as well as humans, and these sex differences are likely affected by early hormone exposure.

Finally, because child-rearing practices vary so greatly among different cultures, anthropologists, psychologists, and sociologists have looked for universal commonalities in the behavior of all children. Studies of sex differences in behavior that emerge consistently regardless of rearing conditions suggest that some such differences—in aggressive behavior, for example—are mediated by biological factors (Hines, 1982, 2004). Although this fourth approach will not be reviewed in great depth here, such behavioral surveys have indicated that several behaviors in humans may have significant biological bases that can override social effects. Of course, one could argue that human parents may universally treat their sons differently from their daughters and induce the sex differences in observed behaviors. This argument is hard to refute, because experimental controls are infrequent in long-term developmental studies of human behavior. Consequently, nonhuman animal studies have generally proved to be superior to human studies for understanding the sex differences underlying behavior, because of the possibility for greater experimental control.

Sex Determination and Differentiation

What is sex? What makes you male or female? There are several different ways to answer this very basic question (**FIGURE 3.5**). At the most basic level is **chromosomal sex**, which is determined by the sex chromosomes an individual receives at fertilization. The **homogametic sex** has homomorphic (similarly shaped) sex chromosomes. In mammals the homogametic sex is female (XX), whereas the heterogametic sex (with differently shaped chromosomes) is male (XY). In birds and some retiles, the homogametic sex is male (ZZ) and females are the heterogametic sex (ZW). Chromosomal sex is fundamental during the process of sexual differentiation and determines **gonadal sex**: the possession of either ovaries or testes. Females have ovaries, whereas males have testes. Gonadal sex is related to **gametic sex**. Gametic sex forms the fundamental basis underlying the two sexes. The ovaries of female animals produce comparatively small numbers of large, immobile, resource-rich gametes called ova or eggs; the testes of male animals produce extraordinary numbers of small, mobile gametes called sperm. Females and males also differ on the basis of **hormonal sex**. Females of most, but not all, vertebrate species tend to have high estrogen-to-androgen ratios of circulating steroid hormone concentrations; males have the opposite pattern. **Morphological sex** refers to the differences in body type between males and females. Male mammals are typically larger than females and possess different external genitalia. In addition to differing in size, males of many species differ from females in coloration; the presence or size of horns, antlers, and other ornamentation; and body shape. **Behavioral sex** can be discriminated on the basis of male-typical and female-typical behaviors. For example, females of many species often care for young, whereas males, especially male mammals, rarely provide parental care (see Chapter 7). Male and female birds of many species share equally in parental care, but they display other types of behavioral sex differences. For example, males of many avian species sing and defend territories, whereas the female conspecifics do not.

Additional categories of sex classification exist among humans. For example, **gender identity** reflects the sex, or gender, that individuals feel themselves to be;

chromosomal sex   The sex of an individual as determined by the sex chromosomes that an individual receives at fertilization.

homogametic sex   The sex that has two similar sex chromosomes. Except for birds and some reptiles, female vertebrate animals are the homogametic sex because they have two X chromosomes.

gonadal sex   The sex of an individual as determined by the possession of either ovaries or testes. Females have ovaries, whereas males have testes.

gametic sex   The sex of an individual as determined by the production of ova by females and sperm by males.

hormonal sex   The sex of an individual as determined by the concentration of androgens and estrogens. Males tend to have higher androgen concentrations, while females tend to have higher estrogen concentrations.

morphological sex   The sex of an individual as determined by body form.

behavioral sex   The sex of an individual as discriminated on the basis of male-typical and female-typical behaviors.

gender identity   The psychological self-perception of being either male or female.

FIGURE 3.5   Levels of sex determination Chromosomal sex, which is determined at conception, determines which gonads form in the embryonic individual. Gonadal sex determines the hormonal environment in which the fetus develops, and it steers morphological development in a male or female direction. The resulting sex differences in the central nervous system and in some effector organs lead to the behavioral sex differences observed in later life. There is some evidence that chromosomes may also directly influence specific sexually dimorphic brain anatomy and function (dashed line).

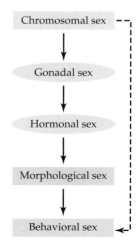

gender role   The collection of behaviors and attitudes that are considered appropriate or normal within a specific culture for each sex.

sexual orientation   The process of developing an erotic sexual attraction for other people. This term suggests that the process is mediated primarily by biological factors.

sexual preference   The process of developing an erotic sexual attraction for other people. This term suggests that the process is mediated primarily by learning and conscious choices.

legal sex   The official designation of sex, which is heavily influenced by morphological sex at birth but is also influenced by chromosomal and gonadal sex.

parthenogenesis   A type of asexual reproduction in which eggs can develop into offspring without fertilization.

gender identity usually corresponds to the expression of a **gender role**, a culturally based summary of sex-specific behaviors. **Sexual orientation** or **sexual preference** can also categorize males and females. Males generally prefer female sexual partners, whereas females generally prefer male sexual partners. Finally, there is **legal sex**. You are recognized by governmental agencies as male or female because of an *M* or *F* on your birth certificate, driver's license, or some other official document. If individuals sporting *M* identification documents enter a women's rest room, they can be arrested in most parts of North America, even if they are exhibiting female-typical behavior (e.g., wearing a bridal gown). And in many sports, individuals who were assigned an *M* on their birth certificates cannot compete as women later in life regardless of their hormonal state or pattern of body development during puberty or beyond. Sex differences occur at each of these systematic levels.

Ultimate Causes of Sex Differences

Most of the animals with which you are familiar engage in sexual reproduction. Indeed, most animal species currently on the planet engage in sexual reproduction. However, a survey of the entire animal kingdom reveals that a number of animals, especially insect species, breed asexually (Rhen and Crews, 2008). There are several forms of asexual reproduction. The process of asexual reproduction among animals is called **parthenogenesis** (also see Chapter 6). In parthenogenetic vertebrates, there is only one sex: female. Parthenogenetic females produce genetically identical eggs that develop into female offspring that are all 100% genetically identical to their mother. Females that breed sexually dilute their relatedness to their offspring on average by 50% by incorporating the genes of the father into their offspring. From the Darwinian perspective, reproductive success reflects the amount of genetic material an individual contributes to subsequent generations. Thus, asexual reproduction may seem like an extremely efficient system. This mode of breeding must have some distinct disadvantages, however, if so many animals breed sexually. One hypothesis about why asexual reproduction is rare among vertebrates is that asexual individuals, because of their identical genotypes, provide little variation on which natural selection can act. Thus, if the environmental conditions in which the clones live change markedly, an asexual species can easily become extinct. Sexual reproduction, through the separation of chromosome pairs into haploid gametes and their recombination in each offspring, provides genetic variability and hence evolutionary flexibility (Howard and Lively, 1994). Those animals and plants that have the option of either sexual or asexual reproduction usually opt for sexual reproduction when the environment becomes unstable. By analogy, would you rather have 100 lottery tickets with the same number or 50 tickets, each with a slightly different number? Another problem that can burden asexual species is the likelihood that pathogens may become specialized to exploit a single genotype (Heitman, 2006). Because pathogens reproduce faster than their hosts, they can rapidly evolve ways to override the hosts' immunological defenses (Judson, 1997; Ladle et al., 1993). By shuffling the genetic material, host species reduce the odds that pathogens will be preadapted to exploit their offspring. Importantly, the evolution of sex remains an unsolved issue and far from settled among evolutionary biologists.

Sexually reproducing species have two sexes: male and female. Why do the two sexes differ in appearance and behavior (Rhen and Crews, 2008)? In other words, what are the ultimate causes of the behavioral differences between males and females? We cannot travel back in time to watch the slow evolution of sexual dimorphism in a given species and note the ecological or social factors associated with the development of sex differences. But we can address these "why" questions by examining present-day species that show little or no sexual dimorphism and comparing them with species that are sexually dimorphic. When these comparisons are made, a striking relationship between sexual dimorphism and mating system

(A) Prairie voles

(B) Elk

FIGURE 3.6 **Sex differences are reduced in monogamous species.** (A) It is virtually impossible to tell the male (right) from the female monogamous prairie voles without a close examination of their genitalia. (B) Male and female polygynous elk are readily distinguishable—males have antlers and are much larger than females.

becomes obvious. Species that are **monogamous** (have a single mating partner) display less sexual dimorphism than species that are **polygamous** (have multiple mating partners) (Trivers, 1972) (**FIGURE 3.6**). In polygamous species, in which members of one sex compete to mate with the other sex, sexual selection may act to favor certain behavioral or morphological traits in the competing sex (Andersson, 1994).

Sexual selection is a subcategory of natural selection (Andersson, 1994; Trivers, 1972). Generally, the rule among animal species is that males compete and females choose. For instance, unlike most birds, bowerbirds are typically polygynous, with females building the natal nest and raising offspring alone. Because the male's contribution to the offspring is simply his genetic material, females must choose males wisely based on behavioral and morphological characteristics. To prove their worth, male bowerbirds build elaborate structures called bowers and adorn them with colorful objects (**FIGURE 3.7**). Males compete with other males, often stealing colorful objects from each other, necessitating careful watching and defending of bowers. Males attract females to their bowers through courtship displays. Females

monogamous Species that form a pair bond in which a male and female mate and raise offspring exclusively with each other.

polygamous Species that mate with more than one individual.

sexual selection A subset of natural selection that occurs when individuals within a population differ in their abilities to compete with members of the same sex for mates (intrasexual selection) or to attract mates of the opposite sex (intersexual selection).

FIGURE 3.7 **Male bowerbirds and sexual selection** A male Vogelkop bowerbird collects colorful flowers and fruits to decorate his cone-shaped bower in the Arfak Mountains of West Papua, Indonesia.

typically visit several bowers before making a final decision and entering a bower to mate. Male bowerbirds' plumage reflectance is associated with internal parasitic infection (i.e., duller coloration = higher internal parasite load), whereas bower quality is associated with external parasitic infection (i.e., more elaborate bower = fewer parasites) (Doucet and Montgomerie, 2003a,b). Consequently, females indirectly select high-quality males by choosing those with bright coloration that make bowers with numerous, colorful objects—in other words, males with good genes. In general, because males typically compete for females, successful males have evolved to be bigger, more colorful, and more aggressive than females. In species in which the sex roles are reversed and females compete with one another for males (**BOX 3.1**), the females are typically larger and more colorful than their male conspecifics (Trivers, 1972). Thus, sexual selection favors sexual dimorphisms, and probably amplifies them over time (Zahavi and Zahavi, 1997).

Although monogamy is asserted to be the most common mating system practiced by humans (*Homo sapiens*) in Western societies, this assertion is not consistent with the data that suggest humans are mildly to strongly polygynous; that is, each male may mate with more than one female (Alexander et al., 1979; Daly and Wilson, 1983; Martin and May, 1981; Murdock, 1967). Approximately 700 out of 850 human societies described in an extensive ethnographic catalog practiced polygyny (Murdock, 1967). Furthermore, the sex differences observed among humans are atypical for monogamous animals but common in polygynous and promiscuous species. For example, human sexual dimorphisms include larger body size and strength (Alexander et al., 1979), later puberty (Bronson, 1988; Tanner, 1962), and higher mortality rates (Shapiro et al., 1968) in men than in women. Importantly, cross-cultural studies of humans have revealed behavioral sexual dimorphisms that are consistent with those of other polygynous species, including increased courtship activity (Daly and Wilson, 1983), elevated levels of aggression (Moyer, 1976), and reduced parental care (Clutton-Brock, 1991) in males as compared with females. Thus, the morphological, physiological, and behavioral differences between men and women may reflect the evolutionary history of the most common human mating pattern, namely, polygyny.

Again, we cannot go back in time to test these ultimate hypotheses, but we can use them to make predictions about current behaviors, and we can conduct animal experiments designed to test our predictions. For example, males of polygynous species typically move around over larger areas than conspecific females or males of monogamous species, presumably because wandering around increases their chances of finding additional mates. One might predict that females and males of monogamous species will have poorer direction-finding skills or spatial aptitudes in general than males of these wide-ranging polygynous species. This prediction appears to be true when tested. Males of polygynous species, including rats, mice, meadow voles (small field mice, *Microtus pennsylvanicus*), and humans, are superior in spatial aptitudes to females of the same species (see Chapter 12). Moreover, male meadow voles are superior in spatial abilities (navigating a maze) to male pine voles (*Microtus pinetorum*), a monogamous species of the same genus (Gaulin and FitzGerald, 1986). Interestingly, these differences in spatial ability are associated with sexual selection for brain dimorphisms in structures important for spatial navigation, such as the hippocampus (see Chapter 12); males of polygamous species have larger hippocampi than female conspecifics, whereas this brain structure is monomorphic in monogamous pine voles (Jacobs, 1996).

The ultimate level of explanation (i.e., the "why" questions) is useful for guiding predictions about the proximate mechanisms (i.e., the "how" questions) that cause males and females to behave differently. The remainder of this chapter will review the proximate processes of sex determination and sexual differentiation. In other words, how do sexually dimorphic behaviors arise?

BOX 3.1 *Behavioral Sex Role Reversals*

In virtually every mammalian and avian species studied, males are more aggressive than their female conspecifics. They also tend to weigh more, are (particularly among mammals) more likely to establish and defend breeding territories, and are less likely to provide parental care to the young. There are several notable exceptions to this rule, however, and the study of these unusual cases is useful for shedding light on the more typical situation, as well as for understanding how far the "generalities" of the interaction between hormones and behavior can be relied on.

Female spotted hyenas (*Crocuta crocuta*) are socially dominant: in addition to eliciting submissive postures and vocalizations from males, they are also allowed first access to food (Frank, 1986; Kruuk, 1972). In addition to their masculinized behavior, females have masculinized external genitalia. Indeed, the species was once thought to be hermaphroditic because all individuals, even nursing mothers, possess scrota and penis-like structures. The photographs at right show external genitalia of male (top) and female (bottom) hyenas. The vaginal labia in spotted hyenas are fused to form a fat-filled pseudoscrotum. The clitoris develops into a pseudopenis through which the urogenital tract passes. Females urinate, copulate, and deliver young through the urogenital tract. The pseudopenis possesses full erectile function, and both males and females routinely display erections as part of their social interactions (Glickman et al., 1987). Erectile function in both sexes is observed from infancy. The extreme masculinization of female behavior and morphology appears to be organized by high maternal concentrations of ovarian androstenedione in pregnant females, which is converted to testosterone by the placenta (Glickman et al., 1987, 1992). However, exposure to antiandrogens in utero does not block the development of a pseudopenis in female hyenas (Drea et al., 1998). It is possible that some other factor stimulates the androgen receptor in female hyenas, leading to external masculinization, but the androgen receptors appear to be relatively unaltered (Catalano et al., 2002). Adult males exhibit higher androgen concentrations than adult females. Thus, adult concentrations of androgens do not appear to account for the difference in social dominance (see Chapter 8).

Spotted sandpipers (*Actitis macularia*) are birds that display atypical sex roles. Females establish and defend a feeding territory and engage in mate competition with other females for access to males (Fivizzani and Oring, 1986). Males incubate the eggs and brood the young with little or no assistance from the female. Prior to incubation, blood plasma concentrations of testosterone and dihydrotestosterone are substantially higher in males than in females. As incubation proceeds, testosterone levels in males plummet 25-fold. Mated females exhibit testosterone concentrations that are 7 times those of unmated females (Fivizzani and Oring, 1986). These hormone profiles are similar to those of other avian species in which males assist with care of the young. Thus, the reversal of sex roles in spotted sandpipers appears to be unrelated to adult hormonal effects.

Photographs courtesy of Stephen Glickman.

Proximate Causes of Sex Differences

Biologists are interested in phenotypic differences because phenotype, the observed trait, is the result of genes and the environment, including the microenvironment in which individuals develop. Because behavioral sex differences are so ubiquitous among animals, and because of the previous beliefs that sex differences were fairly discrete and nonoverlapping, behavioral endocrinologists have focused significant

organizational/activational hypothesis   The proposition that sex differences in behavior arise from two fundamental processes. Hormones early in development act to differentiate the nervous system in a male or female direction (organizational) while hormones act on these differentiated circuits later in life to drive behavior in a sex-typical manner (activational).

disorders of sex development (DSD)   Congenital conditions in which development of chromosomal, gonadal, hormonal, or anatomical sex is atypical.

germinal ridge   A thickened ridge of tissue on the ventromedial surface of each mesonephros of an embryo that has the potential to develop into either a testis or an ovary.

SRY gene   Sex-determining region of the Y chromosome; the gene that is responsible for the transformation of the undifferentiated gonad into a testis.

effort on studying phenotypic differences. One very important concept developed to guide this effort is the so-called **organizational/activational hypothesis**. This fundamental hypothesis on how hormones guide behavioral sex differences will be presented within its historical context. Basically, the original organizational/activational hypothesis, framed about 50 years ago, suggests that behavioral sex differences result from (1) differential exposure to hormones that act early in development to organize the neural circuitry underlying sexually dimorphic behaviors and (2) differential exposure to sex steroid hormones later in life that activate the neural circuitry previously organized. The workings of this process in several animal models commonly used to study behavioral sex differences will be described in detail below. Sex differences in brain structures, how these differences arise, and how these differences might mediate behavioral differences between males and females will also be reviewed in this chapter, as well as in Chapter 4.

A number of clinical syndromes exist among humans and nonhuman animals that cause anomalies in the process of sexual differentiation. These syndromes are collectively referred to as **disorders of sex development** (**DSD**) (Lee, 2005). Many of these syndromes are congenital; others are the result of endocrine treatment or exposure to endocrine mimics during gestation. The behavioral consequences resulting from these developmental irregularities in humans, as well as from animal studies in which these clinical syndromes were simulated, will be presented in this chapter. Issues of gender identity, sex role, and sexual orientation among humans, as well as cognitive and affective sex differences, will also be explored in Chapter 4.

There are real and substantial differences between males and females. Some of these sex differences may be apparent at birth; others appear later in development. Our goal is to understand how behavioral sex differences develop and are maintained. But in order to do this, it is necessary to understand sexual differentiation in general. If we limit our discussion to mammals and birds, then basically, chromosomal sex determines gonadal sex, and virtually all subsequent sexual differentiation reflects differential exposure to gonadal steroid hormones. Thus, gonadal sex determines hormonal sex, which in turn influences morphological sex. Morphological differences in the central nervous system, as well as in some effector organs, lead to behavioral sex differences (see Figure 3.5). To understand the specifics of how sexually dimorphic behaviors arise, a brief discussion of embryology is necessary. Therefore, the next section will begin with embryology, with an overview of Sexual Differentiation in Birds later in the chapter. An understanding of embryology will yield a rationale for the principles underlying behavioral sex differences.

Mammalian Sexual Differentiation

The primary step in the process of mammalian sexual differentiation occurs at fertilization. An ovum can be fertilized by a sperm bearing either an X or a Y chromosome (**FIGURE 3.8**). This event, called sex determination, has far-reaching consequences for the differentiation of the embryonic gonads, as well as for subsequent behavioral differences. Each individual embryonic mammal, whether XX or XY, exhibits a thickened ridge of tissue on the ventromedial surface of each mesonephros (protokidney), known as the **germinal ridge** (Jost, 1979) (**FIGURE 3.9**). At this stage, this primordial gonad is said to be indifferent or bipotential. In most mammals studied to date, whether the germinal ridge will develop into a testis or an ovary is determined by the cellular expression of a gene known as **SRY** (**s**ex-determining **r**egion on the **Y** chromosome) in the indifferent gonads (Berta et al., 1990). SRY was the first-identified member of the SOX (SRY-related high mobility group [HMG] box) family of transcription factor genes (Bowles et al., 2000). Expression of SRY produces testis determination factor (TDF). When TDF is present with the SF-1 (steroidogenic factor 1) protein, the two form a transcription factor that regulates expression of another member of the SOX family, SOX9 (SRY-related HMG box 9)

(A)

(B)

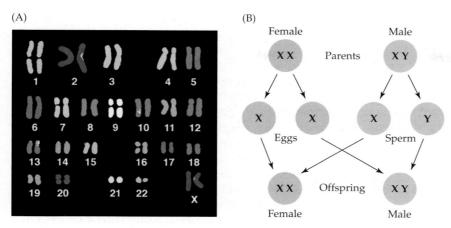

FIGURE 3.8 Chromosomal sex determination (A) Humans have 23 pairs of chromosomes, with one pair being the sex chromosomes. (B) During reproduction, female gametes always contribute an X chromosome, and the sex of the child is determined by whether the sperm contributes an X or Y chromosome.

(Harley and Goodfellow, 1995; Harley et al., 2003; Sekido and Lovell-Badge, 2008). When the protein products of these two genes are produced, the middle (medulla) of the germinal ridge develops and a testis forms (Berta et al., 1990). If products of the *SRY* or *SOX9* genes are not produced, or the genes are not expressed in the required sequence, then the outer part of the germinal ridge (the cortex) develops and an ovary is formed, or in some cases neither testes nor ovaries are formed. It is possible for the *SRY* and *SOX9* genes to be expressed in one gonad but not in the other, which leads to unilateral differentiation: in other words, a testis develops on one side while an ovary develops on the other side, suggesting that TDF functions only locally and is not a blood-borne agent. Partial expression of the *SRY* or *SOX9* gene can lead to incomplete gonadal differentiation, yielding an ovotestis. Mice that are chromosomal XY males but do not have the *SRY* gene develop ovaries; similarly, XX transgenic mice into which an *SRY* gene has been inserted develop testes (Goodfellow and Lovell-Badge, 1993; McElreavey et al., 1995). In humans, XY women lacking *SRY* develop gonadal streaks, not ovaries. This condition is called Swyer syndrome. The first case of an XY woman carrying a pregnancy to term was a woman with Swyer syndrome (Bianco et al., 1992; McCarty et al., 2006). In nonmammalian vertebrates, *SRY* is not a testis-determining gene. Although it is generally assumed that the ovaries are formed in the absence of active gene regulation, more recent lines of evidence suggest that expression

(A)

(B)

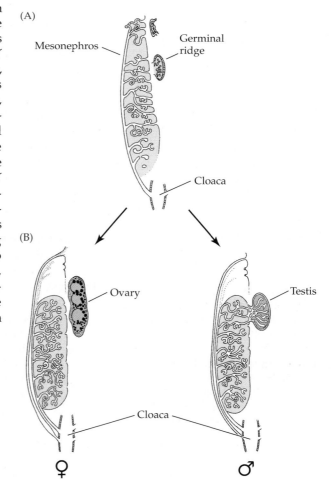

FIGURE 3.9 Gonadal development of the human embryo (A) Each individual, regardless of chromosomal sex, develops a thickening called the germinal ridge on the ventromedial surface of each mesonephros (protokidney). The germinal ridge is a bipotential primordial gonad; it can become either an ovary or a testis. (B) If the *SRY* gene is expressed and the testis determination factor protein is present, the medulla of the germinal ridge develops, forming a testis. If no *SRY* gene is expressed and testis determination factor is not present, the cortex of the protogonad develops, and an ovary is formed.

anlagen The primordial substrate in a developing individual.

accessory sex organ The internal organs of the male and female reproductive tract that connect the gonads to the external environment.

Müllerian duct system A duct system present in both sexes during embryonic development that connects the gonads to the exterior. During normal development, the Müllerian duct system develops into the accessory sex organs in females and regresses in males.

Wolffian duct system A duct system present in both sexes during embryonic development that connects the gonads to the exterior. During normal development, the Wolffian duct system develops into the accessory sex organs in males and regresses in females.

Müllerian inhibitory hormone (MIH) A peptide hormone produced in the Sertoli cells in the developing testis that suppresses development of the Müllerian duct system, which prevents development of the uterus and cervix. Also called *Müllerian inhibitory factor (MIF)*.

of a gene called *Wnt4* (wingless-related MMTV integration site 4) is required for normal ovarian development (Jameson et al., 2012; Jeays-Ward et al., 2004). In the absence of *Wnt4*, expression of *SOX9* is up-regulated, even in the absence of the *SRY* gene, and the gonads of XX null mice exhibit partial masculinization.

Hormonal secretions from the developing gonads determine whether the individual develops in a male or female manner. The mammalian embryonic testes produce androgens, as well as peptide hormones, that steer the development of the body, central nervous system, and subsequent behavior in a male direction. The embryonic ovaries of mammals are virtually quiescent and do not secrete high concentrations of hormones (but see Arnold and Breedlove, 1985; Döhler et al., 1982). In the presence of ovaries or in the complete absence of any gonads, morphological, neural, and later, behavioral development follow a female pathway. As we will see, however, low estrogen concentrations are probably required for typical female neural and behavioral development (e.g., Bakker et al., 2002, 2006). Thus, the prevailing hypothesis about the initiation of sexual differentiation indicates that the gonads are differentiated by genetic influences (*SRY* and *SOX9*) and that all other sexual differentiation reflects hormonal mediation. However, it is possible that some sex differences in brain and behavior might be mediated more directly by gene expression in nongonadal tissue (Arnold, 2009). For example, the *SRY* gene is transcribed in the hypothalamus and midbrain of adult male mice (Lahr et al., 1995). Indeed, sexually dimorphic transcription of over 50 genes was observed in the brains of mice 10.5 days postconception, before the gonads had developed (Dewing et al., 2003). Because only genetic males possess a Y chromosome, any gene located on the Y chromosome that is involved in neural development is a candidate to mediate sex differences in brain and behavior directly, without invoking an endocrine messenger. Mice can be genetically engineered to differ in their sex chromosomes (i.e., XX or XY) but to possess the same type of gonads (i.e., ovaries or testes). Such mice show subtle differences in certain brain cell types. For example, mice with ovaries, regardless of sex chromosomes, have fewer cells expressing tyrosine hydroxylase in the anteroventral periventricular nucleus of the preoptic area than mice with testes (Arnold et al., 2004). Sex chromosomes also appear to influence the density of vasopressin-containing fibers in the lateral septum (DeVries et al., 2002) and some aspects of aggression (e.g., Gatewood et al., 2006). Additional work is required to determine the importance of these examples on the general development and expression of sexually dimorphic behaviors. It is also possible that "leaky" X chromosome inactivation can be another nonhormonal, genetic source of sex differences.

In contrast to the single, bipotential primordial gonad, dual **anlagen** (primordia) for the accessory sex organs are present early during ontogeny (**FIGURE 3.10**). The **accessory sex organs** connect the gonads to the outside environment. The **Müllerian duct system** develops into the female accessory sex organs: the fallopian tubes, uterus, and cervix. The **Wolffian duct system** develops into the male accessory sex organs, which connect the testes to the outside environment via the penis. Later-developing components of the Wolffian duct system include the seminal vesicles and vas deferens. During normal sexual differentiation, the Wolffian duct system develops in males, whereas the Müllerian duct system regresses. Conversely, in females, the Müllerian duct system develops, whereas the Wolffian duct system regresses. In humans, this process occurs during the first trimester of gestation.

In the presence of ovaries *or in the complete absence of gonads*, normal development of the Müllerian ducts is accompanied by complete regression of the Wolffian duct system. Again, no hormones are necessary to permit essentially normal female development among mammals. Male development of the accessory sex organs requires two products from the embryonic testes: testosterone and a peptide hormone called **Müllerian inhibitory hormone (MIH)**. Testosterone is necessary to stimulate Wolffian duct development. Müllerian inhibitory hormone, as its name implies, causes the regression of the Müllerian duct system. If testosterone is absent early in

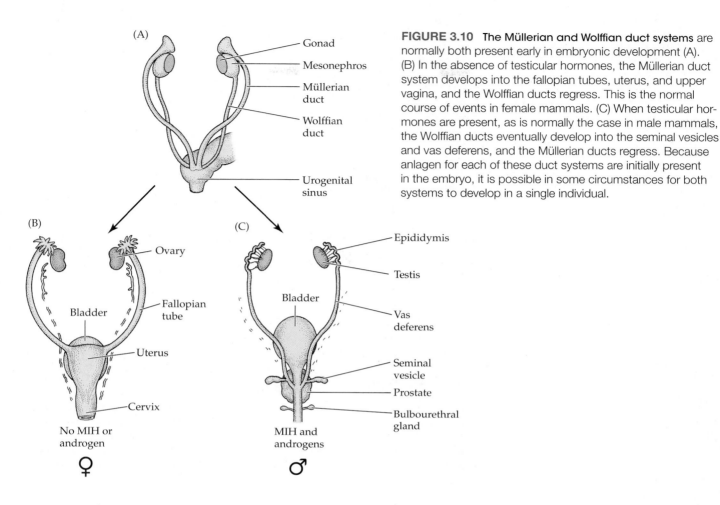

FIGURE 3.10 The Müllerian and Wolffian duct systems are normally both present early in embryonic development (A). (B) In the absence of testicular hormones, the Müllerian duct system develops into the fallopian tubes, uterus, and upper vagina, and the Wolffian ducts regress. This is the normal course of events in female mammals. (C) When testicular hormones are present, as is normally the case in male mammals, the Wolffian ducts eventually develop into the seminal vesicles and vas deferens, and the Müllerian ducts regress. Because anlagen for each of these duct systems are initially present in the embryo, it is possible in some circumstances for both systems to develop in a single individual.

development, then Wolffian duct development fails to occur. If MIH is not secreted at the proper time, then the Müllerian duct system develops. Because of the twin anlagen, it is possible for both systems to develop in a single individual or for neither system to develop.

In order for female morphological development of the accessory sex organs to occur, the embryo must become feminized (Müllerian duct development), as well as demasculinized (Wolffian duct regression). Male development requires both masculinization (Wolffian duct development) and defeminization (Müllerian duct regression). In other words, sexual differentiation of the accessory sex organs proceeds along two continua: (1) a masculinization-demasculinization scale and (2) a feminization-defeminization scale (**FIGURE 3.11**). **Masculinization** is the induction of male traits; **feminization** is the induction of female traits. **Demasculinization** is the removal of the potential for male traits, whereas **defeminization** is the removal

masculinization   The induction of male traits.

feminization   The induction of female traits.

demasculinization   The removal of the potential for male traits.

defeminization   The removal of the potential for female traits.

FIGURE 3.11 Typical development of the accessory sex organs occurs along two dimensions. Females must become feminized (Müllerian duct development) as well as demasculinized (Wolffian duct regression). Males must become masculinized (Wolffian duct development) as well as defeminized (Müllerian duct regression). Thus, sexual dimorphism in accessory sex organs, as well as in many behaviors, requires development along two separate continua, a masculinization-demasculinization continuum and a feminization-defeminization continuum. Male-typical behavior is usually masculinized and defeminized.

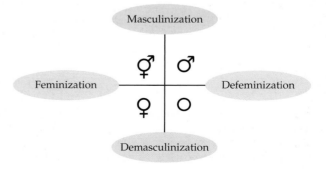

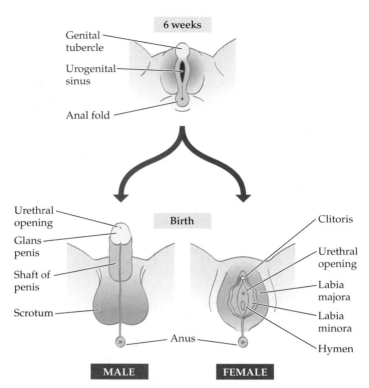

FIGURE 3.12   Embryonic development of human external genitalia During development, a genital tubercle forms in front of the urogenital sinus. The urogenital ridges are flanked by two flaps of skin called the genital folds. In the absence of hormonal influences, a clitoris develops from the genital tubercle, and the genital folds become the vaginal labia. In the presence of androgens, the genital tubercle develops into a penis, and the genital folds fuse into the scrotum.

genital folds   A fold of skin on each side of the genital tubercle that develops into the labia minora in females and the urethral groove and scrotum in males.

genital tubercle   The region of the embryo that develops into male or female genitalia.

of the potential for female traits. This nomenclature will be important for describing behavioral sex differences, as well.

The difference in external genitalia is the most obvious difference between the sexes at birth and has been used for generations to assign the sex of humans. During embryological development, the urogenital sinus is surrounded on both sides by long, thickened urogenital ridges that are flanked by two flaps of skin called the **genital folds** (**FIGURE 3.12**). In front of (anteroventral to) the urogenital opening, the two ridges meet to form a median outgrowth called the **genital tubercle**. The genital tubercle and folds are common to both sexes and develop into the external genitalia. Female humans, as well as many other species of mammals, possess a clitoris and vaginal labia, which develop from the genital tubercle and genital folds, respectively. Males possess a penis, which develops from the genital tubercle, and a scrotal sac, which results from the fusing of the genital folds and eventually contains the testes. Consequently, development of one type of genitalia occurs at the expense of the other type. In other words, a single continuum of masculine to feminine external genital development exists (**FIGURE 3.13**). Typically, males develop along

FIGURE 3.13   Standard development of the external genitalia proceeds along a single masculine-feminine continuum. Because there is a single anlage for female and male external genitalia, the development of one type of genitalia precludes the development of the other.

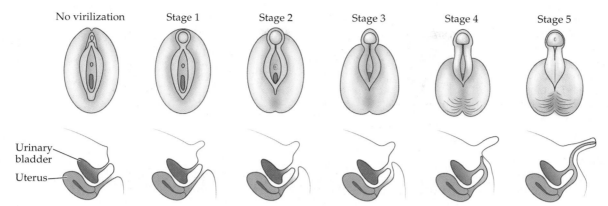

FIGURE 3.14 **Prader scale for scoring degrees of genital virilization** The Prader scale is a scoring system for grading the degrees of genital masculinization. The Prader scale starts at 0, which is an unvirilized female, and ends at 5, which is a completely virilized female (a female who appears externally male at birth with the labial/scrotal sac empty since there are no testicles).

the penis end of the continuum, whereas females develop along the clitoral end of the continuum. Although the two sexes are generally binary, genital development can fall anywhere between these two outcomes (ambiguous genitalia; see below) (Speiser and White, 2000) (**FIGURE 3.14**).

Androgens are responsible for the differentiation of the external genitalia. In the absence of hormones, a clitoris develops from the genital tubercle, and the vaginal labia develop from the genital folds. In the presence of androgens, the urethral groove fuses, the genital tubercle develops into a penis, and the genital folds fuse into the scrotum (Wilson et al., 1981). One of the androgenic metabolites of testosterone, **5α-dihydrotestosterone** (**DHT**), is critical for this process of genital fusing. Testosterone is converted to DHT by an enzyme called **5α-reductase**, which is locally abundant in the embryonic genital skin of both females and males (Wilson et al., 1981). If unusually high concentrations of androgens are available to a female fetus, then DHT conversion in the genital skin occurs, and the development of male-typical external genitalia proceeds. Males that congenitally lack the 5α-reductase enzyme undergo incomplete differentiation of the external genitalia and may be considered female at birth (see Figure 3.20). Females that lack 5α-reductase have female-typical external genitalia because typical female genital development occurs in the absence of sex steroid hormones.

Anomalous Mammalian Sexual Differentiation

The process of mammalian sexual differentiation is summarized in **FIGURE 3.15** (MacLaughlin and Donahoe, 2004). This process is complex, and as the case of 5α-reductase deficiency shows, the potential for error is present. People and nonhuman animals that have undergone anomalous sexual differentiation are of interest to behavioral endocrinologists because they can serve as "experiments of nature," and, as such, they can provide important information about the workings of the standard process of sexual differentiation.

Departures from typical sexual differentiation have been recognized by humans since early in our history. One very old idea was that male babies came from the right testis and females came from the left, and **hermaphrodites**, individuals who possess both ovaries and testes, were believed to arise when both testes simultaneously contributed to the offspring. All human babies born with ambiguous genital development used to be called hermaphrodites (Ellis, 1945), or **pseudohermaphrodites**

5α-dihydrotestosterone (DHT)
A potent androgen that is derived from testosterone and binds more strongly to androgen receptors than testosterone. There are both 5-alpha and 5-beta forms of DHT.

5α-reductase An enzyme necessary to convert testosterone to 5α-dihydrotestosterone.

hermaphrodite An individual who possesses both ovaries and testes. In some species, the possession of both types of gonads occurs simultaneously, whereas in other species it occurs sequentially.

pseudohermaphrodite An individual, especially a human, born with ambiguous external genitalia.

FIGURE 3.15 Sexual differentiation in humans is complex, and there are several stages where errors can occur. Chromosomal sex determination takes place when an egg is fertilized by a Y- or X-bearing sperm. The normal developmental pathways for females and males are indicated by the solid lines; common developmental errors are indicated by the dashed lines, which show where individuals can be "shunted" onto the developmental pathway of the opposite chromosomal sex.

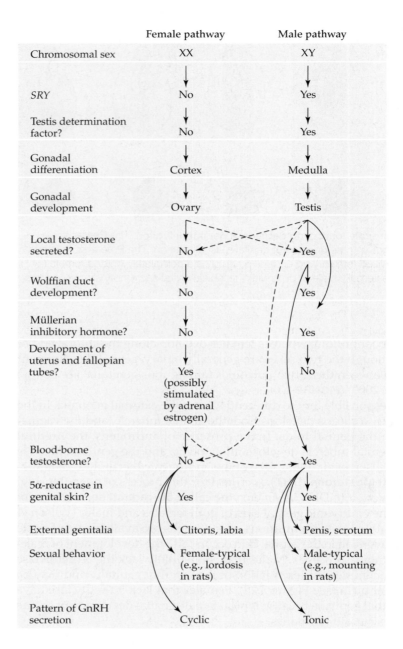

	Female pathway	Male pathway
Chromosomal sex	XX	XY
SRY	No	Yes
Testis determination factor?	No	Yes
Gonadal differentiation	Cortex	Medulla
Gonadal development	Ovary	Testis
Local testosterone secreted?	No	Yes
Wolffian duct development?	No	Yes
Müllerian inhibitory hormone?	No	Yes
Development of uterus and fallopian tubes?	Yes (possibly stimulated by adrenal estrogen)	No
Blood-borne testosterone?	No	Yes
5α-reductase in genital skin?	Yes	Yes
External genitalia	Clitoris, labia	Penis, scrotum
Sexual behavior	Female-typical (e.g., lordosis in rats)	Male-typical (e.g., mounting in rats)
Pattern of GnRH secretion	Cyclic	Tonic

because only one set of gonads is usually present. The common term used today to describe such individuals is intersex (see Chapter 4). Today such individuals are considered to be affected by disorders of sex development (DSD) (Lee et al., 2006). True hermaphrodites, with two complete sets of gonads, are extremely rare among humans. **FIGURE 3.16** represents a person with female breasts and male genitalia—a phenotype that is never observed in true hermaphrodites; such individuals have either female or ambiguous external genitalia, despite what the Greeks told us.

DSD IN FEMALES   The female organization is basic among mammals. Because females are the so-called neutral or default sex, neither ovaries nor hormones are necessary for female development of the body prior to puberty. However, it is becoming increasingly clear that low concentrations of estrogens are critical for typical female development of the brain (Bakker et al., 2006; Döhler and Hancke, 1978;

FIGURE 3.16 **Hermaphrodites** have been of great interest to artists and writers for centuries even though true hermaphrodites are extremely rare. This statue is on display in the Louvre museum in Paris.

Döhler et al., 1982; Toran-Allerand, 1984). Because sexual species appear to evolve from asexual ones, it has been hypothesized that females are the ancestral sex and that males are the derived sex (Crews, 1993).

One out of about 3000 live human births exhibits **Turner syndrome**, characterized by a congenital lack of, or damage to, the second X (or a Y) chromosome (XO) (Stochholm et al., 2006) (**FIGURE 3.17**). Individuals with Turner syndrome are unambiguously sexed as girls at birth. The gonads rarely develop completely, but they are clearly recognizable as ovaries. The dysgenic ovaries fail to produce steroid hormones, however, so girls with Turner syndrome must be treated with sex steroid hormones in their midteens to induce puberty. The consequences of missing a second sex chromosome are widespread and are not limited to sexual differentiation. Additional endocrine problems associated with Turner syndrome are reflected in the slow growth rates of affected girls. Both neural and nonneural tissues are also affected; hearing loss and intellectual developmental disabilities, as well as kidney dysfunction and webbing of the neck, are observed in some individuals born with Turner syndrome. These individuals are of interest to behavioral endocrinologists because they are not exposed to steroid hormones prenatally or postnatally until the age of 16 or 17, when exogenous hormonal treatments generally begin.

One intriguing study was conducted that examined the role of gene imprinting on behavior in girls with Turner syndrome. Because a female normally inherits one X chromosome from her mother and another X chromosome from her father, one of the X chromosomes in each cell is usually disabled so that normal transcription can occur. The process of inactivating either maternal or paternal genes is called **gene imprinting**. Girls with Turner syndrome have only a single X chromosome, which is either maternal (X^m) or paternal (X^P). X^mO girls tend to suffer from neurodevelopmental disorders of social cognition (e.g., autism) more than X^PO girls (Skuse

Turner syndrome   A congenital condition in which individuals lack an X chromosome (XO). These individuals have a female external appearance, but ovarian development is usually limited, and they do not attain puberty without medical attention.

gene imprinting   Genes expressed in a parent-of-origin-specific manner. If the allele inherited from the father is imprinted, it is silenced and only the allele from the mother is expressed.

FIGURE 3.17 **Turner syndrome** results from a congenital absence of one of the X chromosomes. With appropriate hormone therapy, these individuals undergo typical puberty. This woman (center), who has been diagnosed with Turner syndrome, has an MD and works as a genetic counselor to assist others with disorders of sexual development.

congenital adrenal hyperplasia (CAH)   A genetic deficiency that results in the overproduction of androgens by the adrenal glands. This syndrome has no reported effects on genital differentiation in males but causes various degrees of masculinization of the external genitalia in females, which may lead to erroneous assignment of sex at birth.

et al., 1997). Because the X chromosome of all males necessarily comes from the mother, these results suggest that the vulnerability of males to cognition and social adjustment problems is not necessarily due to the presence of specific genes on the Y chromosome but could rather be due to genes on the maternal X chromosome (which presumably act independently of sex steroid hormones). Alternatively, it is possible that pieces of the Y chromosome might be expressed in neural tissue to cause these behavioral difficulties, because many individuals with Turner syndrome are so-called genetic mosaics (Henn and Zang, 1997), possessing cells with differing genetic contents. This issue will probably go unresolved for some time because it is virtually impossible to observe the chromosomal makeup of brain cells in living people (Skuse and Jacobs, 1997), but it is apparent that neither physical stature nor lymphatic, renal, or cardiac development is affected by X-linked genomic imprinting (Bondy et al., 2007).

The most common reason for anomalous sexual differentiation in human females is prenatal exposure to androgens, from either exogenous or endogenous sources. Exogenous androgen exposure most commonly occurs during treatment of the pregnant mother with steroid hormones to maintain the pregnancy. Exposure to the artificial steroid hormones diethylstilbestrol (DES) and medroxyprogesterone acetate (MPA), for instance, often causes masculinization of reproductive function and subsequent behavior in the exposed children (see Chapter 4). Endogenous androgens are most likely to be secreted from one of two sources: the ovaries or the adrenal glands. For example, both males and females afflicted with **congenital adrenal hyperplasia (CAH)** possess fetal adrenal glands that produce high concentrations of androgens instead of cortisol. As you may recall from Chapter 2, the production of aldosterone and glucocorticoids in the adrenals requires the 21-hydroxylase enzyme. Individuals with CAH lack this enzyme, resulting in overproduction of adrenal androgens, the only pathway available in the absence of 21-hydroxylase. CAH does not cause sexual development problems in genetic males but results in moderate to severe masculinization of the genitalia in affected females (**FIGURE 3.18**). The clitoris can be enlarged into a penis-sized structure, and the labia may be fused into a scrotum-like structure. The anomalous genitalia can be reshaped by surgery, and the endocrine disorder can be treated by lifelong cortisol treatments if desired by the individual.

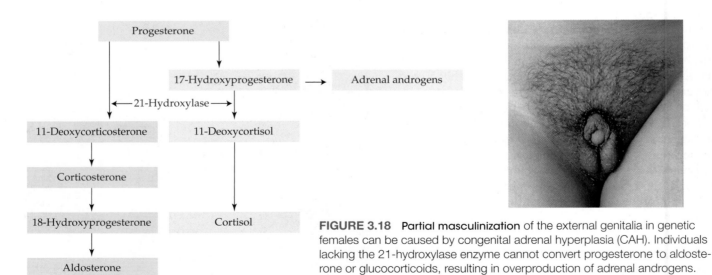

FIGURE 3.18 **Partial masculinization** of the external genitalia in genetic females can be caused by congenital adrenal hyperplasia (CAH). Individuals lacking the 21-hydroxylase enzyme cannot convert progesterone to aldosterone or glucocorticoids, resulting in overproduction of adrenal androgens. Congenital adrenal hyperplasia, a condition in which the adrenal glands secrete high levels of androgens, can cause varying degrees of masculinization of the external genitalia in genetic females, including clitoral enlargement and fusing of the urethral groove.

DSD IN MALES   There are more steps that require physiological intervention in male than in female sexual differentiation, and consequently more clinical problems in male sexual development can occur. For example, some XY individuals look and act like males throughout their lives, but during exploratory surgery for abdominal cramps, a uterus and small fallopian tubes are discovered. These individuals lack either MIH or the receptors that respond to this hormone; all other components of their sexual differentiation are male-typical. This sort of error in sexual differentiation does not have important consequences for male behavior, but in other cases, as we will see next, anomalous sexual differentiation produces dramatic behavioral effects.

Anomalous sexual differentiation occurs in XY humans with **androgen insensitivity syndrome (AIS)**, a condition also known as testicular feminization mutation (TFM) in rodents. AIS can be complete (CAIS) or partial (PAIS). The tissues of individuals with CAIS do not possess functional androgen receptors. A genetic mutation on the X chromosome involving a single base pair substitution in the gene for the androgen receptor causes this insensitivity to androgens in rats (Yarbrough et al., 1990). Genetic XX females with this mutation have a second X chromosome that contains the normal gene for androgen receptors, so they suffer no ill effects from this condition. However, in genetic XY males, because a Y chromosome is present, the *SRY* gene is activated and testicular development proceeds, accompanied by significant prenatal and postnatal androgen secretion. The testes also produce MIH, which causes the regression of the Müllerian duct system. However, the Wolffian duct system is generally underdeveloped, even in the presence of androgens (Salmasi et al., 2008). In humans, there are several mutations that cause androgen insensitivity (Brinkmann et al., 1996). XY individuals born with CAIS have perfectly normal-appearing female external genitalia and are sexed and reared as girls. The condition is usually discovered during adolescence when menstruation fails to occur. Upon examination, the vagina is discovered to be reduced in length (blind vagina). Because the Müllerian ducts failed to develop in these individuals, there are no uteri or fallopian tubes, and they are sterile. Usually the testes are removed surgically, vaginoplasty is performed, and estrogen treatment is provided, although this treatment has been questioned by some individuals who have received it (see Chapter 4). Genetic male XY individuals with CAIS display typical female body shapes and regard themselves unequivocally as female (Wisniewski et al., 2000) (**FIGURE 3.19**).

Behavioral endocrinologists are interested in CAIS (TFM) because this genetic anomaly has been discovered in several nonhuman species, including rats, mice,

androgen insensitivity (AIS)
A condition in genetic males, in which functional androgen receptors are absent. AIS is caused by a genetic mutation on the X chromosome.

FIGURE 3.19 Complete androgen insensitivity syndrome (CAIS) is a condition caused by the absence of functional androgen receptors in genetic male (XY) individuals. Because individuals with CAIS completely lack androgen receptors, the functional ratio of estrogens to androgens is high, and puberty, including development of secondary sexual characteristics, proceeds in a feminine direction. Although individuals with CAIS exhibit typical female body morphology, their gonads are testes, and the internal duct organs do not develop normally, resulting in sterility. Because these individuals usually grow up with strong female gender roles and identity, these women often marry and adopt children. Individuals may also display partial androgen sensitivity (PAIS). Pictured are members of a support group for individuals diagnosed with CAIS.

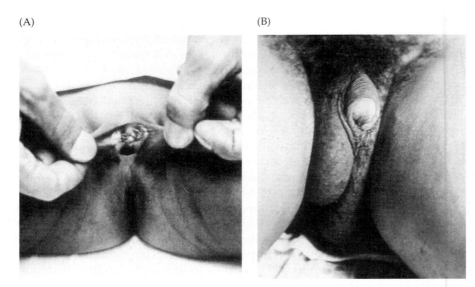

(A)   (B)

FIGURE 3.20   5α-reductase deficiency results in incomplete genital masculinization. (A) Note the incomplete fusing of the urogenital groove, the lack of penile development, and the presence of hypospadias, the opening of the urethra on the underside of the penis. Most individuals with 5α-reductase deficiency are sexed as girls at birth. (B) The same individual at puberty. Although DHT is still not present, high blood concentrations of other androgens at puberty can activate androgen receptors and cause delayed and partial masculinization of the external genitalia. Despite pubertal penile development, hypospadias remains, which contributes to infertility. Because these androgen-induced changes in the external genitalia are accompanied by a change to a male-typical body type, some individuals with 5α-reductase deficiency who have been raised as females may take on a male gender identity and gender role at puberty. Courtesy of Julianne Imperato-McGinley.

cattle, and chimpanzees (Olsen, 1992), allowing experimental study of its physiological mechanisms. Also, individuals with CAIS have normal receptors for, and normal concentrations of, the nonandrogenic hormones (such as estrogens) involved in sexual differentiation and thus provide researchers with the opportunity to separate the contributions of androgenic and nonandrogenic hormones to typical behavioral sexual differentiation. In Chapter 4, you will learn that, at least in rodents and nonhuman primates, estrogen acts in the brain to masculinize and defeminize many aspects of behavior. Because testicular androgens can be further converted into estrogens in the brain in utero, it is intriguing that women with CAIS virtually always identify as females and exhibit female-typical behavior during development and adulthood. These observations suggest that human brain and behavior differentiation may be different from that of other well-studied species or that parental and cultural influences strongly shape sexual identity and behavior.

As noted above, another genetic dysfunction that leads to anomalous sexual differentiation is 5α-reductase deficiency. Genetic males (XY) with 5α-reductase deficiency are born with ambiguous genitalia and small, undescended testes. They are usually considered females at birth and reared as females. At puberty, testosterone masculinizes the body, which develops male-typical musculature and axillary hair growth, and the genitalia develop to resemble a male-typical penis and scrotum (**FIGURE 3.20**). The urethra usually opens at the base of the penis; this condition, called **hypospadias**, substantially reduces fertility. Because these individuals are exposed to male-typical hormones pre- and postnatally but are reared as females until puberty, behavioral endocrinologists have studied them in order to understand the contribution of hormones versus rearing to human behavioral sexual differentiation.

hypospadias   A condition where the urethral opening is not at its typical location at the tip of the penis.

Trisomic anomalies

Occasionally, babies are born with extra chromosomes. Approximately one infant in every 600 live births is born with **Klinefelter syndrome** (Nielsen and Wohlert, 1990). These individuals possess an extra X chromosome (XXY). The presence of the Y chromosome is sufficient for the *SRY* gene to be activated and masculinization to occur, and these individuals are sexed as males at birth. Although the testes develop sufficiently to cause masculinization, these individuals are usually sterile because of reduced sperm production. Learning disabilities, often severe, are also commonly observed among individuals with Klinefelter syndrome. The disorder seems to mainly reflect variation in the androgen receptor (polyglutamine [AR CAG_n]) repeat length (Zinn et al., 2005).

Approximately one infant in every 850 live births possesses an XYY genotype (Nielsen and Wohlert, 1990). These individuals are considered male at birth, but in common with XXY individuals, XYY men may be sterile. The XYY genotype was once thought to result in increased aggressiveness, because a survey of prison populations revealed that a disproportionately large number of these individuals were represented (Hook, 1973; Jacobs et al., 1965). It was proposed that the Y chromosome was responsible for aggressiveness in normal males, and it was hypothesized that individuals with two Y chromosomes therefore displayed elevated aggression, which led to their imprisonment. Further analyses revealed that individuals with XYY genotypes were not necessarily more aggressive than XY males but that they possessed two other traits that increased the likelihood of criminal prosecution: they were less intelligent than average, and they were much taller than average. Thus, these individuals may not engage in more criminal activities than average, but apparently they tend to be apprehended and identified more readily (Witkin et al., 1976).

In sum, in people with trisomic anomalies, possession of a Y chromosome sets off a chain reaction that leads to the differentiation of the testes. Hormonal secretions from the testes lead to masculinization and defeminization. In the absence of these hormonal events, feminization and demasculinization occur. It is difficult to draw strong conclusions regarding sexual differentiation of behavior from trisomic individuals, given that the addition of an extra chromosome leads to confounding behavioral variables associated with intellectual deficits. In the following sections, the similarities and differences in the process of sexual differentiation among mammals, birds, and other animals will be presented.

Klinefelter syndrome A congenital condition in humans in which individuals possess an extra X chromosome (XXY) and are externally and internally masculinized.

Sexual Differentiation in Birds

Studies of nonmammalian species offer intriguing insights into our own species by demonstrating alternative solutions to common problems of adaptation. The process of avian sexual differentiation is similar to that of mammals, but with several interesting differences. Among birds, females are the heterogametic sex (ZW), whereas males are the homogametic sex (ZZ). In the case of copulatory behavior, males are the default sex: in the absence of gonadal hormones, the masculine developmental trajectory is followed, whereas the female pattern of development is attained only by active hormonal secretion (Balthazart and Adkins-Regan, 2002) **(FIGURE 3.21)**. Although there are general rules about the hormonal programming of sex differences in mammalian and avian behavior, different behaviors are mediated by different patterns of early hormone exposure in birds. For example, the sexually dimorphic avian neuromuscular system underlying singing behavior requires estrogens to exert a masculinizing effect on singing. The absence of hormonal stimulation leads to the feminine pattern of no birdsong, but birdsong and the song system do not seem to differentiate as does copulatory behavior in some species (e.g., Figure 3.21); the precise mechanisms for sexual differentiation of the neuronal system underlying birdsong remain unspecified. For yet other aspects of sexual dif-

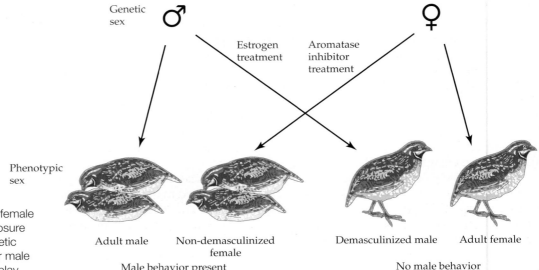

Genetic sex

Estrogen treatment   Aromatase inhibitor treatment

Phenotypic sex

Adult male   Non-demasculinized female   Demasculinized male   Adult female

Male behavior present   No male behavior

FIGURE 3.21 Male-typical copulatory behavior is lost in female quail following embryonic exposure to ovarian estrogens. The genetic sex of birds in the egg is either male or female. The potential to display male-typical behavior (mounting) develops in the male embryo in the absence of any hormonal influence and is lost in the female embryo if she is exposed to estrogens produced by her ovary before day 12 of incubation. If estrogen is given to a genetic male bird in the egg, then he is demasculinized. If a genetic female bird is given an aromatase inhibitor in the egg, preventing the formation of estrogens, she is not demasculinized and shows male copulatory behavior as an adult. After Balthazart and Ball, 1995.

ferentiation, the default condition in birds is neither male nor female; rather, ovarian or testicular hormones must exert feminizing or masculinizing effects, respectively, during the normal course of typical sexual differentiation (Adkins-Regan, 2007).

At the present time, no known sex-determining gene has been identified in birds. The presence of the W sex chromosome appears to cause the primordial gonad to secrete estrogens. The estrogens stimulate proliferation of the germinal epithelium in the left gonad, leading to ovarian cortical development. Only the left ovary of birds usually develops (Nalbandov, 1976). If chicken (*Gallus gallus domesticus*) eggs containing ZZ chromosomal males are injected with estrogen, then gonadal tissue develops into ovarian tissue. Similarly, when the embryonic gonads of one sex are grafted into an embryo of the other sex, or when embryonic gonads are grown together in culture dishes, ovaries are observed to feminize testicular development, but the presence of testes does not affect ovarian development (Haffen and Wolff, 1977).

Normal sexual differentiation of the avian Müllerian duct system provides an example in which neither the male nor the female pattern of development can be regarded as neutral. As in mammals, avian embryos of both sexes initially possess both Müllerian and Wolffian duct primordia. The Müllerian duct system develops in female chickens to form the oviduct and the shell gland (**FIGURE 3.22**) and regresses in male chickens during days 8–13 of incubation. Only the left duct develops in female chickens; the right duct regresses during days 9–18 of incubation. Thus, feminization of the accessory sex organs requires development of only the left components of the Müllerian duct system. If embryonic chickens or ducks are gonadectomized by focal X-irradiation prior to day 8 of incubation, then both duct systems persist; in other words, neither defeminization (regression of the Müllerian duct system) nor feminization (development of the left components of the Müllerian duct system) occurs in the absence of gonadal influences (Wolff and Wolff, 1951).

The discovery of a rare, bilateral gynandromorphic zebra finch suggested that, at least in some bird species, genes likely guide some central and peripheral sex differences, regardless of hormonal conditions. In this single bird, half of its body was genetically male (ZZ) and the other half genetically female (ZW) (Agate et al., 2003) (**FIGURE 3.23**). Because both halves of this bird developed under identical hormonal conditions due to the fact that hormones circulate throughout the brain and periphery, this model could be exploited to determine whether or not aspects of sexual differentiation are guided by sex chromosome–linked genes. This finch had male plumage on its right side and female plumage on the left, a gonad resembling a testis on the right and an ovary on the left, and brain structures controlling song

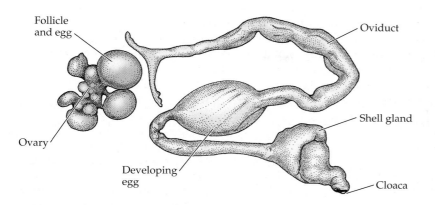

FIGURE 3.22 Ovary and oviduct of a chicken
Eggs (ova) at different stages of preovulatory development are shown in the ovary. Chickens ovulate virtually every day, and the egg travels down the oviduct to the shell gland, where a calcium-rich shell is laid down prior to oviposition (egg laying). Other birds have not been bred to be as prolific in their egg-laying behavior as chickens; typically, most, but not all, songbirds and seabirds lay only 1–4 eggs per clutch and rear 1–2 clutches per year. After Nalbandov, 1976.

that were masculinized on the right and feminized on the left. Thus, in the finch, genetic mechanisms contribute to some aspects of sexual differentiation, although complementary contributions of hormones also participate.

Sexually dimorphic avian behavior also reflects this variation in hormonal influences. In some cases, as in copulatory behavior, the masculine behavior pattern

(A)

Male plumage   Female plumage

(B)

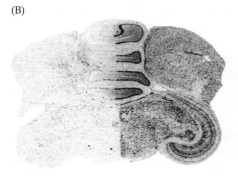 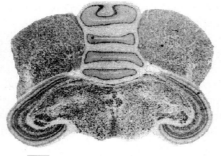

ASW   *PKCIZ*

FIGURE 3.23 Zebra finch gynandromorphy (A) Zebra finch gynandromorph with male plumage on its right side and female plumage on its left side. A few black male feathers can be seen on the left breast. (B) Photomicrographs of in situ hybridization in brain sections using probes specific for Z and W chromosomes. Autoradiograms were photographed in dark field and then black-white inverted; thus dark areas show label. The mRNA encoding the W chromosome gene, *ASW* (left), was ubiquitous on the left side but virtually absent on the right. The dividing line of high and low expression is sharp and follows the midline of the brain. The mRNA encoding the Z-linked gene, *PKCIZ* (right), was ubiquitous but higher on the right side of the brain, compatible with the idea that the brain was ZW on the left and ZZ on the right. (Bar = 1.0 mm.) From Agate et al., 2003.

is the default condition, whereas the feminine pattern is produced by hormonal activation that causes demasculinization. In the case of other behaviors, testicular hormones exert a defeminizing or masculinizing effect, whereas the absence of hormonal stimulation leads to the feminine pattern.

Environmental Sex Determination in Reptiles and Fishes

In mammals and birds, sex is determined by the presence or absence of sex-specific genes. If homologous sex chromosomes are present, then female mammals or male birds develop; if heterologous sex chromosomes are present, then male mammals or female birds develop. Sex determination is dependent only on genotypic differences. Mammals and birds evolved from reptilian ancestral forms about 325 million and 150 million years ago, respectively. Like mammals and birds, some modern reptilian species display genotypic sex determination. In some of these species males develop if homologous sex chromosomes are present, and in other species females develop if homologous sex chromosomes are present. However, in some lizards, most turtles, and probably all crocodilian species, environmental factors, not genotypic information, direct sex determination (Crews, 2003b; Rhen and Crews, 2002, 2008). Indeed, sex chromosomes are generally absent in these species (Crews and Bull, 2009).

The environmental factor most commonly involved in reptilian sex determination is temperature (Bull, 1980; Korpelainen, 1990), although water potential (concentration of salts) may also mediate sex determination in some species (e.g., the painted turtle, *Chrysemys picta*) (Gutzke and Paukstis, 1983). The embryos of a species with **temperature-dependent sex determination** are bipotential and can develop into males or females solely on the basis of the temperature at which the egg incubates. Relatively high temperatures (>30°C) produce males, and cool temperatures (<28°C) produce females in some lizard species, as well as in alligators (Crews et al., 1988a) (**FIGURE 3.24**). The opposite pattern of temperature effect on sex determination is observed among many turtle species. Yet another pattern of temperature-dependent sex determination has been reported for snapping turtles and crocodiles: females are produced at the high and low extremes, whereas males are produced at intermediate temperatures (Bull, 1983). This mechanism could allow the mother to determine the sex of her offspring by varying the temperature of the nest in which her eggs are incubated. Although this is an extremely exciting possibility, there is no clear evidence thus far that sex ratio is manipulated by parental care (Clutton-Brock, 1991; Navara and Nelson, 2009), nor is there any evidence that temperature exerts its effects by means of differential mortality in either sex (Crews, 2003b). Rather, incubation temperature determines whether the primordial gonad develops into a testis or an ovary. The primordial gonad in reptiles consists of distinct cortical and medullary tissue. If the cortical portion of the gonad develops, then an ovary develops; if the medullary portion of the gonad develops, then a testis develops. The physiological mechanisms by which temperature determines which portion of the gonad develops are beginning to be unraveled (Ramsay and Crews, 2009; Shoemaker and Crews, 2009).

As in birds, steroid hormones influence gonadal differentiation, and steroid treatment can override temperature effects on gonadal development. That is, if eggs are incubated at male-producing temperatures but given estrogens, females develop; conversely, if eggs are incubated at female-producing temperatures but given androgens, males develop. The mechanism by which temperature affects steroidogenesis remains unknown. Presumably, the enzymatic conversions necessary for steroid metabolism are temperature sensitive. It is possible that temperature controls the activity of aromatase (which converts testosterone to estradiol) or reductase (which converts testosterone to dihydrotestosterone) in reptilian gonads (Crews and Bull,

temperature-dependent sex determination A process that occurs in animals without sex chromosomes in which sex is determined solely on the basis of the temperature at which the egg incubates.

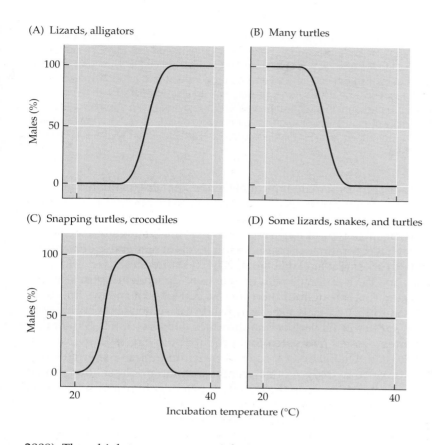

FIGURE 3.24 Temperature-dependent sex determination in reptiles (A) Exposure to relatively high ambient temperatures during incubation results in male-typical development among the offspring of some lizards and alligators. (B) In many turtle species high temperatures during incubation result in female-typical offspring development. (C) Moderate temperatures result in male offspring in snapping turtles and crocodiles, while exposure of eggs to either high or low temperatures results in female offspring in these species. (D) Sex determination in some reptilian species is unaffected by incubation temperatures. Because mammals and birds are kept at relatively constant temperatures during their embryonic development, the role of ambient temperature in the sex ratio of offspring in these species is unknown. After Crews et al., 1988a.

2009). Thus, high temperatures might inactivate enzymes necessary for converting androgens to estrogens in some species, whereas low temperatures could have the same effect in other species. The development of the reptilian gonads into testes or ovaries may start a cascade of events that results in subsequent male-typical or female-typical behavior, respectively, in the adult reptile. Alternatively, aromatase activity in the brain may differ between the putative sexes. For example, at the start of the temperature-sensitive period in red-eared slider turtles (*Trachemys scripta*), the pattern of aromatase activity in the gonads/adrenals was found to be similar between the sexes, but in the brain, turtles destined to become females displayed significantly higher concentrations of aromatase than turtles destined to become males. However, aromatase activities waned by the time of hatching, so sex differences in enzymatic activities were no longer present (Willingham et al., 2000). These data suggest that the brain is the primary site of the aromatase response to temperature, which affects estradiol concentrations, which in turn may affect the neuroendocrine events regulating sex steroid hormone production (Willingham et al., 2000). Although conceptually attractive, the idea that incubation temperatures are the physiological equivalent of sex hormone milieus has since been disproven (Radder et al., 2007; Huang et al., 2008).

What happens if reptile eggs are maintained at intermediate temperatures? Based on the outcome of one study of leopard geckos (*Eublepharis macularius*), intermediate temperatures can have interesting consequences for adult sexual behavior (Gutzke and Crews, 1988). In this species, temperatures of 32°C produce mainly male geckos, but a few female offspring are also produced; temperatures of 26°C produce only females. When females incubated at these two temperatures, as well as a third, intermediate temperature (29°C), were compared as adults in mating tests, female geckos from all three groups elicited equivalent amounts of courtship from males. Females from the low-temperature group responded to male courtship with female-typical behavior. However, females from the high-temperature group responded to

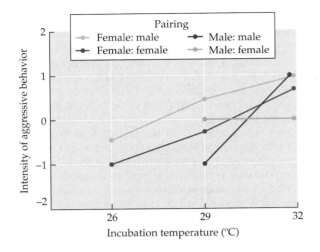

FIGURE 3.25 **Aggression in adult female geckos** can be influenced by incubation temperature. Relatively high temperatures (32°C) produce few female offspring, and relatively low temperatures (26°C) produce only female offspring in geckos. Females produced at low incubation temperatures display low levels of aggression as adults, compared with females incubated at high temperatures, which display male-like aggression as adults. For intensity of aggressive behavior, −2 = fleeing, −1 = low posture, 0 = no response, +1 = high posture, +2 = attack. After Gutzke and Crews, 1988.

courtship with male-typical behavior. Females incubated at intermediate temperatures displayed adult sexual behavior intermediate between the two extremes, showing some female-typical and some male-typical courtship behaviors. Interestingly, incubation at high temperatures increased adult levels of aggressive behavior in both sexes (Sakata and Crews, 2004) (**FIGURE 3.25**).

Like mammals and birds, animals with temperature-dependent sex determination remain the same sex throughout their lives (Crews, 2003b; Crews and Bull, 2009). However, some other animals, especially fishes, can switch sexes during their lifetimes! Several species of fish are hermaphrodites (Demski, 1987). **Simultaneous hermaphrodites** possess **ovotestes** that produce both eggs and sperm, and they alternate between two behavioral roles in providing eggs or sperm during spawning. There are also two types of **sequential hermaphrodites**: animals that begin life as one sex, then change to the other sex as adults in response to social, environmental, or genotypic factors (de Mitcheson and Liu, 2008; Demski, 1987; Grober and Rodgers, 2008). Several species of sequential hermaphroditic reef fish have been identified, including wrasses, sea basses, gobies, anemonefishes, and parrotfishes (Bass, 1996). **Protogynous** types begin life as females, then change into males; **protandrous** types are first males, then change into females. Such sequential sex changes involve a change in gonadal type and function, a change in the dominant gonadal steroid secreted, a change in morphology (body type), and a change in behavior (**FIGURE 3.26**). Clownfish (*Amphiprion percula*), as depicted in the popular children's movie *Finding Nemo*, defend an anemone home. The typical family unit consists of a mating pair and one to three juveniles. Unlike in the movie, however, if the mother disappears, the father undergoes a dramatic transformation to become the egg-laying female, and the oldest juvenile grows rapidly to become the male mate (Buston, 2003).

Although many species undergo sex changes, the specific trigger varies. In some cases, it appears to reflect an attainment of a certain size. For example, a meta-analysis of about 80 species of sex-switching fishes, crustaceans, mollusks, echinoderms, and polychaete worms indicated that they change sex when they attain 72% of their maximal size for their given species (Allsop and West, 2003). Over 90% of the variance in the timing of adult sex changes could be accounted for by this body mass set-point rule. Although such a high degree of consistency regarding the average timing of adult sex changes may indicate that similar life history events underlie the decision to switch sexes, specific social factors show variation in their timing (Perry and Grober, 2003). Presumably, models of "ultimate" factors driving the decision to switch sexes are based on "proximate" factors underlying the process.

Stoplight parrotfish (*Sparisoma viride*) are coral reef fish that begin life as females and change into males (Cardwell and Liley, 1991a,b); in other words, these fish are protogynous. In many cases, the sex change is accompanied by a striking change in body coloration, from the female-typical "initial phase" coloration to the male-typical "terminal phase" coloration. Some individuals, however, undergo the sex change from female to male without the change in coloration. These female mimics compete with terminal-phase males by using a "sneaker" mating tactic. Terminal-

simultaneous hermaphrodite An animal that possesses ovotestes that produce both eggs and sperm and alternates between two behavioral roles in providing eggs or sperm during spawning.

ovotestes A gonad consisting of both ovarian and testicular tissue, capable of producing both ova and sperm.

sequential hermaphrodite An animal that begins life as one sex, then changes to the other sex as an adult in response to environmental or genotypic factors.

protogynous A form of sequential hermaphroditism in which individuals begin life as females, then change into males.

protandrous A form of sequential hermaphroditism in which individuals begin life as males, then change into females.

(A)

(B)

FIGURE 3.26 **Sequential hermaphroditism** in the striped parrotfish. (A) Young females of this species have bold stripes and defend territories along the edges of reefs. (B) As females mature and grow in size, they change sex and adopt male-typical coloration and behavior, joining other males in defending large territories encompassing several "harems" of young females.

phase males establish territories from which they exclude other males and in which they court females. If a courted female releases her eggs, then a female mimic may enter the territory undetected and fertilize some of the eggs. This alternative reproductive tactic is maintained in the population because of its occasional success in attaining fertilizations.

The sex change in parrotfish is accompanied by changes in the pattern of circulating steroid hormones. Females have undetectable concentrations of the primary fish androgen 11-ketotestosterone, moderate concentrations of testosterone, and high concentrations of 17β-estradiol. During the transition from initial to terminal coloration phases, concentrations of 11-ketotestosterone rise dramatically and estrogen concentrations decline. Males have high concentrations of 11-ketotestosterone and testosterone but low concentrations of estrogen. Injection of adult females with 11-ketotestosterone causes a precocious change in gonadal, gametic, and behavioral sex. Female mimics, which maintain the initial-phase coloration, do not display the increase in blood concentrations of 11-ketotestosterone.

Alternative Reproductive Tactics and Male Polymorphism

There are other situations in which the default condition is neither male nor female but, rather, ovarian or testicular hormones must exert feminizing or masculinizing effects, respectively, during normal sexual differentiation of behavior. The previous sections have assumed, for the most part, that there are two distinct sexes—male and female. Within some species, however, there are multiple types (or **morphs**) of the same sex, as with the sneaker fish mentioned above. Different male morphs often look very distinct, and they often exhibit quite dissimilar behavioral patterns, as well as alternative mating tactics. In some cases, a subset of males within a population resemble females, whereas the alternative male morph differs from females in appearance and behavior; in other cases, there are several different male morphs (polymorphism) within a population, all of which differ from females in appearance and behavior (Moore et al., 1998). Different male morphs often pursue alternative tactics to achieve reproductive success. Some morphs are territorial and exclude

morph Individuals of a species that differ in form or function but are capable of interbreeding.

FIGURE 3.27   Different male morphs of the plainfin midshipman fish This nest contains a type I male (center), a female (right), and type II males (far right and lower left). Also shown on the left are newly hatched fry attached to a small rock by an adhesive disk at the base of the yolk sac. During the breeding season, male plainfin midshipman fish (*Porichthys notatus*) build nests under rocky shelters along the intertidal and subtidal zones of the western coast of the United States and Canada. Photograph by Margaret A. Marchaterre, courtesy of Andrew Bass.

other males from (and attempt to attract females to) their defended territories. Other morphs are "satellite" or "sneaker" males. Satellite males usually loiter near the edges of a territorial male's property and attempt to mate with females that are attracted to his territory. Sneaker males often resemble females; they "sneak" into a territorial male's property along with visiting females, then attempt clandestine matings with the females before the resident male discovers the deception.

Males that change phenotypes, either permanently or temporarily, during their lives are said to have plastic phenotypes (Moore, 1991). For example, male spring peepers (frogs of the genera *Pseudacris*, *Rana*, and *Hyla*) display one of two alternative mating tactics: they either vocalize to attract females or remain silent near calling males and attempt to intercept females that are moving toward the callers. Calling is energetically expensive, and males can switch between these behavioral strategies on different nights (Lance and Wells, 1993).

Male morphs that permanently differentiate into a single phenotype for life are said to have fixed phenotypes (Moore, 1991). For example, male ruffs (*Philomachus pugnax*, a type of sandpiper) become either darkly colored and highly territorial or lightly colored with the behavioral characteristics of satellite males (Lank et al., 1995). Several species of fishes, including sunfishes, swordtails, platyfishes, and midshipmen, display male polymorphism in appearance and mating tactics (Bass, 1996). One of the most interesting examples of alternative male phenotypes comes from the midshipman fishes.

There are two types of male plainfin midshipmen (*Porichthys notatus*) (**FIGURE 3.27**). Type I males build nests and attract females to their nests by generating an advertisement call, which sounds like a series of long-duration hums. If you walk along a Pacific beach anywhere from Northern California to the Canadian border on a summer night, you are likely to hear the "songs" of type I midshipman males calling females to their nests (Bass, 1996). A responding female inspects the nest, and if it meets her specifications, she deposits her eggs. After the female lays her eggs, the type I male fertilizes them, then maintains a vigilant defense of the clutch and the nest site against rivals. While guarding the eggs, he emits an aggressive call (or grunt) to warn away potential intruders (Bass, 1996). On average, type I males are two to three times larger than type II males, which physically resemble females (Bass, 1996). Type II males never build nests, guard eggs, or vocalize to attract females; rather, they have evolved an alternative reproductive tactic as sneaker/satellite males. They swim into nest sites guarded by type I males and release sperm. Presumably, the type I males do not challenge them because they resemble females.

Type II midshipman males undergo sexual maturation nearly a year earlier than type I males, and this precocious puberty differentiates the two male phenotypes. It has not yet been established whether the difference in the timing of puberty is the primary determining factor in the developmental pathway leading to the different male morphs, but it appears that differential steroid concentrations in adulthood are important. Both types of males (and females) have detectable testosterone concentrations in their blood, with type II males displaying the highest blood testosterone concentrations, followed by females, then type I males (Brantley et al., 1993). The primary teleost fish androgen, however, is 11-ketotestosterone. The 11-ketotestosterone concentrations in type I males are up to 20 times higher than their testosterone concentrations; neither type II males nor females have detectable 11-ketotestosterone levels (Bass, 1996). Treatment with 11-ketotestosterone causes the vocal muscle morphology of type II sneaker males to resemble that of the larger type I males but does not appreciably change their courtship behavior (Lee and Bass, 2005; Oliveira et al., 2005). Addition of 11-ketotestosterone, but not testosterone, activates the vocal pattern generator in the brain of type I males so quickly that they emit a neural pattern signature of "song" within 5 minutes! In contrast, addition of testosterone, but not 11-ketotestosterone, activates the vocal pattern generator in type II males and females (Remage-Healey and Bass, 2006). Only females have any detectable circulating estrogens, but the behavioral effects appear to depend more on testosterone than estradiol. In females only, the rapid actions of testosterone are eliminated by inhibition of aromatase, but not by pharmacological blockade of androgen receptors. Presumably, these effects in females reflect testosterone effects that are the result of rapid conversion to estradiol in the vocal pattern generator. Although also activated by testosterone, the receptor mechanisms appear reversed in type II males; that is, activation of the vocal pattern generators is eliminated by blockade of androgen receptors but not affected by aromatase inhibition (Remage-Healey and Bass, 2007). This same steroid receptor response is observed in type I males to 11-ketotestosterone. As a final interesting twist, cortisol, the primary glucocorticoid in this species, also shows differential effects. Relative to type I males, cortisol treatment increases activation of the vocal pattern generator of females and decreases activation in type II males. Thus, different patterns of steroid hormones activate different types of steroid receptors in various neural tissues involved in growth, reproductive behavior, and vocalization (Bass and Remage-Healey, 2008).

In several lizard species, as well, males exhibit alternative behavioral mating strategies and body types. For example, male tree lizards (*Urosaurus ornatus*) display striking polymorphisms in the color of a body structure called a dewlap (Moore et al., 1998). The dewlap is a flap of skin attached to the throat of a lizard; males extend the dewlap during courtship and aggressive encounters. Dewlaps of male tree lizards may be solid colors (typically orange, yellow, blue, or violet) or have a central spot surrounded by a contrasting background color (e.g., an orange spot surrounded by blue) (Hews et al., 1997). Nine different color morphs have been identified among tree lizards in Arizona, but most populations consist of two or three different male phenotypes. One well-studied population contains two types of males that are present in nearly equal proportions: (1) territorial males that have an orange dewlap sporting a blue spot and (2) nonterritorial males with a solid orange dewlap (Thompson and Moore, 1992). The nonterritorial males display one of two dominant behavioral patterns: (1) sedentary satellite behavior or (2) nomadic behavior. The dewlap color and behavioral polymorphisms appear to be permanently organized early during post-hatching development (Moore et al., 1998). If immature males are exposed to high testosterone and progesterone concentrations, then territorial orange-blue males result; if they are not exposed to high testosterone and progesterone concentrations, they develop into nonterritorial males with orange dewlaps (**FIGURE 3.28**). However, the nonterritorial tactics of the orange morphs appear to be affected by environmental conditions. Stressful ambient conditions

FIGURE 3.28 Three types of male tree lizards coexist in some Arizona populations: (1) territorial males, (2) sedentary nonterritorial (satellite) males, and (3) nomadic nonterritorial males. The territorial males develop an orange dewlap with a blue spot; this morph results from early post-hatching exposure to high testosterone and progesterone concentrations. In the absence of high testosterone and progesterone concentrations, males develop a solid orange dewlap and become nonterritorial. In adulthood, if stressful environmental conditions result in high corticosterone concentrations, and thus lowered testosterone concentrations, nonterritorial males become nomadic; if low corticosterone concentrations, and thus higher testosterone concentrations, are present, nonterritorial males become sedentary. Territorial orange-blue males remain territorial regardless of environmental conditions and corticosterone concentrations. After Moore et al., 1998.

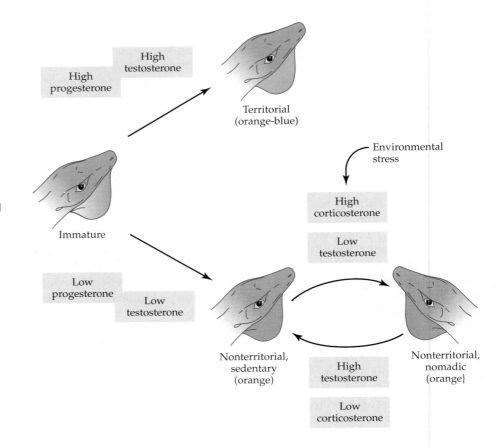

(e.g., drought) cause sustained corticosterone secretion, which promotes nomadic, wandering behavior (Moore et al., 1998). Thus, the two male phenotypes are permanently fixed by early hormone conditions, whereas the flexibility of tactic switching (i.e., sedentary versus nomadic) among males with orange dewlaps is mediated by the temporary effects of corticosterone concentrations during adulthood. Importantly, to date, alternative reproductive tactics and multiple morphs have not been described for females. Whether this is a true sex difference or simply represents a failure of discovering these alternatives among females remains unknown.

The Effects of Hormones on Sexually Dimorphic Behaviors

As we have seen, the initial step in sex determination—the development of a testis or an ovary—triggers a cascade of events that results in sexually dimorphic behaviors (see Figure 3.15). In order to understand the interaction between hormones and behavior, behavioral endocrinologists have studied several animal models that display distinct behavioral sex differences. By studying the development, neural and hormonal bases, and molecular mechanisms of a simple behavior that is displayed by one sex but not by the other, researchers hope to elucidate general principles that can be expanded from these simple systems to explain more complex behavioral sex differences, such as those displayed by humans.

The Organizational/Activational Hypothesis

In 1959, W. C. Young (**BOX 3.2**) and his colleagues published a classic study on the effects of prenatal and early postnatal androgen treatment on female reproductive behavior (Phoenix et al., 1959). This experiment rivals Berthold's study with roost-

BOX 3.2   *William C. Young*

William Caldwell Young was an important pioneer in behavioral endocrinology. Young received his undergraduate degree at Amherst College, where he worked with Professor Harold H. Plough. He published his senior thesis on the effects of high temperature on fertility in *Drosophila* (Young and Plough, 1926). Young attended the University of Chicago for his graduate training and worked in the laboratory of Carl R. Moore in the zoology department.

Carl Moore had earned his doctorate at the University of Chicago working in the laboratory of Frank Lillie. Moore had published a series of 11 papers with the generic title "On the Physiological Properties of the Gonads as Controllers of Somatic and Psychic Characteristics." He noted in his studies that although castration of male guinea pigs resulted in rapid and nearly uniform degeneration of the epididymis and seminal vesicles, the timing of the cessation of sexual behavior varied enormously among individuals. Moore interpreted these results to suggest that reproductive behavior was "utterly capricious, unordered by hormonal events, and unrelated to variables of significance to reproductive biology" (Goy, 1967).

Young produced a classic study of epididymal sperm transport for his dissertation project and was awarded his doctorate in 1927. During the course of these studies, Young became interested in the hormonal control of female mating behavior, but his mentor, Professor Moore, actively discouraged behavioral research because his own experience suggested that the variation inherent in behavioral studies was daunting.

Young joined the biology department at Brown University in 1928 and submitted a grant application to continue his work on the reproductive morphology and physiology of guinea pigs. While waiting for the funding agency's decision, he had "nothing better to do than investigate the inexpensive problem of the morphological changes associated with female sexual behavior in the guinea pig" (Goy, 1967). By the time he received the news that his grant application was not to be funded, Young and his research group had already started a productive line of research that used behavior as an indirect measure of ovarian activity (Dempsey, 1968). In 1939, Young moved to the Yerkes Laboratories of Primate Biology in Orange Park, Florida, where he interacted with R. M. Yerkes and other psychologists during his 4-year tenure. His research began to include behavior as a primary object of study.

Apparently, Young felt isolated in a nonacademic research setting (Goy, 1967) and left the Yerkes laboratory in 1943 to teach at Cedar Crest College. He then accepted an offer to set up an endocrinology laboratory in the anatomy department at the University of Kansas. This laboratory was very active, and

William C. Young (1899–1965)

studies of hormonal control of reproductive function, including mating behavior, were conducted there by a stellar team of graduate students and postdoctoral fellows, including M. Diamond, H. Feder, A. Gerall, R. Goy, J. Grunt, C. Phoenix, W. Riss, and E. Valenstein. The famous study of the organizational effects of prenatal androgen on guinea pig mating behavior was conducted in Young's Kansas laboratory (Phoenix et al., 1959). This study has been one of the cornerstones of modern behavioral endocrinology research. While at Kansas, Young also edited the third edition of *Sex and Internal Secretions*, published in 1961, which was the bible for reproductive biologists at that time and continues to be an important sourcebook 55 years later.

In 1963, Young moved to the Oregon Regional Primate Research Center, where he became chairman of the reproductive physiology department. There, his organizational/activational hypothesis of behavioral sexual dimorphism was examined in rhesus monkeys (Goy and Phoenix, 1972; Goy and Resko, 1972). William C. Young is one of the most important figures in behavioral endocrinology because of his many significant research contributions; his theoretical contributions, which were profoundly important in framing research problems; and the graduate and postdoctoral students trained in his laboratories, who continue to make important contributions to the field (Beach, 1981).

lordosis A female sexually receptive posture in which the hindquarters are raised and the tail is deflected to facilitate copulation.

mounting A behavior observed among males of many species with internal fertilization in which the male assumes a copulatory position but does not insert his penis (or other intromittent organ) into the female's vagina (or urogenital opening).

ers (see Chapter 1) in theoretical importance to behavioral endocrinology (Gerall, 2009; Phoenix, 2009; Wallen, 2009). Because of the profound effect of Young's study on shaping the field, this study will be described in detail.

Females and males of many species show sexually dimorphic mating postures. Female rodents stand immobile with arched backs and allow males to mount them. This mating posture is called **lordosis** (see Chapter 6). Males, on the other hand, mount females. Females rarely exhibit **mounting** behavior, the masculine behavior pattern, and males typically do not assume the lordosis posture, the feminine behavior pattern, when mounted by other males.[1]

Mating behavior in both sexes is under the control of gonadal steroid hormones. For example, castration of males stops mounting behavior, and testosterone replacement therapy restores mounting behavior to its original levels (see Chapter 5). Logically, we might conclude that testosterone causes mounting behavior. However, injection of adult females with testosterone does not increase their mounting behavior to male-typical levels. Females somehow lose the potential to exhibit male-typical behavior during development; in other words, the behavior of females is demasculinized. Similarly, castration of adult males and subsequent treatment with estrogens and progestins does not lead to the appearance of female-typical mating behavior. Males become defeminized during development; that is, they lose the potential to display female-typical behavior.

Professor Young and his research group sought to understand how these behavioral differences in hormonal response were mediated. They reasoned that hormonal events early in development must be responsible for the induction of feminine and masculine behavioral patterns in general, as well as for the shifting of the probabilities of masculine and feminine mating behaviors in females and males in the presence of the appropriate stimulus. In the experiments designed to address this hypothesis, testosterone propionate was administered to pregnant guinea pigs throughout most of their 69-day gestation period. Some pregnant females were given large doses of the hormone. At birth, some of the female offspring from these pregnancies possessed external genitalia that were indistinguishable from those of their brothers or of normal males. These females were labeled "hermaphrodites" by the researchers. Another group of females was exposed to smaller doses of the androgen prenatally; these females had no visible abnormalities of the external genitalia and were referred to as "unmodified females." The researchers waited for the guinea pigs to mature to examine their behavior in the second phase of the study.

In adulthood, both groups of androgen-exposed females, as well as androgen-exposed male and control male and female guinea pigs, were gonadectomized and then injected with estrogen and progesterone to stimulate female sexual behavior. Each of these animals was paired with a stud male guinea pig. Some time later, all of the animals were injected with androgens to stimulate male sexual behavior and paired with a standard conspecific female that was in mating condition. The results were impressive. Androgens given to guinea pigs prenatally (1) decreased the tendency of both experimental groups of females to display lordosis in adulthood and (2) enhanced the tendency of both experimental groups of females to display mounting behavior in response to testosterone therapy but (3) caused no deleterious effect on mounting behavior or other masculine behavioral patterns in males similarly treated.

Not only were the data of considerable interest, but the conceptual framework in which the authors chose to cast them was rich and wide. Professor Young and his colleagues made the following speculations (Feder, 1981; Phoenix et al., 1959):

---

[1] It should be noted here that this yes/no dichotomy is presented for clarity's sake; in reality, males of some strains of rats show lordosis regularly, and females of some rat strains display frequent mounting behavior. A sex "difference" is often one of frequency, behavioral threshold, or the quality of the behavior.

1. A clear distinction can be made between the prenatal actions of hormones in causing differentiation, or organization, of neural substrates for behavior and the actions of hormones in adulthood in causing activation of these substrates. This is a very important point and provides the basis for the organizational/activational hypothesis of sexually dimorphic behaviors. During development, the sex steroid hormones organize, or "program," the components of the nervous system that will be needed for subsequent male- or female-typical behaviors. In adulthood, these same hormones activate, modulate, or inhibit the function of these existing neural circuits.

2. Critical periods of perinatal development exist during which an animal is maximally susceptible to the organizing effects of steroids on neural tissue. (We now know that the timing of organizational effects of steroids may be broader in scope than originally formulated by Young and his collaborators.)

3. Organization of the neural tissues mediating mating behavior is in some ways analogous to the differentiation of the accessory sex organs. That is, the nervous systems of males are normally masculinized and defeminized during development, whereas the nervous systems of females are normally feminized and demasculinized.

4. The organizing effects of steroid hormones on prenatal neural tissues are subtle and reflect alterations in function rather than structure, because even females whose external genitalia are not physically masculinized demonstrate behavioral masculinization and defeminization. (As you will soon learn, however, during the past 30 years or so, it has been established that changes in neural structures are associated with sexually dimorphic behaviors.)

5. The idea that prenatal hormones act to organize the neural substrates for behavior has possible implications for the study of behavior in primates, including humans.

This study profoundly affected the way behavioral endocrinologists conceptualized the interactions of hormones and sexually dimorphic behaviors. This groundbreaking study did not arise out of thin air, however, but was built on three separate, but related, lines of research, involving (1) embryological studies showing that prenatal androgen exposure results in masculinized external genitalia, (2) studies of the effects of blood-borne substances in masculinizing the female twins of male cattle, and (3) endocrine studies investigating the control of ovulation. Anatomists had studied the sexual differentiation of the body and had discovered what many of us have observed: the most striking sexual dimorphism in most species is that of the external genitalia. An early study demonstrated that injection of pregnant rats with androgens throughout their pregnancy affected the external genitalia of the offspring (Hamilton and Gardner, 1937). Female rats whose mothers had received androgens during pregnancy were born with masculinized external genitalia: in other words, they developed a penis. This study, and studies of the regulation of ovulation, contributed to the development of the organizational/activational hypothesis by demonstrating that early endocrine treatments could masculinize or feminize anatomical and functional features. Given this context, it is perhaps not surprising that the canonical behavioral endocrinology experiment was conducted by Professor Young and colleagues in an anatomy department.

Because studies examining the hormonal control of ovulation have continued to shed light on the mechanisms of sexual differentiation, they will be described in detail. Female mammals display cyclic gonadal function, whereas males have more or less tonic reproductive function: that is, ovulation, the expulsion of a mature

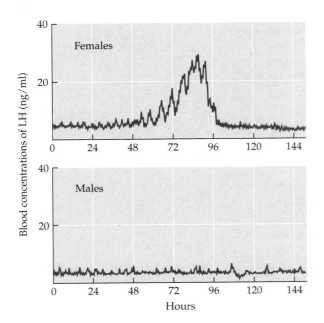

FIGURE 3.29 **LH profiles of female and male rats** In both male and female rats, LH is released in a pulsatile fashion from the anterior pituitary in response to pulses of GnRH from the medial basal hypothalamus. In females, the pulse frequency and amplitude increase around the time of ovulation, as negative feedback mechanisms are temporarily overwhelmed by increasing blood estrogen concentrations and positive feedback mechanisms are engaged.

egg from the ovary, occurs cyclically, whereas sperm production is constant throughout the breeding season. The reproductive behavior of the sexes follows these fundamentally different patterns of gamete production, with females displaying cycles of mating behavior and males displaying more or less continuous willingness to mate.

What causes these patterns? Gonadal function is driven by gonadotropins secreted from the anterior pituitary (see Chapter 2), but what drives the gonadotropins? Gonadotropin-releasing hormone (GnRH) secreted from the median eminence of the hypothalamus determines the pattern of release of luteinizing hormone (LH), a gonadotropin, from the anterior pituitary. In both males and females, this process begins when a series of LH pulses—20–40 minutes apart in rats and 60–120 minutes apart in humans—are released into the circulation in response to pulses of GnRH from the hypothalamus; these pulses of LH often precede pulsatile releases of gonadal steroid hormones (**FIGURE 3.29**). Thus, the hypothalamus provides a pulsatile delivery of GnRH in both males and females, which subsequently drives the anterior pituitary, which eventually drives gonadal function. As circulating concentrations of LH and sex steroid hormones rise, they feed back to suppress further GnRH secretion (negative feedback). Similarly, the injection of steroid hormones suppresses GnRH and gonadotropin secretion in a dose-dependent manner. Differential half-lives of four types of hormones (GnRH, 2–4 min; LH, 20–30 min; follicle-stimulating hormone, 3 h; gonadal steroids, 6–8 h) (Hayes and Crowley, 1998), which permit fine-tuning of reproductive function in the face of challenging or opportunistic conditions, contribute to the multilevel pulsatile organization. Recall from Chapter 2 that GnIH inhibits GnRH and gonadotropin secretion (Kriegsfeld et al., 2010; Tsutsui et al., 2000). GnIH neurons express estrogen receptors and seem to mediate steroid negative feedback regulation of reproductive function, likely inhibiting GnRH secretion until the time of the LH surge (Gibson et al., 2008; Kriegsfeld et al., 2006).

In females, there is a steady increase in the amount of estrogen produced by the ovaries against the backdrop of continuous pulses of GnRH secretion and negative feedback endocrine regulation. These pulses increase in both frequency and amplitude. Female rodents escape from rigid negative feedback control. As estrogen accumulates in the blood, a signal from a putative "surge center" in the anteroventral periventricular nucleus (AVPV) of the hypothalamus drives GnRH secretion. The surge of GnRH causes a surge of LH and follicle-stimulating hormone (FSH) secretion, which in turn stimulates ovulation via the positive feedback mechanism, likely through secretion of the stimulatory neuropeptide, kisspeptin (Smith et al., 2006; Williams et al., 2011), illustrated in **FIGURE 3.30**. Ovulation may be controlled by the release from negative feedback of GnIH, allowing the positive drive to dominate (Gibson et al., 2008; Russo et al., 2015). Additionally, γ-aminobutyric acid (GABA) switches from a negative to a positive regulator at the time of the surge (Christian and Moenter, 2007). Kisspeptin neurons of rodents are located in the rostral periventricular area of the third ventricle (which includes the AVPV) and are positively activated by estrogen during positive feedback (Smith et al., 2006). A similar re-

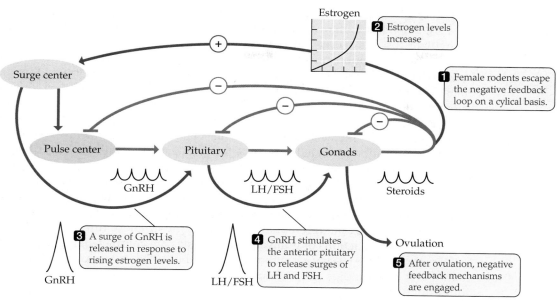

FIGURE 3.30   Positive feedback and the control of ovulation Steroid secretion in both males and females is usually regulated by negative feedback (red lines), whereby increasing gonadal steroid concentrations feed back to the gonads, anterior pituitary, and hypothalamus to slow secretion of GnRH, gonadotropins, and gonadal steroids. However, on a cyclical basis, females escape this rigid negative feedback control (green lines).

sponse likely occurs in kisspeptin neurons located in the mediobasal hypothalamus of primates and sheep. The majority of GnRH neurons express the receptors for kisspeptin, and kisspeptin evokes activation of these GnRH-containing cells. Kisspeptin administration in vivo causes immediate and prolonged release of LH in all mammalian species examined to date (Clarkson and Herbison, 2009). These findings indicate that kisspeptin neurons located in the rostral periventricular area of the third ventricle that project to GnRH neurons are an essential component of the surge mechanism in rodents.

The sexually dimorphic pattern of gonadotropin secretion can be demonstrated in the following manner. Providing an ovariectomized rat with low doses of estrogen causes a reduction of GnRH and LH concentrations via negative feedback; providing an ovariectomized rat with chronically high doses of estrogen, however, causes an increase in GnRH and LH every 4–5 days (i.e., the normal time of the ovulatory cycle) through the process of positive feedback (Legan and Karsch, 1975). Thus, evoking a positive feedback response in most rodents requires attaining a threshold value of estrogen. Providing a castrated male rat with low amounts of estrogen also causes reduction of GnRH and LH concentrations due to negative feedback, but estrogen does not induce a positive feedback response. It has also been documented that injections of even pharmacologically high doses of estrogens never result in a positive feedback response in male primates (Karsch et al., 1973). In monkeys, the preovulatory gonadotropin surge does not require elevated GnRH from the hypothalamus; the positive effect of estrogens on LH and FSH secretion in primates seems to require a specific pattern for an extended period of time to change numbers of GnRH receptors (Ganong, 2006).

What is the basis of the sex difference in the regulation of endocrine function? Initially, it was proposed that the pituitary gland itself differs between the sexes. Females were thought to possess pituitaries that displayed cyclic function, whereas males were believed to possess pituitaries that displayed tonic function (Pfeiffer, 1936). According to this logic, a male does not normally ovulate because his pitu-

precocial Born or hatched at an advanced stage of development so that little or no parental intervention is required for survival.

altricial Born or hatched at an early stage of development. Altricial offspring are generally quite helpless and require substantial parental care to survive.

itary does not display cyclic function—and more obviously, because he does not have an ovary. But if an ovary is transplanted into an adult male rat, he still does not ovulate. A series of classic papers reporting on the physiological control of ovulation in rabbits demonstrated that pituitary function is indeed controlled by the hypothalamus (Harris, 1937, 1948, 1955). These studies also demonstrated that the "male" pituitary can, under the right conditions, sustain ovulation. If the pituitary is removed from a female rat and replaced by a pituitary from an adult male, then ovulation occurs, provided that vascular connections with the hypothalamus are established (Harris and Jacobsohn, 1952). Thus, the sexual dimorphism in the ability to support ovulation is not at the level of the pituitary but, rather, reflects changes induced by early androgen exposure upstream in the hypothalamus.

In contrast to the studies by Professor Young's group, many investigations of the process of sexual differentiation have used rats rather than guinea pigs because investigators do not have to make endocrine manipulations via the mother but can influence the sexual differentiation of each individual rat directly after birth. The masculinizing actions of guinea pig fetal testes are completed approximately halfway through the 69-day gestation period, or about 35 days postconception (Goy et al., 1964). Guinea pigs are **precocial** animals, which means that the young are born fully furred, able to walk about, and able to thermoregulate. In contrast, rats are **altricial** animals: their gestation period is only about 21 days, and they are born in a very immature state, blind and hairless and unable to walk about or thermoregulate. Sexual differentiation in rats occurs, in part, during the first 10 days or so after birth, again about 35 days postconception. This developmental pattern allows researchers to make endocrine manipulations in individual newly born rats. In rats, there is a critical period for sexual differentiation, or more properly, a period of maximal susceptibility to the effects of the hormones that induce behavioral sexual dimorphisms. If a male rat is castrated at 1 day of age and implanted with an ovary as an adult, ovarian cycles that are identical to female cycles are observed. However, if a male rat is castrated at 20 days of age and implanted with an ovary as an adult, no cycles in ovarian function are observed (Pfeiffer, 1935, 1936). Further studies have indicated that castration after 3 or 4 days of age also fails to preserve the potential for cyclic ovarian function in adult males. The secretion of testosterone by the male during the first several hours of life destroys forever the potential for the cycling that is seen in females.

The blood testosterone concentrations of male rat pups approach adult concentrations by about 6 hours after birth. This elevation in blood testosterone concentrations has been attributed to (1) release of the infant's testes from negative feedback suppression by placental gonadotropins and (2) retarded steroid clearance rates as steroid metabolism shifts from maternal systems to the infant's own liver function (Baum et al., 1988). This perinatal surge of testosterone appears to permanently alter the neuronal circuitry involved in the release of surges of GnRH from the hypothalamus, and thus it permanently eliminates the potential for feminine positive feedback effects. In the absence of high concentrations of gonadal steroids, the neural circuitry involved in GnRH surge generation is spared. Male human babies also display this surge in blood testosterone concentrations at birth (Forest and Cathiard, 1975). However, they retain the ability to show positive feedback responses of gonadotropin release when injected with estrogens. In other words, the presence of positive feedback mechanisms associated with the hypothalamic-pituitary-gonadal axis is not a sexually dimorphic trait in humans, or in other primates examined (see Chapter 4) (Clarkson and Herbison, 2009; Hodges and Hearne, 1978; Karsch et al., 1973; Norman and Spies, 1986).

Where in the brain does the rodent sex difference in positive feedback occur? Recall that both males and females release LH in pulsatile bursts (see Figure 3.29). This pulsatile release of LH follows pulsatile bursts of GnRH in both sexes. In addition to these pulses of GnRH, females also show large, cyclic surges of GnRH that are not seen in males. The pulsatile release of gonadotropins in both males and females appears to be the result of packets of hormone release triggered by the arcuate nuclei and the ventromedial nuclei of the hypothalamus, which are often collectively considered to be part of the medial basal hypothalamus. However, most of the GnRH cells in females are located in the rostral aspects of the preoptic hypothalamus, that is, in front of the optic chiasm (Chappel, 1985). The surge generator is located in the region of the preoptic and suprachiasmatic nuclei (Pierce, 1988) (**FIGURE 3.31**). As you will learn in Chapter 8, there are biological timekeepers located in these regions that control ovulation. A daily "minisurge" of GnRH is elicited by one of these clocks, and when this minisurge coincides with high estrogen concentrations, females' GnRH cells release large and rapid pulses of GnRH, resulting in a GnRH and LH surge. Destruction or surgical isolation of these timekeeping cells prevents the surge of GnRH in response to estrogen treatment, but these procedures do not

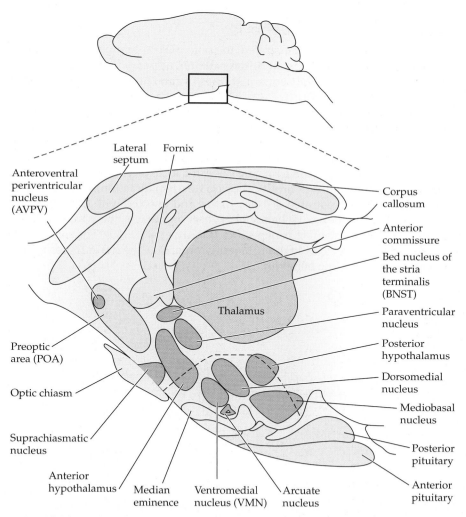

FIGURE 3.31 The surge and pulse centers of the hypothalamus Schematic sagittal view of rat brain showing the hypothalamic nuclei involved in the regulation of gonadotropin pulses and surges. Pulsatile gonadotropin secretion remains normal after isolation of the dorsomedial and mediobasal hypothalamus in females (below the dotted line), but the periovulatory surges observed in normal females no longer occur, indicating that the female surge center is located in the hypothalamic nuclei adjacent to the preoptic area (POA) of the hypothalamus, in the suprachiasmatic nucleus and AVPV.

perinatal Around the time of birth, typically a few days before or after birth in rodents or a few weeks before and after in humans.

affect negative feedback; negative feedback in both males and females of some rodents appears to be regulated in the medial basal hypothalamus.

Early exposure to androgens has been hypothesized to be what destroys the neural connections between the surge generators and the pulse generators. For example, kisspeptin cells in the AVPV are sexually dimorphic, with males having few cells and females having an abundance of kisspeptin expression in this region (Kauffman et al., 2007b). An alternative hypothesis states that androgenization may diminish pubertal estrogen binding to cytosol receptors such that surges are not observed (Gerall and Givon, 1992). Either hypothesis is consistent with the observation that no amount of estrogen treatment in adulthood can evoke a GnRH surge in male rodents or in female rodents treated with androgens **perinatally** (around the time of birth, i.e., in the late prenatal or early postnatal period): the underlying neural machinery is either not present or nonfunctional. In some cases, early androgen treatment promotes death of neurons; in other cases, early androgen exposure spares neurons from death.

Sexual Differentiation and Behavior

As Young and his colleagues demonstrated, the potential for feminine or masculine behavior, like other aspects of sexual differentiation, appears to be organized by early exposure to hormones. Subsequent studies of rats, mice, and other rodents have confirmed this view (**FIGURE 3.32**). Female rats that are ovariectomized as adults and injected with androgens do not exhibit male-typical mounting behavior in the presence of other females that are sexually receptive. However, if female rats are injected with androgens prior to 10 days of age and injected again with androgens as adults, they do display male-typical mounting behavior in the presence of receptive females. Similarly, if male rats are castrated at 20 days of age and injected with estrogens and progestins as adults, they do not display feminine mating postures. But if male rats are castrated at 1 day of age and injected with estrogens and progestins as adults, female sexual behavior is observed; that is, these males exhibit lordosis when mounted by male conspecifics (Grady et al., 1965). Thus, exposure to androgens prior to day 20 of life permanently organizes the brain to permit the later expression of masculine behavior.

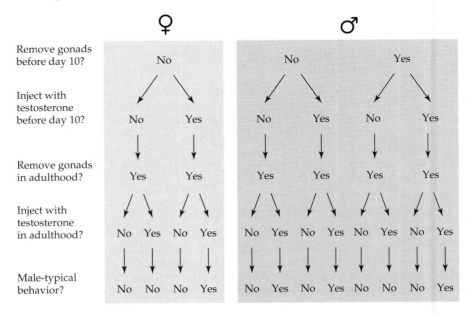

FIGURE 3.32 Experimental protocol for determining organizational versus activational effects of androgens on sexually dimorphic mating behavior in rodents.

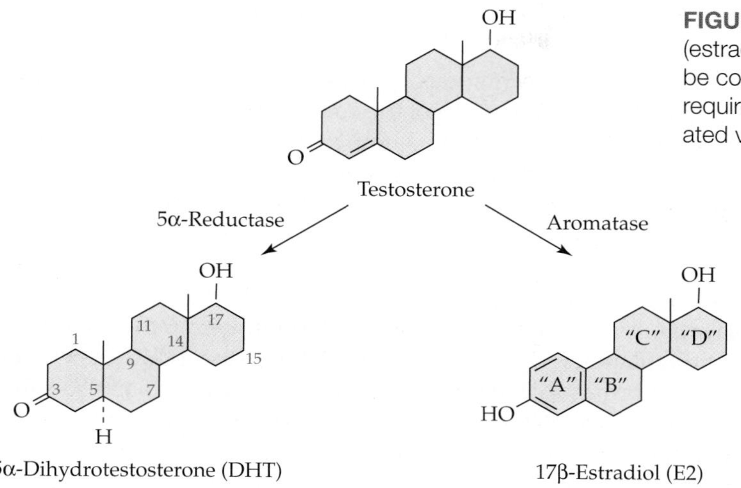

OH

Testosterone

5α-Reductase   Aromatase

OH

11   17
1   14
9   15
3   5   7

O
H

5α-Dihydrotestosterone (DHT)

OH

"C" "D"
"A" "B"

HO

17β-Estradiol (E2)

FIGURE 3.33 **Testosterone is a prohormone** for an estrogen (estradiol) and for an androgen (dihydrotestosterone) that cannot be converted into an estrogen. Thus, additional studies are always required to determine whether the effects of testosterone are mediated via estrogen or androgen receptors.

In addition to mating behavior, many adult behavioral sex differences in rats (e.g., aggressive behavior, taste preferences, and parental behavior) are organized by steroid hormones perinatally and activated by steroid hormones in adulthood. The presence of such adult sexually dimorphic behaviors can be manipulated in a predictable way in infancy. Masculinization and defeminization of subsequent behavior occur when rats are exposed to androgens prior to 10 days of age; feminization and demasculinization of subsequent behavior occur when rats are not exposed to androgens prior to 10 days of age. Different sexually dimorphic behaviors do vary slightly in their organizational requirements. Small variations in the timing and dosage of androgen exposure do not influence all sexually dimorphic behaviors in rats equally; however, most behaviors are masculinized by androgen exposure on or before day 10 (Grady et al., 1965). Masculine behaviors are activated in adulthood by androgens; feminine behaviors are activated in adulthood by estrogens and progestins.

It is not androgen per se, however, that is responsible for the masculinization of neural organization. There is now overwhelming evidence that testosterone is aromatized to an estradiol in the brain and that many of its masculinizing effects upon behavior are dependent on this cellular conversion (Gorski, 1993; Reddy et al., 1974) (**FIGURE 3.33** and see below). Indeed, an injection of estrogens before 10 days of age masculinizes later sexual behavior among rats even more effectively than an injection of androgens (Booth, 1977; Feder and Whalen, 1965).

You may be wondering, if estrogens cause masculinization of the nervous system, then why aren't all females masculinized? The ovaries of pregnant rats produce high concentrations of estrogens during gestation. Estrogens, like other fat-soluble steroids, could theoretically pass the blood-placental barrier easily, enter the fetal circulation, and masculinize female fetuses. However, perinatal rats produce large quantities of a protein called α-fetoprotein, which actively binds circulating estrogens; the bound estrogens are removed through the placenta and metabolized by the maternal liver. The α-fetoprotein does not bind androgens effectively, however, so testosterone from the gonads of a male fetus reaches its brain, where it is aromatized to estradiol and masculinizes behavior. The α-fetoprotein protects female fetuses from estrogenic steroids, and because females normally have low circulating concentrations of androgens, neither masculinization nor defeminization occurs (Bakker et al., 2006). However, some artificial estrogens do not bind very well to α-fetoprotein (e.g., DES), and these artificial estrogens, as we saw above, can have masculinizing effects on female morphology and behavior as well as long-term ill effects on female health.

Early Effects of Androgens Mediated by Activational Effects of Sex Steroids

Genetics and molecular biological techniques have been applied to the problem of sexual differentiation in rat brains. The results of these studies demonstrate the importance of neural estrogen receptors in masculinization and defeminization (McCarthy and Arnold, 2008). For example, mice with targeted deletions (knockouts [KO]) of the gene for the α estrogen receptor (ERα), a ligand-activated transcription factor, were produced (αERKO mice) (Korach, 1994). Because these mice developed with ERα missing throughout life, one might predict that the males would not display normal masculine mating behavior. However, their behavior was only party changed: male αERKO mice displayed normal mounting behaviors, though with reduced levels of intromissions and no ejaculations (Ogawa et al., 1997, 2000). The αERKO males were also less aggressive than normal wild-type (WT) males. But because many so-called estrogen-dependent processes remained functional in the αERKO mice, the researchers reevaluated their hypotheses about the role of estrogen receptors in the development of sexually dimorphic behaviors. It was soon discovered that an alternative form of the estrogen receptor (termed β estrogen receptor; the originally characterized estrogen receptor was named α) persisted in αERKO mice (see Chapter 5). Male mice that had the gene for the β estrogen receptor disabled (βERKO mice) retained virtually all components of sexual behaviors (Ogawa et al., 1999). Still other mice were generated that lacked both the ERα and ERβ genes (αβERKO mice). It was discovered that male αβERKO mice failed to display any components of sexual behaviors, including mounting behaviors and ultrasonic vocalizations (Ogawa et al., 2000). These double-knockout mice displayed the reduced aggressive behaviors of single-knockout mice (αERKO). Supporting a redundancy in function, these results suggest that either one of the estrogen receptors is sufficient to maintain mounting in male mice. In contrast, offensive aggression specifically requires the presence of the ERα gene (reviewed in Nelson and Trainor, 2007).

Recent studies, however, suggest that the contribution of functional steroid receptors to sexually dimorphic behaviors is even more complicated. If the masculinizing effects of testosterone are exerted through its conversion by brain aromatase into estrogens that activate one of the estrogen receptors, then deletion of androgen receptors should not affect attainment of sexually dimorphic behaviors. However, male androgen receptor knockout (ARKO) mice showed marked reductions in male-typical reproductive and aggressive behaviors (Sato et al., 2004). Female ARKO mice displayed normal female sexual behaviors. Although treatment with the nonaromatizable androgen DHT failed to normalize male mating behaviors in male ARKO mice, DHT partially restored impaired male aggressive behaviors, suggesting the possibility of a second androgen receptor subtype. Interestingly, DHT treatment restored male-typical behaviors in αERKO mice (Sato et al., 2004).

More recently, mice have been developed that lack androgen receptor (AR) only in their nervous systems (Raskin et al., 2009); AR levels and distribution are normal in the peripheral tissues, so genital development is normal and these animals are fertile. Nevertheless, sexual and aggressive behaviors are impaired in these mice despite the presence of normal numbers of ERα-positive cells (Raskin et al., 2009). These results suggest that different patterns of sexually dimorphic behaviors require different patterns of functions by steroid receptor genes (Garey et al., 2003). Additionally, the sex difference in body size also appears to depend in part on the presence of AR in the nervous system; mutant mice did not display increased body size relative to females as wild-type males do.

Epigenetic Influences on Sexual Differentiation

epigenetic regulation   Changes in gene transcription resulting from modifications in the structure of chromatin, typically through DNA methylation and histone acetylation/deacetylation events.

Epigenetic regulation is the alteration in gene transcription resulting from the modification in the structure of chromatin, the complex of DNA and proteins that forms chromosomes within the nucleus of eukaryotic cells. Perhaps the most commonly explored epigenetic modifications are those resulting from DNA methylation and histone acetylation/deacetylation (**FIGURE 3.34**). **DNA methylation**, as the name implies, is the addition of methyl groups to DNA via a reaction catalyzed by

DNA methylation An epigenetic mechanism of gene regulation whereby methyl groups are added to DNA to reduce gene expression.

(A)

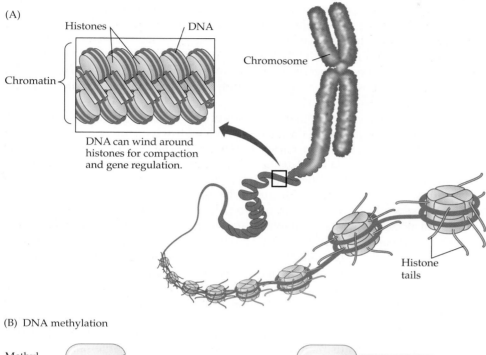

DNA can wind around histones for compaction and gene regulation.

(B) DNA methylation

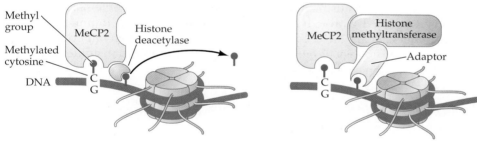

Acetyl group removed from DNA

Methyl group added to DNA

(C) Histone methylation/acetylation

Inaccessible nucleosomes: Histone tails largely methylated

Accessible nucleosomes: Histone tails largely unmethylated and acetylated

FIGURE 3.34 **Epigenetic regulation** through modification of chromatin (A) structure. When DNA is methylated (B), through the addition of a methyl group to a cytosine base, gene transcription is silenced. Methylated histones lead to chromatin modifications that can either increase of decrease gene transcription. Histone acetylation is associated with chromatin relaxation and increased gene transcription.

histone acetylation   An epigenetic mechanism of gene regulation whereby an acetyl group is added to residues protruding from the histone core. Acetylation increases access to genes and thereby their transcription.

histone deacetylation   An epigenetic mechanism of gene regulation whereby an acetyl group is removed from residues protruding from the histone core. Deacetylation decreases access to genes and thereby their transcription.

DNA methyltransferases (DNMTs). The resulting conversion of cytosine bases to 5-methylcytosine results in modified cytosine residues that usually lie next to guanine bases (i.e., CpG methylation). DNA methylation is typically associated with reduced gene expression. **Histone acetylation/deacetylation** is the process by which an acetyl group is added (acetylation) or removed (deacetylation) to/from a residue protruding from the histone core; the reactions are catalyzed by histone acetyltransferase (HAT) or histone deacetylase (HDAC) enzymes, respectively. Histones are proteins found in eukaryotic cell nuclei that package DNA into structural units by acting as spools around which DNA winds. Acetylation results in the "relaxation" of chromatin, more ready access to genes, and increased gene transcription. The opposite occurs following deacetylation, with chromatin condensing and reducing gene transcription (see Figure 3.34).

Both of these processes appear to be involved in sexual differentiation, with early findings demonstrating that neonatal male mice have more acetylation and methylation than females in the cortex and hippocampus on embryonic day 18, the day of birth, and 6 days later (Tsai et al., 2009). Such epigenetic regulation appears to be an important contributing factor in typical sexual differentiation; treatment of mice with an HDAC inhibitor in the first 2 days of life prevents the masculinization of a highly sexually dimorphic brain region, the bed nucleus of the stria terminalis (Murray et al., 2009). In rats, similar neonatal treatment blocked the masculinization of male sexual behavior (Matsuda et al., 2011). These findings suggest that the suppression of particular genes during a sensitive period of development is required for brain masculinization. In contrast, neonatal pharmacological inhibition of DNMTs in rats results in females that exhibit male sexual behavior in adulthood but has no impact on males (Nugent et al., 2015). These findings imply that masculinization of the female brain is prevented through suppression of genes by DNA methylation events. Indeed, neonatal male rats have lower DNMT expression in the preoptic area of the hypothalamus than females, and masculinization of female rats by estradiol is associated with reduced DNMT expression relative to unmanipulated females (Nugent et al., 2015). Together, these studies point to an important role for hormone-guided epigenetic events in altering gene expression to guide sexual differentiation of brain and behavior.

Environmental Influences on Mammalian Sexual Differentiation of the Nervous System

As noted above, the majority of behavioral sexual differentiation occurs postnatally in altricial rodents such as rats, mice, and hamsters. However, small and very subtle developmental events that occur in the egg (**BOX 3.3**) or in utero can also result in significant behavioral effects in adulthood. In addition to the effects of the intrauterine environment, differences in maternal care and exposure to environmental chemicals can also affect sexual differentiation. These effects are discussed in this section.

EFFECTS OF THE INTRAUTERINE ENVIRONMENT   Although much of the process of sexual differentiation occurs postnatally, some sexual differentiation processes begin in utero for rats. For example, the position in the uterine horn where a female rat gestates can have important effects on subsequent adult physiology and behavior. Fetal rodents lie adjacent to one another in the uterine horns much like peas in a pod (**FIGURE 3.35**). Because the sexes are arranged randomly, a female fetus may be located between two sisters (a position designated 0-M, for no males), between a sister and a brother (1-M, for 1 male), or between two brothers (2-M) (Clemens et al. 1978; vom Saal, 1979). This is an excellent natural preparation for investigating whether there are postnatal effects on physiology and behavior of rodents due to varying intrauterine differences. In these studies, rat pups are delivered by cesarean

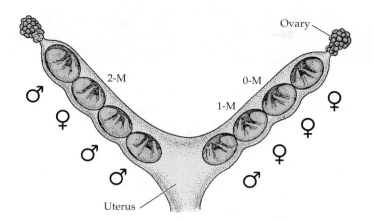

FIGURE 3.35 **Rat pups gestating in utero** are packed into the two uterine horns like peas in a pod. The sex of any given pup's neighbors in utero is entirely random. Thus, a female may gestate between two brothers (a position signified as 2-M), between a brother and a sister (1-M), or between two sisters (0-M). A female's uterine position in relation to male siblings can exert subtle influences on several behaviors later in life because it determines the degree of her exposure to androgens in utero.

section and their intrauterine positions noted. Because behavior reflects the interaction between genes and environment, these studies emphasize that the environmental influences begin before birth or hatching.

Only a summary comparing female mice from two positions, 0-M and 2-M, will be presented here. Ultimately, there is no difference in reproductive capacity between 0-M and 2-M female mice in the laboratory; 0-M and 2-M females both become pregnant and produce equivalent numbers of offspring. However, interfemale aggression is higher in 2-M females than in 0-M females. Males spend more time with 0-M females than with 2-M females; that is, 0-M females are more attractive to males than 2-M females. The reproductive cycles of 0-M females are more easily inhibited by exposure to other adult females than those of 2-M females. The 2-M females have longer ovarian cycles than 0-M females. The 2-M females have male-like anogenital distances, indicating more exposure to androgens compared with 0-M females (Hurd et al., 2008). Thus, intrauterine position can affect several physiological and behavioral characteristics of adult female rodents. Interestingly, uterine blood flow proceeds from the direction of the cervix to the ovary, and females downstream of male siblings in the uterine horn are more vulnerable to the masculinizing effects in utero (Meisel and Ward, 1981). In nature, enhanced aggressiveness, lengthened reproductive cycles, and reduced attractivity could significantly affect fitness (Ryan and Vandenberg, 2002).

Maternal stress can also affect subsequent adult reproductive behavior of offspring. When pregnant rats are stressed by restraint under bright lights several times per day, their male fetuses produce less androgen than control males (Ward and Weisz, 1980). In adulthood, the mating behavior of these male rats is adversely affected (Grisham et al., 1991; Ward and Reed, 1985), and certain parts of the nervous system are more female- than male-typical (see Box 4.2 and Chapter 11). In addition to these changes in copulatory behaviors, male rats that are prenatally stressed show reduced infanticidal behaviors, increased parental behaviors, and reduced aggressiveness (Ward, 1992). The duration of rough-and-tumble play in prenatally stressed males is comparable to that in females (Ward and Stehm, 1991) (**FIGURE 3.36**).

EFFECTS OF MATERNAL CARE   Sex steroid hormones can affect the way in which maternal care is delivered, which in turn can further affect sexual differentiation of behavior. Mother rats routinely lick the anogenital regions of their newborn pups. The primary function of licking the pups is to stimulate the elimination of wastes, but newborn males require maternal licking if they are to develop normal adult mating behavior. Mother rats spend more time licking male pups than female pups (C. L. Moore, 1984, 1986; Moore and Morelli, 1979), apparently

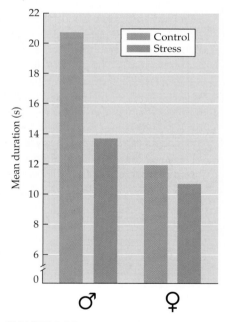

FIGURE 3.36 **Rough-and-tumble play** is demasculinized in males by stress in utero. When pregnant rats were stressed by exposure to bright lights during the last trimester of gestation, the average duration of rough-and-tumble play (at 31 days of age) in their male offspring was similar to that in females. After Ward and Stehm, 1991.

BOX 3.3 Epigenetic Effects on Sexual Dimorphism: Direct Maternal Provisioning of Steroids to Offspring

Maternal hormones can be transferred directly to the offspring via the egg yolk (Adkins-Regan, 1981; Schwabl, 1996). The extent to which provisioning eggs with steroids influences sexually dimorphic behaviors (or even causes sex reversals in the developing young) remains controversial (Pike and Petrie, 2003). However, it is now well established that the amounts of steroids deposited into eggs vary, and this variation reflects factors ranging from environmental to social to maternal conditions.

Testosterone concentrations in canary (*Serinus canaria*) eggs were found to increase as a function of the laying order; regardless of chromosomal sex, eggs that were laid last in a clutch were provisioned with more testosterone than eggs laid first (Schwabl, 1993). This variation in testosterone had functional effects on the offspring. The social rank of hatchlings was positively correlated with the testosterone concentrations in the eggs, suggesting that differential androgen levels in the eggs affected subsequent behaviors. These results were the first to demonstrate that mother birds could provision their offspring with hormones to alter subsequent behavior. This epigenetic mechanism was hypothesized to account for some of the variation in offspring behavior (Schwabl, 1993).

Why would females sequester varying amounts of hormones into their eggs? Androgens speed growth and development of the offspring, and they increase food-begging behaviors (Schwabl, 1996). One adaptive functional reason that mothers would differentially supply eggs with sex steroid hormones would be to allow the mothers to gain the upper hand in parent-offspring conflicts (Trivers, 1974). There is an inherent conflict of interest between parents and offspring. Because parents share about 50% of their genes with each offspring, each has equal value and parents attempt to equalize resources that they provide to the offspring. However, each offspring values

itself twice as much as it values its siblings. (It "shares" 100% of its genes with itself but shares only 50% of its genes with its siblings, and only about 25% of its genes with half siblings.) Thus, it is in the interest of each offspring to compete with its siblings for parental resources and to get as large a share of those resources for itself as it can. As a result, offspring will always demand more resources than their parents are willing to provide (Trivers, 1974).

Provisioning the eggs with anabolic androgens can reduce the conflict between the chicks that hatch first and their siblings that hatch later, by enhancing growth and development. Otherwise, in clutches of eggs that hatch asynchronously, later-hatched siblings would be at a disadvantage when begging for food. To test the hypothesis that maternally provisioned androgens hasten growth, first-laid black-headed gull (*Larus ridibundus*) eggs were used to create artificial clutches of three eggs each that varied in androgens (Eising et al., 2001). In some clutches, all the eggs received a control treatment with an oil vehicle for the androgen, whereas other clutches were experimentally manipulated so that clutches had eggs with different concentrations of testosterone—constant low, low supplement, or high supplement. Testosterone-treated eggs hatched an average of 0.5 days earlier than oil-treated eggs (Eising et al., 2001). Androgen treatment did not affect survival but did enhance growth (Eising et al., 2001). Androgen-treated, last-hatched gull chicks with experimental high androgen supplementation had higher body mass and longer legs than last-hatched gulls treated with oil only. Moreover, having two younger androgen-treated siblings retarded the growth and development of the first-hatched (nonsupplemented) gulls. Thus, it appears that differential transfer of steroid hormones by the mother can "level" the competition among siblings in the nest.

because mothers prefer the chemosensory cues associated with male pup urine. Testosterone contributes to this preference (female rat pups injected with testosterone are licked as often as males). Mother rats that are made anosmic (unable to smell) do not lick their male offspring more than daughters, and these males display altered patterns of copulation in adulthood (see Box 4.2). Differential parental treatment of male and female infants has been reported for several primate species as well, including humans (Stewart, 1988). These differential behavioral interactions, as well as maternal stress, can have significant modifying effects on the neural tissues that may underlie sexually dimorphic behaviors (see Chapter 4).

ENVIRONMENTAL ENDOCRINE DISRUPTORS Combustion products from plastics and a number of commercial chemical agents, including the many pesticides that contain some types of polychlorinated biphenyls (PCBs), can have pronounced estrogenic effects on animals (Anway and Skinner, 2006; Ottinger and vom Saal, 2002;

The advanced time of hatching may reflect, in part, accelerated development of the hatching muscle (musculus complexus) (Lipar and Ketterson, 2000). This muscle is important for breaking open the shell during hatching and for dorsal flexion of the neck during begging. In red-winged blackbirds (*Agelaius phoeniceus*), yolk androgen concentrations were found to increase with laying order regardless of sex, and the size of the hatching muscle increased as a function of the order of laying, which is positively correlated with testosterone concentrations in the egg. Direct injections of testosterone into eggs increased the size of the hatching muscle, whereas treatment with the testosterone antagonist, flutamide, decreased the relative mass of this muscle (Lipar and Ketterson, 2000).

In addition to the order of egg laying, social factors can influence maternal contribution of steroids to the eggs. Attractiveness of male zebra finches (*Taeniopygia guttata*) can easily be manipulated by providing leg bands of different colors. Females preferentially mate with red-banded males and avoid green-banded ones (Gil et al., 1999). Manipulation of color bands has a greater effect on male attractiveness than any other measured male characteristic thus far discovered (Cuthill et al., 1997). In one study, male zebra finches were randomly fitted with either red or green leg bands (Gil et al., 1999). Females were randomly assigned to the "attractive" red-banded males or the "undesirable" green-banded males. Their eggs were removed immediately after laying for hormone analyses and replaced with dummy eggs. At the end of laying, the fake eggs were removed and the females were provided with new males with different-colored leg bands. At the end of the study, it was discovered that, in general, when a female mated with a red-banded male, she placed more testosterone and DHT in the eggs than she did when paired with a green-banded male (Gil et al., 1999).

Social rank of leghorn hens affected the amount of testosterone in their eggs. The eggs of low-ranked hens had about equal concentrations of androgens, whether carrying male or female embryos (Muller et al., 2002). However, dominant hens allocated significantly more androgens to male than female eggs. In contrast, subordinate females transferred more androgens to female than male eggs. The investigators attribute this pattern to the benefits of high reproductive fitness of high-status roosters and low reproductive fitness of low-status roosters. Low-status males achieve virtually no reproductive success, but females, regardless of their social status, attain nearly identical reproductive success. Thus, dominant females would benefit by producing sons that would become high-status roosters, whereas subordinate females would benefit by producing daughters.

It remains controversial whether maternal allocations of steroid hormones can reverse the sex of offspring after fertilization and sex determination have occurred (e.g., Pike and Petrie, 2003). Although it is theoretically possible, no compelling evidence currently exists to suggest that maternal postfertilization manipulations can alter offspring sex ratio factors by hormonally reversing sex determination to alter sexual differentiation in birds. However, in reptiles it appears that maternal allocation of steroid hormones can influence sex. In eggs from painted turtles (*Chrysemys picta*), seasonal changes in yolk steroid concentrations appear to influence the sex of the offspring. The hatchling sex ratio at 28°C was found to shift from 72% male to 76% female seasonally, which corresponded to a seasonal change in the estradiol-to-testosterone concentration ratio in the eggs (Bowden et al., 2000). The ability of females to control the sex of their offspring may be an important adaptive function to maintain environmental sex determination in some species. Importantly, these yolk steroids can have long-lasting (organizational) effects on behavior (e.g., Groothuis et al., 2005). Obviously, these maternal steroids can program adult behavior without interfering with the endogenous sexual differentiation process, likely by acting on different targets during different developmental epochs. Thus, understanding how these prehatching hormones are regulated is important in understanding avian behavior.

Raloff, 1994a,b). Although these substances are not steroids, they mimic estrogens and bind to estrogen receptors (Crews and McLachlan, 2006). Other **endocrine-disrupting chemicals** (**EDCs**) mimic the effects of androgens or thyroid hormones. One of the first demonstrations that these chemical agents could affect reproduction was the link made in the 1950s between the now-banned pesticide DDT and the thinning of eggshells in many avian species. As you probably know, animals at the tops of food chains ingest all of the toxic chemicals that have accumulated in the bodies of the animals they consume. Birds that consume fish, reptiles, and insects are particularly at risk for contamination. Many bird species, including bald eagles, were put at risk of extinction by DDT, which caused abnormally thin-shelled eggs that parents inadvertently crushed during incubation.

DDT had other dramatic effects on reproduction in birds. One California gull population (*Larus californicus*) on Santa Barbara Island, off the coast of California, was heavily contaminated with DDT. When eggs did manage to hatch, the morphol-

endocrine-disrupting chemicals (EDCs)   Chemicals that mimic the effects of hormones or disrupt hormonal systems.

ogy of the offspring was markedly atypical. As you will recall, female birds normally develop only the left ovary and oviduct, but young females on Santa Barbara Island displayed some development of the right reproductive tract as well. Young males also developed oviducts, and the right gonad often developed as an ovotestis (Fry and Toone, 1981). The behavior of adults was also atypical. Two parent gulls are required to obtain sufficient food to rear offspring successfully, but on Santa Barbara Island, most males were not engaging in reproductive behavior. Breeding males had become scarce in the population, which led to females predominating on the island; apparently many females mated with the scarce reproductively competent males, then shared nests in female-female pairs. This rise in so-called lesbian gulls was thought to reflect the estrogenic effects of DDT on male mating behavior, because when eggs were experimentally treated with estradiol or DDT, males hatching from those eggs demonstrated the same feminized structures and reduced sex drive as the males on Santa Barbara Island (Fry and Toone, 1981). After the banning of DDT in 1972, the gull sex ratio on Santa Barbara Island began slowly returning to normal levels, and the incidence of morphological and behavioral abnormalities began waning. However, given the massive reduction in the gull and other bird populations in Southern California resulting from DDT exposure, along with new challenges faced through the introduction of PCBs and other endocrine-disrupting chemicals, monitoring and restoration programs are required to ensure continued success of bird populations in these and other affected regions.

On the other side of the continent, biologists have been concerned with the dwindling numbers of the Florida panther (*Felis concolor coryi*). One reason for the decline in the number of panthers is human encroachment into their habitats, but these panthers also seem to exhibit increasingly high rates of cryptorchidism, a condition in which the testes remain in the abdominal cavity after birth (Raloff, 1994a). Normally, the testes develop near the kidneys and descend into the scrotum through the inguinal canals (small openings in the pelvis) around the time of birth. The mammalian scrotal sac has evolved a number of adaptations in mammals to maintain the testes at temperatures less than the core body temperature. Mammalian sperm are very sensitive to high temperatures and may be damaged by temperatures above 37°C. Failure of the testes to descend into the scrotum is associated with infertility because a high proportion of the sperm are damaged.

In 2008, only about 80–100 Florida panthers were estimated to remain in the wild, and the incidence of cryptorchidism was thought to be due to a genetic bottleneck, or reduction in genetic variation, in the dwindling population. Recent data do not rule out that possibility, but they also suggest that environmental estrogenic pesticides may be responsible for the increase in the incidence of cryptorchidism. When blood samples from Florida panthers were analyzed for steroid hormone levels, investigators discovered that several cryptorchid males had unusual hormone profiles showing higher circulating concentrations of estrogens than androgens, and that at least one female had higher circulating concentrations of androgens than estrogens. Investigators suspected that steroidogenic agents in the environment were responsible for the unusual steroid levels, and consequently, approximately 100 wildlife preserves in the southeastern United States that are managed by the U.S. Fish and Wildlife Service are now forbidden from using any known estrogenic chemicals, including pesticides and herbicides.

More recently, a study led by the U.S. Geological Survey and U.S. Fish and Wildlife Service reported that an alarmingly high percentage of largemouth (27%) and smallmouth (85%) bass examined from 19 National Wildlife Refuges in the Northeast were intersex, possessing testicular oocytes and abnormal hormone concentrations (Iwanowicz et al., 2016). The prevalence of intersex populations of bass was associated with high concentrations of estradiol in the water samples obtained, suggesting that estrogenic contamination contributed to the incidence of intersex individuals in the populations sampled. This is one of the first, large-scale studies of

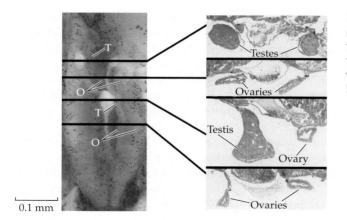

FIGURE 3.37 Atrazine exposure causes testicular malformations in frogs. The most severely malformed testes failed to produce any sperm but appeared to function as ovaries and displayed ova after tadpoles were treated with various concentrations of atrazine. From Hayes et al., 2002b.

its type and indicates a need for intervention, restoration and monitoring programs not only to prevent the decimation of a variety of species, but to promote a future where environmental contamination is not further exacerbated.

One of the most common herbicides in use in the world is atrazine (2-chloro-4-ethylamino-6-isopropylamine-1,3,5-triazine). Atrazine is a widely used herbicide in the United States, and though it is generally considered to be safe because of its relatively short half-life and lack of bioaccumulation, it can affect reproductive development across species, including fish, amphibians, reptiles, and mammals (Hayes et al., 2011). Importantly, atrazine has been detected in virtually every U.S. waterway examined, as well as in groundwater. Early laboratory studies indicated that sexual development in frogs (*Xenopus laevis, Rana pipiens,* and *Hyla regilla*) is significantly impaired by modest, ecologically relevant levels of atrazine (Hayes et al., 2002a) (**FIGURE 3.37**). At study sites in the western and midwestern sections of the United States, 10%–92% of male frogs were observed to have testicular abnormalities. The most severe testicular malformations displayed were ova in the testes rather than sperm (Hayes et al., 2002b). Female malformations were not noted. Some of these testicular malformations could be induced in laboratory studies using various concentrations of atrazine (Hayes et al., 2002b, 2003). More recently, it was shown that atrazine exposure could completely feminize male frogs, resulting in sex-reversed males (ZZ females) that were only capable of producing male offspring (i.e., ZZ females crossed with ZZ males always resulted in ZZ males) (Hayes et al., 2010). It has been suggested that endocrine-disrupting chemicals may contribute to the worldwide reduction in amphibian populations (Hayes et al., 2006, 2010). In response to a series of recent lawsuits by the Center for Biological Diversity, the U.S. Fish and Wildlife Service will begin studying the effects of four commonly used herbicides, including atrazine, on the health of 1500 endangered species in the United States. Given that 80 million pounds of atrazine are used in the United States each year, it is critical to establish the effects of this and other herbicides before the damage is irreparable.

Remarkably, some pollutants in the water are not hormone mimics but hormones (Kolpin et al., 2002)! The estrogen 17α-ethinylestradiol (EE2) is commonly used in birth control drugs and is excreted in the urine, usually as sulfate of glucuronide conjugates. There are now sufficient numbers of women on oral contraceptives that these steroids are entering the waste systems of cities. During sewage treatment these EE2-conjugated molecules are hydrolyzed and re-form the parent EE2 molecules. Because the molecules are too small for the filters used, these steroids remain in the treated water downstream from major cities and have been measured in the range of 1–9 nanograms per liter (ng/L) (Flores and Hill, 2008). A more recent study in Argentina revealed concentrations as high as 43 ng/L in the "Girado" stream (Valdés et al., 2015). If this treated water is used for drinking by people downstream, then unsuspecting individuals may be exposing themselves to steroid hormones (Kolpin et al., 2002). Unfortunately, the solution is not to avoid tap water and drink more bottled water. As described below, some plastic bottles also leach estrogenic chemicals into their contents.

Are steroidogenic agents affecting human reproduction? Probably. Thus far, disruptions in breeding attributed to environmental hormones have been reported for severely contaminated populations of amphibians, reptiles, birds, and mammals throughout the world. Humans, residing atop our food chain, may be ingesting far more of these steroidogenic agents than we suspect. For instance, bisphenol A (BPA) is used in the synthesis of polycarbonate (PC), a type of polymer used in producing plastic food containers, including baby bottles, the linings of food and beverage cans, and bottles for water and virtually anything that was previously sold in glass bottles (vom Saal and Hughes, 2005). This substance has several estrogenic effects in animals. A number of tests demonstrated that BPA was released from 1990s PC flasks at concentrations of 10–25 millimolar (i.e., 2–5 ng/ml) (Krishnan et al., 1993) and that such doses evoked toxic reproductive responses in mice, including accelerated puberty and reduced fertility (vom Saal et al., 1998). Human exposure to BPA tends to increase with temperature; thus, heating baby bottles to sterilize them has caused much concern. Tests of PC bottles revealed that addition of boiling water released doses of BPA resulting in concentrations between 0.0002 and 0.0022 mg/kg body mass/day, which is below the established "tolerable daily intake" of 0.05 mg/kg body mass/day established by the European Food Safety Authority (Hengstler et al., 2011; Maragou et al., 2008). However, the migration of BPA from PC containers into their contents after microwave exposure appears facilitated. Infants appear more at risk than human adults. Because the majority of BPA exposure occurs through ingestion, laboratory animal studies that use the oral route of administration are considered the most useful in assessing potential effects in humans. Most early laboratory animal studies of BPA, however, used subcutaneous routes of administration to deliver the chemical, making direct links to the human condition difficult. More recent work using low-dose oral BPA administration has demonstrated that perinatal exposure to BPA can masculinize the brains of female rats and demasculinize the brains of male rats (McCaffrey et al., 2013). Importantly, BPA exposure in this study was well below the current no observed adverse effect level (NOAEL) of 0.05 mg/kg/day. Although the U.S. Food and Drug Administration has reported that BPA levels found in U.S. products appear to be safe, this conclusion has been questioned by its own panel of experts. Canada banned the use of BPA in baby bottles in 2008. In May 2009, Chicago's city council became the first in the United States to ban the sale of baby bottles and "sipper cups" containing BPA, with 13 other states following with similar legislature. In July, 2012, the U.S. Food and Drug Administration announced that it would no longer allow BPA in baby bottles and children's drinking cups, although no restrictions have been placed on other consumer products.

As in the Florida panthers, the rate of cryptorchidism showed a marked increase during the last century (Carlsen et al., 1992); the incidence in the 1950s of about 1.6% of live births had nearly doubled by the 1970s to 2.9% in Western Europe. The incidence of hypospadias, an abnormality in which the urethra opens on the underside of the penis, which can be considered the result of an incomplete masculinization of the external genitalia (see Figure 3.20), more than doubled in Great Britain between 1964 and 1983. Even more disturbing, testicular cancer, possibly associated with endocrine factors, has been increasing sharply in several European, North American and Asian countries: the rate of testicular cancer has nearly doubled since the 1960s, and the incidence appears to be increasing in industrialized countries (Giwercman and Skakkebaek, 1992; Shanmugalingam et al., 2013). Plastics and pesticides contain endocrine-disrupting chemicals that can interfere with mammalian development (Gray et al., 2000). For example, exposure of developing rodents to EDCs at doses

(A)

(B)

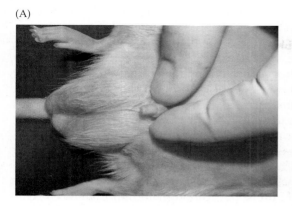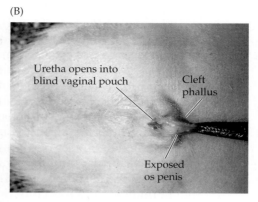

Uretha opens into blind vaginal pouch

Cleft phallus

Exposed os penis

FIGURE 3.38 **External genitalia of adult male rats** that were prenatally exposed to (A) corn oil (control procedure) or (B) vinclozolin, a commonly used fungicide and antiandrogen. Exposure to vinclozolin early in development results in abnormal sexual phenotype and multiple reproductive malformations, including hypospadias, cleft phallus, female-like anogenital distance, ectopic (undescended) testes, vaginal pouches, and small or absent sex glands. Not surprisingly, a number of behavioral impairments are observed in such rats. Courtesy of L. E. Gray, U.S. Environmental Protection Agency.

likely experienced by humans has been seen to advance puberty and alter reproductive function (Howdeshell et al., 1999) (**FIGURE 3.38**). The reproductive effects that have become apparent in humans over the last century are consistent with those seen in animals after exposure to high doses of EDCs, such as increased incidence of genital abnormalities in boys and earlier puberty in girls.

Human fertility also seems to have waned in recent years. Although undescended testes can be moved to their correct location in the scrotum by surgical means, boys with this condition at birth often suffer fertility difficulties later in life. Across human populations, sperm counts appear to be declining. In 1940 the average density of human sperm was 113 million per milliliter of semen; in 1990 this figure had dropped to 66 million per milliliter in the United States and Western Europe. Researchers also estimated that the volume of semen produced by men dropped about 20% during that time, reducing sperm count per ejaculation even further (Carlsen et al., 1992). Between 1981 and 1991, the ratio of normal spermatogenesis decreased significantly from 56.4% to 26.9%, with a parallel increase in the incidence of partial and complete spermatogenic arrest (Pajarinen et al., 1997). During this period, the size of seminiferous tubules decreased, the amount of fibrotic tissue in the testes increased, and testicular mass decreased significantly. These alterations in testicular characteristics over time could not be explained by changes in body mass index or in tobacco, alcohol, or other drug use. The authors of this study suggested that deteriorating spermatogenesis might be one important factor in the explanation of the declining sperm counts observed worldwide. Sperm count and fertility are affected by estrogens.

Other endocrine disruptors may cause sex reversal of male Chinook salmon (*Oncorhynchus tshawytscha*) as they develop, contributing to the rapid and extraordinary population decline of this species (Nagler et al., 2001). In addition to conjugated hormones re-forming as parent steroids, some pollutants are known to biotransform to potent hormones. For instance, it was discovered that female eastern mosquitofish (*Gambusia holbrooki*) were masculinized in a polluted river in Florida. To determine the source of the masculinizing chemical, water was collected from this river and analyzed with sophisticated chemical tools. It was determined that the mixture of pollutants in the Fenholloway River was producing trace amounts of an environmental androgen (Jenkins et al., 2001). What was surprising was that this androgen was identified as androstenedione, a relatively mild anabolic androgenic steroid that has been linked to performance enhancement among U.S. major league baseball players. In the sediment of the river, even higher concentrations of androstenedione, as well as progesterone, were detected (Jenkins et al., 2003). These two hormones have relatively low androgenic activities and were unlikely to account for the masculinization of the female mosquitofish. Additional analyses of the water revealed additional androgenic substances. These studies hinted at an additional environmental risk from hormones that can be synthesized de novo from the toxic brew of chemicals that many of our rivers and creeks have become.

In addition to mimics of estrogenic and androgenic steroid hormones, several other endocrine-disrupting chemicals have been discovered in a wide variety of common chemical compounds. These include substances that interfere with thyroid hormones, growth factors, and prolactin. Although an important book, *Our Stolen Future* (Colborn et al., 1997), motivated the U.S. federal granting agencies to begin funding systematic studies on the toxicology and developmental effects of endocrine disruptors, the effects of these chemicals on behavior remain, for the most part, unknown. Certainly, the extent to which human behavior has been affected by environmental steroidogenic agents remains unknown. BPA has been linked to obesity in some studies (Newbold et al., 2006). Are aggressive, parental, or sexual behaviors in humans altered by the more than 500 measurable chemicals in our bodies that were not present prior to the twentieth century? No one knows for sure. It seems prudent to curtail the use of these substances until their effects on the reproduction and health of humans and nonhuman animals are understood.

Conclusions

Three main principles of the sexual differentiation of behavior can be distilled: (1) gonadal steroid hormones have organizing effects upon behavior, (2) the organizing effects of steroid hormones are relatively constrained to a particular time during development, and (3) an asymmetry exists in the effects of testes and of ovaries on the organization of behavior (but see Bakker et al., 2002). The early effects of hormones are considered to cause permanent, irreversible behavioral characteristics (Phoenix et al., 1959; Wallen, 2009); for example, early androgen treatment causes irreversible and permanent masculinization of rodent copulatory behavior.

These early hormonal effects can be contrasted with other, reversible behavioral influences called activational effects (Phoenix et al., 1959). For example, androgens provided in adulthood activate male copulatory behavior by acting upon the structures organized earlier by these same hormones. The activational effects of hormones on adult behavior are temporary and usually wane soon after the hormone is metabolized. The organizational and activational effects of hormones may actually be quite similar when considered at the molecular level. The permanency of the effects of early exposure to androgens may reflect events unique to a limited period of development. For example, in rats less than 10 days of age, gonadal steroid hormones may prevent neuronal death or promote neuronal survival during a period of cell death (**apoptosis**) that is limited either temporally or developmentally (Gorski, 1993).

The notion of a critical period for organizational effects arises from the observation that these effects occur only during a specific temporal window of development. The mating behavior of rats, for example, can be masculinized by physiological concentrations of androgens only prior to about day 10. Masculinization can be induced between days 10 and 20 with pharmacological doses of androgen, but at some point (about day 25) no amount of androgen treatment can cause masculinization. This critical period reflects developmental processes that can be altered by steroid hormones only during particular stages of ontogeny; some of these developmental processes will be described in Chapter 4. The number of reported examples

apoptosis Programmed, orderly cell death that avoids immune system activation.

of organizational effects on postpuberty behavior has increased in recent years (Adkins-Regan et al., 1989; Bloch and Gorski, 1988; Cherry et al., 1990; Commins and Yahr, 1984; DeVries et al., 1985), suggesting again that the organizational and activational effects of hormones may be similar at the level of genetic mechanisms.

Finally, the asymmetry of gonadal effects on behavioral organization is striking. In the absence of gonads or steroid hormones, female-typical behavior patterns emerge in mammals; that is, behavior is feminized and demasculinized. Exposure to androgens causes the organization of male-typical behaviors; that is, behavior is masculinized and defeminized. This observation has led to the idea that females are the neutral or default sex in mammals, but recent studies indicate that hormones and gene expression may be necessary for normal development of feminine behavior. Studies of avian sexual behavioral differentiation suggest that male birds are the default or neutral sex (see Box 4.3). To some extent, the asymmetry of testicular and ovarian effects on behavioral sexual differentiation in birds and mammals reflects the differential sensitivities (i.e., receptors) of the underlying neural tissue to estrogens and androgens. However, in both cases, estrogens ultimately act at the cellular level to masculinize and defeminize sexual behaviors.

More recently, adjustments to the organizational/activational hypothesis have been suggested (Arnold, 2009; Schulz et al., 2009; Wallen and Baum, 2002). For example, altricial species appear to rely more on aromatization for masculinization than do precocial mammalian species. Another issue is the importance of hormones in demasculinization of female brain and behavior in the process of becoming a female, and in defeminization of male brain and behavior in the process of becoming a male (Wallen and Baum, 2002). Also, because of the substantial programming of adult behavior during puberty (Sowell et al., 2003), it has been suggested that the organizational temporal window should be extended to the peripubertal period (Schulz et al., 2009; Sisk and Foster, 2004). These ideas will be explored in more depth in Chapter 4.

Summary

1. Behavioral sex differences are common in humans and in nonhuman animals. Because males and females differ in the ratio of androgen to estrogen concentrations in their blood plasma, behavioral endocrinologists have been particularly interested in the extent to which behavioral sex differences are mediated by sex steroid hormones.

2. Individuals of asexual vertebrate species produce only one sex: females. Production of offspring by asexual reproduction is very efficient, but such species risk extinction if environmental conditions change drastically, because there is no genetic variation among the offspring. The recombination of genetic material during sexual reproduction produces genetic variation. Sexual species produce two sexes: females and males.

3. The ultimate cause of sex differences appears to reflect sexual selection, a subcategory of natural selection. Animals with polygynous mating systems display more sexual dimorphism than monogamous animals. Humans, who are mildly to moderately polygynous, display several sexual dimorphisms, including larger body size, delayed puberty, increased courtship activity, elevated aggression, and reduced parental care in men as compared with women.

4. The process of becoming female or male is called sexual differentiation. The primary step in sexual differentiation occurs at fertilization. In mammals, the ovum (which usually contains an X chromosome) can be fertilized by a sperm bearing either a Y or an X chromosome; this process is called sex determination. The

chromosomal sex of homogametic mammals (XX) is female; the chromosomal sex of heterogametic mammals (XY) is male. Chromosomal sex determines gonadal sex. Most subsequent sexual differentiation is normally the result of differential exposure to gonadal steroid hormones, although some genetic influences are apparent. Thus, gonadal sex determines hormonal sex, which regulates morphological sex. Morphological differences in the central nervous system, as well as in some effector organs, lead to behavioral sex differences. Some processes of behavioral sexual differentiation appear to be directly mediated by sex chromosomes in the absence of hormones.

5. The gonads of both sexes develop from the same primordial anlage; once they develop, these organs differ between males and females along a continuum of masculinity and femininity. The same is true of the external genitalia. In contrast, there are dual anlagen for the accessory sex organs. Normal female development of these organs requires feminization (Müllerian duct development) as well as demasculinization (Wolffian duct regression). Normal male development requires masculinization (Wolffian duct development) as well as defeminization (Müllerian duct regression). Thus, sexual differentiation of the accessory sex organs proceeds along two continua: a masculinization-demasculinization scale and a feminization-defeminization scale. Masculinization is the induction of male traits. Feminization is the induction of female traits. Demasculinization is the removal of the potential for male traits, whereas defeminization is the removal of the potential for female traits. This nomenclature is also appropriate for describing behavioral sexual differentiation.

6. The process of sexual differentiation is complex, and the potential for errors is present. Perinatal exposure to androgens is the most common cause of anomalous sexual differentiation among females. The source of androgen may be endogenous (as in congenital adrenal hyperplasia) or exogenous (exposure to DES or MPA). Turner syndrome results when the second X chromosome is missing or damaged; these individuals possess dysgenic ovaries and are not exposed to steroid hormones until puberty. Female mammals are the "neutral" sex; additional steps are required for male differentiation, and more steps bring more possibilities for errors in differentiation. Some examples of male anomalous sexual differentiation include 5α-reductase deficiency (XY individuals are born with ambiguous genitalia because of a lack of dihydrotestosterone and are reared as females, but masculinization occurs during puberty) and androgen insensitivity syndrome, called TFM in rodents (XY individuals lack functional receptors for androgens and develop as females). By studying these individual "experiments of nature" in which the process of sexual differentiation is atypical, behavioral endocrinologists glean hints about the process of typical sexual differentiation.

7. The process of sexual differentiation in birds is different from that in mammals; the homogametic sex is male (ZZ), whereas the heterogametic sex is female (ZW). Males appear to be the "neutral" sex among birds in most aspects of sexual differentiation. Estrogens have the ability to feminize the embryonic testis.

8. Some reptilian species are like birds in that the male is homogametic; other species resemble mammals in that the female is homogametic. In yet other reptilian species, sex chromosomes are absent and sex determination occurs in response to incubation temperature. Substantial variation in this process exists; high ambient temperatures evoke male development in some species but female development in others. Some fish species possess the ability to undergo sex changes in adulthood in response to social or physiological cues.

9. In some species, alternative mating strategies among males are associated with differences in body type and behavior, which are often regulated by changes in hormone secretion.

10. Gonadal steroid hormones have organizing effects upon behavior. The organizing effects of steroid hormones are relatively constrained to the early stages of development. An asymmetry exists in the effects of testes and ovaries on the organization of behavior in mammals. Hormone exposure early in life has organizational effects on subsequent rodent mating behavior; early steroid hormone treatment causes relatively irreversible and permanent masculinization of rodent copulatory behavior. These early hormone effects can be contrasted with the reversible behavioral influences of steroid hormones provided in adulthood, which are called activational effects. The activational effects of hormones on adult behavior are temporary and may wane soon after the hormone is metabolized.

11. Females undergo cycles of reproductive physiology and behavior that correspond to the cyclic release of eggs during the breeding season; males produce sperm at relatively constant rates throughout the breeding season and exhibit relatively constant reproductive behavior. The cyclic nature of female reproductive function is driven by the cyclic release of GnRH from surge generators located in the anterior hypothalamus. Both males and females display pulsatile release of GnRH from the medial basal hypothalamus. Exposure to androgens early in development abolishes forever the potential to generate GnRH surges, either by destroying the neural connections between the pulse and surge generators or by reducing estrogen receptor availability in the surge generator tissues.

12. Environmental factors can influence sexual dimorphism. These environmental factors include temperature, intrauterine position and conditions, and chemicals that mimic hormones. Because the combination of these factors is usually complex, determining the individual contribution to atypical sexual characteristics is complicated. Another potential complication contributing to sexually dimorphic characteristics in birds and some reptiles is variable maternal contribution of hormones to the egg yolks. This variation may reflect diverse maternal conditions, including social rank, food availability, and season of the year. The extent to which these maternal hormones affect the brain and behavior of the offspring remains unknown.

Questions for Discussion

1. List and describe some behavioral differences that you have noticed between boys and girls. What causes girls and boys to choose different toys? Do you think that the sex differences you have noted arise from biological causes or are learned? How would you go about establishing your opinions as fact?

2. Why might disorders of sexual development be more common in males than females?

3. How might we study the roles of hormones in the sexual differentiation of human behavior without performing experiments where hormones or other physiological parameters are manipulated?

4. What can we learn about the process of human brain/behavioral sexual differentiation from studying rodents? What are some concepts that were learned from studying rodents that are likely applicable to humans? Are there any examples where findings from rodents are not applicable to human brain/behavioral sexual differentiation?

5. Discuss the following proposition: the process of developing sexually dimorphic behaviors is conceptually similar to the development of sexually dimorphic accessory reproductive organs, and it is dissimilar from the development of sexually dimorphic external genitalia.

6. Discuss the role of intrauterine environment in sexual differentiation, particularly how steroid hormones from adjacent siblings can alter sexual development in males and females.

Suggested Readings

Arnold, A. P. 2009. The organizational-activational hypothesis as the foundation for a unified theory of sexual differentiation of all mammalian tissues. *Horm. Behav.*, 55:570–578.

Balthazart, J., Arnold, A. P., and Adkins-Regan, E. 2009. Sexual differentiation of brain and behavior in birds. In D. W. Pfaff, et al. (eds.), *Hormones, Brain, and Behavior*, Vol. 2, pp. 1745–1789. Academic Press, New York.

Becker, J. B., et al. (eds.). 2008. *Sex Differences in the Brain: From Genes to Behavior.* Oxford University Press, New York.

Crews, D., and Gore, A. C. 2012. Epigenetic synthesis: A need for a new paradigm for evolution in a contaminated world. *F1000 Biol. Rep.*, 4:18.

Hines, M. 2011. Gender development and the human brain. *Annu. Rev. Neurosci.*, 34:69–88.

Krentzel, A. A. and Remage-Healey, L. 2015. Sex differences and rapid estrogen signaling: A look at songbird audition. *Front. Neuroendocrinol.*, 38: 37–49.

McCarthy, M. M., et al. 2012. Sex differences in the brain: The not so inconvenient truth. *J. Neurosci.*, 32:2241–2247.

McCarthy, M. M. and Arnold, A. P. 2011. Reframing sexual differentiation of the brain. *Nat. Neurosci.*, 14: 677–683.

Phoenix, C. H., et al. 1959. Organizing action of prenatally administered testosterone propionate on the tissues mediating mating behavior in the female guinea pig. *Endocrinology*, 65:369–382.

Schulz, K. M., et al. 2009. Back to the future: The organizational-activational hypothesis adapted to puberty and adolescence. Special issue on the 50th anniversary of the publication of Phoenix, Goy, Gerall, and Young. *Horm. Behav.*, 55:597–604.

Wallen, K. 2009. The organizational hypothesis: Reflections on the 50th anniversary of the publication of Phoenix, Goy, Gerall, and Young (1959). *Horm. Behav.*, 55:561–565.

Sex Differences in Behavior:
Animal Models and Humans

4

Learning Objectives

This chapter discusses neural, molecular, and behavioral sex differences in humans and animals. By the end of this chapter you should be able to:

- describe how sex differences in brain and behavior emerge.
- explain how one designs studies to explore the mechanisms responsible for sex differences.
- understand the significance of these differences from ecological/adaptive and functional perspectives.

Walk through any major toy store and you will see a couple of aisles filled with pink boxes and the complete absence of pink packaging of toys in adjacent aisles. Remarkably, you will also see a strong self-segregation of boys and girls in these aisles. It is rare to see boys in the pink aisles and vice versa. The toy manufacturers are often accused of making toys that are gender biased, but it seems more likely that boys and girls enjoy playing with specific types and colors of toys. Indeed, toy manufacturers would immediately double their sales if they could sell the same toys to both sexes. Boys generally prefer toys such as trucks and balls, and girls generally prefer toys such as dolls. Although it is doubtful that there are genes that encode preferences for toy cars and trucks on the Y chromosome, it is possible that hormones might shape the development of a child's brain to prefer certain types of toys or styles of play behavior. It is commonly believed that children learn which types of toys and which styles of play are appropriate to their gender. How can we understand and separate the contribution of physiological mechanisms from that of learning to understand sex differences in human behaviors? To untangle these issues, behavioral endocrinologists often use animal models. In contrast to humans, in which

(A)   (B)

FIGURE 4.1 Sex differences in monkey play Female (A) and male (B) vervet monkeys prefer dolls and toy cars, respectively, as do their human counterparts. Courtesy of Melissa Hines.

sex differences are usually only a matter of degree (often slight), in some animals, members of only one sex display a particular behavior. For example, often only male songbirds sing, or generally only male dogs lift a back leg while urinating. Studies of such strongly sex-biased behaviors are particularly valuable for understanding the interaction among behavior, hormones, and the nervous system.

For example, a study of vervet monkeys (*Cercopithecus aethiops*) calls into question the primacy of learning in the establishment of toy preferences (Alexander and Hines, 2002). Female vervet monkeys preferred girl-typical toys, such as dolls or cooking pots, whereas male vervet monkeys preferred boy-typical toys, such as cars or balls (**FIGURE 4.1**). There were no sex differences in preference for gender-neutral toys, such as picture books or stuffed animals. Presumably, monkeys have no prior concept of "boy" or "girl" toys. Young rhesus monkeys (*Macaca mulatta*) also showed similar toy preferences (Hassett et al., 2008).

What, then, underlies the sex difference in toy preference? It is possible that certain attributes of toys (or objects) appeal to either males or females (Alexander, 2003). Toys that appeal to boys or male vervet or rhesus monkeys—in this case, balls and toy cars—are objects that can be moved actively through space, toys that can be incorporated into active, rough-and-tumble play (Alexander, 2003). The appeal of toys that girls or female vervet monkeys prefer appears to be based on color. Pink and red (the colors of the doll and pot in the study) may provoke attention to infants (Zemach et al., 2008).

Human society may reinforce such stereotypical responses to gender-typical toys. The sex differences in toy preferences emerge by 12 or 24 months of age and seem fixed by 36 months of age (Alexander et al., 2009; Ruble et al., 2006), but are sex differences in toy preference present during the first year of life? It is difficult to ask preverbal infants what they prefer, but in studies where the investigators examined the amount of time that babies looked at different toys, eye-tracking data indicate that infants as young as 3 months showed sex differences in toy preference (Alexander et al., 2009); girls preferred dolls, whereas boys preferred trucks. Color preference does not appear until 2 years of age in boys and girls, suggesting that, although toy preference may be dependent on early androgen exposure, color preference might emerge from experience with the world, including associations made with sex-typical coloration of children's toys (Jadva et al., 2010; LoBue and DeLoache, 2011; Wong and Hines, 2015). Another result that suggests, but does not prove, that hormones are involved in toy preferences is the observation that girls diagnosed with congenital adrenal hyperplasia (CAH) played with masculine toys more often than girls without CAH. Additionally, there was a dose-response relationship between the extent of the disorder (i.e., degree of fetal androgen exposure) and degree of masculinization of play behavior (van de Beek et al., 2009). Are the sex differences in toy preferences or play activity, for example, the inevitable consequences of the differential endocrine environments of boys and girls, or are these differences imposed by cultural practices and beliefs? Are these differences the result of receiving gender-specific toys from an early age, or are these differences due to some combination of endocrine and cultural factors? Again, these are difficult questions to unravel.

What happens when individuals adopt a preference for atypical gender toys or activities? In the past, there have usually been strong sanctions against children's cross-gender activities from parents, teachers, friends, siblings, and clergy. Little girls have been told to "act like a young lady" if they engaged in rough-and-tumble play, and young boys have been told to "be a man" if they cried or tried to wear their mothers' high heels and skirts. We will explore how sex differences become established and what underlies atypical gender identification or gender role. The goal of this chapter is to examine the complex factors that cause male and female brains to develop along distinct pathways underlying cognitive and behavioral sexual dimorphisms. We will explore these issues in humans but also examine some important animal models in which behavioral sex differences are studied to understand the underlying mechanisms. Finally, we will examine some of the cognitive and perceptual sex differences commonly observed between men and women.

Recall that Phoenix, Young, and their colleagues proposed the organizational/activational hypothesis of hormonal sexual differentiation (see Chapter 3), based on their discovery in guinea pigs that neonatal castration of males reduced the incidence of adult male-like behaviors and increased the incidence of adult female-like behaviors. Additionally, they reported that treating neonatally castrated males and females with testosterone maintained male-like adult behaviors and eliminated female-like adult behaviors. Thus, the organizational effects of hormones were considered relatively permanent changes evoked in response to exposure to hormones early in life, whereas activational effects of hormones were considered reversible and occurred during adulthood when hormones activated neural circuits that were previously developed. After five decades of research, the organizational/activational hypothesis remains remarkably viable in explaining sex differences, with a few minor adjustments. For example, as mentioned in Chapter 3, it is now clear that gene products encoded by the sex chromosomes participate in sexual differentiation of brain and behavior (Arnold, 2012; McCarthy and Arnold, 2011) (**FIGURE 4.2**). Likewise, because of substantial programming of adult behavior during puberty, it has been suggested that the organizational temporal window should be extended to the peripubertal period (Schulz et al., 2009; Sisk and Foster, 2004) (**FIGURE 4.3**).

FIGURE 4.2 Twenty-first-century model of sex differentiation In this view of sexual differentiation of the brain, the importance of genetics and environment are incorporated along with the effects of hormones to provide a more nuanced portrayal of the types of variables that cause sex differences. Included in this view are the principles that hormones, sex chromosome genes, and sex-specific environments have independent parallel differentiating effects that can interact with each other, often synergistically, to cause sex differences in the brain. However, there are also compensatory sex-specific variables that act to reduce sex differences rather than induce them. The result is that some aspects of male and female brain, behavior, and physiology differ from each other, whereas others are highly similar. From McCarthy and Arnold, 2011.

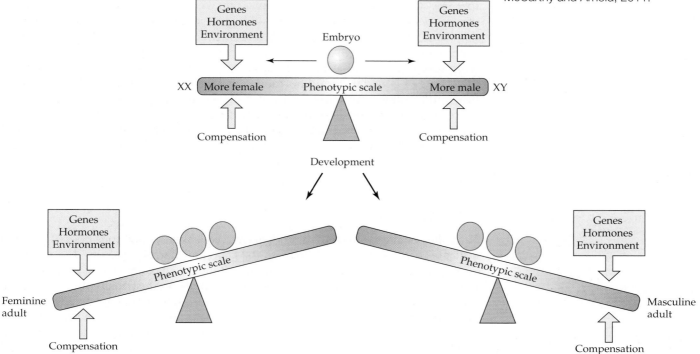

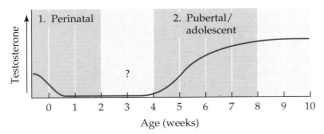

FIGURE 4.3 Two-stage model for organizational effects of steroids on behavior Exposure to androgens during the perinatal (1) and peripubertal (2) periods act in concert to affect mating behavior in adult hamsters. The green line reflects relative testosterone production during development. The question mark emphasizes the lack of knowledge about processes during the period between the perinatal and peripubertal periods that affect adult brain and behavior. From Schultz et al., 2009.

In their classic 1959 paper, Phoenix and colleagues drew an analogy between the effects of early testosterone exposure on the development of the accessory sex organs and its effects on the neural tissues underlying mating behavior. Because exposure to hormones early in life was discovered to change the probability of specific behaviors, and because all behavior is mediated by the nervous system, it was reasonable to suggest that hormones caused changes in the nervous system. The authors warned, however, that, unlike the developmental biologists who had reported pronounced structural changes in the reproductive organs in response to perinatal androgen exposure, behavioral biologists interested in the effects of androgens on neural tissues were unlikely to find alterations so drastic. Instead, it was expected that more subtle changes, in function rather than structure, would be eventually described (Phoenix et al., 1959). Therefore, most behavioral endocrinologists in the 1950s and 1960s believed that structural changes in the central nervous system mediated behavioral differences between the two sexes but assumed that any underlying changes in brain tissue would be beyond the technical abilities of the day to observe. Despite the lack of any empirical data showing direct evidence of changes in neural tissue that mediated sexually dimorphic behaviors, hypothetical models of neural modulation of behavior in response to early hormone exposure flourished. Because the evidence of hormonally induced neural changes was indirect, other researchers resisted the temptation to speculate on mechanisms beyond their data. They explained changes in the adult copulatory ability of neonatally castrated rats, for example, as effects of sensory deficiencies that resulted from inadequate penile development due to androgen deprivation (Beach, 1971). Thus, the results of perinatal steroid hormone manipulations on subsequent adult behavior were initially explained as indirect effects on genital (nonneural) morphology.

In the early 1970s, however, researchers discovered subtle, microscopic sex differences in the neural connections of the hypothalamus, and soon thereafter macroscopic sex differences in brain organization were reported. Remarkably, these sex differences in brain organization could be reversed by early hormonal manipulation. Even the staunchest critics of the organizational/activational hypothesis were eventually persuaded that early hormone treatment changed neural tissues underlying sexually dimorphic behaviors and that these behaviors could be activated by the effects of gonadal steroid hormones on these same tissues in adulthood (e.g., Beach, 1975). It is now known, however, that hormonal effects on the nervous system can also be indirect; hormones may act upon nonneural tissues, such as penile or syrinx development, and especially those that potentially change sensory input to affect neural development (DeVries and Simerly, 2002; reviewed in DeVries and Södersten, 2009; Simerly, 2002). Some hormonal effects can be subtle and long lasting (**BOX 4.1**).

Why Study Sex Differences?

Since the behavioral findings of Phoenix and colleagues, numerous lines of research indicate that sex differences exist in the CNS and periphery, from differences in brain structures and their connectivity to differences in complex biological systems that underlie health and disease. Although intellectual curiosity and a desire to understand the world around us are acceptable reasons for exploring any question of interest, investigating sex differences has important political, medical, and ecological implications. For example, until 1973, homosexuality was listed as a mental health disorder in the *Diagnostic and Statistical Manual of Mental Disorders* second

BOX 4.1 *Sex Ratio of Litter Affects Adult Behavior*

Development is continuous, but scientists often view development as the accumulation of discrete segments. Although the stages are somewhat arbitrary, and some traits can span conventional stages, among mammals we often consider a series of stages including the prenatal (intrauterine), postnatal (until weaning), adolescent (after weaning), peripubertal, sexually mature, and reproductively senescent stages. Each stage has its own characteristic interactions among hormones, brain, and behavior and its specific contributions to the adult behavioral phenotype. It is possible to deconstruct early life events and study each stage, both in its own right and in how it interacts with the other stages.

In the field of behavioral endocrinology, complex behavioral traits such as mating and aggression are typically studied in adults. The formative environment for social and anxiety-related behaviors is the family unit among mammals; in the case of rodents, this family unit is the litter and the mother-young bond (Fleming et al., 2002; Meaney, 2001; Moore, 1995). Typically, investigators study individuals without consideration of the litter in which they were born. However, each litter is a structured unit involving the mother and her life history, as well as the pups as they interact with one another and with the mother. Research has demonstrated that much of adult behavior has its antecedents early in life, especially in hormone-behavior interactions.

One important factor in this early environment is the sex ratio of the litter. Recent studies have untangled this confounding variable and demonstrated separate and distinct effects on the nature and quality of individuals' behavior later in adulthood, as well as metabolic activity in brain nuclei that underlie these behaviors (Crews et al., 2004, 2006, 2009). Functional neural systems can be reorganized depending upon the composition of the litter in which the individual develops!

Typically, litter composition reflects the sex ratio produced at birth, but there is evidence that prenatal environment (who your fetal neighbors are) and the postnatal period (the nature and quantity of maternal care—see Chapter 7) also affect the adult behavioral phenotype. Unfortunately, few studies of prenatal or postnatal environments have disassociated these two periods. Most previous research demonstrating that the intrauterine sex ratio influences adult behavior failed to control for the sex ratio of the litter after birth. Similarly, most research demonstrating that the sex ratio of the litter influences maternal behavior has not considered the prenatal sex ratio of the pregnant mother.

However, and contrary to the literature, deconstructing these sequential experiences reveals that the sex ratio of the litter postnatally, and not the intrauterine position or maternal behavior as previously believed, affects sexuality in adult male rodents (Crews et al., 2006; deMederios et al., 2010). When prenatal sex ratio is controlled for, it can be seen that males raised in female-biased litters display less male behavior and are less attractive to females than males raised in litters of equal sex ratio or in male-biased litters. These differences are not erased by sexual experience, suggesting that the effects of the sibling environment are permanent. Taken together, these findings indicate that litter composition during the preweaning period must be considered, as it can affect the development of behavior and the neural network responsible for the regulation of important behaviors.

edition (DSM-II), the standard classification system used by mental health professionals. Despite its removal from the DSM-II, many retained the notion that homosexuality was a mental health issue, or "choice," that could be reversed through therapy or acceptance of a higher power. As you will see later in this chapter, brain differences between heterosexual and homosexual men have been discovered, suggesting a biological basis to partner preference. These findings fueled significant debate and inevitably set the stage for broader acceptance of the LGBTQ (lesbian, gay, bisexual, transgender, and questioning [or queer]) communities.

Although it is convenient to think of sex as a binary dimension with males on one side and females on the other, as you learned in Chapter 3, sex is exquisitely complicated, with incongruencies among chromosomal, gonadal, hormonal, morphological, and behavioral sex being common. Some difficult questions arise when deciding the best way to raise a child born with ambiguous genitalia or counseling an individual whose gender identity is different from his or her morphological sex, for example. Without an understanding of the ways that hormones and other factors affect sex, it is impossible to make decisions that are best for the psychological health of those in question. Early studies suggested that psychosexual development is driven by a child's upbringing, leading physicians to surgically alter ambiguous genitalia soon after birth, based upon whichever surgery would be easiest (see Box 4.4). We now know that psychosocial sex results from interactions between biology and the environment, allowing such decisions to be better informed.

Until 1993, when the U.S. National Institutes of Health Revitalization Act required enrollment of female participants in federally supported, phase III clinical trials, most pharmacological studies principally assumed that the female dose could simply be adjusted for body weight. The exclusion of female subjects, or the failure to analyze findings by sex when females are included, puts women at risk when using drugs only tested on men, and both sexes are put at risk when sex is not considered. Such risks recently came to light with the sleep aid Ambien (known generically as zolpidem). Drug metabolism differs between the sexes, and Ambien reaches 45% higher peak levels in women, leaving women using the original recommended dose with impairing levels of the drug in their systems upon waking. This observation led the FDA to cut the suggested dosage for women by 50% relative to the male dose. In addition to the dangers of sex differences in the response to pharmaceutical agents, substantial differences exist in the prevalence of a variety of diseases, including cardiovascular and autoimmune diseases (e.g., multiple sclerosis and rheumatoid arthritis). Even clinical presentation of disease can be different in men and women; men typically experience radiating sternal pressure and nausea with a myocardial infarction, whereas women might experience fatigue, isolated shortness of breath, numbness of the arm, and jaw pain (McSweeney et al., 2003). In common with clinical studies, animal research in the biological sciences is extraordinarily sex biased, particularly in the neurosciences, with females being grossly under-represented (Beery and Zucker, 2011). Fortunately, in 2014, the National Institutes of Health initiated policy changes to mandate the inclusion of female cell lines and animals in preclinical trials to ensure the appropriate study of sex differences as these fields move forward. The recognition that sex differences in disease rates exist often helps to guide research into their etiology and treatment as well as identify life-threatening events when symptomology is unique between the sexes.

Finally, understanding sex differentiation can have important ecological implications. As you learned in Chapter 3, considerable diversity exists within the animal kingdom, with sex determination being temperature-dependent in some species, others species able to switch sexes, and still others having multiple phenotypes within a sex. Like the parrotfish, many species of fish start their lives as female and change sex to male when they are large enough to defend territory. Commercial fishing removes the largest fish from the population, potentially skewing the sex ratio and negatively affecting population growth. Likewise, you can imagine a scenario in which a breeding season for reptiles is unseasonably warm or cold, significantly distorting the sex ratio. Finally, endocrine-disrupting chemicals in our environment can negatively affect the brain, physiology, and behavior of males and females differentially, even altering the sex of some species, as you saw in Chapter 3. As a result, the careful study of both sexes is necessary to fully appreciate the implications these chemicals have for the future of the environment. By understanding the potential impact of such perturbations, we can implement interventions before the survival of a species is irrevocably impacted.

Neural Bases of Mammalian Sex Differences

If we speculate on what changes might be provoked by hormones in a developing brain that could account for sex differences in adult behavior, then there are several logical possibilities. Hormones might affect neuronal survival by either promoting or protecting against cell death. Hormones might influence connectivity; that is, hormones might change dendritic branching and patterning or axonal projections (McCarthy, 2008). On a cellular level, hormones might affect the number or distribution of hormone receptors in specific brain regions or change the neurochemistry (including neurotransmitters) in specific brain regions (Morris et al., 2004). The

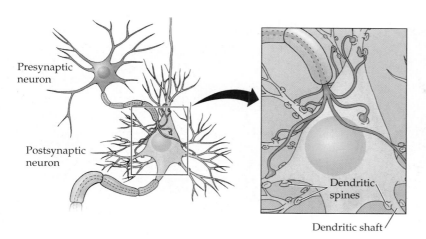

FIGURE 4.4 Synapses may form either upon dendritic spines or upon the shaft of a dendrite. In the MPOA, male rats tend to have more synapses from nonamygdaloid neurons on dendritic shafts and fewer synapses on dendritic spines than females; females have more synapses on dendritic spines and fewer synapses on dendritic shafts than males. Hormone manipulations immediately postpartum can affect this pattern of neuronal connectivity.

net result is that these differences in neuronal survival and physiology would be expected to cause observable structural changes. Sex differences in the brain can be broadly categorized as either volumetric or connective (McCarthy, 2008). Volumetric sex differences refer to size differences in the brains of males and females of specific brain regions or collections of neuronal cell bodies (nuclei). Connective sex differences refer to the type or number of synapses or the size of a particular type of projection within the brain (McCarthy, 2008).

The first clear-cut, though minuscule, sexual dimorphism found in the brain was a connective sex difference. During electron microscopic examination of synapses in the **medial preoptic area** (**MPOA**), an area just anterior to the hypothalamus in rats, a sex difference in the type of connections was discovered (Raisman and Field, 1973a) (see Figure 3.32). Because previous studies had shown that lesions or stimulation of the MPOA altered sexual behavior (see Chapter 5), the possibility of the existence of sex differences in the neural organization of this area was particularly intriguing. The researchers carefully counted and categorized the synapses in the MPOA that survived after axons projecting from another area of the brain, the stria terminalis, had been cut. They discovered that females had more synapses on dendritic spines and fewer synapses on dendritic shafts than males, whereas males had more synapses on dendritic shafts and fewer synapses on dendritic spines (Raisman and Field, 1973a). Dendritic spines are small outgrowths along the dendritic shafts that give dendrites possessing them a "rough" appearance. These spines have become the focus of much research, especially on learning and memory, because their number and function may vary in response to experience (**FIGURE 4.4**). In male rats castrated on day 1 of life, the female pattern of synapses was observed (Raisman and Field, 1973b). Similarly, in females injected with testosterone prior to 4 days of age, the male pattern of synaptic organization was observed. The functional meaning of these data remains unknown; in other words, how the observed sex differences in synaptic organization mediate behavior, or even if they mediate behavior, remains unresolved. However, this observation began to fulfill the prediction made years before that a "more subtle change reflected in function rather than visible structure" was involved in mediating sex differences in behavior (Phoenix et al., 1959).

Since this early report of a connective sex difference, volumetric structural sex differences have also been observed in mammalian brains. Because of its prominent role in the mediation of male mating behavior in several species, the **preoptic area** (**POA**) of the hypothalamus has received special attention. For example, the dendritic arrays of POA neurons differ between male and female hamsters (Greenough et al., 1977). Also, there is a collection of cell bodies (a nucleus) in the medial preoptic area of rats that is five to seven times larger in males than in females (Gorski et al.,

medial preoptic area (MPOA)
A subdivision of the anterior hypothalamus implicated in the control of homeostatic processes and motivated behaviors, including sexual behavior and gonadotropin secretion.

preoptic area (POA) A region of the brain anterior to the hypothalamus. This region is usually divided into the lateral and medial preoptic areas.

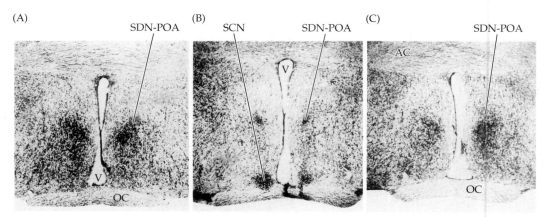

(A) SDN-POA

(B) SCN SDN-POA

(C) SDN-POA

AC

V

V

OC

OC

FIGURE 4.5 The bilateral sexually dimorphic nucleus of the preoptic area (SDN-POA) in rats is shown in cross section in micrographs of the brains of a male (A), a female (B), and a female treated with testosterone as a newborn (C). Note that the SDN-POA volumes of the male are substantially larger than those of the untreated female but are equal in size to those of the testosterone-treated female. OC = optic chiasm; SCN = suprachiasmatic nucleus; V = third ventricle. Courtesy of Roger Gorski.

sexually dimorphic nucleus of the preoptic area (SDN-POA) A set of cell bodies anterior to the hypothalamus that is larger in male than in female humans and rodents. The functional significance of this brain dimorphism is unknown.

testicular feminization mutation (TFM) A genetic disorder in which XY individuals are insensitive to androgens.

1978)! The difference is so prominent that rat brains can be accurately classified as either male or female by examining thin slices dissected through the hypothalamus with the naked eye (**FIGURE 4.5**). This region of the preoptic area has been termed the **sexually dimorphic nucleus of the preoptic area** (**SDN-POA**) (Gorski et al., 1978). The SDN-POA of females treated early in life with androgens can approach the size of the masculine SDN-POA, whereas the size of the feminine SDN-POA can be attained only in males that are neonatally castrated (Gorski, 1984). Presumably, a sex difference in the size of a nucleus or other brain region may reflect differences in cell number or in cell size between males and females. Male and female rats start out with similar numbers of sexually dimorphic nucleus (SDN) neurons. The sex difference in the size of the SDN-POA is due to a decreased number of cells in females and castrated males; androgens, or more precisely their estrogenic metabolites, protect neurons from apoptosis, programmed cell death (Dodson and Gorski, 1993; Forger, 1998; Rhees et al., 1990). Rats with complete **testicular feminization mutation** (**TFM**) (called androgen insensitivity syndrome in humans), which have deficient androgen receptors but normal estrogen receptors, display female-typical genitalia but male-typical SDN-POA (Jacobson, 1980). Thus, it is possible that the presence of the Y chromosome, and not androgens per se, drives these sex differences. Alternatively, because aromatase is induced by androgen receptor activation and POA aromatase activity is reduced in TFM mice (Roselli et al., 1987) and reduction of postnatal aromatase demasculinizes the POA (Lund et al., 2000), it is possible that this process is steroid-dependent rather than genetic, as previously thought.

The functional significance of the sex difference in the size of the SDN-POA is not well established. Lesions to the entire POA disrupt normal mating behavior in a wide variety of species, including rodents and primates (Hart and Leedy, 1985). If only the SDN-POA is lesioned in females, they continue to display normal reproductive cycles (Arendash and Gorski, 1983). If only the SDN-POA is lesioned in males, they also continue to display normal mating behavior or, in some cases, exhibit temporary and mild copulatory dysfunction (Arendash and Gorski, 1983; DeJonge et al., 1989). Similar results have been documented with other animals. Although it is attractive to hypothesize that a larger male brain structure likely serves to facilitate a masculine behavior, two lines of evidence suggest that the larger SDN-POA of males might act to inhibit female sexual behavior. First, lesions of the entire POA lead to the expression of female-typical sexual behavior (see Chapter 6) when males are treated with estrogen and progesterone (Hennessey et al., 1986). Similarly, treatment of newborn male rats that reduces the expression of *steroid receptor coactivator-1* (*SRC-1*), a gene whose protein acts to increase sex steroid actions on gene expression, leads to a reduction in the size of the SDN-POA and the expression of female sexual behavior (Auger et al., 2000). Although these findings do not provide a conclusive link between the SDN-POA and sexual behavior, they provide an important caveat for consideration when exploring sex differences in the brain—when a nucleus is bigger in one sex, it does not always mean that this locus is positively driving a behavior.

In rats, the cell-dense central core of the medial preoptic nucleus is the most sexually dimorphic part of this complex; males display more neurons than females, and these neurons are rich in androgen receptors (Madeira et al., 1999). Thus, these two examples—the sex differences in the connectivity pattern of dendrites (in the MPOA) and the size of the SDN—represent two of the main structural brain sex differences. In the absence of androgens, these neurons undergo apoptosis (Morris et al., 2004).

Volumetric sex differences have been reported in many other brain structures of rodents and other mammals. For example, the volume of the medial amygdala and the medial posterior area of an associated part of the limbic system called the **bed nucleus of the stria terminalis** (**BNST**) are about 20% larger in males than in females (del Abril et al., 1987; Mizukami et al., 1983). The amygdala is an almond-shaped structure in the brain that is often involved in aggression or reproductive behavior. These two brain regions appear to be part of a sexually dimorphic neural circuit that includes the SDN-POA and the rostral aspects of the preoptic area of the hypothalamus, such as the **anteroventral periventricular nucleus** (**AVPV**) (Simerly and Swanson, 1986). Recall that the AVPV regulates ovulation, and it is the source of a sexually dimorphic projection to the arcuate nucleus (Simerly, 2002). In contrast to the cell groups mentioned thus far, in the AVPV the volume is larger in females than in gonadally intact males. Males castrated before 10 days of age have AVPV volumes that resemble those of females rather than intact males (Simerly, 2002). Thus, two points can be made here. First, testosterone or its metabolites can have opposite effects on promoting or inhibiting apoptosis in clumps of neurons in the nervous system (testosterone promotes apoptosis in the AVPV but inhibits apoptosis in the SDN-POA) (**FIGURE 4.6**). Thus, in the cells of these two brain regions targeted by testosterone or its metabolites, molecular mechanisms must differ (Morris et al., 2004). Second, a brief temporal window exists during which testosterone can induce its effects on apoptosis, so whatever difference in cellular/genetic machinery exists in the AVPV and SDN-POA exists for only a few days during early life.

Several sexual dimorphisms in the central nervous systems of humans have also been described (**TABLE 4.1**). One of the earliest morphological sex differences noted was that women have smaller brains than men. Initially, this observation was considered evidence supporting the intellectual inferiority of women and rationalizing the lack of educational opportunities afforded them in the late eighteenth and early nineteenth centuries. It was eventually noted, however, that when the larger male body mass is taken into consideration, the relative brain sizes of women and men are equivalent. Studies using a new three-dimensional MRI device found more folding (i.e., gyrification and fissuration) of the brain surface in women than in men (Luders et al., 2004). This increased complexity of folds provides more cortical surface area in the frontal and parietal lobes,

bed nucleus of the stria terminalis (BNST) A limbic forebrain structure that mediates autonomic, neuroendocrine, and behavior responses.

anteroventral periventricular nucleus (AVPV) A small region of the anterior preoptic area that is abundant in nuclear hormone receptors and participates in the control of sex-typical behavioral and endocrine responses.

TABLE 4.1 *Structural sex differences in the central nervous system of humans*

Brain region	Difference
Hypothalamus	
SDN-POA	♂ > ♀
Interstitial nucleus of the anterior hypothalamus-3 (INAH-3)	♂ > ♀
Bed nucleus of the stria terminalis (BNST)	♂ > ♀
Suprachiasmatic nuclei (SCN)	♂ < ♀[a]
Spinal cord	
Onuf's nucleus (no. of motor neurons)	♂ > ♀
Structures associated with language	
Planum temporale	♂ < ♀[b]
Dorsolateral prefrontal cortex	♂ < ♀
Superior temporal gyrus	♂ < ♀
Structures connecting the hemispheres	
Corpus callosum (posterior portion)	♂ < ♀[c]
Anterior commissure	♂ < ♀
Massa intermedia of thalamus	♂ < ♀

Source: After Forger, 1998.
[a]More elongated in ♀.
[b]Left and right more symmetrical in size in ♀.
[c]More bulbous in ♀.

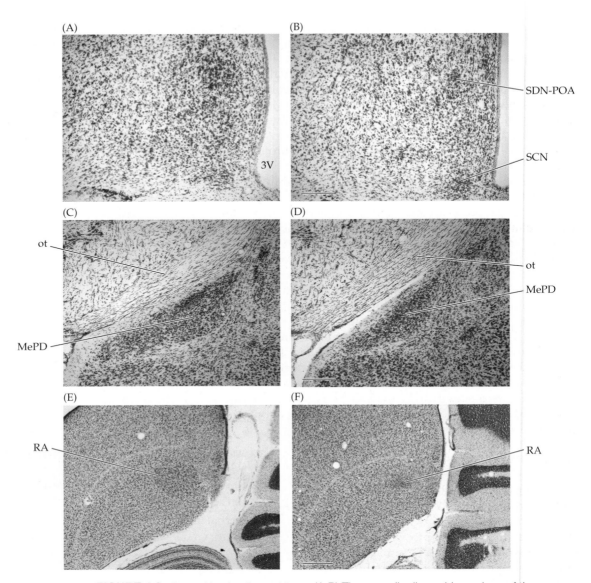

FIGURE 4.6 **Sexual brain dimorphisms** (A,B) The sexually dimorphic nucleus of the pre-optic area (SDN-POA) is larger in male rats (A) than in females (B) because the testes secrete testosterone during the perinatal sensitive period. After that time, testosterone has little effect on SDN-POA volume. (C,D) In contrast, the volume of the rat posterodorsal medial amygdala (MePD), which is about 1.5 times larger in males (C) than in females (D), retains its responsiveness to testosterone throughout life. (E,F) In zebra finches, the robustus archistriatum (RA) nucleus is crucial for song production and has a greater volume in males (E) than in females (F). As with the rat SDN-POA, exposure to steroid hormones early in life is essential for development of a masculine phenotype RA. For the RA, however, the steroids are synthesized de novo in the brain, rather than originating from the testes. SCN = suprachiasmatic nucleus; 3V = third ventricle; ot = optic tract. All scale bars = 250 μm. From Morris et al., 2004.

which may compensate for the smaller female brain size and account for some of the behavioral differences between males and females (see below).

In common with other mammals, humans were discovered to have a sexually dimorphic nucleus in the POA (Swaab and Fliers, 1985). Because this nucleus resembles the SDN-POA of rats and is larger in males than in females, it was also named the SDN-POA. There has been some controversy, however, about the boundaries of the human SDN-POA and the consistency of the observed sex differences in its volume (e.g., see Allen et al., 1989). In other studies, the nuclei of the human POA have been subdivided into four smaller regions called the **interstitial nuclei of the anterior hypothalamus** (**INAH**), abbreviated INAH-1, INAH-2, and so on (Allen et al., 1989). Under this neuroanatomical classification scheme, INAH-1 was considered to be equivalent to the SDN-POA, and, in contrast to the previous report, no sex differences were observed in this tiny brain region. The volumes of INAH-2 and INAH-3, however, were reported to be larger in men than in women (Allen et al., 1989) (**FIGURE 4.7**). In another study, a sex difference in nuclear volume was reported in INAH-3, but not in INAH-2 (Byne et al., 2001; LeVay, 1991).

interstitial nuclei of the anterior hypothalamus (INAH) Four regions of neuronal cell bodies in the anterior hypothalamus and preoptic area of humans. Sex differences have been reported in INAH-2 and INAH-3. INAH-1 has been considered to be equivalent to the SDN-POA in rats.

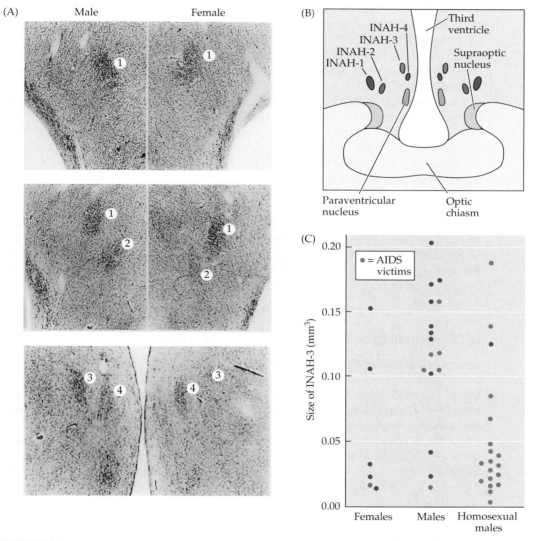

FIGURE 4.7 **The interstitial nuclei of the anterior hypothalamus** (A) Micrographs showing the interstitial nuclei from a male (left column) and a female (right column). The male examples were taken from the left side of the brain, female examples from the right side at the same level. (1) INAH-1, (2) INAH-2, (3) INAH-3, (4) INAH-4. INAH-4 is well represented in both male and female, whereas INAH-3 is clearly less distinct in the female. (B) These nuclei in humans are seen in the same part of the hypothalamus where the SDN-POA is found in rats. (C) INAH-3 is larger in men than in women, and larger in straight men than in gay men. Although most of the gay men in this study had died of AIDS, note that heterosexual men who died of AIDS still had a larger INAH-3, indicating that the differences between straight and gay men are not due to AIDS. A from Allen et al., 1989; B,C LeVay, 1991.

Because brain tissue from humans is obtained at different times after death and is fixed with a variety of methods, it is not particularly surprising that contradictory results have been obtained. The report by LeVay (1991) generated enormous debate because, in addition to the observation that INAH-3 was smaller in women than in men, INAH-3 was reported to be smaller in homosexual men than in heterosexual men. Although sexual orientation/preference has not traditionally been part of medical records, the sexual preference of the homosexual men in LeVay's sample was included in their health records because the vast majority of these men had died from complications resulting from AIDS. Their brains were compared with those of men whose sexual orientation was unknown but assumed to be heterosexual and who had died primarily from other causes. However, not all of the obvious potential confounding variables—HIV infection, age, body size (people infected with HIV often have reduced body weight), brain size, and testosterone concentrations (males infected with HIV often show end-stage reductions in plasma testosterone concentrations)—have been ruled out as causative factors underlying the differences in INAH-3 size between the heterosexual and homosexual men (Byne and Parsons, 1993; Byne et al., 2001; Swaab et al., 2001).

In addition to the INAH-3, the nucleus in the brain responsible for daily rhythms in physiology and behavior, the suprachiasmatic nucleus (SCN) (see Chapter 10), has shown a volumetric difference. It is considerably larger and contains over twice the number of cells in homosexual men relative to a reference group of males of unestablished sexual orientation (Swaab and Hofman, 1990). In humans and other mammalian species, the SCN contains sex steroid receptors (Fernandez-Guasti et al., 2000; Karatsoreos and Silver, 2007; Kruijver and Swaab, 2002), suggesting that androgens and/or estrogens might act early in development to modify this brain clock. Whether or not changes in SCN morphology contribute to human sexual orientation cannot be experimentally examined, but at least in rats, lesions of the SCN do not alter male sexual behavior (Kruijver et al., 1993). These findings have fueled the debate on whether sexual orientation/preference is mediated primarily by biological or by environmental factors, a debate that will be considered later in this chapter.

Molecular Sex Differences in the Brain

One possible explanation for why adult hormone treatment elicits different sexual behaviors in males and females involves sex differences in the number and distribution of neural estrogen and androgen receptors. In most early studies, no differences in steroid hormone binding sites were reported; however, recent studies using more sophisticated techniques have revealed some modest sex differences (Brown et al., 1992). For instance, sex differences in the distribution of corticosteroid receptors in rat brains have been reported. Three days after both gonads and adrenal glands had been removed, mineralocorticoid binding in males was higher than in females throughout the hippocampus, although glucocorticoid binding in the brain was equivalent between the sexes (MacLusky et al., 1996). These results may reflect sex differences in neural stress responses.

Also, and more to the point, there are sex differences in the distribution of androgen and estrogen receptors throughout the nervous system (MacLusky et al., 1996). The highest density of sex steroid hormone receptors is in the hypothalamus or parts of the limbic system that connect to the hypothalamus (DeVries and Simerly, 2002). There is significant overlap among the distributions of neurons that express progesterone receptors, androgen receptors, and the two estrogen receptors (ERα and ERβ) (FIGURE 4.8). Androgen receptor binding and mRNA expression appear to be higher in the medial amygdaloid nucleus, bed nucleus of the stria terminalis, preoptic periventricular nucleus, and ventromedial nucleus of the hypothalamus of male compared to female rats (DeVries and Simerly, 2002). Estrogen and proges-

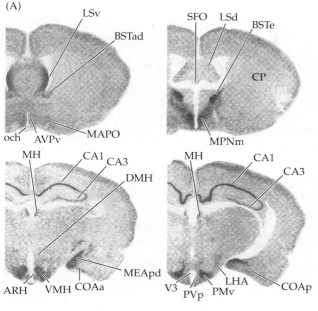

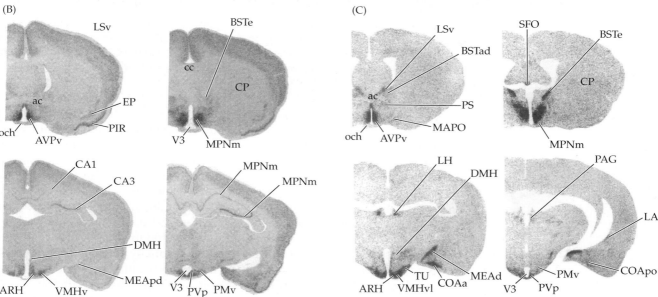

FIGURE 4.8 Receptors for different sex steroids overlap significantly in the brain. Cross sections of rat brain show dark spots that indicate androgen receptors (A), α estrogen receptors (B), and progestin receptors (C). ac = anterior commissure; AVPv = anteroventral periventricular nucleus; ARH = arcuate nucleus; BSTad = anterodorsal nucleus of BNST; BSTe = encapsulated nucleus of BNST; CA1/ CA3 = fields of hippocampus; cc = corpus callosum; COAa = cortical nucleus of the amygdala (anterior) ; COApo = cortical nucleus of the amygdala (posterior); CP = caudoputamen; DMH = dorsomedial hypothalamic nucleus; EP = endopiriform nucleus; LA = lateral nucleus of the amygdala; LH = lateral habenula; LSv = lateral septal nucleus (lateral part); MAPO = magnocellular preoptic nucleus; och = optic chiasm; PAG = periaqueductal gray; PIR = piriform cortex; PS = parastrial nucleus; PVp = posterior periventricular nucleus; SFO = subfornical organ; TU = tuberal nucleus; V3 = third ventricle. From Simerly, 2002.

terone receptor binding and mRNA expression appear to be higher in the preoptic periventricular nucleus, medial preoptic nucleus, and ventromedial nucleus of female than of male rats (DeVries and Simerly, 2002). Sex steroid receptor gene expression is regulated, in part, by circulating steroid hormone concentrations, although this regulation may be region-specific. For example, testosterone up-regulates androgen receptors in the medial amygdala, but down-regulates those receptors in the medial preoptic nucleus (Burgess and Handa, 1993; Simerly, 1993).

Several studies that reveal sex differences in the distribution or regulation of neurotransmitters or their receptors have been reported. Only indirect links have been established between sex differences in neurotransmitter distribution and in the ability of steroid hormones to evoke adult sexual behavior, however. For example, in the AVPV, which is larger in female rodents than in males, dopamine-containing neurons are more plentiful in females than in males. The number of neurons expressing tyrosine hydroxylase (a convenient marker of dopaminergic neurons) is

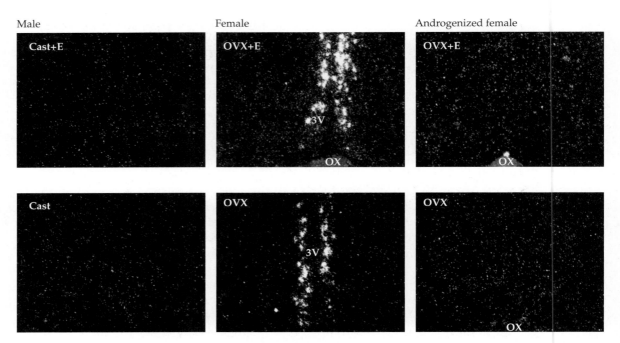

FIGURE 4.9 Sexual dimorphism in kisspeptin neurons in AVPV of rats Dark-field photomicrographs showing *Kiss1* mRNA-expressing cells (indicated by the presence of *white clusters of silver grains*) in sections of the AVPV of males, females, and females treated with testosterone early in development. Cast = castration; OX = optic chiasm; OVX = ovariectomized; E = estrogen replacement. From Kauffman et al., 2007b.

equivalent in male and female rats between birth and postnatal day 2. In the presence of testosterone or estrogens, however, the tyrosine hydroxylase mRNA decreases in males, leading to dramatic sex differences by postnatal day 10 (reviewed in DeVries and Simerly, 2002). Mice with an androgen receptor mutation display this sex difference, whereas male mice genetically engineered to lack the α estrogen receptor do not show this decrease in the number of dopaminergic neurons; thus, the sex difference appears to be a result of the organizational actions of estrogens.

Because the AVPV nuclei are important in the secretion of GnRH (see Chapter 2) and because the regulation of GnRH differs substantially between the sexes, the AVPV is a reasonable brain region in which to expect sex differences. Indeed, some neurons in the AVPV express *KiSS1* mRNA and its gene product, kisspeptin (Dungan et al., 2006), and female mice have about ten times more kisspeptin neurons in the AVPV than males (Clarkson and Herbison, 2006). In rats, the sex difference is exaggerated, as virtually no kisspeptin neurons are observed in the AVPV of males (Gonzalez-Martinez et al., 2008; Kauffman et al., 2007) (**FIGURE 4.9**). Along with other neural components, kisspeptin is likely involved in the circuit mediating the estrogen-mediated LH surge (DeVries and Södersten, 2009; Williams and Kriegsfeld, 2012).

The innervation of several brain regions, including the lateral septum, by neurons that release vasopressin shows marked sex differences among vertebrates (DeVries and Panzica, 2006). In addition, male rats have two to three times the number of vasopressin-expressing neurons than females in the BNST and medial amygdala (DeVries and Södersten, 2009; DeVries et al., 1983; van Leeuwen et al., 1985). These regions of the brain are involved in sexual behaviors in males and females, and the vasopressin projections of the BNST and medial amygdala may be indirectly involved in these behaviors. The sex difference is based on the organizational effects of sex steroid hormones (DeVries and Panzica, 2006). Despite correlations between sexual behavior and vasopressin expression in response to the presence and absence of sex steroid hormones, the functional meaning of sex differences in vasopressinergic neuronal number and projections remains somewhat unspecified. Vasopressin injected into the ventricles of the brain inhibits lordosis in female rats (Devries and Södersten, 2009). It is possible that the increased vasopressin in the brains of males is responsible for the lack of male lordosis in adult rodents. Sex differences in vasopressin correlate strongly with sex differences in social behavior that are influenced by vasopressin. For example, in male rat aggressive behavior, castration leads to both a slow reduction in vasopressin content in the projections from the BNST and the medial amygdala and an associated reduction in male aggression (DeBold and Miczek, 1984); injection of vasopressin into the medial amygdala elevates aggressive behavior in male rats (Koolhaas et al., 1991).

In contrast to the somewhat vague role of vasopressin in rats, a nanopeptide related to vasopressin, **arginine vasotocin (AVT)**, has been shown to modulate several aspects of sexually dimorphic behavior in bullfrogs (*Rana catesbeiana*) (Boyd, 1997). Only male bullfrogs give the so-called mate call, and only females respond to mate calls by moving toward the source of the call (phonotaxis). Males respond to other males' mate calls by emitting their own mate calls. Both sexes give "release calls" when mounted inappropriately. Injection of males, but not females, with AVT increases the rate of vocalizing. Injection of AVT increases female attraction to the source of a call (a male frog or a speaker). Six separate populations of AVT-releasing neurons have been found in bullfrog brains, and receptors for AVT are located in brain regions that are linked to important reproductive behaviors, including vocalization, phonotaxis, and locomotor activity. Sex differences exist in the numbers of AVT receptors in the amygdala, hypothalamus, pretrigeminal nucleus, and dorsolateral nucleus (**FIGURE 4.10**). More importantly, steroid hormones affect AVT receptor availability. Estradiol modulates AVT receptor numbers in the amygdala in both sexes, and both estradiol and dihydrotestosterone (DHT) affect AVT receptor numbers in the pretrigeminal nucleus of males. Thus, in bullfrogs, AVT seems to function as a neurotransmitter for reproductively relevant behaviors, and AVT activity is modulated by steroid hormones in bullfrogs. Sex differences in AVT in other species mediate sexually dimorphic social behavior. Some of these will be discussed in Chapter 8.

arginine vasotocin (AVT)
A neuropeptide homologous to mammalian oxytocin and vasopressin that is found in non-mammalian vertebrates and mediates social and sexual behavior.

(A)   (B)   (C)

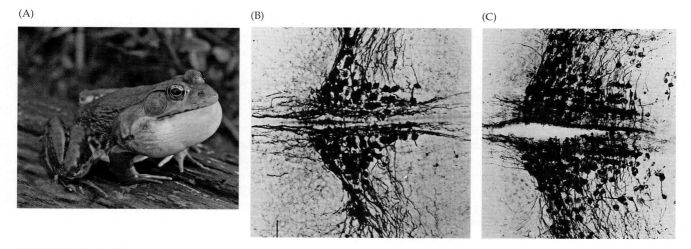

FIGURE 4.10 Sex differences in bullfrog brains mediate calling behavior. (A) A male bullfrog. Calling behavior attracts potential mates and wards off competing males. Immunocytochemistry reveals smaller numbers of neuronal cell bodies and fibers containing arginine vasotocin (AVT) in the preoptic area of a female bullfrog brain (B) than in the same region of a male brain (C). B,C from Boyd et al., 1992.

Aggression in mammals is often mediated by the neurotransmitter serotonin. There are at least 14 different types of serotonin receptors in mammals, and activation of one of 3 or 4 different receptors modulates aggressive behavior. In one study using positron emission tomography (PET) and a selective radiotracer that binds only to the type 2 serotonin receptor, the distribution of this receptor was mapped in living, age-matched men and women (Biver et al., 1996). Significantly higher numbers of type 2 serotonin receptors were found in the brains of the men (Biver et al., 1996). More recently, a similar PET study on living people has reported significantly higher serotonin 1A receptor binding potential and greater serotonin 1A receptor distribution in women than in men (Parsey et al., 2002); these data confirmed previous postmortem binding data. The mechanisms by which sex steroids influence serotonin or vasopressin receptor numbers and distribution have not yet been discovered.

As noted in Chapter 2, testosterone serves as a prohormone for the production of either estradiol or DHT in many mammals and birds. One strategy for understanding the role of testosterone in evoking sex differences in neural tissue is to identify neurons containing testosterone receptors as well as enzymes that convert testosterone to other hormones (Hutchison and Beyer, 1994; Schlinger, 1997). Neurons that contain androgen receptors and aromatase or 5α- or 5β-reductase are likely candidates for part of a circuit mediating sexually dimorphic behavior(s) (Pinckard et al., 2000; Roselli et al., 1996, 1997). There are substantial sex differences in aromatase activity in several brain regions of rats, including the BNST, the medial preoptic nucleus, and the ventromedial nucleus (VMN) of the hypothalamus; aromatase activity has been found to be two to four times higher in males than in females in these areas (Roselli et al., 1997). Aromatase activity appears to be regulated by androgen receptors in the preoptic area and the hypothalamus; testosterone and DHT, but not estrogens, maintain aromatase activity in these regions in castrated rats. There is no sex difference in aromatase activity or aromatase mRNA in the amygdala, and neither aromatase levels nor aromatase mRNA expression have been found to be affected by steroid hormones in that area. These results suggest that adult sex differences in responsiveness to androgens may reflect differences in gene expression in neural circuits that are involved in regulating sexually dimorphic behaviors or in some other process (see the next section) (Balthazart and Ball, 1998; Celotti et al., 1997; DeVries and Simerly, 2002; Pinckard et al., 2000; Roselli et al., 1997; Schlinger et al., 2001). One process that can be studied to understand brain sexual dimorphisms is called epigenetics (see Box 3.3). Another strategy is to identify neural cells that function as endocrine cells and produce estrogens de novo (McCarthy et al., 2009). We will learn more about neurons that produce estrogens in the context of bird brains and song.

As discussed in Chapter 3, epigenetic regulation is required for sexual differentiation of the brain during development (Forger, 2016). In addition, pronounced sex differences have been observed in adult levels of DNA methylation and histone modification, pointing to epigenetic control of sex differences in gene regulation. One early study demonstrated that perinatal sex steroid exposure leads to differential DNA methylation of sex steroid receptors in rats, with males exhibiting greater ERα promoter methylation than females at several CpG sites in adulthood (McCarthy et al., 2009; Schwartz et al., 2010) **(FIGURE 4.11)**. Cytosines in CpG dinucleotides can be methylated via DNA methyltransferases and can change gene expression. Similarly, a genome-wide analysis of the BNST and the POA in adult male and female mice revealed that approximately 1000 genes are differentially methylated (Ghahramani et al., 2014) and 248 genes and loci exhibit differential histone modification (Shen et al., 2015). Sex differences in adult levels of gene methylation were dependent on early life hormone exposure, with neonatal testosterone exposure masculinizing the pattern of methylation (Ghahramani et al., 2014). Despite marked sex differences, gene expression patterns were not associated with epigenetic modi-

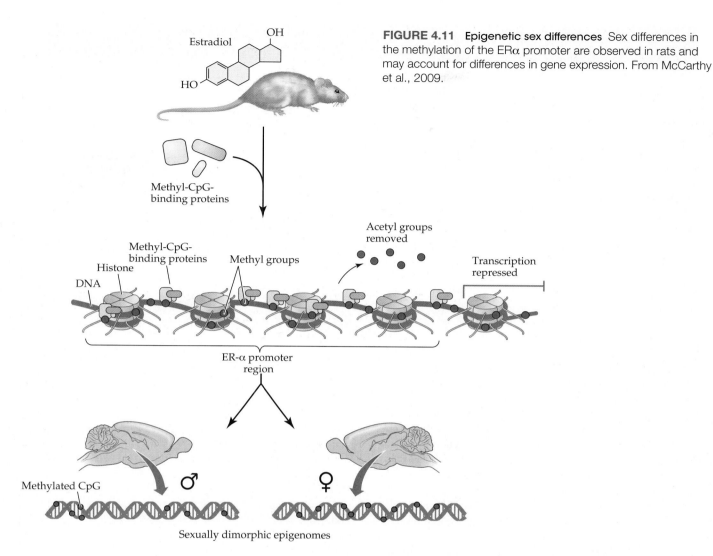

FIGURE 4.11 Epigenetic sex differences Sex differences in the methylation of the ERα promoter are observed in rats and may account for differences in gene expression. From McCarthy et al., 2009.

fications in either study. It is possible that, under basal conditions, sex differences in gene expression are not apparent and are more likely to emerge when these brain structures are activated to drive sex-specific behavior.

Animal Models for Sexually Dimorphic Behaviors

Because male and female humans show significant overlap in their behavioral repertoires and because it is difficult or ethically impossible to conduct the appropriate experiments in people, it is useful to study the effects of hormones on sexually dimorphic traits in animals for which only one sex displays the behavior all or most of the time (**BOX 4.2**).

Birdsong

Birds provide the best evidence that behavioral sex differences are the result of hormonally induced structural changes in the brain (Balthazart and Adkins-Regan, 2002; Nottebohm and Arnold, 1976). In contrast to mammals, in which structural differences in neural tissues have been only indirectly linked to behavior, structural differences in avian brains have been directly linked to a sexually dimorphic behavior: birdsong. A subset of birds belonging to the order Passeriformes (the Oscines,

BOX 4.2　Urinary Posture in Canines

The difference in urinary posture between male and female dogs is a well-known sexually dimorphic behavior. The difference in body posture during urination is observed not only among domestic dogs but also among wild canids (Martins and Valle, 1948). Although this might seem at first to be a silly topic for research, this sexually dimorphic behavior has provided endocrinologists with a useful measure in studies of sexual differentiation. If you were challenged to assign the sex of a dog 100 m away, your task would be immediately simplified if you saw the dog raise one of its rear legs and urinate. If you had observed many dogs, then you would also be in a position to state that the male dog had undergone puberty, because only male dogs that are sexually mature regularly display the raised-leg urinary posture. Females very rarely raise a leg when urinating, although adult males occasionally assume the squatting posture characteristic of female dogs. The important features of this behavior are that (1) it is sexually dimorphic, (2) the sexual dimorphism appears around the time of puberty, and (3) it is not a reproductive behavior per se. Behavioral endocrinologists have formalized these observations during controlled studies to elucidate the role of sex hormones in mediating this sexual dimorphism. The figure at right shows a clear sex difference seen in domesticated dogs that has been exploited in studies of sexual differentiation. Adult male dogs usually raise a rear leg and orient the stream of urine toward some target to mark it; adult females usually adopt a squatting posture. Puppies of both sexes usually assume a squatting position during urination, although male dogs begin to show a "lean-forward" urinary posture around the time of puberty (Beach, 1974b).

In a study that followed in the conceptual footsteps of the classic experiment conducted on guinea pigs by Phoenix and coworkers (1959), beagle puppies were subjected to several different early hormonal environments (Beach, 1974b). Beagles have a gestation period of about 58–63 days, and sexual differentiation begins late in gestation and continues for 10–15 days postnatally. In a study of hormonal effects on behavioral differ-

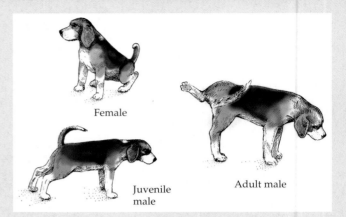

Female

Juvenile male

Adult male

entiation, some females were injected with testosterone 1–3 days after birth. The timing of the treatment for this experimental group was equivalent to that of the androgen treatment typically given to newborn rats to masculinize their mating behavior. Females of a second experimental group were exposed to testosterone in utero when their mothers were injected with this steroid hormone late in pregnancy. This experimental treatment was reminiscent of the early endocrine treatment of guinea pigs, a species for which sexual differentiation occurs prenatally. A third experimental group simulated more closely what normally occurs for male dogs: female pups were exposed to testosterone in utero as well as immediately postpartum. Additional experimental groups included normal females that were ovariectomized in adulthood, males castrated at birth, and males castrated in adulthood.

With no additional hormone replacement therapy later in life, postpubertal female dogs that were exposed to testosterone both in utero and postpartum displayed the male urinary posture about 50% of the time. Many of their reproductive behaviors were also masculinized and defeminized. Their external genitalia, but not their internal sex organs, were masculinized; these females had a penis through which the urogenital opening passed.

or songbirds) produce complex vocalizations that, for the most part, are learned during development. These complex, learned vocalizations are referred to as song.

In most species of songbirds, song production is sexually dimorphic. Males usually sing more than females, although the expression of this sex difference varies across species. Male zebra finches (*Taeniopygia guttata*), like many male songbirds, sing in order to attract females and ward off competing males. Female zebra finches never sing, even after testosterone treatment in adulthood (Adkins-Regan and Ascenzi, 1987). In contrast, no sex difference in the singing behavior is observed in bay wrens (*Thryothorus nigricapillus*), a tropical duetting species in which males and females participate equally in producing two-bird song (Brenowitz, 1997; Brenowitz and Arnold, 1985, 1986; Brenowitz et al., 1985). Other species, such as canaries

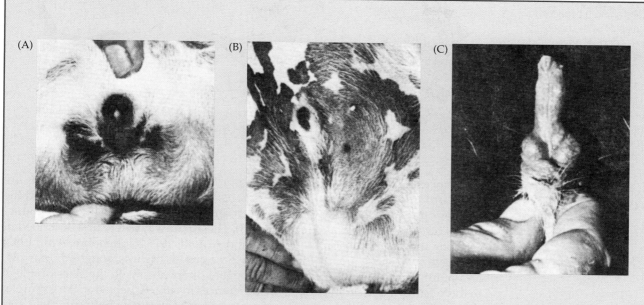

(A) (B) (C)

In the figure above, panel A shows the external genitalia of a normal, untreated female. In panel B, a female treated with androgens in utero shows labial swelling and clitoral enlargement. In panel C, a female treated with androgens in utero and immediately after birth shows a clitoris formed into a structure that is indistinguishable from a penis; this pseudopenis displays erectile function. Despite this masculinization of the external genitalia, these females have structurally normal ovaries and derivatives of the Müllerian duct system, and they show estrous bleeding through the pseudopenis if treated with estrogen in adulthood (Beach et al., 1983).

Control females and females that were exposed to testosterone for shorter durations rarely displayed the male-typical urinary posture. Males, even if castrated in infancy, began shifting from the juvenile squatting posture to the male-typical posture at about 4–6 months of age, the usual time of puberty (Beach, 1974b; Ranson and Beach, 1985). These experiments show that the sex difference in canine urinary posture is organized by sex steroid hormones but does not require their presence for activation of the behavior.

An interesting facet of the hormonal mediation of urinary posture in dogs is the way this behavior develops (Ranson and Beach, 1985). The developmental pattern of this behavior indicates that the male puppy's perception of his world changes as he experiences puberty. Initially, male and female puppies display similar squatting urinary postures. Females do not exhibit place preference for urination around the time of puberty, but as males mature, they begin to spend much time sniffing and exploring vertical objects in their environment. Objects with certain dimensions are preferred. As males become sexually mature, they lift a rear leg and direct the stream of urine onto these vertical objects (Ranson and Beach, 1985). These behaviors are the antecedents of the territorial marking behaviors that males will engage in throughout their adult lives. The process by which certain vertical objects become worthy of investigation and marking by males or perinatally androgenized females, but not typical females, remains unspecified, but it appears that hormones affect the perceptual focus (or attention) of young dogs so that they attend preferentially to objects of certain dimensions when marking.

(*Serinus canaria*), fall somewhere between these two extremes; that is, females sing, but they sing less frequently and produce less complex songs than males (**FIGURE 4.12**). This natural distribution of sexually dimorphic behavior permits investigation of the mechanisms underlying song. In the case of birdsong, sex differences in behavior reflect sex differences in the neural centers of the brain that control singing (Ball and Balthazart, 2010; Balthazart and Adkins-Regan, 2009; Schlinger, 1998; Schlinger et al., 2001).

NEURAL BASES OF SEX DIFFERENCES IN BIRDSONG In contrast to the early predictions of subtle, hormonally induced changes in brain structure (Phoenix et al., 1959), the volumes of several brain regions in songbirds display substantial sex

FIGURE 4.12 Singing in female songbirds falls along a broad continuum: females of some species, such as zebra finches, never sing in nature; females of other species, such as bay wrens, sing as frequently as male conspecifics. Most species are intermediate between these two extremes. For example, female canaries sing, but not as frequently as males, and their songs are generally less complex than those of males. After Brenowitz, 1997.

differences. Some of the sex differences in the nervous systems of songbirds are listed in **TABLE 4.2**. Two major brain circuits, the efferent motor pathway and the auditory transmission pathway, have been implicated in the learning and production of birdsong (Arnold and Jordan, 1988). These pathways were first described in canaries and zebra finches (Nottebohm and Arnold, 1976; Nottebohm et al., 1982) and have been subsequently identified in three groups of birds: songbirds, parrots, and hummingbirds (Nottebohm, 2005). Sexual dimorphisms in the sizes of nuclei in these pathways seem to parallel sex differences in singing behavior. For example, there are large size differences in several song control nuclei between male and female zebra finches (Bottjer et al., 1985; Nottebohm and Arnold, 1976), but these dimorphisms are less extreme in canaries, and they are undetectable in bay wrens (Brenowitz, 1991, 1997; Brenowitz and Arnold, 1986; Brenowitz et al., 1985).

The efferent motor pathway is necessary for the production of song in adult birds. This pathway consists of the interconnected brain areas that control neural output to the syrinx (the avian vocal production organ). The locations of the song control nuclei in this pathway for a "generic" songbird brain are illustrated in **FIGURE 4.13**. The "high vocal center" (HVC) sends an efferent projection via the posterior descending pathway to the robust nucleus of the archistriatum (RA). A projection from the RA travels to the tracheosyringeal division of the nucleus of the hypoglossal nerve (nXIIts), either directly or indirectly via the dorsomedial (DM) portion of the nucleus intercollicularis (ICo). From the nXIIts, motor signals travel by way of the tracheosyringeal nerve to the syrinx. The posterior descending pathway is necessary for both song acquisition and the production of learned song (Nottebohm, 2005). Lesions of the HVC and RA result in song production deficits in adulthood (Nottebohm et al., 1976, 1982).

Information from the HVC can also reach the RA through a more circuitous route (Bottjer et al., 1989; Okuhata and Saito, 1987). This second route, the anterior forebrain pathway, has been called the "recursive loop" (Nottebohm et al., 1990). Information in the recursive loop travels from the HVC to area X (a forebrain nucleus located in the parolfactory lobe), then to the medial nucleus of the dorsolateral thalamus (DLM), to the lateral magnocellular nucleus of the anterior neostriatum (lMAN), and finally to the RA. This anterior forebrain (recursive) pathway has been implicated in the process of song learning.

The song-learning process occurs in two stages. During the sensory stage, a young bird hears and memorizes the song(s) of adult birds. The sensory stage is followed by a sensory-motor stage, in which the bird tries to reproduce the song that is stored in its memory. Learning at this stage

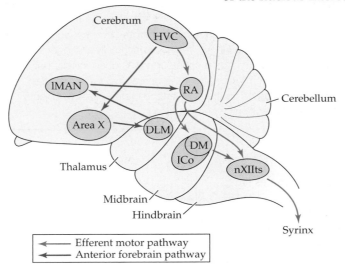

FIGURE 4.13 The neural basis of birdsong, shown in a "generic" songbird brain. In species in which large sex differences in song frequency are observed, the nuclei involved in song brain circuits are larger in males than in females.

TABLE 4.2   *Sexual dimorphism in songbird brains*

Brain structure	Species
Volumes of song system nuclei IMAN, DM, and nXIIts[a]	
IMAN volume (♂ > ♀)	Zebra finch, starling, dark-eyed junco
DM volume (♂ > ♀)	Zebra finch
nXIIts volume (♂ > ♀)	Zebra finch, canary, red-winged blackbird
Number of neurons	
HVC and RA (♂ > ♀)	Zebra finch, bush shrike
RA neurons (♂ slightly > ♀)	White-browed robin chat, bay wren, buff-breasted wren
IMAN (♂ > ♀)	Zebra finch
Size of neurons	
Neuronal somata in HVC (♂ > ♀)	Zebra finch, Carolina wren, bush shrike
Neuronal somata in RA (♂ > ♀)	Zebra finch, Carolina wren
Neuronal somata in RA (♂ = ♀)	White-browed robin chat, bay wren, buff-breasted wren
Neuronal somata in IMAN (♂ > ♀)	Zebra finch
Dendritic fields in some HVC neurons (♂ > ♀)	Canary
Dendritic fields in RA (♂ > ♀)	Zebra finch and canary
Dendritic field sizes in RA (♂ = ♀)	Buff-breasted wren
Dendritic fields in IMAN (♂ > ♀)	Zebra finch
Number of neurons with sex steroid receptors	
Cells with androgen receptors in HVC and IMAN (♂ > ♀)[a]	Zebra finch
Cells with androgen and estrogen receptors in HVC (♂ > ♀)	Canary
Cells with androgen receptors in HVC and IMAN (♂ = ♀)	Bay wren, rufous-and-white wren
Connectivity	
HVC neurons projecting to RA (♂ > ♀)	Zebra finch
HVC neurons projecting to area X (♂ > ♀)	Zebra finch
IMAN neurons projecting to RA (♂ > ♀)	Zebra finch
Neurochemistry	
RA activity induced by GABA$_A$ receptor antagonist (♂ = ♀)	Zebra finch
Ascending catecholaminergic and enkephalinergic projections to area X (♂ > ♀)	Zebra finch
Acetylcholinesterase staining in area X (♂ > ♀)	Zebra finch

Source: Balthazart and Adkins-Regan, 2002.

[a] IMAN = lateral magnocellular nucleus of the anterior nidopallium; nXIIts = tracheosyringeal division of the nucleus of the hypoglossal nerve
HVC = high vocal center; RA = robust nucleus of the archistriatum, aka robustus archistriatum; area X = a forebrain nucleus located in the parolfactory lobe

proceeds by trial and error. The sensory-motor stage ends when the bird can reproduce full adult song. In some species, such as zebra finches, song is considered crystallized and is relatively impervious to change, although there are many species of birds that continue to modify their songs and learn new ones throughout their lives. Damage to the recursive loop in zebra finches, especially area X and IMAN, before species-typical song is crystallized results in song abnormalities (Bottjer et al., 1984; Mooney, 1999; Scharff and Nottebohm, 1991; Schlinger, 1998).

FIGURE 4.14 Singing in zebra finches is organized by estrogens but activated by androgens. Only females that are injected with estradiol after hatching and injected with either DHT or testosterone in adulthood show neural development comparable to that of males and display singing behavior. Thus, early exposure to estradiol is necessary for androgens to have the song-activating effects seen in adult male birds. The plus signs indicate the degree of increase in neuron number and size compared with normal females. After Gurney and Konishi, 1980.

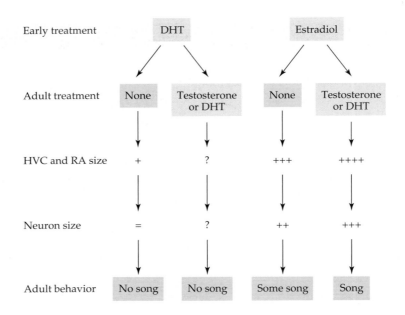

HORMONAL INFLUENCES ON SONG CONTROL CENTERS Because sexual dimorphisms in size of their song control areas are so conspicuous, zebra finches have proved to be an excellent model species in which to study the effects of sex steroid hormones on the neural structures involved in song (Arnold et al., 1987). The HVC and RA of male zebra finches are three to six times larger than those of female conspecifics, and one song control region, area X, cannot even be discerned in females (Nottebohm, 1991; Nottebohm and Arnold, 1976). The larger size of these nuclei in males is due to the larger, more numerous, and scattered neurons in these nuclei (Arnold and Gorski, 1984; Arnold and Matthews, 1988). Although castration of adult zebra finches leads to a reduction in singing, it does not reduce size in the brain nuclei controlling song production. Similarly, androgen treatment of adult female zebra finches does not induce changes either in singing or in size of the song control regions. Thus, activational effects of steroid hormones do not account for the sex differences in singing behavior or in brain nucleus size in zebra finches.

The sexual dimorphisms in brain nucleus size and in the subsequent singing behavior of zebra finches are organized early in development. Adult singing is activated by testosterone acting on the male-typical neural structure (Gurney and Konishi, 1980) (**FIGURE 4.14**). Both male and female zebra finches have been studied, but only the results of endocrine manipulations of females will be presented here. Females treated with DHT soon after hatching and given no endocrine therapy as adults exhibited increased numbers of neurons in the RA and HVC, but these nuclei were approximately the same size as those of untreated females. These females did not sing. If females were injected with DHT post-hatching, then treated with testosterone or DHT in adulthood, the RA and HVC were larger and had more neurons than those of typical females but were smaller and had fewer neurons than those of typical males. These females also failed to sing as adults. Females that were injected with estradiol post-hatching but not treated with hormones as adults did produce some song. In them the RA and HVC were larger in size and had more and larger neurons than those of untreated females, but these brain regions were still smaller and had fewer neurons than those of untreated males. If females were injected post-hatching with estradiol, then treated with either testosterone or DHT in adulthood, the RA and HVC sizes approached those of untreated males, and they sang!

The failure of hormonal manipulations to produce females indistinguishable from males in neural structure size and behavior has provoked the hypothesis

BOX 4.3   *The Organization of Avian Copulatory Behavior*

Birds have been useful models for the study of neural sexual differentiation because they allow researchers to avoid one confounding factor that is present in the study of mammals: treatments that masculinize behavior in mammals usually masculinize the external genitalia of mammals as well. For this reason, researchers found it inappropriate to assume that sex differences in behavior reflect changes in the nervous system. In other words, the sex differences in behavior might simply be due to the changes in external genital morphology (Beach, 1971). One way to resolve the controversy about the contributions of neural and nonneural changes to the development of sex differences in behavior is to discover structural changes in the nervous system that correspond to behavioral differences. Although sex differences in neural structure, neurotransmitter systems, and neuronal numbers have been reported in the mammalian nervous system (Breedlove, 1992), these morphological differences have not been linked directly to the regulation of sexually dimorphic behaviors (Balthazart et al., 1996).

Another approach to this issue has involved studies of hormone-behavior interactions during the development of birds. Males and females of most avian species do not differ in external genital morphology: both sexes have a single cloacal opening. Thus, neural and genital morphological changes are not confounded in birds as they are in mammals (Adkins-Regan, 1987). Studies of avian sexual differentiation of behavior have provided the most convincing evidence that early hormone exposure changes the neural structures that control adult sexually dimorphic behaviors.

The Japanese quail (*Coturnix japonica*) is the avian species most commonly studied to gain understanding of the hormonal bases of mating behavior. Mating behavior is sexually dimorphic in quail. Males strut and crow before and after copulatory mounting (Adkins, 1978). Castration of males reduces these male-typical behaviors, and testosterone therapy restores

them (Adkins, 1975). Females never display copulatory mounting behaviors, and they crow and strut less frequently than males even when they are injected in adulthood with androgens (Adkins, 1975; Balthazart et al., 1983). Generally, estrogenic metabolites of androgens activate copulatory behavior in adult males, whereas androgenic metabolites of testosterone activate the strutting and crowing behaviors (Adkins, 1978; Adkins-Regan, 1996; Balthazart et al., 1985).

If eggs containing male quail embryos are injected with either testosterone or estradiol, the males exhibit fewer male-typical copulatory behaviors as adults than untreated males (Adkins-Regan, 1987). In other words, the males are demasculinized. These demasculinizing effects of testosterone or estradiol occur only prior to day 12 of the 17-day incubation period. If eggs containing female quail embryos are injected with androgens or estradiol, adult female behavior is relatively unaffected (Adkins-Regan, 1987). In other words, the females are neither defeminized nor masculinized by the endocrine manipulations. When female quail in the egg prior to day 9 of incubation were treated with an antiestrogen (a substance that binds to estrogen receptors and prevents natural estrogens from binding), adult copulatory behavior was masculinized (Adkins, 1976). In other words, antiestrogens prevented the demasculinization that is produced by the endogenous estrogens (Balthazart and Foidart, 1993).

Male and female quail do not differ in their concentrations of circulating androgens immediately post-hatching, but females do exhibit higher circulating estrogen concentrations during the last few days before hatching occurs (Balthazart and Foidart, 1993). Taken together, these results suggest that the estrogens secreted from the ovaries normally demasculinize the copulatory behavior of female quail. Male quail apparently do not secrete sufficient quantities of sex steroid hormones to demasculinize their own behavior.

that genes may have direct effects on sexual differentiation in birds (Arnold, 2004; Wade, 2001) (see Chapter 3). In any case, early exposure to estradiol certainly increases sensitivity to androgens in adulthood. This pattern of hormonally mediated organizational effects in birds is very different from that underlying other avian behaviors, such as quail copulatory behavior (**BOX 4.3**). The precise reasons underlying this difference remain unknown. In addition, the source of the early estrogen during standard male development is uncertain. Presumably, the gonads produce androgens or estrogens that normally masculinize male zebra finches. However, castration fails to prevent masculinization of male zebra finches (Adkins-Regan and Ascenzi, 1990). Furthermore, the presence of functional testicular tissue does not masculinize the development of the song system in genetically female zebra finches (Wade and Arnold, 1996).

Significant evidence suggests that the organizational/activational hypothesis that was developed to explain mammalian sexual differentiation accounts for the sexual differentiation of the zebra finch song system:

- Female hatchlings treated with estradiol undergo substantial masculinization of song neural circuitry and singing behavior, as we have just seen.

- Male nestlings have significant circulating estradiol concentrations.

- Some aspects of male song circuitry are demasculinized by treatment with a 5α-reductase inhibitor (Balthazart and Adkins-Regan, 2002).

However, compelling evidence that the organizational/activational hypothesis falls short of explaining the sexual differentiation of zebra finch song also exists, as you can see from the following examples:

- Effective masculinizing doses of estradiol are high, often toxic, and some females are not masculinized even by very high doses of estradiol.

- Males castrated as hatchlings sing normally.

- The song control nuclei have few estrogen receptors during early development.

- The sex differences in neuron size and number in the HVC are present by post-hatching day 9, despite the lack of estrogen receptors at that age.

- Treatment of hatchling males with antiestrogens, antiandrogens, or aromatase inhibitors fails to demasculinize the song system or singing behavior.

- Females hatched from eggs injected with fadrozole, an aromatase inhibitor, have testes or ovotestes but still possess female-typical song systems and no singing behavior (Balthazart and Adkins-Regan, 2002).

Taken together, these findings suggest that although hormones can masculinize the song control nuclei of female zebra finches, nonhormonal factors, perhaps specific activation of genes on the Y chromosome, normally induce masculinization of the zebra finch song system (Arnold, 2002; Wade, 2001).

PHOTOPERIOD EFFECTS   Because the incidence of birdsong shows a strong relationship with the breeding season and because most temperate zone songbirds breed in spring or early summer, the possibility of seasonal changes in the brain regions that regulate song was explored (Nottebohm, 1980a,b). Seasonally breeding songbirds such as canaries also display sex differences in song production. Female canaries sing much less frequently than males, and their song is much less complex than that of males. However, the frequency of female singing can be increased to nearly male levels by injecting adults with androgen, which also causes a dramatic size increase in the adult female canary HVC and RA (Nottebohm, 1980a,b, 1989). Male canaries sing more frequently in spring than in winter, and they appear to lose components of their songs after each breeding season and incorporate new components each spring (Leitner et al., 2001). Their song production is mediated by day length, or **photoperiod** (the number of hours of light per day). Day length increases in the spring, the testes grow and secrete androgens, the frequency of singing increases, the song repertoire enlarges, and the HVC and the RA double in size in the laboratory. In autumn, the photoperiod decreases, the testes regress in size, androgen production virtually stops, the frequency of singing decreases, the song repertoire shrinks, and the HVC and RA regress in size as well (Nottebohm, 1989). Of course, these correlations do not establish definitively that day length affects birdsong via androgens. Experimental treatment with testosterone in autumn mimics spring hormonal conditions and supports song production. The seasonal plasticity in behavior appears to reflect seasonal changes in brain morphology induced by activational hormonal exposure (Barnea, 2009; Tramontin and Brenowitz, 2000). Several of the brain nuclei in the birdsong system express androgen and estrogen receptors (Brenowitz, 2008).

photoperiod   Day length, or the amount of light per day.

Estrogens appear to be necessary to activate the neural machinery underlying the song system in birds. The testes of birds primarily produce androgens, which enter the circulation. The androgens enter neurons containing aromatase, which converts them to estrogens. Aromatase is generally localized in neurons lying near other neurons with estrogen receptors in the hypothalamus and preoptic area of songbird brains, as well as in limbic structures and in the structures constituting the neural circuit controlling birdsong (Balthazart and Ball, 1998; Schlinger, 1999). Indeed, the brain is the primary source of estrogens, which activate masculine behaviors in many bird species (Arnold and Schlinger, 1992; Balthazart et al., 2009; London et al., 2009; Remage-Healey et al., 2010; Schlinger et al., 2001).

White-crowned sparrows (*Zonotrichia leucophrys*) display seasonal cycles of androgen secretion and song production but do not exhibit a seasonal cycle of changes in song system nuclear volume (Baker et al., 1984). Studies of canaries in their natural habitat verified the seasonal changes in song complexity in the absence of seasonal changes in the gross anatomy or ultrastructure of HVC or RA (Leitner et al., 2001). The source of the seasonal plasticity in song complexity in these birds remains unspecified.

Melatonin may be one hormone that affects song behavior and adult neuroplasticity. Many species of songbirds display melatonin receptors in neurons comprising the song nuclei (Ball and Balthazart, 2010). Castrated European starlings (*Sturnus vulgaris*) continued to show photoperiod-driven changes in HVC in the absence of testicular androgens, and this response was blocked by implants of constant-release melatonin (Bentley et al., 1999). Recall from Chapter 2 that melatonin is only secreted at night. Thus, a relatively long duration of melatonin secretion corresponds with a long night and short day (i.e., winter). House sparrows (*Passer domesticus*) treated with long nightly durations of melatonin displayed small song nuclei compared with birds treated with short nightly durations of melatonin (Cassone et al., 2008). These results suggest that melatonin may have direct effects that contribute to the effects of steroid hormones on song nuclei volumes.

Courtship Behavior of the Plainfin Midshipman Fish

As described in Chapter 3, there are two very different types of male plainfin midshipman fish (see Figure 3.21). The so-called type I males are large and olive gray, they build nests and guard them, and they attract females to their nests with a persistent humming sound, which has earned these fish the nickname "canary bird fish." These males have high testosterone and 11-ketotestosterone concentrations. Their sonic muscles and the motor neurons that innervate them are large, and the motor neurons exhibit a high discharge frequency matching the rhythm of the sonic muscles' pacemaker cells (about 20% higher than in females or type II males) (Bass, 1996). Importantly, the duration of the vocalizations is modulated by steroids, and the sonic organs of these fish respond rapidly to steroids, suggesting a nongenomic mechanism of action (Remage-Healey and Bass, 2004).

In contrast, the type II males do not build nests, guard eggs, or vocalize to attract females. Rather, type II males are characterized as "sneaker" males. They follow females into type I males' nests and release sperm when the females release their eggs. Because type II males resemble females in size and color, the type I males do not exclude them from their nests effectively (Bass, 1996). The sonic system musculature and innervating motor neurons of type II males are small and resemble those of females (**FIGURE 4.15**). The primary circulating steroid hormone in type II males is testosterone, and that in females is estradiol. Females are physically larger than type II males, but they also do not engage in much vocal behavior (Bass and Remage-Healey, 2008).

Communication requires a sender and a receiver. Hormones not only affect the sender, but can also affect the perceptual mechanisms of the receiver that are nec-

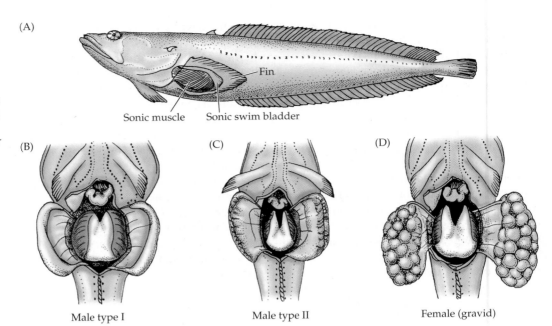

FIGURE 4.15 The sonic organs are used by type I male midshipman fish to attract females to their nests. (A) The sonic organs comprise a pair of sonic structures attached to the swim bladder; contraction of the sonic muscles vibrates the swim bladder like the skin of a drum. The sonic organs of type I males (B) are well developed compared with those of type II males (C) or females (D). The ratio of sonic muscle mass to total body mass is 6 times greater in type I males than in type II males. In contrast, the gonad-to-body-mass ratio is 9 and 20 times higher in type II males and gravid females, respectively, than in type I males. After Bass, 1996.

Sonic muscle   Sonic swim bladder   Fin

Male type I   Male type II   Female (gravid)

essary to respond to the sender's signals (Sisneros et al., 2004). For many species, the peak sensitivity for each sensory modality is closely correlated with biologically important signals. For example, in the túngara frog (*Engystomops pustulosus*) there is a match between the emphasized frequencies in the mating call and the tuning of the frog's two inner ear organs (Ryan, 1985). One can imagine that it could be adaptive to adjust the peak sensitivity of the sensory organs to reproductive stimuli during the breeding season, and perhaps to predator stimuli outside of the breeding season. Such a system has been described in the midshipman fish. Nonreproductive female midshipman fish treated with either testosterone or 17β-estradiol increase their sensitivity to the frequency of male vocalizations (Sisneros et al., 2004). In other words, steroid hormones secreted during the breeding season mediate the seasonal plasticity of the perceptual mechanisms. This sensory plasticity provides an adaptable mechanism that enhances coupling between sender and receiver in vocal communication (Sisneros et al., 2004).

The steroid hormone 11-ketotestosterone is produced only by type I males. This hormone is particularly effective in stimulating development of the sonic musculature and neural circuitry. The endocrine cascade leading to puberty occurs 3 to 4 months earlier in type II males and in females than in type I males, precluding development of the sonic musculature and neural circuitry (Bass, 1996). The existence of two distinct male forms within a population exhibiting marked differences in behavior provides a terrific opportunity to study hormone-behavior interactions (see Chapter 3 and Figure 3.21).

Rough-and-Tumble Play in Primates

In rhesus monkeys and many other mammalian species, males engage in much more play behavior than their female peers throughout development (Hinde, 1966; Paukner and Suomi, 2008; Pellis et al., 1997; Wallen and Hasset, 2009). A number of other play-associated social behaviors are also sexually dimorphic in rhesus monkeys. Males, using specific gestures, initiate play more often than females. Males also engage in more threat behaviors than females. A larger proportion of male play behavior involves simulated fighting or rough-and-tumble play as compared with the play behavior of females. Finally, males engage in pursuit play at higher rates than females (Goy and Phoenix, 1972). To further understand these sex differences in play behavior, as well as other components of primate behavior, a series of studies was conducted on two populations of rhesus monkeys (Goy, 1978; Goy and Phoenix, 1972) and one population of marmosets (Abbott, 1984) treated prenatally with steroid hormones. The studies of rhesus monkeys (Goy, 1978) will be described below.

When pregnant rhesus monkeys were injected with androgens, the external genitalia of their female offspring were masculinized. When the behavior of these pseudohermaphroditic females was compared with that of females and males resulting from nonmanipulated pregnancies, it was found that males engaged in much more threat behavior, play initiation, rough-and-tumble play, and pursuit play behavior than normal females (**FIGURE 4.16**). The pseudohermaphrodites engaged in these behaviors at frequencies that were between the observed rates for males and females (until the age of 4) (Goy and Phoenix, 1972). This sex difference in behavior is not dependent on activational effects of hormones; in other words, it is organized prenatally. This sex difference is also not dependent on the presence of altered genitalia. By a change in the timing of the androgen treatment, juvenile play behavior could be affected independently of any hormonal effects on the external genitals (Goy et al., 1988). Castration or other postnatal endocrine manipulation did not affect the amount of threat, play initiation, rough-and-tumble play, or pursuit play behavior. Interestingly, in order for these sexually dimorphic behaviors to be expressed at all, appropriate social stimulation had to be present during development. Rhesus monkeys that were reared in social isolation with access to only surrogate mothers did not develop the appropriate patterns of play. These results suggest that organization by hormones interacts with environmental factors to produce normal play behavior (Wallen, 1996).

As noted in the introduction to this chapter, human boys and girls also differ in the amount of rough-and-tumble play in which they engage, and there is some evidence suggesting that this difference, too, is organized prenatally by steroid hormones. In one series of studies, aggression was examined in children who had been exposed prenatally to the synthetic progestin medroxyprogesterone acetate (MPA) provided to their mothers to prevent premature labor (Reinisch, 1981). This progestin reportedly has androgenic effects but does

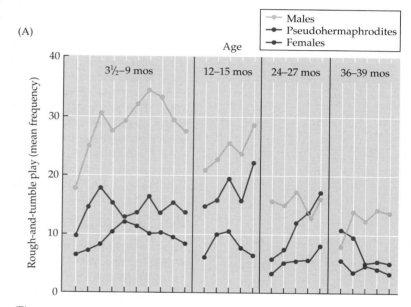

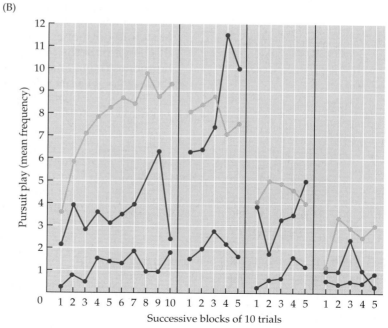

FIGURE 4.16 The frequency of rough-and-tumble and pursuit play is affected by early exposure to androgens. Rates of rough-and-tumble play (A) and pursuit play (B) at different ages are shown for normal males, normal females, and pseudohermaphroditic females treated in utero with androgens. Males engage in these play behaviors more frequently than normal females, but pseudohermaphrodites are intermediate between males and females, indicating that, in addition to the external genitalia, play behavior is masculinized by early androgen treatment. After Goy and Phoenix, 1972.

not usually cause masculinization of the external genitalia at low therapeutic doses; in some instances, prenatal exposure to MPA enhances feminine traits.

Seventeen female and eight male exposed children were compared with their unexposed, same-sex siblings using their responses to paper-and-pencil tests as well as questionnaire data obtained from friends and family members (Ehrhardt et al., 1977). Girls exposed to prenatal progestins were considered ultrafeminine for some traits. They were very interested in clothes and playing child-rearing games and were less often characterized as tomboys by themselves or by their peers than were unaffected girls. Despite this so-called enhanced feminization, girls exposed to MPA engaged in higher-energy play activities and excelled at athletic endeavors as compared with control females. In another study, both males and females exposed to MPA scored higher on aggression on paper-and-pencil tests than their unexposed siblings (Reinisch, 1981). However, although paper-and-pencil tests of aggressive behavior provide interesting data, direct observations of aggressive behavior provide more valid results (see Chapter 9).

Girls born with congenital adrenal hyperplasia (CAH), which results in exposure to high androgen concentrations early in development, also displayed elevated rates of energetic play, as well as initiation of fighting and rough-and-tumble play (Ehrhardt and Money, 1967; Ehrhardt et al., 1968a). In a later study, girls with CAH were found to be masculinized and defeminized in several ways; compared with their sisters, they played more with boy-typical toys, were more likely to use aggression when provoked, and showed less interest in infants than typical girls (Berenbaum et al., 2000). Sex-atypical behavior appeared to be significantly associated with the degree of inferred prenatal, but not postnatal, excessive androgen exposure. Considered together, the evidence suggests that gonadal steroid hormones may contribute to behavioral sex differences, especially in play behavior, among humans and other primates (Collaer and Hines, 1995).

Sex Differences in Human Behavior

We have seen that many sex differences in behavior arise because the neural substrates of sexually dimorphic behaviors are organized by hormones early in development and the behaviors are activated by hormones later in development (Breedlove et al., 2002). The mating behavior of male rodents, for example, is both organized and activated by steroid hormones. Other sex differences, such as rates of rough-and-tumble play in rhesus monkeys, arise only from organizational effects of steroid hormones. Still other behavioral sex differences, such as the electrical discharge patterns of electric fishes, may result only from activational effects of hormones (Landsman, 1991). However, some sex differences in behavior, such as the learning of a sex role in humans, may be unrelated to hormones (**FIGURE 4.17**). Behavioral endocrinologists aim to disentangle the contribution of hormones from the contribution of the environment to determine the cause of such behavioral sex differences.

As noted in Chapter 3, researchers cannot ethically manipulate hormone concentrations in developing humans to observe their effects on brain and behavior. Consequently, the effects of hormones on human brains and behavior must be inferred by observing the outcomes of so-called experiments of nature, situations in which individuals have been exposed to atypical levels of hormones during some developmental period of their lives. Early exposure to MPA provides one example, and several other such conditions were described in Chapter 3. The primary goal of studying the effects of unusual hormone exposures on human brains and behavior is to understand the effects of more typical endocrine events. As we review studies on human gender identity, gender role, and

	Organizational effects	
	Yes	No
Activational effects Yes	Rodent sexual behavior	Yawning in rhesus monkeys
Activational effects No	Primate rough-and-tumble play behavior	Human gender role learning

FIGURE 4.17 Contributions of activational and organizational effects of hormones to behavior Sexually dimorphic behaviors may be organized and activated by hormones, organized but not activated, activated but not organized, or not influenced by hormones.

sexual orientation, it is important to appreciate that at first glance, these studies provide powerful evidence that gender identity and gender role are learned. But they do not rule out the potential effects of early hormone exposure. When a child is born with ambiguous external genitalia, for example, the decision for surgical correction in a male or female direction is not based on the whim of the surgeon; historically, if there was substantial genital development, then a medical decision was made to modify the genitals in the male direction and rear the child as a boy; if there was little genital development, then surgical modifications were made in the female direction and the child was reared as a girl (**BOX 4.4**). The extent of genital development probably covaries with the extent of androgen exposure, so again, the sex of rearing is confounded by early hormone exposure.

As suggested above, the assignment of sex at birth in the case of ambiguous genitalia is a complicated issue requiring parental consultation with trained psychologists and social workers. Since 1993, guidance has also been available from the Intersex Society of North America (ISNA), founded in an effort to advocate for patients and families who felt they had been harmed by their experiences with the health care system. The ISNA recommends that, following consultation, a gender be assigned based upon the gender the child is most likely to identify with after growing up. However, the society recommends that gender assignment should not involve surgery that will "cement" this assignment in newborns. Instead, it is recommended that the choice to make the genitals either male or female, or to perform surgery at all, not be made until the child is old enough to make a mature, informed decision. These suggestions are based on the experiences of those in the community who felt they would have been best served by making their own decisions instead of having choices imposed upon them (also see Box 4.4). Another benefit of delaying a decision is that it allows the individual to speak with others in the intersex community to determine the most appropriate course of action based on the experience of others. This perspective further underscores the complexity of genetic, hormonal, and environmental factors in guiding gender identity and the conclusion that a one-size-fits-all approach is not sensible. A contrast of this patient-centered approach versus a "concealment-centered" model is outlined by the ISNA in **TABLE 4.3**.

Sexual differentiation in humans occurs early during gestation, near the end of the first trimester and throughout the first few weeks of the second trimester of pregnancy. Using the models developed in rodents, dogs, and rhesus monkeys, we can predict that exposure to high concentrations of sex steroid hormones during this time will masculinize and defeminize human brains and behavior, whereas low concentrations of steroid hormones early in development will tend to feminize and demasculinize brains and behavior. Two basic clinical populations have been examined in this regard: (1) individuals with congenital disorders that expose them to unusually high or low hormone concentrations during development, such as CAH, Turner syndrome, 5α-reductase deficiency, and complete or partial androgen insensitivity syndrome (CAIS or PAIS); and (2) individuals whose mothers were treated with steroid hormones during pregnancy for medical reasons (see Chapter 3). Exposure to prescribed hormones almost always occurs prenatally and may involve natural or artificial estrogens (such as diethylstilbestrol [DES]), as well as progestins (such as MPA).

Compared with the animal studies previously described, these clinical studies have many inherent flaws. In animal studies, individuals from inbred strains of genetically identical animals can all be treated with equal amounts of steroid hormones at the same time during development and examined under standard test conditions. The human clinical studies, on the other hand, are summaries of individual cases that may differ in the severity and timing of the disorder, or in the type, dose, and timing of the exposure to prescribed steroid hormones. Often the effects of prescribed hormones are confounded with the effects of the medical

BOX 4.4   *Ambiguous Genitalia: Which Course of Treatment?*

As we saw in Chapter 3, there are occasional developmental anomalies in sexual differentiation that result in ambiguous external genitalia at birth. Prior to the twentieth century, intersex individuals received no surgical treatment as newborns, and some earned their living displaying their bodies in sideshows. The figures (next page) show one such "bearded lady," Marie-Madeleine Lefort, in youth and in old age. Lefort, who possessed masculine and feminine traits, worked in carnivals throughout Europe in the 1800s (Dreger, 1998). It later became standard practice to surgically alter ambiguous genitalia shortly after birth, but the decisions involved in such procedures are far from simple.

Most studies, including those described in this book, include large numbers of subjects in an effort to ensure that their findings will be generalizable to many individuals. In medical settings, physicians often base treatment decisions on guidelines that emerge from clinical trials that sometimes include thousands of patients. Sometimes this is impractical, however, because particular conditions occur only rarely. Physicians study rare cases in depth and sometimes publish their findings as "case studies" or "case histories," which preserve patients' confidentiality and sometimes present hypotheses about the causes of a condition and the effectiveness of a given treatment.

It is fairly rare when a baby is born with ambiguous genitalia and physicians and parents must make treatment decisions based on a body of knowledge that has been gleaned from only a small number of cases. Although it is relatively easy to debate this issue from the comfort of the classroom, in the clinical setting a decision must be made quickly and in an emotionally charged atmosphere.

What are the options? One can determine the newborn's genetic sex and make surgical (and later endocrine) alterations so that the external genitalia match the genetic sex. This strategy assumes that genetic sex is supreme in determining psychosexual attributes such as gender identity or gender role. In contrast, one might assume that prenatal hormonal effects on the brain are reflected in genital development. According to this view, if the genitalia appear more female- than male-typical, then corrective surgery that enhances the female genital characteristics should be performed, and the individual should be raised as a female, and vice versa if the genitalia appear more male- than female-typical. These courses of action would be pursued regardless of chromosomal or gonadal sex and would be based solely on genital appearance—an "anatomy is destiny" approach that assumes that environmental (i.e., rearing) factors are more important than early biological factors in determining psychosexual development. Alternatively, and more often, parents wait until the affected individual grows up and let the child choose to have surgery or not.

So imagine you are the physician working in the maternity ward, and a beautiful baby has been born with atypical genitalia. The parents are asking you what they should do. Until recently, virtually all physicians opted for the easiest surgical procedure and rearing the child in a sex-specific manner that matched the altered genitalia, regardless of chromosomal sex; and these decisions were based on the classic and influential work of Dr. John Money and his colleagues at The Johns Hopkins University. Money's work on individuals born with ambiguous genitalia (reviewed in Money and Ehrhardt, 1972; follow-up studies are discussed in Money et al., 1986, and Money and Norman, 1987) had convinced him that babies are born neutral with respect to psychosexual development: if a child is raised unambiguously as one sex or the other, that child will develop a gender identity to match the sex assignment. Of course, for the sex of rearing to be unambiguous, the genitals must match the assigned sex. One classic case, now known as the "John/Joan case," provided some of the strongest possible evidence for Money's position. But that case has received much scrutiny (including a feature in *Rolling Stone* magazine [Colapinto, 1997]) because the conclusions drawn in Money's original case study (Money and Ehrhardt, 1972) differ sharply from those of a follow-up study reported nearly 25 years later (Diamond and Sigmundson, 1997).

The original case study described a little boy, given the pseudonym *John*, who had his penis severely damaged during circumcision at 8 months of age; essentially, the penis was burned almost completely off. John was brought to Johns Hopkins Hospital several months later for a consultation, and it was decided that he should be reared as a girl (called "Joan" in the literature). A complete penectomy was performed: at the time, reconstructive penile surgery had not yet been (and still has not been) perfected. The fact that John was genetically male and had been born with typical male genitalia made his case a particularly strong clinical test of the "sex-of-rearing" hypothesis. He also had a twin brother who could serve as a sort of "baseline control" in assessment of the treatment's success. John became Joan at 17 months of age, which was, according to Dr. Money, within an acceptable window of "early re-assignment." A series of follow-up reports indicated that Joan had successfully adopted a female gender identity, although she clearly displayed many "tomboyish" traits such as "abundant physical energy" and a "high level of activity" and was "often the dominant one in a girls' group" (Money and Ehrhardt, 1972). Around the time of puberty, Joan and her family decided to end her participation in the study, and no more follow-up examinations were conducted by the Johns Hopkins research group.

Diamond and Sigmundson (1997) presented a startling report that, 25 years after the original report, Joan was living as a man

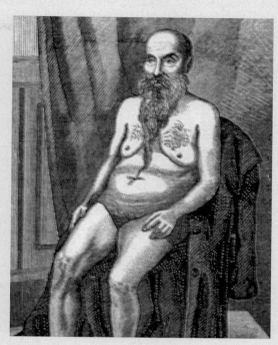

Courtesy of the Wangensteen Historical Library, University of Minnesota, Minneapolis, MN.

who had had reconstructive surgery with a penile prosthesis, was married to a woman, and was a father to adopted children. In other words, his gender role and identity were firmly male. Known again in the literature as "John," he also reported that he had experienced substantial mental anguish during childhood and adolescence and a growing sense that he was not a girl. These feelings culminated in a decision at age 14 to reverse his gender role and identity. The authors of this follow-up study claimed that this outcome showed that biological factors are extremely powerful in psychosexual development. Essentially, Diamond and Sigmundson's report was the last installment in a long series of doctrinal debates on this topic between Drs. Money and Diamond about the primacy of environmental versus biological factors in psychosexual development (Zucker, 1996). Tragically, both twin brothers committed suicide, suggesting that John struggled, even with life as a male.

Clearly, there is a strong interaction between biological and environmental factors in determining psychosexual development, and the truth is likely to lie somewhere in between the two extreme positions. Unfortunately, this is not particularly helpful to physicians and parents agonizing over how to help babies born with ambiguous genitalia to attain the best quality of life. Those of us who are used to conducting experimental studies never rely on a single incident or an "N of 1" (Favreau, 1993) to draw a firm conclusion. Additional studies on human psychosexual development are being conducted to help inform sound clinical decisions in cases of anomalous sexual differ-

entiation. Thus, it is essential to understand the base rate of behavioral outcomes. Some percentage of people who do *not* undergo sexual reassignment surgery tragically also commit suicide. The contented sex-assigned people typically do not. Only the dramatic cases such as John's make the news and, as such, may influence the perceptions that this is a common outcome in the absence of critical evidence.

The two options for treatment presented above suggest an acceptance of the division of humanity into only two sexes and an assumption that making individuals fit into one of the two "normal" categories is a desirable goal of the medical profession. A third option is more daring and has rarely been chosen in the past 40 years: that is, do nothing, in the belief that intersexuality is not an "error" but simply unusual. Recently, vocal spokespersons for intersex individuals have expressed hostility toward surgical treatments. The imposition of "normality" by surgical means is often seen in hindsight as a judgmental assertion of abnormality, and intersex individuals demand acceptance as born. This position was declared most elegantly by an anonymous author who noted, "I was born whole and beautiful, but different. The error was not in my body, nor in my sex organs, but in the determination of the culture, carried out by physicians with my parents' permission, to erase my intersexuality. 'Sex error' is no less stigmatizing than 'defect' or 'deficiency.' Our path to healing lies in embracing our intersexual selves, not in labeling our bodies as having committed some 'error.'"

TABLE 4.3 *Shifting the paradigm of intersex treatment*

Key points of comparison	Concealment-centered model	Patient-centered model
What is intersex?	Intersex is a rare anatomical abnormality which is highly likely to lead to great distress in the family and great distress for the person with an intersex condition. Intersex is pathological and requires immediate medical attention.	Intersex is a relatively common anatomical variation from the "standard" male and female types; just as skin and hair color vary along a wide spectrum, so does sexual and reproductive anatomy. Intersex is neither a medical nor a social pathology.
Is gender determined by nature or nurture?	Nurture. Virtually any child can be made into a "boy" or a "girl" if you just make the genitals look convincing. It doesn't matter what the genes, brain, hormones, and/or prenatal life are/were like.	Both, surely, but that isn't the point. The point is that people with intersex conditions ought to be treated with the same basic ethical principles as everyone else—respect for their autonomy and self-determination, truth about their bodies and their lives, and freedom from discrimination. Physicians, researchers, and gender theorists should stop using people with intersex conditions in "nature/nurture" experiments or debates.
Are intersexed genitals a medical problem?	Yes. Untreated intersex is highly likely to result in depression, suicide, and possibly "homosexual" orientation. Intersexed genitals must be "normalized" to whatever extent possible if these problems are to be avoided.	No. Intersexed genitals are not a medical problem. They may signal an underlying metabolic concern, but they themselves are not diseased; they just look different. Metabolic concerns should be treated medically, but intersexed genitals are not in need of medical treatment. There is no evidence for the concealment paradigm, and there is evidence to the contrary.
What should be the medical response?	The correct treatment for intersex is to "normalize" the abnormal genitals using surgical, hormonal, and other technologies. Doing so will eliminate the potential for parents' psychological distress.	The whole family should receive psychosocial support (including referrals to peer support) and as much information as they can handle. True medical problems (like urinary infections and metabolic disorders) should be treated medically, but all non-essential treatments should wait until the person with an intersex condition can consent to them.
When should treatments designed to make a child's genitals look "normal" be done?	As soon as possible because intersex is a psychosocial emergency. The longer you wait, the greater the trauma.	ONLY if and when the intersexed person requests them, and then only after she or he has been fully informed of the risks and likely outcomes. These surgeries carry substantial risks to life, fertility, continence, and sensation. People with intersex conditions should be able to talk to others who have had the treatments to get their views.
What is motivating this treatment protocol?	The belief that our society can't handle genital ambiguity or non-standard sexual variation. If we don't fix the genitals, the child with an intersex condition will be ostracized, ridiculed, and rejected, even by his or her own parents.	The belief that the person with an intersex condition has the right to self determination where her or his body is concerned. Doing "normalizing" surgeries early without the individual's consent interferes with that right; many surgeries and hormone treatments are not reversible. The risks are substantial and should only be taken if the patient has consented.
Should the parents' distress at their child's condition be treated with surgery on the child?	Yes, absolutely. Parents can and should consent to "normalizing" surgery so that they can fully accept and bond with their child.	Psychological distress is a legitimate concern and should be addressed by properly trained professionals. However, parental distress is not a sufficient reason to risk a child's life, fertility, continence, and sensation.
How do you decide what gender to assign a newborn with an intersex condition?	The doctors decide based on medical tests. If the child has a Y chromosome and an adequate or "reconstructable" penis, the child will be assigned a male gender. (Newborns must have penises of 1 inch or larger if they are to be assigned the male gender.)	The parents and extended family decide in consultation with the doctors. This approach does not advocate selecting a third or ambiguous gender. The child is assigned a female or male gender but only after tests (hormonal, genetic, diagnostic) have been done, parents have had a chance to talk with other parents and family members of children with intersex conditions, and the entire family has been offered peer support.

This section is continued on facing page.

TABLE 4.3 *Shifting the paradigm of intersex treatment* (continued)

Key points of comparison	Concealment-centered model	Patient-centered model
How do you decide what gender to assign a newborn with an intersex condition?	If the child has a Y chromosome and an inadequate or "unreconstructable" penis according to doctors, the child will be assigned a female gender and surgically "reconstructed" as such. If the child has no Y chromosome, it will be assigned the female gender. The genitals will be surgically altered to look more like what doctors think female genitals should look like. This may include clitoral reduction surgeries and construction of a "vagina" (a hole).	We advocate assigning a male or female gender because intersex is not, and will never be, a discreet biological category any more than male or female is, and because assigning an "intersexed" gender would unnecessarily traumatize the child. The doctors and parents recognize, however, that gender assignment of infants with intersex conditions as male or female, as with assignment of any infant, is preliminary. Any child may decide later in life to change their gender assignment; but children with intersex conditions have significantly higher rates of gender transition than the general population, with or without treatment. That is a crucial reason why medically unnecessary surgeries should not be done without the patient's consent; the child with an intersex condition may later want genitals (either the ones they were born with or surgically constructed anatomy) different than what the doctors would have chosen. Surgically constructed genitals are extremely difficult if not impossible to "undo," and children altered at birth or in infancy are largely stuck with what doctors give them.
Who should counsel the parents when a child with an intersex condition is born?	Intersex is a psychosocial emergency that can be alleviated by quick sex assignment and surgery to reinforce the assignment. Professional counseling is suggested but typically not provided. Peer counseling is typically not suggested or provided.	Intersex is a community and social concern requiring understanding and support. Counseling should begin as soon as the possibility of intersex arises and/or as soon as the family needs it. Professional counselors trained in sex and gender issues, family dynamics, and unexpected birth outcomes should be present. Families should also be actively connected with peer support.
What should the person with an intersex condition be told when she or he is old enough to understand?	Very little, because telling all we know will just lead to gender confusion that all these surgeries were meant to avoid. Withhold information and records if necessary. Use vague language, like "we removed your twisted ovaries" instead of "we removed your testes" when speaking to a woman with AIS.	Everything known. The person with an intersex condition and parents have the right and responsibility to know as much about intersex conditions as their doctors do. Secrecy and lack of information lead to shame, trauma, and medical procedures that may be dangerous to the patient's health. Conversely, some people harmed by secrecy and shame may avoid future health care. For example, women with AIS may avoid medical care including needed hormone replacement therapy.
What's wrong with the opposing paradigm?	Parents and peers might be uncomfortable with a child with ambiguous genitalia. Social institutions and settings like locker rooms, public restrooms, daycare centers, and schools will be brutal environments for an "abnormal" child. The person with an intersex condition might later wish that her or his parents had chosen to have her or his genitals "normalized".	The autonomy and right to self determination of the person with an intersex condition is violated by the surgerycentered model. In the concealment model, surgeries are done without truly obtaining consent; parents are often not told the failure rate of, lack of evidentiary support for, and alternatives to surgery. Social distress is a reason to change society, not the bodies of children.
What is the ideal future of intersex?	Elimination via improved scientific and medical technologies.	Social acceptance of human diversity and an end to the idea that difference equals disease.
Who are the proponents of each paradigm?	John Money and his followers, most pediatric urologists and pediatric endocrinologists, and many gynecologists and other health care practitioners.	Intersex activists and their supporters, ethicists, some legal scholars, medical historians, and a growing number of clinicians.

Source: Alice Dreger, the Intersex Society of North America.

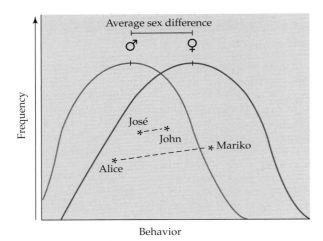

FIGURE 4.18 Average sex differences in behavior often reflect significant overlap between the sexes. There are often greater differences in behavior between individuals of the same sex (e.g., between Alice and Mariko in the figure) than between individuals of the opposite sex (e.g., between John and Mariko in the figure).

condition (e.g., toxemia) that prompted treatment of the mother in the first place. Furthermore, parental expectations may have an effect (see Box 4.4).

It is important to remember that there is more variation *within* each sex than *between* the sexes for virtually all human behaviors (**FIGURE 4.18**). That is, there is considerable overlap between males and females for most behaviors. With a sufficiently large sample size, however, relatively small differences in the performance or the frequency of a given behavior can be statistically significant, and these differences are reported in the scientific and popular presses as "significant sex differences." Because there is often more variation within each sex than between the sexes, it is appropriate to talk about the "effect size," a measure of the variation between sexes corrected for the variation within each sex (Collaer and Hines, 1988; Forger, 1998; but see Cahill, 2006). The effect size is "moderate" when the average difference between the sexes is about half the size of the standard deviation of the scores within each sex (**TABLE 4.4**). For example, the sex difference in height between 16-year-old male and female humans has a moderate effect size (Collaer and Hines, 1988; Kimura, 1992). We will typically be discussing only slight behavioral sex differences as we discuss humans; this is very different from the research strategy using animal models in which only one sex displays a particular behavior. These caveats should be borne in mind as we discuss what these studies have revealed.

gender role The collection of behaviors and attitudes that are considered appropriate or normal within a specific culture for each sex.

Gender Role

The most prominent behavioral sex differences between men and women are observed in gender role, gender identity, and sexual orientation/sexual preference. Most, but certainly not all, women assume a feminine gender role, perceive themselves as female, and are sexually attracted to men. Similarly, most, but not all, men assume a masculine gender role, perceive themselves as male, and are sexually attracted to women. Estimates of the number of individuals who do not fall into these categories vary.

Every society has a set of expectations for the behavior of males and females. Children learn these expectations through their play activities and through shaping by their parents, caregivers, siblings, and peers. Young males may be scolded because "boys don't cry," or a young girl may be disciplined more harshly for fighting at school than her brother. The assumption of culturally based behavioral patterns that are specific to one's own sex is the adoption of a **gender role**. Gender roles are learned early in life, and it is difficult to reverse this early learning. For example, among the Nuer people of western Africa, the men tend cattle and the women cook meals (Evans-Pritchard, 1963). Men never cook in this society, and women never work with livestock. For these two tasks, the gender roles are distinct: cooking is considered a feminine gender role, whereas tending cattle is considered a masculine gender role. In North American society, gender roles are less distinguished by occupation than they were 30 years ago, but they still exist. Because gender roles vary substantially among

TABLE 4.4	*Effect size for behavioral sex differences in humans*
Behavior	**Approximate effect size**[a]
Aggression	Moderate (♂ > ♀)
Rough-and-tumble play	Moderate–large (♂ > ♀)
Childhood activity levels	Moderate–large (♂ > ♀)
Overall verbal abilities	Negligible–small (♂ < ♀)
Speech production	Small (♂ < ♀)
Verbal fluency	Moderate (♂ < ♀)
Perceptual speed	Moderate (♂ < ♀)
3-D visual rotation	Large (♂ > ♀)
2-D visual rotation	Small (♂ > ♀)
Spatial perception	Small–moderate (♂ > ♀)
Overall quantitative abilities	Small–moderate (♂ > ♀)
Quantitative problem solving	Small–moderate (♂ > ♀)

Sources: After Collaer and Hines, 1988; data from J. Cohen, 1977; Forger, 1998; Kimura, 1992.

[a]Effect sizes of ≥0.8 standard deviations are considered large, of ~0.5 standard deviations, moderate; of ~0.2, small; and of <0.2, negligible.

human cultures and over time in the same culture, it has sometimes been assumed that gender roles are entirely mediated by environmental factors. Nonetheless, subtle influences of early endocrine conditions on subsequent gender roles can be demonstrated.

Girls born with CAH, for example, display varying degrees of masculinization at birth. Typically, the endocrine dysfunction can be managed by exogenous hormone treatment and the masculinized genitalia can be surgically corrected. However, these girls display some degree of behavioral masculinization; as described by their siblings and parents, as well as in self-reports, they

- engage in increased physical activity with higher levels of rough-and-tumble play;

- are characterized as "tomboys";

- prefer male playmates;

- prefer male-typical to female-typical toys;

- engage in fewer games of simulated maternal behaviors;

- display reduced interest in infant care;

- are less likely to be interested in hairstyles, makeup, or jewelry;

- engage in fewer fantasies about marriage and maternity, as compared with their unaffected sisters (Ehrhardt and Baker, 1974; Ehrhardt et al., 1968a,b).

Remember that no such study can be conducted in an "unbiased" way, because the parents, and often the child, know that there was a hormone dysfunction that required surgical modification of the genitalia. This knowledge may lead to subtle ambiguities in perception of the individual's gender and may result in exaggerated reports of masculine behavior.

Researchers addressed the issue of parental bias by secretly observing unsupervised play sessions among girls with CAH and their unaffected sisters and first cousins (Hines, 2004; Hines and Kaufman, 1994). The play behavior of CAH girls was significantly masculinized. In other words, the CAH girls played with toys typically preferred by boys. Given a choice of transportation and construction toys, books, board games, dolls, or kitchen supplies, CAH girls preferred to play with the toys generally preferred by boys and avoided by their unaffected female relatives. Of course, this preference for masculine toys could still reflect the biases of the parents or other environmental influences. However, one might expect that parents would be as likely to encourage feminine preferences in toys for their CAH daughters as for their unaffected daughters.

In the draw-a-person test (a psychological test during which a child is asked to draw a person; drawing a person of the same sex is considered an indication of satisfaction with gender role), both females and males with CAH drew the sex-appropriate picture (Hines, 1982). This was typically viewed as a good outcome by their parents. Incidentally, boys exposed to high prenatal androgen concentrations engaged in higher physical activity levels and more rough-and-tumble play, and were more likely to excel in aggressive sports, than their unaffected brothers (Money and Ehrhardt, 1972). Although one may quibble about the relevance of the gender role identifiers used in this study 25 years ago to discriminate boys from girls (e.g., preference for dolls as play objects), a subset of the results is strikingly similar to the behavioral data obtained with early androgen treatment of female rhesus monkeys (Goy and Phoenix, 1972) and more recent data in vervet monkeys (Alexander and Hines, 2002).

Imperato-McGinley and her colleagues (Imperato-McGinley et al., 1974, 1979b) described a group of Central American males in whom an adolescent gender role change appears to be common. In the Santo Domingo region of the Dominican Republic live several families with a high incidence of 5α-reductase deficiency. The affected individuals are XY chromosomal males who lack 5α-reductase, the enzyme that converts testosterone to DHT (Savage et al., 1980). These individuals have ambiguous external genitalia and small, undescended testes at birth. They are generally reared as girls until puberty, when testosterone masculinizes their bodies and genitalia (see Figure 3.17). Most individuals with this condition successfully switch gender role from female to male at puberty. Of the 21 individuals studied in the original reports, only 2 retained the female gender role, and one of these was known to frequent a local female prostitute. Because these individuals were exposed to testosterone during development and puberty, the authors of the study argued that hormones are more powerful than rearing in determining gender role.

Before this interpretation of the supremacy of hormonal factors over rearing conditions can be accepted, however, the process of change and the particular developmental and cultural backgrounds of these individuals must be carefully examined. In the Dominican Republic, these individuals have been given the colorful Spanish name *guevedoces*, which literally translates into "eggs at 12." In Papua New Guinea, the frequency of individuals with 5α-reductase deficiency is also relatively high, and this population has also been the subject of study (Herdt and Davidson, 1988). Individuals in the Papua New Guinea study population with 5α-reductase deficiency also apparently undergo successful change in gender identity and develop a heterosexual male sexual orientation after puberty. The pidgin nickname for these individuals is *turnim-man* (Herdt and Davidson, 1988). The assignment of a special nickname for this syndrome in both cultures suggests that the nature of 5α-reductase deficiency is well known, and it is possible that rearing was not unambiguously female for these individuals. Furthermore, these individuals may have been motivated to switch gender roles because of the greater prestige and power afforded to males as compared with females in both societies.

As we have seen, early androgen exposure seems to result in male-like patterns of play. These findings occur cross-culturally and among different species (Goy and Phoenix, 1972; Hines, 1982; Meany, 1988; Pellis et al., 1997). However, virtually all other aspects of gender role agree with the sex of rearing. For example, boys (Meyer-Bahlburg et al., 1977) and girls (Ehrhardt et al., 1977) that were exposed in utero to MPA, an artificial progestin with androgenic effects, were completely satisfied with the male and female gender role, respectively.

Gender Identity

The process by which individuals come to view themselves as either male or female reflects the development of **gender identity**. Gender identity has generally been considered by clinicians to be irreversibly established by 2 years of age (Green, 1987; Money, 1988; Money and Ehrhardt, 1972; Wisniewski et al., 2001; but see Diamond, 1996, and Diamond and Sigmundson, 1997, for opposing views) (see also Box 4.4). To what extent is gender identity the result of parental influences and cultural expectations, and to what extent is it the result of perinatal hormonal influences?

Until recently, it was generally accepted that the sex of rearing is the dominant feature mediating gender identity, that is, that the gender identity of children reflects the sex of rearing regardless of early endocrine environment. For example, girls born with CAH often display clitoral enlargement to the extent that visual assignment of sex at birth is difficult. Generally, the genitalia are corrected surgically and sex is assigned by the parents as female, and previous studies reported that these girls develop normal female gender identity (Ehrhardt and Meyer-Bahlburg, 1981). More recent work reports that girls with CAH exhibit an increase in cross-gender identification independent of gender role (Paterski et al., 2015). Increased cross-gender identification in girls with CAH may be more prevalent in developing

gender identity   The psychological self-perception of being either male or female.

countries where diagnosis and the beginning of cortisone treatment (a treatment to reduce adrenal androgen production) is delayed, suggesting a potential contribution of postnatal androgen exposure to gender identity (Chowdhury et al., 2015). These new findings suggest that a more informed approach is necessary when considering sex assignment and that delaying assignment might be appropriate for XX individuals with the highest genital virilization.

A potential problem with the notion that gender identity is primarily the result of parental influences is raised by the studies of *guevedoces* in the Dominican Republic. As described above, these genetic male individuals had been reared as girls and had established a female gender identity but changed their gender identity from female to male when their bodies became masculinized at puberty (Imperato-McGinley et al., 1974, 1979a). Change of gender identity was observed even among a few individuals who had married men in their early teens and then remarried women after puberty. These observations suggest that biological factors—namely, the presence or absence of androgens—mediate gender identity regardless of the sex of rearing. However, this conclusion must be tempered by the same two considerations that pertain to using these individuals to draw conclusions about gender role. First, as noted above, it is not at all clear that the sex of rearing was unambiguously female (Rubin et al., 1981). Because the 5α-reductase deficiency syndrome was so well known in this village, parents may have known that an unusual metamorphosis was possible at puberty, and they may have treated the affected individuals differently from genetic females, preparing them for a gender identity change. Furthermore, the society in this region of the world is strictly sexually segregated, and opportunities for work, education, and so forth are limited for women. Consequently, these individuals may have been motivated by social factors to change their gender identity from female to male. In other cases, changing gender identity is a long and difficult psychological process (Green, 1987). Thus, the extent to which gender identity is mediated by early hormone exposure or parental influences remains uncertain.

In an effort to control for degree of masculinization at birth, two studies were conducted in which chromosomally male infants born with ambiguous genitalia were matched for genital phenotype. Some were raised male and some were raised female; these choices were made according to who the attending physician was, the religious/cultural background of family, and other factors. The children in the first study had congenital micropenis. The other study was of boys with truly ambiguous genitalia resulting from a variety of causes. Gender identity was consistent with the sex of rearing in most cases, and in the relatively rare cases in which dissatisfaction with the sex of rearing occurred, it occurred as often in those raised male as in those raised female (Migeon et al., 2002; Wisniewski et al., 2001).

Sexual Orientation/Sexual Preference

In most cases there is a marked sex difference in erotic attraction among humans: males are generally attracted to females, and females are generally attracted to males. But this is not always true. The process of developing an erotic preference for same-sex partners is as complex as the process of developing an erotic preference for opposite-sex partners (Gorman, 1994). Very little is known about how heterosexuals form sexual attractions, and even less is understood about how homosexuals form sexual attractions. This section has a dual title because the terms used in discussions of this issue connote subtle beliefs about causality. The term **sexual orientation** suggests that homosexuality is the result of biological factors. The term **sexual preference** indicates to some that homosexuality is a lifestyle, a choice of same-sex erotic partners that is learned. The two terms will be used interchangeably here because, as with heterosexuality, both environmental and biological factors are likely to be involved in the development of homosexuality. This statement is based on the observation that monozygotic twins (with identical genes) do not always display the same

sexual orientation The process of developing an erotic sexual attraction for other people. This term suggests that the process is mediated primarily by biological factors.

sexual preference The process of developing an erotic sexual attraction for other people. This term suggests that the process is mediated primarily by learning and conscious choices.

sexual orientation (e.g., Bailey and Pillard, 1991; Buhrich et al., 1991). The evidence suggests that homosexuality, in common with heterosexuality, is a biologically hard-wired trait. There is no evidence that homosexuals "choose" homosexuality as a trait; not surprisingly, there is no evidence that heterosexuals "choose" heterosexuality.

Because erotic attractions typically begin at puberty, sex steroid hormones have been assumed to be involved in their development (McClintock and Herdt, 1996). One common, but largely unsubstantiated, hypothesis about the cause of homosexuality is that the hormone concentrations of homosexuals are different from those of heterosexuals; that is, heterosexual men and homosexual women are attracted to women because of high androgen concentrations (or low estrogen concentrations), and heterosexual women and homosexual men are attracted to men because of low androgen concentrations (or high estrogen concentrations). However, many studies have failed to find any consistent evidence that adult homosexual men or women differ from their heterosexual counterparts in blood concentrations of androgens or estrogens. Some studies have reported lower blood androgen values in homo-sexual than in heterosexual men, other studies have reported no differences, and a few studies have indicated that homosexual men have higher blood androgen levels than heterosexual men (reviewed in Bancroft, 1984; Meyer-Bahlburg, 1984). Similarly, there has been no consistent indication that hormonal imbalances under-lie transsexuality, the feeling in an anatomically typical individual that he or she is actually a member of the other sex (Gooren, 1990).

Some studies have suggested a difference in adult neuroendocrine regulatory mechanisms between heterosexual and homosexual men. For example, the positive feedback response to estrogen treatment was reported to be greater in homosexual than in heterosexual men (Gladue et al., 1984). As we saw in Chapter 3, low doses of estrogens usually have a negative feedback effect on the secretion of gonadotropins in both sexes (Lacroix et al., 1979; Tsai and Yen, 1971). However, treatment with high doses of estrogens evokes a surge of LH and FSH release in women after the initial suppression (a positive feedback response) (Tsai and Yen, 1971). The greater positive feedback response in homosexual men generated substantial interest because the results suggested that the brains, or at least the control mechanisms of gonadotropin secretion, of homosexual men are feminized relative to those of heterosexual men. These results seemed to be in accord with the previous studies of feminization and demasculinization of the neuroendocrine regulatory mechanisms associated with ovulation in rats (see Chapter 3). However, the sex difference in steroid effects on gonadotropin release is obvious in rats (but not in rhesus monkeys) (e.g., see Karsch et al., 1973). Male rats never show positive feedback effects of estrogen treatment un-less they are castrated at birth and do not receive steroid hormone replacement treat-ment. Other studies of humans have noted a positive feedback effect in men under various experimental conditions (Barbarino et al., 1983; Kastin et al., 1972; Kuhn and Reiter, 1976). Several subsequent experiments have failed to replicate the original finding that homosexual and heterosexual men differ in their neuroendocrine re-sponses to estrogen treatment (e.g., Gooren, 1986; Gooren et al., 1984; Hendricks et al., 1989). Thus, it appears that homosexual and heterosexual men cannot be reliably discriminated by their gonadotropin response to estrogen treatment.

If hormones are implicated in mediating human sexual preference, then expo-sure to hormones early in development may be involved. Again, it is not possible to manipulate early hormonal environments, or even to obtain blood samples from a human fetus without substantial risk to its well-being, and animal models are generally of limited use in understanding sexual orientation (Adkins-Regan, 1988) (BOX 4.5). Consequently, experiments of nature must be examined to see whether changes in sexual orientation arise after unusual hormonal exposures. Studies of this type show that individual sexual preference does not necessarily reflect early endocrine events. For example, some XY individuals exhibit partial androgen in-sensitivity and are born with ambiguous genitalia. If they are surgically altered and reared as girls, then these individuals are generally sexually attracted to men; if they are surgically altered and reared as boys, then these individuals are generally sexually attracted to women (Migeon et al., 2002; Money and Ogunro, 1974). Similarly, if XX individuals with CAH are surgically altered and reared as boys, they develop a male-typical sexual orientation; females with CAH who are surgically altered and reared as girls typically develop a sexual attraction to men (Money and Dalery, 1976) (but see below).

An example of hormones affecting sexual preference is observed among the XY individuals with 5α-reductase deficiency discussed above. Despite being reared as girls, and in some cases married to men at an early age, most of these individuals switch gender roles and gender identities after puberty (Imperato-McGinley et al., 1974, 1979a). Furthermore, the vast majority of individuals in this group display an erotic orientation toward women. Again, the sex of rearing may not have been unambiguously female (Rubin et al., 1981).

More recent studies have reported a slightly higher than typical rate of bisexual and homosexual fantasy, or less sexual activity with a partner, in CAH women compared with those without CAH (Wisniewski et al., 2004). Likewise, there is consistent evidence that women with CAH tend to report more sexual attraction to, and encounters with, the same sex compared with non-CAH women (Frisen et al., 2009; Hines, 2011; Meyer-Bahlburg et al., 2008). DES, a synthetic estrogen used to prevent miscarriages, has been reported to cause significant masculinizing and defeminizing effects in nonhuman animals (Hines, 1991), but the extent of behavioral effects of DES in humans remains somewhat controversial. For example, prenatal exposure to DES in humans may slightly increase the incidence of bisexual and homosexual activities to about 25% from a 15%–20% incidence in nonexposed women. Despite this finding, it is important to note that the majority (about 75%) of the women in this study who were exposed to an unusual prenatal endocrine milieu reported exclusively heterosexual behavior (Ehrhardt et al., 1985). Taken together, these studies indicate that prenatal sex steroid hormones may not play a primary role in sexual orientation. However, the incidence of homosexuality and bisexuality among the general population is not really known. The "increase in incidence" to about 25% is based on classic data that have recently been called into question (Kinsey et al., 1948). An alternative perspective would suggest that the early hormonal environment is involved in sexual orientation, but the effects of elevated endogenous adrenal androgen levels or exogenous steroid treatment may not mimic the fetal conditions of high local hormone concentrations or the specific timing necessary for producing an effect.

As noted previously, INAH-3 size is correlated with sexual orientation in adults, but this observation does not provide a biological basis for homosexuality, nor does it suggest any "mechanism" underlying homosexuality. It is possible that homosexual men are genetically determined to have a smaller INAH-3 than heterosexual men. Or the differences in INAH-3 size between homosexual and heterosexual men could be due to organizational influences of hormones. It is also possible that homosexual behavior decreases INAH-3 size (Breedlove, 1997; LeVay, 1991). A study in which male rats were paired with individual ovariectomized females provides support for such a hypothesis (Breedlove, 1997). Some males were paired with ovariectomized females that were hormonally primed, and they engaged in frequent mating behavior. Other males were paired with females that did not receive hormone replacement therapy, and they never mated. The motor neurons in the spinal nucleus of the bulbocavernosus (SNB) mediate penile erection in rats (see Box 4.5). Microscopic sections of SNB tissue from these rats were stained with a Nissl stain, the same histological stain used in human postmortem studies to highlight cell bodies (LeVay, 1991). Adult male rats that had engaged in sexual behavior had smaller neuronal cell bodies and nuclei in the SNB than did noncopulators (Breedlove, 1997). These results indicate that adult sexual behavior can affect neural morphology.

BOX 4.5 *The Spinal Nucleus of the Bulbocavernosus Muscle*

One way to overcome the problems inherent in understanding the functional significance of neural sex differences is to study a sexually dimorphic system with a very simple function. One such mammalian system that has been studied extensively is located in the spinal cord of rats. The spinal motor neurons that innervate the muscles attached to the base of the rat penis are located in a particular position in the spinal cord, and collectively they are referred to as the spinal nucleus of the bulbocavernosus (SNB) (Breedlove, 1992). These neurons control the striated bulbocavernosus and levator ani muscles that are responsible for penile erection in rodents, as well as for the control of the external anal sphincter (**Figure A**). The SNB is larger and has more neurons in males than in females because the SNB in females, and the muscles that control erectile function, are diminished in size or completely absent in adult female rats (Breedlove and Arnold,

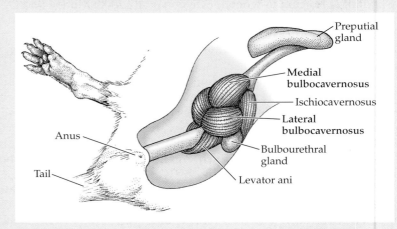

Figure A

1983a,b). Humans also have the bulbocavernosus muscle, but the sex difference is much less pronounced in humans than in rats (Forger and Breedlove, 1986). In men, the bulbocavernosus muscle has a similar function to that in rats, contracting rhythmically during erection and ejaculation. Women retain a bulbocavernosus muscle, albeit smaller and modified in form. The motor neurons of Onuf's nucleus, the human homologue of the rat SNB, are more numerous in men than in women (Forger and Breedlove, 1986).

During fetal development, female rats have bulbocavernosus and levator ani muscles similar in size to those of males, and these muscles, which connect to the base of the clitoris

in females, are innervated by the SNB (Rand and Breedlove, 1987). However, these muscles atrophy and the SNB motor neurons die in females around the time of birth. Androgen treatment spares the muscles and secondarily spares the SNB. Once the muscles have regressed, androgen treatment cannot restore the muscle cells, so the critical period of androgen effectiveness in sparing motor neurons in the SNB is defined by the rate of muscular atrophy. The muscle cells, but not the motor neurons of the SNB, possess androgen receptors during the time of fetal sexual differentiation (Fishman et al., 1990). Thus, androgens act on the neural tissue of the SNB indirectly by preventing apoptosis in the muscles. Androgens, but not estrogenic metabolites of androgens, prevent cell death. This

---

Bilateral lesions of the so-called male nucleus (MN) of the MPOA/anterior hypothalamus caused male ferrets to prefer males in choice tests (Cherry and Baum, 1990). The male nuclei are present only in males and depend on the organizing effects of early androgen exposure. These nuclei were subsequently discovered to process chemosensory information, so lesioned males could not discriminate between male and female odors (Alekseyenko et al., 2007). Presumably, male-typical attraction toward females requires sensory processing of a variety of inputs through the MPOA/anterior hypothalamus.

Studies in African cichlid fish (*Astatotilapia burtoni*) also provide an excellent example of how behavior feeds back to influence brain structures (White and Fernald, 1997). There are two types of adult male cichlids: those with and those without territories. Territorial males are brightly colored, with blue or yellow basic body coloration. In contrast, nonterritorial males are cryptically colored, making them difficult to distinguish from the background and from females, which are similarly camouflaged (**FIGURE 4.19**). Individual males may change from one type to the other. When males become territorial, the GnRH neurons in the POA increase in size; when they lose their territories, their POA neurons shrink (Fernald 2002; Insel and Fernald, 2004). These data indicate that social experience can provoke neuronal size changes (Robinson et al., 2008).

Male

Female

Anogenital distance

Figure B   Photographs courtesy of Nancy Forger.

assertion is based on the observation that genetic XY males with testicular feminization mutation, who lack functional androgen receptors but retain functional estrogen receptors as well as aromatase activity, exhibit a feminine SNB and associated musculature (Breedlove and Arnold, 1981).

Environmental effects can also influence the size of the SNB. Mother rats spend more time licking and attending to the perianal regions of male than of female pups. Anosmic mothers reduced the time spent licking their male offspring, and these males exhibited a 10% reduction in the number of motor neurons in the SNB (Michel and Moore, 1995; Moore et al., 1992). This reduction in SNB size may have contributed to the adult deficits in male mating behavior observed in these males. In utero stress and other factors can also feminize the SNB of male rats (Ward, 1992).

The sex difference in the SNB has been detected in all rodent species examined—except one (Peroulakis et al., 2002). Naked mole rats (*Heterocephalus glaber*) are hystricomorph rodents found in eastern Africa. In the wild these animals live entirely underground in colonies of 60–90 individuals. They subsist on buried tubers. Their reproductive biology is unusual for mammals because each colony has a single breeding female, called the queen, and one to three breeding males. All other individuals in the colony, called subordinates, are reproductively inactive. This social organization is common among eusocial insects, such as ants, bees, and termites, but extremely rare among vertebrates. Subordinate males have very low testosterone concentrations, and they have never been observed to engage in mating behavior. Indeed, no behavioral sex differences have ever been observed among the subordinate individuals of this species (Lacey and Sherman, 1991). The external genital anatomy of subordinate male and female mole rats is indistinguishable (**Figure B**), and there are no sex differences in the perineal muscles or the perineal motor neurons (Peroulakis et al., 2002).

In any case, attempts to study human sexuality are often emotionally charged for a number of reasons, not all of which are rational. Variation in sexuality likely represents variation in underlying biological mechanisms. To remove the moral considerations of studying human sexual orientation/preference, an animal model is required in which all the individuals are reared in identical conditions but the physiological mechanisms can be examined. Domesticated rams (male sheep) naturally display four mating types: exclusively heterosexual, bisexual, no libido, and exclusively homosexual. Among domesticated breeds, about 8% of rams consistently prefer mounting males rather than females (Roselli and Stormshak, 2009) (**BOX 4.6**). Neither male- nor female-oriented males display LH surges akin to those of females after estradiol treat-

FIGURE 4.19   Cichlid fish change cell size in response to social conditions.   When male African cichlid fish (*Astatotilapia burtoni*) change type, their color change is accompanied by a size change in their GnRH neurons. Courtesy of R. D. Fernald.

BOX 4.6   *Hormonal Influences on Mate Choice*

Although there are enormous species differences in the type and extent of sexual dimorphism observed, nearly all animal species exhibit the following sex difference: females are generally attracted sexually to males, and males are generally attracted sexually to females (Adkins-Regan, 1998). Despite the fact that this sex difference in sexual attraction is a critically important component of individual fitness, little is known about the mechanisms that account for it. Studies at the ultimate level of analysis have investigated species preferences and individual partner preferences, but surprisingly few data have been collected that address the problem of sexual partner preferences (Adkins-Regan, 1998). In most cases, mate preferences have been experimentally determined using a two-choice test in which one individual (the "test" individual) can choose between mates A (e.g., a male conspecific) and B (e.g., a female conspecific); usually individuals A and B are tethered in some way so that the test animal can move freely between them. The animal with which the test individual spends the most time is assumed to be the animal it prefers as a mate. Recent evidence suggests that hormones can affect sexual preferences but possibly via an indirect path.

The activational role of hormones on mate preference or mate choice remains ambiguous; when given a choice between a male and a female, gonadectomized test males usually lose their preference to spend time with females. Similarly, gonadectomized test females usually lose their preference to spend time with males. Hormone replacement therapy typically restores the heterosexual preference. Importantly, however, no endocrine treatment in adulthood has been shown to reverse sex preferences. Thus, it seems that the activational effects of hormones function on sexual motivation, rather than on sexual preference.

However, some interesting studies on sheep have revealed that different hormone concentrations might account for differences in sexual preference (reviewed in Roselli and Stormshak, 2009). Researchers at a USDA sheep-breeding facility discovered that up to 16% of male sheep never mate with females during the breeding season. Approximately 6% of these males never show any sexual activity, but another 10% prefer males over females; that is, they are homosexual rams. Homosexual ewes have not been identified. Homosexual rams display a level of estrogen binding in the amygdala that is similar to that of females and much less than that of heterosexual rams (Perkins et al., 1995). (The amygdala is an almond-shaped structure in the brain that is often involved in aggression or reproductive behaviors.) The level of aromatase in the preoptic area of the brain is also lower in homosexual than in heterosexual rams (Perkins et al., 1995). Furthermore, homosexual rams have lower circulating testosterone concentrations than

heterosexual rams (Perkins et al., 1995). As noted in the text, the ovine sexually dimorphic nuclei in male-oriented rams more closely resemble those in females than in female-oriented males (Roselli and Stormshak, 2009). Considered together, these results indicate that steroid hormone concentrations, receptors, and converting enzymes differ between male sheep that prefer females and those that prefer males. It is not known to what extent the difference in the brain is caused by behavior or vice versa. No studies have been conducted on humans to determine whether there is a similar difference in hormone binding between male heterosexual and homosexual individuals.

Studies of the contribution of the organizational effects of hormones to partner preferences were conducted in zebra finches (*Taeniopygia guttata*), which are monogamous (Adkins-Regan, 1998; Adkins-Regan et al., 1997). Female zebra finches were either exposed to early treatment with estradiol (during the first 2 weeks post-hatching) or given no treatment, then housed for the next 100 days in an all-female or a mixed-sex aviary (Mansukhani et al., 1996). These females were then given testosterone in adulthood and tested for "social" partner and sexual partner preferences. Females reared in all-female groups were more likely to have a social preference for other females in a two-choice test, regardless of their early hormone treatment. However, females that were both exposed to early estradiol treatment and reared in an all-female group not only had a social preference for other females but also formed sexual pairs with females in the aviary. Perhaps females must interact with adult males to learn to choose them later in adulthood. In any case, these data suggest that, in contrast to adult hormone manipulations, steroid hormone manipulations early in life can reverse sexual partner preference.

An interesting finding demonstrated the importance of the interaction between environment and genes in the sexual behavior of fruit flies (*Drosophila*) (Zhang and Odenwald, 1995). These flies were genetically manipulated so that a tryptophan/guanine transmembrane transporter gene was activated. The activation of this single gene caused males to vigorously court other males (Zhang and Odenwald, 1995). Mutations that removed this gene appeared to reverse this behavior. Notably, when wild-type flies lacking the mutation were courted by homosexual males, they altered their behavior and sexual preference and actively participated in the male-male courtship behaviors (Zhang and Odenwald, 1995). Thus, in *Drosophila*, both genetic and environmental factors can be shown to affect male sexual preference.

Taken together, these results suggest that hormones interact with environmental conditions to elicit homosexual preferences. This may also be the case for humans, but again, it is difficult to conduct tightly controlled studies with humans.

(A)

(B)

(C)

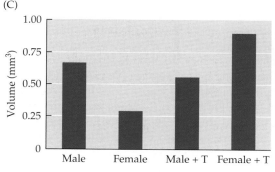

(D)

Behaviors	Female-oriented rams		Male-oriented rams	
	Estrous stimulus ewe	Ram stimulus	Estrous stimulus ewe	Ram stimulus
Precopulatory behaviors[a]	33.4	9.4	2.6	37.0
Mount attempts[b]	0.4	0.1	0	0.4
Mounts	9.2	0.5	0	11.1
Ejaculations	2.8	0	0	0.6

FIGURE 4.20 Rams display four types of sexual preference. Most male sheep prefer females (female-oriented), but some rams are attracted to males and females (bisexual), some show no preferences, and some males exclusively prefer other males (male-oriented). (A) Rams are tested for sexual partner preference in the device depicted showing two male and two female sheep in a four-way stanchion (see insert). (B) A male-oriented ram mounting another male. (C) Sex difference and effects of prenatal testosterone (T) on oSDN volume in sheep. (D) The table depicts behavioral responses of female- and male-oriented rams after exposure to two estrous females and two rams. From Roselli and Stormshak, 2009.

Note: Before partner preference tests, rams were given performance tests with estrous ewes for a total of 9 h. Male-oriented rams did not mount ewes in any test.
[a]Precopulatory behaviors include the sum of: genital sniffs, foreleg kicks, vocalizations and flehmen responses (lip curls).
[b]Mount attempts signify unsuccessful mounts in which both front feet left the ground but the ram did not become firmly positioned on the ewe's rump.

ment or adult female sexual behavior (Roselli and Stormshak, 2009). Although exposure to females induces rapid increases in LH and testosterone in female-oriented males (the so-called ewe effect), male-oriented males do not show this endocrine change in response to males or females. An ovine (sheep) sexually dimorphic nucleus (oSDN) was discovered in the MPOA/anterior hypothalamus of sheep. The oSDN is larger in female-oriented males than in male-oriented males (Roselli and Stormshak, 2009). These data are similar to the results reported for the INAH-3 in men. Importantly, this model system provides the potential tool to allow researchers to ask whether organizational effects of steroids are responsible for these differences or whether adult behavior feeds back to influence sexual preference. At this time, technical limitations do not allow early examination of oSDN size to determine whether it is predictive of sexual partner preference (Roselli and Stormshak, 2009). However, treatment of pregnant ewes with testosterone from days 30–90 of gestation resulted in enlarged oSDN of females (**FIGURE 4.20**), suggesting that prenatal androgens might predispose rams to be attracted to either females or other males.

Although it is challenging to find a direct link between sex differences in early life hormone exposure and sexual preference/orientation, the finding that the ratio of the second digit (the "pointer" finger) to the fourth digit (the "ring" finger) is larger in men than women (Manning et al., 1998, 2003) and reflects early life androgen exposure (Brown et al., 2002) provides a mechanism for associating early life androgens with sexuality in humans. Using this approach, researchers found that finger ratios were masculinized in homosexual women (Grimbos et al., 2010; Williams et al., 2000). In contrast, finger ratios were not different between homosexual and heterosexual men (Grimbos et al., 2010; McFadden et al., 2005). These findings are intriguing because they suggest the possibility that, while prenatal androgen exposure might alter sexual orientation in women, early life androgen exposure might not account for differences in male sexual orientation. It is more likely that neural targets on which androgens act during development might account for sexual orientation in men.

Despite the importance of sexual dimorphisms in brain structure size as gross indicators of sex differences in brain function and behavior, structural differences in neural tissues have not been directly linked to behavior, especially in mammals. These relationships remain correlations, which may or may not be causally linked. The critical questions regarding which features in the brain are necessary and sufficient to account for sex differences in the ability of sex steroid hormones to activate adult sexual behavior remain, for the most part, unanswered (DeVries and Simerly, 2002; DeVries and Södersten, 2009). In addition to studies of nuclear volume, behavioral endocrinologists have examined sex differences in neurochemistry, neural connectivity, enzyme activation, hormone and neurotransmitter receptor distribution, and gene expression in the brains of males and females in an attempt to answer these questions.

Considered together, sexual orientation or sexual preference is the result of a complex interaction between biology and environment, but there is no strong evidence that prenatal steroid hormone exposure directly orchestrates sexual orientation. The development of homosexual erotic attraction remains as mysterious as the development of heterosexual erotic attraction (Gorman, 1994).

Sex Differences in Cognitive Abilities

Sex differences in human brain size have been reported for years (Crichton-Browne, 1880; Swaab and Hofman, 1984), and, as described above, specific differences between male and female humans in the size (volumetric) or shape of certain brain regions have also been reported. These differences in brain structure are subtle but can be readily discerned in most cases (Hampson, 2008; Luine and Dohanich, 2008). Male and female humans certainly behave differently, and if human behavior reflects some manifestation of central nervous system activity or organization, then differences in brain activity or structure are to be expected. But because male and female humans overlap substantially in their behavioral repertoires (see Figure 4.18), any sex differences in the brain are expected to be subtle. Logically, as was the case for birdsong, sex differences in human brain morphology should be found in humans in regions where behaviors that are clearly sexually dimorphic are processed. Thus, an important strategy for studying human behavioral sex differences is to study behaviors that are sexually dimorphic and to map these behavioral differences onto sex differences in brain organization. The roles of the dimorphic brain regions in mediating behavior can then be assessed by examining patients who sustain damage to the designated areas.

It should be emphasized here that there is no direct evidence that the sex differences in brain morphology thus far discovered mediate human behavioral sex differences. Similarly, there is no direct evidence that they do not. A further complication exists, as we saw above in the case of sexual orientation: if brain structural differences that correspond to behavioral differences do exist between males and females, it remains uncertain whether they are the cause or the effect of the behavioral dimorphisms.

With these disclaimers in mind, there are several sex differences in cognitive abilities that are consistently observed cross-culturally and hence are good candidates to be differences mediated primarily by physiological factors, namely, sex steroid hormones. Corresponding sexual dimorphisms in the brain regions that are involved in these cognitive processes have also been found. This section presents a brief review of sex differences in perception and sensory abilities, lateralization of cognitive function, verbal skills, and mathematical and visuospatial abilities among humans (Hampson, 2008; Luine and Dohanich, 2008; reviewed in Velle, 1987).

Perception and Sensory Abilities

Sensation and perception are possibly the most basic cognitive functions. **Sensation** is the initial processing of sensory information as it enters the nervous system through the sensory receptors. **Perception** is the transduction of this sensory information into biologically meaningful information. Sex differences have been widely reported in both sensation and perception. There are many subtle and a few marked differences between males and females in sensory and perceptual abilities.

Three general aspects of sensory and perceptual function have been the subject of research: sensitivity, discrimination, and preference. In a study of sensitivity, an experimental participant is usually presented first with no stimuli, then stimuli are presented and increased in small incremental steps until the person reports a sensory experience. For example, someone may be placed in a dark room and asked to stare at a wall and push a button whenever he or she perceives a pulse of light. The experimenter may initially flash only one or two photons of light but continue to provide stronger stimuli until the participant reliably reports the presence of the light. In studies of discrimination, sensory stimuli that are closely related are presented to the subject and are made increasingly different by the experimenter until the participant reports the presence of more than one stimulus. For example, two cups containing equimolar sucrose solutions may be provided to the person, who should not report any difference in taste. The experimenter then covertly increases the concentration of sucrose in one of the cups very slightly until the participant reports a difference between the two solutions. Preference can be determined in a straightforward manner. For instance, a participant might be water deprived for 24 hours, then provided with cups of saline solution of varying concentrations and asked to sample all of the cups. The experimenter simply records the volume consumed from each cup to determine the preferred concentration.

PAIN   Sex differences in pain responsiveness are common (Berkley, 1997). Although a number of factors can influence pain, including type of painful stimulus, location of pain, age, culture, and menstrual cycle (Mayer et al., 2008), females generally respond with lower thresholds and display less tolerance to painful stimuli than males. The sex difference in pain responsiveness appears especially reliable, albeit small, in cutaneous pain responses (Riley et al., 1999). Women also display greater sensitivity to visceral pain, in terms of both intensity and frequency (Murphy et al., 2009). In women, natural variations in adult hormone levels are associated with pain tolerance, suggesting activational effects of sex steroids in pain perception (Bartley et al., 2015).

The extent to which the sex difference in pain response reflects underlying mechanisms or cultural/learning influences remains unspecified in humans. For example, prolonged painful stimuli engage the endogenous opioid systems, whereas acute, transitory painful stimuli typically do not engage the endorphin system. Using positron emission tomography and a μ opioid receptor–selective radiotracer to examine activation of the opioid system in response to pain, researchers found

sensation   The initial processing of sensory information as it enters the nervous system through sensory receptors.

perception   The transduction of sensory information entering the nervous system into biologically useful information.

FIGURE 4.21 Effect of estradiol on μ-opioid receptor binding and on responses of μ-opioid receptor-mediated neurotransmission to a stress challenge. (Left) Three-dimensional representation of μ-opioid receptor binding in a representative healthy volunteer, superimposed over an MRI image. Binding potential values are represented by the pseudocolor scale in the lower part of the figure. (Right, top) Baseline μ-opioid receptor binding is increased in the thalamus (THA), ventral basal ganglia (NAC), and amygdala (AMY) during times of high estradiol compared with the low-estradiol condition. (Right, bottom) Stress-induced activation of the μ-opioid system was greater in the THA, NAC, and AMY in the high-estradiol condition. From Smith et al., 2006.

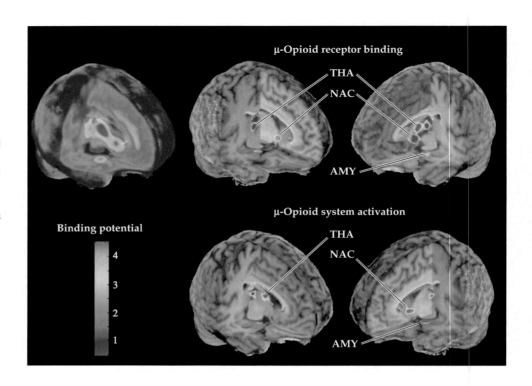

that men exhibited larger opioid system activation than women in the anterior thalamus, ventral basal ganglia, and amygdala (Zubieta et al., 2002). Activation of the μ-opioid system was dependent on menstrual cycle stage, with high estrogen being associated with higher pain tolerance than low estrogen (Smith et al., 2006) (**FIGURE 4.21**). These findings are consistent with the notion that women experience more pain due to reduced opioid system activation relative to men and that this sex difference is due to hormonal state. Men do not always exhibit increased pain tolerance; in contrast to visceral and cutaneous pain, men display more muscle pain than women after exercise (Dannecker et al., 2005). Importantly, psychosocial factors might also account for sex differences in pain (Robinson et al., 2001; Wise et al., 2002). In most cultures, men are expected to tolerate pain more than women, and this gender role may affect results in experimental pain studies. When men are primed with female gender roles, they report greater pain (Fowler et al., 2011).

OLFACTION The olfactory sensory system (the sense of smell) transduces information about airborne chemicals into central nervous system signals. Sex differences have been reported in human olfactory brain circuits and activation patterns, as revealed by functional magnetic resonance imaging (fMRI) (Garcia-Falgueras et al., 2006). Importantly, these differences in activation patterns reflect differences in function, as important sex differences in olfactory sensitivity and odor identification ability exist. Women are approximately 1000 times more sensitive to musk-like odors (e.g., pentadecanolide and oxohexadecanolide) than men. The increased sensitivity of women to these odors begins at puberty and appears to be estrogen-dependent (Koelega and Koster, 1974). Indeed, sex differences in chemosensory detection, when they exist, typically favor women (Doty and Cameron, 2009).

In another study, olfactory stimuli (eugenol, phenyl ethyl alcohol, or phenyl ethyl alcohol alternating with hydrogen sulfide) were delivered to the nostrils of young men and women while their brains were scanned using fMRI (Yousem et al., 1999). The women's group-averaged brain activation maps showed up to eight times more activated voxels (units of brain volume activation) than the men's for specific regions of the brain (frontal and perisylvian regions). Generally, more women than men showed activation. The functional meaning of these results remains unknown.

Olfactory information can also affect mood, and these mood effects may differ between the sexes (Jacob et al., 2001, 2002). For example, Δ4,16-androstadien-3-one, but not other musky odors such as androstenol or muscone, affects psychological state, reducing negative mood and increasing positive mood (Jacob et al., 2001, 2002). Women tended to experience an immediate increase in positive mood when in the presence of a male tester, whereas the responses of men were unaffected by the sex of the experimenter (Jacob et al., 2001). It is not apparent whether these differences are organized or activated by hormones.

For other odors, however, such as amyl acetate, a sex difference appears before puberty; girls are far superior to boys at detecting this odor at low concentrations. Periovulatory women, as well as women in early pregnancy, display enhanced olfactory sensitivity. Menstruating women and women tested late in pregnancy exhibit lowered olfactory sensitivities. Women are better than men at all ages at identifying odors, and this sex difference has been demonstrated in cross-cultural studies (Doty and Cameron, 2009). These consistent and reliable sex differences in olfactory acuity, as well as the variation in olfactory sensitivity observed across the menstrual cycle, during pregnancy, and in individuals with clinical endocrine disorders, strongly suggest that sex steroid hormones influence olfactory sensitivity. For example, a study of women with irregular menstrual cycles showed that these women exhibit reduced olfactory sensitivity compared with women with regular menstrual cycles; fully 20% of the subjects were completely unresponsive to odors, but many of them did not recognize that they possessed a sensory impairment (Marshall and Henkin, 1971). The mechanism by which hormones affect olfactory sensitivity in most people remains unspecified.

An olfactory deficit in one clinical population indicates that olfaction and hormones may be only indirectly related in these individuals. Men with **Kallmann syndrome** possess small testes, are infertile, and are anosmic (cannot detect odors). Their olfactory deficit results from a congenital lack of olfactory bulb development during early ontogeny. Embryological studies have indicated that the hypothalamic neurons that secrete GnRH originate in the olfactory bulbs, then migrate to the hypothalamus (Schwanzel-Fukuda and Pfaff, 1989) (**FIGURE 4.22**). In Kallmann syndrome, the lack of olfactory bulb development interferes with the normal migration of the GnRH neurons, so reproductive difficulties ensue (Schwanzel-Fukuda et al., 1989). Thus, the sensory deficit is not affected directly by hormones in this case but rather by a congenital condition that blocks normal olfactory bulb development as well as normal endocrine function.

TASTE The gustatory sense (taste) provides information to the nervous system about chemicals in solution. On tests of taste perception, women, on average, display more sensitivity than men (Doty, 1997). Typically, a drop of a sweet, sour, salty, or bitter solution is placed on the tongue and subjects are asked to identify the flavor. Solutions commonly used include sucrose, citric acid, sodium chloride, and quinine sulfate (Fikentscher et al., 1977). Women are superior to men in naming tastes and in discriminating tastes, especially bitter tastes (Doty, 1978). The physiological bases for these sex differences in the sensation and perception of taste in humans are unknown. Differential sex steroid hormone concentrations are suspected to be involved, because the sex differences in taste perception arise after puberty, are exaggerated during pregnancy and the follicular phase of the menstrual cycle, and are diminished somewhat after menopause (Doty, 1978; Fleming, 1988; Fleming and Pliner, 1983; Kuga et al., 2002).

Sex differences in taste preferences have also been reported in many species of laboratory animals. In the case of rats, the effects of hormones in mediating this sex difference are well known (Krecek, 1973; Valenstein et al., 1967; Wade, 1972; Zucker,

Kallmann syndrome A congenital condition in humans characterized by the inability to smell and lack of gonadal development, caused by a lack of olfactory bulb development and GnRH cell migration from the bulbs to their normal location in the hypothalamus during early development.

(A) (B)

(C) (D)

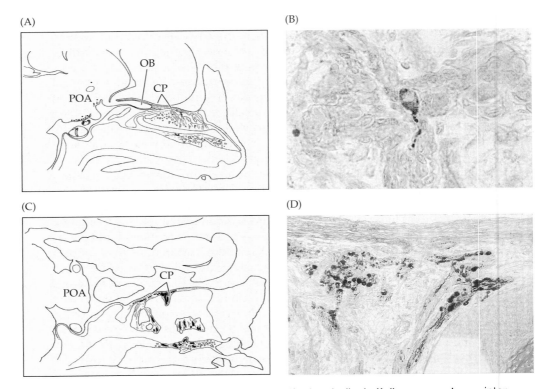

FIGURE 4.22 **Congenital absence of the olfactory bulbs in Kallmann syndrome** interferes with the migration of GnRH neurons to their proper destination in the hypothalamus. (A) Microprojection drawing of a sagittal section through the brain and nasal region of a normal 19-week-old human fetus showing olfactory bulb (OB) development and a normal distribution of GnRH-immunoreactive cells (black dots) in the nose and preoptic area (POA) of the brain. (B) Photomicrograph of the same section at higher magnification, showing a single GnRH-immunoreactive cell in the nose tissue, in a ganglion of the terminal nerve. (C) Microprojection drawing of the same section from another fetus, also 19 weeks old, with Kallmann syndrome. Note that the olfactory bulbs are absent and that no GnRH immunoreactivity is visible in the brain. GnRH-positive cells are seen as dots and heavy black lines in the nose, between the meninges, and on the dorsal surface of the cribriform plate (CP), the bony shelf on which the olfactory bulbs are normally located. (D) Photomicrograph of this brain section, again at higher magnification, shows thick clumps and clusters of GnRH-immunoreactive cells in the nose. Courtesy of Marlene Schwanzel-Fukuda.

1969). Females display estrogen-dependent preferences for sweet tastes (e.g., sugar or saccharin) (reviewed by McCaughey, 2008), organized by the lack of perinatal androgens and activated by estrogens in adulthood.

AUDITION Sound pressure changes are perceived by the auditory sensory system (hearing). There is ample evidence that women are more sensitive than men to sound. Women hear pure tones at lower thresholds than men; this is particularly true at higher frequencies and occurs at all ages (Corso, 1959). Similarly, tolerance for white noise (noise composed of all sound frequencies; an example of white noise is the hiss of an FM radio not tuned to a station) is significantly lower in females than in males. In children ranging in age from 5 to 12, the average noise tolerance level was about 82 decibels (dB) for boys and 73 dB for girls (Elliot, 1971); among college students ranging in age from 18 to 26, the average noise tolerance level was about 83 dB for men and 76 dB for women (McGuinness, 1972). (Recall that decibels are measured on a log scale; a difference of 10 dB represents a doubling of perceived loudness.)

In one interesting study of babies 12–14 weeks of age, the infants were trained by operant conditioning (rewarded for the appropriate behavior) to maintain visual fixation on a white circle (Watson, 1969). Both sexes could perform the task equally well under the right circumstances. In addition to demonstrating that human babies were capable of learning at a much earlier age than previously believed, this study also demonstrated a sex difference in reward contingencies. Girls could maintain visual orientation when a low-frequency tone was provided as the reward but not when a visual stimulus was presented as the reinforcement. Baby boys performed the task better when the reward was visual. This study suggests that at a very young age, females react to auditory information preferentially, whereas males respond better to visual information. One might conclude from this study that physiological factors must mediate these effects in such young children; however, this conclusion must be tempered by the observation that parents interact with baby girls differently than with baby boys and that this difference in interaction begins as soon as the sex of the child is known. Whatever the cause of the reinforcement preference, this auditory propensity in girls may be related to the increased verbal abilities displayed by girls relative to boys (see below). One recent study reported that men preferred women's voices of elevated pitch (i.e., feminized female voices), whereas women preferred men's voices of low pitch (i.e., masculinized male voices) (Jones et al., 2009).

In addition to hearing sounds, the ear also produces faint, echolike noises generated by the cochlea of the inner ear, called click-evoked otoacoustic emissions (CEOAEs) (McFadden, 2002). These emissions are present from birth and remain relatively stable throughout life (in the absence of ear damage). They can be measured by inserting a very small speaker/microphone into the outer ear, sending a series of clicks into the ear, and recording the responses. Women generally have louder CEOAEs than men, a sex difference that is present from birth, suggesting that this phenomenon is organized by early hormone exposure. In support of this notion, earlier studies reported that women with twin brothers had more male-like "quiet ears" (McFadden and Loehlin, 1995), presumably in response to exposure to prenatal androgens. One study reported that homosexual and bisexual women produced weaker CEOAEs than heterosexual women (McFadden and Pasanen, 1998). CEOAEs did not differ among male homosexual, heterosexual, and bisexual men. Importantly, there are few data suggesting that androgens from a male twin affect the brain and behavior of a female twin, or that there is an increase in the prevalence of homosexuality among females with twin brothers. Furthermore, because there is significant overlap in CEOAE volumes between heterosexual and homosexual/bisexual women, it is not possible to predict homosexual behavior simply by measuring female CEOAEs. However, it appears that oral contraceptives masculinize CEOAEs in women (McFadden, 2000), and women with CAH have masculinized CEOAEs whereas 46,XY CAIS females had CEOAEs similar to those of XX females (Wisniewski et al., 2014). This information may be useful in guiding the course of treatment for children born with ambiguous genitalia. As noted previously, treatment is often directed by the degree of masculinization of the external genitalia, which may or may not correspond to the extent of masculinization of the central nervous system. It may be possible to assess the degree of brain masculinization at a very early age with little risk or expense because CEOAEs are already routinely measured to assess hearing in infants (McFadden, 1999).

Nonhuman animals display similar sex differences in otoacoustic emissions. For example, CEOAEs of rhesus monkeys were greater in females than males, in common with humans (McFadden et al., 2006a). The sex differences were greater during the autumnal breeding season than at other times. A slight sex difference in CEOAEs was also reported in sheep; prenatal exposure of females to testosterone reduced (i.e., masculinized) CEOAEs compared with females treated with vehicle only (McFadden et al., 2009). Because female spotted hyenas are normally exposed to high androgen concentrations in utero, a sex difference in CEOAEs was hypothesized to be reduced or eliminated (McFadden et al., 2006b), and experimental results supported this predicted outcome; that is, the sex difference in CEOAEs in hyenas was greatly reduced. Considered together, studies of CEOAEs have high value for assessing phenotypic changes associated with activational hormone effects.

VISION   The visual system transduces light energy into the electrochemical signals of the nervous system. As we have just seen, baby boys find visual information more rewarding than auditory information. With few exceptions, visual acuity is better in men than in women; that is, men see better than women. Sex differences also exist in tolerance of light intensity; on average, women tolerate higher levels of light intensity than men. Conversely, when subjects with good visual acuity are tested, women undergo dark adaptation more quickly than men (McGuinness, 1976). Visual perception, especially in regard to visuospatial abilities, is markedly better among males than females at all ages.

In rats, males have about 20% more neurons in the primary visual cortex than females (Nunez et al., 2000, 2001). In one study, females were implanted with DHT or estradiol capsules on postnatal day 1. Females exposed to DHT showed the male pattern of developmental cell death, whereas females exposed to early estrogen treatment were indistinguishable from normal females in apoptosis (Nunez et al., 2000). These results indicate that perinatal androgens inhibit cell death in the primary visual cortex of rats.

Lateralization of Cognitive Function

The two cerebral hemispheres of the brain are somewhat specialized for processing different types of cognitive tasks (Wisniewski, 1998). In right-handed individuals, generally the right side of the brain specializes in spatial processing, whereas the left hemisphere is better at processing verbal information (Hines, 1982; Kimura and Harshman, 1984). This tendency for cognitive skills to be concentrated in one hemisphere is called cerebral specialization, or **lateralization**. In left-handed indiviuals, this lateralization is less pronounced. Males and females differ in the extent to which cognitive function exhibits cerebral lateralization: males tend to be more lateralized than females. That is, different cognitive functions tend to be more confined to separate hemispheres in males, whereas female cognitive function is generally more evenly distributed between both hemispheres.

Cerebral lateralization can be measured in several ways. Researchers take advantage of the fact that auditory information enters one ear, and visual information enters one visual field, and the information is then processed by the contralateral hemisphere. For instance, auditory signals can be presented via headphones to one ear or the other. Commonly, a brief tone or a word is embedded in white noise, and the subject must indicate as quickly as possible when the signal is present. A variation of this technique involves presenting two signals (words) simultaneously to both ears; again, the subject must react as quickly as possible. The discrepancy in response speed or accuracy between the two ears reflects the degree of lateralization. A similar type of technique using a special apparatus called a tachistoscope to present visual stimuli to only one visual field has been employed to assess lateralization of visual processing.

People typically can detect sounds better with the right ear; that is, auditory processing is better in the left than in the right hemisphere. This facility has been referred to as the right-ear advantage. Perhaps not surprisingly, the processing of language and speech for most people occurs predominantly in the left hemisphere. However, there is a sex difference, with men being much slower, and making more

lateralization   The tendency for the neural substrate for cognitive skills to be confined to one cerebral hemisphere; can also be called cerebral specialization.

mistakes, in responding to auditory information arriving at the left ear than women. Women show less discrepancy than men in both response speed and response accuracy between the two ears and between the left and right visual fields. In other words, the brains of women are less lateralized than those of men for auditory and visual information processing. Additional support for this view comes from the clinical literature on verbal deficits caused by cerebral hemorrhages (strokes) (McGlone, 1980). In general, men who have suffered a stroke on the left side of the brain exhibit verbal deficits, but women with cerebral vascular damage on the left side may or may not exhibit verbal deficits. If men suffer a stroke on the right side of the brain, their visuospatial abilities are affected. In many cases, women who suffer strokes on the right side do not exhibit any obvious decrement in cognitive or behavioral abilities. Thus, the masculine pattern of cognitive processing involves distinct lateralization of function, whereas the feminine pattern exhibits more equal distribution of cognitive function between the two hemispheres.

Prenatal steroid hormones can affect lateralization patterns. Women with Turner syndrome do not secrete steroid hormones prenatally and do not exhibit lateralization of auditory information (Gordon and Galatzer, 1980; Netley, 1977, 1983). These women may have other atypical features, however, such as reduced mental development, which may affect cognitive processing tasks independently of hormones. In contrast, women exposed to DES in utero displayed the male-typical pattern of increased lateralization of auditory and visual information as compared with their unexposed sisters (Hines, 1991).

Sex differences have also been reported in the lateralization of human brain morphology. The left hemisphere is slightly larger and weighs more than the right hemisphere of the human brain, but the weight difference between the two hemispheres is less pronounced in females than in males. The two hemispheres of the brain communicate with each other through several fiber pathways; one of these links is the corpus callosum. Sex differences in the size and shape of the corpus callosum, detected by magnetic resonance imaging and other techniques, suggest a neuroanatomical correlate that could account for the sex differences in lateralization of cognitive function (**FIGURE 4.23**), but there are many conflicting reports that fail to find a morphological sex difference in the corpus callosum (Allen et al., 1991; Crichton-Browne, 1880; deLacoste-Utamsing and Holloway, 1982; deLacoste et al., 1986; Wada, 1976).

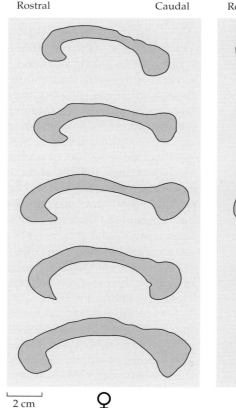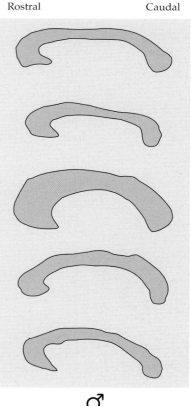

Rostral   Caudal   Rostral   Caudal

♀   ♂

2 cm

FIGURE 4.23 **Possible sex difference in the human corpus callosum** is shown in these drawings based on midline cross sections. In females, the caudal portion of the corpus callosum is more bulbous than in males. It has been suggested that some sex differences in the lateralization of cognitive function might be accounted for by differential numbers of axons in the caudal corpus callosum (splenium). Because this section of the corpus callosum connects the occipital lobes, which process visual information, sex differences in visual processing have also been attributed to sexual dimorphism in this structure. These attributions are controversial. After deLacoste-Utamsing and Holloway, 1982.

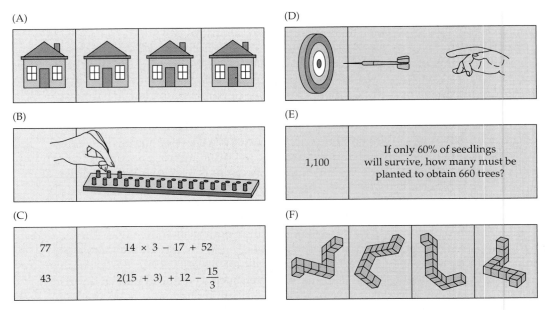

FIGURE 4.24 Performance on certain tasks favors one sex over the other. Specifically, women tend to outperform men on tests of perceptual speed, such as (A) finding the match to the house on the far left as quickly as possible. Women also do better than men in manual tasks that require fine motor coordination, such as (B) placing pegs on a board as quickly as possible. Women also excel over men on mathematical calculations (C). Men, on the other hand, are more accurate than women in target-directed motor skills such as catching a ball or (D) throwing a dart, regardless of previous sports experience. Men also do better than women in mathematical reasoning (E). Men excel over women at mentally rotating an object (F). After Kimura, 1992.

Verbal Skills

There are no sex differences in scores on modern standardized tests of intelligence (Hines, 1982). That is, boys and girls do not differ predictably in IQ. However, some subsets of the skills and abilities measured on intelligence tests show consistent, though small, sex differences in performance. On average, females excel at verbal tasks, perceptual skills, fine motor skills, and mathematical calculations, whereas males outperform females on targeted directed motor skills (e.g., guiding or interception of a projectile), quantitative tasks, and visuospatial abilities, including map reading, sense of direction, and mathematical reasoning (Bryant, 1982; Gladue et al., 1990; Hines, 1982; Kimura, 1992; Velle, 1987) (**FIGURE 4.24**).

Females generally display better language comprehension, faster language acquisition (both first and additional languages), and better spelling, verbal fluency, and grammar skills than males (Hines, 1991; Netley, 1983). Many of these sex differences in verbal performance arise after puberty, which makes it likely that they are mediated by hormonal effects (Maccoby and Jacklin, 1974); however, social and other environmental factors cannot be ruled out. No consistent effect of prenatal endocrine dysfunctions on subsequent verbal abilities has been demonstrated (reviewed in Hines, 1982).

Several studies have suggested a neuroanatomical basis for these sex differences in performance. In most people, the planum temporale, a flattened area of the temporal lobe, is larger in the left cerebral hemisphere than in the right. Based on earlier case studies of individuals with brain damage restricted to the planum temporale, it has been concluded that this brain region is involved in speech. The asymmetry between the right and left planum temporale is less marked in women than in men (Wada et al., 1975). In other words, its size is less lateralized in females. In another

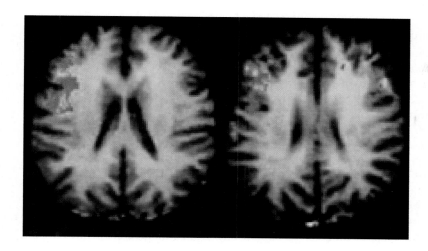

FIGURE 4.25 **Men and women use different parts of their brains to solve similar language tasks.** Among males (left), fMRI reveals that brain activation during rhyming tasks is restricted to the left inferior frontal gyrus. In females (right), both the left and right inferior frontal gyri are activated, and the pattern of activation is more diffuse. From Shaywitz et al., 1995, courtesy of NMR Research/Yale Medical School.

study, the volume of the superior temporal cortex and the cortical volume fraction of Broca's area, which is also involved in speech, were about 20% larger in female than in male brains (Harasty et al., 1997), a finding that corresponds well with findings on sex differences in verbal function.

With the advent of new imaging tools such as fMRI, it is now possible to view the living, awake brain and monitor specific brain region activity during the performance of a particular task. One recent study using fMRI revealed that men and women use different parts of their brains to solve similar phonological tasks. Nineteen males and 19 females were asked to report whether or not two nonsense words rhymed. Among males, brain activation during this rhyming task was concentrated in the left inferior frontal gyrus region. In contrast, both the left and right inferior frontal gyri were activated in females performing the rhyming task, and the pattern of activation was more diffuse than for males (Shaywitz et al., 1995) (**FIGURE 4.25**). These striking data provide evidence that the brains of men and women operate differently when processing certain features of language.

Mathematical Reasoning and Visuospatial Abilities

Sex differences in performance on mathematical reasoning tasks have been consistently observed within the general population for decades. In general, males outperform females on tests of mathematical reasoning ability, such as the mathematics section of the Scholastic Aptitude Test (SAT-M) (Benbow and Stanley, 1983; Gouchie and Kimura, 1991). This sex difference increases dramatically at the high end of performance: the sex ratio of seventh-grade boys to girls receiving SAT-M scores of 500 or above is 2.1:1; for scores of 600 or above, the ratio is 4.1:1; and for scores of 700 or above, the ratio is 12.9:1 (Benbow and Stanley, 1983). The activational effects of hormones are not likely to mediate this sex difference, because it is observed prior to the onset of puberty (Wisniewski, 1998). However, it remains possible that the difference in math performance reflects differences in being judged by the negative stereotype that women possess poorer math skills. When women are told prior to a math test that there are sex differences in performance, they tend to do worse than women who are told prior to a math test that there are no sex differences in performance (Spencer et al., 1999).

On average, males perform visuospatial tasks better than females (McGee, 1979). Visuospatial tasks include mental rotation of objects, map reading, mental visualization of relationships among objects in space, solving maze problems, and shape recognition (Hines, 1991) (see Figure 4.24). The difference in visuospatial abilities between boys and girls is small or absent prior to puberty but present after puberty, suggesting that hormonal influences could be involved. However, it is important to note that in contrast to other species, there is no direct evidence to date that human brain morphological or behavioral sex differences have any hormonal bases.

Visualization of space, objects, or relationships among objects in space is a common test of visuospatial abilities. For example, in a test of verbal abilities, an individual may be asked to go through the alphabet mentally as fast as possible and count the number of letters containing the sound "ee," including the letter *e* (Coltheart et al., 1975). Females are faster than males at this verbal test. In contrast, in a visuospatial test a person is asked to go through the alphabet mentally as quickly as possible and count all of the uppercase letters with a curve in their form (Coltheart et al., 1975). Males perform better than females at this task. However, in a reaction-time fMRI study of a visuomotor response task (such as tracking), no sex differences in brain volume activation were reported in the right visual, left visual, left primary motor, left supplementary motor, or left anterior cingulate areas. The authors concluded, based on these results, that sex seems to have little influence on fMRI brain activation when performance on a simple reaction-time task is compared between men and women (Mikhelashvili-Browner et al., 2003). However, if visual processing in an emotional context is assessed with fMRI—for example by using pictures from the International Affective Picture System—then obvious sex differences emerge (Wrase et al., 2003). Given that many visual stimuli have negative or positive emotional content, it seems prudent to consider the sex differences in brain activation revealed by these fMRI studies (Wrase et al., 2003; Sabatinelli et al., 2004).

As with visuospatial tests, males perform better at map reading and directional tasks. In one study, college students were placed in a windowless room and told to imagine that they were facing the front of a familiar building—the college administration building, for instance. With this imaginary orientation in space, they were requested to point to other familiar landmarks, such as the stadium or the clock tower. When the degrees of error in the students' estimated orientation reports were computed, it was found that men made fewer errors in estimation of direction than women (Bryant, 1982, 1991). Of course, college men may have more experience in navigating through space than college women. Boys may have been allowed to range farther from home than girls as they were growing up, or allowed to drive more frequently than girls. Alternatively, this sex difference may be due to activational effects of hormones in adulthood.

Some postmenopausal women were treated with estradiol, and others with methylated testosterone, for 3 months. The women receiving testosterone supplements performed better than the estrogen-treated women in a map memory test (Wisniewski et al., 2002). In another study of "navigation," men and women were asked to navigate a virtual maze while undergoing fMRI (Grön et al., 2000). Performing this task activated the medial occipital gyri, lateral and medial parietal regions, right hippocampus, and posterior cingulate and parahippocampal gyri in both sexes. In addition to the common brain regions activated, males also activated the left hippocampus, whereas females also activated the right parietal and right prefrontal cortex (Grön et al., 2000) These findings point to a novel neural locus potentially responsible for sex differences in navigation (**FIGURE 4.26**).

Active

Control

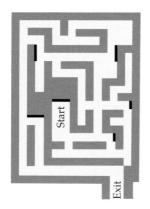

Start

Exit

FIGURE 4.26 Men and women use different parts of their brains to solve navigation tasks. Usually, visuospatial navigation is studied using maze exploration. Because fMRI requires subjects to lie very still, researchers developed a virtual maze on a computer screen that people could navigate while remaining in the fMRI device. During the control condition, the screen was frozen at the last position of the active condition. Two white bars above and below indicated the control phase. During the control phase subjects subjects performed a reaction time task. From Grön et al., 2000.

ANIMAL MODELS OF VISUOSPATIAL SKILLS Because it is so difficult to account for differential experiential effects in humans, animal models, in which environmental experiences can be somewhat equalized, have been employed to understand sex differences in visuospatial abilities. There is no perfect animal model for human visuospatial skills. However, animals can be taught to run mazes, a task that incorporates visuospatial (or perhaps olfactory-spatial) skills. A consistent sex difference in maze-running ability is observed among many rodent species (reviewed in Gaulin and FitzGerald, 1986; Haaren et al., 1990): males learn mazes faster and make fewer errors than females (McNemar and Stone, 1932) (see Chapter 12). This sex difference in maze learning is thought to be mediated by hormonal effects on the hippocampus, a structure in the brain that is important for spatial learning (McEwen, 2001). Recall from Chapter 3 that male meadow voles have greater spatial aptitudes than female conspecifics, whereas there is no difference between male and female pine voles (Gaulin and FitzGerald, 1986). The hippocampus of male meadow voles is approximately 10% larger than the hippocampus of females, but hippocampal size does not differ between male and female pine voles (Jacobs et al., 1990). Whether hippocampal size drives the difference in behavior or whether sex-related differences in experience in spatial habitats drive hippocampal size has recently been investigated; the results will be discussed in Chapter 12. Importantly, no differences in performance between male and female rats were observed using a computer-automated behavioral testing system that allowed the animals to nose-poke visual stimuli on a touch screen (Bussey et al., 2008). These results suggest that perhaps sex differences in learning and memory performance might reflect sex differences in the use of sensory information to solve problems.

CLINICAL MODELS OF VISUOSPATIAL SKILLS Sex differences in human visuospatial cognitive behavior have been documented, but how do we gather evidence to determine the contribution of hormones to these differences in human behavior? Clinical models are few. Indirect evidence from people with atypical endocrine function suggests that early hormone exposure influences visuospatial abilities among humans. For example, individuals with Turner syndrome display a marked deficit in visuospatial abilities (Hines, 1982; Netley, 1983). Because these individuals possess dysgenic ovaries and produce no steroid hormones, these results are consistent with the idea that early exposure to androgen (or androgen metabolites) promotes subsequent visuospatial abilities. Also, in some studies of females with CAH, who experience high levels of early androgen exposure, there have been reports of enhanced visuospatial abilities; however, these reports have not consistently shown a clear trend (Hines, 1991; Hines et al., 2003) (**BOX 4.7**). Similarly, exogenous prenatal hormone exposure has not been seen to consistently affect visuospatial abilities. Except for one brief report (Wada, 1976), there have not been reports of sex differences in brain regions that process visuospatial information that correspond to those found in brain regions that process verbal information (but see Sabatinelli et al., 2004; Wrase et al., 2003).

Many similarities exist between the sexes in brain structure, function, and neurotransmission. However, critical differences distinguish healthy male from healthy female brains (Cosgrove et al., 2009): (1) global cerebral blood flow is higher in women than in men; (2) overall brain volume is greater in men than women, but after total volume is controlled for, women have a higher proportion of gray matter, whereas men have a higher percentage of white matter; (3) there are sex differences in regional volumes, though they are less consistent; and (4) sex-specific differences in human dopaminergic markers, serotonergic markers, and gamma-aminobutyric acid (GABA) markers indicate that male and female brains display neurochemical differences. The extent to which these sex differences in neurochemistry predispose individuals to specific mental disorders (e.g., major depression, anxiety disorders, schizophrenia) that display distinct sex differences remains unknown.

The organizational/activational hypothesis suggests that the human central nervous system is ordered in a male or female manner early in prenatal development by the presence or absence, respectively, of gonadal steroid hormones, and that behavioral sex differences arise when these prenatally organized neural circuits are activated by sex steroids secreted at puberty. Thus, sex differences in behavior reflect differential prenatal exposure to steroid hormones. If the time frame of the organizational/activational hypothesis is expanded, then an alternative view

BOX 4.7 Hormones, Sex Differences, and Art

In addition to the sex difference in rough-and-tumble play, boys and girls differ in other aspects of their play behavior. For example, boys tend to play with vehicles and building blocks, whereas girls tend to favor dolls. Freestyle drawings done by boys and girls also differ on a number of parameters, including color and motifs. Girls tend to draw flowers and people in "warm" colors, whereas boys tend to draw vehicles and other moving objects and use "cold" colors (Iijima et al., 2001) (see **Figure A** and the table). In addition, girls tend to line up their motifs at ground level, whereas boys tend to draw from an overhead (bird's eye) perspective and to pile objects on top of one another. Do boys and girls perceive the world differently? Or do they express their similar perceptions from different perspectives? The two pictures on the left in the group of children's drawings were drawn by a 6-year-old boy (B) and a 5-year-old boy (C). Note the vehicular motifs and the overhead view (B) and the piling of objects (C). The two drawings in the center were drawn by a 5-year-old girl (D) and a 6-year-old girl (E). Note that the motifs are lined up at ground level. The two drawings on the right were drawn by a 5-year-old girl (F) and a 7-year-old girl (G) with CAH. Note the vehicular motifs and the piling of objects. When a number of these aspects of children's drawings were calculated, the "feminine index" of pictures drawn by CAH girls was much lower than that of pictures drawn by unaffected girls, whereas the "masculine index" was much higher than that of pictures drawn by unaffected

girls and comparable to that of pictures by unaffected boys (Iijima et al., 2001). These CAH girls have female gender identity and are reared as girls. All of the CAH girls in this study had plastic surgery to make their external genitalia female-typical, had a female gender identity, and were being reared as girls. However, the CAH females appeared to display bisexual traits in their drawings.

Motifs in Children's Drawings

Motif	Boys (%)	Girls (%)
Moving objects (vehicle, train, aircraft, etc.)	92.4	04.6
Person	26.5	96.6
Flower	07.2	57.0
Butterfly	03.2	23.4
Sun	50.8	76.5
Mountain	14.5	03.1
House and building	17.7	33.5
Tree	09.6	23.4
Ground	42.7	57.8
Cloud	25.0	32.8
Sky	41.9	49.2

(A)

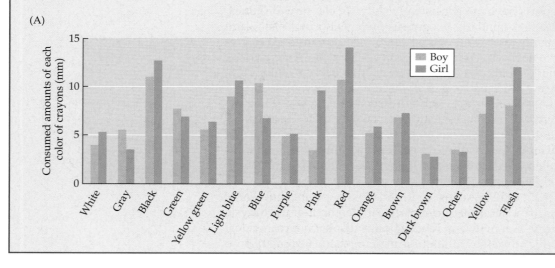

emerges (Lenroot and Giedd, 2010; Sisk and Zehr, 2005). In a very interesting study, individuals who underwent puberty early were compared with individuals who underwent puberty late (Waber, 1976). Regardless of sex, early-maturing adolescents performed better than late-maturing adolescents on tests of verbal abilities. Late-maturing individuals outperformed early-maturing individuals on tests of spatial abilities. Because females typically undergo puberty at an earlier age than males, the differences in cognitive function between males and females could re-

Photographs courtesy of Dr. Yasumasa Arai.

flect differential brain organization mediated by peripubertal sex steroid hormones coincident with differential rates of brain maturation (Waber, 1976).

Conclusions

A final note about sex differences in human cognitive performance: This area of research is highly politicized, both within and outside the scientific community. Some people see the discovery of sex differences in brain function, organization, or morphology as evidence of biological differences between the sexes in ability. Others view sex differences in the human brain as reflecting a social history of differential treatment of the two sexes, and thus as mutable. The data can be used either to maintain the status quo ("women are different biologically and therefore should not be expected to perform as well as men") or to effect change ("women and men are not fundamentally different and complete parity in opportunity should be a societal goal") (Harris, 1980). If career choices are made on the basis of these requirements, then people may sort themselves into career tracks because of their respective test scores. Thus, scientific data can be used to both contribute to and explain the enormous disparity between the sexes in these occupations. Another perspective is that because women are "far more likely to be equally talented in both math and verbal domains," they have more options in nonmathematical occupations than do men (Ceci and Williams, 2009).

It should be emphasized that the range of differences in brain morphology or function is greater *within* each sex than *between* the two sexes (Breedlove, 1994; Crichton-Browne, 1880; McGlone, 1980; but see Cahill, 2006). Are studies of subtle differences in the human brain worthwhile? How are the data to be interpreted? These are difficult questions that require sensitive and carefully reasoned answers. A quote from Mrs. Fawcett, a leader of the women's movement in the late nineteenth century, nicely puts the debate into perspective:

No one of those who care most for the women's movement cares one jot to prove or to maintain that men's brains and women's brains are exactly alike or exactly equal. All we ask is that the social and legal status of women should be such as to foster, not to suppress, any gift of art, literature, learning, or goodness with which women may be endowed. (Quoted in Romanes, 1887)

Summary

Companion Website

sites.sinauer.com/be5e

Go to the
*Behavioral Endocrinology
Companion Website*
for animated tutorials,
videos, web links, and
an online glossary.

1. The organizational and activational actions of steroid hormones cause changes in neural tissue. Sexual dimorphisms in brain structure have been reported for a number of neural regions. Some of these dimorphisms are subtle, such as the differences in synapse patterns in the MPOA, but others are marked, such as the differences in the size of the rat SDN-POA. Other sex differences have been reported in brain structure and in neurotransmitter secretion, receptor numbers, and receptor distribution patterns. In all mammalian cases, these neural sexual dimorphisms can be altered in a predictable fashion by early steroid hormone treatment. Sexual dimorphisms in the brain can be affected by circulating hormones in adults as well. However, the functional significance of sexually dimorphic brain structures in mammals is still under investigation.

2. A strong relationship among hormones, brain structure, and sexually dimorphic behavior has been established in studies of birdsong. The neural pathways underlying the production of birdsong involve several interconnected nuclei, some of which show sexual dimorphism. The HVC and RA of male zebra finches, which sing, are three to six times larger than those of female conspecifics, which do not sing. Birdsong is organized and activated by sex steroid hormones in some species and only activated by hormones in other species. The sexual dimorphisms in brain nucleus size and subsequent singing behavior of zebra finches appear to be organized early in development. In contrast, some female canaries will sing if treated in adulthood with testosterone. Adult androgen treatment increases the size of the song control regions of the brain. Bird species in which both sexes sing exhibit no sex differences in the size of the neural structures making up the song control regions.

3. In rhesus monkeys and many other mammalian species, including humans, males engage in much more play behavior than their female peers throughout development. A larger proportion of male than female play behavior involves simulated fighting or rough-and-tumble play. The sex difference in play behavior is organized prenatally, and castration or other postnatal endocrine manipulation does not affect the amount of threat, play initiation, rough-and-tumble play, or pursuit play among monkeys.

4. Three common sex differences observed in humans are gender role, gender identity, and sexual orientation/preference. Gender role is the sum of culturally based behavior patterns that are specific to one sex or the other. Gender role appears to be primarily learned; however, there is currently great controversy about this topic. Individuals with early endocrine dysfunction may adopt an atypical gender role. Similarly, gender identity, whether individuals view themselves as male or as female, appears to be primarily learned. Studies of individuals with 5α-reductase deficiency who change gender role and gender identity at puberty suggest that hormones, rather than rearing, could determine gender role and/or gender identity.

5. Very little is known about how heterosexuals develop erotic attractions, and even less is known about how homosexuals develop erotic attractions. Because erotic attractions typically begin at the time of puberty, sex steroid hormones have been assumed to be involved. A common hypothesis about the cause of homosexuality is that the hormone levels of homosexuals are different from those of heterosexuals. However, many studies have failed to find any evidence that adult homosexual men or women differ from their heterosexual

counterparts in blood concentrations of androgens or estrogens. Evidence for effects of early exposure to steroids on sexual preference is also inconclusive, but the study of male sheep has provided some insights into the development of partner preferences.

6. Sex differences in human brain size have been reported for years. More recently, sex differences in specific brain structures have been discovered. Sex differences in a number of cognitive functions have also been reported. Females are generally more sensitive to auditory information, whereas males are more sensitive to visual information. Females are also typically more sensitive than males to taste and olfactory input.

7. Women display less lateralization of cognitive functions than men. On average, females generally excel in verbal, perceptual, and fine motor skills, whereas males outperform females on quantitative and visuospatial tasks, including map reading and direction finding. Although reliable sex differences can be documented, these differences in ability are slight; there is more variation within each sex than between the sexes for most cognitive abilities.

Questions for Discussion

1. There is strong evidence for sexual dimorphism of certain neuroanatomical features of mammalian brains. In most cases, it has been difficult to relate the change in anatomy to changes in behavior. Describe the types of experiments one would design to test the role of sex differences in the brain on behavior, and describe the types of evidence that would be necessary to conclude that sex differences in the brain were responsible for sex differences in behavior.

2. You are a counselor at a hospital consulting with parents whose newborn baby is XX with ambiguous genitalia. Based on what you have learned in this chapter, what kinds of tests might you suggest be conducted to help them determine which gender to raise their child. What kind of test results would make you confident that sex assignment and corrective surgery should be immediate, and what would cause you to argue to delay gender assignment until the child is old enough to participate in the decision?

3. What are the advantages and disadvantages of studying animal models to understand human behavioral sexual dimorphisms? Discuss the advantages and disadvantages of three different model systems. What characteristics of an animal model would provide an ideal experimental system for understanding human behavioral sexual dimorphisms?

4. Using organ discharge patterns in electric fishes, discuss the proposition that hormones affect perception. Can you conceive of some possible ways in which this might occur, using a proximate level of explanation? Can you conceive of some possible reasons why this might occur, using an ultimate level of explanation?

5. Apart from animal experiments, what studies would you conduct to help tease apart the impact of social and biological factors in the regulation of sexually differentiated behavior, gender role, and gender identity in human children.

6. Some individuals are born with genitalia that are neither definitely male nor female. Physicians and parents often must make choices about treatment and may make a sex assignment at birth. Some adult individuals who were born with ambiguous genitalia claim that, in retrospect, they would have been happier "unaltered" than forced into one particular sexual category. Keeping these views in mind, what should physicians do or advise when individuals are born with atypical genitalia?

Suggested Readings

Balthazart, J. 2012. *Brain Development and Sexual Orientation*. Morgan & Claypool, San Rafael, CA.

Balthazart, J., et al. 2009. Sexual differentiation of brain and behavior in birds. In D. W. Pfaff et al. (eds.), *Hormones, Brain and Behavior* (2nd ed.), pp. 1745–1787. Acaemic Press, New York.

Bao, A. M. and Swaab, D. F. 2011. Sexual differentiation of the human brain: relation to gender identity, sexual orientation and neuropsychiatric disorders. *Front. Neuroendocrinol.*, 32:214–226.

Becker, J. B., et al. 2009. *Sex Differences in the Brain: From Genes to Behavior*. Oxford University Press, New York.

Ceci, S. J., and Williams, W. M. 2009. *The Mathematics of Sex: How Biology and Society Conspire to Limit Talented Women and Girls*. Oxford University Press, New York.

Hines, M. 2005. *Brain Gender*. Oxford University Press, New York.

LeVay, S., and Baldwin, J. 2012. *Human Sexuality* (4th ed.). Sinauer Associates, Sunderland, MA.

McCarthy, M. M. and Nugent, B. M. 2015. At the frontier of epigenetics of brain sex differences. *Front. Behav. Neurosci.*, 9:221.

Sandberg, D. E., Callens, N., and Wisniewski, A. B. 2015. Disorders of sex development (DSD): Networking and standardization considerations. *Horm. Metab. Res.*, 47:387–393.

Male Reproductive Behavior

5

Learning Objectives

The goal of this chapter is to describe the interactions between hormones and male reproductive behaviors. By the end of this chapter you should be able to:

- summarize the proximal bases of *sexual behavior* in male animals.

- relay a timeline of the research on *male sexual behavior* and its endocrine correlates.

- describe mating behaviors in male rodents, primates, birds, and reptiles.

- explain some of the brain mechanisms involved in *sex*.

- discuss individual and age-related variations in male reproductive behavior.

Generally, successful sexual reproduction in animals requires bringing the males and females together. Male reproductive behavior, which relies on the hormones involved in gamete maturation, as well as on the powerful motivational force we refer to as sex drive, accomplishes the delivery of male gametes (sperm) to female gametes (ova or eggs). The endocrine and nervous systems interact in mediating male sexual behavior, which comprises two components: sexual motivation and sexual performance. Most of what we know about the physiological mechanisms underlying sexual behavior has been gained through studies of nonhuman animals, especially rodents, so you will learn much about rodent reproduction in this chapter, but you will also learn about male sexual behavior in humans and other primates, as well as in birds and reptiles.

FIGURE 5.1 Elephant seal fitness (A) A dispute over territory between two male elephant seals. Waterfront areas are hotly contested among males of this species because females prefer to have their pups near the water—an easy escape route from terrestrial predators for themselves and their offspring—and thus prefer to mate with males that control these territories. Male elephant seals are highly aggressive: they have been known to accidentally crush their own offspring in an attempt to keep other males away from their territories. (B) There are significant reproductive benefits to being the highest-ranked male elephant seal (>150 offspring sired), whereas all females produce between 5 and 10 pups regardless of rank. (A) courtesy of Burney LeBoeuf.

(A)

(B)

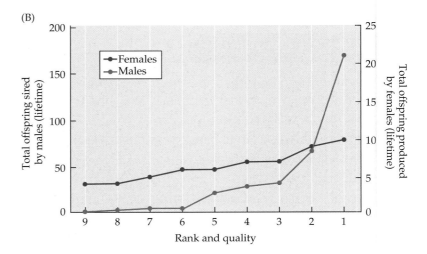

Males of many species, including salmon, marsupial mice, and praying mantises, face certain death in order to mate. Stories abound in the natural history literature describing the heroic journeys of males of these and other species that overcome obstacles and dangers just to gain the opportunity to fight other males for the *possibility* of mating.

Although their competition is less overtly lethal, male elephant seals (*Mirounga angustirostris*) also compete vigorously for the opportunity to mate. They migrate hundreds of kilometers to the Northern California coast in order to set up breeding territories, and they fight ferociously with their neighbors for the best real estate. Beachfront property is the best territory to control, because females prefer locations close to the water, presumably because a pup is safer from terrestrial predators there, and they tend to mate with males occupying these prime spots. Once the territories are established, the high-ranking males cluster around the water's edge, surrounded by lower-ranking males. As females come ashore, the lower-ranking males continually challenge the dominant males for the opportunity to mate with the females (**FIGURE 5.1A**).

Why do male elephant seals expend so much energy fighting among themselves in order to secure a piece of the beach valued by females? The males occupying desirable waterfront territories mate with many more females than do the males located in peripheral areas, because females prefer to mate with the males located in territories that provide the best place to deliver and nurse their pups (LeBoeuf,

1974). The females directly choose the areas in which they want to rear their young, and by doing so, they also indirectly choose males possessing a constellation of genes that promotes the ability to fight against other males and win. The males' proximity to the water provides a reliable indication of these dominance traits. By mating with dominant, so-called alpha males, females increase the probability that their sons will possess the genes associated with reproductive success and thus enhance their own fitness. Males are driven to fight for prime territories because if they fail to secure territories that are preferred by females, then they are unlikely to mate, whereas if they do secure prime territories, then they have the chance to sire many offspring. Thus, the ultimate cause of males' strong motivation to mate is to increase their reproductive fitness. Only about one-third of the males get to mate each year. The top-ranked males account for the vast majority of matings, but they pay a steep price; high-ranking males die within a year or two of their reproductive peak. The reproductive success of most males is zero, and most males die, often from wounds obtained during the fights, before achieving a successful mating.

Males and females differ in their potential rates of reproduction. As we learned in Chapter 3, females produce relatively few, large, resource-rich gametes. Females generally invest much more than males in each offspring. The number of offspring a female can produce in her lifetime is limited to the number of eggs she can produce or the number of young she can rear. A male, on the other hand, may produce billions of gametes in his lifetime, and he invests relatively little energy in each one (see Chapter 7). A female elephant seal, for example, can produce and raise only one pup per year and perhaps 10 in her lifetime, but a male can potentially father many pups per year and more than 100 in total (**FIGURE 5.1B**). Thus, the difference in potential reproductive success forms the basis of the different mating strategies of the two sexes (**BOX 5.1**). According to sexual selection theory, females improve

BOX 5.1 *Battle of the "Sexes"*

As noted in Chapters 3 and 4, most animals are either male or female; that is, they possess either testes or ovaries. Males and females typically have conflicting interests as mating partners, and individuals have evolved behaviors to protect and promote their sex-specific self-interest. However, some animals are true hermaphrodites and possess both types of gonads and produce both eggs and sperm. Yet, even among hermaphrodites, conflicts of interest involving mating arise. For example, hermaphroditic animals often participate in elaborate courtship displays to determine which individual will donate sperm and which individual will donate ova during a particular encounter. In some circumstances, it is advantageous to donate sperm; in other cases, it is advantageous to provide ova.

One dramatic case in which it appears advantageous to donate sperm involves hermaphroditic flatworms (*Cotylea*) that typically mate in pairs. These flatworms rear up and literally fence with their penes (as shown in the figure). Each flatworm thrusts and parries, trying to stab an exposed area of its mating partner's body while trying to avoid getting stabbed (Michiels and Newman, 1998). An individual that successfully pierces the body of its mating partner injects sperm that travel to the partner's ovaries to inseminate its ova. These "fencing" bouts

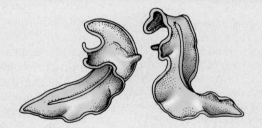

After Michiels and Newman, 1998.

are intense and may last 20–60 minutes before one individual succeeds in inseminating the other. Apparently, the costs of developing ova, and of mending the stab wounds, are sufficiently high to favor the selection of competition among these hermaphroditic flatworms to donate sperm.

These dueling flatworms exemplify the complexity of so-called simple organisms. In contrast to most sexually reproducing animals, individual hermaphroditic flatworms may have identical, but incompatible, interests as mating partners; thus, as you might predict, cooperation between mating partners should be rare, and the mechanisms underlying aggression and reproductive motivation are probably linked.

their fitness by choosing the best males possible with whom to combine their genes; males can often best achieve reproductive success by seeking to mate with as many females as possible. In other words, females have generally evolved to be "choosy," and males have generally evolved to be "ardent."

Of course, men also appear highly motivated to mate. The media are often filled with news of high-profile men in political office, in the corporate world, or with lucrative sports contracts and endorsements who have been discovered to have engaged in multiple extramarital affairs. What drove these married men to risk their jobs, income, families, and possible health for sexual intercourse with additional partners? The obvious answer is that sexual intercourse is fun, exciting, and pleasurable; but, miniature golf is also fun, exciting, and pleasurable, and married men are rarely motivated to play miniature golf with women who are not their partners (unless it is a prelude to sexual activities). However, sexual pleasure can be sufficiently rewarding that some men report being "addicted" to sex, whereas miniature golf addiction has not been reported. Indeed, Tiger Woods, Charlie Sheen, David Duchovny, and others have checked themselves into rehabilitation facilities for their so-called sex addiction. Although the American Association for Marriage and Family Therapy has suggested that as many as 12 million Americans have a sex addiction, there is still widespread disagreement among clinicians about the existence of this disorder.

Animals, including humans, have evolved to respond with sensations of pleasure in response to adaptive signals in the world. For example, we find sugar sweet, babies cute, water refreshing, and sex rewarding. Underlying such rewards is increased dopamine signaling in our brains. Are the evolutionary forces that shape sexual behavior the same in men as in elephant seals? In other words, are the rewarding properties of sexual behavior what is driving males to seek females for sexual union? If so, what drives the sexual behavior of males who have no experience with the rewarding aspects of sexual behavior? Are men consciously trying to improve their fitness by their sexual behaviors? Probably not. Do men who control more resources pursue more mating opportunities? Possibly. Importantly, men do not need to be conscious of their motives in order for high sex drive to be adaptive. They merely need to behave in this adaptive fashion. By analogy, a bird does not need to be conscious of the theory of aerodynamics in order to engage in the adaptive behavior of flying—the bird merely needs to behave as if it understands aerodynamics. Natural selection operates on behavior. Even if men are consciously trying to avoid impregnation of extra-pair women by using contraceptive methods, unconsciously the brain circuits underlying their behaviors may be similar to the brain circuits underlying the sexual drive of male elephant seals and males of other species, and the brain circuits may yield adaptive outcomes. Importantly, the proximate bases of sexual behavior reflect these ultimate, evolutionary factors.

The Proximate Bases of Male Sexual Behavior

As described in Chapter 3, **sex** is associated with a division of gamete types, and **sexual behavior** is behavior that has evolved to bring the two gamete types together. **Male sexual behavior** is defined as all the behaviors necessary and sufficient to deliver male gametes (sperm) to female gametes (ova or eggs). The hormones involved in gamete maturation—namely, the sex steroid hormones—have been co-opted over evolutionary time to regulate the web of behaviors necessary to bring the two sexes together for successful gametic union (Crews, 1984). **Sex drive**, the motivational force that propels individuals to seek sexual union, is a very powerful engine underlying the behavior of all animals, including humans. Sex drive is primitive. Although the nervous system of the nematode worm *Caenorhabditis elegans* comprises only a few hundred neurons (White et al., 1986), *C. elegans* display

sex Condition, property, or quality by which organisms are categorized as female or male on the basis of their chromosomes, hormones, reproductive organs, and other morphology, as well as behavior. Also, the physiological, morphological, functional, and psychological differences that distinguish females and males.

sexual behavior Copulation. Actions directed towards reproduction. Also called *mating*.

male sexual behavior All the behaviors necessary and sufficient to deliver male gametes (sperm) to female gametes (ova or eggs).

sex drive The powerful motivational forces propelling individuals to seek copulation; in humans, often referred to as *libido*.

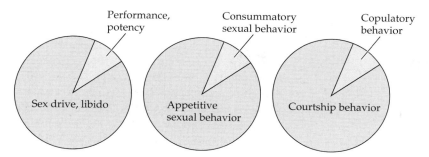

FIGURE 5.2 **Male sexual behavior** can be operationally divided into two phases: the appetitive phase (seeking sexual encounters) and the consummatory phase (engaging in copulation). The behavioral components of the appetitive phase are variously referred to as sex drive, libido, or courtship behavior; those of the consummatory phase are known as performance, potency, or copulatory behavior. Male expend much more time and energy seeking copulation than actually copulating. This division of male sexual behavior into two phases is useful for heuristic purposes as well as in medical diagnoses, because hormones can affect each component differently.

complex patterns of sexual behavior (Barrios et al., 2012). Males engage in a mate-searching behavior that resembles the motivated behaviors of vertebrates. When males are isolated from their mating partners, they will leave an area with plentiful water and food and wander about their environment (in the laboratory, their environment is a petri dish coated with agar and seeded with food [*E. coli* bacteria]), presumably in search of a mate. Searching for mates by male *C. elegans* is regulated by signals from their mates and by endogenous signals indicating nutritional and reproductive status, including genes involved with serotonin, insulin, and the sex determination pathways (Lipton et al., 2004). The pigment-dispersing factor receptor PDFR-1 modulates the circuit that encodes male mating drive that promotes male sex motivation (Barrios et al., 2012). Sex drive tends to be strong in males, and the threshold for mating behavior tends to be low.

For purposes of description here, all male sexual behavior can be divided into two overlapping phases: (1) the appetitive phase and (2) the consummatory phase (Hinde, 1970) (**FIGURE 5.2**). The **appetitive phase** is roughly equivalent to courtship and involves all of the behaviors the male uses to gain access to the female. Behaviors as diverse as searching for or providing food for females, fighting for territory, or advertising may occur during the appetitive phase. Obviously, the neural circuitry underlying so many complex behaviors will differ and will offer different points of hormonal influence. Courtship functions as a communication opportunity during which information about species, readiness to mate, resources, and genetic endowments is shared. The appetitive phase lasts much longer than the second phase, called the **consummatory phase**, during which copulation occurs. Although separating mating behavior into these two phases is likely to divide an integrated behavioral program artificially, this dichotomy remains valuable for understanding the hormonal and neural bases of male reproductive behavior. Thus, the distinction between seeking sex (sex drive, motivation, or libido) and engaging successfully in a mating act (performance, potency) can be useful for heuristic purposes, as well as in medical diagnoses (Meisel and Sachs, 1994; but see Sachs, 2007).

A debate has arisen about the usefulness of these old ethological concepts (**FIGURE 5.3**) in describing male sexual behavior because of the "fuzzy" boundaries between the appetitive phase and the consummatory phase (Ball and Bathazart, 2008; Sachs, 2007, 2008). Certainly, precision in scientific definitions is a goal, but some fuzzy concepts, such as the concept of "species," remain useful in modern biology. One might conceptualize the two behavioral states with substantial overlap

appetitive phase An ethological term, roughly equivalent to *courtship*. All the behaviors an individual displays when attempting to gain access to an individual of the opposite sex for the purpose of mating.

consummatory phase An ethological term that encompasses the completion of a motivated behavior. In terms of sexual behavior, copulation represents the consummatory phase.

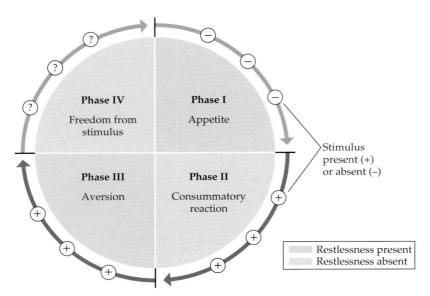

FIGURE 5.3 Early model of "instinctive" behavior In this model of so-called instinctive behavior, most behavior was explained by the strengths of attractions and repulsions. In Phase I, individuals display an intrinsic motivation for a specific stimulus in the absence of that stimulus (e.g., food, sexual partner), which is manifested by restlessness and searching behaviors. During Phase II, the stimulus is present, and increased expression of consummatory behaviors in response to that stimulus occurs. After expression of the consummatory behavior, the stimulus acquires an aversive status, so it is avoided during Phase III. During Phase IV, individuals attain a restful state and are no longer attracted to or repelled by the stimulus, which may be present or absent. Please note that the amount of time for Phase I is greater than that for Phase II. After Craig, 1917.

of the appetitive and consummatory boundaries (Pfaus et al., 2003). Hormones affect both sex drive and sexual performance, but often to differing degrees and via different processes (Hemsworth and Tilbrook, 2007; Katz, 2007). Despite the replacement of ethology by several modern fields of study, some of its concepts, such as the appetive-consummatory distinction, serve a useful heuristic function, and we maintain the distinction here.

A related concept is sexual arousal. Although everyone knows when they are sexually aroused and most know when their sexual partner is aroused, it is difficult to define this state, especially in male animals. Originally, Frank Beach described sexual arousal as the engagement of the mechanisms that increase "sexual excitement to such a pitch that the copulatory threshold is attained" (Beach, 1956). Thus, without appropriate sexual arousal, copulation could not take place. As with any hormone-behavior interaction, it is critical to operationally define the components of male sexual behavior in order to understand the physiological underpinnings. Over time, the operational definition of sexual arousal has evolved. Many researchers still equate arousal with motivation, in line with Beach's original writing (Ågmo, 2008). However, many other definitions have been proposed, and this widening of perspectives has not provided clarity to understanding sexual arousal (Sachs, 2007). To remedy this problem, a more precise definition that can be used for both humans and nonhuman animals has been proposed. According to this definition, male sexual arousal can be inferred only by the presence of an erect penis in a sexual context (Sachs, 2007). This definition, though precise, seems to move sexual arousal away from concepts associated with motivation and closer to the realm of performance. An additional problem is that "sexual context" is a mutable notion. As we will learn, learned associations can be made with sexual behavior and previously neutral stimuli. Thus, an empty cage that previously lacked sexual context for a sexually naive rat becomes a sexual context after the rat engages in multiple mating bouts within the cage. It may be beneficial to limit the operational definition of sexual arousal to genital blood flow, as is currently the case for humans (Ågmo, 2008), especially because such a simplified definition may also be used for both sexes. Additional refining is probably necessary, however. For instance, this definition does not consider men with erectile dysfunction who may report sexual arousal in the absence of penile erection.

Male sex drive is expressed overtly after puberty as the testes become active. The coincidence between the onset of sexual interest and puberty suggests that the testes influence sexual motivation. The observation that removal of the testes typically reduces the frequency of all male mating behaviors provides further evidence that the testes are important in the regulation of male sexual behavior (see Chapter 1). Postcastration treatment with androgens, the principal class of sex steroid hormones produced in the testes, restores reproductive behaviors to precastration levels. Thus, it is reasonable to conclude that androgens cause sexual behavior.

However, the statement that androgens cause sexual behavior requires some qualification. First, recall that hormones change the probability that a particular behavior will be exhibited in a specific context. Second, the effects of experience interact significantly with hormones to affect behavior. These two caveats are important to keep in mind when discussing the effects of hormones on behavior in general and on male sexual behavior specifically. One outdated model of hormone-behavior interactions arose from physiological models—the so-called hydraulic models—once proposed by ethologists to explain innate, reflexive fixed action patterns. According to these simplistic models, hormonal effects on behavior were analogous to a faucet: for example, if the "androgen spigot" was turned on, then male mating behavior or aggression ensued. But hormone-behavior interactions are far more complex than suggested by this model. About half the readers of this book have significant concentrations of androgens in their blood, yet they are reading, not copulating. How can we say, then, that androgens cause sexual behavior? It is more accurate to state that androgens, as well as other sex steroid hormones, appear to affect the likelihood of mating behaviors by reducing the threshold for these behaviors in the presence of the appropriate stimuli in the appropriate social context. All other things being equal, a male with high blood androgen concentrations is more likely to copulate with a conspecific female than is a male with low androgen concentrations. In other words, in terms of a stimulus-response paradigm of sexual behavior, hormones facilitate the male response, probably by affecting the perception and processing of the stimuli associated with the female. As we will see, androgens have many direct effects on the nervous system, such as regulating neurotransmitter levels as well as affecting the availability of neurotransmitter receptors and other proteins that affect neurotransmitter function (Hull and Dominguez, 2013).

Males vary in the frequency of their copulatory behavior, and vast species differences exist in the extent to which male reproductive behavior relies on hormones. Similarly, enormous individual differences exist within any given species in both the frequency of sexual behavior and the extent to which sexual behavior is mediated by hormones. For example, the regulation of rodent sexual behavior is highly dependent on hormones; but in primates, the control of sexual behavior is less dependent on hormones and more dependent on socialization and learning. Compared with rats, then, primates are relatively less reliant on hormones to regulate sexual behavior. However, primates are not unique in this regard, and there is no evidence that species located "higher" on the phylogenetic scale have been emancipated from direct hormonal control of mating behavior as compared with so-called lower species. Examination of the regulation of mating behavior in nonmammalian animals also reveals varying degrees of hormonal dependence. An example of a reptile species (the red-sided garter snake) in which reproductive behavior is completely divorced from hormonal control will be presented to help counter the belief that humans are unique in this regard.

This chapter examines the endocrine mediation of sexual behavior among males and will address many of these comparative issues. The chapter will also describe the ways in which hormones interact with the nervous system in males. Animal models, mainly rodents, have been helpful in gaining an understanding of the physiological mechanisms underlying sexual behavior, both appetitive and consummatory, in men. The results of research based on these models will be presented in detail below. But first, the history of research into the control of male sexual behavior will be briefly reviewed.

Historical Origins of Research on Male Sexual Behavior

Castration virtually eliminates mating behavior among males of many species, a fact that has been known since the earliest recorded history (see Chapter 1). The

New Testament notes, "There are eunuchs who are born so from their mother's womb; and there are eunuchs who are made so by men; and there are eunuchs who have made themselves so for the sake of the kingdom of heaven. Let him accept it who can" (Matthew 19:12). Some people have suggested that this passage indicates that Jesus believed that castration could clear the path to heaven. In the late 1990s members of the San Diego cult Heaven's Gate apparently believed this to be true. Eight of the 18 males, including the cult leader, who committed suicide together prior to their imaginary journey to a waiting "mother ship," reportedly had performed self-castration. There have been many other religious sects throughout history that believed possession of functional testes blocked rational and/or pious thought.

The English word *testicle* is derived from the Latin *testiculus*, a diminutive, but synonymous, form of the Latin term *testis*, which means "witness." The verb *testify* has a similar derivation. Witnesses in ancient Roman courts often covered their testes with their right hands and swore "on their virility" that they were about to state the truth (that is, provide testimony). This practice illustrates that a relationship among the testes, virility, and mating behavior has been well established for many centuries, but many misconceptions have arisen regarding the nature of the interaction between the testes and sexual behavior.

One common misconception about the regulation of male sex drive that persisted through the late 1800s was that distention, or swelling, of the seminal vesicles activated male sexual behavior (Carter, 1974). Neural stretch receptors were recent discoveries in the 1880s, and it was proposed by several researchers of the time that these receptors, activated by bulging seminal vesicles, induced copulation. Variations of the idea that male sex drive was the result of "pressure" sensations from the accessory sex organs that had to be relieved lasted well into the twentieth century (e.g., Ball, 1934a; Nissen, 1929). Anecdotally, many men report "pressure" in their testes or seminal vesicles when they are sexually aroused. A major piece of scientific evidence supporting the "distended seminal vesicle" theory came from work on frogs in mating condition (Tarchanoff, 1887, cited in Steinach, 1894). Male frogs were reported to continue copulating despite removal of major portions of their anatomy, including their testes; after physical separation from their partners, castrated frogs would immediately remount the females. However, draining the seminal vesicles led to the rapid separation of the pairs and loss of subsequent sexual activity for the males. Thus, neural impulses from the full seminal vesicles were thought to generate sexual behavior, or more commonly, sex drive. Apparently unaware of Steinach's research or Berthold's work (see Chapter 1), Cunningham (1900) also suggested that male sex drive was a manifestation of neural impulses from the testes.

Eugen Steinach (**FIGURE 5.4**) was one of the most influential biologists of the early twentieth century. He was the director of the Biological Research Institute of the Academy of Sciences in Vienna, Austria, and was nominated for a Nobel Prize 11 times! He never won a Nobel, but he did win the Lieben Prize (the "Vienna Nobel") twice—once in 1909 for his work on stimulation of the nervous system, and again in 1918 for his experimental analysis of the "puberty gland" in mammals. Steinach was apparently influenced by the writings of fellow Viennese citizen Sigmund Freud when he postulated the existence of an incipient sexuality that existed prior to puberty and was triggered by nervous impulses from the swelling reproductive glands. Steinach believed that once the process was initiated, psychic influences or sensory input could send the mechanisms underlying reproductive behavior into action. He tried to reduce mating behavior in rats by removing their seminal vesicles; however, this procedure had little effect upon their mating behavior (Steinach, 1894). Some of Steinach's views on the regulation of sexual behavior, especially the importance of sensory information, remain part of current hypotheses.

FIGURE 5.4 Eugen Steinach

The pressure hypothesis has fallen out of favor in response to several studies that appear to rule it out; subsequent research has supported the idea that hormones from the testes generate male mating behavior. The presence or absence of gonads, however, is not the only mediating factor in male sexual behavior; sexual experience also affects postcastration responses. Virtually all sexually inexperienced male rats display mating behavior when given the opportunity to interact with estrous females soon after castration, but their interest in females wanes in about 2 weeks. Males with prior sexual experience, on the other hand, display significant variation in how long they maintain reproductive behavior after castration; some males lose interest in females rapidly, whereas others continue to mate for weeks (reviewed in Larsson, 2003). The contribution of experience to the interaction between hormones and sexual behavior remains unspecified.

Steinach and his early-twentieth-century contemporaries were aware that sexual experience affected the rate of postcastration reductions in male sexual behavior in domesticated animals. For instance, tomcats with sexual experience prior to neutering may continue to engage in copulatory behavior for months after the testes are removed, usually to the chagrin of pet owners (Dunbar, 1975). Even Aristotle noted in his *Historia Animalium* that castrated bulls occasionally continued to copulate with cows. It was also well known during the nineteenth century that men who lost their testes through disease or accident maintained sexual behavior for some time, often indefinitely, after the injury. According to Pflüger (1877, cited in Steinach, 1894), one way the difference between human sexual behavior and that of other animals could be explained was on the basis of humans' unique mental faculties, that is, their "psychic qualities, the vigor of men's fantasies, and their powerful memories."

Certainly, "psychic" qualities must be called forth as an explanation for the claims made by Charles Edouard Brown-Séquard, at the Société de Biologie of Paris in 1899 (Brown-Séquard, 1899). Ten years earlier, Brown-Séquard (**FIGURE 5.5**), a prominent researcher, had published findings in the *Archives de Physiologie Normale et Pathologique*, claiming that injections of endocrine extracts had astounding rejuvenating effects on several physical parameters, including sexual vigor. His claim that the injections had amazing restorative effects prompted sales of endocrine extract "treatments" (**FIGURE 5.6**). At the Société in 1899, Brown-Séquard sought to dem-

FIGURE 5.5 Charles Edouard Brown-Séquard Photogravure by Heliog Dujardin.

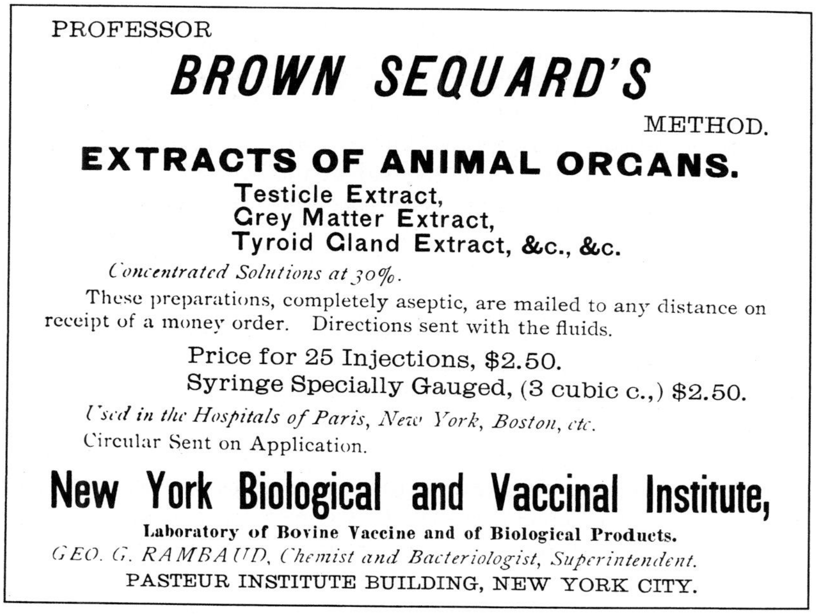

Advertisement, New York Therapeutic Review, *1893.*

FIGURE 5.6 A representative nineteenth-century advertisement for extracts based on Brown-Séquard's fallacious claims. Hoping to capitalize on Brown-Séquard's findings, charlatans sold "rejuvenating" preparations.

FIGURE 5.7   Calvin P. Stone

onstrate his findings: he injected himself with an aqueous solution of homogenized dog and guinea pig testes. However, androgens were later discovered to be lipid-soluble steroid hormones; therefore, water-based injections are unlikely to have produced the behavioral effects reported by Brown-Séquard, because they would have been unlikely to contain many androgen molecules. The improvements in stamina that he noted were probably the result of a placebo effect produced by his belief in the treatment. Although his final studies on himself overshadowed a career of bona fide accomplishments in endocrine research, the furor created by Brown-Séquard's demonstration initiated medical interest in the sex steroid hormones, for which he must be given credit.

As noted in Chapter 3, a masculine or feminine behavior pattern is not determined simply by the presence or absence of a particular behavior but is often a matter of the frequency of, or the threshold for, a certain behavior. Quantitative measures of male sexual behavior are therefore an important means of describing it. One of the earliest attempts at quantification of mammalian sexual behavior was made by Calvin P. Stone (**FIGURE 5.7**), a psychologist, who determined the age at which male rats first exhibited copulatory ability (Stone, 1922). He tested males for mating behavior every day from when they weaned from their mothers (21 days of age) until they were 60 days of age; Stone discovered that the average age at which first copulation was observed was about 50 days (Stone, 1924). Stone also determined that developing male rats maintained copulatory ability for about 14 days after castration (Stone, 1927) and reported that substantial variation exists in the maintenance of intermale aggression and mating behavior after castration. We will return to this issue of variation in responses below.

During the 1920s, "drive theory" was important in shaping North American psychology. The underlying causes of behavior were conceptualized as competing intrinsic drives or motivations. During this time, psychologists developed new ways of measuring the strength of the sex drive, in addition to measuring sexual performance (e.g., Tsai, 1925; Warner, 1927). Given a choice, researchers asked, will a rat prefer to satiate its hunger, thirst, or sex drive? What levels of deprivation are necessary for one biological need to override another? How much work will an individual perform to attain sex? And how much pain will an individual bear to reduce its sex drive? It is interesting that these questions are again being addressed using very simple model species such as *C. elegans*, and elegant genetic tools are being used to discover the regulation of these drives (e.g., Barrios et al., 2012; Lin et al., 2011). The sex drives of individuals of many species were quantified by a battery of motivational tests (e.g., Nissen, 1929; Stone et al., 1935) (see below). Recall that "motivation" is a psychological hypothetical construct; like "learning" or "attention," motivation cannot be measured directly. Only performance on a test designed to indirectly assess such a hypothetical construct can be measured.

Early in the twentieth century, the ablation-replacement technique (see Chapter 1) was used to determine the behavioral effects of sex steroid hormones. For instance, a series of studies suggested that ovarian grafts in castrated young male rats or guinea pigs modified their subsequent behavior and physiology so that they "became" females (Steinach, 1910, 1913). In guinea pigs, growth of the mammary glands and milk secretion were reported, but these findings were never replicated completely. On the other hand, grafts of testicular tissue in young females influenced their development so that they became masculinized as they matured. These latter findings have been replicated many times in several species. A secreted product from the interstitial cells of the transplanted gonad was proposed as the controlling factor in these transsexual changes, because the secondary sex characters of the opposite sex were not manifested unless the implanted gonad developed vascular connections (Steinach, 1940). We now know that the organizing properties of the steroid hormones from the testes cause the appearance of male-like characters in early-treated females (see Chapter 3).

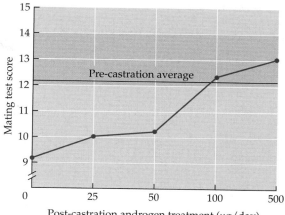

FIGURE 5.8 Testosterone treatment maintains sexual behavior after castration. Mating behavior declines after castration in male rats but can be maintained by testosterone treatment. The maintenance of sexual behavior by testosterone is dose-dependent: in this study, only rats receiving testosterone doses of 100 µg/day or greater displayed sexual behavior at precastration levels. After Beach and Holz-Tucker, 1949.

An obvious refinement in experiments addressing endocrine effects on male sexual behavior was the discovery of the active agents in the testes that were responsible for observed behavioral effects. After the estrus-inducing hormone from the ovarian follicle was discovered to be lipid-soluble, the search for the *andros*-generating hormone began. Injections of an extract of bull testes dissolved in oil produced a rapid regeneration of capons' combs (McGee et al., 1928). Pure crystalline hormone from testicular tissue was soon isolated and named testosterone (David et al., 1935). A year later, preparation of synthetic testosterone from cholesterol became feasible, and large amounts of the hormone rapidly became available for clinical and experimental studies. Several investigators demonstrated the restoration of sexual behavior in castrated male rats after injections of testosterone propionate, a stable, injectable form of testosterone (Moore and Price, 1938; Shapiro, 1937; Stone, 1938a,b, 1939). For example, a dose-response experiment revealed that 50–75 µg of testosterone propionate per day was necessary to maintain adult male mating behavior after castration (Beach and Holz-Tucker, 1949) (**FIGURE 5.8**).

Many early researchers who attempted to link hormones and behavior came to approach their work, both theoretically and methodologically, with a "one hormone equals one behavior" philosophy (reviewed in Beach, 1948). Differences in behavior were thought to represent differences in the underlying hormone that controlled the behavior in question. However, we now know that hormonal effects on behavior rarely reflect this type of unitary relationship. For example, male copulatory behavior can be restored in castrated males by injections of either estrogens or androgens (Ball, 1937; Beach, 1942c). Massive doses of testosterone propionate also can cause either feminine or masculine mating behaviors in castrated males. These results indicate that the action of any particular sex steroid hormone cannot be behavior-specific; every individual probably possesses the behavioral repertoire of both sexes, but one set of responses appears to have a lower threshold for expression in the presence of a particular hormone(s) (Beach, 1948). Indeed, aromatization of androgens into estrogens occurs in the nervous system, which accounts for many of these puzzling results in nonprimates. Indeed, in many species, the brain produces the most estrogens of any organ in the body. Nonetheless, the empirical observation that both estrogens and androgens can support mating behavior in castrated males led eventually to an appreciation and understanding of the neural bases of reproductive behaviors and to the formulation of modern theories of hormone-behavior interactions. Current views about the hormonal regulation of behavior focus on the substrate or target tissues of the hormones, and research is now aimed at elucidating how differences in behavior reflect differences in target tissue sensitivity.

Male Sexual Behavior in Rodents

As with other areas of behavioral endocrinology research, most work on the effects of hormones on male reproductive behavior has been performed on laboratory rats (*Rattus norvegicus*), and many current theoretical considerations have arisen from these studies. Work with animal models has provided useful information that is also applicable to human clinical conditions (Ågmo, 2007, 2011; Giuliano et al., 2006; Hull and Dominquez, 2007, 2013). Consequently, many of the concepts we discuss

FIGURE 5.9 Male sexual motivation can be assessed by determining how much work an individual is willing to do or how much pain or other unpleasantries an individual will endure to obtain access to a female. In this case, the rat must bar-press several hundred times to open a door that separates him from an estrous female.

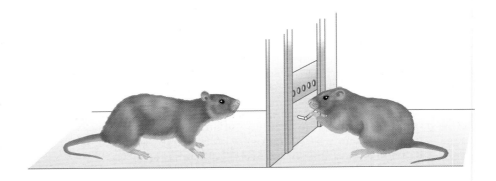

will be illustrated with examples from studies of rat mating behavior. In order to understand what these studies have revealed about the hormonal and neural bases underlying male reproductive behavior, a thorough description of rat mating behavior is necessary.

Male Mating Behavior in Rats: A Description

In rats and many other rodent species, there are three easily distinguishable behavioral components of the consummatory phase of male mating behavior: (1) mounting, (2) intromission, and (3) ejaculation. In most standard mating tests, one male and one female are introduced into a glass enclosure (usually an empty aquarium). Several precopulatory behaviors are observed in male mice before they mount; these behaviors are relatively easy to quantify, and they provide a useful measure of male sexual motivation. Mount latency, for instance, is the time from the introduction of the male and female until the first mount. Sexual motivation is considered high if mount latency is low, and vice versa. Sexual motivation can be tested by placing some sort of obstacle between the male and the female and observing how long it takes the male to overcome the obstacle. This common test of sexual motivation is called an obstruction test. The so-called Columbia University obstruction test, using a physical barrier or an electrified floor, was often used in research of this sort (e.g., Stone et al., 1935; Warner, 1927). In other obstruction tests, the male must run on a treadmill that is moving away from the female, climb a ladder, or press a bar (Plaud and Martini, 1999) (**FIGURE 5.9**). Presumably, high motivation for sex can be inferred if the male passes the obstruction at a high speed or endures great pain. Males unmotivated for sex will not work or suffer to obtain access to a female (Lopez et al., 1999).

Soon after introduction of the pair, the male begins to investigate the female, sniffing her mouth and anogenital region (Stone, 1922). Moments later, he attempts to mount her. If she is in estrus, or mating condition, the female exhibits the lordosis posture, which facilitates an intromission (**FIGURE 5.10A**). **Mounting** is operationally defined as the male assuming a copulatory position but not inserting his penis into the female's vagina. In some cases, males may mount the side or head of the female, and occasionally males may mount other males. In other cases, males may not mount at all. During tests with time limits, 1 hour for example, some males consistently fail to initiate sexual behavior by mounting. Males may fail to mount a female because of low sex drive, decreased penile sensitivity, or reduced erectile potential. One measure used to describe sexual behavior is the **inter-mount interval (IMI)**, or the average time between successive mounts.

Intromission can be defined as the penis entering the vagina during a mount. In rats and mice, intromission is associated with thrusting motions of the hindquarters (**FIGURE 5.10B**), but in many species, thrusting is not observed. For example, male guinea pigs and rabbits ejaculate during the first intromission and complete copulation within a few seconds without thrusting. Counting the number of intromissions

mounting   A behavior observed among males of many species with internal fertilization in which the male assumes a copulatory position but does not insert his penis (or other intromittent organ) into the female's vagina (or urogenital opening). This behavior is androgen-dependent.

inter-mount interval (IMI)   The interval of time between successive mounts by a male during copulation.

intromission   The entrance of the penis into the vagina.

FIGURE 5.10 Sexual behavior in rats A male rat first investigates the anogenital region of a female, and if she is in estrus, he will mount her, with his forepaws clasped against her hindquarters. This tactile stimulation causes her to display the lordosis posture, arching her back and deflecting her tail (A). Lordosis facilitates intromission, or insertion of the male rat's penis into the vagina, accompanied by thrusting of his hindquarters (B). After several seconds, the male dismounts, grooms himself, and soon remounts. After several intromissions, the male ejaculates, forcefully expelling semen into the female rat's vagina (C). Courtesy of Lique Coolen.

(A)

(B)

(C)

prior to each ejaculation provides a useful measure of reproductive behavior for males that exhibit multiple intromissions; however, the utility of this measure is limited because interindividual differences are common. Another common measure of male sexual behavior is the **inter-intromission interval (III)**, the average time between successive intromissions. It is also possible to measure the copulatory motor patterns and make detailed analyses of animals at different ages or in different hormonal conditions (Morali et al., 2003).

Ejaculation is the forceful expulsion of semen from the male's body via the urethra. Ejaculation is behaviorally defined in rats as the culmination of vigorous intravaginal thrusting accompanied by the arching of the male's spine and often the lifting of his forepaws off the female prior to withdrawal (**FIGURE 5.10C**). During ejaculation, a sperm plug is often deposited in the vagina. In some rodent species, this plug effectively blocks intromission by other males until the sperm have had the opportunity to fertilize the estrous female. In laboratory tests, the number of intromissions prior to ejaculation and also the ejaculatory latency, the time from the first intromission to ejaculation, are typically recorded. The mating potential of any given male is determined by the number of ejaculations during a time-limited test or by the number of ejaculations prior to his attaining sexual satiety (Sachs and Meisel, 1988). Most male laboratory rats can ejaculate five to eight times during an unlimited-time mating test (Ågmo, 1997).

Male rats often "sing" after an ejaculation. A special ultrasonic detector is required to hear these vocalizations, which are in the 20–22 kHz range (Fernández-Vargas et al., 2015); however, observers can detect singing by noting the rapid shallow respirations that correspond with the ultrasonic vocalizations. After ejaculation, male rats usually become sexually inactive and rather lethargic. The male may groom his genitals, then lie down and sleep. He virtually ignores the female. This post-ejaculatory sequence of behaviors is not due to ejaculation per se, because artificial electroejaculation does not induce these behaviors.

The time between an ejaculation and the onset of the next copulatory series is called the **post-ejaculatory interval (PEI)**. The PEI is less than 30 seconds in Syrian hamsters (*Mesocricetus auratus*) (Bunnell et al., 1976), about 5–15 minutes in laboratory rats, and as long as hours or days in some other species (Dewsbury, 1972; Fernandez-Guasti and Rodriguez-Manzo, 2003; Money, 1961). The PEI is generally considered to be composed of two separate periods, an absolute refractory phase and a relative refractory phase (Beach and Holz-Tucker, 1949). Males are completely nonresponsive to sexual, mildly painful, and other stimuli during the absolute refractory phase. A new or very potent sexual stimulus may elicit responsiveness in a male rat during the relative refractory phase (see below). A male rat with a PEI greater than 90 minutes is usually considered sexually "exhausted" or satiated (Ågmo, 1997). Studies in other types of animals have revealed interesting diversity in male mating patterns (**BOX 5.2**).

inter-intromission interval (III)
The interval of time between successful intromissions by a male during copulation.

ejaculation The forceful expulsion of semen from a male's body via the urethra.

post-ejaculatory interval (PEI)
The interval of time between ejaculations by a male during copulation.

BOX 5.2   *Diversity of Male Mating Patterns*

Male copulatory behavior in mammals can be classified into several categories based on the presence of four features: (1) copulatory lock, (2) intravaginal thrusting, (3) multiple intromissions, and (4) multiple ejaculations (Dewsbury, 1972). Species can be grouped according to 16 different mating patterns that emerge from this classification scheme (**Figure A**). Animals that show copulatory lock, such as dogs (pattern 3), have a penis that swells after ejaculation, which facilitates sperm transport to the female; this process may take several minutes, during which time it is virtually impossible for the pair to disengage. Males of some species, such as guinea pigs, do not show pelvic thrusting and ejaculate with a single intromission. Male rats, on the other hand, engage in about 20 mounts and 10 to 15 intromissions prior to the first ejaculation, although these values vary among rat strains; additional intromissions are usually required for each subsequent ejaculation (Beach and Jordan, 1956).

As shown in **Figure B**, a male dog first investigates the anogenital region of a female (top). If she is in estrus (mating condition), she will allow the male to mount her (middle left). The hindquarters of the male thrust with increasing intensity until ejaculation occurs some seconds later. After ejaculation, the penis remains "locked" in the vagina, and the male steps over the female as he dismounts (middle right). They remain in this copulatory lock for several minutes to facilitate sperm transport (bottom).

The various patterns of male copulatory behavior have been related to the ecology of particular species, and several broad generalizations can be made (Dewsbury, 1972). For example, predator species are more likely to lock than prey species; prey species cannot risk being immobilized for long periods of time, and there are few prey species that require lengthy sperm transport periods. Animals that mate at night are more likely to engage in copulatory locking than diurnal creatures, presumably because of a lack of predation pressures. Virtually all rodent species that lock (e.g., golden mice, *Ochrotomys nuttalli*, and southern grasshopper mice, *Onychomys torridus*) are nocturnal.

Copulatory lock?	Thrusting?	Multiple intromissions?	Multiple ejaculations?	Pattern
Yes	Yes	Yes	Yes	1
			No	2
		No	Yes	3
			No	4
	No	Yes	Yes	5
			No	6
		No	Yes	7
			No	8
No	Yes	Yes	Yes	9
			No	10
		No	Yes	11
			No	12
	No	Yes	Yes	13
			No	14
		No	Yes	15
			No	16

Figure A After Dewsbury, 1972.

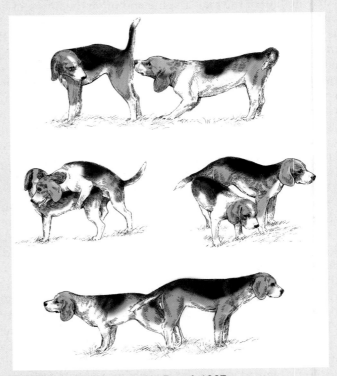

Figure B After Beach and LeBoeuf, 1967.

Hormonal Correlates of Male Mating Behavior in Rodents

As we have seen, testosterone is necessary for the maintenance of mating behavior in male rats. Castration leads to a reduction in sexual responsiveness; both motivation and performance wane. For most rodent species, sexual behavior is markedly reduced immediately after castration (but see below). Sex drive also declines rapidly after the testes are removed. Castrated males will not investigate females, nor will

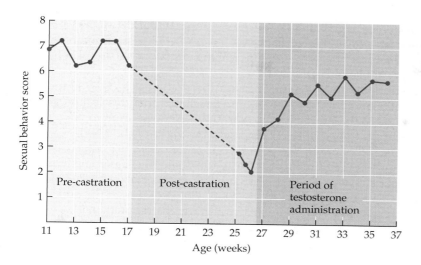

FIGURE 5.11 Sexual behavior can be restored by testosterone therapy. After castration, guinea pigs displayed marked declines in sexual behavior, but testosterone replacement therapy gradually restored sexual behavior to precastration levels. After Valenstein and Young, 1955.

they work or suffer pain to reach them. If castrated rats are examined during daily mating tests, then the timing of the disappearance of components of sexual behavior follows a characteristic pattern. The effects of castration are observed within days. Males first begin to take longer to initiate mounting and intromissions (Hull and Dominquez, 2007; Hull et al., 2002; Meisel and Sachs, 1994). Another early effect of castration is that fewer intromissions occur prior to ejaculation. This may seem paradoxical: fewer intromissions before ejaculation may appear to reflect increased reproductive performance. However, a male that normally has 8 intromissions prior to ejaculation is not necessarily a more efficient or effective copulator than one that typically has 15 intromissions before ejaculation. Fewer intromissions may be less likely to provide the female with sufficient stimulation to induce a progestational state (see Chapter 6), resulting in a failure of blastocyst implantation (Wilson et al., 1965). By a week or two postcastration, rats cannot mate to ejaculation. The inability to ejaculate is soon followed by a decline in the number of mounts with intromissions, and finally the male no longer mounts females.

The effects of castration on male rodent reproductive behavior can be reversed by testosterone treatment (**FIGURE 5.11**). The restoration of copulatory behaviors after sustained androgen therapy mirrors the disappearance of those behaviors: first mounting recurs, followed by intromissions, then ejaculations. Of course, neither intromissions nor ejaculations can occur in the absence of mounting, and ejaculations will not be observed in the absence of intromissions, yet it is theoretically possible that all the behaviors could be restored simultaneously. However, they generally reappear sequentially over the course of several days (Larsson, 1979). This rigid sequential ordering of behavior suggests, although it does not prove, that mounting, intromission, and ejaculation behaviors have different sensitivities to testicular hormones.

If androgen replacement therapy is initiated immediately after castration (maintenance treatment), then lower amounts of hormone are required to maintain reproductive behavior than are necessary to restore sexual behavior sometime later, after it has stopped (restoration treatment) (Davidson, 1966a,b) (**FIGURE 5.12**). Persistent exposure of brain and sensory neural tissue to androgens apparently preserves their responsiveness to these hormones. Of course, testosterone is released in a pulsatile manner (see Chapter 2). Short-duration pulses of testosterone infusions (either one 4-hour dose of 100 µg or two 4-hour doses of 50 µg) were sufficient to maintain sexual behavior in castrated male Syrian hamsters up to 11 weeks postcastration even though circulating testosterone val-

FIGURE 5.12 Maintenance versus restoration of sexual behavior by testosterone therapy The amount of testosterone necessary to restore full sexual behavior is greater if the treatment begins after all sexual behavior stops (restoration regimen) than if it begins immediately after castration (maintenance regimen). Presumably, the restoration regimen requires higher doses because androgen receptors decrease in number if not maintained by circulating androgens. After Davidson, 1966a.

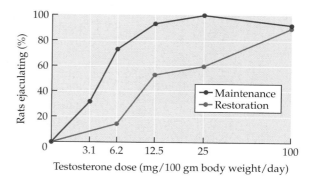

ues were undetectable 7 hours after the infusions stopped (Park et al., 2007). Sexual behaviors waned in vehicle-treated hamsters 3 weeks after castration. Infrequent low doses of testosterone, however, are sufficient to maintain male sexual behaviors in Syrian hamsters (Piekarski et al., 2009).

Seasonal breeders undergo a natural castration each year as they enter their nonbreeding season. Small rodents undergo regression of their testes, and gonadal hormones decline to undetectable concentrations in the autumn in response to shortening day lengths (see Chapter 9). After several weeks of short-day exposure, male Syrian hamsters stop mating behavior (Morin and Zucker, 1978), and castrated short-day male hamsters require more testosterone than long-day male hamsters to maintain sexual behaviors. The threshold for initiation of sexual behavior may be higher in short-day animals (Park et al., 2004). Consistent with the notion that more testosterone is necessary to stimulate mating after castration than is needed to maintain mating behaviors, male Syrian hamsters that develop their reproductive systems in the spring require a larger pulse of androgens to activate the reproductive system than long-day animals need to maintain sexual behavior (Berndtson and Desjardins, 1974).

Two androgens—testosterone and androstenedione, a weakly androgenic precursor of testosterone—can maintain mating behavior in castrated rodents (Sachs and Meisel, 1988). Dihydrotestosterone (DHT), another product of testosterone, does not prevent the postcastration decline in reproductive behavior, regardless of whether it is provided at the time of castration or postcastration (Feder, 1971). In contrast to DHT, estradiol, an estrogen, is very effective in activating mating behavior in castrated male rodents (Davidson, 1969; Södersten, 1973). As you know, both testosterone and androstenedione can be aromatized to estradiol and other estrogens, but DHT cannot be converted into an estrogen (see Chapter 2). Taken together, these findings suggest that testosterone and androstenedione produce their behavioral effects after first being converted to estrogens (Larsson, 2003). Further support for this hypothesis arises from the observation that injecting castrated rats with specific estrogen receptor blocking agents renders subsequent androgen therapy ineffective in sustaining copulatory behavior (Beyer et al., 1976). Also, inhibiting the conversion of androgens to estrogens with a drug that blocks aromatization (fadrozole) reduces both appetitive (searching for females) and consummatory (mounting, intromission, and ejaculation) features of male rat sexual behavior (Roselli et al., 2003). Estrogen treatment overrides the fadrozole effects. DHT is not completely without effect; estradiol plus DHT treatment restores the mating behavior of castrated rats to the level of gonadally intact individuals (Feder et al., 1974). DHT appears to be important for maintaining penile tactile sensitivity (see below). In general, estradiol appears to affect the central nervous system to promote mating behavior, and DHT affects neurons in the periphery to maintain tactile sensory feedback. Thus, testosterone from the testes appears to function primarily as a prohormone, providing estrogens to the CNS and providing DHT to the periphery to regulate sexual behavior. Of course, as we learned in Chapter 4, estrogen can be produced de novo in the brain and may also contribute to the regulation of male sexual behavior. Corticosterone is also elevated during all aspects of male rat sexual experiences, but its regulatory function requires further investigation (Bonilla-Jaime et al., 2006).

Penile responses, in either the presence or absence of females or other contextual cues, can be tested by placing a rat or mouse on its back and retracting the penile sheath to the base of the glans penis (Sachs, 1995a). The pressure of the sheath causes the erection reflex of the glans, which is due to the engorgement of the corpus spongiosum (**BOX 5.3**) with venous blood. An erection of the penile shaft is depicted in **FIGURE 5.13**. If the pressure on the penis continues, then penile reflexes called flips are noted. Flips are due to the action of the corpora cavernosa and the striated penile muscles. Intense glans erections, called cups, are observed after prolonged

BOX 5.3   *Anatomy of the Penis*

There are two important structural components of the mammalian penis, the corpus spongiosum and the paired corpora cavernosa. Both components are critical erectile tissues comprising smooth muscle and blood vessels and are usually associated with a set of striated muscles. The corpora cavernosa and the corpus spongiosum usually function together during tumescence and detumescence, but they may become functionally dissociated.

In humans, the corpora cavernosa are twin "tunnels" of highly vascular tissue that occupy most of the penile body. A muscle called the ischiocavernosus is connected to the base (crus) of each corpus cavernosum. The glans and the central tissue of the penis make up the corpus spongiosum. Some species have a bone (**Figure A**), called the os penis, located within the corpus spongiosum. In rats, the bone is present only in the glans; in other species, such as dogs, the os penis is found in the penile body. In primates, the base of the corpus spongiosum is connected to the bulbospongiosus striated muscle, which is called the bulbocavernosus muscle in other species, including rodents.

There is great diversity in penile morphology across species. In some species the penis is so distinctive that the species can be classified taxonomically by this organ. This species-specific penile morphology has evolved to maximize fertilization of conspecific females. Enormously diverse mechanisms of penile erection have also evolved among mammals, involving different combinations of smooth muscle, vascular tissue, and striated muscles. In rats, penile erections are mainly the result of neural signals that contract striated muscles, causing erection of

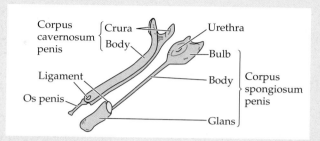

Figure A

the glans penis (**Figure B**). In humans, penile erections are the result mainly of vascular changes that cause the corpora cavernosa to fill with blood, resulting in tumescence of the penile body (Tanagho et al., 1988).

The innervation of the penis and the details of how penile erection in humans is mediated have been established, but the details remain incomplete (McConnell et al., 1982; Tanagho et al., 1988). It has been known for over a century that it is possible to induce penile erections with electrical stimulation of certain pelvic nerves in rats and dogs (Eckhardt, 1863). Direct electrical stimulation of the rat cavernosus nerve results in tumescence of the penile shaft—because of corpus cavernosum blood engorgement—but not tumescence of the glans (Burgers et al., 1991; Quinlan et al., 1989). The latter may be the result of a somatic response produced by the erect corpora cavernosa; contraction of the bulbocavernosus muscle may compress the erect shaft against the os penis in the glans, resulting in straightening of the glans.

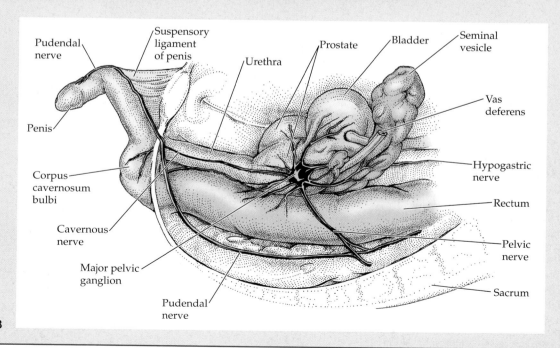

Figure B

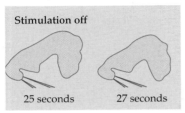

Stimulation on

5 seconds   7 seconds   12 seconds   15 seconds   22 seconds

Stimulation off

25 seconds   27 seconds

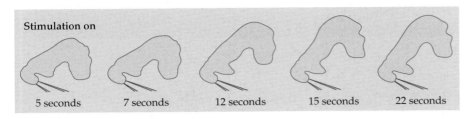

FIGURE 5.13 **Erection in rats** can be induced by bilateral electrical stimulation of the cavernosus nerve, as seen in these drawings of sequential video images of a 22-second stimulation period. Tumescence begins between 5 and 7 seconds after the initiation of stimulation; detumescence is brisk and occurs within 5 seconds of cessation of the electrical current. Courtesy of David Quinlan.

penile stimulation (**FIGURE 5.14**). These three penile responses are similar in form to those observed both during normal sexual behavior (*in copula*) and during artificial stimulation (*ex copula*) (Meisel et al., 1984; Sachs, 1995b). Developmental studies of male rats show a remarkable similarity in the average ages of onset of erections and mounts (40.0 and 40.8 days, respectively), flips and intromissions (44.0 and 43.8 days, respectively), and cups and ejaculations (about 47.5 days in both cases) (Sachs and Meisel, 1979). This coincidence in development between penile reflexes and copulatory behaviors suggests a functional relationship, as well as separate underlying mechanisms and possibly different sensitivities to hormonal regulation for the three components of mating behavior.

If animals fail to mate after castration, then it is difficult to ascertain whether sexual performance, sex drive, or both functions have been affected by the surgery. One way to differentiate between the effects of hormones on sex drive and on mating performance is to isolate the brain—presumably the source of sex drive—from the spinal cord. We know that the entire erectile repertoire is programmed in the spinal cord, because appropriate stimulation causes a rat with his spinal cord severed from the brain to show erections as well as the penile reflexes underlying intromission, thrusting, and ejaculation (Meisel and Sachs, 1994). The term *sex drive* implies that the brain is "driving" behavior through excitatory messages to the periphery via the spinal cord. Although the brain does send some excitatory signals, it acts primarily

FIGURE 5.14 **Reflexive erections in rats can be induced by retraction of the penile shaft.** In A–C, the glans is directed toward the tail, the normal orientation. In D, the glans is oriented toward the head, the position necessary for intromission. The penis also changes color from A–B to C–D. This reflects engorgement with blood. (A) The quiescent rat penis. (B) Tumescence and slight elevation of the penile shaft without glans erection. (C) Intense glans erection ("cup") and penile shaft. (D) Anteroflexion ("flip") of the penis. From Hull et al., 2002.

(A) (B)

(C) (D)

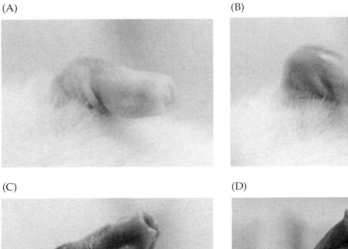

TABLE 5.1 *Frequency of sexual reflexes, latency to first reflex, and plasma testosterone concentrations in intact, castrated, and testosterone-treated male rats*

Treatment	Sexual reflex			Latency (min)	Plasma testosterone (ng/ml)
	Erection	Flip	Cup		
Intact	22.2	4.2	1.3	5.5	1.95
Castrated	12.3	0.5	0.04	9.9	<0.20
Testosterone implant					
2 mm	18.4	2.4	0.04	6.5	0.40
6 mm	22.5	6.0	0.6	5.4	0.79
18 mm	20.8	3.5	1.0	6.5	1.09

Source: Davidson et al., 1978.

to inhibit the spinal mechanisms of erection (Beach, 1967; Sachs and Bitran, 1990). In spinally transected rodents, the stimuli required to induce an erection are much less than the stimuli necessary for inducing erections in intact males. As we shall see, clinical data suggest an inhibitory influence of the human brain on erectile function as well.

If spinally transected rats are also castrated, then their penile reflexes begin to wane after 24 hours and disappear after 12 days (Hart et al., 1983). The loss of penile responses after castration follows an ordered pattern similar to the degradation of postcastration mating behavior: cups, then flips, and finally erections disappear (Davidson et al., 1978). (As discussed previously, however, the order of decline and restoration of copulatory behaviors is somewhat constrained by the nature of the chaining of these processes.) These results suggest that androgens are necessary, but not sufficient, for erections. Appropriate penile stimulation is necessary for penile erection, and androgens reduce the amount of stimuli required for a penile response to be observed.

Normal penile reflexes are maintained or restored by testosterone. In one study, castrated rats were implanted with Silastic capsules of testosterone that varied in length (from 2 to 18 mm). The hormone seeps out of the capsules at a constant rate; therefore, longer capsules result in more testosterone being released into the body tissue fluid per unit of time. Animals bearing capsules greater than 6 mm in length displayed penile reflexes comparable to those of intact males. A 6 mm capsule produced average blood plasma testosterone concentrations of 0.79 ng/ml, well below the average blood testosterone concentrations of 1.95 ng/ml in gonadally intact males (Davidson et al., 1978) (**TABLE 5.1**). Thus, blood plasma testosterone concentrations are typically well above the minimum necessary to maintain copulatory behaviors or penile reflexes, so a substantial decrease, of even 30%, from normal blood androgen concentrations should not be expected to influence mating behavior. Even an average reduction of blood testosterone concentrations of 50% would probably not affect behavior.

Testosterone also does not seem to directly regulate penile responses. Rather, testosterone serves as a precursor to DHT, which directly regulates penile responses. DHT maintains or restores penile reflexes to precastration levels in both spinally transected and spinally intact rats; estradiol, another testosterone metabolite, does not seem to affect penile reflexes (Gray et al., 1980; Hart, 1979; Meisel et al., 1984). Castrated rats implanted with Silastic capsules of estradiol maintained mating behavior at a level comparable to gonadally intact animals; however, the rate at which penile reflexes decreased in estrogen-treated males was similar to that in untreated castrated individuals (Meisel et al., 1984). Thus, it appears that testosterone that is aromatized to estradiol in neural tissue mediates copulatory behavior, whereas testosterone that is converted to DHT mediates penile reflexes and sensitivity to tactile feedback (Meisel and Sachs, 1994). Again, testosterone appears to act as a prohormone from which steroids affecting central nervous system processing and peripheral sensory receptor sensitivities are produced to ensure successful copulation.

Brain Mechanisms of Male Rodent Mating Behavior

Historically, brain lesioning techniques have been used to discover where in the brain sexual behavior is regulated. The logic behind lesioning techniques is that removal of a critical component of the neural mechanism underlying sexual behavior should disrupt sexual behavior. Initially, rather large lesions were performed to study sexual behavior. Perhaps not surprisingly, removing the entire neocortex of rats diminished their sexual behavior; removal of the frontal cortex also effectively disrupted rat copulation (Larsson, 1962; Lashley, 1938). More recently, researchers have tried to limit the scope of brain lesions to locate more precisely the brain areas that regulate sexual behavior.

Essentially, dopamine is released in the medial preoptic area (mPOA) as soon as a male mammal or bird meets a receptive female; dopamine secretion is further elevated during copulation. Stimulation of dopamine receptors in the mPOA contributes to both genital reflexes and sexual motivation. The mPOA is critical for male sexual behavior in all vertebrate species that have been studied thus far, including men. Testosterone, or more commonly its metabolite 17β-estradiol, promotes copulation, in part, by provoking the release of dopamine in the mPOA. Locally produced 17β-estradiol in the brain promotes sexual motivation, but not sexual performance. After ejaculation, dopamine is inhibited in mesolimbic brain regions, partly by the release of serotonin. The evidence for the role of the mPOA, dopamine, and serotonin is provided in the following sections.

THE PREOPTIC AREA The region of the brain anterior to the hypothalamus, especially the preoptic area (POA) (**FIGURE 5.15**), appears to be critical for integrating environmental, physiological, and psychological information prior to and during successful copulation (Crews and Silver, 1985; Sachs and Meisel, 1988). The POA contains several nuclei from which axons project to other brain regions. The mPOA is the region of the POA along both sides of the midline of the brain. Some studies have focused on this specific area of the POA. In virtually all vertebrate species studied to date, lesions of the POA in adult males eliminate sexual performance, although sexual motivation appears unaffected (but see Paredes, 2003): male rats

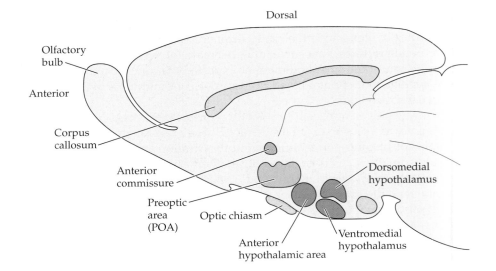

FIGURE 5.15 Regions that are essential to the control of sexual performance in male rats, seen in a schematic sagittal section of the brain. The preoptic area (POA) appears to be especially important for the integration of environmental, physiological, and psychological information prior to and during successful copulation; POA lesions reduce or eliminate male sexual behavior in virtually every vertebrate species examined. The POA apparently regulates endocrine function by interacting with hypothalamic nuclei and mediates parasympathetic functions associated with male copulation. After Pfaff, 1980.

with POA lesions fail to mount females even when tested 8 months after surgery, although they will press bars or run mazes to gain access to females (Ginton and Merari, 1977; Heimer and Larsson, 1966). Neither testosterone treatment nor access to multiple females compensates for POA lesions.

What are the consequences of a POA lesion? Preoptic neurons project to several places in the brain, including the dopaminergic neurons in the periaqueductal gray (PAG) and ventral tegmental areas (VTA). A POA lesion destroys the connections to these dopaminergic neurons and impairs the POA regulation of dopaminergic activity in these brain regions (Hull et al., 1997). Treating POA-lesioned male rats with lisuride, a chemical that mimics dopamine, transiently activates copulation in these animals, with many of them copulating to ejaculation (Hansen et al., 1982). Presumably, the dopaminergic neuronal input destroyed by a POA lesion is part of a neural circuit that integrates and regulates copulatory behavior. In the absence of dopamine-receptor interactions "downstream" from the POA, copulatory behavior is not observed. When dopamine is replaced with an agonist that can interact with and excite neurons downstream from the POA, copulatory behavior is restored. If this hypothesis is correct, then drugs that increase dopamine synthesis or stimulate postsynaptic dopamine receptor sites should also facilitate copulatory behavior among intact male rats, and this has been observed to be true (Ahlenius and Larsson, 1984; Napoli-Farris et al., 1984; Paglietti et al., 1978; Sachs, 1995b). Similarly, one might predict that drugs that suppress dopaminergic activity would reduce male rat sexual behaviors, and this has also been observed to occur (e.g., Ahlenius and Larsson, 1984; Napoli-Farris et al., 1984). The claim that dopaminergic axons are mainly responsible for mediating male copulatory behavior in rats is strengthened by the observation that no other pharmacological treatment, including GnRH or naloxone, an opioid antagonist, reinstates copulatory behavior in POA-lesioned rats. Taken together, these results indicate that projections to dopaminergic neurons that are destroyed by POA lesions are necessary for normal copulatory behaviors in male rats (Mas, 1995).

It appears that activation of μ opioid receptors in the mPOA occurs after male sexual behavior. When male rats were allowed to mate to ejaculation, μ opioid receptors were activated and internalized in mPOA neurons within 30 minutes, and this process continued for 6 hours postcopulation (Coolen et al., 2004). Prior treatment of rats with naloxone prevented the internalization of μ opioid receptors after copulation. These results support the hypothesis that male sexual behavior evokes secretion of endogenous opioids and that the mPOA is part of the brain circuitry mediating the rewarding properties of sexual behavior (Coolen et al., 2004). It is not uncommon for people who abuse opioids to be hypersexual.

Social history can dramatically affect the outcome of POA lesions in young rats. Male rats reared in social isolation and then given POA lesions as juveniles never copulate as adults (Twiggs et al., 1978). But in sharp contrast to the profound copulatory deficits observed in adult rats after POA lesions, there are virtually no effects on adult copulatory behavior of similar lesions in juvenile rats reared in heterosexual groups (Twiggs et al., 1978). Exactly what component of group living ameliorates behavior following POA lesions remains unspecified. A reasonable hypothesis is that social interactions somehow elevate dopamine levels. This result is intriguing because it shows the importance of social conditions in mediating rodent brain plasticity and reproductive function after a substantial neural insult, and because social conditions also play a major role in the development of normal sexual behavior among primates (Hull and Dominguez, 2013, 2015).

Remote cues from females result in so-called noncontact erections in rats (Sachs et al., 1994). These noncontact erections are analogous to psychogenic erections in humans that occur in response to visual, auditory, chemosensory, or imaginative stimuli (Meisel and Sachs, 1994). Thus, studies of noncontact erections should help us to trace the neural circuits involved in sexual arousal or motivation prior to

FIGURE 5.16 The vomeronasal organ (VNO) and other major components of the rodent chemosensory system, seen in a lateral view of the guinea pig snout. This structure is absent in most primate species but is essential to normal rodent reproductive behavior. When male rodents engage in anogenital investigation of females prior to mounting, vaginal chemosignals are maneuvered to the roof of the mouth, then "pumped" through the nasopalatine duct into the opening of the VNO. Other signals may enter via the external nares (nostrils) and may be pulled down to the VNO from the floor of the nares. Neural information moves from the VNO to the accessory olfactory bulbs via the vomeronasal nerve; thus, information originally obtained from activation of VNO receptors is processed by the accessory olfactory bulbs. Information from the olfactory receptors is processed separately in the main olfactory bulbs. After Wysocki, 1979.

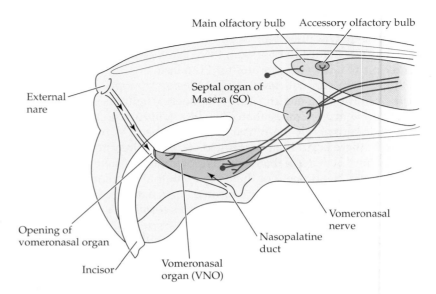

copulation. Lesions of the medial amygdala inhibit noncontact erections; however, lesions of the bed nucleus of the stria terminalis (BNST) or paraventricular nucleus of the hypothalamus (PVN) cause only mild impairments, and lesions of the mPOA have no obvious effect (Liu et al., 1997b).

THE CHEMOSENSORY SYSTEM   Olfaction is critical for successful expression of male reproductive behavior among many rodent species. Chemosensory cues are also critical in mediating many other social interactions. Experimental blocking of the sense of smell usually results in social and reproductive behavioral deficits.

The **olfactory bulbs** are located at the front of the brain (see Figure 5.15) and comprise two anatomically distinct regions, the main olfactory bulbs and the accessory olfactory bulbs (**FIGURE 5.16**). The olfactory neurons are bipolar cells located in the olfactory neuroepithelia at the rear of the nasal cavity. Their axons form the first cranial nerve and terminate in the main olfactory bulbs (Scalia and Winans, 1976). In many mammalian species, a portion of the olfactory neuroepithelium is discretely organized into a **vomeronasal organ** (VNO) (also called Jacobson's organ), an encapsulated structure on each side of the nasal septum located near the floor of the nasal cavity (Moulton, 1967). Rodents have highly developed vomeronasal organs, but this structure is regressed or absent in some primate species (e.g., great apes and humans) and aquatic mammals. The neurons of the VNO connect to the accessory olfactory bulb via the vomeronasal nerves (Alberts, 1974; Moulton, 1967; Wysocki, 1979).

Historically, several methods have been used to impair the chemosensory system in order to ascertain its behavioral and physiological roles (reviewed in Alberts, 1974; Liberles, 2014). The most common technique is olfactory bulbectomy (surgical removal of the olfactory bulbs), but this method has some drawbacks. Removal of the olfactory bulbs destroys approximately 4% of the entire central nervous system in rodents (Cain, 1974). Consequently, substantial neural damage can occur, and separation of the effects of such damage from the effects of sensory loss after bulbectomy is not always possible. Also, the olfactory bulbs integrate nonsensory functions as well as sensory functions (Alberts, 1974), and the proportions of damage to sensory versus nonsensory functions caused by olfactory bulbectomy may vary among species. Finally, the procedure is irreversible.

Several acute, somewhat reversible, methods of impairing olfaction have been used to reduce the neural damage associated with olfactory bulbectomy. One frequently used technique is intranasal infusion of zinc sulfate (ZnSO$_4$) (Alberts, 1974; Alberts and Galef, 1971), which temporarily destroys the olfactory neuroepithelia,

olfactory bulbs   Rounded cigar-shaped structures protruding from the front of the brain that receive input from the olfactory sensory cells in the nose and project to various parts of the brain associated with processing of airborne chemosensory stimuli.

vomeronasal organ   An encapsulated sensory receptive organ located near the floor of the nasal cavity in mammals that receives chemosensory information, which then travels to the accessory olfactory bulbs.

rendering the animal anosmic (unable to smell). The chemosensory receptors in the nasal cavity regenerate after several weeks. Two problems with using $ZnSO_4$ are uncertainty about its side effects and about the extent of the olfactory impairment (Murphy, 1976). Anesthesia of the nasal epithelia is another method used to produce acute olfactory impairment (e.g., Doty and Anisko, 1973).

The results of olfactory bulbectomy have varied among studies and among species. Surgical ablation of the olfactory bulbs of sexually naive rats had no discernible effect on subsequent mating behavior in one early study (Stone, 1922). In contrast, a later study revealed that many bulbectomized rats were sexually impaired; some stopped mating completely after the surgery (Beach, 1942a). Sexually naive rats exhibited profound behavioral deficits after bulbectomy in other studies (Beach, 1942a; Bermant and Taylor, 1969). Further analyses of the impairments in mating behavior following olfactory bulbectomy revealed that male rats failed to achieve ejaculation after a series of intromissions or simply did not initiate copulation at all, suggesting that both sexual performance and motivation were impaired by olfactory bulbectomy (Larsson, 1969). Olfactory bulbectomy completely eliminated sexual behavior in male house mice (*Mus musculus*) (Rowe and Smith, 1972; Whitten, 1956a), but removal of the olfactory bulbs had variable effects on the copulatory behaviors of male guinea pigs (*Cavia porcellus*) (Beauchamp et al., 1977). Local anesthesia of the nasal mucosa (Doty and Anisko, 1973) and olfactory bulbectomy both virtually eliminated sexual behavior in male Syrian hamsters (*Mesocricetus auratus*) (Murphy and Schneider, 1970; Winans and Powers, 1974).

Copulation can be activated in bulbectomized rats by techniques that increase the general level of arousal in the animals. Thus, a mildly painful tail pinch or an electric shock to the flank will stimulate bulbectomized rats to copulate to ejaculation. Such arousal "therapy" is only temporarily restorative; additional arousing stimuli must be administered prior to subsequent mating sessions conducted a few days later (Meisel et al., 1980). These findings suggest that olfactory bulb tissue or neurons that are connected to the bulbs are part of a neural circuit involved in male sexual motivation among rodents.

Inputs from both the main olfactory neurons and the VNO are apparently necessary for rodent mating behavior (Guillamón and Segovia, 1997). Olfactory bulbectomy tends to destroy both the main olfactory bulbs and the accessory bulbs, so differentiation of the contributions of the olfactory and vomeronasal inputs requires manipulations of the respective sensory receptors. While treatment with $ZnSO_4$ alone had no effect, destruction of the vomeronasal nerve alone stopped mating behavior in about one-third of the male hamsters tested (Powers and Winans, 1975). Thus, the VNO has an important, but not critical, role in normal reproductive behavioral function in these animals. In contrast, ablation of the VNO in male house mice and pine voles (*Microtus pinetorum*) eliminated the surges of luteinizing hormone associated with the presence of females and stopped mating behavior (see below) (Lepri and Wysocki, 1987; Lepri et al., 1985; Wysocki et al., 1983). Because the deficits of vole and mouse mating behavior are similar following either olfactory bulbectomy or VNO ablation, the vomeronasal organ/accessory olfactory bulb system appears equally or more important in mediating mating behavior than the olfactory neuroepithelia/main olfactory bulb system.

In mice and rats, two large chemical families of chemosensory receptors (the V1Rs and V2Rs) have been characterized in the distinct VNO regions of the olfactory neuroepithelia (Dulac and Torello, 2003). The VNO neurons express specific receptors and appear to respond either to male or to female urine; other neurons do not discriminate between male and female urine, suggesting that other attributes of the chemostimuli are encoded by these cells (Dulac and Torello, 2003). It appears that a functional VNO is necessary for males to discriminate between males and females during mating (Stowers et al., 2002) and that the main and accessory olfactory systems interact for successful mate recognition and sexual behavior (Keller et al., 2009).

amygdala An almond-shaped structure located near the base of each temporal lobe of the brain. The amygdala is critical for the integration of sensory information that is important in sexual behavior.

THE ROLE OF THE AMYGDALA Projections from the accessory and main olfactory bulbs travel to the **amygdala** (from the Greek for "almond"), an almond-shaped structure located in each temporal lobe of the brain. The amygdala is critical for the integration of sensory information important in sexual behavior. Two regions of the amygdala have been studied in rodents: the basal and lateral collections of neuronal cell bodies (the basolateral nuclei), and the cortical and medial nuclei (corticomedial nuclei) (**FIGURE 5.17**). Removal of the basolateral nuclei of the amygdala generally does not affect the reproductive behavior of male rodents but does reduce sexual motivation (Everitt, 1990). Lesions of the corticomedial nuclei, on the other hand, increase the ejaculation latencies of rats (Giantonio et al., 1970) and completely abolish copulation in male hamsters (Lehman and Winans, 1982). Information from the amygdala is relayed to the mPOA via the stria terminalis and the ventral amygdalofugal pathway. Predictably, lesions of these relay structures produce reproductive deficits similar in nature to those caused by corticomedial amygdala lesions (Giantonio et al., 1970).

Exposure to the chemosignals in the vaginal secretions of female hamsters produces sex-specific behaviors in the recipient animal: females mark over the scent, whereas males initiate copulatory behavior aimed at the source of the scent (Swann and Fiber, 1997). Although these behaviors are markedly different, the responses of both sexes to the chemosignals of female hamsters involve the main olfactory system. In females, the neural circuitry involved includes the medial nucleus of the amygdala and the posterior medial subdivision of the bed nucleus of the stria terminalis. In addition to these two neural components, the magnocellular subdivision of the mPOA is activated in males exposed to female vaginal secretions (Swann and Fiber, 1997). The integrity of this brain region is necessary for normal mating behavior in male hamsters (Swann et al., 2003). The bed nucleus of the stria terminalis of males can be activated by vaginal secretions only if plasma testosterone concentrations are sufficient (i.e., only in gonadally intact males) (Swann and Fiber, 1997).

ELECTRICAL/OPTOGENETIC STIMULATION AND RECORDING STUDIES In addition to lesion studies, researchers have employed electrical stimulation and recording studies to locate the neural circuitry underlying male reproductive behavior. Generally, electrical stimulation of a brain site produces a behavioral response that is opposite from the effect of destroying the area. Recording of the electrical activity in the brain in response to specific stimuli can also reveal what parts of the brain are involved in a behavioral response.

Recall that POA lesions, especially mPOA lesions, disrupt copulatory behaviors. Electrical stimulation of the mPOA accelerates ejaculation in male rats (Malsbury, 1971; Van Dis and Larsson, 1971). The mPOA appears to be crucial for integrating important external and internal information. Prior to making a successful mating response, a male rat must orchestrate and organize a multitude of stimuli. The environmental context, including time of day, plus the stimuli associated with the estrous female and the endocrine state of the male and his memories of previous sexual encounters, if any, must be processed and integrated in the mPOA. Lesions of the mPOA disrupt not only sexual behavior but also several other motivated behaviors, including maternal behavior (see Chapter 7), locomotor behavior (King, 1979), drinking (Mogenson et al., 1980; Rolls and Rolls, 1982), and thermoregulatory behaviors (Satinoff and Prosser, 1988; Szymusiak and Satinoff, 1982).

Male rats must integrate auditory, olfactory, and tactile sensory cues in order to mate successfully (Sternson, 2013). The mPOA appears to be critical for processing this sensory information (Hull et al., 1997; Melis and Argiolas, 1995). Early studies found that adult male rats with no previous sexual experience required at least two of these three sensory inputs to engage in successful copulation, and it was thought that it did not matter which two sensory channels were available. Rats with previous sexual experience were thought to require only one source of

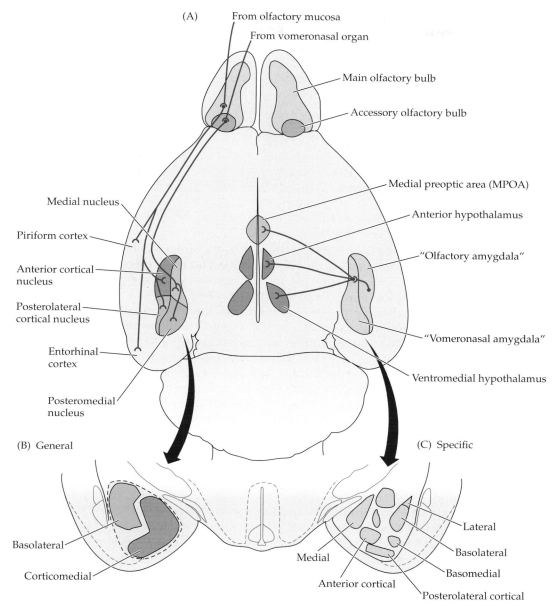

(A) From olfactory mucosa
From vomeronasal organ
Main olfactory bulb
Accessory olfactory bulb
Medial preoptic area (MPOA)
Anterior hypothalamus
Medial nucleus
"Olfactory amygdala"
Piriform cortex
Anterior cortical nucleus
Posterolateral cortical nucleus
"Vomeronasal amygdala"
Entorhinal cortex
Ventromedial hypothalamus
Posteromedial nucleus

(B) General
(C) Specific
Lateral
Basolateral
Basolateral
Medial
Basomedial
Corticomedial
Anterior cortical
Posterolateral cortical

FIGURE 5.17   Neural pathways in the rat olfactory system are shown in a schematic horizontal section (A). Axons from the olfactory mucosa synapse in the main olfactory bulb, where sensory information is sent to the piriform and entorhinal cortices and the anterior and posterolateral cortical nuclei of the amygdala; axons from the vomeronasal organ synapse in the accessory olfactory bulb, which sends axons to the medial and posteromedial nuclei (left side of figure). Because of these projections, the cortical portion of the amygdala can be considered the "olfactory amygdala," and the medial portion the "vomeronasal amygdala." The olfactory amygdala innervates the vomeronasal amygdala, from which signals are sent to central structures, including the medial preoptic area (mPOA), the anterior hypothalamus, and the ventromedial hypothalamus. (B) The amygdala, an almond-shaped structure located in each temporal lobe, seen in a schematic drawing of a coronal section of the rat brain. Two general amygdaloid regions have been studied extensively because they receive neural input from the main olfactory bulbs. Destruction of the corticomedial nuclei, but not the basolateral nuclei, severely affects male copulatory behavior in rodents. (C) The specific nuclei of the basolateral and corticomedial amygdala that receive olfactory input are depicted.

FIGURE 5.18 Castration reduces neural responsiveness in the mPOA. Electrical recording in the olfactory bulbs and mPOA of intact male rats reveals that the urine of estrous females causes increased neural activity in both regions. After castration, estrous urine continues to increase neural activity in the olfactory bulbs, but not in the mPOA. Testosterone replacement therapy restores mPOA responsiveness to estrous urine to the levels seen in intact rats. After Pfaff and Pfaffmann, 1969.

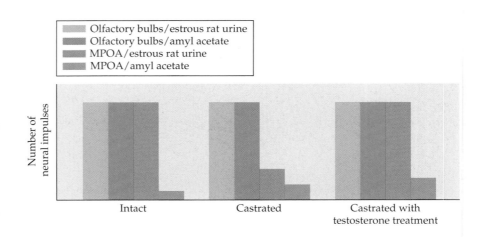

sensory information (Beach, 1942b; Stone, 1923). Current views suggest that olfaction and somatosensation (tactile cues) are critical for the expression of appropriate copulatory behaviors, although the specific somatosensory requirements for male copulatory behaviors remain unknown (Stern, 1990).

As the male's brain processes incoming olfactory sensory information, a sufficiently powerful stimulus evokes a neural response from the mPOA, which results in the appropriate motor output, as well as a burst of GnRH release from the hypothalamus, which begins an endocrine cascade resulting in elevated testosterone secretion (Purvis and Haynes, 1974). Chemosensory stimuli from an estrous female induce electrical activity in the mPOA as well as in the olfactory bulbs of a male rat. Castration of the male does not affect the electrical activity in the olfactory bulbs; in other words, the chemosensory cues associated with the female continue to be processed at this early level of sensory input into the brain. However, the electrical activity of the mPOA, several synapses downstream from the olfactory bulbs, is no longer evoked by estrous female odors. The neurally coded sensory signal from the bulbs no longer influences the output of the mPOA of castrated males (Pfaff and Pfaffmann, 1969). Testosterone replacement therapy appears to amplify the chemosensory signal so that the mPOA again responds with neural activity (**FIGURE 5.18**).

Optogenetic studies have provided precision in identification of the neurocircuitry underlying male sexual behavior. A recent study combined electrophysiology studies with optogenetics to reveal specific neuronal cellular responses to social behaviors in male mice (Lin et al., 2011). Upon an initial encounter with another mouse, male mice generally are primed to attack unless stimuli from estrous females promote sexual mating behaviors. Electrophysiological experiments revealed the existence of a so-called aggression locus within the ventrolateral subdivision of the ventromedial hypothalamus (VMHvl) (Lin et al., 2011); these cells were more active during aggressive encounters. The VMHvl also contained distinct neurons that were active only during mating. Optogenetic stimulation of the VMHvl in the absence of an intruder did not affect behavior, but in the presence of a male intruder it elicited a rapid onset of coordinated and directed attacks (Lin et al., 2011). Because the overall activity in the VMHvl declined during mating, it was believed that inhibition of these neurons prevented aggression toward females during mating. Optogenetic stimulation of these neurons during mating (before mounting, during intromissions, after intromissions, or after ejaculation) resulted in progressively more aggressive attacks on the females (Lin et al., 2011) (**FIGURE 5.19**). Thus, many neurons were identified that were activated during aggressive encounters but inhibited during mating. These data suggest the presence of a close neuroanatomical relationship between aggression and reproductive neural circuits, and a potential neural substrate for competition between mating and fighting (Sternson, 2013).

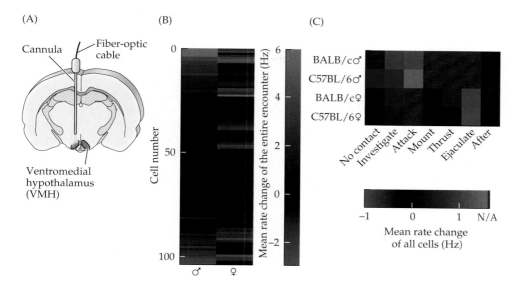

FIGURE 5.19 Optogenetic activation of the VMHvl caused aggressive attacks on male intruders, but a subset of the neurons within this brain region were active during mating behavior. (A) Placement of cannula with fiber-optic cable to stimulate the VMHvl. (B,C) If the cage mate was a female, then the same cells shifted in their firing rates to be less active (red = excited cells; blue = inhibited cells). If these neurons were stimulated optogenetically during sexual encounters, then progressively more aggressive responses toward the females were observed after each type of sexual encounter. B, C from Lin et al., 2011.

IMPLANT STUDIES As we unravel the basic neural circuitry underlying sexual behavior, we hope to discover where exactly hormones interact with the central nervous system to mediate mating behavior. Brain implant studies have pinpointed some of these areas. Implants of crystalline testosterone into the mPOA of castrated male rats facilitated copulation in 100% of the animals; conversely, when the implants were of crystalline cholesterol (a hormonally inert precursor of testosterone), none of the castrated rats mated (Davidson, 1966a). Simultaneous treatment with an androgen aromatization inhibitor during such testosterone implantation resulted in mating frequencies much lower than after implants of estrogen in the same conditions (Christensen and Clemens, 1975). These results again suggest that testosterone exerts its effects on mating behavior via aromatization to estrogen. Systemic injections of low doses of DHT do not affect the reproductive behavior of castrated male rats. However, DHT injections paired with implants of estradiol into the mPOA elicited full copulatory behavior in castrated males, providing additional evidence that estradiol mediates central mechanisms of mating behavior, whereas DHT is important in maintaining peripheral sensitivity in castrated males (Davis and Barfield, 1979). Nevertheless, androgens must be able to interact with central androgen receptors to initiate male sexual behavior. In support of this, sexual behavior was inhibited in males that received intracranial implants of hydroxyflutamide, an androgen receptor blocker, in the POA or hypothalamus, while sexual behavior was not inhibited when hydroxyflutamide was implanted in the amygdala or the septal region, which are parts of the limbic system involved in motivation (McGinnis et al., 1996).

AUTORADIOGRAPHIC AND IMMUNOCYTOCHEMICAL STUDIES To gain additional information about where sex steroid hormones might exert their influence upon

FIGURE 5.20 The distribution of sex steroid receptors, depicted in a hypothetical generalized vertebrate brain. Note that most steroid receptors are clustered in the preoptic area, the lateral septum, the amygdala, the hypothalamus, the hippocampus, and the pituitary. After Morrell and Pfaff, 1978.

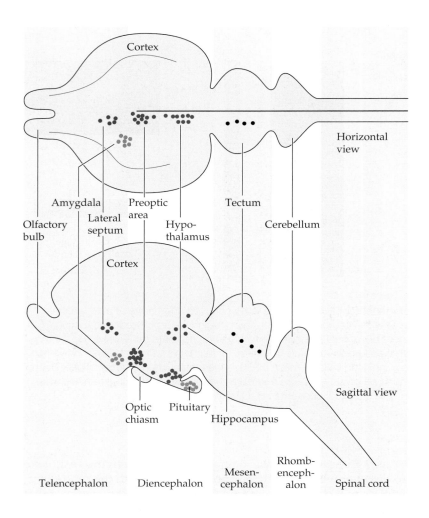

behavior, autoradiographic studies have been used to map the distribution of sex steroid receptors in the central nervous system. After an injection of radiolabeled testosterone, evidence of receptor binding has been found in several specific regions of the rat brain involved in sexual behavior: (1) the mPOA, (2) the bed nucleus of the stria terminalis, and (3) the corticomedial nuclei of the amygdala (Sar and Stumpf, 1977) (**FIGURE 5.20**). Other brain regions, such as the ventromedial nuclei (VMN) and arcuate nucleus of the hypothalamus, were also heavily labeled, but lesion studies suggest that these nuclei are not directly involved in the control of male mammalian mating behaviors. That is, males perform normally in mating tests after lesions of the VMN and arcuate nucleus.

Because testosterone can be converted into other androgens or into estrogens inside of neurons, binding studies that specifically examined estradiol and DHT receptors have also been conducted to ascertain the separate roles of these steroid hormones in specific neural target tissues. The distribution of cells that concentrate labeled DHT in the rat brain is essentially identical to the pattern of testosterone-concentrating cells (Sar and Stumpf, 1977). This is not unexpected, because DHT and testosterone bind to the same androgen receptor. The distribution of estrogen-concentrating cells is more extensive than that of androgen-concentrating neurons (Commins and Yahr, 1985; Sheridan, 1978), extending from the mPOA into the forebrain. As noted, both androgen and estrogen receptors mediate male sexual behavior.

Recall from Chapter 2 that an enzyme called aromatase converts testosterone to estradiol. In rodents, aromatization of testosterone into estradiol in the brain is

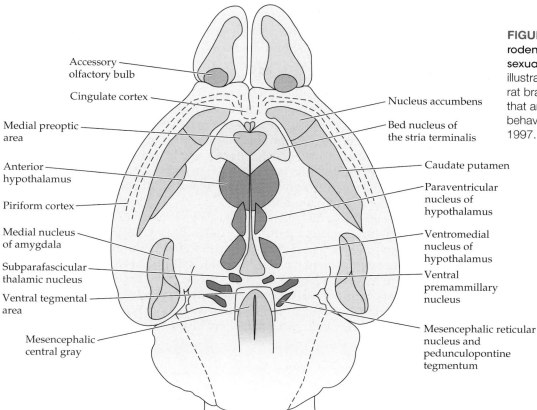

Accessory
olfactory bulb

Cingulate cortex

Medial preoptic
area

Anterior
hypothalamus

Piriform cortex

Medial nucleus
of amygdala

Subparafascicular
thalamic nucleus

Ventral tegmental
area

Mesencephalic
central gray

Nucleus accumbens

Bed nucleus of
the stria terminalis

Caudate putamen

Paraventricular
nucleus of
hypothalamus

Ventromedial
nucleus of
hypothalamus

Ventral
premammillary
nucleus

Mesencephalic reticular
nucleus and
pedunculopontine
tegmentum

FIGURE 5.21 Brain regions in rodents show fos activation after sexual stimulation. This schematic illustration of a horizontal section of rat brain depicts the various regions that are activated during male sexual behavior. After Pfaus and Heeb, 1997.

required for the expression of normal male mating behavior (Christensen and Clemens, 1975; Clancy et al., 1995). A radiolabeled antisense RNA probe for rat aromatase mRNA can be used to show where in the brain aromatase mRNA is present (Roselli et al., 1997). Aromatase mRNA has been detected in many areas of the rat brain; the mPOA, the VMN, and the medial and cortical nuclei of the amygdala are especially rich in aromatase activity (Roselli et al., 1997). Castrating male rats caused aromatase mRNA concentrations in the mPOA and hypothalamus to drop after 7 days; androgen replacement therapy (either testosterone or DHT), but not estrogen treatment, restored aromatase activity and aromatase mRNA concentrations in those brain regions (Roselli et al., 1997). Neither aromatase activity nor mRNA levels in the amygdala were affected by castration. As mentioned above, testosterone serves as a prohormone in mediating male sexual behavior. DHT can regulate aromatase mRNA transcription and/or stability in specific rat brain regions, whereas estradiol can activate neural circuits regulating male sexual behavior.

Much of the neural circuitry involved in mediating male mating behavior has been confirmed and extended by tracking the activation of so-called **immediate early genes (IEGs)** (Hull et al., 2002). In neurons, these genes are activated early during the signal transduction process whereby extracellular signals result in the expression of specific genes. The nature and function of the "activation" of IEGs remain controversial (Hull et al., 2002); nevertheless, the presence of their protein products is thought to indicate the initial activation of the genetic machinery of neurons. The products of IEGs such as the *fos*, *jun*, and *egr-1* families can be detected by immunocytochemical methods. Analysis of IEG proteins in neurons has confirmed that copulatory stimuli activate neurons in several steroid-concentrating brain regions, including the mPOA, lateral septum, BNST, PVN, VMN, medial amygdala, ventral premammillary nuclei, central tegmental field, mesencephalic central gray region, and peripeduncular nuclei (Pfaus and Heeb, 1997) (**FIGURE 5.21**; also see Box 10.3). Although devoid of intracellular sex steroid hormone receptors, the ventral

immediate early genes (IEGs)
Genes that show rapid and transient expression in the absence of new protein synthesis. These genes are expressed immediately after cells are stimulated by extracellular signals such as growth factors or neurotransmitters. By observing the expression of these IEGs, neuron activation in association with specific behaviors can be mapped.

and dorsal striatum and the cortex also display significant activation after sexual behavior. Note that the mPOA, BNST, and corticomedial amygdala are regions of the brain that other methods have shown to be critical for regulating male sexual behavior. Although many nonspecific stimuli can "activate" neurons and increase IEG expression, it is a reasonable strategy to use IEG expression as one of several tools to identify neural circuits involved in sexual behavior. A putative neural circuit of male sexual behavior in rodents is depicted in **FIGURE 5.22**. In Figure 5.22B, the output pathways are depicted. Information is integrated in the mPOA, then projects to the periaqueductal gray area, which in turn projects to the nucleus paragigantocellularis. From here information is transmitted to spinal cord neurons that project to the pudendal musculature and also to cells that control penile erection (Hull et al., 2006; Murphy and Hoffman, 2001).

In one specific example, IEG expression has been used to identify the neural circuitry involved with ejaculation (Hull et al., 2002). The medial part of the parvocellular subparafascicular nucleus (SPFp), which is located in the posterior thalamus, is activated during ejaculation in rats (Coolen et al., 2003a). This region of the brain is ideally located to serve as a processing center for sensory stimuli because olfactory and other sensory information relays through the thalamus. Also, sensory information arrives in the thalamus from the spinal cord. Tract tracing studies revealed that the SPFp receives input from a cluster of neurons in the lumbar spinothalamic

FIGURE 5.22 Schematic depiction of neural activity in circuits underlying male sexual behavior in rodents (A) as indicated by *fos* gene induction. (B) The output pathways that regulate male copulation are depicted. Sensory information is integrated in the medial preoptic area, then projects to the periaqueductal gray area, which in turn projects to the nucleus paragigantocellularis. From here information is transmitted to spinal cord neurons that project to the pudendal musculature and also to cells that control penile erection. aq = aqueduct; AOB = accessory olfactory bulb; BNSTpm = posteromedial bed nucleus of the stria terminalis; CTF = central tegmental field; fr = fasciculus retroflexus; fx = fornix; ml = medial lemniscus; MPN = medial preoptic nucleus; ot = optic tract; PD = posterodorsal preoptic nucleus; sm = stria medularis; st = stria terminalis; v3 = third ventricle; vl = lateral ventricle. A from Hull et al., 2002; B from Murphy and Hoffman, 2001.

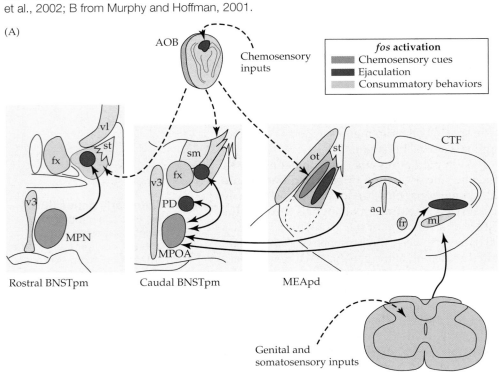

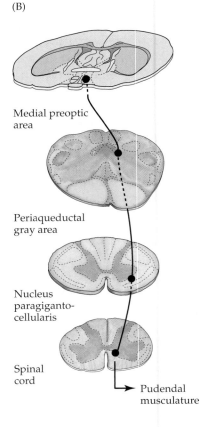

region of the spinal cord (Coolen et al., 2003b). This cluster of neurons is activated only during ejaculation, not during other components of male sexual behavior (Truitt and Coolen, 2002). When these cells were lesioned with a drug that targeted only these specific neurons, rats failed to ejaculate even though all other components of sexual behavior remained intact (Truitt et al., 2003).

THE ROLE OF NEUROTRANSMITTERS   Presumably, neurotransmitter function must be affected if hormones are to influence behavior. In the case of male sexual behavior, dopamine seems to play a central role (Melis and Argiolas, 1995). Although many other neurotransmitters are involved (e.g., glutamate, serotonin, norepinephrine, nitric oxide), a discussion of the effects of hormones on every neurotransmitter system is beyond the scope of this book. We will look at dopamine as an example of how hormones and their receptors function to affect neurotransmission.

Some neurotransmitters act to stimulate sexual behavior, whereas other neurotransmitters act to inhibit it (**TABLE 5.2**). Dopamine appears to facilitate male sexual behavior by removing tonic inhibition (Chevalier and Deniau, 1990) of brain regions that mediate sensorimotor abilities (Hull et al., 1997). Three major integrative dopaminergic systems regulate sexual motivation, genital responses, and body postures during copulation in male rats (Hull et al., 1997): the nigrostriatal tract, the hypothalamic mPOA, and the mesolimbic tract (Putnam et al., 2001). Sensory input from an estrous female before or during copulation evokes the release of dopamine in each of these three tracts (Hull et al., 1995; Mas, 1995). The nigrostriatal tract is the largest dopaminergic system and mediates the initiation of movement. The nigrostriatal tract is damaged in humans with Parkinson's disease, which is characterized by tremors, slow movements, and impairments in the initiation of movement. In rats, the nigrostriatal tract appears to be involved in the muscular movements associated with mounting females (Robbins and Everitt, 1992).

As noted above, lesions of the mPOA impair sexual performance, but spare sexual motivation, in male rats (Everitt, 1990). More-recent research indicates that the mPOA contributes to sexual motivation (Hull et al., 1995, 1997; Paredes, 2003). The mPOA is critical for male sexual behavior in all vertebrate animals thus far studied (Meisel and Sachs, 1994). This structure receives input from and sends output to

TABLE 5.2 *Effects of various neurotransmitters on male sexual behavior*

Neurotransmitter	Effect on copulation	Effect on penile erection
Norepinephrine	α_1 receptor activity ↑ copulation	α_1 receptor activity ↓ reflexive erection
	α_2 receptor activity ↓ copulation	α_2 receptor activity ↑ reflexive erection
	β_1 receptor activity has no effect	β activity inhibits reflexive erection
	β_2 receptor activity ↑ copulation	(β receptor subtype not specified)
Dopamine	Presynaptic activity ↓ copulation	Postsynaptic activity ↑ reflexive erection, but ↓ spontaneous erection
Serotonin (5-HT)	$5\text{-}HT_{1A}$ activity ↑ copulation	$5\text{-}HT_{1A}$ activity ↓ erection
	$5\text{-}HT_{1B/1C}$ activity ↓ copulation	$5\text{-}HT_{1C}$ activity ↑ spontaneous erection
	$5\text{-}HT_2$ activity ↓ copulation	$5\text{-}HT_2$ activity ↓ spontaneous erection
γ-Aminobutyric acid (GABA)	$GABA_{A/B}$ activity ↓ copulation	$GABA_{A/B}$ activity ↑ spontaneous erection
Acetylcholine	Inconclusive	Inconclusive
Endorphins	Activity ↓ copulation	Activity ↓ erection
Neuropeptide Y	Activity ↓ copulation	No effect
Oxytocin	Activity ↑ copulation	Activity ↑ spontaneous erection

Source: Meisel and Sachs, 1994.

↑ = facilitates; ↓ = decreases.

virtually every sensory modality (Hull et al., 1997, 2002). This reciprocity in connections provides a means for the mPOA to modulate sensory processes and for sensory information to affect the integration of sexual motivation. Many dopaminergic neurons within or connected to the mPOA possess receptors for sex steroid hormones (Simerly and Swanson, 1986). The same is true for many neurons in nondopaminergic neurotransmitter systems. Testosterone replacement therapy in sufficient doses to restore copulation in castrated male rats also increased mPOA secretion (Putnam et al., 2001).

In microdialysis, a very small (200–300 µm diameter) probe (hollow tube) is inserted into the brain. The probe is usually filled with cerebrospinal fluid, and neurotransmitters, hormones, and their metabolites diffuse into the tube from the surrounding extracellular fluid. Microdialysis samples are usually obtained continuously while animals are awake and active. The samples can be analyzed using high-performance liquid chromatography (HPLC). Microdialysis has revealed a consistent pattern of increased dopamine concentrations in the mPOA of male rats in the presence of an estrous female rat housed behind a perforated barrier (Hull et al., 1997). A variety of other stimuli, including access to highly palatable food or a male conspecific, do not affect mPOA dopamine secretion. Castration attenuates the female-induced elevation of dopamine in the mPOA (Du et al., 1998). Male rats that continue to copulate after castration continue to elevate dopamine after exposure to females (Dominguez and Hull, 2010). This indicates that testosterone increases the probability that dopamine will be released in the presence of a female, rather than that testosterone release is an all-or-none phenomenon. A similar mechanism might underlie the observation that the percentage of hypogonadal men who can copulate and/or masturbate to ejaculation is similar to the percentage in gonadally intact men. Dopamine appears to regulate the integration of sensorimotor information in the mPOA, resulting in facilitation of male sexual behavior (Hull et al., 2002) (**FIGURE 5.23**).

The mesolimbic tract is important in reward and appetitive behaviors such as brain self-stimulation, drug addiction, and food, alcohol, and water intake, as well as in sexual behavior (Balfour et al., 2004; Hull and Dominquez, 2007; Hull et al., 1997). The mesolimbic tract terminates in the nucleus accumbens, and blocking or stimulating dopamine receptors in this region decreases or restores, respectively, behaviors associated with sexual motivation (Everitt, 1990; Pfaus and Phillips, 1991); however, activation of the nucleus accumbens may only enhance generalized appetitive behavior (Hull et al., 2002). The mesolimbic tract consists primarily of dopaminergic neurons that project from the ventral tegmental area (VTA) in the hindbrain to the nucleus accumbens in the forebrain. Local interneurons that secrete GABA inhibit firing in these dopaminergic neurons; these interneurons are, in turn, modulated by activation of µ opioid receptors (Balfour et al., 2004). The µ opioid receptors were observed to be internalized in neurons in the VTA after copulation or after exposure to sex-related environmental cues. These stimuli also activated dopaminergic neurons in these brain regions (Balfour et al., 2004).

Dopamine also seems to facilitate sexual behavior in primates (Hull et al., 1997; Melis and Argiolas, 1995). Treatment of male rhesus monkeys (*Macaca mulatta*) with a dopamine agonist, apomorphine, resulted in dose-dependent enhancements of sexual responses toward females that males could see, hear, and smell but not touch. For instance, low doses (25–100 µg/kg) of apomorphine caused yawning, whereas moderate doses (50–200 µg/kg) caused penile erections and masturbation, occasionally to ejaculation (Pomerantz, 1990). Interestingly, the males required the presence of a female in order to show these sexual behaviors. These results are reminiscent of the effects of testosterone in facilitating male sexual behaviors in the presence of the appropriate stimuli, and they also suggest that hormones mediate male primate behavior by acting via dopaminergic pathways. Apomorphine also induces penile erections in men with and without erectile dysfunction (Lal et al., 1984, 1987). Ni-

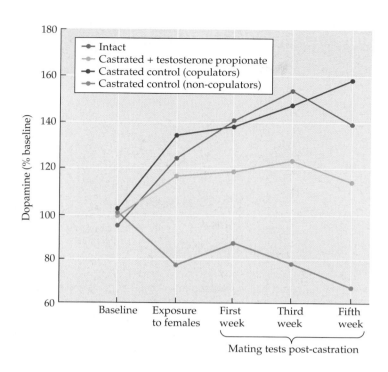

FIGURE 5.23 **Extracellular dopamine in the mPOA is elevated by cues from the female.** Dopamine concentrations in the mPOA of male rats were measured by microdialysis in the presence of an estrous female rat housed behind a perforated barrier. Rats were either gonadally intact or castrated and treated with testosterone or a placebo. Some of the castrated rats copulated when the barrier was removed, but in the absence of the precopulatory rise in dopamine, other males failed to copulate. In contrast, males that showed an increase of approximately 50% in extracellular dopamine in the mPOA copulated with females, regardless of testosterone concentrations. After Hull et al., 1995.

tric oxide (NO) is a well-established neurotransmitter (Nelson et al., 1995), and has emerged as a key mediator in human penile erection (**BOX 5.4**).

In contrast, serotonin tends to inhibit male sexual behavior. One well-known side effect of antidepressant drugs that work by elevating synaptic serotonin levels (so-called selective serotonin reuptake inhibitors [SSRIs]) is sexual dysfunction among men (Baldwin et al., 2013). During ejaculation, increased serotonin secretion in the mPOA functions to indirectly, but effectively, inhibit dopamine, which in turn reduces male sexual responses (Dominguez and Hull, 2010; Hull et al., 2004).

GENE MANIPULATION STUDIES   As described in Chapter 1, new advances in molecular biology make it possible to perform specific genetic manipulations. An increasingly common genetic technique used in behavioral endocrinology studies is the insertion (knockin) or removal (knockout) of the genetic code for a specific hormone or its receptor. The use of genetic manipulations has revealed or confirmed several regulatory mechanisms underlying male sexual behavior in mice. For example, mice that have had the gene encoding the μ opioid receptor deleted display reduced mating activity (Tian et al., 1997). The μ opioid receptor mediates the pain-attenuating features of endogenous and exogenous opioids such as morphine and heroin. The "pleasurable" aspects of copulation may require the μ opioid receptor (van Furth et al., 1995).

In contrast to the serendipitous, unexpected, and somewhat subtle results of the targeted deletion of the genes encoding the μ opioid receptor and other molecules, such as nitric oxide, the deletion of genes encoding androgen or estrogen receptors would be expected to result in predictable, severe defects in male mating behavior. However, early studies of male estrogen receptor knockout (ERKO) mice showed only subtle deficits in male sexual behavior, mainly reduced ejaculations (Eddy et al., 1996; Ogawa et al., 1995); otherwise, they showed mounting and intromission behaviors comparable to those of normal, wild-type mice (Ogawa et al., 1995). Different researchers have, however, reported differences in the behavioral deficits observed in ERKO mice. The specific source of these deficits has not been identified but may relate to differences in experimental conditions in tests for sexual behavior. For example, if male ERKO mice are castrated and implanted with Silastic

BOX 5.4 *Just Say NO (Nitric Oxide) to Erectile Dysfunction with Viagra*

Approximately 50% of men over the age of 40 have some degree of erectile dysfunction (ED). Because penile erections are mainly vascular events, medical problems such as diabetes, high blood pressure, high cholesterol, and heart disease—all of which affect blood flow—are frequently underlying causes. Therefore, it is important for individuals experiencing erectile dysfunction to be screened for these conditions. Furthermore, if these conditions are not treated, there could be a progression of erectile dysfunction.

Androgens are essential for the expression of normal sex drive (libido) in men, but their role in the maintenance of the erectile response in humans is controversial. Castration in rats causes both a loss of penile reflexes and a marked reduction in the erectile response to electric field stimulation of the cavernosal nerve. Both of these effects can be reversed by testosterone or DHT, but not estradiol, replacement (Lugg et al., 1995).

However, nitric oxide (NO) has emerged as a key mediator of erection. The physiological mechanism of penile erection involves a release of NO in the corpora cavernosa (the paired chambers in the penis where blood is trapped) during sexual stimulation (Burnett, 1995). Nitrates such as nitroglycerin are broken down to NO, a very transient and reactive free radical that not only acts as a vasodilator but is vital in the regulation of mitochondrial respiration in both skeletal muscle and other organ systems. NO is normally produced by the vascular endothelial tissues to facilitate blood flow, stimulate cellular respiration, and help prevent plaque formation on interior vessel walls. NO also appears to function as a neurotransmitter. However, NO is a very toxic free radical that can cause substantial tissue damage in high concentrations, especially in the brain. In stroke, for example, large amounts of NO are released from nerve cells and cause damage to surrounding tissues.

Figure A Viagra (sildenafil citrate)

In the penis, NO is released from both neuronal and endothelial sources (Nelson et al., 1997). When NO combines with the enzyme guanylate cyclase, which converts GTP to cyclic guanosine monophosphate (cGMP), the resulting elevation of cGMP concentrations in the penis produces smooth muscle relaxation in the corpora cavernosa, allowing the inflow of blood.

Recall that the loss of penile reflexes in rats following castration can be reversed by testosterone or DHT replacement. Production of the synthetic enzyme (nitric oxide synthase) that produces NO and a by-product, citrulline, from arginine is also dependent on DHT (Lugg et al., 1995) (see also Box 8.3). DHT production wanes in men after the age of 40, so the increased prevalence of erectile dysfunction at this age may reflect the interaction between DHT and NO.

In 1998, the Pfizer pharmaceutical company released the drug Viagra (the generic name is sildenafil citrate) (**Figure A**) for the treatment of erectile dysfunction. Sildenafil acts by potentiating the effects of NO on the mechanism of penile erection; it enhances the effect of NO on cGMP by inhibiting the

capsules filled with testosterone (which leaks out at a constant rate) so that their blood concentrations of testosterone are all similar, then a deficit in the rate and onset of intromissions is observed, as compared with wild-type mice (Rissman et al., 1997b). Interestingly, treatment of the ERKO mice with dopamine agonists such as apomorphine bolsters the earlier evidence that dopamine acts "downstream" of the POA to support male sexual behavior (Wersinger and Rissman, 2000). Of course, it is difficult to tease apart the effects of the missing estrogen receptors on sexual differentiation from the effects of the absence of estrogen on adult sexual behavior.

Based on the results of early injections of estrogen receptor antisense RNA, estrogen receptors appear to be necessary for the organization of masculinization and defeminization of behavior (McCarthy et al., 1993a). How do we reconcile the results of these studies with the observation that male ERKO mouse mating behavior is essentially unaffected (Ogawa et al., 1995)? One hypothesis is that there might be other forms of the estrogen receptor gene that persist in ERKO mice. In vivo autoradiography studies indicated that neurons in ERKO mouse brains continue enzyme phosphodiesterase type 5 (PDE5), which breaks down cGMP in the corpora cavernosa. Individuals can take sildenafil 30–60 minutes prior to sexual activity. When sexual activity stimulates NO release, inhibition of PDE5 by sildenafil causes increased levels of cGMP in the corpora cavernosa, resulting in the desired smooth muscle relaxation and inflow of blood to the corpora cavernosa. Thus, sildenafil does not cause an erection per se but enhances or potentiates an erection. Current evidence suggests that sildenafil does not affect sexual motivation.

Sildenafil at recommended doses (50–100 mg) has no effect on penile erection in the absence of sexual stimulation. At appropriate doses and in the presence of sexual stimulation, however, sildenafil is reportedly very effective. One study showed a covariant relationship of sildenafil dosage to the number of patients reporting improvement in erectile function: with a 25 mg dose of sildenafil, 63% of patients reported improvement, while 82% reported improvement with a 100 mg dose (**Figure B**). Although anecdotal information suggests that sildenafil also enhances female sexual performance, no controlled studies have confirmed this suggestion.

Recent reports to the U.S. Food and Drug Administration Adverse Event Reporting System implicate sildenafil citrate in adverse emotional and aggressive behaviors. They occur because sildenafil acts by inhibiting PDE5. This causes accumulation of cGMP, which is synthesized by guanylyl cyclase, which is directly activated by NO. Elevated concentrations of cGMP have been associated with increased aggressive behavior. The hypothesis that sildenafil citrate may increase aggression via its actions on cGMP and potential feedback inhibition of NO concentrations was tested in male C57BL/6 mice that received thrice-weekly injections of the drug at different doses. No change in agonistic behavior was observed

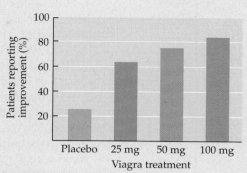

Figure B Effectiveness of sildenafil

in mice during treatment with sildenafil citrate. However, sildenafil-treated mice given the highest dose were generally more aggressive 1 week after cessation of drug treatment than vehicle-treated mice, suggesting that withdrawal or abuse effects of sildenafil could be significant (Hotchkiss et al., 2005).

Shortly after its release, Viagra became the fastest-selling drug in history. At ~$43 per pill (100 mg) in the US, current annual sales for Viagra are approximately $1.5 billion. However, it is estimated that only 13% of men suffering from erectile dysfunction currently seek medication. With the release of two new drugs to treat ED, Levitra (vardenafil) by Bayer and GlaxoSmithKline and Cialis (tadalafil) from Lilly, we can expect the marketing of these drugs to the remaining 87% of men with ED (estimated at 30 million men in the United States) to be fierce.

to concentrate radiolabeled estrogens (Shughrue et al., 1996)! A second isoform of the estrogen receptor, which binds 17β-estradiol with high affinity, was isolated in rat prostate and ovarian tissue (Kuiper et al., 1996); this second estrogen receptor was designated ERβ, whereas the originally described receptor is now called ERα (Shughrue, 1998). All components of male sexual behavior are intact in βERKO mice (Ogawa et al., 1999). Male mice genetically engineered to lack both the α and β estrogen receptors, however, display no male sexual behaviors (Ogawa et al., 2000). These results are in sharp contrast to the generally intact, but reduced, mating behavior displayed by aromatase knockout mice (Honda et al., 1998), which produce no estrogens (Bakker et al., 2004). It follows that the ERKO mice in the study by Ogawa and colleagues (1995) were what would now be called αERKO mice that retained their ERβ genes.

Genetic disorders resulting in the lack of estradiol signaling are quite rare among humans. At this point, only eight men have been discovered who lack the gene for aromatase, and only a single man has been identified who lacks the gene for ERα

(Rochira and Carani, 2009; Simpson and Davis, 2000). A man lacking aromatase activity because of a mutation in the P450 aromatase gene was given a series of hormone treatments, during which time he maintained a diary of his sexual behavior and thoughts (Carani et al., 1999). Psychosexual and sexual behavior evaluations were performed before and during treatment with testosterone or with three doses of estradiol. The gender identity and the sexological interview indicated that the individual was clearly male and that his orientation was heterosexual. Significant modification of the patient's sexual behavior, including increased libido, frequency of sexual intercourse, masturbation, and erotic fantasies, occurred only during estradiol treatment. Treatment with estradiol also reduced his scores on the Beck Depression Inventory (showing improved mood) and reduced scores on Spielberger's State-Trait Anxiety Inventory (Carani et al., 1999). The authors concluded that estrogens do not affect gender identity and sexual orientation in men but may influence male sexual activity (Carani et al., 1999).

How do steroid hormones affect male mating behavior? Taken together, the studies on rodents suggest that steroid hormones activate certain genes in neurons. Recall that a neuron, in common with other cells, has a cell nucleus, and within the nucleus are genes located along the chromosomes. Hormones turn on DNA transcription within neurons to produce proteins (see Chapter 2). Generally, steroid hormones serve as DNA transcription factors, or they activate cell signaling pathways when bound to membrane-bound receptors, which ultimately affect protein production. The result of this genomic expression may be an increase or a decrease in the number of hormone receptors or a change in the presence or amounts of enzymes that affect neurotransmitter or neurohormone production, neurotransmitter receptor production, or even recycling of neurotransmitters. For example, dopamine may not be recycled quickly in some circumstances; increased dopamine concentrations in the mPOA stimulate male sexual behavior (Bitran et al., 1988; Hull et al., 1997, 2002); thus, a genomic signal initiated by steroid hormones that reduced dopamine recycling rates, thereby increasing dopamine concentrations, could stimulate male copulatory behavior in the appropriate social context. New protein synthesis in response to steroidal influences on neuronal genes may allow new neuronal connections to be made, facilitating sensory input associated with estrous females or even memories of prior sexual encounters (e.g., Pfaff and Pfaffmann, 1969; Stern, 1990). For instance, implants of testosterone into the mPOA of rats stimulate dendritic branching and other structural changes there (Meisel and Sachs, 1994).

Recent studies in Japanese quail, which display a briefer temporal pattern of copulation than rodents and do not have an intromittent organ, suggest that both the genomic and nongenomic effects of estradiol are necessary to coordinate male sexual behaviors (Seredynski et al., 2013) (see below). Mating behaviors are very complex, and many endocrine, neural, and environmental stimuli interact to produce successful copulation. Further discoveries of the physiological mechanisms by which hormones affect male mating behavior await our understanding of precisely how a change in protein synthesis in a brain region becomes amplified into a behavioral response.

Social Influences on Male Rodent Mating Behavior

The endocrine and neural mechanisms underlying mating behavior in male rodents have been discussed up to this point. As we know, hormones affect behavior by changing the thresholds at which specific behaviors are displayed in response to particular stimuli. But many environmental factors, including social cues, can modulate hormone-behavior interactions. One environmental stimulus that greatly affects males is the presence of females. Females affect both sexual motivation (appetitive behavior) and performance (consummatory behavior) among males.

If a male rat is placed in a box with an estrous female, he will mate to satiation; that is, he may ejaculate seven or eight times over the course of several hours. He is operationally defined as sated when no mating behavior is observed for 90 minutes or longer. However, if a new female is introduced into the mating arena, the so-called sated male often immediately resumes copulation. This phenomenon has been termed the Coolidge effect, in honor of an anecdote involving the thirtieth president and first lady of the United States (Bermant et al., 1968).[1] The Coolidge effect, the enhanced mating performance of males with novel females, is a striking phenomenon in some species, including rats and cattle, but in general it is not a very robust effect among mammals. Among humans, there are many anecdotal reports of enormous individual differences in the stimulatory effects of novel females on males' copulatory performances but not very many convincing data. There is a complete absence of this phenomenon in some other species. For example, males of some monogamous rodent species do not show the Coolidge effect; for a male prairie vole (*Microtus ochrogaster*), the opportunity to mate with a novel female results instead in resumption of copulation with his mate (Getz et al., 1987; Gray and Dewsbury, 1973). The endocrine bases, if any, of the Coolidge effect remain unspecified. However, its neurobiological bases may involve an augmentation of dopamine release in the nucleus accumbens (mesolimbic tract) during copulation (Fiorino et al., 1997).

In studies of the effects of hormones on reproductive behavior in the laboratory, the physical space in which the animals interact is often simplified. Typically, the mating behavior of rats is assessed in a small, empty aquarium. The rich complexity of the natural habitat, including space, odors, and escape paths, is eliminated to control as many variables as possible during the experiment. This simplification of the physical space in which behavior is examined may make experiments easier to analyze, but it also removes much of the rich environmental context that may play important roles in the regulation of behavior.

Natural sexual behavior may be unintentionally constrained by these simplified testing environments. The stimuli associated with copulation normally induce luteal function and subsequent progesterone production in female rats (see Chapter 6). The timing of the vaginal stimulation caused by copulation may be important for inducing luteal function; thus the interval between, and the pacing of, intromissions varies on a somewhat species-specific basis. The optimal pattern of intromissions for some species has been called the vaginal code (Diamond, 1970). Under natural conditions, female rats control the pacing of reproductive activities to match closely the pattern of physical stimuli necessary for optimal reproductive efficiency. Female rats can adapt to the typical mating arena provided in most behavioral endocrinology studies, in which the pace of mating is faster than the physiological optimum. However, they may produce less progesterone during these behavioral assessments and thus produce fewer offspring than females mating in naturalistic settings. Providing a seminatural environment to rats results in a slower pace of mating behaviors (McClintock, 1987). The reason for this reduction in mating pace is not certain, but the animals appear to interact with the environment and also to move farther away from each other during mating. The running and chasing observed during rodent mating bouts conducted in seminatural enclosures is often qualitatively and

---

[1]According to the story, President Coolidge and his wife were visiting a farm in the Midwest and were given separate tours by the owners. Both President and Mrs. Coolidge noted during their tours that only one rooster was associated with the large flock of hens. Mrs. Coolidge asked the farmer how many times per day the rooster engaged in romance. "Several times a day," the farmer replied. "Please relay that information to the president," responded the first lady, apparently impressed by the rooster's performance. Later, during his tour, President Coolidge was given this same information about the copulatory prowess of the rooster. The president pressed further, "Same hen each time?" "Oh no," replied the farmer, "A different hen each time." "Please relay that information to Mrs. Coolidge."

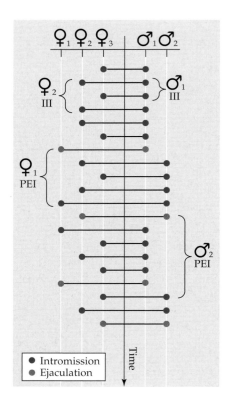

FIGURE 5.24 **Copulatory sequence of rats mating in groups** In this example, three estrous females (left) copulate with two males (right). A mating event is signified by either a blue dot (intromission) or a red dot (ejaculation); the female and male participating in a given event are indicated by a horizontal line. The first mating event is an intromission with male 1 and female 3; then there is an intromission with male 1 and female 2, with male 1 and female 3, then male 1 and female 2 again. Thus, the inter-intromission interval (III) is different for female 2 than for male 1; in a more typical paired mating test, the III would be the same for the two partners. Similarly, the post-ejaculatory interval (PEI) for female 1 is different from the PEI for male 2 but would be identical in a standard paired mating situation. Laboratory assessment of mating behavior in groups more closely approximates field conditions and thus provides data with more ecological validity than that obtained in paired mating tests. The timeline indicates the order and relative temporal relationship of mating events but does not reflect actual temporal intervals. After McClintock, 1984.

quantitatively different from what is observed during typical laboratory mating tests. In many species for which both laboratory and field hormonal data have been collected, hormone concentrations vary substantially between the two situations. In any case, it is clear that the females control the pacing of mounts, intromissions, and ejaculations when in larger enclosures, whereas males control the pacing of sexual behavior in the traditional small enclosures (Larsson, 2003).

Not only the physical environment but also the social environment of rodents is artificially simplified in laboratory studies of hormonal effects on reproductive behavior. Typical studies with laboratory rats pair a single male with a single female and record the resulting behavior. However, rats in nature do not necessarily mate in pairs; several males and females may mate in a group. Sperm competition studies suggest that the male having the most ejaculations with a female, or the last ejaculation during her series of copulations, usually sires the most offspring. Presumably, strategies have evolved for males to compete for copulations and to time their copulatory acts to maximize their chances of fertilizing a female. One interesting advantage for rats mating in groups (a "promiscuous" mating system) is that because the participants can take turns mating with different partners, each sex can mate at a different "optimal" pace for fulfilling its respective neuroendocrine stimulus requirements (McClintock, 1984; see also Chapter 6) (**FIGURE 5.24**).

The stimulus value of the female is another variable that may influence the outcome of behavioral endocrine investigations of male sexual behavior. Males have different mating responses to females in naturally occurring estrus than to females that are in artificially primed estrus (Hardy and Debold, 1971). Males also respond differentially to females brought into estrus with different hormonal treatments. For example, male rats with corticomedial amygdala lesions responded slowly to estrogen-injected females in one intriguing study. However, they responded as quickly as intact males when the female was brought into estrus with both estrogen and progesterone (Perkins et al., 1980). Perhaps the additional hormonal treatment provided females with enhanced stimulus value that overcame the effects of the brain lesion. Additional studies are required to understand the effect of the hormonal condition of estrous females on male mating behaviors.

The presence of female rodents, especially novel females, induces an elevation in blood plasma testosterone concentrations in male rodents during mating (Bronson and Desjardins, 1982a; Purvis and Haynes, 1974). Prior to mating, sensory cues associated with females can cause a rapid increase in circulating luteinizing hormone (LH) and testosterone concentrations in sexually experienced male mice (Batty, 1978). This response can be classically conditioned to previously neutral stimuli (Graham and Desjardins, 1980). A natural stimulus, normally referred to as the unconditioned stimulus, normally causes some reflexive response, called an unconditioned response. In Pavlov's famous studies, food in the mouth was the unconditioned stimulus that naturally caused a dog to increase salivation, which was

FIGURE 5.25 LH and testosterone secretion can be modified by classical conditioning. Upon the first presentation of a neutral stimulus (in this case, wintergreen odor) to male house mice of the CF-1 strain, there was no change in serum hormone concentrations (neutral). The mice were then repeatedly exposed to the wintergreen odor paired with the presentation of a female. After training, conditioned males showed increased LH and testosterone secretion in response to the odor alone at levels close to those shown by unconditioned males in response to a female. After Graham and Desjardins, 1980.

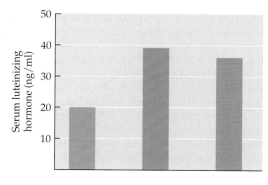

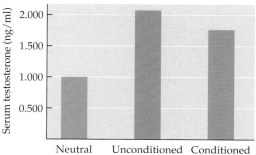

the unconditioned response. If a previously neutral stimulus, one that normally does not cause the biological response, is paired repeatedly with the unconditioned stimulus, then the neutral stimulus becomes a conditioned stimulus that causes a conditioned response. In Pavlov's studies, dogs became classically conditioned to a previously neutral bell tone (conditioned stimulus) that caused salivation (conditioned response) in the absence of food.

Female presence naturally causes a rise in blood LH and testosterone concentrations in males in the CF-1 strain of house mice. Exposure to the odor of wintergreen normally has no endocrine effects in mice. If female presence is repeatedly paired with wintergreen odor, however, eventually the odor will evoke increased plasma LH and testosterone concentrations in the male mice in the absence of a female. In other words, the males will "learn" to increase their hormonal concentrations whenever they experience the odor of wintergreen (**FIGURE 5.25**). Classical conditioning of male sexual behavior has now been shown in several species, including rats (e.g., Kvitvik et al., 2010). The sights and sounds associated with estrous females may promote endocrine changes prior to the onset of mating, because of previous associations between these stimuli and mating behavior. Indeed, sexual experience in a specific location within a cage causes males to establish a conditioned place preference in subsequent visits to the empty cage; that is, males will spend more time in the side of the cage where they copulated than in any other area of the cage (Tenk et al., 2009). The role of learning in the elevation of mating and premating reproductive hormones, and thus in mediating copulatory behaviors, is not yet well understood, but this is one possible mechanism by which experience may interact with the endocrine system to preserve hormone-dependent behaviors in the absence of the hormone (Nyby, 2008). Similar classical conditioning has been reported for men who had previously neutral visual stimuli paired with sexually stimulating material (Lalumiere and Qunsey, 1998; O'Donohue and Plaud, 1999). Indeed, testosterone is often released during male sexual behavior, and this secretion of testosterone may potentially feed back to activate reward or motivational systems, provided that the feedback is sufficiently rapid (Nyby, 2008). Of course, rapid steroid hormone actions require either very fast genomic actions (gene transcription and protein translation) or physiological changes in response to fast nongenomic pathways. As we saw above, rapid effects of steroids affect sexual motivation, but not necessarily sexual performance (Kleitz-Nelson et al., 2010a,b; Seredynski et al., 2013).

A number of recent studies have examined the role of experience in the mPOA. For example, sexual experience was found to influence mating-induced activity in nitric oxide synthase–containing cells in the mPOA of male rats (Nutsch et al., 2014). The number of mPOA astrocytes was negatively correlated with the latency to ejaculate in sexually inexperienced, but not in experienced, male rats (Will et al., 2015). Enhancement of male sexual behavior due to experience was shown to involve dopamine D1 receptors and phosphorylation of phosphoprotein 32, regulated by dopamine and cyclic AMP, in the mPOA of male rats (McHenry et al., 2012). Perhaps not unexpectedly, sexual experience increased the number of androgen receptors in the mPOA of male mice (Swaney et al., 2012).

FIGURE 5.26 Individual differences in sex drive are retained following castration and restoration therapy. Guinea pigs that were classified as having high, medium, or low sex drives based on behavioral assessments were castrated. After castration, the sexual behavior score eventually dropped to the same baseline for all three groups. Both low-dose and high-dose testosterone therapy restored copulatory behavior in the castrated males, and the differences in sexual behavior among the three groups were still observed. This study demonstrated that differences in blood androgen concentrations do not correspond closely to individual differences in sexual behavior, which are more likely due to variation in target tissue sensitivity to androgens. After Grunt and Young, 1952.

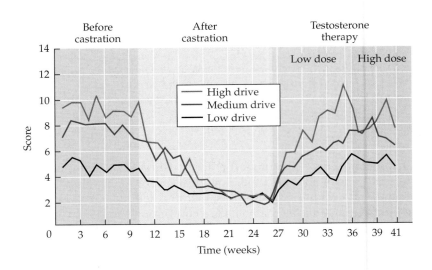

Individual Differences in Male Rodent Mating Behavior

Vast individual differences exist in the amount of sex drive and the sexual performance observed among individuals of many species. That is, the sexual behavior of males falls along a continuum between hyposexual and hypersexual activity. If male rats are tested in typical time-limited mating tests, some will mate several times within the time constraints, while others will not mate at all. An early hypothesis that was proposed to account for individual differences in mating behavior was that animals with high sex drive had higher circulating testosterone concentrations than animals with low sex drive. This hypothesis was tested initially on guinea pigs prior to the availability of direct assays of circulating steroid hormones (Grunt and Young, 1952, 1953). Males were prescreened for sexual activity and categorized as high–, medium–, or low–sex drive males based on their numbers of ejaculations during a time-limited mating test. All the males were then castrated, and their copulatory behavior was tested during the following weeks (**FIGURE 5.26**). Low–sex drive males stopped mating first, followed by the medium– and high–sex drive animals. After 16 weeks, all the males had completely stopped displaying mating behavior. They were then injected with low doses (50 μg/day) of testosterone propionate, after which each male returned to his precastration level of sexual behavior. A similar study examining high and low rates of sexual activity in rats yielded similar results (Larsson, 1966). The results of these studies indicate that animals do not differ in their mating behavior because of different concentrations of hormones. More likely, differences exist in the target tissues that mediate reproductive behaviors.

A similar study was conducted on laboratory rats, and its outcome was in agreement with the earlier study by Grunt and Young on guinea pigs: differences in blood hormone concentrations did not account for the differences observed in the frequency of sexual behaviors. Males were identified as copulators or noncopulators, and blood plasma testosterone was assayed for all the animals. All the males in this study had testosterone concentrations between 2 and 3 ng/ml of plasma. The known copulators were then castrated, and testosterone-filled Silastic capsules of different lengths were implanted in them, resulting in different blood concentrations of testosterone. However, normal sexual behavior was restored in most of the males, even those with very low testosterone concentrations. With only a 2 mm capsule, 72% of the males ejaculated normally, yet the concentrations of their plasma testosterone were much lower than normal values (Damassa et al., 1977) (**FIGURE 5.27**).

This study demonstrates that very low concentrations of circulating testosterone can maintain sexual behavior. Why, then, do males have circulating androgen

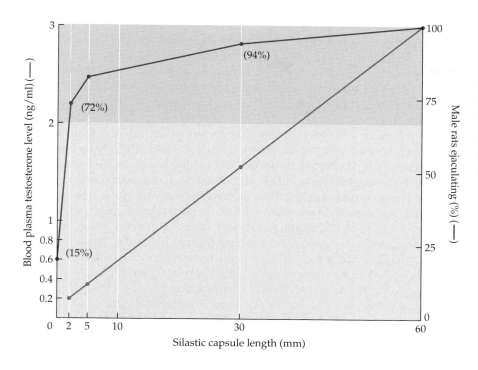

FIGURE 5.27 Clinically low testosterone concentrations can restore mating behavior in castrated rats. Rats that were known copulators and had plasma testosterone concentrations of 2–3 ng/ml (beige area) were castrated. Most of the rats exhibited normal ejaculatory behavior after implantation with a 2 mm Silastic testosterone capsule, even though the capsule treatment resulted in plasma testosterone concentrations that were much lower than those found in intact rats. After Damassa et al., 1977.

concentrations an order of magnitude higher than necessary to maintain sexual behavior? Probably because local testis androgen concentrations must be very high to support spermatogenesis, and mating behavior has evolved to depend on the diluted concentrations of androgens in the general circulation. Thus, large variations in circulating concentrations of testosterone (of even an order of magnitude) will presumably not affect behavior. High androgen concentrations are also important in aggression and in maintenance of other male traits. Indeed, high androgen levels support secondary sex characters that are often the criteria by which females choose mates (Andersson, 1994).

Differences among genetic strains in reproductive behavioral responsiveness to hormones have also been noted. In one study, for example, several strains of mice were examined for male copulatory behavior, and the hybrid B6D2F1 strain was eventually discovered; in this strain approximately one-third of the males continued to copulate for 2 years after castration (McGill, 1962, 1977). Usually mice, like rats, stop mating soon after castration. If different strains of mice, which vary in their genetic background, display varying degrees of mating responses to castration, then genotype appears to be a salient factor underlying the dependency of male sexual behavior upon hormones in mice. But what is the relationship between genotype and behavioral responsiveness to hormones? This question was addressed in a thorough study of this hybrid B6D2F1 mouse strain (Park et al., 2010). Castrated B6D2F1 mice were treated with androgen receptor blockers and an aromatase inhibitor, but sex behavior continued. Treatment with an estrogen receptor blocker also failed to block persistent sexual behavior in these castrated mice, and no differences in the mRNA levels for the genes that encode ERα, androgen receptor, or aromatase enzymes were detected in the POA or BNST (Park et al., 2009). Sexual motivation also persisted in a subset of castrated B6D2F1 mice, although the precise mechanism allowing this variation in response to castration remains unspecified. Previous studies have ruled out adrenal steroids as mediators of the persistent sexual behavior in castrated male mice of this strain.

A similar study was conducted in Siberian hamsters. As noted above, individuals of seasonally breeding species undergo gonadal regression in the autumn; circulating testosterone falls to undetectable concentrations, and mating behavior stops.

However, approximately 40% of both short- and long-day castrated Siberian hamsters maintain full mating repertoires, including the ejaculatory response (Park et al., 2004). Taken together, these results suggest that some steroid-independent factor maintains male sexual behavior in some males of some species. If this factor could be identified, then presumably we would learn something valuable about the regulation of sexual behavior. Likely, a constellation of strain-specific traits accounts for the individual differences.

Reproductive performance and competence decline as mammals, including humans, pass the midpoints of their life expectancies (Bishop, 1970; Vom Saal and Finch, 1988). Reduced reproductive behavior may be due to age-related changes in sexual motivation, perceptual capabilities, attractiveness to the opposite sex, physical prowess, or some combination of these factors. Reductions in the frequency of sexual behavior may or may not correlate with changes in reproductive physiology or morphology. Aged mice (30 months old) have reduced gonadal mass, reduced rates of spermatogenesis, and low average blood plasma LH and testosterone concentrations compared with 6-month-old mice (Bronson and Desjardins, 1982b). Numerous syndromes can be described in which various physiological systems change, leading to decreased reproductive competence. But the most interesting question relating to issues of aging is why some healthy male mice can mate at 30 months of age and others cannot, despite equivalent blood concentrations of testosterone.

We currently do not understand completely the physiological mechanisms underlying individual differences in reproductive activity. Uptake and metabolism of testosterone in the mPOA of the hypothalamus do not differ between sexually active and inactive rats. However, estrogen receptor numbers in the mPOA are significantly reduced in sexually nonresponsive male rats as compared with copulating males (Clark et al., 1985). Perhaps protein synthesis is differentially affected by hormones, causing changes in synthesis of hormones, receptors, or structural proteins necessary for dendritic spines. Rats with inherited insensitivity to androgens lack specific androgen receptors but have normal estrogen receptors; testosterone causes less of an increase in their sexual behavior than in normal rats (Beach and Buehler, 1977). With the exception of receptor numbers in the mPOA, we cannot yet point to any structural difference between the brains of copulators and those of noncopulators. Further analyses are necessary to understand individual, strain, and species differences in reproductive drive and performance, but thus far, the obvious candidates seem not to be important (e.g., Park et al., 2009). As noted above for male Japanese quail, mPOA dopamine levels increased in the presence of a female and returned to baseline after removal of the female; however, quail that failed to copulate did not display this increased release, suggesting that part of the copulators versus noncopulators categorization reflects high versus low dopamine levels in the mPOA (Kleitz-Nelson et al, 2010 a,b). Additional research is necessary to determine whether this is true in mammals as well.

Individual differences in adult sexual behavior may reflect different experiences during development. For example, if pregnant rats are stressed by exposure to bright lights and consumption of alcohol, their male offspring fail to ejaculate as adults (I. L. Ward et al., 1996). Although their adult blood LH and testosterone concentrations are in the normal range, they can ejaculate only with pharmacological testosterone treatment. The effects of prenatal stress and alcohol exposure are maximal if they coincide with days 18 and 19 of gestation, a time when males normally secrete testosterone.

Male Sexual Behavior in Primates

Despite the importance of sexual motivation in human behavior, the physiological components of human sex drive and performance have not been well studied, and with only a few notable exceptions, scientific descriptions of human sexual behavior are rare. The theoretical bases of sexual behavior across humans and nonhumans are rarely linked; investigators in each field have developed separate scientific literatures and rarely interact (Pfaus, 1996; van Anders, 2013; van Anders and Watson, 2006). The best descriptions of the power of sexual motivation among men are often provided by playwrights, poets, and novelists. In literature, however, descriptions of sex drive and performance are masked or presented under the guise of burning passions, emotional imperatives, or even a desperate desire to marry. For example, Shakespeare's Romeo is a classic tragic character because of his nearly obsessive desire for Juliet. Despite a number of obstructions, some social, others truly physical, Romeo is highly motivated to interact with Juliet, and we in the audience share his intense emotions as he risks everything to be with her. Their story is a great tragedy because the audience can see, although Romeo is blind to it, the trajectory of his life as he attempts to overcome the obstructions in his path and obtain his goal of being with Juliet. Romeo's powerful sex drive, couched in terms of passion, overruns his life, and from the beginning of the story, we uneasily sense the sad end of the play. But to what extent does art reflect life, or in this case, hormones and behavior?

The Strength of the Sex Drive in Human Males

In their classic book *Patterns of Sexual Behavior*, Clellan Ford and Frank Beach (1951) combined information about sexual behavior from three major sources: (1) anthropological data on human sexual behavior from non-Western societies, (2) the Kinsey studies on the sexual habits and attitudes of married Americans (Kinsey et al., 1948), and (3) data about sexual behavior in nonhuman animals. This synthesis of knowledge about sexual behavior laid the foundation for much of the subsequent research in human sexual behavior. One striking observation in their book was how powerful the motivation to engage in sexual activities truly is among humans as well as nonhuman animals. For example, young people in every culture examined were found to participate in premarital sexual activities, despite threats in some societies of extremely severe disgrace and punishment if such activities were discovered. This was particularly true among sexually restrictive societies, including at the time North America. In another sexually restrictive society that inhabited the Gilbert Islands in the Pacific, a girl's chastity prior to marriage was required. If a sexual liaison was discovered, both parties were immediately put to death (Ford and Beach, 1951). Examples of instantaneous death sentences for unmarried couples who engaged in sexual intercourse have been reported for many societies, both Western and non-Western. To engage in sexual activities, men often risk injury or death from a woman's disapproving relatives or husband. The lack of sexual restraint in the face of such drastic and immediate threats provides a striking and compelling indication of the power of the motivation driving the sexual behavior of men.

If instant death sentences are ineffective in controlling sex drive, then it may be naive of some policy makers and educators to believe that adolescents will curtail their sexual activities because of the vague possibility of an unwanted pregnancy or contracting a disease such as AIDS that may not have any ill effects for years. Between 1997 and 2008 the U.S. government spent more than $1 billion on abstinence promotion programs in U.S. high schools. An evaluation of students in four states receiving abstinence-only sex education showed that they performed no differently in their sexual attitudes, knowledge, and behavior than teens receiving more traditional sexual education. The abstinence-only teens were no more likely to abstain from sex or wait longer before losing their virginity. The average age of first sexual intercourse was about 15 for both groups. Other studies suggest that individuals who take virginity pledges do not differ from nonpledgers in (1) the age of onset or rate of vaginal, anal, or oral premarital sex; (2) the incidence of sexually transmitted diseases; or (3) the number of lifetime sexual partners (Rosenbaum, 2009).

TABLE 5.3   *Top 50 reasons why men and women have sex*

| | WOMEN | | | MEN | |
REASON	M	SD	REASON	M	SD
1. I was attracted to the person	3.89	1.32	I was attracted to the person	4.03	1.16
2. I wanted to experience the physical pleasure	3.75	1.19	It feels good	3.96	1.28
3. It feels good	3.59	1.39	I wanted to experience the physical pleasure	3.84	1.21
4. I wanted to show my affection to the person	3.58	1.25	It's fun	3.57	1.39
5. I wanted to express my love for the person	3.48	1.30	I wanted to show my affection to the person	3.46	1.26
6. I was sexually aroused and wanted the release	3.30	1.33	I was sexually aroused and wanted the release	3.43	1.28
7. I was "horny"	3.11	1.26	I was "horny"	3.38	1.25
8. It's fun	3.05	1.49	I wanted to express my love for the person	3.26	1.31
9. I realized I was in love	2.92	1.47	I wanted to achieve an orgasm	3.14	1.55
10. I was "in the heat of the moment"	2.89	1.06	I wanted to please my partner	3.11	1.35
11 I wanted to please my partner	2.79	1.32	The person's physical appearance turned me on	2.96	1.44
12. I desired emotional closeness (i.e., intimacy)	2.76	1.25	I wanted the pure pleasure	2.85	1.41
13. I wanted the pure pleasure	2.73	1.42	I was "in the heat of the moment"	2.84	1.09
14. I wanted to achieve an orgasm	2.65	1.46	I desired emotional closeness (i.e., intimacy)	2.79	1.31
15. It's exciting, adventurous	2.49	1.23	It's exciting, adventurous	2.71	1.30
16. I wanted to feel connected to the person	2.44	1.33	The person had a desirable body	2.67	1.44
17. The person's physical appearance turned me on	2.39	1.37	I realized I was in love	2.66	1.46
18. It was a romantic setting	2.39	1.14	The person had an attractive face	2.62	1.47
19. The person really desired me	2.39	1.40	The person really desired me	2.56	1.39
20. The person made me feel sexy	2.37	1.29	I wanted the adventure/excitement	2.45	1.25
21. The person caressed me	2.34	1.31	I wanted to feel connected to the person	2.45	1.37
22. It seemed like the natural next step in my relationship	2.24	1.18	I wanted the experience	2.43	1.27
23. I wanted to become one with another person	2.24	1.33	It was a romantic setting	2.35	1.15
24. It just happened	2.21	1.07	The person caressed me	2.34	1.27
25. I wanted to increase the emotional bond by having sex	2.20	1.28	The person made me feel sexy	2.32	1.32

However, making virginity pledges appears to affect memory; 82% of abstinence pledgers denied making such a pledge 5 years later! Also, recall that 85 years ago the possibility of contracting a horrible venereal disease, namely syphilis, did not really reduce sexual behavior. In fact, the Roaring Twenties were a time of sexual liberation in both North America and Europe (Quétel, 1990), despite the fact that there was no cure for syphilis before the development of antibiotics in the 1940s, and this disease often led to blindness and severe neurological dysfunction prior to a painful death. Treatments of the day included cellular poisons such as mercury and arsenic that, in common with the early AZT treatment of AIDS, had debilitating side effects. Until antibiotics became generally available, sexual abstinence or the use of condoms provided the best protection against syphilis. However, many men and women have reported that during sexual arousal they have been so motivated to engage in sex that the possible consequences of their actions were forgotten or dis-

TABLE 5.3 *Top 50 reasons why men and women have sex* (continued)

REASON	WOMEN M	SD	REASON	MEN M	SD
26. I wanted the experience	2.17	1.24	It seemed like the natural next step in my relationship	2.29	1.19
27. I wanted the adventure/excitement	2.17	1.22	I wanted to increase the emotional bond by having sex	2.27	1.29
28. The person had an attractive face	2.15	1.35	I wanted to keep my partner satisfied	2.25	1.26
29. The person was a good kisser	2.14	1.27	The opportunity presented itself	2.24	1.18
30. I wanted to intensify my relationship	2.14	1.15	It just happened	2.23	1.14
31. My hormones were out of control	2.11	1.17	I wanted to intensify my relationship	2.22	1.25
32. I wanted to try out new sexual techniques or positions	2.11	1.16	I wanted to try out new sexual techniques or positions	2.22	1.16
33. I wanted to feel loved	2.11	1.22	My hormones were out of control	2.20	1.17
34. The person had a desirable body	2.08	1.31	The person was too "hot" (sexy) to resist	2.17	1.26
35. I wanted to celebrate a birthday or anniversary or special occasion	2.06	1.05	I was curious about my sexual abilities	2.17	1.09
36. I wanted to communicate at a "deeper" level	2.06	1.24	I wanted to improve my sexual skills	2.16	1.22
37. I was curious about sex	2.06	1.08	I wanted to become one with another person	2.16	1.36
38. It was a special occasion	2.03	1.03	I saw the person naked and could not resist	2.15	1.27
39. The person was intelligent	1.91	1.23	The person was a good kisser	2.15	1.26
40. I wanted to say "I've missed you"	1.90	0.99	I wanted to feel loved	2.15	1.26
41. I wanted to keep my partner satisfied	1.88	1.12	I wanted to celebrate a birthday or anniversary or special occasion	2.14	1.11
42. I got "carried away"	1.88	1.03	The person was too physically attractive to resist	2.11	1.23
43. The opportunity presented itself	1.87	1.09	It was a special occasion	2.11	1.08
44. The person had a great sense of humor	1.87	1.19	I hadn't had sex for a while	2.10	1.07
45. I wanted to improve my sexual skills	1.87	1.14	The person had beautiful eyes	2.06	1.31
46. I was curious about my sexual abilities			I wanted to communicate at a "deeper" level	2.02	1.22
47. The person seemed self-confident	1.86	1.06	I wanted to experiment with new experiences	2.01	1.14
48. I wanted to make up after a fight	1.84	1.19	The person was intelligent	2.01	1.28
49. I was drunk	1.83	0.98	I wanted to keep my partner happy	2.00	1.21
50. I was turned on by the sexual conversation	1.82	1.10	I was curious about what the person was like in bed	1.94	1.08

Source: Meston and Buss, 2007.
Note: Absolute range, 1–5; *n* = 894–908 for women; *n* = 460–480 for men; M = mean; SD = standard deviation.

counted. Does testosterone contribute to these risky behaviors? Although elevated testosterone has been associated with risky behaviors, a recent study demonstrated the somewhat paradoxical relationship that high testosterone values were correlated with increased attitudes for safe sex (van Anders et al., 2012).

Although it has been assumed that people are motivated to have sex because it feels good (proximate level of explanation) or to reproduce (ultimate level of explanation), a recent study identified the top 50 reasons to have sex reported by its study group (Meston and Buss, 2007) (**TABLE 5.3**) and discussed several more. They included such common explanations as seeking physical pleasure and such lofty explanations as "I wanted to get closer to God." Some people had sex for revenge to hurt a partner, whereas others reported having sex for altruistic reasons associated with making someone feel better about themselves. Altogether, the researchers identified 237 reasons that people wanted to copulate. The extent to which sexual motivation is as complicated for nonhuman primates as it is for humans deserves further attention.

Understanding the physiological bases of the human sex drive seems very important if we hope to reduce the number of unwanted pregnancies or prevent the spread of sexually transmitted diseases such as AIDS. There is something different and possibly unique about sexual motivation, compared with other motivated behaviors such as miniature golf, that impairs decision-making processes. Do hormones contribute to this "clouding of logic" that many individuals experience during sexual arousal? Obviously, an understanding of the physiological mechanisms underlying typical human male sexual behavior is also required before we can understand undesirable behaviors such as rape or sexual molestation. But, as noted above, basic research on human sexual behavior has been relatively rare, and the physiological mechanisms of human sex drive remain obscure. The majority of human sex research has focused on performance, primarily emphasizing the physiology of erectile function (Sachs and Meisel, 1988; Tanagho et al., 1988). With very few exceptions, funding sources have been reluctant to provide money for basic research on human sexual behavior. Sex research currently being conducted on animal models may help us to understand the physiological bases of human sexual behavior, as well as the basic processes and mechanisms underlying all reproductive behavior. Animal research, mainly on rats, provides most of our knowledge of the effects of hormone-behavior interactions. However, basic data on human behavior and physiology would be useful in making informed public policies. Given the fundamental importance of understanding human sexual behavior, remarkably little research is presently being funded, especially in the United States.

Human Male Sexual Behavior: A Description

Before the known physiological mechanisms underlying primate male sexual behavior are described, brief descriptions of human and nonhuman primate male sexual behavior will be provided (see also Chapter 6, which addresses female sexual behavior). Scientific descriptions of human male sexual behavior are available, including well-known reports from Kinsey et al. (1948), Masters and Johnson (1966), and Money (1988), but their utility is somewhat limited. As you may have guessed, human sex researchers, with clipboards and stopwatches in hand, have not placed large numbers of couples in glass-enclosed rooms and recorded the ensuing sexual behaviors. Yet, the sorts of descriptive analyses that have been conducted on rodents are necessary before issues of causation can be addressed in humans. Like male mating behavior in rodents, sexual behavior in men can be divided into two components: (1) sex drive (appetitive), which is sometimes called sexual motivation or libido, and (2) sexual performance (consummatory) or potency. As we discovered in the discussion of rodent mating behavior, both components are required for normal male sexual behavior, and one or both components can fail. Hormones appear to be crucial for maintaining both behavioral components, although much more research is needed to verify this claim.

There is no universal sexual position for humans. In contrast, if you see two dogs copulating at a distance, you can easily assign the sex of each participant with virtual certainty. If the female is in estrus (see Chapter 6), she stands relatively motionless, deflects her tail, and allows the male to mount her. The male mounts her from behind, clasps his forepaws around her sides, and repeatedly thrusts his hindquarters until he achieves intromission (see the figure in Box 5.2). This mating position, with the male mounting the female from the rear, is common among nearly all mammals, and few nonhuman examples of other mating positions exist. Aristotle reported in his *Historia Animalium* that hedgehogs (a European relative of porcupines) mated belly to belly. However, later observations proved Aristotle

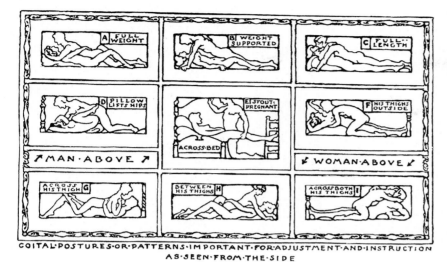

FIGURE 5.28 Human copulation is not constrained to stereotyped positions. This illustration from a 1940s manual used by North American physicians in marriage counseling depicts several possible coital postures, and well-known Eastern works such as the *Kama Sutra* describe many others. From Dickinson, 1949.

wrong. His notion that hedgehogs mated belly to belly was probably due to his disbelief that these beasts could manage to mate and avoid each other's sharp quills in any other fashion. But hedgehogs mate in the same position as dogs; that is, the male mounts the female from the rear (Reed, 1946). Many humans also copulate in this position, although it is not the dominant sexual position in any culture sampled, perhaps because of the lack of clitoral stimulation it affords (Ford and Beach, 1951; Kinsey et al., 1953).

Far from having a stereotyped mating posture, humans copulate in a variety of positions (**FIGURE 5.28**). Generally, in most societies one position for copulation is preferred and dominates but other positions are also practiced. Most humans mate in face-to-face positions.[2] The most common sexual position among humans of all cultures appears to be some version of the woman sitting or squatting on the supine man, although the most common sexual position among Europeans and North Americans is the face-to-face position with the man above the woman, sometimes derisively called the missionary position.

---

[2] The Hebrew word for knowing someone and copulating with someone is the same, *yada*; hence the term *knowing someone in the Biblical sense*. The reason for the two meanings of the word apparently arises from the observation that humans copulate face to face and, unlike other animals, "know" their partners.

FIGURE 5.29 The typical mating posture of nonhuman primates is exhibited by copulating rhesus monkeys. In this posture, the female faces away from the male and bends from the waist to make her genitalia more accessible. The male usually clasps the female around the waist and mounts from the rear as he remains standing.

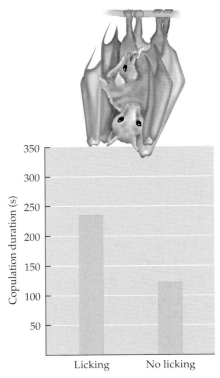

FIGURE 5.30 Short-nosed fruit bats have been observed to engage in fellatio. Mating pairs spend significantly more time in copulation if females lick the genitalia of males. Presumably, extended copulation increases successful fertilization. After Tan et al., 2009.

The point of this shopping list of human sexual positions is that the mere description of human sexual behavior indicates that, in contrast to rodents, stereotyped mating sequences are not observed in humans. There are some basic constraints, but within these constraints many sexual positions exist among humans. Lordosis is not a stereotyped mating posture in women, and copulatory behavior in men cannot be partitioned easily into mounting, intromissions, and ejaculations. The lack of stereotyped behaviors suggests that hormonal regulation of the muscle patterns underlying human sexual behavior is unlikely. Therefore, the hormonal regulation of human copulatory behavior must differ fundamentally from that of rodent mating behaviors, although hormonal control of human male sexual motivation and penile erection, thrusting, and ejaculation may be similar to that in rodents.

Nonhuman Primate Male Sexual Behavior: A Description

In contrast to humans, almost all adult nonhuman primate species have virtually the same mating posture. The female nonhuman primate turns her back to the male and bends forward at the hips. In the nonhuman primate, the vagina is located more posteriorly than in women, and thus intromission from the front is nearly impossible. Typically, the male clasps the female around her waist and copulates while standing (**FIGURE 5.29**). Nonhuman primates have occasionally been reported to employ unusual mating positions in zoos (usually a male sitting while a female backs into his erect penis), but nearly all observations of mating positions among natural populations of nonhuman primates have indicated that copulation occurs only with male entry from the rear. A few exceptions to this pattern have been observed. One great ape, the orangutan (*Pongo pygmaeus*), has been observed in nature mating face to face while hanging upside down by the toes (Mitani, 1985)! Female primates have often been observed to perform fellatio on males (Erwin and Mitchell, 1975). Not only is oral stimulation observed among several nonhuman primates, a species of short-nosed fruit bats (*Cynopterus sphinx*) has also been reported to engage in this behavior (Tan et al., 2009). Bats that engage in oral sex prolong copulation and presumably increase the odds of successful fertilization compared with bats that do not engage in this behavior (Tan et al., 2009) (**FIGURE 5.30**). Thus, the mating patterns of nonhuman primate males (and perhaps even bats) appear to be less stereotyped than those of rodents but more programmed than those of humans.

The primary exception is provided by bonobos (*Pan paniscus*), also known as pygmy chimpanzees. These animals are very closely related to humans (about

98% gene homology), and primatologists have been impressed by their social interactions. Unlike the male-dominated, highly "political" and confrontational nature of common chimpanzee (*Pan troglodytes*) social life, bonobo society is best characterized by the phrase *make love, not war* (de Waal and Lanting, 1997). Bonobos use sexual interactions to resolve a wide range of social conflicts. Importantly, bonobos also have been observed to engage in numerous sexual postures, including the face-to-face position (**FIGURE 5.31**). In fact, most of the copulations observed in captivity (70.1% at the San Diego Zoo) (de Waal, 1987) are face to face. Face-to-face positions are also observed in the wild (29.1%), but not as often as reported in captivity (Kano, 1992). One hypothesis for this difference is that the observers' presence in the wild disturbs bonobos and induces them to climb trees, where face-to-face copulation is more difficult. Importantly, the female genitalia of bonobos are situated more frontally than in other nonhuman primates, facilitating face-to-face copulations.

FIGURE 5.31 Face-to-face mating of bonobos

Hormonal Correlates of Primate Male Sexual Behavior

Prepubescent boys do not engage in sexual activities outside of the context of play. After puberty, sexual behaviors are expressed. The average age of onset of masturbation among North American boys is about 13.5 years (Bancroft, 1978). At age 14, 62.6% of males reported at least one prior occurrence of masturbation, whereas 80% of 17-year-old boys reported ever having masturbated. The incidence of recent masturbation also increased with age in boys: 67.6% of 17-year-olds reported masturbation during the past month, compared with 42.9% of 14-year-old boys (Robbins, et al., 2011). The average age of first intercourse has changed over time—for example, males experiencing coitus before age 19 increased from 45% in the 1940s to 61% by 2003 (LeVay and Valente, 2006)—but frequency of sexual behavior usually peaks during the twenties and slowly declines thereafter throughout life. The general pattern of average androgen concentrations found in men of different ages corresponds to these average levels of sexual activity. Blood plasma concentrations of testosterone peak during the mid and late teen years and remain high throughout much of the twenties (Kaufman and Vermeulen, 2005). Testosterone concentrations typically diminish as men age, usually showing a sharp decline in the sixth or seventh decade of life. The decline in blood testosterone concentrations mirrors the pattern of male fecundity and sperm counts (**FIGURE 5.32**). This decline in testosterone and fertility has been named andropause, and although it is not as prevalent or recog-

FIGURE 5.32 **Plasma testosterone concentrations in human males change with age.** There is great variation among men in plasma concentrations of testosterone, but the general trend is for testosterone levels to increase during the teens and twenties, stay generally stable until the sixties, and then gradually decrease to prepubertal levels in the nineties. Note, however, that 90-year-old individuals may have plasma testosterone levels comparable to those of many teenage males. After Vermeulen et al., 1972.

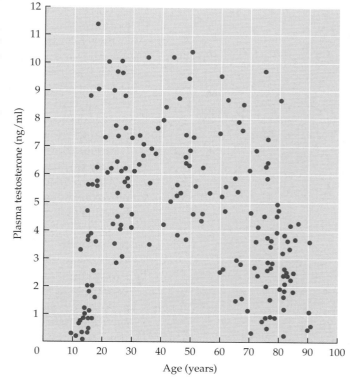

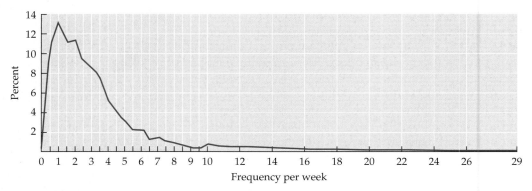

FIGURE 5.33 Individual variation in weekly frequency of sexual outlet in men According to the Kinsey data, most North American men engage in 1–3 sexual acts per week, including heterosexual, homosexual, and autoerotic activities. Less than 1% of men engage in 12 or more sexual events per week. After Kinsey et al., 1948.

nized as menopause, physicians debate whether hormone replacement treatment is warranted to treat a number of maladies, including mood disorders, anemia, and osteoporosis (Wald et al., 2009). Although the frequency of sexual interactions decreases with aging, a stable rate of sexual activities has been reported in elderly men (Lindau et al., 2007).

All of these data suggest, but do not prove, that human male sexual behavior is influenced by androgens. As you probably already have surmised, there is vast individual variation in the age of onset of human sexual activities, as well as in the lifelong frequency of sexual behaviors (**FIGURE 5.33**). Individual variation in the role of the testes in sexual behavior is also large among human males. The effects of castration on men's sexual behaviors vary from absolutely "no loss of sexual capacities and responsiveness" to a "decrease or total loss" (Money, 1961). In one study of men who were castrated for "treatment" or punishment of sex crimes, there appeared to be three classes of behavioral response. More than half of the men stopped exhibiting sexual behavior shortly after castration. In other words, they responded to castration as rodents do, with a rapid cessation of sexual behavior. The frequency of postcastration sexual behavior decreased more gradually in about one-fourth of the men; in some cases many years elapsed before sexual behavior had completely waned. In these men, castration appeared to hasten the normal age-related decline in sexual behavior. The frequency of sexual behavior was reported to be unchanged after castration for about 10% of the men (Heim and Hursch, 1979). The age at castration accounted for some of the variation in behavioral response; older men appeared to show the greatest reduction in the frequency of postcastration sexual behavior. However, the variation in behavioral responsiveness to castration remains largely unexplained for all vertebrates thus far studied.

Hypogonadism induced by injections of leuprolide acetate (Lupron) reduced all sexual behavior in men, and testosterone treatment restored sexual activities to baseline (Schmidt et al., 2009). Leuprolide mimics GnRH. Recall that when GnRH is released in a pulsatile manner, it stimulates the hypothalamus to produce gonadotropins that stimulate the gonads to produce sex steroid hormones. However, constant release of GnRH has the opposite effect and turns off steroid hormone production, as does leuprolide. Not surprising perhaps, leuprolide has also been used to treat male sexual offenders.

Very few studies have directly examined the role of hormones in the sexual behavior of men (Wang and Swerdloff, 1997). One of the best experiments was a double-blind study performed on hypogonadal men at the Stanford University Medical Center. These men met the clinical definition of hypogonadal because their blood plasma testosterone values were <3 ng/ml (Davidson et al., 1982). In the Stanford

FIGURE 5.34 Effects of testosterone treatment on hypogonadal men (A) Men with low concentrations of blood plasma testosterone (<3 ng/ml) received three injections 6 weeks apart: a placebo (oil vehicle alone) and low (100 mg) and high (400 mg) doses of testosterone enanthate, both of which temporarily increased plasma testosterone concentrations in a dose-dependent manner. (B) The patients' self-reports indicated that the incidence of erections and certain sexual behaviors also increased in a dose-dependent manner. After Davidson et al., 1979.

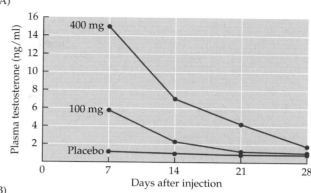

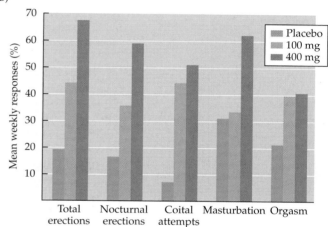

study, six hypogonadal patients received three treatments: (1) 100 mg of a long-lasting androgen called testosterone enanthate dissolved in oil, (2) 400 mg of testosterone enanthate in oil, and (3) the oil vehicle alone. None of the patients received the treatments in the same order; 6 weeks elapsed between treatments.[3] The low and high doses of androgens resulted in blood concentrations of about 6 and 15 ng/ml, respectively; the oil treatment did not change plasma testosterone concentrations from the prestudy average of approximately 1.5 ng/ml. The patients kept daily logs of their erotic thoughts, penile erections, and sexual activities. The researchers found that the incidence of erections depended on the dose and timing of androgen treatment. Peak numbers of erections occurred about 1 week after the onset of the high dose of testosterone enanthate (Davidson et al., 1982). Injections of oil alone did not influence sexual thoughts or behaviors. Low doses of testosterone enanthate caused intermediate behavioral effects (**FIGURE 5.34**). Another more recent study induced hypogonadism pharmacologically in men (in their late twenties) and evaluated their sexual activities (Schmidt et al., 2009). The study used a double-blind, controlled, crossover design in which the men served as their own controls. Reduced testosterone concentrations were correlated with lowered sexual activities. More typically, transdermal patches of testosterone (e.g., Dobs et al., 1999; Wang et al., 2010) or longer-acting injectable formulations of testosterone esters (Jockenhövel et al., 2009) have been used to elevate circulating testosterone and promote typical sexual behavior in hypogonadal men.

Other studies have demonstrated a dose-dependent effect of androgens on sexual fantasies and subsequent sexual arousal resulting from those erotic thoughts (O'Carroll et al., 1985). Interestingly, chronic monitoring of penile girth revealed that erections occurred normally among hypogonadal men in response to sexual fantasies or viewing of erotic films (LaFerla et al., 1978). However, these men did not have spontaneous and nocturnal erections. This study suggests that, in contrast to the findings with rats, androgens in men appear to be unnecessary to increase the probability of a sexual response in the presence of the appropriate stimuli. Or do they? Recall that some castrated rats showed copulatory behavior if dopamine was elevated in the POA (see Figure 5.23). Perhaps these hypogonadal men experience a rise in POA dopamine when they view erotic films.

---

[3] This study is "double-blind" because neither the patients nor the investigators knew which treatment the patients were receiving. Recall that Brown-Séquard knew that he was injecting an aqueous solution of testicular tissue into himself, and his beliefs about its potential effects probably influenced his reports of increased abilities. If someone else had injected Brown-Séquard either with androgens or with the inert vehicle in which the steroid hormone had been dissolved, then the study would have been considered single-blind. That is, the patient would be ignorant of the treatment, but the investigator would be informed. In double-blind studies, neither the subjects nor the researchers are informed, so neither can unconsciously influence the outcome.

Does testosterone affect sexual behavior in humans directly, or does it serve as a prohormone, as it does in rodents? The answer is not clear. Testosterone and DHT were equally effective in improving sexual activity in hypogonadal men. Neither blocking estrogen receptors in normal men nor treating them with an aromatase inhibitor, a drug that blocks the conversion of androgens to estrogens, influenced their sexual behavior (Gooren, 1985). The results of additional studies have hinted that estrogens may influence sexual behavior in men receiving these steroids for treatment of a variety of diseases, but there has been no conclusive demonstration of an effect of estrogen on sexual behavior in non-afflicted human males (Carani et al., 1999; reviewed in Meisel and Sachs, 1994).

TREATMENT OF PARAPHILIAS   Despite a lack of data, assertions of a strong link between blood androgen concentrations and human sexual behavior are common, as is the belief that removal of the source of these androgens will diminish human sexual behavior. This belief has found expression in some legal systems that sentence some sex offenders to "chemical castrations" in lieu of prison sentences (e.g., State of Michigan v. Roger Gauntlett, 1984). The two most common chemical compounds used for these purposes are medroxyprogesterone acetate (MPA) and cyproterone acetate (CPA). Both substances are used for treatment of sex offenders in Western Europe, but only MPA is currently approved for treatment of aberrant sexual behavior in North America. The chemicals have primarily been used to treat "paraphilic disorders," in which individuals have exhibited atypical sexual behaviors such as heterosexual and homosexual pedophilia, sexual sadism, self-mutilation, self-strangulation (asphyxiophilia), lust homicide, voyeurism, exhibitionism, fetishism, transvestitism, and frotteurism (rubbing against persons or objects for sexual stimulation) (Lehne, 1988).

Administration of CPA, a potent antiandrogen, interferes with the binding of androgen to its receptors, and it decreases LH secretion and subsequent endogenous testosterone production. MPA reduces plasma concentrations of testosterone in two ways. First, it reduces LH secretion, and decreased LH secretion leads to reduced secretion of testicular androgens. Second, MPA raises the level of specific enzymes in the liver that metabolize testosterone, accelerating its clearance from the blood (Gordon et al., 1970). Blood plasma testosterone concentrations are usually less than 1 ng/ml after 60 days of MPA administration (Meyer et al., 1985).

Many studies have suggested that MPA treatment is effective in reducing paraphiliac activities (Cooper, 1986). Most of these studies were based on self-reports from patients receiving MPA treatment, either voluntary or court-ordered; in other words, former sex offenders were asked whether they continued to engage in their illegal sexual behaviors, and, perhaps predictably, most reported in the surveys that they did not. Such studies typically did not use control groups. In one controlled, double-blind study, penile engorgement (measured by a device, called a plethysmograph, that monitors pressure changes) in response to erotic slides was not affected by MPA treatment, despite a 68% reduction in plasma testosterone values. Physiological arousal was similar in patients treated with MPA and with a placebo. However, the patient self-ratings revealed a reduction in self-perceived arousal in response to erotic visual stimuli (Langevin et al., 1979). Most clinicians agree that MPA treatment does not actually "cure" paraphiliac behaviors but rather reduces the frequency of paraphiliac fantasies. This reduction in fantasies seems to allow the individual to benefit from counseling therapy (Money and Bennett, 1981).

One study reported that blood plasma LH concentrations were higher in men viewing erotic films than in men viewing nature films (LaFerla et al., 1978). The elevated LH concentrations were positively correlated with self-reports of sexual arousal; that is, men who reported that they were highly aroused by the erotic movies had higher LH concentrations than men who reported less arousal. More recent hormonal treatments include GnRH agonists that, acting through negative feedback, reduce gonadal steroid production (Guay, 2009).

In another study, rapists and nonrapists watched pornographic movie scenes, and both became sexually aroused when viewing depictions of consensual sex. Similarly, both groups of men became sexually aroused when watching scenes of simulated rape in which the women acted as if they were involuntarily experiencing pleasure. However, the rapists, but not the nonrapists, became sexually aroused when viewing rape scenes in which the women appeared to be experiencing displeasure, pain, or suffering. Thus, rapists and nonrapists do not appear to differ in what activates sexual arousal but differ in what normally terminates sexual arousal (Abel et al., 1977; Malamuth et al., 1980). Rapists and nonrapists do not differ in their average blood concentrations of androgens, despite a tendency of violent men housed in prison to have higher average blood values of testosterone than nonviolent prisoners.

NONHUMAN PRIMATE STUDIES Investigations of nonhuman primates have not yielded much more specific information about the hormonal regulation of sexual behavior in primates or in humans specifically. This lack of progress is due, in part, to the fact that most of the primate species investigated, unlike humans, show large seasonal variations in reproductive function. For example, free-ranging rhesus monkeys display seasonal covariation between sexual behavior and androgen-dependent secondary sex characters, such as scrotal sac color (Vandenbergh, 1969). Also, large, inadequately explained interexperimental variations have been reported in the extent of hormonal influences on nonhuman primate male sexual behavior.

Generally, among free-ranging adult male rhesus monkeys, castrated males display fewer sexual behaviors than intact males (Wilson and Vessey, 1968). The effects of castration and testosterone replacement therapy on the sexual behavior of adult male rhesus monkeys have also been examined in captive animals. Prior to castration, all of the males exhibited at least one ejaculation during a mating test. Half the animals ejaculated when tested 6 months after castration, and 30% ejaculated 1 year postcastration. Two of ten males failed to ejaculate after castration. Daily intramuscular injections of testosterone propionate (1 mg/kg) restored mating behaviors to precastration levels (Phoenix et al., 1973). This study demonstrates that the hormonal control of sexual behavior in nonhuman primates is similar to the regulation of human sexual behavior; that is, enormous individual variation exists in the extent to which males are dependent on steroid hormones to initiate mating behaviors. Other studies on nonhuman primate male sexual behavior have revealed the same general outcome (reviewed in Eberhart, 1988).

Brain Mechanisms of Primate Male Sexual Behavior

As stated previously, rodents have been the primary animal model used in studies of reproductive hormone-behavior relationships. However, rodents differ from humans in many important and fundamental ways. Therefore, experiments that are considered unethical to perform on humans have been performed on nonhuman primates, animals that presumably share more characteristics and more genes in common with humans than do rodents. Studies of the brain mechanisms underlying primate sexual behavior have relied almost exclusively on rhesus monkeys (*Macaca mulatta*) (Eberhart, 1988; Michael and Zumpe, 1996; Michael et al., 1992).

Lesions of the mPOA severely disrupt copulation in male rhesus monkeys. Although mPOA lesions in primates produce mating deficits that are superficially similar to those observed in mPOA-lesioned rodents, additional descriptive analyses of the lesioned males revealed that they continued to masturbate, maintain erections, and ejaculate at presurgery rates (Slimp et al., 1978). Clearly, destruction of the mPOA in male rhesus monkeys does not abolish the physiological mechanisms underlying sexual arousal, or even possibly sexual performance, but these lesions severely interfere with the males' ability to copulate with estrous females. As in rodents, the primate mPOA integrates internal and external information relevant to mating behavior. Destruction of the mPOA disables this sensory integration and thus apparently blocks the generation of appropriate sexual behavior in the presence of the appropriate stimuli.

Electrical stimulation of the mPOA causes penile erection in socially isolated male rhesus monkeys (MacLean and Ploog, 1962). Remote electrical stimulation of different brain sites of males living alone and in heterosexual social groups produced various behavioral responses: (1) erections, (2) mounting, and (3) mounting with erections. Of 59 sites within the diencephalic and telencephalic regions of the brain, stimulation of 19 sites, including several hypothalamic areas, evoked erections but did not affect, or in some instances actually decreased, the number of mounts. Stimulation of 8 sites produced mounting behavior in the absence of erections, whereas stimulation of 9 sites produced both erections in social isolation and mounts with erections in social groups (Perachio, 1978; Perachio et al., 1973, 1979). In some sites, stimulation that caused erections also produced behaviors not normally associated with sex, including eating and urination. This finding suggests that no "sex centers" were being activated by the electrical stimulation but that possibly some general level of arousal was increased.

Chemosensory cues are not as important for successful mating in primates as they are in rodents. Removal of the olfactory bulbs has no effect on rhesus monkey mating behavior (Goldfoot et al., 1978). Lesions that interrupt the function of the amygdala have produced mixed results. The most consistent series of studies on the influence of the amygdala on sexual behavior arose from studies of the Klüver-Bucy syndrome in monkeys. Scientists became interested in the influences of the amygdala and temporal lobe on sexual behavior after reports of so-called hypersexuality in primates in which the temporal lobes had been surgically removed (Klüver and Bucy, 1939). Removal of the temporal lobes removes both the temporal lobe cortices and the underlying limbic structures, including the amygdala. Postoperatively, these monkeys became very docile and fearless. Inappropriate behaviors, including ingestion of inedible material and indiscriminate mounting behavior, were observed. Removal of only the temporal cortex did not produce the Klüver-Bucy syndrome, suggesting that deeper, limbic structures were involved in the hypersexuality (Eberhart, 1988).

Autoradiographic studies of steroid hormone binding in male primate brains have revealed that cells concentrating androgens, estrogens, and progestins are most abundant around the ventricles. That is, the hypothalamus and amygdala and the hippocampus, a bilateral forebrain limbic structure of the temporal lobe, show significant numbers of steroid hormone receptors (Eberhart, 1988; Michael et al., 1995). Thus, the pattern of steroid receptors in the male primate brain closely resembles the pattern found in rodents. In fact, the distribution of sex steroid hormone receptors is a rather conserved feature throughout the evolution of vertebrate brains (Balthazart and Ball, 1992). However, the location of steroid-metabolizing enzymes in neural tissue appears to have changed substantially during the evolution of vertebrates.

Because these initial studies of primates generally agreed with the results of studies of steroid receptor and enzyme labeling in rodents, further data on adult primates were not obtained for several years, and subtle differences between primates and rodents may have been missed. For instance, the data for DHT binding came from a single male rhesus monkey (Sheridan et al., 1982), and the data for testosterone binding came from only two males (Bonsall et al., 1985). Although the economy of using the fewest possible animals should be applauded, the danger of this approach is that researchers may accept that steroid binding patterns are identi-

FIGURE 5.35 Activation patterns in the brains of common marmosets exposed to odors from either ovariectomized or ovulating females in cross sections obtained by fMRI at the level of the (A) prefrontal cortex, (B) amygdala, or (C) midbrain. Courtesy of Craig Ferris.

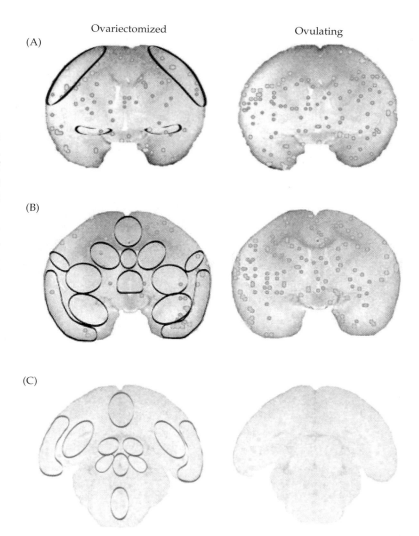

Ovariectomized   Ovulating

(A)

(B)

(C)

cal in disparate groups of animals when the brain regions regulating sexual behavior are only similar. More recent studies have confirmed the patterns of steroid hormone binding and have mapped out the development of these binding sites (e.g., Bonsall and Michael, 1992; Michael et al., 1992).

Electrode recording during testosterone treatment of gonadally intact male rhesus monkeys revealed slow, synchronized electrical activity representing patterns of neural firing among groups of neurons in the anterior and posterior hypothalamus, as well as in the mammillary bodies, structures located just behind the hypothalamus. These wave forms appeared to spread to the amygdala and hippocampal regions during the recording session. Synchronization of neural activity in these brain regions was intensified and accelerated after castration (Mangat et al., 1978a,b). In other studies, androgens appeared to change the speed of neural transmission, as well as the pattern of neural firing (Eberhart, 1988).

Interesting similarities and differences between primates and rodents in the brain regions involved in sexual behavior have been revealed by fMRI studies of primates. For example, when male common marmosets, restrained in an fMRI machine, were exposed to odors from either ovulatory or nonovulatory females, brain activity increased in the POA and anterior hypothalamus (Ferris et al., 2001). In addition to these brain regions, several cortical areas showed significantly increased activity patterns in response to periovulatory odors. These areas included the striatum, hippocampus, septum, periaqueductal gray, and cerebellum, brain regions involved not only with sexual behavior but also with emotional processing and reward (Ferris et al., 2004) (**FIGURE 5.35**). A recent study using fMRI on young men watching either fishing documentaries or pornography showed that although many brain regions seemed to alter blood flow, a consistent "automatic" activation occurred in the pars opercularis, which contains many so-called mirror neurons (Mouras et al., 2008). Mirror neurons have been observed in primates and spike both (1) when an individual acts and (2) when the individual observes the same action performed by another. Thus, the neuron "mirrors" the behavior of the other, as though the observer were acting. All eight of the volunteers developed penile erections watching the pornography, but none did watching the fishing videos. It appeared that the pars opercularis region of the brain was activated prior to penile erection, suggesting that the mirror neurons act as a command area (Mouras et al., 2008).

When positron emission tomography (PET) was used to scan the brains of men while they were brought to orgasm by their female partners, the ventral tegmental area (VTA)—a cluster of cells known to play a key role in reward and euphoria—was activated. Recall that this brain region is important in rodent ejaculation (Bal-

FIGURE 5.36 Some brain regions are strongly activated during ejaculation. The top panel shows external views in the sagittal, coronal, and horizontal planes; the most active areas are the darkest. The bottom panel shows cross-sectional views (A–D); the most active areas are the brightest. Note that the VTA is activated during ejaculation. Courtesy of G. Holstege.

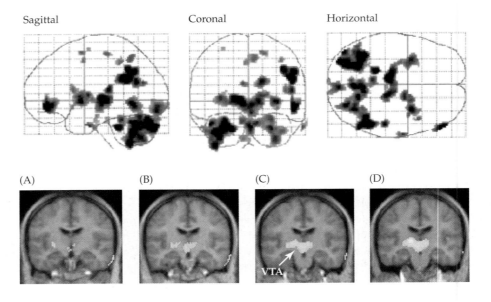

four et al., 2004); it is also part of the reward system activated during a heroin high. Some brain regions that are strongly activated in the brains of rodents at ejaculation are also activated in humans (**FIGURE 5.36**). In particular, activation was noted in the posterior thalamus, including the parvocellular subparafascicular nucleus, further confirming the importance of this thalamic structure and its spinal inputs for ejaculation. However, PET scanning failed to demonstrate ejaculation-related activation in other areas in humans, including the medial amygdala and bed nucleus of the stria terminalis (Holstege et al., 2003). Finally, activation was not observed in the human POA, which shows robust activation during rodent male sexual behavior, although this activation is not specifically related to ejaculation (Coolen et al., 2004; Tenk et al., 2009).

As noted in the introduction of this chapter, some men find sexual activation so rewarding that they develop a so-called sexual addiction. It is more common to call such conditions sexual compulsions or hypersexualities, rather than addictions. One case study provides a description of a 24-year-old man (JMB) with a reported sex addiction associated with the Internet (Bostwick and Bucci, 2008). He presented to a psychiatrist with the assertion that "I'm here for sexual addiction—it has consumed my entire life." He could not control his increasing preoccupation with Internet pornography and in addition spent many hours daily chatting to women online and occasionally meeting with some of these women in person for unprotected sex. Because of these sexual activities, JMB no longer had sexual relations with his wife, because he feared infecting her with a sexually transmitted disease. Despite a wide variety of treatment attempts over 7 years, including antidepressant medication, individual and group therapy, pastoral counseling, and attendance of Sex Addicts Anonymous meetings, he continued to engage in compulsive Internet use and compulsive masturbation. A self-described conservative Christian, he reported to be morally troubled by his own behavior, ascribing it, in part, to "negative influences from the devil" (Bostwick and Bucci, 2008). Psychiatrists at the Mayo Clinic suspected that JMB suffered from an obsessive-compulsive disorder (OCD) and prescribed sertraline (a selective serotonin reuptake inhibitor [SSRI] type of antidepressant). However, sertraline did not provide relief from the pleasure associated with Internet pornography. An adjunct treatment with naltrexone, an opioid antagonist, reduced the feelings of pleasure associated with the porn sites within 7 days (Bostwick and Buccie, 2008). This case report illustrates how an overwhelmed mesolimbic reward center can progress from a brain area that regulates motivated behavior to one that is focused on the addicted responses to the detriment of other adaptive behaviors. Clearly, endorphins are normally involved in sexual motivation and ejaculation, but the neural circuitry underlying these parts of sexual behavior can be dysregulated, often in the presence of androgens (e.g., Johansson et al., 1997). A number of recent studies have confirmed the high prevalence of compulsive Internet use for sexual purposes (e.g., Ross et al., 2012; Scanavino et al., 2016).

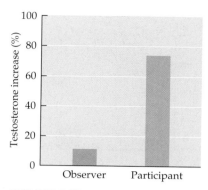

FIGURE 5.37 Testosterone of men watching or participating in sexual behavior increases ~10% or ~70%, respectively, in men attending a sex club. From Escasa et al., 2011.

Social Influences on Men's Sexual Behavior

As we have seen, behavior can feed back to affect hormone concentrations in rodents. Interactions with women can also affect hormone-behavior interactions in men. One isolated scientist, presumably a little bored, maintained daily records of the weight of his beard trimmings in his electric razor (Anonymous, 1970). He noticed that his beard trimmings were heavier immediately prior to and during his visits to his fiancée than at other times. He attributed the increased beard weight to elevated androgen concentrations induced by sexual anticipation and sexual activity. Another study of a single man reported that testosterone was elevated around the time of intercourse compared with other times (Fox et al., 1972). These demonstrations have many flaws as scientific studies, but the general concept that behavior can feed back to affect hormone concentrations has been observed experimentally in several other contexts. A few studies have directly measured androgens prior to, during, or immediately after sexual behavior in men. In one such study, testosterone, as well as DHT and androstenedione, were elevated following masturbation, suggesting that ejaculation per se stimulates steroid hormonal production in men (Purvis et al., 1976). In another study, among men (average age = 40) visiting a sex club, those watching people engaging in sexual activities showed an increase of about 10% in circulating testosterone, whereas men engaging in sexual activities displayed an increase of about 70% (Escasa et al., 2011) (**FIGURE 5.37**). But laboratory studies on steroid hormone–sexual behavior interactions in humans have produced mixed results. Many studies have found no hormonal changes after masturbation or coital ejaculation (e.g., Lee et al., 1974; Lincoln, 1974; Stearns et al., 1973). For example, a recent study suggests that although sexual thoughts increased sexual arousal, testosterone values did not change (Goldey and van Anders, 2012). In this study, nearly 100 men provided a baseline saliva sample from which to assess testosterone, imagined and wrote about a sexual or nonsexual situation, then provided a second saliva sample 15 minutes later, but no changes in testosterone (or cortisol) were observed.

The endocrine effects on men of visual erotic stimuli were investigated in other studies. In one study, 15 adult males viewed either erotic or sexually neutral films. Changes in penile girth, self-reports of arousal, and blood concentrations of testosterone, LH, prolactin, cortisol, ACTH, and β-endorphin were recorded. Sexual arousal, as indicated by both self-assessment and erectile response, was greater in all the men when viewing the erotic than when viewing the neutral films. However, no hormonal changes corresponding to the sexually aroused state were observed (Carani et al., 1990). In another study, heterosexual men were asked to rate pornographic images in terms of arousal, unpleasantness, and closeness to ideal (Brand et al., 2016) (**FIGURE 5.38**). Pictures from the preferred category were rated as more arousing, less unpleasant, and closer to ideal. Ventral striatum response was strongest for the preferred condition compared with nonpreferred pictures. Ventral striatum activity seen in an fMRI was correlated with self-reported symptoms of Internet pornography addiction, supporting the conclusions of previous studies indicating that ventral striatum activity increased when participants viewed pornographic compared with nonpornographic images. A third study example involved a study of young men who were left in a room alone or with either a woman or man. Testosterone concentrations were elevated nearly 10% in the presence of a woman (Roney et al., 2007). It may be

(A)

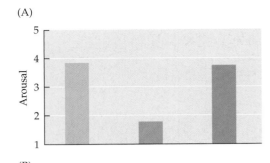

(B)

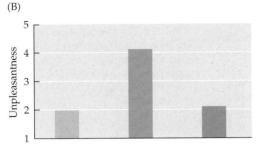

(C)

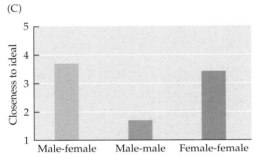

Male-female   Male-male   Female-female

(D)

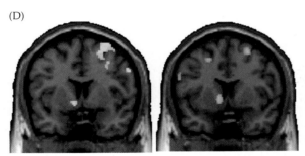

FIGURE 5.38 Brain imaging of heterosexual men observing porno-graphic pictures of male-female, male-male, or female-female interactions. (A–C) Graphs depict ratings of arousal, unpleasantness, and closeness to ideal. (D) Ventral striatal responses were strongest for preferred images and correlated with self-reports of internet pornography addiction. From Brand et al., 2016.

that the elevated testosterone is responsible for some of the subtle, and often unconscious, changes that occur when men interact with women, such as squaring of their shoulders, more use of hands during verbal interactions, and upright posture. This rapid elevation in testosterone may also increase risk taking as part of human courtship behaviors. For example, a field experiment revealed that male skateboarders took more physical risks in the presence of an attractive female than at other times and that the increase in risk taking was associated with an increase in circulating testosterone (Ronay and von Hippel, 2010). Is it the case that young men use physical risk taking as a sexual display or competition strategy?

Individual Variation and Effects of Aging on Male Sexual Behavior

The mechanisms underlying the enormous variation in the sexual behavior of aging men are unknown. A small proportion of aging men with sexual dysfunction have hormonal deficiencies; however, most do not. Men in their sixties start to show decreases in circulating blood concentrations of androgens (see Figure 5.32). However, approximately one-half of healthy men over 80 years of age have plasma testosterone concentrations in the normal range for men 25–59 (Tserotas and Merino, 1998). If an elderly man complains of impotence and his blood plasma testosterone concentrations are below 1 ng/ml, then three possible neuroendocrine problems may be responsible: (1) the hypothalamus may not release sufficient GnRH to start the endocrine cascade that normally stimulates testosterone production, (2) the anterior pituitary may not release sufficient gonadotropins, or (3) the Leydig cells may not produce sufficient androgens in response to gonadotropin stimulation. In most cases, men over the age of 60 exhibiting hypogonadal concentrations of androgens also have elevated plasma concentrations of LH, thus indicating a failure of the Leydig cells to produce sufficient steroid hormones to feed back and maintain normal blood concentrations of LH.

As we have seen, there is great individual variation among men in their dependence on steroid hormones for the maintenance of sexual behavior. It has been suggested that male animals are less dependent on hormones for sexual behavior the higher they are on the phylogenetic scale (Beach, 1947). If experiments on different species in which proven copulators are castrated and later examined for mating behavior are compared, the following observations can be made: (1) most rodents and birds show a decrease in sexual behavior immediately after castration, (2) cats also exhibit a striking decline in sexual behavior after castration, and (3) the postcastration sexual behavior of monkeys and humans is very dependent on prior experience. Dogs typically show no behavioral effects on mating during the first 15 weeks postcastration. But again, the effect of gonadectomy is very dependent on experience even in so-called lower animals. For example, a sexually experienced cat or dog may continue to copulate for a long time after being neutered (Dunbar, 1975;

Rosenblatt and Aronson, 1958). Adrenalectomized, castrated dogs may continue to display complete copulatory behavior for years after the surgery, indicating a lack of dependence on steroid hormones for mediation of sexual behavior (Beach, 1970). The extent of individual differences in postcastration mating behavior is great regardless of species; that is, the variation within species is generally as large as that between species in the reliance of sexual behavior on hormones (Hart, 1974).

When young (3-month-old) and middle-aged (12-month-old) rats were assessed for mating behavior, the middle-aged rats showed impairments in all behaviors assessed (Wu and Gore, 2010). After castration and testosterone replacement therapy, male sexual behavior was restored and there were no longer any differences between the young and middle-aged rats. Hormone replacement therapy also increased the numbers of androgen receptors (fivefold) and the ERα (sixfold) in the anteroventral periventricular and the medial preoptic nuclei (Wu and Gore, 2010). These results suggest that middle-aged brains have the capacity to respond to testosterone therapy with elevated steroid hormone receptor numbers.

The extent to which testosterone replacement therapy is appropriate to treat hypogonadism in aged men remains a topic of debate (Kaufman and Vermeulen, 2005). There is no correlation between blood testosterone concentrations and frequency of sexual behaviors among human males (W. A. Brown et al., 1978). Indeed, in a study of more than 3000 American adults age 58–85, it was reported that many men maintain active, frequent, and rich sex lives well into their eighties. Although frequency wanes somewhat, interest in sexual behavior is maintained into the ninth decade, and frequency of sexual activity is remarkably stable among healthy elderly men (Lindau et al., 2007). One important exception to this typical pattern of male sexual behavior is in the case of frontotemporal dementia—unlike the case with men with early onset Alzheimer's disease, men (and women) with frontotemporal dementia show significant hypersexuality (Mendez and Shapira, 2013).

Peptide Hormones and Male Sexual Behavior

Steroids are the predominant hormones involved in the endocrine regulation of sexual behavior, but other hormones, particularly peptide hormones, appear to modulate their effects (**BOX 5.5**). For example, GnRH has subtle effects on ejaculation latencies in rats (Moss et al., 1975; Myers and Baum, 1980). Elevated prolactin concentrations interfere with male reproductive behavior. Other peptides that have been reported to influence male sexual behavior include vasopressin, oxytocin, GnRH, corticotropin-releasing hormone, and the neurohormones cholecystokinin, vasoactive intestinal polypeptide, galanin, and neuropeptide Y (Hull et al., 2002).

The most consistent reports of peptidergic influences on male reproductive behavior have involved endorphins. Providing male rats with naloxone, an antagonist to endorphins, typically enhances reproductive behavioral performance. When noncopulators, for example, were given either naloxone or saline injections, three-fourths of the naloxone-treated animals, but none of the saline-treated animals, mated to ejaculation in subsequent tests (Gessa et al., 1979). Thus, readiness to mate appears inversely correlated with the amount of endorphin receptors available. Recall that sexually inactive male rats are nonreactive to many stimuli and that a tail pinch is very effective in initiating copulatory behaviors (Meisel et al., 1980; Pfaus and Gorzalka, 1987). Opioids appear to affect the dopaminergic systems involved in the release of GnRH and thus subsequently suppress blood concentrations of LH and androgens (Pfaus and Gorzalka, 1987). Opioids, from endogenous or exogenous sources, tend to inhibit male sexual behavior in humans and nonhuman animals (reviewed in Pfaus and Gorzalka, 1987). Chronic heroin use, for example, suppresses plasma testosterone and LH concentrations. Chronic heroin use among human males throughout puberty does not affect later testosterone or LH blood concentrations after heroin use is discontinued (Mendelson and Mello, 1982). This

BOX 5.5   *Sodefrin, A Female-Attracting Pheromone in Newts*

Recent evidence suggests that amphibians are decreasing in numbers throughout the world. Some suggest that environmental endocrine disruptors are involved, whereas others hypothesize that other types of toxins are affecting reproductive function in these animals. A fungus or other pathogen may also be involved in the declining numbers of amphibians. Whatever the cause of the decline in amphibian populations, it serves as an early warning signal of environmental degradation for humans. We must understand the reproductive physiology and behavior of amphibians in order to understand how they, and we, might be affected by environmental agents. We know that pheromones play a key role in communication in many, if not most, vertebrates, including rodents, but the role of pheromones has been particularly well characterized in newts.

If given a choice, female newts and salamanders (urodele amphibians) appear to be attracted to water in which a male conspecific was recently courting a female. During courtship, male fire-bellied newts (*Cynops pyrrhogaster*) fan the water with their tails. This action tends to move water from the male's cloacal opening to the snout of the female. The female follows the male and keeps her snout in contact with the male's tail (**Figure A**). Upon close inspection, it was noted that a courting male extends small tubules from his cloaca in the presence of females (Kikuyama et al., 1997). These tubules are connected to the abdominal glands. Males without abdominal glands are not successful at courting females (Malacarne et al., 1984). Electrophysiological recordings of the olfactory nerve showed

Figure A   Courtesy of Sakae Kikuyama.

that the neuroepithelial cells of female crested newts (*Triturus cristatus*) became more active when exposed to male odors or extracts of the male abdominal glands (Cedrini and Fasolo, 1970). Taken together, this evidence suggested that male urodeles were emitting a chemical signal that attracted conspecific females.

In an elegant series of experiments, a team of researchers in Japan has isolated, characterized, localized, and quantified the female-attracting agent (pheromone) in male Japanese fire-bellied newts (Kikuyama et al., 1995). Using reverse-phase high-pressure liquid chromatography, they isolated a decapeptide from the abdominal glands of males. This decapeptide, which had no sequence homology with any known peptide, was named sodefrin (Kikuyama et al., 1995).[1]

When small blocks of sponge were impregnated with sodefrin, the minimal effective concentration for attracting females

and other studies suggest that a tolerance for opiates, in terms of sexual behavior, does not develop. Although marijuana is often associated with facilitating sexual motivation, sexual performance may be affected. For example, men who smoked marijuana daily reported premature ejaculation at three times the rate reported by nonsmokers (Pitts et al., 2006).

Male Reproductive Behavior in Birds

Reproductive behavior in male birds, both appetitive and consummatory, is highly dependent on androgens (reviewed in Ball and Balthazart, 2002; Fusani, 2008). Males of most bird species engage in some sort of ritualized courtship behavior, and castration eliminates this behavior. Since Berthold's findings regarding castration in roosters (see Chapter 1), many species of birds have been studied. In virtually all species, mating behavior wanes rapidly after castration, and treatment of castrated male birds with androgens restores courtship and mating behaviors (Ball and Balthazart, 2002; Crews and Silver, 1985; reviewed in Silver et al., 1979). Either testosterone or DHT restores most aspects of mating behaviors to precastration levels in male birds (Adkins and Adler, 1972; Adkins and Nock, 1976; Beach and Inman, 1965; Cheng and Lehrman, 1973; Hutchison, 1970; Silver, 1977). However, DHT does not restore copulation; rather, DHT restores precopulatory displays. In contrast, male pigeons that congenitally lack testes exhibit little sexual behavior as compared with normal males (Riddle, 1924/1925).

Figure B Courtesy of Sakae Kikuyama.

(in 3000 ml of water) was determined to be between 0.1 pM (picomolar) and 1.0 pM. A synthetic version was produced, and its effectiveness in attracting females was similar to that of the native peptide (Kikuyama et al., 1997). This peptide appeared to act through the female's olfactory system, because females whose nostrils were plugged with cotton and petroleum jelly were not attracted to the sodefrin.

An antibody to sodefrin was made in rabbits, and immuno-histochemical and radioimmunoassay techniques were used to locate and measure, respectively, sodefrin in male fire-bellied newts (Kikuyama et al., 1997). Sodefrin was primarily located in secretory granules in the apical portion of epithelial cells in the abdominal glands. Castration and hypophysectomy reduced sodefrin concentrations substantially, and testosterone and prolactin replacement therapy prevented this reduction. Testosterone appears to play a more critical role than prolactin in mediating sodefrin concentrations (Toyoda et al., 1994).

This pheromone seems to show species specificity. Sodefrin from red-bellied newts did not serve as an attractant to female sword-tailed newts (*Cynops ensicauda*), a related species (Kikuyama et al., 1997), and it appears that another pheromone with a different amino acid sequence may act as a chemical attractant in congeneric (belonging to the same genus) species. The sodefrin studies were the first to identify an amphibian pheromone and the first to discover a peptide pheromone among vertebrate animals (Kikuyama et al., 1995). Because of their diversity, and their potential for small changes in amino acid sequence, other peptides could easily serve as chemical signals conveying species-specific messages.

[1]The name was derived from two Japanese words prominent in a well-known poem. Nukada (**Figure B**) was a famous and beautiful poet who married an emperor. One day, she went out with the emperor to the outskirts of the city, but the emperor's brother, who was once her lover, solicited her by waving (*furu*) his sleeves (*sode*). She responded to his unwanted advances with a poem that loosely translates, "Don't be so bold as to wave your sleeves to me. People will say that we are still in love" (Sakae Kikuyama, personal communication).

Birds have some specific features as animal models for the study of hormone-behavior interactions. Blood concentrations of androgens in birds covary with their breeding season; that is, androgen concentrations are typically highest at the beginning of the breeding season and lowest during the summer molt and early winter (Wingfield and Farner, 1980). These changes in steroid concentrations are linked to seasonal fluctuations in day length (see Chapter 9). Additionally, female birds do not provide consistent behavioral stimuli to males following treatment with adequate doses of estrogens eventually associated with progesterone, unlike female rodents. Consequently, the behavior of the male may be less easy to separate from the behavior or responsiveness of the female.

The earliest, and arguably the best, descriptive studies linking testicular steroid hormones with avian reproductive behavior were conducted on ring doves (*Streptopelia risoria*) (Lehrman, 1965). Ring doves, however, may not be an ideal avian model, because several features of the endocrine control of behavior may be unique to the species. One such unusual feature is the nearly complete lack of photoperiodic (day length) effects on the reproductive behavior of male ring doves. Second, ring doves possess a crop sac, a highly specialized adaptation that requires unique hormonal stimulation. Most breeding behaviors in the ring dove have been linked to changes in hormone concentrations (**FIGURE 5.39**). However, there is a gradual shift from the aggressive courtship behavior observed early in the courtship sequence to the nest-oriented courtship behavior observed later that does not reflect a change in hormones but probably reflects testosterone-induced changes in brain

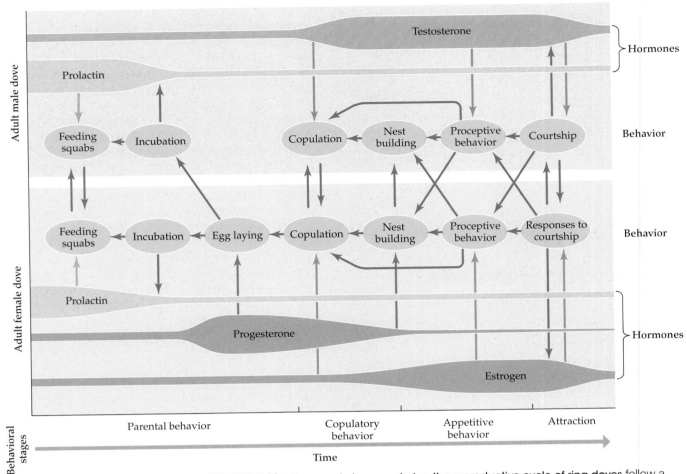

FIGURE 5.39 **Hormonal changes during the reproductive cycle of ring doves** follow a consistent pattern. In females (bottom), ovarian growth and estrogen secretion (pink-shaded area) coincide with courtship behavior; ovulation and rising progesterone levels induce incubation behavior and suppress bowing and cooing courtship behaviors. Prolactin induces the formation of the crop sac and brood patch and also stimulates parental behaviors. In males (top, blue-shaded area), testosterone stimulates courtship behavior, and prolactin appears to be involved in incubation and other parental behavior. Testosterone levels decrease and courtship behavior is suppressed during incubation and paternal care. Progesterone does not appear to be involved in male ring dove reproductive behavior. As soon as one cycle is completed in the laboratory setting, a new cycle begins with the onset of courtship behavior. After Rosenzweig and Leiman, 1989.

aromatase activity. That is, testosterone directly mediates the aggressive courtship behaviors, but it must be converted in the brain to estrogen to mediate the nest-oriented courtship behaviors (Hutchison and Steimer, 1983).

Japanese quail (*Coturnix japonica*) have also been used as a model species to study the hormonal control of male avian sexual behavior (Ball and Balthazart, 2004; Balthazart et al., 2004, 2009a,b). These birds provide a useful animal model for investigating hormone–reproductive behavior interactions because they have been selectively bred to mate quickly, and their other reproductive behaviors have waned; for example, in the laboratory these birds no longer incubate their eggs. Consequently, hormonal effects on their sexual behavior can be separated from effects on other reproductive behaviors. When a sexually mature pair of quail is introduced into a neutral mating arena, copulation usually is initiated within 10 seconds. The male grabs the neck of the female, mounts her, and brings his cloacal area into contact with hers (**FIGURE 5.40**). The male typically ejaculates during this brief cloacal contact period. After copulation, the male struts around the arena, often with a wing lowered toward the female. He may vocalize or crow. Castration eliminates all these behaviors within days, and testosterone therapy restores copulation to precastration levels. DHT is ineffective in restoring copulatory behavior in castrated quail but activates strutting and crowing (Balthazart, 1989).

Studies of Japanese quail have reported that testosterone must be converted to estrogen in the mPOA before it produces an effect on copulatory behavior

(A)

(C)

(D)

(B)

FIGURE 5.40 Copulation in Japanese quail may take only 10 to 15 seconds. In a typical sequence, the male struts around (A), crows (B), then rushes at the female, mounts her (C), and positions his cloaca against hers (D). Because female birds do not exhibit rigid consistency in their behavior from one mating test to the next, as do female rodents, it is difficult to separate factors associated with male behavior from those resulting from the behavior or responsiveness of the female. Courtesy of Jacques Balthazart.

FIGURE 5.41 Aromatase and estrogen receptors in the quail brain shown in camera lucida drawings of sections double-labeled for aromatase and estrogen. Each panel shows an enlarged area of the brain, the location of which is indicated by the inset. (A) Sections of the preoptic area (POA), where only a small proportion of cells expressed both aromatase and estrogen receptor activity. (Top left) Middle part of the preoptic medial nucleus (POM); (top right) POM at the level of the anterior commissure; (bottom) caudal POA and septum at the level of the nucleus striae terminalis. (B) One section in the caudal hypothalamus at the level of the nucleus inferioris hypothalami. Solid circles = cells labeled for estrogen receptors; open stars = cells labeled for aromatase; solid stars = cells double-labeled for estrogen receptors and aromatase. From Balthazart et al., 1991.

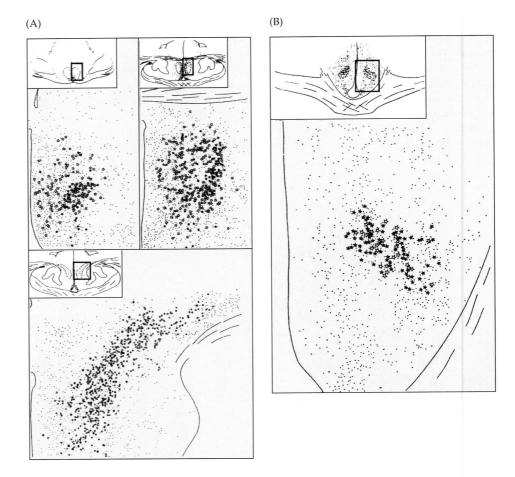

(Adkins-Regan, 1996), although some behaviors such as crowing are influenced exclusively by androgens (Balthazart and Ball, 2007). Blocking aromatase activity or estrogen binding prevents androgens from restoring copulatory behavior to pre-castration rates (Adkins-Regan, 1987; Balthazart, 1989). When immunocytochemical techniques are used, the preoptic area, especially the preoptic medial nucleus (POM), which is analogous to the mPOA in mammals, stains positively for estrogen receptors, as well as for cells containing the enzyme aromatase (Balthazart and Ball, 1993; Panzica et al., 1996). This indicates that androgens are converted to estrogens in these or possibly adjacent cells (Balthazart and Ball, 2007) (**FIGURE 5.41**). Other sites where this aromatization occurs include the nucleus striae terminalis, nucleus taeniae of the amygdala, infundibular hypothalamic nucleus, ventromedial nucleus of the hypothalamus, and mesencephalic substantia grisea centralis (homologous to the periaqueductal gray in mammals) (Adkins-Regan, 1996). Taken together, these data indicate that estrogens locally produced in the brain by aromatization of testosterone play a key role in the activation of copulatory behavior (reviewed in Remage-Healey et al., 2011). They exert these effects by affecting neurotransmitter dynamics and also probably by influencing the growth of neural processes.

Recent studies suggest that in Japanese quail both genomic and nongenomic effects of estradiol play roles to coordinate male sexual behaviors (Seredynski et al., 2013). Central administration of estradiol rapidly increases sexual motivation, as assessed by several measures of sexual motivation in response to the visual presentation of a female, but does not affect sexual performance in male quail. Treatment with analogs of estradiol that cannot cross the cell membranes also increase sexual motivation, suggesting the enhanced motivational effects are initiated at the cell membrane, and not via genomic mechanisms inside of neurons. These rapid estrogenic effects likely stimulate dopamine in the mPOA to promote sexual motivation. Dopamine in the mPOA contributes to sexual motivation, not merely general arousal, in Japanese quail (Kleitz-Nelson et al., 2010 a,b). Dopamine levels increase in the presence of a female and return to baseline after removal of the female from sight; however, quail that fail to copulate do not display this increased release, suggesting that part of "studs versus duds" reflects high versus low dopamine levels in the mPOA.

Estradiol, acting via the traditional genomic pathways, is necessary in these birds to support sexual performance, which requires extensive protein synthesis, neurogenesis, and axonal growth and restructuring—processes that all require significant time. Thus, estradiol works via two mechanisms (i.e., rapid nongenomic and traditional genomic mechanisms) that are coordinated to regulate male sexual behavior over two time scales (deBournonville et al., 2012; Seredynski et al., 2013). Studies such as these that allow a better understanding of the hormonal regulation of the appetitive and consummatory phases of male sexual behavior would likely not be possible with rodents or other traditional animal models and emphasize again the value of comparative studies.

Golden-collared manakins (*Manacus vitellinus*) are tropical birds that produce some of the most striking courtship displays among vertebrates, including acrobatic maneuvers, group displays, and production of loud popping sounds called wing snaps (Fusani et al., 2007) (**FIGURE 5.42**). Their courtship behavior is influenced by the activational effects of androgens, not estrogens. Treatment of courting males with the antiandrogen flutamide reduces courtship activity. Testosterone treatment of females and juvenile males, which typically do not produce wing snaps, will start to produce this behavior (Day et al., 2006). The production of wing snaps is activated by the action of testosterone on specialized motor neurons localized in the spinal cord that control wing movements. These androgen-sensitive neurons represent a unique neural adaptation of manakins related to the development of this unique behavior display.

FIGURE 5.42 Manakins engage in remarkable courtship displays. These displays, including a so-called wing snap, are regulated by the activational effects of androgens, not estrogens. Wing snaps are activated by testosterone actions on specialized motor neurons in the spinal cord that control wing movements. These androgen-sensitive neurons are a unique neural adaptation of manakins related to the development of this unique behavior display. After Day et al., 2006.

Snap!

In quail, as in roosters, crowing is an androgen-dependent behavior, and crowing and copulation occur in close temporal proximity to each other. If a castrated male or a female quail is injected with testosterone or DHT, crowing will ensue. These data suggest (but do not prove) that testosterone must be converted to DHT in order to have a behavioral effect on crowing (Adkins and Pniewski, 1978), but, as stated above, testosterone must be converted to estrogen before it elicits a copulatory behavioral response. The latter conversion appears to occur at a much higher rate in the brains of males than of females: this may explain at least in part why females injected with testosterone never show the mounting behaviors associated with male copulatory behavior (Adkins and Adler, 1972). Copulation is integrated in the POM, and as described above, the aromatase enzyme, which converts testosterone to estrogen, is present in that brain region. Vocalizations during courtship are probably regulated in the nucleus intercollicularis, a mesencephalic brain nucleus. This area of the brain contains the enzyme 5α-reductase, which converts testosterone into 5α-DHT. Thus, the enzymes that produce the behaviorally active metabolites of testosterone responsible for copulatory behavior and for crowing are located in the brain regions that underlie these two separate, but linked, reproductive behaviors (Balthazart and Ball, 1993).

One report has suggested that castration does not affect copulatory behavior in white-crowned sparrows, which naturally breed in the spring when the photoperiod exceeds 12 hours of light per day. (Moore and Kranz, 1983). If male white-crowned sparrows are injected with testosterone before puberty and maintained under short-day light conditions, then as expected, they will not mate with receptive females. After exposure to long days and attainment of puberty, they will copulate. If pre-pubertal males are castrated and then exposed to long days after they mature, they will mate despite a complete lack of assayable testosterone in their blood (Moore and Kranz, 1983). The extent to which male mating behavior in other avian species may be divorced from hormonal control requires further investigation. To this date, this study on white-crowned sparrows is indeed the only one suggesting independence of sexual behaviors from testosterone activation. Other species of sparrows clearly require androgens to elicit copulatory behavior (Balthazart, 1989). In song sparrows, these androgens can be produced in the gonads or directly in the brain by transformation of a steroid precursor called dehydroepiandrosterone (DHEA), which is synthesized in the adrenal gland (see Soma et al., 2008).

Male Reproductive Behavior in Reptiles

Like birds, most male reptiles stop mating after castration (Crews and Silver, 1985). One notable exception is the red-sided garter snake (*Thamnophis sirtalis parietalis*), found on the midwestern Canadian prairies (Mason, 1987). Males of this species emerge from their winter hibernacula several weeks earlier than females and attempt to mate with females as they emerge. Many males court a single female as she moves out of the hibernaculum (**FIGURE 5.43**). Females are much larger than males in this species. The male has two hemipenes, one of which is inserted into one of the female's two vaginae during copulation. Other males stop courting the female as soon as one male achieves an intromission. Apparently, a chemosensory signal is expressed by the copulating female that inhibits court-

FIGURE 5.43 A "mating ball" of male red-sided garter snakes forms when great numbers of males attempt to court and mate with a female, which emerges from the winter hibernaculum several weeks after the males. As soon as one male successfully achieves intromission, the female expresses a chemosignal that disperses the unmated suitors.

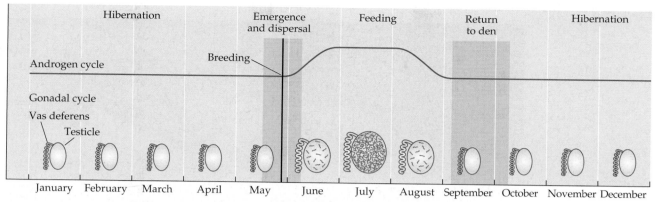

FIGURE 5.44   Red-sided garter snakes display a dissociated reproductive pattern. Male red-sided garter snakes emerge from hibernation and mate with females in the spring; however, the testes and vas deferens are regressed during the mating period, and the testes are not producing sperm or androgens. In midsummer, the testes develop and begin producing androgens and sperm. The gonads regress prior to hibernation in the fall, and sperm produced in summer is stored for the mating period of the following spring. After Crews and Gartska, 1982; © 1982 by Scientific American, Inc. All rights reserved.

ship behavior in the other males (Mason et al., 1989); the exact chemical identity of this substance is currently unknown, but appears to involve copulatory fluid as application of copulatory fluids on unmated females causes males to stop courting (Shine and Mason, 2012).

Most male animals have an **associated reproductive pattern**. That is, during the breeding season, mating behavior coincides with maximal testis size, as well as maximal androgen concentrations and sperm production. The red-sided garter snake, however, exhibits what has been termed a **dissociated reproductive pattern** (Crews, 1984, 1991). When the snakes are mating, the testes remain regressed; no sperm are being produced. The males inseminate females in the spring with sperm stored from the previous autumn. The testes begin to develop, produce androgens, and make sperm in midsummer, after all mating behavior has stopped (**FIGURE 5.44**). The testes then regress again, and the animal enters hibernation. The sperm are stored in a special organ until the following spring. Androgen levels are still elevated when the males emerge from hibernation (Moore et al., 2000, 2001) but decrease along with mating intensity through the spring breeding season (Krohmer et al., 1987). Interestingly, castration has no effect on subsequent mating behavior in this species. Removal of the adrenals, another potential source of androgens, or even the pituitary gland also has no effect on mating behavior in these snakes (Camazine et al., 1980; Crews et al., 1984). Neither treatment with steroid hormones nor treatment with gonadotropins affects copulation in this species (Crews, 1984). However, destruction of the mPOA (Krohmer and Crews, 1987) or removal of the pineal gland (Crews et al., 1988b; Nelson et al., 1987) eliminates mating behavior, probably because these two brain regions integrate the environmental information that allows the snakes to ascertain the appropriate season of the year for mating (Crews, 2010) (see Chapter 10). The finding that mating behavior is divorced from hormonal control among these snakes shows that position on the phylogenetic scale is not a perfect indicator of the independence of sexual behavior from direct hormonal control (cf. Beach, 1947); that is, it is not only humans and large apes with large brains that have their sexual behavior separated from hormonal control.

Male whiptail lizards of the genus *Cnemidophorus* rely on androgens to regulate their reproductive behavior. Courtship is highly ritualized in this species. The male approaches the female from the rear, climbs onto her back, bites her back or foreleg,

associated reproductive pattern   The breeding pattern observed in most vertebrate species, in which reproductive behavior, maximal gonadal size and activity, high steroid concentrations, and gamete production coincide.

dissociated reproductive pattern   A breeding pattern observed in some vertebrate species in which reproductive behavior does not coincide with maximal gonadal size and activity. Instead, copulation occurs when steroid levels and gamete production are low.

(A) (B)

FIGURE 5.45 Copulatory behavior in sexual and asexual species of whiptail lizards is similar. (A, top to bottom) The copulatory sequence in *Cnemidophorus inornatus*, a sexually reproducing whiptail lizard. The male mounts the female, tucks his hindquarters under the female, and finally bites the female's back and achieves intromission in the so-called doughnut posture. (B, top to bottom) Pseudosexual behavior in *C. uniparens*, a parthenogenetic whiptail lizard species that developed from hybrids of species that reproduce sexually. Although both participants are females, the copulatory sequence closely resembles that of the sexual whiptail species, including the performance of the doughnut posture. This behavior has been found to be necessary to maximize ovulation. From Crews and Fitzgerald, 1980.

then brings his tail underneath her to bring their respective cloacal areas together, assuming the so-called doughnut posture (Crews and Fitzgerald, 1980) (**FIGURE 5.45**). The male dismounts after about 10 minutes and leaves the scene.

Some species within the genus *Cnemidophorus* are parthenogenetic; that is, all the members of these species are triploid females, which lay unfertilized eggs that all develop into daughters. These species evolved from hybrids of two sexually reproducing species. Interestingly, the occurrence of "male-like" behavior persists in at least five all-female *Cnemidophorus* species. Captive female *C. uniparens* alternate during the breeding season between displaying male-like pseudosexual behavior and female-like behavior. Female "receptive" behavior is observed before ovula-

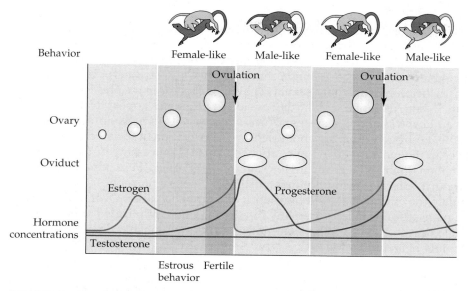

FIGURE 5.46 **Hormones mediate pseudocopulation in parthenogenetic whiptail lizards.**
Females in parthenogenetic whiptail species alternate in performing female and male roles
during pseudocopulation, and this alternation has clear hormonal correlates. The bottom
portion of the figure shows the hormonal cycles and events in the ovary and oviduct in relation to a hypothetical female alternating between female- and male-like behavior (top; dark
lizard). In the preovulatory state, when estrogen levels are increasing, the female behaves in a
female-typical fashion. After ovulation, when her oviducts are full of eggs, blood progesterone
levels increase, estrogen levels decrease, and she exhibits male-like pseudosexual behavior.
This cycle repeats itself throughout the breeding season. Note that these behavioral shifts
have no relation to testosterone levels, which remain constant throughout the cycle, despite
the importance of this steroid hormone in mediating male behavior in sexually reproducing
whiptail species. The neural substrates of male-like courtship and copulatory behavior have
apparently been retained in the parthenogenetic species, but they are mediated by progesterone. After Crews, 1987.

tion, when estrogen concentrations are relatively high (see Chapter 6); at this time,
females allow other females to mount them. Male-like behavior is observed after
ovulation, when blood concentrations of progesterone are elevated (Crews, 1987)
(FIGURE 5.46); postovulatory females court, mount, and assume the doughnut mating posture with periovulatory females. Ovariectomized females injected with progesterone show male-like pseudosexual behavior, and those injected with estradiol
show female pseudosexual behavior. Thus progesterone, rather than androgens,
apparently mediates male-like behavior in these species.

Why do these parthenogenetic lizards engage in pseudosexual behavior (Crews,
1997)? Functionally, females that undergo mounting and pseudosexual mating behavior produce more offspring than females that do not engage in this behavior.
Apparently, the act of pseudocopulation stimulates the release of additional ova.
The reciprocal alternation between male-like and female-like behavior facilitates
breeding in these species (Crews, 1987). This seemingly altruistic behavior is to be
expected when we recall that asexually reproducing animals share virtually all of
their genes in common, so an individual that helps other females to increase their
production of offspring also enhances her own inclusive fitness. These unusual
lizards provide a wonderful demonstration that the structures of the hormones
involved in hormone-behavior interactions do not evolve very much; instead, new
functions for those hormones evolve (Crews, 1997; Godwin and Crews, 2002).

Conclusions

How do hormones affect male sexual behavior? Based on our discussions of different species, a few generalizations can be made. Sex steroid hormones clearly do not act as a "switch" to activate sexual behavior. The presence of testosterone does not automatically stimulate mating behavior; rather, testosterone, or its metabolites, increases the probability that a sexual behavior will occur in the presence of specific stimuli. In both mammals and birds, sex steroid hormones appear to affect sensory input and central nervous system processing, as well as behavioral output. For example, androgens amplify chemosensory information associated with estrous females in the male rodent's brain, allowing further processing of that incoming information (Pfaff and Pfaffmann, 1969; Stern, 1990; Wood, 1997). Steroid hormones are, in turn, affected by environmental stimuli. Peptide hormones also appear to modulate the effects of steroid hormones on sexual behavior. Overall, hormones affect male sexual behavior in many interacting and complicated ways. Several physiological and behavioral systems integrate information in order to enhance the probability of an individual male's reproductive success.

Summary

1. Male sexual behavior consists of all behaviors necessary and sufficient to deliver male gametes to female gametes. Male sexual behavior can be divided into two phases: the appetitive phase (courtship, sex drive) and the consummatory phase (copulation, performance).

2. Sex drive, the motivation to seek sexual contact, becomes extremely powerful and overtly expressed in males after puberty, when the testes begin to secrete androgens. Sexual performance and copulatory ability increase after puberty as well.

3. Castration reduces sexual behavior in some proportion of individuals of virtually all vertebrate species examined. However, there is great individual and species variation in the extent to which sexual behavior is regulated by hormones. Testosterone treatment generally reverses the decrease in frequency of male sexual behavior observed after castration. More testosterone is necessary to restore sexual behavior in castrated males after it has ceased than is required to maintain male sexual behavior.

4. There are three components of male rodent sexual behavior: mounting, intromission, and ejaculation. Corresponding penile responses—erections, flips, and cups—can be elicited from animals independent from higher brain influences. Testosterone does not seem to regulate sexual behavior or penile reflexes directly, but rather acts as a prohormone; metabolic products of testosterone, namely, estrogens and dihydrotestosterone (DHT), appear to be important in mediating copulatory behaviors and penile sensitivity, respectively.

5. An intact chemosensory system is necessary for the proper function of sexual behavior in rodents. Lesions along the neural circuit that mediates olfactory information, from the olfactory bulbs to the amygdala to the medial preoptic area of the hypothalamus (mPOA), result in diminished sexual behavior. Electrical stimulation along this circuit increases the frequency of sexual behavior in male rodents.

6. The mPOA appears to be crucial for integrating sensory and internal stimuli in order for normal copulation to occur. Destruction of the mPOA eliminates copulatory behaviors in virtually all vertebrate males. Implantation of minute amounts of testosterone into the mPOA restores mating behavior in castrated males.

Testosterone must be converted to estrogen in order to have a behavioral effect; DHT implanted into the brain does not stimulate copulation. Mapping the distribution of steroid hormone receptors and aromatase activity has helped to pinpoint exactly where in the brain hormones act to regulate male sexual behavior. The use of mice with targeted deletions of specific genes has yielded some novel, and in some cases contradictory, information about hormone-behavior interactions underlying male sexual behavior.

7. Females can affect hormone concentrations in males and can also affect the frequency and timing of their copulatory behaviors. The Coolidge effect is one well-known example in which novel females have substantial effects on the reproductive behavior of males. Plasma concentrations of LH and testosterone increase in males after exposure to females. This elevation in hormone concentrations can be classically conditioned.

8. Individual differences exist in the frequency of sexual behavior exhibited by males. This difference in sexual activity does not appear to correlate with blood androgen concentrations.

9. In men, sexual behavior does not seem to be as dependent on blood androgen concentrations as it is in some other taxa. However, there is great variation in the frequency of postcastration sexual activities among men. Hypogonadal men treated with a long-lasting androgen showed increases in several sexual behaviors and thoughts, indicating that androgens can affect sexual behavior in humans.

10. The copulatory behaviors of men cannot be classified according to muscular reflexes as in other animals. Other male primates exhibit stereotyped mating positions. Androgens are important in maintaining nonhuman primate male mating behavior.

11. The same brain regions underlying rodent sexual behavior appear to be involved in the hormonal mediation of primate sexual behavior, with the exception of the olfactory system.

12. Female primates, like female rodents, affect sexual behavior and hormone concentrations in males, but the few systematic studies on female rodents comparable to the experiments with rodents report, for the most part, inconsistent results.

13. Opioids appear to inhibit sexual behavior, especially with chronic exposure, whereas treatment with opioid antagonists appears to facilitate the expression of sexual behavior.

14. Birds, like rodents, appear to require androgens to maintain sexual behavior. Androgens are converted into estrogens in the preoptic medial nucleus (POM) to mediate copulatory behavior, or to DHT in other regions to mediate vocalizations.

15. Most male reptiles stop breeding after castration, and mating behavior is restored by androgen replacement therapy. Red-sided garter snakes, however, engage in copulatory behavior when the testes are regressed and no circulating androgens can be detected. The independence of male copulatory behavior from hormone levels in these snakes provides strong evidence that it is not only animals with highly developed brains that copulate without the presence of androgens.

16. Individuals of female parthenogenetic lizard species engage in male-like behavior in order to increase the number of ova released during ovulation. Although male copulatory behaviors in related sexually reproducing species are regulated by androgens, male-like behaviors in the all-female species are mediated by progesterone.

Questions for Discussion

1. What is sexual behavior? What behaviors do you think can reasonably be called male sexual behavior in the following species: rats, ring doves, and humans?

2. "Androgens cause sexual behavior in males." Is this statement really true? Defend your answer.

3. Discuss the advantages and disadvantages of treating male sexual offenders with drugs that decrease testosterone production or activity.

4. How do testosterone and its metabolites (dihydrotestosterone and estradiol) influence male sexual performance and motivation? What are the similarities and differences between the influences of steroid hormones on these two aspects of sexual behavior?

5. The medial preoptic area is an important site regulating mating behavior in male mammals. Discuss the experimental evidence linking the mPOA to male sex behavior, and speculate on how the mPOA controls sexual behavior.

6. Given the role of dopamine in mediating male sexual behavior, would you expect any changes in compulsive sexual behaviors in men taking L-dopa, a precursor to dopamine?

Suggested Readings

Ågmo, A. 2007. *Functional and Dysfunctional Sexual Behavior: A Synthesis of Neuroscience and Comparative Psychology*. Academic Press, San Diego.

Ball, G. F., and Balthazart, J. 2017. Neuroendocrine regulation of reproductive behavior in birds. In D. W. Pfaff, et al. (eds.), *Hormones, Brain and Behavior* (3rd ed.), pp. In press. Academic Press, New York.

Balthazart, J., and Ball, G. F. (eds.). 2012. *Brain, Aromatase, Estrogens, and Behavior*. Oxford University Press, New York.

Crews, D., et al. 2017. Hormones, brain and behavior in reptiles. In D. W. Pfaff, et al. (eds.), *Hormones, Brain and Behavior* (3rd ed.), pp. In press. Academic Press, New York.

Hull, E. M., and Dominguez, J. M. 2015. The neurobiology of male sexual behavior. In E. Knobil and J. Neill, (eds.), *Physiology of Reproduction* (4th ed.), pp. 2211–2286. Elsevier Press, Amsterdam.

van Anders, S. M., et al. 2011. The Steroid/Peptide Theory of Social Bonds: Integrating testosterone and peptide responses for classifying social behavioral contexts. *Psychoneuroendocrinology*, 36:1265–1275.

Veening, J. G., and Coolen, L. M. 2014. Neural mechanisms of sexual behavior in the male rat: Emphasis on ejaculation-related circuits. *Pharmacol. Biochem. Behav.*, 121:170–183.

Female Reproductive Behavior

6

Learning Objectives

The goal of this chapter is to describe the neural and hormonal mechanisms underlying the control of female sexual motivation and behavior. A brief historical overview provides the context to understand why investigations into female sexuality have a shorter past than those of males. By the end of the chapter, you should be able to:

- recap significant early discoveries that guided the study of female sexual behavior.

- compare female mating behavior across well-studied species.

- provide examples that correct historic misconceptions about female sexual behavior.

- distinguish between proceptivity and receptivity and describe the neural substrates that underlie them.

- describe the neural, hormonal, and ovarian mechanisms responsible for the ovulatory cycle.

- describe the neural and hormonal circuitry underlying the control of female sexual motivation and behavior.

During their breeding seasons, male vertebrates are capable of sexual behavior all the time, provided they are sexually mature and not socially inhibited. Female vertebrates must also be sexually mature and not inhibited but, in addition, they show significant fluctuations in sexual activity during their breeding seasons. Syrian hamsters (*Mesocricetus auratus*) provide a good example. The females venture out of their individual burrows around dusk every night to forage alone for food. Female hamsters are usually very aggressive and will wound or even kill male conspecifics (see Chapter 8).

FIGURE 6.1 Estrous females are motivated to seek males. High circulating estrogen concentrations increase the motivation of females to engage in sexual behavior. Female hamsters in estrus seek out males that they otherwise avoid. This estrous female Syrian hamster is shown developing a specific posture called lordosis, which allows the male to mount and successfully copulate with her. She does not behave in this manner when not in estrus.

However, during the vernal and summer breeding season, on certain nights, female hamsters emerge earlier than usual, and they venture farther away from their burrows than usual. On these nights, the females leave fragrant urine trails that attracts male hamsters (Johnston, 1979). A male hamster follows a trail back to a burrow and is soon confronted by the friendly female that eventually mates with the male one or more times (**FIGURE 6.1**); then her behavior radically changes. She again becomes highly aggressive and attacks the male, driving him away from her burrow.

What accounts for the dramatic change in the behavior of female hamsters? When female hamsters seek and permit mating, they are said to be in "heat," or **estrus**. The word *estrus* comes from the Latin word *oestrus*, which loosely translates to "in a frenzy, or possessed by the gadfly" (Feder, 1981). Many pet owners have experienced a dog or cat in heat and are often surprised by the intensity of effort displayed by their pets to mate. They may jump fences or bolt out of slightly open doors or windows. In a laboratory setting, an estrous rat will cross a highly charged electrified floor to gain physical access to a male (Warner, 1927); a female rat in estrus will also diligently depress a lever or poke its nose through an opening many times in order to gain access to a male (Bermant, 1961; Matthews et al., 1997). Female rats (or dogs or cats or hamsters) that are not in estrus will not sustain pain or exert much effort to interact with males. The ovaries are involved in the expression of estrous behavior in rats and dogs. Removal of the ovaries of hamsters in the laboratory eliminates all estrous behaviors, including early emergence from burrows, seeking of males, and mating behavior.

estrus The period during which female mammals will permit copulation.

anestrus The reproductive condition of a female mammal that is not in estrus, or mating condition.

The differences between estrous and **anestrus** (not in estrus) female mammals are striking. First, a female in estrus will seek out males, initiate copulation, and prefer to remain in close proximity to males; the same female will not engage in these behaviors when not in estrus. Second, estrous females are more attractive to males than anestrous females; that is, conspecific males prefer to visit, and exert more effort to maintain close proximity to, estrous rather than anestrous females. The urine and other odors of estrous females appear to be more attractive to male conspecifics than those of anestrous females. Third, males mount estrous females preferentially. Finally, only estrous females will permit mating to occur. Anestrous females will not tolerate male mounting behavior; in fact, anestrous females of many mammalian species will inflict serious injuries on persistent male suitors (**FIGURE 6.2**).

What physiological changes evoke these dramatic changes in a female's behavior as she cycles between an estrous and an anestrous state? Briefly, the hormones associated with maturation of her ova (eggs) have also evolved to affect her nervous system in a number of ways. The resulting neural changes influence her behavior in such a way that the probability of mating, and ultimately the successful production of offspring, is increased. Thus, mating behavior is tightly coupled in time with ovulation and occurs when successful fertilization of ova is most likely. Although analyses of the evolution of hormonal regulation of female sexual behavior are intriguing (Thorton et al., 2003; Wallen and Zehr, 2004), the focus of this chapter will be the proximate endocrine mechanisms underlying sexual behavior in females.

FIGURE 6.2 Nonestrous females are not motivated to mate. In female rodents, low circulating estrogen concentrations are not consistent with motivation to mate. This female mouse is showing disinterest by back kicking a male that is attempting to mount her.

As noted in Chapter 5 with respect to males, reproductive hormones do not "turn on" female sexual behavior per se; rather, hormones change the probability that specific stimuli will elicit particular behaviors that lead to successful copulation. Hormones affect the input systems: the acuity, sensitivity, and efficiency of the sensory systems are enhanced by reproductive hormones. Consequently, estrous females are better able than anestrous females to detect and respond to conspecific males. The central nervous system is also affected by the endocrine changes associated with estrus. Females' motivation, attention, and perception change as sex steroid concentrations fluctuate. Finally, because effectors, too, are affected by hormones, the way that a female moves and reacts to stimuli also changes. Her behavior, as well as the stimuli she emits (e.g., chemosensory agents or auditory signals), affect the way males behave; the males' behavior may also feed back to alter the endocrine state of the female further.

As described previously, sexual behavior is behavior that has evolved to bring the two gamete types together. Female sexual behavior is defined as all behaviors necessary and sufficient to achieve fertilization of female gametes (ova) by sperm. Sex drive provides a powerful motivational force urging females to seek sexual union, just as it does in males. Until recently, however, sexual motivation was not emphasized in studies of female mating behavior. Although male sexual behavior has been the subject of research for much longer than female sexual behavior, in some ways a more detailed understanding of the hormonal correlates and neural bases of sexual behavior has been achieved for females (Blaustein, 1996; Blaustein and Erskine, 2002; Pfaff et al., 2000). For example, most of the neural circuitry underlying one female reproductive behavior—namely, lordosis, the reflexive mating posture of female rats—as well as the specific effects of hormones on this circuit have been elucidated by the exquisite research of Donald Pfaff and colleagues (Micevych et al., 1997; Pfaff et al., 2000).

As noted, female reproductive states typically occur in cycles. Mammalian female reproduction has six components: courtship, mating, ovulation, pregnancy, parturition, and lactation (Everett, 1961). This chapter will be limited to behavior associated with the first three components of female reproduction; the latter three components will be reviewed in Chapter 7, which discusses parental care. In common with the studies on males presented in Chapter 5, most of our knowledge about the physiological mechanisms underlying female sexual behavior has been gained through studies on nonhuman animals, especially rodents, and examples of such studies will be described below. But first, efforts to understand female sexual behavior will be presented from a historical perspective to explain the formal constructs of female sexual behavior. Then female sexual behavior and reproductive cycles will be described. The last part of the chapter is devoted to experimental and correlational data relating hormones, genetics, and the nervous system to female sexual behavior.

Early Discoveries about Female Sexual Behavior

In contrast to the early studies on males, remarkably little progress was made in the study of female sexual behavior until the twentieth century. It is difficult to discern whether this lack of progress was due to the inherent complexity of female sexual behavior or whether it merely reflected a lack of interest on the part of a predominantly male research community that assumed that females were passive participants in copulation (but see Beach, 1976; Doty, 1974). A possible practical impediment to research is that ovariectomy is a difficult surgical operation compared with removal of the testes.[1] In any event, prior to 1900, there were relatively few studies on the effects

---

[1]In the context of females, the terms *ovariectomy*, *gonadectomy*, and *castration* all mean removal of the ovaries.

of female gonadectomy on behavior, in contrast to the wealth of information already available regarding the behavioral effects of male castration. However, in all the early studies, as well as in most subsequent ones, the results were quite consistent: most adult female mammals' mating behaviors stop immediately after the removal of the ovaries (reviewed in Beach, 1948). The development of ideas and methodologies associated with studies of hormonal correlates of female sexual behavior paralleled the studies on male sexual behavior presented in Chapter 5.

A major complicating factor in understanding the physiological mechanisms underlying female sexual behavior is the cyclic nature of that behavior. Adult males are generally able to mate any time they encounter an estrous female during the breeding season, but females of many mammalian species, especially those commonly used in laboratory research, enter and leave estrus on a regular basis. For instance, if a female Syrian hamster (*Mesocricetus auratus*) is placed in a cage with a vasectomized male for a short period each night, she will permit copulation every fourth night. Her estrous cycle is thus said to be 4 days in length. If the male were not vasectomized and copulation continued until ejaculation, her eggs would be fertilized, and she would not display estrous behavior again for 16 days, until immediately postpartum (i.e., after giving birth). Sustained copulation, even with a vasectomized male, would activate the formation of specific ovarian structures that would also disrupt the display of 4-day estrous cycles. The nature of this disruption, termed pseudopregnancy, will be described later in this chapter.

The Development of the Vaginal Cytological Assay

Because estrous cycles stop after ovariectomy, it was surmised that the cycles in estrous behavior reflected cycles in ovarian function, but at the start of the twentieth century, it was difficult to discern these cyclic ovarian changes without surgical intervention. In most cases, after behavioral observations were made, the ovaries were removed and histologically fixed for microscopic examination, and the behavior was correlated with the presence or absence of different ovarian structures, such as follicles or corpora lutea (see Chapter 2). Only limited data could be obtained in this manner. Repeated behavioral tests could not be performed in the same animals, because the behavior in question stopped after ovariectomy. Consequently, the first breakthrough in understanding the cyclicity of female sexual behavior was the technical development of noninvasive external markers that reliably reflected ovarian activity. The demonstration by Stockard and Papanicolaou (1917) that changes in vaginal cytology (cell types) could be closely correlated with changes in ovarian function in guinea pigs was an extremely important advance in the study of female reproductive behavior and physiology. This technique was soon extended to mice (Allen, 1922) and rats (Long and Evans, 1922) and eventually to hundreds of species (Asdell, 1964; Rowlands and Weir, 1984). This powerful tool allowed researchers to correlate mating behavior with ovarian function, without direct surgical examination of the ovaries.

The technique for assessing changes in vaginal cytology is rapid and straightforward. A modified version of this histological test, in which cells from the cervix (instead of the vaginal lumen, or opening) are obtained and examined, is part of a typical gynecological examination and is commonly called the Pap test, after Dr. Papanicolaou (**FIGURE 6.3**). In rodents, the procedure consists of swabbing cells from the vaginal lumen after lavage (sterile wash), then examining those cells microscopically. When applied to rats, this method reveals changes in the cellular contents of the vaginal lumen that recur every 4 or 5 days (Long and Evans, 1922).[2] At one

---

[2]For the sake of simplicity, only 4-day cycles will be considered here, but it is important to note that among rats there are either 4-day or 5-day cycles but no 4.5-day cycles. The 5-day rat estrous cycle includes an additional 24 hours of diestrus, called diestrus III. Older studies sometimes refer to diestrus I as "metestrus."

FIGURE 6.3 **Dr. George Nicholaus Papanicolaou** was born in 1883 in Greece. He attained an MD degree from the University of Athens and a PhD in Munich. Dr. Papanicolaou obtained a position in the department of anatomy at Cornell Medical College in 1913. His wife, Mary, also worked there, as his technician. Dr. Papanicolaou remained at Cornell until a few months before his death in 1962. It was at Cornell that he began examining vaginal smears of guinea pigs to determine the external markers of the 16-day estrous cycle. Eventually, he began to study menstrual cycles in women. In 1933 he published a monograph titled "The Sexual Cycle of the Human Female as Revealed by the Vaginal Smear." It was while doing this work that he noticed cancer cells coming from the cervix. Dr. Papanicolaou's understanding of the significance of these cells as a diagnostic tool was not immediate. After an extensive collaboration with gynecologist Herbert Traut to validate the diagnostic potential of vaginal cells, he published the now famous monograph "Diagnosis of Uterine Cancer by the Vaginal Smear" in 1943. This diagnostic procedure was named the Pap test and has been used to diagnose millions of cases of cervical cancer.

point in the cycle, "cornified" epithelial cells are present; these cells look like corn-flakes under the microscope. This stage, which lasts about 36 hours, is arbitrarily considered the first stage of the cycle and is called **vaginal estrus**. Vaginal estrus is followed by a period during which cornified cells become reduced in number, and leukocytes (white blood cells), as well as a few nucleated epithelial cells, appear. This stage, called vaginal **diestrus**, persists for approximately 48 hours. The first day of diestrus is referred to as diestrus I, and the second day is often called diestrus II. The next phase is characterized by the presence of many nucleated epithelial cells, as well as a dramatic reduction in the number of leukocytes. This final stage, called vaginal proestrus, lasts for about 12 hours. An obvious external marker of vaginal **proestrus** is that the thin vaginal membrane disappears, revealing a patent (open) vaginal canal. This external marker coincides with behavioral estrus, the onset of mating behavior.

These changes in vaginal cytology were soon correlated with ovarian changes (**FIGURE 6.4**). When researchers took vaginal smears from rats, then removed the ovaries from the same individuals, fixed them histologically, and examined them under a microscope, they found that the following correlations between changes in vaginal cytology and ovarian activity could be made (Boling et al., 1941; Feder, 1981):

1. Vaginal estrus is correlated with the presence of recently ruptured follicles following ovulation. In addition, tertiary follicles begin to develop from secondary follicles at this time. The next wave of ova released by the ovaries will eventually come from these tertiary follicles after they develop fully. The antrum of each tertiary follicle is small at this stage. The granulosa cells, the epithelial cells surrounding the follicle, induce the formation of a distinct layer of connective tissue called the theca interna.

2. As the vaginal smear becomes diestrous, the tertiary follicles become larger and the granulosa cells become more numerous. The antrum begins to fill with a clear fluid called the liquor folliculi. The rupture sites where previous ovulations occurred have been repaired, and endocrine luteal cells surround the fluid-filled cavities of the former follicles to form corpora lutea.

3. By diestrus II, the layer of connective tissue surrounding the theca interna differentiates into a layer of spindle-shaped cells called the theca externa. The enlarging tertiary follicles are now referred to as Graafian follicles. The corpora lutea are fully formed; the inner cavity has been filled with endocrine luteal cells and their supporting vascular and connective tissues.

vaginal estrus Directly following mating behavior and ovulation. Characterized by cornified epithelial cells.

diestrus Associated with the development of ovarian follicles and characterized by reduction in the number of epithelial cells and an increase in leucocytes.

proestrus The vaginal cellular condition coincident with mating behavior (estrus) in female rodents.

4. As the vaginal cell cycle becomes proestrous, a growth spurt occurs in the Graafian follicles destined to ovulate (preovulatory swelling). Other follicles that are not going to ovulate regress. The corpora lutea also regress unless specific vaginal stimuli associated with intromission are experienced by the female.

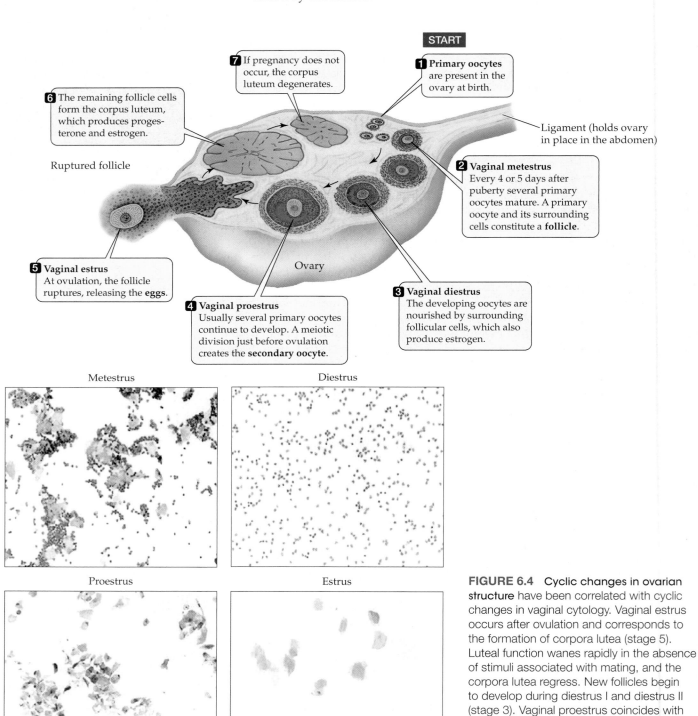

7 If pregnancy does not occur, the corpus luteum degenerates.

1 **Primary oocytes** are present in the ovary at birth.

6 The remaining follicle cells form the corpus luteum, which produces progesterone and estrogen.

Ligament (holds ovary in place in the abdomen)

Ruptured follicle

2 **Vaginal metestrus** Every 4 or 5 days after puberty several primary oocytes mature. A primary oocyte and its surrounding cells constitute a **follicle**.

5 **Vaginal estrus** At ovulation, the follicle ruptures, releasing the **eggs**.

Ovary

4 **Vaginal proestrus** Usually several primary oocytes continue to develop. A meiotic division just before ovulation creates the **secondary oocyte**.

3 **Vaginal diestrus** The developing oocytes are nourished by surrounding follicular cells, which also produce estrogen.

Metestrus

Diestrus

Proestrus

Estrus

FIGURE 6.4 Cyclic changes in ovarian structure have been correlated with cyclic changes in vaginal cytology. Vaginal estrus occurs after ovulation and corresponds to the formation of corpora lutea (stage 5). Luteal function wanes rapidly in the absence of stimuli associated with mating, and the corpora lutea regress. New follicles begin to develop during diestrus I and diestrus II (stage 3). Vaginal proestrus coincides with maximal follicular development (stage 4); behavioral estrus and mating occur during vaginal proestrus. After Feder, 1981; micrographs from Hong et al., 2010.

When ovulation occurs, the cycle begins anew—unless the female mates. If she receives sufficient vaginal stimulation through copulation or simulated copulatory stimuli, then the corpora lutea do not regress. If the mating is fertile and the female becomes pregnant, then the corpora lutea remain large throughout most of the pregnancy. If the mating is sterile and the female does not become pregnant, then the corpora lutea remain large for approximately 14 days before regressing. Because it causes a number of physiological changes that resemble those of pregnancy, this state of sustained corpora luteal function is called **pseudopregnancy**. The estrous cycles are suspended during pregnancy or pseudopregnancy.

The linkage of vaginal cytology to ovarian structural changes enabled researchers to make a very good guess about ovarian function simply by observing cells obtained from the vaginal lumen. As these studies continued, other research was proceeding that linked mating behavior with vaginal cytological changes (see Figure 6.4). A classic monograph by Long and Evans (1922) provided an excellent description and partial quantification of the sexual behavior of female rats correlated with vaginal cytology. Long and Evans found that mating behavior is observed only when the vaginal smear shows many nucleated epithelial cells; in other words, as noted above, behavioral estrus coincides with vaginal proestrus. Female rats generally stop mating by the time vaginal estrus occurs. This unfortunate duplicity of terms has confused students for decades. Remember that behavioral estrus coincides with vaginal proestrus; vaginal estrus follows behavioral estrus.

As a result of these studies, vaginal cycles in cell types could be correlated with cycles of estrous behavior, and thus, logically, estrous behavior could be correlated with ovarian function through observations of vaginal cytology. Because the cycles of both vaginal cytology and estrous behavior stop after ovariectomy, researchers reasoned that the ovaries must produce a cyclic signal that drives the changes in both vaginal cell types and behavior. Because the cycles continue if the ovaries are denervated, it was reasoned that hormones must be mediating the cyclic signal. The next part of the puzzle involved understanding the endocrine products associated with the various ovarian structural changes. Relating these endocrine changes to behavioral alterations provided the framework for the modern era of sex research on females (Beach, 1981).

Research in the Twentieth Century

The two types of ovarian structures that were considered most likely to be producing hormones that influenced estrous behavior were the follicles and corpora lutea. Researchers tested these hypotheses by injecting laboratory animals with extracts from ovaries obtained from slaughterhouses. When chemical extracts derived from the follicles of hog ovaries were injected into ovariectomized mice, they caused four physiological changes that are normally observed in estrous female rodents: hyperemia (vascular development) of the reproductive tract, uterine growth, hypersecretion in the genital tract, and growth of the mammary glands (Allen and Doisy, 1923). Mating behavior was also observed in ovariectomized mice injected with the extract. These four physiological changes, as well as the presence of mating behavior, served as important bioassays in the attempts to isolate and identify endocrine products from the ovarian follicles.

The substance in the follicles that produced these effects was called estrogen, a generic term for "estrus-generating substances." Estrogens were the first steroid hormones to be chemically isolated when Doisy and coworkers (1929) and Butenandt (1929) independently succeeded in crystallizing the first known estrogenic material, now known as estrone, from the urine of pregnant women. Isolation of estrogens directly from ovarian tissue occurred a few years later (Doisy and MacCorquodale, 1936), with the use of hormone isolation techniques that are quite crude by today's standards. For example, MacCorquodale obtained approximately

pseudopregnancy   The luteal phase of the estrous cycle, or any period when there is a functional corpus luteum and buildup of the endometrial uterine layer in the absence of pregnancy.

12 milligrams of relatively pure 17β-estradiol by processing over 3800 kg (4 tons) of sows' ovaries! However, the availability of even small amounts of these relatively pure hormones ushered in a new era for behavioral endocrinology and allowed the first direct correlations to be made between hormones and behavior.

Researchers soon established the role of estrogens in stimulating female sexual behavior. It was found that the fluid within the Graafian follicles is rich in estrogenic hormones, which are secreted into the general blood circulation. Rapidly increasing estrogen concentrations during the day of proestrus induce behavioral estrus, as well as cornification of vaginal epithelial cells. These findings were originally reported in mice (Allen and Doisy, 1923; Allen et al., 1924; Wiesner and Mirskaia, 1930), rats (Boling and Blandau, 1939), and guinea pigs (Dempsey et al., 1936). However, although estrogen injections induced estrous behavior in most ovariectomized rodents, in all these early studies a substantial minority (approximately 40%) of ovariectomized females failed to mate after estrogen treatment, regardless of dosage (Ring, 1944). It should be noted that the doses of estrogen provided in these studies were typically in a pharmacological, rather than physiological, range. The observation that many animals did not mate even after receiving large doses of estrogen prompted several researchers to suggest that a supplemental factor might be working in concert with estrogen to induce behavioral estrus (Wiesner and Mirskaia, 1930).

When chemical extracts from corpora lutea, also obtained from slaughterhouses, were injected into ovariectomized rabbits, they effectively prepared the uterus for pregnancy and maintained pregnancy (Corner and Allen, 1929). The luteal steroid hormone responsible for these effects was called progesterone, so named because it produced a progestational condition (i.e., supportive of pregnancy) in the uterus. Progesterone was identified and isolated from ovarian tissue in the mid-1930s (Turner and Bagnara, 1971). It was not identified initially in urine because pregnanediol, the urinary metabolite of progesterone, is biologically inactive and thus difficult to quantify with bioassays.

Progesterone was discovered to be the supplemental factor that operates in concert with estrogen to induce behavioral estrus. In a series of papers, Young and his collaborators (e.g., Dempsey et al., 1936; Young et al., 1935, 1938, 1939) demonstrated that estrogen alone was insufficient to produce behavioral estrus in guinea pigs. Because one of the ovarian changes associated with the onset of estrus is preovulatory swelling, and because injections of luteinizing hormone (LH) cause preovulatory swelling, Young and his associates reasoned initially that LH was the substance acting in concert with estrogen to cause estrus. However, subsequent experimentation revealed that LH does not act directly with estrogen to cause behavioral estrus. Rather, LH causes the formation of corpora lutea; in turn, the developing corpora lutea secrete progesterone, which acts synergistically with estrogen to cause behavioral estrus (Dempsey et al., 1936).

Progesterone exerts biphasic effects on sexual behaviors, and these biphasic effects appear to differ among species. Initially, studies reported that progesterone was important, although not required, for causing behavioral estrus in rats (Boling and Blandau, 1939) and a number of other species (Ring, 1944). Subsequently, progesterone has been discovered to be important in mediating estrous behavior during natural estrus in rats (Feder, 1981). However, Ball (1941) reported that progesterone administered to estrogen-primed, ovariectomized monkeys decreased sexual behavior. This counterintuitive finding was explained when the biphasic effects of progesterone on female mating behavior were eventually discovered. First, progesterone, in concert with estradiol, initiates female sexual behavior in rats. This preovulatory progesterone comes from the Graafian follicles. As the cycle continues after copulation and estrogen concentrations fall, the corpora lutea secrete larger amounts of progesterone, and elevated concentrations of progesterone in the blood inhibit female sexual behavior. The importance of progesterone in sexual behavior varies among species, as we will see below. These differences have likely evolved because of the coincidence of ovulation with elevated progesterone secretion in most rodents, a pattern not observed in higher primates (see description of the menstrual cycle later in the chapter).

In rats and certain other rodent species, elevated estrogen secretion accompanies follicular development during diestrus II and proestrus, stimulating cornification of vaginal epithelial cells as well as estrous behavior. As just described, progesterone is also needed for the full expression of female sexual behavior in many species. In several rodent species, including rats, mice, guinea pigs, and hamsters, progesterone concentrations increase abruptly prior to ovulation to induce mating behavior. After ovulation, the corpora lutea secrete progesterone at high rates, which often serves to terminate estrous behavior. The neural and endocrine events that drive this cycle of estrogen and progesterone secretion, and thus drive the cycle of estrous behavior, will be described later in this chapter. But first, a description of female mating behavior, as observed in the laboratory, will be presented.

lordosis A female sexually receptive posture in which the hindquarters are raised and the tail is deflected to facilitate copulation.

Mammalian Female Mating Behavior: A Description

Description should always precede mechanistic analyses. Thus, to study the mechanisms that underlie female mating behavior, we should first provide a thorough description of the behavioral parameters under study.

Rodents

If an adult female rat is placed with an adult vasectomized male in a typical laboratory cage for 30 minutes every evening, a very consistent behavioral pattern will emerge (Long and Evans, 1922). Every fourth (or fifth) night, the female will be in behavioral estrus. The most prominent aspect of her estrous behavior is the assumption of the mating posture called **lordosis** (**FIGURE 6.5**), a name derived from a medical term that refers to curvature of the spine. When touched on or near the

(A)

(B)

FIGURE 6.5 Lordosis, the characteristic mating posture of estrous female rodents, as seen in (A) rats and (B) Syrian hamsters. The female arches her back and deflects her tail to allow a male to gain intromission. Lordosis occurs in response to tactile stimulation of the flanks and anogenital region, usually provided by a mounting male; in (B), the female exhibits lordosis in response to the male's investigation of her anogenital region and his previous tactile stimulation of her flanks. The female will maintain the lordosis posture for some time after a male has dismounted. A courtesy of Robert Meisel; B courtesy of Robert E. Johnston.

FIGURE 6.6 Lordosis makes successful copulation possible, as shown in these drawings based on X-ray images of female rats. (A) When the female is standing in her normal posture, it is impossible for the male to intromit. (B) During lordosis, the vaginal opening is accessible and the vagina is horizontal. Because rats have no manual dexterity, this precise postural adjustment on the part of the female is necessary for the male to intromit successfully. After Pfaff et al., 1978.

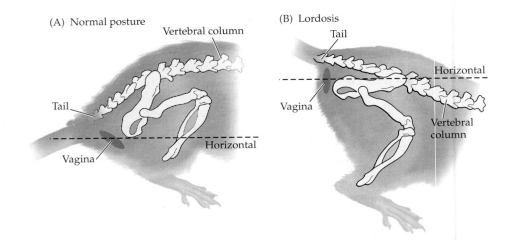

flanks, an estrous female rat will arch her back, deflect her tail, and stand completely immobile to aid the male's penile insertion (a behavior called intromission). In the absence of lordosis, intromission and ejaculation are impossible (**FIGURE 6.6**) (Diakow, 1974; Pfaff et al., 1978). In order to initiate or maintain mounting behavior by the male, the female may approach him, then dart away. Hopping a short distance away, waiting, moving back, and wiggling (rapidly moving) the ears are all behaviors that serve to attract male rats; males are motivated to follow and usually mount a female performing these behaviors (Erskine, 1989; Georgescu and Pfaus, 2006) (**FIGURE 6.7**). After an intromission, the female will abandon the mating posture and groom herself or the male, walk about the cage, or perhaps rest.

Mice, hamsters, voles, lemmings, and many other rodent species display patterns of female copulatory behavior similar to those of rats. However, guinea pigs differ strikingly from other laboratory rodents in their mating behavior. Guinea pigs have a longer latency to ejaculation (Young et al., 1938, 1939). Male guinea pigs mount females, intromit, and ejaculate immediately; there is no pelvic thrusting (see Chapter 5). Consequently, it is not necessary for female guinea pigs to display lordosis for sustained periods of time, although they may maintain the lordosis posture for over 4 seconds in response to male mounting behavior in the laboratory and, if stimulated by manual palpation of their flanks, may maintain lordosis for 10–20 seconds (Goy and Young, 1956/1957).

Canines

The estrous cycle of canines is about 7–8 months in duration but recurs more frequently in unmated females (Asdell, 1964). From an evolutionary perspective, one might expect that the intensity of female sexual motivation would be high because a female that missed becoming pregnant would have to wait another 7–8 months for another opportunity. Indeed, female canines in estrus persistently seek out potential mating partners. Estrus persists for a week or

Full solicitations

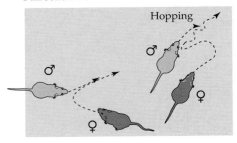

Partial solicitations

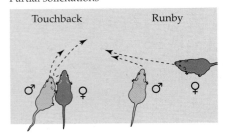

Interception

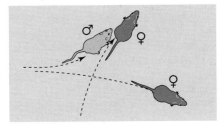

FIGURE 6.7 Female initiation of sexual interactions in rats often involves solicitational behaviors. In so-called full solicitations, a female rat will dart toward the male and run or hop away; the male often follows. During partial solicitations, the female may pause in front of the male (touchback) or run past (runby) the male. In mating situations involving multiple animals, interceptions may occur, whereby a female darts in front of a male that is following another female and distracts him. After McClintock, 1984.

FIGURE 6.8 Dogs and other Canidae, including wolves, often lock together after copulation. This ensures sperm transmission and fertilization. Only carnivorous species can afford to engage in this behavior, as they are quite helpless and defenseless at this time.

10 days. Termination of estrus is signaled when the female refuses to be mounted by males. Estrus is followed by about 2.5 months of diestrus, during which corpora lutea persist. After the corpora lutea regress, the female enters anestrus, which continues for about 4–5 months. The follicles begin to grow and secrete estrogens during proestrus, which lasts about 10 days. Vaginal bleeding is often observed during proestrus; the female will not mate during this time. The onset of estrus coincides with the female's acceptance of a male.

Female mammals in estrus have often been portrayed as "out of control" because they appear to be indiscriminate about their mating partners, but part of this portrayal results from the laboratory testing situations used, especially for rodents. Dogs, and probably individuals of most other mammalian species (especially primates), display substantial selectivity when in estrus (LeBoeuf, 1967). An estrous dog may absolutely refuse to mate with a male to whom she is not attracted, and there is substantial individual variation among female dogs in mate choice. Females may or may not choose their mates by rank in the pack; the alpha males of domestic canine packs do not appear to possess mating advantages over lower-ranked dogs (Beach and LeBoeuf, 1967).

An estrous dog is likely to seek out males to whom she is attracted. Male dogs are likely to seek out estrous females because, as in hamsters, a chemosensory cue in the urine of estrous females is very attractive to them (Beach and Gilmore, 1949). When an estrous female and a male meet, she will orient her hindquarters toward his muzzle and deflect her tail. The male will lick her vulva, sometimes so vigorously that he lifts her hindquarters off the ground (Beach and LeBoeuf, 1967). The male then mounts the female and inserts his erect penis into her vagina; the female may assist the male by backing into him as he thrusts. She may also compensate for missed intromissions by changing her position slightly. After a brief series of intromissions, the male ejaculates and then dismounts. The two animals are locked together for some minutes as seminal fluid is transferred to the female (**FIGURE 6.8**, and see Figure 5.12). An anestrous female dog will not allow a male to mount. She will sit down, try to move away, or growl and snap at or even bite the male.

Primates

Early research conducted at the Yerkes Laboratories of Primate Biology in Orange Park, Florida, provided a very complete quantification of the sexual behavior of

FIGURE 6.9 Sexual posture among chimpanzees is rather stereotyped, with the male mounting the female from behind. It is not necessary for her to hold a stationary posture as in rodents, as a male chimpanzee has sufficient manual dexterity to manipulate his penis to compensate for postural differences among females.

chimpanzees in a laboratory setting. This description of chimp copulatory behavior was quite lively:

> *What happens when a male and female meet, under the conditions of our experiment, has been found to depend upon individuality, physiological status, social relations, and environmental circumstance.… [Various] postures and gestures [by the male] evidently are intended as appeals for sexual contact. If perchance the female does not respond to his solicitations, the male goes to her, usually examines her genitalia, and thereupon either attempts to copulate or turns away. Ordinarily, however, she responds instantly, when she sees the male … by running quickly to him and crouching low or even flat upon the ground, with limbs flexed and genitalia directed toward him. To this female presentation [the male] bends over her back, with his hands on her shoulders or sides, or touching the floor. In this posture, he presses forward against her genital swelling and forces the long slender penis into the vagina.… Insertion is followed by pelvic thrusts [which] may vary from as few as four or five to as many as twenty or thirty in our observation. Successful and mutually satisfactory copulation may be followed by manual, oral, or olfactory self- or mutual examination of the genitalia, and by grooming. (Yerkes and Elder, 1936)*

Obviously, some of the researchers' remarks, including "mutually satisfactory copulation," are inferences, but on the whole, their description is very accurate.

The mating posture of female chimpanzees is rather stereotyped; there is little variation among females of this species (**FIGURE 6.9**). In contrast, as noted in Chapter 5, humans often seek variety in copulatory postures (Masters and Johnson, 1966). Variation in the sexual posture of some other nonhuman female primates has also been noted; for example, the ventral-ventral, or face-to-face, position associated with humans has been observed in gorillas and orangutans (Nadler, 1976, 1988). Thus, among primates, there are species in which female sexual behavior is highly stereotyped (e.g., chimpanzee and marmoset) and other species (human, gorilla, bonobo, and orangutan) that tend not to exhibit stereotyped female copulatory patterns.

Some primates, such as marmosets, have clearly defined estrous cycles, and mating behavior is limited to the time of estrus. Other female primates, including rhesus monkeys, bonobos, and humans, do not limit sexual activity to a particular time and thus do not possess an estrous cycle per se (de Waal, 1995). There has been recurring controversy about the extent to which copulatory behavior in female humans and other so-called higher primates is regulated by ovarian hormones. Some investigators contend that because higher primates can copulate at any time during the ovarian cycle or even after ovariectomy, hormones are not involved in mediating female sexual behavior. Others have noted that under the appropriate circumstances, female primate sexual behavior shows a clear reliance on gonadal hormones. The controversy remains unresolved, although some consensus has emerged suggesting that sexual behavioral motivation in relation to fertility remains coupled to hormones, whereas sexual behavioral motivation for social goals is uncoupled from hormones in female anthropoid primates (Wallen, 2001; Wallen and Zehr, 2004).

Are Females Active Participants in Sexual Behavior?

Prior to the mid-1970s the consensus among sex researchers, especially laboratory researchers, was that females were more or less passive recipients of male sexual attention. Although this perspective continues to dominate bird sexual research (see Cheng, 1992; van Tienhoven, 1983), Beach (1976) addressed this issue in mammals by noting that females often initiate sexual activities. We now know that females indeed take a very active role in initiating sexual activities and in many species virtually always act as the initiators of copulation (reviewed in Erskine, 1989; Wallen, 1990; Wallen and Zehr, 2004). The sex drive of females may equal or even exceed that of male conspecifics but may be expressed only in very specific spatial, temporal, or social contexts. Recall that the number of offspring a female can produce in her lifetime is limited, as compared with males, who can potentially sire a large number of offspring. Thus, females generally have evolved to provide more resources to their offspring than males do, because females have a larger stake in the successful outcome of each breeding effort than males, who typically invest little in each reproductive effort (Clutton-Brock, 1991). Consequently, females exhibit much greater selectivity than males in their choice of mating partners. This choosiness, which can easily be explained at an ultimate, evolutionary level of analysis, should not be invoked at the proximate level to suggest that females have less sex drive than males. Rather, the sex drive of females has evolved to maximize the reproductive success of each individual.

In retrospect, it may seem surprising that sex researchers "forgot" that *estrus* means "in a frenzy." And it may also seem surprising that they failed to notice the highly motivated behavior of their female pets in their attempts to copulate. Of course, the behavior of pets provides only anecdotal evidence at best, but there were many scientific reports, from field settings, of females that were highly motivated to engage in sexual behavior. For example, one study of a seminatural population of chimpanzees revealed that females risked physical attack whenever they approached males. Nevertheless, in most cases females were the initiators of copulation:

> *During her receptive period, her social status in the group shifts and she becomes a sexual incentive for the group's males. She actively approaches males and must overcome their usual resistance to close association; hence she becomes an object of attacks by them. Even other females attack her as a result of her shifted social status.... Females 49, 105, 126, 144, "f.n." and 109 were all severely wounded during their estrous periods. Female 105 lost parts of both ears, was cut severely on the arm and received a network of wounds over her face and muzzle. Female 144 had a leg wound which compelled her to walk on three legs for several days. Female 144 was deeply cut on the thighs. Female "f.n." had a badly bruised nose while female 109 had a long, deep gash and her infant was wounded so severely that it died. (Carpenter, 1942b)*

This account indicates that these females initiated copulation despite the threat of severe physical punishment and social disruption. Even the earliest laboratory accounts of primate mating (Ball and Hartman, 1935; Yerkes and Elder, 1936) indicated that females were highly motivated to copulate:

> *Under the conditions which we have specified, copulation is determined and controlled almost entirely by the female. The male is suitor and servitor, not lord and dictator. There may be no suggestion of compulsion. The female ignores his solicitations if she sees fit; terminates the sexual union when she will—and that may be before orgasm and completion of ejaculation. (Yerkes and Elder, 1936, 10)*

What accounted for the failure of subsequent laboratory researchers to note the initiatives of females in copulation? As noted in Chapter 1, observer bias can adversely affect behavioral observations. Because female sexuality was widely assumed to be of a passive nature, it is possible that cultural constraints limited the interpretations of feminine sexual behavior observed in the laboratory. And in all fairness to those earlier sex researchers, one of the most striking aspects of female rodent sexual behavior in the laboratory test situation is the adoption of the rigid mating posture, lordosis. Maintaining immobility during copulation does indeed appear passive. It is also likely that sex researchers were victims of their own methods, born of their desire to control as many variables as possible during behavioral tests. Fieldwork produces highly valid results, but it is difficult and expensive and occurs under uncontrolled conditions. Moving sex research into the laboratory permitted a high level of experimental control but inadvertently removed important environmental and social variables that mediate female sexual behavior in nature. For example, pairing a single female with a single male has been the most common testing situation used in studies of rodents and primates, but it completely ignores the social reality of these animals. When a female is confined in a small space with a single male, her behavior may be more passive than it would be if she could control the pacing of mating behavior or choose her mating partner, as is often the case in nature.

Components of Female Sexual Behavior

The knowledge that estrogens and progestins influence feminine sexual behavior is important but is insufficient for students of behavioral endocrinology. In order to understand in greater detail how these hormones relate to behavior, researchers have been conceptually partitioning female sexual behavior into smaller and smaller component parts. Beach (1976) proposed the concept of dividing female sexual behavior into three components: (1) attractivity, (2) proceptivity, and (3) receptivity. **Attractivity** is the stimulus value of a female for a given male, a hypothetical construct that must be inferred by observation of a conspecific's behavior and must always be measured in relational terms. If a male will expend effort to come into contact with a particular female, then she is more attractive than something else; perhaps she is more attractive to the male than being alone, an empty box, food, or another female. **Proceptivity** is the extent to which a female initiates copulation. It reflects her overt behavior, as well as her underlying motivational state. **Receptivity** reflects the stimulus value of the female for eliciting an intravaginal ejaculation from a male conspecific; in other words, receptivity is her state of responsiveness to the sexual initiation of another individual (Beach, 1976).

Proceptivity and receptivity overlap conceptually, as well as in practice. For example, a proceptive female rodent may initiate copulation by assuming the lordosis posture; this mating posture would also indicate her receptivity. The conceptual separation of proceptive behavior from receptive behavior was an important means of clarifying and operationalizing observations of female sexual behavior. Prior to Beach's classification scheme, hormonal effects on female "receptive" behavior, from assumption of the lordosis posture in rats to solicitation of copulation by rhesus monkeys, appeared to vary immensely. In retrospect, it is not surprising that few

attractivity The stimulus value of a female for a particular male. Attractivity is a hypothetical construct that must be inferred by observation of a conspecific's behavior.

proceptivity The extent to which females initiate copulation.

receptivity The stimulus value of a female for eventually eliciting an intravaginal ejaculation from a male conspecific.

FIGURE 6.10 Estrogen mediates proceptivity, attractivity, and receptivity in rhesus monkeys. Female rhesus monkeys were taught to press a bar 250 times within 30 minutes to gain access to a male for a 1-hour behavioral test. (A) The average amount of time it took females to press the bar 250 times is plotted across the menstrual cycle, showing a marked decrease around day 16. Ovulation would have occurred on about day 15 for these females. (B) Measures of proceptivity (mean access time for 250 bar presses), attractivity (male mounting rate), and receptivity (number of ejaculations and time to ejaculation) show that these components of female sexual behavior are maximal when plasma estradiol concentrations peak near ovulation. After Bonsall et al., 1978.

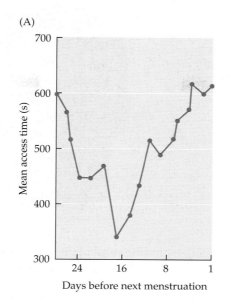

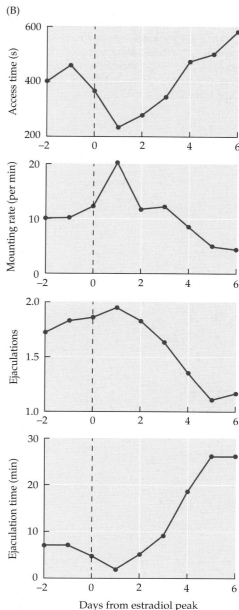

general principles arose relating hormonal influences to such poorly defined female sexual behavior. Beach's scheme of separating female sexual behavior into these three components contributed to the acknowledgment of female sexual initiation, facilitated the study of female sexual behavior, provided a conceptual framework that equalizes the sexes in terms of sexual motivation and responsiveness, and thus facilitated the identification of hormone-behavior relationships underlying female sexual behavior. Sex steroid hormones, especially estrogens, affect all three components of female sexual behavior (**FIGURE 6.10**). Sorting out the degree to which hormones affect attractivity, proceptivity, and receptivity has led to an increased understanding of the complex interactions between hormones and behavior and has also provided clues about the underlying physiological mechanisms.

Again, these categories interact and overlap in the real world. For example, an economic study of female dancers working in a gentleman's club revealed that the women made more money in tips around the time of ovulation than at other times of the menstrual cycle (Miller et al., 2007). Dancers averaged $335 per 5-hour shift during midcycle (6 days around ovulation) but only $260 per shift during the luteal phase. Tips were even lower during menstruation, averaging only $185 per shift (Miller et al., 2007). Dancers who were taking contraceptive pills showed no significant variation across the 60-day study in the amount of their tips. Thus, hormones likely affected this economic interaction. In terms of categorization of this phenomenon, further studies would be necessary to determine whether the tips reflect that the male clients found the dancers more attractive during ovulation, that the dancers were more proceptive during ovulation and thus became more attractive to the men, or that some interaction among attractivity, proceptivity, and potentially receptivity accounts for these data. There are certainly data suggesting that choice of clothing and attractiveness of voice change in response to ovulation in women (e.g., Durante et al., 2008; Pipitone and Gallup, 2008).

Women's preferences for male traits vary across the menstrual cycle. During the follicular phase, women tend to prefer men exhibiting traits associated with testosterone, traits that are not necessarily preferred during other times of the cycle (Gangestad et al., 2004, 2007; Penton-Voak and Perrett, 2000). Studies indicate that estrogens and androgens provoke women's preference for mas-

(A)

(B)

FIGURE 6.11 Women in the follicular phase are attracted to more masculine faces such as the one on the left. Examples here are versions of a composite male face that has been computer-manipulated to (A) increase and (B) decrease the masculinity of a man's face. Courtesy of Benedict Jones and Lisa DeBruine, Face Research Laboratory, University of Aberdeen.

culine men, including masculine faces (**FIGURE 6.11**), voices, bodies, video behavioral displays, and odors (Gildersleeve et al., 2014; Jones et al., 2008; Roney and Simmons, 2008; Welling et al., 2007). Women differed in neural activation in response to masculine men across the cycle; these differences correlated in some brain regions with the estrogen-to-progesterone ratio (Rupp et al., 2009). Progesterone is also a hormone that is relevant to women's mate preferences. Women in the luteal phase (or pregnant), when progesterone is elevated, tend to prefer feminine faces (e.g., Jones et al., 2005; Perrett et al., 1998). This response has been interpreted to mean that women who are pregnant seek out affiliation with individuals who might provide support and care during pregnancy (Jones et al., 2008). All of these cyclic preferences tend to disappear in women taking oral contraceptives (e.g., Penton-Voak et al., 1999). Finally, when women consider partners, preference for masculine faces is greater for short-term relationships than for long-term relationships, suggesting that hormones of the menstrual cycle drive females to seek masculine characteristics when fertile, to maximize the health of their offspring (Jones et al., 2008). In sum, women's proceptive behavior (seeking out males) tends to be increased during the follicular phase, and preferences for masculine and feminine characteristics vary across the menstrual cycle, presumably to maximize reproductive success.

Other researchers have divided female sexual behavior into two phases: the precopulatory phase and the copulatory phase (Madlafousek and Hlinak, 1977). The precopulatory phase roughly corresponds to proceptive behavior in Beach's scheme. The precopulatory phase also corresponds to the appetitive phase described earlier for males; it may also be called courtship. The precopulatory phase involves all of the behaviors that allow a female to attract a male and initiate copulation. Behaviors as diverse as searching for males, emitting a chemical attractant, or assuming a mating posture and soliciting copulation may occur during courtship. Courtship functions as a communication opportunity during which information about species, readiness to mate, resources, and genetic endowment is shared. As with males, the precopulatory phase lasts much longer than the second phase, copulatory behavior, which corresponds roughly to receptive behavior in Beach's scheme. Although this dichotomy, like any other classification scheme, may artificially divide a unified behavioral program, such partitioning can be valuable for elucidating the hormonal bases of female reproductive behavior, and possibly for discriminating the underlying neural mechanisms. As in males, sexual motivation in females, as represented by proceptive behaviors, may be regulated by different hormones than sexual performance, as represented by receptive behaviors, or it may be regulated by the same hormones to a different extent.

A third classification system has been proposed for female sexual behavior. A strong argument has been made that the term *female sexual initiation* should be used for any feminine behavior that facilitates mating and that *female sexual motivation* should be used for the state underlying sexual initiation or accommodation (Wallen, 1990; Wallen and Zehr, 2004; Zehr et al., 1998). Under this nomenclature, behaviors such as lordosis that facilitate copulation would be separated from solicitational behaviors that indicate sexual motivation. Hormones could affect these two components of female sexual behavior in the same way or differently. For example, female rodents differ from some female primates in their reliance on hormones for the expression of sexual behavior. Under laboratory conditions, female rodents appear to require ovarian hormones to maintain both facilitatory and motivational behaviors. In contrast, many primates appear to require hormones only for maintenance of female sexual motivation. Sex steroid hormones allow the expression of lordosis among female rodents in response to male tactile stimulation during mounting. As we have seen, lordosis is necessary for rodent copulation, because penile insertion is impossible unless the female stands immobile. Because of their manual dexterity, primates do not require the female to maintain a rigid mating posture to facilitate successful copulation. Female primates may permit copulation at all times during their ovarian cycle, but this copulation may not reflect their sexual motivation, because female primates, especially those confined in the laboratory with a male, may copulate for a variety of reasons. Thus, the only valid measure of primate sexual behavior would be female-initiated mating, because primate facilitatory behaviors are somewhat unnecessary.

Recently, a descriptive system has been proposed that parses female sexual behavior into (1) copulatory behaviors, (2) paracopulatory behaviors, and (3) progestative behaviors (Blaustein and Erskine, 2002). Copulatory behaviors are similar to receptive behaviors described by Beach and include all behaviors that facilitate successful transfer of sperm to the ova. Paracopulatory behaviors are courtship-like behaviors that stimulate a male to mount and initiate copulation and are similar to the proceptive behaviors previously described by Beach. Progestative behaviors are those behaviors that promote reproductive success and include species-typical copulatory patterns and other activities that maximize fertilization (Blaustein and Erskine, 2002). Although many of the arguments for new terminology are valid and help to sharpen researchers' definitions and interpretations of behavior, especially the behavior of primates, Beach's nomenclature will be used in this chapter because of its enduring descriptive strengths.

Attractivity

What exactly is attractivity? Both nonbehavioral and behavioral components sum together to form the stimulus bases of attractivity (Beach, 1976). Female attractivity is usually measured in terms of preference, that is, the extent to which a male prefers to be near one female as compared with others (**FIGURE 6.12**). In other words, attractivity refers to how attractive the female is to males, rather than to whom the females are attracted. As indicated in Chapter 5, the stimulus basis of male attractivity remains for the most part unspecified. As for females, nonbehavioral bases of attractivity include morphological changes that coincide with ovulation. For example,

FIGURE 6.12 A three-chamber preference test is used to determine attractivity. All three chambers contain food and water. Females are tethered in the outer two chambers, and a male is free to move among all three chambers. He will spend the majority of the test period with the female to which he is more attracted. Courtesy of Sabra Klein.

(A)

FIGURE 6.13 Estrogen increases attractivity. (A) Male olive baboons find the swelling of the female's perineum during estrus, induced by high estrogen concentrations, very attractive; they spend more time looking at and approaching females with swollen perinea than other females. (B) The proportion of solicitations by a female monkey that result in male mounting behavior is called the male acceptance ratio. Males are more likely to mount an ovariectomized female after she is injected with estrogen than after she is injected with a biologically inert substance. Note the enormous individual differences in mounting behavior among males and thus in the attractivity of the test female to specific males. Male 1 rarely mounted the female in the absence of estrogen, but male 6 regularly mounted this female regardless of her hormonal condition. B after Dixson et al., 1973.

(B)

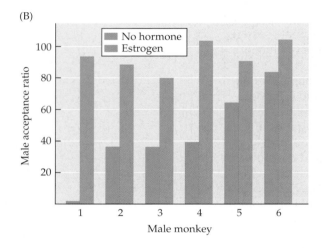

female primates in estrus experience a swelling of the perigenital skin. The visual stimulation provided by this conspicuous swelling attracts male attention (Carpenter, 1942b) (**FIGURE 6.13A**). Subordinate males in a troop of primates may not be permitted to get sufficiently close to females to have a real opportunity to mate, but even these males spend more time looking at estrous females than at anestrous females (Dixson et al., 1973).

Recall that bringing the two sexes together (attraction) when both are potentially fertile is the primary function of sexual behavior. Therefore, it should not be surprising that hormones associated with ovulation also mediate attractivity in females. In general, estrogens enhance attractivity. One way to test the attractiveness of females is to confine them separately and measure how much time a male spends with each of them. The assumption is that the duration of visitation by the male reflects the attractiveness of the female (Phoenix, 1973). In this situation, males always spend more time in close proximity to estrous than anestrous females (reviewed in Beach, 1976). Ovariectomized females are rarely attractive to males. However, their attractivity is greatly enhanced by estradiol treatment. When spayed female dogs were injected with estradiol, the average duration of visits by males was increased sixfold (Beach and Merari, 1970). Similarly, ovariectomized female monkeys are rarely mounted by males. However, if ovariectomized female monkeys are injected with estradiol, then they are mounted at a much higher frequency by males (Wallen, 1990) (**FIGURE 6.13B**).

In nature, high blood estradiol concentrations correspond to the time of maximal fertility. From an evolutionary perspective, it is predictable that females would be considered most attractive by male conspecifics when they are maximally fertile. Attracting males in order to mate is especially important for a solitary animal such as a cat or hamster, which must signal its fertile condition to males over great distances. In a number of species, estradiol-induced attractivity is reduced or abolished by progesterone treatment, which is also predictable because high concentrations of progesterone are often associated with pregnancy or other nonfertile (from the male's perspective) states.

Chemical cues are also important in forming the stimulus bases of female attractivity throughout the animal kingdom. For instance, chemosensory cues emanate from the urinary and vaginal secretions of estrous females (**BOX 6.1**). Males sniff and lick females' external genitalia and vagina prior to copulation in many species of mammals, and males are much more likely to engage in this behavior with estrous than with anestrous females (Beach and Merari, 1968). Males of many mammalian

FIGURE 6.14 **The flehmen response**, seen here in two male horses (stallions), is common in many male mammals, especially carnivores, ungulates, and rodents. In response to chemosignals obtained during anogenital investigation, the male extends the neck, curls the upper lip to reveal the gums, and usually presses the tongue against the roof of the mouth to force the chemosignals into the vomeronasal organ.

species, especially carnivores, ungulates, and rodents, discriminate estrous from anestrous females on the basis of chemosensory signals that are processed through the vomeronasal organ (see Chapter 5). Male ungulates commonly display a flehmen response when sexually excited, extending the neck and curling the upper lip to reveal the upper gums (**FIGURE 6.14**), which allows the female chemosignal to be delivered to the vomeronasal organ (Dulac and Torello, 2003 Wysocki, 1979) (see Figure 5.18). Historically, the vomeronasal organ (VNO) has been thought to be reduced or absent in higher primates, and humans are notoriously poor among mammals in their olfactory abilities. However, recent studies of human cadavers revealed the presence of VNO openings with connections from VNO cells to capillaries, suggesting potential functional significance (Wessels et al., 2014) (**FIGURE 6.15**). Likewise, endoscopic examination of human volunteers has uncovered the presence of a nasopalatine duct, the gateway to the VNO across well-characterized species (Jacob et al., 2000). Despite the likely presence of a VNO, blocking the putative human VNO does not alter the ability to detect pheromones in humans, sug-

(A)

(B)

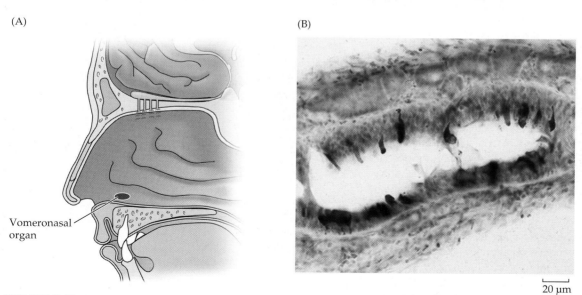

Vomeronasal organ

20 μm

FIGURE 6.15 **The human vomeronasal organ** (A) Relative location of the adult human VNO in the nasal septum. (B) Stained cells demonstrate thin protrusions that reach the lamina that surrounds the VNO. From Wessels et al., 2014.

BOX 6.1 Chemosignals and Courtship in the Red-Sided Garter Snake

An interesting twist to the story of chemical signals in courtship is provided by the red-sided garter snake (*Thamnophis sirtalis parietalis*) described in Chapter 5. Recall that the males of this species emerge from their winter hibernacula earlier than females, then attempt to mate with females as they emerge over the next several weeks. Females emerge one at a time, so many males court a single female as she leaves the hibernaculum, forming a large, writhing mating ball of snakes (**Figure A**).

How does a courting male identify the female in such a tangle of snakes? One possibility is that males discriminate by size; females are larger than males of this species. But size is not the primary cue male snakes use. They mainly rely on chemosensory information. Males produce one type of chemical signal, a squalene, that acts to identify them as males. Females produce another type of chemical signal, composed of methyl ketones, that males find very attractive. When males are courting, they flick their tongues along the dorsal surface of the female. As their vomeronasal systems are stimulated by the female "attractiveness" cue, they begin to rub their chins on the female until one male gains intromission. As soon as an intromission occurs, the male expresses another chemical cue that immediately "turns off" the courtship behavior of the other males. Thus, female attractiveness is mediated directly by chemical factors: males are attracted to females emitting one chemosignal indicating readiness to mate and are repelled by males emitting another chemical cue signaling that mating has already occurred (Mason et al., 1989). Estrogen is necessary for the production of the "attractive" chemical; however, injection of estrogen into adult males does not cause them to be courted by other males. In other words, estrogen alone is not the basis of female attractiveness in snakes.

In nature, however, most newly emerged males in a mating ball are briefly courted by other males; that is, other males are observed slithering along their scales, tongue-flicking and chin-rubbing. What causes these males to be attractive objects of courtship? The courted males might have picked up the chemical attractant from a female that they were courting. But when researchers wiped off courted males with a chemical solvent and released them into a mating arena, this treatment did not reduce the incidence of courtship behavior directed at them (Mason, 1987; Shine et al. 2001). Chemical analyses of the skin secretions of courted males revealed that they produce the same attractant chemical that females do and none of the male-identifier chemosignal. These "she-males" have higher testosterone-to-estrogen ratios than typical males (blood plasma testosterone levels about 2.5 times higher than those of "he-males" and more than 3000 times higher than those of females) and have higher mating success (**Figure B**) and also have very high concentrations of aromatase, the enzyme that converts testosterone to estradiol, in their skin.

Figure A Courtesy of Robert T. Mason.

These differences may account for the she-males' producing the female attractant chemosignal.

But why have male snakes that are attractive to other males evolved, and how are they maintained in the population? The answer appears to be that these she-male snakes have evolved under selective pressures from natural selection and not sexual selection. When male garter snakes first emerge in the spring, they are very cold and sluggish. Thus, they are poor courters, and they are also exposed to predators, mostly corvids. By attracting other males' courtship, these she-males are covered by the warmer males that have emerged earlier in the season. The newly emerged she-males gain an advantage by "stealing" the body warmth of the courting males, thus warming faster themselves than they would if left in isolation. By warming sooner, these she-males are able to begin courting females faster. In addition, while the cold, newly emerged she-males are being courted, they are effectively covered by the courting males and thus protected from bird predators. Within an hour these attractive she-males lose their attractivity to other males and begin to actively court females. An ongoing mystery is that a small subset of she-males maintain their attractivity, and the maintenance of this morph may be based on developmental events and not strictly genetically inherited traits.

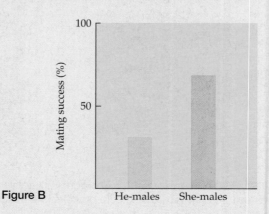

Figure B

FIGURE 6.16 **Female rhesus monkey presenting to a male** One measure of proceptivity among nonhuman primates is the number of solicitations made prior to sexual contact. Solicitations take the form of assuming the mating posture or standing in front of a male and exhibiting genitalia. Virtually all social contacts between males and females prior to copulation in nonhuman primates are initiated by females. Courtesy of Kim Wallen.

gesting that the primary olfactory system is sufficient for pheromonal processing in humans (Frasnelli et al., 2011). Whether or not higher primates utilize the VNO to select partners under natural circumstances remains debatable.

In addition to physiological and morphological stimuli, various types of behavior may also increase the attractiveness of females. For example, females that actively solicit copulations have a higher stimulus value for males than females that do not. As noted above, females of many nonhuman primates present their genitalia by backing their hindquarters toward a male (**FIGURE 6.16**); males spend more time with females that engage in this presentation behavior than with females that do not present (Dixson et al., 1973). Female rats also solicit mounts from males as described above by darting, hopping, and crouching behaviors and by running away from and returning to the male. As we will see below, in seminatural or natural settings, these female behaviors set the pace of the copulatory sequence because virtually all male mounts follow female solicitation (Coopersmith et al., 1996; Erskine, 1989).

All of these factors associated with attractivity, both behavioral and nonbehavioral, appear to involve sex steroid hormones. However, there are also nonhormonal factors that affect attractivity. Individual preferences exist among many species. For example, even when several ovariectomized female dogs are treated with equal amounts of estradiol, some consistently evoke more sexual responses from males than others (Beach and Merari, 1970; LeBoeuf, 1967). There is also sexual "favoritism" among male monkeys, apes, and humans (Herbert, 1970; Michael et al., 1972). A female may be very attractive to one male but unattractive to another. This variation is consistently observed in the "Coolidge effect" (see Chapter 5), in which the stimulus value of a female is reduced for a male that has already copulated with her several times. She remains attractive to other males that have not just mated with her, but she has temporarily lost her stimulus value for the first male.

Understanding the stimuli underlying attractivity in various animal species is a daunting task. To get some idea of the complexity involved, think about the various components of individuals to whom you are attracted. Even though you can use language and can describe the features important in forming an attraction, it is very difficult to assign a value to each feature. Several traits can be influenced by the hormones of ovulation in women. For example, voice, dress, and scent are judged as more attractive around the time of ovulation (e.g., Durante et al., 2008; Haselton et al., 2007; Kuukasjärvi et al., 2004; Pipitone and Gallup, 2008). Yet, to some individuals, honesty may be a very important characteristic; to others, a clear complexion is important. How do you assign weight to each characteristic? If you ask your friends to describe attractive people, their responses will vary. How do you account for the vast differences among individuals in attraction? There is no reason to assume that the stimulus basis for attractivity is any less complicated in nonhuman animals (but see Grammer et al., 2003).

Proceptivity

Proceptive behavior comprises all of the appetitive activities shown by females. In other words, proceptivity is indicated by sexually solicitous behaviors that initiate sexual union, but it is not copulatory behavior per se. Proceptivity reflects a female's underlying motivational state in much the same way libido or sex drive reflects a male's motivational state (see Chapter 5). The female hamster's journeys from her burrow and visits to her male neighbor's territory indicate proceptivity. Estrous females, as well as being the most attractive to males, are also the most attracted to males.

Several behavioral measures have been used to assess proceptivity in females. The most common assay of proceptivity has been assessment of affiliative behaviors—efforts by females to establish and maintain proximity to males, which is a universal response of proceptive females. Female rhesus monkeys rarely interact with males except to initiate mating (Carpenter, 1942a,b). In one study, more than 80% of all proximate social interaction between male and female monkeys was initiated by females prior to mating (Cochran, 1979; Wallen et al., 1984). Another behavioral measure of proceptivity is the number of solicitations made before intromission, such as assumptions of the mating posture or presentations of the genitalia to the male (reviewed in Wallen, 1990) (see Figure 6.16). Such solicitations are commonly observed in primates but are also observed in many disparate taxa, including birds, reptiles, and fishes. Vocalizations and head bobbing are also observed among monkeys that are soliciting copulations (Ball and Hartman, 1935; Carpenter, 1942a; Michael, 1972). A study of rhesus females was conducted during the nonbreeding season, when males are not responsive to females. Estradiol treatment during this time increased initiation of contact with males by ovariectomized female rhesus monkeys despite the lack of behavioral feedback from males (Zehr et al., 1998) (**FIGURE 6.17**).

Another female behavior that is highly proceptive is alternating approaches and withdrawals. This pattern is commonly observed in rodents and is also part of ungulate, canine, and primate copulation sequences. The female approaches the male, and if he follows her, she may pseudoretreat, but eventually she allows him to investigate her. If the male does not follow her, then she approaches him again. This pattern of approach and withdrawal is very stimulating to most conspecific males and is in no way indicative of nonreceptivity or disinterest on the part of the female.

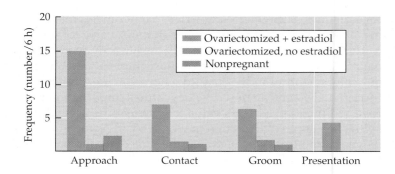

FIGURE 6.17 Estradiol enhances proceptivity in the absence of male interest. Estradiol treatment of ovariectomized rhesus monkeys during the nonbreeding season, when males are not responsive to females, increased the frequency of female sexual initiation. After Zehr et al., 1998.

Females may also initiate physical contact by investigating the male's anogenital region. Occasionally, mounting by highly proceptive females is observed (Beach, 1968). Females may mount males or other females, and these mounts are accompanied by thrusting pelvic movements (Beach, 1942d). In fact, ovulation may result from female-female mounting behavior among rabbits (Fee and Parkes, 1930). After being mounted by a female several times, the male often mounts the female in turn.

A final determinant of female proceptivity is the attractiveness of the male mating partner. As noted above, females do not initiate copulation with males to whom they are not attracted. Castrated male rhesus monkeys, dogs, and hamsters elicit fewer approach responses by females than gonadally intact males in two-choice tests (reviewed in Beach, 1976). Female proceptivity is especially critical in species such as gorillas and rhesus monkeys because most copulation is a result of the females' initiative and mate selection (Cochran, 1979; Pomerantz and Goy, 1983; Wallen et al., 1984) (see Figure 6.16). Beach (1976) maintained that presentation to males by females is highest during midcycle, when ovulation occurs. This observation was based on laboratory, zoo, and natural populations of animals. In all species examined, high concentrations of estrogens facilitate proceptive behavior.

Receptivity

Receptivity, the consummatory phase of mating behavior, can be defined as those female reactions that are necessary and sufficient for fertile copulation with a potent male. As Beach (1976) said, "Sexual receptivity is distinguished equally by the ubiquity of its usage and the infrequency of its definition." Prior to the development of Beach's classification scheme, behavioral measures of either receptivity or proceptivity were taken as evidence of receptivity.

Receptivity is indicated by a species-specific mating posture in all nonprimate mammals examined. For example, sows tread backward during copulation to help the boar gain intromission. Female rodents display the lordosis posture in response to tactile stimulation by the male. Females of several primate species back into males and literally seize the penis (reviewed in Wallen, 1990). Virtually all nonmammalian species also have a characteristic female mating posture (Crews and Silver, 1985). Most behavioral measures of receptivity are expressed in terms of ratios between a male's attempts to mate with a female and his success in doing so. This ratio is expressed in rats as a lordosis quotient (LQ), in dogs as a rejection coefficient, and in primates as an acceptance ratio.

It has been proposed that female ringdoves initiate their own receptive behavior by hearing themselves cooing. Cooing is usually performed by females in response to behavioral stimuli provided by males (Lehrman, 1961). It was first thought that the male induced receptivity in the female. However, the male actually induces the female to emit cooing vocalizations, and her behavior feeds back to affect her endocrine state and to initiate receptivity (Cheng, 1986; Cheng et al., 1998). If females are induced to coo in the absence of males, their follicles develop and secrete estrogens, and if females are devocalized by any of several means, including brain lesions, their ovaries do not develop in response to male stimulation. If the females' cooing vocalizations are recorded prior to devocalization and played back to them, even in the absence of males, the follicles develop and estrogens are secreted, inducing further receptive behavior (Cheng, 1992). Thus, ringdoves present an interesting case of behavior in one individual inducing a behavioral change in the receiving animal that stimulates hormonal changes that cause further behavioral changes. In fact, part of the neural circuitry involved, located in the midbrain vocal nucleus, thalamus, and neuroendocrine hypothalamus, has been identified (Cheng and Zuo, 1994). Specific hypothalamic neurons have been identified that respond to the female nesting coo and induce the secretion of LH (Cheng et al., 1998). Although the ringdove is the first species for which this sort of interactive feedback has been demonstrated, these kinds of complex social-behavioral-hormonal interactions are probably common and awaiting discovery. For example, engaging in sexual activity and "cuddling" increases testosterone in women (van Anders et al., 2007b). The functional significance of this change in testosterone remains unspecified; however, as detailed below, testosterone is linked to sexual motivation in women. So it is possible that sexual activity feeds back onto women's hormones in a similar manner.

There is abundant evidence that estrogen stimulation is very important in receptivity. For example, the display of the mating posture disappears in ovariectomized females of virtually all species examined. As noted below, lordosis can be induced in rodents by injections of estradiol and progesterone or sometimes estradiol alone (Feder, 1981). Rabbits, as well as rhesus monkeys and women, are maximally sensitive to tactile stimulation when the stimulation is concurrent with high blood concentrations of estrogen, but individuals of all these species will copulate at all stages of the ovarian cycle, which has led some researchers to believe that hormones do not influence female sexual receptivity among primates (Wallen, 1990).

FEMALE CONTROL OF COPULATION Much has been made of the so-called constant receptivity reported for humans and other primates. Their ability to copulate at any time during the ovarian cycle, or even in the complete absence of ovarian steroid hormones, caused many sex researchers to conclude that the sexual behavior of many primate species is not under hormonal control. However, as suggested above, the behavior of a female primate accepting copulation may not reflect the same motivational state as the behavior of a female rodent accepting copulation. A male rodent or canine cannot successfully copulate without female cooperation; the female must maintain a rigid posture. Primates do not exhibit this constraint, and copulation is mechanically possible without the female's cooperation. Although forced copulation is rare among most nonhuman primates, it has been consistently observed among orangutans (Mitani, 1985).

In a traditional laboratory test of paired partners, female primates require little sexual motivation to copulate. Frankly, there is little else to do. A male is provided in a small room, and there are no other animals with which to interact. Under these test conditions, a female primate's sexual behavior is unrelated to her ovarian cycle or endocrine state (Wallen, 1990). If animals are tested in more complex social conditions—that is, in the presence of multiple males and females—then females risk aggression from other females when they actively solicit males for sexual contact, especially if they are low-ranking females (Carpenter, 1942b; Wallen et al., 1984; Wallen and Zehr, 2004). Presumably, attacks by other females are aversive, and sexual motivation must be high to overcome this aversion. When female primates are tested in such group settings, copulatory behavior is tightly coupled to endocrine state (Wallen, 1990) (**FIGURE 6.18**).

Is the sexual receptivity (or proceptivity) of women affected by hormones? This question has not been adequately answered, in part because the definitions of receptivity and proceptivity have become entangled and in part because social factors are not appropriately considered. Virtually all studies of human sexual behavior over the menstrual cycle involve self-reports by couples in long-established, usually marriage, relationships. Under these circumstances there is little change in the frequency of copulation over the ovarian cycle (Adams et al., 1978; Udry and Morris, 1968), although some studies have revealed a peak in human female sexual activity around the time of ovulation. Ovulation is said to be "hidden" in women, by which it is meant that few women, and presumably fewer men, know precisely when ovulation occurs; however, the validity of this assumption remains unknown. Diaries of erotic thoughts or autosexual activities by women show a peak around the time of ovulation, suggesting an endocrine effect on sexual motivation (Adams et al., 1978).

Studies that report a peak in sexual behavior among married couples around the time of ovulation usually have not controlled for the possibility that males find

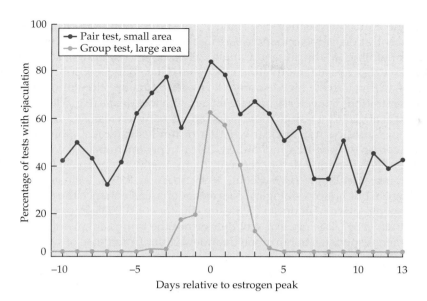

FIGURE 6.18 Endocrine control of receptivity can be affected by social factors. If female rhesus monkeys are tested with one male in a small area, there is no close relationship between estrogen concentration and receptivity (as measured by the number of tests with ejaculations). However, a clear relationship between receptivity and estrogen concentration emerges when females are tested in mixed social groups in large areas. Pair test after Goy, 1978; group test after Wallen et al., 1984.

periovulatory females more attractive and, hence, that men may initiate more sexual contacts around the time of ovulation. One study controlled for this possible confounding variable by examining the frequency of sexual activities among lesbian couples (Matteo and Rissman, 1984). This study reported a small peak in sexual activity around the time of ovulation, along with a secondary, perimenstrual peak. Other studies of heterosexual couples have also suggested a secondary perimenstrual peak in sexual behavior (e.g., Harvey, 1987; Sherwin, 1988a,b; Slob et al., 1991, 1996; Van Goozen et al., 1997). A study of sexual arousability over the menstrual cycle used both subjective self-reports and objective (labia minora temperature) measures to discover cycles in erotic responsiveness (Slob et al., 1996). This study revealed that the order of testing (i.e., whether the test was first administered during the luteal or the follicular phase) could affect subjective reports of erotic arousal. Thus, caution must be exercised when gathering self-reports, to make certain that multiple cycles are followed.

Part of the confusion about the role of hormones in the sexual behavior of women stems from imprecise assessment of ovulation. When the preovulatory surge of LH was pinpointed, it became clear that women were more sexually active on the days immediately before, and on the day of, the preovulatory LH surge (the time of maximal fertility). This pattern was pronounced when women initiated sexual contact but not when sexual activity was initiated by their male partners, suggesting that women were more motivated to engage in sexual behavior but not necessarily more attractive or receptive to their male partners (Bullivant et al., 2004).

Testosterone is also associated with sexual behavior in women (van Anders, 2009; van Anders and Gray, 2007). For example, women in monogamous relationships display reduced testosterone levels compared with women involved with multiple partners (van Anders et al., 2007a) or single women (van Anders and Watson, 2006). It appears that women who have multiple partners have elevated testosterone in comparison with women who have a polyamorous approach to relationships but do not have multiple partners at the time of blood sampling (van Anders et al., 2007a). These results suggest that cues associated with partners, rather than sexual desires or intentions, mediate testosterone concentrations (van Anders et al., 2007a). Additional support for this perspective is the observation that women in same-city relationships have reduced testosterone compared with single women, whereas women in long-distance relationships display intermediate testosterone concentrations, again suggesting that cues associated with partner presence mediate the lower testosterone values in partnered women (van Anders and Watson, 2007). Testosterone concentrations appear to increase in women in new relationships but decrease after a brief time (Marazziti and Canale, 2004). Low circulating testosterone is associated with low sexual motivation in women (Guay and Jacobson, 2002). Birth control pills with relatively high estradiol levels tend to cause circulating free testosterone concentrations to decrease and are linked with low desire (e.g., Davison et al., 2008; Greco et al., 2007). Despite these associations between testosterone and sexual behavior or fantasies, it is unclear whether or not testosterone, alone, enhances libido in women (Cappelletti and Wallen, 2016). In postmenopausal women, replacement of estrogen to periovulatory concentrations, without concurrent testosterone treatment, increases libido (Davis et al., 1995; Sherwin, 1991). Testosterone, at supraphysiological but not physiological concentrations, can enhance the effects of low-dose estrogen replacement on sexual desire (Buster et al., 2005; Panay et al., 2010; Sherwin et al., 1985). It is unclear whether or not the brain regions of postmenopausal women responsive to hormone treatment differ from those of women actively producing sex steroids, necessitating further studies aimed at determining the mechanisms underlying sexual motivation in premenopausal women. In naturally cycling women, estrogen is positively associated with sexual desire (Grebe et al., 2016; Roney and Simmons, 2013). Additionally, estrogen is positively associated, and progesterone negatively correlated, with sexual attraction to men other than one's primary partner. However, progesterone is associated not with decreased sexual interest generally, but with sexual desire being redirected to one's primary partner (Grebe et al., 2016). These findings might reflect an evolutionary-adaptive motivation to conceive at the time of maximal fertility while seeking a more stable, nurturing relationship during pregnancy.

The effect of hormone contraceptive pills on sexual motivation and performance in women is a topic that is often of interest to college-age readers. Throughout the 1950s, a common societal perception was that women's sex drive was low compared with that of men. The "Kinsey report" began to chip away at that misperception. It was assumed that women were less sexually motivated because they were afraid of becoming pregnant. With the virtual certainty of full contraception that resulted from the widespread use of "the Pill" in the 1960s, it was expected that the sex drives of men and women would equalize. Certainly, during the sexual liberation that swept Europe and North America in the 1960s, it appeared to be the case. Upon closer inspection, however, most studies report that use of hormonal contraceptive pills reduces, rather than increases, sexual motivation (Caruso et al., 2004; Davison et al., 2008; Dei et al., 1997), although many studies reported the opposite pattern (e.g., Caruso et al., 2005; Guida et al., 2005). More evidence for dysregulated testosterone in women taking hormone contraceptives comes from one study exploring the impact of sexual thoughts on hormonal changes. When women were asked to imagine a positive sexual encounter with an attractive partner, women not taking hormone contraceptives exhibited an increase in testosterone not seen in women on oral contraceptives (Goldey and Van Anders, 2011). Likewise, taking oral contraceptives decreases female preference for masculine faces relative to predilections prior to commencing oral contraception use (Little et al., 2013). Oral contraceptive pills with relatively high estradiol levels tend to reduce circulating free testosterone concentrations (e.g., Davison et al., 2008; Greco et al., 2007). Thus, women taking high-estrogen pills may display sexual motivation, whereas women taking low-estrogen pills may see increased libido. In other words, the Pill might decrease concerns about unwanted pregnancies, which could increase sexual motivation by minimizing a social deterrent, but hormonal contraceptives also reduce testosterone, which could decrease sexual motivation in some women. To complicate matters, there are clearly individual differences in the responses of women to hormone contraceptive pills. For example, about half of women taking pills with either 35 µg or 25 µg of ethinylestradiol who reported changes in sexual motivation had increased libido,

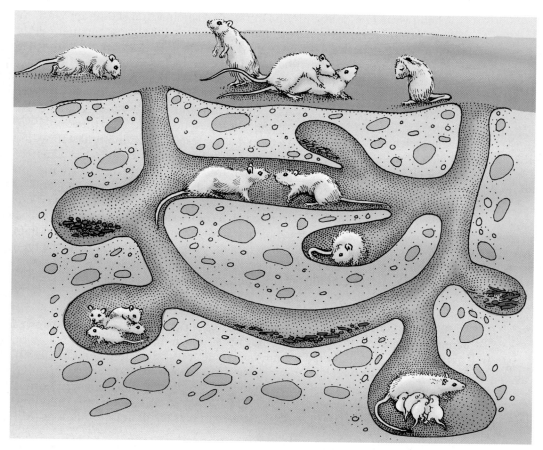

FIGURE 6.19   A breeding deme, the typical social organization of wild rats, consists of a small group of animals that includes a few adult males, several adult females, and many subadults. In this social setting, the females may undergo estrous cycles synchronously and mate with several males sequentially. The burrows and runway systems in the rats' natural habitat promote a slower mating pace than is typical in a laboratory setting. From McClintock, 1987.

whereas the other half reported decreased libido (Greco et al., 2007). The source of this individual difference in response to estrogen remains to be studied.

FEMALE PACING OF COPULATION   Sex steroid hormones are necessary and sufficient for normal sexual behavior among female rodents in the laboratory. There does not seem to be much selectivity of mating partners among estrous female rats when they are tested in the typical laboratory apparatus with a single male. Under these conditions, an estrous rat will mate with virtually any adult male with which she is paired. But estrous rats do not normally mate with a single male in an enclosed space. Wild rats and mice typically live in small breeding units, called demes, consisting of one or two adult males, several females, and their offspring (**FIGURE 6.19**). The animals often mate in groups, and the pacing of mating behavior is usually under the control of the females. Group-living females often come into estrus together, and two or more estrous females may compete to copulate with two or more attendant males (Bronson, 1979; Calhoun, 1962a; McClintock and Adler, 1978). Because the first and last males to ejaculate with a female in a group mating situation sire proportionally more of her offspring than other ejaculating males, a female can to some degree choose the sires of her offspring by her choice of males for these roles (see Figure 5.25).

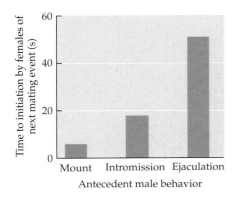

FIGURE 6.20 Female pacing of copulation Female rats in paced paired mating tests, in which they are provided with an "escape" area away from the male, return to the male more slowly following an ejaculation than after an intromission or mount, indicating that they can discriminate among different types of vaginal stimulation. After Erskine, 1985.

When researchers tested groups of rats in a seminatural setting in which female rats could control the pace of mating behavior, the temporal pattern of rat copulatory behavior began to emerge (McClintock, 1987; McClintock and Adler, 1978). The natural pace of mating can also be simulated in a single-pair mating test by using a setting that allows the female to escape from the male between mating events (Erskine, 1985). Under conditions that allow females to pace copulation (paced tests), the intervals between intromissions are longer than those observed in the more typical artificial settings of nonpaced tests (Erskine, 1985; McClintock and Adler, 1978). In group mating tests in a seminatural setting, the female retires to her burrow or moves behind some barrier for approximately 3 minutes after each intromission. In contrast, the average inter-intromission interval during standard paired rat mating tests is less than 1 minute. Females paired with a single male in a standard mating arena but able to dart in and out also show different timing than females in nonpaced tests: females in paced paired tests stay away from the male for a longer time after an ejaculation than after an intromission, demonstrating that they are able to discriminate the type of vaginal stimulation they have received (see Yang and Clemens, 1996) (**FIGURE 6.20**). Anesthesia of the perianal region disrupts this discriminative ability (Bermant and Westbrook, 1966).

The larger size of the mating arena in natural (Calhoun, 1962a) or seminatural (McClintock and Adler, 1978) settings permits the full expression of female solicitation behaviors, including approach-and-withdrawal behavior, that are often missing or altered in standard mating test situations (Erskine, 1989). Approach-and-withdrawal behavior appears as the hopping and darting observed in typical laboratory settings. This behavior is an important component of normal rat sexual behavior and precedes 90% of intromissions in natural or seminatural settings. In contrast, only 3% of male-initiated contacts result in intromissions (McClintock, 1987).

The temporal pattern of copulatory events has an important role in rodent reproduction, namely, the induction of corpora luteal function. In Chapter 5, various rodent copulatory patterns were presented. In some species, such as the guinea pig, males ejaculate on the first intromission, and there is no pelvic thrusting. In rats and mice, males mount a number of times, and there are multiple intromissions before ejaculation. Why have multiple intromissions? Physiologically, multiple intromissions stimulate sperm transport after ejaculation. But there are other important coadaptations between the physiology of females and the behavior of male conspecifics. If no mating stimuli, or insufficient stimuli, are received, a female undergoes recurrent estrous cycles of 4 or 5 days. The corpora lutea regress soon after being formed and do not secrete sufficient progesterone to build up the uterine endometrium to support pregnancy. Multiple intromissions maintain luteal function so that the fertilized ova can implant in the uterine wall. The sensory input from the multiple intromissions stimulates secretion of prolactin from the anterior pituitary in a characteristic twice-daily pulse. The secretion of prolactin in this manner supports the corpora lutea for about 10–12 days (Gunnet and Freeman, 1983). The corpora lutea then persist until the end of pregnancy without further prolactin support. Unlike a female guinea pig, a female rat cannot become pregnant with a single intromission and ejaculation—unless corpora luteal function has been activated by artificial vaginal stimulation.

The female's pacing of copulation may be a means of ensuring that she receives a pattern of stimulation as close as possible to the "vaginal code"—the so-called optimal pattern of stimulation for producing offspring—for her species (see Chapter 5) (Erskine et al., 2004; Lehmann and Erskine, 2004). In standard nonpaced mating tests of rats, approximately ten intromissions are required to induce luteal function and ensure successful pregnancy. In a paced mating test, in which the female controls the timing and duration of the copulatory activity, only five intromissions are

FIGURE 6.21 Paced mating enhances reproduction. The slower mating pace seen in female-paced mating tests optimizes reproduction: in this study, five male intromissions in a paced test resulted in more successful pregnancies than did ten intromissions, and both paced tests resulted in more pregnancies than did the nonpaced tests. After Erskine, 1985.

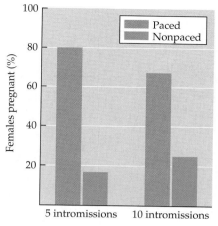

necessary to induce corpora luteal function, and more females are impregnated after five intromissions than after ten intromissions (**FIGURE 6.21**). Males also need fewer intromissions to ejaculate in paced than in standard laboratory mating tests (Erskine, 1985). Presumably, his interaction with a female displaying the approach-and-withdrawal behavior pattern increases the male's arousal such that fewer intromissions are required prior to ejaculation (Erskine, 1989). It appears that the number, rather than the timing, of prior intromissions affects subsequent mating behavior and termination of estrus in rats (Coopersmith et al., 1996). Furthermore, paced mating appears to be more effective than non-paced mating in inducing the expression of *c-fos* genes in neurons that are part of the neural circuitry underlying female sexual behavior (Erskine and Hanrahan, 1997). Paced mating changes pain thresholds in rats (Lee and Erskine, 2000) but does not seem to be involved in mating-induced analgesia. A role of proper pacing of mating behavior in the reproduction of other species has been identified only in mice (Garey et al., 2002). Pacing is unnecessary in guinea pigs. Male guinea pigs ejaculate on the first intromission, but female guinea pigs have spontaneous corpora luteal activity, so multiple intromissions are unnecessary. Such coadaptation between male and female copulatory behavior and reproductive physiology is a fundamental characteristic defining a species.

The pattern of intromissions, important in the induction of the corpus luteum, plays another role as well. Female rats seek a specific pattern of intromissions that is most rewarding, further indicating that female rodents are active participants in the sexual encounter and find the experience pleasurable. If artificial vaginocervical stimulation (VCS) is administered to female rats in the interval preferred, they will develop a conditioned place preference for the location in which it was administered (Meerts and Clarke, 2009). That is, females will associate the environment in which VCS was delivered with reward and prefer to spend time in that context even in the absence of a male. In addition to developing a conditioned place preference to VCS, female rats that experience paced mating with a "scented" male will exhibit more solicitations toward a male exhibiting this scent in future choice tests, suggesting that partner preference can be conditioned with properly timed stimulation (Coria-Avila et al., 2005). In addition to VCS, genital to genital contact during copulation results in clitoral stimulation in female rats, suggesting an additional reward mechanism. If the clitoris is anesthetized with lidocaine prior to copulation, rats spend less time in contact with males and the pacing of mating is disrupted, indicating that VCS under these conditions is insufficient to pace mating and that anesthesia significantly reduces the rewarding value of copulation (Meerts et al., 2015; Parada et al., 2014. The fact that a specific pattern of vaginal stimulation is both rewarding and important for the formation of the corpus luteum argues for the coevolution of this behavioral pattern with sensory, reward, and neuroendocrine circuitry required for sexual motivation and successful pregnancy.

Female Reproductive Cycles

The durations of estrus and the intervals between estrous periods vary from species to species (**TABLE 6.1**). Rats, as we have seen, come into estrus every 4 or 5 days. For some species, like the golden-mantled ground squirrel (*Spermophilus lateralis*), the estrous period may last only a few hours per year during a single morning. In other species, such as rabbits, females will permit mating at any time during the breeding

TABLE 6.1 *Typical length of the estrous cycle of several common species when living under optimal conditions*

Common name	Taxonomic name	Cycle length (days)
Laboratory rat	*Rattus norvegicus*	4–5
House mouse	*Mus musculus*	4–6
Guinea pig	*Cavia porcellus*	16
Golden hamster	*Mesocricetus auratus*	4
Deer mouse	*Peromyscus maniculatus*	4–5
Cotton rat	*Sigmodon hispidus*	4–20
Domestic cat	*Felis catus*	9–10, 2/year
Domestic dog	*Canis familiaris*	10, 2/year
Sheep	*Ovis aries*	16
Goat	*Capra hircus*	21
Cow	*Bos taurus*	21
Pig	*Sus scrofa*	22

Source: Asdell, 1964.

season. Female mammalian reproductive cycles can be classified into several types based on how and when ovulation and pseudopregnancy occur. Although these types will be presented here as if they were discrete categories, keep in mind that reproductive cycles actually vary along a continuum. The description of reproductive cycles that follows is largely based on the classification system put forth by Conaway (1971).

Types of Reproductive Cycles

The **follicular phase** of an ovarian cycle occurs prior to ovulation, when the follicles are developing. The **luteal phase** is that part of the cycle after ovulation during which the corpora lutea are active and producing lots of progesterone. Of course, the ovaries are producing progesterone around the time of ovulation, too. Successful fertilization usually occurs in the fallopian tubes, as the egg travels from the ovary to the uterus. Progesterone—the "progestational" hormone—typically induces the buildup of the uterine endometrium in preparation for the implantation of a **blastocyst**—the small mass of dividing cells that develops into an embryo—and supports the uterus during pregnancy. If a luteal phase occurs during a rodent's cycle when no mating, or a sterile mating, has taken place, then a pseudopregnancy will occur as the uterus is prepared for blastocyst implantation. Estrous cycles are suspended during pregnancy, pseudopregnancy, and lactation. Pseudopregnancy is considered spontaneous if the formation of functional corpora lutea always follows ovulation; if the formation of functional corpora lutea does not automatically follow ovulation but requires some sort of additional stimulus, as in rats, then pseudopregnancy is considered induced. In Conaway's classification system (**TABLE 6.2**), pseudopregnancy is defined as "the occurrence of any functional luteal phase in a non-pregnant cycle" (Everett, 1961). Although the luteal phase of the ovarian cycle is hormonally identical to pseudopregnancy, the term *luteal phase* is reserved mainly for describing primate ovarian cycles. Exceptions include guinea pigs and sheep, which both display spontaneous luteal phases.

The reproductive cycles of female anthropoid primates, including humans, are not technically estrous cycles because, as described previously, mating behavior is not confined to a particular phase of the ovarian cycle. Women and females of a few other primate species may copulate on any day of the cycle (Wallen and

follicular phase   The portion of the primate menstrual cycle that begins at the end of menstruation and ends at ovulation, characterized by high blood levels of estrogens and the development of follicles.

luteal phase   The portion of the primate menstrual cycle that begins at ovulation and continues until the onset of menstruation and is characterized by corpora luteal function and high blood levels of progesterone.

blastocyst   A fluid-filled sphere of cells that develops from a zygote. The embryo usually develops from the cluster of cells in the center of the blastocyst, whereas the external wall of the blastocyst develops into the placenta.

Zehr, 2004). The ovarian cycle displayed by most primates is called the menstrual (moon) cycle because of the recurring period of menstruation (sloughing off of the uterine endometrium) that typically occurs during each cycle, about once a month in humans (**FIGURE 6.22**). Dogs and some other mammals discharge blood from the vagina prior to estrus, but this discharge is fundamentally different from menstrual bleeding. Menstruation occurs when blood concentrations of estrogens and proges-

(A) Gonadotropins secreted by the
     anterior pituitary

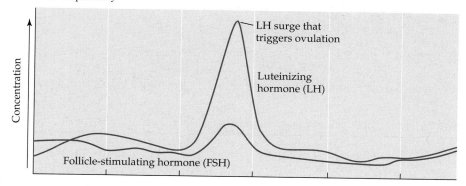

(B) Events in the ovary

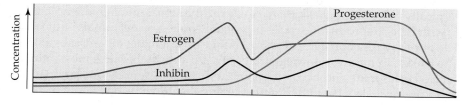

(C) Ovarian hormones

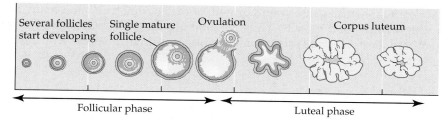

(D) Events in the endometrium of the uterus

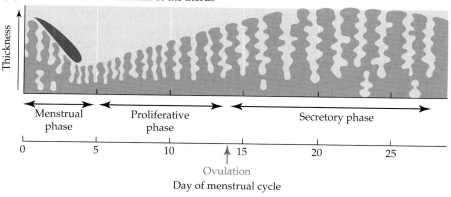

FIGURE 6.22 The human menstrual cycle After menstrual bleeding has ceased, blood concentrations of LH and FSH increase gradually (A), stimulating the development of estrogen-secreting follicles in the ovary (B). When estrogen concentrations are high, a positive feedback response occurs, causing a surge of gonadotropins that induces ovulation (A). After ovulation, negative feedback returns gonadotropin concentrations to baseline values, and estrogen concentrations wane (C). Corpora lutea form (B) and secrete progesterone (C). If a woman is not pregnant, the corpora lutea regress, progesterone concentrations sharply decrease, and menstruation begins (D).

TABLE 6.2   *Types of female reproductive cycles in mammals*

Cycle	Length	Features	Examples
Type 1			
Subtype 1.1.A	2–5 weeks	Spontaneous ovulation and pseudopregnancy; copulation limited to periovulatory period	Guinea pigs/other hystricomorph rodents
Subtype 1.1.B	2–5 weeks	Spontaneous ovulation and pseudopregnancy; copulation may occur throughout cycle	Great apes, including humans
Subtype 1.2	>5 weeks	Spontaneous ovulation and pseudopregnancy; copulation limited to periovulatory period	Dogs and other canids
Type 2			
Subtype 2.1	3–5 weeks	Induced ovulation, but spontaneous pseudopregnancy	Rabbits and hares; lemmings and voles
Subtype 2.2	>5 weeks	Induced ovulation, but spontaneous pseudopregnancy	Cats, minks, ferrets, and skunks
Type 3			
	<1 week	Spontaneous ovulation, but induced pseudopregnancy	Rats, mice, and hamsters

Source: Conaway, 1971.

terone are basal. The endometrial layer of the uterus, no longer supported by the sex steroid hormones, is shed, and the corkscrew-shaped blood vessels that remain leak blood into the uterine lumen. The blood discharged by proestrous or estrous dogs, on the other hand, results from estrogen-induced stimulation of the uterine wall (hyperemia), which causes rapid growth of the endometrium and many tears in the supporting blood vessels. Thus, vaginal bleeding in canines results from steroid stimulation, whereas menstrual bleeding in primates results from steroid hormone deprivation.

The Ecology of Reproductive Cycles

Table 6.2 describes the several different kinds of reproductive cycles in mammals. The type 3 reproductive cycle was once considered to be the pattern most typical of mammals because of the enormous amount of research that was conducted on species—typically rodents—that exhibit it. However, the actual number of mammalian species with type 3 reproductive cycles is probably quite low. Mammals with type 3 cycles do not have functional luteal phases if they do not mate; this ensures a rapid return to estrus. In nature, nonpregnant cycles are a rarity because most animals with type 3 cycles mate and become pregnant during a spontaneous postpartum estrus and thus gestate a new litter while nursing the previous one.

    Why are there so many different types of reproductive cycles? From an ecological perspective, each species' cyclic pattern can be seen as an adaptation for increasing its reproductive success. The cyclic pattern increases the probability that mating will occur when the female is fertile and that offspring will be produced and survive. Keep in mind that female mammals in the wild are typically pregnant, lactating, or in seasonal diestrus, that is, reproductively quiescent. Frequent estrous cycles are laboratory artifacts that are unusual in free-ranging mammals. Except in primates, sterile copulation is probably very rare in nature (Nalbandov, 1976). Repeated, sterile estrous cycles represent an abnormal state that females in the wild cannot afford (Conaway, 1971).

    What are the relative advantages of the various reproductive cycle types? One correlation that is immediately apparent is that short-lived prey species (e.g., rodents and lagomorphs [rabbits and hares]) display either subtype 2.1 or type 3 reproductive cycles, which minimize the time spent in a nonpregnant condition. Animals that live longer, such as predators, do not require as many adaptations to reduce nonpregnant intervals and can focus more effort on rearing fewer offspring successfully. Another loose correlation occurs between induced ovulation and solitary living. Many of the solitary carnivores are induced ovulators; this adaptation ensures that ovulation occurs only when males are present. In some species of induced ovulators, behavioral estrus is also induced by the presence of male conspecifics.

In many species of lagomorphs, behavioral estrus is induced by synchronized courtship displays by the males in the population (Conaway and Wight, 1962). In this case, group synchrony in mating probably confers individual advantages because births will be synchronized, and the chance of any one offspring becoming the victim of predation will be much less than if births were randomly timed throughout the breeding season. In contrast, many large group-living mammals display spontaneous ovulation. A social organization such as a herd probably guarantees that males will be present whenever a female comes into estrus.

Female prairie voles (*Microtus ochrogaster*) do not display regular estrous cycles but are induced into behavioral estrus by the presence of a conspecific, fertile male or exposure to his urine (Richmond and Stehn, 1976). Undisturbed, isolated female prairie voles never display the cycles in vaginal cell types observed in mice and rats. When a male is present, the female may ingest a few drops of his urine during mutual anogenital investigation. The urine is delivered to the VNO (reviewed in Wysocki, 1979; Wysocki and Lepri, 1991). As described in Chapter 5, this chemosensory organ connects with the accessory olfactory bulb of the brain via the vomeronasal nerves. In many rodent species, the cell bodies of neurons that secrete gonadotropin-releasing hormone (GnRH) are in the olfactory bulb (Dluzen and Ramirez, 1983); these neurons project to the median eminence of the hypothalamus. The delivery of male urine to the VNO of the female stimulates a cascade of endocrine events. Within an hour, GnRH is released from the olfactory bulb, which stimulates secretion of LH, and probably follicle-stimulating hormone (FSH), from the anterior pituitary gland (Dluzen et al., 1981). The secretion of gonadotropins results in follicular development and subsequent production of estrogen. Elevated estrogen concentrations cause estrous behavior within 24 hours (Carter et al., 1986). Ovulation occurs approximately 12 hours after mating and is induced by copulation.

The behavior of a female prairie vole directly influences her endocrine state. If the female does not engage in anogenital investigation, then she will not be induced into estrus. When female voles are housed with their fathers or brothers, they do not engage in anogenital investigation, are not induced into estrus, and thereby avoid incestuous mating (Carter et al., 1980). Because the ovaries are quiescent prior to the induction of estrus, proceptive behavior (anogenital investigation) is not mediated by ovarian steroid hormones in this species (Moffatt and Nelson, 1994). Note that this pattern is reminiscent of the ringdove story.

In nature, the first estrus of the breeding season in prairie voles is induced by males, but subsequent mating occurs during a spontaneous postpartum estrus (Nelson, 1985; Richmond and Conaway, 1969). Most pregnancies among natural populations of rodents are the result of mating during postpartum estrus. Rats ovulate about 3–6 hours after delivery of their young, and postpartum estrus occurs within 24 hours of the onset of parturition. The hormonal milieu of parturition is similar to the endocrine state associated with ovulation during an estrous cycle (Connor and Davis, 1980a,b). A female in postpartum estrus is attractive and signals males to mate with her (Greef and Merkx, 1982). Typically, she becomes pregnant again within a day after giving birth and gestates a new litter while nursing the previous one. At about the time the current litter of pups is weaned, a new litter arrives, the female again enters estrus, and the sequence is repeated until the end of the breeding season (see Chapter 10). Thus, this reproductive pattern decreases the interval between successive litters and effectively doubles reproductive output. If a female fails to become pregnant during postpartum estrus, she enters a lactational diestrus and does not enter estrus again until her young are weaned 25–30 days later. This type of reproductive pattern is common among many mammalian groups, including marsupials, mustelids (e.g., mink, ferrets, skunks), and rodents. Despite the preponderance of pregnancies in the wild that arise from postpartum matings, little is known about the physiology of, or behavioral changes associated with, postpartum estrus (Blandau and Soderwall, 1941; Connor and Davis, 1980a,b; Everett, 1961; Greef and Merkx, 1982; Lu et al., 1976).

If estrous cycles such as those observed among laboratory rodents do not result in increased production of offspring, then why have estrous cycles evolved? Estrous cycles are probably an adaptation that allows a female to enter reproductive condition at the beginning of the breeding season or reenter estrus after a failed reproductive attempt. If nutritional availability wanes, or some other disruption of reproduction occurs, the estrous cycle returns the female to reproductive condition as soon as possible when conditions improve.

Social and Environmental Effects on Reproductive Cycles

Social conditions and environmental factors can dramatically affect female reproductive cycles, as several of the examples in the previous section demonstrate. Several effects of the social environment on reproductive cycles have been observed in laboratory studies. For example, female house mice (*Mus musculus*; type 3 cycle in Table 6.2) that are housed together in groups of four or more often enter a period of anestrus. If a male conspecific, or his odor, is introduced into such a group, the females ovulate synchronously 3 or 4 days later (van der Lee and Boot, 1955; Whitten, 1956b). Thus, the organization of estrus among house mice can resemble that of prairie voles under the appropriate social conditions. These social effects on female reproductive cycles appear to be mediated by chemosensory cues from conspecifics. Four related chemosensory-mediated effects that have been observed in the laboratory are described in **TABLE 6.3**.

THE ROLE OF PHEROMONES There appear to be two pheromones that are responsible for social effects on female reproductive cycles. One of these chemical signals comes from females and tends to suppress ovarian function. Depending on the reproductive condition of the recipient animal (prepubertal or cycling) and the strength of the stimulus, exposure to the female chemosignal either inhibits puberty or suspends estrus. This chemosignal probably acts by suppressing gonadotropin release from the anterior pituitary. The other chemical signal is emitted by males and, depending on the reproductive condition of the recipient female (prepubertal, suspended estrous cycling, or pregnant), accelerates puberty, induces estrus, or interrupts pregnancy. The male chemosignal appears to induce an abrupt release of LH, which stimulates follicular growth. Prolactin appears to interfere with the induction of LH release; for example, lactating females that become pregnant during postpartum estrus are protected against pregnancy block due to male chemosignals (Komisaruk et al., 1981).

As in males (see Chapter 5), an intact chemosensory system is critical for successful female reproduction. Although it is commonly believed that the main and accessory olfactory systems are separate sensory systems, because they innervate different parts of the brain and process different types of signals (Meredith, 1991), it is becoming increasingly clear that information moves between these two systems (Baum and Kelliher, 2009; Keller et al., 2009).

From where do these chemical signals emanate? The entire body can, in theory, provide a multitude of chemical signals, but probably the most important source of chemical signals in rodents is the urine and feces. Recently, by examination of vomeronasal neurons that respond to female, but not male, urine, a new class of vomeronasal ligands was identified in female mouse urine, called steroid carbox-

TABLE 6.3 *Four related chemosensory-mediated effects that have been observed in laboratory mice*

Effect	Physiology	Cue	Reference
Lee-Boot effect	When housed 4/cage with no males present, female mice display longer estrous cycles due to lengthening of diestrous stage.	Chemosensory	van der Lee and Boot, 1955
	Considered comparable to the pseudopregnancies induced by sterile matings, because growth of the uterine lining was sometimes observed (decidual reaction).		
Whitten effect			Whitten, 1956b, 1957
(1) Estrus induction and synchronization	Presence of a male or his odors induces estrous behavior within 48 h in group-housed female mice. Exposure to male urine induces GnRH release and estrus.	Chemosensory (androgen-dependent substance in male urine)	
(2) Suppression of estrus	When housed >20/cage with no males present, female mice suspend estrous cycles. Exposure to female urine suppresses GnRH release and estrus.	Chemosensory (androgen-dependent substance in male urine)	
Bruce effect	Pregnant females abort or resorb their fetuses if exposed to a male that was not the sire for >48 hours. Exposure to male urine induces GnRH release and estrus. This combination of endocrine events is incompatible with pregnancy.	Chemosensory (androgen-dependent substance in male urine)	Bruce, 1959, 1960; reviewed in Heske and Nelson, 1984
Vandenbergh effect			Vandenbergh, 1967, 1983, 1994
(1) Acceleration of puberty	Female juvenile mice exposed to adult males mature earlier than those not exposed to adult males. Exposure to male urine induces GnRH release and puberty.	Chemosensory (androgen-dependent substance in male urine)	
(2) Delay of puberty	Female juvenile mice exposed to adult females mature later than those not exposed to adult females. Exposure to female urine inhibits GnRH release and puberty.	Chemosensory	

ylic acids. These ligands stimulate vomeronasal neuron activity, are necessary for normal levels of male investigatory behavior of female scents, and are sufficient to trigger mounting behavior (Fu et al., 2015). There is good evidence that the primer pheromones produced by male mice are androgen-based components of urine; urine from castrated or prepubertal males is not very effective in producing estrus in females. One identified compound found in male urine, 6-hydroxy-6-methyl-3-heptanone, can accelerate puberty in female mice (Novotny et al., 1999). Additionally, like other mammals, male mice mark territory with urine containing a variety of pheromones. One component of male mouse urine, darcin, stimulates neurogenesis in female mice, suggesting a mechanism for social identification of males in the region (Hoffman et al., 2015).

The effects of social factors on ovarian cycles are not limited to rodents. In one study, for example, women who lived together for extended periods of time exhibited greater synchrony in their ovulatory cycles (McClintock, 1971). Records of menstrual cycles obtained from undergraduate women attending Radcliffe College showed that menstrual synchronization is more likely among roommates than among women who live in the same dormitory building and that approximately 7 or

BOX 6.2 *Human Pheromones*

Although there have been many claims of the existence of human pheromones—chemical signals that are released by one person and travel through the air or water to affect the physiology or behavior of another person—until recently there was no solid evidence of such substances. Nevertheless, one can buy perfumes, bearing such provocative names as Lure, Scent, and Primal Instinct Pheromone, purported to contain human pheromones specifically formulated to attract the men or women of one's choice. The best part of these sales pitches (for those selling these "naked emperor" fragrances) is that the pheromones are essentially odorless (buyers can mix them into their favorite perfumes or colognes) and affect the behavior of recipients without their conscious awareness. One such product claims to have 50 "known" human pheromones as ingredients. Despite these widespread claims for their existence, no human pheromones have been isolated and characterized, and until very recently, their existence was unproven (Stern and McClintock, 1998).

One study established the existence of two human pheromones produced by women that affect women—one produced prior to ovulation during the follicular phase, which shortens the ovarian cycle in recipients, and a second one produced around the time of ovulation, which lengthens the ovarian cycle in recipients. These pheromones mediated a specific neuroendocrine response in women without the recipients' conscious awareness (Stern and McClintock, 1998). Women between the ages of 20 and 35 took part in the study. Nine of these women provided chemosensory samples during different times of their menstrual cycles by wearing absorbent pads under their arms for at least 8 hours daily. The pads were quartered and stored frozen until tested on other women. The pads were wiped under the noses of the recipient women. Pads obtained from donor women during the follicular phase accelerated the periovulatory surge of LH and shortened the menstrual cycles of the recipient women by 1–14 days over two menstrual cycles (lower curve in the figure) (Stern and McClintock,

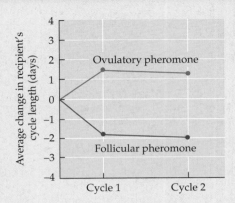

1998). Pads obtained from donor women around the time of ovulation delayed the periovulatory LH surge and lengthened the menstrual cycle of recipient women by 1–12 days (upper curve in the figure). Approximately 70% of the recipient women responded to the pheromones. Because the same donors provided all the chemosensory samples, this study demonstrated that the timing of ovulation in women could be manipulated, and it provided the first definitive evidence of human pheromones. This work opens the door to a more "natural" way of manipulating the timing of ovulation, which could help in birth control and fertility treatments.

A similar study used compounds collected from lactating women and their breastfeeding infants. These pheromones increased the sexual motivation of other women, in terms of self-reported sexual desire and fantasies (Spencer et al., 2004). Interestingly, the increased sexual motivation took different forms depending on whether or not a woman had a regular sexual partner. Women with regular sexual partners reported increased sexual desire, whereas women without regular partners reported more sexual fantasies (Spencer et al., 2004). These results indicate that imperceptible chemical cues can affect hormone-behavior interactions in humans.

8 months of cohabitation is required before menstrual cycles become synchronized. This phenomenon may be mediated by chemosensory signals, but the experiments necessary to determine this cannot be conducted on humans. Analogous studies have, however, been conducted on rats, demonstrating that rats living in groups show a similar estrus-synchronizing phenomenon, with chemosensory cues providing the stimuli allowing synchronization of the estrous cycles (McClintock, 1978). Olfaction is probably a very important component of normal human sexual behavior, but it has only recently become an area of scientific study (**BOX 6.2**). Clinical reports on women with congenital absence of the olfactory bulbs revealed a markedly increased incidence of ovarian hypoplasia (nondevelopment) (Schwanzel-Fukuda et al., 1989), but this condition probably reflects the lack of GnRH neuronal migration rather than the loss of olfactory ability. It is likely that menstrual synchrony is part of a larger phenomenon of social influence on human ovulatory cycles (McClintock, 1998) similar to the chemosensory influences on female mouse repro-

ductive physiology and behavior (see Table 6.3). Certainly, smelling androstenol, a derivative of anabolic steroids, as well as 4,16-androstadien-3-one can activate the hypothalamus of women (Savic and Berglund, 2010). Likewise, smelling androstadienone, a component in male sweat thought to be a pheromonal chemosignal, is associated with increased physiological and sexual arousal, enhanced mood, and higher cortisol concentrations in women (Wyart et al., 2007). The extent to which this brain activation affects sexual behavior in women remains to be determined. However, exposure to androstadienone triggers similar activation in the hypothalamus of heterosexual women and homosexual men, but not in heterosexual men or homosexual women (Berglund et al., 2006). Somehow this effect seems to be linked to gender, sexual orientation, or gender of partner.

ENVIRONMENTAL EFFECTS Environmental factors have an enormous influence on ovarian cycles. Lack of proper nutrition, stress, or lack of appropriate habitat can adversely affect ovarian cycles (Schneider et al., 1998; Wade et al., 1997). Stressful events ranging from starting college to imprisonment can suspend menstrual cycles in women (Bachman and Kemmann, 1982; Bass, 1947). One study found that premenopausal women awaiting their execution on death row were not experiencing any menstrual cycles (Pettersson et al., 1973) (see Chapter 11).

In most mammals, estrous cycles occur only during the breeding season. The breeding season represents the "temporal fit" among many selective forces—including food availability, thermoregulatory pressures, climatic factors, and the species' mating system and gestation length—that best ensures reproductive success. The environmental factors that turn the ovaries on and off at the beginning and the end of the breeding season will be discussed in Chapter 10. As indicated in Chapter 3, perinatal events can also affect subsequent estrous cyclicity. Recall that proximity to brothers in the uterine horn during gestation increased estrous cycle length and reduced attractiveness in female rats and mice as compared with individuals gestated between two sisters (vom Saal and Bronson, 1980). Illness can also affect female sexual behavior (**BOX 6.3**).

Experimental Analyses of Female Sexual Behavior

By now you have noted that a tremendous amount is known about estrous cycles. The research efforts aimed at understanding the temporal characteristics, physiological mechanisms, and adaptive functions of estrous cycles have been enormous. However, as the previous discussion has revealed, most laboratory studies examining female reproductive physiology and behavior have been conducted on females undergoing repeated estrous cycles. Although a strong case was made above that the chronic estrous cycles observed and studied in the laboratory are merely artifacts, a great deal of valuable information has been gained by studying those cycles: virtually all that we know about the regulation of female sexual behavior has been derived from studying cycling female rodents. The development of oral contraceptives for human use was accomplished by understanding the endocrinology of cycling rodents and nonhuman primates; all of our understanding of the relationships among the nervous system, hormones, and female sexual behavior has been achieved by studying cycling rodents and nonhuman primates. Therefore, despite their lack of ecological validity, laboratory studies of estrous cycles have been valuable. The final sections of this chapter detail the endocrine-neural interactions underlying female sexual behavior that have been revealed by such studies.

Attempts to localize the neural bases of female sexual behavior have followed, in many cases, the same sequence as attempts at localization in males. However, it is much easier to quantify receptivity in females in the form of lordosis than it is to quantify "receptivity" in males in the form of appetitive behavior. As is the case for males, there have been two major lines of research dealing with the interac-

BOX 6.3   *Illness Suppresses Female Sexual Behavior*

Physical condition, including body mass and blood concentrations of specific metabolic fuels, has dramatic effects on female sexual physiology and behavior. Females with low energy, or otherwise in poor condition, are usually not receptive or proceptive toward males, and males are generally less attracted to females in poor condition than to females in good condition. Similarly, females that are ill are generally less receptive, proceptive, and attractive than females that are not ill.

The behavioral cues associated with illness are probably well known to you. An entire constellation of so-called sickness behaviors, which occur in response to systemic diseases or localized infections, has been documented in humans and several other mammalian species. Obvious behavioral changes observed in sick individuals include lethargy, hypersomnia, malaise, anorexia, loss of interest, and reduction in goal-directed behaviors (Hart, 1988). To induce "sickness behaviors" experimentally, animals are treated with endotoxin (which consists of heat-inactivated shells of *E. coli*) or lipopolysaccharide (LPS, which is the major molecular component of the cell walls of *E. coli*); both treatments activate the immune system but do not give the animals a replicating infection.

Activation of the immune system is communicated to the neuroendocrine system by chemical messengers called cytokines. Cytokines are released by activated macrophages during immunological responses to infections. Several of these chemical messengers, including interleukin-1β (IL-1β), interleukin-6 (IL-6), and tumor necrosis factor-α (TNF-α), affect neuroendocrine processes in the hypothalamus and pituitary (Segreti et al., 1997). Administration of IL-1β causes fever, hypersomnia, and slow-wave sleep, as well as reductions in locomotor activity, exploratory behaviors, food intake, and social contact

(Yirmiya et al., 1995; Avitsur et al., 1997). Treatment with IL-1β also inhibits GnRH gene expression in the hypothalamus, decreases GnRH release in rats on the afternoon of proestrus, and decreases circulating LH concentrations in ovariectomized rats and monkeys, as well as inhibiting steroid hormone synthesis in the ovaries and testes (Rivest and Rivier, 1993; Yirmiya et al., 1995).

Administration of IL-1β to female rats significantly reduced their sexual receptivity and proceptivity (Yirmiya et al., 1995). IL-1β–treated females also lost their preference for sexually active male rats. Surprisingly, IL-1β treatment of males did not diminish their sexual behavior. Both males and females displayed reduced locomotor activity after receiving IL-1β, which suggests that the sex difference in responsiveness to IL-1β is limited to sexual behavior. IL-1β also affected attractivity of female, but not male, rats: When males had a choice between estrogen-treated, ovariectomized females injected either with IL-1β or with saline, males preferred saline-injected females (Avitsur et al., 1998); that is, IL-1β reduced attractiveness in females (**Figure A**). In contrast, when presented with a choice of males that had been injected either with IL-1β or with saline, females did not discriminate between these males except at high doses (**Figure B**).

Taken together, these studies suggest that cytokines have direct and dramatic effects on behavior. Furthermore, the effect of IL-1β on sexual behavior shows a clear sex difference. The ultimate cause of this sex difference probably reflects the differential effects of illness on the reproductive success of males and females. As these studies show, the interactions between the immune and endocrine systems that affect behavior are becoming a rapidly expanding area of research.

(A)

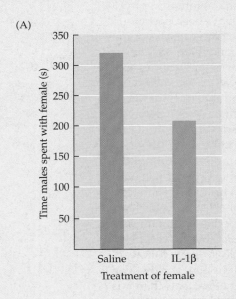

(B)

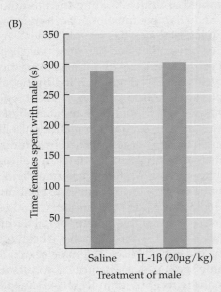

tion of female sexual behavior and hormones. The physiological line of research has attempted to determine the sources of the signals generating sexual behavior, that is, to discover the loci of the interaction between sex hormones and behavior (e.g., Bard, 1936; Beach, 1944b; Brookhart et al., 1941). As with males, early research established that the interaction does not take place at the level of the gonads; consequently, much of the subsequent work has focused on the central nervous system. The second line of research has considered sexual motivation. The strength of the female sex drive has been tested and quantified using a variety of motivational tests (e.g., Nissen, 1929), and in some cases, the neural bases of female sexual motivation have been discovered inadvertently during studies of receptivity. Pioneering sex researchers faced social pressures against positing a sex drive for females, as opposed to the "obvious" sex drive manifested by males. Then, as today, sexual behavior was a politically charged scientific topic. More recently, female sexual motivation has been quantified in terms of proceptive behavior (Erskine, 1989; Pfaff, 1999; Wallen, 1990).

The next section will review the hormonal events associated with female ovarian cycles in rats and rhesus monkeys. The following section will present the neural bases of female sexual behavior.

Hormonal Correlates of Female Reproductive Cycles

Recall from Chapter 2 that there is a dynamic relationship among the gonadal sex steroid hormones, the gonadotropins, and the hypothalamic releasing hormones. Basically, this relationship is one of reciprocal inhibition. The hypothalamus secretes pulses of releasing hormones, which stimulate the release of gonadotropins from the anterior pituitary. Pulses of gonadotropins drive the release of sex steroid hormones by the gonads. Negative feedback works in the following way: as sex steroid hormone concentrations increase, secretion of gonadotropins is reduced, which results in decreases in gonadotropin-stimulated steroid hormone synthesis. Removal of the ovaries causes the well-known **castration response**: the removal of the source of steroid hormones removes the negative feedback that regulates gonadotropin secretion, resulting in sustained elevated gonadotropin concentrations, as well as elevated releasing-hormone secretion. The simplified version of the relationship between gonadal sex steroid hormones and the gonadotropins is reflected in the metaphor of a seesaw (Moore and Price, 1932).

THE OVARIAN CYCLE IN RODENTS   GnRH is released by the hypothalamus in brief pulses (Christian and Moenter, 2010). These pulses of GnRH stimulate cells in the anterior pituitary to release FSH and LH (**FIGURE 6.23A**). Follicle-stimulating hormone (FSH), as its name implies, causes the follicles of the ovaries to grow. As the follicles develop, they produce estrogens and progestins. During the diestrous and proestrous periods of the rat estrous cycle, the follicles are stimulated to produce sex steroid hormones in increasing concentrations (Blaustein, 2008). On the afternoon of proestrus, the pulse amplitude and pulse frequency of GnRH release, and subsequently the pulse amplitude and pulse frequency of LH and FSH release, increase. Under these conditions, negative feedback fails momentarily, and the follicles release a large surge of estrogen and, soon thereafter, a smaller surge of progesterone. The temporary removal of negative feedback occurs, at least in part, through the removal of GnIH (gonadotropin inhibitory hormone; see Chapter 2) inhibition of the reproductive axis at this time (Gibson et al., 2008; Russo et al., 2015). This preovulatory LH surge stimulates ovulation, reflecting the positive feedback feature of the hypothalamic-hypophyseal-gonadal control mechanism (see Figure 3.27). The elevated estrogen and progesterone blood concentrations also stimulate estrous behavior. Estrogen concentrations fall back to baseline rapidly, but the blood proges-

castration response   The increase in gonadotropin concentrations following removal of the gonads and consequent release from negative feedback effects of sex steroids.

terone concentration remains high for many hours if no mating occurs, or for many days if mating does occur. The elevated progesterone concentrations act eventually to terminate estrous behavior (Goy and Young, 1956/1957; Zucker, 1966, 1968).

The tonic release of GnRH throughout most of the estrous cycle is mediated by the medial basal hypothalamus, as it is in males (see Chapter 3). The release of increasingly higher pulses of GnRH is mediated by this so-called pulse generator. A neuronal pathway made up of neurons located in the anterior hypothalamus, preoptic area, and suprachiasmatic nucleus, as well as the arcuate nucleus, is involved in providing a daily signal for ovulation if the appropriate endocrine milieu is present. The master circadian clock in the suprachiasmatic nucleus (see Chapter 10) normally attempts to stimulate the GnRH system every afternoon to initiate the LH surge that stimulates ovulation (Legan and Karsch, 1975); that is why there are 4- or 5-day estrous cycles in rats, but no 4.5-day cycles. Experimental destruction of the suprachiasmatic nucleus or its output pathways eliminates the LH surge of most rodents, whereas temporary disruption of this daily signal through anesthestic suppression of neuronal activity on the afternoon of proestrus delays estrus for another 24 hours. Only when the daily signal for a large surge of GnRH is coincident with proestrus concentrations of estrogen will the positive feedback mechanism be engaged (Gibson et al., 2008; Silver and Kriegsfeld, 2006).Until relatively recently, the neural locus at which estrogen and circadian signaling were integrated to initiate the LH surge remained mysterious. With the discovery that kisspeptin cells were located in the anteroventral periventricular nucleus (AVPV), a brain region known to be critical for the LH surge in rats (Le et al., 1997), along with the fact that these cells expressed estrogen receptor (Smith et al., 2005), researchers began to explore whether kisspeptin cells might be the elusive integration site. Indeed, it was soon found that these kisspeptin cells are activated at the time of the LH surge (Robertson et al., 2009; Smith et al., 2011; Williams et al., 2011) and receive SCN input (Williams et al., 2011; Vida et al., 2010). The combined observations that AVPV kisspeptin cells express estrogen receptor, receive SCN input, and are activated concomitantly with GnRH/LH surge provide strong evidence that these cells integrate estrogenic and circadian signaling to time the LH surge and ovulation (**FIGURE 6.23B**).

Soon after ovulation, the negative feedback mechanism is restored, and low concentrations of GnRH, gonadotropins, and steroid hormones are secreted during early diestrus. The cycle resumes when pulses of GnRH stimulate brief pulses of gonadotropins, which stimulate follicular development anew. The 2 days of diestrus and 1 day of proestrus can be considered the follicular phase of the rat estrous cycle because follicular development occurs in anticipation of ovulation. Because the corpora lutea are not maintained after ovulation in unmated rats, there is no luteal phase. Thus, natural estrous behavior is the result of prolonged, high concentrations of estrogen followed by high concentrations of progesterone. Behavioral estrus can be induced in ovariectomized rats and guinea pigs with appropriately timed injections of estradiol and progesterone (Blaustein, 1996; Feder, 1981; Pfaff et al., 1994). In other species, such as Old World primates, a preovulatory GnRH and LH surge also occurs but is not necessary for ovulation.

Although the sequential *elevation* of estradiol (and other estrogens) and then progesterone is necessary to induce full estrous behavior in rats and guinea pigs, it is the sequential *presence* of estradiol and progesterone is necessary to induce estrus in sheep (Robinson, 1954). In other species, such as prairie voles (*Microtus ochrogaster*) and Siberian hamsters (*Phodopus sungorus*), progesterone is unnecessary for the expression of estrous behaviors (Carter et al., 1987; Wynne-Edwards et al., 1987). Female musk shrews (*Suncus murinus*) secrete testosterone from their ovaries around the time of ovulation. The testosterone enters the circulation and is aromatized to estradiol in neurons located in the preoptic area and in the hypothalamus. The intracellular interaction of estradiol with its receptors produces behavioral estrus (Rissman, 1991). Testosterone and other androgens have been shown to be

(A)

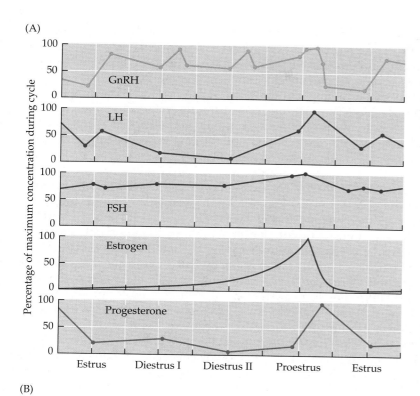

FIGURE 6.23 The ovarian cycle in rats (A) GnRH stimulates the secretion of LH and FSH, which cause a steady increase of estrogen until the afternoon of proestrus. Then the pulse amplitude and frequency of GnRH release increase, causing a rapid increase in LH and FSH concentrations and a corresponding surge of estrogen and progesterone that leads to ovulation and estrous behavior. Estrogen concentrations decline rapidly at vaginal estrus, but progesterone concentrations decline more gradually, especially if mating has occurred. (B) *Kiss1*-expressing neurons appear to mediate both positive and negative feedback effects of sex steroids on GnRH release. Kisspeptin increases GnRH release and consequently increases pituitary gonadotropins and sex steroid hormones. Sex steroids regulate *Kiss1* gene expression differently in the arcuate and anteroventral periventricular nuclei (AVPV). In the arcuate, sex steroids inhibit *Kiss1* expression, which in turn reduces kisspeptin input to the GnRH neurons and reduces GnRH and gonadotropin release in both sexes. However, in females, estrogens can stimulate *Kiss1* gene expression in the AVPV and thus increase kisspeptin stimulation of GnRH neurons, leading to increased gonadotropin release. A after Ganong, 2005; B redrawn from Popa et al., 2008.

(B)

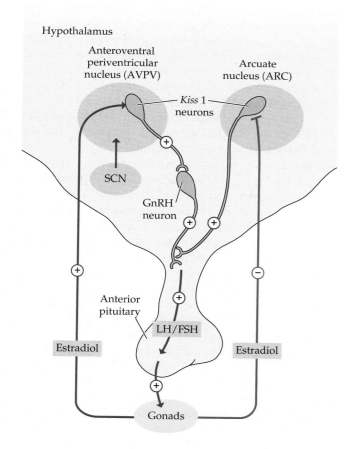

important in mediating female sexual behavior in several vertebrate species (Staub and De Beer, 1997). Thus, most female mammals require ovarian steroid hormones associated with ovulation to evoke behavioral estrus. However, the pattern of steroid hormone secretion is species-specific (Blaustein, 1996).

Estradiol provokes a doubling of lipocalin-type prostaglandin D synthase transcript levels (Mong et al., 2003a). The effects of estradiol on female sex behaviors in mice can be mimicked by reducing prostaglandin D synthase in the POA (Mong et al., 2003b), indicating that this molecule is important in the post–estrogen receptor pathway regulation of sexual behavior in rodents.

THE OVARIAN CYCLE IN PRIMATES The ovarian cycle of rhesus monkeys is virtually identical to that of humans (see Figure 6.22). In women and rhesus monkeys, only one follicle usually develops during each cycle. The corpus luteum is maintained after each ovulation (subtype 1.1B cycle in Table 6.2) and persists for about 14 days in a nonpregnant cycle. The endometrial lining of the uterine wall develops in anticipation of blastocyst implantation. If the ovulated ovum is not fertilized in the fallopian tube and there is no blastocyst to implant, the endometrial lining is shed, and menstrual bleeding occurs. The follicular phase is more variable among individuals, ranging between 10 and 20 days. Variation in menstrual cycle length is almost always due to variation in the length of the follicular phase.

If a female rhesus monkey has a 28-day cycle, then the following endocrine profile occurs (Knobil and Hotchkiss, 1988): Blood plasma concentrations of FSH and LH slowly increase for approximately 10 days following the end of menstrual bleeding. Under the stimulation of FSH, the primary ovarian follicle secretes estrogen. Estrogen (primarily estradiol) concentrations increase gradually during the first week after the onset of menstrual bleeding, then increase sharply during the following week. Estrogen concentrations display a periovulatory surge, which stimulates a surge of LH release and a lesser surge of FSH release from the anterior pituitary. The gonadotropin surge stimulates ovulation of the ripe ovum. After ovulation, plasma estrogen concentrations plummet to basal levels, and gonadotropin concentrations also diminish. As the corpus luteum begins to function, plasma concentrations of progesterone increase. In a nonpregnant cycle, the corpus luteum begins to regress, and progesterone concentrations fall back to baseline approximately 10–12 days after ovulation. The low progesterone concentrations evoke menstruation, and the cycle recurs. This cycle is similar to the human menstrual cycle.

Androgens seem to be critical in mediating sexual behavior in women. The source of androgens in females appears to be the ovaries and adrenal glands. Blood concentrations of these androgens fluctuate during the menstrual cycle. In a study that assayed plasma concentrations of free estradiol, testosterone, and progesterone at weekly intervals, it was discovered that only free testosterone correlated positively with sexual desire, sexual thoughts, and anticipation of sexual activity (Alexander and Sherwin, 1993). Treatment of surgically induced menopausal (ovariectomized) women with several steroid hormones in double-blind studies revealed that androgen treatment was most effective in restoring sexual desire (Sherwin, 1988a; Sherwin and Gelfand, 1987; Sherwin et al., 1985). These results are reminiscent of the effects of androgens on sexual motivation among hypogonadal men (see Chapter 5) (Davidson et al., 1979).

As in hypogonadal men, hormone concentrations above a certain threshold that maintains sexual behavior do not further increase the frequency of sexual behavior in ovariectomized women (Sherwin, 1988b). One study compared several aspects of sexual behavior in women using oral contraceptives and in nonusers (Alexander et al., 1990). Nonusers displayed higher blood plasma concentrations of testosterone than oral contraceptive users, and they also displayed perimenstrual decreases in plasma testosterone concentrations. This was associated with a reported drop in the level of sexual desire. There was no significant difference reported in the frequency of autosexual activities, but users of oral contraceptives reported more frequent and more satisfying sexual experiences than nonusers (Alexander et al., 1990). Of course, as described above, these results may reflect a relaxation of pregnancy fears rather than endocrine events. More recent studies suggest that although low-estrogen-dose contraceptive pills improve mood, they do not affect sexual desire (e.g., Graham et al., 2007; Greco et al., 2007). Taken together, these findings suggest that androgens induce sexual motivation, receptivity, and satisfaction in some women (Bancroft et al., 1991a,b; Sherwin and Gelfand, 1988). Clinical trials with androgens have convincingly demonstrated that pharmacological doses of testosterone increase libido in postmenopausal women. The long-term safety of such doses is unclear (Seagraves and Baron, 2003). Androgens appear to enhance receptive and proceptive behaviors in female rhesus monkeys as well (e.g., Everitt and Herbert, 1971; Herbert and Trimble, 1967; Wallen and Goy, 1977). As mentioned previously, whether androgenic or estrogen therapy is more effective at restoring libido in postmenopausal women is unclear. Likewise, the fact that libido is only increased in postmenopausal women by supraphysiological doses of androgens calls into question whether androgens mediate sexual arousal in women of reproductive age (Cappelletti and Wallen, 2016).

Much of the evidence linking androgens with sexual motivation in women is based on the correlation of the midcycle peak in testosterone and elevated sexual motivation. Estrogens and progesterone, as well as their ratio, change much more dramatically than testosterone across the menstrual cycle and have also been linked to changes in women's sexual motivation (e.g., Bullivant et al., 2004; Thornhill and Gangestad, 2008; Harvey 1987; Tarin and Gomez-Piquer, 2002; Wilcox et al., 2004). Although additional studies are needed to fully understand the importance of hormones in regulating women's sexual motivation, some surprising observations have been made so far. For instance, women and men do not differ in how much time they spend looking at photographs of naked women (Rupp and Wallen, 2008). What may also be surprising is that when eye-tracking studies were conducted on people watching either a pornographic or a nonpornographic movie, both women and men looked most frequently at the actress's face (Tsujimura et al., 2009). Men as well as women taking oral contraceptives rated images of genitalia as not particularly attractive (Renfro et al., 2015; Rupp and Wallen, 2009). The women using contraceptives looked less at the genitals, but their subjective ratings did not differ. These women also looked more at the contextual aspects of the pictures than did men or women not taking the Pill.

The fluctuating concentrations of gonadal, pituitary, and hypothalamic hormones in female mammals complicate somewhat the understanding of hormone-behavior interactions. Generally, slowly rising concentrations of estrogen seem necessary to prime mammalian females for the subsequent elevated progesterone concentrations that induce behavioral estrus. As the ratio of estrogen to progesterone in the blood is reversed, progesterone often acts to stop estrous behavior. The hormonal correlates of the estrous cycle of rodents and of the menstrual cycle of primates differ in a few important ways. Ovulation and peak estrogen concentrations roughly coincide in both rats and primates. However, rats display a periovulatory progesterone peak that is reduced or absent in primates. In rodents, and probably other nonprimate species, both sexual motivation and sexual performance are mediated by sex steroid hormones; copulation does not occur unless there are high blood concentrations of estrogen. In contrast, the ability to copulate is not linked to hormones in primates, but motivation to copulate appears to be linked to a periovulatory peak in androgen concentrations. The Neural Mechanisms Mediating Female Sexual Behavior section further below reviews how these fluctuating hormones affect neurons directly to change female behavior.

THE OVARIAN CYCLE IN EWES   Ewes (female sheep) are used as a model system for the study of reproduction for several reasons. First, due to their large size, it is possible to gather frequent blood samples from the hypophyseal portal system to gain insight into the specific pattern of gonadotropin pulse frequency and amplitude across the ovulatory cycle. By comparing patterns of gonadotropin secretion with neuroendocrine brain cell activity, insight can be gained into the neural control of reproduction. Additionally, ewes are seasonal breeders, allowing for an increased understanding of reproduction through examination of neuroendocrine differences between anovulatory and ovulatory animals during the nonbreeding and breeding seasons, respectively (see Chapter 10). Finally, due to their agricultural importance, there is significant interest in understanding ewe reproduction to maximize breeding and milk production.

As in rodents and primates, increasing estrogen during the follicular phase of the cycle inevitably leads to the LH surge and ovulation in sheep (Clarke et al., 1989; Moenter et al., 1991). Until the recent discovery of kisspeptin, the neural mechanisms responsible for triggering the GnRH system to initiate the LH surge remained enigmatic (Caraty et al., 2010). In ewes, the reproductive axis is restrained throughout most of the ovulatory cycle through negative feedback actions of estrogen and progesterone (Goodman and Karsch, 1980). As in other species, during the late follicular phase of the cycle, estrogen acts via positive feedback to drive the GnRH/LH surge that leads to ovulation (Clarke, 1987). The mediobasal hypothalamus (MBH) and POA have been implicated in estrogen negative and positive feedback, but, until recently, the cell phenotype on which estrogen acts was unknown (Smith, 2013).

In sheep, kisspeptin neurons located in the POA and arcuate nucleus (Arc) express estrogen receptors, providing a direct target for estrogen positive and negative feedback regulation (Franceschini et al., 2006). Across species, the majority of Arc kisspeptin cells coexpress the positive and negative regulators of the reproductive axis, neurokinin B (NKB) and dynorphin, respectively (Goodman et al., 2007; Lehman et al., 2010). These triple-phenotype neurons are now commonly referred to as KNDy, pronounced "candy" and denoting kisspeptin (K), NKB (N), and dynorphin (Dy) neurons (Lehman et al., 2010). KNDy neurons project upon GnRH neurons, providing a direct means of stimulation or inhibition, depending on the neurochemical released (i.e., kisspeptin, NKB, or dynorphin) (Lehman et al., 2010). KNDy neurons are reciprocally connected and express receptors for NKB and dynorphin, providing the ability to propagate stimulatory or inhibitory signaling (Lehman et al., 2010). KNDy neurons also express progesterone as well as estrogen receptors, providing a mechanism for mediating steroid negative feedback (Foradori et al., 2002; Smith et al., 2007). Estrogen negative feedback likely acts through reductions in *Kiss1* expression, whereas progesterone feedback is likely mediated through actions of dynorphin. Recent studies suggest that NKB-responsive neurons in the retrochiasmatic area of sheep act via KNDy cells to stimulate the LH surge (Grachev et al., 2016). Together, these results point to an important role for KNDy neurons in the ewe ovulatory cycle and further underscore the importance of the discovery of kisspeptin in advancing our understanding of the neuroendocrine control of reproduction.

Neural Mechanisms Mediating Female Sexual Behavior

Virtually everything that is known about the endocrine effects on neural tissue that mediate female sexual behavior has come from studies on the neural and endocrine control of lordosis in rats. As we have seen, lordosis is a receptive behavior, a sexual reflex observed in female rats. Estrogen and progesterone prime females for this behavior, and it occurs in response to tactile sensory information normally provided by a copulating male. Thus, sensory input is one aspect of the behavior on which hormones can be predicted to act (**FIGURE 6.24**).

FIGURE 6.24 Receptive fields in the flanks increase in size during estrus. By recording sensory nerves, the area of the skin that causes increased sensory nerve firing can be mapped during light tactile stimulation. (A) Relative size of the receptive field of a flank sensory neuron in an anestrous rat. (B) Relative size of a receptive field in an estrous rat. The receptive fields of the flank sensory neurons expand under the influence of estrogen.

(A)

(B)

How does sensory information get to the hypothalamus? Relevant sensory input enters the female rat's nervous system during mating via cutaneous receptors on the flanks, rump, and perineum. Information from the stimulated skin receptors and from pressure-responsive sensory neurons enters the spinal cord, where the motor neurons controlling the muscles involved in lordosis are located, and is sent to the medullary reticular formation (Pfaff and Schwartz-Giblin, 1988) (**FIGURE 6.25A**). This pathway to the brain stem is necessary, but not sufficient, for lordosis to occur.

Hormones can also be predicted to act on the central brain mechanisms integrating the endocrine, social, and environmental stimuli coincident with mating. Several brain sites mediate lordosis (**FIGURE 6.25B**). Researchers found that lesions of the ventromedial nucleus of the hypothalamus (VMN) or destruction of its afferent

(A) Sensory and motor pathways

(B) Brain regions

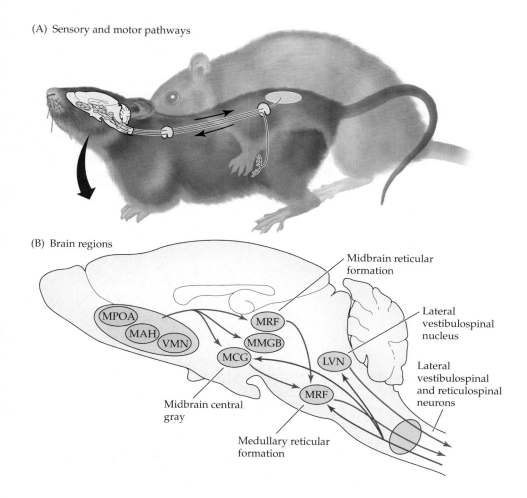

Midbrain reticular formation

Lateral vestibulospinal nucleus

Lateral vestibulospinal and reticulospinal neurons

MPOA

MAH

VMN

MRF

MMGB

MCG

LVN

MRF

Midbrain central gray

Medullary reticular formation

FIGURE 6.25 The neural basis of lordosis (A) Male mounting behavior causes activation of pressure receptors in the female's flanks; axons from these receptors form a sensory nerve that projects to the dorsal root ganglion of the spinal cord. From the spinal cord, the sensory signals travel to the medullary reticular formation in the hindbrain and the midbrain central gray area (lower arrow). When estrogen concentrations are high, various brain regions activate the spinal motor neurons innervating the deep back muscles (upper arrow), resulting in the characteristic postural changes of lordosis. (B) Brain regions activated by estrogen and involved in lordosis include the ventromedial nucleus of the hypothalamus (VMN), the medial preoptic area (MPOA), and the medial anterior hypothalamus (MAH). Signals from these regions reach the midbrain central gray, midbrain reticular formation, and medial geniculate body (MMGB); the midbrain reticular formation and MMGB ultimately activate the spinal motor neurons innervating the back muscles involved in lordosis behavior. After Pfaff et al., 1994.

and efferent fibers typically reduced the frequency of lordosis (Clark et al., 1981; Kennedy, 1964; Yamanouchi, 1980; but see Emery and Moss, 1984), demonstrating that the VMN is critical to the lordosis response. In order to map the neural circuit involved in lordosis, the incoming and outgoing fibers then had to be traced. Certain fibers leaving the VMN via a sweeping lateral posterior pathway were found to be necessary for lordosis, whereas other exiting fibers were less critical (Pfaff et al., 1994). The essential axons descend to the midbrain central gray region; lesions of this region were found to reduce lordosis (Sakuma and Pfaff, 1979). Destruction of the midbrain ascending ventral noradrenergic bundle (VNAB) completely abolished the appearance of lordosis (Hansen et al., 1980, 1981). Neurons in the midbrain central gray region project axons to the medullary reticular formation in the brain stem. This region of the hindbrain controls motor neurons for axial muscles, especially the deep back muscles, which are critical for lordosis (Pfaff and Schwartz-Giblin, 1988). The connection of this brain stem region with the descending fibers from the midbrain central gray region permits lordosis only when sex steroid hormones are available to neurons in the midbrain or to cells in the VMN. **FIGURE 6.26** is a detailed diagram of these neural circuits.

What is the mechanism of action of estrogens and progestins on these brain regions? The steroid hormone receptors found in the brain are chemically similar

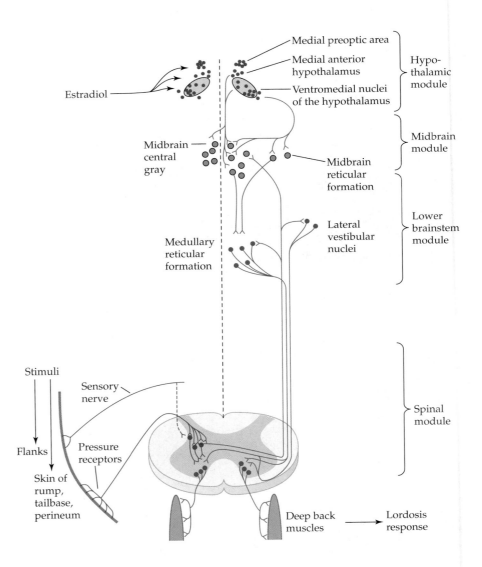

FIGURE 6.26 A detailed view of the neural circuitry mediating lordosis in rats. The neural circuits outlined in Figure 6.25, separated into structural and functional neural modules. After Pfaff et al., 1994.

to those found in the uterus. As described in Chapter 2, steroids can stimulate production of their own receptors as well as production of other steroid receptor types. Because all the steroid hormones are structurally similar, elevated estrogen concentrations can stimulate the production of both estrogen and progestin receptors in the cytosol of neurons throughout the nervous system. Thus, high concentrations of estradiol (injected by an experimenter, for example) can induce the production of progesterone receptors. Antisteroids—that is, substances that occupy steroid receptors without producing any biological effect—block the occurrence of lordosis (Blaustein and Olster, 1989; Delville and Blaustein, 1991; Pfaff, 1980; Pfaff et al., 1994). Additionally, high doses of estrogen alone can induce lordosis, although this effect is independent of progesterone receptors.

Cells that concentrate estradiol and progesterone have been discovered throughout the vertebrate brain. These target cells show virtually the same distribution regardless of taxon, and they correspond closely with the distribution of receptors for androgens (see Figure 5.21). The areas with the highest density of estradiol- and progesterone-concentrating cells are located in the forebrain, including the medial preoptic area, the anterior hypothalamus, and the ventromedial-ventrolateral hypothalamus, as well as the amygdala and midbrain central gray area (Blaustein, 1996; Pfaff and Conrad, 1978) (**FIGURE 6.27**). Many lesion studies and electrical stimulation studies have revealed that these regions are involved in the regulation of female sexual behavior.

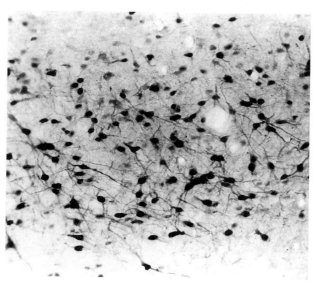

FIGURE 6.27 **Estrogen receptor immunoreactivity** shows that neurons in the hypothalamus have estrogen receptors (shown here with dark staining) in all parts of the cell (i.e., cytosol, nucleus, cellular processes). Courtesy of Jeffrey Blaustein.

There are hormone manipulations that can mimic the hormonal profile of natural estrus. One way to bring an ovariectomized mouse or hamster into estrus is to inject her with estradiol early one morning, then inject her with progesterone about 48 hours later. In about 6–8 hours, the female will display lordosis in response to the appropriate tactile stimulation. Behavioral estrus is observed approximately 4 hours after the progesterone injection. Another way to bring an ovariectomized rat into estrus is to implant under her skin a Silastic capsule of estradiol, which will secrete estradiol at a constant rate that varies with the length of the capsule. If the female is then injected with progesterone about 4–8 hours prior to her pairing with a male, estrous behavior will ensue when the male is present.

Several experiments have demonstrated that estrogens must prime the central nervous system for further estrogen and progesterone exposure in order for estrous behavior to be exhibited. Implants of crystalline estradiol into the VMN induce lordosis in ovariectomized rats (Barfield and Chen, 1977; Lisk, 1962), but this lordotic behavior is relatively weak and infrequent compared with that observed among female rats in natural estrus. However, if crystalline estradiol is implanted into the VMN and the animal is then injected systemically with progesterone (or if crystalline progesterone is implanted into the VMN and the animal is then injected systemically with estradiol), virtually all female rats display lordosis that resembles that observed in females in natural estrus (Rubin and Barfield, 1983). A variety of techniques, including microimplants of protein synthesis inhibitors, transcription inhibitors, and antiestrogens, have demonstrated that the VMN is critical for estradiol priming in rats (Blaustein and Olster, 1989). Thus, it can be concluded that estrogen treatment primes the central nervous system for subsequent treatment with estrogen or with estrogen and progestin (Parsons et al., 1979; Walker and Feder, 1977, 1979), in part through the induction of progesterone receptors (Parson et al., 1981). At least in guinea pigs, virtually all cells in the VMN that express progesterone receptors (PRs) also express ERα (α estrogen receptor) (Blaustein and Turcotte,

FIGURE 6.28   Estrogen priming induces progesterone receptor expression. Photomicrographs of PR immunoreactivity (right) and ERα immunoreactivity (left) coexpression in the VMH of an estradiol-primed, ovariectomized guinea pig show that virtually all estradiol-induced PR cells also coexpress ERα immunoreactivity. Arrowheads point to cells containing both estradiol-induced PR immunoreactivity and ERα immunoreactivity. From Blaustein and Turcotte, 1989.

ERα-immunoreactivity   PR-immunoreactivity

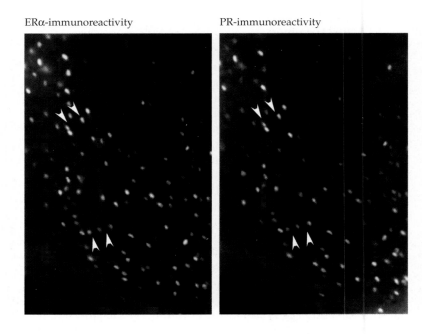

1989) (**FIGURE 6.28**). Estrogen priming requires about 24 hours unless doses are very high, in which case the first lordosis response occurs in about 18–20 hours. More recently, estrogen has been shown to have rapid effects via a membrane-bound receptor in addition to classic genomic actions (Watson et al., 2007). Estradiol acts on membrane-bound receptors in the VMN to enhance histaminergic (e.g., Dupré et al., 2010) and NMDA neuron depolarization, a process that allows genomic actions of estradiol to synergize with rapid estrogen signaling to facilitate the lordosis (Kow et al., 2016). As with sexual differentiation (see Chapter 3), epigenetic events initiated by estradiol act to alter chromatin structure in cells of the VMN, presumably to facilitate changes in gene transcription required for appropriate female sexual behavior, including lordosis (Gagnidze et al., 2013).

Progesterone facilitates estrus. Occupied progesterone receptors in relevant neurons mediate many of the behavioral effects of progesterone by serving as gene transcription factors (Blaustein, 1996). In many species, including rats and guinea pigs, progesterone initially facilitates estrous behavior, but eventually a refractory period occurs. In other species, especially reptiles, progesterone inhibits female receptive behavior (Godwin et al., 1996). The physiological explanation for the termination of estrous behavior is the down-regulation of progesterone receptors.

Once estrogen binds to nuclear receptors in the hypothalamus and elsewhere, the estrogen-receptor complex attaches to the nuclear DNA and serves as a gene transcription factor. Thus gene transcription and translation are either activated or, in some cases, decreased by estrogen treatment. Predictably, protein synthesis inhibitors block the effects of steroid hormones on estrous behavior. Over the course of the next few hours, estrogen causes electrophysiological changes in the pattern and frequency of firing rates of neurons in the VMN, especially in slow-firing neurons in this region (Pfaff and Schwartz-Giblin, 1988). Electron microscopy studies have revealed that estrogen binding and subsequent DNA transcription promote RNA synthesis. Growth-like processes occur in and around the VMN in response to estrogen treatment, which is consistent with the observed increases in RNA and structural protein synthesis after estrogen exposure. Conversely, treatment of the hypothalamus with protein synthesis inhibitors eliminates lordosis (Meisel and Pfaff, 1984). Thus electrophysiological and structural changes occur in the VMN in response to estrogen priming, and continued exposure to high estradiol or progesterone concentrations induces the expression of lordosis in response to appropriate sensory input. Furthermore, intermittent exposure to estrogens is sufficient to prime ovariectomized rats and guinea pigs to respond behaviorally to progestins (Clark and Roy, 1983; Olster and Blaustein, 1988).

Many neurotransmitters have been implicated in the neural mediation of hormone-induced estrous behavior. For example, there is evidence that norepinephrine, dopamine, acetylcholine, serotonin, and GABA (each acting through its own specific receptor subtypes), as well as GnRH, prolactin, oxytocin, and substance P, facilitate estrous behavior (Blaustein, 1996). Serotonin (acting through the 5-HT$_{1A}$ receptor), dopamine, β-endorphin, and corticotropin-releasing hormone (CRH) may inhibit lordosis. Interestingly, estrogen receptor binding in the medial preoptic area (MPOA) may inhibit lordosis and genetic suppression of estrogen receptor gene transcription facilitates lordosis behavior (Spiteri et al., 2012). The effects of hormones on estrous behavior likely reflect their effects on these and other neurotransmitters. Estradiol mediates many neurotransmitters that facilitate female sexual behavior (McCarthy and Pfaus, 1996); for example, estradiol evokes oxytocin and enkephalin gene expression and increases the numbers of many types of postsynaptic neurotransmitter receptors (Flanagan-Cato and Fluharty, 1997). However, no clear pattern of neurotransmitter and steroid hormone receptor co-localization has been found in the brain. That is, knowing that a particular neuron has estrogen or progestin receptors does not tell us the type of neurotransmitter used by the neuron in question. However, recent work suggests that there can be "cross talk" between certain neurotransmitters (e.g., dopamine) and steroid hormone receptors (e.g., progestin). A dopamine D1 receptor agonist, but not a dopamine D2 receptor agonist, mimicked the effects of progesterone in facilitating sexual behavior in female rats (Mani et al., 1995). If the rats were treated with a progesterone antagonist, then the facilitatory effects of dopamine were blocked. These results suggest that neurotransmitters may affect in vivo gene expression and behavior by means of cross talk with steroid hormone receptors in the brain (Mani, 2001, 2003; Mani et al., 1995).

Can these data from rats be helpful in increasing low sex drive in women? There appears to be an excitatory system that is involved in sexual motivation that is composed of the brain dopamine systems (both mesolimbic and incertohypothalamic) that link the limbic system with the hypothalamus (Pfaus, 2009). This excitatory system includes norepinephrine, oxytocin, and melanocortins. The inhibitory components of sexual motivation appear to involve brain serotonin, opioid, and endocannabinoid systems. Thus, drugs that activate hypothalamic dopamine or suppress endocannabinoids or serotonin may enhance sexual motivation in women as they do in rats (Pfaus, 2009).

In terms of nonhumans, two primary hypotheses regarding the role of estrogen in promoting lordosis have been proposed: the trigger hypothesis and the maintenance hypothesis (Pfaff et al., 1994). The trigger hypothesis states that one brief pulse of estrogen sets off a chain of events that continues to the end of the program with the display of lordosis (**BOX 6.4**). This hypothesis was generated in response to data indicating that a relatively brief exposure (approximately 30 minutes) to estrogen could result in lordosis (e.g., Bullock, 1970; Johnston and Davidson, 1979). However, the esterified estrogens used in these studies have relatively slow clearance rates and probably stayed in the blood and affected neural tissue for much longer than 30 minutes (Clemens and Weaver, 1985). The maintenance hypothesis contends that estrogen must be present continuously from the beginning of estrogen treatment throughout the behavioral test in order for lordosis to be displayed. However, tests using estradiol implants that could be inserted and removed rapidly revealed that two discontinuous exposures to estrogen could facilitate progesterone-evoked lordosis (Södersten et al., 1981). Researchers using a variety of temporal schedules of estradiol exposure reported that only 2 hours of total estrogen treatment were

BOX 6.4 *Nongenomic Behavioral Effects of Steroid Hormones*

Traditionally, the behavioral effects of steroid hormones have been assumed to be mediated via intracellular receptor-ligand interactions that ultimately affect gene transcription (Flanagan-Cato and Fluharty, 1997). However, an alternative mechanism of steroid action emerged in the mid-1990s (Moore and Orchinik, 1994). It was reported that corticosterone administration could rapidly interfere with mating behavior in a species of newt (*Taricha granulosa*) (Moore and Orchinik, 1994; Orchinik et al., 1991). Membrane-bound corticosterone receptors have been located in neuronal membrane fractions from these newts (Moore et al., 1995). The discovery of the membrane-bound steroid receptors and the rapidity of the response suggested that the genetic machinery could not have been engaged, and it was hypothesized that a nongenomic mechanism must mediate this rapid behavioral effect of steroid hormones.

Additional evidence of nongenomic effects of steroid hormones on behavior has been provided in mammals. For example, rapid onset of sexual receptivity can be induced in estrogen-primed female golden hamsters (*Mesocricetus auratus*) by providing progesterone that has been conjugated with a protein that presumably prevents the steroid from entering cells

and interacting with intracellular receptors (DeBold and Frye, 1994; Frye and Debold, 1993; Frye et al., 1992).

Other research has demonstrated that estradiol evokes rapid electrophysiological effects in the CA1 neurons of the hippocampus and that the rapid effects of estradiol on hippocampal neurons can be blocked through interference with protein kinase A or with G protein receptors (Gu and Moss, 1996; Wong and Moss, 1992; Wong et al., 1996). More recent studies have shown that progesterone and neurosteroids modulate lordosis by acting in the ventral tegmentum and ventromedial hypothalamus via nongenomic effects (Frye, 2001a,b; Frye and Petralia, 2003).

Steroid hormones also bind to the GABA receptor–chloride ion channel complex (Majewska et al., 1986), as well as other membrane-bound receptors (Ke and Ramirez, 1990), to affect neurotransmission (Becker, 1990). Taken together, these findings suggest that steroid hormones can affect behavior both through traditional genomic actions and via alternative membrane-bound receptors. It appears that both mechanisms could act in concert to increase or decrease the likelihood of a particular behavior in a specific context (Frye 2001a; Frye et al., 1996).

sufficient to increase progesterone receptor numbers in the hypothalamus, as well as to permit lordosis. The second estrogen treatment had to begin at least 4 hours after the end of the initial estrogen exposure but not more than 13 hours later (Parsons et al., 1982).

A cascade hypothesis has been proposed to explain the endocrine events underlying lordosis. According to this hypothesis, specific and discrete events occur within the neurons of the VMN as a result of initial estrogen-receptor binding, and these events are required for later estrogen-dependent events to occur. This hypothesis differs from the maintenance hypothesis because continuous estrogen receptor occupation is not required; rather, estrogen must occupy receptors at specific, critical times in order for lordosis to be expressed (Pfaff and Schwartz-Giblin, 1988). When the two-pulse experiment described above was replicated, it was found that anesthesia (Roy et al., 1985) or protein synthesis inhibition (Meisel and Pfaff, 1984; Roy et al., 1985) prior to either pulse of estrogen (Parsons et al., 1982) or between the two pulses interfered with the facilitation of lordosis. These results suggest that electrophysiological events (suppressed by anesthesia), new protein synthesis, and incoming sensory information are all critical components of a cascade of events that begins with the initial exposure to estrogen and ends with the onset of the lordosis response. The cascade hypothesis is reminiscent of the organizational/activational hypothesis presented in Chapter 3 to explain sex differences in neural function. Recall that sex steroid hormones organize neural structures perinatally in a masculine or feminine pattern and that subsequent postpubertal hormonal stimulation activates these previously organized neural circuits, resulting in sexually differentiated behaviors. The cascade hypothesis is fundamentally the same as the organizational/activational hypothesis. There is a much shorter time course between the organizing effects of the initial estrogen exposure—during late diestrus II in the rat—and the activating effects of estrogen and progestin during late proestrus, but the principles are the same. Many of the early events associated with estrogen action likely involve membrane-initiated estrogen signaling, because they can be induced with estradiol bound to molecules that cannot cross the cell membrane and prime the system for slower genomic actions of estrogens (e.g., Vasudevan et al., 2001). The cascade hypothesis, along with the wonderfully detailed data on cellular and subcellular mechanisms now available (Pfaff et al., 1994), suggests that the organizational/activational principles proposed in 1959 may be the fundamental principles underlying all hormone-behavior interactions.

Gene Knockouts

As noted in previous chapters, studies of mice that have had specific genes deleted (knocked out) can be very useful in analyzing hormone-behavior interactions. In most cases studied, production of progesterone receptors is induced when estradiol interacts with estrogen receptors. Thus, many of the effects of progesterone on reproductive physiology and behavior could actually be due to a combination of progestins and estrogens. To separate out the effects of these two steroids, a strain of mice was generated that lacked functional progesterone receptors (PRs) (Lydon et al., 1996). Both male and female PR gene knockout (PRKO) mice (with genotype PR−/−) develop to adulthood; males are fertile, but females are sterile. Female PR−/− mice display uterine hyperplasia and minimal mammary gland development, and they are anovulatory even when stimulated with exogenous gonadotropins (Lydon et al., 1996; Mani et al., 1997). When ovariectomized, neither PR−/− mice nor wild-type (PR+/+) mice displayed lordosis after treatment with estradiol. Treatment with progesterone induced lordosis in virtually all of the estrogen-primed PR+/+ mice tested but in none of the PR−/− females (Lydon et al., 1996) (**FIGURE 6.29**). These results with PRKO mice support previous work in which lordosis could not be elicited in estrogen-primed rats that received infusions of progesterone receptor antisense oligonucleotides into the VMN (Ogawa et al., 1994).

Knockout mice have also been developed for both α and β subtypes of estrogen receptors (Lubahn et al., 1993; Ogawa et al., 1996a,b; Rissman et al., 1997a; Tetel and Pfaff, 2010). When female α estrogen receptor gene knockout (αERKO) mice and wild-type (WT) mice were ovariectomized, then given equivalent doses of 17β-estradiol, only the WT mice displayed lordosis when tested with a wild-type male in a neutral arena (Rissman et al., 1997a). Progesterone treatment did not facilitate lordosis in αERKO females (Rissman et al., 1997b). When these αERKO females were given foster pups, induction of maternal behavior was also impaired (Ogawa et al., 1996a).

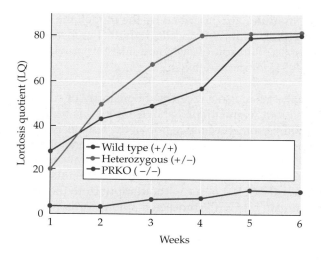

FIGURE 6.29 Lordosis does not occur in progesterone receptor knockout (PRKO) mice. Treatment with progesterone after estrogen priming induced lordosis in virtually all of the estrogen-primed wild-type progesterone receptor (PR+/+) female mice tested but in none of the progesterone receptor knockout (PR−/−) females. After Lydon et al., 1996.

In a neutral mating arena, males mounted both αERKO and WT females, suggesting that mice of both genotypes were attractive to males. When tested in a three-chamber preference apparatus, males spent equivalent amounts of time with αERKO and WT females (Rissman et al., 1997b). When the conditions under which the female αERKO mice were tested were changed, however, a different pattern of results emerged (Ogawa et al., 1996a,b). When ovary-intact αERKO mice were placed in the males' home cages, some lordosis was observed. However, males often responded with aggressive attacks against the αERKO females (suggesting that the αERKO females were not particularly attractive to them). Males responded to male intruders into their home cages with similar aggressiveness but never responded to WT females in this manner.

Taken together, the results of these behavioral analyses of steroid receptor knockout mice suggest that the presence of a functional estrogen receptor is necessary for female-typical reproductive behavior. Both estrogen receptor subtypes, ERα and ERβ, which bind to estradiol with similar affinity, have been identified in numerous sites in the brain (Mitra et al., 2003; McDevitt et al., 2008; Shughrue et al., 1997). For example, both receptor subtypes are present in the arcuate nucleus and the POA, whereas ERα is present in the VMN and ERβ in the paraventricular nuclei. These regions in and around the hypothalamus are important in sexual behavior, thermoregulation, and feeding behavior. Both estrogen receptor subtypes also are present in the amygdala and hippocampus, where they may mediate short-term memory and emotional responses. ERβ has also been identified in the cerebellum and in cortical regions (Mitra et al., 2003). The α estrogen receptor seems critical for mediating lordosis. Female mice missing both estrogen receptor subtypes (αβERKO mice), like αERKO mice, failed to display lordosis after appropriate hormonal priming (Kudwa and Rissman, 2003). Female βERKO mice, however, displayed lordosis to the same extent as WT female mice (Kudwa and Rissman, 2003).

A Neural Model of Lordosis

Despite its inherent complexity, the neural regulation of lordosis has been modeled (Pfaff and Schwartz-Giblin, 1988; Pfaff et al., 2008), and a summary of all the components contributing to the regulation of lordosis will be provided in this section. The comprehensive and extraordinarily detailed model developed by Pfaff and colleagues is based on the idea that several neural modules (specific subsections of the nervous system) function together to mediate the lordosis response. This model should be celebrated as the first complete circuitry map of a mammalian hormone-behavior interaction. Pfaff and colleagues mapped the sensory input, central integration, and effector pathways involved in lordosis and documented their interactions with hormones. Five modules are described by the model: the spinal cord module, lower brain stem module, midbrain module, hypothalamic module, and forebrain module. A brief synopsis of the role of each module is provided below (**FIGURE 6.30**; refer to Pfaff et al. [1994] for more details).

SPINAL CORD MODULE   The spinal cord module receives the majority of somatosensory information during copulation. As mentioned above, lordosis is triggered by sensory input from the rump, flanks, and perianal region of the female. In addition to initially processing the sensory input, the spinal cord module generates the motor neuronal output that results in lordosis. Although the behavioral program of sensory input and motor output is located in the spinal cord, female rats differ from males in that the sexual response will not occur without input from the brain (Meisel and Sachs, 1994). Thus, female rats with transected spinal cords will not display lordosis.

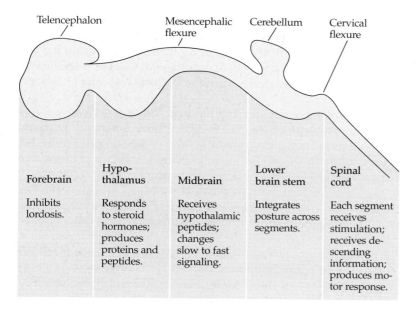

FIGURE 6.30 Five neural modules that mediate lordosis. The components of the nervous system that mediate lordosis in rats can be separated into five modules. The forebrain normally inhibits lordosis, but estrogen plus tactile stimulation disinhibits the behavior, as do lesions of the forebrain. Nuclei of the hypothalamus are either inhibited (the MPOA) or activated (the VMN) by estrogens and produce proteins and other peptidergic hormones that interact with the midbrain, which serves to transduce these relatively slow endocrine changes into fast neural signals. The lower brain stem is critical for the postural changes involved in lordosis, and the spinal cord is responsible for moving sensory information associated with male mounting behavior to the brain and bringing motor signals from the brain to the deep back muscles that directly cause lordosis. After Pfaff et al., 1994.

LOWER BRAIN STEM MODULE   Integration of information about posture and moment-to-moment corrections to posture are mediated in the lower brain stem module. Input from the vestibular organs and from proprioceptors throughout the body is necessary for maintaining a rigid posture and making corrections to maintain the weight of the mounting male.

MIDBRAIN MODULE   The midbrain module receives input from the hypothalamus and elsewhere in the brain, and it translates and integrates these signals to mediate firing rates in the reticulospinal neurons in the lower brain stem module. Peptides are transmitted from the hypothalamus to the central gray region of the midbrain module, where these typically slow neuroendocrine signals (on the order of hours) are transduced to neural signals. If the midbrain module is not activated by peptidergic information from the hypothalamus and by steroid hormones, lordosis will not occur. Lordosis is steroid-dependent, and it is the midbrain module and, even more extensively, the hypothalamic module where the action of steroids is critical.

HYPOTHALAMIC MODULE   The effects of estradiol and progesterone on the electrophysiological properties of neurons, RNA transcription, and the synthesis of new structural and other proteins are primarily mediated in the hypothalamic module. Components of this module are either inhibited (the MPOA) or activated (the VMN) by estrogens.

FOREBRAIN MODULE   The forebrain module exerts primarily inhibitory effects on lordosis. Large frontal cortical lesions, as well as lesions to the olfactory bulbs or septum, facilitate lordosis. In the presence of estrogen, tactile stimulation disinhibits lordosis behavior.

According to this model, sex steroid hormones, as well as several peptide hormones, including GnRH, prolactin, β-endorphin, and substance P, modulate lordosis by acting on one or more of the neural modules during normal or experimentally induced estrus. When females with estrogen concentrations insufficient to evoke lordosis by themselves are primed with GnRH, prolactin, or substance P, lordosis results. GnRH is transported to the midbrain central gray region along axons from the medial basal hypothalamus and, in the presence of estrogen, stimulates excitatory responses in central gray neurons (Moss and McCann, 1973). Experimental treatment with GnRH antibody in the central gray region caused reductions in the lordosis response in rats (Sakuma and Pfaff, 1980). Application of CRH or β-endorphin to the central gray region also led to a decrease in the lordosis response (Pfaff and Schwartz-Giblin, 1988).

In contrast to the comprehensive model that has been developed for receptive behavior, the neural loci mediating proceptive behavior have been only partially identified. Because lordosis is such a prominent feature of female rat mating behavior, the vast majority of brain lesion studies and hormone implant studies have used the presence or absence of lordosis as a behavioral assay in much the same way that mounting and intromission have been employed in studies of the neural bases of male copulatory behavior. However, during the course of behavioral analyses of brain-altered females, changes in proceptive behaviors have occasionally been reported (Erskine, 1989).

As described above, implants of estradiol alone into the VMN induced lordosis in ovariectomized rats, but at a low frequency. Proceptive behaviors were never observed during mating tests under these conditions (Rubin and Barfield, 1983). However, a full complement of proceptive behaviors, including hopping, darting, and ear wiggling, was observed among estrogen-injected ovariectomized female rats that received progesterone brain implants into the VMN; it was not observed in those that received implants into the POA, midbrain central gray region, hippocampus, or medullary reticular formation (Rubin and Barfield, 1983). Infusions of progesterone into the VMN facilitated lordosis in less than 2 hours, suggesting that changes in electrophysiological parameters, rather than structural changes or protein synthesis, mediate the effects of progesterone (Glaser et al., 1983; McGinnis et al., 1981). The VMN is involved in the mediation of female sexual behavior across a wide range of taxa, including parthenogenetic whiptail lizards (*Cnemidophorus uniparens*) (see Chapter 5) (Kendrick et al., 1993).

Lesions of the VMN, or destruction of the afferent and efferent VMN fibers, typically reduce the frequency of lordosis. Proceptive behaviors also appear to be affected by VMN lesions. As described above, projections from the VMN to the midbrain are important parts of the neural circuitry mediating lordosis (Kow and Pfaff, 1998). However, the midbrain appears to be less involved in the mediation of proceptive behaviors (Erskine, 1989). In fact, proceptive behaviors remain intact, or in some instances are enhanced, after destruction of the ascending VNAB, a procedure that completely abolishes lordosis (Hansen et al., 1980, 1981). Thus, different brain regions may mediate receptive and proceptive behaviors. This possibility suggests that different neural substrates underlie sexual motivation and sexual performance in both males and females.

Neural Mechanisms Underlying Primate Sexual Behaviors

The brain mechanisms underlying primate sexual motivation and performance appear to be similar to those in rodents (Pfaus et al., 2003). For example, lesions of the anterior hypothalamus of estrogen-treated common marmosets (*Callithrix jacchus*), which extended to varying degrees into the medial hypothalamus, virtually abolished proceptive tongue-flicking and staring displays. Tongue flicking during copulation also decreased, but the females did not increase the number of mounts that they refused or terminated, with the exception of one animal that had received more extensive damage to the medial hypothalamus (Kendrick and Dixson, 1986). These results suggest a neuroanatomical distinction between hypothalamic mechanisms that regulate proceptivity and those involved in receptivity in primates.

To determine the neural mechanisms underlying sexual behavior in female monkeys, single-neuron activity in the ventromedial hypothalamus (VMH) and the MPOA was recorded during sexual interactions with a male partner (Aou et al., 1988). Proceptive presentation behavior with no mating evoked activity changes in about 40% of neurons tested in the VMH (mainly excitation) and MPOA (mainly inhibition). When the male's mating acts occurred, about 50% of VMH cells and about 90% of MPOA cells changed firing rates during presentation behavior; MPOA cells significantly increased excitatory firing rates. As copulation progressed, activity in about 40% of VMH and 70% of MPOA cells was observed. These findings suggest that the VMH and MPOA regulate primate sexual behavior in different ways: excitation of the VMH and inhibition of the MPOA are related to presentation behavior (proceptive behavior), whereas excitation of the MPOA is related to copulation with a male partner (receptive behavior). Furthermore, they suggest that the sexual behavior of a male partner modulates activity in both VMH and MPOA neurons of the female (Aou et al., 1988).

In women, recent work has examined the neural correlates of orgasm. As of yet, no definitive explanation for what triggers orgasm has emerged. The first studies of brain imaging (PET, coupled with MRI) during orgasm in women were reported in 2002 (Whipple and Komisaruk, 2002; Komisaruk et al., 2002). Increased brain activation during orgasm, compared with that during pre-orgasm sexual arousal, was noted in the following brain regions: paraventricular nucleus of the hypothalamus, periaqueductal gray region of the midbrain, hippocampus, and cerebellum (Whipple and Komisaruk, 2002). Further studies that compare brain areas activated by orgasm with those activated during sexual arousal without orgasm are needed to assess whether there are specific brain regions responsible for triggering orgasm in women (Meston et al., 2004). Research on hormonal correlates of orgasm reveals some surprising details. Testosterone is positively correlated with women's reports of relaxing and peaceful orgasm experiences, rather than more intense sexual pleasure as might be expected. In contrast, estradiol is positively correlated with reports of the physical sensations of orgasms (e.g., "flooding" or "spreading"). These correlations are consistent with previous findings; that is, testosterone is linked to psychological or motivational sexual states, whereas estradiol is linked to the physical aspect of sexual responses (van Anders and Dunn, 2009).

In terms of sexual motivation, women are generally less interested in and responsive to visual sexually arousing stimuli than are men (Rupp and Wallen, 2009). Functional MRI revealed that the amygdala and hypothalamus were less strongly activated in women than in men viewing identical sexual stimuli (**FIGURE 6.31**). These results were the same even when women reported greater arousal than men (Hamann et al., 2004). Men and women showed similar activation patterns across several other brain regions, including ventral striatal regions involved in reward. These experimental results suggest that the amygdala mediates sex differences in responsiveness to appetitive and biologically salient stimuli; the human amygdala may also mediate the reportedly greater role of visual stimuli in male sexual behavior, paralleling prior animal findings. One can also gain insight into the neural mechanisms underlying female sexual motivation by examining neural

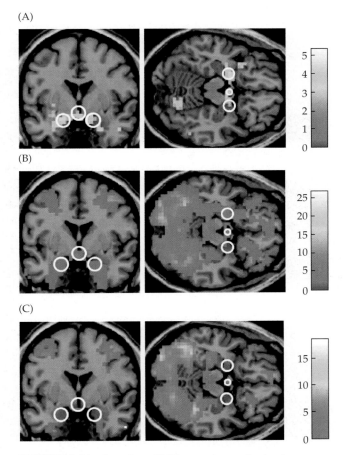

FIGURE 6.31 Functional MRI reveals greater brain activation in the amygdala and hypothalamus in men than women. Regional activation maps indicate the brain activation contrasts between men and women exposed to visual erotic stimuli involving couples (B and C) as compared with fixation contrast (A). Left panels show a coronal image; right panels give an axial view showing additional right cerebellar activation. White circles approximate the regions of interest. There is higher bilateral amygdala and hypothalamic activation for males (B) than females (C). From Hamann et al., 2004.

activity differences in women diagnosed with hypoactive sexual desire disorder (HSDD) versus controls. Women diagnosed with HSDD exhibit lower activation in brain areas involved in the processing of erotic stimuli, including intraparietal sulcus, dorsal anterior cingulate gyrus, and ento-/perirhinal region. In addition, HSDD participants exhibit higher activation in brain areas associated with higher-order social and cognitive functions, such as inferior parietal lobule, inferior frontal gyrus, and posterior medial occipital gyrus (Bianchi-Demicheli et al., 2011). These findings show that the brain areas involved in processing erotic stimuli are hypoactive in HSDD as one might expect, but HSDD might be potentiated by hyperactivity in brain regions that lead to altered cognitive processing of such stimuli.

To summarize, hormones affect female sexual behavior by affecting the input, central integration, and output functions of the central nervous system. Estrogens affect sensory input by increasing the receptive field size in sensory cells (Kow et al., 1979). Estrogens affect protein synthesis, the electrophysiological responses of neurons, and the appearance of growth-like processes on neurons (Pfaff and Schwartz-Giblin, 1988). Finally, estrogens affect the muscular output that results in lordosis in rodents, as well as chemosensory stimuli important in attracting a mating partner (Beach and Gilmore, 1949).

Summary

1. Copulatory behavior in nonprimate females usually coincides with ovulation. In females that ovulate periodically and whose copulatory behavior is observed in cycles, those cycles are called estrous cycles and females are said to be in estrus when they permit copulation.

2. Female sexual behavior has been the subject of formal study for much less time than male sexual behavior. Despite this disparity, much is known about the mechanisms underlying the hormone-behavior interactions involved in the regulation of female copulatory behavior in rodents. Ovariectomy consistently results in decreased sexual behavior in females from all vertebrate taxa.

3. Cyclic changes in vaginal cytology have been correlated with changes in ovarian structure and subsequently with behavior. In rats, the vaginal estrous cycle consists of 2 or 3 days of diestrus followed by a proestrous phase of 12–18 hours and then an estrous period of 24–36 hours. Behavioral estrus and mating occur near the end of proestrus and end as the vaginal smear becomes estrous. Ovulation occurs near the beginning of vaginal estrus.

4. Mating behavior coincides with the presence of a Graafian follicle; chemical extraction of this ovarian structure led to the discovery of the estrogen class of steroids. Mating behavior often stops with the onset of activity of the corpora lutea; chemical extraction of these ovarian structures led to the discovery of progesterone. Replacement studies using these steroids on ovariectomized animals demonstrated that estrogens and progesterone were required for mating behavior in guinea pigs, mice, rats, and many other species. In most species, in order to stimulate behavioral estrus, ovariectomized individuals had to be "primed" with estradiol, an estrogen, for about 24 hours, then progesterone had to be provided 4–8 hours prior to the display of the behavior. This injection paradigm mimicked closely the endocrine environment of natural estrus.

5. Females of most vertebrate taxa display species-specific mating postures. In rodents, the characteristic mating posture is called lordosis. Females in lordosis arch their backs, deflect their tails, and remain immobile to allow male intromission. Female dogs, cats, and many other mammalian species deflect the tail

and display a virtually rigid mating posture. With the notable exception of rhesus monkeys, primates typically do not display stereotypical mating postures.

6. Females have historically been portrayed as passive recipients of male sexual attention. However, in many species, especially primates, females initiate virtually all sexual interactions. In an attempt to reduce variation in behavioral tests, researchers have traditionally studied female copulatory behavior in single-pair tests. In this context, females appear rather passive. However, when they are tested in social groups that simulate natural conditions, females' initiation and control of copulatory activities become evident.

7. Female sexual behavior can be divided into three components: (1) attractivity, (2) proceptivity, and (3) receptivity. Attractivity is the stimulus value of the female for a given male. Proceptivity is the extent to which females initiate copulation; it reflects overt behavior as well as the underlying motivational state. Receptivity reflects the stimulus value of the female for eliciting an intravaginal ejaculation from a male conspecific; in other words, receptivity is the state of responsiveness to the sexual behaviors of another individual. Proceptivity and receptivity overlap conceptually, as well as in practice. Generally, estrogens enhance attractivity, proceptivity, and receptivity, and progestins reduce these parameters. Female receptivity and control of copulation vary among species; some females copulate even when not in estrus, and others reject certain males even when in estrus. Pacing of copulatory behavior by female rats has important physiological consequences for induction of corpora luteal function and subsequent maintenance of pregnancy.

8. Female reproductive cycles have been categorized into three basic types. In type 1 cycles, ovulation and pseudopregnancy are spontaneous. Humans and other primates display type 1 cycles. In type 2 cycles, ovulation is induced by copulation or other vaginal stimulation, but pseudopregnancy is spontaneous. Cats and ferrets display type 2 ovarian cycles. Both ovulation and corpora luteal formation are spontaneous in animals with type 3 cycles, but pseudopregnancy is induced via the release of prolactin following copulation. Mammals with type 3 cycles do not have functional luteal phases in nonpregnant cycles. Rats, mice, and hamsters have type 3 ovarian cycles.

9. Reproductive cycles have evolved so as to maximize reproductive output, and thus they vary with the ecology of the species. Repeated estrous cycles are laboratory artifacts and occur infrequently in free-ranging mammals. Females in nature are typically pregnant, lactating, or in seasonal diestrus. Most pregnancies in nature are the result of mating during postpartum estrus.

10. Reproductive cycles can be influenced by a number of social and environmental factors. Four examples of social effects on murine estrous cycles are the Lee-Boot, Whitten, Bruce, and Vandenbergh effects. The Lee-Boot effect is the interruption of regular estrous cycles in mice by prolonged diestrous periods when females are housed in groups. The Whitten effect involves two different effects of conspecific females on one another: estrus induction and synchronization, and suppression of estrus. The ability of a strange male to interrupt pregnancy and cause a return to estrus is the basis of the Bruce effect. The Vandenbergh effect reflects the retardation of first estrus in female mice housed in the presence of adult females and the acceleration of first estrus in female mice housed with adult males. All of these effects on estrus are mediated by chemosensory factors.

11. The effects of social factors on ovarian cycles are not limited to rodents. Women who live together for extended periods of time also may synchronize their menstrual cycles.

12. Ovulation and peak estradiol concentrations coincide in both rats and primates. However, rats exhibit a periovulatory peak in progesterone that is reduced or absent in primates. Primates of many species, including humans, often display periovulatory peaks in androgen concentrations. Motivation to copulate appears to coincide with blood concentrations of androgens in primates.

13. Several brain sites are necessary for lordosis. Lesions of the ventromedial nucleus of the hypothalamus (VMN) or destruction of afferent and efferent VMN fibers reduces the frequency of lordosis. Lesions of the central gray region also reduce lordosis behavior. Destruction of the midbrain ascending ventral noradrenergic bundle (VNAB) completely abolishes lordosis. The medullary reticular formation in the brain stem controls motor neurons innervating axial muscles, especially the deep back muscles that are critical for lordosis.

14. Sensory input enters the female rat's nervous system during mating via cutaneous receptors on the flanks, rump, and perineum. Information from these skin receptors and from pressure-responsive neurons enters the spinal cord and is sent to the medullary reticular formation. Interaction of these ascending sensory messages with descending fibers from the midbrain central gray region, which carries information from the VMN, permits lordosis only when sex steroid hormones are available to cells in the central gray region and to cells in the VMN.

15. Estrogen promotes estrogen and progesterone receptor formation in the VMN, as well as stimulating RNA transcription, protein synthesis, electrophysiological changes in neurons, and delivery of peptides to the midbrain central gray region. According to the cascade hypothesis, estrogen induces these changes over several hours, or "primes the nervous system" for subsequent estrogenic facilitation of lordosis. The cascade hypothesis is similar to the organizational/activational model of sexual differentiation; hormones affect subsequent behavior by causing structural changes prior to evoking electrophysiological or other fast-acting changes.

16. A comprehensive model of the regulation of lordosis has been proposed, based on five neural modules (specific subsections of the nervous system)—namely, the spinal cord module, the lower brain stem module, the midbrain module, the hypothalamic module, and the forebrain module—that function together to mediate the lordosis response. Sex steroid hormones, as well as several peptide hormones, modulate lordosis behavior by acting on one or more of these neural modules.

17. The neural and endocrine bases of proceptive behaviors are different from those of lordosis, a receptive behavior. Males and females are similar in that sexual motivation and sexual performance are organized separately in the nervous system.

Questions for Discussion

1. Discuss the proposition that a female mammal can be sexually receptive without being sexually attractive. Also provide examples of a female that is attractive but not receptive. Would such observations negate a role for hormones in the mediation of attractivity and receptivity?

2. Document the following assertion: Hormones play a lesser role in mediating sexual behavior in female primates than in female rodents. Is it reasonable to state that the sexual behavior of women is unaffected by sex steroid hormones?

3. Why might estrogen and progesterone have been co-opted over evolutionary time to drive sexual motivation in rodents while estrogen alone enhances sexual motivation in higher primates?

4. Discuss the implications of the following quote in terms of the study of female sexual behavior: "It is an unfortunate accident that studies of reproductive physiology and behavior have been limited to a few domesticated species because our conceptual limits in the understanding of the regulation of female reproductive processes have become compressed and distorted" (Beach, 1978).

5. Given what you know about the ovulatory cycle of rodents, how might a dependence of the LH surge on high concentrations of estrogen and circadian (daily) signaling act to maximize female reproductive success?

6. Some clinicians and researchers are convinced that testosterone is the female equivalent of Viagra. What assumptions are built into the search for a female Viagra and the possibility that testosterone is it? What is the research that might support this?

Suggested Readings

Beach, F. A. 1976. Sexual attractivity, proceptivity, and receptivity in female mammals. *Horm. Behav.*, 7:105–138.

Blaustein, J. D. 2008. Feminine reproductive behavior and physiology in rodents: Integration of hormonal, behavioral, and environmental influences. In D. Pfaff, et al. (eds.), *Hormones, Brain and Behavior* (2nd ed.), pp. 67–107. Academic Press, New York.

Cappelletti, M., and Wallen, K. 2016. Increasing women's sexual desire: The comparative effectiveness of estrogens and androgens. *Horm. Behav.*, 78:178–193.

Clayton, A. H. 2008. Epidemiology and neurobiology of female sexual dysfunction. *J. Sex. Med.*, 4:260–268.

Pfaff, D. W. 1999. *Drive: Neurobiological and Molecular Mechanisms of Sexual Motivation*. MIT Press, Cambridge, MA.

Pfaff, D. W., et al. 2008. Reverse engineering the lordosis behavior circuit. *Horm. Behav.*, 54:347–354.

Pfaus, J. G, et al. 2015. Female sexual behavior. In T. M. Plant, et al. (eds.), *Knobil and Neill's Physiology of Reproduction* (4th ed.), pp. 2287–2370. Academic Press, New York.

Vasudevan, N., and Pfaff, D. W. 2008. Non-genomic actions of estrogens and their interaction with genomic actions in the brain. *Front. Neuroendocrinol.*, 29:238–257.

Parental Behavior

7

Learning Objectives

This chapter provides an overview of the neuroendocrine mechanisms responsible for maternal and paternal behavior in vertebrates. The chapter begins by considering parental investment and style based on the developmental state of offspring at birth and their growth trajectory. The chapter continues with a review of the hormones and neural mechanisms underlying parental care in birds and mammals. After reading this chapter, you should be able to:

- explain why *paternal behavior* is common in birds and relatively rare among mammals.

- outline the hormones and neurochemical systems responsible for parental behavior in birds and mammals.

- differentiate the requirements for the onset of *maternal behavior* in mammals from the requirements for its maintenance.

- elucidate some challenges to gaining insights into the mechanisms underlying human and higher primate maternal behavior.

In the autumn of 1996, a 3-year-old boy climbed over the retaining wall around the gorilla exhibit at the Brookfield Zoo in Illinois and fell 6 meters into the enclosure. As the other gorillas approached the semiconscious child, an 8-year-old female western lowland gorilla named Binti Jua (Swahili for "daughter of sunshine") growled at her cohorts, who backed away, and she picked up the boy (FIGURE 7.1). She gently carried the boy to the back of the enclosure, where the zookeepers could retrieve him and get him to medical care, where he quickly recovered. During the dramatic rescue, the lactating Binti Jua had her own 17-month-old baby, Koola, clinging to her back.

(A)

FIGURE 7.1 Different outcomes from similar zoo incidents; maternal care across species. (A) Binti Jua, an 8-year-old female gorilla, is shown in an image from television rescuing a toddler who fell into the primate exhibit on August 16, 1996, at Brookfield Zoo in Brookfield, IL. (B) Harambe, a 17-year-old male gorilla at the Cincinnati Zoo was filmed after a boy sneaked into his enclosure. He is seen aggressively dragging the boy through the water of the moat in the middle panel.

(B)

This incident is in stark contrast to a more recent event at the Cincinnati Zoo that occurred a few months before this book went to press. In the spring of 2016, a 3-year-old boy slipped into the enclosure of a 17-year-old male western lowland gorilla named Harambe. While his mother was distracted, the boy went under a rail, through wires, and over a moat wall to get into the enclosure. The gorilla roughly dragged the boy through water while the onlookers cried out and zookeepers were quickly deciding how to rescue the child from the 450-pound animal. The zookeepers inevitably made the painstaking decision to shoot and kill the gorilla rather than risk tranquilizing him, a process that could be slow and dangerous. Although injured, the child survived. But, following the event, there was public outcry over the death of Harambe and the assumed irresponsibility of the child's mother. Most experts on gorilla behavior agreed that the correct decision was made by the zoo, and no charges were filed against the child's mother.

Why did the two events lead to such radically different outcomes? The former story demonstrates the two, seemingly opposite, features of parental care that promote offspring survival: gentle caregiving and aggressive behavior. The latter incident, unfortunately, involved a nonparental, dominant male. It is common for parents of many species to become protective of their young. Indeed, pet owners are often surprised by the aggressive behavior of their formerly docile dogs or cats if their owners get too close to puppies or kittens. This form of parental aggression can be surprising and dangerous to unsuspecting pet owners or hikers who inadvertently come between wild animals and their young. Protection from harm; provision of food, water, and warmth; and instruction for successful adult competition are all part of parental care. Indeed, Binti Jua had been hand-reared at the San Francisco Zoo. Hand-reared primates often fail to show good parental care as adults; therefore, Binti Jua had been sent to Chicago to learn how to be a mother by observing other gorillas. It is probably safe to assume that she learned her lessons well.

This chapter will focus on the endocrine mechanisms underlying the development and maintenance of parental care. Thus far we have focused on the interactions between hormones and mating behavior in reproduction. Mating behavior is obviously critical for reproductive success because it brings the two sexes together in order to combine their genetic material. However, successful mating is insufficient for reproduction to be successful. From an evolutionary perspective, the only currency of reproductive success is the production of successful offspring, that is, offspring that themselves manage to survive and produce descendants. The offspring of many animal species require assistance from one or both parents in order to attain maturity and reproduce themselves.

Parental Investment Theory

The amount of assistance that parents provide varies widely, both among and within species, and reflects an optimal evolutionary strategy for maximizing fitness. The optimal strategy for each parent is to provide sufficient care but no more than is absolutely necessary to produce successful offspring. Parental investment, the extent to which parents compromise their ability to produce additional offspring in order to assist current offspring, may result in a conflict of interest between parents and young. That is, parents usually share about 50% of their genes with each offspring, whereas each offspring is 100% related to itself and acts accordingly! Species and individuals can adjust their fitness by altering the amount of parental investment they put into their offspring. Generally, the sex making the larger investment in feeding and protecting the offspring is the choosier about potential mates, whereas individuals of the sex that contributes fewer resources to offspring success compete among themselves to be chosen (Trivers, 1972). In most species of mammals, females are generally the choosier sex and invest the most parental care. The sexes generally face a trade-off between reproductive and parental care investment. For example, if a single female can provide offspring with sufficient resources and protection to survive, then it is in the best interest of the male to make additional reproductive investments to increase his fitness. Of course, if both parents abandoned the young, fitness of both parents would suffer. In most cases, the fitness of males will generally improve with paternal care only if the offspring require care and protection from two parents. At one end of the parental care continuum are the numerous vertebrate species that provide absolutely no parental care. Females of many fish species, for example, simply release hundreds or even thousands of eggs from their bodies to be fertilized, then leave them to face the vagaries of the cold, harsh world on their own (**FIGURE 7.2A**). Females of most reptilian species merely cover their newly deposited eggs with dirt and other debris and provide no additional parental assistance. These young must fend for themselves immediately upon hatching. Parental care, ranging from rudimentary to complex, is observed among invertebrate animals, mainly in the form of nest defense or provisioning the young with food. Parents of many other vertebrate species go further, providing food, shelter, and protection from harm as their offspring mature (**FIGURE 7.2B**). Humans represent the other

(A)

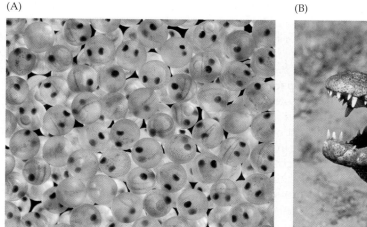

(B)

FIGURE 7.2 **Some species provide little or no parental care.** (A) Brown trout (*Salmo trutta*) newly hatched alevins and eggs ready to hatch. The eggs remain where they fall, and no parental care is provided. The sheer number of eggs released ensures that some offspring will survive despite the absence of parental protection. (B) Female Nile crocodiles protect their newly hatched young by gently carrying them to the water in their mouths. Aside from nest building, this is the extent of parental care in this species; males make no parental contribution.

FIGURE 7.3 Women's ability to produce and nurture new life was accorded great respect in many early human societies. This mother-and-child sculpture from neolithic Croatia (Vinca group), about 5500–4500 BCE, celebrates the nurturant power of women, while depicting a nearly universal image of human maternal behavior.

parental behavior Behaviors performed in relation to one's offspring that contribute directly to the survival of fertilized eggs or offspring that have left the body of the female.

maternal behavior Parental behavior typically performed by the mother or another female.

paternal behavior Parental behavior typically performed by the father or another male.

altricial Born or hatched at an early stage of development. Altricial offspring are generally quite helpless and require substantial parental care to survive.

precocial Born or hatched at an advanced stage of development. Precocial young require little or no parental intervention for survival.

end of the parental care continuum, often providing substantial care and resources to their children for years and, more recently, for decades.

What is parental behavior? **Parental behavior** can be broadly defined as any behavior performed in relation to one's offspring (Rosenblatt et al., 1985); more specifically, parental behavior is any behavior that contributes directly to the survival of fertilized eggs or offspring that have left the body of the female. If the mother performs parental behavior, then a more specific term, **maternal behavior**, is typically used; similarly, parental behavior performed by the fathers is called **paternal behavior**.

Why is parental care an important topic to study? Parental care is critical for infant survival among many species, including humans, and hence is critical for the reproductive success of the individual parent(s). Parental care plays an important role in the evolution of competition for mates, because individuals may seek mates that can best provide care for their offspring; the intensity of mate competition within each sex influences the selection pressures operating on behavior, physiology, and morphology (Clutton-Brock, 1991). Parental care influences the course of physical and psychological development of offspring and is also important among many species in the socialization of young. Individual humans display a wide range of parenting skills; it would be useful to discover any endocrine correlates of poor parenting, because poor parenting is associated with numerous social problems for the offspring. The importance of mothers as nurturers of new life has been an inspiration to artists for eons (**FIGURE 7.3**).

As you will see, not only is there a wide range of parental behavior within a species, there is a wide diversity of parental care strategies among vertebrates. Some of this diversity is due to variation in the developmental maturity of the offspring when they are produced. Two broad categories of offspring development are found among vertebrates. In the first, females produce large numbers of immature and helpless, or **altricial**, young. Females that engage in this reproductive strategy may or may not display parental care. In the second, females produce a few **precocial** offspring that are well developed and may be able to survive with little or no parental intervention (**FIGURE 7.4**). There are trade-offs between these two strategies. If we consider the costs and benefits of producing precocial or altricial young for similar-sized individuals, precocial young require a greater initial investment per individual offspring, as the female must invest more energy in their development before birth or hatching, but less parental investment is usually required after birth. Altricial young require less prenatal investment, but if parental care is provided, more is necessary. Some species, rather than giving parental care to their altricial offspring, rely on the production of large numbers of offspring to ensure that at least a few will survive. Other species, including humans, produce semiprecocial young that always demand significant parental care at birth but can thermoregulate and cling to the mother. It should be noted that although human infants retain the grasp reflex, clinging to their mothers is not a very effective strategy to ensure maternal care or protection, as it is in most other primates. Human mothers must be much more proactive in carrying their young to ensure survival. Furthermore, human mothers display a wide variation of parenting behaviors that range from constant vocal and physical interactions to inattention and neglect. Successful mothers do not reflect a single phenotype, but rather they require appropriate experience during their development, as well as appropriate stress and coping styles, affective responses, and attentional and executive function, plus the complex interaction among genes, various hormones, and neural substrates that underlie maternal caregiving. In studies of such things, it is virtually impossible to tease out causative factors, so many experiments use rodents to understand how single hormones or neural sites affect maternal behavior.

In animals that display parental care, ideally the behaviors must be performed correctly, with little margin for error; they initially must be performed without pre-

(A)

(B)

FIGURE 7.4 **Extent and nature of parental care depends on the development of the offspring.** There are vast differences in the developmental stages of offspring. The young of guinea pigs (A) are precocial, born fully furred and mobile. They require different types of parental care than altricial young, such as rat pups (B), which are born without the ability to move about or thermoregulate.

maternal aggression A type of aggressive behavior observed among new mothers when they fiercely defend their young from intruders.

vious experience, and they must usually begin immediately after the hatching or birth of the offspring. Given these constraints, the onset of parental behavior is often remarkable for its precision and suitability, at least to most casual human observers. There are important experiential effects (detailed below), and upon closer look, maternal behavior is often not performed particularly well during the first attempt, especially in some species of primates. Even among rodents, the litter size, survival, and the efficiency of maternal care are better for subsequent litters after the first litter is weaned.

Nonetheless, the apparent confidence with which first-time mother dogs attend to their newly arrived pups is impressive. A day or two prior to giving birth, a pregnant dog builds a nest (often using only the best shirts, towels, or sweaters available) into which her puppies will be delivered. The pups are born about 20 to 60 minutes apart. As each pup is born, the mother behaves solicitously toward it, licking off the amniotic fluid and membranes and also vigorously licking the anogenital region, which functions to stimulate the elimination of wastes and other physiological processes. After consuming the placentas, she lies on her side and the pups can attach to her nipples to nurse (**FIGURE 7.5**). The altricial puppies are blind and partially deaf, their coats are not completely established, and their thermoregulatory and locomotor abilities are not fully developed. During the first days of their lives, the mother continues to groom her pups as they nurse, and she also keeps them warm. She will retrieve pups by the scruff of the neck should they wander too far from the nest, and she may move the entire litter if there are too many disturbances. If another dog, a well-known human acquaintance, or even the father of the litter comes too close to the pups, then the mother may act very aggressively and can inflict serious damage on the intruder. Again, the ferocity of this **maternal aggression** in previously docile animals can be surprising and dangerous to unsuspecting pet owners.

Ordinarily, female dogs do not act in a solicitous and protective manner in the presence of newborn

FIGURE 7.5 **Females of many species provide their offspring with food, shelter, and protection from harm.** Mammals, such as this female dog, have evolved to provide a specialized secretion, milk, to feed the young. Because male mammals do not lactate, only females can meet the nutritional demands of the young. In some mammalian species, the male contributes by feeding the female while she nurses. In very rare cases, male mammals participate more fully in parental care.

puppies; however, female dogs that have just delivered their own pups virtually always behave maternally. What triggers the set of maternal behaviors in dogs? While one might suppose that the stimuli, neural or otherwise, associated with the birth process initiate the onset of parental behavior, this hypothesis can be rejected because dogs that give birth by cesarean section (C-section) also behave maternally toward their puppies as soon as they recover from anesthesia. Indeed, many correlational studies in dogs, rabbits, and other mammals, especially rats, have demonstrated that it is the hormones associated with pregnancy and lactation that regulate the onset of mammalian parental behavior. In other vertebrate orders, hormones involved in egg production, nest building, egg laying, and incubation may activate parental behavior. In any case, hormones affect motivation to engage in parental care, and hormones are thus important to initiate maternal care.

The hormones that trigger parental behavior wane soon after the arrival of the young. What factors serve to maintain parental behavior? If you observe mother dogs as their puppies mature, you will notice that their maternal behaviors change over time. Nest building and pup retrieval behaviors wane, and the durations of nursing and play behaviors increase. Many maternal behaviors, including nursing, completely disappear after a few additional weeks. How are these changes in parental behavior coordinated with changes in the pups? What role, if any, do hormones play in the maintenance and termination of parental behavior? These questions will be answered in detail in this chapter.

Sex Differences in Parental Behavior

With the exception of most bird and some fish species, paternal behavior is rather rare in the animal kingdom; maternal care is much more common. Why does this sex difference exist? As described in Chapter 3, the two sexes produce different types of gametes. Females produce relatively few, large, immobile, resource-rich gametes (eggs), whereas males produce large numbers of small, mobile gametes containing few or no resources (sperm). One male can produce enough sperm to fertilize many more eggs than one female can produce. For example, a single ejaculation from a typical man (about 5 ml of semen) contains sufficient sperm, in theory, to fertilize all the women (~265 million) in North America. In contrast, a woman produces only a few hundred eggs in her lifetime. Associated with this difference in reproductive potential, males and females differ fundamentally in how they can best maximize reproductive success.

Reproductive effort can be divided into mating effort and parental effort (Trivers, 1972). Males tend to concentrate their reproductive effort on mating, because locating and fertilizing as many different females as possible is the best way for males to achieve maximal reproductive success. Females tend to put the majority of their reproductive effort into parental care, because each offspring represents a substantial proportion of a female's lifetime investment of time and resources. A female can best increase her reproductive success by turning food into eggs or successful offspring at a faster rate. Mating with additional males while pregnant or lactating typically does nothing to increase her reproductive success unless those copulating males provide resources to the female or to the female's existing offspring. Consider human females. Pregnancy lasts 9 months, and lactation-induced infertility can delay further reproductive efforts for another year or two. During this same time, a man could potentially fertilize hundreds of women.

The various factors limiting male and female reproductive success were first documented experimentally by Bateman (1948). He put equal numbers of male and female fruit flies in a large bottle and scored the number of matings and the number of offspring produced by each individual. Bateman was able to use specific genetic markers to assign parentage. He found that some males fertilized many females, while others never fathered offspring; however, all the females fared about equally well. The reproductive success of a male depended on the number of females he fertilized, whereas the females achieved maximal reproductive success, in most cases, with a single copulation.

A male forgoing additional mating opportunities to help raise his offspring is typically at an evolutionary disadvantage relative to a nonparental conspecific male. The reproductive success of the nonparental male will be higher than that of the parental male—that is, unless the offspring cannot survive without parental assistance from two adults. Only in those situations in which two adults are required to guarantee the survival of the young, as is the case for many avian species, will parental males achieve higher reproductive success than nonparental males. Given these theoretical considerations, it is not surprising that paternal care is rare. Presumably, animals that have pursued existing reproductive strategies have been more successful than animals that have not. It is not necessary for these strategies to be consciously directed, even among humans, to be successful. By analogy, birds do not require a conscious understanding of aerodynamic theories to fly. But birds that behave as if they understand the theories of flight increase their reproductive success. Similarly, birds (or people) that behave as if they understand parental investment theory increase their reproductive success.

This chapter describes patterns of parental behavior in various species, the hormonal correlates of parental behavior, and the cues that are necessary and sufficient to elicit parental care. In addition, what is currently known about the neural foundations of parental behavior will be reviewed. As you will see, there is an enormous variety of parental behaviors among vertebrate taxa. Although parental care has been well studied in numerous species, little is known about its endocrine mechanisms in any but those few well-studied species. The vast majority of research addressing the hormonal correlates of parental behavior has been conducted on ringdoves, sheep, and laboratory rats. Parental behaviors in birds are described first, followed by a description of the hormone-behavior interactions underlying them. Birds are interesting to study because more is known about the endocrine correlates of paternal behavior in birds than in mammals. A discussion of parental behavior in mammals then follows.

Parental Behavior in Birds

Birds display enormous diversity in parental behavior (Rosenblatt, 2003). Some avian species are so-called nest parasites that never engage in parental behavior. Female cuckoos and cowbirds deposit their eggs secretly into the nests of other birds, and the unknowing "adoptive" parents provide parental care for their "guests," incubating the eggs and feeding and protecting the hatchlings. In other avian species, such as chickens, only the female provides parental care. In some rare cases, only the male provides parental care. Mallee fowl and jacana males build and maintain nests and incubate the eggs deposited in them. The females compete with one another to lay eggs in different males' nests. Such instances of sex role reversal are interesting to study, because they provide clues about the selective pressures driving the evolution of parental care. Biparental care, in which both male and female birds provide virtually equivalent care, is the most common pattern of avian parental care (**FIGURE 7.6**). Nearly 90% of avian species are putatively monogamous, and in contrast to parenting in mammals, paternal care is a common avian trait.

FIGURE 7.6 Biparental care is common in birds. In most bird species, both parents make approximately equal parental investments, in the form of nest building, incubation, feeding, and protection of the young. Immature birds require nearly continuous food intake to survive and develop successfully, and in most cases two parents are required to meet their needs, as in the mallard ducks (*Anas platyrhynchos*) shown here.

Parental behavior in birds typically includes nest building, incubating the eggs, brooding the newly hatched nestlings, and taking care of the young until they are ready to live independently. The extent to which the young are cared for depends on their developmental state at hatching. Altricial young are generally helpless after hatching and require substantial attention, feeding, brooding, and protection, whereas precocial young generally require only supervision. Many fowl, including chickens, pheasants, and ducks, produce precocial young. Maternal care in chickens involves nest building, incubation, and broody behavior, which consists of clucking and hovering over the chicks and nest for protection. The hen may stimulate the chicks to feed by pecking at grains herself; she calls attention to the potential food by emitting a species-specific sound. But generally, the chicks are fully capable of feeding themselves after a day or two. If the chicks are threatened by an intruder, a broody hen will chase it with her wings extended and emit loud squawking sounds. Birds that produce altricial young, such as robins and starlings, also build nests and incubate eggs, but they must provide their newly hatched young with food for several weeks. Regardless of whether altricial or precocial young are produced, many birds (sometimes both sexes) develop a brood patch on the breast, which loses feathers and becomes highly vascularized during incubation, facilitating heat transfer from the parent to the egg.

Males contribute some parental care in approximately 60% of avian subfamilies; in 20% of these subfamilies, the males provide virtually all of the parental care (Buntin, 1996). Some male birds, such as roosters, provide little or no paternal care. Males of other species, such as flycatchers, titmice, pigeons, and doves, are more or less equal partners in rearing their offspring. Male spotted sandpipers and Wilson's phalaropes, like male jacanas and Mallee fowl, provide all the parental care to their young. Males may assist in one, several, or all of the parental tasks (Silver et al., 1985).

Why is paternal care common among birds? At an ultimate level of causation, as we have seen, males care for their offspring when they can better increase their own reproductive success by continuing to invest in those offspring than by seeking additional mates and fathering additional offspring (Angelier et al., 2016). Most young birds are helpless at hatching and require constant food and warmth to develop sufficiently to leave the nest in just a few weeks. If males did not help to feed them, then the hatchlings would die, and the males' fitness would suffer. In most cases, male birds are as capable as females of providing parental care in the form of nest construction, incubation of the eggs, and feeding of the young. This ability of avian fathers to feed their young—usually by regurgitating the results of recent foraging trips—contrasts sharply with most mammalian species, in which only the mother can meet the nutritional demands of the infants in the wild. Paternal care is observed in bird species in which males guard their mates while the females are fertile and thus have a reasonable, albeit not perfect, chance that parental efforts are being directed at their own offspring.

In some birds, care of nestlings is provided through **alloparental behavior**, with male parental "assistants" caring for offspring in addition to the parents (Emlen, 1978; Skutch, 1935). These helpers are usually elder brothers that are unable to set up their own breeding territories because of scarce resources, and they increase their reproductive fitness indirectly by helping their younger siblings.

Behavioral endocrinologists have traditionally focused their studies on two groups of birds—namely, the Galliformes (e.g., chickens) and the Columbiformes (e.g., pigeons and doves)—probably the two most atypical representatives of the class Aves (Buntin, 1996). Chickens have been studied because of their economic value, even though galliform birds are highly unusual in that only the mother provides any care. The pattern of avian parental behavior on which most endocrine investigations have focused, however, is one of the rarest: a unique mode of providing food to the young, observed only among members of the family Columbidae. In

alloparental behavior Caregiving to offspring that is provided by individuals other than their genetic parents.

this family, both sexes engage in full parental care. The male brings nest material to the female, which does most of the nest construction. Both parents incubate the eggs, and both help feed the young, which are called squab, after they hatch. So far, this pattern of behavior is not unusual among birds. What makes the pigeons and doves unique is that both parents produce a substance called crop milk, which is fed to the young. The crop milk, which resembles small-curd cottage cheese, is produced in a specialized exocrine gland called the crop sac. The parents regurgitate the crop milk to feed the squab (Horseman and Buntin, 1995) (**FIGURE 7.7**). Immediately after hatching, the squab are fed crop milk exclusively, but a mixture of seeds, insects, and crop milk is provided by the parents as the squab grow older. This unique avian adaptation of providing the young with "milk" is sufficiently similar to mammalian behavior to suggest that common underlying physiological mechanisms may be involved. Thus, pigeons and doves have proved to be attractive avian animal models in which to study hormonal effects on parental behavior.

Endocrine Correlates of Avian Parental Behavior

Parental behaviors, often performed by both mothers and fathers, are extensive among birds (Rosenblatt, 2002). The hormonal correlates of avian parental behavior are described in the following sections.

AVIAN MATERNAL BEHAVIOR Which hormones mediate maternal behavior in birds? Hens exhibit maternal behavior, or broodiness, by making "clucking" vocalizations and by persistent incubation or "nesting" behavior (**FIGURE 7.8**). The term *broodiness* can refer either to sitting on eggs in a nest or, more commonly, to protecting, covering, and warming the young under the wing. When hens become broody, they stop laying eggs, so there has been significant research effort among poultry scientists aimed at preventing broodiness in order to increase egg production. Nearly 90 years ago, it was discovered that blood serum from a broody hen could induce a nonincubating hen to sit on a clutch of eggs (Leinhart, 1927). Oscar Riddle and his colleagues provided compelling early evidence that prolactin induces broodiness in pigeons and chickens (Riddle et al., 1935a,b). Increased blood concentrations of prolactin are associated with broodiness in all female birds studied to date (see Angeliers et al., 2016; Goldsmith, 1983; Riddle et

FIGURE 7.7 **Domestic white pigeon chicks feed on crop milk,** which is produced by both males and females in response to stimulation by prolactin. As the squab get older, a greater and greater proportion of the adult diet of seeds and insects is mixed with the crop milk, until eventually only the adult diet is consumed and parental crop milk production wanes.

FIGURE 7.8 **An extreme example of broodiness** After maternal behavior has been initiated by hormones, virtually any contact, even when provided by the young of another species, is sufficient to maintain normal broody behavior in the hen.

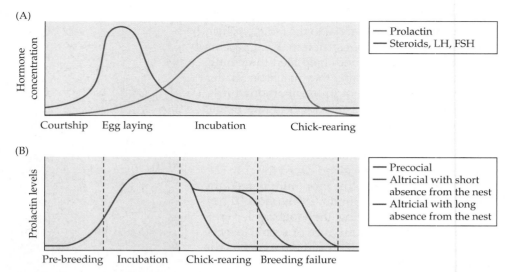

FIGURE 7.9 Generalized endocrine profile of north temperate zone birds (A) While individual birds in a population may display different concentrations of reproductive hormones on any given sampling date, if the blood samples are arranged according to reproductive activity, a clear pattern of hormone concentration and reproductive function is observed. Sex steroid hormones usually increase coincident with the onset of courtship behavior, peak during the time of egg laying (oviposition), and rapidly decrease to baseline prior to incubation. Prolactin concentrations begin to increase at the time of egg laying, remain high during incubation, then drop off gradually to baseline concentrations during post-hatching care. (B) A schematic representation of the prolactin cycle of breeding birds with different reproductive modes (precocial as in ducks, geese, and other fowl; altricial with short absence from the nest as in gannets, starlings, and doves; altricial with long absence from the nest as in penguins, albatrosses, and petrels). A after Ball, 1991; B from Angeliers et al., 2016.

al., 1935b; Silverin and Goldsmith, 1983) (**FIGURE 7.9A**). Although all avian species display elevated prolactin concentrations during incubation, in many precocial species, prolactin concentrations decline at the time of hatching, while in altricial species prolactin concentrations remain high throughout chick rearing (Angelier et al., 2013; Dawson and Goldsmith, 1982; Etches et al., 1979; Hall and Goldsmith, 1983; Hector and Goldsmith, 1985; Riou et al., 2010; Sharp et al., 1979) (**FIGURE 7.9B**). Even in nest parasite species such as cowbirds, which lay their eggs in other birds' nests and never show broodiness or any other parental behavior, blood prolactin concentrations increase after egg laying (Rissman and Wingfield, 1984). Because the parental behavior of cowbirds differs substantially from that of other birds despite the similar hormonal profile, it is plausible that these behavioral differences are due to differences in the sensitivity of the central nervous system to hormones; experimental evidence supporting this proposition will be presented below.

The vast majority of studies on endocrine correlates of avian maternal behavior have been conducted on ringdoves (*Streptopelia risoria*) (Buntin, 2010). Female ringdoves, which were studied extensively by researcher Daniel S. Lehrman (**BOX 7.1**), undergo a stereotyped sequence of mutually exclusive behaviors during their reproductive cycle (Lehrman, 1965). The cycle begins with courtship, which is followed by nest building, incubation, feeding the young, and finally resumption of courtship behavior. Changes in hormone concentrations correlate with the different stages of this cycle. Incubation is initially evoked by progesterone (against a background of high estradiol concentrations), but around midincubation, it is sustained by prolactin, which is secreted in response to ventrum (belly) stimulation from contact with the eggs. Ovariectomy eliminates nest building and incubation behavior.

BOX 7.1   *Daniel S. Lehrman*

Daniel S. Lehrman made major contributions to behavioral endocrinology, particularly by untangling the complex interactions among social, psychological, and hormonal stimuli that control courtship behavior in ringdoves (e.g., Lehrman, 1965). An avid bird watcher, Lehrman worked as a volunteer research assistant at the American Museum of Natural History for Dr. G. K. Noble while completing his undergraduate education at the City College of New York. At the museum, he was encouraged by Frank Beach and Ernst Mayr to study animal behavior. After completing U.S. Army duties, he returned to the museum in 1946 and met Theodore C. Schneirla, a well-known comparative psychologist, with whom he completed a doctoral degree in 1954. Lehrman joined the faculty at Rutgers University and founded the Institute of Animal Behavior in 1958; the institute has been an important research establishment and home to many prominent behavioral endocrinologists. Indeed, the primary award for mentoring in the Society for Behavioral Neuroendocrinology was named after Dr. Lehrman.

Dr. Lehrman's primary contribution in behavioral endocrinology was extending the well-established relationship that hormones could affect behaviors to demonstrate that behaviors could feed back to affect hormone secretion. Most of his work was conducted to understand courtship and parental behavior in ringdoves.

Despite his seminal work in behavioral endocrinology, Lehrman was probably most widely known for firing a major salvo at the European ethologists in 1953, in his "A Critique of Konrad Lorenz's Theory of Instinctive Behavior." Ethologists focused on "instinctual" behaviors, whereas comparative psychologists focused on learning. Although the publication of this

Daniel S. Lehrman (1919–1972).
Courtesy of Rae Silver.

biting attack on Lorenz's notions of "hard-wired" behavioral programs initially caused a number of caustic debates between North American comparative psychologists and European ethologists, the net effect of the paper was to bring the two schools together, setting up an eventual synthesis between the two scientific disciplines (Dewsbury, 1984).

Lehrman was a member of the National Academy of Sciences and is remembered by his students for his outstanding ability to communicate his ideas to scientists and nonscientists alike: he was famous for jumping onto tabletops and performing enthusiastic imitations of courting ringdoves bowing and cooing.

Injections of either estradiol or progesterone fail to restore nest building or incubation behavior, but treatment with both steroid hormones restores these behaviors to normal values (Cheng and Silver, 1975). Prolactin is critical for stimulating brooding and development of the crop sac in ringdoves (Silver, 1978) (**FIGURE 7.10**). Prolactin secretion wanes by the time the squab are 20 days old, at which time the mother no longer participates in the feeding of her brood. Although the female and male begin to court and build a new nest at this time, the male continues to secrete prolactin and provide crop milk to the squab. Thus the onset, maintenance, and termination of parental behavior in pigeons and doves appear to depend primarily on prolactin concentrations. Stress caused by low food availability or unfavorable ambient conditions can affect whether or not parents continue to raise their offspring or abandon a nest and await better conditions (Wingfield et al., 2016). Treating parental black-legged kittiwakes (*Rissa tridactyla*) with corticosterone for just 2 days reduced prolactin by 30% and impaired parental care (Angelier et al., 2009). These results suggest that the suppressive effects of stress on reproductive success may operate via corticosterone (Buntin, 2010; Rensel et al., 2009; Schoech et al., 2009), in part by decreasing prolactin secretion. Stress may inhibit reproduction, at least in part, through release of gonadotropin inhibitory hormone (GnIH) (Calisi, 2014; Calisi et al., 2008). In house sparrows (*Passer domesticus*) acute stress increases the number of

FIGURE 7.10 Plasma prolactin, crop development, crop contents, and parental food intake are related in ring-doves. Plasma prolactin concentrations increase post-laying and are associated with elevated food consumption by the breeding pair, presumably to support foraging for insects for the squab. As prolactin falls, the crop mixture changes from crop milk at hatching to mainly seeds and insects by 14 days post-hatching. After Horseman and Buntin, 1995.

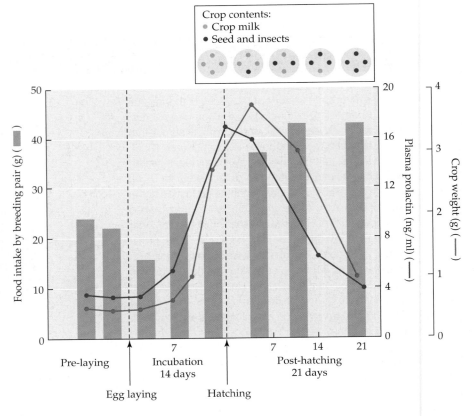

GnIH cells seen with immunohistochemical labeling. Because glucocorticoids receptors are expressed in GnIH neurons (Kirby et al., 2009; Son et al., 2014), it is likely that corticosterone acts directly on this inhibitory cell population to suppress breeding when conditions are unfavorable.

AVIAN PATERNAL BEHAVIOR   Despite the wide variety of parenting patterns found among male birds that provide parental care, there have been relatively few studies of the endocrine correlates of avian paternal behavior in noncolumbid birds (Ketterson and Nolan, 1994; Lynn, 2008). Early research on the endocrine bases of parental behavior focused on sex differences in the expression of parental care in species in which males normally do not provide any paternal assistance. Roosters typically do not exhibit paternal care, but a castrated rooster, or capon, becomes broody almost to the same extent as a hen when provided with foster chicks (Goodale, 1918). Tom turkeys also do not display paternal care, but males restrained so that they are forced to sit on a clutch of eggs eventually show incubation behavior (Taibell, 1928).

Generally, nest building and incubation behaviors by male passerine (i.e., perching) birds are observed after courtship and mating and correspond to a sharp decline in blood concentrations of androgens (Lynn, 2008; Lynn et al., 2016; Pinxten et al., 2007) and sometimes progesterone. Prolactin concentrations generally increase at the onset of incubation behavior (Angeliers et al., 2016; Ball, 1991; Silverin, 1990). However, in field populations of sparrows, in which males may sire multiple broods, paternal behavior is observed while the birds modulate blood concentrations of testosterone (Lynn and Wingfield, 2008; Wingfield and Moore, 1987). Although baseline testosterone concentrations are low at this time, these birds can increase testosterone rapidly in response to a territorial challenge (Goymann et al., 2007). Elevated androgen concentrations are necessary to maintain the territorial defense behaviors required for successful rearing of the young. Males of species that display sex role reversal, such as the spotted sandpiper (*Actitis macularia*) and Wilson's phalarope (*Phalaropus tricolor*), display the typical pattern of reduced steroid and increased prolactin concentrations; usually their prolactin concentrations exceed those of female conspecifics (Oring et al., 1986a,b).

In common with research on maternal care, the majority of research on hormonal correlates of avian paternal behavior has been accomplished on ringdoves in laboratory settings (Buntin, 1996, 2010). During the reproductive cycle, male ringdoves first exhibit courting behavior; after copulation, they engage in nest building. After the eggs are laid, males begin to incubate them, and after the squab hatch, males assist in feeding them for the first 3 weeks or so of their lives (Lehrman, 1965). These behaviors occur sequentially (see Figure 7.10), and hormones are important in the transition from one behavior to the next.

Although testosterone is required for courtship, this steroid hormone is not necessary for the onset of nest-building behavior in male ringdoves. Castrated males treated with daily injections of testosterone either courted females or built nests; which behavior they chose was solely dependent on the behavior of the females (Silver, 1978). Thus, in contrast to maintenance of nest-building behavior of females, that of males is independent of hormonal status. This example makes the interesting point that virtually identical behaviors can have markedly different physiological bases in the two sexes. Apparently, stimuli from the female, rather than hormonal changes, also induce the male to begin incubation behavior (Silver, 1978). In both sexes, prolactin is required to stimulate broody behavior and production of crop milk (Lehrman and Brody, 1961). Testosterone, but not progesterone, appears necessary for the onset of incubation behavior in castrated male doves (Lea et al., 1986; Ramos and Silver, 1992).

In addition to sex steroids and prolactin, the avian homologues of oxytocin and vasopressin, vasotocin and mesotocin, are likely to be involved in avian parental behavior (Kelly and Goodson, 2014). In female zebra finches, peripheral administration of an oxytocin receptor antagonist reduced nest building in females, but it had no effect in males. In contrast, peripheral treatment with a vasopressin receptor antagonist reduced nest building in both males and females. In contrast to expectation, central administration of the vasopressin antagonist did not influence nest building in either sex, suggesting indirect effects on peripheral systems that inevitably feed back to the central nervous system to influence nesting behavior (Klatt and Goodson, 2013).

The endocrine correlates of alloparenting have been studied in Florida scrub jays (Schoech, 2001). In male helpers, testosterone and prolactin concentrations were lower than in fathers (**FIGURE 7.11**). Although the prolactin values of female helpers showed a pattern similar to those of male helpers, their blood estradiol patterns were more complicated. During the prenesting period, breeding females had higher estradiol concentrations than helper females, but female helpers' estradiol concentrations increased when the breeders were building nests and incubating. This increase in estradiol may prepare the helper females to strike out for their own breeding opportunities (Schoech, 2001).

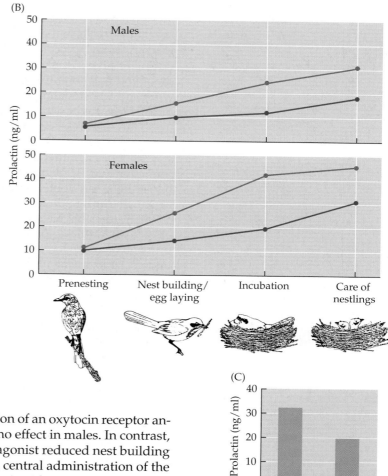

FIGURE 7.11 Prolactin concentrations correlate with the amount of care provided to the offspring in Florida scrub jays. (A) A male helper at the nest. (B) Breeding males and females (red) have higher prolactin values than helpers (blue). (C) Helpers have higher prolactin concentrations than nonhelpers. B from Schoech, 2001.

NEURAL REGIONS ASSOCIATED WITH AVIAN PARENTAL BEHAVIOR   Relatively few studies have investigated the neural substrates of avian parental behavior (Buntin, 2010). However, in the few studies performed, a consistent pattern has emerged indicating that the preoptic area (POA) anterior to the hypothalamus is essential for the expression of parental behavior (Erikson and Hutchison, 1977; Komisaruk, 1967; Lea et al., 2001; Slawski and Buntin, 1995; Ziegler et al., 2000). Most of these studies have involved lesioning the POA and observing the resulting behavioral deficits (Buntin, 1996). In birds, the POA is interconnected with a variety of brain regions known to be implicated in social behavior, including the medial amygdala, bed nucleus of the stria terminalis, and ventral tegmental area (Balthazart et al., 1994; Goodson and Kigsbury, 2013; O'Connell and Hofmann, 2011), and these regions are generally more active (express more Fos in nesting zebra finches (Hall et al., 2014). The brain areas in this network express the neuropeptide vasoactive intestinal polypeptide (VIP), a neurochemical implicated in social behavior, suggesting that VIP cells in these neural loci might underlie nesting behavior. In support of this possibility, VIP cells in all of these brain areas exhibit increased FOS expression during nesting in male and female zebra finches (Kingsbury et al., 2015). Together, these findings point to a potential role for this interconnected social-behavior network and VIP signaling in nest building, although further studies are necessary to directly test this possibility. Relative to nest building, the neural circuitry underlying incubation behavior remains unspecified (Buntin, 1996).

Similar strategies have been used to explore avian parental behavior in other species. For example, by using autoradiography and expression patterns of the immediate early gene *c-fos*, it was determined that the POA and the nucleus tuberis, the avian homologous structure of the mammalian arcuate nucleus, were activated during parental behavior in ringdoves (Georgiou et al., 1995; Sharp et al., 1996). Studies have also been conducted to determine which hormone receptors are activated during parental behavior and where these receptors are located. Expression of androgen receptors in ringdoves is high during courtship but virtually undetectable during parental behavior, a pattern corresponding to that of hormone concentrations (Lea et al., 2001). Prolactin receptors decreased in the nucleus tuberis in parental birds of both sexes, whereas in the POA, prolactin receptor expression was high throughout courtship and brooding (Lea et al., 2001).

Another approach that has been useful in understanding the neural substrates of avian parental behavior has employed comparisons of prolactin receptors in the brains of bird species that differ in their parental behaviors. This comparative approach has yielded data suggesting that differences in parental care are mediated not by differences in hormones per se but by differences in receptor numbers. For example, prolactin binding sites were compared in the brains of female cowbirds, red-winged blackbirds, and European starlings. Cowbirds, as you will recall, do not show parental care, but they exhibit prolactin profiles similar to those of other birds. In some brain areas, the pattern of prolactin binding was similar among all three species; however, the cowbirds displayed reduced prolactin binding in the POA compared with the species that exhibit parental care (Ball, 1991). Thus, it seems reasonable to conclude that species differences in parental behavior may be mediated by differences in target tissue sensitivity, rather than differences in blood concentrations of hormones.

In another study, male dark-eyed juncos (*Junco hyemalis*) were implanted with testosterone-filled or empty capsules, then evaluated for paternal behavior. Specific binding of radiolabeled prolactin at brain sites previously implicated in the regulation of avian paternal behavior, namely, the POA, the ventromedial nuclei, and paraventricular nuclei (PVN) were investigated (Schoech et al., 1998). Testosterone-treated males reduced their parental contributions to their offspring, but prolactin concentrations were not affected by the elevated testosterone concentrations. Furthermore, no differences were observed in the capacity for prolactin binding.

These results indicate that testosterone does not block parental behavior by suppressing prolactin concentrations in the blood or by reducing prolactin receptor binding in brain regions that mediate paternal behavior (Schoech et al., 1998).

One important question regarding the hormone-brain relationship in avian parental behavior is how prolactin, a relatively large protein hormone, crosses the blood-brain barrier to interact with prolactin receptors on neurons. Short-term studies using intravenous injections of radiolabeled prolactin into the blood of ringdoves revealed that somehow prolactin does cross the blood-brain barrier and accumulates in brain neurons that have prolactin receptors (Buntin et al., 1993). Presumably, some sort of transport system exists to move prolactin into the brain, where it interacts with receptors on the surface of neurons in the hypothalamus and POA (Buntin, 1996).

Parental Behavior in Mammals

Mammals have evolved specializations for taking care of their young (Bridges, 1990; González-Mariscal and Kinsley, 2009; Rosenblatt, 2003). The development of mammary glands, which provide nourishment to the young after they are born, makes mammals unique among vertebrates. Parental care—specifically maternal care—is a particularly important mammalian characteristic (Numan and Insel, 2003).

Mammalian Maternal Behavior

Among mammals, species exist that produce offspring at virtually every developmental stage. The **marsupials** have specialized in the production of highly altricial young that at birth resemble embryos more than offspring. A marsupial mother has a pouch that contains the mammary glands and also serves as a receptacle for the young. Most marsupials, including wallabies and kangaroos, have temporary or permanent pouches in which the young are carried for several months (**FIGURE 7.12A,B**). When the young reach a certain species-specific age, they leave the pouch, but they return to the mother to nurse. Other marsupial species, such as opossums and koalas, bear young that cling to the mother's fur after they have left the pouch and are carried in this manner as the mother forages for food (**FIGURE 7.12C**). These patterns of maternal care are adaptations based on the mothers' need to remain mobile, both to obtain food in their usually barren habitats and to escape predators (Sharman, 1970; Tyndale-Biscoe and Renfree, 1987). The young, in turn, are adapted to remain attached to the mother, either in the pouch or outside of it; should they become dislodged, the mother does not attempt to reattach them, and they invariably perish. Thus, marsupials do not invest

marsupial A mammal belonging to the subclass Metatheria that lacks a placenta, such as opossums and most Australian mammals. Most marsupials have a pouch (marsupium) in which the mammary glands are located and the young are transported.

(A)

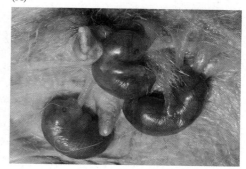

(B)

(C)

FIGURE 7.12 Maternal behavior in marsupials Marsupials have specialized in the production of altricial young and have developed means for the mother to stay mobile and forage while the young are nursing. (A) A red-necked wallaby, *Macropus rufogriseus*, suckling in the pouch. (B) In marsupials, such as Bennett's wallaby, a subspecies of the red-necked wallaby (*M. rufogriseus*), the female has a pouch in which the mammary glands are located and that also serves as a carrier for the young. (C) In other species of marsupials, such as this opossum (*Didelphis virginiana*), the young stay in the pouch only briefly and are carried by the mother, as they cling to her fur, until they are weaned.

FIGURE 7.13 Monotremes display maternal care. This duck-billed platypus (*Ornithorhynchus anatinus*) is shown with her two altricial young in her den. When pregnant, a female of this species builds a den in which she lays her eggs.

in gestation per se but instead invest in postpartum maternal care, which does not include extensive maternal behavior. Their unreliable habitat favors this arrangement because marsupial mothers can jettison a pregnancy, or even their young, if conditions turn bad. Although it may sound harsh, because of the short gestation period they can replace these young quickly when conditions improve.

Another group of mammals, the **monotremes**, produce young that are born at an even earlier developmental stage than are the marsupials: as eggs. These odd creatures are considered to be modern representatives of very ancient forms of mammals that have retained the reptilian egg-laying trait (oviparity). In terms of maternal behavior, monotremes represent a transitional stage between reptiles, which lay eggs and may or may not bury them, and the much more solicitous modern mammalian species (Burghardt, 1988). As with the marsupials, there are two basic patterns of maternal care among the monotremes (Nowak and Paradiso, 1983; Rosenblatt et al., 1985). The first is evident in the duck-billed platypus (*Ornithorhynchus anatinus*) (**FIGURE 7.13**). The female of this species constructs a grass-lined burrow in which she lays her eggs. She then seals herself in the burrow with the eggs and incubates them until they hatch. In the sealed burrow containing the nest, she cares for the young and provides them with milk, which drips from the hair surrounding her mammary glands. Females of this species do not develop a pouch. The second pattern is seen in the echidnas (spiny anteaters) *Tachyglossus aculeatus* and *Zaglossus bruijni*, which produce a single egg and carry it in a special pouch that develops at the time of egg delivery. The offspring, when it hatches, lives in the pouch and obtains milk from a milk-secreting gland that lacks a nipple.

The widest variety of maternal care patterns has evolved among the **eutherian** (*eu*, "true"; *therion*, "beast") mammals, which have placentas during pregnancy. There are three basic patterns of maternal care among eutherian mammals; the patterns are related to several characteristics of the species but mainly reflect the developmental status of the newborn (Rosenblatt et al., 1985). Eutherian mammals, in contrast to the marsupials and monotremes, live and reproduce in more stable and reliable habitats and therefore have invested in relatively long gestations, which allow for greater development of the young before birth. Thus, mechanisms have evolved in all mammalian species to provide resources necessary for offspring development regardless of whether or not maternal behavior is required.

In the first pattern of maternal care, the mother provides offspring with food, care, and shelter. This pattern is characteristic of dogs, as described above (see Figure 7.5), as well as of other carnivores, rats and most other rodent species, and insectivores (such as shrews). Females exhibiting this pattern of maternal care give birth to altricial young that require a great deal of care: Prior to the birth the mother must build a nest. Once she deposits the young there, she must visit her offspring frequently to feed them[1] and protect them from predators (**FIGURE 7.14**). Recall that mother dogs usually choose a site for the nest and construct it before the young are born.

After parturition, a mother dog eats the placenta (placentophagia also occurs in other mammalian species [Kristal, 1980]; e.g., see Figure 7.27) and licks the amniotic fluid off the puppies. In dogs, and probably in other mammals as well, this cleaning behavior is crucial for maternal acceptance of the newborns: if pups are removed

monotreme   A primitive egg-laying mammal, such as the duck-billed platypus and the spiny anteater, or echidna.

eutherian   The subclass of mammals that possess a placenta during pregnancy.

---

[1] Rabbits and hares show a similar pattern, except that they typically visit their litters only once daily to nurse the young; the rest of the day is spent foraging.

from the nest immediately after birth, washed, and returned to the mother, she will reject them and will not provide any maternal care (Abitbol and Inglis, 1997). A mother dog also nurses her young (see Figure 7.5) and continues to lick them to stimulate various physiological processes.

In dogs and many other mammalian species, the mother will retrieve the young if they wander from the nest, but this is not always the case. Rabbit mothers, for example, will not retrieve young that leave the nest (González-Mariscal and Kinsley, 2009). Mammalian mothers that retrieve their offspring often display fierce maternal aggression, attacking any animal that approaches their nests or young.

The parental competence exhibited by dogs and other nonhuman animals can lead to a powerful impression among human observers that nonhuman parents always perform parental behavior perfectly, and it is perhaps for this reason that comparatively few studies have examined the development of parental behavior. Early studies revealed no differences between mothers that were primiparous (first-time mothers) and multiparous (mothers of multiple litters) in several dimensions of maternal care in rats (Beach and Jayne, 1956; Moltz and Robbins, 1965; but see Wang and Novak, 1994). In all fairness to human parents, however, the "decisiveness" with which dogs and other nonhuman mothers seem to perform their parental behaviors is often an illusion. Upon close observation, errors are observed, especially by inexperienced mothers, and it is seen that trial-and-error learning often occurs during the onset of maternal behavior (reviewed in Numan and Insel, 2003). Little is known about how first-time mothers do in the wild. It is probably fair to say that if challenged by adverse environmental conditions such as weather, food availability, or predation, then first-time mothers are more likely to abandon their young than experienced females (e.g., French et al., 1999). Indeed, in some populations of primates, infant mortality in the first litter can be 60% greater than in later litters of the same mother (Hrdy, 1999). Parental "instinct" is not completely hardwired, or innate, and one can observe variation from parent to parent within the same species. Although this species-specific parental variation likely provides the grist upon which natural selection acts and is thus important for the reproductive success of individuals, the behavioral patterns of parents within a species share much in common. If you think of our own species, there are certainly components of care that differ between mothers, but there are certainly components of care that are observed among virtually all vigilant mothers.

The many maternal behaviors described above can be classified according to whether or not a particular behavior is directed toward offspring (Bridges, 1996). In this scheme, nest building, consumption of the placenta, and defense of pups are classified as non-pup-directed; pup-directed behaviors include grouping the pups together in the nest, huddling with them to provide warmth, retrieving them if they wander, licking their anogenital regions, and providing other forms of tactile stimulation. There may be different mechanisms underlying pup-directed versus non-pup-directed behaviors (González-Mariscal and Poindron, 2002).

In a second pattern of maternal care among eutherian mammals, females bear precocial young that are capable of a high degree of independent activity when they are born, though they may be confined to a nest at birth and for a few days afterward. Some hoofed mammals, such as white-tailed deer, cows, and horses, give birth to one or two precocial offspring. These species are characterized as hider-type animals because the young remain hidden at the nest site for 7–10 days (Geist, 1971). The mother spends most of her time away from the nest, foraging for food, but visits

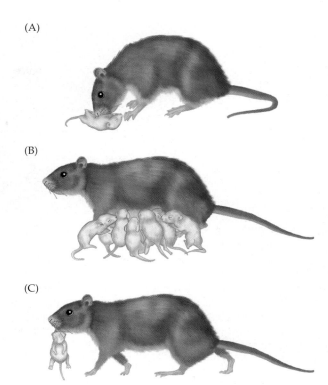

(A)

(B)

(C)

FIGURE 7.14 **Rat maternal care has three major components.** Like mother dogs, rat mothers ("dams") must engage in three major behaviors in order for their altricial offspring to survive. First, they must lick their pups after birth to clean off the amniotic fluid and to stimulate elimination of wastes (A). Second, they must adopt a nursing posture, huddling above the pups to allow access to the ventrum and to provide warmth and protection (B). Third, they must also bring the pups back to the nest if they wander away (C). After Alberts and Gubernick, 1990.

(A)

(B)

FIGURE 7.15 **Some mammalian species bear precocial offspring.** Unlike dogs and rats, some mammals bear young that are quite well developed. In most mammalian species that bear precocial offspring, an exclusive bond forms between mother and young. (A) Hider-type young, such as white-tailed deer (*Odocoileus virginianus*) fawns, are born in a nest and may be sequestered there for a few days. Hider-type young eventually leave the nest and follow their mothers about. (B) Follower-type young follow their mothers about from birth. Mother giraffes (*Giraffa camelopardalis*) nurse their offspring and watch for danger, leading the young away from impending trouble.

her offspring to nurse them. Hider-type offspring eventually grow mature enough to leave the nest and follow the mother about. Other hoofed and nonhoofed species, including sheep, goats, elephants, and many species of whales, have offspring that follow the mother about from birth; these species are characterized as follower-type animals (**FIGURE 7.15**). The mother nurses her young and maintains constant vigilance, leading them away from danger and protecting them from predators.

Maternal care in many species that bear precocial young is noted for the exclusive bond that forms between the mother and her offspring (Gubernick and Klopfer, 1981; Nowak et al., 2011; Numan and Young, 2016; Poindron et al., 2007a,b). This bonding occurs soon after birth, which takes place in a secluded location away from the social group. Sheep and goat mothers that have just given birth emit characteristic low-pitched bleats in the presence of their newborns, which appear to attract the offspring to their mothers. In these species, the mother initially licks her offspring and allows them access to her udders. If a mother is separated from her newborn, she does not form a maternal bond with that specific offspring. She continues to behave maternally for about 24 hours but is nonexclusive about which lambs/kids are permitted to nurse. After this temporal window closes, then she actively rejects any young other than her own that attempts to nurse (Lévy et al., 2004). Thus, there appear to be two distinct processes in sheep maternal behavior: (1) maternal responsiveness and (2) maternal selectivity (Lévy et al., 1996; Poindron et al., 2007a). Both processes are dependent on cues from the lamb; anosmia interferes with the ewe's selective responses to her own lambs, though not with maternal responsiveness to lambs in general (Poindron and Le Neindre, 1980). In this sense, the mechanisms mediating maternal responsiveness in the precocial ewe and, as we will see below, the altricial rat are similar (Lévy et al., 2004; Numan et al., 2006).

Many other eutherian mammalian species bear young that are neither precisely precocial nor precisely altricial; such offspring are usually described as semiprecocial. The offspring of humans and several other primate species are essentially helpless at birth, but they can cling to the mother in order to move about with her (**FIGURE 7.16**). In this third maternal care pattern, mothers in some species alternate between carrying the young and placing them in a nest or crib; in other species, the mother may deposit her young in a tree nest, where they remain during their early development. Galagos (bush babies) hide their young while foraging during the day and return to carry them during the night.

Mammalian Paternal Behavior

Among mammals, paternal care is relatively uncommon, but it is observed in certain carnivore, rodent, and primate species (Kleiman and Malcolm, 1981). If it is assumed that paternal behavior occurs when it increases male reproductive success, then there should be obvious and compelling selective factors among the species displaying paternal care. Thus far, no such generalities have emerged, except the assumption that females would be unable to rear offspring successfully without the additional support of the male. Another supposition is that certainty of paternity must be very high in order for paternal care to occur (Werren et al., 1980). Males clearly would not increase their reproductive success by relinquishing the opportunity for additional matings in favor of rearing the offspring of other males. It could also be argued that continued proximity to the female after mating improves the male's chances of paternity and is a factor in fostering paternal care (Crowe et al., 2009; Gowaty, 1996). Therefore, paternal behavior should be observed only in species that have a high degree of mating exclusivity between males and females.

FIGURE 7.16 Many primate species produce semiprecocial young. The offspring of several primate species are neither precocial nor altricial. These young are virtually helpless at birth but can cling to the mother as she moves about. Young orangutans cling to their mother as she forages.

Historically, paternal care was reported in fewer than 6% of rodent genera, and even in those relatively rare cases, the behavior was poorly documented with small sample sizes (e.g., one or two individuals) in artificial laboratory environments (Gubernick and Alberts, 1987). These findings led some to question how often, if ever, paternal behavior is actually exhibited among mammals. Although it remains clear that paternal care is rare among mammals, recent studies have convincingly demonstrated paternal behavior in a number of species. Among rodents, paternal care has been documented in laboratory studies of several species of deer mice (*Peromyscus*) (Gubernick and Alberts, 1987; Hatton and Meyer, 1973; McCarty and Southwick, 1977); Syrian hamsters (*Mesocricetus auratus*) (Marques and Valenstein, 1976); house mice (*Mus musculus*) (Priestnall and Young, 1978); grasshopper mice (*Onychomys torridus*); and two vole species (*Microtus ochrogaster, M. pinetorum*) (Gruder-Adams and Getz, 1985; Hartung and Dewsbury, 1979; Oliveras and Novak, 1986; Thomas and Birney, 1979; see Elwood, 1983, for review). California mice (*Peromyscus californicus*), for example, exhibit a biparental system of care. These animals form long-term pair bonds in the wild and in the laboratory and remain together throughout both the breeding and nonbreeding seasons (Ribble and Salvioni, 1990). Furthermore, these animals are exclusively monogamous (Ribble, 1990). Males and females exhibit the same parental behaviors to the same extent, with the obvious exception of lactation (**FIGURE 7.17**). Males spend as much time in the nest as females, help build nests, and carry young. Males also groom the pups and lick the anogenital regions of the pups to stimulate urination (Gubernick and Alberts, 1987). Indeed, paternal hamsters as-

FIGURE 7.17 Male California mice display paternal behavior. With the exception of lactation, males of this species exhibit the same parental behaviors as females, and to the same extent, males spend as much time with the pups as females do. This species is reported to be monogamous in both the laboratory and the field. Courtesy of David Gubernick.

sist with the birthing process (e.g., Gregg and Wynne-Edwards, 2006). Importantly, however, removal of the father may not lead to offspring mortality, as removal of the mother does, although removal of fathers may lead to altered growth or increased stress responses among the offspring.

Another well-studied biparental species is the common marmoset (*Callithrix jacchus*), a New World primate that also displays a monogamous mating system. The male assists during birth, chews food for the babies, and except during nursing sessions, always carries the young (Hampton et al., 1966). Other nonhuman primates, including tamarins (*Leontocebus midas*), Japanese macaques (*Macaca fuscata*), gibbons (*Hylobates lar*), and siamangs (*Symphalangus syndactylus*), also show paternal involvement in the care of the young (Yogman, 1990; Ziegler et al., 2000). In humans, individual males vary from providing no parental care to providing substantial care to their young. In the limited confines of the laboratory setting, many species of rodents and primates exhibit paternal behavior even though they never display these behaviors in nature (Elwood, 1983; Redican and Taub, 1981; Suomi, 1977).

Endocrine Correlates of Mammalian Parental Behavior

The endocrine correlates of the onset, maintenance, and termination of maternal behavior are probably better understood in rats than in any other species. Because the onset of maternal behavior coincides with the birth of the young, the hormones associated with pregnancy and lactation were historically considered likely candidates for causing maternal behavior. In many respects, lactation is the key to mammalian maternal behavior, but it is just one element in a complex system. Because prolactin and lactation are closely linked, prolactin was initially considered to be the critical hormone underlying maternal behavior (Riddle et al., 1935a), but a number of endocrine manipulations have since revealed that several additional hormones are involved, namely, oxytocin, β-endorphin, cholecystokinin, prostaglandins, relaxin, progesterone, and several estrogens (Bridges, 1996; Nelson and Panksepp, 1998). Virtually all mammalian species display elevated estrogen concentrations around the time of birth, and these hormones are important, if not critical, for the onset of maternal behavior (González-Mariscal and Kinsley, 2009; González-Mariscal and Poindron, 2002).

Pituitary prolactin and placental lactogen (a prolactin-like hormone) play leading roles in maternal behavior, but how they are related to other hormones in the regulation of maternal behavior has not yet been specified (Rosenblatt, 1990). Although some straightforward relationships between hormone concentrations and behavior have been reported, there are many subtle endocrine interactions as well. For example, although the induction of maternal behavior seems to be dependent on hormones, especially among first-time parents, some components of maternal behavior are virtually independent of hormonal influences.

SENSITIZATION, OR PUP INDUCTION An experimental paradigm often used to explore the occurrence and hormonal correlates of rat parental behavior is the presentation of foster pups. Researchers present pups of differing ages (typically 1–10 days of age) to adult females (and males) in different endocrine states; then they observe whether, and how quickly, the adults begin to behave parentally toward them. During the first day of exposure to pups, castrated or intact male rats normally ignore them, or in some cases attack them. Adult females that are not pregnant or pseudopregnant also ignore or attack the pups initially. Pregnant females, however, soon begin to behave maternally toward foster pups if they are first exposed to them during the last few days of their pregnancy (typically starting between day 16 and day 18 of the 22-day pregnancy) (**FIGURE 7.18**). Pseudopregnant rats may also show a rapid onset of maternal behavior at the end of their 12–13 day pseudopregnancy. Once a female rat has weaned pups of her own, she retains an enhanced sensitivity

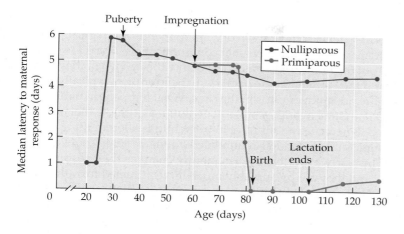

FIGURE 7.18 Latency to maternal behavior in rats Prior to puberty, rats behave maternally on the first day of exposure to foster pups. After puberty, 5–6 daily exposures to novel pups are required to elicit maternal behavior; that value gradually drops to about 4 days as rats age. Pregnant rats do not show maternal behavior during most of the gestation period, but during the last 2–3 days of pregnancy there is a rapid drop in the latency to display maternal behavior in response to pups. This sensitivity to pups remains high for some weeks after weaning. After Bridges, 1990.

to rat pups and will show a reduced latency to behave maternally in future tests (Bridges, 1990).

If foster pups are presented to an adult female rat that has never been pregnant (a nulliparous female) for several hours each day, then she begins to behave maternally after 5 or 6 days. This phenomenon is called **concaveation** (Rosenblatt, 1967; Wiesner and Sheard, 1933), sensitization (LeBlond, 1938), or pup-induced parental behavior (Fleming et al., 1996). All the behaviors, except maternal aggression in defense of the nest, that are typically observed in a rat that has just given birth are observed in these "sensitized" females; they even adopt a nursing posture, albeit an imperfect one in the absence of suckling by the pups (of course, they do not lactate without the proper hormonal priming). Remarkably, male rats also show this response to exposure to rat pups, although they take more time to achieve the level of maternal behavior observed in females, and the behavior is less consistent than that shown by females (Lubin et al., 1972; Mayer et al., 1979). Concaveation appears to have little or nothing to do with hormone concentrations, because the effect persists after the removal of the gonads, pituitary, or adrenal glands; the behavioral changes appear to be induced by the mere presence of the pups (Rosenblatt, 1967), likely mediated by neurochemical pathways, especially the dopamine system (Afonso et al., 2008, 2009; Hansen et al., 1991, 1993) (see below). An examination of the pattern of *fos* activation in the presence of pups revealed that maternal behavior induced by concaveation activated the same brain regions in virgin females as in mothers (Kalinichev et al., 2000).

Mother rats, or dams, on the other hand, behave maternally toward their own pups as soon as they are born, and this rapid onset of maternal behavior is hormonally mediated. Normally, adult laboratory rats are fearful of pups; they approach them very tentatively, sniff them, and withdraw quickly. One way in which the hormones associated with pregnancy and lactation predispose the new mother to behave maternally is by reducing the fear associated with the presence of rat pups (Fleming, 1986; Fleming and Luebke, 1981), as we will see below. Continued exposure to her pups also appears to allow the dam to overcome her initial fear of newborns as she becomes accustomed to them.

Males may require longer exposure to pups than females to behave maternally in concaveation tests, because as open field tests and other evaluations have shown, males are generally more timid than females (Gray and Lalljee, 1974). As noted above for dogs, rats that give birth by C-section typically behave maternally toward their pups as soon as they recover from anesthesia if they receive some time with the pups. However, if C-sectioned or normally parturient mother rats are not permitted this initial interaction with their pups, maternal responsiveness to pups wanes during the first week after birth (Bridges, 1977; Orpen and Fleming, 1987). By the tenth day postpartum, dams show the same latencies to respond to foster pups as nulliparous females do.

concaveation The process of becoming sensitized to newborn animals so that full maternal behavior is expressed. Also called pup induction or sensitization.

It is important to emphasize that most mammals studied in laboratory environments have an abnormal developmental history that prevents the typical juvenile experience with neonates (J. Lonstein, personal communication). Pups are usually weaned and taken from the home cage/natal nest before the age when they would typically disperse, or if they remain in the natal nest, their mothers typically do not mate again, so there are no younger pups in the cage. What happens in natural settings and has shaped parenting over the course of evolutionary time is that juveniles are typically attracted to neonates and thus gain tremendous alloparenting experience with their younger siblings (and also unrelated young in some cooperatively breeding species). This early experience permanently changes their responses to neonates later in life, and they are presumably much more attracted to, rather than fearful of, offspring. There is probably little requirement for relief from neophobia (fear of new things—in this case, neonates) in "real" animals outside the laboratory. This is also presumably true for spontaneously parental animals, even in cases where adults have no previous parenting experience but are still not fearful of pups (e.g., male prairie voles and many strains of laboratory mice).

MOTIVATION AND MATERNAL BEHAVIOR Like mating behavior, parental behavior can be divided into two components: motivation and performance. Hormones affect both the motivation to engage in parental care and the performance of specific actions required for parental care.

To untangle the effects of hormones and brain regions on maternal behavior, several studies have been conducted on rats. For example, female rats that were either postpartum or cycling (but had previous experience as mothers) were given the opportunity to press a bar to get access to a pup (Lee et al., 2000). Females were also exposed to pups in their home cages. Different groups of these female rats had previously received lesions of the medial preoptic area (MPOA), the lateral amygdala, or the nucleus accumbens; other rats with sham lesions served as controls. Both postpartum and cycling females with MPOA lesions showed a reduced rate of bar pressing for pups compared with control females (Lee et al., 2000). In postpartum females, amygdala lesions also reduced bar pressing. Rats in all the lesioned groups displayed decreased maternal behavior in the home cage. Taken together, these results indicate that the MPOA is part of a circuit that mediates both stereotyped maternal behaviors and motivation to perform them, but they also suggest a dissociation of mechanisms mediating expression of the species-typical maternal behavior and those mediating motivation (Lee et al., 2000).

In another series of studies, the maternal motivation of rat dams was tested by determining whether they preferred a chamber previously associated with either cocaine or pups. This process is called conditioned place preference and is used commonly to understand the rewarding properties of various stimuli, including addictive drugs. During the early postpartum period (i.e., 8 days after birth), most dams preferred the chamber that had previously held their pups. In contrast, later in the postpartum period (i.e., 16 days after birth), most dams preferred the chamber in which they had received a shot of cocaine (Mattson et al., 2001). On postpartum day 10, however, the numbers of dams that preferred the cocaine-associated and the pup-associated chambers were nearly equal. Thus, postpartum day 10 appeared to be a midpoint in the shift in motivation of rat dams or in the reward properties that rat pups had for dams (Mattson et al., 2001). Regardless of their preference, the dams displayed equivalent levels of maternal behavior (Mattson et al., 2003). These studies indicate that differences in motivational state can be observed even while performance of maternal behavior remains the same. The factors, endocrine or otherwise, that underlie this distinction remain unspecified.

EXPERIENTIAL INFLUENCES ON MATERNAL BEHAVIOR The effects of various hormones and neuropeptides on maternal behavior change as a function of experience.

In general, experienced mothers are "better" mothers. Females that have given birth previously display maternal care toward foster pups within one day regardless of their hormonal status (Bridges, 1996). Furthermore, rats undergoing their second pregnancy respond to pups with maternal care within one day during midgestation, in contrast to primiparous (pregnant for the first time) rats, which require 7 to 8 days (Bridges, 1978). Even hypophysectomy appears to have little effect on the maintenance of maternal behavior (Erskine et al., 1980a). Thus, hormones appear to be important in priming first-time mothers to behave maternally at the end of their pregnancy. Subsequently, experiential factors appear to mediate maternal care for future offspring (Bridges, 1996).

It seems that a "maternal memory" that depends on experience with pups is normally formed immediately postpartum and that this memory serves to reduce the latency to display maternal behavior (Bridges, 1975). Alison Fleming and her colleagues tested this hypothesis by administering cycloheximide, a protein synthesis inhibitor that interferes with memory formation in other contexts, to rat dams immediately before or after allowing them a 2-hour postnatal maternal experience with their pups. They found that these treatments blocked the expression of later maternal behavior toward foster pups (Fleming et al., 1990a). In order to specify the neural circuits involved in maternal memory, two subregions of the nucleus accumbens, the shell and the core, were lesioned. Lesions of the shell region of the nucleus accumbens either before or shortly after a brief maternal experience substantially disrupted maternal memory (Li and Fleming, 2003b). However, lesions in this brain area had no effect if the dam had more than 24 hours experience with pups. Lesions of the core of the nucleus accumbens did not affect maternal memory (Li and Fleming, 2003b). Furthermore, when cycloheximide was infused into the shell region of the nucleus accumbens (but not elsewhere) of dams immediately after a single 1-hour interaction with their pups, maternal memory was disrupted. The accumbens shell receives dopaminergic fibers from the mesocortical dopamine system, the primary dopaminergic reward system in the brain, and infusion of D1 and D2 receptor antagonists block this maternal memory (Parada et al., 2008). Additionally, as you will see below, oxytocin is released around the time of parturition and participates in the formation of this maternal memory by acting on the nucleus accumbens (D'Cunha et al., 2011). These results indicate that the shell, but not the core, of the nucleus accumbens is part of the brain circuitry mediating maternal memory, likely through dopaminergic and oxytocinergic stimulation (Li and Fleming, 2003b).

Cycloheximide apparently blocks the formation of a rat dam's memory of her early experiences with her pups by preventing the consolidation of new information (Davis and Squire, 1984). Precisely what new information is normally being consolidated is not known, although there are many hypotheses. Most likely, an association between stimuli correlated with the pups and the maternal response is stored during normal attachment. We know that protein synthesis is necessary for the formation of new memories. This protein synthesis may represent new growth of neural processes or an increase in neurotransmitter or receptor production. Thus, the protein synthesis inhibitor might prevent the consolidation of information by blocking either structural changes in or the enhancement of the efficacy of certain neurons. Based on chemical lesion studies, intracerebroventricular injections, microdialysis, and gene manipulations, researchers believe that the neurotransmitters involved in maternal behavior include dopamine, norepinephrine, and serotonin (Bridges, 1996; Nelson and Panksepp, 1998; Thomas and Palmiter, 1997).

THE ONSET OF MATERNAL BEHAVIOR The natural endocrine profile of late pregnancy and pseudopregnancy in rats includes a precipitous drop in blood plasma concentrations of progesterone after a dramatic increase throughout pregnancy; a steady, gradual increase in blood estradiol concentrations; and an increase in prolactin concentrations at the end of pregnancy and immediately postpartum

FIGURE 7.19 Hormone profile during pregnancy in rats and humans (A) In rats, after blastocyst implantation, which occurs about 5 days after insemination, blood concentrations of progesterone begin to rise, peaking on days 15 and 16, then drop precipitously at the end of gestation. Blood estradiol concentrations remain stable during the first part of pregnancy, then rise dramatically at the end. Prolactin concentrations are high during the first half of pregnancy, due to daily pulses of this hormone, but then decrease until the end of pregnancy, when they rise again; this hormone is necessary to support lactation and is important in mediating some maternal behaviors. (B) In humans, prolactin concentrations (not shown) increase gradually until parturition and stay elevated until nursing is completed. Concentrations of progesterone increase dramatically during the first trimester, then continue to increase until just prior to parturition. Estrogen (primarily estradiol) concentrations show a slow, continuous rise until the last few weeks of pregnancy, then quickly drop prior to parturition. After Rosenblatt et al., 1979.

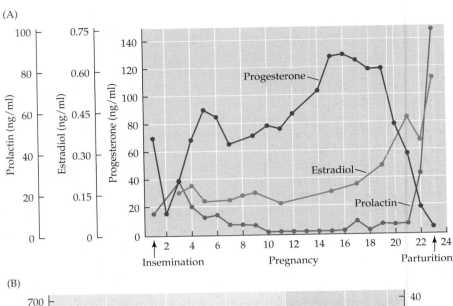

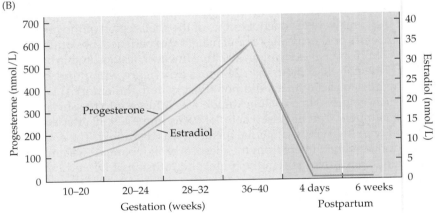

(Bridges, 1990; Lonstein et al., 2014, 2015) (**FIGURE 7.19A**). This endocrine pattern is also evident in near-term pregnant mice (McCormack and Greenwald, 1974), rabbits (Challis et al., 1973), and sheep (Chamley et al., 1973). In contrast, pregnancy in Old World primates, including humans, is characterized by high concentrations of both estradiol and progesterone throughout pregnancy, followed by a precipitous drop in the concentrations of both steroids at parturition (Coe, 1990; Warren and Shortle, 1990) (**FIGURE 7.19B**). Oxytocin and endorphins increase around the time of parturition; oxytocin is important in the smooth muscle contractions necessary for giving birth (Bridges, 1996). The role of opioids remains controversial; they may reduce pain during childbirth, and they may be involved in the mediation of maternal behavior. Both stimulatory and inhibitory roles of β-endorphin in maternal behavior have been reported (reviewed in Bridges, 1996; González-Mariscal and Kinsley, 2009).

Primates also increase concentrations of ACTH and cortisol throughout gestation. The elevation of cortisol concentrations may serve to lower progesterone concentrations in addition to suppressing immune reactions of the mother toward her fetus (Coe, 1990). Elevation of glucocorticoids is typically associated with increased stress responsivity; however, increased cortisol in late gestation in mothers does not seem to make these mothers more stressed, probably because of differential receptor availability in the hypothalamic-pituitary-adrenal axis.

Research on the topic of endocrine induction of maternal behavior in rats has fallen into two general categories. One approach has attempted to induce maternal

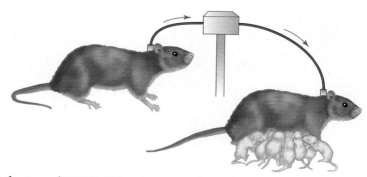

FIGURE 7.20 A blood-borne factor induces maternal behavior in nulliparous rats. When the blood of a new mother was transfused into a nulliparous rat, the recipient showed maternal behavior within 24 hours. Normally, 4–6 days of sensitization are required to induce maternal behavior in nulliparous females. After Terkel and Rosenblatt, 1968.

behavior in nulliparous females via the administration or removal of hormones associated with pregnancy and lactation. Techniques used in such endocrine induction studies have included hormone replacement therapy and the transfusion of blood between pregnant and nonpregnant animals. This approach has also been used in other mammals. The other type of study has attempted to induce maternal behavior by terminating pregnancy at various stages. The logic behind these pregnancy termination studies is that (1) hormones change during pregnancy, (2) maternal behavior is caused by the hormones associated with pregnancy, and (3) because pregnancy termination leads to the rapid onset of maternal behavior before its normal onset at parturition, correlating the onset of maternal behavior with the coincident endocrine profile will reveal the hormonal cause of these behaviors.

Nearly 100 years ago, Calvin P. Stone exchanged the blood of a female rat that was behaving maternally with the blood of one that was not, by connecting their circulatory systems in what is called a parabiotic preparation. In this manner, Stone attempted to induce maternal behavior in the nonmaternal rat, but he was unsuccessful (Stone, 1925). Many years later, Terkel and Rosenblatt (1968, 1972) set up a transfusion system whereby the blood of one female could be exchanged with that of another while they were free to walk around and, apparently, behave normally (**FIGURE 7.20**). In one such experiment, the blood of a female that had just delivered a litter was exchanged with that of a nulliparous female. Virtually complete maternal behavior was observed in the nulliparous female within 24 hours of her receiving blood from the mother rat. This now classic study demonstrated conclusively that a blood-borne factor is important in the induction of maternal behavior in rats.

The vast majority of work on the effects of pregnancy termination on the onset of maternal behavior has been conducted by Jay Rosenblatt and his colleagues (e.g., Bridges et al., 1978a; Rosenblatt and Siegel, 1975; Siegel and Rosenblatt, 1975, 1978) (**FIGURE 7.21**). Female rats normally do not behave maternally toward foster pups in early or mid pregnancy but are intensely maternal at the end of pregnancy. The rationale behind these studies was to find out whether prematurely terminating pregnancy would induce the endocrine changes observed at birth and consequently induce maternal behavior. The researchers found that surgical removal of the uterus, fetuses, and placenta (hysterectomy) induces maternal behavior. Rats hysterectomized between days 16 and 19 of pregnancy respond rapidly with maternal behavior if they are presented with newborn foster pups 24–48 hours after surgery (Bridges et al., 1978b). Recall that nonpregnant female rats—with or without a uterus—require 5 or 6 days of periodic exposure to pups before they behave in a maternal manner.

From a hormonal perspective, the removal of the placenta is probably the main causative factor in the induction of maternal behavior in hysterectomized rats. The removal of the placenta eliminates the source of placental lactogen, which supports the corpora lutea during mid to late pregnancy in rats. Consequently, removal of the placenta during hysterectomy leads to rapid regression of the corpora lutea and subsequent reductions of blood concentrations of progesterone. The rat placenta is also the source of a gonadotropin that typically suppresses ovarian estrogen production until very late in pregnancy. Removal of this source of estrogen inhibition results in a rapid pulse of estrogen secretion, which normally results in postpartum

FIGURE 7.21 Jay Rosenblatt, a pioneer in the study of hormones and maternal behavior.

FIGURE 7.22 A dwarf rabbit (*Oryctolagus cuniculus*) plucks hair from herself to line her nest. A specific combination of estradiol, progesterone, and prolactin regulates this fur removal behavior and also regulates the loosening of her fur.

estrus. Thus, mid- to late-pregnancy termination via hysterectomy results in an endocrine profile resembling that found in a normal rat immediately prior to parturition.

In other studies of the hormonal bases of maternal behavior, attempts have been made to mimic the endocrine patterns of pregnancy in ovariectomized females by injecting them with different hormones in various sequences (Bridges, 1990, 1996; González-Mariscal, 2001; Moltz et al., 1970; Rosenblatt et al., 1998; Zarrow et al., 1971).

Two of these early studies will be described in detail. In one study, nulliparous rabbits that were injected with estradiol for 18 days and received progesterone injections on days 2 through 15 exhibited nest-building behavior (Zarrow et al., 1963; reviewed in González-Mariscal and Rosenblatt, 1996). Maternal behavior is relatively difficult to assess in rabbits because of its brevity. The energetic demands on a lactating rabbit doe are enormous, and foraging demands virtually all of her time. Consequently, a rabbit doe does not engage in as much maternal behavior as other species that produce altricial young; for instance, a mother rabbit nurses her litter for only about 3–4 minutes once per day (Ross et al., 1959; Zarrow et al., 1965). Thus, the maternal behavior of rabbits that is most commonly assayed in the laboratory is nest building. Near the time of birth, the pregnant doe builds a nest of straw and grass and lines it with her own fur, which loosens progressively throughout pregnancy, so it can be easily removed at this time (**FIGURE 7.22**). This fur loosening is dependent on hormonal changes. The increased estrogen-to-progesterone ratio at the end of pregnancy probably stimulates the release of prolactin from the anterior pituitary, as it does in rats and sheep. Treatment of pregnant rabbits with dopamine agonists (e.g., ergot compounds), which block prolactin release, suppresses nest building; concurrent treatment with prolactin reverses the suppression (Zarrow et al., 1971). Thus, the maternal nest building observed at the end of pregnancy in rabbits correlates with an increased estrogen-to-progesterone ratio in the blood, as well as with elevated prolactin titers (González-Mariscal, 2001; González-Mariscal et al., 2005).

In contrast to rabbits, house mice and golden hamsters build nests during early or mid pregnancy. High concentrations of both estrogens and progestins induce maternal nest building in these species (Lisk, 1971; Richards, 1969; reviewed in González-Mariscal and Rosenblatt, 1996). External factors interact with hormones in mediating maternal nest building in rabbits (González-Mariscal et al., 1998). The endocrine profile during pregnancy and parturition is very different from the endocrine profile during nursing. Yet, the quality (and perhaps quantity) of maternal care in rabbits remains constant. As in other mammalian species, maintenance of rabbit maternal behavior appears to require sensory stimulation (e.g., olfactory, tactile, acoustic, and visual) that is provided by the offspring (González-Mariscal, 2007; reviewed in González-Mariscal and Poindron, 2002).

In another study, ovariectomized female rats were injected with estradiol for 11 consecutive days, progesterone on days 6 through 9, and prolactin on days 9 through 11 (Moltz et al., 1970). This pattern of hormone treatment caused full maternal behavior within 35 hours of exposure to pups. Although the induction of complex maternal behavior with a certain pattern of hormone injections is impressive, normal maternal behavior begins at or immediately before parturition, not 35 hours later. There must be other factors, endocrine as well as nonendocrine, involved in the induction of normal postpartum maternal behavior, or else the presentation of the hormones via systemic injections was insufficient to engage the neural machinery underlying this behavior. Infusions of prolactin directly into the MPOA of steroid-primed rats induce maternal behavior very quickly (Bridges, 1996; Bridges and Freemark, 1995; Bridges et al., 1996).

The role of progesterone in the induction of maternal behavior is not precisely understood (Numan and Insel, 2003). Progesterone appears to have two functions in rats. It probably acts with estradiol early in pregnancy to facilitate subsequent maternal behavior (both motivation and performance), but later in pregnancy it inhibits maternal behavior. That is, progesterone needs to be withdrawn prior to parturition if maternal behavior is to be displayed (Sheehan and Numan, 2002).

Other studies suggest that placental lactogen may mediate the reduced latency to maternal behavior that occurs during pregnancy prior to parturition. Infusion of placental lactogen into the MPOA of steroid-primed rats was as effective as prolactin infusion in stimulating maternal behavior (Bridges et al., 1995, 1996). It appears that the conceptus (the fetus plus placenta) secretes placental lactogen, which can stimulate maternal behavior during and at the end of the pregnancy (Bridges et al., 1996). Thus, the endocrine communication between the developing conceptus and the mother ensures that maternal behavior will occur as soon as possible after birth (Bridges, 1996). This intriguing "manipulation" of maternal endocrine function is in the best interest of the fetus but also benefits the mother's long-term fitness.

Other experiments have suggested a role for oxytocin in mediating the onset of rat maternal behavior. In all mammalian species that have been investigated, oxytocin concentrations increase during parturition (Fuchs and Dawood, 1980; Fuchs and Fuchs, 1984). Oxytocin causes the uterine and vaginal contractions of birth, as well as milk letdown, processes that may induce other physiological changes leading to the onset of maternal behavior. If oxytocin is injected directly into the ventricles of the brain in estrogen-primed ovariectomized rats, maternal behavior is observed within 1 hour (Pedersen and Prange, 1979; C. A. Pedersen et al., 1982). Oxytocin appears to act as a neurotransmitter or neurohormone in the brain, because systemic injections of oxytocin into estrogen-primed ovariectomized rats do not induce maternal behavior (Insel, 1990a). However, rats are very sensitive to the testing environment, and differences in apparatus and test procedures may mask the effects of oxytocin on maternal behavior. Of course, the relevance of oxytocin released during milk letdown for the onset of maternal behavior remains unspecified because maternal behavior must be present before pups suckle and milk letdown occurs, not after. It is also important to note that oxytocin does not cross the blood-brain barrier, so oxytocin released from the posterior pituitary to the general circulation does not get back into the brain to affect behavior.

It is possible that vaginal stimulation during parturition causes oxytocin secretion, which in turn stimulates further contractions as a sort of feed-forward mechanism that ultimately leads to high circulating oxytocin concentrations. It is possible that sufficient oxytocin could leak into the brain via the cerebrospinal fluid and affect maternal behavior. To test this hypothesis, multiparous (having previously given birth several times) nonpregnant sheep were injected with a hormone regimen that included 12 days of progesterone followed by a large dose of estradiol; then they were tested for maternal responsiveness to newborn lambs (Keverne et al., 1983). Half of the ewes received vaginocervical stimulation with a vibrator 5 minutes prior to the presentation of the lambs. Vaginocervical stimulation elevated oxytocin concentrations in the cerebrospinal fluid (Keverne and Kendrick, 1994). Only 20% of the nonstimulated ewes showed maternal behavior during a 1-hour test, but 80% of the stimulated ewes displayed maternal behavior. These results suggest that oxytocin is important in the induction of maternal behavior in sheep (**BOX 7.2**). More recent evidence suggests that parturition activates the immediate

BOX 7.2   *Maternal Behavior in Sheep*

Research on sheep has been especially informative about the hormone-brain-behavior interactions associated with maternal behavior. Sheep are seasonal breeders, and most lambs are born early in the spring to coincide with the maximal availability of green vegetation for food. Sheep form feeding flocks and graze over a common home range (Lévy et al., 1996). When pregnant ewes are about to give birth, they seclude themselves away from the flock. The mother and her highly precocial lamb form a strong social bond within the first hour after birth. During this time, the mother learns to discriminate her lamb from the other lambs in the flock. This discrimination appears to be based on olfactory cues emitted by the lamb (Kendrick et al., 1992). Ewes normally permit only their own lambs to approach their udders and suckle. This discrimination is important from an evolutionary perspective because ewes that permitted other lambs to nurse would give up resources that could go to their offspring (Lévy et al., 1996). Such misdirected parental care would have strongly negative consequences for fitness if there were insufficient milk for the ewes' own lambs. In fact, ewes are highly rejecting of approaching lambs with which they have not formed a social bond (Lévy et al., 1996). Thus, the establishment of an exclusive bond during the first hour is a critical component of sheep maternal care.

Importantly, establishment of the exclusive bond is separate from maternal responsiveness, a suite of behaviors that is directed toward any lamb immediately after parturition. Olfactory cues are also important in making lambs attractive stimuli to ewes. Both maternal responsiveness and establishment of the exclusive social bond characterize maternal behavior in sheep (Lévy et al., 1996).

As in other mammals, parturition in sheep is preceded by an increase in the ratio of estradiol to progesterone in the blood circulation. If nulliparous ewes are hormonally primed with estra-

diol and progesterone to mimic the conditions of the last week of pregnancy and presented with newborn lambs, the ewes are either indifferent or aggressive toward the lambs. However, nulliparous ewes hormonally primed and given vaginocervical stimulation display a rapid onset of maternal behavior. The vaginocervical stimulation simulates parturition and evokes the release of oxytocin (Keverne and Kendrick, 1994). In vivo microdialysis studies of stimulated ewes revealed that oxytocin concentrations were elevated in the cerebrospinal fluid, as well as in the olfactory bulbs, medial preoptic area, paraventricular nuclei of the hypothalamus, and substantia nigra (reviewed in Lévy et al., 1996), all brain areas that are important in sheep maternal behavior. When oxytocin is injected directly into the cerebrospinal fluid of nonpregnant ewes, the full complement of maternal behaviors is observed (Keverne and Kendrick, 1994). These results suggest that oxytocin is important for both maternal acceptance and other maternally motivated behaviors in sheep. The relevance of these findings to humans is potentially great.

early genes *fos* and *fosB* in neurons expressing oxytocin receptors in the MPOA, the piriform cortex, and the bed nucleus of the stria terminalis (BNST), as well as central oxytocinergic neurons (Lin et al., 2003). As we will see below, these neurons are critical for proper expression of maternal behavior.

Oxytocin plays an interesting role in pig maternal responses. When a sow lies on her side to initiate nursing, she starts to grunt. This grunting provokes the piglets to attach to her nipples and begin to suckle. In response to this activity by the piglets, oxytocin is released, which provokes the sow to emit a different kind of grunting sound. This new type of grunting provokes the piglets to suckle more vigorously than before and promote additional milk letdown (Algers and Uvnäs-Moberg, 2007).

A suite of hormones, neuropeptides, and neurotransmitters is responsible for the initiation and maintenance of maternal behavior in mammals. In rats, the factors that appear to have the greatest effects on maternal behavior are estrogens and lactogenic hormones (i.e., prolactin and placental lactogens) (Bridges, 1996). The supportive roles of prolactin, progesterone, oxytocin, cholecystokinin, and probably β-endorphins in maternal behavior are estrogen-dependent (Bridges, 1996; Insel, 1990b) (see Figure 7.19A).

Several neurotransmitter systems are involved in the mediation of rat maternal behavior, but the dopaminergic system seems particularly important (Afonso et al., 2008, 2009). As you likely know, the dopamine system is composed of three distinct pathways: (1) the nigrostriatal pathway, which originates in neurons within the substantia nigra of the midbrain and whose axons project into the striatum region of the forebrain to control motor functions; (2) the mesolimbic system, which involves neurons in the ventral tegmental area of the midbrain that project mainly to the nucleus accumbens, amygdala, and hippocampus to regulate stimulus salience and behavioral activation; and (3) the mesocorticoid system, which projects from the midbrain through the forebrain and frontal cortex and is involved in human "executive" functioning (Tobler, 2009). As noted above, maternal care is a motivated behavior, as are sexual behaviors; motivated behaviors generally have a rewarding component that involves the dopamine system.

Activation of the mesolimbic dopamine system appears necessary for appropriate maternal behavior (see Numan and Insel, 2003; Numan and Stolzenberg, 2009). Maternal retrieval behavior in rat dams is disrupted when a dopamine receptor antagonist (D1 and D2) is infused into the nucleus accumbens of these animals (Li and Fleming, 2004a,b), whereas maternal behavior is enhanced by infusion with a dopamine receptor agonist (D1) (reviewed in Numan and Insel, 2003). Importantly, the dopaminergic system can be stimulated and inhibited by lactogenic hormones and inhibited by endogenous opioids (Bridges, 1996). For example, hormonally induced reduction of baseline dopamine transmission appears to provide an important mechanism underlying the immediate expression of maternal behavior in postpartum rats (Afonso et al, 2009). When ovariectomized rats with no pup experience are treated with progesterone and estradiol (which induces maternal responsiveness to foster pups), they display reduced basal responses and increased response to pup presentation, prior to the actual expression of maternal behavior, that are seen in postpartum intact mothers (Afonso et al., 2009). It appears that cues (e.g., olfactory, vocal, visual) from the pups are sufficient to induce dopamine release into the nucleus accumbens, and female participation in maternal behavior is not required to elicit this response. If pups are presented to hormone-primed females in a box with perforations that allow visualization, hearing, and smell (but not direct interactions), dopamine release occurs as it does with interacting mothers (Alfonso et al., 2013). Microdialysis has indicated that the speed with which a rat displays maternal behavior is negatively correlated with basal dopamine levels prior to pup exposure. Thus, hormones that facilitate maternal responsiveness in inexperienced rats have effects on dopamine that are similar to those observed in intact postpartum experienced female rats; importantly, hormone-induced basal dopamine suppression is related to elevated maternal responsiveness.

Dopamine systems outside the primary ascending pathways are also important for maternal behavior (Miller and Lonstein, 2009). As with male sexual behavior, blocking dopamine receptor function within the POA disrupts maternal behavior (Miller and Lonstein, 2005), and the primary dopaminergic projections to the POA are not from the ventral tegmental area or substantia nigra (Miller and Lonstein, 2009).

As noted above, virgin and multiparous female rats that are cycling will also show maternal behavior when given foster pups over several days (Rosenblatt, 1967). What is the role of the dopamine response in the animal that is not hormonally primed? Although hormones augment dopamine responsiveness, they are not necessary for the dopamine response, because postpartum, cycling multiparous rats display elevated dopamine in response to pups (Afonso et al., 2008). Essentially, all categories of dams with previous maternal experience display elevated extracellular dopamine concentrations, as compared with inexperienced virgin rats. But there is a hierarchy of responses; that is, dopamine appears to be additive: pups are most rewarding to females that have had both experience with pups and exposure to hormones, followed by females with experience alone or hormones alone, followed by females with no experience with pups and no hormone treatments (Afonso et al., 2008).

Is the dopamine response specific to pups, or does any salient stimulus provoke similar dopamine responses? Typically, there is a specificity, or fit, between motivational state and stimulus salience, such that food is most salient to hungry individuals, estrous females are most salient to sexually active males, and pups are most salient to new mother rats (Kelley and Berridge, 2002). Based on this assumption of specificity, behavioral and dopamine responses to pups and food (Froot Loops) were compared for different groups of animals, and it was found that in a choice test, mothers preferred pups almost exclusively, whereas nulliparous rats preferred food. The nulliparous females displayed higher dopamine responses to food than to pups, whereas new mothers (and hormonally primed female rats) displayed the opposite pattern (Afonso et al., 2009).

MATERNAL AGGRESSION Protection of offspring from predators or infanticidal conspecifics is an important component of parental care (Gammie and Lonstein, 2006; Lonstein and Gammie, 2002). Maternal aggression is one mechanism by which female mammals protect their offspring. The onset of maternal aggression appears to be regulated by hormones. However, the hormonal control of maternal aggression appears to differ from the hormonal control of other components of maternal behavior. Maternal aggression is rarely observed in the absence of the offspring.

Most of the research on maternal aggression has been conducted on house mice—more specifically, maternal aggression by house mice directed toward male conspecific intruders. However, substantial work on the interaction of hormones and the somatosensory aspects of maternal aggression has been conducted on rats. Laboratory strains of mice and rats are rather docile and do not usually attack conspecifics. However, beginning in the middle of gestation and peaking in intensity during the first week after birth, mouse dams react to intruding males by displaying intense threat and biting behavior. Prior to parturition, progesterone appears to induce maternal aggression (Svare, 1990). Four converging lines of evidence point to a role for progesterone in mediating maternal aggression in pregnant mice. First, progesterone treatment elevates the rate of aggressive behavior in nulliparous mice (Mann et al., 1984). Second, pseudopregnant females become more aggressive as blood concentrations of progesterone increase (Barkley et al., 1979). Third, pregnant females begin to show signs of maternal aggression when peak concentrations of progesterone occur (Mann et al., 1984). Finally, surgical pregnancy termination, which dramatically reduces progesterone concentrations, eliminates maternal aggression when performed on day 15 of pregnancy, and progesterone replacement therapy partially restores maternal aggression in hysterectomized females (Svare et al., 1986). However, other hormones are also probably involved in maternal aggression, because progesterone treatment alone never induces the level of aggression in nulliparous females that is observed in newly parturient mice. Furthermore, maternal aggression is very high at the time of birth, when progesterone concentrations are relatively low, suggesting that other factors mediate aggressive behavior after the birth of the young.

The results of other studies suggest that in mice, and to a lesser extent in rats, suckling by the young stimulates postnatal maternal aggression (Svare and Gandelman, 1976). Intense maternal aggressive behaviors are observed in mice after 48 hours of suckling, and thelectomized (nipples surgically removed) mice display lower levels of maternal aggression than normal postpartum mice (Svare, 1990). Because suckling was found to be a critical stimulus for the expression of maternal aggression, it was logically suspected that prolactin was responsible for the induction of this behavior. However, this hypothesis was ruled out because neither postpartum hypophysectomy nor treatment with prolactin-inhibiting ergot compounds affected the occurrence of maternal aggression (Erskine et al., 1980b; Mann et al., 1980; Svare et al., 1982). Furthermore, no relationship has been found between blood plasma concentrations of prolactin and the initiation, maintenance, or decline of maternal aggression in house mice (Broida et al., 1981). However, prolactin does mediate maternal aggression in white-footed mice (*Peromyscus leucopus*) (Gleason et al., 1981) and Syrian hamsters (Wise and Pryor, 1977).

Thus, ovarian hormones present during pregnancy appear to regulate maternal aggression in mice and rats in two ways. First, ovarian steroids directly promote aggressive behavior during gestation. Second, these hormones indirectly induce aggressive behavior by stimulating nipple development for attachment and suckling by the young (Lonstein and Gammie, 2002). Whether ovarian hormones exert additional effects on postpartum aggression remains unresolved.

Nursing-induced postpartum aggressive behavior coincides with elevated levels of serotonin, and treatment with a serotonin antagonist reduces maternal aggression (Ieni and Thurmond, 1985). Endorphins, oxytocin, vasopressin, and nitric oxide also may play a role in maternal aggression (Lonstein and Gammie, 2002). Decreased norepinephrine signaling in the lateral septum facilitates maternal aggression (Scotti et al., 2011). Corticotropin-releasing hormone (CRH), an activator of fear and anxiety, regulates maternal aggression (Gammie et al., 2004). Intracerebroventricular injections of CRH inhibited maternal aggression but not other maternal behaviors. When the gene encoding the binding protein for CRH was deleted, then maternal, but not intermale, aggression was impaired (Gammie et al., 2008). These results suggest that decreased CRH is important for maternal aggression and may act by adjusting brain activity in response to an intruder (Gammie et al., 2004, 2008).

When the paraventricular nuclei of rat dams were destroyed by a chemical (ibotenic acid) lesion, maternal aggression increased at day 5 postpartum, a time when maternal aggression is normally high (Giovenardi et al., 1998). Recall from Chapter 2 that the neurons of the PVN are a source of oxytocin. To ascertain that oxytocin modulates maternal aggression, oxytocin antisense oligonucleotides were infused into the PVN on the fifth day postpartum, and maternal aggression was elevated (Giovenardi et al., 1998).

Maternal aggression per se does not seem to be a typical component of human maternal care, because human mothers rarely express aggression to protect children. However, the lack of regular expression of maternal aggression does not necessarily indicate that human mothers would not act aggressively, if necessary. Human mothers are highly protective, and stories of mothers acting quickly to defend or rescue their children permeate popular culture. The ability to quickly defend offspring at great personal risk is a commonality between human parental protective behavior and maternal aggression observed in other taxa. Experiments on humans are rarely conducted because of ethical considerations; consequently, correlational studies are usually preferred. In one study, women with high concentrations of circulating prolactin due to prolactin-secreting tumors reported higher levels of hostility in paper-and-pencil tests than normal controls; treatment with prolactin-inhibiting ergot compounds reduced these high hostility scores (Buckman and Kellner, 1985; Fava et al., 1981). In another study, new mothers rated themselves as more hostile on day 7 postpartum than did control females (hospital employees) (Mastrogiacomo et al., 1982/1983).

One can imagine nonendocrine explanations for the increased hostility scores of newly parturient women, but studies on women differ fundamentally from the assessment of maternal aggression in other animals. Reliance on hostility scores, rather than on the aggressive behaviors themselves, reduces the likelihood that accurate information about endocrine correlates will be obtained. Paper-and-pencil tests of hostility are rarely validated to ascertain whether they truly correlate with the likelihood of agonistic behavior. Assessment of maternal aggression among nonhumans, as can be seen from the discussions above, is always conducted in the presence of offspring cues or offspring themselves. Mouse dams, for instance, rarely display maternal aggression outside of the nest area. Women, however, are generally separated from their babies during questionnaire testing. Direct tests of maternal aggressive behavior in the presence of their infants and concurrent measurements of hormone concentrations have not been performed on humans (but see Fleming, 1990).

MAINTENANCE AND TERMINATION OF MATERNAL BEHAVIOR   Hormones are clearly necessary to trigger maternal behavior when the offspring are first born. Yet maternal behavior persists after parturition and long after the high hormone concentrations of pregnancy have returned to baseline levels. Are hormones involved in maintaining maternal behavior? Furthermore, mothers act less maternal as their offspring grow older (**FIGURE 7.23**). Are hormone concentrations changing, or are the young less effective in stimulating maternal care?

These questions have been addressed in rats, which display three stages of maternal behavior, but the answers remain speculative. It is important to emphasize that at each stage, the pups are trying to get food from their mother, and the pups' suckling behavior induces maternal nursing behaviors. During the first stage, the majority of the maternal behaviors are initiated by the dam. She builds the nest, delivers the young into it, and retrieves any pups that wander away from it. She huddles over her litter in the nursing posture. The pups must attach themselves to a nipple and stay attached, but the dam provides cues for the pups to promote the initial nipple attachment: she licks her vulva and ventrum during birth, spreading amniotic fluid across the front of her body, and the odor of the amniotic fluid attracts the newborn pups to the nipples. If the amniotic sacs of fetuses are injected with lemon oil during pregnancy, the pups are attracted to the odor of lemon oil after birth (Pedersen and Blass, 1982). As the pups age, the odor of their own and their littermates' saliva and that of their mother keeps attracting them back to the nipple. At an early age, nutritional state does not particularly influence the time it takes for pups to attach to a nipple, but as the pups age, the length of time since the last meal does influence the latency to reattach to a nipple.

In the second stage of rat maternal behavior, there is more mutually initiated contact. The dam may initiate care, but the pups often approach her for contact. Stimuli associated with the pups are critical for maintaining maternal care at this stage (**BOX 7.3**). If a mother rat is provided with new 4- or 5-day-old foster pups every few days, she continues to build nests and behave maternally (Södersten and Eneroth, 1984). This behavior is maintained by tactile and other sensory stimuli from the young pups. In the normal situation, however, maternal care eventually wanes as the pups mature.

Maternal rejection of the pups and subsequent separation from them constitutes the third stage of maternal behavior in rats. The dam makes herself less available to the pups by "hiding" her ventrum

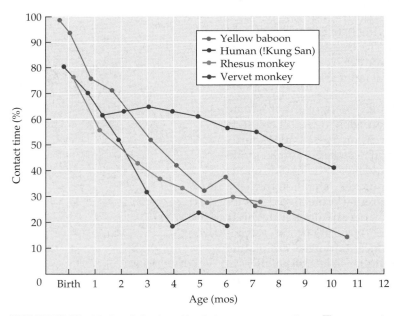

FIGURE 7.23 Mother-infant contact decreases over time. The percentage of time that mothers and their young spent in close contact each day is plotted over the first year of the lives of the offspring for four primate species. When young are first born, virtually all of a mother's day is spent in contact with them, but in nonhuman primate species, this value drops to 10%–30% of the day after 6 months. At 10 months, approximately 40% of a human (!Kung San) mother's time is spent in contact with her baby; this may reflect the slower maturation rate of humans or the increased solicitousness of human mothers. After Altmann, 1980.

BOX 7.3 *Offspring Behavior and the Maintenance of Maternal Behavior*

Research by Judith Stern has established the importance of somatosensory (tactile) feedback from pups for maintaining maternal care in rats (Stern, 1996). Most rat maternal behaviors, including nest construction, licking, and pup retrieval, involve the mouth. During the course of nuzzling or sniffing the pups, the female receives somatosensory input that stimulates further maternal behavior. Many maternal behaviors can be reduced or abolished by cutting or anesthetizing the nerves that innervate the area around the mouth (Stern, 1990). For example, a mother rat that has had her muzzle desensitized with a local anesthetic exhibits reductions in nest building, nest repair, pup retrieval, pup licking, and even biting of intruders.

Somatosensory information from the pups is also important for maintaining nursing behavior. Virtually all mammalian newborns arrive equipped with reflexes that allow them to find and attach to a nipple and ingest milk. Mothers' assistance of their offspring's nursing behavior ranges from the "passive tolerance" of marsupial mothers to the active participation in feeding seen in humans and other primate species (Stern, 1990; Stern and Johnson, 1990). In rats, ventral somatosensory information maintains the maternal nursing posture, an immobile, upright crouching posture in which the female stands over the pups. If the nipples are anesthetized or removed, then even an entire litter cannot stimulate the female to exhibit a normal nursing posture (Stern et al., 1992). Similarly, if the mouths of the pups

are anesthetized so that they no longer root up against the mother, trying to locate her nipples, an unanesthetized dam will fail to adopt the nursing posture. Thus, tactile stimuli from the pups are important in maintaining nursing behavior in mothers.

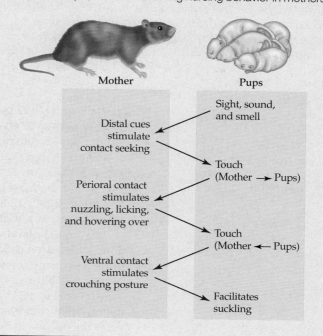

Research by Judith Stern has established the importance of somatosensory (tactile) feedback from pups for maintaining maternal care in rats (Stern, 1996).

from them, by rejecting them, or by remaining out of their reach (Reisbick et al., 1975). What are the signals that reduce maternal care as the pups grow older?

One such signal might be changes in the body temperature of the dam or the pups. Rat pups are born blind, deaf, hairless, and unable to regulate their body temperatures. Rat pups are considered to be poikilothermic, like reptiles; the body temperature of an isolated rat pup is only slightly higher than the ambient temperature. However, although an individual pup cannot thermoregulate, a litter of pups can. After 4 hours of exposure to a 24°C ambient temperature, an individual pup possesses a body temperature of 26°C, while individuals in a huddle of four pups maintain a body temperature of 37°C (Alberts and Brunjes, 1978). Researchers examined the percentage of time that a rat pup spent on the outside of a huddle and found that there was considerable competition among littermates for inner and outer positions within the huddle. In one study, in which litters were culled to four, all four pups kept switching their positions within the litter. In another experiment (Alberts and Brunjes, 1978), one of the four pups in each litter was anesthetized, and the huddle was placed in either a hot or a cold environment (**FIGURE 7.24**). In the cold environment, the anesthetized pup spent up to 90% of the time exposed to the cold at the outer fringes of the huddle. In the hot environment, the anesthetized pup spent a considerable amount of time on the inside of the huddle.

Thermoregulation may play a major role in modulating mother-pup contact time during the third stage of rat maternal behavior, and hormones may underlie the physiological orchestration of changes in contact behavior. The amount of time a mother rat spends with her litter decreases as the pups get older. The dam initially spends about 75% of the day in contact with her litter. The bouts of time she spends

FIGURE 7.24 **Thermoregulation in rat pups** An isolated rat pup's body temperature soon falls several degrees below the normal body temperature of 37°C, but pups in groups can maintain their temperatures at 37°C because individuals move in and out of the huddle to maintain their body temperature in an ideal range. This behavioral thermoregulation can be demonstrated by adding an anesthetized pup to the huddle. (A) At warm ambient temperatures, the pups' maneuvering leaves the anesthetized pup in the center of the huddle and becoming overheated. (B) At cool ambient temperatures, the anesthetized pup is shoved to the outside of the huddle. After Alberts and Brunjes, 1978.

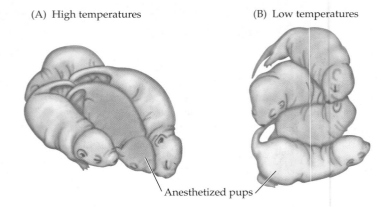

(A) High temperatures   (B) Low temperatures

Anesthetized pups

on the nest decline progressively during the first 2 weeks postpartum; that is, the number of nest bouts remains constant, but the length of each nest bout decreases. Mother rats secrete progressively increasing amounts of prolactin during days 1–14 of lactation (Leon et al., 1990). When Adels and Leon (1986) treated mother rats with bromocriptine, an ergot compound that blocks prolactin production and secretion, they found that nest time did not decrease during the first 2 weeks of lactation but remained high. Adels and Leon suspected that prolactin was acting through another hormone, and in a series of ablation experiments, they showed that removal of the adrenal glands proved to be most effective in blocking the decrease in nest time. If the adrenal glands were removed, time on the nest did not show the normal decrease during days 1–14 of lactation, but removal of the adrenal medulla alone did not block the decline in nest time. Consequently, the researchers surmised that the decrease in nest time must be due to glucocorticoids (e.g., corticosterone) rather than mineralocorticoids (e.g., aldosterone). To discover which hormone would reverse the decline in nest time, they injected adrenalectomized dams with corticosterone, aldosterone, progesterone, or a control treatment (the oil vehicle in which the injected steroids were dissolved). By this means, they eventually discovered that corticosterone was the critical hormone responsible for the decline in nest time. Normally, ACTH increases during the first 2 weeks of lactation and induces increased concentrations of corticosterone in the blood; the increased blood concentrations of corticosterone in turn lead to a reduction in nest bout time.

How do these hormones influence nest bout time? One possibility is that hormones could affect the efficiency of milk transfer. Mothers might regulate the amount of milk that their pups receive by utilizing cues associated with milk delivery to regulate nest time; the pups might become more efficient with age and remove a given amount of milk in less time. Faster transfer of nutrients would allow more time for the mother rat to forage for food. But this hypothesis can be dismissed because the decline in nest bout time is also observed in dams with surgically closed nipples (Leon et al., 1978). Alternatively, the dam might monitor the pups' body temperatures and stay on the nest long enough to keep them warm. As the pups aged and began to thermoregulate on their own, she would need to spend less time with them. This hypothesis can also be rejected because the body temperature of the pups does not directly affect nest bout time (Leon et al., 1978).

Another possibility is that mother rats monitor their own body temperatures to decide when to leave the nest. Glucocorticoids increase the metabolic rate and thus chronically elevate the body temperatures of mother rats (Leon et al., 1990). They cannot dissipate their own body heat when crouching over a litter, so if they stay with the pups for too long, they are in danger of suffering hyperthermia and resultant brain damage. As the pups get older, they retain heat more efficiently, requiring dams to regulate their own body temperature by spending shorter bouts of time on the nest. When pups were experimentally heated or cooled, dams spent less time with hot pups than with cold pups (Woodside and Leon, 1980). When mother rats were shaved, they showed less of a decline in nest time than did furry mothers. Furthermore, direct heating of the MPOA in the dams induced immediate termination of a nursing session (Woodside et al., 1980).

Thus, the researchers concluded that the suckling pups stimulate the secretion of prolactin by the dam, which in turn stimulates increased corticosterone production. Elevated glucocorticoid concentrations increase the mother's basal metabolic rate, which causes a rise in her body temperature. The dam's increased body temperature leads to a decline in time spent with the pups.

The results of some of these studies, however, are subject to alternate interpretations. It is possible that the overheated pups failed to induce nursing behavior in their mothers (Stern and Lonstein, 1996). It can be argued that the high temperatures used in these experiments, which rat mothers and pups do not normally experience in their natural habitats, had confounding effects. That is, hyperthermic pups usually do not suckle, and suckling is critical to inducing maternal behaviors. Because these studies were automated and the time dams spent on the nest was assessed using photocells, no other behavioral changes were recorded. Another potential confounding variable is that the boxes in which the dams were tested at high temperatures were too small to allow them to adopt "heat-dissipating" nursing postures (Stern and Lonstein, 1996). Thus, the apparatus used in these studies might have altered the behavior under study in a manner reminiscent of the way in which paired nonpaced mating tests altered female rat mating behavior (see Chapter 6) (e.g., Erskine, 1989).

The third stage of maternal care involves not only maternal rejection but also separation initiated by the pups. At about 16 days of age, rat pups begin leaving the nest to feed on their own. How do they find their way back to the nest? They use odors. In home orientation tests using odor cues, pups orient to the nest during days 12–14 or so, then start orienting toward their mother. This switch from nest to mother is an important change that frees the pups from the nest. Beginning on day 15 or 16 of lactation and continuing through day 27, mother rats emit a chemosensory signal that pups find very attractive. Leon and Moltz (1972) tested the attractiveness of odors from nests of lactating dams compared with the nest odors of nulliparous females. They found that older pups have a stronger preference for the odors of lactating dams than do younger pups: 5-day-old pups showed no preference, but 15-day-old pups showed a strong preference. However, this preference is not specific to the odor of the pups' own mother (Leon, 1980).

What is the source of this attractive chemosensory signal? It is released in the anal excreta of mother rats—their urine does not attract pups. In addition to feces, rats excrete small pellets of partially digested food matter, called *caecotrophs*, which they usually reingest. Caecotrophs are distinguishable from feces in the caecum, and they are the source of the mother rat's attractive odor. Young rats consume their mother's caecotrophs as an energy-saving measure. In addition, a pup's digestive system is not very efficient, and it benefits from the bacteria found in caecotrophs in building its own internal gut fauna to aid in digestion, particularly digestion of cellulose (Moltz and Kilpatrick, 1978). Caecotrophs taken directly from the caecum of a lactating female attract young rats. Interestingly, caecotrophs taken from the caecum of a nulliparous female rat work almost as well as those of mothers in attracting pups. A nonlactating female, however, normally reingests all of her caecotrophs. A lactating female experiences an increase in appetite and food intake, stimulated by prolactin (Leon et al., 1990), and thus produces so many caecotrophs that some are left near the nest. Thus it is not a specific chemical agent found only in lactating females' caecotrophs, but the emission rate, that is responsible for attracting pups. If prolactin secretion is blocked in the mother rat, then the attractiveness of her nest odor is decreased, probably because she then consumes all the caecotrophs she produces, just like a nonlactating female. Pups lose interest in mothers' caecotrophs at about 28 days of age, when mothers reduce caecotroph production and the pups are about to be weaned.

If nulliparous female rats are sensitized to pups so that they behave maternally and if they are prevented from ingesting their caecotrophs, then eventually the caecotrophs from these females are attractive to other rat pups (Leon, 1992). It requires about 14 days after concaveation for there to be sufficient chemical stimuli to attract pups. As with mothers, the attractiveness of the caecotrophs to pups increases as the pups age. Unlike in lactating females, the blood prolactin concentrations of these rats do not change; again, it is the buildup of sufficient numbers of caecotrophs in the nest that makes the nest attractive to the pups, rather than a special chemical agent produced only by lactating females. The mechanism underlying this phenomenon in concaveated females is unknown.

Endocrine Correlates of Primate Parental Behavior

The endocrine correlates of maternal behavior among primates generally, and humans specifically, remain largely unknown. The reasons for this are varied but probably reflect an assumption by researchers that primate maternal care depends primarily on experiential, not hormonal, factors (**FIGURE 7.25**). However, recent studies have indicated important roles for estradiol in nonhuman primate motivation to engage in maternal behavior, for cortisol and the pattern of estradiol and progesterone secretion in mediating maternal behavior in women, and for prolactin and a decrease in testosterone concentrations in mediating paternal behavior in men (Lonstein et al., 2015; Saito et al., 2015).

Maternal experience seems to play an important role in primate maternal behavior. In one study, adult female rhesus monkeys were presented with an infant for 1 hour daily on 5 consecutive days. Some of the females were nulliparous; others had previously given birth to several offspring. Some of the multiparous females were bilaterally ovariectomized; others were intact; and others were aged, postmenopausal animals. Essentially, the nulliparous females avoided the infant, whereas the multiparous females, regardless of endocrine status, immediately accepted the baby rhesus (Holman and Goy, 1980). One possible conclusion from this study is that hormones are involved in the onset of maternal behavior in first-time mother rhesus monkeys but may not be necessary to stimulate maternal behavior in experienced females. Stimuli associated with primate infants, primarily visual, can trigger appropriate maternal behavior in multiparous females (Coe, 1990).

We know that hormones associated with pregnancy, although not necessary for initial induction of maternal care (Saltzman and Maestripiri, 2011), facilitate interest in infants, with many female primates interacting with other females' infants as pregnancy progresses (Maestripiri and Wallen, 1995; Maestripiri and Zehr, 1998). The hormones of lactation, prolactin and oxytocin, appear to be less important for maternal interaction with infants than is true for rodents, although only a few studies have examined the role of these hormones directly (Saito et al., 2015). In test situations in which primigravid common marmosets were able to press a bar to receive sensory stimuli associated with infants, the rate of bar pressing increased at the end of pregnancy in association with increasing estradiol concentrations. In the same study, the pregnant marmosets pressed the bar at high rates to turn off the recorded cries of an infant (Pryce et al., 1993). A high rate of bar pressing continued postpartum even though estradiol values were decreasing (**FIGURE 7.26**). This correlational study suggests that estradiol primes females to behave in an appropriately maternal manner. Indeed, administration of progesterone and estradiol to marmosets changed their rates of bar pressing

FIGURE 7.25 Maternal behavior in bonobos Female bonobos (*Pan paniscus*) engage in extended maternal care of their semiprecocial offspring. This female bonobo carries her infant and holds it to allow it to nurse.

(Pryce, 1996). An alternative interpretation is that these females are interested in hearing these stimuli, not to cuddle with infants, but to kill them! In both the field and the lab, pregnant, especially late-pregnant, marmosets have been observed to kill infants. Because marmosets are cooperative breeders, there is typically a single breeding female per group; infanticide is typically seen in groups in which a subordinate female has "escaped" from reproductive suppression by the alpha female and presumably views other infants as reproductive competition (Saltzman and Abbott, 2005). When multiparous late-pregnancy female common marmosets were allowed to interact with infants, they showed little or no maternal responsiveness; rather, these females behaved aggressively toward the infants. Both studies (Pryce et al., 1993; Saltzman and Abbott, 2005) report that hormonal changes in pregnancy alter the responsiveness of marmosets toward infants, but for vastly different goals. Whether elevated aggression during late pregnancy is unique to cooperative breeding primates or represents a more common pattern requires additional research.

MATERNAL BEHAVIOR IN HUMANS Among human mothers, it is assumed that hormonal factors facilitate the initial postpartum expression of maternal care, but data to support this assumption are minimal. In fact, hormones are neither necessary nor sufficient for the appearance of basic parental behaviors (Fleming, 1990). Adoptive parents, siblings, grandparents, other relatives, and caregivers can grow attached to infants during a process that appears identical in qualitative and temporal character to the process observed in the biological mother. Obviously, the endocrine profiles of biological parents, adoptive parents, and other caregivers will vary in the presence of virtually identical behavioral patterns. There may be parallels between concaveation and parental care in adoptive parents or caregivers.

Another issue in the study of endocrine correlates of human maternal behavior is that, in contrast to rats, humans have no clear-cut universal set of maternal behaviors. Human mothers typically provide most of the care for their infants, carry them, and nurse them, but this is by no means ubiquitous. There does not seem to be a single set of behaviors, or even attitudes, that characterize human maternal behavior. For example, consuming the placenta and umbilical cord after birth is virtually universal among nonhuman primates (Coe, 1990) (**FIGURE 7.27**), but there is great variation in the occurrence of this behavior among human societies (Kristal et al., 2012). Placentophagia might be adaptive in that it reduces the likelihood of infection and of hemorrhage in the infant. Thus, establishing hormonal correlates of human maternal behavior is difficult when the behavior itself eludes precise definition.

Information about human mothers' perceptions of their behaviors, attitudes, and feelings is typically collected on questionnaires; however, there is generally no consensus about endocrine correlates of the attitudes observed in such studies (reviewed in Krasnegor and Bridges, 1990). Items on questionnaires are usually designed so

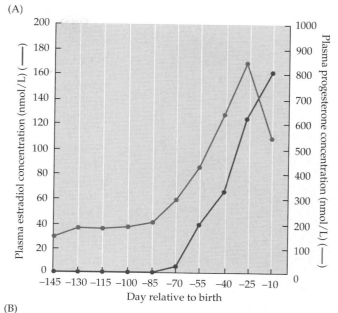

(A)

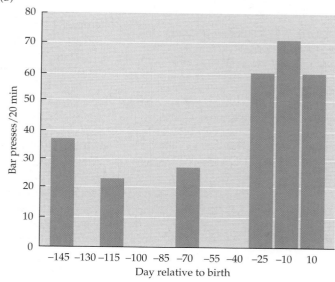

(B)

FIGURE 7.26 During pregnancy, female marmosets increase bar pressing to receive infant sensory reinforcement. (A) Plasma concentrations of estradiol (red line) and progesterone (blue line) over the course of pregnancy in common marmosets. (B) The number of bar presses made by females to gain infant sensory reinforcement. After Pryce et al., 1993.

FIGURE 7.27 Placentophagia in the pig-tailed macaque Eating of the placenta, or placentophagia, is an important component of maternal care among nonhuman primates. Females consume the placenta and umbilical cord up to the ventrum (belly) of the infant. Consuming the placenta and umbilical cord rids the nest of a source of infection for the parents and offspring. Courtesy of Leonard Rosenblum.

that the answers are marked on a five- or seven-point scale reflecting a range of responses from "strongly agree" to "strongly disagree" (Fleming, 1990). Blood samples are sometimes obtained, or correlations between obvious endocrine status (e.g., in midpregnancy or menstruation) and self-reports are made. However, as we have seen, associations between self-reports of attitudes and actual behaviors are not always evident, and experiments to test behavior itself are difficult to perform on humans. These difficulties seriously impair the ability of researchers to ascertain the endocrine correlates of human maternal behavior.

Self-report studies have found differences in attitudes and feelings between new mothers and nonmothers. For example, the hedonic values of a variety of infant-associated odors (e.g., general body, urine, feces) and non-infant-associated odors (e.g., cheese, spices, and lotions) were rated by individuals in four distinct experimental groups: (1) new mothers, (2) mothers who were 1 month postpartum, (3) nonparent women, and (4) nonparent men (Fleming et al., 1993). The odors were rated on a scale that ranged from "extremely pleasant" to "extremely unpleasant," and all of the participants completed several attitude questionnaires, as well. As in studies on nonhuman animals (e.g., Lévy et al., 1996; Poindron and Lévy, 1990), new mothers found infant-associated odors more pleasant than nonmothers did. New mothers also reported more nurturant attitudes and feelings (Fleming et al., 1993). Similar studies indicate that several postpartum factors, including hormone concentrations and learning, are important in the establishment of a mother's attraction to her newborn infant's odors (Fleming and Corter, 1995; Fleming et al., 1993; Schaal et al., 1980).

In another series of studies, new mothers were asked to identify, in a two-choice test, T-shirts that had been worn by their own infants (Fleming et al., 1995). This task was easily performed by virtually all new mothers. Similarly, new mothers can identify their infants based on their cries (Formby, 1967) and tactile features (Kaitz, 1992). The ability of new mothers to discriminate their infants from others appears to rely primarily on experience with the infants, although hormones may potentiate or enhance the effect (e.g., Fleming et al., 1995). Both mothers and fathers could discriminate between the odors of two samples of amniotic fluid—both parents could identify the amniotic fluid associated with their own infant (Schaal and Marlier, 1998).

A series of elegant experiments by Alison Fleming and her collaborators (e.g., Fleming, 1990; Fleming et al., 1987, 1990b) examined the endocrine correlates of the behavior of human mothers as well as the endocrine correlates of maternal attitudes as expressed in self-report questionnaires. In one such study, behavioral responses of new mothers to their 3-to-4-day-old infants were recorded. Responses such as patting, cuddling, or kissing the baby were called affectionate behaviors; talking, singing, or cooing to the baby were considered vocal behaviors. Both affectionate and vocal behaviors were considered approach behaviors (Fleming, 1990). Basic caregiving activities, such as changing diapers and burping the infants, were also recorded. In these studies, no relationship between hormone concentrations and maternal attitudes, as measured by the questionnaires, was found (Fleming, 1990). For example, most women showed an increasing positive self-image during early pregnancy that dipped during the second half of pregnancy but recovered after parturition (**FIGURE 7.28A**). A related dip in feelings of maternal engrossment occurred during late pregnancy but rebounded substantially after parturition in most women (**FIGURE 7.28B**). However, when behavior, rather than questionnaire responses, was compared with hormone concentrations, a different story emerged (Fleming et al., 1987). Blood plasma concentrations of cortisol were positively associated with approach behaviors. In other words, women who had high concentrations of blood cortisol, in samples obtained immediately before or after nursing, engaged in more physically affectionate behaviors and talked more often to their babies than mothers with low cortisol concentrations. Additional analyses from this study revealed that

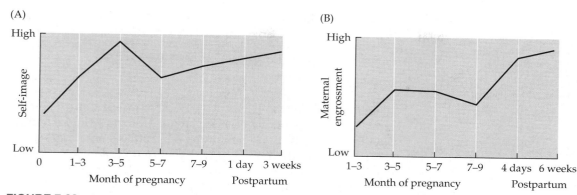

FIGURE 7.28 **Changes in self-image and maternal preoccupation during and after pregnancy** Feelings of maternal self-image (A) and maternal engrossment (B) change in women across pregnancy and the early postpartum period. After Fleming et al., 1990.

the correlation was even greater for mothers who had reported positive maternal regard (feelings and attitudes) during gestation. In fact, nearly half of the variation in maternal behavior among the women could be accounted for by cortisol concentrations and positive maternal attitudes during pregnancy (Fleming et al., 1987).

Presumably, cortisol does not induce maternal behaviors directly, but it may act indirectly on the quality of maternal care by evoking an increase in the mother's general level of arousal (Mason, 1968) and thus increasing her responsiveness to infant-generated cues (Fleming, 1990). For example, new mothers with high cortisol concentrations were also more attracted to their infants' odors, were superior in identifying their infants, and generally found cues from infants highly appealing (Fleming et al., 1997b) (**FIGURE 7.29**). Although there have been a few examples of glucocorticoid involvement in the onset of maternal care in nonhuman animals (e.g., Keverne and Kendrick, 1992), it is possible that cortisol might simply reflect other endocrine changes involving oxytocin, CRH, and opioids, all of which affect maternal responsiveness in nonhuman animals (Fleming et al., 1997b) and all of which are secreted in concert with the glucocorticoids. Perhaps not surprisingly, experiential factors also affect maternal responsiveness in humans; experienced mothers find infants more attractive than do nonmothers and react to infant cues earlier in pregnancy than do first-time mothers (Fleming et al., 1996). Moreover, the relation between cortisol and attraction to infant odors is found only in first-time mothers, in whom hormonal effects would presumably be most necessary.

Recent studies that have examined both human maternal behavior and hormone concentrations have revealed more surprises. Mothers who displayed a positive shift in the ratio of estradiol to progesterone during pregnancy were found to have more positive attachment to their infants than mothers who showed a negative shift (or no change) in the ratio of these two steroid hormones during pregnancy

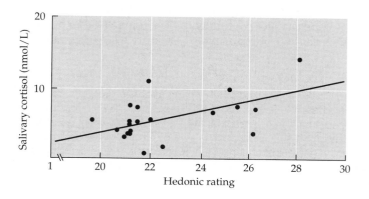

FIGURE 7.29 **Hedonic ratings of mothers' own infants' odors are positively correlated with cortisol concentrations.** Saliva samples of cortisol from first-time mothers were compared with their hedonic ratings (1–41) of their infants' T-shirt odors. Mothers with higher cortisol concentrations found their infants' odors more appealing than did mothers with lower concentrations. After Fleming et al., 1997b.

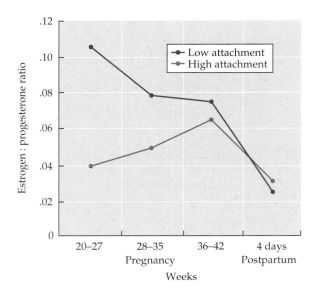

during pregnancy (i.e., an increase in the ratio) show more positive attachment to their infants than mothers whose pregnancy endocrine profiles show a negative shift (or no change). After Fleming et al., 1997a.

(Fleming et al., 1997a) (**FIGURE 7.30**). More recent studies point to a role for oxytocin in maternal behavior. Mothers with the highest oxytocin concentrations exhibit the most affectionate contact and social gaze in a 10-minute test with their 4-to-5-month-old infants (Apter-Levi et al., 2014). Similarly, women with the greatest increases in oxytocin as their pregnancies progress show the highest levels of maternal bonding when observed with their infants (Feldman et al., 2007). In common with these findings, women with differing polymorphisms in the gene encoding the oxytocin receptor might be predisposed to be higher- or lower-quality caregivers. Mothers judged to exhibit high-quality parenting were examined years later through genetic screening and neural imaging (Michalska et al., 2014). Mothers with the genotype associated with highest oxytocin receptor expression had higher positive parenting scores and greater neural responses to images of their children than women with polymorphisms associated with lower oxytocin receptor expression. Taken together, the results of these studies on endocrine correlates of human maternal behavior suggest that a greater emphasis on observing behavior in human mothers is more likely to yield meaningful endocrine correlates than are scores from questionnaires (Fleming et al., 1996). These studies, in common with the studies described for sheep and rats, also emphasize the importance of early contact between mothers and infants at birth for optimal maternal behavior (Klaus and Kennel, 1976). Importantly, there is a bidirectional effect between mother-infant contact and oxytocin levels, and this positively affects offspring growth and development (e.g., Schanberg et al., 1984).

PATERNAL BEHAVIOR IN HUMANS Studies of the endocrine correlates of paternal behavior in mammals that display this behavior in nature have been limited to a few species, including California mice, prairie voles, dwarf hamsters, gerbils, tamarins, and marmosets (Bales and Saltzman, 2016; Storey and Zeigler, 2016). In this section, we will first consider the findings of these experiments before addressing human paternal behavior. As described above, male California mice provide extensive paternal care to their offspring. In one study (Gubernick and Nelson, 1989), the parental behavior of fathers, expectant fathers (males living with their pregnant partners), and unmated males was assessed. The males were exposed to a novel 1-to-3-day-old pup during a 10-minute test. Relatively few

(A)

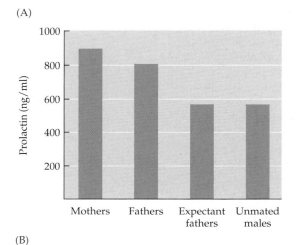

(B)

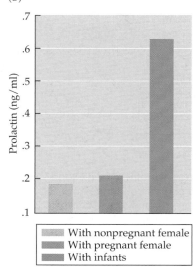

FIGURE 7.31 Marmoset and California mouse fathers have increased prolactin concentrations. (A) Blood samples were obtained from California mouse (*Peromyscus californicus*) mothers and fathers 2 days postpartum, from expectant fathers within 10 days of parturition, and from unmated males. Males of this species engage in virtually all aspects of parental care, and fathers show concentrations of blood prolactin comparable to mothers. (B) Prolactin concentrations increased in male marmosets (*Callithrix jacchus*) with infants in their cages. After Dixson and George, 1982, and Gubernick and Nelson, 1989.

unmated males displayed parental behavior (19%) as compared with fathers (80%) or expectant fathers (56%). Plasma concentrations of prolactin were higher in fathers than in expectant fathers or unmated males (**FIGURE 7.31A**). A similar phenomenon has been observed among male marmosets (**FIGURE 7.31B**). Assessment of oxytocin levels revealed an increase immediately postcopulation, but there were no detectable changes in oxytocin levels after the pups were born, when the males behaved paternally (Gubernick et al., 1995). Testosterone concentrations did not differ among the three groups of males.

Unlike in birds and most mammals, testosterone appears necessary for paternal behavior in California mice. Castration reduced their paternal behavior, whereas testosterone replacement maintained high levels of paternal behavior (Trainor and Marler, 2001) (**FIGURE 7.32**). Testosterone promotes paternal behavior in these mice through its conversion to estradiol (Trainor and Marler, 2002). California mouse fathers have more aromatase activity than nonfathers in the MPOA, a brain area known to regulate maternal care (Trainor et al., 2003).

Examination of plasma concentrations of prolactin in male rats that had undergone concaveation revealed no relationship between prolactin concentrations and paternal behavior (Samuels and Bridges, 1983; Södersten and Eneroth, 1984; Tate-Ostroff and Bridges, 1985). In male gerbils exposed to pregnant females or pups, prolactin values increased throughout pregnancy and remained elevated during the first 10 days after birth; plasma testosterone concentrations rose during pregnancy, then showed a steep decline in paternal males after their pups were born (Brown et al., 1995). However, there is substantial intraspecific variation in testosterone responses in gerbils; males seem to follow one of two reproductive tactics. Either testosterone remains elevated and males pursue additional copulations, or testosterone values decrease and males behave paternally (Clark et al., 1997). Studies on common marmosets have also found that males behaving paternally show a fivefold increase in blood concentrations of prolactin and reductions in blood testosterone concentrations, compared with nonpaternal males (Dixson and George, 1982). In marmosets, exposure to the scents of their own infants is sufficient to reduce testosterone concentrations, suggesting that odor is an important signal for offspring recognition in these fathers (Prudom et al., 2008). Similar findings have been reported for paternal dwarf hamsters (*Phodopus campbelli*) (Reburn and Wynne-Edwards, 1998; Wynne-Edwards, 1998). Other studies have not seen these endocrine changes in the onset of paternal care (e.g., Wynne-Edwards and Timonin, 2007).

The hormonal correlates of human paternal behavior resemble the factors associated with paternal behavior in other mammals, namely, testosterone, prolactin, and cortisol. Plasma prolactin concentrations were elevated in fathers just prior to parturition (Storey et al., 1998). Men who responded physiologically to the sounds of babies crying also displayed elevated prolactin concentrations compared with men who did not respond to infant cries (Elwood and Mason, 1994; Storey et al., 1998). Testosterone concentrations were lower in new fathers relative to men examined soon before their babies were born (Storey et al., 2000). The dynamics of cortisol secretion are similar between men and women around the time of parturition (Storey et al., 1998). Recall that elevated cortisol concentrations in new mothers are linked with the establishment of social bonding between mothers and infants (Fleming et al., 1997b). Cortisol concentrations were highly correlated between men and women partners during pregnancy and birth (Storey et al., 1998). In common with other paternal mammals, men displayed depressed testosterone values (−33%) immediately postpartum (Storey et al., 1998). Women experience elevated testosterone levels near the end of pregnancy but typically display a significant reduction in testosterone concentrations postpartum (Fleming et al., 1997a).

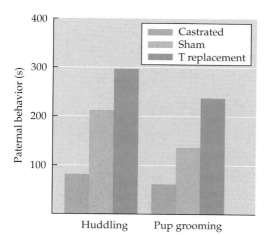

FIGURE 7.32 **Testosterone is necessary for paternal care in California mice.** Unlike most species of birds and mammals, *Peromyscus californicus* males require high testosterone concentrations to display paternal care. Castrated males displayed no huddling or pup-grooming behaviors, but testosterone (T) replacement restored this behavior in castrated males to the level of intact fathers. After Trainor and Marler, 2001.

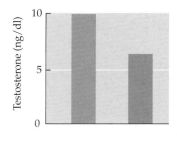

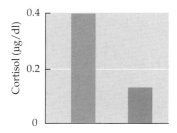

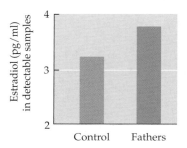

FIGURE 7.33 Expectant human fathers display reduced testosterone and cortisol concentrations, as well as increased circulating estradiol concentrations. After Wynne-Edwards, 2001.

Another study observed endocrine changes in men who were becoming fathers for the first time (Berg and Wynne-Edwards, 2001). Men were recruited from prenatal classes to give saliva samples until the third month after their babies were born. Male volunteers from the general population were also chosen to provide samples, which were age matched and obtained at the same time and season as those from the expectant fathers. Expectant fathers displayed lower testosterone and cortisol concentrations and a higher proportion of samples with detectable estradiol concentrations than control participants (**FIGURE 7.33**). The physiological importance of these hormonal changes in men, if any, is not known, but these hormones have been shown to influence maternal behavior (Berg and Wynne-Edwards, 2001).

In one study investigating changes in perception coincident with parenthood, new fathers and nonfathers were exposed to recorded infant cries and to control stimuli. Heart rate and endocrine responses, including salivary testosterone and cortisol, as well as blood prolactin concentrations prior to and after the stimuli, were assessed. Fleming and her coworkers reported that (1) fathers hearing the recorded crying felt more sympathetic and more alert than nonfathers, (2) fathers and nonfathers with low testosterone concentrations felt more sympathy and the need to respond to the infant cries than did fathers with high testosterone concentrations, and (3) fathers with high prolactin concentrations were more alert and more responsive to the cries. The study also found endocrine differences between new and experienced fathers (Fleming et al., 2002). In common with previous experiments on biparental species, these studies of men indicate that human fathers are more responsive to infant cues than are nonfathers and that the responses of fathers to infant cues are associated with both hormone values and previous caregiving experience (Fleming et al., 2002). When interacting with a RealCare computer-controlled doll that would stop crying when "comforted," testosterone concentrations declined in men provided with a computer-controlled bracelet that responded to effective parental care (Van Anders et al., 2012). When the bracelet was not provided, testosterone concentrations did not change. Similarly, lower concentrations of testosterone in fathers have been associated with higher numbers of positive interactions with infants (Weisman et al., 2014). These findings indicate that hormone concentrations during early fatherhood are not absolute but reflect dynamic interactions between father, child, and context.

As noted, the neuropeptides oxytocin and vasopressin have recently been implicated in paternal behavior. Compared with nonfathers, fathers with 1-to-2-year-old children have higher oxytocin concentrations (Mascaro et al., 2014), and these concentrations increase during the first 6 months of parenthood (Gordon et al., 2010). Intranasal oxytocin administration enhances father-child interactions, including increased positive affect, social gaze, and touch (Naber et al., 2013; Weisman et al., 2014). As in mothers with polymorphisms in the gene encoding the oxytocin receptor (described above), such polymorphisms are predictably associated with paternal interactions (Feldman et al., 2012). As with oxytocin, new fathers have higher vasopressin concentrations (Gray et al., 2007); however, nasal oxytocin administration leads to increased vasopressin (Weisman et al., 2012), making it unclear whether associations between vasopressin and paternal behavior may be due to associated increases in oxytocin. Finally, it is unclear whether blood or salivary concentrations of oxytocin and vasopressin are reflective of neural signaling by these hormones; further study is required to clarify their potential role in paternal behavior.

Neural Changes Associated with Mammalian Parental Behavior

The influences of hormones on the neural bases of parental care will be presented in this section. Again, most of the research on this topic has been done on maternal behavior in rats. There are very few studies addressing the neural control of parental behavior in nonmammalian species. Studies on rats indicate that estrogen promotes maternal behavior by enhancing pup-stimulated neural activity in the MPOA, the bed nucleus of the stria terminalis, and the dorsal and intermediate lateral septum, brain regions considered part of a neural circuit underlying maternal behavior (Sheehan and Numan, 2002). In contrast, progesterone may inhibit maternal behavior in rats by inhibiting neural activity in parts of this brain circuitry (Sheehan and Numan, 2002; Sheehan et al., 2001).

MATERNAL BEHAVIOR Michael Numan, Alison Fleming, and Judith Stern have provided much insight into the interactions among the nervous system, hormones, and parental behavior. The first attempts to elucidate the neural bases of maternal behavior were made by Beach (1937) and Stone (1938c). Beach made multiple neocortical lesions in rats and found that small lesions failed to disrupt the onset or maintenance of rat maternal behavior, but larger lesions seriously interfered with the expression of most components of maternal care. Later, certain hypothalamic lesions were shown to seriously disrupt maternal behavior (Numan, 1990) (**FIGURE 7.34**). Recently, several experiments have implicated the MPOA as a critical component of maternal behavior (Numan, 1988, 1990; Numan and Insel, 2003). Lesions of the MPOA eliminate performance of maternal behavior in rats (Numan, 1974; Numan and Sheehan, 1997).

Of course, the elimination of a behavior after the destruction of a brain region does not necessarily indicate that the destroyed brain area mediates the behavior in question. It is always possible that the destruction of axons of cell bodies originating outside of the lesioned area caused the change in observed behavior. One way to address this issue is to perform selective lesions of the neuronal cell bodies in a specific brain area. The excitotoxic N-methyl-D-aspartic acid (NMDA) is an amino acid that selectively kills neuronal cell bodies but spares the axons near to the injection site. When NMDA was injected bilaterally into the MPOA of normally behaving mother rats 4 days postpartum, maternal behavior was severely curtailed. Bilateral NMDA injections into the lateral preoptic area and adjoining regions, called the substantia innominata, also severely interfered with the display of maternal behavior (Numan et al., 1988). Estrogen implants into the MPOA stimulate maternal behavior in male rats (Rosenblatt and Ceus, 1998; Rosenblatt et al., 1996). Other brain areas are also involved in maternal behavior in rats. For instance, neurons in the lateral preoptic area contribute to pup retrieval, nest building, and nursing behavior (Numan, 1990). There are data suggesting that the POA is also involved in mediating parental care in hamsters (Miceli and Malsbury, 1982b), rabbits (González-Mariscal, 2001), and ringdoves (Komisaruk, 1967). One pathbreaking study suggests that the MPOA changes its role in the regulation of maternal behavior (Pereira and Morrell, 2009). Using a reversible technique to inactivate the MPOA at different points postpartum, it was discovered that, as described above, the MPOA initially facilitates maternal behavior, but later in the postpartum period, the MPOA appears to inhibit maternal behavior (Pereira and Morrell, 2009). These data suggest that the MPOA may orchestrate maternal behavioral onset, maintenance, and termination.

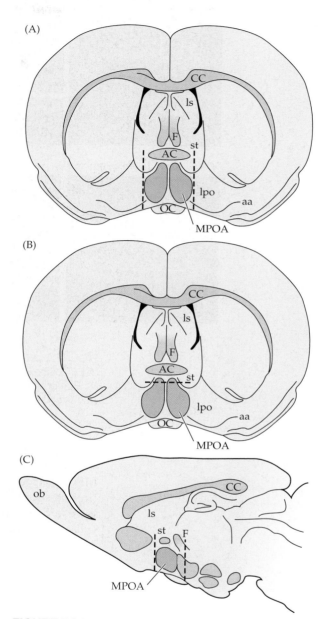

FIGURE 7.34 Lateral projections from the MPOA are critical in rat maternal behavior. MPOA lesions severely disrupt the onset of maternal behavior in rats. (A) Coronal section of a rat brain at the level of the MPOA, showing lesions (dashed lines) that sever the lateral connections of the MPOA to the rest of the brain. (B) Coronal section showing a lesion that severs the dorsal connections of the MPOA. (C) Sagittal section showing that lesions cause anterior and posterior isolation. Only cuts severing the lateral connections interfere with maternal behavior. CC = corpus callosum; OC = optic chiasm; ob = olfactory bulb; MPOA = medial preoptic area; lpo = lateral preoptic area; aa = anterior amygdaloid nuclei; AC = anterior commissure; F = fornix; ls = lateral septum; st = bed nucleus of the stria terminalis. After Numan and Insel, 2003.

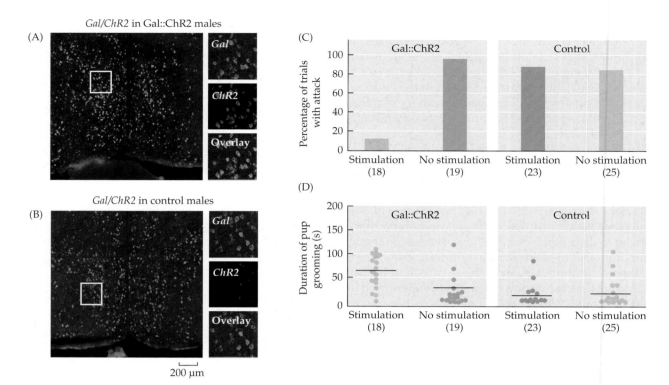

FIGURE 7.35 Optogenetic stimulation of galanin-expressing neurons in the MPOA (A,B) Colabeling showing ChR2 expression in experimental (A) but not control (B) males. (C) Percentage of trials with attacks of pups by virgin males. (D) Pup grooming in the tests with virgin males From Wu et al., 2014.

Recent findings suggest that galanin-expressing cells in the MPOA are key mediators of parental behavior in mice (Wu et al., 2014). Galanin neurons in the MPOA express Fos when male and female CF-1 mice exhibit parenting behavior (in this strain of mice, males can show parental behavior). By using galanin-Cre mice, a Cre-dependent neurotoxin was delivered to the MPOA to ablate galanin cells specifically. The quality of parental care in males and females was reduced by MPOA galanin cell targeting, with parental behavior markedly suppressed when more than 50% of cells were depleted. In virgin males, optogenetic stimulation of MPOA galanin cells leads to reductions in pup-directed attacks and induces pup grooming (**FIGURE 7.35**). These findings suggest that galanin represents a phenotypic cell marker for MPOA cells critical for parental care and suggests that males and females may possess similar circuitry underlying parental behavior. Whether similar results are seen in virgin females or if optogenetic suppression of MPOA galanin-expressing cells suppresses maternal behavior in lactating females requires further investigation. Likewise, whether galanin-expressing cells are directly responsive to hormones such as estrogen, progesterone, and oxytocin or integrate with neurons expressing these receptors in the MPOA or elsewhere remains to be determined.

The nucleus accumbens (NA) appears to play a crucial modulatory role in the performance of maternal behaviors in rats (Li and Fleming, 2003a). Lesions of specific parts of the NA revealed that removing the shell, but not the core, of the NA disrupted pup retrieval. Females with lesions to the shell of the NA required more time to collect all the pups than rats that were not lesioned. However, the latency to first pup retrieval was not affected by lesions of the NA, suggesting a specific deficit in performance. No other component of maternal care was affected by these lesions.

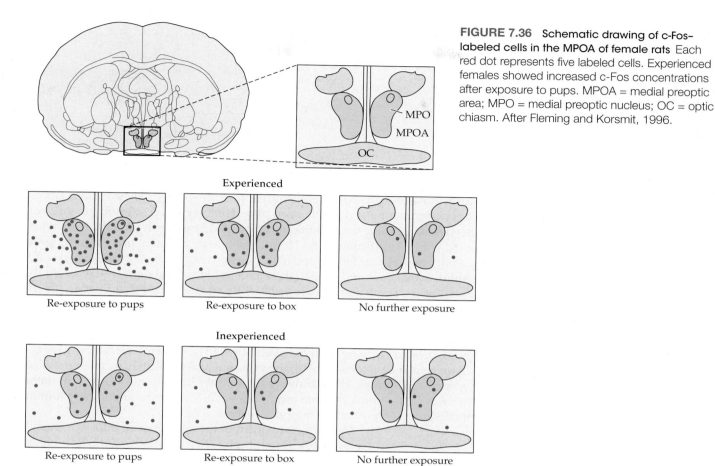

FIGURE 7.36 Schematic drawing of c-Fos–labeled cells in the MPOA of female rats Each red dot represents five labeled cells. Experienced females showed increased c-Fos concentrations after exposure to pups. MPOA = medial preoptic area; MPO = medial preoptic nucleus; OC = optic chiasm. After Fleming and Korsmit, 1996.

These results suggest that the shell of the NA may be required for maintenance of maternal attention or motivation (Li and Fleming, 2003a).

Additional evidence supporting the importance of specific brain regions in maternal behavior has been provided by immunocytochemical visualization of c-Fos, the protein product of the immediate early gene *c-fos*, as an indication of neuronal activity. Several studies have reported an elevation in c-Fos production in the MPOA in rat dams (e.g., Fleming et al., 1994, 1996; Lonstein et al., 1998; Numan and Numan, 1994; Numan et al., 1998). In one study, female rats with and without experience as mothers were allowed to interact with pups in a perforated box, then re-exposed to pups in the box or to the box alone or left in the home cage without further stimulation (Fleming and Korsmit, 1996) (**FIGURE 7.36**). Experienced rats showed increased Fos levels in the MPOA, the basolateral amygdala, the parietal cortex, and the prefrontal cortex (Fleming and Korsmit, 1996) in response to pup exposure. In another study using Fos as a marker for neural activity, dams were separated from their 5-day-old offspring for 48 hours to down-regulate the *c-fos* gene. The dams were then reunited with pups that were capable or incapable (due to anesthetized snouts) of suckling. In a third study, dams were presented with pups housed in a double wire mesh box so they could see, smell, and hear but not touch them. Two additional control groups were included in this study: one group of dams that were presented with the wire mesh box alone, and a group of females that had no further stimulation (Lonstein et al., 1998). Physical interaction with rat pups induced high Fos levels in the MPOA, regardless of whether or not the pups nursed (Lonstein et al., 1998). Expression of Fos was relatively low in the three control groups. These results indicate that the MPOA is involved in maternal behavior but not in response to neuroendocrine changes or sensory inputs.

FIGURE 7.37 The VNO-MPOA pathway
Information from the vomeronasal organ (VNO) travels directly to the accessory olfactory bulbs, then to the medial nuclei of the amygdala via the lateral olfactory tract. Via the stria terminalis, information from the VNO eventually reaches the bed nucleus of the stria terminalis (BNST) or the medial preoptic area (MPOA). Information from the BNST is also relayed to the MPOA. Lesions anywhere along this pathway will interfere with chemosensory processing and will hasten the onset of maternal behavior in rats. After Numan, 1990.

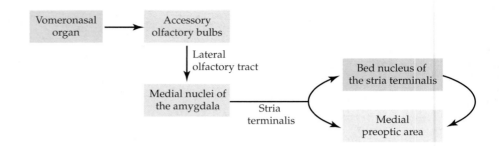

As previously described, rats are quite neophobic—that is, they fear novel stimuli in their environment—and newly born pups are truly novel stimuli. Juvenile rats are often less neophobic than adults, and they readily perform parental tasks when presented with pups (Brunelli and Hofer, 1990). After an initial bout of sniffing the pups, adult nonpregnant female and male rats first react to them in one of two ways. Most animals make a rapid retreat, then tend to ignore and deliberately avoid the squeaking pups. Some animals are apparently so frightened that they attack the pups and may even cannibalize them. As we saw above, newly parturient rat dams overcome their timidity and behave solicitously toward their offspring. One function of hormones in mediating the onset of maternal behavior may be reduction of the fear associated with the newly arrived pups. In fact, hormones not only reduce the negative valence associated with the pups but also separately increase the positive valence of the pups, thus drawing the mother into close contact with them. In other words, the pups become attractive stimuli, a phenomenon new human parents frequently report about their new babies.

A major component of the avoidance of pups is a chemosensory-based repulsion (Lévy and Keller, 2011; Rosenblatt, 1990). The repulsiveness of the pups' odors appears to be overcome by exposure to maternal hormones or by repeated experience with pups during the process of concaveation. This repulsion can also be overridden by making nulliparous females anosmic. As described in Chapter 5, rats have two sets of chemosensory receptors, the olfactory receptors and the vomeronasal organ. Chemosensory information from both inputs is relayed from the primary and accessory olfactory bulbs to the cortical and medial nuclei of the amygdala. The amygdala projects, via the stria terminalis, to both the BNST and the MPOA; the BNST also projects to the MPOA (Fleming and Rosenblatt, 1974) (**FIGURE 7.37**). Lesioning both types of olfactory receptors with intranasal infusions of $ZnSO_4$ results in female nulliparous rats that do not avoid pups and that begin behaving maternally with a short latency.

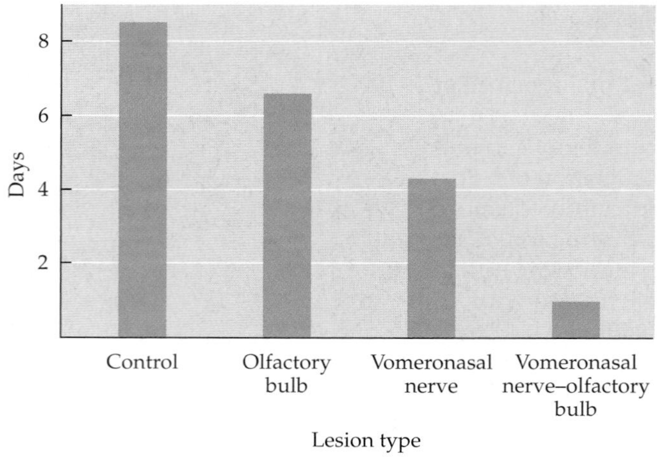

The amygdala appears to inhibit maternal behavior in rats (Fleming et al., 1996; Sheehan and Numan, 2002). Lesions of the medial nuclei of the amygdala accelerate concaveation in nulliparous females (Fleming et al., 1980). Lesions anywhere along the pathway from the vomeronasal receptors to the amygdala also facilitate the onset of maternal behavior in nulliparous rats (Fleming and Rosenblatt, 1974; Fleming et al., 1979, 1980, 1983) (**FIGURE 7.38**). Other parts of the inhibitory circuit of maternal behavior include the ventromedial hypothalamus, septum, and periaqueductal gray region (Bridges, 2008). Taken together, these results suggest that both olfactory and vomeronasal inputs to the MPOA normally inhibit

FIGURE 7.38 Latency to maternal behavior is reduced after lesions to the chemosensory organs. Adult female rats that cannot smell pups will behave maternally toward them almost as quickly as newly parturient mothers. Control rats began to behave maternally after about 8 days of exposure to pups. Lesions of the olfactory bulbs and vomeronasal nerve resulted in latencies of about 7 and 4.5 days, respectively. If both the olfactory bulbs and vomeronasal nerve are damaged, female rats will behave maternally after only 1 day of exposure to pups. These results suggest that the hormones associated with the onset of maternal behavior function by inhibiting chemosensory stimuli from the pups that adults usually find noxious. After Fleming et al., 1979.

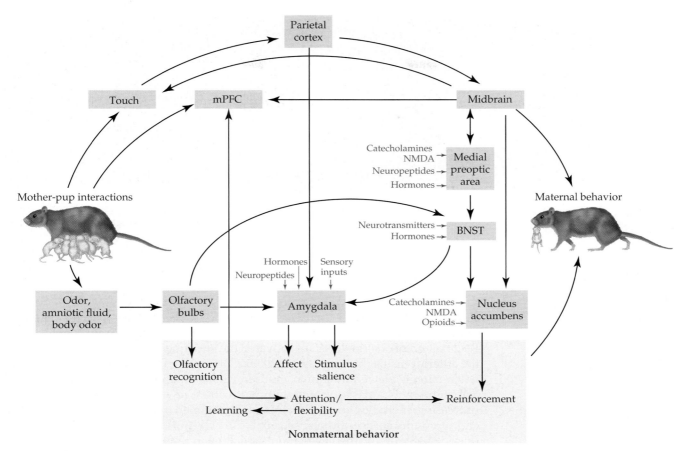

FIGURE 7.39 Functional neuroanatomical model of mammalian maternal behaviors
Neuroanatomical structures involved in maternal behavior in mammals include the olfactory
bulbs, amygdala, nucleus accumbens, bed nucleus of the stria terminalis (BNST), medial preoptic area, ventromedial hypothalamus, midbrain, and parietal cortex. Relevant neurochemicals include the catecholamines (e.g., norepinephrine and dopamine), neuropeptides, and
opioids. After Fleming and Gonzalez, 2009.

maternal behavior in rats and that maternal behavior occurs when the MPOA and
other components of the inhibitory circuit are released from this inhibition. The
medial amygdala projects to the anterior/ventromedial hypothalamic nuclei in a
neural circuit that inhibits maternal behavior; the principal bed nucleus of the stria
terminalis, ventral lateral septum, and dorsal premammillary nucleus also may be
involved in this inhibitory circuit (Sheehan et al., 2001). Selective lesions along the
vomeronasal organ–amygdala pathway disinhibit the MPOA and allow the expression of maternal behavior in both virgin and pregnant rats. A model of brain regions
associated with maternal behavior is summarized in **FIGURE 7.39**.

The use of functional magnetic resonance imaging (fMRI) has revealed some
important neural sites involved in maternal responsiveness among human mothers. In one early study, using only four participants, mothers listened to recorded
infant cries and white-noise control sounds while they underwent fMRI of the brain
(Lorberbaum et al., 1999). Only the anterior cingulate and right medial prefrontal
cortex showed significant changes in response to the infant cries as compared with
white noise. More recently, fMRI was used to determine brain response to infant
crying and laughing in mothers and fathers of young children and in women and
men without children (Seifritz et al., 2003). Regardless of parental status, women,
but not men, displayed neural deactivation in the anterior cingulate cortex in re-

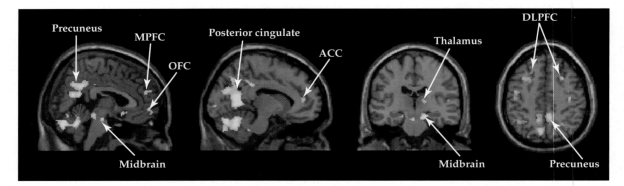

FIGURE 7.40 Mother's hemodynamic brain activations in response to photographs of her own versus an unrelated child. Hemodynamic increases in the midbrain, dorsal putamen, thalamus, anterior cingulate, and prefrontal cortices were observed in fMRI scans of a mother when she viewed her own child, relative to a stranger's child. MPFC = medial prefrontal cortex; OFC = orbitofrontal cortex; ACC = anterior cingulate cortex; DLPFC = dorsolateral prefrontal cortex. From Michalska et al., 2014.

sponse to both infant crying and laughing. Regardless of sex, parents displayed increased activation in the amygdala and other limbic areas (Seifritz et al., 2003). Recognition of one's own infant activated the periaqueductal gray region, as well as the anterior insula (Noriuchi et al., 2008). Contrasting the pattern of activation seen when parents viewed their own children versus images of other children revealed activation in regions associated with motivation, reward, and emotion regulation processing, including the midbrain, dorsal putamen, thalamus, anterior cingulate, and prefrontal cortices (Michalska et al., 2014) (**FIGURE 7.40**). Interestingly, parents (independent of sex) displayed more activation in response to infant crying, whereas nonparents displayed more activation in response to infant laughing! In another recent study, each new mother viewed photographs of her own baby, another baby, and adult faces while undergoing fMRI (Nitschke et al., 2004). Mothers displayed significant bilateral activation of the orbitofrontal cortex while viewing pictures of their own, as compared with unfamiliar, infants. While in the scanner, mothers rated their moods more positively when viewing pictures of their own infants than when viewing unfamiliar infants or adults or at baseline. Thus, activation of the orbitofrontal cortex correlated positively with pleasant mood ratings. Areas of the visual cortex also displayed differential activation in response to the mothers' own babies versus unfamiliar infants; this activation, however, was unrelated to mood ratings (Nitschke et al., 2004). These data suggest that the orbitofrontal cortex activation represents the affective responses of a mother to her infant (Nitschke et al., 2004). Similar results were obtained when movies, rather than still photos, were shown to mothers during fMRI (Ranote et al., 2004).

But let us return to the central question of this chapter: How do hormones stimulate the onset of maternal behavior? In light of the results described above, one possibility is that hormones act on the MPOA to disinhibit maternal responsiveness (Numan and Stolzenberg, 2009). In the presence of the appropriate hormonal priming, implants of estradiol into the MPOA trigger maternal behavior in rats. Similar implants into other neural regions do not stimulate maternal behavior (Fahrbach and Pfaff, 1986). As one might expect, the number of estrogen receptors in the rat MPOA (**FIGURE 7.41**) increases during pregnancy (Giordano and Rosenblatt, 1986). The protein products produced by cells in the MPOA in response to estrogen stimulation have yet to be fully characterized, but one of these products is oxytocin receptors (Champagne et al., 2001). In rats, central oxytocin receptor levels are functionally linked to behavioral differences in maternal care (Champagne et al., 2001; Francis et al., 1999; Insel and Shapiro, 1992).

FIGURE 7.41 Estradiol receptors in the rat MPOA In this schematic coronal section of a rat brain, each red circle represents a cell in the preoptic area that binds estradiol and projects through or to the ventromedial midbrain. BNST = bed nucleus of the stria terminalis; MPOA = medial preoptic area; ot = optic tract; V = third ventricle. After Fahrbach et al., 1986.

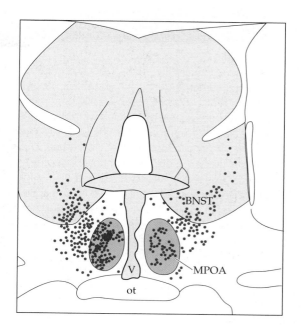

As with human mothers, maternal care varies among rat mothers, and quality of maternal care may be transferred through epigenetic mechanisms across generations (**BOX 7.4**). In rats, central oxytocin receptor levels are functionally linked to behavioral differences in maternal care (Champagne et al., 2001; Francis et al., 1999; Insel and Shapiro, 1992), and oxytocin receptor binding in the MPOA is increased in lactating females that exhibit high levels of licking and grooming as compared with lactating females displaying a low level of these behaviors (Champagne et al., 2001; Francis et al., 1999). Estrogen regulation of oxytocin receptors in the MPOA requires the α estrogen receptor (Young et al., 1998). Upon further examination, the individual differences in maternal licking and grooming reflected the variation in the expression of the α estrogen receptor but not the β estrogen receptor in the MPOA (Champagne et al., 2003). Oxytocin secretion by the PVN also appears to be important in the control of maternal behavior in sheep (DaCosta et al., 1996).

There is also evidence that synapses in the hypothalamus are restructured during maternal behavior (Hatton and Ellisman, 1982; Modney and Hatton, 1990). Performing the electron microscopic technique of freeze-fracture analysis on the PVN and supraoptic nuclei (SON) of the hypothalamus of rats that had behaved maternally demonstrated the presence of a unique postsynaptic specialization in those animals. Restructuring of neural connections, as well as changes in the numbers of neurons and the types of neural connections and coupling mechanisms, have also been reported in juvenile rats that have behaved maternally (Modney and Hatton, 1990). As described in Chapter 2, magnocellular neurons in the PVN and SON produce vasopressin and oxytocin. Nearly all of the morphological changes in neural organization observed in rat dams are reversed approximately 1 month after their pups are weaned. It is likely that the secretion of oxytocin associated with parturition and lactation accounts for these changes in neuronal structure, but it remains possible that the change in postsynaptic specialization reflects oxytocin-mediated effects on maternal behavior, which in turn cause the neural changes. Presumably, progesterone and prolactin also affect neuronal structure or function underlying rat maternal behavior. The ultrastructural changes that are observed in the PVN and SON of rat dams are also observed in nonlactating, nulliparous females that behave maternally after undergoing concaveation (Modney and Hatton, 1990). Other studies of neurons in the SON have demonstrated that oxytocinergic neurons show a reduction in dendritic length because of decreased branching (approximately 40% reduction) during lactation (Stern and Armstrong, 1998). In contrast, SON neurons containing vasopressin show an approximate 50% increase in dendritic length during lactation (Stern and Armstrong, 1998). Thus, merely behaving maternally causes structural changes in the brain independently, not involving hormonal influences. In addition to oxytocin systems changing in response to parenthood, prolactin systems also change. There are several examples of these changes in postpartum rats, but more surprising are changes in prolactin receptor systems in sensitized virgin rats (e.g., Sakaguchi et al., 1996; Sugiyama et al., 1996).

Pregnancy stimulates neurogenesis in the subventricular zone of the forebrain in mice (Shingo et al., 2003); these new neurons migrate to the olfactory bulbs. Exposure to male chemosensory factors stimulates the prolactin-induced neurogenesis and promotes the development of maternal behavior in mouse dams (Larsen et al., 2008).

BOX 7.4 *Nongenetic Transmission of Parenting Styles*

Stable individual differences among rats in pup licking and grooming emerge during the first week postpartum (Champagne et al., 2003). Such naturally occurring variations in maternal behavior are associated with differences in estrogen-inducible oxytocin receptors in the MPOA (Champagne et al., 2001). Offspring of mothers that display high levels of pup licking and grooming display attenuated hypothalamic-pituitary-adrenal axis responses to stress and also display enhanced cognitive ability (Caldji et al., 1998; Champagne, 2008, 2009; Francis et al., 1999; Liu et al., 1997, 2000). Amazingly, these individual differences in maternal care are transmitted across generations; offspring of mothers that engage in licking and grooming at a high rate exhibit a high rate of licking and grooming as mothers themselves, whereas the offspring of mothers expressing a low rate of licking and grooming become mothers that display a relatively low rate of licking and grooming their offspring (Francis et al., 1999). Similar natural variation has been reported for various strains of mice (Champagne et al., 2007) and primates, including humans (Champagne, 2008). The mechanisms underlying this brain organization have been recently elucidated in a series of elegant studies by Michael Meaney, James Curley, Francis Champagne, and their colleagues.

High levels of pup licking, grooming, and arched-back nursing organize the brain of the recipient offspring so that they are resistant to stressors as adults, and female pups adopt the type of maternal behavior that they received as infants (Weaver et al., 2004). The immediate consequence of the high levels of pup licking/grooming and arched-back nursing style is an increase in the glucocorticoid receptor (GR) gene expression in the hippocampus, which seems to be critical for the reduced stress effects observed later in adulthood (McCormick et al., 2000). But how can these transient effects on GR gene transcription have permanent organizational effects on brain and behavior? The answer appears to involve two epigenetic processes that affect gene expression: methylation and histones (see Figure 11.16). Methylation is a process of long-term gene silencing and involves attaching a methyl group to the promoter region of a gene (Egger et al., 2004). Thus, demethylation often results in significant gene expression (Egger et al., 2004). The DNA of animals is wrapped around proteins called histones; DNA plus histones comprise the chromatin. The histones can bind tightly to the DNA so that transcription factors cannot access promoter sites. Specific types of maternal care evoke changes in methylation and chromatin structure, resulting in increased GR gene expression (Weaver et al., 2004). These changes emerge in early life, can be reversed by cross fostering to mothers that display low levels of licking/grooming and arched-backed nursing, and persist into adulthood. Thus, these epigenetic influences of maternal care persist into adulthood and can be passed on to subsequent generations.

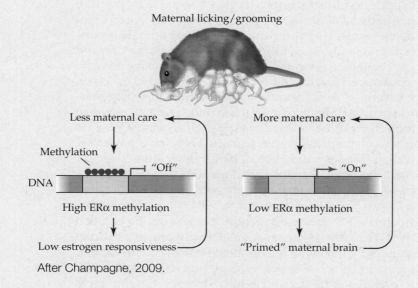

After Champagne, 2009.

You will recall from Chapter 1 that mice with a specific gene that has been selectively disrupted are called knockout mice. Mice lacking the immediate early gene *fosB* display little maternal behavior (J. R. Brown et al., 1996). The lack of maternal behavior among *fosB* knockouts (FosB$^{-/-}$) does not correspond to a lack of fertility or the ability to lactate. FosB$^{-/-}$ mothers appear to have endocrine profiles similar to those of wild-type (WT) dams, but they fail to display nest building, cleaning and retrieving of pups, nursing, or protective crouching postures (J. R. Brown et al., 1996). It is not clear through what mechanism(s) the *fosB* gene affects maternal behavior, although expression of its protein products occurs in brain regions considered part of the maternal behavior neural circuit (Numan and Insel, 2003).

As we saw above, oxytocin (OT) is an important mediator of maternal behavior. It was therefore surprising that in two studies, female oxytocin knockout mice (OT$^{-/-}$) showed the full complement of normal maternal behaviors (DeVries et al., 1997; Nishimori et al., 1996). OT$^{-/-}$ females, however, failed to eject milk in response to suckling, so their pups had to be cross fostered to WT mothers to survive. How do we interpret these data? Do we now conclude that oxytocin is not involved in maternal behavior? Not necessarily. There are alternative explanations for the results of both studies of OT$^{-/-}$ animals. It appears that maternal behavior is easily induced, simply by brief exposure to pups, in the particular strain of mouse used in the first study (Young et al., 1997). Thus, knocking out the *oxytocin* gene in rats might be a better test of the hypothesis that OT is necessary for maternal behavior. The other OT$^{-/-}$ mouse study also had problems; the *oxytocin* gene was only partially deactivated in this knockout. In addition, vasopressin concentrations were lower than normal because the neurophysin molecule was also damaged in this knockout (DeVries et al., 1997). Consequently, additional research must be conducted to clarify the role of oxytocin in maternal behavior (Winslow and Insel, 2002; see also Macbeth et al., 2010; Pedersen et al., 2006).

In contrast to the disquieting results associated with the OT$^{-/-}$ mice, mice with the prolactin receptor (PRLR) gene (*Prlr*) deleted displayed defective maternal behavior, as expected (Lucas et al., 1998). Specifically, pup-induced maternal behaviors were disrupted in both PRLR$^{-/-}$ and PRLR$^{+/-}$ females, and primiparous PRLR$^{+/-}$ females displayed dramatic deficiencies in maternal care of foster pups (Lucas et al., 1998). These studies clearly indicate that the prolactin receptor is critical in mediating maternal behavior. ERKO female mice have no estrogen receptors and are infertile, and so it is not surprising that maternal behavior cannot be evaluated in them. When the sensitization technique was used, ERKO females showed no maternal behavior and indeed displayed vigorous aggression toward pups to such a degree that tests had to be stopped (e.g., Ogawa et al., 1996a, 1998). Gonadectomized ERKO females continued to show elevated rates (50%) of attacks on, as well as poor retrieval of, pups after sensitization.

One final example from knockout mice adds an evolutionary twist to the role of genes in maternal care. *Mest* (also known as *Peg1*) is an imprinted gene, meaning that it is expressed only from the paternal allele during development (Keverne, 2001). *Mest*-deficient females displayed impaired maternal behavior and impaired placentophagia. These results provide evidence for the involvement of an imprinted gene from the father in the control of adult behavior of female offspring (Lefebvre et al., 1998). The effects of other gene manipulations on maternal behavior have been extensively reviewed (Leckman and Herman, 2002).

The genetics of human parenting behavior have not been studied extensively. However, few genes have been linked to human parenting style. For instance, as mentioned previously, there is a common polymorphism in the oxytocin receptor gene. A glycine replaces an alanine residue, possibly reducing the ability of the receptor to signal. Mothers carrying this glycine residue exhibit lower sensitivity scores, a laboratory measure of maternal behavior (Bakermans-Kranenburg and van Ijzendoorn, 2008). Similarly, other genes associated with monoamine neurotransmitters have also been linked to parenting style. Mothers who have polymorphisms in the dopamine D4 receptor and catechol-O-methyltransferase genes are less sensitive to their children in the face of daily hassles (van Ijzendoorn et al. 2008), and variants in the dopamine transporter have been related to negative parenting behaviors, particularly in the mothers of disruptive children (Lee et al., 2010).

These observations potentially open up a new area of inquiry into the mechanisms underlying hormonal mediation of maternal behavior. Behavioral studies of knockout mice may also evoke questions about established hormonal relationships. The missing genes may have subtle effects on maternal behavior. Indeed, most knockout mice studied to date are successfully raised by their knockout mothers. The extent to which the altered behavior of knockout mice reflects atypical maternal behavior remains unknown (Caldji et al., 1998; Kinsley, 1994; Winslow and Insel, 2002). Cross-fostering studies comparing the behavior of knockout mice reared by WT dams with that of knockout mice reared by knockout mothers will be critical in the future to further untangle the roles of extrinsic (environmental) and intrinsic (hormonal) factors in maternal behavior.

PATERNAL BEHAVIOR Recall that behaving maternally causes structural changes in the brain that are independent from hormonal influences. Do similar structural brain changes occur in males that behave in a paternal manner? This question is best addressed in a species that normally shows paternal behavior. Perinatal exposure to androgens suppresses parental responsiveness in many species of rodents (Kinsley, 1990). As we have seen, androgens organize sex differences in anatomical structures in several brain areas of rodents and primates, including the MPOA (see Chapter 4). Are these structural differences in the organization of the MPOA, for instance, responsible for the sex difference in propensity to behave parentally? There is a sex difference in the size of the MPOA in California mice; the volume of the MPOA in virgin males is larger than in nulliparous females. Paternal behavior in California mice was seen to be associated with a decrease in the number of neurons in the MPOA (Alberts and Gubernick, 1990) and consequent shrinking of MPOA volume to approximately that of a female (**FIGURE 7.42**). There was no change in the size of the MPOA in females when they became mothers; this suggests that hormones act in females of this species, as in rats, to disinhibit maternal behaviors. The reduction in the number of neurons during paternal behavior suggests that the circuitry underlying this behavior is typically inhibited unless hormones activate some process leading to neuronal death, possibly by destroying the inhibitory neurons themselves. As noted above, the main endocrine correlates of paternal behavior thus far discovered are an increase in blood prolactin and a decrease in blood testosterone concentrations, but it has not been established whether prolactin or some other hormone causes the cell death associated with paternal behavior in this species. Also, administration of vasopressin into the cerebral ventricles of naive male voles stimulated, whereas administration of vasopressin receptor blockers inhibited, paternal behavior (Bales et al., 2004).

More recently, several studies have shown that fatherhood is associated with neural plasticity in several rodent species. In prairie voles, fatherhood is associated with reduced cell survival in the amygdala, dentate gyrus, and hypothalamus while cell proliferation is unaffected (Lieberwirth et al., 2013). These findings suggest that fatherhood does not reduce the amount of new cells being produced in the brain, but changes their survival and incorporation into these brain structures. Similarly, hippocampal neurogenesis is reduced in the hippocampus of California mouse fathers relative to males without pups (Glasper et al., 2011). Another study in California mice revealed that fathers have higher levels of nestin staining in the CA2 and CA3 regions of the hippocampus compared with pup-exposed virgins and pup-naive virgins (Lambert et al., 2011). Nestin is a protein involved in axonal growth, suggesting that hippocampal reorganization occurs with fatherhood in this

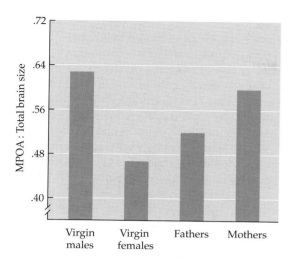

FIGURE 7.42 Effects of parental behavior on MPOA volume in California mice There is a sex difference in the size of the MPOA in California mice: the volume of the MPOA of males without sexual experience is larger than that of nulliparous females. Paternal behavior caused the number of neurons in the MPOA to decrease and its overall size to diminish to approximately that found in females. The MPOA volume of females does not change significantly when they become mothers. After Alberts and Gubernick, 1990.

species. Together, these findings suggest that, like motherhood, the transition to fatherhood is associated with neural reorganization of the brain.

Other studies have used lesion and early immediate gene studies to map the neural circuitry underlying paternal behavior in California mice. Such studies have indicated that, as with maternal behavior, the MPOA, basolateral amygdala, lateral septum, medial bed nucleus of the stria terminalis, and posterior medial amygdala are critical components of a paternal behavior neural circuit (De Jong et al., 2009; Lee and Brown, 2002, 2007). MPOA and basolateral amygdala lesions were most disrupting to paternal behavior (Lee and Brown, 2007). The onset of paternal behaviors in California mice appears to be mediated by the medial preoptic nucleus and stria terminalis (de Jong et al., 2009).

Conclusions

A good understanding of the manner in which parental behavior is affected by hormones has recently been gained in a few species, but the parental behaviors shown by individuals in the various orders and families of birds and mammals are extremely diverse. Are the underlying endocrine mechanisms and the hormones associated with them equally varied, or do just a few select hormones produce this diversity of parental responses? Too few species have been studied to answer this question at this time. However, it is reasonable to propose that a combination of common hormonal signals is paired with a variety of extrinsic cues to elicit the species-appropriate constellation of parental behaviors.

As with other behaviors we have thus far examined, hormones affect parental behavior at the level of input, integration, and output systems. Sensory inputs related to the perception of rat pups appear to be changed by hormones in parturient rat dams. Nonparental rats fear pups, but hormones alter mothers' perceptions of their pups to make them attractive stimuli. Sensory input associated with nursing (and likely with contact between nonnursing mothers and pups) probably is perceived as rewarding via the actions of oxytocin, dopamine, and endogenous opioids. The effects of hormones on central nervous system processing have been well documented in rat maternal behavior. Restructuring of neural connections, as well as changes in numbers of neurons and the types of neural connections and coupling mechanisms, has been reported in mother rats. Maternal behavior is integrated and consolidated in the MPOA and inhibited in the amygdala. Finally, hormones affect output systems to mediate maternal behavior. For instance, steroid hormones stimulate mammary gland development in mice; without mammary gland development, suckling stimuli could not trigger the onset of maternal aggression in this species. In birds, prolactin stimulates development of the brood patch, and feedback from this morphological feature encourages further incubation behavior.

Thus, parental behaviors are mediated by hormones via their effects on input, integration, and output systems, as well as the interactions of those systems with experiential factors. Although much has been learned about this important topic, there is still a great deal left to learn. Parental care is fascinating to study because of its fundamental importance to the survival and reproductive success of individuals and because of the role of hormones in the plasticity of brain and behavior. The diversity of parental care patterns found in nature provides an opportunity for comparative studies that will reveal how different animals have evolved different solutions to the common problem of increasing the odds of offspring survival and reproductive success.

Summary

1. Parental behavior is any behavior that contributes directly to the survival of fertilized eggs or offspring that have left the body of the female.

2. There are many patterns of mammalian parental care. The developmental status of the newborn is an important factor driving the type and quality of parental care in a species. Maternal care is much more common than paternal care.

3. Birds show great diversity in parental care, ranging from nest parasite species that show absolutely no parental care to species in which both sexes build nests, incubate the eggs, and feed and protect the young.

4. Most studies on hormonal correlates of avian parental behavior have been performed on ringdoves, which share the parental chores more or less equally and also produce a protein-rich crop milk that is regurgitated and fed to the squab. Ovariectomy eliminates nest building and incubation behaviors in female ringdoves. Estradiol and progesterone replacement restores these behaviors. Prolactin mediates brooding and stimulates development of the crop sac in both sexes. Gonadectomy does not affect nest building or incubation behaviors in male ringdoves; behavioral cues from the female elicit these behaviors in males.

5. The vast majority of research on the hormonal correlates of mammalian parental behavior has been conducted on rats. Rats bear altricial young, and mothers perform a cluster of stereotyped maternal behaviors, including nest building, crouching over the pups to allow nursing and to provide warmth, pup retrieval, and increased aggression directed at intruders.

6. Sensitization of adult nonparental rodents to pups by daily exposure causes them to behave maternally, but several days are required in order for maternal behavior to be observed. This process is called concaveation and appears to serve to reduce the adult rats' fear of pups.

7. The onset of maternal behavior in rats is mediated by hormones. Several methods of study, including pregnancy termination, hormone removal and replacement therapy, and parabiotic blood exchange, have been used to determine the hormonal correlates of rat maternal behavior. A precipitous decline in blood concentrations of progesterone in late pregnancy after sustained high concentrations of this hormone, in combination with high concentrations of estradiol and probably prolactin and oxytocin, induces female rats to behave maternally in the presence of pups. This hormone profile at parturition overrides the usual fear response of adult rats toward pups, and it permits the onset of maternal behavior.

8. Laboratory strains of mice and rats are usually docile, but mothers can be quite aggressive toward animals that venture too close to their offspring. Progesterone appears to be the primary hormone that induces this maternal aggression in rodents, but species differences exist. The role of maternal aggression in women's behavior has not been adequately described or tested.

9. Female rats become less maternal as their pups mature, and they spend less time with the pups during each nursing bout. Prolactin stimulates corticosterone secretion, which increases metabolic rate and subsequently raises the mother's body temperature. As the pups grow larger and produce more heat, they block the mother's ability to dissipate her own body heat. When her brain temperature rises acutely during nursing, she leaves the litter to reduce her heat load and avoid hyperthermia.

10. Rat pups at 2–3 weeks old are attracted to the nest odors of lactating dams. The excess production of caecotrophs by lactating dams attracts the young to the nest or to their mother until they are fully weaned.

11. With the exception of cortisol, few clear-cut endocrine correlates of human or other primate maternal behavior have been discovered. Behavior per se is rarely tested in humans; rather, responses to questionnaires or surveys are used to study hormone-behavior interactions. A further confounding variable is a lack of consistent or universal definitions of human maternal care.

12. Elevated prolactin concentrations appear to mediate paternal behavior in the two best-studied mammalian species, California mice and the common marmosets. Reduction in blood concentrations of testosterone is also associated with paternal behavior in marmosets.

13. The medial preoptic area is critical for the expression of rat maternal behavior. The amygdala appears to tonically inhibit the expression of maternal behavior. Adult rats are fearful of pups, a response that is apparently mediated by chemosensory information. Lesions of the amygdala or afferent sensory pathways from the vomeronasal organ to the amygdala disinhibit the expression of maternal behavior. Hormones or concaveation probably act to disinhibit the amygdala, thus permitting the occurrence of maternal behavior.

14. There is evidence that structural changes in neural organization occur during natural maternal and paternal behavior. These changes are reversible and also occur in animals exhibiting parental behavior after concaveation.

Questions for Discussion

1. Discuss the interactions among hormones, maternal care, and stage of development of mammalian offspring. Would you expect that hormones associated with parturition would be more or less important in mediation of maternal care of altricial offspring? Why or why not?

2. A common endocrine correlate of the onset of paternal behavior is a reduction of blood concentrations of androgens. Why do you think this is true?

3. Discuss the proposition that hormones are important for the onset of maternal behavior, but not its maintenance. Is this true across species? Is the circuitry involved in parental care that is hormonally activated the same as that controlling experience-dependent maternal care? Why might evolution have favored such mechanisms of control across species?

4. Are studies of the hormonal correlates of paternal care in birds and mammals useful for understanding the mechanisms of paternal care in humans? Why or

why not? Does the phenomenon of adoptive human fathers behaving paternally provide any insights? How can we account for individual differences in paternal care among men?

5. Do concaveation studies tell us anything about the neural circuits mediating maternal behavior in rats? If so, what sort of information is revealed?

6. Why has it been so difficult to determine the neural and hormonal mechanisms underlying human parental care? How would you design an experiment to test whether or not the same neuroendocrine mechanisms are responsible for parenting behavior in genetic and adoptive parents?

Suggested Readings

Bales, K. L., and Saltzman, W. 2016. Fathering in rodents: Neurobiological substrates and consequences for offspring. *Horm. Behav.*, 77:249–259.

Bridges, R. S. 2015. Neuroendocrine regulation of maternal behavior. *Front. Neuroendocrinol.*, 36:178–196.

Buntin, J. D. 1996. Neural and hormonal control of parental behavior in birds. *Adv. Study Behav.*, 25:161–213.

Feldman, R. 2016. The neurobiology of mammalian parenting and the biosocial context of human caregiving. *Horm. Behav.*, 77:3–17.

González-Mariscal, G., and Kinsley, C. H. 2009. From indifference to ardor: The onset, maintenance, and meaning of the maternal brain. In D. W. Pfaff et al. (eds.), *Hormones, Brain and Behavior* (2nd ed.), pp. 109–136. Academic Press, New York.

Lonstein, J. S., et al. 2015. Common and divergent psychobiological mechanisms underlying maternal behaviors in non-human and human mammals. *Horm. Behav.*, 73:156–185.

Numan, M. 2015. *Neurobiology of Social Behavior*. Academic Press, San Diego, CA.

Stolzenberg, D. S., and Champagne, F. A. 2016. Hormonal and non-hormonal bases of maternal behavior: The role of experience and epigenetic mechanisms. *Horm. Behav.*, 77:204–210.

Hormones and Social Behavior

8

Learning Objectives

The goal of this chapter is to describe the interactions between hormones and various types of social behavior, notably affiliation and aggressive behaviors. By the end of this chapter, you should be able to:

- describe the different aspects of affiliation and aggressive behaviors.
- understand seasonal, sex, and individual differences in aggression.
- explain the roles of hormones in the regulation of social interactions.

Female Syrian hamsters (*Mesocricetus auratus*) are typically more aggressive than males (Payne and Swanson, 1972). A female will attack a male intruder (or cage mate), and if the male is not allowed to escape, then a female can fight a male to death. However, when females are in estrus, they do not fight males but will form social affiliations, albeit just sufficiently long enough to mate. After mating, the male is often chased out of the female's territory. How are these social interactions mediated? What determines whether aggression or affiliation ensues when two individuals meet? As you will see, hormones are important in biasing such social interaction toward either aggression or affiliation.

Social behavior encompasses interactions between individuals from which one or more of the individuals benefit (see Wilson, 1975). This definition is purposely very broad and includes aggressive behavior, particularly in the context of territorial defense, as well as nonhostile interactions, including affiliation, courtship, and parental behaviors. Because the effects of hormones on courtship and parental behaviors were described in previous chapters (see Chapters 5, 6, and 7), this chapter will emphasize the influence of hormones on affiliative and aggressive behaviors.

affiliation A form of social behavior that involves an individual's motivation to approach and remain in close proximity with a conspecific.

aggression A form of social interaction that includes threat, attack, and fighting.

territorial behavior Actions that defend physical areas that may (or may not) contain valuable resources or mating partners.

Animals display a wide range of social behaviors. Some animal species are highly solitary and have few social interactions; in fact, after they have been weaned, their only social interactions may occur during mating. Individuals of other species live together in large colonies where social interactions are frequent. On an ultimate level, there are numerous costs and benefits to living in groups (Alexander, 1974). The most common costs to group living include (1) increased ease of disease transmission; (2) increased competition for resources (food, mates, nesting sites); and (3) increased conspicuousness to predators. In order for group living to occur, presumably these costs must be outweighed by the benefits of group living, which include (1) antipredator detection, defense, and dilution; (2) elevated foraging efficiency; (3) group defense of resources; and (4) increased mating opportunities (Alexander, 1974). Individuals of some species can move between solitary living and social groups in response to environmental factors, including daily or seasonal factors, or in response to different developmental stages or resource availability.

Social behaviors that bring animals together are referred to as **affiliation** (Carter, 2014). Social behaviors that keep animals apart are often expressed as **aggression** (threat, attack) or **territorial behavior** (aggression in defense of physical areas). Although these two categories of social behaviors have the opposite effects on social interactions, the neural and endocrine mechanisms underlying affiliation and aggression do not have opposite effects on a single neural substrate; indeed, many of the same limbic and hypothalamic areas influence both aggression and affiliation (Goodson, 2005; Lin et al., 2011; Newman, 1999).

Individuals of some species engage in one type of social organization throughout life, whereas individuals of many species change their social organization dramatically across the year or even throughout the day. For example, some bird species forage alone throughout the day but come together in large social groups in the evening to roost. Another example involves similar behaviors among vampire bats (*Desmodus rotundus*). Vampire bats, especially the females, live in communal societies during the day, but they tend to hunt alone during the night. The social group usually consists of related females and a dominant male lodged in a cave or hollow tree. These animals attack large mammals (other species of vampire bats specialize in birds) and must consume 20–30 ml of blood every 60 hours to avoid starving to death (Wilkinson, 1984). It is often difficult for the offspring, one of which is born each year, to learn to find a prey, land softly on the tail or other part of the prey's body undetected, slice open a 1 cm cut in the skin, and suck out sufficient blood within 15–20 minutes to maintain the bats' very high metabolism rate (Wilkinson, 1984). When offspring are not successful in hunting, females have been observed to regurgitate their blood meals to share with their offspring. This is critical to help them survive until the next night of hunting. Perhaps this is not surprising and simply reflects good parental behavior. What is surprising is that unrelated animals often engage in a similar behavior (Wilkinson, 1985). Roost mates will share their blood meals with near-starving animals, which can add another 12 hours of life and one more chance to find food. This behavior relies on excellent social memory, strong social bonds, and reciprocity; a vampire bat that received a donation in the past cooperates and feeds the donor when necessary (Wilkinson, 1985). This example suggests that some social behaviors likely evolved from parental behavior. Thus, hormones associated with the regulation of parental behavior may have been co-opted over evolutionary time to serve as modulators of some features of prosocial behaviors.

Other individuals change their social organizations in response to the time of year, especially in relation to the onset and termination of their breeding seasons. Thus, individuals of many species may vary from living isolated lifestyles at one time of year to living in large groups at other times of year. For example, males of several species of songbirds maintain territories and interact aggressively toward their neighbors only during the spring and summer breeding seasons. In contrast,

FIGURE 8.1 **Territories in female meadow voles** (A) During the summer breeding season, female territories do not overlap. Females avidly patrol borders and aggressively exclude interlopers. (B) During the winter, reproduction ceases and females develop overlapping territories. Indeed, females develop same-sex partner preferences. A from Madison, 1980; B from Madison et al., 1984.

(A) Female territories in summer

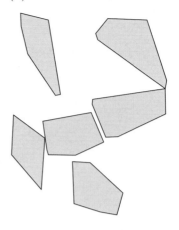

(B) Female territories in winter

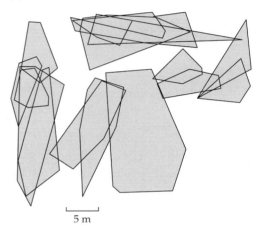

5 m

these individuals affiliate in large feeding flocks during the winter, when they can benefit from group living. Many rodent species show a similar seasonal change in social organization. During the summer breeding season, male and especially female meadow voles (*Microtus pennsylvanicus*) display strong individual territorial defense (Madison, 1980; Webster and Brooks, 1981) (**FIGURE 8.1**). Social interactions during the breeding season tend to be aggressive against same-sex conspecifics, as the territories often abut. If the two neighbors are of opposite sex, however, then courtship and subsequent sexual encounters become the primary social interaction (Beery et al., 2009). During the winter, when reproductive function stops and sex steroid hormone concentrations are barely detectable, the territories collapse in size and the solitary lifestyle observed during the breeding season dissolves. Under short day lengths in the lab or during autumn in nature, voles develop tolerance for other animals and often form mixed-sex sleeping clusters of 3–10 animals (Madison and McShea, 1987). Presumably, the savings of heat from huddling outweighs the costs of social grouping, and this dramatic change in social structure from solitary to group living likely enhances survival. During short days, female meadow voles form social bonds with both kin and nonrelated females (Beery et al., 2009; Parker and Lee, 2003) (**FIGURE 8.2**). High circulating sex steroid hormone concentrations tend to be associated with low tolerance for close proximity of same-sex conspecifics, whereas the absence of circulating sex steroid or reduction in concentrations permits social tolerance and prosocial interactions. Some of this effect is mediated directly by sex steroids, as estrogen treatment of short-day females prevents formation of social bonds; however, ovariectomy of long-day voles does not promote formation of social bonds (Beery et al., 2008). Again, peptides associated with parent-young bonding, especially oxytocin, may interact with steroid hormones or directly be involved. Day length substantially affects the number and distribution of oxytocin receptors of the brains of female meadow voles (Parker et al., 2001). Thus, there is often a tension between affiliation and aggression; sometimes these tensions are influenced by time of year, puberty, or other environmental or social factors. Scientific interest in affiliation blossomed in the 1990s, whereas formal studies of aggression have been common since the 1920s. The role of hormones, especially nonapeptides and sex steroid hormones, in mediating affiliative and aggressive behavior will be explored in this chapter.

Affiliation

As noted, affiliation is generally considered to have evolved from reproductive and parental behaviors, whereby short-term associations have evolved into long-term social bonds (Anacker and Beery, 2013; Bosch and Neumann, 2012; Crews, 1997). Both reproductive and parental bonds are critical for individual reproductive success in most species. Not surprisingly, then, the hormones that are important in promoting affiliative behaviors appear to have

FIGURE 8.2 **Female meadow voles form partner preferences during the winter.** During the summer, females fight other females that wander into their territories. Courtesy of Annaliese Beery.

FIGURE 8.3 Evolutionary tree of the nonapeptide hormones in vertebrates Courtesy of James Goodson.

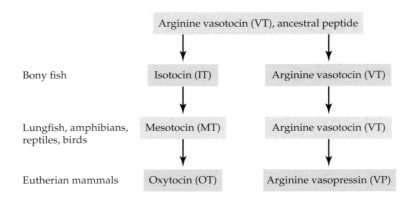

been co-opted from their regulatory roles in reproductive and parental behaviors. Perhaps the best example of this comes from the nonapeptides, the nine-amino-acid neuropeptide family that includes arginine vasopressin and oxytocin in mammals. Nonapeptide neurons share a common ancestry across both vertebrates and invertebrates (Tessmar-Raible et al., 2007); these neurons regulate water and mineral balance, as well as egg laying in taxa ranging from annelid worms to lizards, and even regulate parturition in mammals (the extreme in delayed egg laying!). Built upon this basic functional profile, nonapeptide systems have evolved to regulate diverse social interactions ranging from pair-bonding in voles to flocking in songbirds and to mother-infant bonding and trust in humans (Bartels and Zeki, 2004; reviewed in Donaldson and Young, 2008; Goodson, 2013; Goodson and Thompson, 2010; Insel and Young, 2001; Kendrick, 2000; Pedersen, 1997) (**FIGURE 8.3**).

Imaging Studies of Humans

Parents of newborns or newly adopted children often report that they not only love their offspring "at first sight," but also "fall in love with them" over time (Leckman and Mayes, 1999). Such a statement is reminiscent of romantic love with a long-term partner. Indeed, the highly conserved behavioral and neural systems underlying romantic and parental love have been linked to both addiction (Insel, 2003) and obsessive-compulsive disorders (Leckman and Mayes, 1999). Given their commonalities, the relationship between romantic and parental love has been investigated on a neurobiological level.

In one study, the brain activity of human participants who were "deeply in love" was monitored by fMRI while they looked at pictures of their love interests or pictures of friends whose age, sex, and duration of relationship were similar to those of their partners (Bartels and Zeki, 2000). Brain activation in response to the pictures of romantic partners occurred in the medial insular and anterior cingulate cortices, as well as in subcortical regions including the caudate nucleus and putamen. Significant deactivation was observed in the posterior cingulate cortex and amygdala. Because these brain regions are different from those associated with emotion in previous studies, it remains possible that they are part of the specialized circuitry underlying the affective state of "love" (Bartels and Zeki, 2000).

An additional study by the same research team compared the neural correlates of maternal and romantic love directly (Bartels and Zeki, 2004). Using fMRI as previously described for the study of adults in love who looked at pictures of their partners and nonromantic friends, the researchers had new mothers look at pictures of their babies or familiar infants (Bartels and Zeki, 2004). Romantic and maternal love resulted in some overlapping areas of brain activation, including the putamen and caudate nucleus as well as the medial insular and anterior cingulate cortex (**FIGURE 8.4**). Romantic love specifically activated the dentate gyrus/hippocampus,

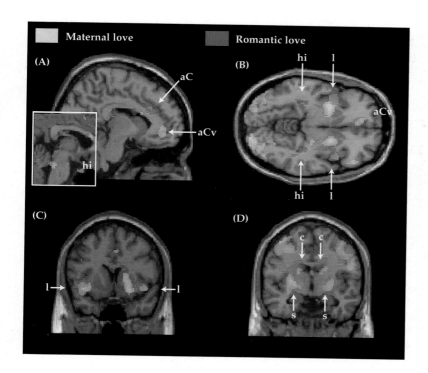

FIGURE 8.4 Romantic and maternal love evoke similar brain activity. The red pseudocolor reflects activation in the brains of women viewing pictures of their romantic partners as compared with pictures of friends, whereas the yellow regions reflect activation in the brains of mothers viewing pictures of their infants as compared with pictures of other babies with whom they were acquainted. The overlapping areas of activation (orange) include the anterior cingulate cortex (aC), the ventral anterior cingulate cortex (aCv), the medial insular cortex (l), the caudate nucleus (c), the hippocampus (hi), and the striatum (s). From Bartels and Zeki, 2004.

hypothalamus, and ventral tegmental area. Maternal love specifically activated the orbitofrontal cortex and the periaqueductal gray (PAG) area. Interestingly, the brain regions that showed the most activation either are part of the human brain's reward circuitry (Kelley and Berridge, 2002) or contain a high density of receptors for the nonapeptides oxytocin (OT) and vasopressin. We will return to the role of oxytocin and vasopressin in regulating social bonds.

In addition to changes in the pattern of brain activation, feelings of positive regard for a romantic partner are associated with changes in OT concentrations. For instance, OT was assayed in 60 new couples, as well as 40 nonattached single people. Individuals in new relationships had elevated OT concentrations compared with singles (Schneiderman et al., 2012) (**FIGURE 8.5**). Elevated OT concentrations remained elevated 6 months later and correlated with the couple's so-called interactive reciprocity; interactive reciprocity includes social focus, positive affect, affectionate touch, and synchronized dyadic states, which parallels interactions during parent-infant bonding. Furthermore, OT levels obtained during the first assessment

FIGURE 8.5 Couples displaying high interactive reciprocity scores had elevated plasma OT concentrations 3 months into the relationship. Individuals in couples had higher OT concentrations than singles. From Schneiderman et al., 2012.

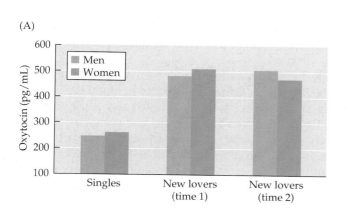
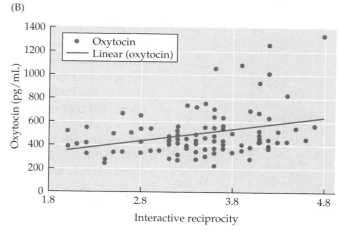

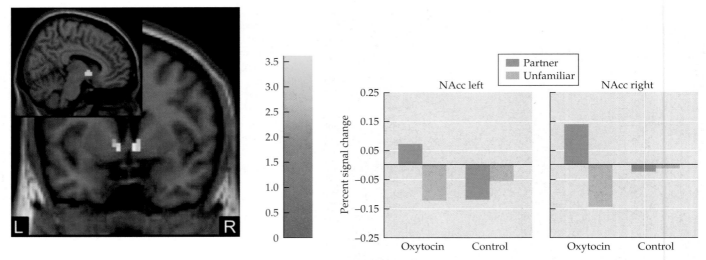

FIGURE 8.6   Oxytocin influences perception of partners. OT treatment biased men to perceive and rate their female partners' faces as more attractive than those of unfamiliar women while increasing the activation of the nucleus accumbens (NAcc), part of the reward neurocircuitry in the brain. From Scheele et al., 2013.

predicted which couples would be together 6 months later. In other words, couples with the highest levels of OT tended to stay together (Schneiderman et al., 2012).

In another study, men in stable romantic relationships were given either an intranasal OT or a control nasal spray treatment, then asked to rank the attractiveness of pictures of unfamiliar and familiar women, including their partners. Men treated with OT ranked their female partners' face as more attractive compared with unfamiliar women; OT had no effect on the attractiveness of other familiar women (Scheele et al., 2013). Functional MRI imaging of these men revealed that compared with their reactions to unfamiliar women, enhanced positive partner perception was paralleled by increased responses to partner stimuli in brain reward regions, including the ventral tegmental area and the nucleus accumbens (Scheele et al., 2013) (**FIGURE 8.6**). Taken together, these results suggest that OT might contribute to romantic bonds formed by men by enhancing the attractiveness and intrinsic reward value of their partners compared with other women (Scheele et al., 2013).

Adaptive Function of Affiliation

Formation of long-term pair bonds is critical for the reproductive success of some monogamous species, usually because both parents are required to rear the offspring. Because both parents have a 50% stake in the success of each offspring, they have evolved to cooperate; their offspring would die if either one abandoned the family. Hormones that evoke affiliation serve as the proximate means of bringing about this cooperation.

From the individual's perspective, the requirement for increased proximity during sexual reproduction may be potentially dangerous. Not only might the individual be attacked and maimed by a potential consort, but as noted above, the potential for disease and parasite transmission increases during social gatherings (Alexander, 1974; Crews, 1997). Mating behavior is a series of approach-avoidance behaviors, like maternal behavior in rats. In order for laboratory rats to engage in successful maternal behavior, the inclination to flee from the frightening or aversive stimuli connected with pups must be suppressed, and the rats must approach the pups that previously elicited these aversive responses (Carter et al., 1997a; Gammie, 2005). As noted in Chapter 7, neural-behavioral systems involving the medial amygdala have been implicated in avoidance behaviors, and neural-behavioral systems underlying approach behaviors include the medial preoptic area and the ventral portion of the bed nucleus of the stria terminalis (Newman, 1999).

Voles have been important animal models in studies of affiliation. Voles are rodents, and although they are sometimes referred to as field mice, they are more closely related to lemmings than to laboratory mice. Voles inhabit much of the Northern Hemisphere, occupying a variety of habitat niches. Despite their similar habitats, different species of voles display very different types of social organization. For example, prairie voles (*Microtus ochrogaster*), which inhabit grasslands throughout much of the midwestern United States, are most often socially monogamous. Meadow voles (*M. pennsylvanicus*), a closely related species, inhabit similar habitat throughout much of the eastern United States but typically display a highly polygamous social system (reviewed in Klein and Nelson, 1998). Individuals of another closely related species, montane voles (*M. montanus*), inhabit grasslands in the western portion of the United States and are also usually polygamous. Prairie voles are typically highly tolerant of other individuals, whereas meadow and montane voles are intolerant of individuals other than their mates during the breeding season (Wolff, 1985). What are the endocrine bases of these differences in social organization?

Hormones and Affiliation

The evolutionary importance of the relationship between hormones and affiliation is suggested by considering a single hormone, testosterone, and the strong correlations among blood testosterone concentrations, testis size, sperm production, and social systems (i.e., monogamy vs. polygamy) (Dixson, 1997; Wingfield et al., 1997). Males of polygamous species generally have larger testes, higher sperm numbers, and higher testosterone concentrations than males of monogamous species (Dixson, 1997; Klein and Nelson, 1998). Plasma testosterone concentrations in male prairie voles are about half of those in meadow or montane voles (Klein and Nelson, 1998). However, supplemental testosterone treatment of male prairie voles does not make them polygamous, and castration of male meadow or montane voles does not make them monogamous (Gaines et al., 1985; Roberts et al., 1996). So this correlation does not reflect a direct causal relationship.

Oxytocin has been implicated in several forms of affiliative behavior, including parental care, grooming, and sexual behavior (Carter et al., 1992, 1995). The locations of OT receptors in the brains of monogamous prairie voles and polygamous montane voles have been characterized using in vitro receptor autoradiography (Insel and Shapiro, 1992). In prairie voles, OT receptor densities were highest in the prelimbic cortex, the bed nucleus of the stria terminalis, the nucleus accumbens, and the lateral aspects of the amygdala; OT receptors were not evident in these brain regions in montane voles (Insel and Shapiro, 1992) (**FIGURE 8.7**). A similar pattern of social organization–dependent OT receptor distribution was observed in the brains of monogamous mice (*Peromyscus californicus*) and polygamous mice (*P. maniculatus*) (Insel et al., 1991), as well as in the brains of monogamous pine voles (*Microtus pinetorum*) and polygamous meadow voles (*M. pennsylvanicus*) (Insel and Shapiro, 1992). The differences in OT receptor distribution appear around the time of weaning (Wang and Young, 1997).

Differences in the patterns of vasopressin receptor distribution in the brains of prairie and montane voles have also been reported (Insel et al., 1994). Compared with montane voles, monogamous prairie voles have higher numbers of the 1a subtype of vasopressin receptors (V1aR, the primary vasopressin receptor subtype

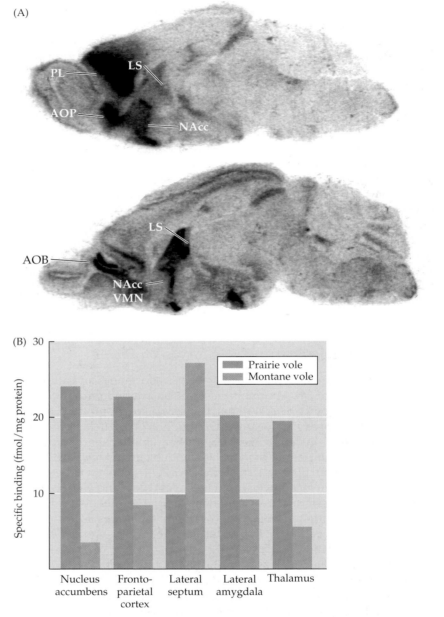

FIGURE 8.7 **The pattern of oxytocin binding differs between monogamous and polyga-mous male voles.** (A) In these autoradiograms, the dark regions represent ¹²⁵I-oxytocin antagonist binding in sagittal sections of the brains of a monogamous prairie vole (top) and a polygamous montane vole (bottom). In the prairie vole, oxytocin receptor densities are high-est in the prelimbic cortex (PL), nucleus accumbens (NAcc), and anterior olfactory nucleus (AOP); in the montane vole, receptors are not evident in these areas. LS = lateral septum; AOB = accessory olfactory bulb; VMN = ventromedial nucleus of the hypothalamus. (B) Levels of oxytocin binding in different brain regions of adult male prairie voles and montane voles. A from Insel, 1997; B after Insel, 1997.

in the brain) in the ventral pallidum, medial amygdala, and mediodorsal thalamus (**FIGURE 8.8**).

The difference in adult affiliative behaviors is reflected in the responses of infant prairie and montane voles to separation from their families (Shapiro and Insel, 1990). When prairie vole pups were isolated from their families for 5 minutes, they

(A) Oxytocin receptors

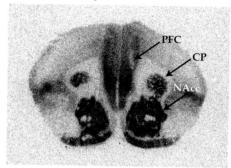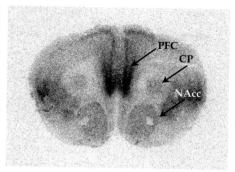

(B) Arginine vasopressin receptors

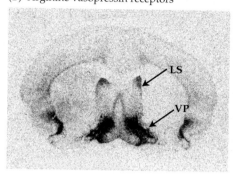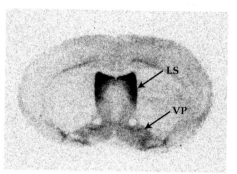

FIGURE 8.8 Distribution of oxytocin receptors (A) and arginine vasopressin receptors (B) in monogamous prairie voles (left two brains) and non-monogamous meadow voles (right two brains). Note the substantial numbers of oxytocin receptors in the NAcc of prairie versus meadow voles. VP = ventral pallidum; PFC = prefrontal cortex; CP = caudate putamen; NAcc = nucleus accumbens; LS = lateral septum. From Hammock and Young, 2006.

emitted over 300 distress vocalizations when they were 4–6 days old and approximately 600 distress calls at 8–10 days of age. Plasma corticosterone concentrations were elevated fourfold to sixfold in isolated prairie vole pups. When montane vole pups were socially isolated, they did not emit any distress vocalizations, and there were no changes in their blood corticosterone concentrations (Shapiro and Insel, 1990). If montane vole pups were stressed by tail suspension (being held by the tail) or vapors of halothane (a gaseous anesthetic), they emitted distress vocalizations and showed elevated corticosterone concentrations. This latter observation indicates that the montane vole pups were capable of responding to stress but apparently did not find social isolation stressful (Shapiro and Insel, 1990).

Separation anxiety such as that displayed by prairie vole pups is part of the phenomenon of **attachment** (Ainsworth, 1972; Bowlby, 1969), in which one individual (usually an infant) strives to maintain proximity to a specific other individual (usually the primary caregiver). Generally, attached individuals display distress if separation or loss is experienced, and they are motivated to reestablish contact after separation (Mendoza and Mason, 1997). The concept of attachment was developed for human infant-parent interactions, but it has been applied to nonhuman animals as well. Social bonding occurs in many species and is particularly salient in parent-offspring interactions (Pedersen, 1997) (see Chapter 7). Even when all their physiological requirements are met—for example, with full stomachs in a warm, dry environment—young animals of some species respond to social isolation promptly with characteristic distress vocalizations. In other words, babies cry when unattended (Kalin et al., 1988; Zimmerberg et al., 1994). The reaction of infants to social separation is fast and quite consistent across many disparate species (Panksepp, 2005; Panksepp et al., 1997).

A series of fascinating comparative studies of New World primates has provided new insights into the hormonal bases of attachment behavior. This research has focused on squirrel monkeys (*Saimiri sciureus*) and titi monkeys (*Callicebus moloch*), two arboreal, omnivorous New World primate species. Squirrel monkeys are

attachment A strong emotional bond that develops between infant and caregiver, which is important for subsequent emotional stability.

(A)

FIGURE 8.9 Infant titi monkeys receive most of their contact comfort from their fathers. (A) An infant titi monkey rides on the back of its father. (B) The graph shows the percentage of the observation time during which infants were carried by their fathers or their mothers under several conditions: in the home cage at baseline, after a disturbance, and after mate separation; and in a novel cage in a triad (infant, mother, and father) and after mate separation. Note that most of the time, fathers carried the offspring, even during times of stress. A courtesy of DeeAnn Reeder; B after Mendoza and Mason, 1986.

(B)

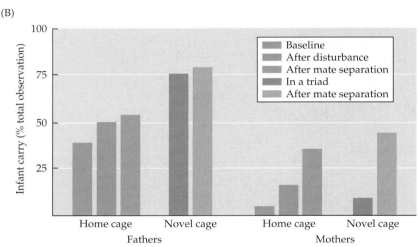

polygynous and live in large social groups containing individuals of both sexes and all ages. With the exception of mother-infant interactions, squirrel monkeys typically interact within same-sex cohorts (Mendoza and Mason, 1997; Mendoza et al., 1991). Titi monkeys are socially monogamous; they live in small family groups, and the males provide substantial parental care (Mendoza and Mason, 1986). The infants spend more than 90% of their time riding on the backs of their fathers, transferring to their mothers only to nurse. Not surprisingly, titi infants form very strong bonds with their fathers (**FIGURE 8.9**).

If a squirrel monkey mother and her infant are separated for 30–60 minutes, then each individual shows a robust increase in cortisol concentrations (Coe et al., 1978). Because separating a mother and infant causes substantial commotion and distress among their cage mates, a control procedure was conducted in which all of the steps involved in separating the mother and infant were taken but the pair was reunited within seconds. In this case, there was no increase in cortisol in either the mother or infant (Mendoza and Mason, 1997). Separation of pairs of adult animals, regardless of their relationship within the social group, did not influence their cortisol values, although cortisol concentrations were markedly decreased during the initial formation of female, but not male, pairs (Saltzman et al., 1991).

A different pattern of results was obtained in similar studies of the socially monogamous titi monkeys (Mendoza and Mason, 1997). Separation of titi infants from their fathers for 60 minutes caused a significant increase in cortisol concentrations even if their mothers were present; separation from their mothers, however, did not affect cortisol concentrations in the infant titi monkeys (Hoffman et al., 1996). Separation from the titi infant did not affect cortisol values in either parent. These different attachment patterns could contribute to the different social structures of these New World primate species (Fernandez-Duque et al., 2009), or they could be the result of these different social structures. These patterns may also serve to inform us about the different patterns of human social behavior.

The formation of social bonds has also been studied in socially monogamous prairie voles (Carter and Keverne, 2002; Carter et al., 1995). Male and female prairie voles form long-term pair bonds characterized by a social preference for a familiar partner and, in some cases, selective aggression directed toward unfamiliar conspecifics (Getz and Carter, 1996; Winslow et al., 1993). Social preferences for a familiar partner are not restricted to heterosexual pairs; partner preferences can form between animals of the same sex and animals of the opposite sex following non-sexual cohabitation (Beery et al., 2008, 2009; DeVries et al., 1995a). In the laboratory, social preferences can develop when socially naive animals encounter and interact with strangers of the opposite sex (Carter et al., 1995). These social preferences can be determined in the three-chamber preference apparatus described in Chapter 6. Typically, when socially naive prairie voles meet, they engage in a brief session of olfactory investigation, followed by prolonged periods of sitting in close proximity (Gavish et al., 1983; Moffatt, 1994). Separation by a wire screen barrier prevents the development of partner preferences, suggesting that physical contact or another form of active interaction is critical for the development of social preferences (Shapiro et al., 1986). It is important to note that social preferences must remain stable during pair separation among monogamous species (Drickamer and Vessey, 1982; Wittenberger and Tilson, 1980); that is, individuals must retain a memory for their preferred partner, or every time the pair was separated, they would have to reestablish their social bond upon each reunion. Partner preferences of heterosexual prairie vole pairs remain stable for up to 6 days in males and for up to 8 days in females (DeVries et al., 1995b).

Prairie voles display very high basal corticosterone concentrations (600–1000 ng/ml) without any of the negative consequences normally associated with chronic glucocorticoid excess (Taymans et al., 1997). The resting corticosterone concentrations of prairie voles are 10–100 times higher than those of laboratory rats or mice (Taymans et al., 1997), and these concentrations can be elevated further in stressed animals. Corticosterone appears to contribute to partner preferences in prairie voles but in a sex-specific manner (DeVries et al., 1996). In socially naive males, both injections of corticosterone and the stress of being forced to swim facilitated the development of partner preferences (**TABLE 8.1**). Adrenalectomized males did not form partner preferences unless injected with corticosterone (DeVries et al., 1996). In socially naive female prairie voles, adrenalectomy facilitated partner preferences; partner preferences were formed within 1 hour of cohabitation among adrenalectomized females (DeVries et al., 1995b). In contrast to males, corticosterone treatment or endogenous corticosterone elevation after swimming stress inhibited pair bond formation in females. It appears that corticotropin-releasing factor receptors in the nucleus accumbens modulate partner preference in this species (Lim et al., 2007).

Corticosterone also appears to be important in social behaviors of birds (Remage-Healey and Bass, 2006; Remage-Healey et al., 2003). Mate separation and reunion was studied in zebra finches (*Taeniopygia guttata*). Plasma corticosterone concentrations and behavioral changes were recorded following an individual's separation from its mate, and again upon reintroduction to the mate or to an opposite-sex cage mate. Corticosterone concentrations were elevated during separation from the mate (even in the presence of same-sex "friends"). The corticosterone concentrations returned to baseline levels upon reunion with the original mate, but not with the cage mate of the opposite sex (Remage-Healey et al., 2003). These results indicate that

TABLE 8.1 *The effects of steroid hormones on prairie vole partner preference*		
Treatment	**Males**	**Females**
Gonadal steroid hormones	0	0
Corticosterone	+	–
Stress	+	–
Adrenalectomy	–	+

Source: After Carter et al., 1997b.

+ = increased partner preference; – = decreased partner preference; 0 = no change

(A) Female prairie voles

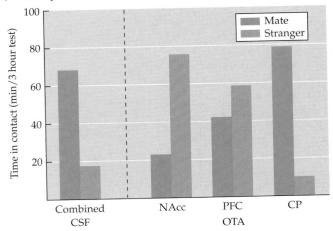

(B) Male prairie voles

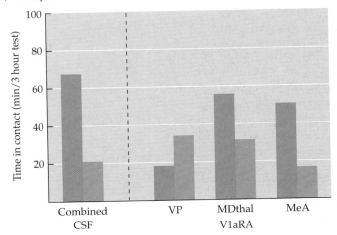

FIGURE 8.10 Social bonding is mediated by oxytocin and vasopressin in prairie voles. (A) When treated with cerebrospinal fluid (CSF) (control treatment), female prairie voles prefer to spend more time with a social partner than with a stranger. This partner preference is abolished by infusion of a specific oxytocin receptor antagonist (OTA) into the nucleus accumbens (NAcc) and the prefrontal cortex (PFC), but not into the caudate putamen (CP). (B) Mating-induced partner preference in male prairie voles is disrupted by infusion of a specific V1a vasopressin receptor antagonist (V1aRA) into the ventral pallidum (VP), but not into the mediodorsal thalamus (MDthal) or the medial amygdala (MeA). After Young and Wang, 2004.

zebra finches display hormonal responses to separation and reunion specifically with a bonded mate and not with other familiar conspecifics. In addition, alterations in behavior during separation and reunion were consistent with the monogamous pair bond maintenance behaviors observed in rodents (Remage-Healey et al., 2003).

In addition to glucocorticoids, nonapeptides appear to play an important role in partner preference formation, although the peptide involved in partner preference differs between the sexes. Sexual experience facilitates partner preference formation in both sexes of voles (Carter et al., 1997a). Treatment with vasopressin, or vasopressin agonists, facilitates pair-bonding in sexually experienced male voles; vasopressin also promotes the onset of aggression that is observed in male voles after mating (Gobrogge et al., 2009; Winslow et al., 1993). Conversely, treatment of males with a vasopressin antagonist that binds to the V1a receptor (the most common type of vasopressin receptor) blocks the effects of vasopressin or sexual experience in facilitating pair-bonding in males (Winslow et al., 1993). Unmated female prairie voles develop a partner preference following OT infusions but not after vasopressin or cerebrospinal fluid infusions. Females treated with a selective OT antagonist display normal mating behavior but do not establish a pair bond (Insel and Hulihan, 1995). Treatment with a vasopressin antagonist failed to block pair bond formation in sexually experienced females. These results suggest that OT, released during mating, may be critical to the formation of a pair bond in female prairie voles; vasopressin appears to be more important for pair-bonding in the male of this species. As noted in Chapter 7, OT is important in the formation of the exclusive bond between mothers and offspring in several species (Kendrick, 2000; Keverne and Kendrick, 1992). Centrally administered OT facilitates the onset of partner preferences in sexually naive female prairie voles; OT antagonists reverse the behavioral effects of OT infusion (Williams et al., 1994). The interaction between nonapeptides and corticosterone in social bonding remains to be specified.

Although exogenous administration of both OT and vasopressin facilitates pair bond formation in both sexes, *endogenous oxytocin* seems to be more important in pair bond formation in females, as demonstrated through the blockade of receptors, whereas *endogenous vasopressin* appears to be more important for males (Young and Wang, 2004). The mechanism underlying this sex difference is mysterious because the distribution of OT and vasopressin receptors is similar in both sexes of prairie voles. Mating-induced partner preference can be blocked by infusions of an oxytocin receptor antagonist into the nucleus accumbens and prefrontal cortex, but not the caudate putamen (Young et al., 2001) (**FIGURE 8.10A**). Blocking the V1a receptors in the ventral pallidum, but not the mediodorsal thalamus or medial amygdala, also blocks partner preference formation in male voles (Lim and Young, 2004) (**FIGURE 8.10B**). Taken together, the prefrontal cortex, nucleus accumbens, and ventral pallidum are part of the pair bond neural circuitry. Probably not coincidentally, these regions are critical components of the brain's reward circuitry, suggesting that pair bond formation is rewarding (Young and Wang, 2004; Young et al., 2001).

Monogamy has evolved independently many times across vertebrate species, and it is therefore important to determine whether mechanisms such as those just described for prairie voles have evolved in other pair-bonding species. To date, no direct experimental evidence is available from other rodents. However, whereas a high density of V1a receptors in the ventral pallidum is required for the expression of pair bonds in prairie voles, and prairie voles have higher V1a receptor densities in the ventral pallidum than do polygamous vole species, the mating system does not predict variation in V1a receptor genes across 8 species of *Peromyscus* mice (Turner et al., 2010) or in 25 rodent species (Fink et al., 2006). The limited replication of the prairie vole story in other species does not necessarily mean that vasopressin does not influence pair-bonding in other rodent species. Outside of the rodents, direct experimental evidence is available only for the monogamous zebra finch, which typically pair-bonds for life. In this species, chronic antagonism of V1a-like receptors has no effect on male pair-bonding, although it does reduce aggressive competition for partners (Kabelik et al., 2009). In humans, genetic variation (repeat polymorphisms) in the V1a receptor gene is associated with human pair-bonding behavior, including partner fidelity, perceived marital problems, and marital status, as well as marital quality as perceived by the partners (Walum et al., 2008). Thus, brains can evolve in multiple ways to generate a monogamous male.

Dopamine, released into the medial nucleus accumbens, appears to mediate the rewarding properties of many addictive drugs, including nicotine and cocaine. This same reward mechanism might drive social contact in prairie voles (Cascio et al., 1998). Oxytocin receptors are located on the surfaces of some neurons in the medial nucleus accumbens. Brain injections of dopamine agonists facilitated pair bond formation in female voles, whereas brain injections of dopamine antagonists blocked pair bond formation. When the natural production of dopamine was measured by microdialysis in the brains of prairie voles during mating, a dramatic elevation in the concentration of this neurotransmitter was observed (Gingrich et al., 1998). As noted in Chapter 5, mating evokes these changes in dopamine in male rodents such as rats and mice, which do not form pair bonds. What may differ between prairie voles and other rodents is the interaction among dopamine, oxytocin, and vasopressin in the reward circuitry (Young and Wang, 2004; Young et al., 2001) (**FIGURE 8.11**). Recall that meadow voles are closely related to prairie voles but are polygamous. Although the distribution of dopamine receptors seems to be similar in the two species, the V1a receptor is expressed at higher levels in the ventral

FIGURE 8.11   Neurocircuitry involved in pair-bonding in prairie voles This model depicts the neurobiology of pair bonding. Mating activates the ventral tegmental area (VTA), which increases dopamine activity in the prefrontal cortex (PFC) and nucleus accumbens (NAcc). Simultaneously, olfactory signals from the mate are transmitted via the olfactory bulb to the medial nucleus of the amygdala (MeA) where oxytocin acts; AVP acts in the lateral septum (LS) to facilitate olfactory learning and memory. The experience of mating also increases extracellular oxytocin concentrations in the PFC and NAcc of females, as well as vasopressin in the ventral pallidum (VP) of males. The source of oxytocin projections to the NAcc, MeA, and PFC remain unspecified and are depicted by dotted lines. Glutamatergic projections from the PFC to the NAcc are likely important for reward and therefore potentially important in establishing pair bonding. From Young and Wang, 2004.

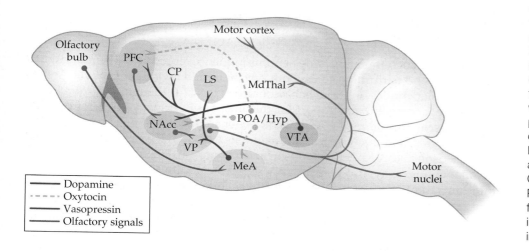

Dopamine
Oxytocin
Vasopressin
Olfactory signals

forebrain of the monogamous prairie vole than in the polygamous meadow vole (Insel et al., 1994). In one study, male meadow voles had a viral vector carrying a V1a receptor gene injected into the ventral forebrain, which caused them to over-express the V1a receptor gene. These males spent a larger proportion of a 3-hour test period huddling and engaged in side-by-side contact with a partner (a female with which they had been housed previously for 24 hours) than did males that had received a viral vector carrying the *lacZ* gene (serving as a control for viral vector expression) or males that were inadvertently injected with the V1a receptor gene outside of the ventral pallidum (Lim et al., 2004). These results suggest that altera-tions in the expression of a single gene may be sufficient against the background of extant gene and neural circuitry to alter social behavior (Lim et al., 2004), and they also suggest that vasopressin is released during mating even in nonmonogamous species. Indeed, recent experiments in nonmonogamous male lab mice report that vasopressin neurons in the bed nucleus of the stria terminalis display a substantial Fos response to copulation (Ho et al., 2010).

In addition to facilitating the rewarding properties of sexual behavior and the formation of pair bonds, OT and vasopressin may be part of a social recognition system (Choleris et al., 2003; Young and Wang, 2004). In order for an animal to form social relationships, either positive or negative, it is critical that it maintain social memory and social recognition. Female mice with the genes for OT, OT receptors, or the α or β estrogen receptor subtypes knocked out display social deficits (Cho-leris et al., 2003, 2004). These genes have been proposed to serve as a four-gene "micronet," an interacting network of genes that serves to link the hypothalamic and limbic forebrain regions in the neural control of estrogen over OT mediation of social recognition (Choleris et al., 2003, 2004). Male V1a receptor knockout mice display deficits in social recognition (Winslow and Insel, 2004), but mice with the 1b subtype of vasopressin (V1b) receptors knocked out display mild deficits in social interactions and decreased aggression (Wersinger et al., 2002). Whether these nona-peptides operate on sensory input, central processing functions such as memory, or some other cognitive function such as perception or attention remains to be determined. Also, the role of these peptides in human social recognition and pair-bonding remain unspecified. Although there are no reports of people with diabetes insipidus displaying altered social behavior, Brattleboro rats, which have no antidi-uretic hormone and serve as an animal model of diabetes insipidus, display reduced social investigation behavior relative to individuals of wild-type Long-Evans rats, and blocking V1 receptors reduces social investigation in the wild-type Long-Evans rats (Engelmann and Landgraf, 1994). Vasopressin increases social investigation in both genotypes.

Evolutionary Basis for Social Effects of the Nonapeptides

As noted, homologous nonapeptide neurons influence reproductive behaviors such as egg laying and parturition across both vertebrate and invertebrate phyla. Are the effects of nonapeptides on social behavior also ancient? Although data from inver-tebrates are lacking, broad support for this idea has been generated from a wide range of species, including vocalizing and sex-changing fishes, newts, frogs, toads, fowl, songbirds, and many species of mammals (**BOX 8.1**) (Donaldson and Young, 2008; Goodson and Bass, 2001; Goodson and Thompson, 2010).

Nonapeptides may also play an important role in differentiating the behavior of flocking and territorial finch species. It was found that following exposure to a same-sex bird through a wire barrier (which elicits little in the way of overt behav-ior), arginine vasotocin (AVT) cells in the medial bed nucleus of the stria terminalis exhibited species-specific Fos responses. Fos activity was increased in highly gre-garious species, such as zebra finches, and was decreased in territorial species, such

BOX 8.1 *Nonapeptides and Fish Social Behavior*

Fish provide an interesting system for study, because they display the basic nonapeptide cell groups of the preoptic area and hypothalamus, which in all vertebrates project to the pituitary and basal forebrain. Fish also possess long descending projections to the hindbrain and spinal cord; but in contrast to four-limbed terrestrial vertebrate species, fish lack extra-hypothalamic cells (DeVries and Panzica, 2006; Goodson et al., 2003). Basic social approach in goldfish is facilitated by the oxytocin-like peptide isotocin but inhibited by arginine vasotocin (AVT), the homologue and evolutionary precursor of vasopressin (Thompson and Walton, 2004). The AVT effect is mediated via the regulation of hindbrain substance-P neurons

that project to the periphery. Although the peripheral target of substance P has not yet been identified, the behavioral effects of centrally administered AVT are completely blocked if a substance-P receptor antagonist is administered peripherally (Thompson et al., 2008). Hence, AVT reduces goldfish affiliation behavior via effects on body states that then feed back to the brain. Accumulating evidence in mammals, including humans, suggests that nonapeptides similarly modulate affective states and behavior through coordination of central behavioral processes with peripheral physiology (Carter et al., 2008; Goodson and Thompson, 2010).

as violet-eared waxbills (*Uraeginthus granatina*). Further experiments demonstrated that Fos activity in the AVT neurons increased only following exposure to a positive, affiliation-related stimulus and that it may even decrease following exposure to a negative stimulus. For instance, in territorial violet-eared waxbills, the percent of AVT cells expressing Fos decreases with a same-sex stimulus but increases dramatically when the subject is reunited with its pair bond partner (Goodson and Wang, 2006) (**FIGURE 8.12**). This is observed in both sexes, and interestingly, homologous vasopressin neurons in mice display a similar profile (Ho et al., 2010). Signals coming out of these cells may be magnified in the more gregarious species, because individuals of such species have about ten times more AVT cells than the territorial species (Goodson and Wang, 2006) and display much higher densities of AVT V1a-like receptors in the lateral septum (Goodson et al., 2006), a major projection

(A)

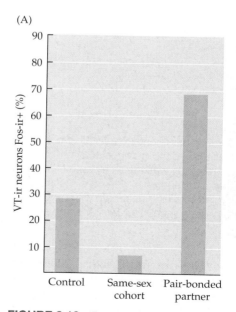

(B)

FIGURE 8.12 Fos expression increases in vasotocin neurons in response to positive, but not negative, stimuli. (A) Graph depicts the number of neurons in the medial bed nucleus of the stria terminalis that express Fos in response to a control situation, a same-sex cohort, or the individual's pair-bonded partner in asocial violet-eared waxbills (B). Increased Fos expression indicates higher neuronal activity. A after Goodson and Wang, 2006.

(A) Novel-familiar choice

(B) Sociality test

(C)

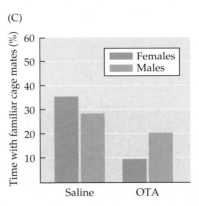

FIGURE 8.13 **Apparatus to test social preferences in zebra finches** (A) The test bird was maintained in the center area with seven perches that allowed the individual to spend time near familiar or novel birds. (B) Using the same setup, sociality was tested by determining whether the test bird preferred to be proximal to 10 or 2 conspecifics. (C) Zebra finches were tested in a novel/familiar task as the ones shown in this figure after treatment with oxytocin antagonists (OTA) and nonapeptides. OTA reduced the time spent near familiar same-sex cage mates. After Goodson et al., 2009a.

target of the AVT neurons in the bed nucleus (DeVries and Panzica, 2006). The flocking finch species also display significantly elevated densities of oxytocin-like receptors in the lateral septum as compared with territorial species. Following peripheral, intraventricular, or intraseptal delivery of an oxytocin receptor antagonist, zebra finches decrease their preferred group size (**FIGURE 8.13**), which suggests that oxytocin-like receptors may play an important role in the evolution of grouping behavior (Goodson et al., 2009a). Oxytocin may play a beneficial role in health as well (**BOX 8.2**).

BOX 8.2   *Beneficial Effects of Social Support on Health*

Social support in humans and social affiliation in gregarious nonhuman animals can have profound effects on health and well-being (DeVries et al., 2007; Repetti et al., 2002). Indeed, a lack of social integration is associated with increased mortality for both men and women across a variety of disease states (Holt-Lunstad et al., 2010). The negative effects of social isolation are perhaps best documented in the context of cardiovascular disease. Social isolation and social stress confer increased risk of coronary heart disease in humans (Smith and Ruiz, 2003) and facilitate the development of atherosclerosis in nonhuman primates (Watson et al., 1998) and rabbits (McCabe et al., 2002). Likewise, socially isolated mice that experience cardiac arrest sustain more neurological damage and harmful inflammation in the brain than mice housed with partners (Norman et al., 2010b, 2011). Social isolation also facilitates the development of depression and cardiac autonomic dysregulation after cardiac arrest in mice. Thus, social environment influences cardiovascular function and over time can modify the risk of heart disease.

The important question is "How does social environment alter physical health?" One possible mechanism involves the release of OT during social contact. Social isolation in prairie voles increases basal heart rate, reduces heart rate variability (low heart rate variability is predictive of poor health and increased mortality), and induces depressive behaviors (Grippo

et al., 2009). Each of these three measures can be improved by pairing a vole with a partner or giving it OT. Administering OT also reduces the development of atherosclerosis in socially isolated mice (Nation et al., 2010). In other words, administration of OT can reproduce the beneficial effects of social interaction on cardiovascular function; thus, in the future, treatment with OT could override the effects of loneliness or the perceived lack of social support. Oxytocin also mediates the anti-inflammatory effects of affiliative social interaction on the brain and periphery (Nation et al., 2010; Norman et al., 2010a).

The serotonergic system, which has a well-documented role in mental health and well-being, may be another mechanism through which social environment influences health. In a positive environment, people with two copies of the short allele of the serotonin transporter (short/short genotype) are more psychologically healthy than those with two copies of the long allele (long/long genotype). However, the reverse is true in the absence of social support; individuals with the short/short genotype are at increased risk for a variety of negative health outcomes (Way and Taylor, 2010). These data are important because they highlight that social environment and experiences can influence whether a given genetic polymorphism would be considered adaptive or maladaptive. Whether serotonin and oxytocin act independently or in concert to mediate the effects of social environment on health remains to be determined.

Oxytocin also modulates social bonds in nonreproductive contexts. A recent study of companion dogs indicated that OT treatment evokes positive social behaviors toward not only conspecifics, but also human partners. Specifically, when sprayed in the nose with OT, dogs showed higher social orientation and affiliation toward other dogs than when sprayed with a placebo (Romero et al., 2014). Remarkably, dogs also showed higher affiliation and approach behaviors toward their human owners when sprayed intranasally with OT compared with the placebo (**FIGURE 8.14**). Additionally, positive social interactions with other dogs provoked the release of endogenous OT, indicating a potential involvement of OT in the development of social relationships in domesticated dogs (Romero et al., 2014). Indeed, human-asso-

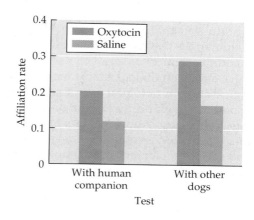

FIGURE 8.14   Affiliation rate in dogs with their human companion (A) versus other dogs (B) after being treated with intranasal oxytocin or saline. From Romero et al., 2014.

FIGURE 8.15 **Behavior and urinary oxytocin levels** among long-gaze dogs, short-gaze dogs, and wolves during the first 5 minutes of interaction (A). Changes of urinary oxytocin concentrations after a 30-minute interaction in human companions (B), and in dogs or wolves (C). After Nagasawa et al., 2015.

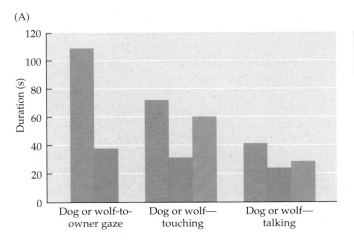

(A)

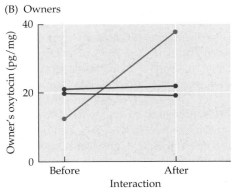

(B) Owners

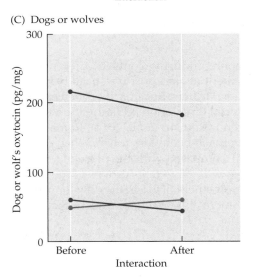

(C) Dogs or wolves

ciated modes of social communication, including mutual gaze, may have been co-opted during the process of canine domestication (Nagasawa et al., 2015) (**FIGURE 8.15**). Gazing behavior from dogs, but not wolves, increased urinary OT concentrations in human companions, whereas elevated OT in the humans facilitated affiliation behaviors and increased OT concentration in their dogs (Nagasawa et al., 2015). Nasal administration of OT increased gazing behavior in dogs, which in turn increased urinary OT concentrations in their humans! These data suggest a novel role for nanopeptides in facilitating close social bonds (**FIGURE 8.16**).

Opioids and Affiliation

Other peptide hormones that are part of the reward circuitry, particularly opioids, are involved in affiliative behaviors. These conclusions were the logical outcome of two observations, namely, that endogenous opioids exist in the brain and that there are remarkable similarities between narcotic addiction and the comfort of social contact. Narcotic addiction and social contact both involve strong emotional attachments, and both processes have characteristic psychological and physiological symptoms during withdrawal. Physiological symptoms common to withdrawal from narcotics and removal of the attachment figure include crying, depression, inability to eat or sleep, and general irritability (Panksepp et al., 1980b). Endogenous opioids mediate isolation-induced distress vocalizations, and social contact increases endogenous opioid concentrations (Panksepp et al., 1997). These similarities suggest a common physiological mediation.

FIGURE 8.16   Gaze into my eyes. Elevated OT in humans facilitated affiliation behaviors and increased OT concentrations in their dogs.

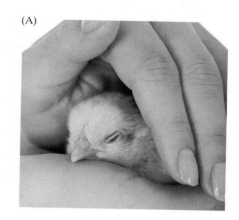

(A)

If opioids mediate contact comfort, then treatment with naloxone or naltrexone, both opioid antagonists, should block the onset of comfort. Young chickens display a characteristic sign of contact comfort; when one is snuggled next to its mother or cupped in a human hand, it rapidly closes its eyes (**FIGURE 8.17A**). Treatment with naloxone reduces the effectiveness of contact comfort in causing chicks to close their eyes (Panksepp et al., 1980a) (**FIGURE 8.17B**). In rodents, treatment with naltrexone blocks the effect of contact comfort in reducing the rate of distress vocalizations (Panksepp et al., 1980b). Treatment with opioid antagonists does not appear to block the rewarding properties of social interactions in adult rats (Panksepp et al., 1997). It is possible that social interactions among adult rats are not rewarding. Thus, it remains possible that opioids are important in the rewarding properties of social bonds in young rats but that some other system maintains social bonds in adulthood.

Opioids are important in the development of social bonds in rhesus monkeys (Kalin et al., 1988). Treatment with opioid antagonists decreases maternal bonding and play behavior and increases distress vocalization in infant rhesus monkeys (Kalin et al., 1995). Opioids also mediate social grooming in rodents and primates. Social grooming is very important in maintaining social contact and serves to bond individuals. Treatment with opioid antagonists reduces the time primates spend in social grooming (Benton and Brain, 1988; Keverne et al., 1989).

Having a "heartwarming" social experience of feeling interpersonally connected to others has been linked with physical warmth. This so-called social warmth (Panksepp, 1998) may be linked to physical temperature, because both experiences are supported by similar neural mechanisms (Panksepp, 1998). In an interesting recent study, naltrexone was administered to people to examine the role of opioids, previously shown to alter temperature and social bonding behavior, in perceived thermal intensity, general positive affect, and feelings of social connection from physical warmth. Study participants received either naltrexone or a placebo and completed a temperature manipulation task (held a warm pack, cold pack, and neutral object) during the treatment (Inagaki et al., 2015). Holding a warm (vs. a cold or neutral) object increased feelings of social connectedness, and blocking opioids reduced this effect. These results suggest

(B)

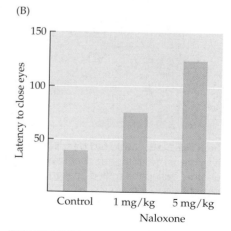

FIGURE 8.17   Contact comfort in chicks is mediated by opioids. (A) When nestled next to a hen or held in a person's cupped hands, a chick will rapidly close its eyes. (B) The eye-closing response can be blocked by administration of the opioid antagonist naloxone. B after Panksepp et al., 1980a.

(A)

(B)

(C)

FIGURE 8.18 **Male red deer fight vigorously for control of rutting areas.** (A) Male red deer use their antlers to battle with one another during the rutting season, and they attempt to wrestle their opponents to the ground (B). The loser of the aggressive encounter leaves the area (C), and the winner retains control of the rutting location and access to fertile females. Courtesy of Fiona Guinness.

that social and physical warmth share opioid receptor mechanisms (Eisenberger, 2012; Inagaki et al., 2015).

In sum, the mechanisms underlying hormone-behavior interactions during affiliation are similar to those underlying mating and parental behavior. Many of these hormones appear to blunt the "stress" or fear of social contact—aversive responses—and allow animals to come together and engage in social behavior or mating behavior.

Aggression

Although aggression may seem superficially to be the opposite of affiliation, the regulation of these two types of behaviors occurs at least partially through distinct circuits, rather than being mediated entirely by the differential activity of the same sets of neurons. Nonetheless, some neuropeptide and dopamine cell groups are known to be important for both, and some of the same nuclei of the basal forebrain and hypothalamus are essential players in both affiliation and aggression (Newman, 1999). We have seen that hormones acting in these brain areas are important in the expression of affiliative behaviors. In the remainder of this chapter, we will see that hormones are also important mediators of aggressive behaviors.

A population of red deer (*Cervus elaphus*) has been studied on the island of Rhum, Scotland, since 1968 (Lincoln et al., 1972). The animals making up the main study population inhabit an area of about 12 km². During most of the year, the males live together in bachelor groups, grazing peacefully near the female herds. But beginning in late summer as their antlers come into so-called hard horn, the males move to traditional rutting areas, usually located in large patches of grasses and sedges. Males fight vigorously for control of these rutting locations throughout September and October. The battles are often fierce, with the males locking their antlers and attempting to inflict serious physical damage on one another (**FIGURE 8.18**). Nearly a quarter of the red deer stags on Rhum are wounded during the rutting season (Clutton-Brock et al., 1979); some animals may even die of their wounds. The social rank of a male and the size of the turf he controls are linked to his ability to win these battles. The oldest males, typically between 7 and 10 years old, are the most experienced fighters and sport fully developed antlers. Age and weaponry have their rewards: these senior males tend to hold the highest rank and win control of the largest rutting areas. After the rutting season has ended in late autumn, males shed their antlers, their levels of aggression are substantially reduced, and they return to a relatively peaceful coexistence in their bachelor herds.

What is the goal of the stags' aggressive behavior? What makes this real estate so valuable that they risk life-threatening injuries? The ultimate explanation is probably somewhat predictable to you. Like the elephant seals described in Chapter 5,

FIGURE 8.19 A red deer stag with his harem The victor in the rutting battles controls an area of grassland on which females graze. It is in the best interest of a male to control as large a parcel of grassland as possible, because it can support a large number of females, and the male will mate with all the females grazing on his territory. It is in a female's best interest to graze in a plot of grassland that is sufficient to support her and her offspring after it is born.

these males are fighting for the opportunity to mate. Each male is apparently trying to control a large tract of pastureland in order to attract and eventually to mate with females. The females, which are called hinds, gather in the victors' rutting territories to feed on the grasses there. Each territorial male keeps other males away from his "harem." Stags can maintain large harems only if they manage to win control of sufficiently large patches of green vegetation to support females and their subsequent offspring. Otherwise, the hinds stray from the harem in search of better food and subsequently mate with other males.

Males have been selected to maximize the number of females that graze on their hard-won territories because most of the females come into estrus, or rutting condition, for just 3 weeks or so during autumn (Guinness et al., 1978). It is relatively easy to explain, on an adaptive level, why males behave in an aggressive manner prior to the onset of the females' estrous season. A stag impregnates most of the hinds in his harem (**FIGURE 8.19**). A large territory can support more hinds than a small one, and the more hinds a stag has on his "property," the greater his reproductive fitness relative to males with access to fewer females (see Chapter 5). In many other cases, the adaptive, or ultimate, function of a seasonal cycle in aggressive behavior also appears to involve control of resources or mates to increase reproductive fitness. The remainder of this chapter, however, focuses on proximate causes, such as the physiological mechanisms underlying this remarkable transformation in social organization and behavior. This part of the chapter will also explore some of the ways in which hormones influence, regulate, and mediate aggression and other social interactions.

There is little doubt that the animals described above are behaving aggressively. But what do we really mean by this? Aggression is overt behavior with the intention of inflicting damage or other unpleasantness on another individual (Moyer, 1968, 1971). Intent is the key to differentiating aggressive behavior from other activities. For example, if you inadvertently kill hundreds of insects with your windshield while driving, your behavior cannot be considered aggressive, because your intent is merely to move at high speeds, and the death of the insects is an incidental occurrence. However, if you rampage through your apartment, spraying insecticide after being bitten by a mosquito, your actions can be considered aggressive because of your intent to destroy insects. So, different behaviors leading to the same outcome may or may not be considered aggressive, depending on the context in which the behaviors appear. Of course, it can be tricky to attribute intention to animals, but by careful observation of the circumstances and outcomes of behaviors, the goals of animals' behaviors can be ascertained.

TABLE 8.2 *Types and tests of aggression*	
Types of aggressive behavior	
Predatory	Predatory attack
Intermale	Self-defensive behavior
Fear-induced	Parental defensive behavior
Irritable	Social conflict
Territorial	
Maternal	
Instrumental	
Common laboratory tests of aggression	
Muricide (mouse killing) by cats or rats	
Shock-elicited fighting	
Isolation-induced aggression	
Resident-intruder aggression	
Maternal aggression	
Brain stimulation–induced aggression (hypothalamus)	
Dominance-related behavior	
Visible burrow stressor	

Sources: After Moyer, 1968 and Brain et al., 1983.

Aggression has been divided into various types for ease of classification (Moyer, 1968, 1971), and these different types of aggression appear to have different physiological causes and are expressed in different environmental and social contexts (**TABLE 8.2**). Maternal aggression and its underlying hormonal mediation have already been described in Chapter 7. Hormonal changes associated with production of offspring—especially the relationship among blood concentrations of estrogens, progestins, and prolactin—are correlated with the onset of maternal aggression. Steroid hormones also underlie other types of aggressive behavior. Intermale aggression and territorial aggression, as well as sex-related and rank-related aggression, all appear to be mediated by androgens (Bouissou, 1983). Predatory aggression is performed in the context of obtaining food. Hormones may be involved in this type of aggression, but few studies have examined this possibility.

Other types of aggression are most commonly evoked and studied in the laboratory (see Table 8.2). Learned aggression and irritable aggression are often studied in the form of restraint aggression, which results after an animal is held motionless. Another type of aggressive behavior commonly studied in the laboratory is fear-induced aggression. Many laboratory studies on aggression use albino house mice, which are normally quite docile. Consequently, the mice must be put into situations that promote frustration, fear, or psychological stress—for example, they are housed in isolation or given an electric shock. More commonly, mice are tested in a so-called resident-intruder test of aggression. Prior to the test, the resident mouse remains in its cage for 2 weeks or more. This causes the odors and other stimuli to become familiar to the resident male, which then defends his "territory" against the intruder, a mouse that is simply dropped into the resident's cage (Chamero et al., 2007; Stowers and Marton, 2005). Typically, the resident has a "home court advantage" and defeats the intruder mouse. Female mice housed in groups will also attack a novel lactating female. Examples of these types of experiments will be provided below, but it is important to keep in mind that the hormonal control of aggression in these contrived situations is likely to differ from the endocrine correlates of natural expressions of aggressive behavior.

The possibility for aggressive behavior exists whenever the interests of two or more individuals are in conflict (Svare, 1983). Conflicts are most likely to arise over limited resources such as territories, food, and mates. A social interaction decides which animal gains access to the contested resource. In many cases, a submissive posture or gesture on the part of one animal avoids the necessity of actual combat over a resource. Animals may also participate in threat displays or ritualized combat in which dominance is determined but no physical damage is inflicted. In order to facilitate the study of aggressive interactions, the term **agonistic** was adopted to describe the entire behavioral repertoire of both aggressive and submissive actions within the context of a social interaction involving a conflict of interest (Scott and Fredericson, 1951). In the strict sense, however, submissive behaviors are not aggressive behaviors; consequently, hormonal mediation of the aggressive and the submissive components of an agonistic interaction may be different (Leshner and Moyer, 1975). Aggression and submission may represent the end points of a single behavioral continuum; alternatively, they may represent independent, but interacting, dimensions of the behaving individual (**FIGURE 8.20**). This is not a trivial semantic issue but rather a conceptual issue that influences the manner in which the neural and endocrine bases of agonistic behavior are studied (Schlinger and Callard, 1990).

There is overwhelming circumstantial evidence that androgenic steroid hormones mediate aggressive behavior across many species. First, seasonal variations in blood plasma concentrations of testosterone and seasonal variations in aggression coincide. For instance, the incidence of aggressive behavior peaks for red deer stags in autumn, when their gonads are secreting large amounts of testosterone (**FIGURE 8.21**). Second, aggressive behaviors increase at the time of puberty, when the steroidogenic component of the testes becomes active and blood concentrations of androgens rise. Juvenile red deer do not participate in the fighting during the rutting season. Third, in any given species, males are generally more aggressive than females. This is certainly true of red deer; relative to stags, red deer hinds rarely display aggressive behavior, and their rare aggressive acts are qualitatively different from the aggressive behavior of rutting males. Finally, castration typically reduces aggression in males, and testosterone replacement therapy restores aggression to precastration levels. There

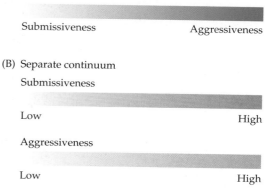

FIGURE 8.20 Two models of agonistic behavior Aggressive and submissive behaviors can be seen as opposite ends of a single behavioral continuum (A), or they can be thought of as two separate aspects of an individual's behavior (B). Each model makes different predictions about how hormones might influence agonistic behavior.

agonistic Referring to any behavior associated with fighting, including aggression, submission, and retreat.

FIGURE 8.21 Seasonal changes in red deer stags At the end of summer, testosterone levels (red line) begin to increase, and they peak in midautumn. These rising androgen levels are accompanied by antler growth (blue line); the antlers come into "hard horn" in November, and the males begin to display aggressive behavior (green line). Mating behavior occurs for about 2 weeks in midautumn (shaded area). After mating, testosterone levels begin to diminish, aggressive behaviors wane, and the males engage in few agonistic interactions. When blood androgens reach low values in January and February, the antlers are cast.

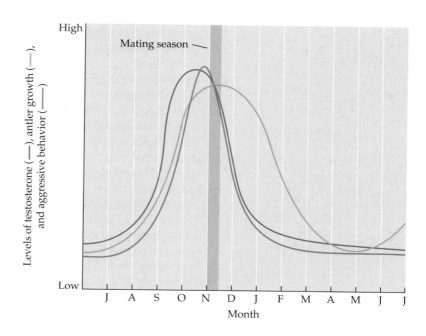

are some interesting exceptions to these general observations; however, such exceptions will be described later in this chapter.

Seasonal Changes in Aggression

As noted, animals that are preparing to mate, or have recently mated, require resources for their offspring and are far more likely to behave aggressively than are nonbreeding individuals. We have already discussed the fierce protective behaviors seen in females in defense of their young. Many animal species breed on a seasonal basis (see Chapter 10); consequently, a seasonal pattern of aggressive behavior is commonly observed. Several experiments have recently been conducted to investigate seasonal changes in aggression and the role of androgens in this temporal variation. This section describes some of those studies and presents examples of this issue in several animal species.

Aggression and the Breeding Cycle: Red Deer

Red deer stags were the subject of one such experiment. Castration of stags during the winter caused them to plummet in social rank (Lincoln et al., 1972). Their reduction in social status mainly reflected the loss of their weapons: castrated stags promptly cast their antlers and acquired velvet antlers. Normally, antlers develop throughout the summer. During the course of their development, the new antlers are covered by a mossy, soft, and highly vascularized tissue called velvet; thus, the deer are said to be in velvet horn during antler development. The velvet is shed at the end of the summer, when high blood testosterone concentrations destroy the blood supply to the velvet tissue and it dies. The antlers gain their familiar bony appearance as the velvet is shed, and the animals are said to be in hard horn. After rutting, the testes regress during the winter, and low blood concentrations of testosterone cause the stags to cast their antlers in late winter (see Figure 8.21). Thus, wintertime castration mimicked the normal vernal (springtime) reduction in testosterone and caused the stags to cast (i.e., shed) their antlers prematurely. In this study, castrated males regained some of their position in the dominance hierarchy when the gonadally intact males also shed their antlers. However, they did not regain all of their former social rank.

Not only does the frequency of agonistic encounters change on a seasonal basis, but the quality of the encounters and the style of fighting also change. Red deer stags use their antlers as both offensive and defensive weapons during the rutting season, but aggressive behavior among males lacking antlers is mainly expressed by kicking with their forelegs. Females typically use their forelegs in agonistic interactions throughout the year.

Some castrated stags in the study were implanted with slow-release testosterone capsules, either in the winter or in the summer (Lincoln et al., 1972). Winter-implanted males retained their antlers, were more aggressive than other males, and climbed in social rank throughout the spring and summer. Without antlers, the normal stags were easily intimidated by the antler-bearing, testosterone-treated stags. The continuous supply of testosterone across seasons permitted the stags to maintain their antlers and evoked aggressive behavior. However, not all androgen-dependent behaviors were supported by the chronic androgen exposure. For instance, the testosterone-treated males showed mating behavior only during the appropriate autumnal breeding season, suggesting either that estrous females generate a cue that normally stimulates mating behavior in stags or that the neural substrate controlling reproductive behavior in this species is responsive to androgens only at a particular time of year.

Stags implanted with testosterone in the summer began to climb in social rank even before the androgen could stimulate antler development, indicating that their aggressive behavior increased in response to androgen treatment even without the external morphological changes. In other words, these males behaved aggressively even in the absence of weapons to fulfill their threats. However, the antlers are the main factor controlling social dominance Amputating the antlers of gonadally intact stags caused an immediate change in their social status without any change in endocrine state (Bouissou, 1983). Thus, steroid hormones affect social status in red deer stags in two ways: first, by acting directly on the brain to promote aggressiveness, and second, by acting on the antlers, the effectors of aggressive behavior. Males of other ungulate species differ from red deer; for example, castrated horses (Tyler, 1972) and reindeer (Espmark, 1964) may still dominate other male conspecifics. It is not yet known what accounts for this variation among species.

Aggression and Winter Survival: Birds

Many migratory birds must compete with resident birds for food and shelter in their winter habitat. Research with migratory redstarts (*Setophaga ruticilla*) demonstrated that the future reproductive success of migrants depends on the quality of the wintering habitat (Marra et al., 1998). At low latitudes, the resident birds are in reproductive condition during the winter and are extremely territorial. Although first reported as anomalous behavior, territoriality has been reported among some wintering migrants, as well, and may be common among passerines (perching birds) that winter in the Neotropics (Greenberg, 1986; Marra et al., 1998). Wintering migrants are not in reproductive condition, and their gonads are not producing any measurable amounts of steroid hormones.

In European stonechats (*Saxicola torquata*), vernal territorial aggression was reduced by using both flutamide (an antiandrogen) and an aromatase inhibitor to block the conversion of testosterone to estrogen. However, the same treatment did not affect territorial behavior in winter, suggesting that in stonechats territoriality is regulated by different hormonal mechanisms at different times of the year (Canoine and Gwinner, 2002). There appear to be substantial species differences in the endocrine regulation of aggressive behavior in birds during the nonbreeding season (Canoine and Gwinner, 2002; Moore et al., 2004; Wingfield et al., 2005). In male song sparrows, for example, field studies found that castration reduced aggression in the summer, but not during winter (Wingfield, 1994). Also, flutamide and an aromatase inhibitor significantly reduced territorial behavior in this species during autumn and winter (Soma and Wingfield, 1999; Soma et al., 1999a,b). Similar results were obtained when an aromatase inhibitor (fadrozole) was used alone (Soma et al., 2000a,b). Fadrozole treatment in combination with estradiol implants as hormone replacement therapy completely restored territorial aggression (Soma et al., 2000a). Considered together, these results suggest that estrogens, presumably aromatized from androgens in the brain, are involved in the regulation of territorial behavior outside the breeding season in song sparrows (Soma et al., 2000a,b). These results emphasize that estrogens, resulting from aromatization of androgens and acting through estrogen receptors, are important in the control of territorial aggression in autumn, whereas androgen receptor–mediated mechanisms appear less important at this time. Given that androgen and estrogen concentrations tend to be low in autumn and winter, what is the source of these steroids? We now know that steroids are produced de novo directly in the brain. Several studies have indicated that the avian brain can produce such neurosteroids at high levels, suggesting that androgens are produced in the brain and converted by neurons into estrogens to regulate aggression outside of the breeding season (Baulieu, 1998; Saldanha and Schlinger, 2008; Saldanha et al., 1999). Not only does this appear to be the case, but the activity of steroidogenic enzymes and the neural production of testosterone are rapidly increased in nonbreeding males in response to a simulated territorial intrusion (Pradhan et al., 2010). Using in vivo microdialysis techniques, local estradiol concentrations were found to rapidly elevate in the forebrain in male zebra finches during social interactions with females. Exposure to other males' songs caused brain estradiol concentrations to increase and testosterone concentrations to decrease in a brain region that is analogous to the mammalian auditory cortex (Remage-Healey et al., 2008). This suggests that avian forebrain steroid concentrations are acutely and differentially regulated during social behavior in a region-specific manner and in a rapid time course similar to regulation of traditional neuromodulators.

Additional studies have linked dehydroepiandrosterone (DHEA), a biologically weak steroid, to regulation of aggressive behaviors in birds (Soma et al., 2008). DHEA is produced by the adrenal glands in significant amounts. The enzymatic machinery exists in the avian brain that can convert circulating DHEA to androstenedione, which in turn can be converted to testosterone or aromatized to estradiol (Labrie et al., 1995). DHEA appears to play an important role in territorial aggression during the nonbreeding season in song sparrows (*Melospiza melodia morphna*) (Soma and Wingfield, 2001) and spotted antbirds (*Hylophylax naevioides*) (Hau et al., 2004). Implants of DHEA into male song sparrows increased singing, one component of territorial aggression, and also resulted in growth of the high vocal center, a song-control nucleus in the telencephalon (Soma et al., 2002). It should be noted that the neurosteroid and circulating-DHEA-precursor hypotheses are not mutually exclusive, so both processes could be operating to provide steroids to regulate territorial behavior (Soma et al., 2008).

Aggression and Winter Survival: Rodents

Individuals of many rodent species shift from a highly territorial social strategy during the breeding season to a social, and highly interactive, existence during the winter. These species undergo reproductive regression at the end of the breeding season in response to short days (see Chapter 10); the resulting lower concentrations of androgens may enable this shift. There are adaptive benefits that accrue from changing social systems on a seasonal basis. During the breeding season, animals benefit from controlling resources to promote their own survival and that of their offspring, and they defend those resources aggressively. However, rodents may benefit from group living during the winter, because this strategy conserves energy and enhances survival during this time of low temperatures and reduced food availability. Many species of rodents conserve energy during the winter by forming aggregations of huddling animals (West and Dublin, 1984). These aggregations, like winter feeding flocks of birds, may consist of different sexes and different rodent species (Madison, 1984).

As noted in the introduction of this chapter, even in the absence of huddling behavior, animals may tolerate one another at close quarters during the winter, whereas interspecific commingling is not tolerated during the breeding season. For example, meadow voles (*Microtus pennsylvanicus*), as their name implies, occupy grasslands during their breeding season; the males are highly territorial at this time. Red-backed voles (*Clethrionomys gapperi*) prefer to breed in spruce forest habitats. But during the winter months, meadow voles move from open meadows into the forest habitats occupied by the red-backed voles, presumably to take advantage of the protective cover provided by the trees. In some cases, they occupy nests with other rodent species. Individual meadow voles trapped during the winter and tested in paired encounters in a small neutral arena exhibit less interspecific aggression than summer-trapped voles (Turner et al., 1975). The winter reduction in aggressiveness allows habitat sharing during harsh conditions. As the animals enter breeding condition in the spring, they once again establish mutually exclusive territories.

Some individual male rodents do not undergo reproductive regression when exposed to short days; rather, these males maintain testicular function and produce sperm and androgens during simulated winter conditions (Nelson, 1987; Prendergast et al., 2001). Males capable of continuous breeding would appear to be superior in fitness to individuals whose reproductive apparatus regresses, because the former are capable of siring offspring at any time of year. Though the advantage of continuous mating ability is obvious, it must incur some hidden costs, because only a minority of individuals adopts that strategy. If there were no costs to a strategy of continuous breeding, then continuous breeders would eventually replace the seasonally breeding animals in any population. One possible cost is that nonregressed males, with their elevated androgen concentrations, may remain too aggressive during the winter to benefit from communal huddling, and thus they may give up substantial energy savings, relative to reproductively regressed males, in order to be reproductively competent all year long. The high behavioral and energetic costs associated with maintenance of the reproductive system would compromise survival and may explain why nonregressive types do not normally predominate in temperate or boreal zone populations of rodents (Nelson, 1987; Nelson et al., 1989).

A field experiment on the winter nesting behavior of meadow voles supports this contention (McShea, 1990). Most voles in the population were reproductively inactive during the winter and formed groups of huddling individuals. However, there were two males in the population that remained in breeding condition and were never observed to huddle with other animals. In pairwise tests of aggression, these reproductively competent males were much more aggressive than reproductively quiescent individuals. Laboratory studies of prairie voles revealed that adult castration does not significantly affect aggression in that species (Demas et al., 1999). In another laboratory study on a related species, reproductive status influenced odor preferences of meadow voles maintained in simulated winter day lengths (Gorman et al., 1993). Males that retained reproductive function in winter-day-length conditions preferred the odors of females that also did not inhibit reproduction during short days. This preference may facilitate the sporadic occurrences of winter breeding frequently reported for this species (reviewed in Nelson, 1987; Prendergast et al., 2009).

Although the results of most rodent studies to date suggest that low circulating testosterone concentrations reduce mating and aggressive behaviors (reviewed in Knol and Egberink-Alink, 1989; Rubinow and Schmidt, 1996), males of some rodent species (e.g., wood rats [*Neotoma fuscipes*], prairie voles) and a growing list of other nondomesticated species do not reduce aggression after castration. For example, castration does not decrease aggressiveness in male red-sided garter snakes (*Thamnophis sirtalis parietalis*) (Crews and Moore, 1986), European starlings (*Sturnus vulgaris*) (Pinxten et al., 2003), or Mongolian gerbils (*Meriones unguiculatus*) (Christianson et al., 1972). Both Syrian hamsters (*Mesocricetus auratus*) and Siberian hamsters (*Phodopus sungorus*) display increased aggressive behavior under short-day conditions despite decreased circulating gonadal steroids (Badura and Nunez, 1989; Garrett and Campbell, 1980; Jasnow et al., 2000) (**FIGURE 8.22**).

Adrenal steroid hormones appear to be involved in the short-day aggressive phenotype in several species of rodents and birds (Soma et al., 2015). Both male and female Siberian hamsters housed in short day lengths were seen to undergo gonadal regression and reductions in circulating gonadal steroids but exhibit substantial increases in aggression, compared with animals in long days (Jasnow et al., 2000; Scotti et al., 2007). Replacement of gonadal steroid hormones such as 17β-estradiol in short-day females (to mimic long-day concentrations) did not reduce aggression to summer levels (Scotti et al., 2007). Thus, another neuroendocrine mediator was sought. Recently,

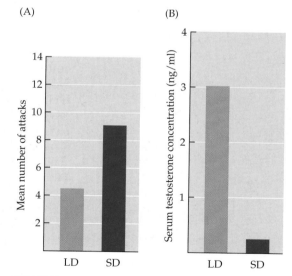

FIGURE 8.22 **Effects of estrogen on hamster aggression change in response to day length** In Siberian hamsters housed under short-day (SD) conditions, the number of attacks is increased (A) and the latency to attack is decreased, as compared with those under long-day (LD) conditions. These day lengths simulate winter (see Chapter 10). Gonads are reduced in size and function, and circulating blood testosterone concentrations are very low (B). After Jasnow et al., 2000.

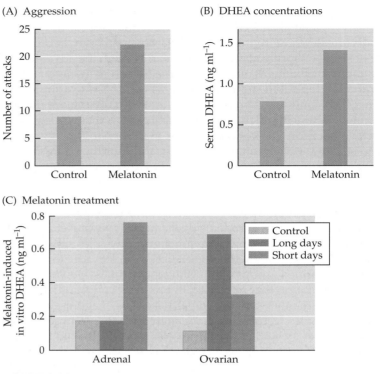

FIGURE 8.23 Melatonin treatment of female Siberian hamsters increased (A) aggression and (B) serum DHEA concentrations; (C) melatonin treatment of short-day female hamster adrenal glands in vitro increased DHEA production but in long-day hamsters ovarian DHEA responses increased. After Rendon et al., 2015.

it was reported that melatonin, which is secreted only at night and so provides an internal marker of night length, bolsters DHEA secretion from adrenal glands in culture (Rendon et al., 2015) (**FIGURE 8.23**). Furthermore, long-day hamsters provided with short-day melatonin doses displayed increased aggression and elevated DHEA concentrations (Rendon et al., 2015). These results suggest that DHEA is a key peripheral regulator of aggression and that melatonin coordinates a "seasonal switch" from gonadal to adrenal regulation of aggression by direct action on the adrenal glands. Other studies suggest that nitric oxide might also be involved in the seasonal mediation of aggression (reviewed in Bedrosian and Nelson, 2014; Bedrosian et al., 2012).

Another approach has revealed a novel mechanism regulating elevated aggression in short-day conditions. Evidence from several species suggests that seasonal changes in aggressive behavior are mediated in part by estrogen signaling (Trainor et al., 2007a, 2008). Under summerlike long day lengths, estrogens inhibit aggressive behaviors in male oldfield mice (*Peromyscus polionotus*). However, if the same mice are housed under winterlike short days, then estrogens exert the opposite behavioral response and increase aggression! This effect cannot be explained by seasonal changes in alpha estrogen receptor (ERα) or beta estrogen receptor (ERβ) expression. This is because drugs that selectively activate ERα and ERβ have similar behavioral effects: decreasing aggression under long days and increasing aggression under short days. The differential effects of estrogens on behavior appear to be due to a shift in the molecular actions of estrogens. A single injection of estradiol increases aggression within 15 minutes in mice housed in short days. If the mice are housed in long days, then an injection of estradiol has no overt behavioral effects in the short term. The time frame is significant because estrogen-dependent changes in

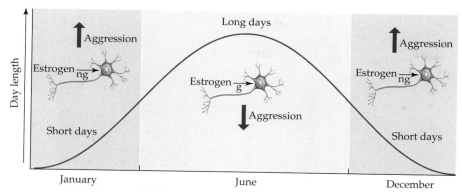

FIGURE 8.24 Effects of estrogen on oldfield mouse aggression change in response to day length. Estrogens increase aggression in beach (aka oldfield) mice (*Peromyscus polionotus*) through nongenomic (ng) mechanisms during the short days of winter, whereas during the long days of summer, estrogen inhibits aggression via genomic (g) hormone mechanisms. After Pfaff and Silver, 2007.

gene expression typically require several hours to occur. Translation of messenger RNA transcripts into biologically active proteins takes even longer. This suggests that the rapid effects of estradiol on aggression in short-day mice are mediated by the so-called nongenomic mechanisms discussed in Chapter 2, which include phosphorylation of kinases and regulation of neurotransmitter release. In contrast, the inhibitory effects of estrogens on aggression in long days may be mediated by changes in gene expression (**FIGURE 8.24**). In support of this hypothesis, estrogen-dependent gene expression in the bed nucleus of the stria terminalis is elevated in mice housed in long photoperiods.

These results are consistent with field studies on song sparrows, which reported that aggression outside of the summer breeding season is not dependent on testosterone (Soma et al., 2008). As in oldfield mice, aggression outside of the summer breeding season is often regulated by estrogens. When male sparrows are treated with an aromatase inhibitor, aggressive behavior is reduced within 24 hours, suggesting a potentially rapid effect of estrogens on behavior. Subsequent studies have suggested that during the nonbreeding season, estrogens regulating aggressive behavior are produced de novo in the brain. Not only do song sparrows express all of the steroidogenic enzymes necessary to produce estrogens within the brain, recent evidence demonstrates that steroid production is rapidly regulated. Nonbreeding song sparrows exposed to aggressive challenges rapidly increased androgen production within the brain (Pradhan et al., 2010). These data are consistent with the hypothesis that estrogen-dependent aggression in the nonbreeding season is regulated by rapid nongenomic pathways.

Male song sparrows display estrogen-dependent territorial aggression throughout virtually the entire year (Wingfield and Soma, 2002). Although territorial aggression in response to a territorial intrusion appears similar throughout the year, what happens after territorial aggression varies seasonally. During the breeding season, territorial residents continue patrolling their territories and display spontaneous song for hours, whereas during the nonbreeding season, resident birds stop behaving aggressively within minutes (Wingfield, 1994b). Thus, breeding territorial aggression is persistent, whereas nonbreeding territorial aggression is transient. It appears that estrogen varies in function by season as in *Peromyscus* described above. Captive song sparrows in either breeding or nonbreeding conditions were provided with wax moth larvae. Some of the larvae were injected with doses of estradiol; this was a clever way to provide estradiol to the birds quickly without the stress of hormone injections. Birds provided with estradiol-laced larvae increased aggres-

FIGURE 8.25 Song sparrows treated with estradiol outside of the breeding season increased aggressive behaviors within 20 minutes of treatment, suggesting a rapid nongenomic mechanism of action. Barrier contacts represent the number of times the male birds flew at and contacted the wire mesh barrier—it is considered an aggressive act. Proximity score indicates the time spent in close association to a cage-mate. Birds examined during the breeding season did not show the rapid onset of aggression in response to estrogens. From Heimovics et al., 2015.

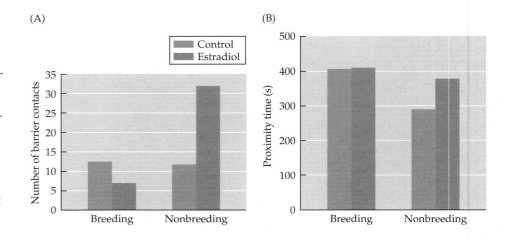

sive behaviors within 20 minutes of treatment, indicating that estrogens increase aggression during the nonbreeding season via a rapid nongenomic mechanism of action (Heimovics et al., 2015) (**FIGURE 8.25**). Birds in breeding condition did not show this rapid onset of aggression in response to estradiol. In song sparrows and other small animals (see below), transient expression of aggressive behavior during the nonbreeding season is presumably highly adaptive as it minimizes energy expenditure and maximizes the amount of time available for foraging (Heimovics et al., 2015).

In addition to the change in blood plasma androgen concentrations, seasonal changes in androgen receptor sensitivity occur in rodents. Consequently, it is not possible to override the wintertime reduction in aggressiveness merely by injecting testosterone. This seasonal shift in responsiveness to androgens has not been demonstrated in voles, but it has been investigated in another seasonal breeder, the Syrian hamster. Injections of testosterone in reproductively regressed male golden hamsters do not elevate the number of aggressive encounters to the level exhibited by hamsters in breeding condition. Presumably, the ineffectiveness of testosterone in stimulating aggressiveness reflects a lack of androgen receptors in the brain regions responsible for organizing aggressive behavior during the nonbreeding season. As with mating behavior, very high blood androgen concentrations are required to stimulate aggressive behavior immediately after the hamsters regrow their reproductive systems, as compared with those necessary to sustain aggressiveness in breeding animals (Berndtson and Desjardins, 1974). Desensitization of receptor tissues to steroid hormones is common after a prolonged absence of the hormone (Morin and Zucker, 1978; Powers et al., 1989), and this may be the mechanism by which seasonal changes in the sensitivity of central nervous system tissue are mediated (see Chapter 10). This last statement is somewhat speculative, however. Seasonal changes in receptors are only one of several factors, including changes in metabolizing enzymes, that may mediate seasonal changes in tissue sensitivity.

Testosterone and the Energetic Costs of Aggression: Lizards

Elevated testosterone concentrations and aggression cause a decrease in survivorship in a number of species. A number of different factors, including injury, energetic costs, exposure to predators, and engaging in more "risky" behaviors, may mediate this effect. In male spiny lizards (*Sceloporus jarrovi*) (**FIGURE 8.26A**), seasonal changes in testosterone concentrations are tightly correlated with seasonal changes in the intensity of aggression, especially territorial aggression (Moore and Marler, 1987). During the autumnal breeding season, when territorial aggression is most fierce, testosterone concentrations are high; conversely, during the winter, when

(A)

(B)

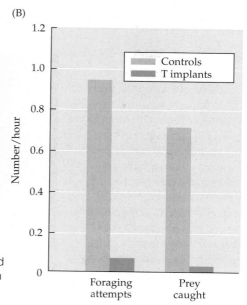

FIGURE 8.26 Costs of aggression in mountain spiny lizards (A) A photo of a male mountain spiny lizard (*Sceloporus jarrovi*). (B) When lizards are treated with testosterone (T), they spend more of their time in aggressive displays and much less time in foraging, resulting in fewer captured prey. B after Marler and Moore, 1989.

little territoriality is observed, testosterone concentrations are at their lowest. High testosterone increases aggression and reduces foraging times and total number of prey captured (**FIGURE 8.26B**). Interestingly, testosterone is highest during summer, just prior to the fall breeding season, in these lizards. Artificial elevation of blood testosterone concentrations by implantation of Silastic capsules during the winter increased aggression above normal summer levels, but not to the level observed during the fall breeding season peak (Moore and Marler, 1987). Males that were implanted with testosterone-filled capsules spent too much time engaged in territorial defense, aggressive displays, and other aggressive behaviors to forage adequately and did not survive as long as males implanted with empty capsules. This decrease in survivorship probably reflects the elevated energetic costs associated with aggressive behavior (Marler and Moore, 1988, 1991). Thus, males behaving aggressively during the winter incur significant costs even in the face of potential reproductive benefits. These costs include the energy expended in increased territorial aggression and displays, as well as longer daily activity levels, which can expose the males to greater predation risks (Marler and Moore, 1988; Marler et al., 1995). When oxygen consumption was measured directly, testosterone treatment did not increase resting, or basal, metabolic rates. The approximately 30% increase in metabolism evoked by testosterone treatment appeared to reflect primarily the energetic costs of territorial defense (Marler et al., 1995). Food supplements were able to compensate for the testosterone-induced costs of aggressive behavior (Marler and Moore, 1991). Other costs of testosterone include interference with paternal care, increased risk of injury, loss of fat stores, and possibly oncogenic effects and impaired immune system function (Wingfield et al., 2001) (**BOX 8.3**).

Do Seasonal Hormonal Changes in Primates Correlate with Aggression?

Seasonal breeding is also observed among many primate species. Intermale aggression may increase during the breeding season in some species, for example, lemurs (*Lemur catta*) (Jolly, 1966) and rhesus monkeys (*Macaca mulatta*) (Michael and Zumpe, 1978, 1996). The frequency of aggressive acts may or may not increase during the breeding season in squirrel monkeys (*Saimiri sciureus*) (Baldwin, 1968;

BOX 8.3   *How Much Testosterone? Just the Right Amount...*

In order to win at the "game of life," Darwin suggested, individuals compete on the level of fitness; in other words, individuals need to produce more successful offspring than their competitors. One strategy might be to become reproductively active right after birth or hatching and continuously produce offspring until death. This strategy will not succeed long term, because producing offspring requires enormous energy and compromises survival. Fitness requires a strategic trade-off in investing in offspring production and survival mechanisms. All things being equal (and they rarely are), (1) long-lived individuals produce more offspring than short-lived individuals of the same species, and (2) making offspring will hasten one's demise. Thus, individuals initially invest in survival mechanisms such as immune function, and then after reproductive maturity they invest in reproductive traits. At what age to undergo reproductive maturation, how many offspring to produce each breeding bout, and how many breeding bouts to have each year are factors that comprise individuals' life history strategies.

Natural selection shapes organisms as integrated sets of traits, but the relative ease with which these traits can be assembled and disassembled in response to selection is a point of contention among biologists. Hormones often underlie the coexpression of traits, and hormonal correlations, in common with genetic correlations, can promote adaptation or delay evolutionary response. The relative importance of phenotypic integration and independence of hormonally mediated traits has significant implications for the evolution of life histories, sexual dimorphism, and population divergence. Integration and independence can be studied via experimental manipulations of hormonal phenotypes, assessment of patterns of natural variation in hormones in relation to phenotype and fitness, comparisons of hormonal phenotypes across populations, and mechanistic studies of hormones and their interaction with target tissues.

The Ketterson Research Group has been addressing these issues by focusing on testosterone and its integrating effect on the physiology and behavior of males and females of a songbird species, dark-eyed juncos (*Junco hyemalis*) (**Figure A**). The long-term goal of their research is to understand the evolution of hormone-mediated phenotypes by taking both an experimental and a correlative approach to the evolution of life histories. Their experimental approach has been simply to manipulate testosterone, then to measure the effects of the manipulation on phenotype and fitness in juncos in both seminatural and natural settings. The main focus has been the trade-offs between mating and parental behavior and between reproduction and survival. For example, testosterone might increase reproductive

Figure A

success by increasing territorial defense and courtship activities but reduce life expectancy because testosterone tends to compromise immune function. Overall, research on the juncos has established that experimental elevation of testosterone reduces viability but enhances fecundity because it increases male mating success (e.g., Casto et al., 2001; Clotfelter et al., 2004; Grieves et al., 2006; McGlothlin and Ketterson, 2008; Zysling et al., 2006). More recently they have been measuring individual variation in the ability to produce testosterone and relating that to traits already known to be affected by experimental elevation of testosterone, and also to fitness. As with experimental elevation, male juncos that naturally produce more testosterone are less parental, are more aggressive, and display compromised immune function (Grieves et al., 2006; McGlothlin and Ketterson, 2008; McGlothlin et al., 2007). Males that naturally produce the most testosterone are less likely to return from year to year; that is, they have reduced survivorship (McGlothlin et al., 2007). Males that naturally produce "average levels of testosterone" have the greatest reproductive success. In short, selection on hormone-mediated traits has proved to be stabilizing, showing that the average male is the best performer (**Figure B**).

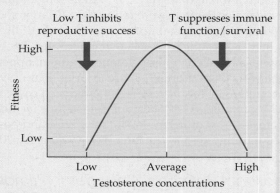

Figure B

Mendoza et al., 1978). Correlations between periods of high androgen production and aggression are interesting but do not demonstrate conclusively that elevated androgen concentrations cause aggression in primates. The results of several studies that addressed the relation between decreases in blood plasma concentrations of androgens and receptor sensitivity to androgens have suggested that these correlations probably do represent causation, despite some notable exceptions. Supportive and nonsupportive evidence that androgens mediate aggressive behavior among primates will be reviewed later in this chapter.

Human males also show seasonal variation in blood testosterone concentrations (Dabbs, 1990; Smals et al., 1976). These seasonal changes have not been shown to cause aggressive behavior. However, this presumption has not been directly tested, despite an abundance of positive correlations, for example, the finding that peak incidences of violent urban crime in North America are associated with high ambient temperatures and peak androgen concentrations in some populations (e.g., Smals et al., 1976). Also, seasonal changes in aggression, as assessed by rule infractions, increased for prisoners maintained in a Maryland prison during the summer as compared with the other three seasons (Haertzen et al., 1993). Of course, these correlations may simply represent increased contact between perpetrator and victim during the warmer weather of summer. However, an analysis of more than 27,000 reports from women in 23 shelters scattered across five locations in the United States who had been abused by their live-in partners (both married and unmarried) revealed an annual rhythm of abuse, with maximal levels occurring during the summer (Michael and Zumpe, 1986). These data suggest that violence by men against women increases during the summer independently of any major seasonal changes in contact between perpetrator and victim. Whatever the causal relationship, such correlations probably reflect factors other than hormone concentrations. As Joan Didion writes in *Slouching towards Bethlehem*, "In Switzerland the suicide rate goes up during the *foehn* [a strong, hot, dry wind], and in the courts of some Swiss cantons the wind is considered a mitigating circumstance for crime" (218–219).

Pubertal Changes in Aggression

There are countless reports of increased aggression in males undergoing puberty. During puberty, the testes grow larger, and under the influence of luteinizing hormone (LH) from the anterior pituitary, the Leydig cells secrete increasing amounts of androgens into the circulatory system. Plasma concentrations of androgens increase at the time of puberty and are associated with the elevation in aggressiveness. Intermale aggression in house mice, as well as isolation-induced aggression, is first observed at the time of puberty (Brain and Nowell, 1969; Levy and King, 1953).

As noted in Chapter 1, male livestock have been castrated prior to puberty since antiquity to make them more docile and manageable. Prepubertal castration is more effective in reducing overall aggression in mice than castration in adulthood (Uhrich, 1938). This observation is not borne out, however, in all species. For example, prepubertal castration of dogs does not necessarily diminish their adult levels of aggression (LeBoeuf, 1970), and prepubertal castration does not preclude male primates from attaining high social status. For instance, Narses (480–574 CE) was a famous Byzantine general and statesman who originally was a eunuch slave in Armenia. He had a reputation for ruthlessness and played an important role in suppressing the Nika riots. Narses served under the emperor Justinian I, who sent him to Italy in 538 CE to fight against the Goths. Eventually, Narses rose to become the exarch of Italy.

Although there are interesting exceptions, it is generally true that aggressiveness increases at puberty. The following sections review some specific examples of associations between hormone concentrations and aggressive behavior that coincide with puberty.

FIGURE 8.27 The type and amount of aggression varies across development. Different types of attacks of resident (R) Syrian hamsters on intruders (I) correspond to different developmental stages, progressing from attacks on (A) face and cheeks to (B) flanks to (C) underbelly and (D) rear end. (E) The frequency of aggressive encounters wanes as the hamsters become older. After Wommack et al., 2003.

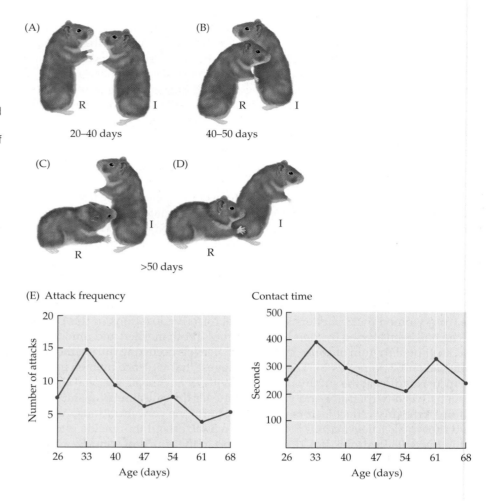

Social Influences on the Development of Aggressive Behavior

One important animal model in studies of social aggression has been Syrian hamsters. Prior to puberty (from 20–40 days of age) male Syrian hamsters engage in agonistic behavior mainly as a form of play, which is characterized by attacking the face and cheeks of their opponents (Wommack et al., 2003). During puberty the frequency of attacks diminishes, and "play fighting" morphs into the adult version of aggression (Delville et al., 2005). From about 40–50 days of age (midpuberty), males undergo a transitional period of behavior during which the attacks are aimed at the flanks. Finally, as they emerge from the pubertal period, males perform adultlike offensive aggressive behaviors, which are characterized by attacks to the underbelly and rear end (Wommack et al., 2003) (**FIGURE 8.27**). Exposure to social stress during puberty alters adult aggressive behavior in at least two ways. Repeated exposure of male peripubertal hamsters to aggressive adults hastens the onset of adultlike offensive, but not defensive, aggression. If the exposure occurrs early in puberty, the young hamsters are most likely to be aggressive, especially toward smaller opponents, postpubertally (Wommack et al., 2003). Furthermore, repeated social stress slows the reduction in attack frequency normally seen during puberty. In contrast to males, female Syrian hamsters display a stable frequency of attacks through puberty and into adulthood. There is no obvious midpubertal transitional period, and cortisol habituates to repeated exposures to aggressive adults (Taravosh-Lahn and Delville, 2004).

Male hamsters do not appear to habituate to repeated exposure to social subjugation (Wommack and Delville, 2003). After 2 weeks of repeated exposure to aggressive adults, male hamsters persistently display elevated plasma cortisol concentrations, an endocrine marker of the maturation of agonistic behavior from play fighting to adultlike attacks (Wommack and Delville, 2003; Wommack et al., 2003). Although castration has well-known effects on aggression in adults, castration of peripubertal hamsters does not affect the transition from play fighting to adultlike fighting (Delville et al., 2005). The maturation of aggressive behavior is also correlated with adrenarche—the maturation of the hypothalamic-pituitary-adrenal (HPA) axis—during puberty, and activity of the HPA axis appears to control preadult agonistic behavior (Delville et al., 2005; Romeo, 2010; Wommack and Delville, 2007). Hamsters exposed to adult aggression begin to show adultlike aggressive behavior earlier in life. These animals undergo normal gonadal development, but they are also very aggressive toward smaller and younger individuals (Wommack et al., 2003). In effect, they become bullies (Hamilton et al., 2008; Newman et al., 2005).

Aggression at Puberty as a Possible Adaptation: Rodents

In one study, a group of peripubertal male prairie voles (*Microtus ochrogaster*) was implanted with slow-release capsules of testosterone, while another group received empty capsules. The testosterone-treated males exhibited a higher level of aggression in pairwise encounters than the control animals (Gaines et al., 1985), presumably because of the elevated concentrations of testosterone. In Syrian hamsters, peripubertal aggression is more intense than adult aggression (Romeo et al., 2003). How might such an increase in aggression at puberty be adaptive? Males of many rodent species, including voles and hamsters, disperse at the time of puberty. Dispersal is a very dangerous time for animals; mortality rates are extremely high during this time. Leaving home exposes the individual to many new threats, including predators and competing males. Dispersing males often find themselves encroaching on other males' territories as they learn to fend for themselves and try to find food, establish territories, and mate with females. Thus, dispersing males have evolved to be aggressive, which presumably increases their odds of survival and success in reproductive competition (Smale et al., 1997).

High blood concentrations of androgens are necessary to elicit dispersal in some mammalian species, but not in peripubertal male Belding's ground squirrels (*Spermophilus beldingii*) (Holekamp and Sherman, 1989; Smale et al., 1997). Male ground squirrels castrated at puberty exhibit dispersal behavior at the same rate and intensity as gonadally intact males. Interestingly, by the time these juvenile ground squirrels disperse, the mating season is over and adult males are no longer maintaining territories with the same intensity as they did at the onset of the breeding season.

What is the ecological significance of accelerated development of agonistic behavior in Syrian hamsters? Hamsters exposed to adult aggression begin to show adultlike aggressive behavior earlier in life (Romeo et al., 2003). These individuals undergo normal gonadal development, but they also become especially aggressive toward smaller and younger individuals (Wommack et al., 2003). The consequences of this enhanced aggression may depend on population density (Delville et al., 2003). The relationship between high population density and elevated aggression is well established. It is likely that juveniles are most likely to be socially subjugated by adults when population levels are high or resources are low. To survive, they themselves likely become more aggressive under these conditions (Romeo, 2010), therefore increasing the level of aggression in the population (Delville et al., 2003). In contrast to early social stressors, social stress during late puberty does not affect the development of aggression. Indeed, hamsters experiencing repeated aggressive encounters in late puberty become submissive and may remain so for life (Huhman and Jasnow, 2005). Such animals are unlikely to compete successfully for mates or resources.

The Timing of Puberty: Birds

In many avian species, reproductive and aggressive behaviors in males are closely linked. Many visual and vocal displays are used to attract females and repel other males simultaneously (Wingfield et al., 1994a). Increasing vernal day lengths trigger reproductive maturation in many birds by stimulating gonadal growth and testosterone production (see Chapter 10). Peak concentrations of plasma testosterone correspond to peak levels of intermale territorial aggression in the late spring. At the end of the nesting period, the testes regress in response to the chronic long day lengths. Because long day lengths no longer stimulate the reproductive system, the birds are said to be refractory to photoperiod (day length), or photorefractory. Exposure to short days is then required to break photorefractoriness and allow the birds to respond to the stimulatory effect of long days the following spring.

The onset of puberty in most avian species is dependent on photoperiod. However, there is substantial variation in the timing of puberty; for example, some birds breed during their first year, other species breed when they are 1 year old, and other species breed after 2 or more years of age (Follett, 1991). This variation in the timing of puberty corresponds with variation among bird species in the timing of first territorial defense and mating. Most nontropical avian species hatch in the late spring and reach adult body size several weeks after hatching but do not breed until the following spring. This is a reasonable strategy from an adaptive, functional perspective, because young males probably could not secure sufficiently suitable territories to induce females to breed. From a physiological perspective, one might ask why long days do not stimulate the birds to undergo puberty in their first summer. There is increasing evidence that birds of species that normally breed at 1 year of age hatch in a photorefractory state (Follett, 1991). That is, these birds must experience short days in order to break photorefractoriness and be stimulated by long days. Thus, unless housed under artificial lighting conditions, these birds cannot undergo puberty until spring, when they first experience long days after a period of short days. As you may know, some birds, such as quail and chickens, undergo puberty when less than 1 year of age (Follett, 1991). These birds are not photorefractory at hatching and can be stimulated by long days to undergo reproductive development during their first year.

When circulating testosterone concentrations increase, aggressive interactions among birds increase in frequency, especially during the establishment of territories or social dominance hierarchies (see below) (Wingfield et al., 1987). Androgens are important in stimulating territorial behaviors, including singing. Experimental implants of testosterone capsules at the onset of territory establishment increased territory size or intermale aggression in several avian species, including the sharp-tailed grouse (*Tympanuchus phasianellus*) (Trobec and Oring, 1972), red-winged blackbird (*Agelaius phoenecius*) (Searcy and Wingfield, 1980), pied flycatcher (*Ficedula hypoleuca*) (Silverin, 1980), and white-crowned sparrow (*Zonotrichia leucophrys*) (M. C. Moore, 1984). Testosterone treatment after territories or social dominance hierarchies were already established, however, usually did not increase territory size or social status (reviewed in Wingfield et al., 1990, but see Cawthorn et al., 1998).

Note that the photoperiodic control of gonadal function is fundamentally different in birds and rodents. Rodents are reproductively "on" unless exposed to short days, which turn them "off." Eventually, the reproductive systems of rodents break free of the inhibitory effects of chronic short days and regain their function. In other words, they become refractory to the inhibitory effects of short days and turn "on" reproductive function. The physiological mechanisms underlying this so-called spontaneous reproductive development are unknown.

Hormones and Dispersal Strategies: Primates

In contrast to what occurs in many animals, the pubertal increase in blood concentrations of testosterone among primates is not always associated with elevated aggression. The onset of puberty in captive rhesus monkeys, for example, does not result in any discernible increase in aggressive behavior (Rose et al., 1978). Similarly, agonistic encounters between young captive male owl monkeys (*Aotus trivirgatus*) and their parents did not change in frequency at puberty, despite large increases in their plasma testosterone concentrations (Dixson, 1980).

As in many avian and mammalian species, puberty is associated with dispersal among many primate species (Carpenter, 1940; Charles-Dominique, 1977; Fossey, 1974). Male rhesus monkeys become targets of increasing aggressive outbursts by adult males as they approach puberty at 3 or 4 years of age. This chronic harassment appears to force the peripubertal males to leave the natal troop and attempt to join a new one. Essentially two strategies exist for joining a new troop: the newcomer may burst right into the group and seize membership status, or he may hang around the periphery and try to sneak into the group. Either strategy has costs, often fatal for the newcomer. Attempts to join a new troop immediately are usually met with strong resistance by the resident males, and a great deal of aggression is aimed at the intruder. Peripheral animals are also in danger, because they may starve to death or succumb to a number of parasitic or stress-related illnesses.

Interestingly, several behavioral and hormonal factors predict which strategy an individual male will attempt in joining a new troop (Virgin and Sapolsky, 1997). Young males that are sons of high-ranking females often have "out-going, risk-taking" personalities (Suomi, 1991). These males venture farther from their mothers and engage in more rough-and-tumble play than do orphans or sons of low-ranking mothers. The sons of high-ranking females exhibit low vagal tone (a measure of autonomic reactivity; these individuals show a steady cardiac output and respiratory rate) and low plasma cortisol concentrations. In contrast, males that are not sons of high-ranking females have high vagal tone (heart rate, respiratory rate, and blood pressure are very reactive) and high blood concentrations of cortisol, suggesting that these males experience more stress in their lives. (In the laboratory, males with high vagal tone and high cortisol concentrations are also more likely to abuse alcohol than males with low vagal tone and low cortisol concentrations [Higley et al., 1991; Suomi, 1991, 1997]). In seminatural conditions, males with low vagal tone and low cortisol concentrations are more likely to employ the strategy of immediately establishing membership in a troop. In contrast, males with high vagal tone and high cortisol concentrations are more likely to try to sneak into a new troop after establishing familiarity from the periphery (Bolig et al., 1992; Cirulli et al., 2008).

In a study of male olive baboons (*Papio anubis*) living freely in stable hierarchies in Africa, some subordinate males displayed elevated basal glucocorticoid concentrations, and they showed a blunted glucocorticoid response and rapid suppression of testosterone concentrations during stress (Virgin and Sapolsky, 1997). These endocrine characteristics were initially interpreted as reflecting the chronic stress of their social position. However, long-term fieldwork revealed that these endocrine characters did not mark all subordinate individuals. Rather, endocrine profiles differed among subordinate males as a function of their individual "styles of social behavior." One of three subsets of subordinate male baboons was identified that had significantly high rates of copulations, a behavior usually shown only by high-ranking males. Such behavior predicted the onset of a transition to dominance, as this subset of subordinate males was significantly more likely than other subordinates to move to the dominant half of the hierarchy over the subsequent 3 years (Virgin and Sapolsky, 1997). A second subset of subordinate males was the most likely to initiate fights and to displace aggression onto an uninvolved third party after losing a fight. Males in this second cohort generally had elevated testosterone and lower basal glucocorticoid concentrations compared with the remaining subordinate cohort. Taken together, these results suggest that variables other than rank alone may be associated with distinctive endocrine profiles and that even in the face of a social stressor (such as social subordination), particular behavioral styles may attenuate the endocrine indices of stress (Virgin and Sapolsky, 1997) (see Chapter 11).

Sex Differences in Aggressive Behavior

Although it is not universally true (**BOX 8.4**), males are generally more aggressive than females. Certainly, human males are much more aggressive than human females. Many more men than women are convicted of violent crimes in North America. The sex differences in human aggressiveness appear very early. At every age throughout the school years, many more boys than girls initiate physical assaults. Almost everyone will acknowledge the existence of this sex difference, but assigning a cause to behavioral sex differences in humans always elicits much debate (see Chapter 4). It is possible that boys are more aggressive than girls because androgens promote aggressive behavior and boys have higher blood concentrations of androgens than girls. It is possible that boys and girls differ in their aggressiveness because the brains of boys are exposed to androgens prenatally and the "wiring" of their brains is thus organized in a way that facilitates the expression of aggression. It is also possible that boys are encouraged and girls are discouraged by family, peers, or others from acting in an aggressive manner. These three hypotheses are not mutually exclusive, but it is extremely difficult to discriminate among them to account for sex differences in human aggressiveness.

What kinds of studies would be necessary to assess these hypotheses? It is usually difficult to separate out the influences of environment and physiology on the development of behavior in humans (see Chapter 4). For example, boys and girls differ in their rough-and-tumble play at a very young age, which suggests an early physiological influence on aggression. However, parents interact with their male and female offspring differently; they usually play more roughly with male than female infants, which suggests that the sex difference in aggressiveness is partially learned (Smith and Lloyd, 1978). This difference in parental interaction style is evident by the first week of life. Because of these complexities in the factors influencing human behavior, the study of hormonal effects on sex-differentiated behavior has been pursued in nonhuman animals, for which environmental influences can be held relatively constant. Animals in which sexual differentiation occurs postnatally are often used as models so that this process can be easily manipulated experimentally. The following sections review the findings of some experiments with such animal models.

Organization and Activation of Aggression: Mice

With the appropriate animal model, we can address the questions posed above: Is the sex difference in aggression due to higher adult blood concentrations of androgens in males than in females, or are males more aggressive than females because their brains are organized differently by perinatal hormones? Are males usually more aggressive than females because of an interaction of early and current blood androgen concentrations? As with humans, these possibilities are difficult to assess in wild animals, but they are relatively simple to examine in laboratory mice, in which sexual differentiation of the brain occurs postnatally. If male mice are castrated prior to their sixth day of life, then treated with testosterone propionate in adulthood, they exhibit low levels of aggression. Similarly, females ovariectomized prior to day 6 of age but given androgens in adulthood do not express male-like levels of aggression. Treatment of perinatally gonadectomized males or females with testosterone prior to day 6 of age and also in adulthood results in a level of aggression similar to that observed in typical male mice (Edwards, 1969, 1970) (see Table 8.2 for typical tests of aggression). Thus, in mice, the proclivity for males to

BOX 8.4   *Sex Role Reversals*

In some species, females are more aggressive than males. It is interesting to examine these species' behaviors because studying them may shed light on aggressive behaviors among species with more typical sex roles.

Some female sandpipers of the genera *Phalaropus* and *Actitis* exhibit brightly colored plumage, in contrast to the dull-colored males of their species (Tinbergen, 1935). Females compete among themselves for access to males, which are the predominant incubators, and are extremely aggressive toward other females (see Box 3.1). These reversals of the typical sex roles are not, however, accompanied by a reversal in the normal male-to-female ratios of blood androgen and estrogen concentrations. Androgen concentrations are six to eight times higher in pre-incubating male than in female Wilson's phalaropes (*Phalaropus tricolor*) (Fivizzani et al., 1986) and spotted sandpipers (*Actitis macularia*) (Rissman and Wingfield, 1984).

Although androgen concentrations are lower in female than in male sandpipers at most times, androgens may still mediate aggressiveness among females. Before pair formation, female testosterone concentrations are quite low and are comparable to values reported for females of other avian species. Females sampled after pairing, however, displayed a temporary sevenfold elevation in blood testosterone concentrations (Fivizzani and Oring, 1986). Thus, female sandpiper territoriality and aggressiveness are not dependent on male-typical blood androgen concentrations, but they may reflect increased sensitivity of brain structures to steroid hormones (Fivizzani and Oring, 1986). There is no sex difference in aromatase levels or in 5α-reductase expression or enzyme activity in the brain, pituitary, or skin of the Wilson's phalarope, suggesting that neural sex steroid hormone receptors or changes in neural circuitry may underlie the sex role reversal observed in this species (Schlinger et al., 1989).

As noted at the beginning of this chapter, adult female Syrian hamsters are often more aggressive than males (Payne and Swanson, 1972). Aggression in these females can be affected by ovariectomy but also by social influences, particularly housing conditions. For example, ovariectomized females housed individually are more aggressive than intact females when they are brought into an arena with another hamster; however, group-housed ovariectomized hamsters fight less than individually housed ovariectomized animals (**Table 1**).

As described in Chapter 3, spotted hyenas (*Crocuta crocuta*) are remarkable in the similarity of the external genitalia of the two sexes (Kruuk, 1972). As is the case for beagles, there is a rigid dominance hierarchy within each sex (Frank, 1983), but in sharp contrast to beagles, female hyenas dominate males in most behavioral interactions. Do hormones regulate social interactions in this species? If so, are blood androgen concentrations higher in females than in males? These questions are unresolved; conflicting reports exist regarding blood androgen concentrations in this species. One study reported no difference in blood androgen concentrations between male and female spotted hyenas (Racey and Skinner, 1979), but the results of another study indicated the usual sex difference in blood androgen concentrations, with males possessing higher concentrations than females. Individual social status was a much better predictor of blood androgen level than sex; resident animals exhibited higher blood serum androgen concentrations than transients (**Table 2**), as did the top-ranking individuals of both sexes (Frank et al., 1985; Hammond et al., 2012; Yalcinkaya et al., 1993).

TABLE 1   Effects of housing condition on aggressive behavior in Syrian hamsters

Endocrine status	Aggressive behavior	
	Housed individually	Group-housed
Females		
Ovariectomized	↑	↓ ↓
Ovariectomized + estradiol and progesterone	↑	↑ ↑
Males		
Castrated	↓	↓
Castrated + testosterone	↑	↑

↑ = increase; ↑↑ = substantial increase; ↓ = decrease; ↓↓ = substantial decrease

TABLE 2   Serum androgen concentrations in Kenyan spotted hyenas

Status	Androgen concentration (ng/ml ± SEM)
Males vs. females	
Adult males	1.93 ± 0.4
Prepubertal males	0.25 ± 0.1
Parous females	0.35 ± 0.1
Prepubertal females	0.18 ± 0.2
Residents vs. transients	
Residents	3.15 ± 0.6
Transients	0.81 ± 0.2

Source: Frank et al., 1985.

act more aggressively than females is organized perinatally by androgens but also requires the presence of androgens after puberty in order to be fully expressed. In other words, aggression in male mice is both organized and activated by androgens. Testosterone exposure in adulthood without prior organization of the brain by steroid hormones does not evoke typical male levels of aggression. The hormonal control of aggressive behavior in house mice is thus similar to the hormonal mediation of heterosexual male mating behavior in other rodent species (see Chapter 3). Aggressive behavior is both organized and activated by androgens in many rodent species, including rats, hamsters, and voles.

The world is much more complex than we often anticipate, however. Even when experimenters use a highly inbred animal model in constant laboratory conditions, it may be discovered that what appeared to be constant conditions in fact contained many variables. Some of these hidden variables may profoundly affect the endocrine-behavior relationships under study. This problem arises in studies of aggression in house mice. In mice, as in other rodent species, fetuses are packed in the uterus like peas in a pod (Clark et al., 1992) (see Figure 3.35) and may thus be influenced by hormones produced by their developing siblings. A female mouse may be situated between two brothers (2-M = 2 males), between a sister and brother (1-M), or between two sisters (0-M). In general, 2-M females are more aggressive than their 0-M sisters. Presumably, androgens produced by their brothers affect these females' nervous systems (see Chapter 3). This example should remind you that many subtle endocrine influences on behavior are possible.

An additional complexity is the observation that additional organization, or programming, of the brain can occur around the time of puberty (reviewed in Schulz et al., 2009). To establish these peripubertal effects, gonadectomy is performed after the typical perinatal brain organization by sex steroid hormones, but before the onset of puberty. Such manipulations in mice reveal changes in play-fighting behaviors (Pellis, 2002).

Testicular hormones during puberty also program adult aggression in hamsters. For example, male hamsters were castrated either before or after puberty; 6 weeks later they were treated with either vehicle or testosterone (Schulz et al. 2006), then aggressive behaviors were tested one week later. Males that were castrated prior to puberty did not attack an intruder and displayed high levels of submissive behaviors, even when given testosterone (**FIGURE 8.28**)! In contrast, males that were castrated after puberty attacked the intruder and rarely displayed submissive behaviors (Schulz and Sisk, 2006). Organizational effects of adolescent hormones on male aggression have also been reported in other species, including the very aggressive male DBA/1Bg mice (Shrenker et al. 1985) and male gerbils (Lumia et al. 1977), that display limited aggression even when treated with testosterone if they are castrated prior to puberty.

Agonistic behaviors in female rodents may also be organized during adolescence. If female mice are ovariectomized at the onset of puberty (30 days of age), treated with testosterone for 3 weeks during adolescent development, and then tested 6 weeks after discontinuation of hormone treatment, aggressive behaviors toward another female in a neutral arena are much higher than in females treated with vehicle (Edwards 1970). Thus, adolescent exposure to androgen has long-term effects on aggression in female mice, and the nervous system remains sensitive to organizing influences of gonadal steroid hormones well into postnatal life, although much higher doses of androgens are necessary to masculinize aggression during puberty than during the perinatal period (Trainor et al., 2016).

Taken together, these results show that sexual differentiation of play fighting and adult aggression is a two-stage process involving gonadal hormone action in the nervous system during perinatal and pubertal periods of devel-

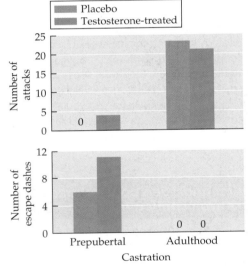

FIGURE 8.28 **Aggressive and submissive behaviors** expressed by male Syrian hamsters in a 10-minute resident-intruder test. Animals were castrated either prepubertally or in adulthood and were treated 6 weeks later with either placebo or testosterone for one week. When endogenous testosterone was absent during adolescence (prepubertal castration group), behavior in adulthood was characterized by fewer attacks and more escapes compared with animals that had endogenous testosterone present during adolescent development. After Schulz and Sisk, 2006.

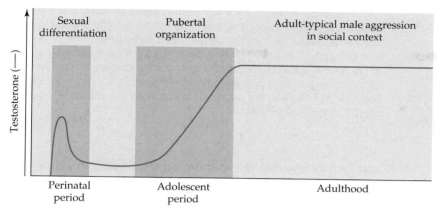

FIGURE 8.29 **Androgens appear to have two temporal windows** to produce organizational effects on adult aggressive behaviors. From Schulz and Sisk, 2006.

opment (Schulz and Sisk, 2006). Both androgens and estrogens regulate the initial process of masculinization and defeminization of circuits underlying juvenile play and adult aggression during the perinatal period. During puberty, both testicular and ovarian hormones reinforce and refine the sexual differentiation of neural circuits to result in sex-typical expression of aggressive behavior in adulthood (Schulz and Sisk, 2006) (**FIGURE 8.29**).

Dispersal: Ground Squirrels

Male Belding's ground squirrels begin the process of leaving home by the time they are about 50 days old. Dispersal is gradual, taking 4–5 weeks to accomplish. It is also a robust sexually dimorphic trait: virtually all males disperse, whereas few (<10%) of the females leave their natal region (Holekamp and Sherman, 1989). This sex difference in dispersal is common among mammals. A sex difference in dispersal also exists among avian species but is reversed; that is, female birds are far more likely to disperse from the natal nesting area than males.

As described previously, peripubertal castration does not affect dispersal in male ground squirrels. If the activational effects of androgens are unimportant in sustaining this behavioral sex difference, then it is reasonable to suppose that it is mediated by early organizational hormonal events. In one test of this hypothesis, pregnant ground squirrels were trapped and caged at an outdoor camp near their home burrows (Holekamp, 1986). Their female offspring were injected with testosterone propionate dissolved in sesame seed oil, or with the oil vehicle alone, several days after birth. Immediately after the injections the families were returned to their home burrows, where the mothers successfully reared their offspring. Twelve of the androgen-treated females were retrapped at 60 days of age or older. Seventy-five percent of them had dispersed from the mother's home burrow to a new nest site, following dispersal routes and traveling distances that were comparable to those of males. Approximately 70% of their male siblings had dispersed by this age. Only 8% of the oil-treated females left the natal area by 60 days of age. These results suggest an important role for early organizational effects of androgens on a complex behavior, namely, dispersal (Smale et al., 1997).

Dominance Status: Canines

Hormonal mediation of sexual differentiation occurs both prenatally and postnatally in dogs (see Chapter 3). Female puppies can be masculinized in two steps, first by treating their pregnant mothers with testosterone propionate during gestation

(A) Male beagle

(B) Pseudopenis of a female beagle

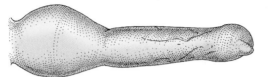

FIGURE 8.30 Perinatal exposure to androgens masculinizes female beagles. (A) The penis of a normal male beagle. (B) The pseudopenis of a female beagle exposed in utero and immediately after birth to androgens. If the penile (or pseudopenile) sheath is retracted, both males and masculinized females display comparable erections. Female dogs exposed to early androgen treatment also display very aggressive behavior and cause social disruption and confusion within small, stable groups. After Beach, 1984.

and then by injecting the newborn puppies with testosterone immediately after birth. Such dogs have highly masculinized external genitalia (**FIGURE 8.30**) and display male-like behavior. The social signals provided by these masculinized females elicit social confusion among beagles living in small, stable groups. The social confusion results because the behavior of a masculinized female is somehow suspect, or she does not emit the appropriate odors or other sensory signals, or possibly some other feature about her is incongruent with her perceived social status.

The dominance hierarchy of a small group of beagles is relatively easy to determine with the right experimental tool. The right tool in this case is a large bone, preferably an oxtail bone, which is simply thrown into the middle of the dogs' pen when all the dogs are present and attending to the "bone provider," namely, the experimenter. During the normal course of events, the highest-ranking dog in a stable group gets the bone, usually with a minimum of conflict, growling threats, or other hostile gestures. To discover which dog is the second in command, one simply removes the number one dog from the enclosure and repeats the bone competition test. In this way, and in pairwise tests between all of the dogs, the dominance hierarchy of a group can be determined (Beach et al., 1972). A variation of this technique, using chicken feed, was first used in classic studies on the pecking order of domestic fowl (Schjelderup-Ebbe, 1922).

Both dogs and chickens have relatively linear dominance hierarchies; that is, the highest-ranking individual, A, supplants all others, whereas the second-highest-ranking animal, B, supplants all others except A, and so on down the line. In some species, especially among primates, dominance status may be inherited and thereby relatively fixed over extended periods of time. In other cases, social organization may be quite plastic as low-ranking individuals continually test and overthrow the status quo. Other species do not have linear pecking orders. Dominance hierarchies among more complex animal societies, especially those of primates, may be circular; for example, A is dominant over B, who is dominant over C, who is dominant over A. Other dominance systems involve complex and dynamic cooperative coalitions; for example, A supplants B only with the aid of C (Bernstein, 1981). In general, dominance hierarchies represent a social adaptation that arose over evolutionary time owing to two factors: (1) not all individuals are equal in securing resources, and (2) it is a waste of time and energy to continually reestablish this inequality among group members (Wilson, 1975).

In one study of beagle social organization, the dominance hierarchies were separately determined for a group of five male beagles, a group of five female beagles, and a group of five masculinized female beagles injected with testosterone in adulthood (Beach et al., 1972). Dogs from the different groups were then paired, and their status was determined by which dogs won two-dog bone competitions over several consecutive days of testing. In general, normal females, regardless of their rank within their own dominance hierarchy, gave way to males, although the bottom one or two male dogs often lost to the top one or two female dogs. Female beagles that had not been exposed to testosterone also yielded to the masculinized females. Possession of the bone in virtually all of these interactions was determined without any overt aggressive behavior: if a female got the bone first, she would drop it when the male or masculinized female approached her. These social interactions became more interesting when males and masculinized females were paired in the bone competition. A masculinized female would not yield to a male if she obtained the bone first. The male behaved as if he expected the female to give up the prized bone; he would growl menacingly at her and eventually attack her when she refused to give up the bone. If the male obtained the bone first, the masculinized female would attack him and continue to harry him until he relinquished the bone or counterattacked. The social signals providing information about the masculinized females' status, or their understanding of canine social rules, whatever they may be, were somehow affected by the early hormonal treatment.

The inclination toward higher levels of aggression in male dogs, as in house mice, requires both early organizational exposure to androgens and activation in adulthood by these steroid hormones (see Chapter 3). Aggressive behavior in males of these species is thus organized and activated by androgens. Early androgen exposure alone elevates the incidence of aggressive behaviors in perinatally castrated males and in females above the level observed in normal females, but it does not increase aggression to the levels of normal males.

Play Behavior: Primates

Although work with altricial rodents has provided remarkable insights into the process of sexual differentiation of behavior, the data generated with these rodents have some fundamental limitations in their application to understanding the process of sexual differentiation of human behavior. People undergo most sexual differentiation in utero, not postpartum. Consequently, the organization of sexual differentiation in rodents, in which the hormonal effects occur postnatally, may differ fundamentally from the process in humans. Also, masculinization in rodents depends on aromatization of androgens to estrogens, whereas the aromatization of androgens does not appear to be important in the development and expression of masculine behaviors in primates (Balthazart and Ball, 1998; reviewed in Resko and Roselli, 1997). Although work with nonhuman primates is difficult and expensive, such work is more likely to provide insights into the sexual differentiation of humans than are studies of rodents.

Several fascinating studies that explored the role of gonadal steroid hormones in primate aggressive behavior have been reported. As is the case in humans, males of many nonhuman primate species are more aggressive than female conspecifics. This sex difference in behavior manifests itself early in development during the expression of play behavior. As noted previously, males engage in more rough-and-tumble play, more chasing, and more threatening behavior, and they initiate play more often than females (see Chapter 3). The increased proclivity for aggression, either real or in the context of play behavior, in male as compared with female rhesus monkeys appears to require only prenatal exposure to androgens. Castrated male rhesus monkeys, for example, do not differ from intact males in the amount of threatening behavior, rough-and-tumble play, chasing, and play initiation they display (Goy and Phoenix, 1971). In contrast, many rodent species require androgens for both early organization and later activation of aggressive behavior. As described in Chapter 3, treatment of pregnant female rhesus monkeys with testosterone propionate produces female offspring that display male genitalia and male-typical behavioral styles. These androgen-treated females display threatening behavior, initiate play activities, and engage in rough-and-tumble play at frequencies intermediate between those of normal males and normal females (Goy, 1966, 1978; Phoenix, 1974; Phoenix et al., 1968). Thus, the expression of sex differences in play behavior in rhesus monkeys requires the organizational effects of androgens, but not the activational effects.

The role of early androgen exposure in the mediation of sex differences in human aggressiveness has also been examined in "experiments of nature." Girls exposed to high concentrations of androgens in utero because their adrenal glands malfunctioned were reported by their mothers to engage in more rough-and-tumble play than their sisters who did not have congenital adrenal hyperplasia (CAH) (Reinisch, 1974). Although these reports are interesting, observations of this type are less reliable in distinguishing cause-effect relationships than controlled experiments in which researchers are uninformed about the treatment condition of any individual. Recall that because the mothers of the girls were aware of their daughters' medical condition, it is possible that their ratings of the girls' behavior may have been inadvertently biased (see Chapter 3).

Individual Differences in Aggression

We all learn early in life that there are large individual differences in the expression of aggressive behavior. Some individuals resort to aggressive tactics with very little provocation, while others virtually never behave aggressively. You may have discovered this variation in preschool when you met your first bully, or you may have learned about it on your paper route when some dogs greeted you happily with wagging tails, whereas other dogs' raison d'être seemed to be to gnaw off your leg. What accounts for these differences in aggressiveness? Are individual differences in aggressive behavior explicable on the basis of blood plasma testosterone concentrations? In other words, are some animals more aggressive because they have higher blood concentrations of androgens, or do these aggressive animals have higher androgen concentrations because they are more aggressive?

Individual differences in aggressive behavior do not correlate with blood testosterone concentrations in mice (Barkley and Goldman, 1977; McKinney and Desjardins, 1973), although they do in rats (Schuurman, 1980). One experimental test of this question first rated male mice as aggressive or not aggressive. All the animals were then castrated, and they all became equally passive. The castrated mice were all provided with equal doses of testosterone and tested for aggressiveness again. Males that were previously aggressive became aggressive with testosterone replacement therapy, and previously nonaggressive males remained docile after testosterone treatment. This study indicates that high circulating concentrations of testosterone are necessary, but not sufficient, for stimulating aggressive behavior. These individual differences in aggressive behavior were probably due to differences in receptor sensitivity or in the ability of androgens to alter the perception of an aggression-evoking stimulus.

There are certainly strain differences among house mice in the extent to which aggressive behaviors are expressed and in the extent to which these aggressive behaviors are mediated by androgens. One systematic study in a Swiss strain of albino mice investigated the effects of castration on predatory, shock-induced, maternal, and isolation-induced aggression. Isolation-induced aggression was generally reduced after castration; postgonadectomy treatment with testosterone, 5α-dihydrotestosterone (DHT), or estradiol restored this form of aggression (reviewed in Haug et al., 1986). In sharp contrast, castration increased territorial aggression toward lactating females, and treatment with testosterone, DHT, or estradiol reversed the elevated rate of aggressive responses in this situation (Brain et al., 1983). These results strongly imply that steroid hormones do not merely "trigger" aggression but act to affect the animal's perception of and response to aggression-provoking stimuli (Haug et al., 1986).

In another series of experiments (Whalen and Johnson, 1987), male mice were pitted against either lactating females or males from which the olfactory bulbs had been removed (reviewed by Johnson and Whalen, 1988). Olfactory-bulbectomized males are used in these types of studies because they elicit, but do not initiate, aggressive behavior. Gonadally intact males and castrated males treated with testosterone attacked the bulbectomized males but did not attack lactating females. Untreated castrated males tended to display tremendous individual differences in aggressiveness, with some attacking either type of opponent, others attacking only one type of opponent, and others failing to attack any opponent. Because castration was associated with large individual variation in aggressive response, and because androgen treatment reduced that variation, Johnson and Whalen (1988) proposed that testicular steroid hormones act to induce "behavioral homogenization"; in other words, androgens reduce variability in male house mouse aggressiveness. This is an intriguing hypothesis to account for the disparate aggressive responses of males to different aggression-provoking stimuli, although further experiments are necessary to evaluate it fully.

Dominance in more complex social organizations may not be related to blood concentrations of testosterone, especially in stable groups. For example, dominant dogs or squirrel monkeys can be castrated without affecting their position in the dominance hierarchy (Dixson, 1980). Also, treatment of low-ranking individuals with androgens does not change their status in these species.

Experience is also important in the relationship between hormones and aggressive behavior (Miczek and Fish, 2005). Castration and hormone replacement studies of males representing several species of reptiles, fishes, and birds clearly demonstrate reduced postcastration levels of aggression and restoration of aggression after testosterone treatment (e.g., Crews and Moore, 1986; Wingfield et al., 1987). In mammals, the effects of androgens in supporting aggressive behavior depend largely on experience. Castrated mice and rats without prior aggressive experience rarely fight when tested with a male conspecific (Christie and Barfield, 1979). If the animals are castrated after aggressive encounters have been experienced, however, aggressive behavior declines, but it endures long after the surgery (e.g., Christie and Barfield, 1979; DeBold and Miczek, 1981, 1984). Rather than having an *obligatory* role in the regulation of aggression, as in fishes, reptiles, and birds, androgens appear to exert a *modulatory* effect on mammalian aggressive behavior (Johnson and Whalen, 1988; Miczek and Fish, 2005).

Hormones and Behavior

Although we often emphasize that hormones affect behavior, it should be emphasized that behavior, in turn, can feed back and affect hormone concentrations. In the following section we will examine studies that examine the territorial behavior of birds and hamsters, followed by human competitive behavior. The final section will explore the brain regions involved in the expression of hormones and the regulation of emotion.

Social Experience Feeds Back to Influence Hormone Concentrations

Hormones obviously affect behavior, but it should be emphasized that behavior, in turn, can feed back and affect hormone concentrations. Tests of male mice in paired aggressive encounters revealed that their androgen levels were suppressed if they lost the fight, and the same was found for Syrian hamsters (Huhman and Jasnow, 2005; Lloyd, 1971; Solomon et al., 2009). This hormonal suppression lasted for many days after the defeat. Similarly, rhesus monkeys that were defeated by higher-ranking males had profoundly reduced testosterone concentrations for weeks after the defeat. In contrast, winning males' circulating testosterone concentrations quadrupled within 24 hours of the victory (Bernstein et al., 1974).

TABLE 8.3 *Home field advantage for English soccer leagues, 2000–2001*

Division (Number of teams)	Average home wins	Average away wins	Proportion of wins at home	Average home goals	Average away goals
Premiership (20)	09.20	4.75	0.66	29.35	20.25
Division 1 (24)	10.29	6.54	0.64	32.54	24.67
Division 2 (24)	10.08	6.62	0.61	35.08	26.00
Division 3 (24)	11.38	5.08	0.70	35.13	23.08

Source: Neave and Wolfson, 2003.

Similar phenomena occur in humans. In sports, there is a so-called home field advantage. Home field advantage has been reported for several levels of competition, from elementary school to professional sports (Neave and Wolfson, 2003) (**TABLE 8.3**). There are several explanations for this advantage, including the home team's familiarity with the playing field, travel fatigue and disruption of routine for the visiting team, and the fact that home team crowd noises inspire and encourage the team as well as influence referee calls. Indeed, U.S. professional football teams with enclosed stadiums are noisier and appear to have an enhanced home field advantage (Zeller and Jurkovac, 1989). All of these factors, as well as the possibility that humans defend a home "territory" in a sporting event in the same way many animals defend their home territory, may be mediated by hormones. In one series of studies, salivary testosterone concentrations were assessed in football (soccer) players in the United Kingdom and were significantly higher before home games than before away games (Neave and Wolfson, 2003). The perceived rivalry with the opposing team influenced testosterone concentrations: testosterone was more elevated before playing a "challenging" rival than a more "moderate" rival, especially among defensive players, such as the goalies (Neave and Wolfson, 2003). Because these games neither attracted large, noisy crowds nor required overnight travel or significant disruption of routine, it appears that a change in testosterone is a primary mediator of the home field advantage, though much additional research is required.

Studies of California mice (*Peromyscus californicus*) have illuminated the relationship between androgens and winning at home. In this species, winning a fight increases a male's subsequent motivation to fight and enhances his ability to win, but only if the previous winning experience was in the home cage (i.e., not an "away game") (Fuxjager et al., 2009). This "winner effect" is mediated by a surge of androgens (**FIGURE 8.31**) and is associated with an up-regulation of androgen receptors in brain areas that mediate incentive and reward processes, such as the ventral tegmental area and the nucleus accumbens (Fuxjager et al., 2010). Males of a related species, white-footed mice (*Peromyscus leucopus*), do not display this winner effect; that is, after winning an agonistic encounter, testosterone does not elevate and future winning behavior is not affected (Fuxjager et al., 2011). However, if white-footed mice are given a surge of exogenous testosterone, then they win future encounters and the "induced" winner effect in white-footed

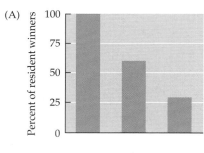

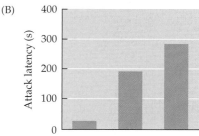

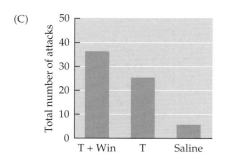

FIGURE 8.31 **Reinforcing winning with testosterone increases future wins.** (A) Nearly 100% of mice receiving testosterone (T) injections after winning an aggressive encounter won their final test encounter, whereas only about 30% of mice receiving saline won their final encounter. (B) Latency was very short in mice receiving testosterone injections after winning an aggressive encounter, in comparison with mice receiving saline. (C) Total number of attacks was significantly increased in mice receiving testosterone injections after winning an aggressive encounter, compared with mice receiving saline treatment. After Gleason et al., 2009.

mice qualitatively matches the winner effect that develops naturally in California mice (Fuxjager et al., 2011). There is evidence of a "winner effect" in humans (Zilioli and Watson, 2014), which is described below.

The Challenge Hypothesis: Birds

The influence of social experience on avian hormone concentrations has been studied in a number of different species (Gleason et al., 2009; Goymann et al., 2007; Pradhan et al., 2010; Wingfield et al., 1997). In one elegant field study, male redwinged blackbirds were trapped under two different conditions. In one condition, a live decoy male was placed in a spring-loaded net trap located near the center of the target male's territory. A tape recorder repeatedly broadcast a specific male "advertising" song to ensure an aggressive response from the resident male. As you might imagine, the presence of a male intruder apparently singing with great abandon elicited a rapid behavioral response from the resident male. First, the resident increased his rate of singing behavior. Then, he exhibited the species-specific wingspread display, showing off his bright red epaulets (**FIGURE 8.32**). Because the tape continued to play and the intruder remained in place, the resident male approached and finally attacked the decoy, activating the net trap. A blood sample was immediately obtained from the resident. Other territorial males were trapped while foraging, without the use of a decoy, for comparison. Blood testosterone concentrations were more variable in the birds caught during an escalating aggressive episode than in the foraging males, suggesting that the frequency of pulsatile androgen discharges in the aggressively behaving birds was increasing. There were no significant differences in blood concentrations of corticoids (Harding and Follett, 1979). This study demonstrated that behavior or environmental stimuli can affect hormone concentrations.

It is difficult to discern whether aggressive behavior per se or simply the perception of aggression-provoking stimuli is critical in mediating hormonal responses. Another study on a different avian species addressed this issue (Wingfield and Wada, 1989). Like red-winged blackbirds, male song sparrows (*Zonotrichia melodia*) exhibit endocrine changes in response to territorial disputes. Again, territorial intrusion was simulated by placing a live, caged conspecific in the center of a male's territory and broadcasting a tape of the conspecific song over a loudspeaker. Responding resident males were caught 1–4 minutes, 5–10 minutes, or 10–60 minutes after the onset of aggression-provoking stimuli. Control birds were trapped while they were foraging and were not actively engaged in territorial disputes. Blood samples were obtained from all captured birds and later assayed for testosterone and LH concentrations. Neither LH nor testosterone concentrations differed between foraging birds and birds involved in territorial disputes sampled 1–10 minutes after the onset of the agonistic interaction. Both testosterone and LH concentrations, however, increased in aggressively behaving birds sampled 10–60 minutes after the agonistic encounter began (**FIGURE 8.33**). The initial pulse of testosterone in response to an intruder appeared to be independent from LH regulation, but persistently elevated testosterone concentrations appeared to be mediated by LH in the usual manner (see Chapter 3). Laboratory tests confirmed these field observations. Thus in song sparrows, testosterone appears to increase persistence of aggression following an intrusion, rather than to activate aggression per se. This would be highly adaptive in the breeding season when reproductive success is at stake but would not be adaptive in autumn when other strategies (switch territories, float) are possible (Wingfield et al., 2005).

Additional laboratory studies examined the nature of the stimuli eliciting this behavioral-endocrine response in more detail (Wingfield and Wada, 1989). Simulated territorial intrusion by a heterospecific, a house sparrow (*Passer domesticus*), did not elicit any behavioral or hormonal response in resident song sparrows. Further

FIGURE 8.32 Male red-winged blackbird in the wingspread display This behavior shows off the bird's bright red epaulets and is an aggressive territorial signal to conspecific male intruders.

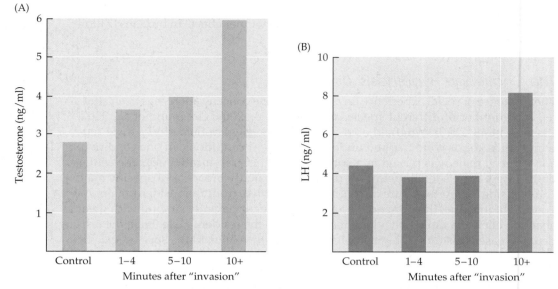

FIGURE 8.33 Effects of an intruder on resident song sparrows' hormone concentrations
After a simulated "invasion" of a male song sparrow's territory, plasma testosterone concentrations begin to rise (A). Note that the rise in testosterone levels 5–10 minutes after the detection of the intruder is not accompanied by a corresponding rise in LH (B) but that the sustained elevation in testosterone seen after 10 minutes appears to be mediated by LH. After Wingfield and Wada, 1989.

experiments dissected different sensory modalities in order to ascertain the contributions of various sensory inputs in affecting the endocrine system. Tactile cues did not influence hormone concentrations during aggressive encounters among male song sparrows. Song sparrows behaved similarly in response to a tape-recorded song (auditory channel), a voiceless conspecific male intruder (visual channel), or a combination of both stimuli. However, a tape recording alone or a devocalized male alone were less effective in stimulating elevations of LH and testosterone concentrations than a combination of both auditory and visual stimuli (Wingfield and Wada, 1989). In other words, although the males behaved similarly in response to various sensory stimuli that simulated a territorial intrusion, a combination of auditory and visual stimuli was necessary to provoke endocrine changes. Had these studies not been designed so well, it might have been concluded that behavior and hormones were not correlated.

A lack of association between hormone concentrations and aggressiveness in birds has been reported in a number of studies. This inconsistency may be explicable on the basis of timing. For example, captive groups of house sparrows were studied over a 2-week period, during which stable social dominance relationships were formed (Hegner and Wingfield, 1987). High-ranking birds were very aggressive during the first week, when the dominance hierarchy was being formed; high-ranking birds had higher blood testosterone concentrations, but not DHT or corticosterone concentrations, than low-ranking individuals during this time. High-ranking males continued to behave more aggressively than low-ranking males during the second week of the study, but their testosterone concentrations no longer differed from those of the low-ranking individuals. These results suggest that social rank (attained via agonistic interactions) and blood testosterone concentrations are correlated when social status is being established (Hegner and Wingfield, 1987) or is being actively challenged (e.g., Harding and Follett, 1979; Wingfield and Wada, 1989). This may also be true of primates. Hormonal mediation of social status may wane after the initial relationships are formed and stabilized, and that status may

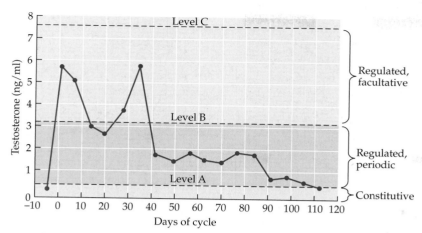

FIGURE 8.34 **The challenge hypothesis** predicts that testosterone will be elevated only during specific times of an individual's life history. Under challenging conditions, testosterone concentrations should be facultatively increased (from level B to level C) during specific events. In field studies, testosterone of song sparrows (brown line) is raised to these high values only when they are setting up territory and initially guarding the first brood. During the rest of the breeding season, testosterone is regulated between levels A and B. After the breeding season ends, plasma testosterone concentrations fall into the constitutive range (below level A). After Wingfield et al., 2001.

then be maintained by nonendocrine factors. Thus, analyses of plasma hormone concentrations after dominance relationships have been established overlook the importance of hormones in mediating agonistic encounters during the formation of those relationships.

Field observations support these laboratory findings. A caged intruder will elicit ferocious fighting and huge surges in testosterone secretion in territorial males during the early part of the breeding season, when territorial boundaries are being established. An intruder may still elicit aggressive behavior later in the season, when territorial boundaries are more stable, but it is less intense and less sustained and may not cause an increase in androgen production. However, local production of steroids in the brain is rapidly increased in response to territorial challenge during the nonbreeding season (Pradhan et al., 2010), suggesting that behavior may be modulated in a specific, targeted manner that does not involve hormone production in the gonads. Such responses have not yet been examined in the context of breeding.

Taken together, these observations of birds have led to the formation of the so-called **challenge hypothesis** to explain the role of androgens in aggressive behavior. Basically, the challenge hypothesis suggests that androgens are elevated and associated with aggressive behavior only when intermale competition is high; that is, androgen concentrations are elevated in a male by a challenge from another male (Wingfield, 1988; Wingfield et al., 1987) (**FIGURE 8.34**). In another example, laboratory tests of aggression in long-term competition between paired Japanese quail showed that testosterone concentrations were elevated in winners during the first 3 days after pairing, but by the fifth day, plasma concentrations of testosterone were indistinguishable between winners and losers (Ramenofsky, 1984).

Generation of the challenge hypothesis has come mainly from comparative studies of avian aggressiveness and hormone concentrations in field-trapped birds (Wingfield et al., 1997). If blood concentrations of androgens and LH are measured in wild male house sparrows, then a seasonal change in these two hormones is observed in the population, with high concentrations from about March until late July (Wingfield et al., 1987). In house sparrows, however, as in many other species of

challenge hypothesis The notion that an individual's androgen production responds to its social interactions such that testosterone is high during aggressive encounters during the breeding season, but not at other times.

FIGURE 8.35 Seasonal changes in blood LH and testosterone concentrations in house sparrows (A) When testosterone and LH concentrations from populations of free-living birds are plotted against a yearly calendar, a smooth population-wide seasonal pattern emerges, with a clear elevation in concentrations of these hormones from about March until late July. (B) When blood samples are linked to stages of the breeding cycle, a different pattern emerges: both hormones increase during the sexual stage of the breeding cycle and diminish prior to and during the parental stage of the breeding cycle. Thus, it might be expected that males are more aggressive when they are establishing territories and beginning a breeding effort than at other times. After Wingfield et al., 1987.

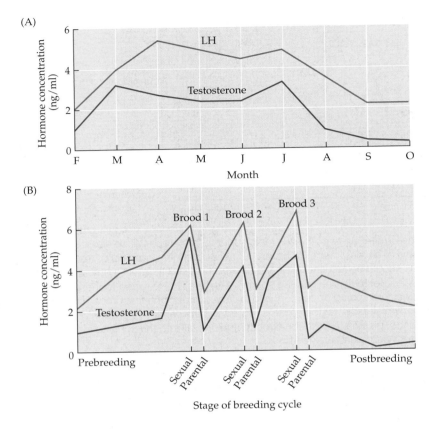

birds, a clear relationship between hormone concentrations and aggressive behavior has been difficult to uncover, because different birds in the population are engaged in different reproductive activities at any one time. House sparrows breed multiple times throughout the season, and they do not synchronize their reproductive efforts. When blood samples are linked to the stage of the breeding cycle, a clear pattern emerges, showing that LH and testosterone concentrations are elevated during the sexual stage and diminished during the parental stage (**FIGURE 8.35**).

FIGURE 8.36 compares blood concentrations of testosterone for several avian species. Two peaks of testosterone are observed among song sparrows; the first corresponds to the establishment of the territory, and the second corresponds to the mating period, during which the male guards his sexually receptive mate from other males. Male European blackbirds (*Turdus merula*), like male song sparrows, show no change in blood testosterone concentrations during the second mating episode of the season (Wingfield et al., 1987); this lack of androgen secretion has been hypothesized to reflect that little competition exists for nest sites in these species at this time. Some other species, such as European starlings (*Sturnus vulgaris*) and house sparrows, nest in holes, which are scarce, and are extremely competitive; males of these hole-nesting species exhibit an increase in testosterone secretion during each egg-laying period. In contrast, the western gull, like many colonial species, is long-lived, and there is often a skewed sex ratio with excess females; thus, there is little intermale competition. These birds may form pair bonds that last 20 years. There is little seasonal change in the blood plasma testosterone concentrations of male western gulls.

The challenge hypothesis suggests something fundamental about how androgens mediate aggressive behavior, and it may account for much of the variation in the relationship between aggression and circulating androgen concentrations found in many species. Numerous studies on additional species suggest that the challenge

FIGURE 8.36 **Blood testosterone concentrations in birds may reflect competition.** The green bars correspond to periods when male-male aggressive interactions are frequent. The first testosterone peak in the song sparrow's breeding season coincides with territory establishment, and the second corresponds with female guarding at the time of mating. The second clutch is not associated with a testosterone spike in song sparrows or European blackbirds, as it is in European starling, which nest in relatively scarce holes. The western gull is a colonial species that displays little male-male competition, and there is little change in androgen concentrations during the breeding season. After Wingfield et al., 1987.

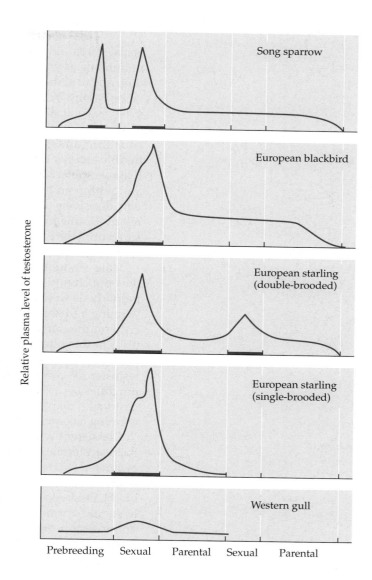

hypothesis may explain aggression in several species (e.g., Cardwell et al., 1996; Gleason et al., 2009; Goymann et al., 2007; Hirschenhauser et al., 2003; Thompson and Moore, 1992; Trainor et al., 2004).

Conditioned Social Defeat

As mentioned, in most encounters of matched combatants, the resident has a home field advantage. After defeat in the home cage of an aggressive conspecific, male Syrian hamsters (*Mesocricetus auratus*) will fail to defend their own home territory, even if the intruder is a smaller, non-aggressive male (Huhman et al., 2003). This phenomenon, which has been called **conditioned defeat** or conditioned social defeat, appears to evoke a stress response via fear conditioning (Huhman and Jasnow, 2005). The physiological effects of defeat include elevated HPA axis activity, such as increased plasma ACTH, β-endorphin, cortisol, and corticosterone concentrations, as well as decreased plasma testosterone and prolactin concentrations (Huhman et al., 1990, 1991; Solomon et al., 2009). This endocrine profile is observed among previously defeated hamsters upon reexposure to another male—even when the new opponent is blocked by a physical barrier (Huhman et al., 1992). This latter finding suggests that this endocrine response is a response to a psychological stressor, and not to the pain or anxiety of the combat itself. Social defeat also affects immune system responses (Fleshner et al., 1989; Jasnow et al., 2001). Corticotropin-releasing factor (CRF), and possibly related neuropeptides such as urocortins, act at CRF 2 receptors to promote the development of defeat-induced changes in social behavior, whereas CRF 1 signaling and glucocorticoid receptors do not appear to play an important role in this process (Cooper and Huhman, 2010). The physiological and behavioral consequences of conditioned social defeat persist for at least 33 days (Huhman et al., 2003) and perhaps throughout adulthood (Delville et al., 1998). Few female hamsters exhibit conditioned social defeat, although ACTH concentrations have been found to be reduced in females that display low levels of submissive/defensive behavior (Huhman et al., 2003; Solomon et al., 2009). In contrast to males, the females' conditioned defeat response does not persist beyond the first test. These results suggest that in male hamsters conditioned defeat is a profound, persistent behavioral change characterized by a total absence of territorial aggression and by the frequent display of submissive and defensive behaviors, as well as marked reductions in sexual behaviors (Bastida et al., 2014; Huhman and Jasnow, 2005; Jeffress and Huhman, 2013).

conditioned defeat The condition in which, after losing an aggressive encounter, an individual is more likely to lose in future encounters.

Hormones, Competition, and Violent Behavior: Humans

Social status and agonistic behavior may feed back to affect hormone concentrations in humans as well. The testosterone concentrations of male primates fluctuate as their social status changes; blood concentrations of testosterone tend to increase when dominance is achieved or defended, and to decrease after defeat (Dixson, 1980). Several studies suggest that a similar effect exists among human males.

Participation in competitive sports is one way in which aggressive behavior is ritualized among humans. In one study, male graduate students participated in doubles tennis matches (Mazur and Lamb, 1980). The team winning the best of five sets split a $200 prize. Blood samples were obtained an hour prior to the match and within an hour of its conclusion. The majority of players whose teams had won decisively displayed postgame elevations in blood testosterone concentrations relative to the losers. Winners of close matches, in which the outcome was not assured until the end, did not differ from losers in their postgame plasma testosterone concentrations.

Male graduate students also participated in another study in which they had the opportunity to win money, but not through any effort on their own part. These individuals were paired, then each member of the pair was given a 50% chance of winning a $100 prize based on a lottery drawing; obviously the men had no influence on the outcome of this contest. A blood sample was obtained immediately prior to the lottery drawing and at four hourly intervals after the recipient of the prize had been determined. The act of becoming a "winner" did not affect blood testosterone concentrations in this situation; blood testosterone concentrations did not differ between winners and losers (Mazur and Lamb, 1980). These results suggest that a man's blood androgen concentrations are more likely to be affected by winning a contest if its outcome is due to his own effort.

Consistent with this hypothesis are the intriguing results of a study in which the testosterone concentrations of five new male recipients of the MD degree were evaluated (Mazur and Lamb, 1980). Blood samples were obtained for several days before and after the graduation ceremony. The samples revealed an elevation of blood androgen concentrations 1 to 2 days after graduation. Whether this increase in steroid hormone concentrations reflected the graduates' change in social status or the disappearance of a stress-induced decline in gonadal function requires clarification. Certainly, the stress of intense physical competition can reduce androgen concentrations—even among winners. For example, blood concentrations of testosterone were reduced in both winners and losers of a 26-hour ice hockey cup tournament (Tegelman et al., 1988). In general, mood elevation was related to increased blood androgen concentrations in all of these studies.

The relationship among mood, competitive outcome, and androgen and cortisol concentrations was examined in college varsity tennis players. Saliva samples were obtained before and after six tennis matches, and saliva concentrations of steroid hormones, which reflect blood concentrations of steroid hormones, were measured (Booth et al., 1989). The players' moods were evaluated prior to play as well as after the match. Most players experienced a prematch anticipatory increase in salivary testosterone concentrations. Testosterone was further elevated in winners, especially those winners who reported positive moods, as compared with losers. Performance carried over to the next match in the sense that winners displayed higher, and losers lower, prematch testosterone concentrations compared with their concentrations prior to the previous match. Winning or losing a match did not affect levels of cortisol, a hormone released during stress. Perhaps not surprisingly, top-seeded individuals had lower cortisol concentrations than low-ranking players; cortisol gradually decreased in all players as the season progressed.

Even the vicarious experience of winning or losing can affect testosterone concentrations among fans at sporting events. In one study, self-identified Brazilian and Italian fans provided pre- and postmatch saliva samples before and after watching their national teams compete in the final match of the World Cup soccer tournament. Mean testosterone concentrations increased among fans of the winning team and decreased significantly among fans of the losing team (Bernhardt et al., 1998). Thus, the performance of sports fans' favorite teams has the capacity to affect more than just civic pride; the testosterone concentrations of the fans can be affected as well. Indeed, spousal abuse by men has been known to increase in the Washington, DC, area after the Washington Redskins win football games (White et al., 1992). It is possible that increased testosterone concentrations, evoked by the vicarious experience of winning, can trigger some men to cross the line into violence.

Studies like those just described, that link hormones and behavior directly in humans, are valuable because they are comparable to animal studies. However, the vast majority of research on hormones and social behavior in humans has relied on methods quite different from those used for nonhumans. This is not to diminish the value of these other types of correlational studies but to remind you that conclusions about hormone-behavior interactions in humans are often derived from data that are fundamentally different from the data generated from nonhumans.

Although the organizational and activational roles of testosterone in aggression have been fairly well established in several species, such as mice and rats (Simon, 2002), the evidence is not compelling in other species, including humans (reviewed in Albers et al., 2002; Harris, 1999). Most studies of hormones and human aggression have been based upon three sources of data, namely, hostility questionnaires, interviews, and criminal records. A blood sample may be analyzed and compared with test scores for aggressive tendencies or feelings. These procedures are very different from those used in research on nonhuman animals, because the aggressive act is separated in time (by years, in many prison studies) from the measurement of endocrine variables. Consequently, many contradictions have arisen about the role of hormones in human aggression. For example, meta-analyses indicate a positive weak correlation between testosterone and aggression in humans (Archer, 2006; Book et al., 2001). Self-reported measures of aggression in criminal and noncriminal populations, however, do not consistently correlate with testosterone concentrations (reviewed in Harris, 1999). Indeed, one study reported a negative correlation between aggressive behavior and testosterone in women (Gladue, 1991). Clinical, randomized, placebo-controlled studies have also yielded mixed results. In some studies, androgen administration in supraphysiological amounts to eugonadal men (normally functioning testes) has not resulted in anger and aggression (Anderson et al., 1992; O'Connor et al., 2002; Tricker et al., 1996). In other studies, a positive association between androgen administration and aggressive behavior has been observed (Kouri et al., 1995; Pope et al., 2000; Su et al., 1993).

In general, studies that have used psychological rating scales to quantify levels of aggressiveness or hostility have reported no relationship between blood or saliva androgen concentrations and aggressiveness (Doering et al., 1975; Monti et al., 1977; Persky et al., 1977). However, relationships between blood testosterone concentrations and behavior have been reported among aggressive, violent, and antisocial individuals, especially those incarcerated in prison (Ehrenkranz et al., 1974; Kreuz and Rose, 1972). Prison inmates exhibiting high circulating concentrations of testosterone, usually defined as the top 5% or 10% of the normal distribution, have committed more violent crimes (Dabbs et al., 1987, 1989; Ehrenkranz et al., 1974), have been more unruly in prison, and have been judged more harshly by their parole boards (Dabbs et al., 1987, 1989). High testosterone concentrations have also been associated with male juvenile delinquency (Olweus, 1983). Although some studies of criminal populations show no association between plasma testosterone and violent behavior (e.g., Matthews, 1979), the consensus is that violence among prison inmates and blood androgen concentrations are positively correlated. A similar relationship was observed among female prison inmates (Dabbs and Hargrove, 1997) (**FIGURE 8.37**).

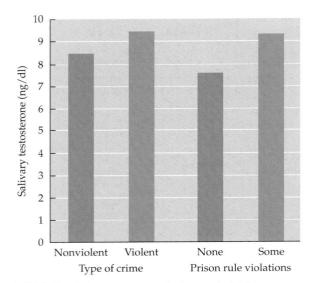

FIGURE 8.37 Relationship between testosterone concentrations in saliva and behavior of female prisoners High salivary testosterone concentrations are linked to violent crimes and to elevated prison rule violations. After Dabbs and Hargrove, 1997.

Two related hypotheses have been proposed to explain the association between high androgen concentrations and human antisocial behavior as observed in delinquent or criminal populations: first, that androgens directly mediate the antisocial activities; and second, that androgens promote a constellation of traits, including social dominance, competitiveness, and thrill seeking, that may be expressed either as antisocial or as prosocial behavior, depending on the individual's resources and background. For example, the same constellation of traits might be expressed as assaultive behavior in a gang fight among high-testosterone individuals living in an economically depressed neighborhood, or as team-spirited competitive behavior among high-testosterone individuals on a college football team. To distinguish between these two possibilities, 4462 U.S. military veterans were examined beginning in 1985. Psychological and medical evaluations and exhaustive laboratory tests, including measurements of blood androgen concentrations, were performed on these men. Analyses of their psychological profiles and saliva concentrations of testosterone indicated that androgens directly mediate antisocial behavior in human males, although socioeconomic status has a small moderating effect (Dabbs and Morris, 1990).

Taken together, these studies suggest that androgens can affect human male aggressiveness and dominance. Some intriguing observations support this contention, albeit in a somewhat indirect manner. Satisfaction with family functioning at midlife, defined as 39–50 years of age in one study, is associated with nonaggressive tendencies among men. Certain psychological factors are also related to men's satisfaction with family life at midlife, including androgynous characteristics, marital satisfaction, parent-offspring communication, and emotional expressiveness. Multiple regression analysis revealed that adoption of androgynous behaviors—behaviors that are both masculine and feminine—was linked to low blood concentrations of testosterone. Similarly, marital satisfaction and the quality of the father-child relationship were negatively correlated with testosterone concentrations. In other words, low testosterone concentrations were associated with high marital and family satisfaction. According to this study's authors, dominance, independence, aggressiveness, and competitiveness may not be valuable male traits for maintaining stable family environments (Julian and McKenry, 1989). A similar finding was reported in a study of testosterone concentrations in men with different occupations (Dabbs et al., 1990). The only statistically significant difference was between NFL football players and ministers (**FIGURE 8.38**).

As in other vertebrates, in humans the effects of winning appear to mediate subsequent agonistic behavior. In one recent study, male and female college students played a video game that was programmed to win against some and lose to others, with the students randomly assigned to win or lose (Carré et al., 2013). After playing the video game, participants moved into a separate room, where each was paired with a same-sex opponent and played the point subtraction aggression paradigm (PSAP), a validated behavioral assay of provoked aggression. Winning increased testosterone concentrations in men, but not women.

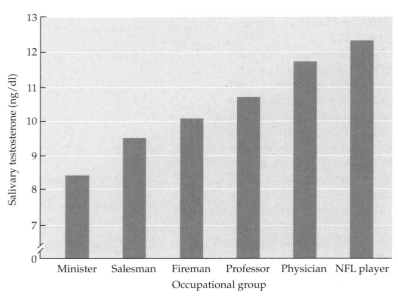

FIGURE 8.38 Salivary testosterone concentrations among men in six different occupations After Dabbs et al., 1990.

(A)

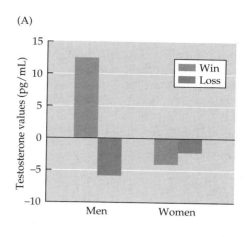

(B)

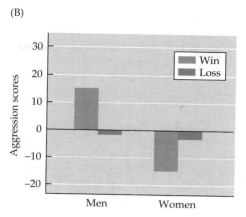

FIGURE 8.39 Testosterone reactivity and aggressive behavior as a function of sex and competitive game outcome. Winning elevates testosterone concentrations relative to losing in men, but not women (A). Importantly, testosterone reactivity to competition mediates the winner effect on subsequent aggression behavior in men, but not in women (B). After Carre et al., 2013.

As in other animals displaying the winner effect, men who displayed increased testosterone in response to winning the video game were more likely to beat the second-game opponent. This mediation effect was not observed in women (Carré et al., 2013) (**FIGURE 8.39**).

It is always possible that the winner effects represent differences in baseline circulating testosterone in males and that after provocation, testosterone values simply rise equivalently from different baseline levels. This was controlled for in California mice by castrating the mice prior to testosterone treatment to equalize testosterone baseline values—a procedure that is not acceptable for men. Thus, to examine this possibility of differential baseline testosterone concentrations, healthy young men were first given an anti-GnRH drug ("AndroGel") that lowered circulating testosterone concentrations to hypogonadal baseline levels (Goetz et al., 2014). Later

that same day, the men then received either testosterone or a placebo and were shown either neutral or threatening faces during functional imagining. Testosterone treatment of the pharmacologically induced hypogonadal men rapidly increased circulating levels and provoked neural activation of the amygdala, hypothalamus, and periaqueductal gray regions of the brain in response to threatening (angry) faces (Goetz et al., 2014) (**FIGURE 8.40**). These results suggest that testosterone rapidly activates the neural circuitry mediating agonistic responses in men as it does in other animals.

Few studies have addressed the role of androgens in aggressive behavior in women, and no consistent correlation has been reported (Dabbs and Hargrove, 1997; Dabbs et al., 1989; Persky et al., 1982). However, subtle effects of androgens may influence aggression in women. Saliva testosterone concentrations did not differ between female prison inmates and female college students. But further analyses discovered that testosterone concentrations were highest in women prisoners convicted

(A)

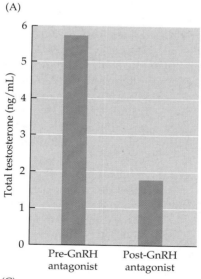

(C)

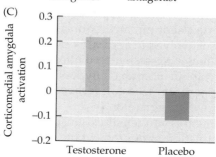

(B)

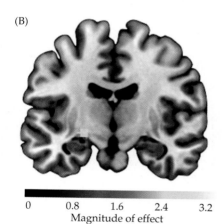

FIGURE 8.40 Treatment with **AndroGel** increased serum testosterone concentrations above the placebo condition within 30 minutes of drug application (A). AndroGel administration also increased corticomedial amygdala (CMA) reactivity to angry faces compared with neutral faces (B). fMRI activation of the CMA was elevated after testosterone treatment compared to placebo treatment (C). From Goetz et al., 2014.

of unprovoked violent crimes and lowest in women convicted of "defensive" violent crimes, such as killing abusive husbands (Dabbs et al., 1989).

Other data suggest that androgen concentrations in women, although much lower than those in men, may influence or be influenced by social status. For example, blood testosterone concentrations of female undergraduate students and professional, managerial, and technical workers are higher than those of female clerical workers and housewives (Purifoy and Koopmans, 1979). As is the case in males, saliva testosterone concentrations are higher in female attorneys than in female teachers and nurses (Schindler, 1979).

Physiological Mechanisms Mediating Hormonal Effects on Aggressive Behaviors

A neural circuit comprising several regions of the prefrontal cortex, amygdala, hippocampus, medial preoptic area, hypothalamus, anterior cingulate cortex, insular cortex, ventral striatum, and other interconnected structures has been implicated in the regulation of emotion, including impulsivity and aggression, and at least the subcortical components of this network are shared across most vertebrate groups (Goodson, 2005). The following sections review the regions of the brain and the hormones and receptors involved in this circuit.

Brain Regions Associated with Aggression

Functional or structural abnormalities in one or more of these brain regions, or in the interconnections among them, can increase the susceptibility for impulsive aggression and violence (Davidson, 2000). Although the brain systems mediating aggression appear to be fairly constant among mammals, many details of the regulatory pathways involved are species-specific. **FIGURE 8.41** diagrams the brain areas involved in aggression for rodents and nonhuman primates. As another species-specific example, Syrian hamsters exhibit *c-fos* immunoreactivity in the medial amygdala, bed nucleus of the stria terminalis (BNST), ventrolateral hypothalamus, and dorsolateral part of the PAG after displaying offensive aggression toward an intruder (Delville et al., 2000). Because these brain regions have direct and indirect connections with the anterior hypothalamus, an integrated network centered on the anterior hypothalamus has been suggested as a regulator of offensive aggression (Nelson and Trainor, 2007). Lesions of the nucleus accumbens lessen testosterone-dependent aggression in male rats (Albert et al., 1990). Androgens also stimulate the hypothalamic tracts to promote aggressive behavior in primates (reviewed in Dixson, 1980).

A neural circuit involving the medial hypothalamus and PAG has been identified that mediates defensive rage behavior in cats (Gregg and Siegal, 2001). The hippocampus, amygdala, BNST, septal area, cingulate gyrus, and prefrontal cortex interconnect these structures and thus can modulate the intensity of attack and rage (Gregg and Siegal, 2001). In rats, attack behavior can be elicited by electrical stimulation of the intermediate hypothalamic area and the ventrolateral pole of the ventromedial hypothalamic nucleus, collectively termed the "attack area" (Kruk, 1991). Afferent and efferent connections to the attack area, including the amygdala, prefrontal cortex, septum, mediodorsal thalamic nucleus, ventral tegmentum, and PAG, are also involved in aggressive behavior (Gregg and Siegal, 2001). Importantly, neurons in these aggression-mediating areas are rich in both steroid hormone receptors and serotonin receptor subtypes 5-HT_{1A} and 5-HT_{1B} (Simon et al., 1998). Although it has been recognized for decades that electrical stimulation of the hypothalamus can provoke aggression in cats and rats, the specific nuclei underlying the regulation of aggression remained unspecified until recently. Optogenetic, but not electrical, activation of neurons in the ventromedial hypothalamus (VMH), specifically the

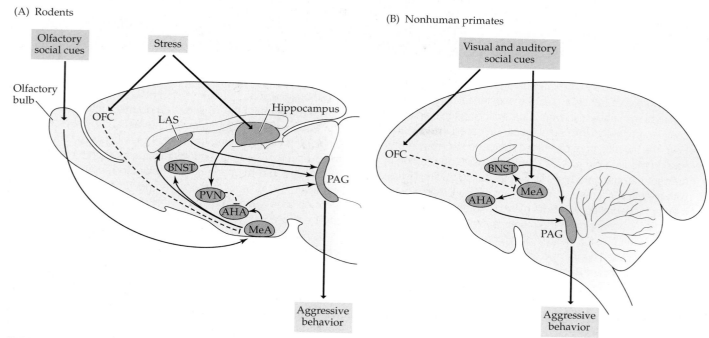

FIGURE 8.41 **Components of rodent and primate brains involved in aggression** This schematic cross section shows the major components known to be involved in aggression in rodents (A) and nonhuman primates (B). (A) In rodents, information from the olfactory bulb is processed by the medial amygdala (MeA) and sent to the lateral septum (LAS), the bed nucleus of the stria terminalis (BNST), and the anterior hypothalamic area (AHA). These brain areas seem to prompt the periaquaductal gray (PAG) into promoting species-specific aggressive behaviors. Stress (from either previous losing or other environmental or social factors) can inhibit aggression via inhibitory inputs from the orbital frontal cortex (OFC), the hippocampus, and the paraventricular nucleus (PVN). (B) In nonhuman primates, aggression is typically evoked by vocal or visual signals. Activation of the MeA is thought to result in activation of the BNST and AHA, which in turn activate the PAG. In general, the OFC appears to be important for the interpretation of social cues, and inhibitory inputs from the OFC might inhibit aggression by reducing responsiveness in the amygdala. Thick arrows represent inputs and outputs to and from the brain; thin arrows represent connections within the brain; dashed lines represent inhibitory connections. After Nelson and Trainor, 2007.

ventrolateral subdivision (VMHvl) of the VMH, provokes male mice to attack male and female conspecifics, and even inanimate objects (Lin et al., 2011) (**BOX 8.5**)!

With the use of fMRI in nonhuman animals, we are discovering the neural circuitries underlying aggression. In one study of male rats, each was presented with both its female cage mate and a strange male in the bore of the magnet while being imaged (Ferris et al., 2008). Brain regions previously associated with aggression—for example, the medial basal amygdala and lateral hypothalamus—were activated. Treatment with a selective vasopressin V1a receptor antagonist (SRX251) or fluoxetine (a selective serotonin reuptake inhibitor) generally suppressed the neural circuit activation associated with aggressive motivation (Ferris et al., 2008) (**FIGURE 8.42**).

Brain Steroid Hormone Receptors

A series of studies that examined sex and strain differences in responses to steroid hormones, as well as studies that employed enzymatic inhibitors and steroid receptor blockers, revealed that testosterone and its major metabolites, estradiol

BOX 8.5 *Optigenetic Control of Aggression in the Ventromedial Hypothalamus*

The neural circuitry associated with male mating behavior and aggressive behavior displays substantial overlap. Recent research may have discovered the switching function in adjacent neurons within the neural circuitry in mice (Lin et al., 2011). First, the investigators examined the gene expression of the early immediate gene *c-fos* during offensive aggression in a resident-intruder paradigm, as well as during mating behavior with an estrous female. Expression of *c-fos* RNA is a general marker for neural activity. Both mating and aggression evoked *c-fos* RNA expression in the medial amygdala, medial hypothalamus, and BNST. Despite significant overlap in the neural circuitry between aggressive and mating behaviors, it was not obvious whether the same neurons were activated during both types of behaviors. To examine that question, the researchers allowed male mice to engage in the two types of behavior sequentially, in two bouts of the same behavior, or in only one of the behaviors. The sequential behavioral bouts were separated by 30 minutes. In mice engaged in two successive episodes of the same behavior, most cells expressing nuclear *c-fos* transcripts also expressed *c-fos* mRNA in the cytoplasm (**Figure A**, green and red bars), indicating activation during both behavioral episodes, because it requires about 20 minutes for this material to migrate from the nucleus to the cytoplasm. Mice that sequentially engaged in different behaviors also expressed both nuclear *c-fos* RNA and cytoplasmic *c-fos* transcripts, blue and purple bars). These results suggested that mating and

fighting may recruit overlapping but distinct sets of neurons in these brain regions.

The researchers then discovered diverse patterns of neuronal cell activation during social interactions by measuring single-unit activity during behavior. They discovered that the VMHvl neuronal activity tended to increase when a male was introduced into the cage of an implanted mouse, whereas activity in the majority of monitored neurons showed a transient increase when a male first encountered a female but then declined.

Using an optogenetic approach, stimulation of VMHvl provoked a rapid onset of coordinated and directed attack. Importantly, whereas male mice rarely spontaneously attack females or castrated males, 11 of 16 males expressing channelrhodopsin-2 attacked such intruder animals. Turning off the fiber-optic light almost immediately stopped the aggression toward females but not toward castrated or intact males (see Figure 5.19). Both the *c-fos* and single-unit recordings from the VMHvl during aggression or mating revealed overlapping, yet distinct, neuronal subpopulations involved in these behaviors. Aggressive behavior could be driven by stimulating neural cells. Neurons activated during attack were inhibited during mating, suggesting a potential neural substrate for a switch underlying affiliative and aggressive behaviors such as those observed in the female hamsters described at the beginning of this chapter.

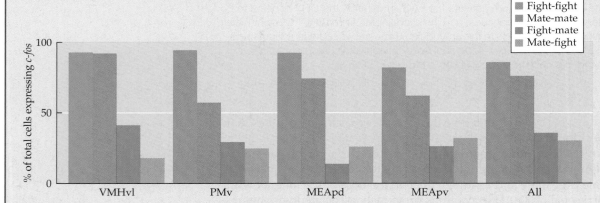

Figure A   Neuronal activation as assessed by the early immediate gene, *c-fos* during social interactions in various brain regions. After Lin et al., 2011

and DHT, are important in regulating aggressive behavior (Simon, 2002). Four distinct regulatory pathways have been discovered through which testosterone promotes the display of aggression in adult males (Simon, 2002; Simon et al., 1996, 1998): (1) an androgen-responsive pathway, which responds to testosterone itself or its 5α-reduced metabolite, DHT; (2) an estrogen-responsive pathway, which responds to estradiol derived by aromatization of testosterone; (3) a synergistic or combined pathway, in which both the androgenic and estrogenic metabolites of

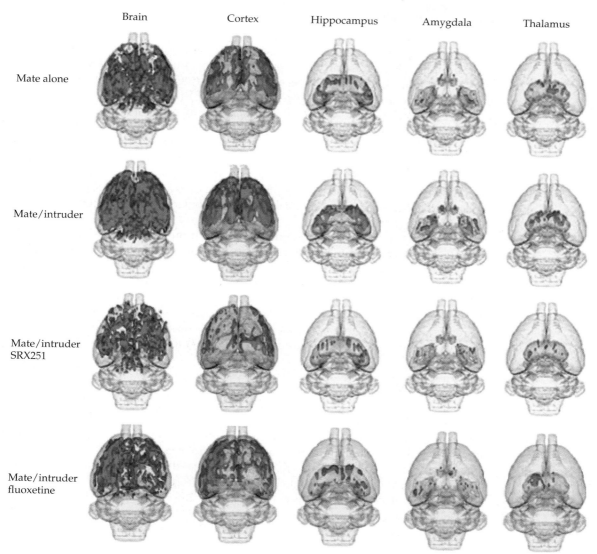

Brain   Cortex   Hippocampus   Amygdala   Thalamus

Mate alone

Mate/intruder

Mate/intruder
SRX251

Mate/intruder
fluoxetine

FIGURE 8.42 **Rat brain activation is increased by a male intruder,** as seen in this fMRI representation. Viewed from the caudal/dorsal perspective, the color red depicts localization of activated voxels a unit of graphic information that defines a point in 2-d space interpolated into a 3-D volume of activation for four experimental conditions: mate alone, mate plus a male intruder, and pretreatment with the V1a receptor blocker SRX251 or fluoxetine followed by the aggressive provoking stimuli of a male intruder in the presence of the resident male and his mate. The volumes of activation for each experimental condition represent ten males. From Ferris et al., 2008.

testosterone facilitate aggressive behavior; and (4) a direct testosterone-mediated pathway, which utilizes only testosterone. Not all of these regulatory pathways are necessarily present in every male of a species. Indeed, the functional pathways appear to be determined by genotype; strain differences and possibly individual differences in aggressive behavior may reflect the presence of certain functional pathways (Simon, 2002). The estradiol-responsive pathway appears to be the one most commonly used to mediate aggression. This observation suggests that aromatization of testosterone to estradiol is a critical step in regulation of aggressive behavior. Not surprisingly, both estrogen and androgen receptors are important in the control of aggression.

Estrogen Receptors

Different estrogens can bind to different estrogen receptor (ER) subtypes, of which there are at least two, ERα and ERβ. Most of what is known about the effects of these receptors on aggression comes from a series of studies on gene knockout mice. ERα is important in mediating aggression in mice (Ogawa et al., 1997, 1998, 1999). Gonadally intact mice lacking the gene for ERα (αERKO mice) displayed virtually no aggressive behavior (Ogawa et al., 1998). Even when castrated and given timed-release implants of testosterone, αERKO mice rarely displayed offensive aggression. This experiment demonstrated that these mice lacked androgen-responsive regulatory pathways mediating aggressive behavior (Ogawa et al., 1998). After the β estrogen receptor subtype was discovered, knockout mice were developed that lacked that receptor subtype. These βERKO mice displayed normal aggressive behavior, indicating that aggressive behavior is mediated by the α estrogen receptor subtype (Ogawa et al., 1999).

Although ERβ does not appear to be involved in murine aggression, it may be important in primate agonistic behavior. Cynomolgus monkeys (*Macaca fascicularis*) were fed diets either high or low in soy phytoestrogens, which bind preferentially to ERβ (Simon et al., 2004). After 15 months, male monkeys fed the diet that was high in soy phytoestrogens were more aggressive than males fed the diet low in soy phytoestrogens (Simon et al., 2004). These behavioral results might represent decreased serotonin function in the dorsal raphe nucleus, where ERβ is the sole estrogen receptor subtype thus far detected in primates (Simon and Lu, 2005).

Androgen Receptors

Using autoradiographic and immunocytochemical methods, the distribution of androgen receptors has been mapped in the brain (Simon and Lu, 2005). Androgen receptors are found in the following brain regions of rodents: (1) bed nucleus of the stria terminalis, (2) medial preoptic area, (3) lateral septum, and (4) medial amygdala (Simon, 2002). It is probably no coincidence that these same brain regions were identified as part of an "aggression brain circuit" in studies using lesions, hormone implants, and electrical stimulation (reviewed in Simon, 2002). It is still not known precisely how activation of androgen receptors contributes to aggressive behavioral output, but interaction with serotonin appears to be important (Trainor et al., 2016).

Serotonin

Although nearly every neurotransmitter system has been reported to contribute in some way to aggressive behavior, serotonin (5-HT) is clearly the major regulator of aggressive behavior (Nelson and Chiavegatto, 2001). At least 14 different 5-HT receptor subtypes have been identified, but the 5-HT_{1A} and 5-HT_{1B} receptor subtypes appear to be critical mediators of aggression. Essentially, low 5-HT function or receptor activation is associated with high aggression, whereas high 5-HT function or receptor activation is associated with low aggression (reviewed in Albert and Walsh, 1984; Nelson and Chiavegatto, 2001; Olivier and Mos, 1992; Olivier et al., 1995; Simon and Lu, 2005). Depletion of 5-HT increases both offensive and defensive aggression (Vergnes et al., 1986). Brain 5-HT depletion increases behavioral responsiveness to sensory and painful stimuli (e.g., Lorens, 1978; Telner et al., 1979). Aggressive behavior in response to a wide variety of stimuli can be suppressed by 5-HT or by any treatment that elevates 5-HT (Ieni and Thurmond, 1985; Olivier and Mos, 1992). These relationships have been demonstrated in animals as diverse as lobsters, mice, hamsters, cats, monkeys, and even humans (Simon and Lu, 2005).

Testosterone and its metabolic by-products, estradiol and DHT, may support aggression by influencing serotonin function in one or several brain regions that are part of the brain circuitry underlying aggression (Simon, 2002). The distributions of steroid hormone receptors and serotonin receptors overlap in several distinct regions of the brain that are part of the neural circuit regulating intermale aggression, including the lateral septum, medial preoptic area, medial amygdala, and bed nucleus of the stria terminalis. Androgens and estrogens modulate 5-HT$_{1A}$ and 5-HT$_{1B}$ receptor function during offensive aggression (Cologer-Clifford et al., 1997, 1999). Serotonin agonists, in the presence of androgen, were much more effective in reducing aggression than were serotonin agonists plus estrogen treatment. Thus, serotonin appears to be able to modulate the ability of testosterone to support aggression. Similar modulatory effects of neurochemicals on hormone-dependent behavior have been observed in studies of reproductive behavior (Etgen, 2002; Etgen et al., 1999; Hull et al., 1999), as well as anxiety and mood disorders (Bethea et al., 2000, 2002). Presumably, steroid hormones can affect serotonin receptor function by changing receptor gene expression, by exerting nongenomic effects on the receptors, or by indirectly influencing serotonin availability by acting on its synthesis, reuptake, or metabolism (Simon and Lu, 2005). Several studies have also implicated nitric oxide (reviewed in Bedrosian and Nelson, 2014), GABA, and vasopressin (see below) as modulators of male aggression, either directly by acting on the aggression neural circuitry or indirectly by affecting serotonergic function (Nelson and Chiavegatto, 2001).

Vasopressin

Microinjections of arginine vasopressin (AVP) into the anterior hypothalamus of male Syrian hamsters and mated male prairie voles increase offensive resident-intruder aggression (Ferris et al., 1997). Castration reduces vasopressin V1a receptor binding in the ventrolateral hypothalamus, a brain region involved in aggression, and testosterone treatment reverses this effect. However, similar microinjections in female Syrian hamsters *decrease* resident-intruder aggression (Gutzler et al., 2010). In male mice, in contrast to male hamsters and voles, Fos activation of hypothalamic vasopressin cell groups is negatively correlated with aggression (Ho et al., 2010). Furthermore, microdialysis studies in male rats show that during aggressive encounters, vasopressin release in the bed nucleus of the stria terminalis is negatively related to aggression, whereas the release of vasopressin is positively related to aggression when it occurs in the lateral septum (Veenema et al., 2010), and the patterns of release in the lateral septum additionally reflect the rat's anxiety phenotype (Beiderbeck et al., 2007). Thus, while it is clear that vasopressin is an important modulator of aggression across multiple rodent species, there is much diversity across sexes, phenotypes, species, and brain areas, and perhaps across contexts, as well.

Similarly, in male songbirds, arginine vasotocin (AVT) promotes male aggression in the presence of a potential mate (termed "mate competition aggression") but decreases aggression in territorial contexts. Territorial aggression is negatively correlated with Fos activation of hypothalamic AVT neurons (as just described for mice), and highly aggressive males may actually suppress AVT neuron activity during aggressive encounters (Beiderbeck et al., 2007). Consistent with this observation, treatment with a V1a receptor antagonist has no effect on aggressive males but facilitates aggression in less aggressive males, apparently by releasing aggression in those males from inhibition by endogenous AVT (Goodson et al., 2009a).

Arginine vasotocin may also mediate aggressive behaviors in a context-dependent manner in fishes. Bluehead wrasse (*Thalassoma bifasciata*) are female-to-male (protogynous) sex-changing fish, and males of this species display two distinct phenotypes: nonterritorial males and large, colorful, territorial, terminal-phase males. AVT reduced the number of aggressive behaviors emitted by territorial males, whereas it increased aggressive behaviors in nonterritorial males (Semsar et al., 2001). The use of an AVT receptor antagonist had the opposite effects; that is, it caused territorial males to behave like nonterritorial males (Semsar et al., 2001). Thus, manipulation of the AVT system could shift social behavior from one state to another (Semsar and Godwin, 2004).

Several drugs that affect both AVP and the 5-HT systems reportedly reduce aggression. For example, systemic treatment of humans with nicotine increases blood AVP concentrations and central 5-HT release while reducing aggression (reviewed in Morrison and Melloni, 2014). It appears that development can impact the effects of V1a receptors on aggression. V1a knockout mice have normal levels of aggression after isolation, whereas V1b knockout mice reduce aggression (Morrison and Melloni, 2014; Wersinger et al., 2002). These results suggest that genetic deletion of V1a results in a compensatory developmental effect in aggression circuits, possibly a greater role for V1b receptor.

Conclusions

How do hormones affect social behavior? Hormones affect social behavior at the level of input systems; for example, androgens affect the perception of aggression-promoting stimuli associated with intermale agonistic interactions (Johnson and Whalen, 1988; Wingfield et al., 2005). Behavior can feed back, as in the case of territorial encounters between house sparrows, to affect hormonal and subsequent behavioral responses to intruders. Androgens, as well as peptide hormones, affect the central processing of stimuli associated with aggressive responding (Panksepp et al., 1980b; Simon and Lu, 2005). Steroid hormones also affect social behavior by influencing the effectors involved in aggressive behavior. In the case of red deer, androgens influence social interactions by acting on the antlers (Lincoln et al., 1972). Hormones, particularly endogenous opioids, may also provide reward properties to social contact or other social interactions.

Summary

1. Social behavior involves interactions between individuals in which one or more of the animals benefit from the interaction. Affiliation refers to behaviors that bring animals together. Aggression is overt behavior with the intention of inflicting damage on another individual. Agonistic behavior is observed when the interests of two individuals are in conflict.

2. Affiliative behaviors are affected by peptide hormones such as vasopressin and oxytocin, as well as by glucocorticoids, all of which also influence parental behaviors. These hormones appear to function in affiliation by affecting the neurotransmitters dopamine and serotonin. Opioids also mediate affiliative behavior, especially in the context of social grooming and social contact.

3. Androgens are linked to aggressive behavior by several kinds of circumstantial evidence: Seasonal changes in blood androgen concentrations and aggression covary. Aggression is correlated with the onset of puberty, when androgen concentrations rise. Aggression is more common among males than females of most vertebrate species. Castration reduces aggression in males, and androgen treatment restores it.

4. The interaction among behavior, hormones, and self-perception of one's place in the social hierarchy is complex and subtle for some species. Among rodents, dramatic seasonal changes in social organization occur in response to blood concentrations of androgens.

5. The onset of puberty heralds the initial display of aggression in males of many species. Pubertal aggression is linked to dispersal in many avian and mammalian species. Dispersing individuals must be aggressive at this time in order to compete within new social contexts.

6. Males are generally more aggressive than females. In rodent species, the sex difference in aggressiveness is organized by androgens via estrogens perinatally and also requires activational actions of androgens in adulthood for expression. The sex difference in aggressiveness among primate species appears to be organized prenatally and does not require androgen stimulation later in life for expression.

7. Females of some species are more aggressive than males. Female sandpipers do not usually have higher blood concentrations of androgens than males; however, females show large elevations in blood concentrations of androgens after pairing, suggesting that testosterone may play a role in their aggressive behaviors. Female hyenas are also more aggressive than males; androgen concentrations in adults do not account fully for the behavioral sex reversal.

8. There are great individual differences in aggressiveness. In some species, such as mice, aggressive behaviors do not correlate with blood testosterone concentrations, but in other species, such as rats, the degree of aggressiveness and blood concentrations of testosterone are related.

9. Social experience feeds back to influence androgen concentrations. Winning an agonistic encounter produces a sustained elevation in blood androgen concentrations in rodents and primates. In contrast, losing results in a chronic reduction of blood androgen concentrations.

10. The act of fighting an intruder can elevate blood concentrations of testosterone in many species of birds. Obtaining blood samples during an aggressive encounter increases the likelihood that androgen concentrations will correlate positively with aggressive behavior, especially during the breeding season. The challenge hypothesis suggests that androgens mediate aggressive encounters only during the establishment of territories, or whenever males are highly competitive. Aggression at other times does not elicit the same kind of endocrine response and probably is not mediated by androgens.

11. Social experience in competitive sports can feed back and affect human androgen concentrations. Elevation in social status is also associated with high blood androgen concentrations among humans.

12. Assessments of human aggression are typically different from studies of aggression in nonhuman animals, because the aggressive act is generally removed in time from the blood hormone assessment. Typically, aggression in humans is quantified on the basis of questionnaires or interviews. Nonetheless, prison inmates who have been convicted of violent crimes tend to have high concentrations of androgens.

Questions for Discussion

1. Suppose that you have obtained blood samples from matadors and bulls immediately after a number of bullfights. You notice that a matador's blood androgen concentration is elevated whenever he decisively defeats a bull and that a bull's androgen concentration is elevated if he gores the matador. Is "winning" the critical factor in determining blood androgen concentrations? What other endocrine events might account for these data?

2. Design an experiment to test the proposition that professional football players are more aggressive than spectators because they have elevated thyroid hormone concentrations. Remember that hormones affect behavior and that behavior can feed back to affect blood hormone concentrations.

3. Many species will vacillate from affiliative to aggressive behavior based on time of year or environmental circumstances. What are the selective pressures and underlying hormonal mechanisms driving this change in behavior?

4. Imagine that you are called to consult on treatment options for repeat aggressive offenders who are due to be released from prison. Based on what you learned about aggression across species, how might you study prisoners to determine whether or not their aggression is hormonally motivated? Would you suggest treatment options aimed at altering hormonal concentrations?

5. How might hormones affect the perception of a threat? How might hormones affect mood in such a way that stimuli become irritating? Design a test of your notions.

6. Compare and contrast the endocrine modulation of social affiliation and parental behaviors.

Suggested Readings

Carter, C. S. 2014. Oxytocin pathways and the evolution of human behavior. *Ann. Rev. Psychol.*, 65:17–39.

Ellison, P. T., et al. (eds.). 2009. *Endocrinology of Social Relationships*. Harvard University Press, Cambridge, MA.

Goodson, J. L., et al. 2012. Evolving nonapeptide mechanisms of gregariousness and social diversity in birds. *Horm. Behav.*, 61:239–250.

Johnson, Z. V., and Young, L. J. 2015. Neurobiological mechanisms of social attachment and pair bonding. *Curr. Opin. Behav. Sci.*, 3:38–44.

Nelson, R. J. (ed.). 2005. *Biology of Aggression*. Oxford University Press, New York.

Nelson, R. J., and Trainor, B. C. 2007. Neural mechanisms of aggression. *Nat. Rev. Neurosci.*, 8:536–546.

Soma, K. K., et al. 2015. DHEA effects on brain and behavior: Insights from comparative studies of aggression. *J. Steroid Biochem. Mol. Biol.*, 145:261–272.

Stoesz, B. M., et al. 2013. Neurophysiological mechanisms underlying affiliative social behavior: Insights from comparative research. *Neurosci. Biobehav. Rev.*, 37:123–132.

Trainor, B. C., et al. 2016. Hormones and the development and expression of aggressive behavior. In D. W. Pfaff, et al. (eds.), *Hormones, Brain and Behavior* (3rd ed.), Vol. 1 (In press).

Homeostasis and Behavior

9

Learning Objectives

The goal of this chapter is to describe the relationship among hormones, homeostasis, and behavior. Homeostasis is the ability to maintain optimal conditions in the body, and hormones are critical to this process. The chapter focuses on the regulation of fluid and sodium balance, as well as energy balance. By the end of this chapter you should be able to:

- describe the conceptual bases of homeostasis.

- integrate the interactions among hormones, behavior, and sodium and water balance, a model physiological homeostatic system.

- understand the effects of hormones and behavior on energy balance, eating, and body mass regulation.

- describe the hormone-behavior interactions controlling specific hungers.

In October 1859, 12 pairs of European rabbits (*Oryctolagus cuniculus*) were sent to a newly immigrated rancher from England in Victoria, the southeasternmost state in Australia. The homesick rancher had been an avid rabbit hunter back in England—spending much of his free time engaged in this activity. These rabbits quickly escaped the confines of his Victoria ranch, and because the animals had no natural predators in Australia, the population soon grew exponentially. Just 5 years after rabbits were introduced to the continent, one hunting drive successfully killed over 20,000. But the rabbits kept multiplying, and by 1900 they presented a serious problem for Australia; the rapid spread of rabbits destroyed large tracts of vegetation, leading to the extinction of many plant species. The loss of vegetation caused soil erosion as exposed soil was washed or blown away, leading to loss of valuable soil nutrients required for new plants to develop. The lost soil was deposited in waterways, causing siltation and destroying aquatic ecosystems.

This large-scale destruction of Australian habitat contributed to the demise of many native marsupial species, such as the bilby and the bandicoot, as their native food sources were swallowed up by marauding rabbits. In addition to being very prolific, rabbits are extremely efficient foragers. Forty years after the introduction of the initial 12 pairs, hundreds of millions of their descendants had spread throughout Australia and had destroyed valuable pastures and rangelands required for grazing sheep. Just seven rabbits can eat as much forage as a single sheep. Given the importance of the production of wool in Australia, the annual economic cost of the rabbit infestation there is between 110 and 600 million U.S. dollars per year. Even today rabbits are considered the single most important factor causing loss of native animal and plant species in Australia.

After several failed attempts by the government to reduce the number of rabbits by using poisons, predators, and other pest control procedures, the myxoma virus (which causes myxomatosis, a disease fatal to rabbits) was first tested in 1937 (**FIGURE 9.1**). A myxomatosis epidemic broke out and killed over 99.9% of the rabbits. Only a few myxomatosis-resistant animals survived. However, these initially rare myxomatosis-resistant animals repopulated the continent once again. In some areas, only 2 years were necessary to restore the decimated populations. Australian government scientists have also introduced a new rabbit virus that causes rabbit hemorrhagic disease (RHD). In some cases, rabbit mortality has been very high (90%–95%), but in other cases only about half of the rabbits in a population have succumbed to RHD. A new concern in areas of Australia where RHD has drastically reduced the number of rabbits is that introduced foxes and feral cats will start killing native Australian species for food. An emergency program to kill foxes and feral cats has been instigated to reduce the damage from this new ecological imbalance. The "experts" hope that in the long run, everything will balance out, but there is a reasonably high chance that RHD-resistant rabbits will soon repopulate Australia. Several organizations (e.g., Foundation for Rabbit-Free Australia) and government programs now advocate an integrated approach of rabbit extermination that includes warren destruction, introduction of predators, poison, introduction of parasites, and explosives.

During their colonization of Australia, the European rabbits were confronted with a broad set of environmental conditions. The rapid spread of the animals throughout the Australian continent attests to their adaptation to markedly diverse habitats, including tropical forests, harsh deserts, fertile plains, and barren seacoasts. Besides undergoing the obvious climatic and reproductive adaptations, these pioneering rabbits had to cope with greatly varying levels of nutrient availability; for example, the prevalence of water and sodium differed widely across habitats and across seasons. Because all physiological systems operate best within a very narrow range of conditions, rabbits living in diverse habitats were forced to make very different biological adjustments depending on the habitat they encountered. For example, maintaining a certain level of sodium chloride, the salt that is common in your diet, is critical for sustaining life. Sodium chloride is scarce in some Australian habitats,

FIGURE 9.1 **The first field trial of myxomatosis** occurred on Wardang Island, South Australia, in November 1937, conducted by the Council for Scientific and Industrial Research. This early pilot study was the proof of principle for the subsequent and broader 1950s release of the myxoma virus throughout Australia. The myxomatosis program was among the first in the world to try biological control of mammalian pests, initially reducing rabbit numbers from 600 million to 100 million in just 2 years before resistance developed and repopulation occurred. From National Archives of Australia, www.naa.gov.au/whats-on/online/showcases/memory/rabbits-around-waterhole.aspx.

and rabbits that colonized these areas were successful only to the extent that they coped with the sodium shortages. Rabbits that settled in sodium-rich habitats, such as in the desert or near the beach, survived only if they could rid their bodies of excess sodium.

Individuals are motivated to maintain an optimal level of water, sodium, and other nutrients in the body. Claude Bernard, the nineteenth-century French physiologist (**FIGURE 9.2**), was the first to describe the ability of animals to maintain a relatively constant internal environment, or *milieu intérieur*. For instance, humans maintain an optimal body temperature between 36°C and 38°C; there are also optimal blood concentrations of sugars, proteins, sodium, potassium, and many other blood constituents, as well as an optimal blood pH. In 1929, Walter B. Cannon named the process by which the body maintains this relatively constant internal milieu; he called it **homeostasis** (from the Greek for "standing" or "staying similar"). Outside of reproduction, hormones are most commonly associated with homeostatic processes.

Many homeostatic systems are completely physiological processes. However, many maintenance systems combine processes. The homeostatic system that maintains water and salt balance, for example, has a behavioral component in that drinking and the desire to drink (thirst) play a role in maintaining the critical balance of water and sodium. In yet other cases, physiological mechanisms normally maintain homeostasis, but behavioral processes may be activated when the normal physiological regulatory systems are unable to restore equilibrium. If both adrenal glands are removed from a rat, for example, then it will usually perish within a week. However, if salt water is made available, then the adrenalectomized rat will drink it and will survive just as well as intact laboratory rats (Richter, 1936). Under normal conditions, when the adrenal glands are present, physiological homeostatic systems maintain sodium balance through the action of aldosterone; this steroid hormone, secreted from the adrenals, acts on the kidneys to conserve sodium (Denton, 1982). Without the adrenals, the animal cannot retain enough sodium to sustain its life; however, it can compensate for the missing physiological sodium conservation mechanism by ingesting increased amounts of sodium. Prior to adrenalectomy, a rat, just like you, will avoid drinking seawater (an approximately 3.5%–7% sodium solution), but after adrenalectomy, a rat will avidly drink a saturated saltwater solution. When physiological homeostatic systems fail, behavioral homeostatic processes are often engaged to sustain life.

Many anecdotal reports describe children, apparently suffering from some sort of nutritional deficiency, who consume seemingly bizarre items to maintain their health. For instance, a child suffering from a calcium deficiency might eat chalk or wallpaper paste in an unconscious attempt to ameliorate the calcium shortage. In the recent past, concerned parents admitted such children to the relatively sterile environment of the hospital, where they might be treated for pica, a disorder in which people eat inedible items. Tragically, many of these patients died because they were no longer able to maintain homeostasis behaviorally (e.g., Wilkins and Richter, 1940). Even in situations in which the physiological homeostatic systems are undeveloped, homeostasis can be maintained by behavior (recall the behavioral thermoregulation of rat pups described in Chapter 7).

Many homeostatic systems, such as those maintaining fluid and energy balance, normally require both physiological and behavioral mechanisms to orchestrate a relatively constant internal condition in the face of varying external conditions. Although the various homeostatic processes are presented here as isolated events for ease of explanation, it should be remembered that any physiological challenge is met with overlapping, redundant physiological responses. Concurrent physiological and behavioral responses are often mediated or signaled by changes in the release of multiple hormones acting in concert or in opposition. Individual hormones may have multiple physiological and behavioral effects.

FIGURE 9.2 Claude Bernard (1813–1878), a French physiologist who developed the concept of *milieu intérieur*, which we now call homeostasis.

homeostasis The maintenance of a steady state within an organism by means of physiological or behavioral feedback control mechanisms.

This chapter will describe the hormonal and behavioral regulation of several homeostatic systems. Chapters 3–7 have emphasized the parsimonious relationship in which the hormones that mediate physiological reproductive processes have been co-opted during evolution to regulate mating and parental behaviors as well. Similarly, the hormones associated with physiological homeostatic mechanisms appear to also mediate behaviors critical for homeostatic maintenance. In many cases, there are reciprocal relations and overlapping neural circuitries between hormones associated with sexual behavior and hormones involved in energy balance. Also, different species use different hormonal signals to solve similar problems or challenges to their homeostatic processes. In other cases, different species rely on the same hormone to mediate very different solutions to similar problems. For example, female rats and hamsters have evolved two very different ways of coping with the energetic challenges of pregnancy. Rats increase their food intake and gain body fat during pregnancy, whereas hamsters do not change their food intake appreciably; rather, they utilize most of their established fat stores to meet the energetic demands of pregnancy (Schneider and Wade, 1987; Shirley, 1984; Wade et al., 1986). The same hormone, progesterone, elicits opposite, but similarly adaptive, responses in these two rodent species.

The conceptual bases of homeostasis will be presented in this chapter. Then, the interaction among hormones, behavior, and sodium and water balance will be described as a model physiological homeostatic system. The effects of hormones and behavior on energy balance, eating, and body mass maintenance will also be discussed. Finally, the hormone-behavior interactions controlling specific hungers will be described.

Basic Concepts in Homeostasis

set point A reference value for a regulated physiological variable.

The archetypal homeostatic device is a thermostatically controlled heating and cooling system. The system in your home is probably controlled by a thermostat (**FIGURE 9.3**). A reduction in ambient temperature below the setting on the thermostat (e.g., 20°C) will activate the furnace, which in turn will raise the temperature of the area controlled by the thermostat. When the ambient temperature increases to the "set" temperature, the thermostat will shut off the furnace (an example of negative feedback). If the ambient temperature rises above the set temperature, then the cooling system will be activated, turning off when the area becomes too cool. The thermostat acts to keep the room temperature within a relatively narrow range around the **set point**. The deviation in room temperature from the set point must be a few degrees before the furnace or air conditioner is activated or turned off; for example, the thermostat set at 20°C may keep the room between 18.5°C and 21.5°C. Otherwise, the system would be continuously engaging and turning off with only minor changes in temperature.

Similarly, rabbits, humans, and most other mammals maintain an internal body temperature of about 37°C, but temperatures in a range between 35°C and 38°C are not life threatening. However, a rapid elevation or reduction in body temperature of just 5°C would

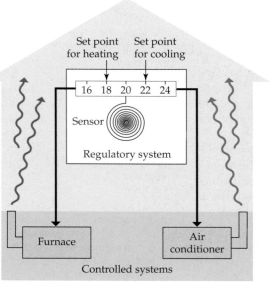

FIGURE 9.3 The thermostat is a common homeostatic device. A thermostat has a means to assign a set point and a detector mechanism to determine deviations from the set point and activate corrective measures. In this example, when the temperature decreases sufficiently from the set point, a signal is sent to activate the heating system; conversely, when the temperature increases sufficiently, the cooling system is engaged. Most physiological regulatory systems operate by similar negative feedback control loops.

seriously endanger the individual. Mammals make physiological, morphological, and behavioral adjustments to maintain body temperature within this relatively narrow range. In common with a thermostat, an animal can have a different optimal set point depending on prevailing conditions. An alternative model of homeostasis is called allostasis, the process of maintaining stability via physiological or behavioral changes. It is achieved through alteration in hypothalamic-pituitary-adrenal axis hormones, the autonomic nervous system, cytokines, or a number of other systems and is generally adaptive in the short term (McEwen and Wingfield, 2003, 2010). Among free-ranging animals, allostatic load is primarily reflective of the availability of food, water, and shelter (see Chapter 11 for a discussion of allostasis in the context of stress). As you will learn in Chapter 10, a daily program exists that reduces body temperature significantly during an animal's inactive period, presumably by changing the set point.

When we have a systemic bacterial infection, our body temperature set point usually changes as well. We often develop a fever, which is an adaptive response because higher temperatures inactivate or kill the microbial invaders producing the illness. Iguanas provide a good example of this phenomenon. Lizards are poikilothermic, unable to maintain their body temperature physiologically. Nonetheless, they can regulate their body temperatures by behavioral means. To demonstrate this phenomenon, a terrarium can be set up in such a way that there is a warm end and a cool end, with a relatively smooth temperature gradient in between (**FIGURE 9.4**). When healthy lizards were placed in such a terrarium, they settled along the temperature gradient so that their body temperature was 37°C (Kluger, 1978). If the reptiles were infected with bacteria, then they chose to be feverish; infected lizards positioned themselves in the terrarium so that their body temperatures were elevated a few degrees. In other words, there was a behaviorally mediated change in the set point as a result of the infection. Again, the behavioral generation of a fever has important adaptive consequences. When the infected lizards were prevented from elevating their temperatures, their chances of surviving the infection were reduced (Kluger, 1986). This elegant interplay between physiology and behavior enhances survival.

The thermostat analogy helps us to understand the basic concepts behind homeostasis, but there are several aspects of the control of food and water balance, discussed later in the chapter, that cannot be described adequately by the thermostat analogy. For example, feed-forward mechanisms, anticipation, and learning that occurs with ingestion may modify the basic thermostatic model. The concept of set point makes sense for systems that must be regulated in a narrow range (e.g., body temperature in active animals or intracellular fuel availability in most organisms); however, set points are probably not useful to regulate systems that can endure wide variation among individuals and over a lifetime. Body fat stores, for example, are not analogous to body temperature, in that individuals can survive with very low or very high body fat levels. In fact, during a famine, the fat store is not maintained but readily utilized to provide energy for survival. An animal that defended an intermediate value of body fat instead of breaking down and mobilizing those fat stores

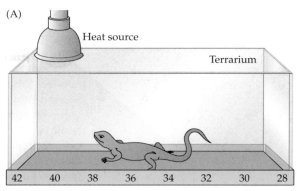

(A)

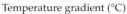

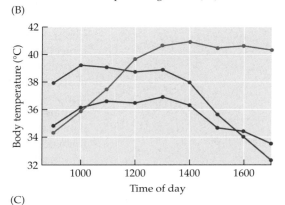

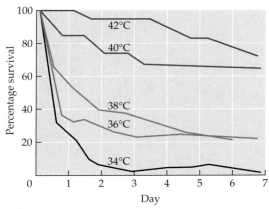

FIGURE 9.4 **Behavioral thermoregulation in iguanas**
(A) If an iguana is placed in a terrarium with a heat source at one end that produces a temperature gradient, it will tend to settle at that place along the temperature gradient where it can maintain a body temperature of about 37°C. (B) The behaviorally selected body temperatures of seven green iguanas placed in such a terrarium over the course of day 1 (green); on day 2, after each lizard received an injection of dead bacteria at 0900 h (red); and on day 3 (blue). Note that the lizards' body temperatures were raised about 3 hours after the injection and that the rise persisted until about 1500 h on day 3. (C) The percentage of iguanas injected with live bacteria and maintained at temperatures ranging from 34°C to 42°C that survived the treatment; note that the number of animals surviving is highest at the highest ambient temperatures. After Kluger, 1978.

would not survive. Thus, some variables, such as food intake and body weight, are controlled in the service of maintaining homeostasis in other variables, such as energy availability.

In order for any system to maintain homeostasis, several systemic properties are needed. First, a *reference value* (the set point) for the regulated variable is necessary. Second, some sort of *detection mechanism* to detect any deviation from the reference value is required. Third, the homeostatic system must be able to *mobilize* the organism to make changes that will return the variable to the normal range when deviation occurs. Finally, the detection mechanism must be able to recognize when the desired change occurs and shut down the mobilization process through a negative feedback mechanism. Homeostasis requires work, and work requires energy; thus, homeostasis requires energy.

Fluid Balance

Unicellular creatures living in the ocean rely upon seawater to provide them with the nutrients, oxygen, water, and basic electrolytes (e.g., Na^+, Cl^-, and K^+) necessary to sustain their life processes. These simple animals are at the mercy of the composition and temperature of the seawater; small deviations in water salinity, for instance, may be fatal. To some extent, the evolution of more-complex multicellular organisms has required the compartmentalization of "seawater" within the body, in the form of extracellular fluid. Essentially, we all carry within us a remnant of the seas in which unicellular organisms evolved—albeit a markedly diluted remnant—to bathe our cells. Homeostatic mechanisms have evolved to maintain the composition and temperature of this extracellular fluid at a relatively constant level. The processes regulating intake and excretion of water and sodium, the two main components of extracellular fluid, are closely linked so that they are maintained at ideal levels within relatively narrow ranges. The ability to maintain this relatively constant internal environment despite variable external conditions has allowed the radiation of multicellular animals into virtually every niche on the planet. The maintenance of a relatively constant internal environment liberated animals from the sea, or as Claude Bernard stated, allowed la vie en liberté, the free life (Bernard, 1856).

Animals are watery creatures. By weight, mammals are approximately two-thirds water. The proportion of body water varies widely among individuals; in humans, body water content ranges from about 45% to 70% (Rolls and Rolls, 1982). The cells of animals require water for virtually all metabolic processes. Additionally, water serves as a solvent for sodium (Na^+), chloride (Cl^-), and potassium (K^+) ions, as well as sugars, amino acids, proteins, vitamins, and many other solutes, and it is therefore essential for the smooth functioning of the nervous system and for other physiological processes. Because water participates in so many processes, and because it is continuously lost through perspiration, respiration, urination, and defecation, it must be replaced periodically. Unlike minerals or energy, very little extra water is stored in the body. When water use exceeds water intake, the body conserves water, mainly by reducing the amount of water excreted from the kidneys. Eventually, physiological water conservation can no longer compensate for water use and incidental water loss, and the animal searches for water and drinks it. Animals appear to coordinate physiology and behavior so as to maintain body water concentration at some ideal range or set point.

The regulation of sodium intake and of water intake are closely linked to one another (Fluharty, 2002; McCormick and Bradshaw, 2006; Stricker and Verbalis, 1990b). Part of the reason for this is the way in which the kidney uses sodium to conserve water (**BOX 9.1**). But sodium is also important in the movement of water between the two major fluid compartments in the body, namely, the extracellular and the intracellular compartments (Daniels and Fluharty, 2004). Approximately two-thirds of the total body fluid content is located in the intracellular compart-

BOX 9.1 *Vertebrate Renal Function*

The kidneys are remarkable organs. The human kidneys filter about 30 L of blood each hour. About 1% of this filtrate is removed as waste and sent to the bladder for elimination. The rest of the blood plasma is reabsorbed in the kidney and returned to the circulation. The kidneys contribute to the maintenance of fluid balance by either conserving water or eliminating excess water, depending on the body's needs.

The functional unit of the kidney, the nephron (shown in the figure), is where the reabsorption of water occurs. There are about a million nephrons in each human kidney. As the filtrate passes into the nephron at high pressure, it enters a long, convoluted tubule that comprises several sections, each with a specific function: the proximal tubule; the loop of Henle, with its descending and ascending limbs; the distal tubule; and the collecting duct. Water flows passively out of the descending limb into the surrounding tissue, and sodium ions enter because there is a high concentration of sodium in the surrounding regions. The sodium concentration of the filtrate is greatest at the bottom of the loop of Henle; in humans the concentration is about 2%. As the filtrate moves out of the loop into the ascending limb, the sodium is actively pumped out into the surrounding tissue. The ascending limb is impervious to water, so water cannot passively follow the sodium into the surrounding tissue. The filtrate is thus extremely dilute as it leaves the ascending limb of the loop of Henle. As it enters the distal tubule, water flows into the surrounding tissue and then into the capillaries by osmosis. The waste filtrate flows into the collecting duct and eventually moves to the bladder to be voided.

Vasopressin, or antidiuretic hormone (ADH), conserves water by acting on the distal tubules to increase their permeability to water and hence return more water to the circulation. Without ADH, the distal tubules become less permeable, resulting in diuresis, an increase in the amount of water eliminated in the urine.

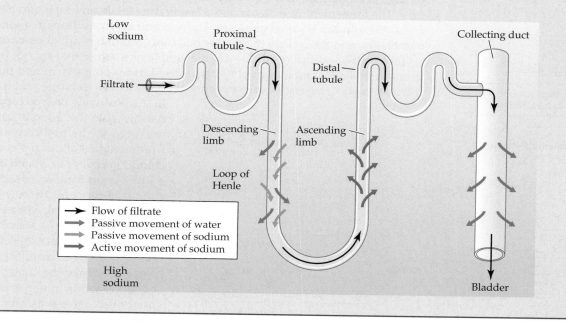

ment. The other one-third is in the extracellular compartment, which comprises two separate but interacting parts: (1) the interstitial (between the cells) fluid and (2) the blood plasma. In the extracellular compartment, about 7% of the total body fluid is in the blood plasma, and 26% is in the interstitial fluid (**FIGURE 9.5**). The distinction between the intracellular and extracellular compartments is not merely one of location. The fluids in the two compartments are fundamentally different in composition. Most of the body's sodium and chloride ions are located in the extracellular

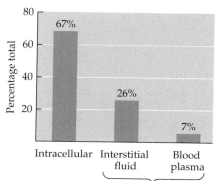

FIGURE 9.5 Body fluid is maintained in separate, but interacting, compartments. Approximately 33% of the total body fluid content is located outside the cells, about 7% in the blood plasma, and 26% in the interstitial fluid. The other two-thirds of the total body fluid content is located inside the cells.

osmosis Process of movement of a solvent through a semipermeable membrane (e.g., in a living cell) into a solution of higher solute concentration that tends to equalize the concentrations of solute on the two sides of the membrane.

osmolality The concentration of solutes in a solution.

osmoregulation The physiological and behavioral control of osmolality.

compartment, whereas most of the potassium ions are located in the intracellular compartment. The differences in fluid composition result from the properties of the cell membranes and blood vessel walls.

Mechanisms exist to balance both the intracellular and extracellular fluid levels. After mammals ingest water, most of it leaves the large intestine and eventually flows into one of the body's fluid compartments, which are separated by membranes. The blood vessel (capillary) walls act as a barrier between the blood plasma and the interstitial fluid and permit the flow of all constituents of the plasma except proteins into the interstitial fluid. Cell membranes are the barriers between the extracellular and the intracellular fluid compartments. A number of physiological mechanisms are engaged to maintain the extracellular-intracellular differences in sodium and potassium concentrations.

In order to understand the dynamics between sodium and water, and how they affect the behavioral manifestations of thirst, it is necessary to remember the concepts of osmolality, osmoregulation, and the regulation of blood plasma volume. Water can pass freely through semipermeable biological membranes, but many solutes, which are chemical substances dissolved in the solvent (water), cannot. When one compartment has a greater concentration of solutes than the other, the water will tend to distribute itself so that the solute concentration on both sides of the membrane is equalized (**FIGURE 9.6**). In other words, water moves across the biological membrane to the compartment that has the higher concentration of solutes. The movement of water across a semipermeable membrane into a more concentrated solution is called **osmosis**. The concentration of solutes in a solution is its **osmolality**, and the control of this osmotic concentration is called **osmoregulation**.

Table salt—sodium chloride—is an example of a solute that cannot pass easily through biological membranes. (Although chloride can move in and out of cells, it tends to stay outside of cells because it has a negative charge and is attracted to the positively charged sodium ions dissolved in the interstitial fluid.) In most cases, the body's extracellular fluid contains about 8.5 g of sodium chloride per liter or, stated differently, a 0.85% concentration of sodium chloride; this concentration is variously called physiological, isotonic, normal, 0.14M NaCl, or 0.9% saline. If an isotonic saline solution is injected into an animal, then it has no effect, because it does not change the concentration of sodium chloride in the animal's interstitial fluid. However, an injection of hypertonic saline, a solution in which

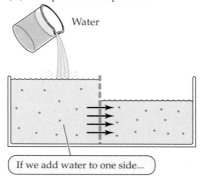

(A) Unequal osmotic pressure

(B) Equal osmotic pressure restored

...water molecules pass through semipermeable membrane, leading to equal concentration of solute on both sides. Concentration of solute is lower (on both sides) than it was before.

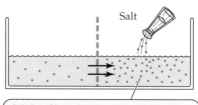

...water molecules on left cross membrane to approach equal solute concentration on both sides, despite the influence of gravity.

FIGURE 9.6 Osmosis The differences in fluid composition in the different fluid compartments of the body are the result of properties of the cell membranes and blood vessel walls. If compartments containing a dilute and a concentrated solution are separated by a membrane that allows only water to pass through (A), water will flow into the compartment of the concentrated solution until the osmotic pressure between the compartments becomes equal (B).

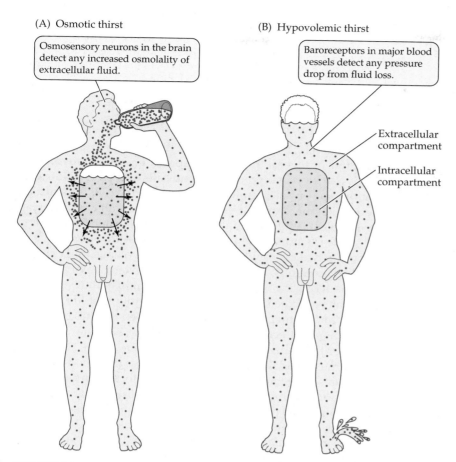

(A) Osmotic thirst

Osmosensory neurons in the brain detect any increased osmolality of extracellular fluid.

(B) Hypovolemic thirst

Baroreceptors in major blood vessels detect any pressure drop from fluid loss.

Extracellular compartment

Intracellular compartment

FIGURE 9.7 **Two types of thirst result from different osmotic conditions.** (A) Osmotic thirst is caused by cellular dehydration—which can occur after ingestion of a salty snack or drink—when increased interstitial osmolality occurs and draws water out of the intracellular compartment. Water quenches osmotic thirst. (B) Hypovolemic thirst is caused by the loss of fluids and solutes—such as after hemorrhage. Replacement of both water and solutes is necessary to quench hypovolemic thirst.

the concentration of sodium chloride exceeds 0.9%, will increase the sodium chloride concentration in the interstitial fluid. The resulting increase in interstitial osmolality will draw water out of the cells, thus inducing cellular dehydration, a potent stimulus for thirst (**FIGURE 9.7**). This type of thirst is called **osmotic thirst** and is an experience that is well known to anyone who has consumed salty foods. Consumption of sugary foods also causes osmotic thirst because the excess glucose molecules in the interstitial fluid also pull water out of cells and induce cellular dehydration.

Vasopressin acts to conserve water as blood moves through the kidneys (Stockland, 2010) (see Box 9.1). If more water is consumed than needed, plasma osmolality is decreased. Reduced plasma osmolality inhibits thirst and suppresses the release of vasopressin from the posterior pituitary. Inhibition of vasopressin release causes diuresis in the kidney: water is lost from the blood plasma and sent to the bladder for elimination (Stockland, 2010).

In addition to the osmoregulatory mechanisms that regulate intracellular and interstitial fluid balance, a second important fluid regulatory system maintains blood plasma volume. Reduction of blood volume produces a potent stimulus for thirst. This type of thirst is called **hypovolemic thirst**, or volemic thirst, and it is manifested in the extreme by individuals experiencing hemorrhage; excessive perspiration, diarrhea, or heavy menstrual bleeding can also trigger volemic thirst (Fitzsimons,

osmotic thirst Motivation to consume water caused by increased osmolality in the brain.

hypovolemic thirst Thirst induced by lack of blood volume; hypovolemic thirst can be ameliorated by water intake.

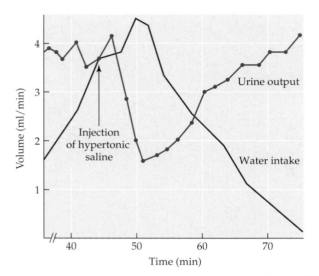

FIGURE 9.8 **Osmotic thirst** An injection of hypertonic saline, a solution of saline in which the concentration of sodium chloride exceeds 0.9%, increases the sodium chloride concentration in the interstitial fluid. The resulting increase in osmolality draws water out of the cells, thus inducing cellular dehydration and osmotic thirst and resulting in increased water intake. After Stricker and Verbalis, 1990b.

1998; Stachenfeld, 2008; Stricker et al., 1987). Volemic and osmotic thirst differ in several important respects. During **hypovolemia**, which is low blood volume, water and salts and other solutes are lost without necessarily pulling water out of the cells. Quenching osmotic thirst merely requires the ingestion of water, but alleviating hypovolemic thirst requires replacement of water, sodium, and other solutes (Kalman and Lepeley, 2010) (**FIGURE 9.8**).

There are two major ways to induce hypovolemic thirst experimentally (Fitzsimons, 1998). Inflicting a controlled hemorrhage has been the traditional method of causing hypovolemic thirst in animals; however, only acute behavioral changes can be studied with this method. In order to study gradual, long-term changes in behavior, another technique was developed that has been very useful in the study of hormonal effects on thirst and drinking behavior (Stricker, 1968): subcutaneous (under the skin) injection of polyethylene glycol (PEG). Because PEG is a relatively large colloidal molecule, it cannot cross the blood capillary membranes and thus remains in the interstitial fluid. The colloidal particles cause an "equi-osmotic" sequestration of fluid; that is, both water and solutes are removed from the body fluids, reducing blood plasma volume without significantly changing blood solute content or inducing severe hypotension (i.e., low blood pressure). The degree of hypovolemia is directly related to the amount of colloidal material injected. When subcutaneous injections of PEG are given to rats, they begin drinking 1–2 hours later, when their plasma volume deficits approach 5%, and they continue to drink in short bouts for several hours thereafter (Stricker and Verbalis, 1988).

Hypovolemia compromises kidney function. The reduced blood volume and resulting low blood pressure prevent the kidneys from extracting water effectively. Consequently, hypovolemic rats consume water but cannot completely correct their blood plasma volume because the ingested water enters all of their fluid compartments. The resulting combination of body fluid dilution and reduced water removal by the kidneys results in reduced blood plasma osmolality, a potent stimulus to stop drinking. Consequently, the rats stop drinking before attaining normal fluid balance. A hypovolemic individual requires salt to restore body fluid osmolality to normal levels. If given access to salt water or salty food, then a hypovolemic rat will ingest the proper combination of water and salt to restore blood volume and osmolality to normal levels. Similarly, athletes often ingest salty beverages such as Gatorade when they are experiencing hypovolemic thirst after heavy perspiration (Kalman and Lepeley, 2010). During the normal course of events—that is, during minor dehydration—the experience of thirst is a psychological manifestation of both osmotic and blood volume changes.

Thirst is defined here as a motivation to seek and ingest water (Fitzsimons, 1998; Stricker and Verbalis, 1988). Because thirst is a psychological hypothetical construct, we cannot measure it directly but can infer it from behavior. In nonhuman animals, the degree of thirst can be operationally determined by the amount of effort an individual expends to drink. Individuals will work harder and endure greater noxious stimuli to obtain water as the length of water deprivation increases. Investigations of human thirst allow the added dimension of verbal reports; people can be asked to rate and describe their thirst (**FIGURE 9.9**). In humans, several parameters of thirst

hypovolemia The state of low blood volume.

thirst Motivational state provoking water intake.

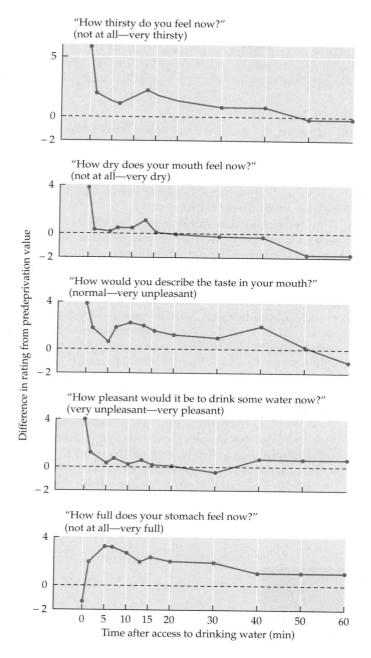

"How thirsty do you feel now?"
(not at all—very thirsty)

"How dry does your mouth feel now?"
(not at all—very dry)

"How would you describe the taste in your mouth?"
(normal—very unpleasant)

"How pleasant would it be to drink some water now?"
(very unpleasant—very pleasant)

"How full does your stomach feel now?"
(not at all—very full)

Difference in rating from predeprivation value

Time after access to drinking water (min)

FIGURE 9.9   Rating of thirst after water deprivation A rating scale can be used by human participants to provide a measure of thirst and other sensations associated with fluid intake. People were asked to rate their thirst, then deprived of water for 24 hours. They were then asked to rate their thirst again before and after access to drinking water, and their ratings were compared with their ratings on the same measures before they were deprived of water. Within 5 minutes of drinking, their thirst sensations were ameliorated, and the participants reported that their stomachs felt full. After Rolls and Rolls, 1982.

can be identified and described. For example, water-deprived humans rate the taste of water as more pleasant than do people who are not water deprived (Rolls and Rolls, 1982).

Endocrine Regulation of Fluid Balance and Thirst

Antidiuretic hormone (ADH) (which is structurally identical to vasopressin—see below) acts on the renal tubules to retain water (see Box 9.1). Occasionally, a genetic error occurs in humans or rats so that ADH is not produced. Individuals lacking ADH suffer from diabetes insipidus (*diabetes*, "run through"; *insipidus*, "weak"), a condition that forces them to ingest copious amounts of water because they are

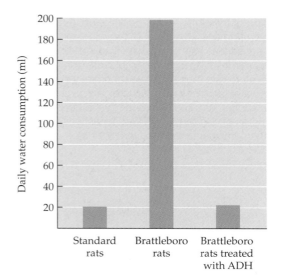

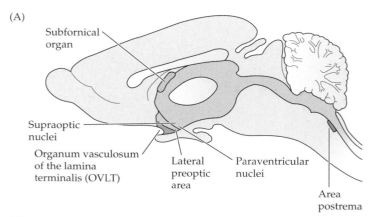

(A)

Subfornical organ

Supraoptic nuclei

Organum vasculosum of the lamina terminalis (OVLT)

Lateral preoptic area

Paraventricular nuclei

Area postrema

FIGURE 9.10 Vasopressin (ADH) mediates water consumption. Standard rats drink about 20 ml of water per day, but rats of the Brattleboro strain, which congenitally lack ADH, drink nearly ten times as much water and also excrete about ten times the volume of urine of standard rats. After ADH treatment, Brattleboro rats display typical levels of water consumption and urinary output.

almost constantly urinating. Essentially, all of their extracellular fluid is lost each day and must be replaced. Rats with this mutation, known as Brattleboro rats, urinate 200 ml/day and must drink about that amount daily to maintain their fluid balance. If these rats are injected with ADH, then their water intake and urine output drop to the normal levels of about 20 and 15 ml/day, respectively (**FIGURE 9.10**).

Two types of stimuli associated with the need to balance body fluids normally provoke the release of ADH from the posterior pituitary. One of these stimuli is the intracellular dehydration of cerebral osmoreceptors. Although virtually all cells in the body shrink in size as water moves into the interstitial space during osmotic dehydration, only these particular cells in the brain signal this condition to the paraventricular nucleus (PVN) and supraoptic nucleus (SON) of the hypothalamus, where ADH is made. These osmoreceptors are generally located in several brain structures located near the third ventricle, including the lateral preoptic area, the subfornical organ, and the organum vasculosum of the lamina terminalis, as well as in the area postrema in the brain stem (Blass and Epstein, 1971; Peck and Novin, 1971) (**FIGURE 9.11**). Two different messages are sent from these cerebral osmoreceptors in response to different levels of dehydration. A signal to release ADH from the posterior pituitary occurs in response to mild cellular dehydration. If dehydration persists after maximal reclamation of water has been achieved in the kidneys, then a second signal from the brain os-

(B)

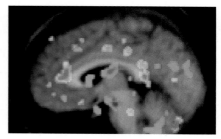

Maximum thirst

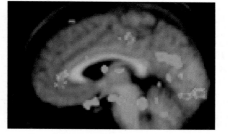

Thirst with wet mouth

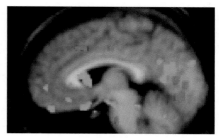

Three minutes after drinking

FIGURE 9.11 Brain structures involved in the mediation of thirst and water intake (A) Cerebral osmoreceptor cells respond to dehydration and shrinkage by signaling the paraventricular and supraoptic nuclei to synthesize vasopressin. These osmoreceptors are found in the circumventricular organs seen in this schematic drawing of a midsagittal section of the rat brain: the subfornical organ, the area postrema, the organum vasculosum of the lamina terminalis (OVLT), and the lateral preoptic area. (B) These are composite fMRI images showing brain activity in individuals experiencing different levels of thirst. The top left image was taken after individuals received an infusion of a concentrated saline solution into the blood to stimulate thirst; regions of activity light up several brain regions of thirsty people, especially the cerebellum and cingulate cortex. When the people simply wetted their mouth (top right scan) the activation was reduced slightly. However, drinking a glass of water quenched their thirst, and brain activity was dramatically reduced (bottom). Yellow and orange areas indicate the most brain activity. B from Denton et al., 1999.

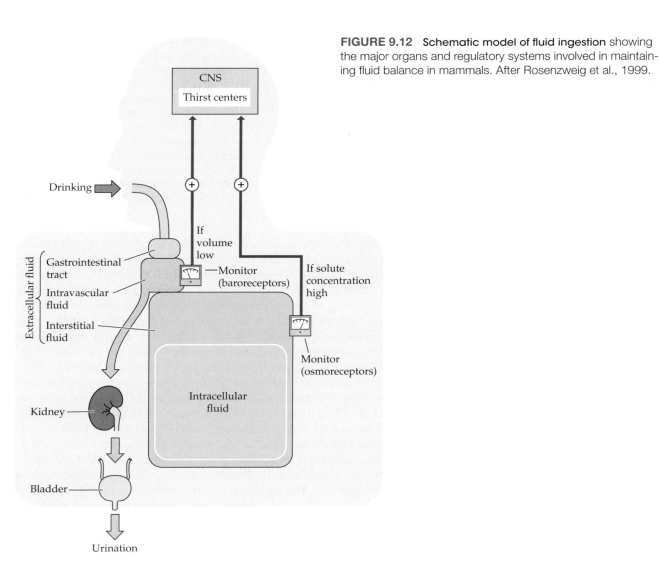

FIGURE 9.12 Schematic model of fluid ingestion showing the major organs and regulatory systems involved in maintaining fluid balance in mammals. After Rosenzweig et al., 1999.

moreceptors stimulates drinking behavior. This dual control allows physiological water-saving systems to be engaged prior to behavioral responses and thus frees individuals from the need to drink frequently. ADH does not inhibit drinking behavior directly; rather, it causes the kidneys to retain water, which decreases blood plasma osmolality. Reduced plasma osmolality, in turn, inhibits drinking.

Another stimulus that triggers the release of vasopressin is a reduction of blood plasma volume. A loss of blood volume is detected by stretch receptors, called baroreceptors, in the walls of the cardiac blood vessels. These receptors signal the PVN and SON to release ADH, which acts as a vasoconstrictor (reduces the diameter of blood vessels) to increase blood pressure (Gauer and Henry, 1963). Hence, the same hormone has two distinct, but related, functions that work in concert when blood pressure drops, and it possesses two common names: antidiuretic hormone (ADH), referring to its effect on the kidneys, and vasopressin, referring to its effect on the blood vessels. The cardiac baroreceptors also signal the brain directly via the vagus nerve[1] to stimulate thirst. The regulation of fluid intake behavior is depicted in **FIGURE 9.12**.

---

[1] The vagus (Latin for "wandering") nerve is one of the cranial nerves that make up part of the peripheral nervous system. It extends far from the head and innervates the heart, lungs, digestive tract, and liver, carrying information between these organs and the central nervous system.

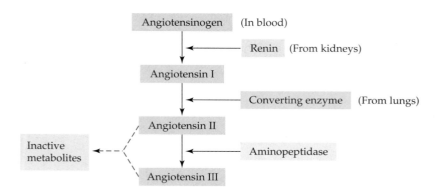

FIGURE 9.13 Synthesis of angiotensin in humans The drop in blood pressure that occurs during hypovolemia initiates the formation of the potent vasoconstrictor angiotensin by stimulating the brain to signal the kidneys to make renin. Renin is an enzyme that converts the blood-borne substance angiotensinogen to three forms of angiotensin: angiotensin I, II, and III. Angiotensin II is the most biologically potent of the angiotensins, but all three exert some effects on water and sodium balance. The kidneys can also make renin in response to low blood pressure without any neural input. After Ganong, 1993.

Hypovolemia also stimulates the formation of another potent vasoconstrictor, angiotensin (Popkin et al., 2010). Angiotensin is a hormone that comes from an unusual source: the blood. Because angiotensin is not produced by any endocrine gland, it is often considered to be a parahormone, secreted from paracrine cells. In any case, a drop in blood pressure during hypovolemia stimulates the brain to signal the kidneys to make an enzyme called renin; the kidneys can also make renin in response to low blood pressure without any neural input. Renin converts a blood-borne substance called angiotensinogen into the various forms of angiotensin, including angiotensin II, the form involved in this response (**FIGURE 9.13**). Angiotensin stimulates drinking behavior in rats; systemic injections of angiotensin (Fitzsimons and Simons, 1969) or injections directly into the subfornical organ (Simpson et al., 1978) increase drinking behavior (Moran and Sakai, 2002).

It is well documented that angiotensin also stimulates the release of aldosterone from the zona glomerulosa of the adrenal gland. Aldosterone is another hormone critical for maintaining fluid balance. Aldosterone promotes the retention of sodium in the kidney by stimulating sodium pumping in the ascending limb of the loop of Henle (see Box 9.1). The resulting retention of sodium at high concentrations in the kidneys causes water to be reabsorbed from the blood as it flows through the nephron, and it thereby reduces the amount of water sent to the bladder for excretion. Without aldosterone, the kidney would route enormous amounts of water and sodium—approximately 30 L of water per day in humans and about 200 mmol salt/L/day—out of the body to be lost in urine.

Pharmacological tools have revealed two distinct types of angiotensin receptors in the brain: type 1 and type 2. Using specific receptor antagonists, it was discovered that only the type 1, and not the type 2, receptors are the mediators of angiotensin II–related thirst and sodium intake (Fluharty and Sakai, 1995). Furthermore, intracerebroventricular (ICV) administration of angiotensin type 1 receptor antisense oligodeoxynucleotides diminishes drinking behavior in rats (Sakai et al., 1995). It was also discovered that ICV administration of mineralocorticoid receptor antisense oligonucleotides reduces sodium appetite in rats (Ma et al., 1997; Sakai et al., 1996) (**FIGURE 9.14**). These results of blocking the expression of either the angiotensin or mineralocorticoid receptors demonstrate the role of

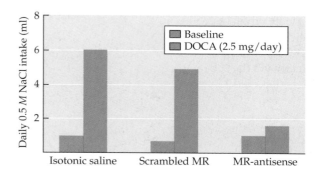

FIGURE 9.14 Antisense oligonucleotides for mineralocorticoid receptors block elevation in saline intake induced by deoxycorticosterone acetate (DOCA). A synthetic mineralocorticoid with about 3% aldosterone activity, DOCA causes an increase in salt appetite when injected systemically, as shown by the increase in saline ingestion by animals treated with this substance. If the treated animals are also infused with isotonic saline or scrambled mineralocorticoid receptor (MR) mRNA into the amygdala, then saline intake is unaffected. If DOCA-treated animals are treated with an MR-antisense infusion, then saline intake is reduced. After Sakai et al., 1996.

endogenous angiotensin II and aldosterone in mediating water and sodium ingestion, respectively, as well as the importance of their actions in the central nervous system. Angiotensin II regulates blood pressure and sodium balance (see below) by acting on both peripheral and brain targets. In the brain, angiotensin binds to the angiotensin type 1 receptor to stimulate thirst and sodium appetite (Daniels et al., 2009; Felgendreger et al., 2013).

Sodium Balance

Humans who consume modern diets, and animals maintained on commercial laboratory diets—both of which provide plenty of sodium—have relatively large reservoirs of sodium in the interstitial fluid (Daniels and Fluharty, 2004, 2009). This sodium reserve probably serves to buffer the brain from wide fluctuations in sodium availability during large variations in daily sodium intake and loss. When the sodium reservoir is depleted, individuals are motivated to seek and ingest sodium. Sustained sodium deprivation interferes with neural functioning and can rapidly lead to death. The detectors for blood levels of sodium appear to be located in the brain (Daniels and Fluharty, 2009; Stricker and Verbalis, 1990b; Weisinger et al., 1982).

Herbivores obtain all of their sodium and much of their water from the plants that they eat. Because there is a wide range of sodium content in plants, herbivores may exposed to wide variation in sodium availability. Carnivores are not usually under the same sodium pressures as herbivores, because the animals that they consume must maintain a relatively consistent sodium level. Essentially, carnivores have the problem of excreting sodium after a meal because their meals tend to be sodium rich, whereas herbivores are adapted to retain sodium and excrete potassium after their meals.

Recall that European rabbits in Australia are confronted with environments that vary substantially in sodium availability. These rabbits must cope with variation in sodium availability in order to survive and reproduce. Rabbits inhabiting the Snowy Mountains in Australia are exposed to an environment that is extremely low in sodium; analyses of the soil and plants in this alpine region have revealed a profound lack of sodium (Blair-West et al., 1968). The rain is virtually free of sodium, and the spring snowmelt further reduces sodium availability by leaching it deeper into the ground. In contrast, the food plants of rabbits living in the harsh desert of central Australia are very high in sodium content. Similarly, rabbits inhabiting ocean coastal regions in Victoria are exposed to relatively high levels of sodium in plants because of the high concentrations of sodium in the coastal rain. Researchers have observed differences among the rabbits in these three regions in the quantities of water consumed and urine produced, as well as in other physiological parameters (**TABLE 9.1**).

The Australian rabbits occupying opposite ends of the sodium availability continuum are faced with a situation analogous to that of freshwater versus saltwater fishes. A freshwater fish is essentially a bag of saline surrounded by dilute water,

TABLE 9.1 *Comparison of sodium regulatory indices of rabbits living in three different habitats in Australia*

Habitat	Na+ in urine (mmol/L)	Aldosterone (ng/100 ml)	Adrenal mass (g)	Zona glomerulosa size (as % of total adrenal cortex)
Snowy Mountains	0.53	69.0	0.12	22.6
Coast	18.00	21.0	0.11	15.6
Desert	139.00	9.0	0.13	15.3

Source: After Blair-West et al., 1968.

which creates an osmotic gradient favoring the movement of sodium out of the fish. Freshwater fishes have evolved effective sodium-retaining mechanisms to combat sodium depletion. A saltwater fish, on the other hand, is essentially a bag of freshwater surrounded by a concentrated saltwater solution. There is a high osmotic gradient favoring the movement of sodium ions into saltwater fishes, but they have evolved mechanisms to keep sodium out and to remove it from their bodies efficiently.

Modern bony fishes, called teleost fishes, are thought to have evolved in freshwater, then radiated to environments with vastly different degrees of salinity. Some fishes, termed *stenohaline* species, have adapted to specific saline environments and cannot tolerate salinities beyond very specific ranges. In contrast, *euryhaline* species can tolerate wide ranges of salinity. Euryhaline fishes in nature may be exclusively saltwater fishes (e.g., the starry flounder, *Platichthys stellatus*) or exclusively freshwater fishes (e.g., the tilapia, *Sarotherodon mossambicus*), or they may be capable of exploiting their tolerance for a wide range of environmental salinities by migrating between salt water and freshwater (e.g., Pacific salmon, *Oncorhynchus* spp., or Atlantic eels, *Anguilla* spp.). Those euryhaline fishes, such as salmons and eels, that move between fresh and salt water rely on hormones—most notably, prolactin, cortisol, and thyroid hormone—to adapt to their changing sodium requirements, and their ability to survive these changes involves a complex interaction among reproductive maturity, day length, and hormonal responses. The extent to which changing hormone levels themselves induce migration or are secondary to other maturational factors remains somewhat controversial.

The Australian rabbits are confronted with the same basic problem as fishes, namely, how to survive in habitats with markedly different sodium availabilities. Several physiological adaptations are evident in rabbits living in sodium-poor habitats. Snowy Mountain rabbits excrete very little sodium in their urine, although there is a notable seasonal cycle of average urinary sodium excretion, which is greater in winter than in summer (**TABLE 9.2**). Average blood plasma concentrations of aldosterone mirror the seasonal urinary sodium excretion cycle, as does the average proportion of the adrenal gland made up by the zona glomerulosa, which varies nearly 50% in size. What is the reason for these seasonal variations? During spring and summer, the rapid growth of lush plants further reduces sodium concentrations per gram of plant material in the Snowy Mountains region. Herbivores living under these conditions must consume enormous quantities of food to maintain sodium at a level consistent with proper physiological functioning. Pregnancy and lactation increase this demand even further. During the spring and summer, rabbits living in the alpine regions of Australia display an avid salt appetite. When wooden pegs impregnated with various salts are made available to the rabbits, they clearly prefer $NaCl$ and $NaHCO_3$, but they will also ingest $MgCl_2$ and KCl in smaller amounts (**FIGURE 9.15**) (Myers, 1967). Thus, these animals possess physiological, morphological, and behavioral adaptations to obtain and to conserve sodium.

TABLE 9.2   *Seasonal changes in sodium regulatory indices of rabbits inhabiting the Snowy Mountains of Australia*

Season	Na+ in urine (mmol/L)	Aldosterone (ng/100 ml)	Adrenal mass (g)	Zona glomerulosa size (as % of total adrenal cortex)
Spring	0.59	130.0	0.18	34.4
Summer	0.53	69.0	0.12	22.6
Autumn	2.60	—	0.14	17.3
Winter	6.40	74.0	0.14	17.8

Source: After Blair-West et al., 1968.

FIGURE 9.15 Rabbits inhabiting sodium-deficient habitats have voracious sodium appetites. This telescopic photograph shows rabbits living in sodium-deficient alpine regions of Australia devouring wooden pegs impregnated with sodium. Rabbits in sodium-rich habitats are never observed ingesting sodium-treated pegs. Photograph by E. Slater, CSIRO Wildlife Division, Canberra.

In contrast to Snowy Mountain rabbits, rabbits living in the desert inhabit a sodium-rich environment, and their physiological challenge is to limit sodium intake and reduce sodium levels in their bodies. These animals excrete consistently high levels of sodium throughout the year and have concomitant low plasma aldosterone concentrations (see Table 9.1). The zona glomerulosa makes up only about 15% of the adrenal cortex. Rabbits living in desert or seashore habitats have never been observed to ingest salt from salt licks provided by experimenters. These results support the notion of the plasticity of the adrenal glands.

Regardless of sodium availability in the environment, each rabbit (and every other mammal, including you) must maintain the sodium levels in its body within precise limits. In rabbits and humans, sodium levels are maintained between 135 and 145 mmol/L in the blood plasma. Obviously, animals living in sodium-rich habitats must excrete excess sodium to maintain blood sodium levels in the optimal range, whereas animals living in low-sodium environments must avoid losing precious sodium. Australian rabbits provide an example of how physiology, morphology, and behavior are linked to bring about fluid balance and maintain homeostasis.

Although many animals are generalists to some extent, most animals have evolved to inhabit specific environmental niches. Some animals have evolved in habitats that regularly experience sodium shortages, whereas others have evolved where sodium is plentiful. Like rats, Syrian hamsters (Mesocricetus auratus) will perish if subjected to bilateral adrenalectomy. Unlike adrenalectomized rats, however, adrenalectomized hamsters provided with salt water to drink will refuse it and die. Hamsters survive adrenalectomy only if provided with a solution of saline mixed with saccharin. Apparently, the sweet taste of saccharin masks the salty taste of the saline. When provided with a choice between a saccharin solution and a salt-water solution, adrenalectomized hamsters will drink the saccharin solution exclusively and invariably perish. Do these facts indicate that hamsters are less intelligent than rats? No. These puzzling results become immediately explicable in light of the fact that Syrian hamsters evolved in the desert, where sodium levels are high and water is scarce. They have evolved physiological and behavioral strategies to avoid sodium. It is unlikely that Syrian hamsters have ever had a need during their evolution to ingest sodium; consequently, behavioral homeostatic strategies in response to sodium loss from the kidneys are not available to this species. The difference in salt appetite between rats, rabbits, and humans on the one hand and Syrian hamsters on the other demonstrates the importance of understanding the evolutionary history of the animals in question when trying to understand the complex web of physiological and behavioral interactions mediating homeostatic processes.

preference threshold The first detectable preference displayed by an individual for any substance or solution.

detection threshold The concentration at which an individual can tell the difference between two substances or stimuli.

Kangaroo rats (*Dipodomys merriami*) are desert rodents that rarely have access to water in their native habitat and probably never drink it if they do find it. Their water needs are met by chemically liberating water from the seeds they eat. Kangaroo rats have evolved to conserve water very effectively; they rarely urinate, and when they do, the urine is highly concentrated. These small rodents have the longest kidney tubules of any mammal, which accounts for their extreme efficiency in retaining water. Another mammal that has an unusual method of obtaining water is the elephant seal (*Mirounga angustirostris*). During their 4-to-5-month mating season, elephant seals engage in territorial and reproductive behaviors along the shoreline but do not eat or drink. All the water they need is liberated metabolically by hydrolysis of their substantial fat reserves. Elephant seals, like other marine mammals, have evolved to live in the sea, but their adaptation is limited in that they are no more capable of surviving on seawater than humans. During the nonbreeding season, they get all their water from the fish they consume (LeBoeuf, 1974). Kangaroo rats and elephant seals have adapted to their particular niches over the course of many eons of evolution. The rabbits invading Australia have not been there very long (in evolutionary time), and new mechanisms to balance water and sodium levels have yet to evolve; consequently, behavioral adaptations, mediated in part by hormones, are critical for their continued survival. Indeed, sodium balance in many vertebrates may be regulated by extra-renal regulatory mechanisms (Titze, 2014).

How Do Hormones Regulate Drinking Behavior?

The hormones that maintain fluid balance interact with the sensory systems, or input systems, associated with water intake. For example, adrenal hormones influence the firing rate of sensory neurons that respond to salt. In a typical study of these interactions, an animal is given a choice between two different drinking bottles (**FIGURE 9.16**). For example, a rat may be given a choice between tap water and an isotonic saline solution. The rat's fluid intake is measured daily, and a preference is calculated. For example, the rat might ingest 9 ml of tap water and 12 ml of saline during a single 24-hour period. In this case, we would say that saline is preferred over tap water by 75% (9/12). To examine the nature of this preference, the saline can be diluted by half to a 0.45% sodium concentration. If the rat still drinks more of the diluted saline than the tap water, an inference is made that the animal can detect the difference between the two and has a preference. In this manner, a **preference threshold** can be determined by serial dilutions. The preference threshold is the lowest concentration at which preference for the solution over water can be maintained. Obviously, animals will display different preference thresholds for different substances; for example, the preference threshold for sucrose solutions and for sodium solutions is different among most individuals. The **detection threshold** is the concentration at which the animal can tell the difference between solutions. These two parameters are not necessarily identical. Note in Figure 9.16 that the detection threshold for sodium is not different for adrenalectomized and intact animals, although the sodium-deficient animals drink more sodium at low and high concentrations.

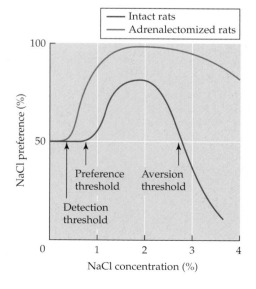

FIGURE 9.16 Adrenalectomy affects saline preference thresholds. The concentration at which an animal responds differently to different solutions is called the detection threshold. Intact rats (blue line) prefer about a 1% solution of saline over water (the preference threshold), but as the concentration of sodium increases, the rats' preference changes to plain water (the aversion threshold). The red line plots the saline preference pattern for adrenalectomized rats, which lack aldosterone. Note that adrenalectomized rats tolerate sodium solutions that intact rats or people would find extremely unpleasant; this change in sodium tolerance helps the adrenalectomized animal maintain behavioral homeostasis.

Adrenal-intact rats can discriminate among different low-sodium concentrations in a test in which they must do so to avoid electric shocks. Presumably, the differences among low-sodium solutions make a difference only to the adrenalectomized animals. Interestingly, the firing rate of the sensory neurons in the mouth as they respond to sodium applied to the tongue is reduced in an adrenalectomized rat. Perhaps adrenal hormones mediate the aversive taste of salt by increases in the firing rate of sensory neurons, and this is why adrenalectomized rats are able to ingest water with such high, normally aversive, concentrations of salt (e.g., Dietz et al., 2006; Garcia et al., 2008).

The hormones associated with fluid balance also mediate behavior by acting on the central processing systems. As described above, during mild cellular dehydration, ADH affects central drinking mechanisms indirectly by causing the kidneys to retain water, which results in reduced blood plasma osmolality; reduced plasma osmolality inhibits drinking. After persistent dehydration, ADH, aldosterone, and angiotensin II all increase drinking behavior by acting directly or indirectly on the central nervous system. Aldosterone stimulates sodium retention by the kidneys and thus maintains osmotic balance, but aldosterone affects drinking behavior only indirectly via its influence on osmotic thirst. Aldosterone may act directly on the central nervous system to regulate sodium appetite in conjunction with angiotensin. Pharmacological doses of angiotensin elicit drinking behavior, presumably by acting on the subfornical organ in the brain (Simpson et al., 1978; Zigmond et al., 1991). Increased plasma osmolality signals osmosensors in the hypothalamus to release ADH. Increased ADH binds to ADH membrane receptors in the renal collecting duct, which causes stored aquaporin protein to be inserted into the plasma membrane to form water channels. This action elevates water reabsorption by the kidney tubules, which thus restores plasma osmolality to ideal levels (McCormick and Bradshaw, 2006). The output systems—the effectors—of water ingestion are essentially unaffected by hormones. Hormones do not appear to increase the efficiency of water intake or otherwise affect the output systems of drinking behavior in any appreciable way.

Sex steroid hormones may also affect water and sodium regulation. For example, administration of estrogen-containing oral contraceptive pills decreased the osmotic threshold for arginine vasopressin (AVP) and stimulation of drinking during hypertonic saline infusion, as well as during dehydration of young women (Stachenfeld and Keefe, 2002). Estradiol also increases plasma volume, whereas progestins tend to decrease plasma volume (Stachenfeld, 2010). Both estradiol and progesterone can influence the complex and integrated neural and hormonal systems that have evolved to regulate thirst, fluid intake, sodium appetite, and renal fluid and sodium regulation (Stachenfeld, 2010). Estrogen receptors are present in the hypothalamic nuclei of animals that produce AVP (Paech et al., 1997).

Energy Balance

Animals eat food to meet the needs of the structural part of the body, that is, to obtain the raw materials to make bone, muscle, and other structures. Animals also eat food to obtain energy to fuel the body. Providing energy to the cells is absolutely critical for moment-to-moment survival. Consequently, homeostatic mechanisms exist to ensure that there is a continuous supply of metabolic fuels even though most organisms do not eat continuously. Many organisms have a predisposition toward storing metabolic fuels to survive food shortages, rather than toward expending excess energy stored as fat. Even at rest, all animals need energy to maintain their cellular processes necessary for life. The central nervous system, particularly the human brain, is a major consumer of metabolic energy.

All the vital systems require energy to carry out their functions, and significant energy is necessary to maintain mammalian body temperatures at 37°C. Despite this persistent need for energy, there are fluctuations in the energy requirements of every individual, as the rate of energy use varies throughout the day, as well as over the seasons. There are also fluctuations in energy acquisition. The balance between the amount of energy stored in the body, energy expenditure, and energy intake is most certainly controlled, but it is not "regulated" in the same sense that water and sodium balance or body temperature are regulated (Friedman, 2008). Whereas body temperature and sodium balance must be maintained within a relatively narrow window, the amount of energy stored in the body can vary widely among individuals of some species. In such species, individuals need a minimum of stored energy for survival and reproduction, but they may survive and reproduce especially well with surplus amounts of stored energy—that is, body fat. Over the course of evolution, this stored fat likely enhanced survival in environments in which energy availability fluctuated, and it allowed individuals to engage in courtship, mating, gestation, lactation, nest defense, and other reproductive behaviors that conflict with eating, foraging, and hoarding food. Those individuals with large fat stores would have been more likely to survive harsh winters, droughts, or famine and to enjoy reproductive success despite the high energetic costs of reproductive processes and behavior. Thus, it should not be surprising to find that in some species, including humans, there are fewer mechanisms to stop eating (satiety signals) and weight gain than there are to promote eating (hunger signals) and weight gain.

As in water balance, the central problem is that eating tends to be episodic, even though the need for energy is more or less continuous (Stricker and Verbalis, 1988). (In common, mealtime drinking tends to be episodic, although the need for water is also somewhat continuous). Accordingly, energy acquisition and energy expenditure are never perfectly balanced. Individuals cannot eat continuously to meet moment-to-moment changes in energy demands; they must occasionally sleep, mate, or acquire food. Also, food availability is not constant; seasonal and daily cycles in food availability exist. All of this leads to a dynamic relationship between energy acquisition and energy expenditure. When more food is consumed than required, the excess energy is stored in the form of **adipose tissue**, or fat. This stored energy is later tapped when the steady delivery of metabolic fuel from the intestines wanes after a meal.

Animals have homeostatic mechanisms that ensure long-term energy balance. These mechanisms function to keep body mass within a relatively fixed range over weeks, months, or even years. Other related mechanisms also exist to regulate short-term energy balance, switching on or off feeding behavior. Multiple redundant mechanisms exist to control energy intake and expenditure, which makes the endocrine and neuroendocrine control of energy balance confusing to understand. Historically, experiments targeting a single hormonal or neuropeptide system have ultimately fallen short because another system has kicked in to reverse the effects of the manipulation of the regulatory system.

Another complicating factor in the study of energy balance is that although many different hormones may be directly involved in the control of food intake, many other substances may indirectly affect food intake, perhaps by increasing general arousal (orexin is an example because animals treated with this hormone that increase their food intake also tend to sleep less) or by making the individual too sick to eat (e.g., pharmacological cholecystokinin [CCK] treatment appears to make individuals nauseated and thus reduce food intake). All of these caveats should be kept in mind as we review the complex interaction between hormones and energy balance.

An additional caveat is that modern humans rarely rely solely on endogenous signaling factors to stimulate eating. In many cases, food intake is divorced from homeostatic processes and relies on nonhomeostatic processes such as experience, habits, and availability; even anticipation of food can affect hormones associated with food intake (Begg and Woods, 2013) (**FIGURE 9.17**). For example, many environmental factors such as specific social situations (e.g., attending a movie in a

adipose tissue Connective tissue in which fat is stored.

FIGURE 9.17 **Endocrine anticipation of food** After several days of receiving a discrete "meal" at time 0, rats begin to show anticipatory endocrine responses 1–2 hours in advance of the learned meal time. This phenomenon contributes to our feeling of hunger when we see that it is noon if we normally eat at that time or in response to other environmental factors such as the sight or smell of food. From Begg and Woods, 2013.

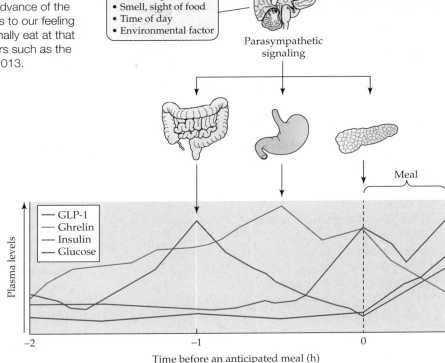

theater), time of day (e.g., seeing 12:00 on a clock at lunchtime), convenience (e.g., passing a candy machine), habit (e.g., walking past a cookie jar), or stress (e.g., craving high-fat food while studying for an exam) all contribute to the onset of food intake somewhat independently of circulating glucose levels (Woods and D'Alessio, 2008). These factors tend not to be mediated by homeostatic mechanisms and thus can contribute to wide fluctuations in caloric intake and body mass. It is likely that nonhomeostatic factors, such as clumped food distribution or safe havens for eating, have contributed as much to the onset of eating in humans as endogenous factors have throughout much of human evolution (Woods and D'Alessio, 2008). Hormones, however, do influence the number of calories consumed, or size of a meal, after the meal has commenced (Begg and Woods, 2013; Grill, 2009). Again, the physiological roles of these hormones have been co-opted over evolutionary time to serve a behavioral function. Several gut hormones mainly function to increase fuel absorption, oxidation, thermogenesis, and body temperature and are generally secreted in proportion to the calories consumed, that is, in response to meal size (Field et al., 2010). Thus, these same hormones have evolved to serve as satiety signals when a certain caloric intake is achieved. Given the importance of anticipatory body fat storage for survival and reproduction, it is not surprising that these "satiety peptides" fail to keep all individuals lean, but the existence of such peptides provides encouragement to look for ways to prevent or curtail obesity and diabetes.

One of the challenges to behavioral endocrinologists interested in food intake has been the vast array of hormones and other chemical messengers that change with fasting and refeeding. All of them can be seen, at first glance, to be candidates for control of food intake. As animals fluctuate between a well-fed and a fasting state, correlated changes occur in the secretion of hormones, neurotransmitters, and neuromodulators. In chronically well-fed animals, such as most U.S. and European humans and many domesticated animals, blood concentrations of glucose, amino acids, insulin, and leptin are all relatively high. Stores of body fat in adipose tissues and glycogen in the liver are high, as are lipogenic (fat-synthesizing) enzymes. Central nervous system neuropeptides released in well-fed animals include CCK, α-melanocyte-stimulating hormone (a cleavage product of pro-opiomelanocortin), cocaine- and amphetamine-regulated transcript, and in at least some species, GnRH-II. In contrast, well-fed animals have relatively low blood concentrations of glucagon, glucocorticoids, free fatty acids, lipolytic enzymes (which break down fat), ketone bodies, and circulating ghrelin and also relatively low hypothalamic

TABLE 9.3	Signaling molecules involved in regulation of energy balance

Molecule	Regulation by adiposity signals
Orexigenic	
NPY (neuropeptide Y)	↓
AgRP (agouti-related protein)	↓
MCH (melanin-concentrating hormone)	↓
Orexin A and B (hypocretin 1 and 2)	↓
Galanin	?
Noradrenaline	?
Anorexigenic	
α-MSH (α-melanocyte-stimulating hormone)	↑
CRH (corticotropin-releasing hormone)	↑
TRH (thyrotropin-releasing hormone)	↑
CART (cocaine- and amphetamine-regulated transcript)	↑
IL-1β (interleukin-1β)	↑
Urocortin	?
Glucagon-like peptide 1	?
Oxytocin	?
Neurotensin	?
Serotonin	?

Source: After Schwartz et al., 2000.

concentrations of orexigenic peptides such as neuropeptide Y (NPY), melanin-concentrating hormone, orexin, corticotropin-releasing factor, and catecholamines. Among fasting animals, the relative concentrations of signaling molecules are reversed (**TABLE 9.3**). As Table 9.3 suggests, determination of the one factor that controls food intake is difficult, especially if elimination of one factor results in compensatory action by the others.

As noted in Chapter 1, an important test of the contribution of a hormone in any hormone-behavior interaction is the use of a specific hormone receptor antagonist to block the effects of the hormone on the behavior under study. Some hormones are still awaiting this "acid test" in the study of ingestive behavior.

Finally, although not as well studied as the consummatory act of eating, the motivation to obtain food also has hormonal influences (Bartness and Clein, 1994; Buckley and Schneider, 2003; Schneider et al., 2007). As with sexual behaviors, it is probably instructive to separately examine the effects of hormones on both appetitive and consummatory aspects of food intake. For example, in Syrian hamsters (*Mesocricetus auratus*) food deprivation increases hoarding of food but does not increase food intake, and similarly in Siberian hamsters (*Phodopus sungorus*) food deprivation has greater effects on food hoarding than on food intake. While treatment of rats and mice with leptin decreases their food intake, in Syrian and Siberian hamsters leptin treatment appears to act on the motivation to procure food; that is, leptin treatment of hamsters decreases food deprivation–induced increases in food hoarding (Buckley and Schneider, 2003; Keen-Rhinehart and Bartness, 2008; Schneider et al., 2007). Rats getting ICV treatment with NPY eat, but if they are given NPY in intraoral food, then they do not eat. Thus, NPY appears important in the appetitive, but not consummatory, phases of eating (Drazen et al., 2006a).

Metabolism during the Well-Fed State

After a meal, there are two phases of energy utilization and storage: (1) the postprandial phase and (2) the postabsorptive phase. The metabolic interactions that occur in a well-fed individual are outlined in **FIGURE 9.18A**. The postprandial phase occurs immediately after the ingestion of food. When you eat a meal, a supply of **metabolic fuels**, in the form of simple sugars (e.g., glucose), fatty acids, and amino acids, enters the bloodstream almost immediately. Unless you are running a marathon immediately after eating, there tends to be an energy surplus after a meal. The excess energy is stored during the postabsorptive phase. The protein hormone insulin acts to promote the uptake of glucose into tissues for oxidation and storage. In doing so, insulin lowers the levels of metabolic fuels in the blood.

During the postabsorptive phase, insulin secretion rises while glucagon secretion falls. In the liver, insulin stimulates the conversion of glucose to glycogen, a stored form of sugar. Glycogen is stored in the liver and in muscle. Insulin also facilitates the transport of glucose into muscle and fat cells, as well as the transport of amino acids into muscle cells. In the liver, amino acids are converted into

metabolic fuels The normal sources of energy for individuals, usually consisting of simple sugars (e.g., glucose), fatty acids, ketone bodies, and amino acids.

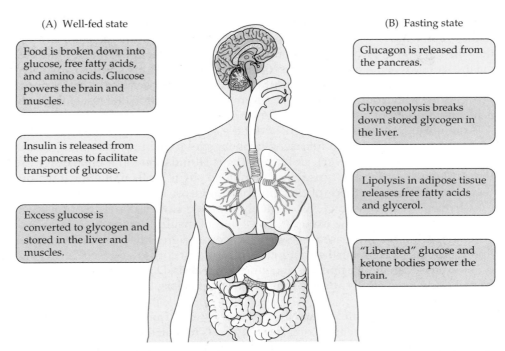

(A) Well-fed state

Food is broken down into glucose, free fatty acids, and amino acids. Glucose powers the brain and muscles.

Insulin is released from the pancreas to facilitate transport of glucose.

Excess glucose is converted to glycogen and stored in the liver and muscles.

(B) Fasting state

Glucagon is released from the pancreas.

Glycogenolysis breaks down stored glycogen in the liver.

Lipolysis in adipose tissue releases free fatty acids and glycerol.

"Liberated" glucose and ketone bodies power the brain.

FIGURE 9.18 Metabolic interactions among the major components of energy balance in (A) the well-fed state, and (B) the fasting state. After Schneider and Wade, 2000.

ketone bodies. In peripheral cells, insulin is necessary for glucose oxidation and lipogenesis, processes that result in the storage of fat in adipose tissue. Insulin also prevents the breakdown of glycogen in both muscle and liver cells, as well as the mobilization of metabolic fuels from adipose tissue. Although insulin is the sole hormone responsible for energy storage in vertebrates, many other hormones play a role in energy metabolism. These hormones include epinephrine, norepinephrine, glucocorticoids, thyroid hormones, growth hormone, somatomedin, and glucagon (Lopez et al., 2013).

There are two phases of insulin release: the cephalic phase and the gastrointestinal (GI) phase. During the cephalic phase, a neurally triggered release of insulin from the pancreatic β-cells occurs as a result of the sensory stimuli associated with food intake (Steffens et al., 1990). So even before any new nutrients have arrived in the digestive system, an insulin-induced reduction in blood levels of metabolic fuels may be associated with an increase in hunger. You have probably experienced the cephalic phase of insulin release when the sights or smells of a favorite meal caused you to feel noticeably hungrier. The primary storage of excess nutrients taken in during a meal occurs in the GI phase, when insulin is released in response to the absorption of nutrients from the gut.

Metabolism during the Fasting State

Eventually, the influx of energy from the gut no longer exceeds the body's energy usage requirements. The body must then shift from putting energy into storage to getting it out of storage. This shift in the energy balance occurs, for example, after strenuous exercise or after a prolonged fast. Most of us are confronted with this situation every morning when we awaken and need to break the nighttime fast, or eat *breakfast*. Energy reserves are mobilized from storage to meet your energy needs as you become active, even prior to eating your first food of the day.

Basically, the metabolic system is designed to provide sufficient levels of energy to the brain, which must receive a constant supply of energy, and then to the rest of the body. In a strict priority system, the brain is at the front of the line for glucose, via the blood. When glucose is scarce, the peripheral tissues are able to oxidize free fatty acids, sparing glucose for the central nervous system because the brain cannot process fatty acids for fuel. During long-term food deprivation, the rest of the body is literally starved of glucose to feed the brain.

After fasting, ketones are formed, and these can also be used by the brain when glucose is scarce. Glucagon release, gluconeogenesis (the production of glucose from amino acids in the liver), and sympathetic stimulation of fat breakdown are the most common mechanisms for raising blood sugar levels without eating, but there are additional methods of elevating blood glucose levels during emergencies to keep a relatively constant level of energy supplied to the brain. After prolonged fasting or very demanding exercise, low levels of insulin, sympathetic release of norepinephrine, and increased levels of glucagon and growth hormone can trigger lipolysis in the fat cells. Furthermore, corticosterone or cortisol released during vigorous exercise can induce lipolysis and gluconeogenesis. During stress, epinephrine from the adrenal medulla acts to stimulate **glycogenolysis**, the breakdown of stored glycogen in the liver.

During the fasting state, cells in the periphery switch from metabolizing glucose for ATP production to metabolizing free fatty acids mobilized from the lipids stored in adipose tissue. The switchover to using free fatty acids spares glucose for the brain. This same mode of metabolism occurs not only when we are fasting but when we are not consuming carbohydrates. Thus, the fasting metabolism is characteristic of individuals on low-carbohydrate diets.

Because the brain receives a relatively constant supply of glucose, you might guess that the detectors for changes in blood sugar levels might not be found in the brain, but rather in the periphery, where blood glucose changes are more pronounced. Logical as this assumption may be, there are several lines of evidence that suggest that there are CNS cells that can sense changes in glucose oxidation, although metabolic fuel detectors are located in the brain and liver, muscle, and fat cells.

There are several physiological methods of getting energy out of storage and into the bloodstream during a fast. The metabolic interactions that occur in a fasting individual are shown in **FIGURE 9.18B**. First, glycogenolysis breaks down stored glycogen in the liver and provides a rapid supply of glucose to the blood. Under extreme conditions, such as during strenuous exercise, glycogenolysis in muscle provides the extra energy for the physical work. Second, **lipolysis**, the breakdown of triglycerides stored in adipose tissue into free fatty acids and glycerol, provides oxidizable fuels for peripheral tissues. During fasting, the protein hormone glucagon is released from the α-cells of the pancreas, whereas the secretion of insulin from the pancreas is inhibited (Steffens et al., 1990). Glucagon induces both lipolysis and glycogenolysis.

Stored energy in the body can also be released via the sympathetic nervous system. The sympathetic system generally acts as an emergency system, although input to all organs can shift to favor the sympathetic or parasympathetic system in day-to-day regulation as well. Sympathetic nerves that innervate the fat cells can induce lipolysis (Steffens et al., 1990). The liver is also innervated with sympathetic nerves that may signal it to release stored glycogen (Sawchenko and Friedman, 1979).

Another backup system that is used during fasting is a process called **gluconeogenesis**, in which glucose is produced from amino acids. Gluconeogenesis takes place entirely in the liver and results in the production of ketone bodies as a side reaction; ketone production also results from the incomplete oxidation of free fatty acids (Friedman, 1990). Prolonged fasting, during which muscles are used for energy, produces toxic levels of ketone bodies, a condition called ketosis; the most

glycogenolysis   The breakdown of stored glycogen in the liver or muscles to provide a steady supply of glucose for energy.

lipolysis   The breakdown of adipose tissue into free fatty acids.

gluconeogenesis   The production of glucose from amino acids, a process that occurs in the liver in response to mild fasting.

serious effect of ketosis is the resulting change in blood pH, which has a deleterious effect on neural function. Diabetics with uncontrolled blood sugar levels can also enter ketosis when insufficient insulin is provided and may suffer serious consequences if blood pH fluctuations are prolonged. Similarly, people on long-term carbohydrate-free diets can enter ketosis.

Deranged Energy Metabolism

Problems with getting energy into cells (where it is either oxidized or stored) are common. Again, insulin is the major actor in this physiological drama, and many metabolic difficulties occur if there are any problems with insulin secretion or insulin-receptor interactions. The best-known such disorders are the two types of diabetes mellitus: type 1 and type 2. Type 1 diabetes (also referred to as insulin-dependent diabetes) is an autoimmune disorder in which the β-cells of the pancreas are destroyed by the immune system and an insulin deficiency results. Type 1 diabetes usually has a rapid onset. It is most common among children and young adults and in the past was commonly called childhood diabetes. Type 2 diabetes begins when some tissues develop insensitivity to insulin, the hormone that is required for glucose uptake into cells. When the cells that are critical for daily activity become insensitive to insulin, the intracellular energy deficit triggers increased insulin secretion. Adipose tissue cells are usually the last to become insensitive to insulin, thus when nonadipose tissue cells in liver and muscle become insensitive to insulin, the increased insulin shunts fuels into storage in adipose tissue. This combination of intracellular energy deficit and predisposition toward lipogenesis increases appetite, food intake, and body weight gain. Type 2 diabetes usually develops slowly in adults, and during the early stages this disorder can be controlled by diet; insulin treatment is usually not required. Indeed, most type 2 diabetics have higher than average concentrations of circulating insulin. This type of diabetes is associated with obesity, stress, or menopause. Although the onset of type 2 diabetes is usually after the age of 40, the incidence of type 2 diabetes is rising among increasingly younger obese individuals (**FIGURE 9.19**). Thus, the terms *juvenile* and **adult** *onset* are no longer useful to distinguish the diabetes types. With the worldwide increase in childhood obesity rates, type 2 diabetes is becoming epidemic. In 2005, type 2 diabetes accounted for 45% of new cases among adolescents (Pinhas-Hamiel and Zeitler, 2005); contemporary estimates suggest that more than 60% of new cases of diabetes among children and adolescents are type 2.

Individuals with either type of diabetes have difficulty moving surplus glucose out of the blood into tissues where it is oxidized. Consequently, diabetes is characterized by several conditions: **hyperphagia** (elevated appetite); extremely high levels of glucose remaining in the blood, a condition that is commonly known as high blood sugar (hyperglycemia); and increased thirst and urination. High glucose concentrations in the blood are highly toxic and damaging to both the nervous and circulatory systems, which can lead to neuropathy, poor circulation, and blindness. Some of this excess glucose is excreted in the urine, giving the urine of diabetics a characteristic sweetness; hence the name of the disorder (*diabetes*, "run through," and *mellitus*, "sweet"). Left uncontrolled, type 2 diabetics can cause the pancreas to stop producing insulin, requiring the use of exogenous insulin.

Insulin has been used to illustrate the role of peripheral metabolic fuels in control of appetite and food intake. For example, because diabetic animals have difficulty moving glucose out of the blood and into tissues to be oxidized, diabetic animals can be used as experimental subjects to examine the importance of fuel oxidation in control of food intake. Is food intake controlled by the amount of fuels in circulation or, alternatively, by the intracellular availability of oxidizable fuels? If oxidizable fuels are the most important variable controlling food intake, then it would be expected that food intake would be vastly increased in animals fed diets high in fuels

hyperphagia   Excessive hunger or elevated appetite

(A)

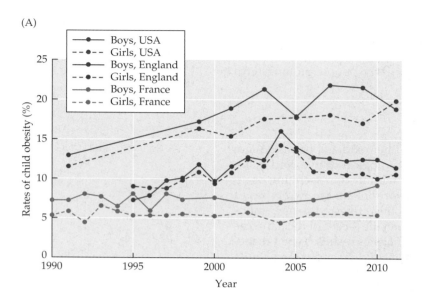

FIGURE 9.19 Incidence of obesity is increasing worldwide. (A) The incidence of obesity is increasing in children at an alarming rate. (B) Obesity in the adult population is increasing rapidly across the United States. The colors indicate the percentage of obese adults in each state. A after OECD Obesity Update, 2014; B after CDC Behavioral Risk Factor Surveillance System, 2014.

(B)

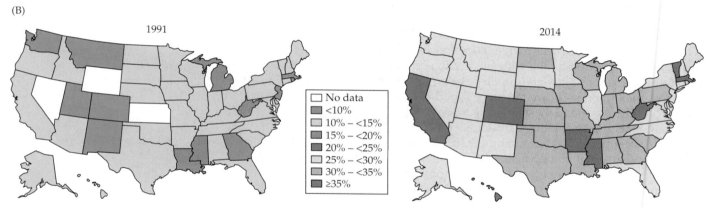

that cannot be oxidized, and food intake would be restored to normal in animals fed readily oxidizable fuels. Diabetic animals, lacking insulin, cannot transport glucose into cells for oxidation, but they readily oxidize fatty acids. Indeed, diabetic animals overeat (are hyperphagic) on a high-carbohydrate diet but eat normally on a high-fat diet, consistent with the idea that food intake is responsive to those fuels that can be readily oxidized, rather than to fuels circulating in the bloodstream (Friedman, 1978; Tepper and Friedman, 1991). The importance of oxidizable fuels is reinforced by the observation that food intake increases in rats treated with 2-deoxy-D-glucose, a glucose analog that inhibits glucose oxidation as it increases glucose concentrations in the blood circulation (Friedman and Tordoff, 1986).

In contrast to diabetes mellitus, a condition exists in which individuals produce too much insulin, called hyperinsulinemia (Friedman, 1990). Hyperinsulinemia that is not due to insulin resistance results in increased glucose uptake, inhibited lipolysis, and concomitant low blood sugar. Hyperinsulinemia also usually leads to marked obesity because individuals with this condition are always hungry, have difficulty losing body fat, and eat frequently. Do these hyperinsulinemic individuals have high levels of insulin because they are obese and somewhat insulin resistant (see below), or are they obese *because* they have high levels of insulin? It should be emphasized here that not all obese people are hyperinsulinemic. There is no straightforward answer to this question in humans, and the issue remains unresolved. Certainly there is evidence that some people may be overly responsive to the cephalic phase of insulin release and become obese because they actually experience greater "hunger" at mealtime than individuals with normal cephalic insulin responsiveness. The appetite of such patients is huge, and they eat larger and longer meals than individuals with a normal cephalic insulin response. There also may be hyper-responsiveness to the GI phase of insulin release in some obese patients. Problems with the mobilization of fat stores, or with the monitoring of blood glucose levels or adiposity signals, may also be involved in obesity (Friedman, 1990; Seeley and Woods, 2003; Woods and D'Alessio, 2008). The obese person or animal may not be able to mobilize normally the fat stores already present, so these individuals must eat frequently to meet their normal energy demands, and thus they continue to deposit more and more fat. Nonetheless, it is becoming increasingly clear that the immune, endocrine, and metabolic systems are tightly integrated, and obesity deranges the coupling among these systems, leading to impaired metabolic signaling and function (Kalin et al., 2015; Osborn and Olefsky, 2012). Tumor necrosis factor (TNF), for example, is a pro-inflammatory cytokine that suppresses food intake. This molecule was originally called cachectin because it was associated with the cachexia (dramatic reduction in food intake and wasting body mass) associated with major infections or cancer (Tracey and Cerami, 1990). TNF administration reduces intake of food whether it is given centrally or peripherally (Begg and Woods, 2013).

Many hormones are involved in maintaining energy balance, and presumably, some of these hormones affect the behavioral systems that are important in maintaining energetic homeostasis. However, despite considerable progress during the past decade, the precise role that hormones play in mediating food intake and body mass has not been completely identified. Our inability to link hormones to ingestive behaviors is due to a lack of consensus regarding the stimuli eliciting hunger, as well as to the discovery of a seemingly endless supply of new peptides involved in the regulation of food intake.

In summary, the fasting state is characterized by low circulating concentrations of certain hormones (insulin and leptin) and elevated concentrations of other hormones (glucagon and glucocorticoids) as well as neuropeptides (NPY), corticotropin-releasing hormone (CRH), and metabolic substrates (free fatty acids and ketone bodies). Eating results in a reversal of all of these parameters. All of these changes in metabolic fuels, hormones, and neuropeptides are correlated with one another. Which aspects of these changes serve as signals to the neural mechanisms that control energy balance? Do one or all of these factors elicit hunger or control ingestion? Recent work has provided a detailed model of regulation of food intake in mammals (see below) and has confirmed that several overlapping, redundant systems are involved in the regulation of food intake and energy balance (Field et al., 2010; Moran, 2009; Woods and D'Alessio, 2008).

Primary Sensory Signals and Secondary Mediators

One way to make sense of all this complexity is to organize the signals into three categories: (1) preparatory factors, (2) primary sensory signals, and (3) secondary mediators or modulators. Preparatory or anticipatory factors cause changes in plasma concentrations of hormones such as NPY and ghrelin before a meal (Drazen and Woods, 2003; Drazen et al., 2006b). Primary sensory signals are those biochemical changes that result when fuels are metabolized to generate cellular energy. For example, changes in glucose metabolism might serve to generate the primary sensory signal that controls insulin secretion. Other metabolic sensory stimuli include changes in the availability of free fatty acids and ATP.

Several studies indicate that individuals on fixed meal schedules (such as most individuals in school or work environments) produce a significant anticipatory increase in circulating ghrelin. For example, rats given their daily food provisions during a 4-hour window displayed a marked increase in plasma ghrelin (Drazen and Woods, 2003). Humans, both obese and of normal weight, also show a similar response (Cummings et al., 2001, 2002). Individuals who have undergone a gastric bypass procedure fail to show the anticipatory ghrelin elevation, which may be related to the reduction in meal size and altered satiety (Cummings et al., 2002). Indeed, gastric bypass patients tend to have five to seven small meals distributed throughout the day, which may eliminate the anticipatory ghrelin responses. Importantly, many of the symptoms of type 2 diabetes resolve virtually immediately after bypass surgery, but prior to loss of significant body mass (Cummings et al., 2004).

The primary sensory signals control the secretion of secondary modulators: the neuropeptides and hormones that influence food intake. Hormones and neuropeptides may have direct effects on mechanisms that control food intake, or they may have indirect effects on food intake via their effects on energy metabolism. Another way to organize the endocrine signals regulating food intake is to categorize them as either *peripheral* (originating outside the nervous system) or *central* (originating inside the nervous system). But even this classification system has issues, as many gut hormones can both provide peripheral signals from the digestive tract and serve as neuromodulators in the brain. Thus, the categories below are not mutually exclusive.

Control of Food Intake

What regulates food intake? We eat because of a variety of external and internal cues, many of which we learn to associate with meal intake. How much food, what kind of food, when we start a meal, and when we stop a meal are all important questions when considering the control of food intake. Other extrinsic factors, such as who is eating with us, where we are eating, time of day, and stressors we are experiencing, can also affect food intake (Moran, 2009; Woods and D'Alessio, 2008). Researchers seem to be reaching a consensus that obesity is not the result of gluttons overeating and consequently becoming fat, but rather, it is the other way around: the process of getting fat makes individuals very hungry. It starts out by people eating the wrong types of calorically dense foods that derange hormonal homeostatic processes, setting off a pattern of cravings, hunger, and more overeating (Walsh et al., 2013). Even genome-wide association studies (GWAS) have revealed more than 32 candidate obesity genes, most of which are expressed in or act on the brain (Yeo and Heisler, 2012). Perhaps these genes are involved in driving the consumption of sugar or fatty foods that drives the increased hunger; obviously additional research is necessary to definitively sort out the regulation of food intake.

An American television show called *The Biggest Loser* chronicles the rapid weight loss of several obese individuals over the course of several months. Participants are guided in a regimen of reduced food portions and increased exercise by enthusiastic and demanding trainers and dieticians. All of the participants on the show lose substantial amounts of body mass. A recent study of individuals after their experience on the show revealed persistent metabolic adaptations 6 years later in 14 of the original 16 participants (Fothergill et al., 2016). The average weight loss was about 60 kg per individual, although some individuals lost much more. Six years after their dramatic body weight losses, virtually all of the contestants had gained back an average 70% of their lost weight, and some had gained additional weight (**FIGURE 9.20**). More troubling is that the people who had lost substantial weight displayed reduced metabolic rates. Indeed, some of the folks who had lost the most weight displayed the slowest metabolic adaptation (Forthergill et al., 2016)—essentially, one Big Mac would be sufficient to account for the entire resting (or basal) metabolic rate (~550 kcal/day) in some of these dieters. Thus, their brains were directing their bodies to work very hard to regain the former body mass. This and previous studies (e.g., Rosenbaum et al., 2008) suggest that the body develops a set point that it defends vigorously. If a man weighing 136 kg (300 pounds) drops his body mass to 91 kg (200 pounds), then his metabolic rate will likely slow down

FIGURE 9.20 Body weight loss is difficult to maintain Sean Algaier, a minister from North Carolina, weighed in at 200 kg (444 pounds) prior to the show and weighed 131 kg (289 pounds) at the finale. As of 2016 he weighed 204 kg (450 pounds), and his resting metabolic rate burned 458 kcal less than is typical for a man his size.

until the original body mass has been regained. If exercise is added, it appears, metabolic rate will fall in response to defend this body mass. This defense of set point is a cardinal feature of homeostasis. The average person will consume between 900,000 and 1,000,000 kcal per year, and most will burn all those calories with great precision until middle age when about 3000–6000 kcal per year will not be burned, leading to 0.5–1 kg body weight increase per year. This is a highly precise, complex homeostatic system involving several satiety hormones as well as hunger hormones. Environmental factors such as time of day or stressors can also influence hormones that may derange energy homeostatic processes.

Eating is an extraordinarily complex process that involves several intrinsic inputs, including the amount of fat stored in the body, the levels of glycogen stored in the liver, the biochemical qualities of the food being digested, neural and endocrine signals from the gut, and even the perceived pleasantness of the food (Morley et al., 1985a). Extrinsic factors, such as food availability and, particularly among humans, psychological and cultural influences, also regulate food intake. All of these intrinsic and extrinsic factors are integrated in the central nervous system to mediate feeding behavior. The difficulty of inducing hunger experimentally stands in sharp contrast to the ease with which thirst can be induced and has prompted the hypothesis that no single stimulus or set of stimuli exists for hunger (Stricker, 1984). **Hunger**, a strong motivation to seek out and ingest food, can thus be broadly considered the psychological state experienced by individuals as satiety from a previous meal wanes. Somehow the body monitors long-term energy stores as well as food intake in relation to energy utilization. As we will see below, the endocrine system is central in this behavior (see Table 9.3).

Peripheral Signals

Animals are able to maintain body mass and energy stores and monitor incoming and expended energy. How does the brain monitor energy and regulate food intake? Two main hypotheses emerged in the mid-20th century. One suggested that the hypothalamus monitors the storage and use of triglycerides (the "lipostat" hypothesis) (Kennedy, 1953). A competing hypothesis suggested that the hypothala-

hunger Motivational state provoking food intake.

mus monitored the storage and use of glucose (the "glucostat" hypothesis) (Mayer, 1955). Synthesis of these two ideas has led to the "metabolic" or "energostatic" hypothesis, which posits that food intake is responsive to the final common metabolic events in metabolism leading to the phosphorylation of ATP (Friedman, 2008).

Although the field has moved beyond the notion that food intake is regulated in service of maintaining *either* a particular body weight *or* a particular level of circulating glucose, *The Biggest Loser* contestants' altered metabolic resting states suggest that the body does seem to defend a specific level of body fat once attained. We have progressed to the idea that food intake is regulated in service of intracellular metabolism. In other words, there is a sensory system that monitors metabolic fuel oxidation and changes food intake, energy expenditure, and body fat storage and breakdown to maintain a constant supply of metabolic fuels for intracellular oxidation. Recent work has linked food intake control to various "nutrient sensing" substrates and enzymes involved in metabolic steps leading to changes in ATP concentrations, such as adenosine monophosphate-activated protein kinase (AMPK) and the mammalian target of rapamycin (mTOR) (Kahn and Myers, 2006; Minokoshi et al., 2004). Investigators studying AMPK and mTOR have noted that these compounds are sensitive to intracellular fuel availability and actually mediate some of the feeding effects of hormones, such as leptin, and neuropeptides, such as α-melanocyte-stimulating hormone (α-MSH) (Hayes et al., 2009; Maya-Monteiro and Bozza, 2008). Researchers who had previously focused exclusively on hormonal signaling have now turned their attention to the integration of metabolic sensory systems and the hormonal signals that control ingestive behavior (Seeley and Woods, 2003; Stefater and Seeley, 2010).

Recall from Chapter 1 that leptin is an **adipokine** hormone (produced by the adipose cells) that was heralded as a "satiety hormone." It has only limited use as a treatment for obesity and, in nature, is more likely to serve other important functions, including orchestration of sexual and feeding behaviors. Leptin circulates in concentrations that are proportional to the total amount of fat in the body. When stored fat is being used for energy, the blood levels of leptin fall faster than the levels of fat being metabolized; this rapid reduction in circulating leptin suggests that this hormone is more likely a "starvation" signal, that is, a signal that stimulates food intake when leptin levels fall, rather than a satiety hormone that curtails food intake when body fat levels and leptin levels increase (Flier, 1998). The contestants on *The Biggest Loser* started out on the show with leptin concentrations in the normal range. At the finale, they had virtually no detectable leptin at all (Fothergill et al., 2016)—making them ravenously hungry.

Consistent with the notion that leptin is unlikely to be a satiety hormone, years of research show that leptin treatments are unsuccessful in reversing human obesity, except in the very rare cases of congenital leptin deficiency (Dardeno et al., 2010). Leptin treatment does, however, reverse nutritional amenorrhea in women with anorexia nervosa (the side effects of this treatment are as yet unknown) (Dardeno et al., 2010), and it increases sexual motivation in laboratory animals. The effects of leptin on feeding behavior are exaggerated when the experimental subjects have a choice between eating and sex, in line with the idea that leptin, and perhaps other peptides, evolved to orchestrate short-term changes in behavioral priorities (Ammar et al., 2000; Schneider et al., 2007). Although these leptin-induced changes in the preference for food over sex likely increase reproductive success in habitats where energy availability fluctuates, the rise in obesity rates worldwide raises questions about the role of leptin in limiting body weight and adiposity (Schneider et al., 2007). Nevertheless, with the recognition in the mid-1990s that leptin is the protein encoded by the *ob* gene, rapid progress has been made in understanding the signals associated with energy balance.

Leptin receptors are located in several peripheral and brain regions; the arcuate nuclei of the hypothalamus, adjacent to the third ventricle, have the highest con-

adipokine   Cytokines (cell signaling proteins) secreted by adipose tissue. Leptin was the first adipokine discovered in 1994.

FIGURE 9.21 **GI hormones serve as satiety signals that converge on the dorsal hindbrain,** where they are integrated with chemosensory, taste, and other signals. The dorsal hindbrain directly connects to the ventral hindbrain, where neural circuits direct the autonomic nervous system to influence blood glucose and where the motor control over feeding behavior is located. The dorsal hindbrain also sends information about satiation and other factors forward to the hypothalamus and other brain areas that integrate both satiety and adiposity signals with nutrients, previous experience, social context and stressors, time of day, season of year, and other factors. The integrated information then converges and moves back to the ventral hindbrain, as well as to the pituitary, to influence all aspects of energy homeostasis. ARC = arcuate nuclei. After Woods and D'Alessio, 2008.

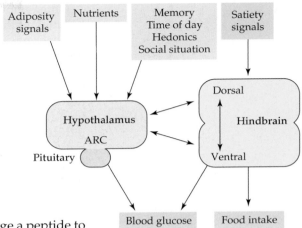

centration of leptin receptors (Schwartz et al., 1996). Leptin is too large a peptide to cross the blood-brain barrier. Thus, an active transport mechanism ferries leptin into the brain. Elevated leptin levels signal the hypothalamus that fat stores are increasing, which inhibits eating, and signal the reproductive system that sufficient calories are stored to support reproduction (Schneider et al., 2007; Tena-Sempere, 2007). The effects of leptin on food intake and reproduction might occur via the well-known effects of leptin on fuel oxidation, because the effects of leptin are blocked by treatments that influence metabolic fuel oxidation or the nutrient-sensing enzyme AMPK (Hayes et al., 2009; Schneider and Zhou, 1999). In contrast, low leptin levels inform the hypothalamus of reduced fat stores, which stimulates eating (Flier, 1998; Seeley and Woods, 2003; Woods and D'Alessio, 2008) **(FIGURE 9.21)**.

Another adiposity signal is insulin, and increased attention has focused on the role of insulin in the mediation of feeding behavior. There is an obvious association between insulin release and meal termination; hunger ensues when insulin levels drop at the end of the postabsorptive phase (Strubbe et al., 1977). Treatment of rats with streptozotocin, a drug that selectively destroys the pancreatic β-cells and induces diabetes, also causes long-term hyperphagia, demonstrating that lack of insulin can interfere with satiety. It has also been proposed that insulin signals the central nervous system about peripheral levels of metabolic fuels via the cerebrospinal fluid (CSF) (Woods and Porte, 1983). Insulin levels increase in the CSF of baboons immediately after a meal or an intravenous glucose injection (Woods et al., 1981), and ICV infusions of insulin reduce food intake and body mass in baboons (Woods et al., 1979).

Several researchers have suggested that tonic levels of central insulin (i.e., insulin in the brain) serve as an important signal to keep body mass and food intake within a healthy range. Thus, obesity might arise from impaired sensitivity to the central insulin signal (Schwartz et al., 1992; Woods et al., 1996). Although insulin concentrations vary substantially before and after a meal, as well as throughout the day, insulin secretion is affected by the amount of stored fat. That is, obese people and animals have relatively high circulating insulin levels, whereas lean people and animals have relatively low circulating insulin levels. Thus, it has been posited that insulin, like leptin, serves as an indicator of fat stores (Schwartz et al., 2000). Infusion of insulin directly into the cerebral ventricles of the brain decreases food intake and causes animals to maintain their body mass at lower levels than before insulin treatment (Chavez et al., 1996). Importantly, insulin receptors are located in the brain, especially in the arcuate nuclei (Baskin et al., 1994). Recall that the brain does not require insulin for glucose to enter cells. Why, therefore, would insulin receptors be located in the arcuate nuclei? It has long been proposed that these insulin receptors monitor metabolic fuels, namely glucose; leptin- and insulin-receptive neurons in the arcuate nuclei integrate this information to affect energy balance by acting on specific hypothalamic circuits (Field et al., 2010; Moran, 2009; Seeley and Woods, 2003).

Other evidence suggests that insulin induces satiety not directly but by its facilitation of the use and storage of ingested carbohydrates (Stricker, 1984) and via feedback mechanisms involving other hormones as well as the autonomic nervous system (Steffens et al., 1990). It is also possible that the oxidation of metabolic fuels itself generates some kind of signal that controls food intake; thus, the storage and mobilization of fat may indirectly affect food intake by changing the rate of oxidation of metabolic fuels. When neither fatty acids nor glucose are available in the blood for oxidation, as monitored primarily by the liver, then feeding might be induced (Friedman, 1990). The evidence for this idea is that plasma insulin concentrations are often correlated with body fat content, and as noted previously in this chapter, it is difficult to determine whether insulin has direct effects on the mechanisms that control food intake or whether it changes food intake through indirect effects on metabolic fuel availability and oxidation.

One way to dissociate the direct and indirect effects of insulin is to measure food intake in diabetic rats fed different diets (Friedman, 1978; Friedman et al., 1985; Tepper and Friedman, 1991). Diabetic rats, of course, have reduced plasma insulin concentrations, and they eat more food than nondiabetic rats. Untreated diabetic rats also eat more food than diabetic rats treated with insulin (considered alone, these data support the notion that insulin acts in the brain to decrease food intake). However, untreated diabetic rats ate more food than normal rats when fed a low-fat, high-carbohydrate diet, but not when fed a high-fat, low-carbohydrate diet. Thus, insulin concentrations were not the critical determinant of food intake, because rats in both groups had equivalent low levels of insulin. The different levels of food intake can be explained by the differences in metabolic fuel availability in the diets fed to the diabetic rats. Insulin is necessary for peripheral glucose uptake and, therefore, for the utilization of carbohydrate fuels. The diabetic rats could readily oxidize fats, but not carbohydrates. Consequently, the diabetic rats on the low-fat, high-carbohydrate diet may have been stimulated to overeat by their inability to oxidize the type of fuels that they were ingesting. In contrast, the diabetic rats on a high-fat, low-carbohydrate diet were better able to oxidize the fuels that they were ingesting and thus did not overeat (Friedman, 1978; Friedman et al., 1985). It is true that when pharmacological doses of insulin are given, metabolic changes in both the body and the brain occur.

Many investigators report significant effects on food intake when the blood-brain barrier is breached and peripheral hormones or antibodies to these hormones are artificially placed into the brain. For example, when antibodies to insulin are infused into the central nervous system, animals eat more with no observable effects on metabolism (McGowan et al., 1990). These results imply direct, rather than indirect, effects of insulin, and yet it is difficult to know whether these results are accurately representative of what occurs in the brain naturally after meals or after fasting.

GHRELIN Virtually all of the GI tract hormones—pancreatic polypeptide (PP), peptide YY (PYY), and glucagon-like peptide 1 (GLP-1)—reduce food intake and body mass (**TABLE 9.4**). However, one hormone from the GI tract, ghrelin, induces profound increases in food intake. Ghrelin came to our attention when small artificial molecules were discovered that could stimulate growth hormone (GH) secretion from the anterior pituitary but were not related to the endogenous growth hormone–releasing hormone released by the hypothalamus. They acted through G protein receptors (Fry and Ferguson, 2010). An endogenous ligand for these so-called GH secretagogue receptors was discovered in rat stomachs and was named ghrelin (Kojima et al., 1999). The name is appropriate for two reasons: its first two letters serve as a mnemonic of GH, and *ghre* is the Proto-Indo-European root for the word *grow*. Soon it was discovered that systemic injections of ghrelin stimulated food intake and increased body mass in rats (Wren et al., 2001). Blood concentrations of ghrelin peaked around the time of meal onset (Cummings et al., 2001). ICV injections of ghrelin strongly stimulated feeding in rats and increased body weight gain (Nakazato et al., 2001). Expression of ghrelin was discovered in a group of neurons adjacent to the third ventricle, between the dorsal, ventral, paraventricular, and arcuate hypothalamic nuclei (Cowley et al., 2001). These neurons send axons onto key hypothalamic circuits, including those producing pro-opiomelanocortin (POMC) products, CRH, and especially NPY/agouti-related protein (AgRP). Ghrelin stimulated activity of NPY neurons in the arcuate nuclei and mimicked the effects of NPY in the PVN (Cowley et al., 2003).

Ghrelin seems to work in opposition to leptin (Tena-Sempere, 2007). The two hormones exert opposite effects on hypothalamic neurons that produce the anorectic neuromodulator α-MSH, as well as on the orexigenic peptides AgRP and NPY. The circulating concentrations of ghrelin and leptin are inversely correlated, and they are tightly associated in the regulation of energy balance, food intake, and body mass (Tena-Sempere, 2007). The two hormones also play opposing roles in the regulation of reproductive function (Shah and Nyby, 2010; Tena-Sempere, 2008). Leptin generally is permissive of reproductive function; high leptin concentrations are an indicator of sufficient metabolic fuels to support successful reproductive efforts. Ghrelin, on the other hand, is inhibitory at every level of the hypothalamic-pituitary-gonadal axis (Tena-Sempere, 2008). Even a single acute exposure to ghrelin is sufficient to suppress male ultrasonic mating calls in male mice (Shah and Nyby, 2010).

As in Syrian hamsters, fasting increases foraging and hoarding but not food intake in Siberian hamsters (*Phodopus sungorus*) (Keen-Rhinehart and Bartness, 2005). Treatment with exogenous ghrelin mimics fasting to increase appetitive behaviors such as foraging and hoarding by Siberian hamsters, but unlike fasting, ghrelin also stimulates food intake in this species (Keen-Rhinehart and Bartness, 2005).

TABLE 9.4	*Gut hormones that affect satiety*
Peptide	**Effect on food intake**
CCK (cholecystokinin)	Decrease
GLP-1 (glucagon-like peptide 1)	Decrease
PYY (peptide YY)	Decrease
Apo (apolipoprotein) A-IV	Decrease
Enterostatin	Decrease
Bombesin/GRP (gastrin-releasing peptide)/NMB (neuromedin B)	Decrease
Oxyntomodulin	Decrease
Amylin	Decrease
Ghrelin	Increase

Central Signals: The Role of the Hypothalamus

How does activation of these insulin, leptin, and ghrelin receptors in the arcuate nuclei affect energy food intake? It was believed for over two decades that mammalian feeding was regulated in a simple way, with two separate centers in the brain controlling hunger and satiety.

A "hunger center" that facilitated eating was hypothesized to reside in the lateral hypothalamus area (LHA), because bilateral destruction of this brain region led to nearly complete **anorexia** (loss of appetite) and subsequent **aphagia** (absence of feeding behavior) in cats and rats (Anand and Brobeck, 1951). Similarly, a "satiety center" that inhibited feeding was hypothesized to be located in the ventromedial hypothalamus (VMH), because lesions of this brain area resulted in hyperphagia and enormous, rapid weight gain (Hetherington and Ranson, 1940). This dual-center theory of the control of feeding was very pervasive in shaping the research and theoretical framework in which experimental outcomes were interpreted (Stellar, 1954). The LHA and the VMH became the key components of putative regulatory systems involving blood glucose (the glucostat hypothesis) and triglyceride (the lipostat hypothesis) levels (Stricker, 1984).

Additional research displaced the dual-center theory of feeding regulation. Bilateral lesions of the lateral hypothalamus were shown to interfere with all motivated behaviors, not just feeding (Marshall et al., 1971). Lesions made anywhere along the dopaminergic tracts that pass through the lateral hypothalamus area from the midbrain to the striatum while sparing the hypothalamic tissue produce behavioral deficits similar to those resulting from lesions of the lateral hypothalamus itself

anorexia   Lack or loss of appetite or lack of voluntary food intake.

aphagia   Inability or voluntary refusal to swallow.

(Stricker et al., 1979). Other evidence suggests that the VMH is not a center for satiety but part of a complex circuit that regulates feeding via the autonomic nervous system and its effects on energy metabolism, as well as mediating many other types of motivated behaviors. Lesions of the VMH suppress sympathetic nervous system activities while increasing parasympathetic nervous activities, resulting in increased storage of fat while inhibiting lipolysis. This excessive storage of energy as fat leaves a shortage of energy to maintain the animal's daily processes. Consequently, VMH-lesioned animals develop voracious appetites, not because a satiety center has been damaged, but in order to maintain a steady delivery of metabolic fuel from the intestines. Eventually, as the animals become obese, the fat cells become insulin resistant—that is, they no longer respond to insulin by taking up more glucose. Thus, food intake and body weight stabilize at this new elevated level, at what is called a new set point. We now know that these lesions disrupt important neural circuits involved in food intake.

The dual-center hypothesis has been replaced by strong evidence for multiple integrated neural circuits that encompass areas of the hind-, mid- and forebrain and receive neural, hormonal, and direct metabolic input from the periphery. In the past, researchers who examined food intake failed to examine energy expenditure, locomotion, and thermogenesis, and those who focused on physiological measures did not examine food intake or other behaviors. Recent evidence, however, indicates that very precise, low-dose infusions of hormones and neuropeptides into discrete brain nuclei affect multiple behavioral and physiological aspects of energy intake, storage, and expenditure; very little separation of function has been found. Thus, ideas about energy intake control in one area separate from energy expenditure control in another are not well supported (Grill, 2006, 2009; Grill and Hayes, 2009).

In addition, the neuroendocrine system that controls food intake does so via both direct and indirect effects on energy partitioning. The direct effect is also known as the metabolic or energostatic hypothesis, the evidence for which has been described above. The oxidation of metabolic fuels creates a signal that is detected by sensory neurons in areas such as the stomach and liver. Signals are sent from these areas via the vagus nerve to the dorsal motor nucleus of the vagus to the area postrema and the nucleus of the solitary tract. From these brain stem areas, signals are sent to the pontine parabrachial nucleus and then to the forebrain, including areas of the hypothalamus. Reciprocal input comes from sensory and higher cortical centers to the hypothalamus. The actions involved in feeding and foraging and the associated physiological events are mediated via descending pathways through hindbrain motor areas.

Research on food intake has focused on the hypothalamus (e.g., the VMH and LHA) and the preoptic area for the past 50 years, although it is now known that areas of the midbrain and brain stem contain many of the same neuropeptides that influence food intake in the hypothalamus. The arcuate nuclei of the hypothalamus contain two opposing sets of neuronal circuitry: (1) a feeding stimulatory circuit and (2) a feeding inhibitory circuit (**FIGURE 9.22**). Both circuits send signals primarily to the PVN but also to other nuclei of the hypothalamus, which then directly modulate feeding behavior. The feeding stimulatory and feeding inhibitory circuits are modulated by peripheral hormonal signals that cross (or are transported across) the blood-brain barrier, such as leptin, insulin, ghrelin, and peptide YY$_{3-36}$ (Gale et al., 2004; Klok et al., 2007).

The feeding stimulatory circuit produces two neurotransmitters: NPY and AgRP, both of which stimulate

FIGURE 9.22 Body adiposity is linked to compensatory changes in food intake. Leptin and insulin signals are secreted in proportion to the levels of fat stored in the body. When elevated, these two hormones act on central effector circuits in the hypothalamus. Leptin and insulin inhibit the anabolic brain circuits that curb energy use and stimulate eating, but they activate catabolic brain circuits that suppress eating and promote energy use. Relatively low leptin and insulin levels during weight loss have just the opposite effect on the anabolic and catabolic brain circuitry. Eating generates neural and endocrine satiety signals in the hindbrain and gut. Leptin and insulin interact with hindbrain satiety circuits to regulate meal size. This accounts for the common experience of following a large meal with a much smaller one to maintain energy balance. After Schwartz et al., 2000.

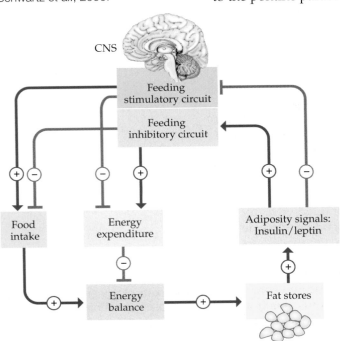

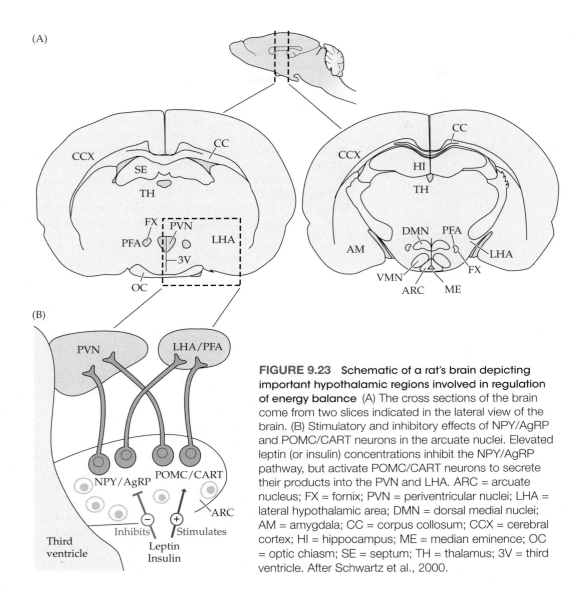

FIGURE 9.23 Schematic of a rat's brain depicting important hypothalamic regions involved in regulation of energy balance (A) The cross sections of the brain come from two slices indicated in the lateral view of the brain. (B) Stimulatory and inhibitory effects of NPY/AgRP and POMC/CART neurons in the arcuate nuclei. Elevated leptin (or insulin) concentrations inhibit the NPY/AgRP pathway, but activate POMC/CART neurons to secrete their products into the PVN and LHA. ARC = arcuate nucleus; FX = fornix; PVN = periventricular nuclei; LHA = lateral hypothalamic area; DMN = dorsal medial nuclei; AM = amygdala; CC = corpus collosum; CCX = cerebral cortex; HI = hippocampus; ME = median eminence; OC = optic chiasm; SE = septum; TH = thalamus; 3V = third ventricle. After Schwartz et al., 2000.

food intake (Schwartz et al., 2000). NPY directly signals the PVN to evoke feeding behavior, whereas AgRP indirectly promotes feeding by blocking the melanocortin type 4 receptor, an appetite inhibitory receptor in the PVN (**FIGURE 9.23**). During an underfed state, leptin and insulin blood concentrations are relatively low. This activates the NPY/AgRP neurons, leading to increased NPY and AgRP secretion, which increases food intake. Once leptin or insulin concentrations in the periphery are elevated, the NPY/AgRP pathway is inhibited.

The feeding inhibitory circuit also has two main signaling molecules: cocaine- and amphetamine-regulated transcript (CART) and POMC. Increased CART secretion in the PVN decreases food intake. POMC produces α-MSH, which operates mainly through the melanocortin type 4 receptor (and to a lesser extent through the melanocortin type 3 receptor) to inhibit appetite. Elevated leptin values activate POMC/CART neurons to secrete their products into the PVN and LHA (Schwartz et al., 2000), and food intake is decreased.

During an underfed state, leptin and insulin blood concentrations are relatively low (**FIGURE 9.24**). This activates the NPY/AgRP neurons and suppresses the POMC/CART neurons in the arcuate nuclei, leading to increased NPY and AgRP

(A) Well-fed state

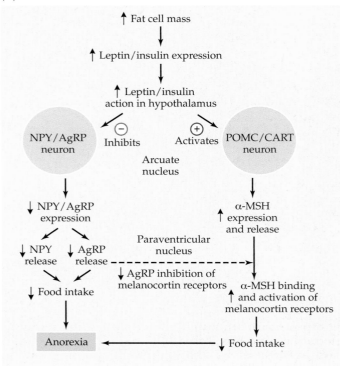

FIGURE 9.24 **Current model of the role of the arcuate nuclei in monitoring metabolic fuels** During the well-fed state (A), the satiety signals, leptin and insulin blood concentrations, are relatively high. The concentrations activate the POMC/CART neurons and inhibit the NPY/AgRP neurons in the arcuate nucleus of the hypothalamus, leading to decreased NPY and AgRP secretion and increased POMC and CART secretion in the PVN, which in turn decrease food intake. Secretion of α-MSH (derived from POMC) in the PVN has an anorexic effect on food intake. During dieting and weight loss (B), the adiposity signals decrease. This stimulates NPY/AgRP neurons and inhibits POMC/CART neurons in the arcuate. NPY release from the PVN has an orexigenic effect, increasing food intake. Unchecked, this process could feed forward, resulting in obesity. After Schwartz et al., 2000.

(B) Reduced food intake

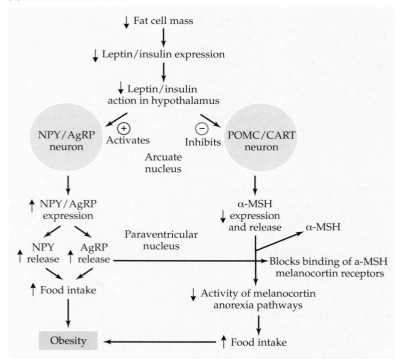

secretion and decreased α-MSH and CART secretion in the PVN, which increases food intake (Gale et al., 2004; Schwartz et al., 2000). This can feed forward, resulting in obesity (Korner and Leibel, 2003).

Ghrelin generally causes the opposite effect as compared with insulin and leptin (Gale et al., 2004). Afferent information about satiety from the liver and from peptides such as CCK or other gut peptides travels via the vagus nerve and sympathetic fibers of the nucleus of the solitary tract. Integration and consolidation of this information leads to termination of a meal. In contrast, reduced adiposity signals (e.g., during restricted caloric intake) may lead to increases in meal size by blocking brain stem responses to satiety signals (Schwartz et al., 2000) (**FIGURE 9.25**).

As noted above, leptin and insulin both interact with receptors on neurons in the arcuate nuclei; thus, the arcuate nuclei are responsive to both circulating adiposity signals. Leptin infused into the arcuate nuclei rapidly suppresses food intake (Satoh et al., 1997). Peptides that act as hormones elsewhere in the body serve as neuromodulators in the arcuate nuclei and have distinct effects on target neurons. Peptides may be anabolic *effectors*, that is, increase appetite and food intake and suppress energy metabolism (**BOX 9.2**). Of course, other peptides are *catabolic effectors*; they tend to decrease appetite and food intake and stimulate metabolism. A few of these anabolic and catabolic effector peptides are briefly described below.

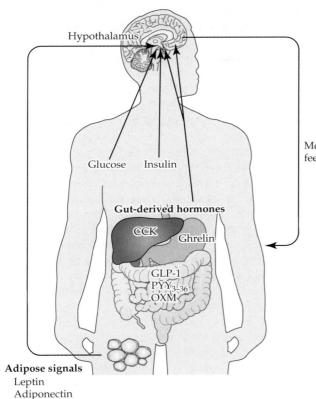

FIGURE 9.25 **Consolidation and integration of endocrine signals regulate food intake** Gut- and adipocyte-derived hormones, reflecting short- and long-term nutritional status, respectively, circulate in the periphery and signal to specific receptors in the brain to regulate food intake. GLP-1 = glucagon-like peptide 1; PYY_{3-36} = peptide YY residues 3–36; OXM = oxyntomodulin; CCK = cholecystokinin. From Yeo and Heisler, 2012.

Central Anabolic Effectors: Peptides That Promote Food Intake

NEUROPEPTIDE Y NPY is a potent activator of food intake in rats and many other species (Levine and Morley, 1984). This **orexigenic** peptide (from the Greek orexis, "appetite") appears to increase motivation to eat; it decreases the amount of food consumed passively (when food is provided directly on the palate), whereas it increases food-seeking and food-hoarding behaviors (Ammar et al., 2005, 2000; Dailey and Bartness, 2009; Flood and Morley, 1991; Woods et al., 1998). ICV injections of NPY, or injections directly into the PVN, evoke marked food and water consumption in rats, both during the day (when these nocturnal animals rarely eat or drink) and at night (Kalra et al., 1991; Levine and Morley, 1984; Stanley and Leibowitz, 1985). NPY interacts with receptors in the PVN to cause hyperphagia. Targeted disruption of the NPY gene reduces hyperphagia and obesity in ob/ob mice (Erickson et al., 1996). NPY neurons project to the PVN, as well as to the LHA. In the LHA, the NPY neurons terminate on neurons that secrete other peptides critical for body mass regulation: orexin and melanin-concentrating hormone (MCH) in the lateral hypothalamus (Elias et al., 1998). There is a reciprocal interaction between NPY and CRH in the hypothalamus. Stress provokes elevated glucocorticoid concentrations, which can interfere with CRH negative feedback on NPY secretion. Thus, stress can cause dysregulation of NPY secretion, leading to overeating and obesity (Dryden et al., 1995); however, treatment of obesity with NPY receptor antagonists has had mixed success at best (e.g., Della-Zuana et al., 2004).

AGOUTI-RELATED PROTEIN The neurons that secrete NPY also secrete another orexigenic peptide with an odd name, agouti-related protein, or AgRP. The path to the discovery that this peptide regulates food intake was circuitous at best. A mouse mutant called *agouti* was instrumental in this discovery. *Agouti* mice have a yellow

orexigenic Substance that stimulates food intake.

BOX 9.2 *Cannabinoids and the "Munchies"*

Marijuana (Cannabis sativa) and derivatives have been used by people for thousands of years (Russo et al., 2008) to provoke a change in mood. To get the active ingredients, including Δ^9-tetrahydrocannabinol (THC), into the body, marijuana is usually smoked or ingested. The subjective effects of smoking marijuana differ across users. For most, relaxation and mood elevation follow ingestion, but some individuals experience stimulation, hallucinations, and paranoia. As with tobacco, there are numerous long-term physical ill effects of smoking this substance. However, one consistent observation among users of marijuana is that THC induces hunger for highly palatable foods.

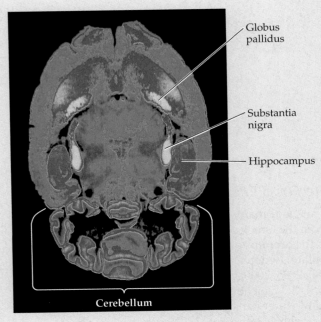

Labels: Globus pallidus; Substantia nigra; Hippocampus; Cerebellum

Cannabinoid Receptors in a Rat Brain   The areas with the highest concentrations of cannabinoid receptors are indicated by warmer colors in this horizontal section of a rat brain. Courtesy of Miles Herkenham, National Institute of Mental Health.

THC interacts with cannabinoid receptors to produce its mood-altering effects (see Figure). So far, two subtypes of these receptors have been identified: CB1 and CB2 receptors (Pertwee, 1997), both of which are G protein-coupled metabotropic receptors. Only CB1 receptors are found in the nervous system. The question arose, of course, of why the brains of humans evolved receptors for THC. Certainly not so college students could elevate their moods in their dorm rooms by smoking marijuana. The hunt was soon on for endogenous ligands to these CB receptors. These substances, termed endocannabinoids, included anandamide (from the Sanskrit *ananda*, which translates as "bliss") (Devane et al., 1992), 2-arachidonylglycerol, and oleamide. Endocannabinoids appear to function to reduce pain responsiveness, protect neurons from excitotoxic damage, modulate learning and memory, and importantly for this chapter, stimulate hunger (DiMarzo, 2008; Heifets and Castillo, 2009).

Given the increasing global problem with obesity, drug companies are looking for an intervention that can increase metabolic rate, block the uptake of dietary fat, or suppress appetite to staunch the rising obesity epidemic. Disrupting endocannabinoid signaling seems like a reasonable target. Indeed, the endocannabinoid system is hyperactive in obese humans and rats. Treatment with anandamide and 2-arachidonylglycerol increases food intake, which provokes fat storage in adipose cells and liver, as well as increased lipogenesis (reviewed in de Kloet and Woods, 2009). Treatment with CB1 antagonists causes body mass loss, as well as improved glucose and lipid parameters (de Kloet and Woods, 2009). Not surprisingly, given the mood-elevating effects of THC, CB1 antagonists tend to depress mood in some individuals. Thus, these drugs as currently formulated have not been approved in the United States as treatment for obesity. However, development of CB1 antagonists that target only food intake centers, but not other brain regions, would be an important advance. Because endocannabinoid receptors show sex differences in several brain regions, it is possible that sex hormones affect food intake and appetite through the CB receptors (de Fonseca et al., 1994).

coat color and are obese. The yellow coat was discovered to be the result of the agouti protein, which when cloned was discovered to antagonize MCH receptors in the skin. The blocked receptors lead to less melanin and a lighter coat color. The mutation also leads to obesity when this protein is overexpressed in the brain. This mutant protein led to the discovery of an endogenous AgRP in the brain. AgRP is a potent stimulator of eating; very small amounts infused into the ventricles of the brain stimulate food intake for up to 6 days (Lu et al., 2001). Low circulating levels of leptin and insulin activate the NPY/AgRP neurons in the arcuate nuclei (**FIGURE 9.26**). Secretion of these peptides activates the NPY/AgRP receptors in the PVN, which stimulate an increase in food intake. Current research is attempting

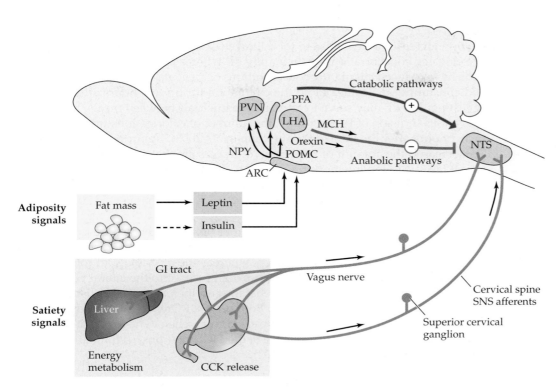

FIGURE 9.26 **Neuroanatomical model** showing the various pathways through which elevated adiposity signals, leptin and insulin, communicate with central autonomic circuits mediating food intake. Leptin and insulin appear to stimulate a catabolic pathway (i.e., POMC/CART neurons) and repress an anabolic pathway (i.e., NPY/AgRP neurons), both of which begin in the arcuate nuclei (ARC) and project to the PVN and LHA. Afferent information about satiety from the liver and from gut peptides such as CCK travels to the brain via the vagus nerve and sympathetic fibers of the nucleus of the solitary tract (NTS). Integration and consolidation of this information leads to termination of a meal. In contrast, reduced adiposity signals (e.g., during restricted caloric intake) may lead to increases in meal size by blocking brain stem responses to satiety signals. Leptin and insulin interact with hindbrain satiety circuits to regulate meal size. This phenomenon accounts for the common experience of following a large meal with a much smaller one to maintain energy balance. PFA = perifornical area. After Schwartz et al., 2000.

to discover ways to block AgRP activity therapeutically to induce negative energy balance and thus combat obesity (Ilnytska and Argyropoulos, 2008).

MELANIN-CONCENTRATING HORMONE (MCH)   Cell bodies of neurons that secrete MCH are located in the LHA. These neurons connect with several brain structures involved in motivation and movement, as well as with spinal neurons that regulate autonomous nervous system function. MCH received its name based on its actions on skin coloration in frogs. In the brains of mammals, it serves as a molecule that signals food intake and reduction of metabolic rate. Injections of MCH into the lateral ventricles or various brain regions evoke feeding behavior (Dube et al., 1999). Deletion of the MCH receptor in knockout mice results in hyperphagia, as expected, but the mice remain lean (Alon and Friedman, 2006). This reflects altered metabolism and hyperactivity (elevated energy expenditure).

PANCREATIC POLYPEPTIDE   Pancreatic polypeptide, or PP, is a hormone that is very similar in structure to PYY and may have evolved from a duplication of the PYY gene (Hort et al., 1995). This peptide is produced by specialized cells in the islets of Langerhans in the pancreas. PP may serve as a satiety signal similar to PYY, as PP secretion increases in response to food intake (Adrian et al., 1976). Obese patients have elevated concentrations of circulating PP, whereas patients suffering from anorexia have reduced circulating concentrations (Zipf et al., 1981; Glaser et al., 1988). Food consumption elevates PP in the circulation for up to 6 hours after the meal, suggesting that PP may serve to regulate the intervals between meals. In humans, intravenous infusion of PP decreased the number of calories consumed at a buffet lunch 2 hours after the infusion (Batterham et al., 2003). Importantly, PP infusions also decreased the amount of food that volunteers ate that evening for dinner *and* at breakfast the following morning. Infusion of PP did not alter circulating ghrelin, PYY, GLP-1, leptin, or insulin concentrations, indicating that the effect on food intake was probably independent of these hormones (Batterham et al., 2003).

OREXIN   Another peptide produced by neurons whose cell bodies are located in the LHA is called orexin. There are two versions of orexin, A and B. Orexin A increases food intake, possibly by inhibiting sleep, whereas the physiological role of orexin B is not known at this time. Like MCH, orexin infused into the lateral ventricles or other brain regions induces feeding behavior and increases metabolism (Dube et al., 1999). This neurohormone is called both orexin, by researchers studying its effects on food intake, and hypocretin, by sleep researchers. The axons of the orexin neurons travel to targets similar to those of the MCH neurons to stimulate a positive energy balance (Seeley and Woods, 2003).

Central Catabolic Effectors: Peptides That Inhibit Food Intake

MELANOCORTINS   Recall that a large precursor molecule called POMC is produced in the hypothalamus and elsewhere. This molecule can be cleaved to make several endocrine products that turn out to be important for regulation of food intake and metabolism: (1) the melanocortins, including α-MSH, β-MSH, and adrenocorticotropic hormone, and (2) the opioids. POMC-secreting neurons in the arcuate nuclei also express leptin and insulin receptors, and both leptin and insulin increase POMC gene expression in these neurons (Cowley et al., 2001). POMC activation increases conversion of white adipose tissue to brown adipose tissue, which is involved in nonshivering thermogenesis but is energetically inefficient; thus, increasing brown fat compared with white adipose tissue increases energy expenditure (Dodd et al., 2014). Thus far, five melanocortin (MC) receptors have been identified; the MC3 and MC4 receptor subtypes are common in the hypothalamus (Seeley and Woods, 2003). Targeted disruption of the gene for the MC4 receptor subtype results in obesity (Huszar et al., 1997).

Mutations or deletions of melanocortin receptors in humans are strongly associated with obesity (Coll et al., 2004, 2007). Nearly 5% of severe obesity in children and up to 2.5% of adulthood obesity is associated with mutations in melanocortin receptors (Hinney et al., 2006; Larsen et al., 2005). Thus, the actions of leptin and insulin to reduce food intake depend on stimulation of POMC-producing neurons to secrete α-MSH, which stimulates MC4 receptors. Activation of MC4 receptors in the PVN is anorexic (Schwartz et al., 2000).

CART   Individuals taking cocaine or methamphetamine become anorexic. It was discovered that a peptide termed cocaine- and amphetamine-regulated transcript, or CART, is expressed in animals given these drugs (Douglass et al., 1995). Neurons in the arcuate nuclei that secrete POMC in the PVN and LHA also secrete the anorexic peptide CART. These CART-secreting neurons possess leptin receptors, and low circulating levels of leptin (and possibly insulin) reduce CART gene expression in the arcuate nuclei, whereas increasing leptin or insulin concentrations can increase CART gene expression. Axons from CART-secreting neurons also travel to other brain regions and to regions of the spinal cord involved in regulation of the autonomic nervous system (Koylu et al., 1998). Activation of CART-secreting neurons also increases metabolic rate. Thus, CART has a net catabolic effect on metabolism. Elevated circulating levels of leptin and insulin activate the POMC/CART neurons in the arcuate nuclei (see Figure 9.24). Secretion of these peptides activates the melanocortin receptors in the PVN, which decreases food intake (see Figure 9.25).

Hindbrain and Brain Stem

Managing the intake and storage of energy is so critical to survival that several redundancies in the regulatory mechanisms have evolved. Although the necessary appetitive components of food intake are controlled in the hypothalamus, several parts of the system do not need the hypothalamus to maintain some components of energy balance. For example, brain regions in the posterior, or caudal, parts of the brain are able to act independently of the hypothalamus to control food consumption (Grill and Kaplan, 2002). The mechanisms that underlie feeding have been studied in animals that have undergone a surgical procedure to isolate the hypothalamus from the rest of the brain; these animals are termed *decerebrate* animals (Grill and Kaplan, 1990). Decerebrate rats display the ingestive motor program that underlies feeding behavior. These studies have demonstrated that even in the absence of information from the hypothalamus, decerebrate rats increase their food intake in response to 2-deoxy-D-glucose (2DG) and mercaptoacetate (MP), which blocks glucose and fatty acid metabolism, respectively, as well as in response to treatment with other orexigenic peptides (Grill and Kaplan, 2002; Grill et al., 1997, 1998; Kaplan et al., 1993, 1998). These results show that the hypothalamus is not required for the control of feeding and that metabolic and endocrine signals can act on other brain regions to control feeding.

There is a rapidly expanding body of data highlighting the importance of the caudal brain stem in the control of food intake (Grill and Kaplan, 2002; Grill et al., 1998). Treatment with metabolic inhibitors that affect food intake increases the activity of neurons in the area postrema and the nuclei of the solitary tract in the brain stem, as well as in forebrain regions such as the PVN (Horn and Friedman, 1998; Ritter et al., 1992). Increases in food intake induced by 2DG are significantly attenuated in rats that receive varying amounts of damage to the area postrema and the medial nucleus of the solitary tract (Bird et al., 1983; Contreras et al., 1982; Hyde and Miselis, 1983; Ritter and Taylor, 1990). Infusions of another potent antimetabolic glucose analogue, 5-thio-D-glucose (5TG), into the fourth ventricle (in the brain stem) but not into the third ventricle (in the hypothalamic area) caused rats to increase their food consumption. Based on these findings, it has been hypothesized that detectors of glucose availability that control food intake may reside in the caudal brain stem. In addition, cells in the caudal brain stem express genes for leptin receptors, ghrelin receptors, NPY, AgRP, and POMC (Grill and Hayes, 2009).

However, there are also detectors of metabolic fuel availability and oxidation in peripheral tissues outside the brain. Their presence was demonstrated by showing that metabolic inhibitors could increase food intake in animals in which the abdominal vagus nerve had been cut. Cutting the vagus nerve severs a connection between the brain and the internal organs. MP-induced, but not 2DG-induced, increases in food intake were abolished in vagotomized animals (Langhans and Scharrer, 1987; Ritter and Taylor, 1989, 1990). One neuroanatomical model of the pathways that regulate meal size is depicted in Figure 9.26.

Protein Hormones That Stop Food Intake

Insulin and leptin levels can regulate long-term patterns of food intake. But what controls the size of individual meals? In general, a large meal is followed by a small

FIGURE 9.27 Neural control of feeding in the blow-fly Satiety in the blowfly is mediated via a simple negative feedback loop. When sufficient food is ingested to overfill the blowfly's crop sac, the overflow distends the foregut and activates neural stretch receptors that signal the brain to stop feeding. If the recurrent nerve between the foregut and the brain is severed, blowflies will continue to eat until they literally burst. After Rosenzweig and Leiman, 1989.

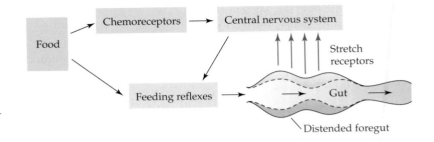

meal, so there must be some sort of metabolic memory, but what factors regulate meal size? Because of the relatively long delay between when nutrients leave the gut and when they begin to be stored or used, there must be factors other than insulin and leptin that signal that eating should stop.

Certainly neural signals of satiety exist. In the blowfly (*Phormia regina*), for example, feeding stops when sufficient food is ingested to overfill the crop sac. The overflow distends the foregut, which activates neural stretch receptors that signal the brain to stop feeding. Cutting the recurrent nerve between the foregut and the brain results in blowflies that continue to eat until they literally burst (Dethier, 1976). Satiety is thus mediated via a simple negative feedback loop (**FIGURE 9.27**). Similarly, neural signals of stomach distension in humans (Cannon, 1929; Thompson, 1980), other primates (Moran and McHugh, 1979, 1982), rats (Davis and Campbell, 1973), and dogs (Janowitz and Grossman, 1949) appear to inhibit feeding. The rate of gastric (stomach) emptying may also affect feeding behavior. A slow rate of gastric emptying would inhibit feeding for a longer time than a fast gastric contraction. In humans, a high-fat or high-protein meal leaves the stomach more slowly than a high-carbohydrate meal. Consequently, you actually may become hungry an hour later, or at least sooner, after eating carbohydrate-rich Chinese food, because the rate of gastric emptying is faster than after a rich, high-fat meal.

More to the point of this chapter, there are endocrine signals that stop feeding behavior. To demonstrate this point, an extra stomach and intestines can be transplanted into a rat. In the absence of neural connections, infusion of a liquid diet into the extra stomach results in a corresponding reduction in feeding behavior, even when the original stomach is empty. This observation suggests that some blood-borne product, possibly a hormone, is secreted in response to gastric distension by food (Koopmans, 1983). Filling the extra stomach with water does not reduce food intake. Further evidence of a blood-borne factor mediating stomach distension signals was obtained from hungry rats that ate much less after receiving blood transfusions from rats that had recently been fed (Davis et al., 1969). People who have had their stomachs surgically removed still report experiencing the sensation of hunger, but they usually reduce their caloric intake nonetheless (Mills and Stunkard, 1976).

Possibly the most salient example of the endocrine regulation of satiety is provided by a mollusk of the genus *Pleurobranchaea* (**FIGURE 9.28**). This sea slug is a voracious cannibal that appears to live by one simple rule: eat it. Anything less than about one-third its size that wanders too close to a *Pleurobranchaea* is devoured. Those of us who yearn for more simple lives can admire the straightforward rules by which this creature conducts itself, but simple lives can also become complicated. *Pleurobranchaea* eggs are small and are therefore, by definition, food. Obviously, any species that incorporates its offspring into its menu has a problem. However, the peptide hormone that stimulates egg laying in this species also stops feeding behavior (Davis et al., 1974). Treatment with the egg-laying hormone stops feeding behavior within 15 minutes and shortly thereafter causes oviposition (egg laying). Simple yet elegant regulatory systems such as that found in *Pleurobranchaea* were thought to be uncommon among vertebrates. As we have seen, there are several complex, yet elegant, levels of endocrine mechanisms, usually involving peptide

FIGURE 9.28 Feeding in *Pleurobranchaea* is tightly regulated by hormones. Normally, this sea slug will eat anything less than about one-third of its size. However, *Pleurobranchaea* avoids eating its own eggs because the peptide hormone that stimulates egg laying in this species also inhibits ingestive behavior.

hormones, controlling feeding behavior in vertebrates. Similarly, there are endocrine mechanisms that signal individuals to stop eating, and in vertebrates many of these hormonal signals come from the gut (see Table 9.4).

CHOLECYSTOKININ Cholecystokinin, or CCK, is considered to be a primary hormonal factor that provokes satiety. CCK is a gastrointestinal peptide hormone that is released during feeding to aid with digestion; it was named for its ability to promote the contraction of gallbladder muscle. CCK is also released from cells in the brain stem and hypothalamus. Administration of CCK to hungry rats, mice, Syrian hamsters, chickens, rabbits, sheep, cats, dogs, or humans decreases their food intake (Morley et al., 1985b). CCK does not suppress water intake in thirsty animals, indicating that its satiating effect is specific to food intake. When CCK is released during a meal, it binds to CCK-A receptors on the vagus nerve that signal the hindbrain that fat/protein has been ingested. This information is integrated in the hypothalamus with the variety of other hormonal signals about metabolic fuels, but it generally serves to stop feeding behavior (Moran, 2009). The effects of CCK on ingestive behaviors can be blocked by cutting the abdominal section of the vagus nerve (Bloom and Polak, 1981) or by treatment with CCK antagonists (Beglinger et al., 2001; Hewson et al., 1988). Because blood concentrations of CCK diminish only slightly as a meal is digested, blood-borne CCK does not seem to mediate satiety. However, CCK concentrations around the vagus nerve vary considerably during the course of a meal, suggesting that local release of CCK mediates satiety via the vagus nerve. It has been proposed that as these satiety signals stop, hunger is experienced again. Although this model is an extreme oversimplification of the endocrine control of vertebrate feeding, it suggests that the feedback principles displayed in the blowfly and *Pleurobranchaea* could theoretically form the basis of satiety in vertebrates as well.

In the absence of language, it is difficult to ascertain whether CCK inhibits feeding via a true satiating mechanism or through secondary aversive effects. We can simply ask people whether CCK makes them feel queasy, or observe them to see if they vomit after CCK treatment, to discover whether CCK causes nausea. But we cannot ask a rat if it is nauseated, and because rats do not vomit, it is difficult to discover whether something is aversive to them. However, learned aversions can be readily established by pairing flavors, such as saccharin, with substances known to produce illness, such as lithium chloride, and presenting the mixture to a rat. Upon subsequent presentations of a saccharin-flavored substance, the animal avoids it, demonstrating that it has learned that the sweet taste predicted the illness induced by lithium chloride. This learned aversion paradigm has been employed to explore the aversive effects of CCK. In some studies, CCK paired with saccharin did not cause rats to develop an aversion to saccharin (Gibbs et al., 1973). Other studies, however, have reported an aversive reaction to CCK in rats (Deutsch, 1982). Other studies with rats have reported that CCK antagonists increase the size of meals consumed after food deprivation, suggesting a physiological role for CCK in normal satiety (Moran et al., 1992). Peripheral treatment with CCK at doses sufficient to inhibit food intake stimulated synthesis of c-Fos, a marker of neuronal activation, in the brain stem, the nucleus of the solitary tract, and the dorsal vagal nucleus (Zittel et al., 1999). There are two CCK receptor subtypes, A and B. Rats lacking functional CCK-A receptors are hyperphagic, diabetic, and obese (Schwartz et al., 1999). This result is species-specific, however, as CCK-A receptor knockout mice display normal body mass (Kopin et al., 1999).

BOMBESIN   Another peptide that mediates feeding behavior is bombesin, a small protein consisting of 14 amino acids that is distributed throughout the mammalian gastrointestinal and nervous systems (M. Brown et al., 1978). It is named bombesin because it was originally isolated from the skin of the European fire-bellied toad, *Bombina bombina* (Anastasi et al., 1971). Experimental injections of bombesin reduce food intake in rats (Gibbs et al., 1979). The mechanism by which this peripheral bombesin treatment affects feeding is unknown; cutting of the vagus nerve does not interfere with the satiating effects of bombesin as it does with CCK (Smith et al., 1981a). The satiating effects of bombesin and CCK are additive, further suggesting that they have different mechanisms of action (Stein and Woods, 1981). ICV infusions of bombesin also reduce food intake in rats, indicating a central nervous system mechanism of action (Morley et al., 1985a). Bombesin treatment inhibits food consumption in humans (Gutzwiller et al., 1994; Lieverse et al., 1993), but treatment of people with bombesin receptor antagonists to assess effects on food intake has not been reported (Woods and D'Alessio, 2008).

AMYLIN   Amylin is also called islet amyloid polypeptide and is released by the pancreatic β-cells in conjunction with insulin. Physiologically, amylin delays gut emptying and gastric acid secretion, reduces glucagon release, and decreases food intake (Ludvik et al., 1997). Treatment with amylin causes a dose-dependent reduction in meal size (Lutz, 2006; Lutz et al., 1995), whereas antagonism of the appropriate central nervous system receptor (a modified calcitonin receptor) provokes increased food intake and body mass (Rushing et al., 2000). Amylin gene knockout mice display elevated body mass. Because amylin belongs to the calcitonin gene–related peptide family, it makes sense that this hormone interacts with a calcitonin receptor (Lutz, 2010). Unlike most gut hormones, amylin does not mediate its effects via the vagus nerve but, rather, directly signals satiety to the area postrema of the hindbrain (Lutz, 2006).

Synthetic amylin is being developed as a therapeutic agent. One version, called pramlintide, is currently available for treatment of type 1 and type 2 diabetes, and clinical trials are examining its potential for obesity treatment (Woods and D'Alessio, 2008). Although pharmacological doses can cause nausea as a side effect, the results of clinical trials provide a proof of principle that satiety hormones can be used effectively as anti-obesity drugs.

CORTICOTROPIN-RELEASING HORMONE   Corticotropin-releasing hormone, or CRH, rapidly reduces food intake and body mass after ICV administration (Arase et al., 1988; Hotta et al., 1991; Rivest et al., 1989). Another regulatory loop appears to exist between NPY, CRH, and the sympathetic nervous system. Discharges of sympathetic nerves to adipose tissues increased after ICV injections of CRH and decreased after ICV injections of NPY (Egawa et al., 1990). These results suggest that these two hormones (neuromodulators) have opposite effects on sympathetic activity (Heinrichs et al., 1992). The sympathetic nervous system may communicate between fat depots and the brain; specific gut endocrine signals may influence the motivation to eat or stop eating, depending on energy stores, energy availability, and energy expenditures. Stressors also motivate eating in many individuals, and CRH dysregulation may be important in stress-evoked food intake (**BOX 9.3**).

GLUCAGON-LIKE PEPTIDE 1 Glucagon-like peptide 1, or GLP-1, is produced both in the gut and in the brain. GLP-1 is released from the L cells in the ileum and colon in response to food, and it interacts with receptors in the brain stem, arcuate nuclei, and PVN (Small and Bloom, 2004). Peripheral administration of GLP-1 stimulates insulin secretion in humans. Administration of GLP-1 directly into the PVN of rats

---

BOX 9.3 *Comfort Food*

When we are not feeling well, we crave a grilled cheese sandwich and tomato soup prepared in a specific manner that our mothers used when we were young boys. Food that makes people feel better is commonly called comfort food. For example, many people eat ice cream or other high-fat/high-calorie food such as macaroni and cheese when distressed (see figure). Research conducted by Mary Dallman and her colleagues (Dallman et al., 2003; Pecoraro et al., 2004) suggests that chronically stressed rats (and perhaps people) crave high-fat food when stressed, in an attempt to reduce anxiety. These mechanisms, the details of which have been worked out in rats, may explain some parts of the epidemic of obesity occurring in Western society.

This model proposes that glucocorticoids work differently in the long term than they do in the short term. Recall from Chapter 2 that stress causes CRH release from the hypothalamus, which stimulates ACTH release from the anterior pituitary, which stimulates the adrenal cortex to secrete glucocorticoids. Normally, high levels of glucocorticoid shut off

CRH and ACTH through negative feedback, but when glucocorticoids are chronically present in the brain and body, those hormones maintain the stress response instead of shutting it down through a feed-forward system (Dallman et al., 2003). CRH and glucocorticoids drive individuals to seek out pleasurable foods and direct the added calories to accumulate as abdominal fat.

In one study, Dallman and her colleagues simulated chronic stress by increasing the brain concentration of corticosterone. As corticosterone concentrations increased, the rats responded by drinking increasingly more sugar water, eating increasingly more lard, and gaining abdominal girth (Pecoraro et al., 2004). Although there was not a net increase in calories, the types of calories plus the high glucocorticoid values put the fat on the abdomen, where it increases the risk for cardiovascular disease and type 2 diabetes in humans. Presumably, reducing stressors would alleviate the hypothalamic-pituitary-adrenal dysfunction of chronic stress and allow a better distribution of stored energy.

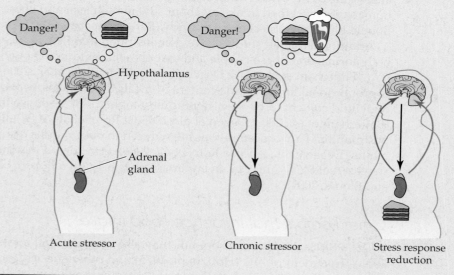

Acute stressor   Chronic stressor   Stress response reduction

significantly suppresses food intake. In contrast, blocking GLP-1 receptors increases food intake (Turton et al., 1996).

Peripheral administration of GLP-1 reduces food intake in humans and rats (Small and Bloom, 2004). In rats, GLP-1 treatment induces *c-fos* expression in the brain stem. These findings plus others implicate GLP-1 in the inhibition of food intake in rodents, acting on the dorsal vagal complex and the area postrema. The extent to which circulating GLP-1 mediates appetite in humans remains unspecified, although infusions of this peptide sufficient to attain normal postmeal concentrations reduce subsequent appetite and food intake (Flint et al., 2001). Because the half-life of GLP-1 is less than 2 minutes in circulation, direct effects of this hormone are unlikely to be mediating its anorexic effects. Additional research is required to see whether drugs targeted for the GLP-1 receptors will have useful therapeutic value, but as with CCK, treatment with GLP-1 receptor agonists causes nausea. This and other evidence, such as the rapid degradation in circulation, suggests that GLP-1 influences food intake via nonhomeostatic mechanisms (Woods and D'Alessio, 2008).

ADIPONECTIN Adiponectin (ADP), like leptin, is a relatively recently discovered adipokine hormone. ADP affects insulin actions in the periphery to facilitate glucose uptake in cells (Seeley et al., 2004). ADP enters the cerebrospinal fluid after intravenous injection, suggesting active transport into the brain (Qi et al., 2004). ICV infusion of ADP decreased body weight mainly by stimulating glucose use. ADP increased expression of CRH in the hypothalamus but did not act on other neuropeptide targets of leptin (Qi et al., 2004). ADP also induced distinct Fos immunoreactivity in brain regions associated with food intake. However, the agouti mice described earlier did not respond to ADP or leptin, suggesting that the melanocortin pathway may be a common target of the two peptides (Seeley et al., 2004). These results suggest that ADP has important central effects on energy balance (Qi et al., 2004). Several other gut peptides have been discovered that contribute to satiety (Pocai, 2014; Wynne et al., 2004).

PEPTIDE TYROSINE-TYROSINE (PYY) PYY_{1-36} is released from the ileum and colon and quickly cleaved to peptide YY_{3-36} (PYY_{3-36}) in response to ingestion of food (Small and Bloom, 2004). PYY_{3-36} decreases food intake by inhibiting hypothalamic NPY- and AgRP-expressing neurons, which releases their inhibition of neighboring POMC-expressing neurons (Gale et al., 2004). In common with leptin, this peptide crosses the blood-brain barrier to act on the arcuate nuclei. Infusion of PYY_{3-36} into humans reduced food intake by about 30% in both lean and obese volunteers in a double-blind, placebo-controlled study (Batterham et al., 2002).

Additional human studies have demonstrated that PYY reduces food intake in both normal and obese people and that obese individuals show dysregulation of PYY (Batterham et al., 2003; Degen et al., 2005; le Roux et al., 2006). PYY secretion is proportional to the caloric content of meals; large meals, especially those with high lipid content, provoke a significantly higher PYY response than small meals (Batterham et al., 2003; Degen et al., 2005; le Roux et al., 2006). Both fasting and postprandial PYY concentrations are reduced in obese adults compared with lean adults (Degen et al., 2005; le Roux et al., 2006). Considered together, these studies suggest that PYY_{3-36} may be an important physiological regulator of appetite (Small and Bloom, 2004).

Other Factors That Influence Food Intake

ENDORPHINS Endogenous opioids may also mediate food intake (Morley et al., 1983). Treatment of rats (Holtzman, 1975) and other species, including humans (Thompson et al., 1982), with the opioid antagonist naloxone reduces food intake.

Apparently, naloxone reduces the hedonic value of food, making its consumption less "rewarding" (Morley et al., 1985a). Ingested sugars and oils are particularly salient cues for the release of endorphins and appear to provide calming and pain-reducing influences (Shide and Blass, 1989). Perhaps this is why we are more likely to reach for a candy bar than broccoli when we are stressed. Endogenous opioids may play a role in desire for comfort food (see Box 9.3).

THE ROLE OF THE LIVER The liver may generate a signal for satiety. This organ is ideally situated to monitor changes in the concentrations of insulin and metabolic fuels (Granneman and Friedman, 1980). It certainly is important in the mediation of insulin-induced feeding, as elegantly demonstrated by Edward Stricker and his colleagues (Stricker et al., 1977). To help you understand their experiment fully, the use of metabolic fuels by the brain and liver will be briefly reviewed.

Two metabolic fuels can be used by the brain: glucose and ketone bodies. As described above, the brain primarily uses glucose, and insulin is not required to get energy into neurons. During prolonged starvation, the brain can function using ketone bodies as fuel. Fructose, like glucose, is a carbohydrate, but unlike glucose, it cannot easily cross the blood-brain barrier; consequently, fructose cannot be used as a fuel for the brain. The liver, on the other hand, can readily utilize fructose as a metabolic fuel, but it is unable to oxidize ketones and use them for energy.

Stricker and his coworkers exploited this disparity in fuel use between the brain and the liver to find out which organ mediated insulin-induced feeding. Rats were infused with (1) saline, as controls; (2) fructose, to "feed" the liver but not the brain; or (3) β-hydroxybutyrate, a ketone, to "feed" the brain but not the liver (Friedman, 1990; Stricker et al., 1977) (**FIGURE 9.29**). All of the rats were also treated with insulin. Insulin treatment of the control animals produced the expected reduction in blood levels of glucose and induced feeding behavior. Infusion of rats with β-hydroxybutyrate did not affect insulin-induced feeding. However, infusions of fructose inhibited the onset of insulin-induced feeding, demonstrating that a "fed" liver, even in the presence of a "starved" brain, was sufficient to block insulin-induced feeding. These results indicate that the liver plays a role in mediating insulin-induced feeding, probably by monitoring its energy stores (glycogen) and communicating this information to the central nervous system via the hepatic branch of the vagus nerve (Friedman and Granneman, 1983; Sawchenko and Friedman, 1979; Steffens et al., 1990; Stricker et al., 1977).

(A)

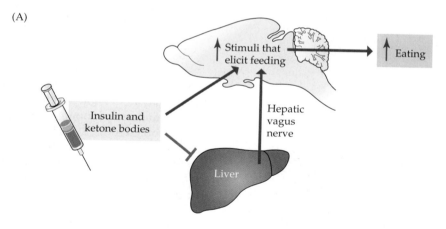

(B)

FIGURE 9.29 The role of the liver in insulin-induced feeding was determined by injecting animals with insulin, which lowers blood glucose levels and induces feeding, and then injecting them with either ketone bodies or fructose. (A) Ketones, which can be used as fuel by the brain but not by the liver, did not inhibit insulin-induced feeding. (B) Fructose, which can be used by the liver but not by the brain, inhibited insulin-induced feeding, indicating that the liver blocks insulin-induced feeding even if fuel levels in the brain are low. After Stricker et al., 1977.

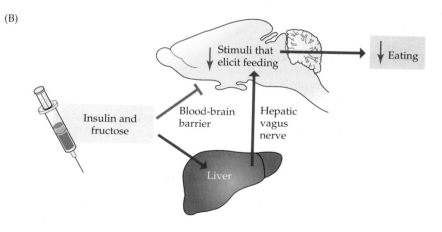

Gonadal Steroid Hormones, Food Intake, and Body Mass

In addition to the peripheral hormones mentioned thus far, gonadal steroid hormones also influence feeding behavior and subsequent body mass. As you have learned in Chapters 3–6, the major role of gonadal hormones is to promote fertility and to synchronize sexual behaviors with the most fertile period. As we shall see, part of this synchronization involves the effects of gonadal hormones on energy intake and storage, in addition to their effects on sexual behavior and fertility (Klingerman et al., 2010). Evidence is accumulating that the mechanisms that control the appetite for food also influence reproductive behavior, thereby optimizing reproductive success in environments where energy availability fluctuates. Reproductive hormones are likely to be important for orchestration of the appetites for food and sex, food intake, body fat storage, and energy expenditure (Schneider, 2006; Schneider et al., 2007). Ovarian and testicular steroid hormones, such as estradiol, progesterone, and testosterone, appear to exert their effects via many of the peripheral hormones and neuropeptides just discussed.

Estrogens and Progestins

After ovariectomy, a female rat increases her food intake and relatively quickly elevates her body mass about 20%–25% as compared with a gonadally intact female. The hyperphagia eventually wanes, and her food intake stabilizes to maintain this new elevated body mass. Most of the increased body weight is the result of increased fat deposition (adiposity) (Leshner and Collier, 1973). Locomotor activity, as measured on a running wheel, is permanently suppressed by ovariectomy (Wang, 1923). In other words, ovariectomy leads to a fat rat. Ovariectomy also promotes obesity in other species, including cats, voles, and mice, although the degree of effect varies with species. The importance of estradiol in body weight, adiposity, and food intake throughout life is illustrated by mutant animals that lack receptors for estradiol. Estrogen receptor α gene knockout (αERKO) mice are hyperphagic and obese, and they display deficits in sexual behavior (Heine et al., 2000; Rissman et al., 1997a). In humans menopause changes fat distribution from the female-like subcutaneous depots to a more male-like pattern, with more fat deposited in the visceral depots. Visceral, but not subcutaneous, adipose tissue is associated with cardiovascular disease (Emery et al., 1993).

Estrogens generally have catabolic effects (increasing energy expenditure, thermogenesis, lipolysis, body fat loss), in contrast to androgens, which, as you know, are generally anabolic (see Chapter 2). Treatment of ovariectomized rats with estradiol benzoate reverses the increase in body mass by inducing a mild, transient hypophagia and a prolonged elevation in activity (Mook et al., 1972). In contrast to the effect of estradiol, treatment of ovariectomized rats with progesterone does not prevent the increase in body mass; progesterone, in the absence of an ovary or estrogen, does not affect food intake, locomotor activity, body fat content, or body mass (Wade and Gray, 1979). In other words, ovariectomized female rats injected with only progesterone are as fat as untreated ovariectomized females. Treatment of an ovariectomized rat with both estradiol and progesterone also fails to prevent the increase in body mass (**FIGURE 9.30**). When gonadally intact females are given progesterone in relatively high doses (e.g., 5 mg/day), they experience a weight gain resembling the weight gain observed after ovariectomy (Hervey and Hervey, 1967). Thus, it is reasonable to assume that progesterone blocks the catabolic effects of estradiol on food intake, adiposity, locomotor activity, and body mass. The effects of ovariectomy and progesterone treatment are virtually

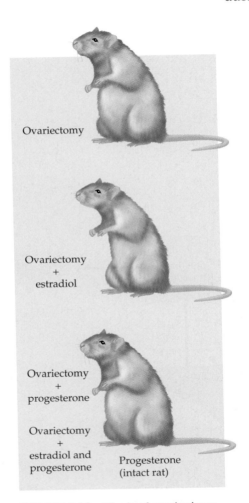

FIGURE 9.30 Effects of ovariectomy and progesterone treatment on body mass Ovariectomized rats increase their food intake and increase their body mass by 20%–25%. Treatment with estradiol reverses these effects, but if estradiol is paired with progesterone, or if progesterone alone is administered, body mass is not reduced. Gonadally intact rats given progesterone increase their body mass in a manner similar to that seen in ovariectomized rats. After Wade and Gray, 1979.

Ovariectomy

Ovariectomy + estradiol

Ovariectomy + progesterone

Ovariectomy + estradiol and progesterone

Progesterone (intact rat)

identical, but nonadditive; that is, both treatments cause the same physiological and behavioral outcomes.

If ovarian steroid hormones have these dynamic effects on food intake and body mass, then predictable changes in eating and body weight should accompany estrous cycles, pregnancy, and pseudopregnancy (Wade, 1986). Furthermore, females undergoing seasonal reproductive cycles should also display seasonal fluctuations in food intake and body mass. Energy balance does appear to oscillate throughout the estrous cycle. Recall from Chapter 6 that rat estrogen concentrations are highest during vaginal proestrus; eating and body mass are reduced immediately after proestrus (Wang, 1924). The low blood plasma estrogen concentrations during diestrus are associated with elevated food intake and body mass (Brobeck et al., 1947). Seasonally acyclic Syrian hamsters increase their body mass when days are short and blood levels of gonadal sex steroid hormones are low (Bartness and Wade, 1985); when the days grow longer and estrous cycles resume, hamsters often display fluctuations in body mass and locomotor activity, and perhaps food intake, similar to those of rats.

Correlations between ovarian steroid hormones and food intake have also been reported for primates. Food intake is higher during the luteal phase, when progesterone levels are high, than at other times during the menstrual cycle in both non-human primates (Czaja and Goy, 1975) and women (Dalvit, 1981). These changes in food intake are attributable to the fluctuations in blood levels of sex steroid hormones; ovariectomized rhesus monkeys show cyclic changes in food intake when injected with estradiol and progesterone in a pattern that mimics the hormonal profile of a normal menstrual cycle (Czaja and Goy, 1975). In the majority of, but certainly not all, studies on women, food intake generally, and carbohydrate intake specifically, is higher during the 10-day period prior to menstruation (the luteal phase) than during the 10-day period immediately following the onset of menstrual bleeding (the follicular phase) (Dalvit-McPhillips, 1983; Fessler, 2003; Wurtman and Wurtman, 1989). Carbohydrate metabolism may increase during the luteal phase, thus triggering an increase in physiological energy needs and subsequent elevated intake of this energy source (Pliner and Fleming, 1983; Wurtman and Wurtman, 1989).

Do these subtle changes in female appetite and energy expenditure over the ovarian cycle have biological relevance? One possibility is that fluctuation in estradiol ensures that females give priority to eating and storing fuels when estradiol is low and that they neglect energy acquisition and storage in preference for sexual behavior only when they are most fertile. If the role of estradiol is related to energetic concerns, then you might expect the estradiol–ingestive behavior link to vary with energy availability. Indeed, sexual behavior is strictly circumscribed to the time of the cycle when estradiol is high only in animals with pressing energetic concerns. The importance of ovarian steroids in control of feeding behavior is masked in animals that live in climate-controlled environments—those with low requirements for energy expenditure and unlimited, high-calorie foods readily available—such as laboratory animals and our own species in modern, Westernized societies. These effects, however, are revealed when animals are raised in seminatural environments that require increased energy expenditure or limit food availability (Klingerman et al., 2010) (**FIGURE 9.31**).

As described in Chapter 6, blood plasma progesterone concentrations gradually increase throughout pregnancy; progesterone is also elevated during pseudopregnancy in rats. Food intake, fat storage, and overall body mass increase during both pregnancy and pseudopregnancy (Slonaker, 1924). Ewes entering their first estrous cycle of the breeding season do not display reproductive behavior; this first estrous cycle of the season is

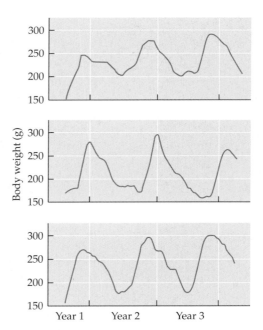

FIGURE 9.31 Annual body mass changes for three ground squirrels housed in a laboratory under constant conditions show approximately 1-year (circannual) fluctuations in weight gain and loss. These fluctuations correspond to seasonal body mass cycles that occur in nature. After Zucker, 1988a.

called a silent heat. However, plasma levels of progesterone are high during the luteal phase of the silent heat, and food intake and body mass escalate accordingly during this time (Sadlier, 1969).

How might ovarian steroid hormones affect food intake and subsequent body mass? The most parsimonious possibility is that ovarian hormones affect the brain sites that control food intake and voluntary exercise. Consequent increases in food intake and decreases in exercise would then lead to adiposity and increased body mass. Alternatively, there might be effects on body mass independent from food intake and exercise. One way to distinguish between these two possibilities is to "yoke" the amount of food available to one animal to the food intake of another. In this paradigm, the yoked animal receives the same amount of food per day as is consumed by a counterpart, usually a littermate. Ovariectomized rats still gain weight when they are fed exactly the same amount that a gonadally intact sister eats. In other words, ovariectomized rats appear almost destined to gain weight, even when provided with only sufficient calories to maintain a normal body mass in a gonadally intact animal. The same result is obtained in ovariectomized rats yoked to ovariectomized females treated with estradiol. Are there changes in metabolic rate? The ovariectomized rats are less active than both intact and estrogen-treated females and thus gain body mass. Another way to examine the direct effects of hormones on body mass is to place hormone implants directly into the central nervous system. Implants of estradiol benzoate into the PVN or VMH of ovariectomized rats reduce food intake and body weight in a manner similar to that of systemic injections of estradiol (Butera and Beikirch, 1989; Wade and Zucker, 1970). Estrogen implants elsewhere in the diencephalon do not reliably affect food intake or body weight.

Adipose tissue metabolism is directly affected by steroid hormones. Alteration of the size of the fat deposits is the main effect of sex steroid hormones upon body mass. Adipose tissue contains receptors for both estrogens and progestins (Gray and Wade, 1979; Wade and Gray, 1978). Estradiol and progesterone affect the activity of lipoprotein lipase (LPL), an enzyme found in fat cells that mediates the uptake of triglycerides (fatty acids) from the bloodstream by the fat cells, as well as other coordinated changes in fat metabolism. LPL activity is high when fats are being stored—for example, after a meal. LPL activity is decreased by estradiol but increased by progesterone. Consequently, fat cells cannot store triglycerides when exposed only to estradiol, but concurrent exposure to progesterone enhances fat storage by increasing the amount of triglycerides sequestered from the blood. Why is the body mass effect of progesterone dependent on estradiol? Recall from Chapter 2 that estrogens turn on genes that code for, among other things, progestin receptors in the uterus and elsewhere. Normally, there are receptors for both estradiol and progesterone in the adipose tissue cytosol. After ovariectomy, progesterone receptors disappear from the fat cells. Within 6–12 hours of an estradiol injection, progesterone receptors again proliferate throughout the cytosol (Gray and Wade, 1979). In this case, the progesterone receptors in the fat cells are dependent on an anabolic effect of estrogens.

Clearly, ovarian steroid hormones can significantly affect food intake and body mass, as demonstrated by ovariectomy and hormone replacement studies. Does this effect of steroid hormones play any functional role in the regulation of food intake and body mass, and in the maintenance of energy balance? The answer is probably yes. Pregnancy causes a great increase in food intake in many mammalian species. Pregnancy, and especially lactation, are very energy-demanding activities. The resting metabolic rate of a pregnant mammal more than triples as compared with the nonpregnant animal (Bronson, 1989). A large increase in food intake is required to maintain the fetuses. Fat deposition, and thus body mass, increases during pregnancy in most mammalian species, probably as a hedge against the coming energetic demands. New mother rats, for example, weigh more just after parturition than they did before becoming pregnant. If a pregnant female cannot find sufficient food or lacks sufficient energy stores, the pregnancy is often aborted. Similarly, a lactating female with insufficient metabolic fuels may kill and eat some or all of her offspring to balance litter size with available metabolic energy supplies (Schneider and Wade, 1989b). Even estrous cycles are suspended if insufficient metabolic fuels are available to the female (Schneider and Wade, 1989a).

There are interesting exceptions to the statement that pregnancy elevates food intake and increases body mass. These exceptions illustrate that the same hormone can have different effects in different species, although both effects lead to reproductive success. For example, Syrian hamsters do not increase their food intake during pregnancy; rather, they draw upon their body fat reserves for energy (Wade et al., 1986). Gonadal steroids and energy deficits influence food hoarding, not food intake, in this species, so estrous females show little or no hoarding during the time of courtship and mating and show high levels of food hoarding near the end of pregnancy (Fleming, 1978; Fleming and Miceli, 1983; Klingerman et al., 2010). Anticipatory food hoarding during pregnancy ensures a food surplus in the mother's nest during lactation, when Syrian hamsters more than double their food intake. In Syrian hamsters and Siberian hamsters, progesterone appears to act on lipolysis in a manner opposite from its actions in rats; that is, progesterone causes a mobilization of fat and substantial decreases in body fat stores in pregnant hamsters (Schneider and Wade, 1987). Furthermore, in hamsters ovarian hormones influence food hoarding in the way that they influence food intake in other species.

Fat deposition increases throughout the first two trimesters of pregnancy in humans. This makes sense when you consider the estrogen and progesterone levels found in the body during pregnancy. But why does fat accumulation virtually stop at the end of the second trimester? The answer to this question is another hormone: prolactin. High blood plasma levels of prolactin inhibit fat production. Prolactin has essentially the same effect as estradiol on fat cells; namely, it reduces LPL activity—except in mammary tissues. Consequently, fat continues to be deposited in the mammary glands through the end of pregnancy.

Androgens

Among vertebrates, males of many species are larger in size and eat more food than females. Much of this difference in size is organized perinatally by androgens, but the activational effects of anabolic steroids also are important in maintaining this sexual dimorphism. In most mammalian species, androgens promote elevated body mass and energy consumption (Wade, 1976). Males generally have more muscle mass than females, and the relatively higher concentrations of circulating androgens in males maintain this sex difference in body mass directly. In males of other species, however, testosterone inhibits growth, and males are generally smaller than females in these species (Cox and John-Alder, 2005; Cox et al., 2009a,b; Crews et al., 1985). Thus, androgens influence sexual dimorphism in size and strength, but not always in the same direction.

Castration decreases food intake and limits weight gain, including muscle mass gain, in rats (Mitchell and Keesey, 1974). The effects of castration on food consumption and body weight can be reversed by low-dose (50–200 µg/day) testosterone replacement therapy (Gentry and Wade, 1976). Bilateral implants of testosterone propionate into the VMH limit food intake in castrated male rats; this action of testosterone presumably reflects the effects of estrogen in this brain region after aromatization of the testosterone. Bilateral implants of dihydrotestosterone, an androgen that cannot be aromatized to an estrogen, into the VMH do not affect food intake (Nunez et al., 1980). These results suggest that androgens have both a central (CNS-induced) and a peripheral (muscle mass) mechanism of action on food intake and body mass in male rats.

As is the case in many aspects of behavioral endocrinology, many of the general principles of androgen action have been generated from data obtained from rats. But many species-specific responses to these hormones have been reported that may require future modifications of the current general principles. For instance, the typical male meadow vole (*Microtus pennsylvanicus*) also eats less food and loses body mass after castration (Dark and Zucker, 1984), but individual voles vary markedly and predictably in their response to castration. Adult male meadow voles of identical age vary in body mass from about 35 to over 60 g; all of the variation is due to differences in body fat stores. Voles heavier than 47 g were seen to lose mass after castration, whereas voles lighter than 47 g gained weight after castration. Males weighing about 47 g at the time of castration did not display substantial body mass changes. Testosterone replacement reversed the effects of castration in the appropriate direction for the heavy and light males. The individual differences in body fat content did not reflect differences in blood plasma levels of testosterone but, rather, appeared to reflect differences in target tissue sensitivity to androgens (Dark et al., 1987b).

As described in Chapter 6, female garter snakes (*Thamnophis sirtalis parietalis*) are larger than male conspecifics; they are about three times heavier. The difference in body size is apparent by 3 weeks of age, a time when plasma levels of androgens are high. Androgens appear to inhibit growth in male garter snakes. The sex difference in body size can be abolished by castration at any age; that is, castrated male snakes grow as large as females. Treatment with testosterone prevents the female-like body size in castrated males (Crews et al., 1985).

In lizard species, testosterone has differential effects on growth, depending on the direction of the sexual dimorphism in size. In male brown anoles (*Anolis sagrei*), for example, males are larger than females, and testosterone treatment reverses castration-induced losses in body weight (Cox et al., 2009a). In *Sceloporus undulatus*, females are larger than males, and castration stimulates males to grow to a female-typical body size. As is often the case, the difference between the species is related to energetics (Cox and John-Alder, 2005; Cox et al., 2005). Reproductive development is more energetically expensive in *Sceloporus*, and males have traded their larger size for reproductive success. It will be interesting to discover the mechanisms through which testosterone inhibits growth. The differential response to testosterone illustrates the ways in which evolutionary adaptation often involves a neuroendocrine solution. How can males and females with a largely shared genome become sexually dimorphic during evolution? The answer is related to their differential response to gonadal steroid hormones. Species differ in their responsiveness to a particular hormone, and males and females with a largely shared genome become sexually dimorphic by secreting different levels of the same hormone.

Inhibition of Reproduction to Maintain Energy Balance

When food is abundant and the energetic demands of thermoregulation and foraging are minimal, there is plenty of energy available for the cellular processes necessary for day-to-day survival, as well as for growth and reproductive activities. However, when food is scarce or energetic demands are high, the activities that are necessary for survival take precedence. Thus, mammals have mechanisms to inhibit reproduction when they fall into negative energy balance (Bronson, 1999). Women who diet or engage in excessive exercise to the point that their body mass is less than 85% of height-typical mass have problems with fertility. Reports of menstrual irregularities, amenorrhea (cessation of menstrual cycles), and diminished sexual desire and sexual activity, as well as infertility, are common among fashion models, women with the eating disorder anorexia nervosa, and athletes or dancers who do not increase their food intake to compensate for their excessive energy expenditure (Schneider, 2004; Schneider and Watts, 2002; Wade and Jones, 2003). The fact that reproductive inhibition occurs among females of all mammalian species and is entirely reversible upon refeeding or relaxation of the energy demands should inform us that this is not a pathology or disease but a biological adaptation for conserving energy in environments in which energy availability may fluctuate (see Chapter 10).

An individual that finds itself hungry in a low-temperature environment must conserve energy and must also find and eat food. Not surprisingly, the inhibition of reproduction in the service of energy balance is controlled by mechanisms that overlap with those that control food intake. Most of the peptide hormones, neuropeptides, and metabolic inhibitors that increase food intake also inhibit reproduction, and many of the same brain regions are involved in both processes (Wade and Jones, 2003). For example, in Syrian hamsters, estrous cycle can be interrupted by a 48-hour fast. Fat, but not lean, hamsters are protected from this fasting-induced anestrus. It was suggested that the fat hamsters were protected by their ability to use fatty acids as fuels by metabolizing lipids from their fat cells. To test this idea, very fat hamsters were either fasted or fed as much food as they wanted (ad libitum). Half of each group was treated with MP, an inhibitor of free fatty acid oxidation. Fat fasted hamsters showed normal estrous cycles, but fat fasted hamsters treated with MP did not. MP treatment had no effect on estrous cycles in hamsters fed ad libitum. Thus, the mechanisms that interrupt estrous cycles are sensitive to signals generated by the oxidation of metabolic fuels (Schneider and Wade, 1989a) (**FIGURE 9.32**). Similarly, pulsatile luteinizing hormone secretion is affected by fasting, insulin, and metabolic inhibitors in rats, sheep, and monkeys (reviewed in Schneider, 2004).

Leptin, insulin, NPY, CRH, CCK, galanin, nitric oxide synthase, GLP-1, orexin, GnRH-II, RFRP (RFamide-related peptide, also known and GnIH), and a variety of other substances are involved in the metabolic control of reproduction. As with the search for the signals that control food intake, the search for the signals that inhibit reproduction is complicated by the fact that hormones may have both direct and indirect influences on reproductive function. As discussed previously, leptin can increase free fatty acid oxidation and can prevent the storage of fat fuels in the form of triglycerides. Does leptin affect reproduction directly, through its effects on brain mechanisms that control estrous cycles, or indirectly, via its known effects on free fatty acid oxidation? To find out, Syrian hamsters were fasted and treated systemically with either leptin or leptin plus MP. Fasting-induced anestrus was prevented by treatment with high doses of leptin. However, leptin treatment did not prevent fasting-induced anestrus in hamsters pretreated with MP (Schneider et al., 1998). These results suggest that exogenous leptin may affect reproduction via indirect effects on fuel oxidation. This idea is born out in recent experiments that show a role for AMPK, a putative nutrient sensor, in leptin's effects on food intake and reproduction (Coyral-Castel et al., 2008; Tosca et al., 2008). Regardless of whether leptin affects reproduction directly or indirectly (or both), the importance of normal daily fluctuations in leptin concentrations will have to be considered in relation to circadian variation in leptin secretion, as well as variation in the spacing of meals. In addition, there are some data that suggest a threshold effect of leptin on normal pubertal development (Cheung et al., 1997). More recently, it has been suggested that ghrelin plays a role in the link between fuel availability and reproduction (Barreiro and Tena-Sempere, 2004).

Specific Hungers

What do we eat? In humans, much of what is consumed is culturally determined: in other words, we learn what to eat (**FIGURE 9.33**). Many nonhuman animals also learn to eat foods that improve their health and to avoid foods that make them ill. For example, rats provided with a diet lacking thiamine (vitamin B_1) do not seek out foods rich in thiamine but instead sample many foods and over the course of several days begin to prefer foods containing thiamine. Humans are no better at

FIGURE 9.32 In Syrian hamsters, estrous cycles can be interrupted by 48 hours of fasting.

FIGURE 9.33 **Depending on your cultural heritage,** you may or may not consider scorpion kebabs to be food, regardless of their nutritional value.

detecting thiamine deficiencies than rats. In the nineteenth century, thousands of people in Southeast Asia died from beriberi, a degenerative disease of the nervous system resulting from thiamine deficiency. The cause of this outbreak of beriberi was the fashion of polishing rice before cooking. The hulls that were removed from the rice contained the thiamine. Once the practice of rice polishing was discontinued, beriberi became rare again. Because humans are unable to recognize thiamine in food, this vitamin has become a common food additive.

In contrast to learned preferences, some physiological requirements seem to elicit specific, unlearned hungers. For example, hungers for sodium and potassium appear to be innate (Milner and Zucker, 1965; Richter et al., 1938). However, even these hardwired specific hungers can be modified by hormones. Most animals, even without prior experience, prefer sucrose-laced water over plain water. This preference is mediated by taste, because preferences also exist for water containing nonnutritive substances such as saccharin or NutraSweet over plain water. An argument can be made that the intrinsic preference for sweet tastes is adaptive because it would increase intake of valuable energy resources. However, the yearning for chocolate is not hardwired at birth but is an acquired taste.

Female mammals, including rats, mice, hamsters, monkeys, and human infants, consume greater quantities of sweet solutions than their male counterparts (Wade, 1976; Zucker et al., 1972). This sex difference is hormonally mediated; sex differences in taste preferences appear to be organized perinatally by androgens and also activated by sex steroid hormones in adulthood. Generally, estrogens stimulate sweet solution preferences; ovariectomy reduces the preference for sweet substances to the level of that in males (Wade, 1976). Castrated males show sweet solution preferences only slightly greater than those of gonadally intact males (Zucker, 1969).

Certainly, the taste for sodium and, to a lesser degree, potassium is innate in many species. Young animals that are sodium or potassium deprived seek out and prefer diets that contain these nutrients; these preferences are immediate and do not require feedback in terms of improvement of health, as in the case of thiamine. Several vertebrate species, including humans, show early and pervasive preferences for a slightly salty solution over plain water (Richter, 1936). One patient, a young boy of 3 or 4, was hospitalized because he was undergoing precocious puberty and experiencing development of secondary sex characters. He refused the bland hospital diet and died after a week in the hospital. An autopsy revealed that his adrenal glands were abnormal: the cells of the zona reticularis, which produce sex steroids, had invaded the zona glomerulosa, which normally produces aldosterone, the major sodium regulator. His parents reported that their son had consumed extremely salty foods and refused most foods that were not very salty at home. In fact, salt was one of the first words that he learned to say (Wilkins and Richter, 1940). Thus, failure of the adrenal glands to produce sufficient aldosterone can promote a powerful specific hunger for sodium.

Conclusions

As already described, many hormonal and neural signals act in concert to balance energy intake and energy expenditure. It appears that hormones affect feeding behavior primarily by affecting the sensory systems related to feeding. CCK has been found to reduce neural activity in the brain regions where sensory information from the taste buds is received (Moran et al., 1983). Similarly, estradiol enhances the neural firing rates of afferent fibers from the tongue. Hormones also probably increase the sensory capabilities of animals hunting for food.

Hormones also have direct effects on the central processing mechanisms controlling food intake. CCK infusions into the brain appear to stop feeding behavior in rats. The hormone's mode of action, and how it would normally cross the blood-brain barrier, are unknown. CCK acts in the periphery by interacting with the vagus nerve (Weatherford et al., 1993). Insulin also exerts direct effects on the central nervous system to stop feeding (Woods and Porte, 1983). Although insulin and leptin are too large to cross the blood-brain barrier, brain capillaries contain receptors for insulin and leptin that enable these hormones to be transported through the capillary walls into the brain interstitial fluid biologically intact (Schwartz et al., 1992). Other peptides, including ghrelin, GLP-1, PYY, and adiponectin, have also been proposed to act centrally to modulate food intake (see Schneider and Watts, 2002, for review). Hormones have not been shown to increase the efficiency of effectors of food intake; that is, hormones do not increase chewing frequency or increase efficacy of the muscles involved in feeding.

Although we know a lot about the endocrine mediation of feeding behavior, particularly in rats, there are many different feeding strategies that probably have very different types of controlling mechanisms. For example, some snakes consume a large prey item and then do not eat again for many days as they digest their meal. Similarly, many cats hunt prey and eat some of it, then leave the remains or carry them to a resting spot. What cues tell snakes and cats that they are fed? What cues indicate hunger? The endocrine mediation of these signals in snakes and cats may very well differ in many respects from that in rats and primates, or it may be identical. Many species go for weeks or even months without eating. Sometimes these fasting individuals are inactive, such as hibernating squirrels, but in other cases the animals are engaged in other activities, as elephant seals are during the breeding season. The endocrine control of metabolism in these long-term fasting animals and the signals that stop them from feeding require further study. All in all, the study of hormones and homeostasis provides a unique opportunity to investigate the complex interactions among physiology, morphology, and behavior.

Summary

1. Individuals are motivated to maintain specific endogenous levels of water, sodium, and other nutrients. The process by which animals maintain a fairly stable internal environment is called homeostasis.

2. Most homeostatic systems operate like a thermostatically controlled heating and cooling system. To maintain homeostasis, a system requires a detection mechanism to note any deviation from a set point. The homeostatic system must also be able to mobilize the organism to make changes to return it to the normal range. Finally, the system must have some way to recognize when the desired change occurs and feed back to stop the mobilization process.

3. In multicellular organisms, water and sodium levels are maintained within narrow ranges by physiological and behavioral systems. Most water is located inside the cells; the water outside the cells is located both in blood vessels and in the interstitial fluid. Sodium is important in the movement of water between the extracellular and intracellular fluid compartments.

4. Movement of fluid out of cells causes cellular dehydration, a potent stimulus for osmotic thirst. Consumption of salty or sugary foods induces osmotic thirst. Cellular dehydration of osmoreceptors in the brain causes ADH secretion from the posterior pituitary, which promotes water conservation by the kidneys. Drinking water alleviates osmotic thirst.

5. Hypovolemic thirst is caused by reduced blood volume (hypovolemia). Quenching hypovolemic thirst requires ingestion of water, sodium, and other solutes.

6. Hypovolemia stimulates the production of angiotensin II, a potent vasoconstrictor. Angiotensin II may also increase drinking behavior.

Companion Website

sites.sinauer.com/be5e

Go to the
*Behavioral Endocrinology
Companion Website*
for animated tutorials,
videos, web links, and
an online glossary.

7. Angiotensin II triggers the release of aldosterone from the adrenals; aldosterone promotes sodium retention and subsequent water conservation by the kidneys. Aldosterone affects drinking behavior indirectly by its influence on osmotic thirst.

8. The need for metabolic fuels is continuous, but food intake is episodic; consequently, energy intake and expenditure are never quite balanced. After a meal, there is a surplus of energy that must be stored for later use. Insulin is the only hormone that promotes energy storage by cells.

9. Although insulin is critical for energy storage, many other hormones, including epinephrine, norepinephrine, glucocorticoids, thyroid hormones, growth hormone, somatomedin, and glucagon, are involved in getting energy out of storage.

10. The stimuli eliciting feeding are numerous and include physiological signals from fat stores, levels of glycogen stores, and the nature and quality of the food, as well as neural and hormonal signals from the gut.

11. Cholecystokinin and amylin are released during ingestion and appear to provide an endocrine signal of satiety, acting to inhibit feeding via the vagus nerve.

12. Endogenous opioids may alter the hedonic value of food. Treatment with opioid antagonists reduces food intake.

13. A complex network of neuropeptides and hormones acts to maintain energy balance. Several peptide hormones, including corticotropin-releasing hormone, leptin, neuropeptide Y, bombesin, and glucagon, influence food intake. Neuropeptide Y, AgRP, MCH, orexin A, and ghrelin are orexigenic, that is, potent inducers of food intake.

14. Insulin may signal the central nervous system about peripheral levels of metabolic fuels via the cerebrospinal fluid. Intracerebroventricular infusions of insulin reduce food intake.

15. Gonadal steroid hormones also act to affect food intake and body mass. Generally, estrogens reduce food intake and body mass, as well as increasing voluntary exercise. Progesterone blocks these effects of estrogen. Androgens generally increase food intake and body mass.

16. Many species must learn what foods to consume, but some physiological requirements elicit unlearned specific hungers. Specific hungers for sodium and potassium appear to be common in terrestrial vertebrates. Hormones mediate some specific hungers.

17. Both leptin and insulin are peripheral adiposity signals that circulate in proportion to stored adipose tissue. Receptors for each hormone are found in the central nervous system, especially in the hypothalamus, and when activated appear to affect food intake. Impaired neuronal signal transduction by either hormone is associated with increased food intake and body fat stores.

18. Insulin and leptin act in the arcuate nuclei of the hypothalamus to suppress expression of neuropeptide Y and agouti-related peptide (NPY/AgRP) in neurons, which promotes an anabolic state (increased food intake; decreased energy expenditure), while stimulating expression of pro-opiomelanocortin and cocaine- and amphetamine-regulated transcript (POMC/CART) neurons that promote catabolic effects (anorexia; elevated energy expenditure).

Questions for Discussion

1. In what ways is a thermostat a poor analogy, and in what ways is it a good analogy, for the control of food intake and body mass?

2. Compare and contrast type 1 and type 2 diabetes mellitus and diabetes insipidus.

3. Discuss the importance of the existence of neuropeptides that regulate energy homeostasis in both the brain and the gastrointestinal system. What are the advantages of having control at the levels of both the brain and the periphery?

4. Morbidly obese people undergoing gastric bypass surgery to lose weight often display improved endocrine responses prior to losing much weight. How might this occur?

5. How are hormones that have central processing effects on feeding behavior different from or similar to neurotransmitters? Are the distinctions between hormones and neurotransmitters applicable when discussing chemical mediation of behavior in the brain?

6. Compare and contrast the conditions of volemic and osmotic thirst and the differential endocrine responses to these conditions.

Suggested Readings

Begg, D. P., and Woods, S. C. 2013. The endocrinology of food intake. *Nat. Rev. Endocrinol.*, 9:584–597.

Daniels, D., and Fluharty, S. J. 2017. Neuroendocrinology of body fluid homeostasis. In D. W. Pfaff, et al. (eds.), *Hormones, Brain and Behavior* (3rd ed.), pp. 259–288. Academic Press, New York.

Grill, H. J., and Hayes, M. R. 2012. Hindbrain neurons as an essential hub in the neuroanatomically distributed control of energy balance. *Cell. Metab.*, 16:296–309.

Hussain, S. S., and Bloom, S. R. 2013. The regulation of food intake by the gut-brain axis: Implications for obesity. *Int. J. Obesity*, 37:625–633.

Knepper, M.A., et al. 2015. Molecular physiology of water balance. *N. Engl. J. Med.*, 272:1349–1358.

Schneider, J. E., and Watts, A. G. 2017. Energy partitioning, ingestive behavior, and reproductive success. In D. W. Pfaff, et al. (eds.), *Hormones, Brain and Behavior* (3rd ed.), pp. 205–258. Academic Press, New York.

Speakman, J. R. 2014. If body fatness is under physiological regulation, then how come we have an obesity epidemic? *Physiology*, 29:88–98.

Biological Rhythms

10

Learning Objectives

This chapter provides an introduction to biological clocks and their significance in coordinating physiological and behavioral functioning. The focus of the chapter is on daily and seasonal rhythms, as these are the most well-studied cycles in behavioral neuroendocrinology. By the end of this chapter, you should be able to:

- differentiate between exogenous and endogenous rhythms.

- explain the importance of rhythms of different durations in guiding behavior and physiology.

- discuss where and how *circadian rhythms* are generated in the brain and how rhythmic information is communicated to the central and peripheral nervous system.

- relate the importance of the circadian system to maintaining optimal health and preventing disease.

- explain how the brain tracks seasonal time to appropriately coordinate physiology and behavior.

As you probably know, some animals (e.g., horses, ground squirrels, and chickens) are **diurnal**, or active during the day, and some animals (e.g., hamsters, raccoons, and owls) are **nocturnal**, or active at night. Other animals (e.g., white-tailed deer and mosquitoes) are **crepuscular**, or primarily active at dawn and dusk. Animals have evolved to restrict many of their behaviors, including feeding, drinking, mating, and locomotor activities, to specific temporal niches in response to a complex web of selective forces. Humans have also evolved to occupy a specific temporal niche; however, with the advent of electric lights about 130 years ago, humans have overcome this temporal constraint, albeit not without significant biological consequences (Foster and Roenneberg, 2008; Roenneberg et al., 2013) (**BOX 10.1**).

BOX 10.1 *Jet Lag*

The temporal niche of humans during the past million or so years has remained quite stable (Moore-Ede et al., 1982); it has been estimated that the time required for the Earth to rotate once on its axis has slowed by only about 20 seconds during the last million years (Rosenberg and Runcorn, 1975). In contrast, the technological changes of the past century have had staggering and unprecedented effects on our temporal environment. The invention of electric lights has permitted round-the-clock shift work, and powerful security lights keep some environments brightly illuminated 24 hours a day. The development of jet travel has led to abrupt phase shifts not previously encountered by east–west travelers (most jet travel occurs on east–west, rather than north–south, routes because many commercial centers in Asia, Europe, and North America are at similar latitudes).

Jet lag, the physiological and behavioral responses to jet travel across time zones, involves phase shifts in all the zeitgebers (i.e., external stimuli that synchronize endogenous rhythms to environmental time) at once. Symptoms include sleep disruption; disruption of digestive processes; impaired psychological processes, including attention, perception, and motivation; and a general feeling of malaise (Office of Technology Assessment, 1991). Most studies indicate that these symptoms are less pronounced when travelers phase-delay (travel west) than phase-advance (travel east). For example, one study discovered that resynchronization of psychomotor performance rhythms took longer for people on eastbound flights than for people on westbound flights, although eastbound travelers could hasten adaptation to local time by being outdoors (Klein and Wegmann, 1974; Moore-Ede et al., 1982). In general, the severity of jet lag symptoms also correlates with the number of time zones crossed. One study showed that physiological adaptation to westbound travel (phase delay) took less time than adaptation to east-bound travel (phase advance) for travelers who crossed four or more time zones. Virtually everyone can easily adapt to 1-hour phase shifts and is adversely affected by 12-hour phase shifts, but there are tremendous individual differences in how temporal phase shifts

affect performance, as well as in the speed of resynchronization following time shifts. Studies also show that elderly people have more difficulty with the effects of jet lag than younger people do. Appropriately timed melatonin treatment may provide some relief from the symptoms of jet lag (Arendt, 1998). Outdoor exercise has also been reported to ameliorate jet lag symptoms (Shiota et al., 1996).

Chronic jet lag can have serious effects on memory function. In one study, flight crews that worked on transmeridian flights were compared with ground crews (Cho et al., 2000). The flight crews showed higher salivary cortisol values than the ground crews. The flight crews also displayed memory deficits. A follow-up study examined two sets of flight crews: one flight crew was designated as "short-recovery" as they had less than 5 days to recover from an international flight (>7 time zones), whereas the other flight crew was designated as a "long-recovery" flight crew and had more than 15 days to recover from such flights. The flight crews were similar in most other ways. Ten female flight attendants were subjected to a functional MRI. Individuals working under the short-recovery schedule had smaller hippocampal volumes than individuals working the long-recovery schedule (A,B in figure). These short-recovery flight attendants also displayed elevated cortisol (C in figure) and significant cognitive impairments (Cho, 2001) (D,E in figure). The hippocampus is where many memory processes occur. These studies indicate that chronic jet lag should be avoided.

However, even a 1-hour phase shift can be significant for some individuals. In many industrialized nations, the entire population undergoes a 1-hour phase shift twice a year with the change from standard time to daylight saving time. It usually requires several days for people to make the adjustment to this biennial time shift in their circadian systems (Monk and Aplin, 1980). In the United States, the rate of traffic accidents increases significantly in the week following the time change (Monk, 1980). Whether this statistic reflects an impairment of attention and psychomotor coordination because of alterations in our circadian systems or whether it is due to missed appointments because of incorrectly set watches is open to question.

diurnal   Active during the day.
nocturnal   Active at night.
crepuscular   Active at dawn and dusk.

This temporal variation in behavior presumably reflects temporal variation in underlying physiology. As we will discover, virtually all physiological processes vary over time. Specific to our interests here, endocrine secretion varies markedly over the course of minutes, over the course of a day, and over the course of a year (**FIGURE 10.1**). Because of this temporal variation in endocrine function, it should not be particularly surprising to you that behavior, especially behavior that is mediated by hormones, exhibits pronounced temporal variation. Much of this temporal variation is regulated by biological clocks. In this chapter, we will focus on daily and seasonal organization of hormone-behavior interactions.

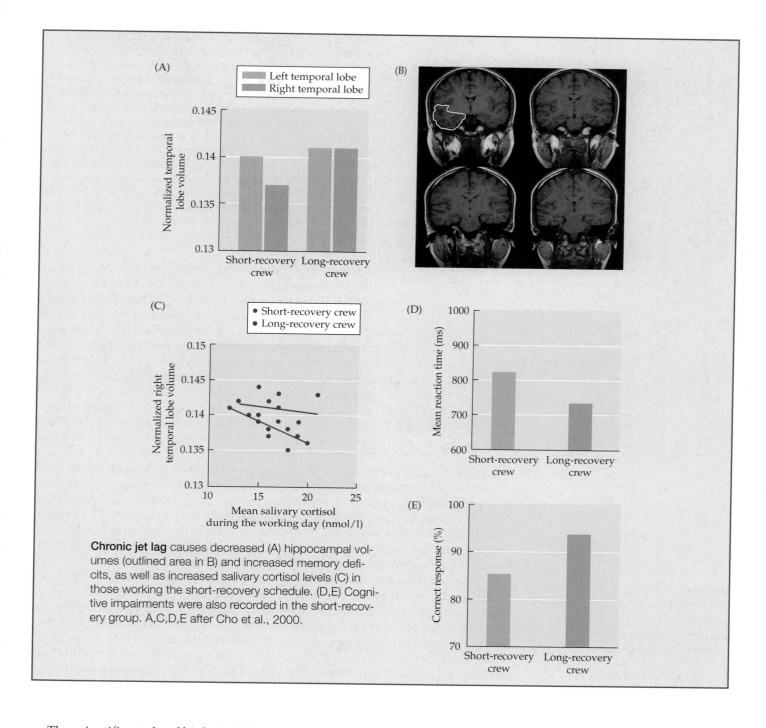

Chronic jet lag causes decreased (A) hippocampal volumes (outlined area in B) and increased memory deficits, as well as increased salivary cortisol levels (C) in those working the short-recovery schedule. (D,E) Cognitive impairments were also recorded in the short-recovery group. A,C,D,E after Cho et al., 2000.

The scientific study of biological clocks and their associated rhythms is called **chronobiology**. Although biological rhythms have been informally recognized by biologists for centuries, the formal study of biological timekeeping began in the 1960s. One reason that chronobiology took so long to develop as a scientific discipline is that it had to counteract the dogma of homeostasis in the biological sciences and medicine. In Chapter 9 we learned that homeostatic processes work to maintain physiological parameters within tightly regulated specific ranges. Biologists and physicians often considered large fluctuations to be pathological, and many resisted the idea of the programmed changes in physiology and behavior that we now un-

chronobiology The study of biological clocks and their associated rhythms. Also referred to as *biochronometry*.

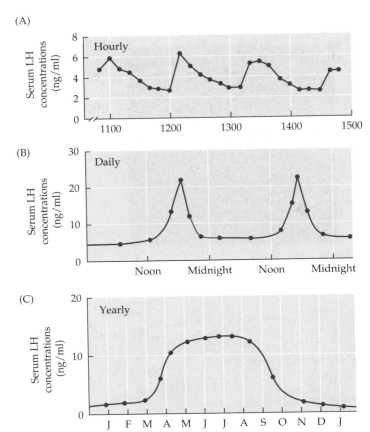

(A) Hourly
Serum LH concentrations (ng/ml)
1100 1200 1300 1400 1500

(B) Daily
Serum LH concentrations (ng/ml)
Noon Midnight Noon Midnight

(C) Yearly
Serum LH concentrations (ng/ml)
J F M A M J J A S O N D J

FIGURE 10.1 Endocrine function shows rhythmic variation over time. Luteinizing hormone (LH) is rhythmically released in hamsters over several different time scales. (A) Assessments every 10 minutes reveal that LH is released in pulses that recur every 30–90 minutes. (B) Samples obtained every 6 hours will not detect 30–90-minute pulses but reveal a daily rhythm of LH release. These daily surges consist of programmed increases in the 30–90-minute pulse frequency and pulse amplitude that result in elevated blood concentrations of LH. (C) Blood samples obtained once a month from hamsters housed in simulated winter conditions do not detect daily pulses, but an annual pattern of LH secretion emerges, showing that blood LH concentrations are generally higher during the breeding season in spring and summer than during autumn and winter.

derstand to underlie homeostatic processes. Many of the specific homeostatic ranges discussed in Chapter 9 are not static but, in fact, change over time. To take these changes into account, the thermostat analogy that we used in that chapter must be updated to an automatic, electronic thermostat that can be programmed to limit heating or cooling to times when people are likely to be home. This temporal variation increases the efficiency of the home heating system. Similarly, biological clocks increase biological efficiency and thus increase fitness. This chapter will describe such temporal variations generally and will focus specifically on the interaction among biological rhythms, hormones, and behavior.

Because the study of biological clocks has revealed properties much like those of physical oscillators, chronobiology has borrowed terms and concepts extensively from engineering disciplines. A **rhythm** is a recurrent event that is characterized by its period, frequency, amplitude, and phase (Aschoff, 1981) (**FIGURE 10.2**). The **period** is the length of time required to complete one cycle of the rhythm in question, for instance, the amount of time required to go from peak to peak or trough to trough. **Frequency** is computed as the number of completed cycles per unit of time (e.g., two cycles per day) and, thus, is the reciprocal of period. **Amplitude** is the amount of change above and below the average value, that is, the distance of the peak or nadir from the average. The **phase** represents a point in the rhythm relative to some objective time point during the cycle. For example, under normal conditions, the phase of onset of the activity portion of a hamster's activity-rest cycle corresponds closely with the onset of dark. Phase relations among various biological rhythms can also be described; for instance, the onset of the low body temperature phase of a hamster's daily body temperature cycle tightly corresponds with the onset of the sleep portion of its sleep-wake cycle.

The goal of this chapter is to describe the characteristics of biological clocks and their associated rhythms in hormone-behavior interactions, as well as to understand the temporal organization of these interactions.

Traditionally, timing has not been considered an important variable in the study of the mechanisms underlying behavior or physiology. Yet, behavioral constructs such as learning, memory, sensation, perception, attention, and especially motivation vary markedly according to the time of day or season of the year. Motivation can be defined generally as why individuals do what they do. From a neurobiological perspective, an animal eats because its hunger circuits are activated by specific neurochemicals. However, the response of neural circuits underlying motivated behaviors varies at different times of day or seasons of the year; therefore, it is es-

rhythm   A recurrent event that is characterized by its period, frequency, amplitude, and phase.

period   The length of time required to complete one cycle of a rhythm, such as the amount of time between peaks in a cycle.

frequency   The number of completed cycles per unit of time; for example, two cycles per month.

amplitude   In biological rhythms, the amount of change in the rhythm above (to the peak) or below (to the nadir) the average value.

phase   A point in a rhythm relative to some objective time point during the cycle, or during the cycle of another rhythm.

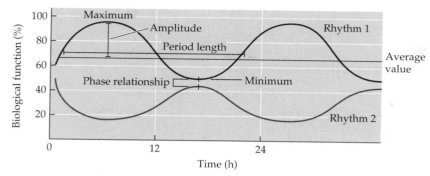

FIGURE 10.2 Components of biological rhythms Rhythms can be analyzed in terms of amplitude, frequency, and period length. The relationship of one rhythm to another is expressed in terms of phase relationships. Both cycles have a period of about 24 hours (frequency = 1/day).

sential to consider timing when asking questions about the biological mechanisms underlying behavior. To add to this example, we can think of an animal's daily schedule as a cycle of rest and wake, starving and feeding, in response to the effects of its internal biological clock on the responsiveness of hunger circuits to specific neurochemical signals. In addition, it is becoming increasingly apparent that disruptions to biological rhythms have pronounced negative impact on our mental and physical health, contributing to the etiology of a number of disease states, including cancer, cardiovascular disease, neural cell death, peptic ulcers, obesity, rheumatoid arthritis, bipolar disorder, depression, and schizophrenia (reviewed in Golombek et al., 2013). For most of us, disruptions to circadian timing are relatively chronic, due to limited exposure to sunlight during the day, use of artificial light at night, and sleeping later on weekends (Dominoni et al., 2016; Roenneberg et al., 2013). Thus, another goal of the present chapter is to consider how dysregulated temporal homeostasis contributes to disease states and how to maximize biological timing given modern constraints.

Exogenous versus Endogenous Control of Biological Clocks

Some behavioral rhythms have been recognized since ancient times, but they have generally been attributed to **exogenous** (outside the organism) factors. For example, the activity-rest rhythms displayed by many species were believed to be caused by daily signals arising from the environment. Thus, one simplistic explanation of how the daily light-dark cycle might drive the activity-rest rhythm of hamsters might be that the light of day is too intense for their eyes, so they rest during the daylight hours and become active after dark. We now know, however, that **endogenous** (inside the organism) timing mechanisms mediate many of the observed rhythms in physiology and behavior.

How is it established whether a rhythm is the result of exogenous factors or an endogenous clock? One type of convincing evidence is provided by isolation experiments. The persistence of a biological rhythm in the absence of environmental cues provides compelling evidence that the rhythm in question is generated within the animal, and not driven by the environment. If a biological rhythm disappears under constant conditions, then it is reasonable to suggest that some cyclic cue in the environment drives the biological rhythm. This logic was first applied to the study of biological rhythms in 1729, when the French astronomer Jean Jacques d'Ortous de Mairan described the tension-relaxation pattern of a heliotropic plant—a plant with leaves that open during the day and close at night—that persisted even

exogenous Relating to a substance or process outside the organism.

endogenous Relating to a substance or process within the organism.

FIGURE 10.3 **De Mairan's experiment** Heliotropic plants isolated from sunlight continued to open and close in synchrony with the day-night cycle, suggesting that this rhythm has an endogenous, rather than an exogenous, source. De Mairan's report is the first recorded observation that biological rhythms can persist in the absence of environmental cues.

when the plant was maintained in the total darkness of a cellar for several days (De Mairan, 1729) (**FIGURE 10.3**). This result was largely ignored for over 100 years until Augustin de Candolle, a French botanist, expanded on de Mairan's initial observation. Mimosa (*Mimosa pudica*) leaf movements also continued in constant dark conditions, but like most other internally generated biological rhythms, these rhythms displayed slight to moderate deviations from 24 hours in period length in the absence of environmental cues (de Candolle, 1832).

Similar examples were reported sporadically over the course of the next 200 years. Although such demonstrations were consistent with the existence of endogenously driven biological clocks, the scientific community largely maintained that these reported rhythms merely reflected rhythms in the environment. From the 1930s through the 1960s, biologists gradually began to accept the existence of endogenous biological clocks, although some scientists continued to argue that the persistent biological rhythms observed when all apparent environmental cues were absent could be explained away as reflecting subtle geophysical forces that simply had yet to be discovered (e.g., Brown, 1972). However, recent evidence has convinced virtually everyone that the clocks driving physiology and behavior are inside the organism and, though often synchronized by the environment, are not driven by the environment. Several types of evidence support this conclusion:

- Animals maintained in constant conditions aboard a spacecraft orbiting far above the Earth, presumably far away from subtle geophysical cues, display biological rhythms with periods similar to those observed on Earth.

- Animals maintained in adjacent, but separate, cages in the absence of environmental cues display biological rhythms with stable but slightly different periods, suggesting that they are not being driven by the same geophysical cues.

- The period (and phase) of the biological rhythms of one individual can be transferred to another individual by means of tissue transplants.

- The period (and phase) of the biological rhythms is heritable and depends on identified genes.

Types of Biological Clocks and Rhythms

Biological timekeeping mechanisms are fundamental characteristics of living cells. This is not a surprising adaptation given the major influence of the daily solar cycle. All animals and virtually all plants studied to date possess endogenous biological clocks that mediate biological rhythms. The periods of biological rhythms display a large temporal range—from the 1-millisecond cycle of enzymatic reactions to the 1-second cycle of the heart beating to the daily sleep-wake cycles to longer cycles, such as the 21-day estrous cycles of cows, the 1-year cycle of ground squirrel hibernation, the 10-year cycle of the thickening of fur in the arctic lynx, or the 100-year cycle of the flowering of certain species of Chinese bamboo (*Phyllostachys bambusoides*) (**FIGURE 10.4**).

circadian rhythm A biological rhythm with a period of about 24 hours.

circatidal rhythm A biological rhythm with a period of about 12.4 hours that is closely tied to changes in tides.

circalunar rhythm A biological rhythm with a period of about 29.5 days that is closely tied to phases of the moon.

circannual rhythm A biological rhythm with a period of about 12 months.

FIGURE 10.4 **The diversity of biological rhythms** The period lengths of biological rhythms range from milliseconds (top) to many years (bottom). The longest known period, the time that elapses between flowerings of certain bamboo species, lasts 100 years. After Aschoff, 1981; Michael and Bonsall, 1977.

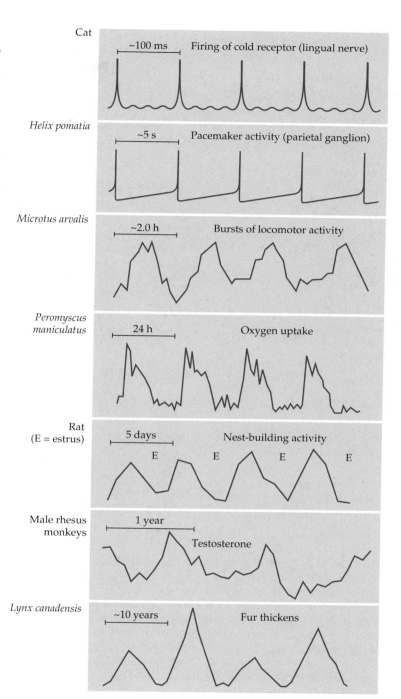

The periods of some biological rhythms, including most central nervous system, cardiovascular, and respiratory rhythms, vary widely within the same individual; for example, the period of heartbeats decreases (i.e., the frequency increases) during exercise because heart rhythms are dependent on activity levels. The periods of other endogenous cycles, such as the ovarian cycle, are largely constant for the same individual, but there may be great interindividual or interspecific variation. However, there are four types of biological rhythms that are typically coupled with environmental cues, and the periods of these rhythms do not vary much under natural conditions. These relatively constant biological rhythms mimic the periods of the geophysical cycles of night and day (**circadian**), the tides (**circatidal**), the phases of the moon (**circalunar**), and the seasons of the year (**circannual**) (Palmer, 1976) (**TABLE 10.1**). These rhythms persist when animals are isolated from the respective environmental cues, but in that case they only approximate the periods of the environmental cycles with which they are normally coupled, as we will see below. Thus, the terms for many biological rhythms use the prefix *circa*, from the Latin word meaning "about" (e.g., *circa*, "about"; *dies*, "day"; circadian, "about a day") (Halberg, 1959). Although conducting an experiment that isolates animals from environmental cues is necessary to determine the extent of endogenous generation of any biological rhythm, it should be emphasized that the environment often exerts permissive effects on endogenously driven biological rhythms. For instance, chronic food restriction, or maintenance in constant bright lights, dampens the expression of estrous cycles in laboratory strains of rats.

TABLE 10.1 *Comparison of biological rhythm types*

Rhythm type	Environmental cycle	Period length	
		Entrained	Free-running
Circadian	Rotation of the Earth	24 hours	22–26 hours
Circatidal	Tides	12.4 hours	11–14 hours
Circalunar	Phases of the moon	29.5 days	26–32 days
Circannual	Seasons of the year	365.25 days	330–400 days

(A)

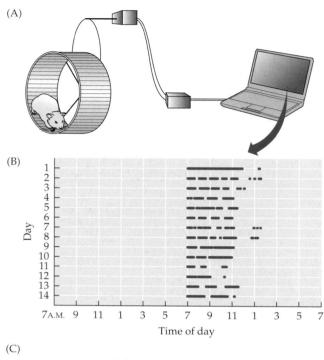

(B)

(C)

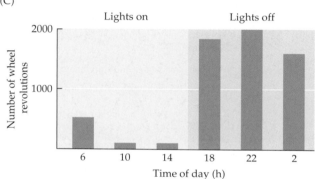

FIGURE 10.5 Collection of data on behavioral biological rhythms (A) A common method of measuring rhythms in loco-motor activity is a wheel-running apparatus that activates data output with each revolution of the wheel. (B) Sustained wheel-running activity appears as a solid bar across the time line for each day. The activity record is read like sheet music, with each line representing 24 hours. The period of the daily biological rhythm can be measured from the onset of activity on one day to the onset of activity on the next. (C) The frequency of activity can be measured by counting the number of wheel revolutions each night. The amplitude is the distance between the peak and the trough of the number of wheel revolutions. Phase could be measured as the amount of time between the onset of running and the onset of darkness.

An important experimental technique used in the study of biological rhythms involves keeping a log of physical activity over time. Basically, monitoring of activity cycles is adapted to the species under investigation. Often small mammals are placed in a cage equipped with a running wheel connected to a counting device that automatically produces a continuous record of the animal's activity (**FIGURE 10.5**). The locomotor activity of small birds is often determined by monitoring perch-hopping activities around the clock. Humans can be equipped with electronic monitoring devices that transmit the movements of an individual to a central monitoring station (**FIGURE 10.6**).

Light serves as a potent environmental time cue, or **zeitgeber** (from the German, meaning "time giver"), for hamsters as well as for most other species (Pittendrigh and Daan, 1976). Temperature is an important zeitgeber for some poikilothermic animals, and possibly a secondary zeitgeber for birds and mammals, but light is the primary zeitgeber among homeothermic animals. If a hamster is placed in constant dim light so that there is no daily zeitgeber, then the onset time of its locomotor activity begins to drift (**FIGURE 10.7**). Without the daily light-dark cycle providing a daily reset, the endogenous clock of the hamster can only approximate 24-hour cycles. If a hamster usually begins to run in its wheel at 7:10 P.M., then in the absence of light-dark cycles, it may begin its wheel-running behavior 15 minutes later each day, with wheel-running activity onset at 7:25, 7:40, 7:55, and so on for subsequent days. Given that there are 1440 minutes in each day, a 15-minute "error" is only an error of about 1%! The variability of the period from cycle to cycle for some species (e.g., flying squirrels and some inbred mouse strains) is <4 minutes out of every 1440 minutes per day. For example, individual mice of the C57BL/6J strain display a free-running period of 23.7 ± 0.1 hour—a daily error of only 0.4% of the period!

Other hamsters may begin their wheel-running activity 10 minutes earlier each day. Biological rhythms such as these that are not synchronized with environmental cues are said to be **free-running**. Each individual displays its own free-running period. After the animals have been in constant dim lighting conditions for about a week, it is possible to observe different individuals housed in the same room running in their wheels at different times throughout the day. Thus, the free-running periods of biological clocks are precise but are not exactly 24 hours. The observation that different hamsters display an array of different free-running periods when housed in the same room suggests that they are not synchronized by one another's behavior and that subtle geophysical cues are not providing any temporal information.

Animals display species-specific times of locomotor activity onset that are often linked to the timing of food intake, water consumption, and reproductive behavior. In the case of hamsters—an animal often used in studies of biological rhythms—locomotor activity begins right after lights are turned off each day. If lights are turned off at 7:00 P.M. each evening, hamsters begin to run in their wheels at about 7:05–7:15 P.M. each evening. More than 99% of their wheel-running activity is confined to

(A)

(B)

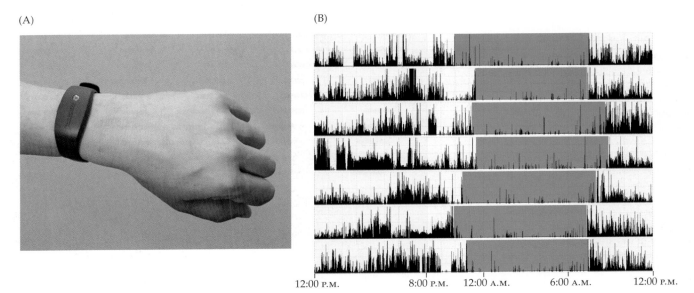

12:00 P.M.   8:00 P.M.   12:00 A.M.   6:00 A.M.   12:00 P.M.

FIGURE 10.6 **Human locomotor activity can be monitored by a small motion detector.** Recording human activity is called actigraphy and is important in studies of circadian biology, including sleep studies. The simplest actigraph is a pedometer, but this does not measure intensity of movement or the timing of movement; thus a more complicated device to assess these parameters is necessary to measure human daily activity. (A) A small recording device can be attached to a wristband, and data can be downloaded via USB port. (B) The blue-shaded areas denote sleep time. The amplitude (height) of the bars depicts the intensity of the movement activity. Each row represents a 24-hour day.

the dark portion of the daily light-dark cycle. Hamsters also confine the majority of their eating, drinking, food hoarding, and sexual behaviors to the dark portion of the daily light-dark cycle. If the environmental light-dark cycles are *phase-shifted* (e.g., lights are turned off 4 hours later, as in Figure 10.7), hamsters adapt their activity rhythms to the new regimen in about four or five cycles. The circadian rhythms of other physiological processes, such as adrenocortical hormone release, body temperature, and blood plasma volume, may require longer to adapt to the new schedule. This process of adaptation to rapid phase shifts in environmental

zeitgeber A potent environmental time cue, or temporal synchronizer.

free-running rhythm A biological rhythm that is not synchronized to its natural zeitgeber and expresses its own endogenous rhythm.

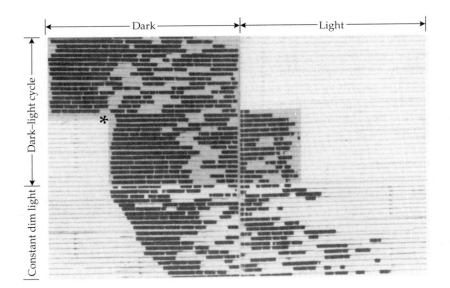

FIGURE 10.7 **Wheel-running behavior of a hamster** When housed in a 12:12 dark-light cycle (lights off for 12 hours, then on for 12 hours), a hamster confines its wheel running to the dark part of the cycle (at top left). If the onset of darkness is shifted ahead by 4 hours (at the asterisk), then the hamster adjusts to the new cycle. If the dark-light cycle is suspended entirely and the hamster is housed in constant dim light, it no longer expresses a 24-hour cycle of activity but free-runs with a period greater than 24 hours (at bottom center). This free-running cycle represents the endogenous circadian rhythm of the individual. From Zucker, 1980.

FIGURE 10.8 Phase-response curve
A free-running nocturnal individual maintained in constant dark conditions was
exposed to a 1-hour light pulse at various times during its subjective day and
night. The blue bars at the top of the
figure are a schematic record of activity
(wheel running), which occurred during
the animal's subjective night. (A) When
the light pulse was given in the middle of
the subjective day, the subsequent activity onset time was unaffected; the middle
of the subjective day is thus called the
dead zone. (B) A light pulse at the end of
the subjective day phase-delayed activity the next day by about 1 hour. (C) With
a light pulse at the start of the subjective
night, a substantial phase delay (3 hours)
was observed. (D) A light pulse given later
during the subjective night caused a substantial advance (4 hours) of activity onset
the next day. (E) Finally, a light pulse at
the start of the subjective day caused a
2-hour phase advance in activity the following day. Light affects the endogenous
circadian rhythms to entrain them to
exactly 24 hours each day. After Moore-
Ede et al., 1982.

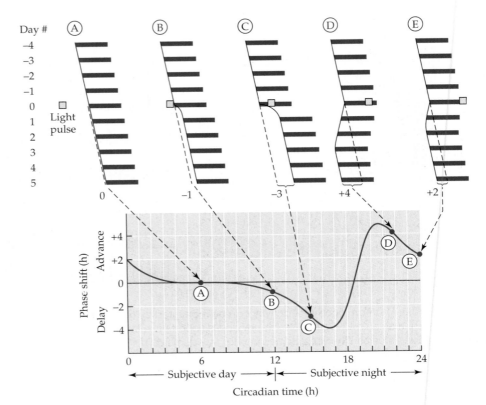

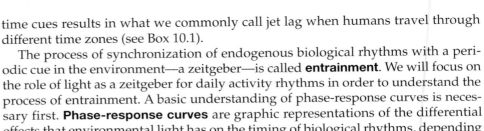

entrainment   The synchronization of biological rhythms to a
periodic environmental cue.

phase-response curves
A graphic representation of the
differential effects that a periodic
environmental cue (usually light)
has on the timing of biological
rhythms.

time cues results in what we commonly call jet lag when humans travel through
different time zones (see Box 10.1).

   The process of synchronization of endogenous biological rhythms with a periodic cue in the environment—a zeitgeber—is called **entrainment**. We will focus on
the role of light as a zeitgeber for daily activity rhythms in order to understand the
process of entrainment. A basic understanding of phase-response curves is necessary first. **Phase-response curves** are graphic representations of the differential
effects that environmental light has on the timing of biological rhythms, depending
on the phase relationship of the light to the circadian organization of the animal
in question (**FIGURE 10.8**). Exposure to light at different times throughout the day
does not result in uniform responses of free-running biological rhythms. If hamsters
(or humans) are maintained in constant dark conditions, their biological rhythms
begin to free-run, with the period of onset of locomotor activity varying slightly
from 24 hours. The circadian period can thus be divided into a "subjective night"
and a "subjective day." Because hamsters are nocturnal, the beginning of activity
usually coincides with the onset of the creature's subjective night, whereas the rest
period begins at the beginning of the animal's subjective day. For diurnal animals,
the onset of activity coincides with the beginning of the animal's subjective day,
and the rest period begins at the beginning of the animal's subjective night. If free-
running hamsters that are housed in continuous darkness are exposed to an hour
of light at any time throughout the middle of the subjective day, then the time of
onset of the next bout of locomotor activity is unaffected; that is, for a hamster with
a free-running period of 24.25 hours, wheel running still begins 24.25 hours after the
start of the previous bout of activity. However, if the 1-hour pulse of light is given
early in the subjective night (or late in the subjective day), then the hamster does
not begin its activity 24.25 hours later, but rather it delays its activity onset for 1–4
hours, depending on when exactly the pulse of light occurs. If the 1-hour pulse of
light is given late in the subjective night (or early in the subjective day), then again
the hamster does not begin its activity 24.25 hours later, but rather it advances its

activity onset by 1–4 hours, depending on when exactly the pulse of light occurs. Thus, the largest phase delays can be produced early during the subjective night, when a nocturnal animal has just awakened and a diurnal animal has just retired, and the largest phase advances can be produced late during the subjective night; light appears to have little effect on the circadian system during the subjective day of either nocturnal or diurnal animals.

Although phase responses to light are best observed in free-running animals, these effects of light also operate on animals that are entrained to a light-dark cycle. Light impinges on the phase-advance and phase-delay portions of an animal's daily cycle of responsiveness to light to reset the biological rhythm to exactly 24 hours—that is, to entrain the rhythm. In an analogous manner, if you owned a wristwatch that gained 15 minutes each day (period = 24.25 hours), you would be the zeitgeber that entrains the watch when you reset it to the correct time each morning. The phase-response curves give clues about what happens when you move across several time zones rapidly (see Box 10.1).

Ultradian (shorter than circadian) and **infradian** (longer than circadian) rhythms are biological rhythms that do not correspond to any known geophysical cycles. These names may seem confusing because *ultra* is synonymous with "higher" and *infra* with "lower," but the terms *ultradian* and *infradian* refer to the frequency of a cycle in relation to a day, rather than to the period. If a circadian cycle has a frequency of one event per day, then an ultradian cycle of one event every 2 hours, or every 1/12 day, has a frequency 12 times higher than the circadian cycle. Ultradian cycles are common (**FIGURE 10.9**); an example is the 90-minute cycle characteristic of REM sleep (Schulz and Lavie, 1985). The pulsatile secretions of several hormones, including gonadotropin-releasing hormone (GnRH), luteinizing hormone (LH), testosterone, growth hormone, and corticosterone, represent ultradian rhythms (Schulz and Lavie, 1985). Ultradian rhythm variation in free estradiol and cortisol concentrations during menstrual cycles may reflect depressive symptoms (Bao et al., 2004) as well as sleep disturbances (Voss, 2004). Ultradian rhythms in locomotor activity, feeding, and metabolism have been reported in a number of high-metabolic mammalian species such as shrews and voles (reviewed in Liu et al., 2007) and may be related to ancient metabolic cell cycles (Lloyd et al., 2003).

Infradian rhythms, less frequently observed than ultradian rhythms, include biological rhythms longer than a day but shorter than a lunar month. There have been

ultradian rhythm A biological rhythm that has a period less than 24 hours (or a frequency greater than once per day).

infradian rhythm A biological rhythm that has a period greater than a day, but shorter than a month (or a frequency less than once per day).

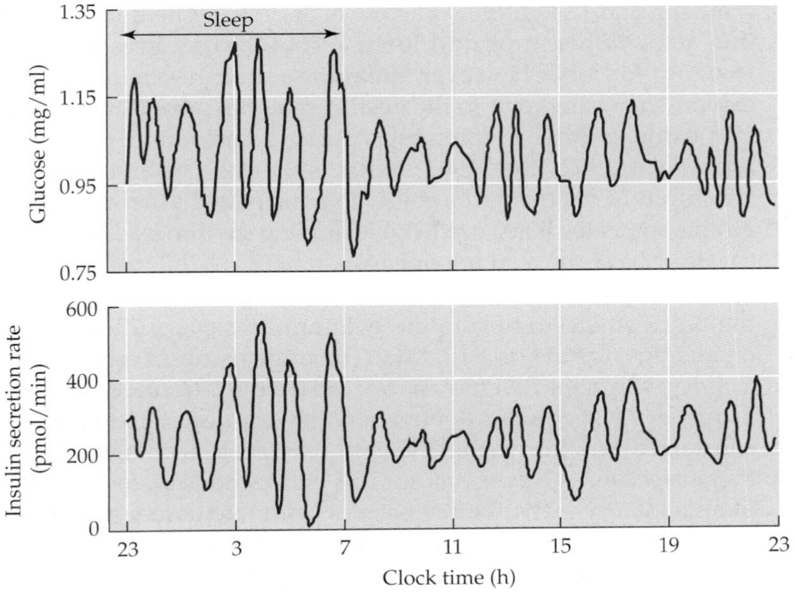

FIGURE 10.9 Ultradian rhythms in humans across 24 hours Human plasma glucose and insulin secretion varies across the day. The mechanism[s] underlying these ultradian oscillations are unknown. After Simon and Brandenberger, 2002.

sporadic reports of a 7-day cycle of excretion of urinary ketosteroids and a 21–28-day cycle of excretion of testosterone in human males, but these findings have not been sufficiently replicated. Infradian testosterone rhythms in human males are probably due to exogenous factors, such as pay schedules or exercise patterns, because these types of rhythms are rarely reported for men isolated from social and environmental cues. Generally, infradian rhythms in testicular function are rare among vertebrates. Dormice (*Glis glis*) have been reported to display infradian rhythms of about 60 days in body mass and body fat content (Grimes et al., 1981; Melnyk et al., 1983). The most common types of infradian rhythms are those associated with ovarian (estrous) cycles. Hamsters have very brief, 4-day estrous cycles. Rats, as you may recall, have estrous cycles of 4 or 5 days. Guinea pigs and sheep have estrous cycles of approximately 16 days. Under the right conditions of adequate food and presence of other favorable environmental factors, these cycles are self-sustaining, endogenously generated biological rhythms that do not correspond to any known geophysical cue. Of course, human menstrual cycles roughly correspond to the period of one revolution of the moon around Earth, the lunar month of 29.5 days. However, the length of the human menstrual cycle seems to be only coincidentally similar to the length of the lunar month, rather than reflecting any adaptive link to the lunar cycle (Knobil and Hotchkiss, 1988).

Examples of Biological Rhythms in Behavior

We can illustrate these principles by looking at examples of the four different types of biological rhythms that occur in nature.

CIRCADIAN RHYTHMS Parental behavior in rabbits shows a distinct circadian rhythm. In the wild, rabbit pups are delivered in a special nursery den that is usually adjacent to the communal warren. The mother doe returns only once a day to nurse her pups, at intervals that at first seemed to field observers to be irregular—a strategy that could serve to deter predators. During the somewhat frenzied 3-to-5-minute nursing bout, the pups ingest an enormous quantity of milk, often exceeding a quarter of their body mass (Hudson and Distel, 1989; Zarrow et al., 1965). The doe does not interact with her pups during the rest of the day, because she is foraging for food. However, the pups anticipate their mother's arrival; they emerge from the nesting material prior to the arrival of the doe in order to commence nursing immediately (Hudson and Distel, 1982; Jilge, 1993). What is the basis of this temporal synchrony? Obviously, the ability to anticipate the arrival of their mother indicates that a predictable nursing rhythm exists and that the pups have the ability to measure time.

In the laboratory, rabbits are born during the light portion of the day. Females return to the waiting litter every 23.15 hours, on average, for the first 10 days. The pups manifest anticipatory activity within the first few days of life (**FIGURE 10.10**). What is the zeitgeber for the pups? Remember, they are normally living in a constantly dark burrow, so the light-dark cycle is not available to them as a cue. The zeitgeber for this endogenous biological cycle of anticipatory activity must be cues from the mother herself. As you will see below, circadian rhythms are controlled by a cellular feedback loop consisting of gene activation and protein product

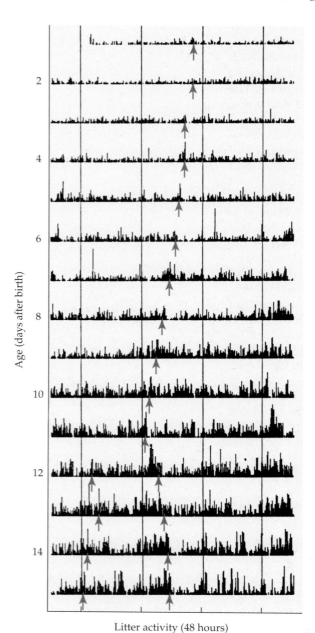

Age (days after birth)

Litter activity (48 hours)

FIGURE 10.10 Development of rabbit circadian rhythms Rhythms of litter activity are double plotted, and the time of nursing is depicted by the arrow. Mother rabbits only nurse their litters once a day for an average of approximately 3.75 minutes per day. Note the anticipatory activity of the litter prior to the mother's return to the nursery cage. From Jilge, 1993.

feedback. In rabbit pups, the time of feeding shifts the phase of cellular clocks in the dorsomedial hypothalamus, suggesting that an endogenous timing system in this brain region synchronizes pup activity to the doe's feeding cycle (Caba et al., 2009). Additionally, a so-called nipple-search pheromone that the mother emits to guide the pups to her teats might act as a supplementary zeitgeber for this internal clock (Montúfar-Chaveznava et al., 2013).

CIRCATIDAL RHYTHMS   An example of an endogenously generated circatidal rhythm can be seen in the locomotor activity pattern of fiddler crabs (*Uca pugnax*) (Palmer, 1990). These crabs are residents of the intertidal zone and can be observed moving along the marsh or beach during low tide, searching for food and mates. The crabs return to their burrows prior to the onset of high tide, when their environment is flooded by the sea. If a fiddler crab is removed to an aquarium, it will retain its cycle of activity, with slight deviations of approximately 2%–3% from the 12.4-hour tidal cycle (Palmer, 1990) (**FIGURE 10.11**). Its periods of locomotor activ-

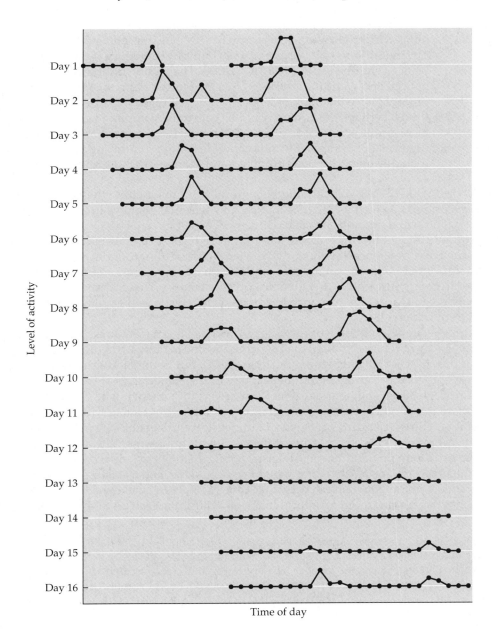

FIGURE 10.11   Circatidal locomotor activity rhythm of fiddler crabs Fiddler crabs maintained in aquaria in constant darkness and constant temperature conditions will become active at approximately the same time that low tide occurs at their capture site and will maintain this endogenous biological rhythm for many months. After Palmer, 1990.

(A)

(B)

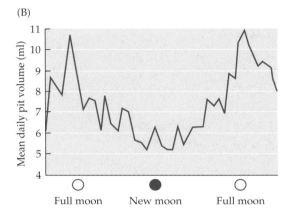

FIGURE 10.12 A circalunar behavioral rhythm (A) The antlion hunts by building a pit to catch passing ants or other insects. (B) Fifty antlions that were fed a single ant per day and maintained in constant conditions exhibited a circalunar rhythm in the average size of the pits they built; they dug larger pits when there was a full moon and smaller pits when there was a new moon. B after Youthed and Moran, 1969.

ity will alternate with quiescence every 12.4 hours, and the locomotor activity will correspond to the occurrence of low tide in the area where it was collected.

CIRCALUNAR RHYTHMS   A few animals have evolved biological rhythms that permit them to time their behavior within the 29.5-day lunar cycle (Richter, 1968). In general, nocturnal predators increase their evening activities around the time of a full moon and decrease their activities around the time of a new moon. Prey species generally show the opposite pattern, avoiding nocturnal activities during evenings with bright moons. Insects may also show this pattern. For example, the antlion (*Myrmeleon obscurus*) hunts by building a pit with steep walls of shifting sands (**FIGURE 10.12A**). The antlion buries itself at the bottom and waits for an ant or other bug to slide into the pit. Its huge pincers pierce the body of its prey, and the antlion sucks out the body fluids. Perhaps the antlion could be called the vampire bug because it increases its activities during the full moon. Even in the constant conditions of a laboratory, the antlion builds a larger pit during full moons than during new moons (Youthed and Moran, 1969) (**FIGURE 10.12B**).

CIRCANNUAL RHYTHMS   Circannual behavioral rhythms include the migratory patterns of birds as well as the hibernation and seasonal changes in body mass observed in several mammalian species. Even when kept in a laboratory for years, birds show 10-to-12-month cycles of premigratory restlessness, weight gain, and reproductive competence (Gwinner, 1986). Mammals such as ground squirrels also show circannual cycles of weight gain, reproductive competence, and (if the temperature is sufficiently low) hibernation (see below). These annual rhythms represent an adaptive response to seasonal changes in energy availability in the environment.

There are also patterns of mixed or hybrid behavioral rhythms. The Pacific palolo worm (*Eunice viridis*) usually spends its time in burrows in the coral reefs off the coast of Fiji and Samoa (Burrows, 1945). But in the months of October, November, and December, on the last day of the last quarter of the moon, at sunrise, a 30 cm segment of each worm breaks off and swims to the surface, where it and other segments explode in unison, forming a slurry of eggs and sperm. The local epicures are aware of this cycle, which enables them to predict the event in advance and arrive at the coral reefs at dawn on the appropriate days to scoop up handfuls of this gastronomic treat. The palolo worms may be consumed raw or roasted, and they have been described as tasting like sushi stuffed with caviar when eaten raw (**FIGURE 10.13**). Human knowledge of cyclic behavior, ranging from grunion "runs" on California beaches to the seasonal

FIGURE 10.13 Palolo worms display a complex reproductive rhythm. These sea worms are native to the South Pacific and move to the ocean surface to exchange sperm and eggs during the months of October, November, and December—but only at sunrise on the last day of the last quarter of the moon. Local residents consider the palolo a delicacy and make use of their knowledge of its complex reproductive patterns in collecting the worms for eating.

migrations of caribou in northern Canada, has allowed the exploitation of many animals for food and other resources.

Adaptive Function of Biological Clocks

Why have these elaborate timekeeping mechanisms evolved? In other words, what is the adaptive function of biological clocks? As the previous examples indicate, biological clocks are useful for synchronizing the activities of animals with conditions in their environments, including their social environments, thus enabling them to prepare for predictable events (e.g., night, winter, or the onset of reproductive function in potential mates), and synchronizing the internal physiological and biochemical processes of animals in order to promote efficient functioning.

One function of biological clocks is to coordinate essential activities both with the appropriate time of day and with other individuals (e.g., DeCoursey and Krulas, 1998). Destruction of the circadian clock in the brain (see below) in free-living ground squirrels increased the likelihood of their being killed by a predator, presumably because of inappropriate timing of their daily activities (**FIGURE 10.14**). Another example of precision in coordinated behavioral activity is the parenting behavior of ringdoves. In ringdoves, males and females share incubation responsibility, taking turns sittings on the nest, ensuring that the eggs are maintained at the appropriate temperature (Wallman et al., 1979). The male takes a shorter "shift" than the female, sitting on the nest for a block of time only during the middle of the day (Ball and Silver, 1983). One question that intrigued researchers was how the male and female knew when it was time to switch nest incubation duties. Such a coordinated parenting strategy could occur through several mechanisms, including social or environmental cues, a circadian timing system in one or both parents, an interval timing system that measures a specific time span in one or both parents, or a combination of these mechanisms. These possibilities were explored by delaying the time that the male was permitted to sit on the nest (Gibbon et al., 1984). If the male uses a circadian timing mechanism, then we would expect him to switch with the female at the usual time of day, despite the truncation of his time on the nest. If he uses an interval timing mechanism, then we would expect that he would delay the switch to account for his late start. Intriguingly, the female in the study returned to the nest at the usual time of day to make the switch, despite the fact that her sitting bout had ended later than usual, indicating that she was using a circadian timing mechanism. In contrast, the male delayed his departure from the nest, attempting to force the female off of the nest, indicating that he was timing his bout based on an interval timing mechanism (Gibbon et al., 1984). Although it is clear that gonadal hormones regulate the expression and timing of ringdove parenting behavior (Ramos and Silver, 1992), the location and mechanism underlying the female circadian timing system and the male interval timing system require further study.

One of the most predictable features of life on Earth is the regular pattern of environmental changes associated with the movement of our planet. Life evolved in a cyclic environment. As one chronobiologist wrote, "The rotation of the Earth on its polar axis gives rise to the dominant cycle of day and night; the revolutions of the Earth around the Sun give rise to the unfailing procession of the seasons; and the more complicated movements of the Moon in relation to the Earth and the Sun give rise to the lunar month and to the tidal cycles" (Saunders, 1977). Except for, perhaps, animals living at the bottom of the ocean or deep within caves, day follows night, and the seasons change. These orderly and predictable changes in the environment have existed since life first began to evolve on this planet. The rotation of the Earth results in periodic exposure to the radiation of the Sun, which causes predictable changes in light and ambient temperatures, as well as associated changes in the relative humidity of the air and in the oxygen levels of aqueous habitats. The biological clocks of animals and plants permit them to start or stop locomotor activities or

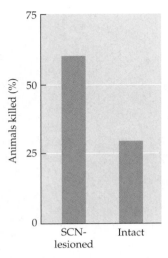

FIGURE 10.14 Antelope ground squirrels with SCN lesions were more likely to be killed by a predator than intact squirrels. Predation by a feral cat was monitored by infrared video camera. After DeCoursey et al., 1997.

FIGURE 10.15 Linnaeus's "flower clock" Linnaeus exploited his knowledge of the activity patterns of heliotropic flowers to design this clock in 1751. He proposed that the clock would operate from 0600 to 1800 (6:00 A.M. to 6:00 P.M.) and that the time of day could be determined by noting which flowers were blooming.

activate photosynthetic machinery, respectively, in preparation for light (**FIGURE 10.15**).

The action of biological clocks in synchronizing the bodily functions of an individual has been compared to the role of the conductor in an orchestra. Internal processes may serve to prepare the body for certain activities to occur later; for example, the elevated adrenal secretions coinciding with the morning onset of activity prepare you for increased activity levels and for breaking your nightly fast. All eukaryotic and most prokaryotic organisms tested to date, from unicellular organisms to humans, display circadian rhythms. Of course, circadian rhythms have not evolved in organisms that live for less than 24 hours. Similarly, circannual rhythms have evolved only in animals that live for a year or more.

Physiological systems show a wide variety of rhythmic changes. For instance, dopamine turnover; body temperature; and blood plasma levels of potassium, sodium, cortisol, androgens, melatonin, and growth hormone all show pronounced circadian rhythms (Halberg, 1977; Rusak, 1989) (**FIGURE 10.16**). Some of these changes may be on the order of 100% to 200% from baseline values. Peak daily cortisol concentrations, for example, which usually occur just prior to or immediately after awakening, coincide with the onset of locomotor activity in the morning. This programmed elevation of cortisol concentrations increases blood pressure and cardiac output prior to the active phase of the day. We know that these increased cortisol concentrations are not driven by the increased activity levels themselves, because the same circadian rhythm is observed in bedridden patients under constant conditions (Aschoff, 1965). In some instances, the production and release of hormones

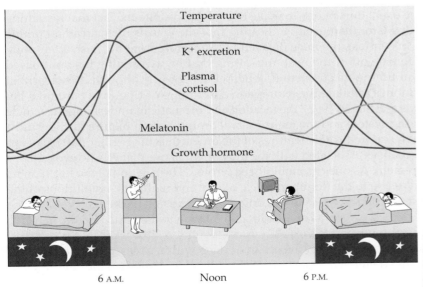

FIGURE 10.16 Circadian rhythms in human physiology and behavior Activity levels, body temperature, urinary potassium excretion, plasma cortisol levels, melatonin, and growth hormone secretion exhibit circadian rhythms that are closely coupled to the sleep-wake cycle. After Richardson and Martin, 1988.

corresponds to the timing of hormone receptor production. Neurotransmitter receptors are manufactured prior to a circadian-programmed increase in neurotransmitter production. Body temperature peaks in midafternoon, when people are most active, but again, muscular activity is not solely responsible for this "heating." If you are inactive in bed under constant conditions, your peak body temperature still maintains a circadian rhythm (Moore-Ede et al., 1982).

Circadian Clocks

Circadian biological clocks have been the subject of intensive study in chronobiology. These biological oscillators are common across phyla and found at every level of organization within an organism (Pittendrigh, 1981; Pittendrigh and Daan, 1976). Several generalizations can be made about circadian biological clocks on a phenomenological level: their period is (1) inherited, (2) relatively independent of temperature, (3) relatively independent of chemical influence, (4) entrained (synchronized) only to limited cycle lengths, and (5) relatively independent of behavioral feedback.

Localization and Characterization of Circadian Clocks

Where in the body are biological clocks located? Biological clocks are found in bacteria, fungi, plants, and animals, so the nervous system cannot be the fundamental level of organization, although you will soon see that biological clocks in the nervous system play a critical role in the temporal organization of the physiology and behavior of birds and mammals. In multicellular species, it was initially assumed that circadian timekeeping is an emergent property of a network of cells operating as a unit, similar to a watch in which timekeeping is lost if one gear, of many, is removed. However, because single-celled organisms exhibit circadian rhythms, it was reasonable to suspect that biological clocks might operate at the cellular level (Ko and Takahashi, 2006) (**BOX 10.2**). From studies of cyanobacteria (Amdaoud et al., 2007), neurons isolated from the snail eye (Michel et al., 1995), and neurons isolated from the mammalian hypothalamus (Welsh et al., 1995), it became clear that single cells have the "machinery" to produce a circadian rhythm. Despite the fact that single cells can produce a circadian rhythm, as you will see below, functional networks of independent cellular clocks operate in the brain and periphery to guide the timing of system-specific functioning.

Once it became clear that circadian function is a cellular property, two general approaches were used to identify the genes and gene products that lead to circadian oscillations. One approach used molecular biological and pharmacological techniques to discover the basic features of the clock. The second approach used classic and molecular genetics to uncover the fundamental properties of the clock. One might simplify the approaches even further as "fishing expeditions" and "finger-pointing." Forward genetics and chemical screens are so-called fishing expeditions that hope to find effects on behavior or physiology without knowing anything about the biology. This approach has yielded important insights into cellular clock functioning, identifying critical genes in flies and mice. Directed knockouts, knockdowns, overexpression, and use of antagonists and agonists are examples of so-called finger-pointing, where the gene or molecule is removed (loss of function) or made overactive (gain of function). This approach has been helpful in moving between model systems and determining whether homologous genes perform a similar function across species. Much of the early work on the genetics of circadian rhythms was performed in fruit flies (*Drosophila melanogaster*) (e.g., Konopka and Benzer, 1971), and this approach was critical in making progress on mammalian clock genes.

Using the first approach, much has been learned about the mechanisms of the cellular clock through the use of chemicals that promote or block specific cellular

BOX 10.2 *Effects of Light on Gene Transcription*

As we have seen, hamsters maintained in constant darkness exhibit free-running activity rhythms, but a pulse of light is sufficient to reset the phase of those rhythms (see Figure 10.8). Light-induced phase shifts are caused by activation of immediate early genes (IEGs) (Kornhauser et al., 1990) (see Chapter 5). To understand this process, it is useful to review the concept of gene transcription.

The process of gene transcription moves the protein-making instructions contained in the DNA molecule (which resides in the cell nucleus) to the protein-manufacturing apparatus, which lies outside the nucleus. The DNA unravels, and one of the exposed strands of DNA provides a template on which a messenger molecule, called messenger ribonucleic acid (mRNA), is formed. The newly transcribed mRNA leaves the cell nucleus and travels to the rough endoplasmic reticulum. After processing to remove extra bases that do not code for proteins (introns), the mRNA represents only the coding regions (exons) of the gene. The mRNA then provides the instructions for production of chains of amino acids through a process called translation. If the resulting chain of amino acids is short, it is called a peptide; if it is long, it is called a protein.

Analyses of the regulation of gene transcription have revealed that several switches are involved in turning transcription on and off. In some cases, hormones or environmental input provide the stimulus to begin or end gene transcription. Each strand of the DNA molecule has a 3′ and a 5′ end. Transcription always proceeds from the 5′ end toward the 3′ end. Upstream from the start of the coding region of a gene are several short segments of the DNA molecule that do not code for proteins; rather, they powerfully affect the rate at which the coding region of the gene is transcribed into mRNA. This *enhancer* region acts like a rheostat switch to control the promoter region of the DNA. The *promoter* region is usually located about 30 bases upstream from the start of the coding sequence and is essential for the actual

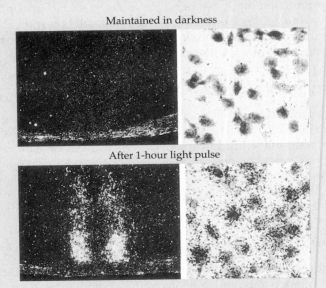

Maintained in darkness

After 1-hour light pulse

Figure A   Photomicrographs courtesy of Jon Kornhauser.

initiation of gene transcription. Steroid hormones and steroid hormone–receptor complexes may bind to specific receptor sequences within the enhancer region and act to repress or activate gene transcription. Approximately six different types of binding areas have been located within enhancer regions of DNA, one of which is called the AP-1 complex.

The first genes activated when a cell receives a signal are the IEGs, which code for a variety of proteins in the Jun family, including Jun-B, c-Jun, and c-Fos. Jun-B and c-Fos bind together to form a dimer that binds to the AP-1 sequences in the enhancer regions of other genes to stimulate gene transcription. Thus, activation of IEGs is often the first indication that the genetic machinery within a cell has been activated by an external or hormonal stimulus. In addition to their effects on

functions (Hastings et al., 2007; Reppert and Weaver, 2002). Typically, a chemical agent is given to an organism that is undergoing regular cycles under constant conditions. For example, providing deuterium oxide (heavy water), which affects cell membrane permeability to ions, to hamsters in constant dark conditions causes them to delay the onset of wheel-running behavior by several hours each night (Richter, 1977; Roberts, 1990). Changes in potassium movement across cell membranes alter some features of biological clocks; lithium, which can replace potassium in some physiological systems, also can affect biological rhythms (Klemfuss, 1992; Sweeney, 1976), although the action of lithium on circadian clocks is now believed to be through kinases and not via changes in membrane potential. Pharmacological studies such as these have indicated that important components of the biological clock include protein synthesis; membrane structures; mechanisms for the transport of calcium, potassium, and other ions; and activation of intracellular kinases (Hall and Rosbash, 1987; Hastings et al., 2007; Reppert and Weaver, 2002; Takahashi et al., 1993).

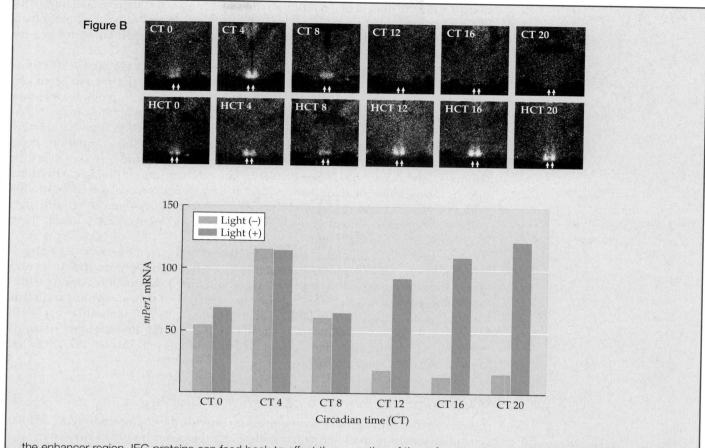

Figure B

the enhancer region, IEG proteins can feed back to affect the promoter region, starting or stopping gene transcription.

Light appears to activate IEGs in the SCN of both nocturnal and diurnal animals (Katona et al., 1998). The photomicrographs shown in **Figure A** are in situ hybridization depictions (see Chapter 1) of the SCN from (top) a hamster maintained in constant darkness and from (bottom) a hamster maintained in darkness and then exposed to a 1-hour pulse of light. Activa-

tion of the *c-fos* gene can be seen in the bottom left panel as light areas and in the bottom right panel as dark spots lying over cells. Light also affects the expression of clock genes in the SCN. Mice receiving a 30-minute pulse of light showed a *Clock*-gated up-regulation in the expression of *mPer1*. Activation of the *Per1* gene is plotted graphically in **Figure B** for various circadian times (CT) throughout the day. From Shigeyoshi et al., 1997.

The second approach to understanding the mechanisms underlying cellular clocks has been to identify the genes that control the clock systems, then to identify the actions of those genes (Konopka, 1987; Reppert and Weaver, 2002; Takahashi, 1993; Takahashi et al., 1994). By studying mutants with unusual free-running circadian rhythms—that is, rhythms with periods substantially greater than or less than 24 hours—and backcrossing these animals with homozygous and heterozygous mates, insights into the locations of the genes that regulate biological clocks can be obtained. Giving mice a drug that promotes gene mutations (e.g., ethylnitrosourea) has become a related strategy to identify genes associated with biological timekeeping. This "forward genetics" (from behavior to gene) strategy has led to the identification of the gene *Clock* and several mutations that produce abnormal circadian rhythms. *Clock* is one of the central components of the circadian machinery described further below. More recently, as part of the Human Genome Project, researchers have conducted a genome-wide small interfering RNA screen of human cellular clocks. This technique identified hundreds of genes that affected the period of circadian rhythms—analyses indicated that genes were likely components of insulin and hedgehog signaling and of folate metabolism (Zhang et al., 2009). Thus, it appears that these important cellular pathways are linked to biological timing.

Biological clock mutants have been discovered in fruit flies (*Drosophila*) (Konopka and Benzer, 1971), Syrian hamsters (*Mesocricetus auratus*) (Ralph and Menaker, 1988), and mice (*Mus musculus*) (Vitaterna et al., 1994), as well as in plants and other animals, including humans (Benca et al., 2009; Hall and Rosbash, 1987). In fruit flies, mutants that display no rhythmicity in their behavior, as well as flies that display 19-hour or 28-hour periods, have been discovered. Most of these mutations have been traced to a single gene called *Period* (*Per*), which affects the period of the clock (Konopka and Benzer, 1971) (see Box 10.2). The mechanisms for biological rhythms appear to be similar for all organisms; that is, they all use molecular feedback loops with a positive regulatory loop and a negative regulatory loop (see below), although some of the specific genes involved differ (Reppert and Weaver, 2002; Takahashi et al., 1993; Yu and Hardin, 2006).

On a physiological level, circadian oscillators and pacemakers have been discovered in several biological systems, mostly by damaging certain structures and observing that biological rhythms disappear after their destruction. Among vertebrates, the eyes of amphibians and the pineal glands of fishes, reptiles, and birds contain circadian oscillators (Cahill et al., 1991; Moore, 1997; Takahashi et al., 1989). Among mammals, the suprachiasmatic nuclei (SCN) of the anterior hypothalamus represent the master circadian clock of the body (Moore and Eichler, 1972; Stephan and Zucker, 1972) (and see below).

Molecular Mechanisms of Circadian Clocks

Similar rhythmic patterns of gene expression provide the engine underlying cellular circadian clocks in many organisms, although the genes involved vary from species to species. Within each cell, this autoregulatory transcriptional/translational negative feedback loop takes approximately 24 hours. Although these genes can be expressed in tissues throughout the body, their expression in the mammalian master clock, the SCN, is critical for integrated temporal coordination in mammals. In mammals, it is generally accepted that CLOCK and BMAL1 (also called MOP3) combine to form heterodimers that activate rhythmic transcription of two *period* genes (*Per1* and *Per2*), two *cryptochrome* genes (*Cry1* and *Cry2*), and two nuclear receptor genes (*Rev-Erbα*) and the retinoid-related orphan receptor gene (*ROR*). The PER and CRY proteins dimerize and move from the cytoplasm into the nucleus to inhibit CLOCK:BMAL1 mediated transcription, thereby closing the negative feedback loop (Mohawk et al., 2012). A secondary feedback loop involves the rhythmic transcription of *Bmal1* that peaks about 12 hours out of phase with the peak transcription of *Per*, *Cry*, and *Rev-Erbα*. The Rev-Erbα protein suppresses *Bmal1* tran-

FIGURE 10.17 The genetics of biological clocks in mammals Constituting the core circadian clock is an autoregulatory transcriptional feedback loop involving the activators CLOCK and BMAL1 and their target genes *Per1*, *Per2*, *Cry1*, and *Cry2*, whose gene products form a negative feedback repressor complex. In addition to this core transcriptional feedback loop, other feedback loops are also driven by CLOCK:BMAL1. One feedback loop involving *Rev-Erbα* and *RORα* that represses *Bmal1* transcription leads to an antiphase oscillation in *Bmal1* gene expression. CLOCK:BMAL1 also regulates many downstream target genes known as clock-controlled genes (Ccg). At a posttranscriptional level, the stability of the PER and CRY proteins is regulated by SCF (Skp1-Cullin-F-box protein) E3 ubiquitin ligase complexes involving β-TrCP and FBXL3, respectively. Two kinases, casein kinase 1ε/δ (CK1ε/δ) and AMP-activated protein kinase (AMPK), phosphorylate the PER and CRY proteins, respectively, to promote their degradation. From Mohawk et al., 2012.

scription, whereas ROR is a transcriptional activator of *Bmal1*. Because the *Clock* gene is constitutively expressed, the rhythmic transcription of relevant genes is driven by *Rev-Erbα/ROR* rhythms in *Bmal1* expression (Buhr and Takahashi, 2013) (**FIGURE 10.17**).

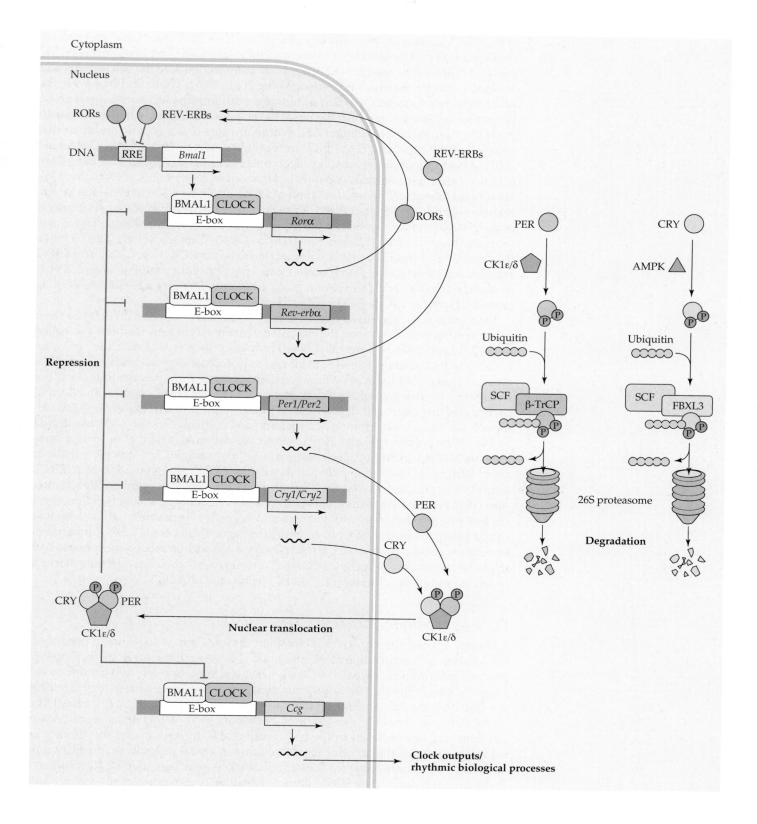

In addition to transcriptional/translational control of cellular clock function, regulatory kinases also play a pronounced role in regulation of circadian periods. The first regulatory kinase was identified through a random mutation found in a Syrian hamster that caused homozygous animals to have an approximately 20-hour period (called *tau* mutants) (Ralph and Menaker, 1988). It was later discovered that these hamsters have a mutation in the casein kinase 1 epsilon (CK1ε) gene (Lowrey et al., 2000). Casein kinase normally phosphorylates PER and "tags" this protein for degradation. The inability of *tau* mutants to use CK1ε to phosphorylate PER makes it more stable, thereby causing a premature feedback to the cell nucleus and evoking a shorter than normal period (Wang et al., 2007). These findings led to the identification of a gene mutation in humans with familial advanced sleep phase syndrome, a disorder in which the onset of sleep is advanced 2–4 hours. Although these individuals had functional CK1ε proteins, they had a genetic mutation that resulted in the production of PER2 protein that could not bind CK1ε (Toh et al., 2001). Affected individuals display sleep onset very early, around 7:30 P.M., sleep duration is normal, and wake-up time is advanced to about 4:30 A.M. Thus, as in the *tau* mutant, abnormal phosphorylation of PER protein by CKIε likely leads to premature negative feedback of PER:CRY heterodimers, thereby speeding the "gears" of the circadian clock. Soon after the discovery of CK1ε, another kinase was found that phosphorylates the PER proteins, called CK1δ (Camacho et al., 2001). Unlike the targeting of the PER proteins indiscriminately by CK1ε/δ, CRY1 and CRY2 proteins are targeted for degradation by unique phosphorylation events; CRY1 is phosphorylated by AMPK1 (Lamia et al., 2009) and CRY2 by a DYRK1A/GSK-3β cascade (Harada et al. 2005; Kurabayashi et al. 2010).

Later evidence suggested a role for a third *Per* gene, *Per3*, in human delayed sleep phase syndrome. For instance, the coding region of the *Per3* gene contains a so-called variable-number tandem-repeat (VNTR) polymorphism. In this case, the *Per3* gene has a motif that encodes 17 amino acids and in humans is repeated either four or five times. A study of individuals who were homogeneous for either the four (*Per3[4]*) or five (*Per3[5]*) *Per3* alleles reported that the polymorphism is associated with "diurnal preference" for sleep and delayed sleep phase syndrome (Archer et al., 2003). Although circadian markers such as melatonin and cortisol secretion were unaffected by *Per3* gene polymorphisms, *Per3[5]* individuals displayed changes in several components of sleep, including sleep homeostasis. For example, *Per3[5]* people fell asleep about 10 minutes faster than individuals with the *PER3[4]* genotype (Viola et al., 2007). Importantly, people with the *Per3[5]* genotype displayed more cognitive deficit after sleep deprivation than individuals with the *PER3[4]* genotype. Taken together, these studies suggest that sleep architecture and cognitive impairment after sleep loss can be predicted by polymorphism in the *Per3* gene (Viola et al., 2007). More recent screens for genetic variants of the *Per3* gene point to additional polymorphisms that might be responsible for people having a "morningness" chronotype (being "larks") or an "eveningness" chronotype ("owls") (Hida et al., 2014).

SCN as Master Circadian Clock

Although it was well known that circadian rhythms are endogenously produced, the location of the circadian clock remained elusive until the early 1970s. One key piece of information, revealed by early tract tracing work, led two groups to explore the possibility that the suprachiasmatic nuclei make up a brain region critical for circadian rhythm generation in mammals. This early tracing work revealed a novel pathway from the eye to the SCN (Moore et al., 1971). Because circadian rhythms can be entrained to the environmental light-dark cycle, and there was no known role for the anterior hypothalamus in visual perception, the SCN represented a candidate locus for the central clock. A year later, two studies showed that bilateral lesions of the SCN eliminate circadian organization of physiology and

(A)

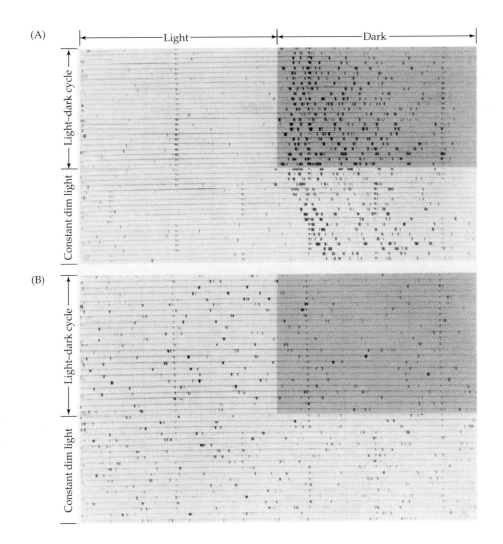

FIGURE 10.18 Disruption of circadian rhythms after SCN damage (A) Drinking behavior of a normal hamster housed in a 12:12 light–dark cycle displays a 24-hour rhythm (top of panel); in constant dim light, a free-running circadian rhythm of 24.25 hours is displayed (bottom of panel). (B) After lesions to both SCN, no temporal organization of the behavior is evident, regardless of lighting conditions. From Zucker, 1980.

(B)

behavior (Moore and Eichler, 1972; Stephan and Zucker, 1972) (**FIGURE 10.18**). These findings provided strong evidence that the SCN was critical for circadian functioning, but because these lesions destroyed the SCN and fibers of passage, it was possible that the SCN was part of a larger neural network generating circadian rhythms or that the circadian clock resided elsewhere with projections proceeding at the site of the lesion. Evidence that neither of these possibilities was correct came from studies demonstrating that neurons in slices of SCN tissue continue to display circadian rhythms of electrical activity even when maintained in a culture dish (Gillette and Prosser, 1988; Nakamura et al., 2002). If the SCN were part of a larger neural network producing circadian rhythms, then the SCN would lose rhythmic function when isolated. Likewise, were the clock located elsewhere in the brain with output fibers coursing through the SCN, this nucleus would not exhibit daily rhythms in neural firing when isolated in culture. Perhaps the strongest evidence that the SCN is the master circadian clock in mammals came from studies showing that SCN tissue transplants restore circadian functioning in an SCN-lesioned recipient, with the period of the recipient's rhythm matching that of the donor (Lehman et al., 1987; Ralph et al., 1990) (**FIGURE 10.19**).

Following these earlier discoveries, the advent of molecular reporter tools for monitoring gene expression made it possible to follow clock gene expression in real time to explore whether rhythms showed a daily oscillation in isolated SCN akin to those of neural firing. The first

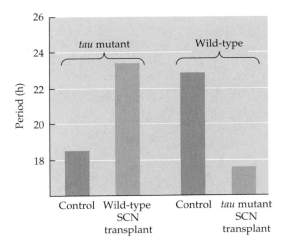

FIGURE 10.19 Restoration of circadian rhythms with the period of the donor by SCN transplants Wild-type hamsters (i.e., with ~24-hour free-running periods) or *tau* mutant hamsters (i.e., with ~20-hour free-running periods) received SCN lesions, then received SCN transplants from the other genotype. In all cases, the recipient hamsters took on the free-running periods of the SCN donors. After Ralph et al., 1990.

FIGURE 10.20 Circadian rhythm of bioluminescence from a cultured SCN explanted from a *Per1*-luc transgenic rat. Black and white bars show the animal's previous LD (light-dark) condition. From Yamazaki et al., 2000.

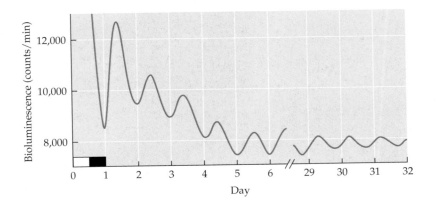

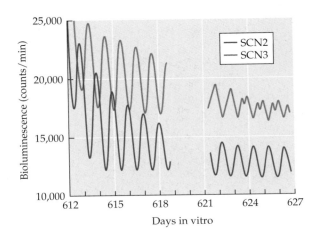

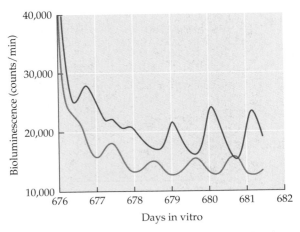

FIGURE 10.21 Circadian rhythms of Per1 bioluminescence from two SCN cultured for 682 days The SCN maintained clear rhythms that only began to degrade after about 676 days in culture. Rhythms from 612 to 627 days show a clear circadian bottom (top). On day 676, the SCN begins to become arrhythmic, likely due to degradation of the culture (bottom). Data kindly provided by Shin Yamazaki, Wataru Nakamura, and Michael Menaker.

studies employed a transgenic rat model in which the *Per1* gene promoter was linked to a luciferase reporter to permit bioluminescent imaging of *Per1* gene expression over time (Yamazaki et al., 2000) (**FIGURE 10.20**). Although rhythms were maintained for over a month in culture, a skeptic could still argue that the SCN might only maintain clock function for a limited time following removal from other essential brain areas. This possibility was refuted by culturing the SCN for almost 2 years and showing that rhythms persisted for 676 days, likely diminishing only due to the viability of the culture (**FIGURE 10.21**). Together, these findings provide undeniable evidence for the SCN as a master circadian clock in the brain.

The SCN are paired clusters of approximately 10,000 neurons on each side, located above where the optic nerves cross in the hypothalamus and below the third ventricle (**FIGURE 10.22**). In humans this area comprises about 600 μm × 600 μm × 600 μm. As mentioned previously, recordings from individual SCN neurons reveal that circadian timekeeping is a cellular property with each cell capable of generating its own specific circadian rhythm (Welsh et al., 1995) (**FIGURE 10.23**). Since each SCN neuron produces its own intrinsic daily rhythm, it must be networked with other SCN cells to produce coherent synchronized rhythms of activity (Herzog, 2007). A daily rhythm of glucose utilization in the SCN was first observed in rats, a nocturnal species (Schwartz and Gainer, 1977). Autoradiographic studies in which rats were injected with 2-deoxyglucose revealed that the SCN were metabolically active during the light phase of the daily light-dark cycle but relatively inactive during the dark phase (**FIGURE 10.24**). Interestingly, the SCN is metabolically more active in the day for both nocturnal and diurnal animals, suggesting the switch from nocturnal to diurnal behavior resides outside the SCN (Smale and Nunez, 2003). The most likely brain region responsible for this switch is the hypothalamic subparaventricular zone (SPVZ), a brain region that extends dorsally and caudally from the SCN to the ventral edge of the paraventricular nucleus of the hypothalamus (PVN). The SCN sends pronounced projections to the SPVZ (Abrahamson and Moore, 2001; Kriegsfeld et al., 2004), and rhythms of multiunit firing and activity and Fos expression in this structure mirror locomotor activity in diurnal and nocturnal species (Inouye and Kawamura, 1979; Sato and Kawamura, 1984; Schwartz et al., 2004).

(A)

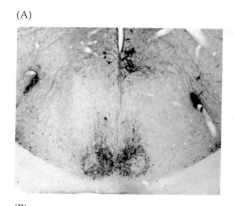

(B)

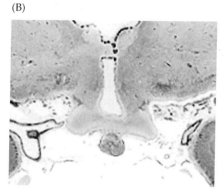

FIGURE 10.22 The SCN in mammals Coronal sections through the anterior hypothalamus in a rodent (A) and a human (B).

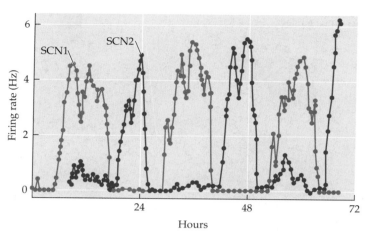

FIGURE 10.23 Individual SCN neurons show precise circadian rhythms. The mean firing rates of two, individual SCN cells in culture (one cell in red and the other in blue) differ. The different periods and phases of these two cells provided the first evidence that individual SCN cells maintain rhythmicity. Were rhythms an emergent property of a network of cells, both cells would exhibit the same period and phase. From Welsh et al., 1995.

(A)

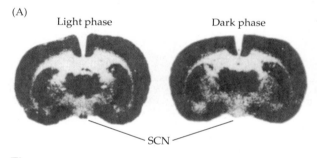

(B)

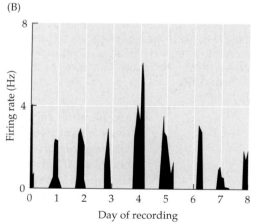

FIGURE 10.24 Activity of the SCN of mammals varies according to the time of day. (A) Autoradiographs of coronal sections through the SCN of rats injected during the light (left) or dark (right) part of the daily light-dark cycle show that energy use by the SCN in these nocturnal animals is higher during the day (dark staining) than at night. (B) Electrical activity in dispersed murine SCN neurons peaks about 4 hours after the lights are turned on (at time 0). A from Schwartz and Gainer, 1977; B after Aujard et al., 2001.

The SCN contain a heterogeneous population of neurons that express several neuropeptides, including neuropeptide Y, AVP, vasoactive intestinal polypeptide (VIP), gastrin-releasing peptide, and somatostatin (Abrahamson and Moore, 2001; Duncan, 1998; Hofman et al., 1996; Huhman et al., 1997; Moore et al., 2002; Silver et al., 1999). Specifically, GABA-releasing neurons in the dorsal "shell" of the SCN express AVP, whereas neurons in the ventral "core" express VIP (Abrahamson and Moore, 2001; Hastings et al., 2003; Moore et al., 2002). It is thought that VIP is critical for the coupling of individual SCN clock neurons so that they oscillate in synchrony (Aton et al., 2005; Maywood et al., 2006; Piggins and Cutler, 2003). Likewise, AVP-expressing cells communicate critical synchronizing cues to the remainder of the SCN, although the nature of this signal has not been determined (Mieda et al., 2015). A more recently discovered neuropeptide, neuromedin S, a peptide expressed throughout the SCN, likely plays a key role in SCN cellular coupling (Lee et al., 2015). The coupling of individual cellular oscillators is unique to the SCN, allowing for the maintenance of circadian rhythms at the tissue level in the absence of intrinsic or extrinsic input. As you will see

(A) Unscheduled

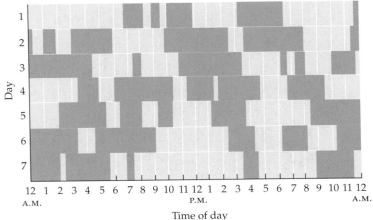

(B) Scheduled

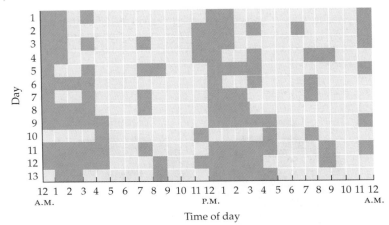

FIGURE 10.25 SCN damage disrupts the daily sleep-wake cycle in humans. (A) The sleep-wake cycle of AH, a woman whose SCN was damaged during surgery, shows little daily temporal organization in an unscheduled environment (waking periods are shown as light areas; green areas represent time asleep). (B) AH's sleep-wake cycle shows daily temporal organization if bedtime, waking time, and meals are scheduled by the nursing staff. Sleep-wake data were obtained every 15 minutes by the nursing staff. After Cohen and Albers, 1991.

below, although circadian timekeeping is likely a property of all cells in the brain and body, this unique coupling ability of the SCN solidifies its position as a master clock.

The central circadian oscillators have been located in several brain sites in birds. The pineal gland is an important circadian clock among many species of passerine (perching) birds (Gwinner et al., 1997; Takahashi et al., 1989; Yoshimura and Sharp, 2010; Zimmerman and Menaker, 1979). Two types of evidence suggest that the avian pineal gland contains circadian oscillators, (1) pineal tissue continues to display circadian rhythms of biosynthetic activity even when maintained in a culture dish (Takahashi et al., 1993), and (2) in some species, if pineal gland tissue is transplanted into a pinealectomized recipient, then the period or the phase of the donor rhythm is imposed on the recipient (Gwinner et al., 1997). For example, a new circadian phase can be imposed in sparrows by implants of pineal glands from donor birds housed under different light-dark cycles than the recipient birds (Meijer and Rietveld, 1989). However, the pineal gland is not required for the expression of circadian rhythms in chickens and Japanese quail. In quail, the eyes control the circadian rhythm of melatonin secretion and they also contribute about 30% of the plasma melatonin. If the optic nerves of quail are cut, their activity rhythms are disrupted, but the ocular melatonin secretion rhythms remain intact (Takahashi, 1992). The role of the pineal gland in seasonal breeding is discussed below.

Although there have not been any clear demonstrations that the SCN mediate circadian organization in humans, several clinical case studies have reported that anterior hypothalamic damage in the vicinity of the optic chiasm was associated with disturbances in the daily sleep-wake or temperature cycle (reviewed in Cohen and Albers, 1991; Schwartz et al., 1986). In one case study of a 34-year-old female patient, AH, a tumor was removed from the inferior region of the anterior hypothalamus that included the SCN (Cohen and Albers, 1991). AH displayed significant disruptions in her daily body temperature and sleep-wake cycles, as well as impairments in cognitive and behavioral function, after the surgery (**FIGURE 10.25**). In aged people, daily rhythms begin to deteriorate, and changes in the wake-sleep cycle, hormone rhythms, and core body temperature are common. Such deterioration in functional physiological and behavioral rhythms is associated with neuronal degeneration of the SCN (Hofman and Swabb, 2007) (**FIGURE 10.26**). In the SCN of hamsters, aging is accompanied by increased numbers of serotonin terminal autoreceptors, 5-HT$_{1B}$ receptors, and serotonin transporter binding sites, alterations that are likely to decrease SCN extracellular serotonin levels (reviewed in Duncan, 2007). Aging also alters serotonin neurotransmission in a midbrain region, the dorsal raphe nucleus, which communicates indirectly with the SCN as well as with many other forebrain regions that may be involved in

FIGURE 10.26 **Effects of aging and Alzheimer's disease (AD) on the human SCN** In patients with Alzheimer's disease, both presenile (<65 years of age) and senile (>65 years of age), the volume of the SCN (A) and the number of AVP-expressing neurons in the SCN (B) are significantly decreased compared with age-matched controls. After Hofman and Swaab, 2007.

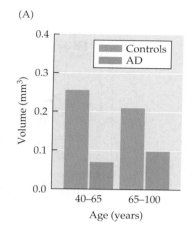

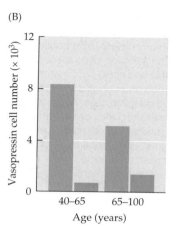

cognition. Among humans, cognitive impairments and depressed mood display higher incidence among the elderly, and this correlation may reflect the degradation of circadian organization (Benca et al., 2009). The effects of aging on the SCN in rodents remain obscure. Some researchers have reported that the firing patterns of individual SCN neurons lost rhythmicity with age (Aujard et al., 2001), whereas other studies have reported no changes with age (Davidson et al., 2008; Gibson et al., 2009; Yamazaki et al., 2002). Additional research is required to resolve this discrepancy.

SCN Inputs and Outputs

In addition to a clock, any biological timekeeping system must have an input system (which usually brings light information to the clock) and an output system, which may be coupled to any number of species-specific physiological and behavioral systems (Abrahamson and Moore, 2001; Reppert and Weaver, 2002; Takahashi et al., 1993) (**FIGURE 10.27**). In some systems, these components may all occur in the same structure. For example, individual pineal cells from chickens possess a photoreceptor, a clock, and melatonin synthesis capabilities in vitro (Bell-Pedersen et al., 2005; Cassone, 1998; Nakahara et al., 1997). Similarly, a photoreceptor protein is located in the clock cells that are located throughout the head, thorax, and abdominal tissues (including the sensory bristles on the wings and legs) of *Drosophila* (Plautz et al., 1997). However, it is generally accepted that only the eyes contain photoreceptors that ultimately influence biological rhythms in mammals (Nelson and Zucker, 1981; Yamazaki et al., 1999). Environmental light entrains the oscillations of the SCN (see Box 10.2). Light information received by light-sensitive ganglion cells in the eyes is transduced into a neural signal communicated to the SCN via a glutamatergic pathway, called the retinohypothalamic tract (RHT), a pathway distinct from the classic visual system (Moore et al., 1971; Pickard, 1982; Rusak and Boulos, 1981). An indirect pathway from the intergeniculate leaflet of the thalamus, the geniculo-

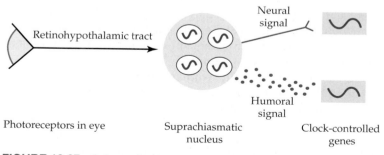

FIGURE 10.27 **Schematic representation of the three main components of a mammalian biological clock system** Environmental light information is transduced from receptors in the eyes to the oscillators in the SCN. Temporal information leaves the SCN via neural and humoral signals to synchronize physiology and behavior. From Kriegsfeld et al., 2001.

FIGURE 10.28 Visual pathway underlying circadian entrainment in mammals Light passes through the ganglion layer and inner retina to rod and cone photoreceptors. The rods and cones send information to ganglion cells. A subset of these ganglion cells, called intrinsically photosensitive retinal ganglion cells (ipRCGs), contain a photopigment called melanopsin that can encode and transmit light information directly. From Lok, 2011.

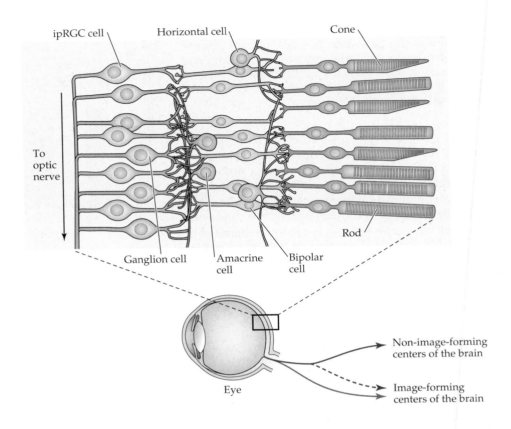

hypothalamic tract (GHT), also carries photic information to the SCN (Stopa et al., 1995). Neuropeptide Y appears to be the primary neurochemical signal from the GHT and may serve to phase-shift the endogenous circadian system (Gillespie et al., 1996; Huhman et al., 1996, 1997; Morin, 2013; Morin et al., 1992; Stopa et al., 1995).

The rod or cone photoreceptors traditionally associated with vision are sufficient, but not necessary, for entrainment (Bellingham and Foster, 2002; Berson, 2003). Mice that congenitally lack rods and cones entrain to light as well as sighted animals (Bellingham and Foster, 2002). Retinal ganglion cells appear to convey photic information to the SCN via the RHT. The photopigment used in the ganglion cells appears to be similar to a frog photopigment called melanopsin (Bellingham and Foster, 2002; Berson, 2003; Berson et al., 2002; Hattar et al., 2002; Van Gelder, 2003). Targeted deletion of the gene for melanopsin in mice impairs circadian entrainment (Panda et al., 2002; Ruby et al., 2002), and loss of melanopsin, rods, and cones abolishes the ability of mice to synchronize to any light cycle (Hattar et al., 2003; Panda et al., 2003). It is striking that loss of the melanopsin cells yields the same result, indicating that all light signaling must go through these specialized ganglion cells for circadian entrainment (Güler et al., 2008). Together, these findings indicate that rods and cones project to light-sensitive, melanopsin-containing ganglion cells to entrain circadian rhythms (Lok, 2011) (**FIGURE 10.28**).

Because lesions of the SCN eliminate all circadian rhythms measured to date, it was generally assumed that the SCN was the only locus capable of sustained rhythmicity and that rhythms in other systems or behavior were driven by broad communication of timing throughout the brain and body by this central pacemaker. However, the observation that cultured fibroblasts exhibit circadian rhythms in gene expression (Balsalobre et al., 1998) caused the field to question this assumption. Soon after this discovery, it became clear that the ability to oscillate was a general property of tissues throughout the central nervous system and periphery (Damiola et al., 2000; Yamazaki et al., 2000; Yoo et al., 2004) (**FIGURE 10.29**). It is now

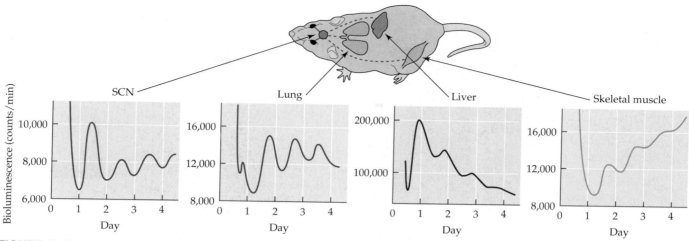

FIGURE 10.29 Central and peripheral oscillators show different phase relationships. Expression of core circadian clock genes is ubiquitous and reflects the presence of circadian oscillators in almost every tissue and cell in the body. To show expression of circadian fluctuations in gene expression, a chemical from fireflies called luciferase is linked to a mouse gene, in this case *Per2*. If cell cultures are recorded with sensitive light detectors, the timing of gene expression can be seen in real time. The SCN expresses robust oscillations of period 2–luciferase fusion protein (PER2::luciferase) activity when isolated in culture, in common with virtually every tissue in the mouse. After Yoo et al., 2004 with permission of Joseph Takahashi.

known that the circadian system is composed of multiple, individual cellular oscillators located throughout the body and most of its organs and glands. But, if clock function is ubiquitous, then why is the SCN unique? The SCN is unique in three respects: (1) as mentioned previously, the network of connectivity among cells within the SCN allows for the synchronization of independent cellular oscillators required for coherent tissue-level clock functioning; (2) the SCN is the only clock with access to environmental light information, allowing internal time to be properly synchronized to environmental time; and (3) through neural and hormonal communication (see below), the SCN synchronizes independent cellular oscillators within a system (e.g., liver) and sets their phase relative to external time. Without the SCN or its outputs, subordinate oscillators within a system lose coherence, leading to tissue-level arhythmicity, despite the observation that individual cells continue to exhibit daily rhythms (Leise et al., 2012; Welsh et al., 2004).

Neural efferents from the SCN appear to be necessary for maintaining most types of endocrine circadian rhythms. It is generally accepted that two different types of output signals emerge from the SCN (see Figure 10.27). One of the largest efferent pathways from the SCN travels to the SPVZ, a region below the PVN. Other direct pathways from the SCN innervate hypothalamic areas that mediate neuroendocrine function. These include the PVN (which mediates the release of corticotropin-releasing hormone [CRH], thyrotropin-releasing hormone [TRH], arginine vasopressin [AVP], and oxytocin [OT]), the supraoptic nuclei (SON, which mediate AVP and OT), and the arcuate nucleus (which mediates TRH, CRH, GnRH, and prolactin inhibitory hormone) (Kriegsfeld and Nelson, 2009; Kriegsfeld and Silver, 2006). Several other pathways directly and indirectly influence neuroendocrine function.

A second type of SCN output appears to be a humoral, diffusible signal. The notion of a diffusible SCN signal emerged from a series of SCN transplant studies. SCN tissue transplanted into the brains of arrhythmic, SCN-lesioned hamsters restores circadian locomotor activity rhythms (Lehman et al., 1987; Ralph et al., 1990) but not endocrine rhythms (Meyer-Bernstein et al., 1999). Because the SCN

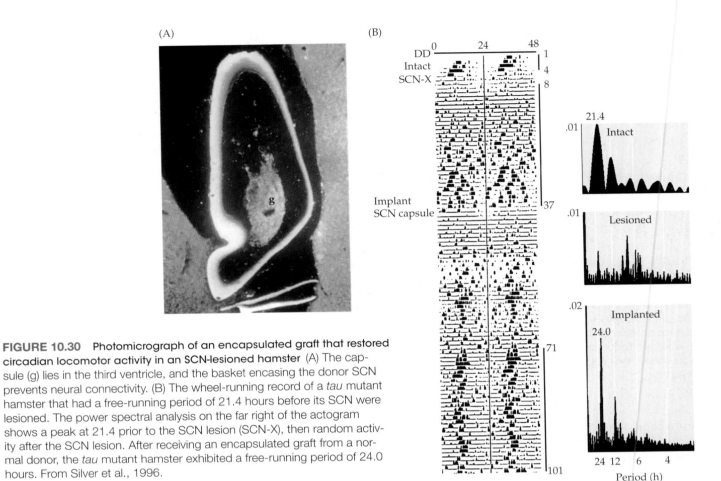

(A)

(B)

FIGURE 10.30 Photomicrograph of an encapsulated graft that restored circadian locomotor activity in an SCN-lesioned hamster (A) The capsule (g) lies in the third ventricle, and the basket encasing the donor SCN prevents neural connectivity. (B) The wheel-running record of a *tau* mutant hamster that had a free-running period of 21.4 hours before its SCN were lesioned. The power spectral analysis on the far right of the actogram shows a peak at 21.4 prior to the SCN lesion (SCN-X), then random activity after the SCN lesion. After receiving an encapsulated graft from a normal donor, the *tau* mutant hamster exhibited a free-running period of 24.0 hours. From Silver et al., 1996.

transplant does not reestablish neural connectivity with the host brain (Lehman et al., 1987), it was hypothesized that rhythms in locomotor activity could be supported by a diffusible SCN output signal. This possibility was tested by sealing SCN transplants into a semipermeable membrane that allowed for diffusible output but not neural outgrowth (Silver et al., 1996). When these encapsulated transplants were implanted into SCN-lesioned hosts, locomotor rhythmicity was restored, indicating that locomotor rhythms can be supported by a diffusible SCN signal (**FIGURE 10.30**). One early candidate for such a signal was AVP. The SCN display a circadian rhythm of AVP release and are responsible for a circadian rhythm of AVP in the cerebral spinal fluid (Majzoub et al., 1991). However, the AVP rhythm is not required for mediating circadian locomotor activity rhythms, because Brattleboro rats, as you recall, lack AVP and they display normal circadian organization (Reppert et al., 1987). Another early candidate diffusible signal was nitric oxide (NO) (Ding et al., 1994); however, mutant mice that lack NO appear to have normal circadian locomotor rhythms (Kriegsfeld et al., 1999, 2001). Additional candidates include prokineticin-2 (PK2) and transforming growth factor alpha (TGFα) (Cheng et al., 2002; Jobst et al., 2004; Li et al., 2012). PK2 is expressed rhythmically in the SCN, and its receptor is present in all major SCN targets (Cheng et al., 2002, 2005). Administration of PK2 during the night (when levels are low) inhibits wheel-running behavior in hamsters. Whether or not this signal normally operates in a diffusible manner and/or is released synaptically requires further examination. In common with PK2, TGFα is expressed rhythmically in the SCN, and its administration inhibits wheel-running behavior. The receptor for TGFα is also expressed in the SPVZ, the major

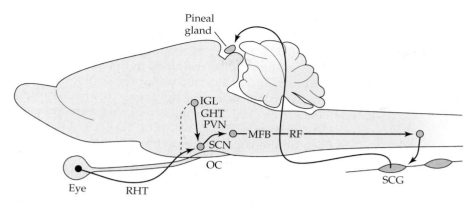

FIGURE 10.31   **Input and output pathways to and from the SCN in mammals** Environmental light information enters the SCN from the eyes via the retinohypothalamic tract (RHT) or geniculohypothalamic tract (GHT) via the intergeniculate leaflet (IGL). One well-characterized output system involves projections from the SCN to the paraventricular nucleus (PVN), from the PVN through the medial forebrain bundle (MFB), and from the MFB to the superior cervical ganglion (SCG). Postganglionic noradrenergic fibers eventually project back into the brain and innervate the pineal gland, where neural information is transduced into a hormonal message. OC = optic chiasm; RF = reticular formation. After Klein et al., 1983.

target of the SCN. Again, the degree to which TGFα is released in a diffusible manner under normal conditions requires further study. Studies in which fiber output is eliminated from the SCN (allowing only for diffusible output), in conjunction with administration of PK2 and TGFα antagonists, are necessary to settle this issue.

Perhaps the best-known output pathway is illustrated in **FIGURE 10.31**. Light information is transduced into an endocrine message in the pineal gland, which secretes the hormone melatonin (see Figure 2.33). The SCN project to the PVN that, in turn, project through the medial forebrain bundle (MFB) out of the central nervous system to the superior cervical ganglion (SCG), a part of the sympathetic nervous system. Cell bodies in the SCG project back into the CNS to the pineal gland. In the dark these neurons secrete norepinephrine, which stimulates the pinealocytes to up-regulate their enzymatic activity to produce melatonin from serotonin when it is dark. This multisynaptic pathway has been confirmed by injecting labeled pseudorabies, a transneuronal retrograde tracer, into the pineal gland (Card, 2000). The pattern of melatonin production and secretion is not a passive response to light and dark but is a programmed rhythm that persists in constant conditions (although continuous bright lights dampen the melatonin rhythm). Lesions of the SCN or any of its output tracts to the pineal gland eliminate circadian rhythms in melatonin production and secretion (Klein et al., 1983; Scott et al., 1995). There is abundant evidence for direct neural SCN control of neuroendocrine cell populations (Kriegsfeld and Nelson, 2009; Kriegsfeld and Silver, 2006). Because these cell populations can regulate neurochemicals that are secreted into the cerebrospinal fluid or general circulation, SCN-derived signals can control widespread systems in the brain and body.

Among mammals, a retinal-SCN axis (with several output pathways, including the pineal gland) appears to underlie the circadian system. Indeed, this axis appears to exist among all vertebrate species, although there is great diversity among species in the extent to which each component contributes to circadian rhythms. There is greater complexity in the contributions of the component parts of the biological rhythm systems of nonmammalian vertebrates than of mammals. For example, multiple input pathways and multiple oscillators have been discovered in different species of birds (Takahashi, 1991). The input pathways may involve photorecep-

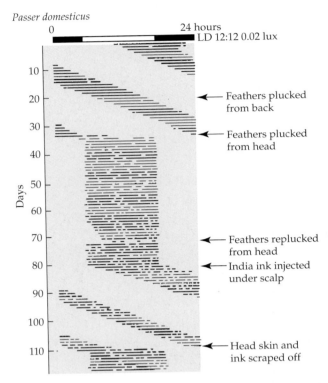

Passer domesticus

Feathers plucked from back

Feathers plucked from head

Feathers replucked from head

India ink injected under scalp

Head skin and ink scraped off

FIGURE 10.32 Circadian locomotor activity in birds is entrained by nonretinal photoreceptors in the brain. If a house sparrow (*Passer domesticus*) is fitted with opaque contact lenses, the bird will continue to be entrained to the daily light-dark cycle (even under dim illumination, 0.02 lux) if the feathers on the head are plucked. As the feathers regrow, the bird will begin to free-run. However, if the feathers are plucked again, re-entrainment will be attained. If ink is injected under the scalp of the bird, it will begin to free-run again because the photoreceptors in the brain necessary for entrainment are blocked. If the ink is removed, entrainment will be observed again. "LD 12:12" means that lights are on for 12 hours and then it is dark for 12 hours. From Groos, 1982.

tors located in the retina or in the pineal gland or dispersed throughout other brain regions. Extraretinal photoreception can be demonstrated by fitting a bird with opaque contact lenses; the bird will continue to be entrained to the daily light-dark cycle. However, if ink is injected under the scalp of the bird, it begins to free-run because the light receptors necessary for entrainment are blocked. If the ink is removed, entrainment is observed again (Groos, 1982) (**FIGURE 10.32**).

Are there different clocks for rhythms of different lengths, or are longer rhythms simply the result of the multiplication of shorter rhythms? For example, is the 4-day estrous cycle of a hamster the result of a 4-day clock cycling once, or a 1-day clock cycling four times? Another possibility does not involve a clock at all but rather assumes that estrous cycles simply reflect the cumulative amount of time required for a specific sequence of physiological processes or stages to occur. These hypotheses were evaluated in a study of rhythms in female hamsters. Phase shifts of the circadian rhythm were accompanied by proportionate shifts in the 4-day (96-hour) estrous cycle. For example, if the daily light-dark cycle was changed to 25 hours, then the 4-day estrous cycle changed to 100 hours (Carmichael et al., 1981; Fitzgerald and Zucker, 1976). Similarly, if the daily light-dark cycle was reduced to 20 hours, then the estrous cycle was shortened to 80 hours. Because estrous and activity onset are coupled temporally, it was suggested that the LH surge and locomotor activity are controlled by either a single, endogenous oscillator or a coupled, multioscillator system that regulates the rhythms of each process independently (Fitzgerald and Zucker, 1976). The former hypothesis postulated that the reproductive axis "tracks" four circadian cycles and ovulation occurs after the count is complete. Converging lines of evidence over the next three decades established that both of these hypotheses are partially correct. We now know that the SCN provides a daily, stimulatory signal to the reproductive axis each day of the estrous cycle, closely preceding the active phase, in most spontaneously ovulating rodents (Legan and Karsch, 1975; Mahoney et al., 2004), indicating that a single clock subserves both processes. However, this signal is only effective at stimulating the GnRH system to produce the LH surge in the presence of estradiol concentrations above a critical threshold (Williams et al., 2012). Prior to the day of proestrus, the developing ovarian follicles secrete insufficient estradiol to fulfill this criterion. As mentioned in Chapter 6, the SCN appears to accomplish this task by signaling estrogen-responsive kisspeptin cells in the anteroventral periventricular nucleus (Piet et al., 2015; Smarr et al., 2012; Vida et al., 2010; Williams et al., 2011) while concomitantly removing inhibition of the reproductive axis mediated by gonadotropin inhibitory hormone (GnIH) (Gibson et al., 2008; Russo et al., 2015).

Circadian Rhythms, Hormones, and Behavior

Hormones may have many effects on daily locomotor activity cycles. As noted previously, hamsters in the laboratory become active 5 to 10 minutes after the lights are turned off. This statement is true of males but only partially true of females. Female hamsters display an interesting pattern of activity onset that has been termed scalloping. Every fourth night, coincident with estrus, females show a spontaneous phase advance in their onset of locomotor activity (**FIGURE 10.33**). As you will

FIGURE 10.33 Estrogen-induced "scalloping" of activity patterns
Free-running female hamsters kept in chronic dark conditions begin locomotor activity at the expected time on most days, but on the day of estrus, the onset of their running behavior is phase-advanced (arrows) by rising levels of estrogens. After Zucker, 1980.

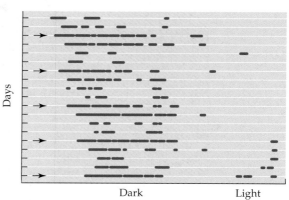

see below, this sex difference results from differences in hormone-responsive SCN target tissues (Bailey and Silver, 2014).

Effects of Hormones on the SCN

Hamsters are solitary creatures, and it has been speculated that the earlier onset of activity during estrus places females above ground earlier in the evening and thus increases the female's odds of locating a male. The scalloping pattern can be eliminated by ovariectomy. Furthermore, estradiol treatment of free-running, ovariectomized hamsters or rats reduces the period of locomotor activity onset, suggesting a direct effect of estrogens on the clock itself (Albers, 1981; Morin et al., 1977). Although there are low levels of estrogen receptors in the SCN (Gundlah et al., 2000; Kruijver and Swabb, 2002), neurons in the preoptic area, amygdala, arcuate nuclei, and bed nucleus of the stria terminalis possess the α estrogen receptor (ERα) in relatively large numbers, and these structures communicate directly with the SCN (de la Iglesia et al., 1999). A direct VIPergic neural connection from the SCN to GnRH-secreting cells (de la Iglesia et al., 2003; Van der Beek et al., 1993, 1997) and projections to kisspeptin cells (Vida et al., 2010; Williams et al., 2011) and GnIH (Gibson et al., 2008; Russo et al., 2015) act to time the LH surge and ovulation (**FIGURE 10.34**).

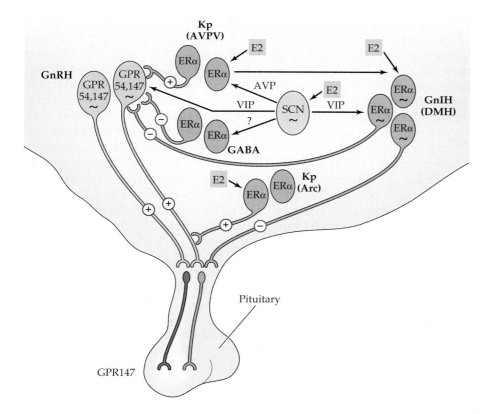

FIGURE 10.34 Model of circadian initiation of the preovulatory LH surge in spontaneously ovulating rodents by major positive and negative regulators of GnRH neuronal activity. Black lines depict monosynaptic projections from the SCN to GnRH neurons and to major positive (kisspeptin, Kp) and negative (GnIH, GABA) neurochemical mediators of the GnRH system that contain estrogen receptors. Kisspeptin cells in the AVPV are active at the time of the LH surge. Neurons containing ERα in the preoptic area and elsewhere are known to project to the SCN and to the vicinity of GnRH neurons and may play a role in mediating the circadian signal to GnRH neurons directly and/or indirectly. Whereas estrogen-responsive cells have not been definitively shown to project specifically to GnRH neurons, the emergence and sexual dimorphism of kisspeptin cells and fibers that project to GnRH cell bodies provide compelling evidence for the direct connection between these two neural phenotypes. Connections between the GnIH and GnRH systems indicate a putative role for GnIH in modulating the negative feedback effects of estrogen, with SCN communication allowing for removal of negative feedback on the reproductive axis during the time of the LH surge. A similar role for SCN-GABA interactions is likely, although SCN projections and ERα expression specific to AVPV GABAergic cells have not been empirically examined. Kisspeptin cells in the Arcuate nucleus likely serve to modify GnRH output at the level of the terminal. After Williams and Kriegsfeld, 2012.

In addition to estradiol, other sex steroid hormones exhibit modulatory effects on biological oscillators. Progesterone lengthens the period of circadian rhythms in females, possibly by counteracting the effects of estradiol (Takahashi and Menaker, 1980). Sex steroid hormones can also affect daily activity rhythms in males. Castration lengthens, and androgen replacement restores, the free-running period of locomotor activity onset in male mice (Butler et al., 2012; Daan et al., 1975). Testosterone also seems to be important in consolidation of locomotor activity rhythms; castrated male rodents increase the duration of and fluctuations in the onset of the daily active period (Ellis and Turek, 1983; Morin and Cummings, 1981). Castrated rodents also reduce the number of daily wheel revolutions (Morin and Cummings, 1981). Testosterone replacement therapy reverses the effects of castration on circadian locomotor activities. Testosterone may have direct effects on the SCN, as androgen receptors have been identified in the SCN of ferrets (Kashon et al., 1996), mice (Karatsoreos et al., 2007), rats (Zhou et al., 1994), and humans (Fernández-Guasti et al., 2000). Females have lower androgen receptor expression than males, and this difference is eliminated by gonadectomy (Iwahana et al., 2008). Alternatively, in some cases, testosterone can be aromatized to estradiol, and estradiol may exert its effects either directly or on neurons that communicate with the SCN (de la Iglesia et al., 1999). In mice, androgen receptors are expressed in the retinorecipient portion of the SCN, and gonadectomy alters the phase-shifting effects of light (Karatsoreos et al., 2007, 2011). Additionally, gonadectomy influences the structure of the SCN, increasing glial fibrillary acidic protein and decreasing the expression of synaptic proteins (Karatsoreos et al., 2011).

Removal of the pituitary gland (hypophysectomy) lengthens the free-running period of circadian locomotor activity onset by about 12 minutes per day (Zucker et al., 1980). However, the endocrine sequelae of hypophysectomy are profound. In addition to disruptions in sex steroid hormone production, alterations in many other endocrine functions occur as a result of hypophysectomy. In order to separate the effects of hypophysectomy from other endocrine consequences of this surgery, endocrine manipulations of other systems mediated by the anterior pituitary have been attempted. Investigators have focused on the thyroid gland because of its obvious and direct effects on metabolic processes. Removal of the thyroid gland results in a shortening of the free-running period of circadian locomotor activity onset in canaries, and thyroid hormone replacement therapy results in a corresponding lengthening of the period (Wahlstrom, 1965). Hypothyroidism induced by the drugs propylthiourea or propylthiouracil has been correlated with lengthened free-running periods of locomotor activity onset in hamsters (Beasley and Nelson, 1982; Morin et al., 1986). It remains unresolved whether alterations in thyroid hormone secretion per se or exposure to the antithyroid drugs accounts for the changes in period length (Morin, 1988). Injections of TRH directly into the SCN had the effect of phase-advancing wheel-running behavior in hamsters (10 and 100 nanomolar doses phase-advanced the behavior 18 and 35 minutes, respectively) (Gary et al., 1996). These hormonal influences on behavioral and physiological cyclic phenomena may eventually provide a key to understanding clock functions directly.

Effects of the SCN on Hormones

GLUCOCORTICOIDS   A strong circadian rhythm of glucocorticoid secretion has been observed in many species of birds and mammals, including humans (Dickmeis, 2009; Kalsbeek et al., 2012). Circadian regulation of glucocorticoid production and release occurs in both the SCN and adrenal biological timekeepers. As noted previously, cortisol secretion begins to rise during sleep, resulting in the daily peak concentrations usually just prior to or immediately after awakening in humans, coincident with the onset of activity in the morning (see Figure 10.16). In rodents and other nocturnal animals, the corticosterone cycle is reversed, but the peak values coincide with the beginning of their active period as night begins (Albers et al., 1985). Central circadian regulation is mediated via the hypothalamic-pituitary-adrenal axis (Kalsbeek et al., 2010) and the autonomic nervous system (Buijs et al., 1999), whereas the adrenal gland clock appears to control sensitivity of the gland to the adrenocorticopic hormone (ACTH). These glucocorticoid rhythms persist in constant conditions in both rodents and primates (Czeisler et al., 1999; Moore and Eichler, 1972). Bilateral SCN lesions eliminate the corticosterone rhythms in rats (Moore and Eichler, 1972) and hamsters (Meyer-Bernstein et al., 1999). The timing of meals can significantly affect the timing of glucocorticoid rhythms (e.g., Wilkinson et al., 1979) and may therefore be another important factor in synchronizing biological rhythms (Balsalobre et al., 2000; So et al., 2009) (see below).

GONADOTROPINS AND SEX STEROID HORMONES   The SCN are important for the appropriate daily timing of gonadotropin secretion. The timing of gonadotropin secretion affects the timing of sex steroid secretion and the onset of reproductive behaviors, especially in females. The SCN send direct and indirect projections to the GnRH system to appropriately time the preovulatory LH surge (Kriegsfeld, 2013). As mentioned previously, this surge generator normally transmits every afternoon in rats (Gay et al., 1970) but only stimulates the LH surge when estrogen concentrations are elevated during proestrus. That is why there are 4- or 5-day estrous cycles in rats but no 4.5-day cycles. Experimental disruption of the surge generator pathway or anesthesia during the afternoon of proestrus prevents transmission of the signal and delays estrus for another 24 hours (Everett and Sawyer, 1950). Bilateral lesions of the SCN block the daily pulse of LH release (Gray et al., 1978). Despite the strong circadian organization of gonadotropin secretion in females, estrogen concentrations do not show consistent circadian rhythms. It appears that the GnRH system exhibits a daily change in sensitivity to neurochemicals that stimulate the LH surge, including kisspeptin and VIP, further ensuring that ovulation is triggered on the afternoon of proestrus (Williams and Kriegsfeld, 2011; Zhao and Kriegsfeld, 2009). Likewise, the GnIH system exhibits time-dependent sensitivity to VIPergic SCN suppression, presumably to time the removal of estrogen negative feedback with the SCN stimulation of the surge (Russo et al., 2015). In contrast, testosterone concentrations in males display clear circadian rhythms that persist in constant conditions (Dibeu et al., 1983; Plant, 1981) despite weak or nonexistent circadian rhythms in gonadotropin concentrations (Veldhuis et al., 1986). In diurnal primates, blood testosterone concentrations begin to rise in the middle of the night and peak around dawn (Velduis et al., 1986) (**FIGURE 10.35**).

MELATONIN   A strong circadian pattern of melatonin secretion is observed in both nocturnal and diurnal animals. As we shall see below, **photoperiod** (day length) can be measured by the duration of melatonin secretion. Melatonin can phase-shift circadian locomotor activity rhythms in mice (Arendt, 1998; Benloucif and Dubocovich, 1996). Melatonin also affects entrainment in birds (Gwinner et al., 1997) and lizards (Bertolucci and Foa, 1998). Importantly, daily treatment with pharmacological doses of melatonin entrains the locomotor activity rhythms of nocturnal rodents, such as rats and mice, but not diurnal chipmunks (Murakami et al., 1997). Despite the diurnal organization of humans, melatonin treatment may be useful in treating jet lag or sleep disorders (Kripke et al., 1998; Waterhouse et al., 1998). Melatonin has also proved effective in treating blind people who are free-running. As you might imagine, this condition causes recurrent insomnia and daytime

photoperiod   Day length, or the amount of light per day.

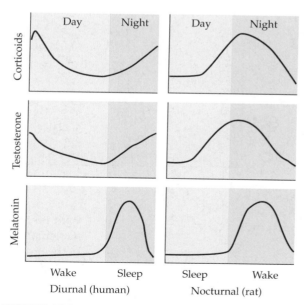

FIGURE 10.35   Daily patterns of testosterone, glucocorticoid, and melatonin in humans and nocturnal rats   After Kriegsfeld et al., 2001.

(A) Pre-treatment assessment

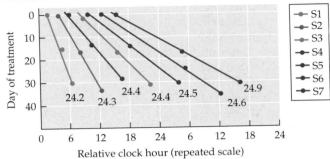

(B) Placebo trial

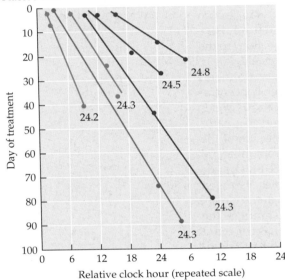

(C) Melatonin trial

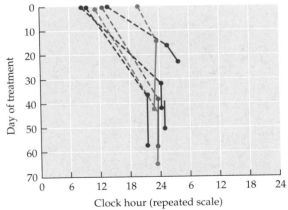

FIGURE 10.36 Circadian rhythms in blind people Seven blind people are depicted with free-running circadian rhythms at baseline and during the melatonin and placebo trials. Each data point represents an assessment of circadian phase as determined by the time at which endogenous plasma melatonin concentrations rose above the threshold of 10 pg/ml. The slopes of the fitted regression lines are indicative of the people's circadian periods (shown in hours below the regression lines for the baseline, placebo, and trial conditions). Treatment with melatonin or placebo began on day 1. In (A) and (B), the regression lines are arranged on a relative time scale in ascending order so that they can be easily compared. In (C), the time scale is absolute and shows the assessments of circadian phase and fitted regression lines for all seven people before (dashed lines) and after (solid lines) the melatonin trial. Treatment with melatonin resulted in entrainment (a circadian period of 24.0 hours) in all but one person, participant 7 (S7); on average, the rise in plasma melatonin after entrainment occurred at 12:18 A.M. After Sack et al., 2000.

sleepiness because the endogenous biological rhythms drift in and out of phase with the typical 24-hour work day. In one study, people who were totally blind (i.e., lacked conscious perception of light) were given either 10 mg of melatonin or a placebo daily for several weeks at 1 hour before their preferred bedtime (Sack et al., 2000). When given the placebo, their sleep-wake cycles free-ran with a period of approximately 24.5 hours. The melatonin entrained the free-running sleep-wake cycle to 24 hours in about 86% of the group (Sack et al., 2000) (**FIGURE 10.36**). These researchers were able to entrain the sleep-wake cycle of blind people with a nightly dose of 0.05 mg of melatonin (Lewy et al., 2001). It is clear that melatonin can influence entrainment in humans. However, the safety, toxicology, and teratogenic effects of melatonin have not been completely determined. Another likely, but as of yet unidentified, problem is that genetic variation among humans yields multiple alleles of melatonin receptors, which may change responsiveness to exogenous melatonin. Melatonin is sold over the counter in the United States as a nutritional supplement but is strictly regulated as a neurohormone in Europe (Arendt, 1997; Guardiola-Lemaitre, 1997).

What is the zeitgeber synchronizing activity in humans? There are several possible candidates, including light-dark cycles, temperature rhythms, and social influences. Social cues do affect the timing of human circadian rhythms. For example, when a group of people is housed in an underground bunker with no time referents, the entire group may adopt a single free-running rhythm (Coleman, 1986). In some cases, the group members adopt the free-running rhythm of the individual with the most dominant personality (Palmer, 1976). In many other studies, the effects of social cues cannot be untangled from other potential zeitgebers, such as meal times or the timing of the sleep-wake cycle. However, as we have just seen with the studies of blind people, melatonin (and likely photoperiod) provides a potent zeitgeber to humans (Lewy et al., 2001).

The importance of light as an entraining agent for human circadian rhythms has been established for rhythms of body temperature and the sleep-wake cycle

(A) Long day

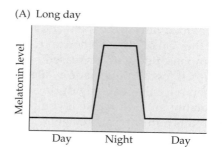

(B) Short day

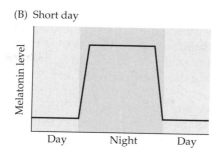

FIGURE 10.37 Melatonin measures night length. Melatonin is secreted only at night in both nocturnal and diurnal animals. Hamsters maintained under long-day (i.e., short-night) conditions display a relatively brief period of melatonin secretion (A), whereas hamsters maintained under short-day (i.e., long-night) conditions display an extended period of melatonin secretion (B). When the duration of melatonin secretion attains some threshold, a short-day response occurs. After Bartness and Goldman, 1989.

(Czeisler et al., 1980; Dinges, 1984). The role of light in human circadian rhythms was emphasized by the discovery that bright light (>2500 lux) suppressed the production of pineal melatonin in humans (Lewy et al., 1980). In a number of mammalian species, including humans, melatonin is normally secreted in a circadian fashion, with an extended peak of secretion occurring at night. The duration of this sustained elevation of melatonin secretion varies with the length of the night (Bartness and Goldman, 1989; Bittman and Karsch, 1984; Illnerova et al., 1985); this variation provides a means of measuring day length and thus discerning the season of the year, as we will see below (**FIGURE 10.37**). Pineal melatonin secretion can be suppressed at night by light, and among many mammalian species, very little light indeed is necessary for this suppression. For example, exposure of hamsters to a very brief (1 ms), dim (0.1 lux—about the illumination provided by a half moon on a clear night) light pulse is sufficient to suppress melatonin production for the entire evening (Milette and Turek, 1986). Thus, exposure to only 1 ms of light per night, strategically placed to occur during the daily melatonin peak, will shorten the length of the nightly bout of melatonin secretion substantially and affect the animal's perception of seasonal cues. It was previously believed that melatonin rhythms in humans are unperturbed by dim light (Czeisler et al., 1989; Lewy et al., 1980). However, recent studies show that short-wavelength "blue" light, even at dim illumination, can alter melatonin and sleep profiles in humans (Cajochen et al., 2005; Chang et al., 2015; Thapan et al., 2001). Given that most screen-based electronic devices emit blue light, and many people use some sort of electronic device near bedtime, many people are likely altering their melatonin profile and adversely affecting their sleep quality.

Because different rhythms may have different light intensity thresholds for entrainment, some rhythms may free-run in low-illumination conditions, whereas other rhythms may remain entrained. Desynchronization of these rhythms during the winter may account for a number of sleep, eating, and mood disorders, including jet lag (Bedrosian et al., 2016). One well-known mood disorder, seasonal affective disorder (SAD), which is associated with dysfunctional biological timekeeping, is described in detail in Chapter 13. In some cases, appropriately timed treatment with bright lights can ameliorate the affective symptoms associated with SAD.

Circadian Regulation of Food Intake

Animals that are nocturnal or diurnal confine most of their food intake to the dark or light part of the day, respectively. Some animals are flexible in the timing of their ingestive behaviors and can eat throughout the day: you have probably had a midnight snack without ill effects. However, the timing of food intake is inflexible in other animals.

CIRCADIAN CONTROL OF FEEDING Syrian hamsters are hardwired to eat specific amounts during the light and dark phases, and they cannot compensate for shortages in one phase during the other. If hamsters eat a total of 10 g of food per day, they might eat 6 g of food at night and 4 g of food during the day. If their food is taken away during the day, then they eat only 6 g of food during the night and lose weight. If their food is restricted during the night, they eat only 4 g of food and lose weight to the point of starvation, rather than compensating with increased food intake during the day (Silverman and Zucker, 1976). If food is only made available during either the light or dark part of the day, then mice that eat only during the daylight become fat (Arble et al., 2009). The regulation of food intake is complex and requires the coordination of several brain circuits and several orexigenic and anorexigenic hormones (see Chapter 9). If the SCN are lesioned in rodents, then food intake is dispersed throughout the day and night. The SCN can presumably affect food intake by several pathways. For example, the SCN communicate directly with all of the hypothalamic nuclei that are involved in the regulation of food intake, including the arcuate nuclei (AN), dorsomedial nuclei (DMN), ventromedial nuclei of the hypothalamus (VMN), and lateral hypothalamus (Kalra et al., 1999). SCN fibers innervate neuropeptide Y (NPY), pro-opiomelanocortin (POMC), and galanin-containing neurons in the AN, and lesions of the AN-PVN may disrupt the circadian pattern of orexigenic and anorexigenic hormones and thus change the pattern of these hormones and the pattern of ingestive behaviors (Kriegsfeld et al., 2002). Neurotransmitters involved in food intake, such as serotonin, norepinephrine, and epinephrine, display circadian variation controlled by the SCN. For example, norepinephrine treatment appears to provoke food intake better at the onset of activity in nocturnal rodents than at other times (Currie and Wilson, 1993). Finally, the SCN can also affect the timing of food intake by affecting secretion of insulin and glucagon. Bilateral lesions of the SCN block the circadian rhythm of insulin and glucagon concentrations in the blood (Yamamoto et al., 1987). It appears that the SCN may stimulate glucagon secretion and inhibit insulin secretion, because glucagon concentrations are lower and insulin concentrations are higher in SCN-lesioned rats than in SCN-intact animals (Yamamoto et al., 1987).

As you might expect given the role of the circadian system in regulating neurochemical systems involved in food intake and metabolism, *Bmal1* knockout mice exhibit dysregulated glucose homeostasis along with decreased gluconeogenesis and increased insulin sensitivity (Marcheva et al., 2010). *Rev-Erbα/β* knockout mice have dysregulated lipid metabolism (Cho et al., 2012). As with clock gene mutations, disruptions to the circadian system lead to irregular eating patterns and an increase in body mass along with reduced rhythms of hypothalamic and liver clock gene expression in mice (Fonken et al., 2013). The impact of dim light at night can be abrogated through wheel-running exercise or subsequent exposure to dark at night (Fonken et al., 2014).

FOOD ENTRAINABLE OSCILLATORS   In some cases, nonphotic cues, such as scheduled handling or injection of saline, can entrain the free-running clocks of adult Syrian hamsters and mice (Hastings et al., 1998) (**TABLE 10.2**). Because many people who are totally blind often show entrainment of their biological rhythms, it is likely that humans also possess the capability for nonphotic entrainment of their circadian clocks. One of the most potent nonphotic zeitgebers is scheduled feeding (reviewed in Stephan, 2002). Not surprisingly, limiting access to food to a specific time of day has dramatic effects on the temporal organization of behavior and physiology. The overt behavioral effect is meal anticipation. Premeal anticipatory behavior, elevation of core body temperature, and elevated serum corticosterone concentrations display dramatic circadian patterns in association with mealtime, and these patterns persist after SCN lesions (Stephan et al., 1979). Although the SCN (and several other CNS sites such as the amygdala, neocortex, hippocampus, and hypothalamus) have been ruled out as the integration site of food-entrainable oscillators (FEOs) (e.g., Stephan, 1983), the search for a specific locus of a separate FEO has been unsuccessful (Marchant and Mistlberger, 1997). Some researchers have suggested

TABLE 10.2   *Nonphotic zeitgebers in mammals*

Zeitgeber	Reference
Mealtimes	Stephan, 2002
Novel running wheels	Reebs and Mrosovsky, 1989
Foraging	Rusak et al., 1988
Social interactions	Mrosovsky, 1988a; Mistlberger and Skene, 2004
Dark pulses	Reebs et al., 1989; Van Reeth and Turek, 1989
Triazolam	Van Reeth and Turek, 1989; Mrosovsky and Salmon, 1990
Brotizolam	Yokota, 2000
Treadmill running	Marchant and Mistlberger, 1996
Limited access to home wheel	Edgar et al., 1991
Cold or refeeding	Mistlberger et al., 1996
Morphine	Marchant and Mistlberger, 1995
Exercise	Mistlberger and Skene, 2005
Temperature	Brown et al., 2002

that BMAL1 protein in the dorsal medial hypothalamus is necessary for this type of timing (Fuller et al., 2008); other research groups have not come to the same conclusions (e.g., Mistlberger et al., 2009). Although it appears that a network of structures is involved (Davidson, 2006), these interconnected brain structures are likely entrained by humoral signals (Carneiro and Araujo, 2009). One candidate for this humoral signal is the stomach hormone ghrelin (LeSauter et al., 2009). Mice lacking ghrelin receptors display reduced food anticipatory behaviors.

The cloning of circadian clock genes and the discovery that these genes are expressed in many CNS structures outside the SCN and in peripheral tissues have led to new strategies for investigating potential loci of an FEO. Clock gene expression has been observed to change in response to changes in periodic food availability in both the CNS and peripheral tissues. For example, food restriction to the light portion of the daily light-dark cycle (or to subjective day) shifted the expression of clock genes in the liver, but not in the SCN, of rats within 1 week (Damiola et al., 2000) (**FIGURE 10.38**). Although the SCN is not required for food entrainment, the FEO likely uses the same cellular clock mechanism, as *Per2* mutant mice do not exhibit food entrainment (Feillet et al., 2006). Because a secondary peak of glucocorticoids emerges at the time of anticipated feeding, glucocorticoids may, in part, mediate food-entrainable circadian rhythms. Restricted feeding alters micronutrient availability and consequent signaling pathways. Taken together, the evidence suggests that the daily light-dark cycle is the most potent zeitgeber for the SCN, whereas food intake appears to be the most important zeitgeber for peripheral oscillators, especially sites involved in metabolism (Kriegsfeld et al., 2002).

Many hormones involved in metabolism are rhythmically expressed, are regulated by the biological clock, and entrain to timed daily food presentation (Patton and Mistlberger, 2013). Clock genes show oscillation in both the SCN and periphery and have been linked to changes in metabolism. Although the central pacemaker does not appear to be affected by diet or mealtime, the peripheral clocks are. For example, restricted feeding affects circadian oscillators in peripheral tissues such as liver, kidney, heart, and pancreas (Damiola et al., 2000). Additionally, a high-fat diet disrupts clock gene expression and leads to increased out-of-phase eating and, ultimately, obesity (Kohsaka et al., 2007). Disrupted peripheral clock expression may be important for shift workers and people with disorders such as night eating syndrome.

FIGURE 10.38 Shifting the time of food intake from night to day changes gene expression in the periphery, but not in the SCN. The panels in the left column depict gene expression of *Per1 and Per2* in the SCN and liver and of the circadian transcription factor *Dbp* in several peripheral organs when mice were given free access to food. Because mice are nocturnal, most of their food intake occurs at night. The panels in the right column show the timing of the same gene expression when food was restricted to the light portion of the day. After Damiola et al., 2000.

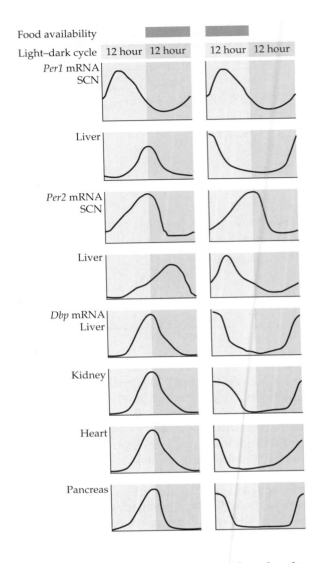

These populations are at increased risk for obesity, which may in part be related to desynchronization of mealtime and clock expression.

Circadian Rhythms in Health and Disease

Virtually all people suffering from mood disorders have significant disruptions in circadian rhythms, and altered sleep patterns are one of the major diagnostic criteria for these disorders, including schizophrenia (Wirz-Justice et al., 1997), major depression (Benca, 1996), bipolar disorder (Benedetti et al., 2008; McClung, 2013), and anxiety disorders (McClung, 2013). Additional evidence for a role of circadian clocks comes from studies showing that polymorphisms in the *Cry2* locus are associated with bipolar disorder (Shi et al., 2008; Sjoholm et al., 2010) and depression (Lavebratt et al., 2010), while the *Per3*, *Cry1*, and timeless (*tim*) genes are associated with schizophrenia and schizoaffective disorder (Lamont et al., 2007; Mansour et al., 2006; Moons et al., 2011; Peng et al., 2007). *Bmal1* and *tim* are associated with bipolar disorder and schizophrenia (Mansour et al., 2006). A postmortem analysis of rhythmic patterns of gene expression in human brain revealed weaker rhythms in patients with major depressive disorder compared with unaffected controls, further suggesting a link between disrupted circadian biology and depression (Li et al., 2013). When circadian dysfunction is present, many of these mood disorders can be treated by manipulating the timing of sleep (Bunney and Bunney, 2013; Kaplan and Harvey, 2013). Another type of therapy for bipolar disorder that shows promise is called interpersonal and social rhythm therapy. This intervention is based on the hypothesis that individuals with bipolar disorders have dysregulated circadian organization and that adherence to a strict daily routine can serve to strengthen their circadian organization. Stabilization of social routines (including sleep-wake and activity rhythms with a presumed effect on underlying endogenous circadian rhythms) is associated with faster recovery from bipolar depression (Miklowitz et al., 2007), has significant protective effects against new episodes of mania and depression (Frank et al., 2005), and is associated with faster improvement in occupational function (Frank et al., 2005, 2008; Miklowitz et al., 2007).

A less well-known clinical condition is called night eating syndrome (Stunkard et al., 1955). The core symptoms include evening overeating and, usually, nighttime awakening and food consumption, associated with behavioral and hormonal phase delays (Allison et al., 2005). Not surprisingly, people with night eating syndrome are generally obese. Treatment with serotonin reuptake inhibitors restores the circadian rhythm and is relatively effective in controlling the episodes of nocturnal eating (Stunkard et al., 2006; Vander Wal, 2014). Recent work suggests that morning bright-light therapy also helps to reduce nighttime eating as well as mood and sleep disturbances in affected patients (McCune et al., 2015).

Along with mood disorders, disruptions to the circadian timing system are associated with a number of disease states, including cancer, cardiovascular disease, neural cell death, peptic ulcers, obesity, rheumatoid arthritis, bipolar disorder, depression, and schizophrenia (Golombek et al., 2013). Not only is disease progression associated with circadian disturbances, but the efficacy of pharmacological disease treatments varies markedly based on the timing of their delivery. Early work in rats and mice, for example, provided evidence that cancer chemotherapy is more effective if delivered at times of greatest drug tolerance (Halberg et al., 1980; Levi, 1987; Reinberg et al., 1987). Likewise, because cancer cells exhibit daily rhythms in mitotic activity and because cytotoxic chemotherapeutic agents are most effective when applied during peak mitotic activity, the timing of chemotherapy has pronounced impact on patient outcome (Ortiz-Tudela et al., 2013). Interruption of melatonin rhythms by either night-shift work or other exposures to low-wavelength lights (blue) has been associated with elevated risk of cancers, especially breast cancer (Hill et al., 2015). Clinical trials for a number of cancers reveal enormous increases in response rate and survivorship and decreased negative side effects when daily timing of chemotherapy is considered. However, it has been challenging to incorporate a chronotherapeutic strategy into oncological practice. Part of the challenge arises from the fact that sex, lifestyle, and genetic background influence the most appropriate time of delivery across individuals (Ortiz-Tudela et al., 2013).

Analogous results indicate that increased efficacy of pharmacological agents, like chemotherapeutic agents, can be gained by considering the timing of delivery. One strategy that has met with success is to administer medication at a time of greatest risk (e.g., myocardial infarction risk is greatest in the morning) or at the daily peak in symptoms of the ailment (e.g., asthma symptoms exhibit marked daily changes) (Bairy, 2013). A more effective strategy is to consider daily changes in drug pharmacodynamics and to deliver medications at a time when the drug is best tolerated and metabolism and elimination are lowest. For over 300 drugs, prominent daily changes in absorption, distribution, metabolism, and elimination have been noted (reviewed in Levi and Schibler, 2007). By considering these daily changes in pharmacokinetics, striking increases in plasma concentrations of a drug can be achieved simply by altering the timing of administration.

Circannual and Seasonal Rhythms

The effects of light on daily melatonin production are critical in mammalian photoperiodism, the use of day length to time annual cycles. A functional circadian clock is required to measure day lengths, and measurement of day lengths is necessary to make seasonal adjustments in behavior. The SCN can serve as both clock and calendar because their function changes in response to photoperiod. As we saw above, the SCN transduces light information from the eyes to the pineal gland, which secretes melatonin when it is dark. The duration of the nocturnal melatonin signal encodes day length, and many species use this information to coordinate physiological adaptations with the yearly climatic cycle (Bartness et al., 1993). The duration of the nightly sustained elevation of melatonin secretion varies with the length of the night; in other words, a relatively brief duration of elevated melatonin secretion codes for short nights, or long days, whereas a relatively long duration of elevated melatonin secretion codes for long nights, or short days (Bittman and Karsch, 1984; Carter and Goldman, 1983a). Hamsters experimentally exposed to a brief pulse of light each night, which shortens the duration of melatonin secretion, display a short-night (long-day) hormone profile. They also exhibit physiological, morphological, and behavioral adaptations consistent with long days, such as maintaining complete reproductive function and their "summer" fur coat. Hamsters maintained in short-day light conditions exhibit longer bouts of elevated melatonin secretion, display reproductive regression, and develop a "winter" coat. Although daily melatonin rhythms are observed in birds and reptiles, the seasonal timekeeping function of these rhythms seems to be less than in mammals.

There appear to be two different types of biological rhythms that account for seasonal behavioral cycles (**FIGURE 10.39**). One reflects a seasonal biological rhythm driven by environmental day length, though it requires an endogenous circadian system to discern day length. The second comprises an endogenous organization in animals that do not have access to environmental cues while they undergo seasonal hibernation in burrows. There appear to be several instances in which both types of biological clocks interact to permit animals to discern the time of year.

Ultimate and Proximate Factors Underlying Seasonality

Most seasonal changes in behavior reflect strategies to manage an annual energy budget. Many animals and plants are exposed to seasonal fluctuations in the quality of their environments. Individuals generally restrict energetically expensive activities to a specific time of the year. Animals migrate or reduce their general levels of activity when food availability is low. Reproduction, preparation for migration, and other energetically demanding activities have evolved to coincide with abundant local food resources or other environmental conditions that promote survival. Precise timing of behavior is therefore a critical feature of individual reproductive success and subsequent fitness. As noted above, animals have evolved to fill temporal, as well as spatial, niches.

In some cases, physiological and behavioral changes that occur in direct response to environmental fluctuations have an obvious and immediate adaptive function. For example, low availability of food or water can inhibit reproductive function (Bronson, 1989; Nelson, 1987) (see Chapter 9). These types of environmental fluctuations have been termed the ultimate factors underlying seasonality (Baker, 1938). Many animals need to forecast the optimal time to breed so that spermatogenesis, territorial establishment, nest construction, or any other time-consuming preparations for reproduction will be complete at the start of the breeding season. Therefore, seasonally breeding animals frequently detect and respond to environmental cues that accurately signal, well in advance, the arrival or departure of seasons favoring reproductive success. The cues used to predict environmental change may or may not have direct survival value and can be referred to as proximate factors (Baker, 1938). The most notable example of such a proximate factor is day length, or photoperiod, a cue that can serve as a very precise reference for the time of year. Under some circumstances, proximate and ultimate factors may be identical (Negus and Berger, 1987). For example, some individuals may not begin breeding until food cues are detected (Bronson, 1989).

The most salient seasonal rhythm expressed by animals is the seasonal breeding cycle. Many animals, including small, short-lived mammals and birds, mate during the spring and rear their offspring during the summer, when food is plentiful; these animals are called *long-day breeders*. Other animals, such as sheep, deer, and cattle,

(A) Type I rhythm
　　Mixed: Driven by endogenous and exogenous
　　signals (e.g., Syrian hamster reproduction)

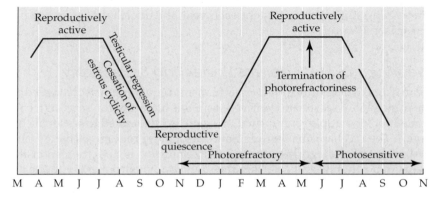

(B) Type II rhythm
　　Endogenous: Product of circannual clock(s)
　　(e.g., ground squirrel body weight)

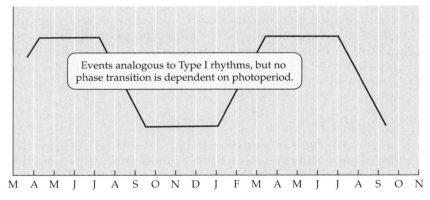

FIGURE 10.39 Schematic representation of two types of seasonal reproductive rhythms in rodents (A) Type I (mixed) seasonal rhythms are mediated by both endogenous (interval timer) and exogenous (ambient photoperiod) components. Decreasing photoperiods in the fall provoke gonadal regression and start an interval timer that eventually (after several months) causes the animals to be nonresponsive to the inhibitory effects of short days and redevelop their reproductive systems. Thus, even animals inhabiting constantly dark hibernacula (burrows) will emerge in the spring with full reproductive functions, rather than waiting 60 days to initiate spermatogenesis or estrus. Exposure to several weeks of long days is necessary to reset sensitivity to the inhibitory effects of short days. (B) Type II (circannual) rhythms are endogenous and have a period of 365 days or less. Photoperiodic information is necessary to entrain Type II rhythms to exactly 365 days. After Prendergast et al., 2002.

mate in autumn and have long gestation periods. These large mammals remain pregnant throughout the winter and, in common with small animals, give birth in the spring, when conditions are most suitable for survival. Animals that mate in autumn are called *short-day breeders*. Thus, many hormone-behavior interactions associated with the breeding season are mediated by biological clocks. Courtship, copulation, parental care, territorial defense, and aggression all exhibit pronounced seasonal fluctuations in occurrence that are linked directly to seasonal rhythms in reproductive function (Moffatt et al., 1993; Prendergast et al., 2009).

Seasonal changes in behavior are observed even among animals living in the tropics, where the annual cycle of changing day length is not as evident as it is at higher latitudes (**FIGURE 10.40**). Despite relatively constant photoperiodic and temperature conditions, seasonal variation in food availability is common for many tropical species. The irregularly timed onset of rain, or some coincident factor, induces tropical birds such as the red-billed quelea (*Quelea quelea*) to breed in East Africa (Disney et al., 1959); consequently, the onset of breeding in quelea there varies from year to year (Murton and Westwood, 1980). In western Africa, where the onset of the rainy season is more consistent each year, the quelea display a predictable breeding season (Ward, 1965).

Neuroendocrine Mechanisms Underlying Seasonality

There is an extensive literature on the mechanisms regulating seasonal breeding cycles. The principles of seasonality derived from this literature can serve as a basis for the examination of the sparser information base directly related to seasonal changes in behavior. The mechanisms that regulate seasonal reproductive changes may be classified under two categories. One set of mechanisms is directly responsible for timing seasonal rhythms and ensuring that they are synchronized with the annual geophysical cycles. In mammals, the pineal gland and its hormone, melatonin, are involved in mediating the effects of day length on the timing of a wide variety of seasonal changes in physiology and behavior (Goldman and Nelson, 1993). A second set of neuroendocrine mechanisms is directly responsible for regulating changes in the reproductive system. For example, changes in the rate or pattern of pituitary hormone secretion are important for driving changes in reproductive hormones. Seasonal changes in reproductive hormones, especially sex steroid hormones, result in a cascade of seasonal changes in steroid-dependent behaviors. These mechanisms will be referred to as activational mechanisms because they generally involve activational effects of hormones (Beach, 1975) (see Chapter 3).

Timing Mechanisms

Studies of seasonal rhythms in reproductive physiology have revealed a variety of timing mechanisms. Photoperiodism has been the most widely studied of these mechanisms. For the purposes of this discussion, photoperiodic mammals may be divided into two categories: (1) those that exhibit endogenous circannual cycles that are entrained, or synchronized, by photoperiodic cues and (2) those that fail to exhibit endogenous circannual cycles in the absence of photoperiodic cues (Prendergast et al., 2002). Deer, an example of the first type, exhibit circannual rhythms of reproductive activity that persist even when the animals are maintained under a constant day length, although these rhythms are not expressed under constant photoperiods of 12 hours or longer. However, changes in day length influence reproductive activity in deer, and natural photoperiodic changes are presumably largely responsible for establishing the seasonal pattern of reproduction (Goss, 1980, 1984; Goss and Rosen, 1973; Plotka et al., 1984). Sheep may also have the capacity to exhibit circannual cycles of reproductive activity in the absence of environmental cues, and these rhythms are clearly responsive to photoperiod under

(A) Temperate zone bird

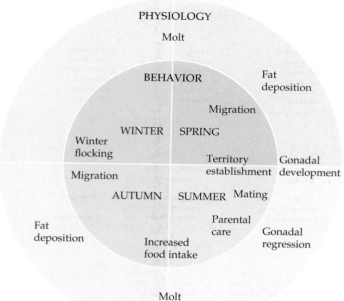

(B) Equatorial bird

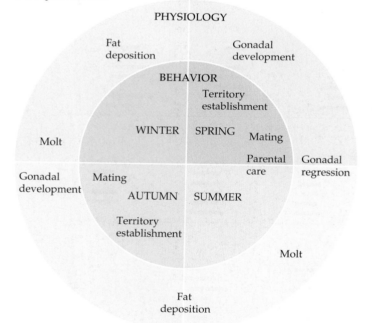

FIGURE 10.40 Annual breeding cycles in birds reflect energy constraints. (A) North temperate zone birds may migrate north in the spring, then become reproductively active, establishing territories, courting, and rearing young. After breeding, the birds molt and increase their body fat stores in preparation for the fall migration south. They feed all winter and undergo another molt prior to the next spring migration. Nonmigratory birds must bear the increased energetic costs associated with thermoregulation during the winter. Thus, molting, migration (or winter thermoregulation), and breeding are separated in time in temperate zone birds so that they can cope with the enormous energetic demands of each activity. (B) Tropical birds may not have the same energetic constraints, so breeding and molting can occur at any time of year, and the frequency of the cycle between these energetic demands is limited only by the physiological capability of the birds.

FIGURE 10.41 Circannual LH rhythms in ewes in a simulated annual photoperiod The sinusoidal line (red) at the top of the figure indicates day length. LH rhythms are shown for (A) intact ewes, (B) pinealectomized ewes, and (C–F) individual pinealectomized ewes treated with winter, spring, summer, or autumn patterns of melatonin replacement therapy. Horizontal blue bars indicate elevated LH concentrations. From Woodfill et al., 1994.

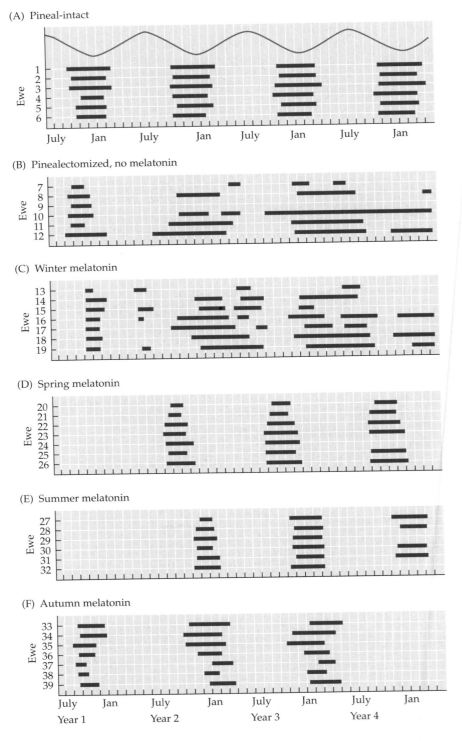

natural or artificial environmental conditions (Karsch et al., 1984; Sweeney et al., 1997) (**FIGURE 10.41**).

Individuals of many species of mammals fall into the second category and fail to exhibit endogenous cycles when housed under a fixed day length. For example, a variety of relatively short-lived rodent species remain reproductively active so long as they are maintained under long photoperiods. The critical photoperiod (i.e., the day length required to maintain reproductive function) for Syrian hamsters is

FIGURE 10.42   *Critical day length for reproduction of male Syrian hamsters* Testicular responses of Syrian hamsters after exposure to various fixed photoperiods for about 3 months. Only day lengths of ≥12.5 hours maintained full gonadal size and function. Thus, the critical day length for this trait in this species is between 12 and 12.5 hours of light per day. After Elliott, 1976.

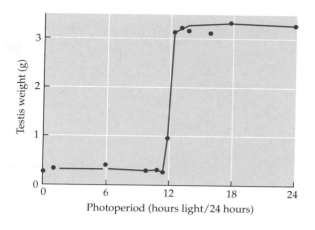

12.5 hours of light per day (**FIGURE 10.42**); other species, particularly those inhabiting high latitudes, have different critical photoperiods. Although these species require photoperiodic changes for the continuance of seasonal cycles, they still display a prominent element of endogenous seasonal timing. Short day lengths (<12.5 hours of light per day) induce reproductive regression, but after several months of exposure to short days, a "spontaneous" activation of the reproductive system occurs. This event seems to be triggered by an endogenous timing mechanism. Many of these species undergo various degrees of torpor in a dark burrow during winter, isolated from environmental cues; this mechanism allows them to prepare for the environmental changes that will take place in the spring (Elliott and Goldman, 1981; Reiter, 1970).

This "spontaneous" activation of reproductive function represents a phenomenon called **photorefractoriness**. In the case of Syrian hamsters, chronic maintenance under short day lengths causes the reproductive system to regress after about 10 weeks. After 20–30 weeks of continuous exposure to short days, however, the reproductive system is no longer inhibited by the short days and is then said to be photorefractory. After this time, the hamsters' reproductive systems become active and remain totally functional, even if the hamsters are kept in total darkness for the rest of their lives. If photorefractory hamsters are switched to long day lengths (>12.5 hours of light per day), after 10 weeks they will be responsive again to the inhibitory effects of short day lengths on reproductive function. In other words, the long days eliminate photorefractoriness. Photorefractoriness is adaptive because it allows preparation of the reproductive system in advance of appropriate breeding conditions.

Perhaps the most striking examples of endogenous timing mechanisms in photoperiodic species are observed in several species of hibernating mammals. Most hibernators undergo gonadal regression before entering hibernation. The gonads shrink, and gamete and sex steroid hormone production stops. Yet when these animals emerge from their hibernacula in early spring, their reproductive systems have been activated, and they are fully capable of breeding. Because the process of spermatogenesis requires several weeks in mammals, reproductive activation in males must begin before emergence from hibernation.

HIBERNATION IN HAMSTERS   Laboratory studies have demonstrated that pituitary gonadotropin secretion and testicular growth begin during the last few weeks of hibernation in Turkish hamsters (*Mesocricetus brandti*). Hibernation is terminated when testosterone levels exceed a certain threshold; this mechanism may serve to coordinate emergence from hibernation with testicular recrudescence (regrowth) (Hall and Goldman, 1980; Hall et al., 1982). The timing of testicular recrudescence in Turkish hamsters is probably accomplished by the same type of seasonal timing mechanism that operates in other photoperiodic rodents. Male Turkish hamsters that are exposed to short days in a warm environment do not hibernate, yet these animals exhibit a cycle of testicular regression and subsequent recrudescence very similar in timing to that observed in hibernating males (Darrow et al., 1987). A similar mechanism for temporal coordination of the seasons of hibernation and reproduction appears to exist in European hamsters (*Cricetus cricetus*) (Darrow et al., 1988) and hedgehogs (*Erinaceus europaeus*) (Saboureau, 1986).

photorefractoriness   The loss of responsiveness to changes in photoperiod.

Males that have just undergone testicular recrudescence produce more androgens and gonadotropins than animals whose reproductive function has been continuously maintained under long day lengths (Berndtson and Desjardins, 1974). This "overshoot" of endocrine activity may have functional behavioral consequences. Recall from Chapter 5 that long-castrated male rodents require higher androgen concentrations to maintain mating behavior than do recently castrated or intact animals (Damassa et al., 1977). The brain centers that control reproductive behavior may require sensitization by androgen exposure after prolonged gonadal quiescence in order to respond appropriately (Morin and Zucker, 1978).

HIBERNATION IN GROUND SQUIRRELS The seasonal organization of reproduction in golden-mantled ground squirrels (*Spermophilus lateralis*) has been the subject of many field and laboratory studies. These squirrels appear to possess an endogenous circannual clock (Berthold, 1837; Gwinner, 1986). When maintained under constant conditions in a laboratory setting, the squirrels display periods of reproductive function every 330–380 days. If the squirrels are exposed to a naturally changing photoperiod, they may entrain their endogenous cycles to exactly 365 days. A typical year in the lives of these squirrels living in Northern California begins with a summer of binge eating and deposition of body fat; body fat levels may double during the weight-gaining period of the summer. The squirrels then enter burrows and go into deep torpor. During torpor, the body temperature approaches the ambient temperature of the hibernaculum, about 2°C–4°C. Contrary to popular belief, the squirrels do not stay in deep hibernation throughout the winter but arouse every few days. They usually do not eat during this time, and their bodies undergo a programmed utilization of fat stores (although other ground squirrel species may arouse and eat at this time) (Dark et al., 1989). The squirrels' reproductive systems become activated during hibernation. In males, blood concentrations of androgens rise and eventually become incompatible with torpor, inducing the final arousal in March. Thus, the onset of testicular androgen production in the spring both terminates hibernation and stimulates subsequent mating behavior. When males emerge from their hibernacula, they are fertile, and their high blood concentrations of androgens cause them to defend territories and court females, which emerge a few weeks later. Virtually all females are inseminated during their first day above ground in the spring, despite the fact that they possess very low fat reserves. A litter is born in late spring, and the young squirrels scramble to increase body mass during their first summer.

These seasonal changes in reproductive function, food intake, and body mass also occur in the laboratory when ambient conditions of temperature, day length, and food availability are maintained at constant levels (Zucker et al., 1991). There is a circannual clock in male and female ground squirrels that regulates gonadotropin-releasing factors (primarily GnRH) and, ultimately, steroid production. In males, the sensitivity of the hypothalamic-pituitary axis to the negative feedback effects of steroid hormones changes; during the end of the hibernation period, the negative feedback mechanisms become less sensitive to steroids, and gonadotropins are released in increasing amounts stimulating greater and greater amounts of steroid production (Zucker, 1988a). In female ground squirrels, the feedback system appears to be switched on and off. Ovariectomy at the beginning of the breeding season results in a pronounced elevation of blood plasma levels of LH, indicating that negative feedback mechanisms are operational at this time. If ovariectomy is performed on females at the end of the breeding season, then there is no postovariectomy rise in plasma LH; the LH concentrations of ovariectomized squirrels remain basal until the following breeding season (Zucker, 1988a) (**FIGURE 10.43**).

The annual cycle of body mass changes, with its corresponding changes in food intake, is also programmed by a circannual clock and persists under constant laboratory conditions. It appears that seasonal changes in food intake are secondary to seasonal changes in fat storage and utilization. If the squirrels are limited to levels

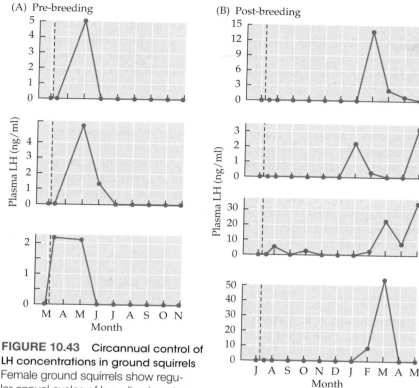

(A) Pre-breeding

(B) Post-breeding

FIGURE 10.43 Circannual control of LH concentrations in ground squirrels Female ground squirrels show regular annual cycles of breeding in nature and a circannual cycle of reproductive condition under constant conditions in the laboratory. (A) Ovariectomy (vertical dashed line) of three female ground squirrels at the beginning of the breeding season led to the classic castration response of increased LH concentrations because it eliminated negative feedback control by steroid hormones. (B) When ovariectomy was performed on four different squirrels after the breeding season, no increase in plasma LH concentrations was observed until the next breeding season, suggesting that the steroid negative feedback mechanism is activated only at certain times of the year. After Zucker, 1988a.

of food availability comparable to what they were ingesting at the end of the hibernation phase, the animals still manage to gain amounts of body fat comparable to those of squirrels fed ad libitum (without restriction). They accomplish this feat by utilizing other components of the body and reducing activity. Even if the fat is removed by surgical aspiration, the animals make new fat cells and are able to catch up to intact control animals in body fat within a year (Dark et al., 1989). Thus, it appears that the circannual clock regulates fat storage and utilization, which causes changes in eating behavior. The exact physiological mechanisms underlying this phenomenon require clarification, but insulin and norepinephrine appear to be involved (Florant et al., 1989; Paul et al., 2008).

Thus, a continuum exists for annual cycles, from those that are completely autonomous and in which environmental cues play a limited role as entraining agents, to those that are driven wholly or in part by environmental factors. Ground squirrels are at one end of the continuum, with annual rhythms that are minimally influenced by environmental factors, except that day length entrains these rhythms. The annual cycles of Syrian hamsters, at the other end of the continuum, are driven by day length. However, during the winter, an endogenous timer appears to activate reproductive function prior to the mating season, which is coincident with, though not caused by, the long days of spring. Both ground squirrels and hamsters spend part of the year underground in relatively constant environments and require endogenous clocks and temporal processes to time part of their seasonal behavioral cycles.

BREEDING SEASONS IN BIRDS Nonmigrating temperate zone birds are exposed to an annual photoperiodic cycle, and much of their seasonal cycle of behavior is driven by that cycle. Like rodents, nontropical birds mate and rear their young during the spring and summer, when days are increasing in length. In contrast to those of rodents, the reproductive systems of temperate zone birds must be stimulated by long days to function, but it is probably more accurate to state that exposure to short days is necessary to "turn on" their reproductive systems. Breeding for most nontropical bird species is completed by the summer solstice. Some species breed more than once during the breeding season, but most undergo reproductive regression in response to the long days of summer. In other words, the previously stimulatory day lengths act to inhibit reproductive function; the birds are said to be photorefractory because long days no longer stimulate reproduction (Nicholls et al., 1988). In order to break photorefractoriness, the birds must experience a period of short days. After exposure to several weeks of short days, the birds are once again responsive to the stimulatory effects of long days on reproductive function (Bentley, 2010; Nicholls et al., 1988).

Neural Mechanisms of Endogenous and Exogenous Seasonal Timekeeping

Virtually no information is available regarding the mechanisms of endogenous seasonal timekeeping in either birds or mammals. Attempts have been made to disrupt circannual rhythmicity by lesioning various brain regions. Neither lesions of the PVN, part of the output pathway from the SCN, nor pinealectomy disrupt circannual cycles of body mass fluctuation in ground squirrels (Dark and Zucker, 1985) (see Figure 10.43). Lesions of the SCN disrupt other patterns of circannual rhythmicity in some individuals; however, most SCN-lesioned squirrels continue to display circannual rhythms, despite the fact that circadian rhythms are absent in these animals (Dark et al., 1985). This observation and others in both ground squirrels and birds suggest that circannual rhythms and circadian rhythms may not be regulated by the same neural substrate (Gwinner, 1986).

In contrast to our lack of understanding of the physiological substrate for endogenous seasonal timekeeping, much has been learned about the neuroendocrine basis of photoperiodism in mammals, especially over the past four decades. In virtually all species of mammals that have been carefully examined, pinealectomy severely interferes with most photoperiodic responses (Goldman, 1983). This was first demonstrated in Syrian hamsters, in which removal of the pineal gland prevented the inhibition of reproductive activity that typically occurs following exposure to day lengths of less than 12.5 hours (Hoffman and Reiter, 1965). This observation led to the common belief that the pineal gland exerts an inhibitory effect on the reproductive system (Reiter, 1970).

As we have seen, the pineal hormone, melatonin, has been shown to be the mediator of pineal effects on photoperiodic responses in a wide variety of mammals (Goldman and Nelson, 1993). Melatonin is secreted at night in both nocturnal and diurnal animals. The rhythm of pineal melatonin secretion is largely regulated by one or more circadian oscillators, probably in the SCN (Darrow and Goldman, 1986; Goldman and Darrow, 1983). The nocturnal pattern of melatonin synthesis and secretion is entrained, but not driven, by the light-dark cycle. The pattern of nightly elevation of melatonin secretion persists in constant lighting conditions and corresponds roughly to the pattern of locomotor activity in nocturnal rodents (Goldman, 2001). In almost all mammals that have been examined, including species (such as the laboratory rat) whose reproductive cycles are generally considered to be nonresponsive to changes in day length, the duration of the nocturnal peak of melatonin secretion increases as the photoperiod decreases (Bartness et al., 1993; Darrow and Goldman, 1986; Illnerova et al., 1986; Karsch et al., 1984). In

Siberian hamsters (*Phodopus sungorus*) and sheep, daily infusions of melatonin have been administered to pinealectomized animals and their reproductive responses have been measured. In both species, responses characteristic of animals exposed to long days (i.e., stimulation of reproduction for hamsters, inhibition for sheep) are elicited by daily melatonin infusions of short duration. Melatonin infusions of longer duration result in short-day responses (Bittman and Karsch, 1984; Carter and Goldman, 1983a,b). In Siberian hamsters, nonreproductive parameters, such as body mass and fat content, are also differentially affected by long-duration and short-duration infusions of melatonin (Bartness and Goldman, 1988a,b). The time of day at which the infusions are given does not appear to be critical in either sheep or hamsters (Bartness and Goldman, 1988b; Carter and Goldman, 1983a; Wayne et al., 1988). Based on these data, it has been proposed that changes in the duration of the nightly melatonin peak serve to convey a photoperiodic message to a variety of physiological systems (Bartness et al., 1993; Bittman, 1993; Goldman, 1983; Goldman and Elliott, 1988). Other species, including Syrian hamsters and white-footed mice (*Peromyscus leucopus*), respond to changes in the duration of the nightly melatonin peak in a manner similar to that reported for Siberian hamsters and sheep (Dowell and Lynch, 1987; Grosse et al., 1993).

In mammals, melatonin-binding sites have been located in several brain areas. In rats and Syrian and Siberian hamsters, for example, the SCN, pars tuberalis, and median eminence display significant melatonin binding, as do several areas of the pituitary, thalamus, hypothalamus, subiculum, and area postrema (Weaver et al., 1989). Interestingly, little melatonin binding was detected in the anterior pituitary glands of adult photoperiodic rodents, despite the profound influence of melatonin on the secretion of gonadotropins (Carlson et al., 1991; Vanecek, 1988). Among three suborders of Rodentia, considerable interspecific variation exists in the sites of high-affinity melatonin binding (Bittman et al., 1994). Among orders of mammals, variation in melatonin binding sites is also noteworthy; for example, numerous telencephalic, diencephalic, hypothalamic, and midbrain structures bind melatonin in sheep, whereas in ferrets only the pars tuberalis and pars distalis of the pituitary bind melatonin, despite the fact that both species respond reproductively to photoperiod (Bittman and Weaver, 1990; Weaver and Reppert, 1990). The pars tuberalis is the only structure that binds melatonin in all mammals and appears to feature prominently in the transduction of photoperiodic information for control of prolactin secretion (Morgan and Williams, 1989). Melatonin may have direct or indirect effects on the release of substances into the hypothalamic-pituitary portal system to regulate LH and follicle-stimulating hormone (FSH) release from the anterior pituitary. Hamsters housed under short-day conditions exhibit reduced expression of LH mRNA, which may or may not be independent from steroidal activation (Bittman et al., 1992).

As previously described, the duration of the nightly peak of melatonin secretion is the critical parameter for transducing the effects of photoperiod on the hypothalamic-pituitary axis. A series of long-duration melatonin signals suppresses anterior pituitary gonadotropin secretion (Bartness et al., 1993; Goldman and Nelson, 1993; Prendergast et al., 2002). Melatonin must suppress GnRH secretion in the hypothalamus, attenuate its ability to stimulate pituitary FSH and LH release, or reduce gonadal responsiveness to gonadotropins (or any combination thereof). Neither in vivo nor in vitro studies provide consistent evidence that either day length or melatonin alters pituitary responsiveness to GnRH in rodents (e.g., Jetton et al., 1994; Martin et al., 1977), but photoperiod plays a significant modulatory role in ruminants (Fowler et al., 1992; Xu et al.,1992). Again, the reproductive effects of melatonin have been most extensively characterized in Syrian and Siberian hamsters. Among hypothalamic nuclei with high densities of melatonin binding, those in the mediobasal hypothalamus, specifically in the DMN, appear to be essential for decoding photoperiod signals. Bilateral DMN lesions blocked the gonadal response to long-duration melatonin infusions in male Syrian hamsters (Maywood and Hastings, 1995; Maywood et al., 1996), and lesions of the adjacent VMN evoked rapid redevelopment of testicular function in Syrian hamsters with regressed gonads (Bae et al., 1999). Because the DMN expresses both melatonin and androgen receptors, it was assumed that melatonin acts in this brain region to increase sex steroid negative feedback. However, more recent studies indicate that DMN lesions that eliminate gonadal regression in response to melatonin do not enhance sex steroid negative feedback (Jarjisian et al., 2013). SCN lesions eliminated the antigonadal effects of long-duration melatonin signals in Siberian, but not Syrian, hamsters (Bartness et al., 1991; Bittman et al., 1979, 1989). Most mammals studied to date reduce prolactin concentrations in short days. DMN lesions spared the lactotropic prolactin response to short day lengths (or long melatonin signals) in Syrian hamsters, even though the responsiveness of gonadotropins to these signals was lost (Maywood and Hastings, 1995). This finding suggests that melatonin signals are transduced in the hypothalamic-pituitary axis via multiple parallel pathways that may be trait-specific (Lincoln, 1990, 1999; Maywood and Hastings, 1995). In support of this notion, SCN lesions that eliminated nocturnal melatonin secretion also abolished the gonadal response to short day lengths, although the prolactin response persisted (Bartness et al., 1991; Bittman et al., 1991). Microinfusions of melatonin into the SCN, the reuniens nuclei of the thalamus, or the PVN each induced testicular regression in juvenile Siberian hamsters, but only infusions into the SCN yielded short-day-like prolactin concentrations (Badura and Goldman, 1992).

As you might expect given their importance in controlling reproduction, the RFamide peptides kisspeptin and GnIH have been implicated in the seasonal control of reproduction. Early studies explored whether GnIH might increase in response to short day lengths or melatonin to suppress reproduction. Contrary to prediction, extended exposure to inhibitory day lengths leads to suppression of GnIH immunostaining and mRNA (Mason et al., 2010; Revel et al., 2008) as well as decreased fiber density and projections to GnRH cells (Mason et al., 2010; Ubuka et al., 2012). Similar results were seen following several weeks of melatonin administration to long-day animals, with pinealectomy preventing the suppression of GnIH in short days (Revel et al., 2008; Ubuka et al., 2012). Analogous seasonal patterns of GnIH expression have been observed in European (Simonneaux et al., 2013) and Turkish (Piekarski et al., 2014) hamsters as well as the jerboa, a semidesert rodent (Janati et al., 2013). In male hamsters, the short-day-induced reduction in GnIH is not the result of low circulating gonadal steroid concentrations; castration of long-day hamsters or testosterone replacement in short-day hamsters does not alter the pattern of GnIH protein or mRNA (Mason et al., 2010; Revel et al., 2008; Ubuka et al., 2012).

Because the pars tuberalis of the anterior pituitary has the highest density of melatonin receptors across species (Bittman and Weaver, 1990; Masson-Pevet and Gauer, 1994) and has been importantly implicated in the control of seasonal breeding (Dardente et al., 2010; Hanon et al., 2008; Nakane and Yoshimura, 2014), recent research has focused on this critical site and on the possibility that GnIH is altered secondary to the actions of melatonin on this neural locus. In hamsters, melatonin acts on the pars tuberalis to inhibit thyroid-stimulating hormone (TSH) synthesis, which in turn acts on tanycytes in the hypothalamic ependymal layer to alter deiodinase activity and, consequently, the conversion of local thyroxine (T_4) to triiodothyronine (T_3) (Barrett et al., 2007; Hanon et al., 2008; Revel et al., 2006b; Stevenson and Prendergast, 2013). As spring approaches and melatonin duration is decreased, increased T_3 acts on downstream circuitry to guide the transition from the winter to summer breeding phenotype. If GnIH is downstream of this mechanism, then exposure of photoinhibited hamsters to TSH or T_3 should lead to increased GnIH expression. Indeed, chronic central administration of TSH or T_3 to short-day hamsters for several weeks restores the LD pattern of GnIH, implicating GnIH as part of this established melatonin-mediated neurochemical circuit (Henson et al., 2013; Klosen et al., 2013).

The role of kisspeptin in seasonal breeding has principally been explored in Syrian and Siberian hamsters (Ansel et al., 2011; Greives et al., 2007, 2008; Mason et al., 2007; Revel et al., 2006a) and sheep (Caraty et al., 2007; Clarke et al., 2009; Goodman et al., 2010, 2014; Lehman et al., 2010; Smith et al., 2008). Across species, kisspeptin is generally elevated during the breeding season and suppressed following exposure to inhibitory photoperiods or appropriately timed melatonin administration. Likewise, infusion of kisspeptin can restore reproductive function to reproductively quiescent hamsters and sheep (Ansel et al., 2011; Caraty et al., 2007). The specific neural pathways by which melatonin impacts kisspeptin cells remain to be determined.

Although seasonal changes in the pattern of melatonin secretion similar to those in mammals also occur in birds, birds do not appear to use the melatonin signal to time their reproductive efforts (Chakraborty, 1995). Thus, the function of the annual fluctuation in the nocturnal melatonin signal in birds remains uncertain, but it has been implicated in the synchronization of circadian activity rhythms (Gwinner et al., 1997; Heigl and Gwinner, 1995; Menaker, 1968) and in seasonal changes in immune function (Bentley et al., 1998). In addition, it may be involved in seasonal changes in the brain areas underlying singing behavior (Bentley et al., 1999). Seasonal neuroplasticity has been documented in several species of songbirds within discrete telencephalic nuclei that are involved in song learning and production (Brenowitz et al., 1991, 1998; Nottebohm, 1981). Increases in the size of these song control nuclei depend largely on seasonal increases in circulating testosterone and its metabolites (Gulledge and Deviche, 1997; Nottebohm, 1980a; Smith et al., 1995), which are directly related to the annual reproductive cycles of these birds (Dawson, 1983). These seasonal changes are associated with changes in cell size and cell number in the various song control nuclei (Smith et al., 1997a) (see Chapter 4).

Despite the well-studied role of testosterone in these seasonal changes in bird brain morphology, there are both gonad- and testosterone-independent seasonal changes in the volumes of song control nuclei (Bernard et al., 1997; Smith et al., 1997b). Thus the annual changes in melatonin secretion may be involved in the regulation of seasonal changes in the structure of the song control system. Presumably, melatonin exerts its effects directly on the neural substrate of the song control nuclei; melatonin-binding sites have been found in the song control systems of three songbird species (Gahr and Kosar, 1996; Whitfield-Rucker and Cassone, 1996). In starlings, the high vocal center (HVC), lateral magnocellular nucleus of the anterior nidopallium (lMAN), area X, and robust nucleus of the archistriatum (RA) all contain melatonin-binding sites (Aste et al., 2001; Gahr and Kosar, 1996; Whitfield-Rucker and Cassone, 1996). As in mammals, melatonin acts to alter GnIH. For example, removal of the pineal gland and eyes, the major sites of melatonin production in birds, leads to decreased expression of *GnIH* precursor mRNA and decreased content of GnIH peptide in the hypothalamus of quail (Ubuka et al., 2005). Melatonin administration to these birds causes a dose-dependent increase in the expression of *GnIH* precursor mRNA and increased production of GnIH peptide. This effect occurs, at least in part, through direct actions of melatonin on GnIH cells, with melatonin binding expressed in GnIH-immunoreactive neurons (Ubuka et al., 2005). Additionally, in vitro studies demonstrate that melatonin administration dose-dependently increases GnIH release from hypothalamic blocks (Chowdhury et al., 2010). These findings suggest that melatonin acts on GnIH cells to coordinate seasonally appropriate behavior and physiology, potentially including reproduction. Taken together, this evidence suggests that although melatonin does not synchronize the reproductive activity of birds to a specific time of year, it is involved in seasonal modulation of aspects of avian physiology and behavior that have the potential to affect reproductive success.

FIGURE 10.44   Seasonal cycle of reproduction in Syrian hamsters
During the summer, both male and female hamsters are reproductively competent and engage in breeding activities. When day lengths fall below some critical value in autumn (12.5 hours of light per day in the laboratory), the negative feedback mechanisms of the hypothalamus are enhanced and become increasingly sensitive to the effects of steroid hormones. Thus, even low concentrations of steroid hormones completely inhibit secretion of GnRH and, consequently, LH, and this suppresses secretion of steroid hormones by the gonads and leads to gonadal regression. Hamsters may spend the winter in torpor in a burrow. In the absence of light, the gonads regrow and begin to produce steroid hormones and gametes again in the early spring. Interestingly, the gonads can become functional again in spring when the day length is much less than what is required to maintain the reproductive systems in the fall. After Zucker, 1980.

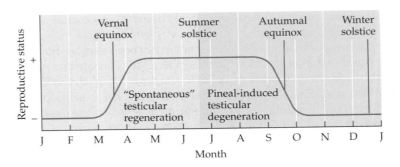

Activational Aspects of Timing Mechanisms

Timing mechanisms interact with the neuroendocrine substrates of reproductive function to ensure appropriate timing of reproductive activities. In mammals, seasonal changes in reproductive activity are generally associated with changes in pituitary gonadotropin secretion. For example, Syrian hamsters, which are long-day breeders, exhibit decreased circulating concentrations of LH and FSH following exposure to simulated winter day lengths (Tamarkin et al., 1976) (**FIGURE 10.44**). In sheep, which are short-day breeders, exposure to short days leads to increased LH secretion, manifested as an increase in the frequency of pulsatile LH release (Karsch et al., 1984). These types of changes in pituitary gonadotropin secretion lead to changes in gonadal growth and sex steroid hormone secretion (Berndtson and Desjardins, 1974). Thus, the current understanding is that the exogenous factors that mediate seasonal changes in reproductive activity do so primarily via actions on the hypothalamic-pituitary axis. Photoperiod can also alter the ability of steroid hormones to activate sexual behavior.

STEROID-DEPENDENT REGULATION OF REPRODUCTION   During periods of reproductive activity, one of the important mechanisms regulating pituitary secretion of FSH and LH is the gonadal hormone feedback system (see Chapter 3). In males, testicular androgens, especially testosterone, are capable of acting on the hypothalamic-pituitary axis to inhibit the secretion of both gonadotropins. In effect, this feedback system helps to maintain appropriate levels of gonadotropins; that is, the gonadotropins stimulate the biosynthesis and secretion of testicular androgens, and the negative feedback effect of the androgens prevents oversecretion of the gonadotropins. In females, a similar negative feedback system utilizes estrogens and progestins to hold FSH and LH concentrations in check. This system is especially important for regulating the number of ovarian follicles that mature during each ovulatory cycle. As follicles become mature, they produce increasing amounts of estrogen, resulting in decreased levels of gonadotropins and a cessation of recruitment of new follicles (Bast and Greenwald, 1977; Bex and Goldman, 1975). In both sexes, a gonadal peptide hormone, called inhibin or folliculostatin, also serves to inhibit the secretion of FSH (Bernard et al., 2001).

One of the mechanisms that inhibits the secretion of pituitary LH and FSH during seasons of photoperiod-induced reproductive quiescence is an increased sensitivity of the hypothalamic-pituitary axis to the negative feedback effects of gonadal steroid hormones (Ellis and Turek, 1980a; Tamarkin et al., 1976; Turek et al., 1975). A return to the lower level of sensitivity in response to stimulatory photoperiods can then return the animal to a state of reproductive activity via increased pituitary hormone secretion. Low concentrations of testosterone are more effective in inhibiting post-castration increases in pituitary gonadotropin secretion in male Syrian hamsters (Tamarkin et al., 1976; Turek and Campbell, 1979) and rams (Pelletier and Ortavant, 1975) when the animals are exposed to nonstimulatory photoperiods. A similar phenomenon has been implicated in the onset of puberty, when a prepubertal decrease in sensitivity to steroid negative feedback leads to increased secretion of

LH and FSH and thus activation of the reproductive system (McCann and Ramirez, 1964; Ramirez and McCann, 1963). The effect of photoperiod on seasonal changes in hypothalamic-pituitary sensitivity is mediated by the pineal hormone, melatonin. Thus, in male Syrian hamsters housed under long-day conditions, administration of melatonin induces an increase in the sensitivity of the hypothalamic-pituitary axis to the negative feedback effects of testosterone (Sisk and Turek, 1982).

STEROID-INDEPENDENT REGULATION OF REPRODUCTION   A steroid-independent mechanism has also been implicated in the regulation of seasonal changes in the rate of gonadotropin secretion. Castrated male snowshoe hares (*Lepus americanus*) display seasonal variation in gonadotropin levels despite the absence of negative feedback from gonadal steroids (Davis and Meyer, 1973). Likewise, castration of male Syrian hamsters results in elevated blood concentrations of LH and FSH under both long-day and short-day conditions, although the postcastration gonadotropin levels are higher in animals housed under long-day conditions (Ellis and Turek, 1980b). A steroid-independent effect of photoperiod on gonadotropin secretion is particularly evident in female Syrian hamsters. Under long-day conditions, female hamsters exhibit an approximately eightfold to tenfold increase in baseline serum LH concentrations following ovariectomy, and LH concentrations can be returned to baseline by administration of estrogen (Yellon et al., 1989). After several weeks of exposure to short days, intact female Syrian hamsters become anovulatory, and their serum LH concentrations are very low during most of the day; however, these anovulatory females show large daily pulses of LH during the afternoon (Seegal and Goldman, 1975). This pattern of LH secretion continues following ovariectomy (Bridges and Goldman, 1975) or after combined ovariectomy and adrenalectomy (Bittman and Goldman, 1979). That is, removal of the source of steroid hormones does not result in any detectable increase in the baseline serum LH concentration in short-day female Syrian hamsters, and daily pulses of LH are still apparent in the steroid-deprived animals. These observations suggest that, in female Syrian hamsters, the effect of short days on LH secretion is mediated primarily via a steroid-independent mechanism. Seasonal variations in circulating and pituitary concentrations of gonadotropins have also been observed after ovariectomy in pony mares (Garcia and Ginther, 1976), ground squirrels (Zucker and Licht, 1983), and snowshoe hares (Davis and Meyer, 1973).

RELATIONSHIP OF BEHAVIOR TO REPRODUCTIVE STATE   The mechanisms that mediate seasonal changes in reproductive state also affect behavior. A wide variety of behaviors vary in relation to an animal's reproductive state. Some of these, most notably mating behaviors, bear an obvious direct relationship to reproduction. In most vertebrates, mating occurs at about the same time as peak gamete production. Because gametogenesis is a steroid-dependent process in all vertebrates, steroid hormone regulation of mating behavior generally provides temporal coordination between gamete maturation and mating (although exceptions exist, as we will see below). Other behaviors, such as territorial behavior and migration, are less directly related to reproduction but are frequently associated in an adaptive way with the reproductive process. It is probably because of the need for a close temporal association between fertility and behaviors that are directly or indirectly associated with reproduction that the regulation of many behaviors by the gonadal steroid hormones has evolved. As one would anticipate, the regulation of behavior by reproductive hormones is most evident for those behaviors most closely associated with reproduction, that is, mating behaviors.

The seasonal changes in the display of mating behaviors in many species are regulated primarily by seasonal changes in the amounts of circulating gonadal steroid hormones. In addition, seasonal fluctuations in behavioral sensitivity to steroid hormones have been observed. In castrated male Syrian hamsters, copulatory behavior can be restored by administration of testosterone; however, larger doses of the steroid are required to elicit the behavior in animals exposed to short day lengths (Campbell et al., 1978; Morin and Zucker, 1978). The various components of masculine sexual responsiveness, including chemosensory behaviors, mounting, intromission, and ejaculation, are not all equally affected by exposure to short days. The effects of short-day exposure on these behaviors in male Syrian hamsters are prevented by pinealectomy (Miernicki et al., 1988). Female Syrian hamsters also exhibit decreased responsiveness to the activational effects of estrogen on lordosis behavior during exposure to short days (Badura et al., 1987). In contrast to males, this decrease in females' behavioral sensitivity to estrogen is not altered either by pinealectomy or by melatonin administration (Badura and Nunez, 1989). It is possible that photoperiod may influence female sexual behavior through a direct neural route. Neural input from the retina to the SCN is probably required for pineal-dependent responses to changes in day length. However, there are also direct retinal projections to the basal forebrain and hypothalamic regions outside the SCN (Pickard and Silverman, 1981; Youngstrom et al., 1987) that concentrate ovarian steroids (Fraile et al., 1987; Morrell and Pfaff, 1978) and may have a role in female sexual behavior.

DISSOCIATED REPRODUCTIVE PATTERNS   Some notable exceptions to the usual association between reproductive hormones and sexual behavior have been reported (Crews, 1984). Some vertebrates exhibit a "dissociated" reproductive pattern, whereby the production of gametes and mating do not occur at the same time of the annual cycle. In the red-sided garter snake (*Thamnophis sirtalis parietalis*), for example, sperm are produced during the summer and are stored in the male reproductive tract through the 8-to-9-month period of winter torpor (see Chapter 5); mating does not occur until the snake emerges from torpor in the spring. Experiments involving castration and treatment with androgens have revealed that the level of androgens present during the mating phase has no influence on the presence or intensity of mating behavior in these snakes (Crews, 1984). Rather, mating behavior, which persists for about 3 weeks, seems to occur only in snakes that have experienced a period of torpor. The pineal gland may be involved in determining when mating will occur, since removal of the pineal gland prior to entry into winter torpor prevents the display of mating behavior in the spring (Crews et al., 1988b; Nelson et al., 1987). A seasonal timing mechanism probably determines the time of mating in this species, and this mechanism may be partially or entirely independent of gonadal hormones. Clearly, for a species that has evolved a dissociated reproductive pattern, it is appropriate for reproductive behavior to be liberated from the influence of sex hormones. In this case, one must suppose that an alternative mechanism is employed to ensure that mating occurs at the proper time.

AGGRESSIVE BEHAVIOR   Perhaps the most general case of seasonal regulation of a behavior by gonadal hormones is exemplified by the male mountain spiny lizard (*Sceloporus jarrovi*), in which a single behavior is largely regulated by testicular androgens during the breeding season in September and October but is expressed independently of testicular hormones during another phase of the annual cycle. The lizard begins to exhibit territorial behavior, expressed as intermale aggression, during the midsummer phase that precedes mating. At this time, castration does not result in a decrease in the level of intermale aggression (Moore and Marler, 1987). During the subsequent mating phase, the level of territorial behavior increases; this increase can be prevented by castration and reinstated by administration of androgens. Castrated mating-phase lizards do not stop showing territorial behavior altogether; rather, aggressiveness declines to a level similar to that exhibited during the earlier, premating phase (Moore, 1987). Yet a third condition occurs in this species, subsequent to the mating phase, in which territorial behavior is completely absent and the animals aggregate, tolerating close proximity and even physical contact by members of the same sex. During this phase, administration of androgens fails to stimulate aggressive behavior. It seems that testicular hormones act on territorial behavior only to regulate its intensity in *S. jarrovi* and that other, as yet unknown, mechanisms determine the overall annual pattern of territoriality.

There are many reports of seasonal changes in agonistic and territorial behavior among birds and mammals. For example, male starlings (*Sturnus vulgaris*) form rigorously defended territories during the breeding season (Feare, 1984). This territorial behavior is correlated with high circulating levels of androgens. At the end of the breeding season, blood androgen levels diminish, and territorial behaviors stop. The reduction in agonistic behavior allows the formation of so-called winter feeding flocks, which appear to confer advantages in predator avoidance and foraging success (Feare, 1984). Small rodents also display seasonal changes in aggressiveness and territorial behavior. Microtine rodents (lemmings and voles), and probably most rodent species in nontropical regions, form winter aggregations. Animals huddling together in the winter presumably benefit by reducing their energetic requirements. Presumably, the lack of circulating androgens permits the social tolerance necessary for this pattern of behavior to appear (see Chapter 8). Even in the absence of huddling behavior, animals may tolerate one another better in close quarters during the winter than during the breeding season. For example, male meadow voles (*Microtus pennsylvanicus*) are highly territorial in the spring and summer and occupy open meadows, whereas red-backed voles (*Clethrionomys gapperi*) breed in spruce forest habitats. During the winter months, meadow voles move into the spruce forest habitats occupied by the red-backed voles, presumably to take advantage of the protective cover provided by the trees. In some cases, they share nests with other rodent species (Madison et al., 1984). Individual meadow voles trapped during the winter and tested in paired encounters in a small neutral arena exhibited less interspecific aggression than voles trapped in summer (Turner et al., 1975). The winter reduction in aggressiveness permits energy-saving habitat sharing. As the animals enter breeding condition in the spring, they reestablish mutually exclusive territories.

In wood rats (*Neotoma fuscipes*), seasonal changes in aggressive behavior are apparently independent of testicular hormones. The level of intermale aggression increases during the breeding season in this species, but this seasonal increase in aggressiveness is also observed in males that have been castrated postpubertally. Furthermore, the increased aggressiveness continues for some time after the breeding season ends. The independence of aggressive behavior from androgens in this species has been hypothesized to have evolved because the greatest threat to reproductive success from conspecific males comes during the breeding season, but the greatest need for nest defense comes later in the year, after the young have been weaned and begin seeking nests of their own (Caldwell et al., 1984). Syrian and Siberian hamsters maintained in short-day conditions or given melatonin treatments to simulate short-day exposure display more aggression than long-day hamsters, despite their low testosterone concentrations (Demas et al., 2004; Jasnow et al., 2000, 2002). This increased aggression is independent of gonadal steroids (Scotti et al., 2007) and associated with seasonal changes in adrenal DHEA release and target tissue response to this hormone (Rendon and Demas, 2016; Soma et al., 2016) (also see Chapter 8). Likewise, in birds, DHEA is correlated with seasonal changes in aggression and might act as a precursor hormone for estrogen synthesis in the brain (Heimovics et al., 2016; Soma et al., 2002, 2016).

DAILY ACTIVITY PATTERNS   Field observations of several species of microtine rodents (e.g., *Microtus agrestis*, *M. oeconomus*, *M. montanus*, *Clethrionomys gapperi*, and *C. glareolus*) have indicated a seasonal shift in activity patterns (Erkinaro, 1961; Herman, 1977; Ostermann, 1956; Rowsemitt, 1986). These animals tend to be nocturnal during the summer and diurnal during the winter (**FIGURE 10.45**). The adaptive

FIGURE 10.45 Photoperiod-mediated shift in activity patterns in montane voles Male montane voles (*Microtus montanus*) maintained under long-day conditions (LD 16:8) change their locomotor activity from a nocturnal to a diurnal pattern if short-day (LD 8:16) conditions are imposed. After Rowsemitt et al., 1982.

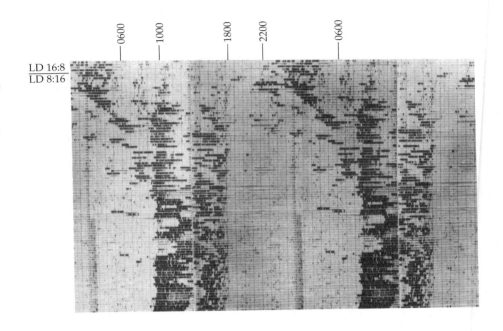

function of this seasonal shift in daily activity patterns probably involves energetic savings. By constraining the majority of its locomotor activity to the daylight hours during the winter, the animal avoids exposure during the coldest part of the day; likewise, bouts of activity during summer nights allow the animal to avoid thermal stress or dehydration (Rowsemitt, 1986; Rowsemitt et al., 1982). Predator avoidance may also contribute to the adaptive significance of this seasonal trait.

Testosterone appears to mediate the seasonal shift in activity pattern in montane voles (*M. montanus*). Adult male voles were either castrated or left intact and maintained in long-day or short-day conditions. Testosterone replacement was given to some of the castrated animals via subcutaneously implanted Silastic capsules. Castrated montane voles showed increased diurnal and decreased nocturnal wheel-running activity compared with intact animals. Castrated voles implanted with testosterone increased their nocturnal activity relative to voles implanted with empty capsules. There was a great deal of individual variation among the experimental animals. Nevertheless, these results suggest that photoperiod primarily mediates this species' seasonal shift in activity patterns by affecting androgen production; that is, short-day animals tend to be diurnal and long-day animals tend to be nocturnal (Rowsemitt, 1986). Other environmental cues, such as temperature and food quality and quantity, may also affect activity patterns.

Although many subtle effects of steroids on the timing of activity have been reported in other rodent species (Ellis and Turek, 1983; Morin and Cummings, 1981; Morin et al., 1977), assessing the functional significance of these effects has been difficult. For example, the number of daily revolutions made in a running wheel significantly declines when Syrian hamsters are moved from long days to short days (Ellis and Turek, 1979). This decline in locomotor activity can be mimicked in long-day hamsters by castration and reversed by testosterone replacement (Ellis and Turek, 1983). Castrated male Syrian hamsters treated with testosterone but maintained under short day lengths do not increase their wheel-running behavior, suggesting that the neural tissues underlying this behavior become insensitive to steroids under short-day conditions (Ellis and Turek, 1983).

BRAIN SIZE AND LEARNING Seasonal changes in brain weight have been reported for several species of rodents and shrews (e.g., *Clethrionomys glareolus*, *C. rutilus*, *Microtus oeconomus*, *M. gregalis*, *Sorex araneus*, and *S. minutus*) (Bielak and Pucek,

(A)

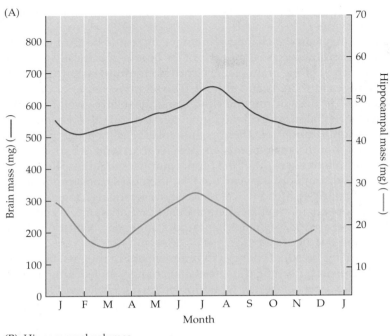

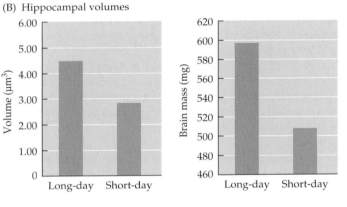

FIGURE 10.46 **Seasonal changes in brain and hippocampal mass** have been reported for several temperate zone mammalian species and are shown here for bank voles (*Clethrionomys glareolus*), corrected for changes in body mass. (A) These changes in brain mass may account for seasonal variation in learning and memory, or they may be related to an energy-saving adaptation. (B) White-footed mice housed in short days show winterlike reductions in brain size and hippocampal volume. These short-day mice perform worse in spatial mazes and (C) have fewer apical dendritic spines in the CA1 region of the hippocampus. After Pyter et al., 2005.

(B) Hippocampal volumes

(C)

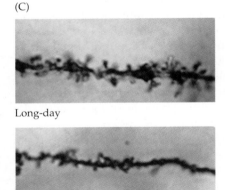

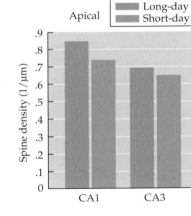

1960; Pucek, 1965; Yaskin, 1984). Brain weights are greater in summer-captured than in winter-captured animals (Pyter et al., 2005; Yaskin, 1984) (**FIGURE 10.46**). The adaptive function of this seasonal variation in brain weight may involve energetic savings. Although the brain constitutes only 2%–3% of the total body mass in rodents and insectivores, it uses over 10% of the total energy expended by the animal. It has been suggested that minor reductions in brain mass could result in substantial energetic savings.

A significant part of this seasonal change in brain weight could be attributable to variation in water content; however, several parts of the brain—specifically, the neo-cortex and the basal portion of the brain (i.e., the corpus striatum)—show seasonal cytoarchitectural changes in rodents and shrews. The relative weight of the fore-brain and hippocampus declines during the winter, and the relative weights of the olfactory bulbs, myelencephalon, and cerebellum increase during the winter. A sex difference in brain weight is observed among bank voles (*Clethrionomys glareolus*) only during the winter months; male brains are heavier than female brains at this time. The absolute and relative weight of the hippocampus is significantly higher in males than in females throughout the year, but the difference is most pronounced during the winter (Yaskin, 1984). Meadow voles also show seasonal changes in brain weight. Photoperiod appears to organize the seasonal fluctuation in brain weight in these animals (Dark et al., 1987b); males kept under short-day conditions have smaller brains than long-day males.

Despite the evidence for seasonal changes in brain weight in rodents, there has been relatively little research investigating seasonal changes in learning among mammalian species. However, short-day white-footed mice (*Peromyscus leucopus*) require longer to learn a spatial maze (Pyter et al., 2005). Short days also decreased brain mass and hippocampal volume compared with mice housed in long days. No photoperiod-induced changes in sensory discrimination or other types of memory were observed despite impairments in spatial learning and memory. Short days decreased dendritic apical spine density in the CA1 region, as well as increasing basilar CA3 spine density (Pyter et al., 2005).

Song learning in birds also fluctuates on a seasonal basis, and the neural tis-sues underlying song learning change seasonally. Photoperiod is important in some avian species for the mediation of these changes, including recruitment of new neu-rons (Nottebohm, 1989); testosterone or its metabolites appear to drive the seasonal changes in brain structure and birdsong production (Bottjer et al., 1986; Nottebohm, 1981).

Three types of evidence exist that support the role of testosterone in mediating the seasonal change in avian singing behavior. First, blood concentrations of testos-terone are highest during the onset of the breeding season, and this peak coincides with maximal singing. Second, song production wanes after castration, and steroid replacement therapy (both androgens and estrogens) reinstates singing behavior (e.g., Harding et al., 1983, 1988; Heid et al., 1985). Third, several of the song control nuclei (see Chapter 4) concentrate steroid hormones; for example, androgen recep-tors have been localized with autoradiographic and immunocytochemical tech-niques in the HVC, RA, lMAN, nucleus intercollicularis (ICo), and tracheosyringeal division of the nucleus of the hypoglossal nerve (nXIIts) (Balthazart et al., 1992; Brenowitz and Arnold, 1992), and estrogen receptors have been localized in the HVC and ICo (Brenowitz and Arnold, 1989; Gahr et al., 1987, 1993).

In addition to the seasonal changes in singing behavior, there are substantial seasonal changes in the morphology of several song control nuclei. For example, the volume of the HVC and RA increased by 99% and 77%, respectively, among male canaries maintained under spring day lengths (>12 hours of light/day) relative to birds housed under autumnal conditions (<12 hours of light/day) (Nottebohm, 1981). Similar results have been reported for several other bird species, including red-winged blackbirds (*Agelaius phoeniceus*) (Kirn et al., 1989), rufous-sided towhees (*Pipilo erythrophthalmus*) (Brenowitz et al., 1991), orange bishop birds (*Euplectes fran-ciscanus*) (Arai et al., 1989), and white-crowned sparrows (*Zonotrichia leucophrys*) (Smith et al., 1991). Estrogens, converted from testicular androgens or produced de novo in CNS neurons (Schlinger et al., 2001), appear necessary to activate the neural mechanisms underlying the song system in birds. Androgens enter neurons containing aromatase, which converts them to estrogens. Aromatase is generally localized in neurons adjacent to other neurons containing estrogen receptors in the hypothalamus and preoptic area of songbird brains, as well as in limbic structures and in the structures constituting the neural circuit controlling birdsong (London et al., 2006). The brain appears to be the primary source of estrogens, which activate masculine behaviors in many bird species (London et al., 2006). Photoperiod is important in some birds to mediate these changes, including recruitment of new neurons (Nottebohm, 2005).

Other avian models of seasonal brain plasticity include annual change in hippocampal volume of food-caching birds (Hoshooley and Sherry, 2007; Smulders et al., 1995) and brood parasitic birds (Sherry et al., 1993). The hippocampus is involved in spatial learning and memory, and generally, species with a larger relative hippocampal volume display better spatial learning and memory (see Chapter 12). Hippocampal size is reduced during the winter in these bird species, when there is a reduction in spatial learning and memory performance associated with food storing (Barnea and Nottebohm, 1994, 1996) and nest parasitism (Sherry et al., 1993). Comparable studies of seasonal brain plasticity in mammals have been relatively rare, despite the prevalence of seasonal breeding in nontropical mammals.

MATERNAL BEHAVIOR AND LITTER SEX RATIOS   Seasonal fluctuations in the capacity to exhibit maternal behavior have not been examined in detail because it has been widely assumed that seasonally induced reproductive quiescence precludes the display of this behavior during part of the year. However, some environmental factors have been identified as having effects on maternal responses. Several avian species are known to adjust clutch size in response to changes in food availability (Lack, 1954). Syrian hamsters (Huck et al., 1986) and house mice (Marstellar and Lynch, 1987) display increased cannibalism of their young during periods of food restriction. The opportunity to hoard food reduces the incidence of, but does not abolish, cannibalism in Syrian hamsters (Miceli and Malsbury, 1982a). Interestingly, food restriction during development can have effects on second-generation offspring; litter survival and growth rate are reduced in hamsters born to a dam that had been food-restricted during development. In addition, the sex ratio of litters born to food-restricted female hamsters is skewed in favor of females (Huck et al., 1986). It is unclear whether this bias reflects a gestational event or an active culling of males via postpartum cannibalism. Montane voles display a similar sex ratio bias toward female offspring when the dam is given 6-methoxybenzoxazolinone (6-MBOA), a plant derivative that is made by young grasses when grazing voles injure the plants during the onset of the breeding season in this species (Berger et al., 1987). Ingestion of 6-MBOA appears to induce the birth of more females during the early portions of the breeding season.

The mechanisms of seasonal changes in maternal behavior may involve photoperiodic changes that modulate behavior through the endocrine system. Increased prolactin levels during pregnancy are required for the induction of the full maternal behavioral repertoire in rats (Loundes and Bridges, 1986) (see Chapter 7). In hamsters, decreased prolactin levels induced by the administration of ergocornine or bromocriptine have been related to decreased maternal aggression toward male intruders, increased aggression toward pups, disruption of pup retrieval behavior, and an increased incidence of maternal cannibalism of pups (Wise and Pryor, 1977). Hamsters and several other species experience seasonal changes in circulating concentrations of prolactin that are largely under photoperiodic control (Blank and Desjardins, 1985; Goldman et al., 1981; Martinet et al., 1982; Smale et al., 1988; Worthy et al., 1985). It is not known whether day length also influences prolactin secretion during pregnancy or lactation. However, it has been reported that whereas pinealectomized hamsters maintained under a natural photoperiod were able to bear litters during the winter, they displayed a high degree of cannibalism (Reiter,

1973/1974). It is possible that cannibalism increased because pinealectomy only partially prevents the effects of short-day exposure on prolactin production in female hamsters, allowing them to reproduce but not allowing them to secrete sufficient prolactin to support maternal behavior (Blask et al., 1986).

In a recent experiment, it was hypothesized that photoperiod may be used to drive the seasonal variation in offspring sex ratios of mammals. Up to 60% of female Siberian hamsters continue to breed during the winter, so sufficient numbers of short-day-breeding hamsters could be produced in the lab. The sexes of weanling hamsters conceived and raised in short, winterlike day lengths were significantly skewed toward males (Navara et al., 2010). Furthermore, these skews occurred before birth; embryos collected from pregnant females maintained in short-day conditions were also significantly male-biased. Thus, photoperiod functions as an effective seasonal cue, stimulating sex ratio skews toward males when day lengths are short.

SEASONAL CHANGES IN COPING WITH STRESS   Reduced food availability, in common with many other energetic challenges, is a potent stressor. The numbers and types of stressors animals encounter vary seasonally (Breuner et al., 1999). Many energetic adaptations have apparently evolved to attenuate the stress response during winter; at this time energy shortages may limit animals' abilities to cope with stress. A comprehensive view of the mechanisms underlying the stress response requires the consideration of its temporal organization (see Chapter 11). Circadian effects on adaptations to stressors have been reported; for example, there is a marked circadian rhythm in glucocorticoid secretion (e.g., Chrousos, 1998a,b; Dallman et al., 1993; Wetterberg, 1999). Increased glucocorticoid release just prior to awakening each day elevates blood glucose concentrations in anticipation of the increased energy demands associated with wakefulness (see Figure 10.35). On this basis, we might expect increased glucocorticoid secretion during the energetically demanding phases of the annual cycle that encompass territorial defense, migration, low temperatures, or food scarcity. Low ambient temperatures and decreased food availability indeed evoke stress responses in mammals (reviewed in Nelson and Demas, 1996).

The primary endocrine components of the stress response are epinephrine and the glucocorticoids, hormones that suppress energy storage and promote energy use from adipose and liver stores (Sapolsky et al., 2000). Although a relatively steady supply of energy is required to sustain biological functions, daily and seasonal fluctuations in energy requirements occur in response to the challenges animals face. Most animals eat discontinuously, storing and accessing energy to maintain cellular function while engaged in nonfeeding activities. Eventually, however, the depletion of energy stores requires their replacement. In most habitats, food availability fluctuates on a daily and seasonal basis. For example, outside the tropics, food availability is generally low during the winter, when thermogenic energy demands are typically high. Consequently, energy intake and energy expenditures are often out of balance. A stress response in the form of secreted glucocorticoids occurs whenever a significant imbalance of energy is detected. The high energy demands associated with reproduction usually elicit stress responses (Nelson and Drazen, 1999). Thus, glucocorticoids are released during territorial defense or courtship behaviors. When energy is insufficient to support both reproduction and thermoregulation, a prolonged stress response can have pathological consequences (Sapolsky, 1998). Glucocorticoids released in response to stressful stimuli can compromise cellular and humoral immune function, reproduction, digestion, growth, and virtually any process that consumes significant energy (Sapolsky et al., 2000).

A direct link between melatonin and glucocorticoid biology has been established (Maestroni, 1993, 1995). Generally, melatonin and glucocorticosteroids enhance and compromise immune function, respectively (Aoyama et al., 1986, 1987). Melatonin can ameliorate the immunocompromising effects of glucocorticosteroids (Persengiev et al., 1991a,b), and glucocorticosteroids can reduce the immunoenhancing actions of melatonin (e.g., Poon et al., 1994). Environmental stressors such as low temperatures elevate blood glucocorticoid concentrations that, in turn, suppress immune function (Ader and Cohen, 1993; Nelson et al., 2002). A positive balance between short-day-enhanced immune status and glucocorticoid-induced immuno-suppression may be essential for winter survival in small mammals (Nelson and Drazen, 1999; Sinclair and Lochmiller, 2000). Overcrowding, increased competition for scarce resources, low temperatures, reduced food availability, increased predator pressure, and lack of shelter may each contribute to immunosuppression. Each of these potential stressors may elevate blood concentrations of glucocorticoids. Winter breeding and the concomitant increase in secretion of sex steroid hormones may also result in immunocompromise (Nelson et al., 2002). Presumably, winter breeding occurs when normal challenges from environmental stressors, such as low temperature and reduced food availability, are ameliorated. The advantages of winter reproduction must be balanced against the increased risks of autoimmune disease and susceptibility to opportunistic pathogens and parasites associated with winter steroidogenesis. Thus, reproductive and immune functions seem intertwined.

In general, studies of captive animals reveal an inverse relation between dominance and glucocorticoid concentrations. However, this may not be the case in the wild. After capture, animals generally increase their secretion of epinephrine and glucocorticoids, and blood concentrations of steroids are generally much higher at this time than several hours later (e.g., Licht et al., 1983; Mahmoud and Licht, 1997; Mendonca and Licht, 1986; Orchinik et al., 1988). Assays of glucocorticoid by-products in the urine or feces of freely behaving dwarf mongooses (*Helogale parvula*) and African wild dogs (*Lycaon pictus*) suggest that high-ranking animals may be under high levels of social stress (Creel and Creel, 1996).

Seasonal variation in glucocorticoid concentrations is influenced by day length. Among Syrian hamsters, blood concentrations of glucocorticoids are lower in animals housed in short than in long photoperiods (De Souza and Meier, 1987; Ottenweller et al., 1987). Decreased glucocorticoid concentrations in short-day hamsters could derive from the suppression of adrenal corticosteroid synthesis (e.g., Mehdi and Sandor, 1977) or from enhanced negative feedback inhibition of glucocorticoid secretion (Motta et al., 1967, 1969). Glucocorticoid receptors in the hippocampus, especially mineralocorticoid receptors (MRs), have been implicated in the negative feedback control of adrenal glucocorticoid secretion during stress responses (e.g., Fischette et al., 1980; Herman et al., 1993; Sapolsky et al., 1984). Changes in circulating glucocorticoid concentrations in short-day hamsters may be caused by alterations in hippocampal MR binding, glucocorticoid receptor mRNA expression, or both (Ronchi et al., 1998). Total hippocampal receptor binding of glucocorticoids was significantly elevated in short-day hamsters, compared with long-day hamsters, after 8 weeks of these light conditions, regardless of gonadal steroid status, primarily due to a significant increase in MR numbers in the former group. MR levels were also significantly elevated in the hypothalamus, but not in cortical tissues, of short-day animals (Ronchi et al., 1998). Basal corticosterone and cortisol concentrations, gonadal mass, and testosterone concentrations did not differ between hamsters housed for 4 weeks in either long or short days (Ronchi et al., 1998). Corticosteroid concentrations were elevated to a similar degree in both long-day and short-day animals after 10 minutes of exposure to ether but returned to baseline values after 60 minutes in short-day, but not in long-day, hamsters (Ronchi et al., 1998). Short days reduced the reactivity of the hypothalamus-pituitary-adrenal axis to the ether stress; this effect was evident after 2 months of short-day exposure (Ronchi et al., 1998). Short-day exposure likewise reduced the magnitude of the stress response elicited by exposure to low ambient temperatures (Demas and Nelson, 1996). Likewise, after only 18 days of exposure to short days, hippocampal MR mRNA expression was increased in short-day compared with long-day hamsters

(Lance et al., 1998). Up-regulation of mRNA expression was associated with increased adrenal gland mass in short-day conditions. Individual differences in stress responses are common, however, and whether individuals are stressed by a change in a specific environmental variable is probably a complex function of individual and species differences (Mason, 1975).

SEASONAL CYCLES OF HUMAN REPRODUCTION   Seasonal rhythms in rates of human conception, mortality, and suicide have been reported (Aschoff, 1981; Becker, 1981; Roenneberg, 2004). In each case, it is generally necessary to sample a large population to obtain statistically significant data, because the fluctuations from season to season are relatively small. Thus, these rhythms are quantitatively different from most of those discussed for other animals, which are far more obvious. Because the human data are derived from populations exposed to both natural and artificial environmental changes, it is clearly impossible to know the underlying causation of these rhythms.

It is interesting to consider the absence of major seasonal fluctuations in human reproductive activity in relation to the selective forces that presumably led to the evolution of reproductive seasonality in other species. Human reproduction is characterized by a relatively long gestation period and an extremely prolonged period of intensive parental care. These energy-demanding processes cannot be compressed into one portion of one year, as is typical for most seasonal species. There may be little selective advantage to beginning this lengthy process at any particular time of year.

With that stated, recent studies have reported a seasonal rhythm in human conceptions. These studies analyzed birth records from many countries from both the Northern and Southern Hemispheres covering over 300 years of monthly data. At high latitudes, where changes in day length are most pronounced, a peak in conceptions (computed by subtracting 9 months from birth records) occurs at about the time of the vernal equinox (Roenneberg and Aschoff, 1990a). The pattern of human conceptions is reversed 6 months in the Southern Hemisphere as compared with the Northern Hemisphere (Roenneberg and Aschoff, 1990b). Temperature has a moderating effect; conception rates are higher than the annual average between 5°C and 20°C, and they are lower than the annual average at extreme temperatures. The influence of photoperiod on conception rates was more pronounced prior to 1930. The authors of the studies conclude that industrialization shielded humans from changes in photoperiod and temperature after that time through artificial lighting and temperature regulation (Roenneberg and Aschoff, 1990b). However, these studies can only be speculative in their conclusions because they are based on correlational data. There are many uncontrolled variables that could provide alternative explanations. However, the possibility of photoperiodic effects on human physiology and behavior remains (e.g., Reiter, 1998; Wehr, 1998).

There are no reports of the existence of endogenous circannual cycles in humans. Collecting such data would be problematic because the studies necessary to test for the presence of circannual rhythms would require the isolation of individuals under constant environmental conditions for periods of more than a year. Clearly, there are major gaps in our knowledge because there are virtually no data that bear directly on the questions of whether humans are either photoperiodic or circannual. Nevertheless, the growing body of data on seasonal mammals may be useful in pointing the way to obtaining such information for humans. Future research into human seasonality might benefit from a consideration of its potential for contributing to human fitness. For example, seasonal changes in human immune function might be mediated by photoperiod, as they are in other mammalian species (Nelson and Demas, 1995).

Conclusions

An understanding of the rhythmic nature of behavior is important for behavioral scientists for two reasons. First, an awareness of the daily and annual variation in many behaviors may minimize any unintended influences of time of day or seasonality on experimental results. Care should be exercised in obtaining experimental animals, in maintaining appropriate lighting conditions, and in the timing of data collection. Second, seasonal and daily changes in many phenomena of interest to psychologists and biologists have been documented. Reliable daily and seasonal variations in learning and memory function, perception, communication, developmental rates, social behavior, parental behavior, and mating behavior have been reported for many species. Few data on the mechanisms underlying these seasonal changes in behavior are available. We do know that many hormone-behavior interactions appear to be linked to reproductive cycles, but virtually no data exist on the mechanisms underlying seasonal phenomena not linked to reproduction.

There is a lack of basic information about human seasonality. For example, it is not known whether humans are photoperiodic or whether they possess endogenous annual cycles. The possibility of seasonal variation in human developmental rates, learning, or perceptual abilities has not been well studied. The extent to which behaviors such as aggression in humans are seasonal and, if so, to what extent these seasonal fluctuations in behavior reflect seasonal changes in human hormone concentrations also remain unknown. Studies on nonhuman mammals should be useful in obtaining information about the functions and mechanisms of seasonal cycles of behavior. In summary, biological clocks can no longer be ignored in describing normal behavior, treating abnormal conditions, or designing experiments.

Summary

1. Endocrine function varies over a wide range of temporal scales. Many of these temporal changes are the result of biological rhythms generated by endogenous biological clocks. The study of biological clocks and their associated rhythms is called chronobiology. Many homeostatic processes show temporal fluctuations over the course of hours, days, months, or years.

2. Some biological rhythms vary in period length, but four general classes of biological rhythms are normally synchronized to the geophysical cycles of day and night (circadian), the tides (circatidal), the phases of the moon (circalunar), and the seasons of the year (circannual). These rhythms persist in the absence of the geophysical cues with which they are normally entrained (synchronized) with a period that approximates that of the geophysical cycle. Ultradian (shorter than circadian) and infradian (longer than circadian) rhythms are also observed but do not correspond to any known geophysical cue.

3. Biological rhythms have evolved to synchronize the activities of individuals with changes in their environment, allowing preparation for predictable events, and to synchronize the internal physiological and biochemical processes of individuals, allowing efficient function.

4. Biological clocks have several formal properties. Biological clocks are inherited, relatively independent of temperature, relatively independent of chemical influence, entrainable only to limited cycle lengths, relatively independent of behavioral feedback, and found at every level of organization within an individual plant or animal.

5. Biological clocks are found in single cells. Within multicellular organisms, the various clocks in the body are linked in a hierarchical organization that allows temporal coordination. The master clock is located in the suprachiasmatic nuclei of the hypothalamus in mammals and in the pineal gland in some species of birds.

6. Hormones can affect daily locomotor activity cycles. Estrogens accelerate clock function, and progesterone lengthens the period of activity cycles. Removal of the pituitary gland and castration also lengthen free-running activity rhythms.

7. Circadian rhythms have important implications for mental and physical health. In many cases, mood disorders are associated with disrupted circadian functioning and can be treated by maximizing circadian health. Circadian disruption is associated with exacerbation of mood disorders and the etiology of a host of physical ailments.

8. Daily rhythms of parental care in ringdoves, and possibly rabbits, are mediated by biological clocks. Ringdoves take care of their young in sex-specific shifts. Adult treatment of castrated ringdoves with sex steroid hormones can result in the sex-specific temporal organization of parental care.

9. Light is important for entraining biological rhythms to geophysical cycles in virtually all species examined, including humans. Light affects the rhythm of melatonin secretion. Melatonin is produced by the pineal gland during the dark phase of the day, resulting in a sustained elevation in blood levels of this hormone. Long nights (short days) are coded by relatively long periods of sustained elevated melatonin levels. Short nights (long days) are coded by relatively short periods of sustained elevated melatonin levels. Animals use the length of this nightly peak of melatonin secretion to assess the time of year.

10. Many annual cycles of hormone-behavior interactions have been observed among animals. Most of these seasonal changes in behavior are correlated with seasonal changes in reproductive function. Thus, steroid-dependent behaviors wane when animals become reproductively quiescent and recur during the breeding season, when reproductive hormones are again secreted.

11. Some annual cycles are the result of endogenous circannual clocks, whereas others are the result of environmental input; day length may be the most widely used cue in the regulation of seasonal rhythms. Seasonal rhythms in mating behavior, parental behavior, territoriality, aggression, and learning have been reported for a variety of species. Seasonal cycles in human conception have also been recently documented.

Questions for Discussion

1. Compare and contrast the concept of homeostasis with the concept of biological rhythms. Are their functions complementary or antagonistic?

2. Circadian clocks are pervasive, potentially existing in every cell of the brain and body. If the SCN contains a master clock, why do we need subordinate clocks everywhere else?

3. Why is it important to have an understanding of biological clocks and rhythms in designing or interpreting behavioral endocrinology experiments?

4. Some have noted that males and females of the same species are quite different animals. Similarly, it can be said that animals examined during the summer are quite different animals from animals of the same species examined during the winter. Defend or refute this statement.

5. Assuming you do not know the nature of the melatonin signal that is important for the neural detection of day length, how might you design an experiment to determine whether it is the duration, phase, or amplitude of melatonin that signals day length?

6. Postulate how disrupted biological rhythms might contribute to disease. Consider how artificial lighting might contribute to the problem. How might dysfunctional biological rhythms be repaired?

Suggested Readings

Buijs, F. N., et al. 2016. The circadian system: A regulatory feedback network of periphery and brain. *Physiology (Bethesda)*, 31(3):170–181.

Butler, M. P., et al. 2009. Biological clocks in the endocrine system. In D. W. Pfaff, et al. (eds.), *Hormones, Brain and Behavior* (2nd ed.), pp. 473–505. Academic Press, New York.

Follett, B. K. 2015. "Seasonal changes in the neuroendocrine system": Some reflections. *Front. Neuroendocrinol.*, 37:3–12.

Hastings, M., et al. 2007. Circadian clocks: Regulators of endocrine and metabolic rhythms. *J. Endocrinol.*, 195(2):187–198.

Nelson, R. J., et al. (eds.). 2010. *Photoperiodism: The Biological Calendar*. Oxford University Press, New York.

Partch, C. L., et al. 2014. Molecular architecture of the mammalian circadian clock. *Trends Cell Biol.*, 24(2):90–99.

Prendergast, B. J., et al. 2009. Mammalian seasonal rhythms: Behavior and neuroendocrine substrates. In D. W. Pfaff, et al. (eds.), *Hormones, Brain and Behavior* (2nd ed.), pp. 507–538. Academic Press, New York.

Silver, R., and Kriegsfeld, L. J. 2014. Circadian rhythms have broad implications for understanding brain and behavior. *Eur. J. Neurosci.*, 39(11):1866–1880.

Stress

11

Learning Objectives

This chapter describes the role of hormones in stress, which is the marked disruption in homeostasis caused by stressors. Stressors may be environmental, physiological, or psychosocial. Stressors are met by a stress response, which is a suite of physiological and behavioral reactions to reestablish homeostasis. By the end of this chapter, you will know the general features of stress, and you should be able to:

- understand the concept of *stress*.
- describe the endocrine contributions to the *stress response*.
- identify the adaptive features of the stress response.
- identify the pathological aspects of the stress response.
- describe the interactions between stress and reproductive, growth, and cognitive functions.

About half (48%) of acute myocardial infarctions (AMIs; heart attacks) can be associated by patients to specific triggers. One study found that the most common triggers were emotional upset (18.4%) and moderate physical activities (14.1%) (Tofler et al., 1990). Wars, natural disasters, and anxiety-provoking events are associated with an increase in AMIs (Leeka et al., 2010). For example, Israeli citizens experiencing the sounds of Iraqi missiles during the start of the Gulf War in 1990 had a much higher incidence of AMIs compared with other time points before the start of the war or with Israelis not experiencing the missile threats in the country (Meisel et al., 1991). The incidence of AMIs increased among individuals during major earthquakes in Athens, Greece (1981); Northridge (near Los Angeles, in 1994); and Hanshin-Awaji, Japan (1995) (Leeka et al., 2010). Fortunately, wars and natural disasters are relatively rare to be major health concerns;

FIGURE 11.1   Cardiac deaths in and around Los Angeles, California (A) The number of cardiac deaths increased for 2 weeks after the Los Angeles Rams, a professional football team, lost the 1980 Super Bowl in the final moments, whereas (B) the number of cardiac deaths decreased after another Los Angeles team, the LA Raiders, won the 1984 Super Bowl. After Kloner et al., 2009.

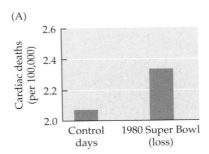

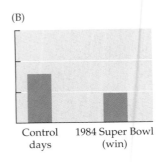

however, seemingly innocuous events such as watching sports can pose significant health risks. Anyone who has attended a sporting event has probably noticed the variety of spectator responses during a close match, ranging from joy to fury. Fans who are screaming and jumping up and down, with sweat pouring down their beet-red faces, and who appear to be on the verge of having a heart attack are not an uncommon sight. Is it possible that such emotional turmoil, even when the personal stakes are so low, could really have fatal consequences? Indeed, emotional stress has been blamed for regional increases in cardiovascular deaths following high-profile sporting events. For example, when the Los Angeles Rams, a National Football League team, lost the Super Bowl in 1980 after maintaining an unexpected lead well into the fourth quarter, there was a significant increase in deaths from heart attacks and strokes over the subsequent 2 weeks within Los Angeles County (Kloner et al., 2009). In contrast, when the Los Angeles Raiders won the Super Bowl in 1984, there was a significant reduction in cardiac deaths reported during the same time period, within the same county (**FIGURE 11.1**). Likewise, the number of deaths from cardiac arrest and stroke increased nearly 50% among Dutch men on the day in 1996 that the Netherlands national soccer team was unexpectedly eliminated from the European Championship by the French team (Witte et al., 2000). No corresponding peak in mortality was observed among Dutch women, French men, or French women (Toubiana et al., 2001; Witte et al., 2000). Such results raise four questions: Why are some groups and individuals affected more severely by a potentially stressful event than others? Are there differences among individuals in perception of stressors, perturbations to homeostasis, and physiological, psychological, and behavioral responses to stressors? Are stress responses always detrimental, or can they be adaptive in some circumstances? How does one measure stress? These four basic questions form the basis of this chapter. We will explore the physiological and behavioral consequences of different types of stressors and how individual differences in response to stress emerge.

Stress and Its Consequences

Life is challenging. For animals living in the wild there is competition for food, mates, and territories, as well as biological stress imposed by the physical environment (e.g., extreme temperatures) and exposure to disease. For humans living in much of the world, stress stems from exposure to the four horsemen of the apocalypse: conquest, war, famine, and pestilence. Yet, even in developed countries—in which resources are plentiful for the majority of the population, shelter protects people against the harsher aspects of the environment, and advanced medical care and sanitation stave off disease—stress still emerges as an important factor affecting health and well-being.

The pressure of survival and reproduction takes its toll on every individual on the planet (**FIGURE 11.2**). The wear and tear of life can compromise reproduction and lead to early death. All things being equal, animals that live the longest tend to leave the most offspring. In the Darwinian "game of life," individuals that leave the most successful offspring win. Although some of the variation in longevity among

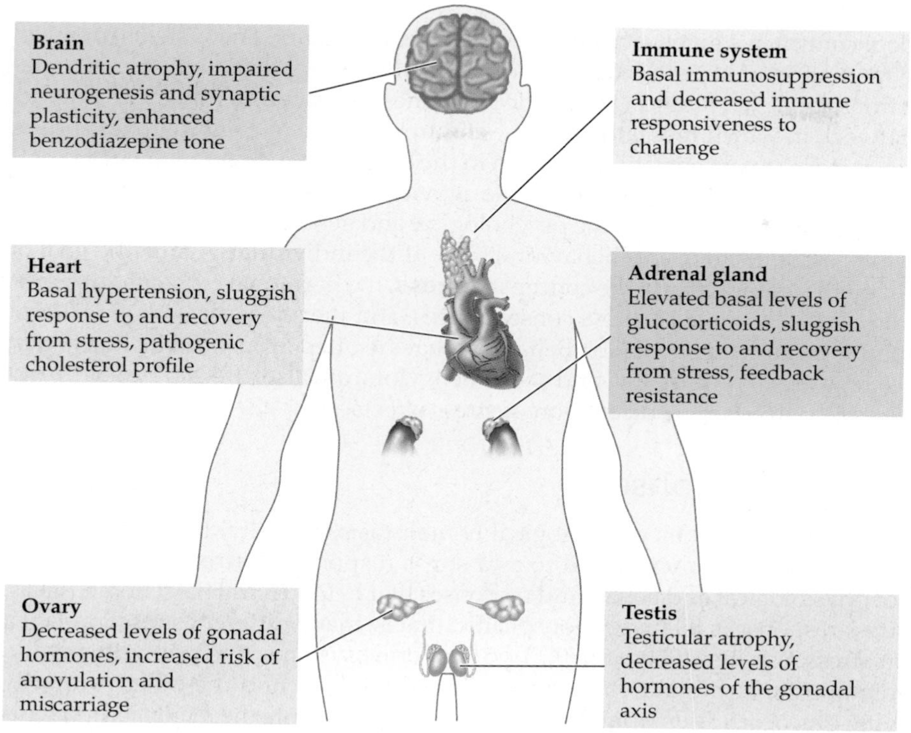

Brain
Dendritic atrophy, impaired neurogenesis and synaptic plasticity, enhanced benzodiazepine tone

Immune system
Basal immunosuppression and decreased immune responsiveness to challenge

Heart
Basal hypertension, sluggish response to and recovery from stress, pathogenic cholesterol profile

Adrenal gland
Elevated basal levels of glucocorticoids, sluggish response to and recovery from stress, feedback resistance

Ovary
Decreased levels of gonadal hormones, increased risk of anovulation and miscarriage

Testis
Testicular atrophy, decreased levels of hormones of the gonadal axis

FIGURE 11.2 Physiological systems and endocrine glands affected by chronic stress From McEwen and Wingfeld, 2010.

individuals of the same species merely reflects genetics and good fortune, a significant part of this variation reflects differences in the ability to cope with the everyday demands of living, whether these demands occur on the African Serengeti, during the daily commute, or on the sidelines of a 12-year-old child's football game.

As described in Chapter 9, all living creatures are vessels of dynamic equilibrium, or homeostasis. Any perturbation to homeostasis requires an animal to expend energy to restore the original steady state. Among birds and mammals, an individual's total available energy is partitioned among many competing needs, such as growth, cellular maintenance, immune function, reproduction, and thermogenesis. During environmental energy shortages, processes that are not essential for immediate survival, such as growth and reproduction, are suppressed and immune function is compromised. If homeostatic perturbations require more energy than is readily available after nonessential systems have been inhibited, then an individual's survival may be compromised.

All living organisms currently exist because they have evolved adaptations that allow individuals to cope with energetically demanding conditions. These demanding conditions range from final exam week for a well-fed college undergraduate in the United States to finding a meal on the African veldt for a wild dog. Surprisingly, similar neuroendocrine coping mechanisms are engaged in both of these cases, as well as in many other potentially stressful situations. Although stressors typically disrupt homeostasis, which affects brain and behavior, it is important to note that the brain itself can perceive psychological factors, such as taking an exam, caring for a chronically ill relative, or giving a classroom presentation, as stressful and evoke a stress response that disrupts homeostasis. Because hormones are important mediators of stress, the stress response emphasizes the bidirectional relationship between hormones and behavior (brain).

There are many sources of stressors. Environmental factors such as temperature extremes or noise are often perceived as stressors. Stressors can also be physiological factors, such as insufficient food quality or quantity or water deprivation. Importantly, psychosocial factors, such as fighting, social subordination, novel situations,

stress Any significant disturbance of homeostasis, as by extreme temperatures or psychological factors.

stressor A condition, agent, or other stimulus that causes stress to an organism.

stress response A suite of physiological and behavioral responses that help to reestablish homeostasis.

fight-or-flight response The automatic and endocrine responses that prepare an individual to battle or flee from real or perceived attack, harm, or threats to survival.

or lack of control in a given situation, can be salient stressors. The systems involved in the mediation of stressors (e.g., glucocorticoids, sympathetic and parasympathetic transmitters, cytokines, metabolic hormones) operate as a nonlinear, interactive network in which mediators down- and up-regulate one another, depending on such factors as concentration, location in the body, and sequential temporal patterning (McEwen, 2006). Importantly, the activity of these mediating systems and mediators is closely coupled to the psychological and genetic makeup, developmental history, social factors, and behavioral state of the individual. Again, the goal of this chapter is to understand the concept of **stress**, the hormonal correlates of stress, the adaptive versus maladaptive consequences, and the effects of both short-term and long-term stress on behavior. Behaviors that are often influenced by hormones, such as reproductive, parental, and social behaviors, are also affected by stress and will be emphasized in the discussion of stress effects.

The Stress Response

When a **stressor** disrupts physiological homeostasis, an individual typically displays what is commonly referred to as a stress response. A **stress response** is a suite of physiological and behavioral responses that help to reestablish homeostasis. The stress response is relatively nonspecific; that is, many different stressors elicit a similar stress response (Selye, 1950). Two endocrine systems, one primarily involving epinephrine (adrenaline) from the adrenal medulla and the other primarily involving glucocorticoids from the adrenal cortex, constitute the major components of the stress response (Stratakis and Chrousos, 1995). Within seconds of perceiving a stressor, the sympathetic nervous system begins to secrete norepinephrine, and both adrenal medullae begin to secrete epinephrine. A few minutes later, the adrenal cortices begin to secrete glucocorticoids.

In 1915, Walter Cannon (**FIGURE 11.3**) proposed his "emergency theory" of the adrenal glands, which suggested that the secretion of epinephrine from the adrenal medulla increases following an exposure to virtually any stressor, as a means of adapting to that stress. Many physiological studies conducted throughout the 1920s and 1930s demonstrated the stimulatory effects of epinephrine on the respiratory and cardiovascular systems. Epinephrine is usually the chemical messenger that acts first because just a doubling of epinephrine from its resting values causes profound changes in respiration and cardiac tone (e.g., heart rate and blood pressure), whereas norepinephrine concentrations must increase fivefold to have similar effects (Ganong, 2005). This immediate, nonspecific component of the stress response was termed the **fight-or-flight response** because the physiological changes in cardiovascular tone, respiration rate, and blood flow to the muscles from the trunk could support either of those behavioral responses (Cannon, 1929). Importantly, the catecholamines (norepinephrine and epinephrine), working through a variety of mechanisms, also increase blood glucose levels. The elevated blood glucose fuels the fight-or-flight response. The catecholamines also increase alertness and, as we will see in Chapter 12, enhance learning and memory.

Modern perspectives on stress are less likely to focus on fight or flight than on a psychological feature of stress, namely, the degree of control the stressed individual has over the situation. For ex-

FIGURE 11.3 **Walter B. Cannon**, a pioneer in stress research, is seen in this photo working in his lab. Cannon established the concept of homeostasis.

(A) Epinephrine concentration

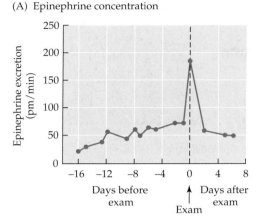

(B) Norepinephrine concentration

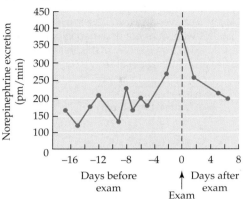

FIGURE 11.4   Catecholamine concentrations peaked on the day of a PhD exam after showing a consistent elevation in the days prior to the exam. Epinephrine (A) and norepinephrine (B) concentrations both peaked on the day of the exam and returned to baseline after successful coping with the stressor (passing the exam). After Frankenhaeuser, 1978.

ample, in one study both epinephrine and norepinephrine concentrations increased in the days prior to a PhD final examination, peaked on the day of the exam, and then slowly returned to basal levels (Frankenhaeuser, 1978) (**FIGURE 11.4**). As the date of the examination neared, the students' confidence and perceived control of the situation waned, and a stress response ensued. After passing the exam, the students' confidence and sense of control returned, and catecholamine and cortisol concentrations returned to typical values.

Other studies report changes not just in epinephrine and norepinephrine but in an entire suite of hormones known to be involved in the mediation of stress over the course of the stress response. The **hypothalamic-pituitary-adrenal (HPA) axis** is activated, and corticotropin-releasing hormone (CRH), adrenocorticotropic hormone (ACTH), and glucocorticoids are released in response to stressors (**FIGURE 11.5**). In one classic study, blood samples were obtained from young military recruits preparing for their first parachute jump (Ursin et al., 1978). Basal blood hormone concentrations were determined prior to the jump. Hormone concentrations on the day of

hypothalamic-pituitary-adrenal (HPA) axis   A complex and interactive system that comprises three endocrine glands: the hypothalamus, pituitary gland, and adrenal gland that constitute a major neuroendocrine system that regulations stress responses.

FIGURE 11.5   The hypothalamic-pituitary-adrenal axis releases several hormones in response to stress. Initially, stress causes the release of epinephrine from the adrenal medulla and of norepinephrine (NE) from the sympathetic nervous system. Moments later, the hypothalamus releases CRH and other releasing hormones, which stimulate ACTH and β-endorphin release from the anterior pituitary gland. ACTH stimulates corticosterone secretion from the adrenal cortex. Prolactin is often released from the anterior pituitary during stress as well. Vasopressin is released from the posterior pituitary.

FIGURE 11.6   Blood hormone concentrations are altered by the stress of parachute jumps. Note that on jump days, cortisol, epinephrine, norepinephrine, and growth hormone concentrations were elevated above their own baseline (pre-jump) values and above values for control individuals who were not engaged in parachute jump training (dashed line). Testosterone decreased on the day of the first jump but rebounded the next day to basal concentrations. After Ursin et al., 1978.

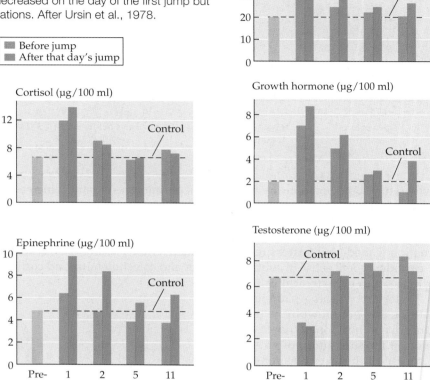

the jump, as well as on days of subsequent jumps, were also measured (**FIGURE 11.6**). Not surprisingly, catecholamine concentrations were high on the day of the first jump, although, as the recruits gained confidence, their stress responses were muted. Cortisol and growth hormone (GH) concentrations were also elevated on the first jump day, while testosterone concentrations were suppressed on the first jump day (Ursin et al., 1978).

Because epinephrine does not cross the blood-brain barrier, and endocrine mediation of the stress response must affect the brain in order to affect behavior, much of this chapter will focus on the effects of glucocorticoids in the stress response. Glucocorticoids are good candidates for mediating behavioral effects of stress because (1) these steroid hormones are released in response to numerous stressors, (2) steroid hormones can easily diffuse past the blood-brain barrier, and (3) there are glucocorticoid receptors in several brain regions.

Within minutes of the onset of a stressor, the adrenal cortex begins to secrete glucocorticoids (e.g., corticosterone in most rodents, birds, reptiles, and fish; cortisol in most primates, large mammals, and carnivores) (Stratakis and Chrousos, 1995). Like epinephrine, glucocorticoids are released in response to virtually any stressor. Hans Selye (**FIGURE 11.7**) discovered this aspect of nonspecificity when attempting to characterize a new ovarian hormone. In Selye's study, some rats were injected with ovarian extracts that were believed to contain the new hormone, and some other rats were injected with saline as a control procedure (Selye, 1937a, 1950). After several days of injections, it was noted that the rats receiving the ovarian extracts developed peptic ulcers and experienced adrenal hypertrophy and regression of key immune system organs (e.g., the spleen and thymus). Unexpectedly, the rats

FIGURE 11.7   Hans Selye (1907–1982) is considered the founder of modern stress research.

that were injected with saline developed the same symptoms. Because injections of extracts from virtually any tissue, as well as inert saline, evoked the same symptoms, Selye reasoned that the unpleasantness associated with the daily injections, and not a specific ovarian hormone, caused these symptoms (Sapolsky, 1992a). It was soon discovered that stressors, originally termed nocuous agents (Selye, 1936), as diverse as frostbite, exposure to formaldehyde, or hemorrhage could also elicit these symptoms (Selye, 1950; but see Kopin, 1995). The common endocrine event underlying these very different stressors was the release of glucocorticoids from the adrenal cortex. Thus, epinephrine and cortisol (or corticosterone) are commonly known as the *stress hormones*, despite the fact that their major endocrine functions involve metabolism and that circadian variation in these hormones occurs even in the absence of exposure to stress (Selye, 1937b).

general adaptation syndrome (GAS) A three-stage reaction to stress proposed by Hans Selye. These stages include the alarm, adaptation (resistance), and exhaustion stages.

General Adaptation Syndrome

One study was particularly important in forming the basis of Selye's thinking about stress response (Selye, 1936). Rats were housed in low-temperature conditions for 2 days, 2 weeks, or 2 months. After 2 days in these conditions, the rats showed hypertrophy of the adrenal cortex, reduced eosinophil (a type of immune cell circulating in the blood) numbers, and atrophy of the thymus, spleen, and lymph nodes. In other words, the rats exhibited a classic stress response. After 2 weeks of low temperatures, the rats no longer displayed these symptoms, suggesting that they had adapted to the stressor. In other words, the rats had become "cold-adapted" and could tolerate even lower temperatures without exhibiting any further stress responses. After approximately 2 months of exposure to low temperatures, the rats "lost" their "acquired resistance" to the low temperatures and died.

This process of coping with stressors was termed the **general adaptation syndrome (GAS)**. The GAS consists of three stages: (1) the alarm reaction, (2) resistance, and finally (3) exhaustion (Selye, 1950) (**FIGURE 11.8**). The stressor is detected during the alarm reaction stage. Coping with the stressor occurs during the resistance stage. The exhaustion stage is characterized by the termination of the stress response and the onset of stress pathology, which in extreme cases leads to death. Although Selye believed that the exhaustion phase was due to the termination of the stress response, current ideas about stress indicate that the pathological effects of stress result from prolonged exposure to the hormones associated with the stress response (Chrousos et al., 1995; Sapolsky, 1992b, 1994).

What Is "Stress"?

Everybody knows what stress is and nobody knows what it is (Selye, 1973a). Everyone has experienced "stress," and most people can give an example of stress. Students particularly complain of stress during final examinations week. However,

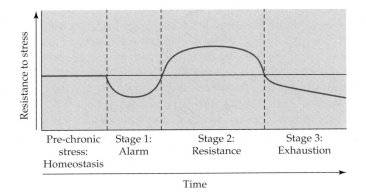

FIGURE 11.8 General adaptation syndrome (GAS) The GAS consists of three stages: (1) the alarm reaction, (2) resistance, and finally (3) exhaustion. During the alarm stage there is decreased resistance to stress and physiological systems may suffer, but during stage 2 there is resistance to stress via increased adrenal function. If the stress is prolonged or the resistance fails, then exhaustion occurs, with physiological and behavioral coping mechanisms failing, and ultimately survival may be compromised.

stress has been a notoriously ethereal concept in biology and medicine, and arriving at a consensus for a precise definition has been difficult. Stress is yet another type of hypothetical construct or concept. We can easily recognize stress in the same way that we can generally recognize "good" and "evil." However, if we try to define the term *stress* precisely, then the concept becomes as slippery as the concepts of good and evil. Consequently, some scientists propose that the term should be abolished altogether (**BOX 11.1**).

The biological concepts and terminology of stress were developed from engineering concepts and terminology. In engineering, the term *stress* has a very specific meaning, namely, forces that act against resistance. In biology, the term *stress* has often been conflated to include the stressor, the stress response, and the physiological intermediates between the stressor and the stress response (Toates, 1995). Despite the confusing array of uses of the term, however, an impressive scientific literature integrating endocrinology, immunology, psychology, and neuroscience has developed around the concept of stress.

What, then, does it mean to say that an individual is under stress? Most definitions employ some of the prevailing homeostatic notions of stress to arrive at a working definition. For example, George Chrousos, an endocrinologist and phy-

BOX 11.1 *Allostatic Load*

A new way to view stress has been proposed recently that takes into consideration both homeostasis and the notion of programmed changes in homeostatic settings. As described in Chapter 9, homeostatic mechanisms work to maintain physiological stability in an animal that is living in a fluctuating environment. Some potentially stressful events, such as the onset of winter or final exams, are predictable and allow the organism to prepare in advance for their occurrence. Other stressors occur without warning and may require the animal to mobilize stored energy or alter its foraging to meet the increased demand. The process of allostasis, achieving stability through physiological or behavioral change, can be carried out via alteration in HPA axis hormones, the autonomic nervous system, cytokines, or a number of other systems and is generally adaptive in the short term (McEwen and Wingfield, 2003, 2010). The cumulative "cost" incurred by the body during allostasis is referred to as allostatic load. Under optimal circumstances, an animal can fairly easily support an increased allostatic load, such as that created among female mice by the birth of their litters in the spring when food availability is at its peak. However, among animals that are already handicapped by malnutrition, poor genes, infection, a harsh physical or social environment, or a hypersensitivity to stressors, the ability to meet the energetic requirements of an increasing allostatic load may be compromised, and demands will ultimately exceed the capacity of the individual to cope with a challenge, resulting in allostatic overload (McEwen and Wingfield, 2003). Sustained exposure to stressors or physiological dysregulation, such as occurs in individuals with Cushing disease, also can lead to allostatic overload.

This squirrel looks miserable, but is probably not experiencing allostatic overload because it appears well-nourished.

Among free-ranging animals, allostatic load is primarily reflective of the availability of food and shelter. In species with rigid social hierarchies, subordinate status may further limit access to these resources. In this scenario, allostatic overload occurs when energetic expenditure exceeds energetic availability (McEwen and Wingfield, 2010), and the animal subsequently enters an "emergency life history stage" that is aimed at ensuring survival through reestablishing the energy balance (Wingfield et al., 1998). In contrast, for most humans living in industrialized countries, food and shelter are abundant year-round, energy acquisition often exceeds energy expenditure, and social conflict becomes the driving force behind allostatic load.

sician, defines stress as "the recognition by the body of a stressor and therefore, the state of threatened homeostasis; stressors are threats against homeostasis; and adaptive responses are the body's attempt to counteract the stressor and reestablish homeostasis" (Chrousos et al., 1998). Similarly, Robert Sapolsky (1994), an ecologist and neuroscientist, defines a stressor as "anything that throws your body out of homeostatic balance—for example, an injury, an illness, subjection to great heat or cold." Considered together, stress is the sum of all nonspecific effects of factors that can act on the body to increase energy consumption significantly above some resting, or basal, level. In the short term, the stress response is adaptive and helps individuals cope with emergency situations; in the long term, the stress response tends to be maladaptive (Sapolsky, 1992b, 1994; Selye, 1936, 1937a). Both short-term and long-term stress responses can affect hormone-behavior interactions.

There are limitations to the homeostatic concept of stress, however. First, it does not address the issue that psychological stressors, such as giving a public lecture or being confined in a tight space, can evoke a full physiological stress response; indeed, this psychological stress response actually *causes* homeostatic imbalance in an individual rather than restores it. Second, the homeostatic concept of stress does not account for individual variation in the perception of stressors. Most people would be terrified to jump out of an airplane with a parachute and would report such an experience as stressful; however, some individuals seek out skydiving for pleasure. In order for a definition of stress to be useful, it must address how the same stimulus can be stressful to one individual and pleasurable to another. One variable to be considered in this regard is the extent to which individuals perceive the stressful situation as being under their control. Individuals that have a sense of control feel less vulnerable to the effects of a stressful condition. Third, some definitions conflate *stress* with *physiological response to stress*, that is, stress activates the adrenal glands to produce epinephrine and glucocorticoids. However, elevated glucocorticoid concentrations and activation of the sympathetic nervous system can be caused by both stressful and pleasurable events, such as winning a lottery or getting married.

Kim and Diamond (2002) proposed a three-part definition of stress that may prove useful in trying to unravel the interaction among stress, hormones, and behavior: (1) Stress is considered to be a condition in which individuals are aroused by aversive stimuli. Stress provokes elevated arousal, which can be assessed by measuring locomotor activity, hormone concentrations (e.g., epinephrine or glucocorticoids), or electrocardiogram (ECG) or electroencephalogram (EEG) activity. (2) Because arousal can increase under both aversive and pleasurable conditions, for an event to be defined as stressful, the individual must perceive it as aversive (Kim and Diamond, 2002). Thus, jumping out of an airplane with a swatch of silk attached to a backpack at 2000 m would provoke arousal; however, parachuting would not be stressful to someone who enjoyed skydiving and did not find it aversive. In contrast, skydiving would be stressful for someone who was afraid of heights or for some other reason perceived skydiving as aversive. The aversiveness would be judged by the extent to which an individual avoided the stimuli if given a choice. For example, a rat placed in a pool of water may be stressed initially, until it learns that there is a hidden platform from which it can escape the water; subsequent experiences with the pool will provoke fewer stress responses as the aversiveness declines with repeated experiences with the easy escape. (3) This final component of the definition of stress encompasses the concept of controllability the extent of the stress is determined by the individuals' perception of their control over the aversive stimuli (Kim and Diamond, 2002) Many studies in both humans and nonhuman animals have indicated that the element of control in an aversive situation, as well as the related element of predictability, significantly ameliorates the long-term negative effects of the stressful experience (see next page).

More recently, Michael Romero and colleagues have developed a reactive scope model to integrate homeostasis, allostasis (see Box 11.1), and stress (Romero et al., 2009). According to this model there are four ranges over which hormones and other mediators respond to perturbations of homeostasis: (1) Predictive homeostasis is the response range that comprises daily and seasonal variation in a given mediator. (2) Reactive homeostasis is the range of mediator fluctuations necessary to respond to threats. (3) Homeostatic overload represents values above the reactive homeostasis range. (4) Homeostatic failure represents mediator values below the predictive homeostasis range. It is useful to think of predictive and reactive homeostasis as the normal reactive scope for a given individual, whereas homeostatic overload and homeostatic failure are pathological and predictive of long-term and short-term health, respectively (Romero and Wingfield, 2016; Romero et al., 2009). One goal of the reactive scope model, as an extension of the allostasis model, is its utility both to biomedical researchers studying laboratory animals and humans and to ecologists studying stress in free-living animals.

Physiological Effects of the Stress Response

Almost immediately after exposure to a stressor, a physiological stress response with several components begins to unfold: within seconds, the sympathetic nervous system secretes norepinephrine, and the adrenal medulla secretes epinephrine. Recall that stress also stimulates increased activity of the HPA axis: the hypothalamus releases CRH, which stimulates release of ACTH from the anterior pituitary gland, and within minutes the adrenal cortex begins to secrete glucocorticoids. Several other hormones, including prolactin, urocortin, glucagon, thyroid hormones, and vasopressin, may also be secreted from various endocrine tissues during a stress response.

Imagine that a rabbit is being chased by a fox. How does the stress response affect the rabbit in this situation? First, the rabbit needs a quick energy supply in order to sustain the sprint back to its warren. In such an emergency, the need for metabolic fuel is acute, large, and unpredictable (Sapolsky, 1992b, 1994). The immediate release of catecholamines raises the rabbit's respiration and cardiovascular rates within seconds; its body requires increased energy availability to sustain these high rates. The most obvious physiological change that occurs in response to a stressor is an immediate increase in available levels of glucose and oxygen in the blood. Epinephrine increases the delivery of oxygen to the tissues and raises sympathetic tone (i.e., the activation level of the sympathetic nervous system). Glucocorticoids, which are secreted within minutes, though probably not until the rabbit is back home, act on metabolic pathways to replenish the energy reserves used to escape the predator. Rapid effects of glucocorticoids operate via nongenomic pathways to affect behavioral stress responses (Dallman, 2005), although genomic pathways mediate some of the long-term effects of stressors. Epinephrine causes blood flow to be temporarily rerouted to the muscles and away from the digestive system or other processes not critical for coping with the emergency situation. In other words, the rabbit's lunch can be digested later (if there is a "later" for our rabbit protagonist). Responses to injuries that might curtail movement (e.g., pain, inflammation) are inhibited by the stress-induced release of endorphins and endocannabinoids. If a rabbit that suffered scrapes and scratches as it darted into the brambles stopped to nurse its wounds, then it would likely become the fox's dinner. Energetically expensive activities such as growth, reproduction, and some components of immune function are also suppressed until after the emergency has passed. Other components of immune function, such as trafficking of immune cells to the skin where injuries might occur, are enhanced during stressful events (Dhabhar and McEwen, 1997, 1999) (**FIGURE 11.9**). Behavioral responses such as suppression of feeding behavior are caused by urocortin binding to CRH receptors in the hypothalamus (Koob and Heinrichs, 1999;

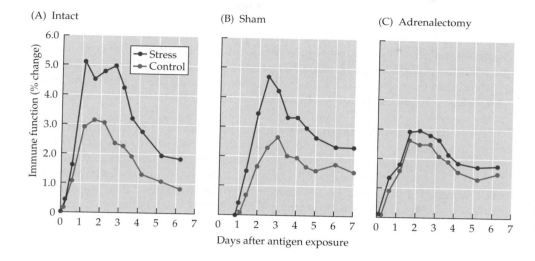

(A) Intact (B) Sham (C) Adrenalectomy

Immune function (% change)

Days after antigen exposure

FIGURE 11.9 Acute stress can improve immune function. Although we often think of stress as only suppressing immune function, acute stressors can enhance some immune functions. For example, restraint stress (blue circles) enhanced a type of immune response in adrenal-intact rodents and in animals receiving a sham adrenalectomy. This effect was abolished by adrenalectomy, suggesting that it was mediated by glucocorticoids. After Dhabhar and McEwen, 1999.

Spina et al., 1996; Vaughan et al., 1995). Well after the rabbit is safe in its nest, the stress response subsides, parasympathetic tone increases, and metabolic rate returns to baseline. In summary, the stress response has many adaptive effects:

- Increased immediate availability of energy
- Increased oxygen intake
- Decreased blood flow to organ systems not necessary for movement
- Inhibition of energetically expensive processes that are not related to immediate survival, such as digestion, growth, immune function, and reproduction
- Decreased pain perception
- Enhancement of sensory function and memory

Importantly, both the predator and the prey are experiencing similar acute stress responses during the chase, despite their disparate roles. This is another example of the nonspecificity of the stress response. If the attempts of the fox to obtain food are unsuccessful and it has not eaten in a long time, then it will experience a chronic stress response. The effects of a prolonged or chronic stress response differ from the adaptive effects described above and will be presented below.

In both the rabbit and the fox in the previous scenario, CRH is released from the hypothalamus into the portal blood system within seconds of perception of a stressor. The CRH travels to the anterior pituitary gland, where it stimulates specific cells to secrete ACTH, which enters the general blood circulation and provokes the adrenal cortex to produce and secrete glucocorticoids. This cascade of endocrine events is often referred to as the HPA response and takes several minutes to be fully engaged.

Recently, it was discovered that in addition to provoking the release of ACTH and, subsequently, glucocorticoids, CRH itself also mediates some aspects of the stress response, both adaptive and pathological (reviewed in Romero and Wingfield, 2016). CRH is found in two brain regions. In the hypothalamus, CRH is mainly involved in regulation of the HPA axis. A second pool of CRH is located in the amygdala, where it is involved in mediating anxiety responses. In rhesus macaques, variation in the *CRH* gene is associated with altered endocrine responses to stress (Barr et al., 2009). It appears that CRH has a role in modulating anxiety under several circumstances (Coste et al., 2001). Transgenic mice that express high levels of CRH are more anxious in a novel environment than control mice. The same is true of wild-type mice and rats that are injected with exogenous CRH. Furthermore, CRH receptor antagonists decrease anxiety normally associated with alcohol withdrawal and social defeat in rats and mice. Similarly, polymorphisms in *CRH* and the CRH receptor genes are associated with increased stress-induced alcohol consumption in primates and rodents (Barr et al., 2009; Hansson et al., 2006). High levels of CRH expressed in transgenic mice also decrease female sexual receptivity, and this is not reversed by adrenalectomy. High CRH levels also impair spatial learning and memory.

Two CRH receptors with distinct binding patterns have been identified, and much of what we know about the influences of CRH and its two receptor types on behavior has been gained through the use of transgenic mice that lack one or both of these receptor types (Zoumakis and Chrousos, 2009). For example, Crh1 knockout mice, which lack functional Crh1 receptors, were less anxious at baseline and after alcohol withdrawal than wild-type mice. Crh1 receptors also appear to mediate the hormonal, behavioral, and nociceptive (pain) responses to stress (Reul et al., 2002) and appear to be involved in negative feedback regulation of the HPA axis (Müller et al., 2003). Mice with conditional *Crhr1* gene deactivation in neurons outside of the hypothalamus and pituitary showed a prolonged elevation in glucocorticoids following stressors. This supports the notion that the hippocampus and possibly the amgydala, where CRH1 receptors are located and presumably inactivated by the conditional gene inactivation (Müller et al., 2003), provide negative feedback during stress responses. Under baseline conditions, the standard negative feedback mechanisms, including those of the hypothalamus and pituitary, are evoked as described in Chapter 2. However, during prolonged stress responses, the hippocampus and possibly the amygdala participate in terminating glucocorticoid secretion.

Urocortin, a CRH-like neuropeptide, has a high affinity for the Crh2 receptor in addition to the Crh1 receptor (Vaughan et al., 1995). Activation of the Crh2 receptor suppresses food intake in food-restricted and freely fed mice and suggests a mechanism for how stress suppresses appetite (Spina et al., 1996). There are three urocortin genes in mammals, and if all three genes are deleted, these triple urocortin knockout mice fail to recover from stress and display enduring anxiety responses (Neufeld-Cohen et al., 2010).

There are two types of corticosteroid receptors in the hippocampus: type I receptors, which are mineralocorticoid receptors (MRs), and type II, which are glucocorticoid receptors (GRs). MRs have higher affinity for circulating glucocorticoids and are usually engaged under baseline conditions. Activation of these receptors is thought to modulate homeostatic balance. However, as glucocorticoids increase during a stress response, the low-affinity GRs are activated, which provides negative feedback and brings the stress response back under control (Mayer and Fanselow, 2003).

The endocannabinoids also are involved in mediating the effects of glucocorticoids on stress responses via synaptic mechanisms (Riebe and Wotjak, 2011). When glucocorticoids bind to membrane-bound glucocorticoid receptors, a G protein signaling cascade induces endocannabinoid ligand production (**FIGURE 11.10**). These ligand molecules are released into the synapse and bind to CB1 cannabinoid receptors on GABA-ergic terminals to inhibit GABA secretion. The decrease in GABA disinhibits norepinephrine secretion and modulates stress responses. Thus, the "mellowing effects" of endocannabinoid signaling may be part of a generalized stress response that affects food intake, emotion, energy balance, pain responsivity, and motivated behaviors such as sex (Di et al., 2003; Hill and McEwen, 2009, 2010; Tasker, 2006).

Chronic stress, genetic differences in corticosteroid receptor numbers or subtype, or other individual differences in endocrine secretion, responsiveness, carrier-binding proteins, or other factors can dysregulate the normal stress response and provoke inappropriate or pathological stress responses (see below). Although ACTH is the pituitary hormone that is most often associated with stress, several other

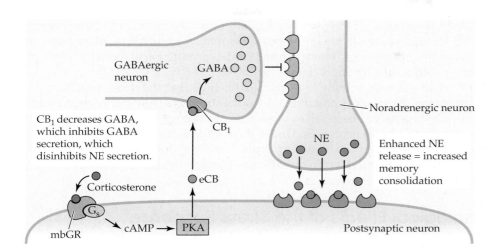

FIGURE 11.10 Model of rapid effects of corticosterone on GABA inhibition and enhanced noradrenaline secretion Corticosterone binds to a membrane-bound G protein-coupled receptor (mbGR), which activates the G_s-cAMP/PKA signal transduction pathway to induce the release of endocannabinoids (eCB) into the synapse. The eCBs bind to CB1 receptors on GABA-ergic terminals, which inhibits GABA secretion. Inhibition of the inhibitory neurotransmitter, GABA, in turn disinhibits norepinephrine (NE), which is then released. After Hill and McEwen, 2009.

pituitary hormones, including vasopressin, prolactin, endorphins, and enkephalins, play important roles. For example, the stress response often includes an increase in blood concentrations of vasopressin, which acts to increase blood volume and blood pressure and makes the delivery of energy to the large muscles more efficient. Vasopressin also directly affects behavior; it enhances memory consolidation and retrieval and increases aggression in defense of a mate. Vasopressin also can work in concert with CRH to augment the release of ACTH from the anterior pituitary (de Kloet et al., 1991). Urocortin can also amplify stress signals by activating CRH receptors. The anterior pituitary gland also secretes prolactin, which functions in the stress response to suppress reproduction temporarily by acting at multiple sites within the hypothalamic-pituitary-gonadal (HPG) axis (Van de Kar et al., 1991) (**FIGURE 11.11**). The α-cells of the endocrine pancreas are stimulated to secrete glucagon. As you will recall from Chapter 2, glucagon serves to increase energy availability. The β-cells of the pancreas are inhibited by glucagon from secreting insulin. Endorphins and enkephalins are often released during stress to provide relief from pain (e.g., Przewlocki, 2009); these hormones also suppress gonadotropin-releasing hormone (GnRH), thereby inhibiting reproductive function. Essentially, all of the

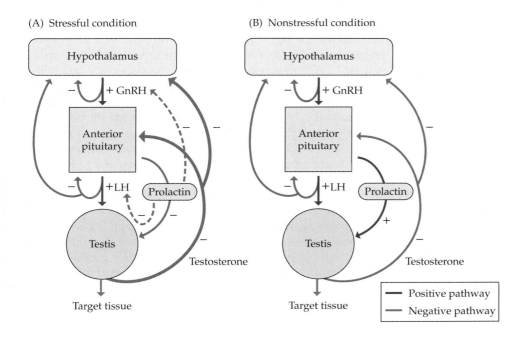

FIGURE 11.11 Prolactin inhibits reproductive function temporarily during stressful conditions by acting at multiple sites within the hypothalamic-pituitary-gonadal (HPG) axis. (A) Under the influence of prolactin, the Leydig cells become less responsive to luteinizing hormone (LH) and produce less testosterone, and the negative feedback mechanisms in the pituitary and hypothalamus are accentuated, so any testosterone produced causes further reductions in GnRH and gonadotropin secretion. (B) Normally, prolactin at low concentrations facilitates testosterone production.

physiological sequelae in the response to a stressor involve making more energy available for immediate use. Again, all processes that are involved in future survival or reproductive success (e.g., energy storage as fat, production of gametes, growth) are put on hold until a future is certain (Sapolsky, 1994).

Thus, when activated acutely, in response to a real threat, the stress response generally improves the chances of survival by orchestrating a shift from nonessential, energetically expensive processes to those that promote immediate survival, such as the muscle and brain processes. Under these circumstances, mounting a stress response is highly adaptive. However, if the stress response is not terminated efficiently, or if it is initiated too frequently or in response to inappropriate stimuli, then pathological consequences may ensue.

Pathological Effects of the Stress Response

In the short term, the stress response is adaptive, and for the most part, the neuroendocrine mechanisms underlying the stress response are conserved across vertebrate phylogeny. Generally, the stress response serves to help an individual cope with an emergency energetic crisis. Ideally, the stress response is initiated by stressful stimuli, then the system is deactivated shortly after the emergency subsides. For example, if a female wild dog were trying to integrate herself into a new pack, she would probably be met by aggressive rebuffs from the females currently in the pack. Whether she decided to stay and fight or to run away, she would experience a short-term stress response that would increase her ability to mobilize and burn energy. If she were accepted into the pack, then a new social hierarchy would be established, fighting would decrease, and the stress response would be terminated. However, if she were driven from the pack, and she had to hunt for food or water alone in an unfamiliar territory, she would probably experience a long-term stress response, especially if her solo hunting success was low.

Prolonged stress shifts the useful, adaptive short-term stress response to a pathological condition that can jeopardize health, economics, and survival (McEwen and Gianaros, 2010; Sapolsky, 1992b, 1994). Stress-related pathologies are a common contributing factor to human disease. The World Health Organization estimates that 5%–15% of individuals living in industrialized societies suffer from stress-related disorders of mood and affect. Prolonged stressors are major contributors to disease onset and progression (Chrousos, 2000; Chrousos and Kino, 2007; McEwen, 2008; Yang and Glaser, 2000); such stressors induce or intensify common human ailments, including cardiovascular disease, cancer, irritable bowel syndrome, and depression. Over a million U.S. employees are estimated to be absent on any given workday because of stress-related medical or psychological complaints (Goetzel et al., 1998). Furthermore, the direct medical expenses of individuals with self-reported chronic stress are elevated by nearly 50% (Goetzel et al., 1998).

Many of us perceive "foxes" (i.e., stressors) all around us—paying the bills, writing textbooks, public speaking, or dealing with our personal relationships may evoke a full-blown stress response. Our bodies remain engaged for emergency action even though we may remain physically inactive. The consequences of this chronic stress are mainly negative (Chrousos, 2009). Some individuals may try to alter their perception of stress-evoking situations by ingesting alcohol or other drugs. Some of us may use various psychological coping strategies, such as visualization, to alter our perception of stressors. Others will go through life seemingly unaware of stressors. And a few will embrace stressors, actually seeking out various experiences that engage the HPA axis, such as working in a big-city trauma center, parachuting, or riding roller coasters. Again, there is a high level of individual variability in perception of and response to stress (McKittrick et al., 2009).

The pathological effects of chronic stress involve cardiovascular, metabolic, reproductive, digestive, immune, anabolic, behavioral, and psychological process-

TABLE 11.1 Pathological effects of long-term stress responses

Acute stress response	Pathological state associated with chronic stress
Shift from energy storage to energy use	Fatigue; myopathy; steroid diabetes
Increased cardiovascular tone	Hypertension
Inhibited digestion	Peptic ulcers
Inhibited growth	Psychosocial dwarfism
Inhibited reproduction	Impotence; anovulation; loss of libido
Altered immune function and inflammatory responses	Impaired disease resistance; cancer
Enhanced cognition	Accelerated neural degeneration during aging
Enhanced analgesia	

Source: After Sapolsky, 1992b.

es (Chrousos, 2009; McEwen et al., 2016; Romero and Wingfield, 2016; Sapolsky, 1992a, 1994) (**TABLE 11.1**). In the case of cardiovascular disease, there are several documented examples of acute natural disasters, such as earthquakes, precipitating heart attacks. Sometimes events that may seem trivial to most people, such as the 1996 elimination of the Dutch national football (soccer) team from the European Championship, are associated with a statistically significant increase in death from cardiovascular incidents. However, it is much more common for stress to cause cumulative damage to cardiovascular health over years. For example, the death of a child is associated with increased incidence of myocardial infarction in the surviving parents beginning 6 years after the loss (Li et al., 2002). Furthermore, the myocardial infarction rate was found to be highest among parents whose children died unexpectedly (e.g., from SIDS).

Social status also influences the development of arteriosclerosis among cynomolgus monkeys (Kaplan and Manuck, 1999). Dominant male monkeys developed more significant arteriosclerosis than lower-ranked individuals when housed in an unstable social group. However, high social status had no effect on arteriosclerotic progression among male monkeys housed in a stable social group (Kaplan and Manuck, 1999). In contrast, low-ranked female monkeys displayed more arteriosclerosis than high-ranked females, regardless of social stability. These results emphasize the sex differences in perception of stress and in outcome of stress on disease progression.

Thus, sympathoadrenal activation, corticosteroid secretion, high pulse rate, and elevated blood pressure are useful for "explosive activities" such as pursuing prey or evading predators, but they are well-established contributors to the development of atherosclerotic plaques leading to heart disease, embolisms, and strokes when activation is abnormally prolonged or repeatedly elicited by daily activities such as paying bills or caring for an ailing relative.

Prolonged glucocorticoid secretion is detrimental to multiple physiological systems. With prolonged glucocorticoid secretion, myopathy (i.e., muscle loss) is inevitable, and in severe cases stress can even induce the irreversible loss of muscle cells in the heart. The stress-induced breakdown of glycogen and lipids to elevate blood glucose concentrations cannot continue indefinitely. Reproductive function is also inhibited by high glucocorticoid concentrations. This has obvious negative consequences for the reproductive success of animals in the wild that are confronted by demanding environmental conditions. An important consequence of stress for reproductive function in humans is that infertile couples often experience an escalating effect of stress on fertility that interferes with the infertility treatment (Agarwal and Haney, 1994; Greenfield, 1997). In other words, the psychological stress of

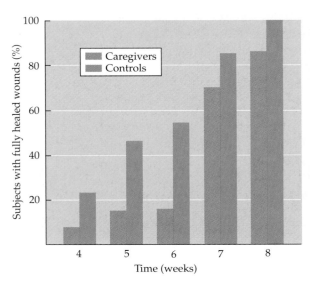

FIGURE 11.12　Wound healing is impaired in stressed caregivers. This graph depicts healing times for a standard-sized punch biopsy wound on the arm in two groups: postmenopausal women who served as caregivers for chronically ill spouses, and control women of the same age. Slower healing increases the risk of infection. After Kiecolt-Glaser et al., 1995.

experiencing infertility, in addition to the stress of the treatments, causes more stress and consequently reinforces the infertility. Prolonged inhibition of digestion during stress can also lead to ulceration and chronic irritable bowel syndrome. Indeed, appearance of gastric ulcers was one of Selye's early indices of chronic stress. Peptic ulcers can develop as a result of suppressed immune function that allows the proliferation of bacteria, especially *Helicobacter pylori*, in the stomach and digestive tract that can attack the lining of the stomach or duodenum. In general, chronic immunosuppression, as seen in AIDS patients, compromises long-term survival. Stress adds to AIDS-associated immunosuppression to reduce the chances of survival (Capitanio et al., 1998; Evans et al., 1997). Chronic stress also inhibits growth and repair processes. You might notice that your fingernails are more likely to be flimsy or brittle, or that your hair grows more slowly, during stressful periods in your life. Indeed, chronic stress delays cutaneous wound healing in humans and rodents (Gouin and Kiecolt-Glaser, 2011), an effect that is mediated by elevated glucocorticoid concentrations and their effects on immune function at the wound site (Detillion et al., 2004). For example, postmenopausal women who served as caregivers for chronically ill spouses displayed high cortisol values and slow wound healing from a biopsy wound on the arm as compared with age-matched control women (**FIGURE 11.12**). Caregivers had fewer lymphocytes in their blood and displayed higher concentrations of cytokines, mediators of the inflammation response, than did non-caregivers (Damjanovic et al., 2007). The stress of caregiving to spouses with Alzheimer's disease or the stress of caring for chronically ill children shortened telomeres (Damjanovic et al,. 2007). Telomeres are the caps on the ends of chromosomes. As cells divide over time, these telomeres shorten as part of the normal aging process. Other experiments have shown that the telomeres in blood cells of caregivers were shorter than those of the controls, and that the level of the telomerase repair enzyme among caregivers was also lower. Chronic stress in children, usually as a result of parental deprivation, abuse, or both, can inhibit GH and can result in a condition called psychosocial dwarfism, as we will see below.

Prolonged exposure to stress and glucocorticoids can also have profound effects on the brain and behavior. Studies on rats and mice have demonstrated that chronic stress alters the structure and function of the brain, especially in the hippocampus, amygdala, and prefrontal cortex. For instance, chronic stress or prolonged exposure to elevated corticosterone concentrations reduces neurogenesis (the birth of new neurons) in the hippocampus (Gould et al., 1990) and causes physical retraction of the dendrites of hippocampal and cortical neurons (Woolley et al., 1990a); however, the same treatment causes physical expansion of dendrites in the basolateral amygdala (Mitra et al., 2005). Chronic stress also increases inflammation in the brain that impairs memory; if the inflammation is reversed by drug treatment, then memory is unaffected by chronic stress (McKim et al., 2016). These changes in the brain following chronic stress are potential ways in which stress can lead to cognitive dysfunction and depression (Magariños et al., 1999; Malberg et al., 2000). These effects may be mediated by changes in brain-derived neurotrophic factor (BDNF), a growth factor that is reduced by stress and is important for promoting neurogenesis and dendritic branching (Malberg et al., 2000; Nestler et al., 2002). Importantly, antidepressant drugs can prevent the development of stress-induced depression, the reduction in BDNF levels, and this type of neural plasticity in the brain (Malberg et al., 2000; Santarelli et al., 2003). Also, drugs that block stress-induced neuroinflammation may also help prevent cognitive decline after chronic stress (McKim et al., 2016).

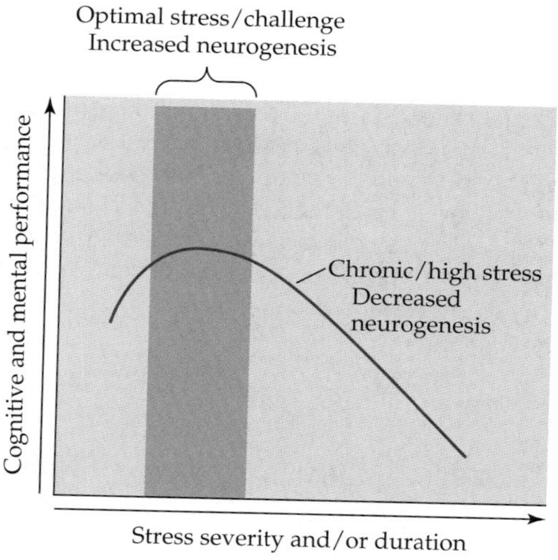

FIGURE 11.13 As with immune function, there are optimal levels of stressors to maintain neurogenesis and cognitive function. However, if stressors persist chronically, then neurogenesis is impaired and learning and memory performance are reduced.

In addition to increasing immune function, stress sometimes causes other positive changes. Acute stress can improve brain function to optimize attentional, behavioral, and cognitive functions. Thus, there appears to be an inverted U-shaped function associated with the severity or duration of an exposure to a stressor (**FIGURE 11.13**). Acute restraint of rats in their cages elevated corticosterone concentrations for a few hours but essentially doubled the proliferation of new neurons from neural stem cells in the hippocampus (Kirby et al., 2013). Acute stress also increased astrocytic *fibroblast growth factor 2* (*Fgf2*) gene expression. Rats tested 2 weeks, but not 2 days, after acute stress had enhanced memory coincident with the timing of enhanced activation of newborn neurons in the hippocampus (Kirby et al., 2013; Shiraz et al., 2015).

Because the hippocampus is one of the key sites of HPA axis negative feedback and is damaged by chronic stress, a vicious cycle can develop (Sapolsky et al., 1984). That is, prolonged elevated glucocorticoids cause hippocampal dysfunction and impair negative feedback, which in turn leads to ever-increasing glucocorticoid concentrations, and so on (Sapolsky et al., 1984). However, there are some nuances to this story in wild baboons. Dominant baboons typically display a much higher initial glucocorticoid response when captured, compared with subordinate conspecifics (Sapolsky, 1990). However, subordinate baboons display resistance to negative feedback, which results in a prolonged, and thus ultimately extended, cortisol response compared with that of the dominant animals (**FIGURE 11.14**).

It remains unspecified where the dividing line is between acute and chronic stressors, that is, the point at which stressors begin to impair, rather than improve,

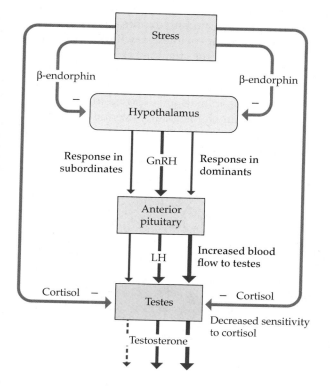

FIGURE 11.14 **Stress has different effects on dominant or subordinate baboons.** After a stressful experience, dominant animals display an elevated cortisol response, but because they possess an efficient HPA axis feedback system, the cortisol concentrations are returned to baseline faster than in subordinate animals. Because of blunted sensitivity of the anterior pituitary to CRH and related hormones among subordinate animals, a similar stressful stimulus results in an initial low cortisol response to stress, but also because of the poor HPA axis feedback regulation, subordinate individuals display long-term elevation of glucocorticoids, which may ultimately harm those individuals. The thickness of the green arrows corresponds to the intensity of the responses. After Sapolsky, 1990.

Acute
Chronic
Minutes to hours
Days to months
Months to years
• Moderate: enhancement
• Intense: suppression
• Traumatic: damage
• Adaptive plasticity
• Loss of resilience
• Decline of resilience with age
• Vulnerability to permanent damage

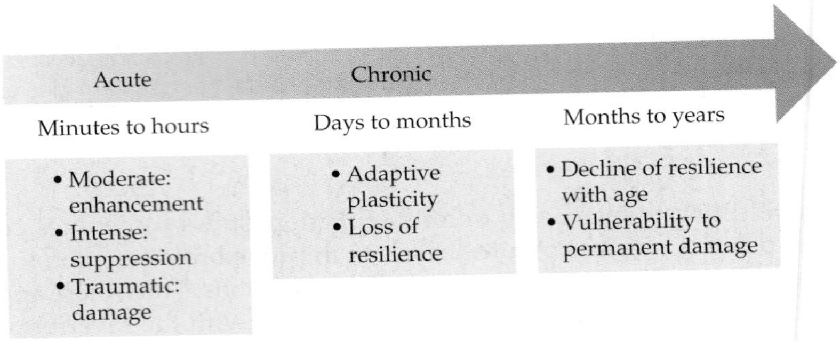

FIGURE 11.15 Acute versus chronic stressors Acute stressors have many beneficial effects, whereas chronic stressors typically produce detrimental effects. Thus far, only broad temporal parameters have been determined to predict when stressors begin to impair, rather than improve, physiology and behavior. Presumably, there are individual differences in this timing, as well as differences in the types of stressors, but additional research is necessary to understand this switch.

physiology and behavior (Bowers et al., 2008) (**FIGURE 11.15**). Of course, there will likely be individual differences in this point. The authors of many studies argue that the peak level of the glucocorticoid response is the key factor in stress responses. The cessation of glucocorticoid secretion is ultimately under negative feedback regulation. However, it appears that both the magnitude and duration of glucocorticoid release is important. Poorly regulated glucocorticoid negative feedback and the cumulative effects of sustained glucocorticoid secretion have been associated with many pathological states (**FIGURE 11.16**). In contrast, rapid glucocorticoid negative feedback of the HPA axis might be associated with improved stress-coping outcomes (Tasker and Herman, 2011).

The pathological long-term effects of chronic stress affect many hormone-behavior interactions. Reproductive function is impaired in chronically stressed individuals (Welsh et al., 1999). It is also known that only the alpha pair of each pack of African wild dogs breeds (see below). A series of studies was conducted to discover why social subordinates do not breed, even though they are reproductively mature (Sapolsky, 1993). It was hypothesized that subordinate wild dogs were reproductively suppressed by stress. These studies were conducted with the hope of reversing the recent population declines in this endangered species (Creel et al., 1996). By collecting feces from individual animals whose social status was known, the investigators were able to assay hormone concentrations (measured indirectly by assaying fecal metabolic breakdown products of the hormones of interest) without disturbing the animals (Monfort et al., 1998). In contrast to the investigators' expectations, these studies, as well as studies of African dwarf mongooses (*Helogale parvula*), indicated that the dominant animals had high glucocorticoid concentrations (Creel et al., 1996) (**FIGURE 11.17**). It is possible that the dominant animals are exposed to the chronic psychological stressor of potentially losing their status. In any event, these results contrasted with the findings of previous laboratory studies that had reported that subordinate rats and mice were more highly stressed than the dominant members

FIGURE 11.16 Glucocorticoid responses to stressors are altered in animals with disrupted negative feedback. In this model, you can see that despite a lower maximal response among disrupted animals, the amount of glucocorticoid (GC) they release over time is increased compared to the amount of GC released by animals with typical negative feedback processes. This response has been observed in both dominant and subordinate wild free-living olive baboons.

Glucocorticoid concentrations
Normal
Disrupted negative feedback
Stressor initiation
Baseline
Time

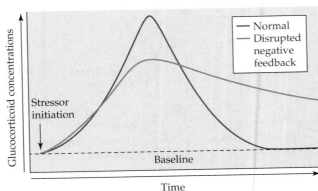

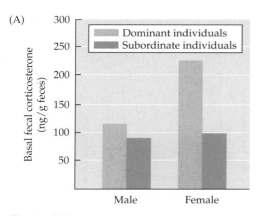

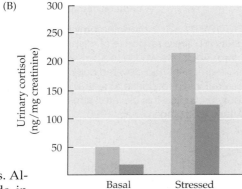

FIGURE 11.17 Corticosterone concentrations are elevated in dominant wild dogs and mongooses. In contrast to the findings in most laboratory animals, the alpha individuals (yellow bars) in groups of (A) free-living African wild dogs and (B) captive mongooses have higher corticosterone values than subordinate animals (green bars). In other words, the dominant individuals appear to be more stressed than subordinate individuals. After Creel et al., 1997.

of their social groups (Sapolsky, 1992b). As noted previously, if primates are representative, then perhaps social organization and stability should be considered when assessing the effects of social status on stress hormones (Sapolsky, 2005).

In an attempt to assess the relative effects of social status and allostatic load, that is, the wear and tear on the body, on free-ranging animals, it was determined that when allostatic load was elevated in dominants compared with subordinates, then the dominant individuals displayed elevated glucocorticoid concentrations (Goymann and Wingfield, 2004). When allostatic load was similar in dominants and subordinates, then glucocorticoid levels were also similar. However, when allostatic load was reduced in dominant group members relative to subordinates, then subordinates had the higher glucocorticoid concentrations (Goymann and Wingfield, 2004).

Factors That Affect Stress Responsiveness

Thus far, we have only considered the activational effects of stress hormones. Although rarely conceptualized as such in the scientific literature, glucocorticoids, in common with sex steroid hormones, can have both organizational and activational effects on brain and behavior. Thus, the effects of early stressors on brain function, hormone concentrations, and hormone receptors, as well as subsequent perception of and ability to cope with stressors, can be enduring and irreversible throughout life.

Perinatal Stress

The brains of stressed fetuses and infants are organized differently from the brains of individuals that do not experience stressors early in development, and they are differentially activated by glucocorticoids in adulthood. These effects of stress can have prolonged consequences throughout life.

PRENATAL STRESS Although we would all do well to try to limit the effects of chronic stress in our lives, sometimes they have already affected us before birth (Herrenkohl, 1986; Takahashi, 1998; Weinstock, 1997). A series of studies have examined the effects of prenatal stress on the physiology and behavior of rat pups. If pregnant dams are placed in clear plastic restraint devices under bright lights for 30–60 minutes each day during days 14–21 of their 21-day gestation, then they respond with increased activation of the HPA axis. Importantly, their offspring display permanent changes in their brain morphology, physiology, and behavior. Maternal stress alters blood testosterone concentrations in fetal male rats, shifting the peak to 2 days earlier than that in nonstressed males (Ward, 1984; Ward and Weisz, 1980). When tested as adults, sons of stressed mothers often failed to ejaculate in mating tests (Ward et al., 1994), even though their adult concentrations of testosterone and luteinizing hormone (LH) were normal (I. L. Ward et al., 1996). The shift in the timing of the testosterone peak blocked the development of the normal sexual dimorphism of the brain, affecting the sexually dimorphic nuclei of the medial preoptic area as well as the spinal nucleus of the bulbocavernosus and the dorsolateral nucleus of the spinal

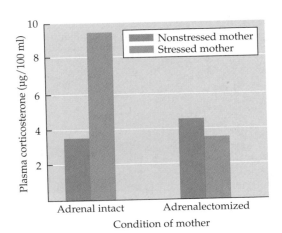

FIGURE 11.18 Adrenalectomy in the dam alters the stress response of offspring stressed in utero. Adult rats whose mothers were stressed while pregnant had elevated corticosterone concentrations in response to restraint. Adrenalectomy prevented this elevated stress response. After Barbazanges et al., 1996.

cord (Kerchner and Ward, 1992; Kerchner et al., 1995). The sex difference in the size of the rostral anterior commissure was also found to be altered by prenatal stress (Jones et al., 1997). Furthermore, when exposed to restraint stress as adults, both male and female rats whose mothers had experienced stress during gestation displayed an attenuated prolactin response (Kinsley et al., 1989), suggesting a permanent effect of prenatal stress on the HPA axis. Prenatally stressed female rats did not display any disturbances in normal estrous cycles, sexual behavior, pregnancy, parturition, pup survival, or maternal behavior when tested as adults (Beckhardt and Ward, 1983; but see Herrenkohl, 1986).

Recall from Chapter 3 that rat dams tend to spend more time licking the anogenital regions of male pups as compared with female pups (Michel and Moore, 1995) and that this sex difference in eliciting maternal attention is mediated by testosterone. If dams are stressed while pregnant, then they show no preference in grooming male versus female offspring (Power and Moore, 1986). Presumably, the prenatal stress affects testosterone secretion such that the male and female offspring do not vary in the critical testosterone-dependent variable that dams normally use to discriminate male from female pups.

Prenatal stress impairs subsequent negative feedback within the HPA axis in adult rats, which often results in elevated basal corticosterone blood concentrations (Henry et al., 1994). Subjecting pregnant rat dams to either stress or exogenous glucocorticoid administration decreases hippocampal GRs in their offspring; this decrease has been hypothesized to account for the impaired negative feedback of the HPA axis in adulthood (Barbazanges et al., 1996). Damage to the hippocampal cells mediating negative feedback results in elevated glucocorticoid levels. Again, the process of prenatal stress is mediated by the HPA axis. If a pregnant female is adrenalectomized prior to stress or corticosterone treatment, the negative feedback mechanisms are not impaired in her adult offspring (Barbazanges et al., 1996) (**FIGURE 11.18**). The offspring of stressed rat dams are more likely to be anxious and to self-administer drugs such as cocaine and amphetamines as adults than peers with nonstressed mothers (Deminiere et al., 1992; Diaz et al., 1995). These results may have important implications for drug abuse in children of stressed parents.

Prenatally stressed human infants have reduced birth weights, experience developmental delays, and also display attentional deficits, hyperanxiety, and impaired social behaviors, and they may have impaired strategies for coping with stressful conditions as adults (Weinstock, 1997). Some studies suggest that prenatal stress may increase the incidence of schizophrenia in adults. For example, the Psychiatric Case Register in the Netherlands provides evidence for an increased incidence of schizophrenia in individuals who were in utero during the 1940 invasion of the Netherlands by the German army (van Os and Selten, 1998). Furthermore, there was a twofold increased risk for schizophrenia among individuals conceived in the western cities of the Netherlands during the height of the Dutch Hunger Winter (1944/1945) (Susser et al., 1996). It also is possible that the same kind of dysregulation of the HPA axis observed in rats exposed to prenatal stress serves as a precursor to the HPA disinhibition observed in many instances of human depression (Weinstock, 1997). As a prenatal stressor, exposure of humans to glucocorticoids in utero has a number of negative consequences, including low birth weight, which in turn is associated with adult cardiovascular and metabolic disorders such as hypertension, insulin resistance, hyperlipidemia, and ischemic heart and brain disease (Nyirenda and Seckl, 1998). There also is limited evidence that human babies exposed to exogenous corticosteroids late in gestation show behavioral problems in childhood and suffer from more cardiovascular disease than unexposed children (Doyle et al., 2000).

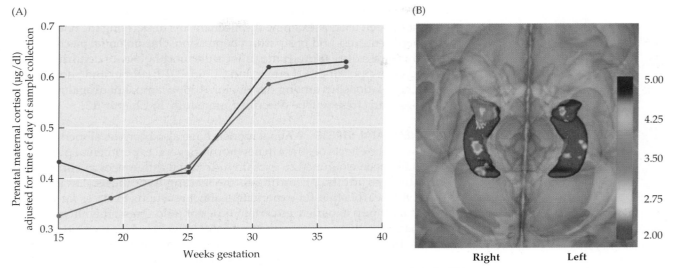

FIGURE 11.19 Elevated cortisol values during early pregnancy were associated with increased right amygdalar development and poor emotional development in girls, but not boys, before puberty. Cortisol values were elevated at 15 weeks of gestation (closed triangles) in some mothers. These high values were correlated with larger right amygdala size (A). The brain scan shows increased amygdalar, but not hippocampal, volumes of girls, indicated by cooler (green) colors. After Sandman et al., 2016.

There is some evidence that stress can have transgenerational effects. Mothers who suffered from PTSD after the September 11 attacks on New York displayed reduced salivary cortisol relative to mothers who were not diagnosed with PTSD. Remarkably, the 1-year-old babies of mothers diagnosed with PTSD also displayed lower salivary cortisol, potentially increasing the babies' risk for developing PTSD themselves (Yehuda et al., 2005).

Because it would be unethical to manipulate stress levels in women in order to observe the effects on their babies, human studies of prenatal stress are, of course, correlational. For example, one recent study correlated maternal cortisol concentrations during early pregnancy and emotional development in human development (Buss et al., 2012; Sandman et al., 2016). Elevated cortisol values during early gestation were associated with increased right amygdala volumes in girls, but not in boys, between the ages of 6 and 9 (**FIGURE 11.19**). The distinctly enlarged right amygdala in girls was correlated with increased affective problems in girls compared with boys. Unlike the rodent models, there was no correlation between maternal cortisol and hippocampal volumes (Sandman et al., 2016).

Long-term studies of monkeys have been used to investigate the long-term consequences of prenatal stress for the behavior and reproductive success of adult primates. The effects of prenatal stress on the human HPA axis have been carefully modeled in rhesus monkeys (Clarke et al., 1994). To induce stress experimentally, pregnant rhesus monkeys were exposed to random loud noises throughout mid to late pregnancy. Their offspring displayed low birth weights, impaired neuromotor development, attention deficits (Schneider, 1992b; Schneider and Coe, 1993), and impaired cognitive function (Schneider, 1992a) compared with their nonstressed peers. Additionally, enhanced stress responsiveness, higher frequencies of abnormal coping behaviors, and impaired social behaviors were observed in the offspring of female rhesus monkeys that were chronically stressed during pregnancy (Clarke and Schneider, 1993; Clarke et al., 1994).

Exposure to stress during pregnancy also negatively affects mothers (Galea et al., 2014; Workman et al., 2012. A strong predictor for postpartum depression (see Chap-

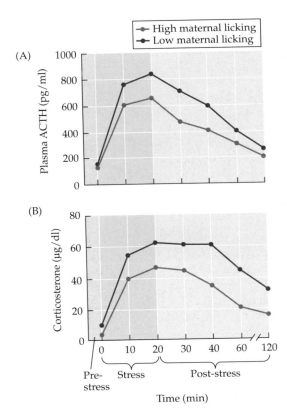

FIGURE 11.20 Stress responses are reduced in rats that received more maternal attention as pups. ACTH (A) and corticosterone (B) concentrations were measured before, during, and after a 20-minute restraint stress (green shaded area). The concentrations were lower in rats that had received a large amount of maternal licking as pups (red circles) than in rats that had received a small amount (green circles). After Liu et al., 1997.

ter 13) is exposure to chronic stress during pregnancy. Rodent models have been used to examine the mechanisms underlying the relationship between stress and postpartum depression. One potential mechanism is that stress during pregnancy affects the morphology of dendritic spines in the hippocampus (Leuner and Gould, 2010; Leuner and Shors, 2013). The relationship among depression, hippocampal neuronal morphology, and stress will be described more fully in Chapter 13.

NEONATAL STRESS   Animal models have also been developed to determine the effects of stress in newborns. Several experimental paradigms have been examined to explain individual differences in coping with stress as adults. According to the leading hypothesis (Levine et al., 1967), early stressful experiences affect reactions to stress later in life. If a rat pup experiences certain types of mild stress, then it appears to be better able to cope with stress later in life. Human handling of pups or brief separation of pups from their mother evokes stress responses in the pups. However, upon the return of the pups to their mother, the rat dam spends extra time licking them. This gentle stimulation appears to reverse the negative effects of the stress on the pups and is responsible for the so-called stress immunization effect that allows the pups to cope with stress better as adults (Liu et al., 1997) (**FIGURE 11.20**). One way this is hypothesized to occur is by changing the pups' densities of hippocampal GRs, which are important in the negative feedback regulatory mechanisms of the HPA axis in adulthood (Liu et al., 1997), as we saw above.

A commonly used experimental paradigm for assessing separation stress involves the separation of infants from their mothers at different ages and for differing periods of time (Levine et al., 1991). Typically, rat pups are isolated in novel test arenas and receive a saline injection; this combined treatment of isolation plus injection is considered to be a mild stressor (e.g., Suchecki et al., 1993). If 6-, 9-, or 12-day-old rat pups are isolated from their mother for 24 hours, their baseline ACTH concentrations are elevated. The elevated ACTH concentrations are significantly higher in stressed than in nonisolated animals, and the magnitude of the increase becomes higher as the pups age (Suchecki et al., 1993). Corticosterone concentrations show a similar effect, and the effect of mild stress on corticosterone concentrations persists for at least 4 days (Rosenfeld et al., 1992). Again, postnatal exposure to mild stressors blunts adult stress responsiveness (Levine et al., 1967; Sapolsky and Meaney, 1986). In contrast, elevated stress responses are observed throughout life in rats that were exposed to moderate or severe stressors as pups (Rots et al., 1996). For example, those severely stressed as pups may have long-term decreases in food intake and body mass in response to endogenous pro-inflammatory cytokines such as interleukin-1β (Kent et al., 1997).

Maternal tactile and feeding cues are sufficient to suppress the elevated concentrations of ACTH and corticosterone resulting from 24 hours of maternal deprivation (van Oers et al., 1998). Interaction with an anesthetized lactating female rat is sufficient to block the elevated corticosterone stress response associated with isolation (Stanton and Levine, 1990). Thus, it appears that the contact comfort of the mother is sufficient to prevent the stress response to isolation, although her grooming and licking behaviors are also important (Liu et al., 1997). Impairment of HPA function is more marked in female than in male rats exposed to isolation stress (McCormick et al., 1995).

While brief maternal separation (e.g., 15 minutes, which is consistent with the amount of time the mother forages in the wild) appears to constrain stress responsiveness in adulthood, and 24 hours of maternal separation causes elevated respon-

FIGURE 11.21 **Epigenetic influences of maternal behavior on offspring** The rat maternal style that includes high rates of licking and grooming as well as arched-back nursing causes changes in two molecular pathways of the pups. First, it increases serotonergic tone in the hippocampus, which increases expression of a transcription factor (NGF1-A). Second, it causes demethylation of the first exon of the glucocorticoid receptor (GR) gene, as well as acetylation of histones adjoining the GR gene in the hippocampus. The net result of these actions is a GR gene that is more readily accepting of the NGF1-A transcription factor, which leads to more GRs in the hippocampus of the offspring as adults and the adoption by the females of their mother's maternal style.

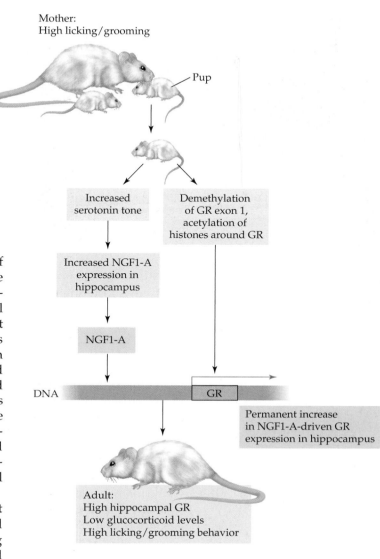

siveness to stress in adulthood, as much as 3 hours of maternal separation has physiological effects that are not obvious from simply measuring circulating corticosterone values (Mirescu et al., 2004). Despite normal basal and post-stress corticosterone concentrations, rat pups that are separated from their mothers for 3 hours show impaired neurogenesis and cell proliferation in the dentate gyrus as adults. If the rats that experienced 3 hours of maternal separation are adrenalectomized as adults, then the suppression of cell proliferation is reversed (Mirescu et al., 2004). These results indicate that prolonged, but not brief, periods of maternal separation cause enduring inhibition of neurogenesis and hippocampal plasticity as adults, caused not by elevated glucocorticoids but by hypersensitivity to normal corticosterone concentrations (Mirescu et al., 2004).

How might early stressors organize the brain so that the activational effects of corticosterone in adulthood are less effective? Recall from Chapter 7 that offspring of mothers that display high levels of pup licking and grooming later display attenuated HPA axis responses to stress and also display enhanced cognitive ability (Caldji et al., 1998; Francis et al., 1999; Liu et al., 1997, 2000). The mechanisms underlying this brain organization have been elucidated in a series of elegant studies during the past few years by Michael Meaney and his colleagues.

High levels of pup licking, grooming, and arched-back nursing organize the brain of the recipient offspring so that they are resistant to stressors as adults, and female pups adopt the type of maternal behavior that they received as infants (Weaver et al., 2004). The immediate consequences of high levels of these maternal behaviors is an increase in the GR gene expression in the hippocampus, which seems to be critical for the reduced stress effects observed later in adulthood (McCormick et al., 2000). But how can these transient effects on GR gene transcription have permanent organizational effects on brain and behavior? The answer appears to involve two epigenetic processes that affect gene expression: DNA methylation and histone modification (**FIGURE 11.21**).

DNA methylation is a process of long-term gene silencing that involves attaching a methyl group to cytosines in the promoter region of a gene (Egger et al., 2004). Thus, DNA demethylation often results in significant increases in gene expression (Egger et al., 2004). The DNA of animals is wrapped around proteins

FIGURE 11.22 Infant rhesus monkeys cling to a cloth "mother" for contact comfort when stressed by a novel toy. These infants were reared with two surrogate mothers: a wire mother that provided nutrition, and a cloth-covered wire mother that provided no nutrition but had a soft surface. From Harlow, 1959.

called histones; DNA plus the histones comprise the chromatin. Histone proteins can wrap DNA tightly, preventing access to promoter regions by transcription factors; alternatively, histone proteins can relax to allow easy access to these gene regions. Specific types of maternal care evoke changes in DNA methylation and chromatin structure that result in relaxed histone proteins and therefore increased GR gene expression (Griffiths and Hunter, 2014; Weaver et al., 2004). These changes emerged in early life, they could be reversed by cross fostering to mothers that displayed low levels of licking/grooming and arched-backed nursing, and they persisted into adulthood. Thus, these epigenetic influences of maternal care persist into adulthood and can be passed on to subsequent generations.

Could such organizational effects of glucocorticoids induced by style of maternal care apply to humans? The studies on isolation-induced stress in rodent pups are reminiscent of the famous biopsychological studies conducted on rhesus monkeys by Harry Harlow and colleagues, in which the factors that represent "motherness" were investigated. In these studies, infants were separated from their mothers immediately following birth. In one series of studies, infants were provided with two surrogate mothers. One surrogate, made of a wire frame, had a nipple protruding from its midsection and gave milk to the infant; the other surrogate mother provided no nutrition, but her wire frame was covered with a soft material to which the infant could cling to derive contact comfort (**FIGURE 11.22**). When stressed by an intruder, the infant ran to the so-called cloth mother (Harlow and Harlow, 1965; Harlow et al., 1971). Neither of these surrogate mothers provided any social instructions, however. When these isolated infants grew up, they were socially inept and generally fearful (Harlow et al., 1971). Only some reversal of this social impairment was possible (Harlow et al., 1971). Some of the best improvements in social behavior in these formerly isolated monkeys were obtained by pairing them with pet dogs (Mason and Capitanio, 1988; Mason and Kenney, 1974). These results suggest that contact with a mother is a powerful HPA axis buffer among nonhuman primate infants and juveniles (Levine and Wiener, 1988).

Social Influences

In common with isolated rodent pups and other animals, human children raised in institutions that provide little social contact develop increased stress responsiveness.

DAY CARE Currently, there is little known about early environmental influences on human brain development. Social and political interests have fueled research over the past several decades into the effects of day care on the physiological and behavioral responses of children; of particular interest are the effects of nonmaternal care on HPA axis activity and emotional development. Of course, because of the nature of these studies, it is not possible to establish a causal relationship between altered cortisol concentrations and behavior. However, a pattern exists in which cortisol concentrations rise from morning to afternoon among children in group day care as compared with children who stay at home; elevated cortisol concentrations are greater in younger children and are often associated with impaired self-control and attention (Dettling et al., 1999). Converging evidence from asthmatic children who are on corticosteroid-based therapy also suggests that elevated cortisol is related to attentional and behavioral deficits (Gunnar, 1998). Furthermore, the nature of the parent-child bond can affect children's corticosteroid responses to potentially fearful stimuli. For example, toddlers with insecure attachments to their parents are more likely to exhibit elevated cortisol than securely attached children when exposed to novel stimuli (Gunnar, 1998). Taken together, these data suggest that parent or stable caregiver interaction is an important determinant of infant reactions to stressors; however, the long-term consequences of early HPA axis activation in humans is not known.

ORPHANS The effects of extreme early adversity have been studied among Romanian orphans (Gunnar et al., 2001; Hoksbergen et al., 2003). War, political turmoil, and economic distress led to stark, minimally sustaining conditions in orphanages in Romania during the end of the twentieth century. As a result, the children often endured malnutrition, sensory deprivation, poor hygiene, exposure to disease, and low levels of social interaction. The orphans were also often characterized as exhibiting mild cognitive deficits, impulsivity, attentional deficits, and social deficits. There is evidence of disrupted circadian rhythms among toddlers in Romanian orphanages; furthermore, cortisol concentration at noon was positively correlated with cognitive deficits (Carlson and Earls, 1997). Several studies suggest that children adopted from Romanian orphanages before reaching the age of 6 months tended to exhibit typical cognitive and social development. In contrast, outcome was more variable among children who spent more than 6 months in these orphanages. Furthermore, the likelihood of long-term behavioral problems and endocrine dysregulation tended to increase with the length of the institutional experience. The average daily cortisol concentrations were higher among Romanian children adopted into Canadian families after 8 months of age than among Romanian infants adopted soon after birth or infants born in Canada (Gunnar et al., 2001) (**FIGURE 11.23**). Furthermore, the longer the Romanian children were under institutional care, the higher their evening cortisol concentrations, and these effects were still

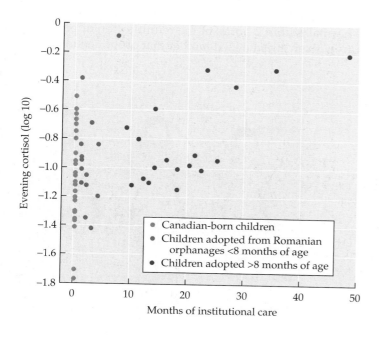

FIGURE 11.23 Cortisol concentrations increase as a function of time in an orphanage. Log scale values of cortisol are depicted for Canadian-born children and for children adopted by Canadian parents from Romanian orphanages, either prior to 8 months of age or after 8 months of age. Hormone concentrations were obtained at 6–12 years of age. Children who spent any time in the Romanian orphanages had higher cortisol levels than Canadian-born children, and the longer the children remained institutionalized, the higher their cortisol concentrations were 6 or more years later. After Gunnar et al., 2001.

present after 6.5 years with their adoptive families. There were no significant differences between the Canadian-born infants and the Romanian children adopted within 8 months of birth. Thus, prolonged orphanage experience may lead to dysregulation of the HPA axis. Among Romanian children adopted by Dutch families, nearly 20% were diagnosed with PTSD (Hoksbergen et al., 2003). A functional magnetic resonance imaging (fMRI) study indicated dysfunction in several brain areas among Romanian orphans (Chugani et al., 2001).

PSYCHOSOCIAL DWARFISM   Institutional experience clearly affected the endocrine function of children from Romanian orphanages; there are well-documented cases of psychosocial dwarfism and precocial puberty among orphanage-reared children (reviewed in Gunnar et al., 2001; Johnson et al., 1992).

Psychosocial dwarfism is a relatively rare syndrome found among human infants who are reared in situations in which they experience little or no physical contact during development, as in orphanages where the staff does not regularly interact with the children (Widdowson, 1951). This syndrome is characterized by lack of growth and development despite adequate nutrition, disruption of normal sleep cycles, a selective disruption of normal patterns of GH secretion, and an absence of tissue responsiveness to exogenous GH (Schanberg and Field, 1987). This last feature of the syndrome distinguishes psychosocial dwarfism from hypopituitary dwarfism, in which treatment with GH restores normal growth. Patients with psychosocial dwarfism, however, usually recover after placement in a hospital or home environment where more social and physical stimulation is available (**FIGURE 11.24**). Like rhesus monkey infants, young humans, too, require tactile stimulation provided by physical contact with their mother (or some other adult) for normal somatic growth and development (reviewed in Romeo and McEwen, 2006).

What are the physiological factors that mediate these stimulatory effects of tactile contact in facilitating growth and development? A series of beautifully constructed studies have addressed this question in rats. When maternal tactile stimulation of rat pups is restricted, either by isolating or anesthetizing the rat dam, the pups' growth is reduced, and at least three biochemical changes occur (Schanberg and Kuhn, 1985). First, levels of the enzyme ornithine decarboxylase (ODC) are sharply reduced immediately after separation from the mother in all tissues examined, including brain, liver, heart, kidney, and spleen (Schanberg and Field, 1987). ODC is the first enzyme required in the synthesis of polyamides, which are involved in the regulation of protein synthesis, and hence in tissue growth and development. ODC concentrations return to normal within 2 hours of the reunification of pups and dam. Placement of the pups with an anesthetized mother that continued to lactate,

psychosocial dwarfism   A grouping of disorders of retarded growth caused by neglect and abuse; this syndrome is also termed failure to thrive.

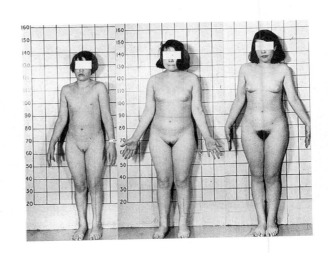

FIGURE 11.24 Psychosocial dwarfism is a rare occurrence seen most frequently in severe cases of child abuse and is usually reversible after termination of the stressors. This girl was drinking from puddles in the street and eating from garbage cans before admission to the hospital at age 15.3 years (left panel). At admission, her height was in the normal range for 9-year-old children, and she displayed abnormal GH release. Both LH and FSH were undetectable. After 1 month in the hospital, she grew 2.5 cm and began to undergo puberty. At age 16 (center panel), she was living in foster care and displaying significant GH release. Growth continued, and at 16.9 years (right panel) she had grown 27.5 cm. Courtesy of Dr. Claude Migeon.

TABLE 11.2 *Effect of stroking on ODC activity and serum GH concentrations in maternally deprived rat pups*

	ODC serum concentration (% control ± SEM)			Serum GH concentration (% control ± SEM)
	Brain	Heart	Liver	
Control	100 ± 13	100 ± 6	100 ± 13	100 ± 20
Deprived[a]	68 ± 8	36 ± 7	32 ± 6	25 ± 7
Deprived and stroked	134 ± 15	93 ± 15	199 ± 41	82 ± 17

Source: From Schanberg and Kuhn, 1985.
[a]$p < 0.05$ or better compared to controls for all values.

provide warmth, and supply all noninteractive maternal cues did not prevent the rapid decline in ODC concentrations in the pups.

Clearly, something that the mother rat does stimulates ODC activity. As previously noted, mother rats retrieve their pups and lick them. When isolated pups were stroked with a damp paintbrush in a way that roughly approximated the tongue movements of the dam, the reduction in ODC concentrations was prevented (**TABLE 11.2**). Other forms of sensory stimulation, such as tail pinching, were ineffective in preventing the decline in ODC concentrations in isolated pups.

The decrease in ODC concentrations in many different body sites suggests that either a general metabolic change or an endocrine signal mediates the effects of tactile stimulation. The second and third biochemical changes observed were that blood plasma concentrations of GH, but not of prolactin or thyroid-stimulating hormone, decreased in pups after maternal separation, whereas blood concentrations of corticosterone increased (Schanberg and Kuhn, 1985). GH regulates ODC activity in the brain and other tissues. Stroking with a wet paintbrush also normalized GH concentrations in isolated pups. In an attempt to counteract the diminished concentrations of ODC after separation, isolated and unstroked pups were injected with GH, but it was discovered that the tissues of these pups were unresponsive to the hormone. Stroking with a paintbrush maintained tissue responsiveness to GH.

After GH is secreted from the anterior pituitary gland, it binds, along with several types of somatomedins, to receptors on the surfaces of cells. Cells that bind GH are stimulated to grow and divide. The physiological mechanisms by which tactile stimuli increase GH secretion from the anterior pituitary, and how they induce tissue sensitivity to GH, are not yet known. But research into this fascinating area should provide more answers about how maternal behavior influences hormone concentrations, growth, and development in the offspring of rats and humans. This research has several practical applications; one important outcome has been the practice of stimulating growth and development in premature infants by increasing handling in perinatal intensive care nurseries (Schanberg and Field, 1987). A low-tech improvement in premature infants' health and the consequent shorter hospital stays are certainly impressive outcomes of these interesting studies in rats.

Glucocorticoids might also be involved in psychosocial dwarfism; however, cortisol concentrations are usually normal or in the low normal range in affected children. As mentioned above, corticosterone concentrations in young rats rise dramatically after maternal separation. In human children, only a doubling of glucocorticoid concentrations is sufficient to arrest growth (Sapolsky, 1994). Glucocorticoids can suppress growth by suppressing GH, inhibiting GH receptor sensitivity, and decreasing protein production and DNA synthesis. A related syndrome is hyperphagic short stature (HSS), which also presents as a failure of growth but is seen in association with hyperphagia without an obvious underlying etiology. It is mostly seen in the context of a stressful environment (Kumaran and Kershaw, 2014). HSS has been associated with emotional and other forms of abuse. Children with HSS eat

TABLE 11.3 *Effects of external events on growth in a child with psychosocial dwarfism*

Event	Plasma GH concentration (ng/ml)	Growth (cm/20 days)	Food intake (g/day)
Hospital admission	5.9	0.5	1663
100 days post-admission	13.0	1.7	1514
Favorite nurse on vacation	6.9	0.6	1504
Favorite nurse returns	15.0	1.5	1521

Source: From Saenger et al., 1977.

excessively and may gorge on food until they vomit. Most show other behavioral problems beyond their relationships with food. The children are typically more than two standard errors below typical heights, and although they display low GH and thyroid hormone concentrations, their cortisol values are typically normal. Whatever is actually suppressing the growth of afflicted children, either with psychosocial dwarfism or HSS, the good news is that removing them from the stress-inducing environment allows a reversal of endocrine markers of an underactive pituitary gland and significant catch-up growth. In **TABLE 11.3**, the effects of emotional factors on growth are obvious in a single boy suffering from psychosocial dwarfism.

Stress Effects on Reproductive Function

Every individual has limited energy resources, which must support maintenance of the body as well as reproduction. Other energetically expensive activities, including immune function and growth, must also be partitioned out of the total energy budget. Consequently, from an evolutionary perspective, there is a trade-off among competing energetic requirements, so growth or immune function may be compromised to support reproduction when energy is somewhat limited (Ots and Horak, 1996). Alternatively, reproduction or immune function (or both, depending on the extent of the limitation) may be compromised when energy availability is significantly reduced.

Reproductive suppression in response to stress occurs on several physiological and behavioral levels and can have potentially severe effects on both humans and nonhuman animals (Welsh et al., 1999). Stress is an important contributory factor in human sexual dysfunction and infertility. Stress-induced reproductive impairments may also have a marked economic impact in domestic animals (Moberg, 1991); stress can reduce milk production in cows and egg production in chickens (Welsh et al., 1999). In sum, the scientific study of the effects of stress on reproductive function has important clinical and practical applications.

Males

A variety of stressors have been reported to suppress male reproductive function. Stress inhibits testosterone production, and low testosterone concentrations reduce both sexual motivation and performance (see Chapter 5). The release of CRH and endogenous opioids can directly suppress the release of GnRH (Hulse and Coleman, 1983; Jacobs and Lightman, 1980; Rasmussen et al., 1983; Rivier et al., 1986). CRH-containing neurons in the paraventricular nucleus of the hypothalamus have been classified into two types: (1) vasopressin-positive and (2) vasopressin-negative neurons. Stress causes certain neurotransmitters to trigger the release of CRH from both types of neurons, and of vasopressin from the vasopressin-positive neurons. CRH travels to the anterior pituitary, where it binds to specific G protein-associated receptors in the ACTH-releasing cells. Activation of these CRH receptors stimulates the protein kinase A pathway, which leads to changes in gene transcription or other cellular functions. CRH and its receptors have also been identified in the testes and ovaries, suggesting that this releasing hormone may also directly inhibit steroid production (Welsh et al., 1999). In the brain, vasopressin binds to its receptor (V1a), which activates the protein kinase C pathway.

Both CRH and vasopressin can stimulate expression of the genes for proopiomelanocortin (POMC) in the anterior pituitary. Recall from Chapter 2 that POMC can be processed by various enzymes to yield several peptides, including ACTH and β-endorphin. There is some evidence that different environmental stressors determine which enzymes are produced, and thus which peptides are cleaved from the POMC precursor molecule (DeWied, 1997). POMC-derived peptides may feed back to inhibit GnRH secretion (Welsh et al., 1999). Indeed, both endogenous and exogenous opioids inhibit secretion of GnRH and LH (Cameron, 1997; DeWied, 1997; Genazzani and Petraglia, 1989; Rivier and Rivest, 1991) (**FIGURE 11.25**). For example, both sexual motivation and performance are impaired in male heroin addicts. More than half of the female heroin addicts interviewed in one study experienced menstrual abnormalities while taking heroin or methadone (Santen et al., 1975; Smith et al., 1982). Detailed endocrine studies revealed impaired gonadotropin secretion in most of these cases (Santen et al., 1975). Naloxone, an opioid antagonist, reverses reproductive suppression by opioids in humans and nonhuman animals (Genazzani and Petraglia, 1989; Gilbeau and Smith, 1985).

ACTH stimulates the production and secretion of glucocorticoids from the zona fasciculata and zona reticularis of the adrenal cortex. Glucocorticoids can inhibit reproduction in several ways. First, glucocorticoids at high concentrations can suppress GnRH and LH secretion (Welsh et al., 1999). Glucocorticoids have also been reported to inhibit the formation of proteins necessary for the production of hormone receptors, steroidogenic enzymes, and several intracellular signaling molecules (Rivier and Rivest, 1991). Cortisol inhibits testosterone secretion in men (Cummings et al., 1983) by acting on testicular LH receptors (Bambino and Hseuh, 1981). Glucocorticoids also suppress spermatogenesis more directly. The testosterone-producing Leydig cells have glucocorticoid receptors that appear to be involved in the normal process of cell growth, metabolism, and energy use. However, when glucocorticoid concentrations are elevated for long periods of time, especially in subordinate animals, an enzyme that normally neutralizes glucocorticoids at basal concentrations is overwhelmed, and testosterone production is curtailed (Ge et al., 1997). The resulting low testosterone concentrations may fail to support spermatogenesis such that sperm counts fall and stressed individuals become infertile (Ge et al., 1997). In contrast, when dominant rats are housed under stressful conditions, their testosterone concentrations increase; it appears that dominant rats have higher levels of the enzyme that counteracts elevated glucocorticoid concentrations to ensure fertility (Monder et al., 1994). Thus, social status appears to affect testicular enzymes that, in turn, mediate androgen production and fertility (**FIGURE 11.26**).

A moderate amount of activity or exercise actually raises testosterone concentrations (Elias, 1981; Grandi and Celani, 1990) (**FIGURE 11.27**). Indeed, mild exercise increases DHT in the hippocampus and may promote neurogenesis, counteracting the effects of stress on this process (Okamoto et al., 2012). However, as one of our

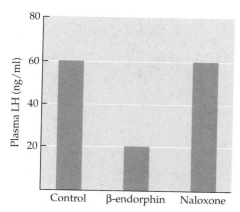

FIGURE 11.25 Opioids suppress gonadotropin production. Plasma LH concentrations are reduced after endorphin treatment; the reduction in LH caused by endorphin is reversed by treatment with the opioid antagonist naloxone. After Kalra et al., 1990.

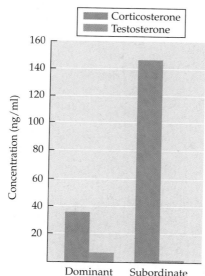

FIGURE 11.26 Dominant male rats have lower corticosterone and higher testosterone concentrations when stressed than subordinate rats. For this experiment, rats were housed in a special seminatural apparatus that allowed investigators to see their social interactions. After Blanchard et al., 1995.

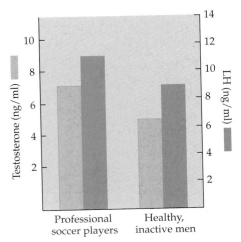

FIGURE 11.27 Exercise elevates testos-terone in men. Professional soccer players display significantly higher testosterone and LH concentrations than healthy but inactive men. However, it remains to be determined whether this statistically significant elevation in hormone concentration is behaviorally significant; that is, do increased testosterone values of 1–2 ng/ml in men make a difference in the number of their aggressive encounters, mating partners, or babies sired? After Grandi and Celani, 1990.

grandmothers used to say, "too much of a good thing is often a bad thing." Excessive exercise can be interpreted by the body as stress; strenuous exercise, such as running a marathon, causes sustained glucocorticoid secretion and leads to low testosterone concentrations in men (Dessypris et al., 1976; Grandi and Celani, 1990; Luger et al., 1987; MacConnie et al., 1986) (**FIGURE 11.28**).

As noted earlier in the chapter, prolactin is released during stress. Elevated blood prolactin concentrations can inhibit male reproductive function in a variety of ways, including enhancement of the sensitivity of the negative feedback mechanisms to testosterone (Bartke et al., 1977a,b; McNeilly et al., 1983). Treatment of hyperprolactinemia in men improves their potency in advance of any enhancement of blood testosterone concentrations (Buvat et al., 1985). The net result of all of these interactions is straightforward: chronic stress inhibits circulating testosterone concentrations. The decrease in testosterone suppresses both sexual motivation and performance and also impairs fertility.

The long-term secretion of epinephrine also interferes with reproductive function. Because sexual behavior can proceed with very low concentrations of testosterone in experienced human males, the most common effects of stress on human copulation typically involve epinephrine and sympathetic signals. Both the sympathetic and parasympathetic nervous systems must act together "in opposition" to generate a penile erection. In order for an erection to be initiated, the parasympathetic nervous system must be activated (Meisel and Sachs, 1994). In some species, such as rats and dogs, activation of the parasympathetic nervous system causes a specific muscle to contract, which pulls up the penile bone (os penis) during sexual excitement. In other species, such as humans, that have hemodynamic penile erections, activation of the parasympathetic nervous system increases blood flow into the penis and blocks blood from draining out via the veins. As the penis fills with blood, it stiffens to permit intravaginal insertion. As copulation proceeds, the rest of the body maintains high sympathetic tone; that is, the sympathetic nervous system increases heart rate, blood pressure, and breathing rate and moves blood

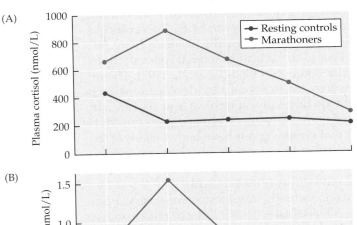

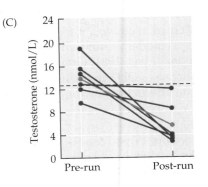

FIGURE 11.28 Prolonged exercise changes hormone concentrations. Male marathon runners have elevated plasma cortisol (A) and epinephrine (B), but their testosterone levels (C) are decreased by half. In (C) the results for individual runners are shown in green; the brown plot shows the mean.

from the periphery to the central trunk. The autonomic input to the genitalia retains its parasympathetic tone until sufficient stimulation occurs, then parasympathetic input suddenly terminates. Simultaneously, the sympathetic inputs to the penis are activated, and ejaculation occurs (Meisel and Sachs, 1994).

Problems with impotence and premature ejaculation are very common during times of stress. During stress, it becomes increasingly difficult to establish parasympathetic activity in the penis because of the stress-induced high sympathetic output (Rous, 1996). In humans, this can result in problems with achieving or maintaining penile erection; that is, stress can cause erectile dysfunction (impotence) (Morokoff et al., 1987; Smith, 1988). If the sympathetic input to the penis is activated too fast, as is also likely during stress, then premature ejaculation often results (Smith, 1988). Premature ejaculation would severely affect the reproductive fitness of males of species in which females require sufficient sexual stimulation to induce ovulation or functional corpora luteal formation (see Chapter 6). The consequences of premature ejaculation for human reproductive fitness have not been evaluated, but premature ejaculation can interfere with sexual relations and represents one of the most common complaints heard by sex therapists. One way for a male to postpone ejaculation is to take a deep breath. Inflating the lungs triggers a salvo of parasympathetic signals that delays the switch from parasympathetic to sympathetic input to the penis (Rous, 1996).

Females

As we learned in Chapter 6, successful ovulation and the onset of mating behavior in females typically depend on the precise timing of neuroendocrine events. Stress, however, often disrupts this timing (reviewed in Chrousos et al., 1998b). Stress can interrupt estrous cycles in laboratory animals, domesticated animals, and zoo animals; in women it may result in cessation of menstrual cycles (i.e., amenorrhea) (Welsh et al., 1999; Xiao and Ferin, 1997). Women with functional hypothalamic amenorrhea (no menstrual cycles and no pulsatile release of GnRH from the hypothalamus), but not other types of anovulation, display elevated cortisol concentrations (Berga et al., 1997). Stress can also interrupt pregnancy or lactation if the stressful conditions are sufficiently severe. Indeed, in female free-ranging snowshoe hares, fecal cortisol values are inversely related to the size of their litters and to offspring birth mass and body size; in other words, elevated cortisol reduces reproductive success and compromises the fitness of the offspring (Sheriff et al., 2009). In a seminatural pen, brief exposure of pregnant snowshoe hares to a predator for 1–2 minutes every other day during gestation significantly increased cortisol concentrations and reduced by nearly 30% the number of viable litters born. This study demonstrating the effects of predator stress on birth rate may explain the observed population cycles in this species.

As noted in Chapter 9, mammals have mechanisms to inhibit reproduction when they fall into a negative energy balance (Bronson, 1999). Women who diet rigorously or exercise strenuously often have problems with fertility (Arena et al., 1995; Constantini and Warren, 1994) (**FIGURE 11.29**). Stress-induced reproductive inhibition occurs among females of all mammalian species and is entirely reversible upon refeeding or relaxation of the energy demands (Cameron et al., 1993).

Fasting increases blood glucocorticoid concentrations and is generally considered to be a stressor. Suppression of reproductive function in the service of energy balance is controlled by mechanisms that overlap with those that control food intake. As we saw in Chapter 9, most of the peptide hormones, neuropeptides, and metabolic inhibitors that increase food intake also inhibit reproduction, and many of the same brain regions are involved in both responses (Schneider and Wade, 2000). Mechanisms that interrupt estrous cycles are sensitive to signals generated by the oxidation of metabolic fuels. For example, treatment of well-fed female hamsters

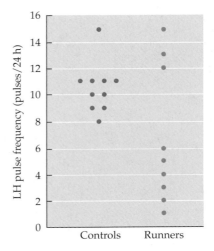

FIGURE 11.29 Effects of exercise on LH pulse frequency LH pulses are less frequent in women who are long-distance runners, which may be related to the high reported incidence of amenorrhea among such women. After Veldhuis et al., 1985.

with 2-deoxy-D-glucose (2DG), which prevents glucose utilization, suspends estrous cycles (Schneider and Wade, 1989a). Thus, stress appears to interrupt estrous cycles by affecting metabolic pathways. It is likely that stress-evoked interruption of menstrual cycles in humans is mediated by the same pathways.

A variety of mechanisms underlie the impairment of female reproduction by stress. All of the neuroendocrine impairments of GnRH and gonadotropin secretion that were described previously for males also occur in females. One additional mechanism of reproductive impairment in females appears to be a side effect of overactive adrenal cortices. In addition to glucocorticoids, the adrenal glands secrete androgens in both males and females. Even though the amount of androgen (primarily androstenedione) released by females' adrenals is only about 2%–3% of male concentrations, it can interrupt female reproductive processes. Many of these androgens are converted to estrogens in fat cells, and during food shortages less estrogen is produced in the fat cells, contributing to the low circulating estrogen concentrations. More importantly, increased androgen concentrations wreak havoc with the negative feedback mechanisms of GnRH and the gonadotropins.

Recently, a study reported a mechanism that may underlie reproductive dysfunction in females (Geraghty et al., 2015). Rats were exposed to 18 days of brief restraint, which ceased 4 days prior to mating. The chronic stress before mating provoked significant reproductive dysfunction, with fewer successful copulation events, fewer pregnancies in those that successfully mated, and increased embryo resorption. Chronic stress exposure also led to elevated expression of the hypothalamic inhibitory peptide, RFamide-related peptide-3 (RFRP3), in regularly cycling females. Genetic silencing of RFRP3 during stress by an inducible-targeted shRNA ameliorated stress-induced infertility in female rats, resulting in mating and pregnancy success rates indistinguishable from nonstressed animals. Development of drugs that reduce RFRP3 may prove an effective treatment for treating stress-evoked infertility (Geraghty et al., 2015).

Sex Differences

Sex differences in the neuroendocrine response to stress have been reported in rats. Female rats normally have higher basal corticosterone concentrations than male rats (Critchlow et al., 1963; Kitay, 1963). In response to stress, female rats generally display higher ACTH and corticosterone concentrations than stressed males do (Handa et al., 1994; Patchev et al., 1995; Viau and Meaney, 1991). These sex differences in stress responses are activated, rather than organized, by hormones; ovariectomy in adulthood eliminates the sex difference in the HPA axis response, and estradiol replacement therapy restores it (Kitay, 1963). Using 2DG autoradiography, it was discovered that stressed female rats display higher glucose utilization than stressed males in several brain regions, including the hypothalamic ventromedial nuclei, arcuate nucleus, and medial preoptic area and the hippocampal CA1 layer and dentate gyrus (Brown et al., 1996) (FIGURE 11.30). Sex differences in stress responsiveness in relation to learning and memory are discussed in Chapter 12.

Individual Differences

One interesting question is what accounts for the individual variation in reproductive response and resistance to stress. Generally, social and other environmental stressors impair reproduction via mechanisms associated with the interaction of the HPA axis with the HPG axis. However, some individuals seemingly ignore the stressor and breed normally. It has been predicted that individuals with a high probability of being able to ignore stressors and breed normally include (1) aged individuals with minimal future prospects for reproductive success, (2) seasonal breeders that have a truncated breeding season because of challenging conditions

(A)

(B)

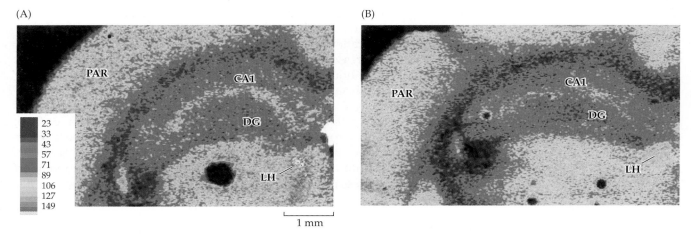

FIGURE 11.30 Sex differences in glucose utilization under stress Females (A) show greater brain utilization of glucose than males (B) under stress. Higher glucose utilization is indicated by warmer colors in these false color images. This difference is seen in all brain regions but is especially prominent in the CA1 region and dentate gyrus (DG) of the hippocampus. From Brown et al., 1996.

at each end of the season, (3) biparental species in which one member of the pair dies, (4) semelparous breeders (one-time breeders such as salmon) that have a single breeding period followed by death, and (5) individuals in plastic social situations in which the window of breeding opportunities is short because of rapidly shifting social organization (Wingfield and Sapolsky, 2003). What are the mechanisms underlying this ability to breed in the presence of stressors? Four mechanisms have been proposed: (1) adjustments within the central nervous system (i.e., individuals no longer perceive the situation as stressful), (2) adjustments at the level of the HPA axis (i.e., to adjust feedback and stimulatory factors to prevent elevating glucocorticoids), (3) adjustments at the level of the HPG axis (i.e., failure of glucocorticoids to impede HPG function), and (4) compensatory adjustments of the HPG axis to counter the inhibitory signals from the HPA axis (Wingfield and Sapolsky, 2003). Understanding these mechanisms will help us understand how wild animals, and perhaps domesticated animals and humans, cope with the stressors in their lives (McEwen, 2014).

Stress and Social Behavior

Research on the effects of social factors on stress arose from ecological research in the 1950s and 1960s investigating the dramatic population cycles observed in voles (*Microtus* spp.), lemmings (*Lemmus* spp.), and wild mice (*Mus* spp.) (e.g., Bronson, 1967; Calhoun, 1961, 1962a; Chitty, 1961; Christian, 1950, 1959; Christian et al., 1965; Clough, 1965; Southwick, 1955a,b; Thiessen and Rodgers, 1961; Wynne-Edwards, 1965). Similar studies of various species of birds emerged at about the same time (e.g., Kluyver and Tinbergen, 1953; Siegel, 1959, 1960). In studies of population cycles in the laboratory, a few animals are generally put in large cages (typically 3 m by 3 m), provided with excess food and water, and allowed to breed and raise their young. Because rodents are particularly well adapted for rapid reproduction, the population in a rodent cage soon increases to amazing levels. But at some point, the population crashes. Why? The crash is not due to a lack of food or water, because these are replenished daily. It is not due to other challenging conditions such as extreme temperatures, inclement weather, or a buildup of predators, which might explain population crashes in the field, because all of these factors are controlled in the lab. The animals that died under these circumstances appeared to have enlarged adrenal glands and showed a variety of problems associated with high circulating glucocorticoid concentrations (Thiessen and Rodgers, 1961).

Were the animals stressed because they had inadequate space as populations increased? If rats were housed individually in cages with about 30 cm^2 of floor space, they did not exhibit any of the signs of stress. If ten rats were housed together in a cage of about 300 cm^2, however, stress responses were evident in the grouped animals, despite the fact that the animals had the same average amount of floor space. In fact, even if the group-housed rats had 32 times more floor space than the individually housed rats, they still exhibited stress responses (Myers et al., 1971). Clearly, something about the increasing social interactions at higher population densities caused the stress responses in the animals.

Population Density and Dispersal

The effects of increased population density have also been studied in European starlings (*Sturnus vulgaris*) (Nephew and Romero, 2003). A resident bird was housed in a cage that allowed the introduction of intruder conspecific birds (one, three, or five intruders) through a special entrance, without humans in the immediate area. The resident bird was implanted with a radio transmitter, which relayed pulse rate information to the investigators while the birds' behavior was videotaped through a two-way mirror (Nephew and Romero, 2003). At the end of each treatment, blood samples were obtained and assayed for corticosterone. Resident and intruder birds reacted differently to the increasing population density in the cage. Corticosterone concentrations did not change in resident birds, whereas corticosterone concentrations increased after 30 minutes in intruders. Heart rate increased significantly in the resident birds, however, when intruders were introduced to the cage, and the extent of the increase in heart rate corresponded directly with the number of intruders introduced. Several indices of behavioral activation were observed among both the resident and intruder birds, including preening, eating, drinking, and aggression. These results indicate that social role and the extent of the elevation of population density influence the corticosterone response to crowding and, also, that behavioral and cardiac activation may be independent of glucocorticoid concentrations (Nephew and Romero, 2003).

To see the kinds of demanding conditions animals must face, let's look at the example of wild dogs more carefully. Despite their common name, African wild dogs (*Lycaon pictus*) are more closely related to jackals than to modern dogs (**FIGURE 11.31**). However, African wild dogs do possess several characteristics typical of domesticated dogs, including group hunting and the formation of strong social bonds. They live in packs of about six to eight adults and several pups. Unlike other canine species, however, wild dogs typically have only one breeding pair per pack (called the alpha pair) (Creel et

FIGURE 11.31 A group of African wild dogs Only the alpha pair of each pack breeds. The other adult members of the pack bring food to the pups and otherwise assist in the breeding efforts of the dominant alpha pair. In contrast to many laboratory animals, the alpha animals have higher corticosterone concentrations than subordinate animals of the pack.

al., 1996, 1997). In one study, 82% of the alpha females bred each year and produced 76%–81% of the offspring; only 6%–17% of the subordinate females produced any offspring (Creel et al., 1997). Thus, the costs and benefits of defined social rank can be highly variable among the members of the group. Not surprisingly, subordinate female African wild dogs tend to leave their natal packs and attempt to become alpha females elsewhere, although some subordinate females stay in their natal packs and attempt to rise through the ranks to alpha status.

In general, dispersal is a demanding time for young animals (see Chapter 8). It requires moving to a new area, where they must learn anew where they can find food and water. Whatever protection they received from their natal pack on their home territory is lost in the new environment, and the dispersing individuals must establish new social relationships. An invading female wild dog faces many challenges when she leaves her natal pack. In order to become the reproductively successful alpha female in a new pack, a new female must attack and dominate the current alpha female of the pack and also defend against the other subordinate females of the group vying for the top position. Thus, intrusion of a newcomer results in increased social instability, and ultimately, dominant dogs attempting to defend their status spend more time in aggressive interactions than subordinate animals. Therefore, it is not surprising that dominant wild dogs have elevated cortisol relative to low-ranked individuals.

Social Dominance

The relationship between corticosteroid concentration and social dominance varies across species and within species, based on social organization, stability of the hierarchy, resource allotment, frequency of agonistic and conciliatory behaviors, and the ability of subordinate animals to avoid dominant animals (Sapolsky, 2005). For example, social instability alters the relationship between cortisol concentration and dominance rank in female rhesus monkeys. Low-ranking female rhesus monkeys in a stable, established group have higher cortisol concentrations than high-ranking females (Gust et al., 1993). In contrast, in a newly formed group with a relatively unstable hierarchy, there is no relationship between cortisol concentration and dominance rank among female rhesus monkeys. An interesting behavioral difference observed between the established and newly formed groups was that the monkeys in the newly formed groups engaged in much more postaggression reconciliatory behaviors, such as grooming, which may have relieved some of the stress associated with losing a skirmish and ultimately resulted in low basal cortisol concentrations in both dominant and subordinate monkeys. Reconciliation following an aggressive interaction may be a behavioral strategy that the aggressors use to ease tensions in unstable social groups in which strong social alliances have not yet been established (Gust et al., 1993). As the hierarchy becomes more stable, the expression of reconciliatory behaviors decreases, subordinate-directed aggression increases, and corticosterone concentrations increase among subordinate individuals.

In general, there is no consistent relationship between stress response and social rank among primates (Abbott et al., 2003) and other social species, although elevated glucocorticoids have been reported for three species of cooperatively breeding carnivores (Creel, 2005). There are also sex differences in stress response. For example, no influence of dominance rank on fecal cortisol levels was observed in female mandrills as in males, suggesting that subordinate females do not suffer chronic stress. This may be because female mandrills have a stable social hierarchy, with low levels of aggression and high social support (Setchell et al., 2008).

Effects of social hierarchy on physiological measures of stress have been reported in a variety of species ranging from zebrafish (Filby et al., 2010) to apes (Sapolsky, 2005). However, in general, for individuals living in a social hierarchy, physiological indicators of stress tend to be state-dependent rather than trait-dependent. In other words, these stress measures are reflective of an animal's position within the social hierarchy at a given point in time, rather than predictive of future social position (Czoty et al., 2009). People who occupy a low socioeconomic status (SES) often report more stress than individuals at higher SES levels. Individual perception of relative standing or ranking in a social hierarchy, formally termed subjective social status, may affect an individual's pattern of emotional, behavioral, and physiological reactivity to and recovery from life stressors, and consequently his or her risk for ill health (McEwen and Gianaros, 2010). Low-SES individuals are at greater risk for psychopathology, cardiovascular and metabolic disorders, and immune dysfunction (McEwen, 2006). Differences in coping or resiliency can overcome these risks.

Several studies have indicated that socially dominant animals have relatively low circulating levels of glucocorticoids, whereas subordinate individuals typically display relatively high circulating glucocorticoid concentrations (reviewed in Sapolsky, 1994). These differences are particularly salient during times of social instability for some species. In some cases, however, as noted with African wild dogs, the dominant individuals tend to have elevated glucocorticoid concentrations compared with subordinate animals (Creel et al., 1996, 1997). Thus, in some cases, it is stressful to be "top dog," and in other cases, being at the bottom of the social ladder is stressful. These differences probably reflect social factors such as the amount of harassment within a social group or the extent to which social positions are out of the control of the participants (e.g., inherited).

Having a history of being bullied as a teenager resulted in increased self-reports of stress and use of avoidant coping strategies in college (Hamilton et al., 2008; Newman et al., 2010). College students who were self-reported victims of bullying were subjected to a stressful experience in the laboratory. The men in this study displayed blunted blood pressure responses to the stressor. There were no physiological effects on the women who were victims of bullying (Hamilton et al., 2008). A sex difference in HPA responses to previous bullying was also reported among 12-year-olds (Vaillancourt et al., 2008), with boys showing blunted cortisol values. Although this may sound adaptive, recall that reduced cortisol concentrations have been linked with vulnerability to PTSD.

This young bullying experience has been modeled in mice. For instance, one model described in Chapter 8 is called the social defeat model. Essentially, a male juvenile mouse is housed with a dominant older male for several minutes over the course of days or weeks. In subordinate animals, chronic social defeat results in a prolonged stress response and chronic activation of the HPA axis that can lead to marked physiological and behavioral changes (reviewed in McEwen et al., 2015). These changes disrupt homeostatic balance and may lead to stress-induced susceptibility to disease that ultimately threatens survival (Huhman et al., 2003). When juvenile mice are tested shortly after experiencing social defeat while still juveniles, they display typical social interactions; that is, they are resistant to the stressful experiences on subsequent social interactions. When these socially stressed juvenile mice are tested later as adults, most display social avoidance. Nonetheless, a minority of these socially stressed mice retains the resistant phenotype and these mice display typical adult social interactions. What accounts for these differences in resilience? Recent work suggests that the mice that seem resistant to the social defeat displayed significantly elevated corticosterone response as juveniles after the first social interaction test, compared with the susceptible mice (Latsko et al., 2016) (**FIGURE 11.32**). These observations suggest that elevated corticosterone during early life may promote coping in adulthood. The molecular mechanisms remain unspecified, but likely neuroendocrine responses to stressors evoke epigenetic adjustments within the neural circuits mediating cognitive, social, and affective responses (Karatoreos and McEwen, 2013; McEwen et al., 2015).

Marmosets and tamarins exhibit an interesting reproductive strategy whereby only one female per social group breeds. The other, subordinate adult females are

(A)

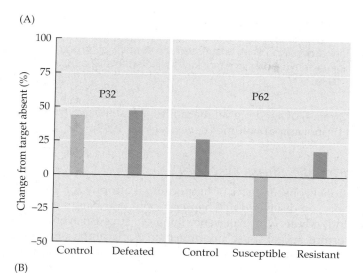

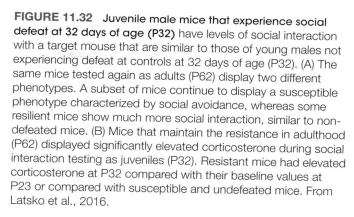

FIGURE 11.32 Juvenile male mice that experience social defeat at 32 days of age **(P32)** have levels of social interaction with a target mouse that are similar to those of young males not experiencing defeat at controls at 32 days of age (P32). (A) The same mice tested again as adults (P62) display two different phenotypes. A subset of mice continue to display a susceptible phenotype characterized by social avoidance, whereas some resilient mice show much more social interaction, similar to non-defeated mice. (B) Mice that maintain the resistance in adulthood (P62) displayed significantly elevated corticosterone during social interaction testing as juveniles (P32). Resistant mice had elevated corticosterone at P32 compared with their baseline values at P23 or compared with susceptible and undefeated mice. From Latsko et al., 2016.

(B)

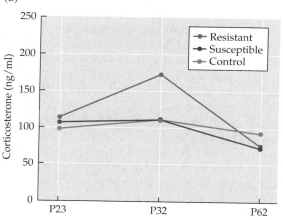

reproductively suppressed by a combination of olfactory, behavioral, and other signals from the dominant female (Abbott et al., 1997; Kuederling et al., 1995; Saltzman et al., 1996). The subordinate females have low circulating estrogen concentrations, but their GnRH levels are indistinguishable from those of dominant females (Abbott et al., 1997). It appears that their anovulation is caused by their inability to generate an LH surge (Abbott et al., 1997). This phenomenon has been termed social castration.

Intense stress can cause brain damage in many species, including primates. This phenomenon was studied in a group of captive vervet monkeys (*Cercopithecus aethiops*) at a primate center in Kenya. In the group-housing enclosures, social hierarchies developed, and the animals at the top of the hierarchies made life miserable for the lower-ranked individuals. The net result of the constant harassment was that many of the monkeys at the bottom of the social hierarchies died at a relatively young age. When these animals were autopsied, it was revealed that their adrenal glands were enlarged, and gastric ulcers were evident. Other signs of chronic stress were apparent upon microscopic examination of the deceased individuals. Neurons in the CA1 region of the hippocampus had atrophied in comparison with those in the same region in high-ranked individuals (Uno et al., 1989) **(FIGURE 11.33)**. Atrophy of brain regions has also been observed in rats that have been subjected to intensely stressful conditions or treatment with very high doses of corticosterone (Sapolsky, 1992b; Sapolsky et al., 1985). Similarly, CAT scan examinations of humans who had been subjected to torture have revealed significant degeneration in some brain regions (Jensen et al., 1982). However, chronic high cortisol treatment (twice

(A)

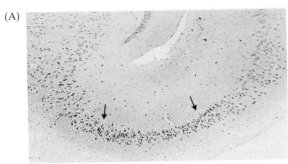

(B)

FIGURE 11.33 Neural degeneration associated with stress The numbers of black spots in the hippocampal regions between the arrows illustrate the normal condition of an unstressed vervet monkey (A) and the large deficit in pyramidal cells in a monkey subjected to stress (B). From Uno et al., 1989.

daily for 2 years) of aged pigtail macaques (*Macaca nemestrina*) did not affect hippocampal volume (Levernz et al., 1999).

Post-traumatic Stress Disorder

The functional consequences of hippocampal atrophy for learning and memory are discussed in Chapter 12, but one example is useful here. Individuals who experience intensely stressful events (e.g., combat, torture, sexual abuse, internment in work camps, or natural or man-made disasters) often suffer later in life from **post-traumatic stress disorder** (**PTSD**), which has a constellation of symptoms (Yehuda et al., 1993). These symptoms include severe behavioral and emotional responses, as well as hormonal dysregulation. Even 50 years after their liberation, individual Holocaust survivors with PTSD displayed low urinary cortisol excretion and impaired memory compared with Holocaust survivors without PTSD or healthy Jewish adults (Golier et al., 2002; Yehuda et al., 1995). Combat veterans from the Vietnam War era displayed similar dysregulation in the HPA axis (Yehuda et al., 1995). In cognitive tests, Vietnam veterans with combat-related PTSD also displayed significant deficits in short-term memory (Bremner et al., 1993). Several fMRI studies have revealed that persons suffering from PTSD have smaller hippocampi than age-matched individuals without PTSD (e.g., Bremner et al., 1995, 1997; Stein et al., 1997). The conclusion of these studies would appear to be that the effects of psychological trauma and accompanying elevated glucocorticoid concentrations were sufficiently significant to reduce the size of the hippocampus in people with PTSD.

However, one provocative study suggested there may be a bit of a chicken-and-egg problem with this conclusion (Sapolsky, 2002). In this study, pairs of monozygotic twins underwent fMRI brain analyses. In each pair, one twin brother had served in combat during the Vietnam War and had been diagnosed with PTSD, whereas the other twin had not served in Vietnam and did not have PTSD (Gilbertson et al., 2002). The severity of the PTSD symptoms was correlated with hippocampal volume in both the combat veteran and his twin (**FIGURE 11.34**). In twin pairs that included a twin with the most severe PTSD symptoms, *both* twins had smaller hippocampal volumes than did twins from pairs suffering less severe PTSD symptoms (Gilbertson et al., 2002). These results suggest that having a small hippocampus puts individuals at risk for PTSD if they encounter trauma during their lives. The factors accounting for variation in hippocampal size remain unspecified for humans.

Veterans with PTSD have fewer GABA$_A$ receptors in the frontal cortex. PET was used to observe benzodiazepine–GABA$_A$ receptor binding and to compare Dutch veterans suffering from PTSD with Dutch veterans without PTSD (but matched for age, region, and area of deployment) (Geuze et al., 2008). Individuals diagnosed with combat-associated PTSD showed reduced benzodiazepine binding throughout the cortex, hippocampus, and thalamus, indicating fewer GABA$_A$ receptors (**FIGURE 11.35**).

Rodent and nonhuman primate studies implicate the medial prefrontal cortex as a target of chronic stress (McEwen and Gianaros, 2010). Long-term stressors provoke structural and functional changes in the anterior cingulate, prelimbic, and orbitofrontal cortices. Importantly, there are individual differences in the effects of stressors on these brain regions, and the dorsal anterior cingulate cortex has been

post-traumatic stress disorder (PTSD) A psychiatric disorder that may occur following the experience or witnessing of life-threatening events such as military combat, natural disasters, or violent personal assaults such as rape. Symptoms of PTSD include reliving the experience through nightmares and flashbacks, sleep disturbances, feelings of detachment, and estrangement.

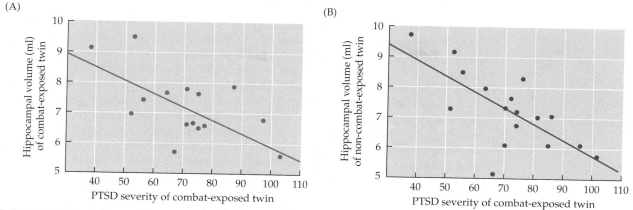

FIGURE 11.34 Correlations of hippocampal volume and severity of PTSD symptoms reveal similar relationships in Vietnam combat veterans (A) and their non-combat-experienced twin brothers (B). The results suggest that having a small hippocampus might be a risk factor for PTSD, rather than a result of PTSD. After Gilbertson et al., 2002.

implicated with regulation of the HPA axis. Based on their findings, the researchers proposed that the level of social support perceived by an individual may influence how specific brain areas, especially the dorsal anterior cingulate cortex, modulate social stress-related cortisol reactivity (Eisenberger et al., 2007). These results may provide a functional explanation for why some people develop more pathology than others in response to stress.

Individuals with stressful events in their childhood are at increased risk for physical and mental health problems in adulthood. The HPA axis is permanently altered by early sexual or physical abuse in people (Neigh et al., 2009), and such individuals are as likely to present with stress-associated mental and physical disorders as are people suffering current abuse (McCauley et al., 1997). Although early life trauma elevates the risk of psychiatric and medical disease, it is important to note that not all exposed individuals demonstrate altered HPA axis physiology, suggesting that genetic or epigenetic variation influences the outcomes of early trauma (Neigh et al., 2009). It is apparent that chronic, intense stress impairs several physiological and behavioral systems. Additional research is necessary to determine the effects of intermittent, moderate stress—the type of stress experienced by most of us—on physiological and behavioral functions.

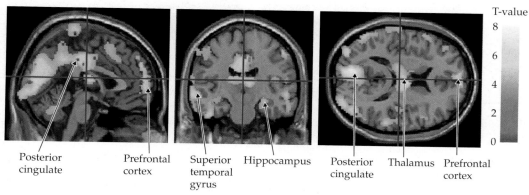

FIGURE 11.35 Veterans with post-traumatic stress disorder (PTSD) showed less GABA$_A$-benzodiazepine binding (yellow areas) in a PET scan throughout the brain, but especially in the hippocampus, insula, and thalamus and the prefrontal, temporal, and parietal cortices. From Geuze et al., 2008.

Seasonal Fluctuations in Stress Responses

The experience of being captured generally causes an animal to experience a rapid surge of epinephrine and glucocorticoids. If blood samples are obtained immediately after an animal is captured, reproductive hormone concentrations are also generally much higher than if they are obtained a few hours postcapture (e.g., Licht et al., 1983; Mahmoud and Licht, 1997; Mendonca and Licht, 1986; Orchinik et al., 1988; Tyrrell and Cree, 1998). Obviously, the interval of time between capture and the blood sample collection is important when trying to determine hormone concentrations in wild-caught animals. Techniques to assay glucocorticoid by-products in urine or feces have allowed the study of the relationship between social dominance and corticosterone values in unrestrained animals, as in the study of wild dogs and mongooses described earlier in this chapter. In any case, multiple blood samples provide a more complete endocrine profile than a single blood sample, which might be obtained at the peak or nadir of a pulse of hormone secretion. Another variable that is important in assessing hormone-stress-behavior interactions is the time of year. A study of greylag geese (*Anser anser*), for example, revealed that a complex interaction exists among social status, stress, and season of the year (Kotrschal et al., 1998). In general, it appears that glucocorticoid concentrations in free-living reptiles, amphibians, and birds, but not mammals, are commonly elevated during the breeding season (Romero, 2002; Romero and Wingfield, 2016).

Redpolls (*Acanthis flammea*) are birds that live in the challenging arctic conditions of Alaska. Both males and females showed the typical marked elevation in blood corticosterone concentrations when held captive for about 1 hour, indicating that they responded to capture as many other vertebrates do (Wingfield et al., 1994a,b). However, the amount of postcapture corticosterone elevation varied across the year. Corticosterone elevations were generally blunted during January, and they were maximal during June, when the birds were breeding. It appeared that individuals with the largest fat stores secreted the smallest amounts of glucocorticoids postcapture (Wingfield et al., 1994). Similar effects have been reported for other birds living at high latitudes, including white-crowned sparrows (*Zonotrichia leucophrys gambelii*) (**FIGURE 11.36**), snow buntings (*Plectrophenax nivalis*), and Lapland longspurs

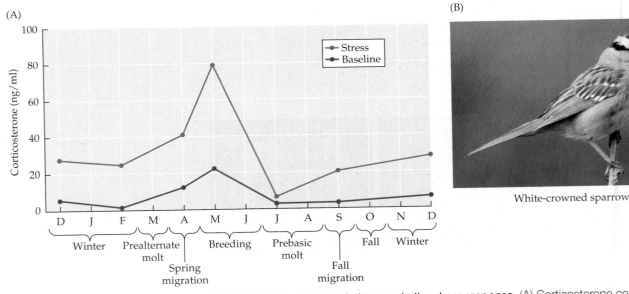

FIGURE 11.36 Seasonal changes in the stress response (A) Corticosterone concentrations were measured in blood samples obtained from white-crowned sparrows both immediately after capture (baseline) and 30 minutes after capture (stress) across the year. Note that the stress response was blunted during the fall and winter. (B) White-crowned sparrow. A after Romero, 2002.

(*Calcarius lapponicus*) (Romero et al., 1997, 1998a–d, 2002). The seasonal modulation of corticosterone secretion appears to be regulated at multiple sites within the HPA axis; during the winter (or during the energetically expensive, feather-replacing molting process), the system appears to be relatively insensitive to the effects of exogenous ACTH in stimulating corticosterone production (Romero et al., 1998a–d).

Because glucocorticoids are released whenever energy requirements rise significantly above baseline, it is reasonable to expect temporal changes in glucocorticoid concentrations. As you may recall from Chapter 10, there is a marked circadian rhythm of glucocorticoid secretion. Glucocorticoids are secreted just prior to awakening each day, to help increase blood glucose levels prior to the onset of activity. Similarly, one might predict that glucocorticoids would be secreted during energetically demanding times across the year, such as molting, migration, or winter. Challenging winter conditions such as low ambient temperatures and decreased food availability can directly evoke a stress response in mammals (reviewed in Nelson and Demas, 1996). In the case of Arctic birds, it appears that special adaptations have evolved to blunt corticosterone secretion during the winter, when the birds' fat stores are too low to power a full stress response.

Winter is a predictable stressor, and animals can use the annual change in photoperiod or other cues to physiologically anticipate adverse seasonal conditions well in advance of those conditions. However, individuals of many species are confronted by unpredictable stressors such as severe storms, floods, or fires. Birds that inhabit high-altitude forests, for example, are often confronted by unexpected poor weather during the breeding season. Unlike other species, birds are highly mobile and can escape adverse conditions at the breeding site and seek out more benign conditions elsewhere (Breuner and Hahn, 2003). There are complex cost-benefit relationships associated with leaving a breeding territory, however, that involve territory size, mate quality, reproductive success upon the birds' return, and survival.

A population of white-crowned sparrows (*Z. leucophrys*) breeds at high elevation in the Sierra Nevada (Breuner and Hahn, 2003). This habitat commonly experiences severe weather at the onset of the breeding season, and in response, the sparrows often temporarily abandon their breeding territories and migrate to lower elevations. Previous studies had indicated that hormonal stress responses modulated the timing of territory abandonment. During severe weather, treatment of the sparrows with exogenous corticosterone provoked movement to lower elevations, and it delayed their return to the breeding site after territory abandonment (Breuner and Hahn, 2003) (**FIGURE 11.37**). During good weather, however, treatment with exogenous corticosterone did not induce territory abandonment, but it did increase the activity range around the breeding site. The level of the endogenous corticosterone response to en-

FIGURE 11.37 Corticosterone influences altitudinal migration in response to inclement weather. (A) Implants of corticosterone (CORT) caused sparrows to move to lower-altitude roost sites in response to late-season snowstorms (clouds). The size of the cloud icon represents the severity of the weather. (B) Corticosterone also caused more activity around the territory during good weather. These results suggest that corticosterone, a proxy for stress, has both costly and beneficial effects. After Breuner and Hahn, 2003.

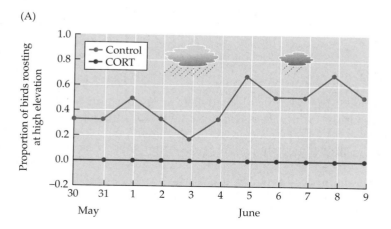

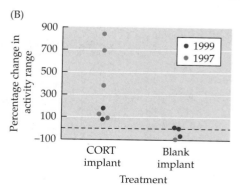

vironmental stressors was inversely related to body condition of these mountain white-crowned sparrows (Breuner and Hahn, 2003). That is, birds in poor condition displayed high glucocorticoid concentrations, whereas birds in good condition displayed low glucocorticoid concentrations (Wingfield and Silverin, 2009).

Rodents also display seasonal changes in stress responses (reviewed in Nelson et al., 2002; Weil and Nelson, 2012). Stressful conditions such as low temperatures and lack of food during winter may weaken immune function and increase an animal's chances of death from hypothermia or starvation. During stressful challenges, it appears beneficial for animals to strengthen their immune function, and for immune system cells to exit the blood and move to areas such as the skin in preparation for potential injury or infection. To test the hypothesis that animals may use photoperiod (day length) to anticipate the onset of seasonal stressors and adjust their immune function accordingly, glucocorticoid concentrations and the distribution of blood leukocytes, as well as a type of immune function called delayed-type hypersensitivity response, were assessed in Siberian hamsters (*Phodopus sungorus*). Hamsters that were exposed to long (i.e., summerlike) day lengths or short (i.e., winterlike) day lengths were tested at baseline and during acute stress (Bilbo et al., 2002). The test for delayed-type hypersensitivity is similar to the skin tuberculosis (TB) screen in which a small amount of antigen is injected under your skin. If you have been previously exposed to TB, then a red wheal will form around the injection site. In experimental tests of delayed-type hypersensitivity, a small amount of antigen is injected under the skin between the shoulder blades of a rodent. A week or so later, the antigen is applied to one of the ears. The resulting inflammation (swelling) is measured and the thickness of the exposed and unexposed ears is compared. Generally, more inflammation indicates a stronger immune response.

In hamsters, acute (2 h) restraint stress induced movement of leukocytes out of the blood and into the skin. This trafficking occurred more rapidly in hamsters housed in short days as compared to long days. Baseline delayed-type hypersensitivity responses were enhanced in the short-day hamsters; this effect was augmented further by acute stress and seemed to reflect a more rapid redistribution of leukocytes. These results suggest that photoperiod may provide a useful cue by which winter stressors can be anticipated so as to adjust the repertoire of available immune cells and increase the likelihood of survival. Energy that might go toward reproductive activities such as defending a territory, engaging in courtship behaviors, or feeding offspring during the breeding season is shunted into immune function during the winter. During the breeding season, animals invest their energy mainly in reproductive efforts, whereas during the nonbreeding season, individuals invest mainly in survival efforts (Nelson, 2004; Walton et al., 2011). Light pollution at night may disrupt these day length signals and block these adaptations. For example, dim light exposure at night (5 lux) was sufficient to block the short-day enhancement of immune responses in Siberian hamsters (Ikeno and Nelson, 2014). The disruption of these seasonal adaptations by modern lighting practices may have long-lasting and dramatic effects on many species of animals (reviewed in Dominoni et al., 2016).

Psychological Factors in Stress and Coping

As described in Chapter 1, the relationship between hormones and behavior is bidirectional. Although most examples of hormone-behavior interactions in this book have demonstrated the effects of hormones on behavior, stress emphasizes the bidirectional relationship between hormones and behavior. We have discussed the effects of hormones on stress responses and behavior: stress causes hormonal changes, which affect brain processes, which affect behavior. However, it is important to note that the brain itself, via memories, perception, and other processes, can elicit a full-blown stress response and evoke the release of glucocorticoids and epinephrine to affect physiology and behavior. It may be crucial to understand how or why the brain (e.g., in anticipation of giving a public lecture) can provoke the same sort of stress responses as a life-threatening situation. It is equally important to understand the variation among individuals in their perception of stressors. For example, approximately 50% of women incarcerated in prison camps during World War II stopped menstruating. Obviously, prison camps are extremely stressful environments. But why were only 50% of the women affected in that way? Is it possible that some individuals were able to perceive the conditions as not stressful?

In many cases of stress (e.g., capture in a net or mild restraint), the actual stressor is psychological, rather than physical. However, the secretion of epinephrine resulting from capture usually increases heart and lung functioning well above baseline, and both of these activities are energetically expensive; the subsequent glucocorticoid secretion several minutes after capture mobilizes energy to power the heart and other muscles normally involved in the fight-or-flight response. The perception of stressors, the amount of epinephrine released in response to perceived stressors, the number of available receptors for epinephrine and glucocorticoids, the number of carrier proteins available to transport adrenal steroid hormones through the blood, and a host of other factors vary from one individual to another. Consequently, individual differences in stress responses are common, and specific causes for individual differences in stress responsiveness are not easily explained. Individual differences in the perception of and responsiveness to stressors—in other words, psychological differences—appear to account for many of the differences among humans responding to stress (Mason, 1975).

As we discovered earlier in this chapter, early individual experiences can modulate stress responses in adulthood. For instance, how children responded to a cold pressor test (a test of physiological reactions to a hand placed in a tub of iced water for 1 minute) in 1934 predicted their health problems as adults (Wood et al., 1984): over 70% of the individuals who "overreacted" to the test as children developed cardiovascular disease as adults, compared with fewer than 20% of the individuals who had displayed little or no reaction to the test 50 years previously (Wood et al., 1984).

One experimenter deprived two monkeys of food to study individual differences in response to stress (Sapolsky, 1992a). Although both individuals were deprived of any nutrition, and both should have shown an equal energy deficit and an equivalent rise in stress hormones, one monkey was fed a nonnutritive flavored placebo. That monkey did not display elevated glucocorticoid secretion, but the other individual did, suggesting that the first monkey did not perceive the situation to be as stressful as the second one did (Sapolsky, 1992a). Most lab studies of rodents house animals individually. However, this takes the artificial environment of the laboratory to an even less valid level (**BOX 11.2**). Most species of rats and mice live in social groups, and individual housing is very stressful for these animals (Bowers et al., 2008). Placing three to four animals in a cage usually leads to the development of a social hierarchy, and as noted above, glucocorticoid concentrations reflect an individual's place within this hierarchy.

Most scientists now accept the power of psychological variables to modulate stress physiology (Sapolsky, 1994). What are these variables? Among individuals of vertebrate species, the main psychological factors that modulate stress responses include (1) control, (2) predictability, (3) outlets for dealing with frustration, and (4) habituation.

Control

Individuals suffer fewer stress-related pathologies if they can control the situation causing the stress (Gatchel et al., 1989). Controlling a stressful situation is a type of coping behavior. Rats were subjected to intermittent electric shocks in one early study (Weiss, 1968). One rat was able to depress a lever to decrease the rate of shocks.

As noted in Chapter 8, rats and mice typically live in large social groups of both sexes and mixed ages. These social groups inhabit interconnected underground burrows that are difficult to study in nature. Thus, rat behavior became characterized within laboratory housing and other standardized environmental factors (Barnett, 1956). In the 1980s, Bob and Caroline Blanchard of the University of Hawaii developed a so-called visible burrow system (VBS) that permitted observation of social interactions of group-living rats (**Figure**). After some revisions, the standard versions of the VBS were 1 m² in size and included a large open area that was under a 12:12 dark-light photocycle. There were also several chambers and tunnels that were maintained in the dark. Animals were implanted with microchips to track individual interactions, and multiple food and water sources were available. Much of the work that emerged provided novel insights into offensive and defensive aggression (Blanchard and Blanchard, 1984). The VBS typically held 4–5 male and 2–3 female rats. The males, but not the females, rapidly established a hierarchy; the dominant rat guarded the food and water sources, and he tried to guard access to females, as well. Under these socially stressful conditions, the subordinate rats lost substantial body weight. Experiments lasted only about 2 weeks; otherwise survival of the subordinate males was at risk.

The VBS was brought to Bruce McEwen's lab at Rockefeller University by Randall Sakai to study the endocrine and neural outcomes of naturalistic chronic social stress. In several measures, both subordinate and dominant males showed similar responses to living in the VBS, despite the difference in their social status (McEwen et al., 2015). For example, both subordinate and dominant male rats displayed increased adrenal mass,

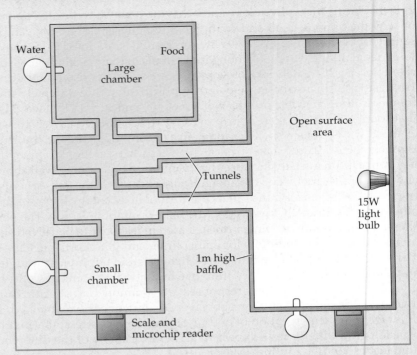

After McEwen et al., 2015

decreased thymic mass, elevated corticosterone concentrations, and decreased corticosterone-binding globulin values (McEwen et al., 2015). Spleen mass was elevated in only the subordinate rats, and some of these subordinate rats failed to respond to novel acute stressors with a corticosterone response, indicating a complicated, individual-based HPA axis dysfunction. It is possible that use of the more naturalistic VBS revealed a valid and reliable window into individual differences underlying stress responsiveness. The blunted corticosterone response to the novel stressor appears to be a direct consequence of diminished synthesis and release of CRH (Choi et al., 2006).

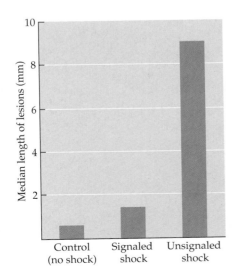

Another rat received a shock whenever the first rat did but could not control the frequency of the shocks. Subsequently, the second rat showed higher glucocorticoid secretion than the rat that could moderate the shocks (Weiss, 1968).

Predictability

In studies comparable to the one just described, predictability reduces the stress responses of individuals. For example, if warning signals are given to rats prior to shocks, then those rats have lower glucocorticoid concentrations than rats

FIGURE 11.38 Predictability of shock determines pathological stress responses in rats. This graph depicts the lengths of gastric ulcerations in rats that were given electric shocks, either signaled or unsignaled by a warning bell. Although rats in both conditions heard the same number of warning bells and received the same number of electric shocks, the contingency of the bell and shocks provided a psychological factor that mediated the physical response to stress. After Weiss, 1972.

(A)

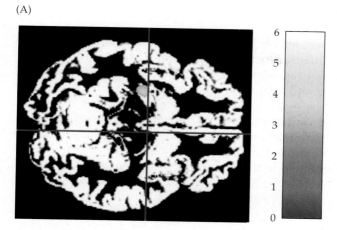

(B)

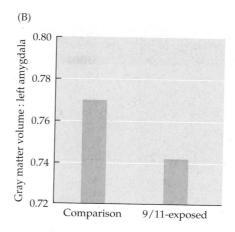

FIGURE 11.39 Proximity to the World Trade Center on 9/11/01 reduced gray matter throughout the brains of otherwise healthy adults. Brain regions with smaller gray matter volumes include the hippocampus, insula, and amygdala and the anterior cingulate and medial prefrontal cortices. In this brain scan, yellow color highlights the left amygdala (A), one area that showed a significant decrease in exposed adults (B). From Ganzel et al., 2008.

that receive no warning stimuli (Sapolsky 1992a) (**FIGURE 11.38**). Thus, predictable stressors are easier to cope with than random presentation of stressors.

An intense but unexpected stressor can have enduring effects on the brain. For example, people who were within 2.5 km of the World Trade Center on September 11, 2001, showed significant reductions in gray matter more than 3 years later (Ganzel et al., 2008). Affected brain regions included the amygdala, hippocampus, insula, anterior cingulate, and medial prefrontal cortices (**FIGURE 11.39**). These data suggest that unpredictable stressors can have long-term consequences on the brain structure (and possibly function) of otherwise healthy individuals (Ganzel et al., 2008).

Outlets for Frustration

The ability to engage in displacement behavior—having an "outlet"—also ameliorates the effects of stress. When rats are shocked, they show relatively low glucocorticoid secretion if they can chew on a piece of wood or attack another rat (Sapolsky, 1992a). It is common knowledge that the effects of stress in humans can be ameliorated by displacement behaviors such as engaging in a hobby or moderate exercise. Even modest activity can lessen the effects of stress. A study of children moving from kindergarten to primary school noted that many children engage in stereotypic "leg swinging" when confronted by the twin stressors of constraint to a desk and learning complex new cognitive skills. Leg swinging appears to induce a shift from sympathetic to parasympathetic nervous system activation. Children engaged in leg swinging display a small, consistent reduction in heart rate during and after this displacement behavior (Soussignan and Koch, 1985) (**FIGURE 11.40**).

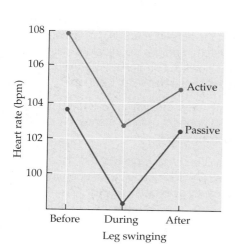

FIGURE 11.40 Leg swinging as a displacement activity reduces heart rate. Leg swinging by first grade children engages the parasympathetic system, which reduces heart rate, regardless of whether the children are involved (active) or uninvolved (passive) in learning activities. After Soussignan and Koch, 1985.

TABLE 11.4	Interventions to reduce the effects of stress on the brain
Regular physical activity	
Mindfulness-based stress reduction	
Social support and integration	
Developing a sense of meaning and purpose	
Never writing a textbook	

Source: After McEwen et al., 2016.

Habituation

Habituation, learning that a stimulus that was originally perceived as a stressor is not a stressor, is an important way to modulate stress responses. Recently weaned ground squirrels appear around my university campus each spring and scurry away at the sight of any student walking by. But eventually, they stop running to hide with every passing student and instead learn that these hulking fellow mammals often are a source of food and should be sought after, rather than hidden from. Similarly, in the paratrooper training study presented earlier (see Figure 11.6), the stimulus is the same each time (jumping off a tower), but the trainees learn that this is not harmful, so they rapidly habituate to the stimulus.

Throughout this chapter we have discussed individual differences in reproductive fitness, how survival and reproductive success are intertwined, and how they both interact with stress. Individual differences in the perception of stressors appear to be among the most important factors that determine the consequences of long-term stressors. Indeed, some individuals who are in extremely stressful situations may avoid PTSD by adopting an illusion of control, such as by carrying a "lucky" charm (Gatchel et al., 1989). A number of interventions have been reported to help the brain change itself (McEwen et al., 2016) (**TABLE 11.4**). Stress is the wear and tear of life. Stress affects us all. How well we cope reflects how well we will age and which diseases we might avoid, and it ultimately affects our reproductive function, as well as our reproductive fitness. In many cases, as your experiences have probably informed you, stress is bad for you. However, as we have discovered in this chapter, stress sometimes causes important positive changes. For example, acute stressors can improve immune function. Furthermore, brief maternal separation in infant rats "immunizes" these animals against prolonged stress responses later in life. What remains unknown is where the dividing line is between acute and chronic stressors, that is, the point at which stressors begin to impair, rather than improve, physiology and behavior.

Summary

1. Serious disruptions in homeostasis are called stressors. Stressors may be environmental, physiological, or psychosocial.

2. Stressors are met by a stress response, which is a suite of physiological and behavioral reactions to reestablish homeostasis. The stress response is nonspecific and consists of epinephrine release from the adrenal medulla, norepinephrine release from the sympathetic nervous system, and glucocorticoid release from the adrenal cortices. The immediate, nonspecific component of the stress response was also termed the fight-or-flight response by Walter Cannon.

3. Hans Selye studied the process of coping with stressors, which he termed the general adaptation syndrome (GAS). The GAS consists of three stages: (1) the alarm reaction, (2) resistance, and (3) exhaustion.

4. Stress is a difficult concept to define precisely. For the purposes of this chapter, stress is defined as all the nonspecific effects of factors that can act upon the body to increase energy consumption significantly above basal levels.

5. The adaptive features of the stress response include an increase in the immediate availability of energy, an increase in oxygen uptake, a decrease in blood flow to areas not necessary for movement, and inhibition of digestion, growth, immune function, reproductive function, and pain perception, as well as enhancement of memory and perception.

6. The pathological features of chronic stress include fatigue, myopathy, cardiovascular disease, gastric ulcers, psychosocial dwarfism, impotence, anovulation, compromised immune function, and potentially accelerated neural degeneration during aging.

7. Prenatal stress can demasculinize male reproductive behaviors but has little effect on female sexual behaviors. Mild stress during infancy can provide "stress immunization" and blunt stress responses later in life. Severe stress during infancy increases stress responses.

8. Psychosocial dwarfism is a rare syndrome found among human children who are raised in very stressful situations. Growth hormone (GH) is suppressed in these individuals; if they are removed from their stressful environments, they can catch up in their growth.

9. Stress impairs male sexual behavior (both motivation and performance) by suppressing testosterone. Stress also affects female sexual behavior by interrupting the precise timing of neuroendocrine events necessary for successful ovulation and sexual behavior.

10. Crowding evokes dramatic stress responses. In some social groups, it appears that the high-ranked individuals display pronounced stress responses, whereas in other social groups, low-ranked individuals display stress responses. These stress responses vary according to time of day and time of year.

11. Individual variation in the stress response reflects variation in many psychological parameters, especially control, predictability, and outlets for dealing with frustration, but also reflects differences in the perception of stressors.

Questions for Discussion

1. Discuss Hans Selye's quote: "Life is stress. Stress is life." Is stress truly a necessary component of life?

2. Why are psychological stressors as effective as physical stressors in evoking a physiological stress response? Is this an evolutionarily adaptive trait in nonhuman animals that has lost its adaptive value among modern humans?

3. Stress interferes with learning and memory. How can the stress response associated with exams be tamed so as not to affect performance?

4. Compare and contrast the roles of the autonomic nervous system and the HPA axis in the stress response, and discuss how the anatomy and physiology of these systems has evolved to support their role in the stress response.

5. Given what you now know about the pathological effects of chronic stress, what sort of pharmacological interventions do you think would help to ameliorate the negative consequences of stress? What sort of psychological interventions?

6. Glucocorticoids bind to two separate classes of receptors (mineralocorticoid and glucocorticoid) with different affinities. Describe the conditions for the activation of these two receptor classes, both at different times of the day and during stress.

Suggested Readings

Blanchard, C. D., et al. 2016. Effects of social stress on hormones, brain, and behavior. In D. W. Pfaff et al. (eds.), *Hormones, Brain and Behavior (3rd ed.)*, pp. 735–772. Academic Press, New York.

McEwen, B. S., et al. 2015. Mechanisms of stress in the brain. *Nat. Neurosci.*, 18:1353–1363.

McEwen, B. S., et al. 2015. Recognizing resilience: Learning from the effects of stress on the brain. *Neurobiol. Stress*, 1:1–11.

Romero, L. M., and Wingfield, J. C. 2016. *Tempests, Poxes, Predators, and People: Stress in Wild Animals and How They Cope*. Oxford Series in Behavioral Neuroendocrinology. Oxford University Press, New York.

Sandi, C., and Haller, J. 2015. Stress and the social brain: Behavioural effects and neurobiological mechanisms. *Nat. Rev. Neurosci.*, 16:290–304.

Sapolsky, R. M. 2004. *Why Zebras Don't Get Ulcers: An Updated Guide to Stress, Stress-Related Diseases, and Coping* (3rd ed.). W. H. Freeman, New York.

Shirazi, S. N., et al. 2015. Glucocorticoids and the brain: Neural mechanisms regulating the stress response. *Adv. Exp. Med. Biol.*, 872:235–252.

Learning and Memory

12

Learning Objectives

The goal of this chapter is to describe the relationship between hormones and learning and memory. There are several types of learning, and many hormones have been reported to affect various aspects of learning and memory. By the end of this chapter you should be able to:

- describe the different components of learning and memory.
- understand the basis for sex differences in learning and memory.
- describe seasonal fluctuations in learning and memory.

Many of us maintain vivid memories of frightening events. A former colleague of ours recounts a terrifying experience that occurred during a childhood game of kickball. He ran after a wayward ball, hoping to stop it before it rolled into the street. He made a valiant rescue attempt but tripped on the curb and sprawled onto the pavement in front of an oncoming car. The driver slammed on the brakes, and the car screeched to a halt, centimeters from him. Fifty-five years later, our colleague insists that he can remember every detail of the incident, including the pattern of the front grille of the car. Now an entomologist, he claims that he can even identify, from memory, the genus of the dead moths that were stuck to the front of the car!

Of course, it is nearly impossible to judge the accuracy of such accounts, but memories of stressful events in our lives seem to be particularly salient. In humans, the phenomenon of vivid memories of important, stressful events has been termed flashbulb memory (Brown and Kulik, 1977). Flashbulb memory is probably not a separate category of memory function; rather, it probably represents a class of memories that are more frequently rehearsed or more strongly encoded. Depending on their age, people are likely to have flashbulb memories of what they were doing when they heard

FIGURE 12.1 Emotionally arousing events are easily and vividly recalled, often with great clarity.

about the terrorist attacks on New York and Washington, the explosion of the Space Shuttle *Challenger*, the death of Prince, or the assassination of President Kennedy (**FIGURE 12.1**). Positive, yet stressful, events such as weddings, births of children, or winning lotteries are also remembered with great clarity (McCloskey et al., 1988). Other memories, however, are more fragile. For example, what you ate for dinner last night should be easily recalled, but you probably cannot remember what you ate for dinner a week ago, unless it made you ill or in some way was stressful for you.

Thus, some memories are relatively permanent, whereas others are fleeting. Generally, important events are remembered better than unimportant events. How are memories tagged as important or trivial? Our friend the entomologist cannot remember the front grille of every car that he has ever seen. The grille pattern of most cars is a trivial detail to him, and probably to you as well. Somehow, the brain sorts trivial and important events, and it has been proposed that hormones released during stress or high arousal may act as a physiological "marker" of importance. You would not want to remember every detail of your life. Unimportant details, such as the color of the shirt that your teacher wore on the forty-third class meeting of the third grade, are probably not useful to retain. Thus, as animals have evolved, memory systems may have co-opted the endocrine signals of physiological stress to signal important events. At an ultimate level of causation, the marking of important events could enhance learning about adaptively significant aspects of the world. Presumably, the entomologist learned about the dangers of running into a street from just one experience, or learning "trial." The hormones secreted as he fell into the street and immediately thereafter notified his brain about the importance of the event. He can confidently claim that he learned from his experience because he never again ventured into the street without first checking for traffic.

Memory is not a unitary process; there are several types of memory systems, and some do not even require a nervous system. For example, the immune systems of vertebrates retain memory for microbes and respond vigorously to previously encountered agents. Likewise, computers and smart phones have sophisticated memory systems. All memory systems share the ability to enter information into storage (acquisition and consolidation), to retain information, and to retrieve information from storage. These three components of memory must operate, or learning will not occur. Hormones can affect any of these components of memory, or they can affect learning directly and thus memory indirectly. However, it is rare to measure learning directly; only the results of learning can be measured and quantified. Consequently, statements about the effects of hormones on learning and memory are typically based on their effects on performance of a task, or observed behavior, but there are other ways by which hormones can affect performance on a learning task.

In addition to using a functional memory system, successful learning involves several psychological components, namely, motivation, attention, and arousal. These components, like learning itself, are hypothetical psychological constructs designed to describe features of behavioral performance. These hypothetical constructs cannot be measured directly; only performance on a test designed to assess one of these constructs can be measured. For example, if your professor gave you an examination to test your learning of behavioral endocrinology but only asked questions about astronomy, you would probably complain, correctly, that the test was not a valid measure of your learning. Sometimes tests cannot discriminate one hypothetical construct from others. If you leave an answer blank on the exam, your professor does not know whether your failure to answer reflects a failure to learn the material, a failure to attend to the material when it was presented in class, or a failure to be sufficiently motivated to answer the question. Probably, your professor will assume that a failure in learning occurred and will assign a grade accordingly.

Learning, motivation, arousal, and attention interact and affect one another. In fact, one of the few laws in psychology states that learning is an inverted U-shaped function of arousal (Yerkes and Dodson, 1908) (**FIGURE 12.2**). That is, learning does not occur in individuals that are too highly aroused (excited, agitated) or insufficiently aroused (exhausted). Hormones are involved in arousal, motivation, and probably also sensation, perception, attention, and emotion. Additionally, hormones can affect the level of anxiety independently from arousal during acquisition or memory testing. The goal of this chapter is to describe several basic components of learning and memory and to describe how hormones can affect these processes as well as affect arousal, motivation, or attention for the salience of learning and memory situations.

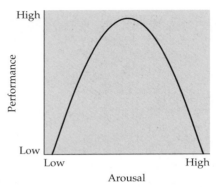

FIGURE 12.2 Arousal and learning
Optimal performance on learning tasks occurs at moderate levels of arousal. If arousal is either too low or too high, learning is adversely affected. Because hormones are involved in arousal, they can have effects on learned performance. After Yerkes and Dodson, 1908.

Components of Learning and Memory

Several recent studies have demonstrated that the endocrine system has an important role in mediating learning and memory. In order to understand these hormonal effects, it is useful to review several components of learning and memory. **Learning** can be defined as a process that expresses itself as an adaptive change in behavior in response to experience. The stages of learning include acquisition, consolidation, retrieval, and extinction. **Memory**—the encoding, storage, and retrieval (or forgetting) of information about past experience—is necessary if learning is to take place. Hormones can affect any one or all of these stages of learning and memory.

Nonassociative Learning

All animals appear to be capable of changing their behavior as a result of experience. **Nonassociative learning** occurs after repeated presentation of a single stimulus. **Sensitization** is one type of nonassociative learning in which a stimulus that originally provoked little or no response begins to evoke stronger responses after several presentations, or a single intense presentation provokes stronger responses to other stimuli. For example, after you experience a loud clanging noise, a slight noise to which you would not have reacted before might elicit a startle response.

Another type of nonassociative learning is **habituation**, a generalized and simple type of learning. Habituation involves learning *not* to respond after repeated exposure to a stimulus. Habituation can be functionally important in all kinds of behavior. When young ground squirrels around the university campus first emerge from their natal burrows in the spring, they seem very fearful. They scurry back home each time someone walks too close or when the shadows of the trees move about on the lawn. Eventually, they habituate to the harmless shadows and the comings and goings of students, and they go about their business of collecting food from the trash barrels. The neuronal mechanism of habituation has been studied in simple invertebrate systems, and in fact, the phenomenon of habituation can be demonstrated in a few cells living in a glass dish. This work has demonstrated that habituation results from a reduction in the amount of neurotransmitter released into the synapses.

Habituation is fundamentally different from fatigue or sensory adaptation. *Fatigue* is loss of efficiency in the performance of a motor act after numerous, rapid repetitions. The loss of response that is experienced after performing several chin-

learning An adaptive change in behavior that results from experience.

memory The encoding, storage, and retrieval of information about past experience.

nonassociative learning Change in the strength of response to a stimulus after repeated exposures.

sensitization Progressive amplification of a response after repeated administrations of a stimulus.

habituation Decrease in response to a stimulus after repeated exposures.

TABLE 12.1 *Types of learning and memory*
Learning
Nonassociative
Sensitization
Habituation
Associative
Classical conditioning
Operant conditioning
Appetitive conditioning: rewarded by attainment of positive reinforcement
Avoidance (aversive) conditioning: rewarded by ending negative reinforcer
Active avoidance: response required
Passive avoidance: suppression of tendency required
Memory
Short-term memory (working memory) (spatial and nonspatial)
Long-term memory (reference memory) (spatial and nonspatial)
Procedural (implicit)
Skill learning
Priming
Conditioning
Declarative (explicit)
Semantic (facts)
Episodic (events

ups, for instance, is due to fatigue in the muscles and is not usually attributable to forgetting how to do chin-ups. *Sensory adaptation* occurs at the level of the sensory receptor: in short, sensory receptors that are repeatedly exposed to a stimulus stop sending nerve impulses to the CNS. Thus, in sensory adaptation, the messages do not reach the CNS; in habituation, the messages reach the CNS, but they are essentially ignored. Sensory adaptation is considered a way for the nervous system to protect itself from being overwhelmed by sensory input (and habituation might serve the same purpose). For example, the pressure of our clothes on hairs wired to cells that sense mechanical pressure is continuous, but sensory adaptation spares us from being overwhelmed by a neural barrage of signals from these cells that would offer little new information about the world.

To date, no studies have directly examined the effects of hormones on a simple cellular learning system, although the effects of gonadal and adrenal steroids (Day and Good, 2005; Kim et al., 2006) on hippocampal long-term potentiation and long-term depression, two critical cellular substrates underlying memory formation (Collingridge et al., 2010; Kullman and Lamasa, 2007), are well described (see below). The direct effects of hormones on the mechanisms of habituation could be studied by the sequential introduction of several hormones, assuming that the appropriate receptors were present; the effects of each hormone on neurotransmitter release could then be catalogued. Presumably, some hormones might facilitate neurotransmitter release, whereas other hormones might inhibit it. In the absence of understanding the mechanisms of hormonal action on the simplest types of learning, one might predict that understanding more-complex types of learning would be difficult; however, as we will see, many attempts to unravel the relationships among hormones, brain, and learning and memory have been successful. Behavioral biologists have developed several ways to study more-complex types of learning (**TABLE 12.1**) in nonhuman animals, and these methods have shown that complex types of learning are affected by hormones.

Associative Learning

Learning about relationships is called **associative learning**. Associative learning is also often called *conditioning*, which refers to the procedure by which this type of learning occurs. One type of conditioning is termed classical conditioning. Ivan Pavlov, a Russian physiologist, discovered this phenomenon while studying the digestive function of dogs (**FIGURE 12.3**). Pavlov noticed that the dogs began to salivate as soon as they saw his assistant arrive to feed them. Most of us probably would have dismissed this observation, but Pavlov designed a study to examine this phenomenon. When meat powder was placed in a dog's mouth, the dog naturally salivated. When Pavlov gave meat powder and sounded a bell simultaneously, salivation resulted. After this sequence was repeated a number of times, the sound of the bell alone produced salivation in the *absence* of any meat powder.

In classical conditioning, a response that was originally elicited by one stimulus can now be elicited by another stimulus that originally had no effect; in other words, learning represents the formation of an *association* (or pairing) between the

associative learning The process by which an association between two stimuli is established.

FIGURE 12.3 Ivan Pavlov first described the phenomenon of classical conditioning. He also was awarded the Nobel Prize in Physiology or Medicine in 1904 for his research about the digestive system.

two stimuli. The first stimulus (the food in the case of Pavlov's dogs) is the one that evoked the response (salivation) without prior experience. This type of stimulus-response pair is considered an innate reflex; the stimulus is called an *unconditioned stimulus* (US) and its response an *unconditioned response* (UCR). For classical conditioning, a second stimulus (the bell) is used that does not initially evoke any response that affects the UCR; this stimulus is termed a *conditioned stimulus* (CS). Over time, Pavlov's dogs associated the sound of the bell (the CS) with the presentation of food (the US). After the CS is presented repeatedly with the US, eventually, when presented alone, the CS can produce a response that is similar, if not identical, to the original UCR; this response is therefore called a *conditioned response* (CR). In our example, when Pavlov sounded a bell (the CS) slightly before the presentation of food and did this repeatedly, his dogs soon began to salivate (the CR) upon hearing the bell.

B. F. Skinner made famous a second type of associative learning, called operant (also known as instrumental, trial-and-error, or Skinnerian) learning. Operant learning occurs when an animal performs an action in the course of appetitive or searching behavior, frequently by accident, which is reinforced or rewarded. Often this single incident does not lead to a direct association of the action (the operant) with its result (reinforcement), but if the act is performed several times, by choice, and is reinforced each time, the association gradually builds. Operant learning, or operant conditioning, can be demonstrated by placing a rat in a box with a lever (**FIGURE 12.4**) and giving it a small food reward each time it presses the lever, either by accident or during exploratory behavior. After a few of these events, the rat will begin to press the lever more and more often. Similarly, you have learned that if you put money into a vending machine, you will receive something to eat or drink in return. If the reward is removed, then the response is rapidly extinguished.

Depending on how behaviors are learned during operant conditioning, the behavior may fade away after only a few trials without reinforcement or it may take many trials. For example, if you put money

FIGURE 12.4 A Skinner box is used to measure instrumental learning (aka operant conditioning). It facilitates assessment of the ability of an animal to form an association between its behavior and the outcome of that behavior.

FIGURE 12.5 **Avoidance behavior** (A) Active avoidance tasks require animals to act to avoid unpleasant stimuli. For example, a mouse might have to move to one side of the box to avoid a foot shock. (B) Passive avoidance tasks require animals to inhibit a behavior that they would otherwise display. In this example, a mouse might have to resist its natural urge to move to the dark part of the box when the light comes on, to avoid a foot shock in the dark compartment.

(A) Active avoidance

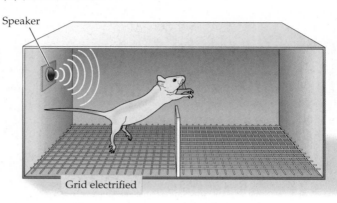

Speaker

Grid electrified

(B) Passive avoidance

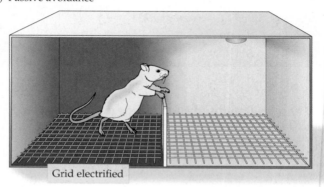

Grid electrified

into a vending machine but received nothing in return, it is likely that you would stop the behavior. You might try again, but only because you have been conditioned to expect a soda, and if you did not receive a soda after a second attempt, you would be highly unlikely to try a third time. In contrast, if you have been conditioned to receive a reinforcement after some *random* number of attempts—for example, by a slot machine—rather than every single time, then you might continue to insert money and pull the handle for a very long time without any reinforcement.

Active avoidance, another type of associative learning, refers to a situation in which an animal must do something—that is, act—to avoid a noxious situation. For example, a mouse may be placed in a box that is divided into two compartments (**FIGURE 12.5A**). A warning bell is sounded, then the mouse receives a mild foot shock. It can escape the foot shock by going to the other compartment. After a few trials, the mouse will learn to move to the other compartment when it hears the bell, thus avoiding the shock. Once the mouse has learned to leave the compartment every time the bell is sounded, it is removed from the test box—called a shuttle box because the animal shuttles back and forth—and receives no more practice. After a period of time, the mouse is returned to the shuttle box, and the strength of the association between the bell and the foot shock—that is, the degree of learning—is assessed. A mouse that leaves the compartment when it hears the bell is said to have a stronger memory than a mouse that does not. The strength of the memory decreases as the interval between training and testing increases. In general, memory fades with time, and a strong foot shock is remembered longer than a mild foot shock.

Note that forgetting (fading memory) differs from extinction. **Extinction** occurs when an individual stops responding to a stimulus following a series of nonreinforced experiences or trials. In the case of extinction, the individual has either

active avoidance A type of learning in which an individual must perform an action to avoid a noxious situation.

extinction The disappearance of a learned response when the response is no longer reinforced.

unlearned what was learned previously or has learned something new to replace the previous information. Forgetting is typically considered to be one of two processes: the decay of a memory trace or the inability to retrieve stored information as a function of the time since learning. A good analogy to keep the two processes of forgetting separate involves books in a library: the ink fading in a book would be analogous to a decay of the memory trace, and the inability to find the book because it had been shelved in the wrong spot would be analogous to retrieval failure. In this scenario, the choice of another book instead would be analogous to extinction.

Passive avoidance refers to a slightly different associative learning situation in which an animal must learn to suppress some behavior that would otherwise be exhibited (**FIGURE 12.5B**). For example, mice prefer dark compartments to illuminated ones. A mouse may be placed in an illuminated compartment that is adjacent to a dark one. When the mouse goes into the dark compartment, which it prefers, it receives a foot shock and must travel back into the illuminated part of the shuttle box to escape the shock. The next time it is put into the illuminated compartment, the mouse should avoid entering the dark compartment if it remembers its past noxious experience there. In other words, the mouse inhibits its inclination to enter the dark compartment of the box and therefore passively avoids the unpleasant stimulus. The length of time the mouse remains in the lighted compartment is an indication of the strength of its memory for the noxious experience.

Both active and passive avoidance learning are examples of aversive conditioning, or **aversive learning**. Fear conditioning, or fear learning, in rodents depends on their natural response to freeze when frightened. For example, when a warning light or sound is paired with a mild foot shock, then rats and mice tend to freeze (**FIGURE 12.6**). After a few pairings, rodents freeze in response to the light or sound without the foot shock. Researchers examine how long this memory persists with various hormonal treatments. Another type of associative learning is called **appetitive learning**. In this situation, an animal learns to perform some task that is rewarded with food, water, or some other pleasant experience. For example, a rat may learn to navigate a maze if it receives a food reward at the end. We learned in Chapter 6 that a female rat or chimpanzee will press a bar to gain access to a male when her estrogen concentration is high.

passive avoidance   A type of learning in which an individual must suppress some behavior that would otherwise be exhibited.

aversive learning   A change in behavior to avoid some noxious outcome.

appetitive learning   Reinforcement of a behavior by a positive outcome.

(1) Warning sound only

(2) Warning sound paired with foot shock—rodents freeze

Grid electrified

(3) Warning sound only—rodents freeze

FIGURE 12.6   **Fear conditioning is often used to test the effects of hormones on memory.** It is easy to perform, quickly learned, and retained for days. Thus, it is used to determine on which stages of memory hormones act. One disadvantage is that the stress of the experience can affect glucocorticoids, epinephrine, and other hormone concentrations that may affect the results. In this model, an individual experiences a tone paired with a foot shock. After a few pairings, the individual is put into a new cage and only the tone is sounded, and the extent to which the animal freezes indicates its memory of the experience.

FIGURE 12.7   The taxonomy of memory

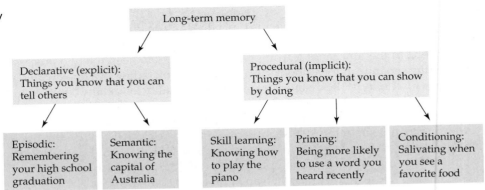

Memory

A memory system is required in order for adaptive changes in behavior to result from experience. Current situations must be compared with prior events that are in some way encoded in memory. Memory has been categorized into several types, to aid in its description and in the study of its mechanisms. However, even with these descriptive labels, there is often disagreement about their definitions and what those definitions tell us about the underlying mechanisms. Memory can be divided, for example, into short-term and long-term memory. *Short-term memory* persists for seconds to minutes. For example, when you look up a telephone number, you usually can retain it sufficiently long to dial the number. If you receive a busy signal, however, you may have to look it up again if you did not rehearse the number to yourself several times. Such *rehearsing* is the best way to move items from short-term into long-term memory. *Long-term memory* lasts for days, weeks, or years. Our long-term memory appears to have no upper limit in capacity or retention, whereas our short-term memory seems able to handle about seven items, give or take a couple—about the number of digits in a telephone number—for up to an hour.

Long-term memory can be divided into several categories as well. For instance, it can be divided into procedural memory and declarative memory (**FIGURE 12.7**). **Procedural memory**, also termed "implicit memory," is essentially your memory for "knowing how." There are three types of procedural memory: for skill learning, priming, and conditioning. Remembering how to play a song on a piano, ride a bicycle, or run in a maze are types of procedural memory for *skill learning*. *Priming* involves a change in memory or processing of a stimulus as a result of previous experience. For example, if a person is exposed to the word *estrogen* on a list of words, then asked to fill in the blank after seeing "est____," then that person is more likely to say *estrogen* than someone who has not been primed. Finally, *conditioning* includes memory for both classical and operant conditioning, as previously described.

Declarative memory, also termed *explicit memory*, is your memory for "knowing what," that is, for knowing facts. Declarative memory can be divided into *semantic memory*, which is your general knowledge of facts and events, and *episodic memory*, which is your memory of personal events (episodes), such as a birthday party. Declarative memory has also been called *verbal memory* in humans, whereas procedural memories are generally nonverbal. Declarative memories are generally formed and forgotten relatively easily, whereas procedural memories, such as knowing how to swim or ride a bicycle, require longer to establish but, once learned, remain easier to retain.

Another way to categorize memory is by dividing it into working memory and reference memory. **Working memory** is similar to declarative and short-term memory in that it typically involves short-term memory for information that changes on a regular basis. It differs from **reference memory**, which generally refers to associations or discriminations requiring repetitive learning, as in learning the rules

procedural memory   Memory that stores long-term information about how to perform procedures, such as walking, swimming, and riding a bike.

declarative memory   Memory for facts or events.

working memory   The part of short-term memory involved with immediate conscious perceptual and linguistic processing.

reference memory   Knowledge for aspects of a task.

of a task or how to navigate around an environment such as a maze. Hormones have significant effects on spatial memory, which can involve both spatial working memory and spatial reference memory. **Spatial memory** can be defined as memory for the location of items or places in space. We usually think about navigation when we think of spatial memory, but spatial memory may include finding a specific reference in this text book, finding your keys before you leave your apartment, or remembering the location of your classrooms on campus.

As noted above, successful learning involves several psychological components, including motivation, attention, and arousal. It is important to note that several animal studies have been conducted in which the influence of these so-called performance factors has been minimized—these studies are discussed later in this chapter. For example, post-training administration of some hormones, particularly water-soluble steroids that are eliminated quickly, prevents the influence of some other exogenous hormones on performance factors. That is, the administered hormones are not bioavailable during training or testing; they are present only during the memory consolidation processes that occur later in the home cage. Thus, careful researchers have minimized the effects of hormones on performance factors, as we will see below.

> **spatial memory** Subcategory of memory that encodes information about the environment and its orientation.

The Effects of Hormones on Learning and Memory

In 1915, Walter Cannon proposed his emergency theory of adrenal function, which suggested that following exposure to stress, the secretion of epinephrine (adrenaline) from the adrenal glands increases as a means of adapting to that stress (see Chapter 11). Many physiological studies conducted throughout the 1920s and 1930s demonstrated the stimulatory effects of epinephrine on the respiratory and cardiovascular systems. Few experimental studies, however, examined the behavioral effects of epinephrine until after the Second World War, when the acute fear "paralysis" that occurred in some soldiers going into combat was thought to be caused by excessive discharge of the adrenal medullary hormones (see Kosman and Gerard, 1955). Aversive conditioning studies were conducted on animals in order to investigate the effects of noxious stimuli on adrenal secretions. In these studies, the effects of adrenal hormones on learning and memory were discovered, and they laid the groundwork for studies of the effects of many other hormones on learning and memory.

Epinephrine

More is now known about the role of epinephrine in learning than about that of any other hormone (Roozendaal et al., 2009). Reliable assays and selective agonists and antagonists have been available longer for epinephrine than for other hormones. One can easily assess the amount of epinephrine released during learning and demonstrate that it is released when learning typically occurs.

In general, epinephrine enhances memory, and the memory-enhancing effects of epinephrine are both dose- and time-dependent. As one would expect based on the U-shaped function of arousal mentioned above, which is known as the Yerkes-Dodson curve, responses to different concentrations of epinephrine follow an inverted U-shaped curve; that is, low and high blood levels of epinephrine impair memory, whereas moderate epinephrine levels enhance memory (Korol and Gold, 2007). Because epinephrine is released in response to stressful events, a reasonable possibility is that epinephrine potentiates the effects of the noxious stimuli used to train animals in active avoidance tasks. Animals perform better in avoidance situations after receiving a moderate rather than a mild foot shock. If epinephrine potentiates the effects of noxious stimuli, then (1) epinephrine should be released when the shock occurs, and (2) epinephrine treatment paired with mild foot shocks should produce

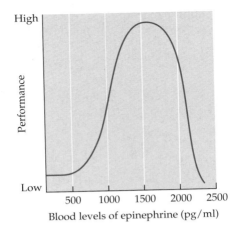

FIGURE 12.8 **Effects of epinephrine on performance** The effectiveness of doses of epinephrine in enhancing performance on memory tasks follows an inverted U-shaped curve. The optimal dose in rats is about 0.1 mg/kg, which yields a blood level of epinephrine of about 1500 pg/ml. After Gold and Van Buskirk, 1975.

learning comparable to that observed in animals experiencing moderate foot shocks. Both of these effects have been demonstrated. For example, the optimal level of epinephrine for avoidance memory enhancement in rats is 1500 picograms per milliliter (pg/ml) of blood serum, and this level is typically observed in rats that show optimal performance in avoidance tasks (Gold, 1987) (**FIGURE 12.8**). If a mild foot shock produces blood epinephrine levels of 1000 pg/ml and this shock is paired with an injection that raises epinephrine levels another 500 pg/ml, then the exogenous and endogenous epinephrine sum together, and the animal exhibits optimal learning (Gold, 1987).

The best time to administer epinephrine is immediately after training; treatment either before training or after a substantial period of time has elapsed since training is not effective in enhancing memory (**FIGURE 12.9**). These temporal constraints are consistent with the hypothesis that epinephrine influences memory by potentiating the effects of noxious events. Our colleague the entomologist was extremely stressed as a boy by observing the car bearing down on him. Possibly, his adrenal glands began releasing large quantities of epinephrine immediately after his learning "trial," and the elevated levels of epinephrine enhanced his memory to the extent that he vividly reports the incident 55 years later.

How does epinephrine enhance memory? Again, learning and memory involve encoding, storing, and retrieving information. Epinephrine, as well as other hormones, may facilitate any or all of these processes. The precise mechanisms of memory have yet to be elucidated, but neuroscientists certainly agree that the memory for active and passive avoidance tasks resides in the brain. However, epinephrine is a polar molecule that does not easily cross the blood-brain barrier, although it is produced by a very few neurons in the brain as a neurotransmitter (Weil-Malharbe et al., 1959). We are faced with an apparent paradox: how can epinephrine secreted by the adrenal glands affect learning and memory processes if it cannot get to the neurons in the brain? Obviously, epinephrine must affect some process outside the brain that subsequently influences the brain. There are currently two working hypotheses regarding how epinephrine affects memory: (1) epinephrine activates peripheral receptors that directly influence brain function, and (2) epinephrine affects memory via its effect on blood glucose levels.

THE PERIPHERAL RECEPTOR HYPOTHESIS One working hypothesis for how epinephrine modulates memory is that it activates peripheral receptors that communicate with the central nervous system (McGaugh, 1989). In order to discover which receptors are involved in the memory effects of epinephrine, specific receptor agonists (mimics) and antagonists (blockers) have been used.

The effects of epinephrine on memory can be blocked by drugs that block both the α- and β-epinephrine (adrenergic) receptors (Sternberg et al., 1985, 1986). For example, rats were injected with an α- or a β-adrenergic antagonist in one study—phenoxybenzamine or propranolol, respectively—30 minutes before they received either an injection of epinephrine or a foot shock (which caused

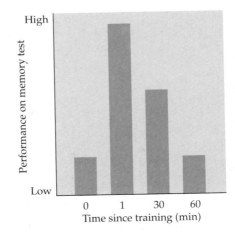

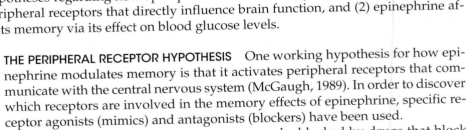

FIGURE 12.9 **The effects of epinephrine on memory are time-dependent.** Injections of epinephrine (1 mg/kg) are most effective in enhancing memory if given 1 minute after training; the beneficial effects of epinephrine diminish 60 minutes after training. After Gold, 1987.

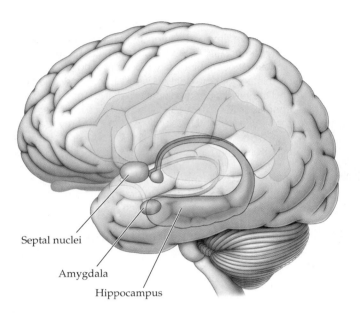

FIGURE 12.10 The amygdala and associated structures seen in a cutaway lateral view of the human brain.

Septal nuclei

Amygdala

Hippocampus

endogenous levels of epinephrine to rise). The results of this study suggest that epinephrine acts on peripheral adrenergic receptors to initiate its effects on memory (McGaugh, 1989).

In addition to acting in the periphery, epinephrine can act directly on neural structures involved in learning and memory. These direct, central effects of epinephrine may reflect endocrine activity, or epinephrine may affect memory directly (perhaps after entering the brain through the cerebrospinal fluid, thus circumventing the blood-brain barrier) by acting as a central neurotransmitter. Of special interest is the amygdala. Although the amygdala has been considered for years to be involved in emotions, this almond-shaped part of the limbic forebrain (at the base of the temporal lobe) is also involved in learning and memory, both directly and indirectly via its close association with the hippocampus (**FIGURE 12.10**). Electrical stimulation of the amygdala can increase memory retention (McGaugh and Gold, 1976). In an elegant series of experiments, it was demonstrated that memory for aversive conditioning can be modulated by post-training injections of epinephrine and norepinephrine directly into the amygdala. The increased retention induced by intra-amygdala injections of norepinephrine can be blocked by concurrent administration of β-adrenergic antagonists such as propranolol (Gallagher et al., 1981). The effect is observed only if the norepinephrine and the adrenergic antagonist are injected on the same side of the brain; in other words, the effect is *stereospecific*. In common with epinephrine, the effect of norepinephrine is dose- and time-dependent. The degree of activation of the amygdala by emotion-arousing stimuli (both positive and negative) correlates directly with subsequent recall of those stimuli. Post-training infusions of adrenergic agonists into the basolateral amygdala (BLA) lead to enhanced memory performance (Lalumiere et al., 2003; Power et al., 2002); conversely, infusions into the BLA of adrenergic antagonists impair memory (e.g., Cahill et al., 2000).

It is possible that peripheral adrenergic stimulation integrates with central, amygdalar stimulation to enhance memory formation. Studies have indicated that peripheral epinephrine acts via β-noradrenergic receptors, which activate ascending neurons in the vagus nerve (Hoyer, 2003; Williams et al., 1998). These neurons travel to the nucleus of the solitary tract (NTS). The NTS projects noradrenergic fibers to the amygdala, especially the BLA. The BLA modulates the memory of emotional experiences by modulating memory consolidation via efferents to other brain regions, including the caudate nucleus, nucleus accumbens, and cortex (McGaugh, 2004).

(A)

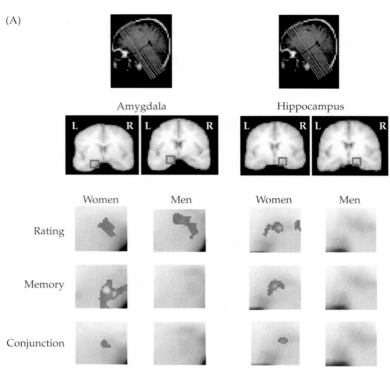

FIGURE 12.11 Colocalization of brain regions associated with emotional-intensity ratings and recognition memory (A) Areas of activation that correlated with highest emotional-intensity ratings (Rating), those that correlated with the best subsequent memory (Memory), and the results of a conjunction analysis of these two conditions (Conjunction) are shown for women and men. Also shown are locations in the left amygdala and right hippocampus in which brain activation correlated with both rating and memory in women, but not men, in overlapping or adjacent brain regions. Oblique slice prescriptions are shown in red, and the slice containing the region of interest is in green. R = right; L = left. (B) Proportion of recognized pictures rated neutral (0) to emotionally very arousing (3) (summed percentage of familiar and remembered pictures) by men and women. From Canli et al., 2002.

(B)

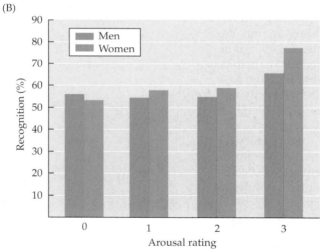

Blocking any part of this pathway prevents the memory-enhancing effects of epinephrine (Gold, 2003).

In one fascinating study of humans, individuals read either an emotionally charged story or a similar story that was judged by other people to be more emotionally neutral (Cahill et al., 1994). Some individuals were treated with propranolol, a potent β-adrenergic antagonist, which significantly impaired memory of the emotionally arousing story but did not affect memory of the neutral story (Cahill et al., 1994). The researchers who conducted this study were able to rule out the possibility that the drug had nonspecific effects on attention or motivation. These results support the hypothesis that highly charged emotional memories require activation of β-adrenergic receptors (Cahill et al., 1994). Treatment with epinephrine or exposure to cold pressor stress (holding a hand in ice water for 2 minutes, which evokes secretion of epinephrine) after participants viewed emotionally charged pictures enhanced the long-term recall of those pictures (Cahill and Alkire, 2003; Cahill et al., 2003).

Imaging work on humans has confirmed and extended the hypothesis that the amygdala is important for encoding emotionally charged memories. Using either PET or fMRI, two studies determined that recall of a series of scenes correlated highly with the activation of the amygdala (Cahill et al., 1996; Canli et al., 2000). Importantly, the association between recall and amygdala activation during learning was highest for the pictures judged to be most emotionally intense (Canli et al., 2000) (**FIGURE 12.11**). Imaging studies of the contribution of emotions to memory consolidation have revealed an important sex difference (McGaugh, 2004). Women displayed enhanced activity in the left amygdala in relation to improved memory recall, whereas men displayed enhanced activity in the right amygdala in the same relationship to memory (Cahill et al., 2001; Canli et al., 2002).

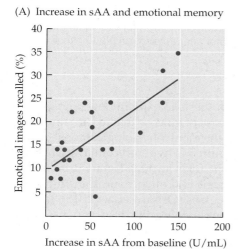

(A) Increase in sAA and emotional memory

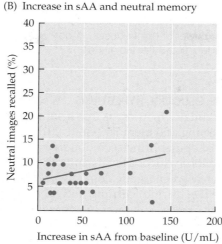

(B) Increase in sAA and neutral memory

FIGURE 12.12 **People catego-rized as responders increased salivary α-amylase (sAA)**, a bio-marker for adrenergic activity, in response to emotional images (A) but not to neutral images (B). After Segal and Cahill, 2009.

In a subsequent follow-up study, salivary α-amylase (sAA), a biomarker for adrenergic activity, was assessed both before and after participants viewed a series of mixed emotional and neutral images (Segal and Cahill, 2009). Endogenous noradrenergic activation, defined as an elevated sAA immediately after the image viewing, occurred in about one-third of the participants. A week later, the participants were invited to return to the lab, where they were given a surprise free-recall test. The increase in sAA and the percentage of emotional, but not neutral, pictures recalled was correlated (**FIGURE 12.12**). Thus, these results suggest a relationship between endogenous noradrenergic activation and long-term memory performance in humans. The vast majority of this relationship was attributed to women; sAA response was found in very few men viewing the emotionally charged images (Segal and Cahill, 2009). More work is necessary to specify the importance of this structural sex difference in emotional processing.

The glucose and peripheral receptor hypotheses of how epinephrine affects memory are not incompatible (Morris et al., 2010). Epinephrine elevates blood glucose concentrations, which increases the amount of glucose that enters neurons in the brain. In turn, these neurons release higher concentrations of acetylcholine into the synapses. Epinephrine also appears to act directly on neurons to enhance their function. There may be other mechanisms underlying memory enhancement by epinephrine as well. During stressful events, additional adrenal hormones (i.e., the glucocorticoids) are secreted. As we shall see, these steroid hormones also have significant effects on learning and memory. In addition, the effects of epinephrine, administered either peripherally or centrally, may hypothetically be mediated via increased release rates of adrenocorticotropic hormone (ACTH). However, the memory-enhancing effect of post-training epinephrine administration is not blocked by dexamethasone, an artificial steroid that blocks the release of ACTH. Therefore, it appears that ACTH does not mediate the memory-enhancing effect of epinephrine (McGaugh et al., 1987), although ACTH and glucocorticoids have their own potent effects on memory.

Possession of enhanced memories associated with arousing experiences is inherently adaptive for avoiding danger in the future. Nonetheless, when memories of fearful situations are intrusive, distressing, and unwanted, they can lead to disorders such as post-traumatic stress disorder (PTSD). The role of epinephrine and norepinephrine in the development and maintenance of PTSD are currently being investigated (reviewed in Wilker et al., 2014). It seems possible that variation among people in their fear-learning and memory mechanisms, as well as their responsiveness to epinephrine and norepinephrine, may contribute to individual variation in susceptibility to PTSD (Wilker et al., 2014).

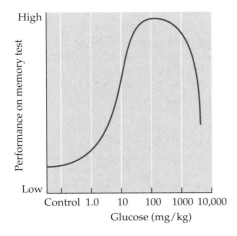

Glucose (mg/kg)

FIGURE 12.13 **Effects of glucose on learning** Optimal performance on a memory task is attained with a dose of 100 mg/kg of glucose provided within 1 minute of training. Lower or higher doses, or doses provided later after training, do not enhance memory function. After Gold, 1987.

THE GLUCOSE HYPOTHESIS   A second hypothesis to explain how epinephrine modulates memory is that it stimulates release of glucose that in turn improves learning and memory (Gold, 2015). One of the many physiological consequences of epinephrine secretion in a stressed animal is hyperglycemia, an increase in blood glucose levels and other metabolic fuels such as lactate used by the increased energetic demands of glutamatergic and other neurotransmitter activities during learning and memory processes (Osburn et al., 2015). In general, glucose enhances memory for avoidance learning; the dose-response curve again resembles an inverted U (Gold, 1986; Parsons and Gold, 1992) (**FIGURE 12.13**). As with epinephrine, the effects of glucose are time-dependent; injections of glucose delayed by 1 hour after training have no effect on retention and performance. The doses of glucose and of epinephrine that are most effective in enhancing memory both result in plasma glucose levels comparable to those found naturally in response to optimal training conditions. Glucose injected directly into the brain also enhances memory (Gold, 2014; reviewed by Korol and Gold, 2007).

Additional evidence that epinephrine produces its effects on memory by raising blood glucose levels is based on negative findings. The memory-enhancing and memory-impairing effects of epinephrine treatment can be blocked by treating animals with adrenergic antagonists—drugs that block peripheral epinephrine receptors—but these blockers have no effect on memory enhancement produced by glucose treatment. These results are consistent with the notion that glucose release is a memory modulation step that occurs subsequent to the release of epinephrine. Because adrenergic antagonists block the receptors by which epinephrine acts, they prevent the effects of epinephrine, as well as those of treatments that act through epinephrine on memory. But the effects of glucose, which are "downstream" from the peripheral epinephrine receptors, remain intact. The agents most effective in enhancing human cognitive performance (i.e., improving learning and memory) share a common feature: they all elevate blood glucose levels (**TABLE 12.2**).

How does glucose produce its effects on memory? As we saw in Chapter 9, the brain requires a constant supply of glucose in order to function. Elevated blood glucose levels permit more glucose to enter neurons, which in turn stimulates an increase in the release of the neurotransmitter acetylcholine from neurons in the brain. Increases in acetylcholine levels in the brain synapses are characteristic of

TABLE 12.2 *Agents that enhance cognitive performance*	
Substance	**Effect**
Nootropics[a]: Aniracetam, piracetam, pramiracetam, oxiracetam	Elevation of glucose
Others: Amphetamine, epinephrine, glucose, hypertonic saline, painful stimuli, stress, vasopressin	Elevation of glucose
Choline, lecithin, physostigmine, phosphatidylserine	Elevation of synaptic ACh, but not glucose
Phlorizin[b]	Inhibition of glucose transport

[a] Pharmacological cognitive enhancers.

[b] Although phlorizin interferes with brain glucose utilization, it still enhances memory performance by some unknown means.

all known cognitive enhancers (see Table 12.2). Thus, cognitive enhancers must work by increasing glucose, which increases acetylcholine release, or by increasing acetylcholine levels directly (McGaugh and Roozendaal, 2009). The neurobiological mechanism(s) by which glucose improves memory do appear to involve acetylcholine release. In a study of rats in a simple T-maze, microdialysis revealed that acetylcholine levels were elevated in glucose-treated rats during memory testing (Ragozzino et al., 1996). The severe memory deficits observed in patients with advanced Alzheimer's disease or AIDS are correlated with a marked reduction in neurons that secrete acetylcholine. Obviously, cognitive enhancers that increase the release of acetylcholine or prolong its half-life have important clinical potential (Gold et al., 2013).

The study of impaired learning and memory represents another approach to understanding the effects of hormones. Memory function in old rats diminishes in a fashion similar to the decline observed in healthy elderly people. Epinephrine enhances the memory of very old rats; however, treatment of elderly human patients with epinephrine to enhance their memories would not be wise, considering the cardiovascular effects of this stimulatory hormone.

Unlike epinephrine, glucose is a relatively safe compound with which to study memory in humans (Smith et al., 2011). For example, in one study, the effects of glucose on memory were tested in a group of healthy 70-year-old people. Individuals of this age typically have memory impairments even if they do not suffer from dementia or other aspects of Alzheimer's disease. These 70-year-olds scored less well on a standard memory test than college students tested at the same time. Following the test of memory, the elderly participants were asked to drink a glass of lemonade that had been prepared with either saccharine or glucose. Another memory test was then administered. Those individuals who had received glucose showed improved memory function relative to those who drank lemonade prepared with saccharine. It was noted that the glucose utilization efficiency of an individual predicted memory function among the aged, but not the young, subjects. Elderly people often have problems regulating their blood sugar levels. The normal decline in memory function during aging may thus reflect a diminishing ability to regulate blood levels of glucose. The extra glucose provided in the study probably allowed the brain cells to function better in the elderly subjects (Hall et al., 1989).

Recent studies have confirmed that glucose enhances both memory storage and retrieval in healthy elderly humans (Manning et al., 1998b; Smith et al., 2011). Glucose also improves learning and memory in people with Alzheimer's disease, as well as in adults with Down syndrome (Korol and Gold, 1998; Manning et al., 1998a). Although earlier studies on college students failed to discover any effects of glucose on performance, subsequent studies revealed glucose enhancement of learning and memory in this age group when the tasks were challenging (Korol and Gold, 1998). In these challenging memory tests on college students, it was demonstrated that glucose augmented memory for material in a paragraph. Glucose seemed to improve attentional skills in the students as well. However, neither face and word recognition nor working memory (defined here as the nonpermanent storage of information that is being processed in a cognitive task) was influenced by glucose treatment (Korol and Gold, 1998).

Insulin

If unregulated blood glucose levels interfere with learning, then diabetic animals and humans should display learning difficulties. Increasingly, more studies are directly addressing the relationship between diabetes and learning and memory in humans. Some studies report no strong correlation between learning and memory and either insulin-dependent diabetes (Crawford et al., 1995; Helkala et al., 1995; Ryan and Williams, 1993; Wolters et al., 1996) or non-insulin-dependent diabetes in humans (Worrall et al., 1996). However, most studies of insulin-dependent diabetes (Amiel and Gale, 1993; Areosa and Grimley, 2002; Langan et al., 1991; Lincoln et al., 1996) or non-insulin-dependent diabetes (Strachan et al., 1997; Zhou et al., 2010) indicate a strong relationship between glucose regulation and cognitive impairment. Verbal memory is the most commonly affected cognitive ability among diabetics. Although the effects of diabetes on cognitive function are most pronounced among aged people, cognitive impairments have been observed among young adult diabetics as well (e.g., Dey et al., 1997). In insulin-dependent diabetes, cognitive impairments appear to be associated with chronic hyperglycemia and the recurrence of hypoglycemia. In non-insulin-dependent diabetes, the onset of cognitive impairments could reflect disruptions of blood glucose metabolism or a number of related problems, including hyperglycemia, changes in insulin concentration, hypertension, and changes in lipid levels (Kumari et al., 2000; Zhou et al., 2010). These symptoms tend to co-occur and are considered to be part of a syndrome associated with obesity and insulin resistance, termed metabolic syndrome. Both insulin-dependent and non-insulin-dependent diabetes negatively affect measures of verbal and numerical reasoning, attention, concentration, verbal and visual memory, and verbal fluency (Kumari et al., 2000). Diabetes may also increase the risk of dementia (Biessels et al., 2006; Park, 2001; Zhou et al., 2010). Impaired insulin signaling has been proposed as important in the development of Alzheimer's disease (Kulscher, 2011). Presumably, even the milder "forgetting" experienced by those of us who have been on the planet for more than five decades is not simply a sign of normal aging dismissed as "senior moments" but represents dysfunctional glucose regulation as we age (Holscher, 2011).

Indeed, decreased cognition is often observed among healthy older adults even in the absence of diabetes. As people age, glucose metabolism often becomes dysregulated, and even slightly dysregulated glucose metabolism can affect memory. For example, a large (179 men and 232 women) study conducted in Sweden examined healthy nondiabetic people who displayed no symptoms of dementia. These individuals participated in cognitive tests of episodic and semantic memory, and their fasting glucose levels were assayed. Elevated plasma glucose was associated with impaired episodic memory in women, but not men (Rolandsson et al., 2008). Similarly, individuals with impaired fasting glucose or impaired glucose tolerance have reported a more profound cognitive decline than subjects without impaired glucose regulation (Xu et al., 2007). Episodic memory is processed through the hippocampus, which is among the brain regions most susceptible to metabolic changes (Cervos-Navarro and Diemer, 1991). Studies in both humans (Convit et al., 2003) and rats (Biessels et al., 1996) have demonstrated that the effects of hyperglycemia on memory are mediated via dysregulated hippocampal function (**FIGURE 12.14**).

Insulin may be produced in the brain, and there are insulin receptors located in the brain, despite the observation that insulin is not necessary for neurons to take up glucose (see Chapter 9). Activation of these insulin receptors in the brain may be important in associative learning (Zhao and Alkon, 2001). Genetic disruption of brain insulin receptors in mice impairs memory (Bruning et al., 2000). Furthermore, abnormal insulin levels and reduced numbers of brain insulin receptors are common among Alzheimer's patients with severe memory impairments (Craft et al., 1998). Treatment of Alzheimer's patients with insulin while maintaining constant blood glucose levels significantly improved memory (Craft et al., 1996). These effects of insulin receptor activation in the brain may reflect improved neurotransmission (Zhao and Alkon, 2001).

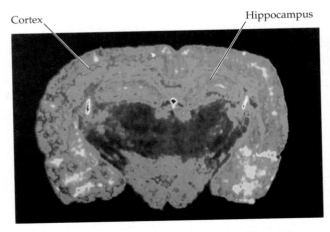

FIGURE 12.14 Insulin receptors (depicted in green) are most concentrated within the cortex and hippocampus. Impaired insulin receptor function correlates with impaired memory. From Hill et al., 1986.

FIGURE 12.15 Streptozotocin impairs performance of passive avoidance tasks. Streptozotocin (STZ) was injected into the ventricles of the brain for the first 18 days of the study. At the initial assessment on day 17, control animals and streptozotocin-treated animals showed little difference in the time they took to step through a door from the brightly lit compartment into the dark compartment. A foot shock was applied on day 18 in the dark compartment. Latency to go from the lit compartment into the dark (preferred) compartment was assessed on days 19, 40, and 80. Note that the rats treated with STZ showed a much shorter latency to enter the box where they previously received a shock. After Hoyer, 2003.

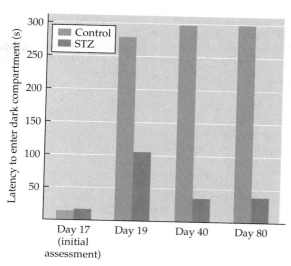

To better understand the mechanisms of cognitive impairment in diabetic humans, several studies have investigated the effects of diabetes on the acquisition of passive avoidance tasks in nonhuman animals. Treatment of rodents with streptozotocin destroys the insulin-secreting β-cells of the pancreas, inducing diabetes (see Chapter 9). Streptozotocin-induced diabetic rodents display modest, but consistent, deficits in passive avoidance learning (Hoyer, 2003; Leedom et al., 1987) (**FIGURE 12.15**). Surprisingly, administration of phlorizin, a drug that inhibits glucose transport into cells, causes significant enhancement of memory performance in diabetic rats in comparison with control rats (Hall et al., 1992). The physiological mechanisms underlying these cognition-enhancing effects of phlorizin remain unspecified.

A common test of spatial learning is the Morris water maze (**FIGURE 12.16**). This water maze consists of a water-filled round tank that is about 1.3 m in diameter and has a small platform below the surface of the water. The tested animal must find and climb onto the platform in order to avoid having to swim (Morris et al., 1982). A rat or mouse is released into the water at different points along the edge of the tank. In order to find the platform on successive trials, the animal must depend on its memory to recall where the platform is located. In the hidden-platform version of the task, the water is milky white and the animal must use its spatial memory to locate the platform in relation to its own current position, with the aid of extra-

(A)

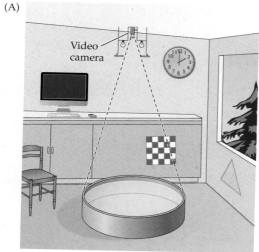

FIGURE 12.16 Spatial memory can be assessed in the Morris water maze. (A) In the Morris water maze, rats must swim to find a submerged platform. The platform is hidden below the surface of milky water. Successfully finding the hidden platform requires relational learning, because the only aids available to guide navigation are large extra-maze cues around the tank. (B) Representative swimming paths of rats in the Morris water maze. Rats learn to navigate to the platform from any position in the tank if they are normal. Each day the rats swim more directly and quickly to the platform or have had their neocortex lesioned. However, if the hippocampus is lesioned, the rat swims aimlessly until it randomly discovers the submerged platform. After Schenk and Morris, 1985.

(B)

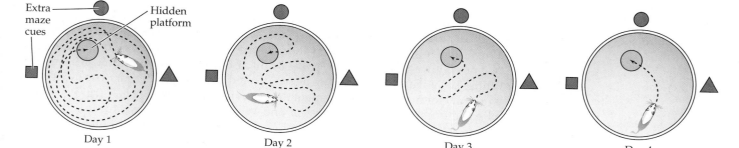

FIGURE 12.17 Impaired glucose metabolism is associated with Alzheimer's disease. (A) Glucose use is reduced in patients with Alzheimer's disease. (B) Regional glucose metabolism is observed in specific brain regions associated with memory in Alzheimer's patients. Early decreases in cortical glucose utilization correspond to the same regions that later demonstrate the greatest density of senile plaques and tangles. From Reiman et al., 1996.

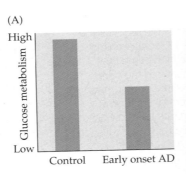

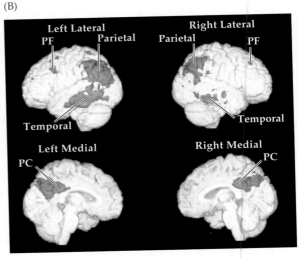

maze visual cues. In a cued version of the task, animals are trained to find a visible platform whose location changes on successive trials; because spatial information is irrelevant to performance of this task, it is often used to control for those aspects of task performance that do not involve memory (e.g., swimming ability and motivation). An animal does not have to be food restricted to learn either version of the task, which has its own built-in motivation—the water is at room temperature and so is unpleasant, and presumably the animal does not want to drown.

Rats rendered diabetic with streptozotocin display deficits in spatial learning in the Morris water maze (Biessels et al., 1996; Lannert and Hoyer, 1998). Streptozotocin-treated rats were tested in the Morris water maze to determine whether their learning deficits could be prevented or reversed by insulin treatment (Biessels et al., 1998). Three experimental groups were evaluated: (1) rats that received streptozotocin but no insulin, (2) rats that received streptozotocin but also received insulin so that diabetes never developed, and (3) rats that received insulin 10 weeks after streptozotocin treatment began (i.e., after the onset of diabetes). In rats treated with insulin early, insulin prevented the streptozotocin-induced deficits in performance. In contrast, if the rats were not treated with insulin until after the onset of diabetes (group 3), then insulin was not effective in reversing the cognitive deficits resulting from the streptozotocin-induced diabetes.

In the next part of the experiment, in vitro long-term potentiation (LTP) in the hippocampus was assessed by monitoring the firing rates of neurons. LTP is an enhancement in the pattern of neuronal connectivity that has been linked to learning (Teyler and Discenna, 1984). The hippocampus is important for processing memory, especially for spatial information. Hippocampal LTP was impaired in the diabetic rats. Insulin treatment that began at the same time as streptozotocin treatment and prevented diabetes also prevented the hippocampal impairments in LTP; insulin treatment that began 10 weeks after the onset of diabetes only partially restored LTP (Biessels et al., 1998). Thus, it seems that insulin affects spatial memory in diabetic rats only if provided from the onset of diabetes.

Other studies have demonstrated that memory can also be enhanced by fructose, a sugar that is not metabolized by the neurons in the brain; other glucose analogues that are not well metabolized by the brain also improved retention (Messier and White, 1987). These latter studies also indicated that a much higher dose of glucose is optimal for memory enhancement than previously reported (e.g., 2.0 g/kg versus 0.1 g/kg in earlier studies) (Messier and White, 1987). The basis for this discrepancy in effective doses is not apparent. Perhaps at high doses these other sugars act at peripheral sites to activate membrane glucose transport mechanisms; at lower

FIGURE 12.18 Recognition memory is related to cortisol concentrations. Treatment with cortisol increased subjects' recall of pictures; negative stimuli were more likely recalled than neutral pictures. After Abercrombie et al., 2003.

doses, the glucose may affect memory more directly via actions on neural function or processing.

If stress is added to the mix, then bad things can happen, at least in an experimental model of Alzheimer's disease. Rats were infused with corticosterone for 2 months, then tested for spatial learning and memory (Osmanovic et al., 2010). Spatial memory was impaired, and gene expression for components of the brain insulin signaling pathway (insulin genes 1 and 2, insulin receptor, and insulin-degrading enzyme) was significantly reduced. Furthermore, gene expression for the tau protein associated with Alzheimer's disease was increased. These data suggest that chronic exposure to high glucocorticoid concentrations affects insulin signaling in the brain and increases tau protein expression, as well as impairs cognition (Osmanovic et al., 2010).

These animal models seem to accurately reflect the cognitive situation in humans with dysregulated glucose. Glucose metabolism is impaired in people with Alzheimer's disease (Salkovic-Petrisic et al., 2009) (**FIGURE 12.17A**). Indeed, glucose metabolism is reduced in brain regions associated with memory (**FIGURE 12.17B**), and brain scans indicate that an early decrease in cortical glucose utilization occurs in the same brain regions that later demonstrate the greatest density of senile plaques and tangles. Considered together, these data indicate that glucose can enhance learning and memory and that impaired glucose metabolism can result in memory problems associated with Alzheimer's disease and other forms of dementia (Salkovic-Petrisic et al., 2009).

Glucocorticoids

This chapter began by describing how memory is enhanced by stressful events. Acute stress appears to promote lasting memories, as does treatment with glucocorticoids. Treatment of people with glucocorticoids prior to learning words or pictures, for example, improves their recall on subsequent memory tests (Abercrombie et al., 2003; Andreano and Cahill, 2006; Buchanan and Lovallo, 2001; Roozendaal et al., 2009) (**FIGURE 12.18**). Chronic stress, however, seems to have the opposite effect. Long-term stress, or long-term treatment with corticosterone, impairs memory (de Quervain et al., 1998, 2009; Luine, 1994; Luine et al., 1994; Oei et al., 2007). Thus, brief exposure to glucocorticoids (i.e., corticosterone or cortisol) enhances learning and memory, whereas chronic exposure to glucocorticoids appears to function as an **amnestic** (an agent that promotes forgetting) in most of the studies reported to date (de Quervain et al., 2009; Roozendaal et al., 2009). Like arousal and epinephrine, glucocorticoid concentrations also provoke an inverted U-shaped curve on learning and memory (**FIGURE 12.19**).

Another common test of learning in rats uses a radial arm maze (**FIGURE 12.20**). This task can be used to test both long-term

amnestic A substance or event that causes forgetting.

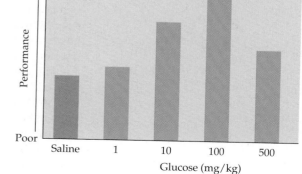

FIGURE 12.19 Learning improves in humans with increasing doses of glucose, but the effect of glucose is limited at higher doses, suggesting that diabetics with elevated circulating glucose levels should be expected to display impaired learning and memory. After Stone et al., 1992.

FIGURE 12.20 **The radial arm maze,** popularized by David Olton, is a common apparatus used in assessments of spatial memory. The maze is open at the top and may have 8, 12, or even 36 arms; the greater the number of arms, the more difficult the maze. During training, the subject learns that only some of the arms are baited (have a food reward) at the end. To solve the maze successfully after training, the subject must make only one trip down each baited arm and avoid exploring the unbaited arms, a task that requires both long-term (reference) memory and short-term (working) memory. The animals navigate using extra-maze cues. After Olton and Samuelson, 1976.

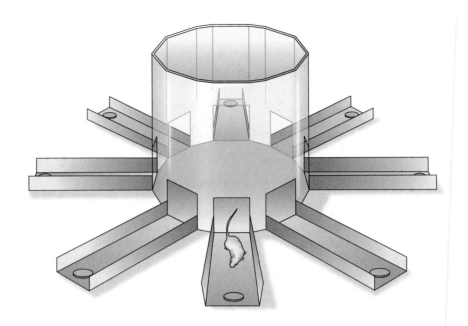

and short-term spatial memory simultaneously. Typically, a radial arm maze has eight runways, four of which are always stocked with a food treat (baited); the other four arms are always devoid of treats (unbaited). The solution to the maze involves making only one trip down each of the baited arms and avoiding the unbaited arms. This task, therefore, requires long-term, or reference, memory (to recall which of the eight arms are always baited); it also tests short-term, or working, memory (to recall which of the four baited arms have already been visited on a particular trial) (Olton and Papas, 1979; Olton and Samuelson, 1976).

Chronic stress generally impairs spatial learning as well as memory, although this statement requires some qualification (Conrad, 2009): chronic stress impairs appetitively motivated tasks (e.g., the radial arm maze) for which arousal tends to be low, but under testing conditions where arousal is increased (such as the radial arm maze filled with water), chronic stress has minimal impairing effects or may even facilitate spatial learning. In one study of spatial learning in the radial arm maze, rats were chronically stressed by being placed in clear ventilated plastic containers, in which their movements were severely limited, for 6 hours per day for 3 weeks (Luine, 1994; Luine et al., 1994). After 21 days of this stress treatment, the rats were food restricted, trained, and then tested on an eight-arm radial arm maze. The performance of the restraint-stressed rats was impaired compared with that of rats that had not been restrained (Luine et al., 1994). In a follow-up study with the same design (Luine, 1994), blood samples were obtained, and blood concentrations of corticosterone were assayed. Rats with the highest corticosterone concentrations displayed the most errors in performance. Similarly, a study that correlated corticosterone consumption (provided in the rats' drinking water) and maze performance indicated that rats consuming the most corticosterone made the most errors in a radial arm maze (Luine et al., 1993). Subsequent studies have shown that long-term corticosterone treatment impairs spatial learning in rats in a variety of testing situations (McLay et al., 1998). Treatment with RU 38486 (a progestin and glucocorticoid receptor antagonist commonly called RU-486) infused directly into the dorsal hippocampus improved the performance of rats in the Morris water maze (Oitzl et al., 1998).

The studies of the effects of glucocorticoids on learning and memory mentioned above were focused exclusively on acquisition and long-term storage. In other studies, acute stressors and corticosterone also appeared to impair memory retrieval

(A)

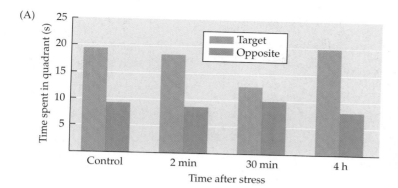

FIGURE 12.21   **Retrieval of spatial learning is impaired by stress.** (A) The amount of time spent in the target quadrant (T; where the platform was formerly located) as compared with the opposite quadrant (O) of the Morris water maze. Rats spent less time in the target quadrant 30 minutes after foot shock, but this impairment was reversed 4 hours after foot shock. (B) Representative swimming paths of a nonstressed control rat and a stressed rat. Note that while the nonstressed rat swam in the general area of the platform, the stressed rat appears to have swum across all areas of the maze randomly. After De Quervain et al., 1998.

(B)

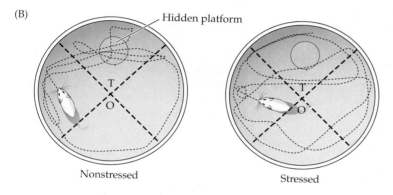

(De Quervain et al., 1998, 2009). Rats were trained to locate a submerged hidden platform in a Morris water maze. After the rats were trained, they received a foot shock (i.e., a mild stressor) 2 minutes, 30 minutes, or 4 hours prior to testing. During the test, the platform was removed. In this situation, rats with good memories typically spend more time swimming over the area of the tank where the platform was previously located. Rats with poor memories swim around somewhat randomly, usually along the edge of the tank, suggesting that they do not recall where the escape platform ought to be. Rats shocked 30 minutes prior to memory testing performed poorly compared with rats tested 2 minutes or 4 hours after the foot shock (De Quervain et al., 1998) (**FIGURE 12.21**). Because electric shocks result in elevated circulating glucocorticoid concentrations about 30 minutes later, these results suggest that elevated glucocorticoid concentrations at the time of memory assessment impair performance.

In some cases, acute stress enhances performance on learning and memory tasks. For example, stress facilitates classical conditioning of the eyeblink response in rats (Shors et al., 1992). Stress-evoked facilitation occurs within minutes and persists for several days. Glucocorticoids appear to be involved in facilitation of both hippocampus-dependent and hippocampus-independent learning and memory. Adrenalectomy blocked the stress-evoked facilitation of learning (Beylin and Shors, 2003). Even when glucocorticoids were replaced at basal levels postadrenalectomy, stress did not facilitate trace conditioning, a type of classical conditioning that is dependent on an intact hippocampus (Beylin and Shors, 2003). Adrenal demedullation, which leaves the adrenal cortex intact and allows glucocorticoid secretion responsive to stressful stimuli, facilitated stress-evoked learning. These experiments, as well as others, indicate that glucocorticoids are both necessary and sufficient for the temporary facilitation of learning caused by acute stressors but cannot sustain these memories 24 or more hours later (Beylin and Shors, 2003).

Single injections of natural or synthetic (e.g., dexamethasone) glucocorticoids mimic acute stress and tend to facilitate memory consolidation (Roozendaal, 2000). Dexamethasone has high affinity for the glucocorticoid receptors (GRs, or type II

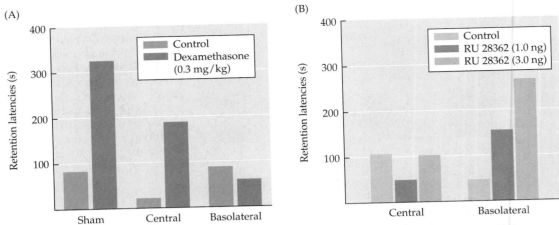

FIGURE 12.22 **The basolateral amygdala mediates stress-evoked learning.** Rats were tested for passive avoidance learning in a light-dark shuttle box. (A) Retention latencies (time to step into the dark compartment where the rat had previously been shocked) were improved by dexamethasone treatment in sham-lesioned rats. However, dexamethasone treatment did not improve latencies when the basolateral amygdala had been lesioned. (B) Rats receiving microinfusions of the GR agonist RU 28362 in the basolateral amygdala showed increased latencies. After Roozendaal, 2000.

receptors). In contrast, natural glucocorticoids, such as corticosterone, have high affinity for the mineralocorticoid receptors (MRs, or type I receptors). Typically, GRs are activated by corticosterone only when concentrations are elevated, such as during stressful events or during the circadian peak of glucocorticoid secretion (Reul and de Kloet, 1985). Therefore, it seems reasonable to hypothesize that GRs mediate the memory-facilitating effects of acute stress. To test this hypothesis, drugs that specifically blocked either GRs or MRs were infused into the brains of rats immediately before or immediately after the rats learned a spatial water maze. Blocking GRs, but not MRs, impaired performance on this spatial memory task (Oitzl and de Kloet, 1992; Roozendaal et al., 1996). The enhancing effects of either acute stress or corticosterone treatment on memory for a passive avoidance task could be blocked by blocking GRs in day-old chicks (Sandi and Rose, 1994a,b). Furthermore, mice lacking the gene for GRs display substantial memory deficits (Oitzl et al., 1998).

The memory-enhancing effects of glucocorticoids appear to involve the amygdala, which modulates the memory consolidation process that probably occurs elsewhere in the brain. The basolateral amygdala (BLA) appears to integrate hormonal information that signals the hippocampus and other brain regions involved in memory consolidation (Roozendaal, 2000; Roozendaal et al., 2009). Specific lesions of the BLA block the memory-facilitating effects of glucocorticoids (Roozendaal, 2003; Roozendaal et al., 2002), and infusions of GR-blocking drugs directly into the BLA impair memory consolidation. Conversely, infusions of GR-activating drugs into the BLA enhance memory consolidation (Roozendaal, 2000, 2003) (**FIGURE 12.22**). Cortisol interferes with extinction of fear learning in men, allowing fearful memories to persist (Merz et al., 2014).

Glucocorticoids are not only important for memory in artificial memory tasks; they appear to have functional significance for survival as well. Several species of birds, in common with many squirrels, hide caches of food in order to survive periods of time when food is scarce (Smulders et al., 2010). These birds rely, at least in part, on spatial memory to find these previously hidden caches. It seems reasonable to assume that the ability to locate these hidden caches becomes critical in harsh habitats where the food supply is generally low or unpredictable. This assumption was tested in captive mountain chickadees (*Poecile gambeli*), half of

(A)

(B)

(C)

(D)

FIGURE 12.23 **Food-caching mountain chickadees** (A) A mountain chickadee in nature. (B) A test box in the lab to test memory in this food-caching bird. (C) Corticosterone is elevated in birds receiving limited and unpredictable food as compared with birds receiving ad libitum food. (D) Performance of birds maintained on a limited and unpredictable food supply and on an ad libitum food supply in a cache-recovery task. Fewer sites inspected indicates better memory performance. C,D after Pravosudov and Clayton, 2001.

which were maintained on a limited and unpredictable food supply while the rest were provisioned with unlimited food supplies for 60 days (Pravosudov and Clayton, 2001) (**FIGURE 12.23**). The birds maintained on an unpredictable food supply were more efficient at cache recovery and performed spatial (but not nonspatial) tasks more accurately than individuals from the same population and species that were fed ad libitum. The birds maintained on an unpredictable food supply displayed moderately elevated corticosterone concentrations compared with the birds provided with unlimited food (Pravosudov et al., 2001). Implanting corticosterone capsules (which increased blood concentrations of corticosterone to the level of the birds with the unpredictable food supplies) into mountain chickadees stimulated food intake and food caching as compared with birds implanted with an inert control pellet (Pravosudov, 2003). Chickadees implanted with corticosterone also displayed improved spatial (but not nonspatial) memory. It appears that challenging environmental conditions evoke corticosterone secretion, which improves spatial memory in food-hoarding birds (Pravosudov, 2005). Thus, moderately elevated corticosterone concentrations appear to be an adaptation to enhance spatial memory (Pravosudov and Smulders, 2010).

Corticosterone causes restructuring of the hippocampus and parts of the so-called hippocampal circuit in mammals and probably in other types of animals as well (Pravosudov and Smulders, 2010) (**FIGURE 12.24**). The hippocampus and related brain structures are rich in glucocorticoid receptors. Treatment of rats with corticosterone or induction of chronic stress decreases the number of pyramidal

FIGURE 12.24 Connections and components of the hippocampal circuit

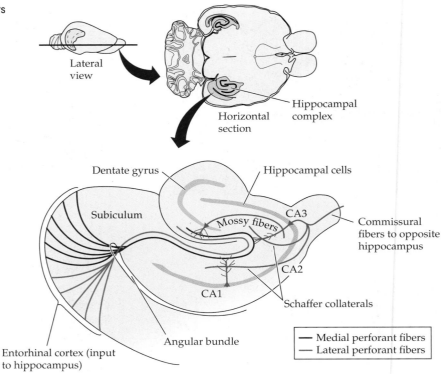

cells, dendrite lengths, and the number of dendritic branch points in the CA1 and CA3 regions of the hippocampus (Sapolsky et al., 1985; Watanabe et al., 1992; Woolley et al., 1990b) (**FIGURE 12.25**). Somewhat paradoxically, very low corticosterone concentrations cause degeneration in the dentate gyrus of the hippocampus (Conrad and Roy, 1992; Sloviter et al., 1989). After adrenalectomy, hippocampal cell numbers decrease by approximately 50% (Conrad and Roy, 1992; Gould et al., 1991; Luine, 1994). Specifically, hippocampal granule neurons decrease in number when corticosterone concentrations are low. Predictably, spatial memory is impaired by adrenalectomy (Conrad and Roy, 1992; Gould et al., 1991). Again, there seems to be an ideal range of corticosterone concentrations, which corresponds to an inverted U-shaped curve, above or below which hippocampal-dependent spatial learning is impaired.

The hippocampus contains the highest density of GRs in the brain and mediates the regulation of the hypothalamic-pituitary-adrenal (HPA) axis (Herman and Cullinan, 1997). Importantly, adult neurogenesis, a phenomenon known to occur in the hippocampal region of rodents and primates, is responsive to glucocorticoid concentrations in the blood. Glucocorticoids and stress inhibit the production of new hippocampal neurons (Gould et al., 1998). It now seems plausible that these new neurons participate in learning and memory in some way. Thus, chronic suppression of neurogenesis or changes in synaptic plasticity resulting from repeated stress may contribute to impaired spatial navigational learning (Gould et al., 1998; Shors et al., 2001, 2004).

Humans with altered glucocorticoid concentrations may display changes in memory. For example, patients with Cushing syndrome, whose adrenal glands produce excessive cortisol, have reduced hippocampal volumes (Starkman et al., 1992). In contrast, patients with Addison disease, whose adrenal glands produce insufficient cortisol, show necrosis of the granule cells in the hippocampus and display impaired memory (Maehlen and Torvik, 1990). These clinical observations in humans support the hypothesis that glucocorticoids can affect memory. Taken

Control: Memory normal

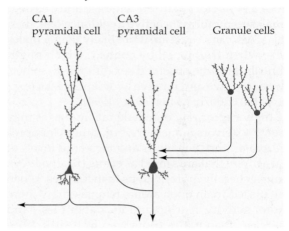

Repeated stress: Memory impaired

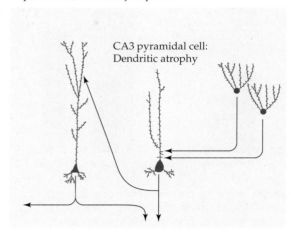

Adrenalectomy: Memory impaired

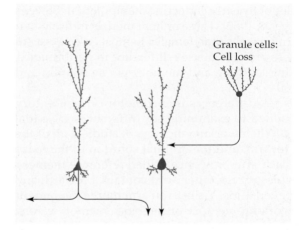

Elevated estradiol: Memory enhanced

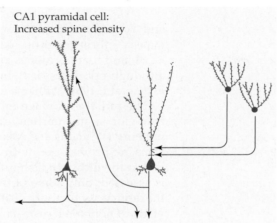

FIGURE 12.25 **Behavioral effects of hormone-induced changes in hippocampal circuitry**
A simple schematic circuit of three hippocampal cell types illustrates structural changes caused by hormones and associated effects on performance in memory tasks. After Luine, 1994.

together, the evidence shows that glucocorticoids modulate cellular morphology and function in the hippocampus, and in some cases their concentrations alter spatial learning and memory. Further research is necessary to determine whether these hormones affect other parts of the brain and other types of learning and to determine the extent to which other hormones affect neuronal morphology and function.

Sex Differences in Learning and Memory

Many studies have demonstrated sex differences in learning and memory performance, but determining whether a sex difference in performance truly reflects learning and memory functions, rather than other hypothetical psychological constructs, is difficult. In general, female rats learn active avoidance tasks faster than male conspecifics, but males do better at passive avoidance tasks (Beatty, 1979; Heinsbroek et al., 1988). These results may not reflect sex differences in learning and memory per se; they may rather reflect a sex difference in general activity levels. Because male rats generally are less active in open-field situations than females, it may be "easier"

(A)

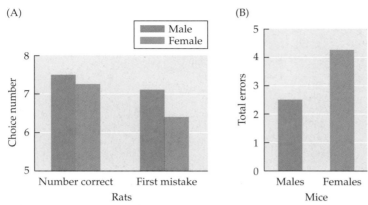

(B)

FIGURE 12.26 Male rats and mice perform better on radial arm mazes than females. (A) Male rats make more correct choices and make mistakes later in their tests (i.e., first mistake) than female rats. (B) Male mice make fewer errors than female mice. Courtesy of V. Luine.

for males to perform a passive avoidance task (i.e., suppress a behavior) than for females, and "easier" for females to perform an active avoidance task than for males. Also, male rats are more likely than females to freeze when frightened by context, which might also contribute to the observed sex differences in performance in active and passive avoidance tasks (e.g., Gresack et al., 2007b; Maren et al., 1994).

The higher error rate of female rats in mazes may represent, not errors in memory, but rather "inappropriate" exploratory behaviors and increased levels of general activity that are scored as errors (Beatty, 1979). Males are generally more anxious than females. When rats are placed in an open arena, females show more locomotor activity, rear up and look about less, and defecate less than males (reviewed in Beatty, 1979; Johnston and File, 1991). These sex differences in behavior can be reduced by anxiolytic drug treatment of males or by early endocrine manipulation (Stevens and Goldstein, 1981; Stewart and Cygan, 1980). These animal models indicate that males perform better on spatial learning tasks than females in most cases (**FIGURE 12.26**) and that hormones are likely to mediate the sex difference in performance, although not necessarily by affecting learning and memory per se (Gaulin and FitzGerald, 1989; Williams et al., 1990).

The radial arm maze minimizes sex differences in locomotor or exploratory behavior, so it is particularly well suited to examining sex differences in spatial memory (Williams and Meck, 1991). When working memory is studied, all of the arms are provisioned with a food reward, and the optimal solution to the maze is that the individual should visit each arm only once. When reference memory is assessed, only some of the arms (e.g., every other arm) contain a reward, and the animal should only visit those baited arms. Visits to an arm more than once or visits to nonbaited arms count as working-memory or reference memory errors, respectively. Males consistently make fewer errors of either type than females on this task, particularly while the rats are learning the task. The different strategies the rats used to solve the radial arm maze were probed by manipulating potential cues in the interior of the maze (called landmarks) and orientation cues outside the maze (geometry). Interestingly, females and feminized males used both landmarks and geometry to solve the maze, whereas males and masculinized females used only geometry. That is, males and masculinized females learned fewer total cues and could master the task faster than females or feminized males (Williams et al., 1990). Male rats and female rats treated with estrogen (or its precursor, testosterone) prior to their tenth day of age learned the radial arm maze faster than female rats or male rats castrated on day 1 (Williams et al., 1990). After the task was learned, there were no differences in subsequent error rates. These results indicate that the sex differences in spatial ability are organized early during development. They are probably mediated by hormonal effects on the hippocampus. Early hormone exposure may influence visuospatial learning among humans as well (see Chapter 4).

Sex differences in learning strategy or cognitive style can influence learning and memory test outcomes even when there are no underlying biological or developmental differences (reviewed in Dohanich et al., 2009). For example, males tend to outperform females on visuospatial cognitive tasks overall (see Chapter 4), but upon closer inspection it becomes apparent that some of these sex differences reflect the male preference for using global information, conceptual processing, and allocentric strategies versus the female preference for using details, perceptual processing, and egocentric strategies (Dohanich et al., 2009; Sandstrom, 2007). Said differently, in spatial learning tasks, males tend to use context configuration or room geometry information, whereas females tend to use positional information or landmarks. In water mazes where landmarks may not be available, males tend to do better. However, in spatial tasks in which multiple strategies can be used to solve the mazes, the differences between males and females tend to decrease (e.g., Herman and Wallen, 2007; Schmitzer-Torbert, 2007).

Whether the sex differences are due to activity levels, problem-solving strategies, or learning styles, males of a variety of species, including rodents, nonhuman primates, and humans, outperform females in a variety of visuospatial tasks, although there are numerous examples of exceptions to this observation (reviewed in Leonard and Winsauer, 2011), as seen in the next section.

Sex Differences and Stress

Animal models show that the effects of sex hormones on learning performance may be indirect and that they may be influenced by a variety of extrinsic and intrinsic factors. One of those factors is stress. Males and females differ in their perception of stressors as well as in their behavioral, morphological, and biochemical responses to stressors. Female rats display higher corticosterone values in response to stress than males (Handa et al., 1994), although other factors such as the number and distribution of glucocorticoid receptors are important. Generally, acute or relatively brief exposures to stressors improve performance on spatial and visual memory tasks by male rats, whereas chronic or relatively long exposures to stressors impair their performance on these tasks (Bowman et al., 2003; Wood and Shors, 1998; Wood et al., 2001). In contrast, females are relatively resistant to the impairing effects of long-term stress. In fact, on several learning and memory tasks in which stress impairs male performance, stress improves performance among females (Bowman et al., 2003) (**FIGURE 12.27**). These sex differences in responding to stress are organized early by perinatal hormonal environments. That is, the presence of androgens early in development organizes the brain so as to enhance learning in adult male rats that experience acute stressors, whereas the lack of androgens results in adult females in which the same acute stressors significantly impair performance (Shors and Miesegaes, 2002). Baseline stress glucocorticoid concentrations, also set by the perinatal hormonal environment, predict stress reactivity glucocorticoid concentrations in adulthood. The sex difference in baselines means that the magnitude of the corticosterone response to stressors is often equivalent in males and females (Park

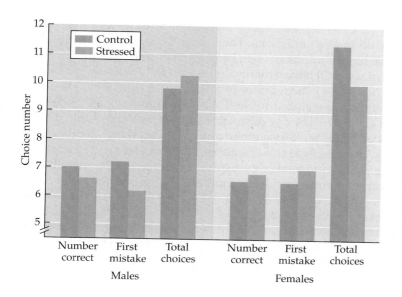

FIGURE 12.27 Sex differences in stress responsiveness Chronic restraint stress impairs male performance and enhances female performance on the radial arm maze. Male performance is impaired by stress; restrained male rats make fewer correct choices and make their first mistakes earlier in their memory tests than control rats do. Females show the opposite pattern. Courtesy of V. Luine.

et al., 2008). Finally, the sex differences in glucocorticoid reactivity in humans appear to depend on a variety of factors, including hormone status, age, and the type of cortisol assay (reviewed by Kudielka and Kirschbaum, 2005).

Male rats exposed to recurring daily restraint (6 hours per day) in a plastic ventilated tube (a chronic psychological stressor) were unaffected in their performance on a radial arm maze after a week of this treatment, but they showed improvement in retention after 2 weeks of restraint, as compared with unrestrained control rats (Luine et al., 1996). If the restraint continued for a third week, however, there was a reversal in performance: the restrained rats displayed worse spatial memory than unrestrained controls (Luine et al., 1994). Restraint of female rats enhanced their performance in the radial arm maze after 3 weeks (Bowman et al., 2001). A similar pattern of sexually dimorphic effects of chronic stress on performance has been reported for other spatial memory tasks and nonspatial visual (object) memory tasks (Beck and Luine, 2002).

Spatial navigation to a hidden goal can be supported by two different orientation systems: a place (or allocentric) system and an egocentric system (e.g., turning left in the T-maze) (O'Keefe and Nadel, 1978). The concepts of multiple memory systems and learning strategies are important contemporary frameworks in learning and memory research and contribute to our current understanding of sex differences in cognition (reviewed in Dohanich et al., 2009) and the contributions of hormones to these sex differences.

Recent research has indicated that stressors and anxiogenic stimuli can bias rats toward using stimulus-response or egocentric strategies (which are based in the striatum) over using a place strategy (which is hippocampus based). It is also known that the amygdala plays an important role in mediating the effects of stress and anxiety on learning strategies (e.g., Packard, 2009). Anxiety can be related to state (e.g., being in an anxiogenic situation such as giving a public presentation), or it can be a trait: some individuals are simply more anxious in many situations than most others, and these individuals are said to have higher trait anxiety. When male rats are categorized as either low or high trait anxiety, then tested on their memory for spatial tasks, males with low trait anxiety levels tend to use a place strategy, whereas males with high trait anxiety levels tend to use a stimulus-response strategy (Hawley et al., 2010).

It is possible that chronic stress differentially affects neural structure or function. For example, after male rats were restrained 21 days, apical dendritic branching and dendritic lengths in the CA3 region of the hippocampus were reduced. In contrast, female rats undergoing the same pattern of daily restraint did not display reductions in apical dendritic branching in the CA3 region (Galea et al., 1997). This dendritic atrophy in males is mediated by corticosterone and can be prevented by blocking glucocorticoid release or actions. There are neural structure differences in the CA1 area of the hippocampus as well. Females in proestrus (when estradiol concentrations peak in rodents) have a higher density of CA1 dendritic spines than males (Shors et al., 2001, 2004). In response to an acute stressor (intermittent tail shocks), spine density was enhanced in the CA1 area in male rats but reduced in females (Shors et al., 2001). The sex differences in hippocampal spine density were correlated with estradiol and testosterone concentrations; however, the stress-evoked spine density changes were not associated with circulating glucocorticoid concentrations. Thus, male and female rats display different densities of dendritic spines in the hippocampus under baseline conditions. In the presence of identical stressors, however, there are opposite responses in the neuronal structure of individuals of the two sexes (Shors et al., 2004).

In common with rats, humans display sex differences in the interactions between stress and memory. In young adults, stress-evoked elevation in cortisol levels was associated with impaired performance on memory tasks in men, but not in women (Wolf et al., 2001). Sex differences in responses to stress persist into old age. Elderly men experiencing psychosocial stress displayed higher HPA responses than elderly women (Kudielka et al., 1998). Sex differences in memory performance in response to stress might reflect sex differences in the activation of the amygdala during emotionally charged learning (Cahill et al., 2001). Importantly, there are several studies showing sex differences in spatial and nonspatial abilities in humans independent of stress. Several studies testing humans in virtual water mazes on computers have shown a consistent male advantage (e.g., Astur et al., 1998, 2004). In contrast, females tend to outperform males on tasks using two- and three-dimensional object arrays in remembering the locations and identities of objects (e.g., Eals and Silverman, 1994). These results have been related to hunter-gatherer theories about why there should be sex differences in memory function among humans (Eals and Silverman, 1994).

It is not the case that males always outperform females in the standard tests of spatial learning and memory; there are several instances of females performing better than males after exposure to either acute or chronic stressors (reviewed in Luine and Dohanich, 2008). Male rats separated from mothers for 3 hours each day during the first 2 weeks of life were impaired in nonspatial and spatial memory compared with males handled by humans but separated from mothers for only about 15 minutes daily. Males separated from their mothers displayed impaired performance on an object recognition task, a Y-maze task, and reference and working-memory versions of the water maze task (Frankola et al., 2010). In contrast, maternally separated females were not impaired, and in some cases they performed better on memory tasks compared with early-handled females. These results strongly suggest that the biological sex of offspring moderated the effects of maternal conditions on several cognitive tasks. Because sex differences were apparent prior to puberty, gonadal hormones probably do not account for these effects on cognition. It is possible that differences in maternal care and attentiveness directed toward male and female pups may provoke these differences (Frankola et al., 2010).

In common with the behavioral effects of stress, the stress-evoked hippocampal structural changes are temporary. Good news for those of us who experience chronic short-term psychological stressors: in rats, both behavioral impairments and hippocampal changes resolve about 5–10 days after the stressor stops (Conrad et al., 1999). Similar results have been reported in nonhuman primates. Psychosocial stressors reduce the numbers of hippocampal pyramidal neurons in subordinate males, but not in females (reviewed in McEwen, 2000). How long recovery takes in humans remains unspecified.

In industrialized societies, humans are no longer tied to the natural light-dark cycle. Because of electric lights and transmeridian air travel, humans experience patterns of light that were never experienced prior to about 120 years ago. To study the effect of one of these patterns—jet lag—female Syrian hamsters were subjected to a 6-hour phase advance every 3 days for about a month (Gibson et al., 2010). No sex differences could be studied in this female-only study, but stress responses were observed. Jet lag inhibited adult neurogenesis and impaired learning and memory (**FIGURE 12.28**). Hamsters exposed to jet lag maintained rhythmic activity patterns but reduced the number of proliferating and surviving cells in the dentate gyrus. Jet lag–mediated differences in cell proliferation, but not cell survival, were mediated by adrenal steroids. In addition to having reduced neurogenesis, these hamsters also reduced performance in a conditioned place preference task. Importantly, the deficits in learning and memory persisted well past the cessation of lighting phase shifts, indicating that this type of disruption has long-lasting and deleterious consequences for normal brain function (Gibson et al., 2010).

Effects of Estrogens

The studies we have just discussed provide convincing evidence that estrogens are neuroprotective against stressors and that they influence learning and memory.

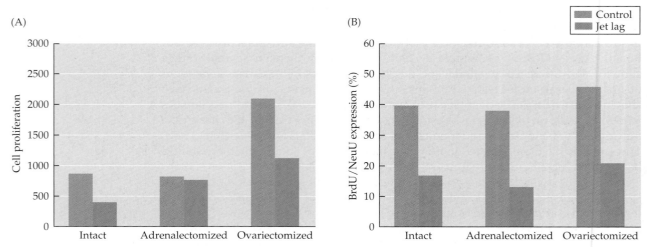

FIGURE 12.28 **Jet lag affects hippocampal neurogenesis.** (A) The number of new neurons in the granule cell layer is affected by the hormonal condition of the animal with ovariectomy and estradiol (OVX + E$_2$) replacement significantly increasing the number of labeled cells as compared to intact hamsters. Simulated jet lag significantly decreased the number of labeled cells in both intact and OVX + E$_2$ hamsters, whereas the number of labeled cells in adrenalectomized (ADX) animals was not affected by simulated jet lag. (B) Chronic jet lag decreased neurogenesis by >50% in intact, ADX, and OVX + E2 hamsters. From Gibson et al., 2010.

Estradiol enhances several aspects of learning and memory in both human and nonhuman animals (Frick, 2008; Luine and Frankfort, 2012) and appears to enhance spatial memory in a reliable, but subtle, manner (Daniel, 2006; Daniel and Bohacek, 2010; Dohanich et al., 2009; Luine, 1994)(**BOX 12.1**). Our understanding of the effects of estrogen on learning and memory has become more nuanced over the past decade and has evolved beyond the simple notion that "estrogen is good for your memory." Current thinking is that the effects of estrogen depend on many factors, including the cognitive process being assessed, the timing of hormone administration, and the gonadal state of the individual being assessed (Daniel, 2006; Daniel and Bohacek, 2010; Dohanich et al., 2009). Although some studies, particularly in mice, report improved spatial memory performance in the standard water maze paradigm (reference memory), most rat studies report that proestrous females or estradiol-treated females are impaired on this task. Gonadal steroids do elevate performance in female rats on a working-memory version of the water maze in which the platform is relocated each day (reviewed by Dohanich, 2002; Dohanich et al., 2009), suggesting that estradiol generally enhances working memory but does not affect or impairs reference memory on some tasks.

Spatial memory in the Morris water maze is better during diestrus than estrus (Frick and Berger-Sweeney, 2001). In addition, several studies in rats and humans have demonstrated that spatial memory is impaired during the periovulatory portion of the ovarian cycle, when estradiol concentrations are normally high (e.g., Frye, 1995; Galea et al., 1995; Korol et al., 1994; Warren and Juraska, 1997). However, in general, estrogens appear to enhance consolidation, and slightly enhance acquisition, in spatial reference memory tasks (Daniel et al., 1997; Fader et al., 1998; Luine et al., 1998) and in two-choice water-escape working-memory tasks (a version of the Morris water maze) (O'Neil et al., 1996).

Estradiol seems to enhance memory when the task is difficult. In one of the first studies of the effects of estradiol on memory, castrated male rats were deprived of food (reduced to 85% of their baseline body mass to motivate them to find food in a maze) and trained on an eight-arm radial arm maze. These males were then

BOX 12.1 Rapid Effects of Estradiol on Spatial Memory

Birds require excellent spatial memory, which, as in mammals, is dependent on the hippocampus. In songbirds, such as zebra finches, the brain is a major source of circulating estrogens. Many neurons produce aromatase that converts androgens to estrogens locally. Neurons in the hippocampus appear to lack aromatase in the cell bodies of neurons but express abundant aromatase at pre- and postsynaptic locations (Bailey and Saldanha, 2015; Peterson et al., 2005). The estradiol produced at the synapses appears to enhance spatial learning in zebra finches through rapid, nongenomic actions. The hippocampi of zebra finches lie near the skull, so a small piece of skull could be removed directly over the hippocampi of these birds. The hippocampi of some birds were treated with small silicone pellets mixed with an aromatase inhibitor (1,4,6-androstatriene-3,17-dione; ATD); other birds received empty silicone pellets, and some birds had their hippocampi lesioned with an excitatory drug (Bailey et al., 2013). After a 3-day recovery period, the birds were tested in an aerial T-maze (**Figure 1**) in which they learned to locate a cup baited with food in one of the two horizontal arms. Birds with lesioned hippocampi or blocked estradiol formation required more trials to learn the tasks and made many more mistakes than birds with intact hippocampi

and normal estrogen synthesis (Bailey et al., 2013) (**Figure 2A** and **2B**, respectively). The estradiol concentrations in the hippocampi of ATD-treated birds were reduced by more than 40%. Taken together, these results suggest that aromatization of androgens to estradiol in the hippocampus is crucial in normal spatial memory.

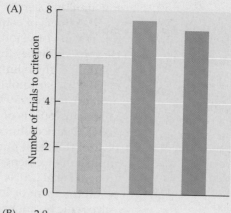

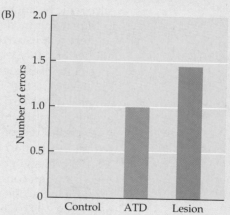

Figure 2 Male zebra finches that received blank silicone pellets (Control) achieved learning criteria (flying to the correct cup within 30 seconds on three consecutive trials) after fewer trials than birds treated with an aromatase inhibitor (ATD) or birds that received hippocampal lesions (Lesion) (A). ATD treatment or hippocampal lesions also caused the birds to make more mistakes than zebra finches in the control group, which made no errors (B). After Bailey and Saldanha, 2015.

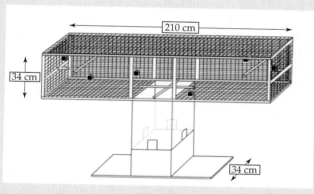

Figure 1 Each experimental bird was food restricted for about 5 hours, then placed in the base of the T-maze and "helicoptered" upward to either the left or right arm of the maze to locate an uncovered food cup. After learning the location of a food cup, each bird was tested 1 hour later for memory of the cup, which at that point was covered with a flap. After Bailey et al., 2009.

implanted with either empty Silastic capsules or capsules containing estradiol benzoate; males implanted with the estradiol capsules had circulating estradiol concentrations of about 90 pg/ml of blood serum (Luine, 1994). Beginning 3 days after capsule implantation, the working memory of the males was assessed over 20 trials. There was no difference between estrogen-treated and control rats in performance (Luine, 1994; Luine and Rodriguez, 1994). In the next eight trials, a 1-hour delay between the fourth and fifth arm choice was added. When the task was made more difficult by the 1-hour delay, the males treated with estrogen exhibited a small, but

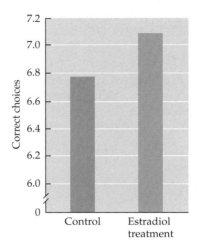

FIGURE 12.29 Estrogen improves spatial memory. Male rats were implanted with either an empty Silastic capsule (blue bar) or a capsule containing estradiol (green bar). The bars represent the average number of correct choices on an eight-arm radial arm maze after a 1-hour delay between the fourth and fifth visits across several trials. After Luine and Rodriguez, 1994.

reliable, improvement in performance as compared with the control animals (Luine, 1994) (**FIGURE 12.29**). In another study, both low (40 pg/ml) and high (200 pg/ml) doses of estradiol resulted in improved choice accuracy in a twelve-arm radial arm maze by young and aged female rats (Williams, 1996). In yet another study, estrogen treatment of ovariectomized female rats augmented working memory but not reference memory (Luine et al., 1998). Similarly, capsules containing estradiol enhanced the performance of ovariectomized female rats during acquisition of an eight-arm radial arm maze when implanted for 30 days, then removed prior to training (Daniel et al., 1997). These results suggest that chronic treatment with estradiol produces an effect on memory and that estradiol may induce changes in neuronal form or function that persist well after the hormone capsule is removed.

The effects of estrogens on spatial memory are probably mediated by the hippocampus. Infusion of a water-soluble form of estradiol directly into the hippocampus enhances the memory of ovariectomized rats for the Morris water maze, but only if given immediately after training (Packard and Teather, 1997; Packard et al., 1996). Estradiol treatment 2 hours post-training did not affect retention (Packard and Teather, 1997). These results and others have demonstrated the memory-enhancing effects of acute estrogen treatment (e.g., Sandstrom and Williams, 2001, 2004). Ovariectomized rats treated with 17α-estradiol, 17β-estradiol, or diethylstilbestrol (DES) 30 minutes prior to, or immediately after, learning trials displayed rapid enhancement of visual and place memory, a special version of spatial memory (Inagaki et al., 2010; Luine et al., 2003). These are tasks in which the individual must recall the form or location of an object encountered on a study trial. When these estrogenic hormones were given 2 hours after learning trials, they were ineffective in improving memory when the animals were tested 4 hours later. These results suggest that estrogens affect learning and memory consolidation processes, but not performance processes. In addition, the rapid effects of estrogens and the nonspecificity of estrogen type suggest that nongenomic mechanisms may be involved (Luine et al., 2003). Estrogen treatment of ovariectomized female rats at supraphysiological doses also increased performance on the hippocampal-dependent task of eyeblink conditioning (Leuner et al., 2004).

Estradiol receptors are located within the hippocampus, especially in the CA1 region but also in the CA3 region and dentate gyrus (Gould et al., 1990; Loy et al., 1988; Maggi et al., 1989) (see Figure 12.24). Estrogen treatment, like naturally high estrogen concentrations around the time of ovulation, is associated with an increase in the density of dendritic spines in the CA1 region (reviewed in Desmond and Levy, 1997; Gould et al., 1990; McEwen et al., 1995; Woolley et al., 1990a) (see Chapter 4). The results of studies that have attempted to correlate hormone-induced changes in hippocampal circuitry with spatial learning performance in rats were initially mixed (Woolley, 1998). However, more recent studies have supported this relationship (Daniel and Dohanich, 2001; Sandstrom and Williams, 2001). For example, hippocampal long-term potentiation (LTP) varies across the estrous cycle in association with these changes in connectivity (Warren et al., 1995). Hippocampal LTP is facilitated by estrogen treatment in awake rats (Cordoba-Montoya and Carrer, 1997). Estrogens also affect basal forebrain cholinergic neurons that might be important in passive avoidance and attentional tasks as well as in spatial learning (Gibbs, 1997). Prenatal gonadal steroids also affect hippocampal cell morphology: males have larger CA1 and CA3 pyramidal cell field volumes and cell body sizes than females (Isgor and Sengelaub, 1998).

Interestingly, estradiol does not increase CA1 dendritic spine density in female mice, as it does in female rats (Li et al., 2004). However, estradiol does increase the growth and maturation of CA1 dendritic spines in female mice and generally improves their spatial memory (Li et al., 2004; Luine and Frankfurt, 2012) (**FIGURE 12.30**). Examination of β estrogen receptor gene knockout (βERKO) mice revealed that the β subtype of the estrogen receptor is necessary for optimal learning and

(A) Spine density

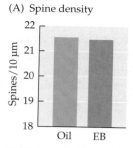

FIGURE 12.30 Estrogens influence CA1 dendritic spine function and spatial memory. (A–C) Treatment with estradiol benzoate (EB) does not increase overall density of dendritic spines in mice. (D–F) This treatment does affect spine maturation, however, as indicated by an increase in mushroom-shaped spines (shown as M in D). Spatial memory (object memory) for new places in ovariectomized (OVX) mice improves with the same dose of EB (F). From Li et al., 2004.

(B) Spine density, oil-treated

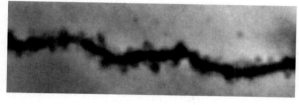

(C) Spine density, EB-treated

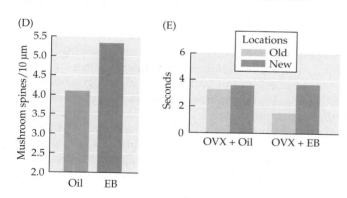

(D)

(E)

memory performance in a spatial task (Morris water maze) (Bodo and Rissman, 2006; Rissman et al., 2002). Ovariectomized βERKO mice given high doses of estrogen replacement therapy failed to learn the task, whereas ovariectomized βERKO mice treated with low doses of estrogens were significantly delayed in learning the water maze. Wild-type female mice, regardless of estrogen treatment, learned the task (Rissman et al., 2002). Estradiol enhancement of hippocampal-dependent object memory involves membrane-bound estrogen receptors (Fernandez et al., 2008).

An additional link between estrogen and spatial memory in mice comes from studies in the water maze showing that the onset of the decline in spatial memory associated with aging occurs earlier in females than in males (and is associated with age-related hormone loss) (Frick et al., 2000) and that estradiol benzoate can significantly improve spatial memory and alter synaptic plasticity in aged female mice (Frick et al., 2002). These latter data, and similar findings, may have important implications for the design of estrogen replacement therapy. Can ovarian hormone therapy prevent or reduce age-related memory decline in menopausal women? Many studies have recently addressed this issue, and although some studies reported beneficial effects of estrogen and/or progestin therapy for certain types of memory in postmenopausal women, other clinical trials suggest that such therapy can increase the risk of cognitive decline and dementia (Frick, 2009; Henderson and

Brinton, 2010). The mechanisms of beneficial estrogen actions on memory will have to be untangled from the cognitive-impairing features if new drug therapies are to be developed. For example, estradiol-induced object memory consolidation in middle-aged female mice requires dorsal hippocampal extracellular signal-regulated kinase (ERK) and phosphatidylinositol 3-kinase (PI3K) activation (Fan et al., 2010). It is possible that failure of estradiol to activate the necessary molecular pathways may underlie the failure of estradiol to enhance object recognition in aged females that was reported in some studies (Gresack et al., 2007a,b).

Estrogen treatment of postmenopausal women has been reported to enhance verbal memory and prevent loss of the ability to learn new material (Sherwin, 1996, 1997, 1998). In contrast, postmenopausal women participating in a short-term estrogen replacement therapy study with a randomized double-blind crossover design showed no significant effects of estrogen treatment on memory (Polo-Kantola et al., 1998). The differences in the results of these studies may reflect differences in the memory tasks assessed. In another study of humans, male-to-female transsexuals receiving estrogen treatment prior to surgical sex reassignment did not differ from women on any tests of learning and memory (Miles et al., 1998). Few studies have examined the extent to which the decline in cognitive abilities and hormonal changes in aging men are related. However, what few data exist seem to support the idea that estrogens may play a role in supporting memory in aging men, as in women (Sherwin, 2003). Estrogen administration has been shown to enhance memory and reduce neuronal losses associated with Alzheimer's disease in postmenopausal women in the short term (Simpkins et al., 1997) and to reduce the damage caused by blood reperfusion (restoration of blood flow) after cerebral ischemia (stroke) (Hurn et al., 1995). Estrogen replacement therapy in postmenopausal women, however, seems to provide inconsistent benefits to cognitive function (Maki and Hogervorst, 2003). Meta-analyses suggest that estrogen replacement protects against the onset of Alzheimer disease. However, studies of randomized trials of estrogen hormone replacement suggest that estrogens do not provide long-term benefits to women who are already stricken with Alzheimer's disease (Maki and Hogervorst, 2003).

The Women's Health Initiative Memory Study (WHIMS) has raised some serious questions about the administration of estrogen replacement therapy as a viable treatment for cognitive decline in postmenopausal women (Daniel and Bohacek, 2010; Dohanich et al., 2009). Several studies have recently suggested that timing is important in estrogen replacement therapy (e.g., Craig and Murphy, 2010; Henderson, 2010; Henderson and Brinton, 2010; Maki, 2006). That is, estrogens should be administered during critical, but limited, periods of postmenopausal life to maximize the positive cognitive effects while minimizing the unwanted side effects of estrogen on health. Several studies in nonhuman animals support the hypothesis that a critical period exists for estrogen replacement therapy to support cognition in the aged (e.g., Bohacek and Daniel, 2010; Daniel et al., 2006; Gibbs, 2000; Rodgers et al., 2010).

Taken together, the evidence suggests that the effects of estrogens on memory may be slight and may affect only certain aspects of spatial memory (Frick, 2012). The extent to which memory is enhanced by estrogen replacement therapy may depend on environmental factors such as cognitive complexity (Gresack and Frick, 2004). A study of ovariectomized female mice given estradiol or a control vehicle examined the effects of long-term exposure to an enriched (complex) environment compared with a standard laboratory environment. Mice were raised from 3 weeks to 6 months of age in standard conditions (housed with cage mates but not exposed to enriching stimuli) or in enriched conditions (also housed with cage mates but exposed to toys and running wheels for 3 hours per day). At 6 months of age, estrogen improved spatial and nonspatial memory only in female mice exposed to the standard, impoverished environment; estrogen did not improve memory in mice exposed to the enriched conditions (Gresack and Frick, 2004). The authors propose that the changes induced by estrogen and environmental enrichment may be associated with similar changes in hippocampal synaptic plasticity (Gresack and Frick, 2004). Importantly, stress can interfere with the effects of estrogen. For instance, water maze training is expected to result in a stress response, but in female rats it completely eliminated the typical estrogen-induced spine density increases observed in the CA1 region of the hippocampus (Frick et al., 2004).

Women often begin showing cognitive decline when their menstrual cycles stop, but because of their side effects, estrogens are rarely prescribed to treat mild cognitive deficits among postmenopausal women. However, work in rats indicates that there may be significant cognitive benefits of acute estradiol treatment in women (Frick, 2012). Thus, it remains possible that new cognitive enhancers might take advantage of these rapid effects of estradiol to improve cognitive function in the future (Frick, 2012).

Effects of Androgens

The effects of androgens on learning and memory have been studied for over 80 years (Tuttle and Dykshorn, 1928). In one of the best early experiments, male rats were castrated at 20, 50, 90, 130, or 170 days of age and later tested for maze-learning ability (Commins, 1932). Castrated and intact animals learned the mazes equally well. An extensive review of these early studies (Stone and Commins, 1936), including the reviewers' own work, in which castration failed to affect performance on a light discrimination task or on three different mazes, led to the conclusion in 1936 that castration does not affect learning in rats.

Many studies since then have investigated the role of testicular androgens in learning and memory, and the results of these studies generally agree with the early pronouncement that gonadal androgens do not affect learning and memory. This appears to be true of human as well as nonhuman animals. For example, neither testosterone replacement therapy in hypogonadal men nor testosterone treatment of typical men resulted in changes in learning and memory performance (Alexander et al., 1998), though castration has had small or subtle effects on learning, especially spatial learning or learning that affects anxiety levels. However, treatment of female rats with testosterone prior to 10 days of age masculinizes the hippocampus and improves spatial memory (Roof and Havens, 1992). It remains unspecified to what extent testosterone or its metabolites influence learning and memory (Leornard and Winsauer, 2011).

As we have seen, female rats generally outperform males in the acquisition of active avoidance tasks, although the difference is small (Haaren et al., 1990). In the laboratory strains of rats used in these studies, neither neonatal nor postpubertal castration affects performance. However, neonatal castration of males treated in utero with the antiandrogen cyproterone acetate raises their performance to levels typical of females, demonstrating that prepubertal organization by sex steroid hormones must be responsible for the difference in performance (Beatty, 1979). Similarly, it has been hypothesized that early organizational effects of androgens account for sexually dimorphic responses to classical conditioning of fearful stimuli (Anagnostaras et al., 1998).

Testosterone does seem to have some positive reinforcing properties. A place preference develops in rats that have testosterone injected into the nucleus accumbens (Packard et al., 1997). A place preference simply refers to the tendency of an animal that receives a rewarding stimulus in one part of a cage to return to the same site later (**FIGURE 12.31**). Systemic treatment with testosterone propionate or nandrolone, but not 17α-methyltestosterone, induces conditioned place preference in adult male mice (Parrilla-Carreo et al., 2009). Similarly, infusion of testosterone or dihydrotestosterone directly into the hippocampus improves performance in an inhibitory avoidance task, such as suppressing the urge to leave a brightly lit cage compartment for a darkened compartment in which an electric shock was delivered previously (Edinger and

FIGURE 12.31 The place preference conditioning apparatus is a box with three compartments; each has distinct stimuli in odor, color, and floor texture. The middle compartment is generally neutral gray and communicates with the lateral compartments through sliding doors.

Frye, 2007). Androgens are also important for frontal cortex–mediated memory, such as novel object recognition, and prefrontal-mediated memory, such as performance of operant tasks (Aubele et al., 2008; Kritzer et al., 2007; Luine, 2007). From an adaptive functional perspective, it makes sense that testosterone would be reinforcing, as this steroid hormone increases in response to mating, and returning to a previous site of mating improves the odds of additional mating opportunities (Paredes, 2009). In terms of human behaviors, the rewarding properties of testosterone might help to explain some of the abuse associated with anabolic androgens (see Chapter 13) or sex addictions (Garcia and Thibaut, 2010; Samenow, 2010).

Seasonal Fluctuations in Learning and Memory

Although androgens do not appear to affect learning in nonseasonal species, studies on seasonally breeding animals have documented a correlation between peak androgen concentrations and peak learning abilities. Goldfish trained in several tasks—including swimming with a tethered float, conditioned avoidance tasks, and maze learning—exhibit seasonal changes in learning ability (Agranoff and Davis, 1968; Shashoua, 1973). Maximal learning occurs between January and March, prior to spawning, when the gonads are developing and blood concentrations of steroid hormones are high. Poor learning is observed during the summer, after the spawning season. Photoperiod may regulate this seasonal cycle of learning ability in goldfish.

A sex difference in spatial learning performance has been reported for meadow voles (*Microtus pennsylvanicus*) and deer mice (*Peromyscus maniculatus*). During the breeding season, males of both species outperform females, but the sex difference disappears when the animals are not in breeding condition (Galea et al., 1996). In female voles, there is a significant correlation between plasma estradiol concentrations and retention, whereas there are no performance differences between males with low and high testosterone concentrations (Galea et al., 1995).

As described in Chapter 10, seasonal changes in brain size in several species of rodents are likely to be mediated by seasonal changes in androgen levels. Changes in learning and memory should correspond to these seasonal changes in brain mass, but this proposition essentially remains untested. In North America, over 95% of learning studies are performed on laboratory rats and mice (Burkhardt, 1987), which are not particularly responsive to seasonal factors.

There is a seasonal change in maze-learning ability in voles, and home range size shrinks during the winter in both meadow voles (*Microtus pennsylvanicus*) and prairie voles (*M. ochrogaster*). In one study, winter-trapped voles were compared with spring-trapped voles on their ability to learn mazes (Gaulin and FitzGerald, 1989). Males captured and tested during the winter made more errors while learning the mazes, and required more trials to negotiate the mazes without making any errors, than males tested during the spring. These results may reflect seasonal changes in brain size; brain weights are proportionally heavier in spring-trapped than in winter-trapped voles (Gaulin and FitzGerald, 1989; Yaskin, 1984).

White-footed mice (*Peromyscus leucopus*) that have been kept in short day lengths require longer to learn the Morris water maze than mice kept in long days (Pyter et al., 2005). Short-day mice also had smaller total brain mass and hippocampal volume than long-day mice. Although spatial learning and memory were impaired, there were no photoperiodic effects on sensory discrimination, locomotor activity, or other types of memory that might have contributed to this impairment. Short days decreased spine density of the apical tips of pyramidal dendrites in the CA1 region, but increased spine density in the basilar tips of dendrites in the CA3 region of the hippocampus (Pyter et al., 2005) (**FIGURE 12.32**).

(A) Hippocampal volume

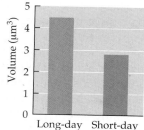

FIGURE 12.32 **Short day lengths shrink hippocampal volume** of the brains of white-footed mice (A). The latency and path length to reach the hidden platform of a Morris water maze (B) is increased in short days as compared with long days. (C) Spine density of the apical tips of pyramidal dendrites in the CA1 region is reduced in short days, and spine density is increased in the basilar tips of dendrites in the CA3 region of the hippocampus. After Pyter et al., 2005.

(B)

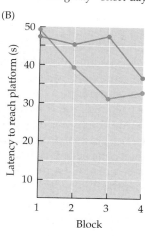
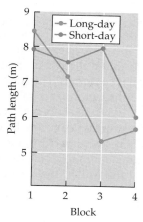

(C)

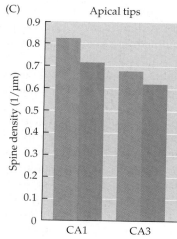
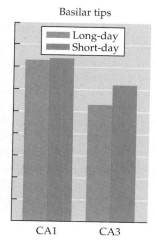

Adrenocorticotropic Hormone (ACTH)

There is convincing evidence that many peptides previously characterized as hormones also function as neurotransmitters in the central nervous system, including vasopressin, oxytocin, the opioids, and cholecystokinin (CCK). Of course, epinephrine and norepinephrine have been known for some time to function as both hormones and neurotransmitters. When there is evidence for a central site of action, as in the case of epinephrine, ACTH, vasopressin, the opioids, and CCK, one must consider the hypothesis that these chemical messengers exert their effects centrally by acting as neurotransmitters or neurohormones, rather than as hormones. This observation may account for the ability of these compounds, which cannot cross the blood-brain barrier, to act in the brain.

In 1950, Hans Selye introduced the concept of the general adaptation syndrome as a model for the physiological coping strategies of an animal enduring stress (see Chapter 11). According to this model, stress causes the release of corticotropin-releasing hormone from the hypothalamus, which stimulates the secretion of ACTH from the anterior pituitary (Krugers et al., 2010); ACTH, in turn, induces the production and release of glucocorticoids by the adrenal cortex. These hormones, along with epinephrine and norepinephrine, presumably prepare an animal to react to threatening stimuli—the so-called fight-or-flight response. In his early work, Selye assumed that the "stress" hormones had a relatively permanent effect on the central nervous system (i.e., learning), as well as affecting the immediate ability to respond (Selye, 1956). Many prominent learning theorists of the mid-1950s attempted to explain avoidance learning in terms of an anxiety reduction model. They hypothesized that an interruption in the "anxiety mechanisms" (i.e., the HPA axis) would disrupt the acquisition of an avoidance response.

The effects of ACTH are independent of its effects on glucocorticoid secretion. In one early study, two groups of rats were subjected to a pole-jump test of active avoidance learning (**FIGURE 12.33**). The pituitary gland had been surgically removed in one group of rats; the control group had received a sham operation. (Recall that the pituitary is also called the hypophysis; the removal of this gland, therefore, is often called a **hypophysectomy**). The control rats learned the avoidance task much faster than the hypophysectomized animals (Applezweig and Baudry, 1955; Applezweig and Moeller, 1959). Injections of ACTH into the hypophysectomized animals restored their performance to the levels of the control animals. It is important to note that ACTH restores performance only in endocrine-deficient animals; ACTH treatment of intact animals does not enhance normal learning and memory performance (Murphy and Miller, 1955). Consequently, this peptide is not a cognitive enhancer.

In general, a deficit in ACTH leads to slower acquisition and poorer retention of information. Remember, however, that the surgical removal of the pituitary gland is not a minor physiological disruption. Hypophysectomy not only reduces ACTH levels but affects many other endocrine and regulatory systems as well (see Chapter 2). DeWied (1964) tried to control for these problems by providing hormone "cocktails" to hypophysectomized rats. The addition of growth hormone and thyroid-stimulating hormone had restorative effects; that is, the animals were much healthier. Without the replacement of ACTH, however, the memory deficits were still observed.

Although studies of hypophysectomized animals point to actions of ACTH independent of the adrenals, the best way to test this possibility is to remove the adrenal glands. ACTH appears to act upon the CNS through a nonadrenal route, because it enhances acquisition of avoidance tasks even in rats that have been adrenalectomized. Because adrenalectomized animals lack feedback control, their ACTH levels rise. Furthermore, ACTH injections in rats lacking both pituitary and adrenal glands also restore learning. Therefore, the effect of ACTH on memory is independent of its classic endocrine effects (DeWied, 1974). It is unclear how ACTH reaches the

hypophysectomy Surgical removal of the hypophysis, or pituitary gland.

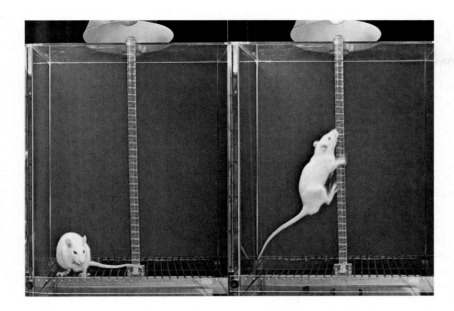

FIGURE 12.33   A test of active avoidance learning In this "pole-jump" apparatus, a rat must jump onto the pole to avoid a foot shock when the light is illuminated. Courtesy of Organon International BV, Holland.

brain to affect memory processes. ACTH consists of 39 amino acids and therefore, in common with epinephrine, is too large to cross the blood-brain barrier.

In addition to ACTH, small pieces of the ACTH molecule that are devoid of any effect on the adrenal glands also affect learning (e.g., DeWied, 1974, 1977). The first hint of this possibility was evident in a number of studies with melanocyte-stimulating hormone (MSH). Administration of α-MSH and β-MSH restored avoidance responses in hypophysectomized rats (Kastin et al., 1975). Recall that ACTH is made from pro-opiomelanocortin (POMC), a giant molecule that is also the precursor of several other hormones, including α-MSH and β-MSH, as well as the endorphins and enkephalins. The α-MSH and β-MSH molecules share the same sequence of amino acids with ACTH at positions 1–13 (see Figure 2.5). Treatment with smaller ACTH fragments, such as $ACTH_{1-10}$ or $ACTH_{4-10}$, which do not affect adrenocortical function, also restored learning (DeWied, 1969, 1974). However, administration of $ACTH_{11-24}$ or $ACTH_{25-39}$ had no effect on avoidance learning (DeWied, 1974). In another series of studies, amino acids were systematically removed from both ends of the ACTH molecule; each ACTH fragment was then tested in vivo to determine its behavioral "potency" (DeWied, 1974, 1980). Through a long series of studies testing various bits and pieces of the ACTH molecule, it was determined that the behaviorally active portion of the ACTH molecule is $ACTH_{4-8}$, which resides at the amino end of the molecule. Artificial analogues of the ACTH molecule have also been produced and examined for behavioral effects. ACTH analogues with a D-isomer of phenylalanine at position 7 of the amino acid sequence exhibit behavioral effects that are opposite to those of comparable ACTH analogues with the normal L-isomer of phenylalanine at position 7: the D-isomer analogue facilitates extinction (i.e., decay of active avoidance responding), while the L-isomer form delays extinction (DeWied, 1980). This kind of dissection of a behavioral response using molecular techniques should prove to be a powerful research tool for probing the physiology underlying avoidance responding.

ACTH can also protect against amnesia, the failure to remember. Substances that protect against forgetting are called **antiamnestics**. Three experimental techniques can induce amnesia: exposing animals to CO_2 immediately after training, administering a strong electric shock after training, or treatment with protein synthesis inhibitors (Quartermain, 1976). ACTH attenuates the amnestic effects produced by these experimental manipulations. If a rat is trained to leave the dark half of a box when it hears a bell, in order to avoid a mild foot shock, and it is exposed to CO_2

antiamnestic   A substance that protects against forgetting.

immediately afterward, the rat will display a low level of memory for the task. If another rat is trained on the same task, given an injection of ACTH, and immediately given CO_2, its memory is less impaired. It is not known whether ACTH is affecting arousal, attention, encoding, retrieval, or some combination of those factors in this paradigm.

As mentioned above, ACTH and its memory-enhancing fragments come from the giant precursor molecule POMC. The precursor molecules of many hormones are cleaved by specific enzymes into two or more pieces: the active form of a hormone is thus liberated from the precursor molecule. It has been hypothesized that different enzyme systems are stimulated by the environment to induce different cleavage patterns of the giant POMC molecule; in this way, various environmental stimuli may produce different hormones. It is also possible that different POMC-cleaving enzymes are made in different cells and that certain environmental factors induce certain cells to produce their specific enzymes.

ACTH has been administered to humans in several studies. In general, ACTH does not affect the performance of typical adult volunteers, children with learning disabilities, or elderly experiment participants on learning tasks. However, $ACTH_{4-10}$ can affect attentional and motivational processes without directly affecting learning in humans (Born et al., 1986; DeWied, 1980).

Another question one can ask is how ACTH (and α-MSH) might increase retention. An easy answer is that ACTH might increase arousal. In other words, the firing rates of neurons might increase, or the likelihood of an action potential might be enhanced by the presence of this peptide. The aversiveness or rewarding properties of a stimulus might thereby be increased. Intraventricular injections of ACTH in rats cause regionally specific changes in cerebral deoxyglucose uptake, an index of brain cell activity (Dunn et al., 1980). ACTH might produce its antiamnestic effect in this way by providing access to weak memory traces. The mechanisms by which ACTH, or hormones in general, affect retention are still largely speculative, and the real answers await advances in the neurobiology of learning and memory. Corticotropin-releasing hormone also influences memory in rats and may account for some of the effects of ACTH on memory, at least in highly emotional states (e.g., Ohmura et al., 2008). Once the biochemical processes of memory are understood, the role of ACTH and other hormones will be more easily described.

Vasopressin and Oxytocin

Oxytocin appears to have a variety of effects on memory, including both enhancing and impairing it. Depending on context, many studies have implicated oxytocin as an amnestic peptide. When given intraventricularly, oxytocin enhances forgetting; rats given oxytocin in this manner forgot the noxious experience associated with an active avoidance task (Bohus et al., 1982). On the other hand, several studies have indicated that systemic injections of oxytocin can enhance memory (DeWied, 1984), though usually only in constrained situations or under specific conditions (Boccia et al., 1998). Furthermore, it appears that the memory-impairing effects of oxytocin are observed only when it is given intracerebrally (Engelmann et al., 1996). Memory for stimuli associated with pups was tested in adult female rats that were treated intracerebrally with oxytocin, an oxytocin receptor antagonist, or an arginine vasopressin (V1) receptor antagonist. All of the rats performed well, as long as the test was performed within 180 minutes of treatment (Engelmann et al., 1998). Intracerebral treatment with oxytocin or the V1 receptor antagonist did not affect performance on this task; however, treatment with an oxytocin receptor antagonist impaired the development of this type of memory after 180 minutes (Engelmann et al., 1998).

Oxytocin promotes smooth muscle contraction and is therefore critical to milk letdown and the uterine contractions of birth. One possible adaptive function of the amnestic properties of oxytocin is the dulling of memories of the pain associated with giving birth, thereby increasing the probability that females will repeat the process (Carter et al., 1992).

More recently, studies have indicated that rodents display improved memory during pregnancy that potentially endures into old age. These changes in pregnancy-mediated memory are associated with changes in hippocampal cell death and birth, as well as increased numbers of spines and neurotropic factors in the maternal brain (Kinsley, 2008; Kinsley and Lambert, 2008; Lambert, 2012; Leuner and Gould, 2010; Macbeth and Luine, 2010; Workman et al., 2012).

In contrast, many women anecdotally report that memory is impaired during or immediately after pregnancy, although the results of several studies have been mixed (reviewed in Brett and Baxendale, 2001). A review of the literature on humans revealed the potential for two separate memory impairment syndromes. First, about 80% of women appear to suffer some slight cognitive impairment during gestation (Brett and Baxendale, 2001). In most women, the memory problems appear to resolve after parturition. In the other syndrome, some memory deficits persist or begin shortly after childbirth and continue for some period of time. In these cases, the most likely endocrine explanation for the memory impairments is elevated cortisol concentrations associated with the stress of pregnancy and infant care (Brett and Baxendale, 2001). According to this hypothesis, pregnancy is similar to a temporary Cushing syndrome, with high concentrations of glucocorticoids inhibiting learning and memory. However, there are no tests of this hypothesis and no animal studies to support this notion.

Oxytocin also appears to mediate memory in the context of social recognition. Social recognition is a critical adaptive trait for social animals (Gabor et al., 2012). Individual recognition can be operationally defined as a change in behavior toward a specific individual based on past experiences with that individual (Gheusi et al., 1994). Individual recognition is important for animals to process social status, health, reproductive status, and kinship, among other important social data. Memory is obviously important for recalling details about specific individuals or even classes of individuals. When oxytocin is provided at physiological doses to mice in a social recognition discrimination task, social memory is improved (reviewed in Gabor et al., 2012). This improvement can be reversed by simultaneous administration of oxytocin receptor antagonists. Mice with the gene for oxytocin deleted fail to show social recognition in a number of circumstances (Choleris et al., 2006; Gabor et al., 2012). This failure of social recognition can be rescued by infusion of oxytocin into the brains of these knockout mice.

As noted in Chapter 8, living in social groups confers a number of advantages, but it has several disadvantages. One major disadvantage of group living is that parasites and diseases are more prevalent than among solitary species. Thus, mechanisms have evolved in social species to detect and avoid individuals that are sick or carrying high parasite loads. This requires social recognition. Mice lacking oxytocin fail to discriminate or avoid parasitized individuals or their odors, in contrast with wild-type mice (Kavaliers et al., 2006). Thus, oxytocin seems necessary for adaptive social learning. Nonetheless, taken together, the effects of oxytocin on learning and memory are inconsistent, sometimes contradictory, context-dependent, and not well understood.

Arginine vasopressin (AVP), as we saw in Chapter 9, promotes water uptake in the kidney tubules and is thus also called antidiuretic hormone (ADH). Brattleboro rats, which have a congenital lack of vasopressin, suffer from diabetes insipidus, a condition that occasionally occurs in humans; human diabetes insipidus is marked by the production of large quantities of dilute urine and concomitant intake of liters of water. In addition to the difficulties that Brattleboro rats have with managing their water economy, these animals have difficulty with shuttle box avoidance tasks (DeWied, 1980, 1984), which they forget very quickly. The deficit in their performance appears to be due to memory problems rather than dysfunctions in learning. Homozygous Brattleboro rats avoid the compartment in which they have been shocked when their retention is tested immediately after the learning trial; however, if a delay occurs between training and testing, they rapidly reenter the compartment in which they have been shocked. Treatment with vasopressin immediately after the learning trial raises the performance level of Brattleboro rats to that of rats that are heterozygous for the Brattleboro mutation, which have normal vasopressin levels. Brattleboro rats also display impaired social memory; predictably, deletion of the AVP type 1 receptor impairs social memory in mice as well (reviewed in Gabor et al., 2012).

As these experiments demonstrate, vasopressin acts as an antiamnestic in Brattleboro rats; like ACTH, it blocks forgetting or prolongs memory. Injections of vasopressin can also prolong memory in normal animals. In contrast to an injection of ACTH, which may delay forgetting for 6–8 hours, vasopressin treatment prolongs memory for noxious experiences by days or weeks (DeWied, 1980). The effects of vasopressin on memory are dose- and time-dependent (DeWied, 1984). The memory-enhancing effects of post-training treatment with vasopressin in normal rats require the presence of an intact adrenal gland or prior treatment with epinephrine (McGaugh, 1989). Vasopressin appears to improve arousal, which might improve learning and memory processes (Croiset et al., 2000).

Injections of vasopressin antagonists directly into the septum (an area of the brain that is rich in neurons in which vasopressin serves as a neurotransmitter) abolish the ability of a male rat to recognize (remember) the odor of a conspecific male that he has previously encountered (Peele and Vincent, 1989). Castration also abolishes this social recognition and reduces the number of vasopressin neurons in the septum. Testosterone replacement therapy reverses these effects of castration. In this case, vasopressin almost certainly functions as a neurotransmitter within the septum, but its influence on social behavior is androgen-dependent in rats and mice (Bluthe et al., 1993). Generally, however, vasopressin facilitates social memory (Caldwell et al., 2008), and vasopressin 1b receptor knockout mice display impaired social memory function (DeVito et al., 2009). Both working (short-term) memory and reference (long-term) memory, as assessed in a radial arm maze, are improved by vasopressin and vasopressin analogues (Dietrich and Allen, 1997a,b), although timing and dosage of treatment can dramatically affect outcome (Engelmann, 2008). Intranasal treatment with vasopressin slightly improved verbal memory in elderly humans (Perras et al., 1997). It is possible that vasopressin metabolites also act to influence memory (Reijmers et al., 1998). Generally, inhibitory avoidance learning was improved by vasopressin and impaired by oxytocin (Boccia et al., 1998).

Endogenous Opioids

Opioids attenuate pain or the emotional response to pain. There is some controversy regarding whether the endogenous opioids, the endorphins and enkephalins, are truly hormones, but they are included here because they seem to fulfill the definition of a hormone as presented in Chapter 2. These substances have clear effects on learning and memory. In general, opioids have amnestic properties in avoidance learning paradigms but seem to enhance the rewarding properties of trial-and-error learning situations. Although true amnestics act directly on memory storage, retrieval, or both, opioids probably ameliorate the noxiousness of an aversive stimulus so that it is not perceived as aversive, thus appearing to act as amnestics.

Opioid receptors likely play a part in reinforcement and reward. This suggestion was first prompted by the observation that exogenous opioids such as morphine and heroin have reinforcing effects that cause some people to become addicted to the drugs. However, it was assumed that opioid receptors in humans did not evolve to permit people to become drug addicts. Consequently, a search for the

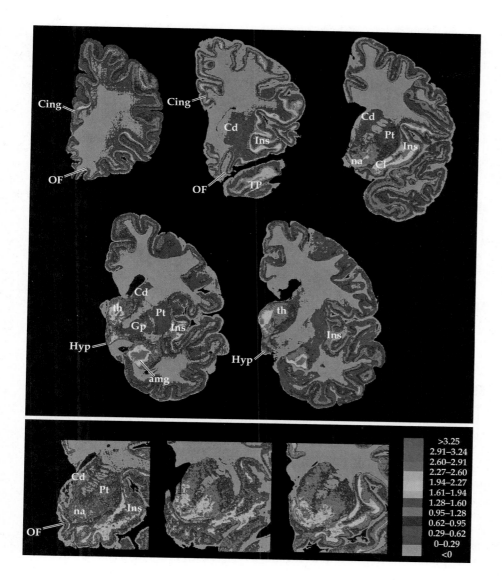

FIGURE 12.34 Increasing densities of κ2 opioid receptors are shown as increasingly bright areas in these darkfield autoradiograms of horizontal (top) and coronal (bottom) sections of rat brain. The locations of these receptors correspond to the locations of brain sites at which electrical stimulation has reinforcing effects. Rats will press a lever repeatedly to cause opiates to be microinjected into these sites, thus activating these receptors. Cing = cingulate; amg = amygdala; Cd = caudate nucleus; Cl = claustrum; Hyp = hypothalamus; Ins = insular cortex; na = nucleus accumbens; OF = orbitofrontal cortex; Pt = putamen; th = thalamus; TP = temporopolar cortex; Gp = globus pallidus. From Staley et al., 1997.

endogenous opioids that fit these receptors began, and the functional significance of these natural, internal "painkillers" was sought. The reinforcing effects of opioids are caused by the activation of opioid receptors in the brain (McGaugh, 1983). Thus, the release of endogenous opioids may play a role in the reinforcement of behavior. Although reinforcing, generally speaking, endorphins (i.e., β-endorphin, α-endorphin, and met-enkephalin) seem to weaken memory consolidation and retention; β-endorphin also impairs memory retention (Roth-Deri et al., 2008).

Neurons that contain opioid receptors are found in several regions of the brain in which electrical stimulation has reinforcing effects, including the hypothalamus, nucleus accumbens, and periaqueductal gray region (**FIGURE 12.34**). Rats will press a lever repeatedly to cause opiates to be injected into their brains, thus activating these receptors. Furthermore, morphine and other opiates increase the rate of responding (bar pressing) for electrical stimulation of these brain areas, whereas naloxone, an opioid receptor blocker, decreases the response rate (Schaefer, 1988). One can imagine situations in which other hormones might have rewarding properties (e.g., rats housed in cold rooms bar-pressing for thyroid hormones); however, there are few reports of animals bar-pressing for non-opioid hormones. Rats also show a place preference in response to systemic injections of

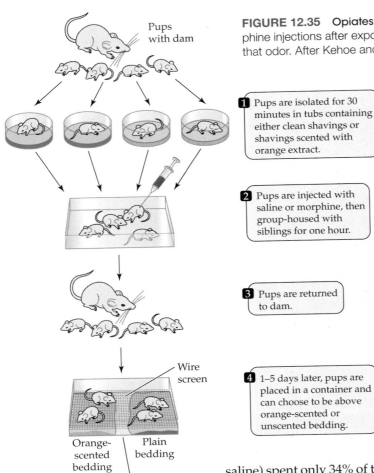

Pups with dam

1 Pups are isolated for 30 minutes in tubs containing either clean shavings or shavings scented with orange extract.

2 Pups are injected with saline or morphine, then group-housed with siblings for one hour.

3 Pups are returned to dam.

4 1–5 days later, pups are placed in a container and can choose to be above orange-scented or unscented bedding.

Wire screen

Orange-scented bedding

Plain bedding

Neutral "start" area

FIGURE 12.35 **Opiates enhance learning in rat pups.** Pups that had received morphine injections after exposure to the novel orange scent showed clear preferences for that odor. After Kehoe and Blass, 1989.

morphine; that is, they prefer the part of a cage where they received morphine injections on previous days (Amalric et al., 1987). This effect is also blocked by injections of naloxone.

Infant rats also experience the positively reinforcing properties of exogenous opioids. Young rats, like many animals, are neophobic; that is, they normally avoid novel experiences. In one experiment, 5-day-old rat pups were isolated from their mother and siblings, placed in the presence of a novel odor (orange extract) for 30 minutes, then injected either with a low dose of morphine (0.5 mg/kg) or with saline. For the next 5 days, these rats were tested to determine their responses to another presentation of the orange odor. Pups were placed in a small cage containing plain bedding chips under one half and bedding chips mixed with orange extract under the other. Testing lasted 10 minutes, and the percentage of time spent in each half of the cage was recorded (**FIGURE 12.35**). Rat pups that had experienced morphine injections after exposure to the novel odor of orange extract spent 73% of their time over the orange-scented bedding. In contrast, control animals (injected with saline) spent only 34% of their time over the orange odor. Pretreatment with naltrexone, another opioid antagonist, before conditioning blocked the positive association between the morphine state and the orange odor (Kehoe and Blass, 1989).

A similar paradigm has been used to test the effects of other substances on learning and memory. When opioid receptor agonists, including morphine, β-endorphin, and enkephalin, were given to adult rats in low doses immediately after training, their memory was impaired in a dose- and time-dependent manner (McGaugh, 1989). Opioid antagonists ameliorate the memory-impairing effects of opioids and their agonists. Studies have demonstrated that retention is enhanced by post-training administration of opioid antagonists, including naloxone, naltrexone, diprenorphine, levallorphan, nalmefene, and β-funaltrexamine (McGaugh, 1989). The memory-enhancing effects of these opioid antagonists are also dose- and time-dependent and have been found in studies using several types of training tasks, including passive avoidance, active avoidance, habituation, and appetitive spatial learning (McGaugh, 1989). Opioid antagonists also block the amnestic effects of electroconvulsive shock therapy (ECT) (Collier et al., 1987) but have had mixed results in human patients with memory disorders (McGaugh, 1989).

The amnestic effects of post-training, peripherally administered met-enkephalin can be blocked by the centrally acting opioid antagonists naloxone and naltrexone, (Zhang et al., 1987). The memory-modulating effects of both central and peripheral injections of met-enkephalin (and peripheral naloxone) are attenuated in adrenal-denervated (or demedullated) animals (Conte et al., 1986). Denervating the adrenal glands prevents the release of epinephrine and norepinephrine. Of course, removal of the adrenal medulla also eliminates the release of many endogenous enkephalins and endorphins (see Chapter 2). Amnesia can be produced in adrenal-demedullated rats if epinephrine is administered prior to training (Conte et al., 1986). Taken together, these results suggest that peripheral injections of opioids affect memory via epinephrine. Predictably, injections of met-enkephalin elevate blood levels of glucose, probably by stimulating epinephrine secretion. This finding may seem contradictory to the results of previous studies indicating that epinephrine and glucose enhance memory. However, recall that the effects of epinephrine and glucose follow an inverted U-shaped curve; levels too high or too low reduce performance on learning and memory tasks. Only moderate levels of epinephrine and glucose enhance learning and memory.

Cholecystokinin

All animals need to find food in order to survive, so it is advantageous for animals to remember where food has been found in the past. Therefore, one might suspect that hormones involved in feeding might modulate memory. At an ultimate level of explanation, it makes sense that hormones involved in feeding and digestion would be co-opted to enhance memory, because the ability to remember the details of successful foraging behavior would have high survival value (Flood et al., 1987).

Cholecystokinin (CCK) is a gastrointestinal hormone that is released during feeding. CCK has been assigned several behavioral functions, including involvement with postfeeding satiety (Smith et al., 1981b). Injection of CCK inhibits feeding by rats via the vagus nerve (Bloom and Polak, 1981; Moran et al., 1992) (see Chapter 9). CCK is also located in the brain.

Cholecystokinin modulates learning and memory. In one study (Flood et al., 1987), two groups of hungry mice and one group of mice with free access to food were given a number of trials to learn to avoid an electric shock in one arm of a T-maze (**FIGURE 12.36**). The mice with free access to food and the mice in one of the food-restricted groups were given access to food immediately after training. The free-access mice tended to eat very little at this time, but the hungry mice feasted. Mice in the other food-restricted group received food 3 hours after training. During the next week, food was provided freely to all the animals. At the end of the week, all of the mice were tested again in the T-maze. Access to food immediately after training enhanced memory retention for the aversive experience in the hungry mice, as compared with both the hungry mice for which feeding was delayed by 3 hours and the mice that received food freely. Presumably, the hungry mice that were fed immediately after training released CCK in response to their meal, which enhanced their memory of the shock. CCK injected intraperitoneally also enhances memory in mice. The memory-enhancing effects of CCK can be blocked by cutting the vagus nerve, which suggests that peripherally administered CCK produces its memory effects by activating ascending vagal fibers (Flood et al., 1987). Mice lacking the gene that encodes for CCK display reduced performance in a passive avoidance task and impaired spatial memory in the Morris water maze (Lo et al., 2008).

Cholecystokinin also affects learning and memory functions in young rats. The normal aversion of young rats to a novel odor

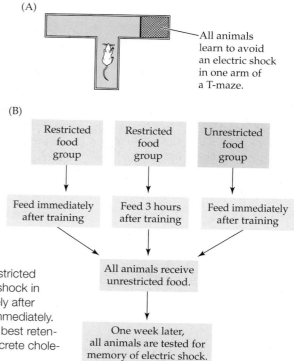

FIGURE 12.36 CCK enhances memory in mice. (A) Mice from two food-restricted groups and from a group that had been fed freely learned to avoid an electric shock in one arm of a T-maze. (B) One of the food-restricted groups was fed immediately after training, and one was fed 3 hours after training; the freely fed group was fed immediately. The food-restricted mice that were fed immediately after training displayed the best retention when tested a week later. Likely, the food caused these hungry mice to secrete cholecystokinin (CCK) shortly after training. After Flood et al., 1987.

can be blunted by pairing such an odor (e.g., orange extract) with injections of CCK, in an experimental design similar to that used to test the effects of morphine (see above) (Weller and Blass, 1988). In one such study, rat pups preferred an orange-scented test arena 24 hours after the CCK injections, whereas pups injected with saline still avoided the orange scent. An antagonist (L-364,718) that selectively blocks peripheral CCK receptors completely eliminated CCK-induced conditioned odor preferences. These results strongly support the hypothesis that CCK affects learning in rats via a peripheral site of action. CCK "conditioning" follows an interesting developmental course: CCK-induced olfactory preferences were observed in rats that were 5, 11, and 22 days of age, but 28-day-old rats failed to exhibit CCK-conditioned preferences (Weller and Blass, 1990). Perhaps the ontogeny of CCK-supported conditioned preferences reflects natural events that correspond to the weaning process.

Cholecystokinin also affects memory consolidation in humans. In one study, people received a nasal infusion of either saline or saline spiked with 40 µg of CCK (Schneider et al., 2009). Compared with the saline, CCK increased encoding and retrieval of memories in the participants. Such studies could benefit from using specific CCK agonists or antagonists applied at different stages of memory processing to evaluate their specific effects on acquisition and retrieval (Schneider et al., 2009).

Considered together, the effects of hormones on learning and memory are usually subtle and often specific to a given situation or task. The precise mechanisms by which hormones affect learning and memory function await additional advances in the understanding of the neurobiological mechanisms of learning and memory. Hormones may change structures in the brain, the activity of specific neural cells, or the uptake or release of neurotransmitters, or they may act in a coordinated way through all of these mechanisms to improve or impair learning and memory processes. Hormones also influence learning strategy or cognitive style, which can influence sex differences in learning and memory performance.

Summary

1. Several types of learning have been documented, including sensitization and habituation, as well as associative learning (classical and operant conditioning, appetitive and avoidance conditioning). There are also several types of memory, including short-term memory (working memory) (spatial and nonspatial); long-term memory (reference memory) (spatial and nonspatial); procedural (implicit) memory, including for skill learning, priming, and conditioning; and declarative (explicit) memory, including semantic (facts) and episodic (events) memory. Hormones affect each type of learning and memory.

2. The hormones that are associated with adaptation to stress enhance learning and memory.

3. There are two hypotheses regarding how epinephrine affects memory: (1) epinephrine may affect memory via its effect on blood glucose levels, and (2) epinephrine may activate peripheral receptors that directly influence brain function.

4. Elevated blood glucose levels facilitate the movement of glucose into neurons. More glucose entering neurons stimulates the release of more acetylcholine into the neuronal synapses.

5. Elevated glucose levels may be a common pathway by which several hormones enhance memory. Hormones may increase blood sugar levels directly (e.g., epinephrine) or act through another agent (e.g., vasopressin) to increase blood sugar levels.

6. Although acute glucocorticoids or stressors enhance learning and memory, chronically elevated glucocorticoids or chronic stress impair spatial learning and memory although interactions with sex steroids are possible. However, if glucocorticoid concentrations are too low, impairments in memory are also observed. Glucocorticoids appear to exert their effects on learning by affecting neuronal structure or function in the hippocampus or amygdala.

7. Sex differences in learning and memory performance are common; however, these differences may be due to sex differences in spatial abilities, exploratory behaviors, or general anxiety levels. Acute stressors tend to improve memory in males but impair memory in females. Chronic stress disrupts memory function in males, but the effects of chronic stress on female memory are not pronounced.

8. Estrogens appear to enhance spatial learning in animals and other forms of memory in humans.

9. In rats, androgens do not have major effects on learning and memory. In some species, enhanced learning and memory are reported during the breeding season, when blood concentrations of androgens are high.

10. Many peptides previously characterized as hormones also function as neurotransmitters in the central nervous system, including vasopressin, oxytocin, CCK, and the opioids. Epinephrine and norepinephrine have been known for some time to function in both roles. When there is evidence for a central site of action of hormones on memory, as in the case of epinephrine, ACTH, vasopressin, the opioids, or CCK, one must consider the hypothesis that these chemical messengers exert their effects centrally by acting as neurotransmitters, rather than as hormones.

11. The lack of ACTH impairs memory formation, and its presence can also protect against amnesia. A small piece of the ACTH molecule, devoid of endocrine activity, contains the features of the molecule that affect memory. The physiological mechanisms underlying the effects of ACTH on memory are unknown.

12. Vasopressin also blocks amnesia and appears to act via its stimulatory effect on epinephrine secretion.

13. Oxytocin may act as an amnestic agent. Both oxytocin and vasopressin contribute to social recognition.

14. Endogenous opioids seem to have amnestic properties in avoidance learning paradigms but appear to enhance rewarding properties in trial-and-error learning tasks.

15. CCK enhances memory but requires an intact vagus nerve to act.

Questions for Discussion

1. Nearly all of the research on the effects of hormones on learning and memory has been conducted on laboratory rats and mice. Discuss the implications and limitations of this approach to studying learning. In your discussion consider the lifestyles of nocturnal rodents and diurnal humans.

2. You learned that hormone concentrations vary on a daily and seasonal basis. It was also documented that performance of several cognitive skills, including learning and memory, varies as a function of time of day or time of year. In most studies on the effects of hormones, learning, and memory, rodents are tested during the experimenters' workday (the rodents' rest period). Discuss the proposition that

hormones affect learning and memory by shifting circadian rhythms of performance. Are seasonal influences usually taken into consideration in field studies of learning and memory?

3. Glucagon, secreted from the α-cells of the pancreas, acts in opposition to insulin and elevates blood sugar levels. Design a study to test the effects of glucagon on learning and memory. Discuss your predicted outcomes.

4. Given what you have learned about the role of insulin, glucose, and CCK on learning and memory, why might it be difficult to study learning and memory in humans if everyone eats at a different time relative to coming to the lab for training or testing?

5. Opioids often act as reinforcers, or rewards, for behavior and consequently have marked effects on learning and memory. Discuss the possibility of other hormones acting as reinforcers and their potential influences on learning and memory. What are these hormones, and under what conditions would you expect them to exert effects on behavior?

Suggested Readings

Daniel, J. M. 2013. Estrogens, estrogen receptors, and female cognitive aging: The impact of timing. *Horm. Behav.*, 63:231–237.

Dohanich, G., et al. 2009. Steroids, learning and memory. In D. W. Pfaff et al. (eds.), *Hormones, Brain and Behavior* (2nd ed.), Vol. 1, pp. 539–576. Academic Press: San Diego.

Frick, K. M. 2009. Estrogens and age-related memory decline in rodents: What have we learned and where do we go from here? *Horm. Behav.*, 55:2–23.

Hamson, D. K., Roes, M. M., and Galea, L. A. M. 2016. Sex hormones and cognition: Neuroendocrine influences on memory and learning. *Compr. Physiol.*, 6:1295–1337.

Luine, V. N., and Frankfurt, M. 2012. Estrogens facilitate memory processing through membrane mediated mechanisms and alterations in spine density. *Front. Neuroendocrinol.*, 33:388–402.

McGaugh, J. L., and Roozendaal, B. 2009. Drug enhancement of memory consolidation: Historical perspective and neurobiological implications. *Psychopharmacology*, 202:3–14.

Pravosudov, V. V., and Smulders, T. V. 2010. Integrating ecology, psychology and neurobiology within a food-hoarding paradigm. *Philos. Trans. R. Soc. Lond. B Biol. Sci.*, 365:859–867.

Wolf, O. T., Atsak, P., de Quervain, D. J., Roozendaal, B., and Wingenfeld, K. 2016. Stress and memory: A selective review on recent developments in the understanding of stress hormone effects on memory and their clinical relevance. *J. Neuroendocrinol.*, doi: 10.1111/jne.12353.

Hormones and Affective Disorders

13

Learning Objectives

The goal of this chapter is to describe the interactions between hormones and various types of affective behaviors. In addition to affecting overt behavior, hormones also affect mood. By the end of this chapter you should be able to:

- describe several mood disorders, including perimenstrual syndrome (PMS), postpartum depression, seasonal affective disorder, eating disorders, and the so-called "roid rage".

- understand the hormonal contributions to these disorders.

Several years ago a young woman was discovered by her mother-in-law trying to drown her 4-month-old twins in a bathtub. She allegedly told authorities that she wanted to kill the babies. Fortunately, the infants were not harmed and the woman was sent to a neuropsychiatric hospital for evaluation. In court, a judge ruled that the woman was suffering from postpartum depression, and she was given probation for 5 years instead of a prison sentence. The judge stated, "This is not a child abuse case. This is a postpartum depression case."

For the vast majority of women, the postpartum period is a time of mother-infant bonding. However, a significant minority may suffer from postpartum depression. Postpartum depression is a well-known outcome of the normal endocrine changes associated with reproductive function (Deakin, 1988; Hendrick et al., 1998; Llewellyn et al., 1997; Rubinow et al., 2002). More accurately, it is an atypical response to typical hormonal fluctuations (O'Hara and McCabe, 2013). All women experience similar endocrine changes during pregnancy and birth, but only some experience significant changes in mood. Many women experience mild to severe depression within a few days of giving birth (O'Hara et al., 1991; Susman, 1996).

affective disorders   Mental disorders characterized by dramatic changes or extremes of mood.

face validity   A reasonable outward representation of a disorder (i.e., behavioral phenotype matching the symptoms of the disorder).

construct validity   Possession of the same underlying mechanisms, or etiology and homology, as a human disorder.

The mildest type of postpartum depression is called maternity blues or baby blues and usually persists for less than a week. A case of maternity blues is usually manifested by periods of crying and sadness; about 50% of women in North America display these symptoms after giving birth. Mild to moderate postpartum depression is experienced by about 15%–20% of women; this type of postpartum depression may last 4–8 weeks. Its symptoms include depressed affect (mood), insomnia, crying, irritability, feelings of inadequacy, reduced coping ability, and fatigue. In very rare cases (less than 0.01% of women giving birth), women display a temporary, but severe, form of depression called postpartum depressive psychosis (Hopkins et al., 1984). Women who attempt to harm their infants are usually suffering from this rare version of postpartum depression. In this chapter we will explore the extent to which hormones can be responsible for the impaired cognition, judgment, affect, and behavior seen in people with postpartum depression and some other disorders. If aberrant hormone concentrations can influence brain function, then should these conditions deserve legal consideration, especially if the hormone fluctuations are not induced by exogenous factors?

As we have seen throughout this book, hormones can affect behavioral thresholds, changing the probability that a given stimulus will elicit a response under specific environmental conditions. In addition, hormones can influence affect, or mood. In some cases, hormones appear to lower the threshold for the appearance of maladaptive behaviors and feelings in humans. It should be apparent from the previous chapters that individuals display a wide range of responses to the same hormone and that there is a substantial range of hormone concentrations that occur normally in both humans and nonhuman species. Individuals who occupy either end of the continuum of endocrine responses or hormone concentrations may display or experience atypical behaviors or moods, that is, **affective disorders**. These affective disorders often require clinical intervention. Hormonal imbalances caused by pathology, inherited predisposition, or the effects of foods, drugs, or toxins may underlie a number of behavioral disorders or cause psychological distress to individuals. Some of the behavioral pathologies that arise because of hormonal dysfunction have been described in previous chapters.

Many mood disorders emerge during adolescence, when hormone concentrations are changing dramatically. The interactions of these hormones with still-maturing brains can trigger dysregulated affective responses in susceptible individuals, who have some combination of genetic and environmental pressures for disordered moods. Mood changes are also associated with other times of substantial hormonal changes, such as after pregnancy. This chapter will focus on a few select examples of the ways in which hormones are involved in affective disorders in humans. The examples that have been chosen have been the most consistently studied and have the best-established relationships between hormones and affect. First, the associations among several hormones and depression will be described; the role of hormones in postpartum depression, specifically, will also be discussed. Second, hormones associated with perimenstrual syndrome (PMS) will be described. Third, the influence of melatonin on seasonal affective disorder, an unusual, recurrent type of annual depression, will be presented. Individuals who abuse anabolic-androgenic steroids often experience a state of nearly psychotic aggressive behavior, commonly called roids rage; the self-inflicted role of these anabolic steroids on mood will be discussed in the next section. Finally, correlations between various hormones and anorexia nervosa and bulimia nervosa will be presented.

Most of the experimental work presented in the previous chapters was based on animal research. Animal models can be useful to understand the endocrine mechanisms underlying affective disorders, but there are limitations in their applicability to humans, especially in the context of disordered mood. Importantly, any animal model for affective disorders must have **face validity**, **construct validity**, and

predictive validity. *Face validity* refers to how well the animal model resembles the human disorder. *Construct validity* refers to the similarity of the underlying mechanisms of the disorder; understanding of mechanisms of the human disorder and development of therapeutic interventions requires construct validity. *Predictive validity* refers to the expected responses to treatment that are effective in humans. Because of the difficulties associated with assessing emotions and mood in nonverbal individuals, many studies of humans, rather than animals, have been conducted to understand the causes and treatments of affective disorders. Consequently, most of the studies described in this chapter employ so-called self-report methods to assess mood. Studies that attempt to correlate human affective changes with endocrine events typically involve people reporting their moods, which are then correlated with measurements of hormone concentrations. The effects of endocrine manipulations or natural endocrine fluctuations can then be assessed.

predictive validity The ability to show a close relationship between test results prior to and after the manipulation in question.

Hormones and Depression

The symptoms of depression can include reduced mood (profound sadness), feelings of worthlessness, general fatigue, feelings of guilt, indecisiveness, disturbances (usually reductions) in sleep and food intake, absence of pleasure, suicidal thoughts/actions, and agitated or retarded motor symptoms (*DSM-5*, 2013). Agitated motor symptoms include pacing or hand-wringing; retarded motor symptoms include slow body movements or speech. In severe cases, delusions and hallucinations may be present.

Patients displaying the symptoms of depression are generally suffering from "clinical" depression. If these symptoms persist for more than 2 weeks, then the patient is diagnosed with major depressive disorder. Those displaying less severe symptoms that last much longer, at least 2 years, are diagnosed with dysthymia.

Another distinction made among types of clinical depression is between bipolar and unipolar depression. Bipolar depression is depression in the presence of at least one episode of mania, or excessively elevated mood, which often involves inordinate feelings of confidence, power, and creative energies. Unipolar depression is depressed affect in the absence of manic episodes. Many of the studies on depression cited below used experimental groups that included individuals diagnosed with either unipolar or bipolar depression. Because the physiological mechanisms underlying these two types of depression may differ, the clumping of all of these individuals into one experimental group may mask hormonal correlates of depression, even though individuals in both groups often respond to the same antidepressant drugs.

Depression is typically considered to be at one end of a mood continuum, with mania at the other end (**FIGURE 13.1**). Depressed individuals vary in both the severity and the duration of their symptoms. The prevalence of depressive symptoms is determined by means of psychological tests such as the Hamilton Rating Scale for Depression, Hamilton Depression Inventory, Beck Depression Inventory, and Zung Self-Rating Depression Scale (Beck et al., 1961; Hamilton, 1960, 1980). Studies of the endocrine correlates of depression use scores on these tests to measure the effects of hormone treatments. A number of endocrine correlates have been associated with depression (Herbert, 2012; Rubin et al., 2002).

| Depression | Melancholia | Normal | Hypomania | Mania |

FIGURE 13.1 Continuum of mood from depression to mania People may display unusual mood elevation or mood depression in response to environmental conditions. When these mood extremes persist and interfere with normal function, they become clinically significant.

Thyroid Hormones

The hormones of the hypothalamic-pituitary-thyroid axis have been implicated in depression (Musselman and Nemeroff, 1996; Sauvage et al., 1998) (see Figure 11.5). It was recognized over a century ago that depressed people tend to have low thyroid function (Bruns, 1888). Administration of thyrotropin-releasing hormone (TRH) stimulates the release of thyroid-stimulating hormone (TSH) from the anterior pituitary gland and subsequent hormone production by the thyroid gland. Administration of TRH to depressed individuals has been attempted in several studies. In one such study, five patients who achieved a certain composite score on psychological tests were considered to be depressed (three were diagnosed as unipolar and two as bipolar) (Kastin et al., 1972). Depression was reduced in four of these five patients by TRH treatment, as indicated by their improved scores on subsequent tests. Amelioration of the depressive symptoms varied in duration from 3 hours to several weeks, and the latency of action of TRH varied from 1 to 72 hours. No improvement of the depressive symptoms was reported when the patients were treated with saline. All of the depressed patients showed a smaller than normal TSH elevation in response to the TRH stimulation, which is unusual in the absence of thyroid dysfunction. Furthermore, although protein-bound iodine levels, basal metabolic rate, and rate of radioactive iodine uptake—all indicators of thyroid function—are usually within the normal range in depressed patients, the thyroid response to TSH is significantly lower in depressed patients than in nondepressed individuals (Ehrensing et al., 1974; Takahashi et al., 1974), suggesting some subclinical endocrine malfunction.

The depressive symptoms of PMS (see below) have also been associated with thyroid function. In one study, the responses of TSH and prolactin concentrations to TRH administration were examined in women who reported PMS symptoms and in women who did not. Previous studies on depressed patients had found both blunted and enhanced TSH secretion in response to TRH administration. TRH had also been found to stimulate prolactin release in nondepressed women but not to affect prolactin levels in depressed women (Roy-Byrne et al., 1987). TRH was given during both the follicular and luteal phases. There were no significant differences between women with and without PMS symptoms in their basal or maximal elevations of TSH or prolactin in response to the treatment, and neither TSH nor prolactin values differed between the luteal and follicular phases. However, the women with PMS showed much greater variation in TSH response to TRH treatment than the control women; that is, sometimes TSH levels were augmented, but other times they were reduced (Roy-Byrne et al., 1987). Women without PMS showed stable responses of TSH to TRH. These results indicate that variable TSH response to TRH could be present in a subgroup of women who suffer depression as part of their PMS symptoms.

As people age, they often become hypothyroid or display subclinical hypothyroidism. Elderly people also display reduced mood more frequently than younger people. Is this correlation between decreasing circulating thyroid hormones and mood linked biologically? One recent study of British elderly patients discovered, after controlling for other factors, that there was a significant link between thyroid hormone concentrations and mood (Roberts et al., 2006). However, although this relationship was statistically significant, the authors deemed the difference not biologically significant. Thus, it remains unclear the extent to which elevated rates of depression are caused by decreasing thyroid function during aging.

In addition to changes in the response of TSH to TRH, studies have reported that depressed patients often exhibit (1) a very high level of antibodies against the thyroid gland, (2) high TRH concentrations in the cerebrospinal fluid, and (3) enhancement of antidepressant efficacy by cotreatment with triiodothyronine (T_3) (Musselman and Nemeroff, 1996; Sauvage et al., 1998). Thyroid hormones can affect serotonin, which influences mood (Lifschytz et al., 2006). Augmentation of serotonin reuptake inhibitor therapy with the coadministration of thyroid hormones (primarily T_3) is a well-documented treatment option for refractory depressed patients (DeBattista, 2006). Because depression is often comorbid with subclinical thyroiditis (an autoimmune disorder), it has been suggested that depression may cause alterations in the immune system or perhaps represent an autoimmune disorder as well (Fountoulakis et al., 2008). Thyroid hormones have been used in conjunction with antidepressant medications since the late 1960s to accelerate clinical responses (Hage and Azar, 2012). Normalization of thyroid hormone concentrations after remission of depression often occurs, but it remains unspecified whether this reflects clinical recovery or a direct effect of antidepressant drug treatment (Hage and Azar, 2012). Future research is needed to discover the extent to which the depression may interact with endocrine and immune functions.

Growth Hormone and Prolactin

Basal growth hormone (GH) concentrations have been reported to be in the normal range in most depressed patients. However, impaired GH responses to insulin-induced hypoglycemia in depressed patients have been reported by many investigators (e.g., Sachar et al., 1973). Depressed patients also display blunted GH responses to serotonin stimulation compared with people not experiencing depression. TRH, which does not affect GH concentrations in normal individuals, evokes an abnormal increase in GH in depressed patients (Maeda et al., 1975). Elevated blood plasma prolactin concentrations have also been reported in depressed patients (Nicholas et al., 1998; Sachar et al., 1973). Although the results of correlative studies linking GH and prolactin to depression are somewhat contradictory (e.g., TRH increased prolactin concentrations in depressed patients in one study [Maeda et al., 1975] and decreased prolactin concentrations in another [Ehrensing et al., 1974]), they point to a fundamental difference in endocrine function between depressed patients and nondepressed individuals and suggest differences in the physiological mechanisms underlying their endocrine feedback control systems (Dinan, 1998; Nicolas et al., 1998). Because stress often provokes depression and affects prolactin concentrations, it is possible that interactions among prolactin, dopamine, and somatostatin in response to stress contribute to some cases of depression (Faron-Gorecka et al., 2013). Importantly, a frequent side effect of antidepressant therapy is hyperprolactinemia; however, few data concerning these effects have been reported (Coker and Taylor, 2010).

Cortisol

Cortisol appears to play a multifaceted role in major depressive disorder (MDD) (Herbert, 2012). First, increased resistance to the feedback actions of glucocorticoids is often observed. Second, daily rhythms in cortisol are perturbed. Finally, resting cortisol concentrations and the postawakening cortisol surge are increased in people at risk for MDD (Herbert, 2012).

The negative feedback features of the hypothalamic-pituitary-adrenal (HPA) axis, shown in **FIGURE 13.2A**, appear to be impaired in depressed patients. Excessive cortisol production has been reported in nearly 50% of depressed patients examined (Carroll et al., 2007) (**FIGURE 13.2B**). These increased serum cortisol concentrations do not appear to reflect the stress of coping with depression, because cortisol concentrations are at their highest 3–4 hours after sleep onset, when stress levels should be lowest, and decrease throughout the daylight hours, when stress levels are presumably highest (Carroll, 1980). Because cortisol is normally secreted in a pronounced circadian pattern, with peak concentrations measured in the early morning, this disturbance

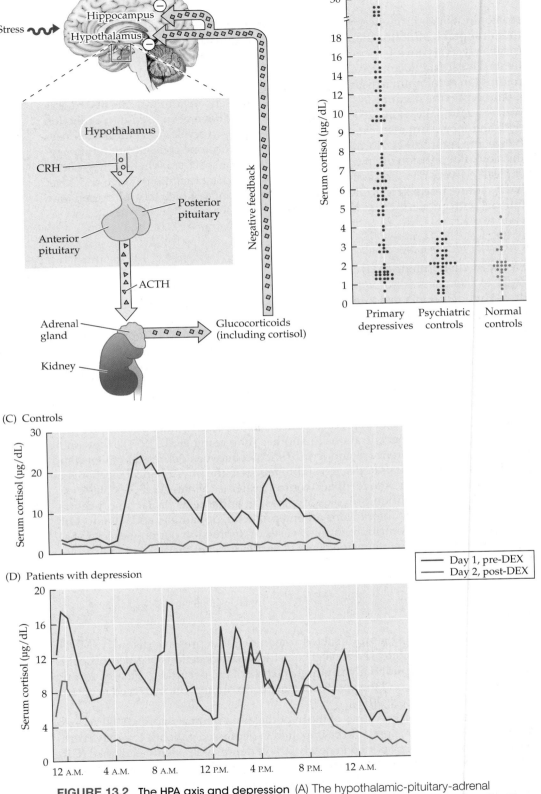

FIGURE 13.2 **The HPA axis and depression** (A) The hypothalamic-pituitary-adrenal (HPA) system. (B) The negative feedback features of the HPA axis appear to be impaired in depressed people, because blood cortisol concentrations are often higher in depressed than in nondepressed individuals. (C) Dexamethasone (DEX) inhibits the normal circadian pattern of cortisol secretion on the first day of treatment. (D) Dexamethasone often fails to suppress cortisol concentrations of depressed individuals. After Breedlove et al., 2010.

of the diurnal rhythm of cortisol secretion suggests an abnormal disinhibition of the neural centers regulating the release of adrenocorticotropic hormone (ACTH), the tropic hormone from the anterior pituitary gland that stimulates adrenal output. Chronic dysregulation of the HPA axis and resultant high cortisol levels are common findings in depression (O'Brien et al., 2004; Thompson, 2007) (**FIGURE 13.3**).

Cortisol normally counteracts the hypoglycemic effects of insulin; however, depressed patients do not show this response. High doses of insulin given during the diagnostic insulin tolerance test suppress blood glucose levels, but glucose levels cannot be restored by cortisol in depressed patients (Carroll, 1980). The function of the HPA axis in depressed patients has also been assessed by means of the dexamethasone suppression test (**FIGURE 13.2C**). Administration of 1 to 2 mg of dexamethasone, an artificial steroid that mimics cortisol, at midnight normally suppresses blood plasma cortisol concentrations for 24 hours via a negative feedback mechanism (Cole et al., 2000). Dexamethasone failed to suppress cortisol production in 46% of depressed patients examined (Carroll et al., 1968). In most cases, plasma concentrations of cortisol were suppressed the morning after dexamethasone treatment but increased shortly thereafter (Carroll et al., 1976) (**FIGURE 13.2D**). This inappropriate response to dexamethasone indicates a failure of the normal neural inhibiting mechanism for ACTH/cortisol secretion. It seems likely that a complex relation between the serotonergic system and the HPA axis (McAllister-Williams et al., 1998) (see Figure 11.5) underlies the hypersecretion of cortisol, the failure to respond normally to dexamethasone by suppressing cortisol production, and the disturbance of the circadian rhythm of cortisol secretion.

FIGURE 13.3 Cortisol secretion is deranged in depressed people. (A) The daily cortisol rhythm is generated by projections from the suprachiasmatic nucleus (SCN) to corticotropin-releasing hormone (CRH) neurons that drive downstream rhythms in anterior pituitary adrenocorticotropic hormone (ACTH). In turn, ACTH acts on the adrenal cortex to stimulate cortisol release. Rhythmic cortisol secretion entrains clock genes in target tissues (including the brain) or acts directly on corticoid-responsive genes. Other peripheral rhythms are entrained independently of cortisol. (B) Ultradian cortisol pulses underlie the circadian cortisol rhythm in control (Con) and depressed (MDD) people. (C) Depressed subjects exhibit hypercortisolemia during depression. Data from O'Brien et al., 2004.

(A)

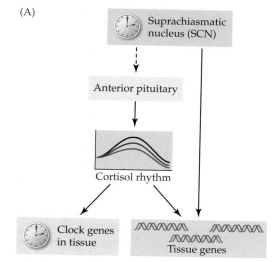

(B)

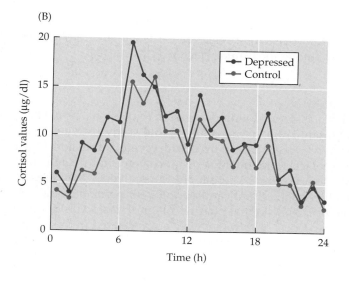

(C)

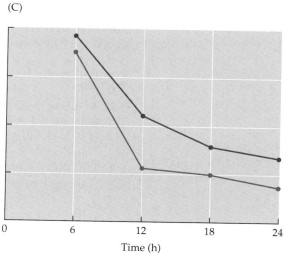

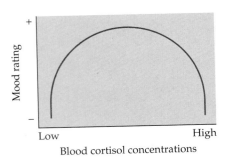

FIGURE 13.4 Cortisol and mood Mood rating in self-reports shows an inverse U-shaped relationship with blood cortisol concentrations, with optimal mood ratings corresponding to moderate blood cortisol concentrations. If blood cortisol concentrations become too high or too low, as in Cushing syndrome or Addison disease, respectively, then mood ratings typically drop into the depressed category.

Taken together, findings in depressed patients of (1) high basal cortisol concentrations due to cortisol hypersecretion, (2) the failure to respond normally to dexamethasone by suppressing cortisol production, (3) high concentrations of corticotropin-releasing hormone (CRH) in the cerebrospinal fluid, (4) a blunted ACTH response to treatment with endogenous CRH, and (5) the disturbance of the circadian rhythm of cortisol secretion appear to indicate a central disinhibition of the HPA axis during depressive episodes (Heuser, 1998; Mitchell, 1998; Musselman and Nemeroff, 1996; Plotsky et al., 1998). These changes in the HPA axis appear to be state-dependent; that is, these factors normalize with the elevation of mood (Murphy, 1997; Plotsky et al., 1998).

In all of these examples of hormonal changes in depressed patients, it is unclear whether depression causes changes in hormone production or whether changes in hormone production cause depression. When depression is secondary to some endocrine or immune dysfunction, then more definitive statements can be made about the direction of causality. For example, individuals suffering from primary hypothyroidism often present symptoms of depressed affect and intellect. However, patients suffering from primary adrenal disorders show conflicting mood responses to cortisol concentrations. For instance, patients with Cushing syndrome have adrenals that produce excessive cortisol, and depression is often a symptom of this disorder; however, patients with Addison disease have adrenal glands that produce insufficient cortisol, and depression is a defining symptom of this disease as well. Thus, an inverted U-shaped function exists for the effects of cortisol concentrations on mood (**FIGURE 13.4**).

Elevated cortisol concentrations inhibit neuronal activity in the brain (see Chapter 11), and normalization of cortisol concentrations often leads to a resolution of depression (Wolkowitz and Reus, 1999). Because thyroid hormones can increase the metabolic clearance rate of cortisol, it has been hypothesized that treatment of depressed individuals with thyroid hormones reduces circulating cortisol levels, thus normalizing serotonin and possibly norepinephrine levels (Thompson, 2007). Thus, it may be the case that the subset of responders to thyroid hormone treatment to ameliorate depression might also present with high circulating cortisol values as a contributory factor to their depression. Additional studies are required to address this intriguing hypothesis. Nonetheless, it is clear that MDD is a multifactorial disorder with many contributory factors; deranged cortisol regulation/actions, however, must be considered among the primary factors (**FIGURE 13.5**).

Estrogens

Deficits in estrogen have been associated with depression (Fink et al., 1996; Halbreich, 1997; Zweifel and O'Brien, 1997). In one double-blind study, estrogen treatment was given to 40 women who were hospitalized with severe depression. None of the women who received placebo treatment showed changes in their affect; in fact, 47% of those patients deteriorated in mood. However, over 90% of the depressed women treated with estrogen significantly improved in mood (Klaiber et al., 1979). It should be noted that substantial pharmacological doses (15–20 times the recommended therapeutic doses) of estrogen were administered in this study. Administration of estrogen in physiological doses improves mood in non-depressed

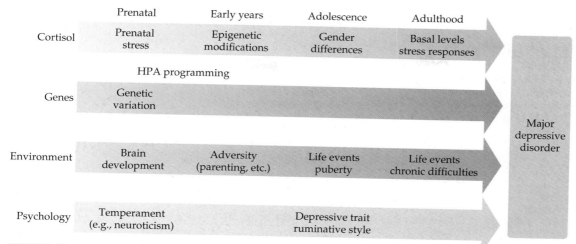

FIGURE 13.5 Role of cortisol in the trajectories that predispose people to major depressive disorder. Traits displayed on four dimensions (arrows) that contribute to the onset of major depressive disorder (MDD). Each arrow represents the lifelong (but variable) influence of four major factors contributing to the risk for MDD. Note that dysregulated cortisol is a major contributing factor. After Herbert, 2013.

women (Sherwin and Gelfand, 1985; Sherwin and Suranyi-Cadotte, 1990) but not in clinically depressed women (Schneider et al., 1977). However, estrogen replacement therapy seems to ameliorate depressed affect in postmenopausal women (Fink et al., 1996; Halbreich, 1997; Pearlstein et al., 1997; Rubinow et al., 1998; Zweifel and O'Brien, 1997). Of course, there are many negative side effects associated with estrogen replacement therapy, so any affective benefits must be carefully considered with a physician in the context of its costs. Nonetheless, a randomized clinical trial has suggested that withdrawal from estradiol in women prone to depression drives the disorder, and the risks associated with depression must be balanced against any negative effects of estrogen replacement therapy.

Sex differences in mood disorders begin at puberty, and generally women are at twice the risk compared with men (Steiner and Young, 2008). Depressed women display significantly reduced estradiol levels compared with nondepressed women (Young et al., 2000). Depressed perimenopausal women undergo earlier menopause and subsequent reduced estradiol concentrations (Harlow et al., 2003). The time around menopause, when reproductive hormones are generally waning in women, is associated with a risk of new and recurrent depression (Schmidt et al., 2015). In light of the similar estrogen level changes with postpartum depression and perimenstrual depression (see below), the notion that withdrawal from the relatively high estradiol concentrations associated with pregnancy and the ovulatory cycles could be involved in depression was tested in an elegant double-blind experiment of two groups of women: those who had no history of depression and those who had such a history. All women received 3 weeks of open-label administration of transdermal estradiol patches (100 µg/day), then were randomized to receive either estradiol (100 µg/day) or matched placebo skin patches for 3 additional weeks under double-blind conditions. The women were given paper and pencil tests for depression, as well as assessments of their blood hormone levels. None of the women reported depressive symptoms during the open-label use of estradiol. Women with past depression who were crossed over from estradiol to placebo patches experienced a significant increase in depression symptom severity; in other words, when estradiol was withdrawn, depression ensued (Schmidt et al., 2015). Women with past depression who continued estradiol therapy and all women in the control group remained

FIGURE 13.6 Estradiol withdrawal precipitation of depressive symptoms Women treated with estrogen skin patches reported no depressive symptoms. However, women with a history of past depression who were crossed over from estradiol to placebo patches experienced a significant increase in depression symptom severity; in other words, when estradiol was withdrawn, depression ensued. From Schmidt et al., 2015.

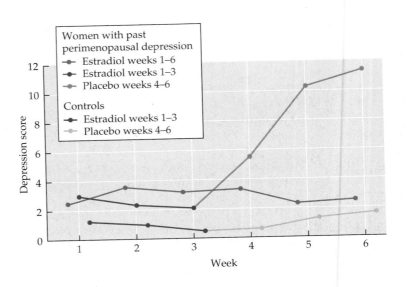

asymptomatic (**FIGURE 13.6**). Women in both groups had similar hot-flush severity and plasma estradiol levels during use of placebo (Schmidt et al., 2015).

It is possible that estrogens play a role in other types of depression associated with the withdrawal of estrogens, including postpartum depression.

Postpartum Depression

Postpartum depression has attracted a lot of attention recently because of several high-profile cases among celebrities. Singer Marie Osmond wrote a popular book entitled *Behind the Smile: My Journey Out of Postpartum Depression* detailing her struggles with depression. Other celebrities, including actresses Hayden Panettiere and Gwyneth Paltrow, have also described their postpartum depression. As noted at the beginning of this chapter, the postpartum period is a time of mother-infant bonding for most women. However, a significant minority may suffer from postpartum depression. Postpartum depression has become a well-known disorder that is the outcome of the typical endocrine changes associated with reproductive function (Deakin, 1988; Hendrick et al., 1998; Llewellyn et al., 1997; Rubinow et al., 2002). However, there is confusion regarding the precise definition of postpartum depression, as well as uncertainty that it is a unique disorder (Hamilton et al., 1988).

Many women experience mild to severe depression within a few days of giving birth (O'Hara and McCabe, 2013; Susman, 1996). As noted above, the mildest type of postpartum depression, called maternity blues or baby blues, typically persists for only 24–48 hours and is characterized by periods of crying and sadness. In North America these symptoms occur in about half of women after they give birth. About 15%–20% of women experience 4–8 weeks of the depressed affect, insomnia, crying, irritability, feelings of inadequacy, reduced coping ability, and fatigue that are common to mild to moderate postpartum depression. Less than 0.01% of women giving birth undergo a temporary severe depression called postpartum depressive psychosis (Hopkins et al., 1984).

The precise precursors of postpartum mood disorders have not been specified, but a combination of biological, social, and psychological factors, including a personal or family history of depression, may be involved. Because dramatic changes in blood concentrations of estrogens, progesterone, HPA axis hormones, and prolactin occur at the time of parturition, most studies of the hormonal correlates of postpartum mood changes have investigated the roles of these hormones (Llewellyn et al., 1997; O'Hara and Zekoski, 1988; Steiner and Young, 2008). For many years, no consistent correlations between mood changes and these hormones were identified

(George and Sandler, 1988; Gitlin and Pasnau, 1989; Kuevi et al., 1983; O'Hara et al., 1991), but a prior case of postpartum depression was the best predictor of subsequent bouts of this mood disorder.

A relationship between opioid peptides, specifically β-endorphin, and postpartum mood changes has been reported (Deakin, 1988; Ferin, 1984; George and Sandler, 1988). Blood plasma concentrations of β-endorphin change during pregnancy: concentrations are relatively constant during the first two trimesters, begin to rise during the end of pregnancy, peak during parturition, and then drop immediately afterward (Newnham et al., 1983, 1984; Smith et al., 1990). Because β-endorphin concentrations plummet within hours of parturition, it has been suggested that maternity blues, and perhaps other, more severe postpartum mood disorders, may result from this "withdrawal" of endogenous opioids (Newnham et al., 1984). In support of this hypothesis, women who displayed the highest incidence of depressive symptoms from gestational week 38 through day 2 postpartum, as well as 3 months postpartum, had the greatest decreases in plasma β-endorphin concentrations after parturition (Smith et al., 1990). Increases in anxiety and tension are also associated with the postpartum decline in plasma β-endorphin levels (Brinsmead et al., 1985). Although several correlative studies have established a relationship between opioids and postpartum mood, direct experimental evidence remains lacking.

As with unipolar and bipolar depression, there has also been a series of studies implicating hormones of the HPA axis in postpartum depression (Steiner and Young, 2008). More recently, elevated midgestation corticotropin-releasing hormone (CRH) concentrations were discovered to be predictive of postpartum depression (Yim et al., 2009). Although CRH typically increases in midpregnancy, the function of this increase remains unspecified. What is clear is that the source of this elevated CRH is the placenta. When pregnant rats are stressed, they exhibit a number of structural modifications in the medial prefrontal cortex, as well as increased depression-like responses and deficient maternal care (Leuner et al., 2014). Additional development of animal models may provide new insights into the mechanisms and treatment options in the future. In summary, however, there appears to be no unifying principle that can be established regarding the contribution of hormones that might affect treatment options for postpartum depression. Rather, there seem to be differences in how individuals respond to the large changes in hormones after parturition. Alternatively, the social dynamics associated with a new person joining the family may contribute to the onset and severity of postpartum depression.

Although a fair amount of descriptive work has been done, only recently have data been collected that seem to indicate that postpartum depression may not reflect only endocrine changes. There are several social changes that occur after the delivery of a baby that may lead to postpartum depression (Hendrick et al., 1998; Nonacs and Cohen, 1998). Indeed, some have asserted that postpartum depression is a disease resulting from our modern lives (Hahn-Holbrook and Haselton, 2014). Hospitalization, for instance, may affect depressive symptoms in some women. The change in status to that of parent can be a significant life event sufficient in itself to cause anxiety and depression (Richman et al., 1991). Women who remain at home with their children are more likely to display depressive symptoms than women who have careers outside the home (Gotlib et al., 1989). Depression resulting from the lack of social support that accompanied a career may be mediated by placental CRH (Hahn-Holbrook et al., 2013); family support was associated with significantly fewer reported depressive symptoms and more gradual increases in placental CRH from weeks 29–37 of gestation. Not surprisingly, perhaps, women bringing unwanted pregnancies to term are more likely to become depressed than women with planned pregnancies. Men are nearly as likely as women to suffer postpartum depressive symptoms within 2 months of a child's birth (68% and 82%, respectively) (Richman et al., 1991).

perimenstrual syndrome (PMS)
A constellation of symptoms, including anxiety, depression, moodiness, and fatigue, that recurs on a cyclical basis and is associated with menstruation.

In one study, repeated measurements of women's moods revealed that 25% exhibited increased depressive symptoms during pregnancy. However, only 10% of the women in this study met the diagnostic criteria for depression, and only 7% could be diagnosed as depressed postpartum (Gotlib et al., 1989). These results indicate that mild depression may be common during and immediately after pregnancy but that debilitating depression is rare. The similar incidence of depression seen in men and the depression seen in women both during and after pregnancy, despite very different hormone concentrations at those times, also suggest that endocrine changes may not be the primary cause of postpartum depression.

Perimenstrual Syndrome

Perimenstrual syndrome (**PMS**) is probably the best-known behavioral phenomenon associated with hormones. Many clinical studies have shown that the normal changes in steroid hormone concentrations associated with the menstrual cycle (see Figure 6.22) are often associated with changes in the behavior and feelings of women. In some instances, the symptoms of PMS appear to be a direct result of those hormonal changes. Other studies suggest that PMS symptoms result from physiological changes that are caused by the endocrine changes. Still other studies suggest that cognitive factors, including social expectations, influence the occurrence of PMS symptoms in the absence of hormonal correlates. Because some symptoms continue or increase in intensity during menstruation, the term *perimenstrual syndrome* is used here instead of the more common term, *premenstrual syndrome*. Use of the word *syndrome* does not imply "abnormal" or "disease" but, rather, refers to a cluster of physiological and emotional symptoms that appear to be linked.

The Social Context of PMS

After one of the 2015 Republican debates, presidential hopeful Donald Trump was annoyed by Megyn Kelly's questions and said on *CNN Tonight*, "You could see there was blood coming out of her eyes. Blood coming out of her wherever." Many people believed that Mr. Trump was referring to menstruation. Later he said that he did not mean to imply that Ms. Kelly was asking tough questions during the debate because she was menstruating. There is no way to know what Mr. Trump meant by his words, but the subtext of his comments was taken to mean that Ms. Kelly was irritable because she was menstruating and suffering from PMS. Even today, much controversy surrounds PMS. As we shall see, the prevalence and the defining symptoms of PMS, as well as the physical and psychological factors associated with it, remain subjects of debate; indeed, the very existence of the syndrome has been questioned by some researchers. Over the past 35 years, PMS has changed from a relatively unknown medical condition to a well-known social phenomenon. North American men and women use *PMS* to communicate a widely shared cultural understanding about the behavior and moods of women. Most North American adults understand that women might become periodically aggressive, assertive, and probably cranky, traits often tolerated or even applauded when displayed by men, because of PMS. It seems probable that assignment of these character traits to PMS trivializes the accomplishments of women.

Perimenstrual syndrome must be considered within a social context because it affects only one sex and because its image is not positive. Feminist social scientists have noted that several cultural phenomena have interacted to establish PMS as a biologically based illness that affects only women and to make it a part of the social fabric (Brown-Parlee, 1990, 1991). For example, the increased awareness of PMS in North America has coincided with an increase of feminist ideas in public forums. A discussion of the meaning of feminism is beyond the scope of this book, but one of its central tenets is that equal opportunities for economic and political power should exist for women and men. This demand is reasonable in the US political system because justice demands equal treatment for individuals who are equal. In theory, women should not have difficulty in making their case for equality. If, however, men and women are not considered biologically equivalent, then making an argument for equal economic and political opportunities for men and women is more difficult (Young, 1990).

Some feminists have argued that the "pathologization" of normal menstruation is an attempt on the part of the male-dominated biomedical community to demonstrate that women and men are unequal in ways that disqualify women from holding positions of economic and political power. Certainly, the biomedical community is not the objective, culture-free, unbiased fellowship of truth seekers that is often portrayed as its ideal. During the first feminist movement early in the twentieth century, scientific "evidence" of the reproductive frailties of women provided by the medical community was used to support the perspective that women should not participate in higher education, vote, or operate automobiles or airplanes. Others argue that many women actively participated in the "conspiracy" to medicalize PMS, apparently embracing it for the advantages of the "sick" role that accompanies it, especially the exemption from accountability for behaviors and feelings for which they would normally be held responsible. According to this argument, some women diagnosed with PMS have thereby been empowered by physicians to be "irrational" or "out of control" and have received subtle cultural acceptance for expressions of aggression and power that are typically unacceptable. The extreme version of this view is evident when PMS is used as a defense against criminal charges. For instance, in France, women defending themselves in court can plead a special form of temporary insanity if their crimes were committed during the late luteal phase of the menstrual cycle, and in Canada, a woman who suffered since adolescence with PMS was found not guilty of shoplifting. In the United States, PMS is not acceptable as a legal defense.

The feminist position does not question the reality of PMS, but it does question the existence of biological mechanisms underlying PMS, and it emphasizes the potential limitations that the acceptance of PMS as a biologically based illness places on women, who are thus assumed to be subject to "raging hormones," "out of control," or "dysfunctional." From a social perspective, the important question is not whether women fluctuate in their moods or even in their levels of aggressive behavior but, rather, whether their functioning is impaired by these monthly fluctuations. The vast majority of research from the social sciences has not detected any significant impairments of this sort (Ussher, 1989). Furthermore, PMS is a so-called culturally bound syndrome described in anthropology that is prevalent in Western societies and virtually nonexistent in non-Western cultures. Viewed this way, PMS may be an appropriate symbolic representation of conflicting expectations that women should be both productive and reproductive (Johnson, 1987; Tseng, 2006).

What Is PMS?

A consideration of PMS from a biomedical perspective reveals several problems with the characterization of this phenomenon. Consequently, understanding the relationship between hormones and the mood changes associated with PMS has proven difficult. The first issue that is often raised in biomedical discussions of PMS is whether PMS is a real phenomenon. Before this issue can be directly addressed, a distinction between illness and disease must be made. PMS is not a disease; it is a response to a natural cycle, and there is no known underlying pathology. However, a woman suffering from symptoms associated with menstruation can visit a physician, receive a diagnosis of PMS, get treatment, and report amelioration of the symptoms (Rapkin, 2003). This scenario suggests that PMS is real and should be considered an illness. One interesting issue, the significance of which remains

TABLE 13.1	**Percentages of women who report perimenstrual symptoms in two tests designed to assess PMS**	
	Test	
Symptom	Menstrual Distress Questionnaire[a]	Premenstrual Assessment Form[b]
Breast pain	35	84
Weight gain	34	83
Swelling	36	77
Backaches	24	74
Sadness	43	76
Anxiety	30	70
Skin blemishes	34	69
Dizziness	5	25

Source: Logue and Moos, 1986.

Note: Tests were administered during the perimenstrual period.

[a]Severity ratings from "mild" to "severe."

[b]Severity ratings from "slight" to "extreme."

unresolved, is the observation that approximately 50% of women who receive placebo treatments for their PMS symptoms report improvements in their symptoms. There are few other illnesses for which this is true. Of course, there is a placebo response for other symptoms not associated with PMS: approximately 30% of both men and women respond to placebo treatments for many symptoms. With PMS, there is reason to believe that the placebo effect wears off after 3 months; however, few clinical investigations of PMS have extended beyond 3 months. As you might expect, correlating hormonal changes with symptoms of PMS is challenging under these circumstances.

If the reality of PMS is accepted, several other problems remain to be addressed. First, estimates of the prevalence of PMS vary widely, despite many cross-cultural studies that have indicated that some women in all societies examined report perimenstrual symptoms. The frequency of perimenstrual symptoms reported in different studies varies between 20% and 90% of North American and European women. A meta-analysis of all published reports yields a prevalence rate of about 45% of all women. Most of these women rate their symptoms as mild; however, some women are debilitated by PMS. The frequency of severe PMS symptoms ranges between 2% and 10% (Logue and Moos, 1986). It is generally accepted that about 3%–5% of women experience PMS symptoms to a degree that interferes with their usual functioning. This variation in prevalence rates is due in part to differences in the criteria used to define the syndrome (Endicott et al., 1981). The prevalence estimates reflect the types of symptoms included in each study (e.g., psychological vs. physiological) as well as the severity of symptoms included (**TABLE 13.1**).

A corollary of this problem is that all of the PMS data are based on self-reports. In some studies, the self-reports are retrospective; in others, they are prospective or concurrent with the symptoms. This is the one area of behavioral endocrinology for which the introspective, or self-report, method is the primary technique used to generate behavioral data to correlate with hormonal data. Obviously, self-reports of PMS symptoms can be influenced by many factors; for example, simply being asked about the symptoms is likely to increase the perceived severity of the symptoms (Brown-Parlee, 1991). Women are also likely to rate their symptoms as more severe when asked about their perimenstrual period after the fact than during the experience.

A second problem with PMS is that neither the premenstrual nor menstrual period is well defined. When should symptoms be considered part of PMS? If they appear 3 days prior to menstruation? If they appear 5 days prior to menstruation? If they appear 10 days prior to menstruation? Furthermore, how long after the onset of menses should symptoms be included? Menstruation may continue for 3 days in some cases or 8 days in others. Is a menstrual period of 3 days equivalent to an 8-day period? Because there is no consensus about which data should be included, there is substantial difficulty in comparing PMS studies with one another.

A third problem with PMS is the lack of consensus concerning its symptoms. PMS was originally described in 1931 as "premenstrual tension." Symptoms of this condition included severe psychological tension, weight gain, headaches, and edema (swelling) that occurred 7–10 days prior to the onset of menses (Frank, 1931). Because these symptoms may also occur in postmenopausal women, as well as in men and children, diagnosis of PMS requires the additional criterion of regular recurrence. Thus, symptoms must manifest themselves on a cyclic basis and end with the onset or offset of menstruation. The current diagnostic criteria for the so-called late luteal phase dysphoric disorder (premenstrual dysphoric disorder [PMDD]) are described in the fifth edition of the American Psychiatric Association's *Diagnostic and Statistical Manual of Mental Disorders*, published in 2013 (*DSM-5*, 2013); they are listed in **BOX 13.1**. Essentially, at least five of these symptoms must be present for a diagnosis of PMDD (Freeman, 2003). With these strict criteria for a diagnosis of PMDD, the prevalence of the disorder drops to between 5% and 10% of women of reproductive age (Halbreich et al., 2003). The 2007 version of the World Health Organization's International Classification of Diseases lists premenstrual tension syndrome as a psychiatric disorder. The defining diagnosis of PMS according to the American College of Obstetricians and Gynecologists requires at least one mood

---

BOX 13.1 *Diagnostic Criteria for Premenstrual Dysphoric Disorder*

A. In most menstrual cycles during the past year, symptoms in B occurred during the last week of the luteal phase and remitted within a few days after onset of the follicular phase. In menstruating females, these phases correspond to the week before, and a few days after, the onset of menses. (In nonmenstruating females who have had a hysterectomy, the timing of luteal and follicular phases may require measurement of circulating reproductive hormones.)

B. At least five of the following symptoms have been present for most of the time during each symptomatic late luteal phase, at least one of the symptoms being either (1), (2), (3), or (4):

(1) marked affective lability, feeling suddenly sad, tearful, irritable, or angry

(2) persistent and marked anger or irritability

(3) marked anxiety, tension, feelings of being "keyed up," or "on edge"

(4) markedly depressed mood, feelings of hopelessness, or self-deprecating thoughts

(5) decreased interest in usual activities, work, friends, hobbies

(6) easy fatigability or marked lack of energy

(7) subjective sense of difficulty in concentrating

(8 marked change in appetite, overeating, or specific food cravings

(9) hypersomnia or insomnia

(10) other physical symptoms, such as breast tenderness or swelling, headaches, joint or muscle pain, a sensation of "bloating," weight gain

C. The disturbance seriously interferes with work or with usual activities or relationships with others.

D. The disturbance is not merely an exacerbation of the symptoms of another disorder, such as Major Depression, Panic Disorder, Dysthymia, or a Personality Disorder (although it may be superimposed on any of these disorders).

E. Criteria A, B, C, and D are confirmed by prospective daily self-ratings during at least two symptomatic cycles. (The diagnosis may be made provisionally prior to this confirmation.)

From: DSM-5, 2013.

FIGURE 13.7 **Average social adjustment scores** of women diagnosed with premenstrual dysphoric disorder (PMDD during luteal or follicular phase) or major depression compared with women representing the community norms. Lower scores indicate better social functioning. After Freeman, 2003.

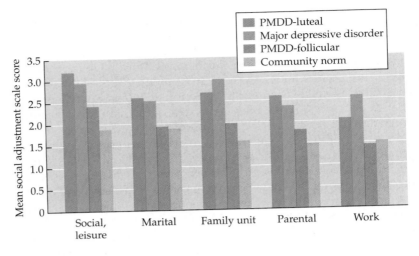

symptom and one physical symptom (Rapkin, 2003). Women with PMDD tend to display impaired daily function in life, as compared with the community norm, and they show social dysfunction similar to that of women with major depression (Halbreich et al., 2003) (**FIGURE 13.7**). Up to 300 different perimenstrual complaints have been reported by women with PMS (Halbreich et al., 1982). Commonly recognized symptoms of PMS have included anxiety, sadness, irritability, bloating, breast enlargement, dysmenorrhea (painful menstruation in the absence of identified pelvic pathology), increased appetite, fatigue, depression, headache, edema, insomnia, emotional lability, dizziness, confusion, asthma, constipation, thirst, nausea, weight gain, aggression, acne, skin abscesses, epilepsy, rhinitis, herpes outbreaks, conjunctivitis, fever, reduced sex drive, increased sex drive, moodiness, impaired motor coordination, craving for sweet or salty foods, and backaches (Brooks-Gunn, 1986; Freeman, 2003; Halbreich et al., 1982, 2003; Sanders et al., 1983; Wurtman and Wurtman, 1989). Obviously, not all of these symptoms are experienced by every woman with PMS, and not all women who experience PMS necessarily have the same symptoms or experience symptoms with the same severity from one period to the next. Thus, the enormous variety and range of symptoms, as well as the varying severity of the symptoms and the difficulty of matching groups of experimental subjects so that their respective symptoms are similar, impede research on the physiological correlates of PMS. All of these caveats necessarily constrain causative statements about PMS and the mood effects of hormones.

Many factors influence the severity of PMS symptoms, but these correlates are not well defined. For example, women with long and heavy menstrual bleeding report more perimenstrual symptoms than women with brief and light menstrual flows (Logue and Moos, 1986). Age also affects PMS symptoms. The severity of PMS symptoms reported by women increases during the late teens and twenties and subsides during the thirties. Women older than 20 who are using oral contraceptives report fewer PMS symptoms than women taking the Pill who are younger than 20 years old. Like *premenstrual* and *menstrual period*, these correlates are not well defined.

Is PMS one syndrome with a single cause, or a number of ailments with differing underlying causes? While occurrence of all of the symptoms together would argue that PMS is one syndrome, generally physiological symptoms are more prevalent during the menstrual phase than during the premenstrual phase of the cycle, whereas psychological symptoms are reported more frequently during the premenstrual than during the menstrual phase (Logue and Moos, 1986). Abdominal swelling and breast tenderness, however, are prominent premenstrual symptoms. Prospective questionnaires (i.e., filled out during the perimenstrual period rather than afterward [retrospective]) based on 19 different symptoms have led to the designation of four major subtypes of PMS (Logue and Moos, 1986): (1) premenstrual tension type A (PMT-A) includes anxiety, irritability, mood swings, and nervous tension; (2) PMT-H includes body weight gain, swelling of extremities, and sensations of bloating; (3) PMT-C includes increased frequencies of headaches, craving for sweet foods, increased appetite, pounding heartbeat, fatigue, and dizziness; and (4) PMT-D includes depression, mild amnesia, crying, confusion, and insomnia. PMT-A and PMT-H are the most commonly occurring subtypes, affecting 57% and 56%, respectively, of the women in one study who scored positive for premenstrual tension (approximately half of the women in the study) (Abraham, 1980). Perimenstrual changes characterized by a depressive syndrome (PMT-D) have been linked to mild or subclinical affective disorders (Endicott et al., 1981). PMS has also been linked to cigarette smoking. In a prospective study, U.S. women age 27–44 and free of PMS were followed for 10 years and their cigarette smoking habits were monitored. Smokers were 2.1 times more likely to develop PMS than women who never smoked (Bertone-Johnson et al., 2008). The results further suggested that cigarette smoking, especially if begun in the teen or young adult years, increased the risk of moderate to severe PMS. Recently, efforts have been made to reach a consensus on diagnostic criteria for PMS and to harmonize the core symptoms of the syndrome (O'Brien et al., 2011). Core symptoms include anxiety/tension, mood changes, aches and cramps, cravings, and disinterest in typical activities (Freeman et al., 2011).

If it is true that different symptoms cluster together, then it seems unlikely that a single hormonal factor associated with the menstrual cycle underlies PMS. The possibility that different subtypes of PMS exist, and that women may experience more than one subtype simultaneously, suggests that several hormonal conditions, sometimes contradictory ones, may be related to PMS.

Hormonal Correlates of PMS

Because most of the mood changes associated with PMS occur during the late luteal phase, when progesterone concentrations in the blood are peaking and estrogen concentrations are decreasing, the first hormonal hypothesis about PMS proposed that progesterone played a role in mood changes (Halbreich, 2003; Parry and Berga, 2002). However, when all studies have been considered together, no consistent differences in progesterone concentrations have been found between women who report PMS symptoms and women who do not (Wyatt et al., 2001). For instance, women who suffer from PMS have higher progesterone concentrations 10 days prior to menstruation than women who do not report PMS symptoms (O'Brien et al., 1979); however, these differences in progesterone concentrations are not evident 4 days prior to menstruation. Perhaps women who experience higher concentrations of progesterone experience greater "withdrawal" from this steroid hormone or its precursors or metabolites.

How might this work? Ovarian hormones modulate synaptic transmission, largely affecting the neurochemical systems involved in emotional and cognitive control, that is, noradrenergic, dopaminergic, serotoninergic, glutamatergic, and γ-aminobutyric acid–ergic (GABA-ergic) systems (Toffoletto et al., 2014). Recall that the major inhibitory neurotransmitter in the brain is gamma-aminobutyric acid (GABA), a simple amino acid that is formed in one step from glutamate. GABA-secreting neurons are found throughout the brain in vertebrates. When GABA interacts with its receptor on a postsynaptic cell, chloride (Cl^-) channels are opened, causing the inside of the postsynaptic neuron to become more negatively charged and less likely to fire an action potential. Neuroscientists have discovered that drugs called benzodiazepines bind to the same GABA receptors as the native ligand, but they do so at a different site on the receptor protein. Thus, benzodiazepines are not traditional GABA agonists but allosteric modulators. Activation of the benzodiazepine receptors appears to enhance the inhibitory effects of GABA on the postsynaptic neuron. The benzodiazepines, which include Librium, Valium, and Xanax, have antianxiety or calming effects, which are presumably the result of enhancement of the inhibitory effects of GABA. These drugs are very effective at therapeutic doses but have potential for abuse and addiction at high doses. Moderate to severe withdrawal symptoms, both psychological and physiological, are associated with the discontinuation of benzodiazepines, and some people display paradoxical symptoms that include elevated moodiness and aggressiveness.

Several steroid hormones, particularly the progestins, have been reported to affect GABA neurons and interact with benzodiazepine receptors (Bitran and Dowd, 1996; Bitran et al., 1995; Majewska, 1987). For instance, both allopregnanolone and pregnanolone positively modulate GABA receptors (Rubinow et al., 2002). Women with severe PMS symptoms display blunted saccadic eye velocity and sedation responses to GABA receptor agonists such as pregnanolone (Sundstrom and Backstrom, 1998) or midazolam (Sundstrom et al., 1997) compared with women with less severe PMS symptoms (Rubinow et al., 2002). Although several studies report low circulating concentrations of allopregnanolone in women with PMS, other studies relate these values to reduced progesterone concentrations at various points in the menstrual cycle or report no differences in circulating progesterone or progesterone metabolites (Rubinow et al., 2002). Women with severe PMS symptoms were given a low-dose GnRH agonist or placebo. Women responding to the GnRH agonist displayed reduced progesterone and allopregnanolone (Nyberg et al., 2007) and an improvement in PMS symptoms. During the placebo treatment, however, women also displayed reduced allopregnanolone levels and PMS symptoms! Thus, manipulations that reduce allopregnanolone may ameliorate severe PMS symptoms. Alternatively, "addiction" to, and withdrawal from, steroid hormones may account for some of the mood-altering effects of these substances—including PMS—but additional studies are necessary.

Progesterone treatment has been reported to alleviate some PMS symptoms (Halbreich, 2003) but certainly not all of them (Backstrom et al., 1983; Daugherty, 1998; Rubinow et al., 1988; Tiemstra and Patel, 1998; Wyatt et al., 2001; Zweifel and O'Brian, 1997). Progesterone vaginal suppositories administered in a double-blind study failed to affect symptoms in women who reported severe PMS symptoms (Maddocks et al., 1986). Combining progesterone with thyroid hormones, however, has been reported to be very effective in alleviating depressive symptoms of PMS.

Blood estrogen concentrations have also been implicated as a factor affecting PMS. Estrogens affect fluid retention, hyperplasia of mammary tissue, and carbohydrate metabolism. Accumulation of estrogen in the limbic system has been hypothesized to account for the emotional and other CNS manifestations of PMS (Reid and Yen, 1981). However, mean serum levels of estrogens and progesterone do not differ between women with severe and mild PMS symptoms (Backstrom et al., 1983), and no data have supported the notion that estrogen treatment ameliorates PMS symptoms, although estrogen therapy is known to elevate mood (Daugherty, 1998) (see below).

Again, physiological abnormalities have not been consistently linked with steroid hormone concentrations associated with the menstrual cycle in women diagnosed with PMS (Schmidt et al., 1991; Young and Korszun, 1998), nor have abnormal responses to normal levels of gonadal steroid hormones been reported (Schmidt et al., 1991). These findings are puzzling because virtually all current biomedical treatments for PMS putatively correct some physiological abnormality associated with the luteal phase of the menstrual cycle; two of the most common courses of treatment for PMS are providing some hormone that is believed to be suppressed in PMS patients and, conversely, suppressing an endogenous hormone in the belief that PMS is a manifestation of elevated hormone concentrations (Schmidt et al., 1991). In summary, no endocrine or other biological disorder has been consistently related to PMS (Rubinow et al., 2002).

The failure to identify any specific physiological aspects of the late luteal phase underlying the symptoms of PMS led one research team to suppress the entire luteal phase of the menstrual cycle in the hope of suppressing the symptoms of PMS. Using the progesterone antagonist mifepristone in a double-blind study, they arrested the luteal phase, causing an artificial follicular phase. If the symptoms of PMS are caused by the endocrine events associated with the luteal phase, then women who do not experience a luteal phase should not experience symptoms. However, women who were treated with mifepristone and did not experience the luteal phase reported no change in either the timing or the severity of their PMS symptoms (Schmidt et al., 1991). These results suggest, but do not prove, that the endocrine events associated with the luteal phase of the menstrual cycle are not directly responsible for the symptoms of PMS, although studies that follow more cycles would be informative.

What, then, is causing the distress of PMS? There is evidence that preventing sex hormone cycling entirely abolishes the symptoms of PMS. Treatment with the GnRH agonist leuprolide, which eliminates menstrual cycles, significantly reduced symptoms in double-blind, crossover studies (Brown et al., 1994; Helvacioglu et al., 1993). It is possible that during the menstrual cycle the target tissue sensitivity to steroid hormones changes differently in women with PMS than in women who do not experience PMS symptoms. In a small but important clinical study, ten women with PMS were given leuprolide, and their symptoms were ameliorated. If leuprolide was accompanied by either estradiol or progesterone, however, the nonmood symptoms returned (Schmidt et al., 1998). Thus, PMS symptoms appear to reflect abnormal responses to normal concentrations of steroid hormones.

As implied above, PMS may reflect a pathological state induced by the chronic fluctuations in hormone concentrations associated with long-term menstrual cycles. That is, women may become dependent upon the elevated steroid hormone concentrations present during ovulation and pseudopregnancy (the luteal phase), and the psychological symptoms associated with PMS may reflect withdrawal of these gonadal steroid hormones. Abrupt withdrawal from gonadal steroid hormones may also be responsible for the postpartum depression reported by many women discussed above. Antidepressants that alter serotonin availability at the level of the receptor appear to be useful in treating depression associated with PMS (Yonkers, 1997). Thus, the current medical therapies of choice include GnRH agonists (usually reserved as a treatment of last resort), benzodiazepines (e.g., alprazolam), and selective serotonin reuptake inhibitors (SSRIs) (e.g., fluoxetine) (Jarvis et al., 2008; Mortola, 1997).

Several SSRIs are used to treat mood-related and physical symptoms of PMS. Two primary medications approved by the U.S. FDA include Sarafem (fluoxetine) and Zoloft (sertraline HCl). Sarafem is essentially repackaged Prozac. Sarafem was marketed heavily for PMDD treatment by its manufacturer, Eli Lilly, which spent more than $33 million promoting the drug to consumers. In the 7-month period after the medication's approval, physicians wrote more than 200,000 prescriptions for Sarafem. About 10 years ago, Zoloft, produced by Pfizer, was also approved to treat PMDD. Some research (Halbreich et al., 2006; Jarvis et al., 2008) suggests that both fluoxetine and sertraline are more effective than placebos in treating PMDD.

Although steroid hormone concentrations, or any hormone concentrations for that matter, do not seem to distinguish between women who suffer from PMS and those who are symptom-free, it is possible that hormones are necessary to trigger symptoms (Rubinow et al., 2002). These two considerations can be reconciled by the results of a study of women who previously had not displayed any PMS symptoms, underwent ovarian hormone suppression, then were provided with steroid replacement therapy so that their hormone concentrations achieved the levels of women with PMS symptoms. These previously symptom-free women continued to

FIGURE 13.8 Optimal human interbirth interval The red line, generated by a computer model, represents the number of surviving human babies for various interbirth intervals, based on a calculation that takes offspring survival into account (reproductive life span/interbirth interval × probability of offspring survival if born at that interval); the dots represent individual cases upon which the model is based. Thus, the optimal birth spacing is about 50 months. The vertical bars represent actual birth intervals in a hunting-gathering society, the !Kung, which roughly correspond to the computed optimum. After Blurton Jones, 1986.

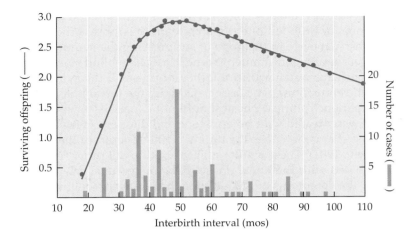

be symptom-free after hormone replacement therapy (Rubinow et al., 2002). These results suggest that women with PMS are differentially sensitive to ovarian hormones and experience mood effects when exposed to changes in steroid hormone concentrations, whereas women who do not experience PMS symptoms are unaffected by these endocrine changes (Rubinow et al., 2002). Perhaps sensitive women have more steroid receptors or a different distribution of one hormone receptor subtype or another. Future research will have to explore such possibilities.

But why would any woman be susceptible to such changes in hormone concentrations? Consider that the hormone fluctuations in present-day Western females are a fairly new phenomenon. Menstrual cycles were probably relatively rare until recently in human history. In extant hunting and gathering societies (**FIGURE 13.8**)—cultures that probably reflect over 99% of human evolutionary history—postpubertal females are either pregnant or lactating for most of their reproductive lives. It has been claimed that PMS had evolutionary advantages including dissolution of pair bonds in infertile couples increasing the reproductive outcomes of afflicted women (Gillings, 2014); that is, couples may break up because of PMS occuring in response to multiple cycles that do not produce offspring allowing women to seek new males who might improve her fertility. Puberty occurs at a later age than in Western civilizations, and because of the high risk of death posed by childbirth, relatively few women survive until menopause. Women are reproductively successful only to the extent that they bear babies, and the high rate of infant mortality demands high pregnancy rates. Each pregnancy interrupts at least nine menstrual cycles. Furthermore, menstruation does not begin immediately after parturition in most cases; lactation also prevents menstruation, so most women experience 2–3 years of lactational amenorrhea between pregnancies. Thus, the reproductive life of a typical woman in such societies lasts for less than 20 years, and within those two decades she experiences probably fewer than 10 to 20 menstrual cycles (Dennis, 1992).

Contrast 10 to 20 menstrual cycles in a lifetime with an extreme, but not uncommon, reproductive scenario for a present-day North American female. If a woman begins menstruating at the age of 12 and continues until her first pregnancy at the age of 35, she will experience nearly 300 uninterrupted menstrual cycles. After the weaning of a single child, this hypothetical woman can expect another 100–150 menstrual cycles before menopause. Thus, PMS may be an unavoidable consequence of Western civilization and the abnormal physiological milieu of chronic, long-term cyclic fluctuations in hormone concentrations that accompanies it. This is not to say that widely spaced pregnancies are not a reasonable goal for individuals and an important means of ameliorating the ecological pressures of the increasing human population on this planet, but those incentives do not negate the possibility

FIGURE 13.9 **Seasonale and Seasonique** birth control pills provide 4, rather than 12, menstrual periods per year. The extent to which the sustained elevated estrogen concentrations improve or impair mood remains to be determined.

that these recent (on an evolutionary scale) changes in the physiological conditions to which the nervous systems of women are subjected could cause changes in behavior and mood. From this perspective, it is remarkable that more women do not report fluctuating mood changes associated with repetitive cycles of hormone surges and withdrawals. A similar explanation involving uninterrupted ovarian cycles has been put forward to explain the increase in the incidence of ovarian cancer (Schildkraut et al., 1997).

The current generation of birth control pills is the extended-regimen pill. Examples are Seasonale and Seasonique (levonorgestrel/ethinyl estradiol tablets), which were approved for use in the United States in 2003 and 2006, respectively. When birth control pills were developed in the 1960s, the drug companies thought that women would not take them if they did not undergo regular menstrual periods. So, each pack of pills included "dummy" pills that contained no hormones and which allowed the uterine wall to be sloughed off each month during the week they were taken. However, there is probably no benefit to women in undergoing monthly menstrual periods other than the reassurance that their reproductive systems are functioning "normally." With the extended-regimen birth control pills, women take daily hormone pills for 3 months, then dummy pills daily for a week, which allows 4 periods of menstruation per year, rather than the 12–13 periods commonly experienced with traditional or no birth control pills (**FIGURE 13.9**). Oral contraceptives have yielded mostly positive results in the treatment of PMS but mixed results in the treatment of PMDD (Pearlstein, 2016; Rapkin and Mikacich, 2013).

One way in which hormones may affect mood indirectly is via food intake. Recall from Chapter 8 that food intake and body mass increase in rodents and primates after ovulation, when blood plasma estrogen concentrations are low and progesterone concentrations are high (Blaustein and Wade, 1976; Bowen and Grunberg, 1990; Czaja, 1978). Women display a similar pattern of caloric intake and body mass change associated with their menstrual cycles. Consumption of carbohydrates, in particular, increases during the luteal phase compared with the follicular phase of the human menstrual cycle (Dalvit, 1981; Kurzer, 1997; Pliner and Fleming, 1983). Specifically, women crave carbohydrate-rich foods more frequently during the luteal phase than during the follicular phase (Davidsen et al., 2007). These carbohydrate cravings occur more frequently during the luteal phase regardless of the occurrence or severity of PMS symptoms (Cohen et al., 1987), indicating that they are a normal component of the menstrual cycle and do not necessarily represent "symptoms" of PPMD (*DSM-V*, 2013; cf. Severino and Moline, 1989).

Leptin appears elevated in women suffering from PMS (Anim-Nyame et al., 2000). A study that examined the eating patterns of overweight women by following food diaries revealed that overweight women with PMS reported a significant increase in fat, carbohydrate, and simple sugar intake during the premenstrual period (Cross et al., 2001). Protein intake decreased at this time. Women without PMS symptoms reported no differences between pre- and postmenstrual nutrient intake when adjusted for energy content. When food intake was analyzed according to food categories, it was seen that women with PMS ate more when premenstrual and increased their intake of cereals, cakes, and desserts, as well as other high-sugar foods (Cross et al., 2001). Women with PMS reported more "episodes of eating" during the premenstrual period than women without PMS (Cross et al., 2001).

Other studies have implicated calcium deficiencies in some women with PMS symptoms (Thys-Jacobs and Alvir, 1995; Ward and Holimon, 1999). Low estrogen concentrations may deplete calcium reserves and affect CNS function. Treatment of PMS with calcium dietary supplements ameliorates many symptoms (Thys-Jacobs and Alvir, 1995; Thys-Jacobs et al., 1998). In one definitive clinical study, 466 women with moderate to severe PMS symptoms were recruited from 12 outpatient clinics across the United States. The women received either calcium (1200 mg elemental calcium/day) or a placebo pill in a randomized double-blind study. In this large study, calcium treatment reduced four separate symptoms (negative mood, water retention, food cravings, and pain) by approximately 50% by the third menstrual cycle of treatment (Thys-Jacobs et al., 1998). Placebo treatment caused a 30% reduction in PMS symptoms after three menstrual cycles. Overall, calcium supplementation seems to be a simple, inexpensive, and effective treatment for PMS (Thys-Jacobs et al., 1998). The roles of calcitonin and parathyroid hormone in PMS symptoms remain unspecified, although a secondary hyperparathyroidism has been reported in women suffering from PMS (e.g., Thys-Jacobs and Alvir, 1995). Blood concentrations of aldosterone vary during the menstrual cycle, and high concentrations of aldosterone during the late luteal phase cause retention of sodium by the kidneys. The retention of sodium leads to water retention and feelings of bloating during the perimenstrual period (Janowsky et al., 1973). There have been reports of other treatments, including magnesium, vitamin B_6, and L-tryptophan supplementation (reviewed in Rapkin, 2003), having better than placebo effects on PMS symptoms. Other types of treatment of PMS that have shown some efficacy include cognitive behavioral therapy and aerobic exercise (Rapkin, 2003).

All of these data indicate that many hormones may be involved at several different levels to cause PMS symptoms. Determining the exact constellation of endocrine events responsible for PMS will require further synthetic research on a number of different experimental levels. Thus far, it has not been possible to identify an animal model that closely mimics the affective and physical components of PMS.

Cognitive Features of PMS

Although negative mood changes are commonly associated with PMS, some women report positive mood changes and improved cognitive performance during the perimenstrual phase of the menstrual cycle (Logue and Moos, 1988; Parlee, 1980). Approximately 5%–15% of women experience elevated energy levels and an enhanced sense of well-being during the perimenstrual phase. Some women reporting reduced energy and activity levels during the perimenstrual phase may not accurately report their activities. In one study, women wore electronic activity monitors and also answered questionnaires. Despite their reports of lethargy during the perimenstrual period, the women's actual behavior indicated an increase in activity (Endicott and Halbreich, 1982).

A significant minority of women also report increased performance on particular types of tasks during the perimenstrual phase. For example, a battery of cognitive tasks, including tests of reaction time and mental arithmetic skills, was administered every other day to women undergoing normal menstrual cycles. Reaction times and speed of mental calculations improved during the late luteal phase (Wuttke et al., 1975). Similar results have been reported for some women for perceptual motor skills, critical thinking abilities, and intelligence test scores (Cormack and Sheldrake, 1974; Jensen, 1982; Logue and Moos, 1988; Wuttke et al., 1975).

Finally, many women report an increase in sexual interest during the perimenstrual phase (Halbreich et al., 1982; Logue and Moos, 1988; Taylor, 1979). A heightened sex drive may represent reduced concern about unwanted pregnancies during the perimenstrual phase. However, women taking oral contraceptives also report an

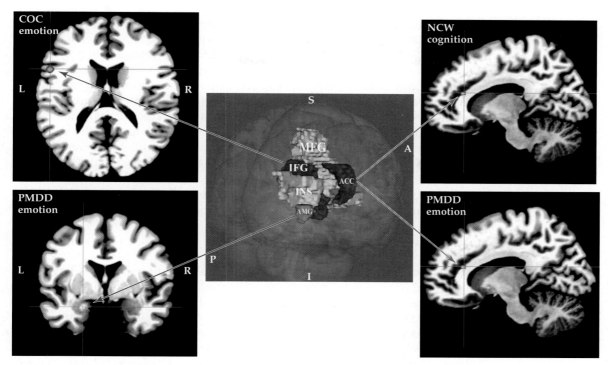

FIGURE 13.10 **Brain regions modulated by ovarian and exogenous steroid hormones**
Functional MRI data from the anterior cingulate cortex, amygdala, inferior frontal gyrus,
insula, and middle frontal gyrus are represented. Central panel: automated anatomical par-
cellation of anterior cingulate cortex (ACC), amygdala (AMG), inferior frontal gyrus (IFG), insula
(INS), and middle frontal gyrus (MFG). Lateral panels: significant clusters in naturally cycling
women (NCW), combined oral contraceptive users (COC), and patients affected by premenstrual dysphoric disorder (PMDD) obtained from the meta-analytical analysis of aggregated
coordinates. A = anterior; I = inferior; L = left; P = posterior; R = right; S = superior. From
Toffoletto et al., 2014.

increase in sexual activity premenstrually, as well as during the time of ovulation
(Englander-Golden et al., 1980) (see Chapter 6).

Preliminary analyses of functional brain imaging to determine the effects of estrogens and progestins in women indicate that the typical fluctuations of ovarian
hormones over the menstrual cycle influence the activation of both cortical and
subcortical brain regions associated with mood and cognition (Comasco and Sundstrom-Poromaa, 2015; Toffoletto et al., 2014) (**FIGURE 13.10**). Most of these studies
had too few participants to make strong conclusions; however, sex steroid hormones associated with oral contraceptives also affect functional changes in neural
activity. From these meta-analyses, it seems that PMS and PMDD reflect impaired
ovarian hormone–mediated sensitivity of neural activation patterns in affective and
cognitive brain networks (Toffoletto et al., 2014). Better-powered and multimodal
neuroimaging studies are required to identify the neural mechanism of functional
brain changes provoked by sex steroid hormones.

Obviously, both endocrine and cognitive factors interact to influence PMS. As
we have seen, the symptoms of PMS can be affected by social expectations and can
be improved by placebo treatments (Koeske, 1980; Parlee, 1982; Ruble, 1977). These
facts, along with the lack of consistent endocrine correlates of PMS symptoms, have
led some researchers to suggest that these symptoms are "all in the head" of the suf-
ferer. However, the interaction of complex endocrine signals with cognitive factors
is not unique to PMS. By analogy, recall that rat maternal behavior can be elicited

after many days of exposure to pups, immediately after parturition, or after several days of specifically timed hormonal treatments involving at least three different hormones (see Chapter 7). In the last case, the endocrine manipulations must still be combined with several days of exposure to pups prior to the onset of maternal behavior. Adults can overcome their fear of pups and begin acting maternally by means of frequent exposure to pups, the endocrine environment of pregnancy, or some combination of hormones and behavior. In other words, there is an interaction between cognitive factors (reduction in fear) and endocrine factors (the hormones that reduce the processing of fear-inducing chemical stimuli). Additional research should focus on this interaction, keeping in mind that various subtypes of PMS are probably mediated by different underlying causes. A more holistic, integrative approach to the study of PMS may be required before the physiological, behavioral, and social causes of PMS are understood.

Seasonal Affective Disorder

Seasonal changes in behavior are legion in animals and humans (see Chapter 10). One seasonal rhythm in humans that has received much attention during the past three decades is winter depression, or seasonal affective disorder (SAD) (Lewy et al., 2009). SAD is characterized by depressed affect, lethargy, loss of libido, hypersomnia, excessive weight gain, carbohydrate cravings, anxiety, and inability to focus attention or concentrate that occur during the late autumn or winter (Rosenthal et al., 1988). In the Northern Hemisphere, symptoms usually begin between October and December and go into remission during March. These symptoms do not merely reflect the holiday blues, because individuals suffering from SAD in the Southern Hemisphere display symptoms 6 months out of phase with Northern Hemisphere residents (Terman, 1988). With the onset of summer, SAD patients regain their energy and become active and elated, often to the point of hypomania or mania. Three features atypical of depression—hyperphagia, carbohydrate cravings, and hypersomnia—set SAD apart from nonseasonal depression. SAD is frequently diagnosed as "bipolar II" depression or "atypical bipolar disorder," particularly if hypomania or mania is present (*DSM-5*, 2013).

Prevalence rates in the population range from 1% to 10%, with higher prevalence rates reported at higher latitudes (Rosenthal, 1993). Women seem to be affected by SAD more often than men (Kasper et al., 1989): the sex ratio of SAD prevalence in one epidemiological study was 3.5 women to 1 man. Over 80% of respondents to newspaper advertisements recruiting experimental subjects with SAD are women (Rosenthal and Wehr, 1987). Among menstruating women suffering from SAD, PMS is common during the fall and winter; often their PMS symptoms are reduced during the summer (Thase, 1989).

Seasonal changes in mood and behavior may be closely related to alcoholism (Sher, 2004). A subset of individuals with alcoholism display seasonal patterns in their alcohol misuse. It is possible that such individuals are self-medicating an underlying seasonal affective disorder with alcohol or manifesting a seasonal pattern of alcohol-induced depression (Sher, 2004). Family and molecular genetic studies suggest the existence of a genetic link between SAD and alcoholism. In any case, the comorbidity of alcoholism and SAD suggests a link that could be causal in nature and that should be considered by both mental health and drug and alcohol professionals when identifying, managing, and referring patients with comorbid alcoholism and SAD (Haffmans et al., 2008; Sher, 2004).

A potential diagnostic tool for SAD may be the presence of a reduced threshold for chemosensory detection (Postolache et al., 2002). People with SAD and control individuals were subjected to a detection threshold test in which phenylethyl alcohol was administered to each side of the nose in a counterbalanced order; the opposite nostril was occluded during the test (Postolache et al., 2002). Individuals

FIGURE 13.11 Bright light therapy may ameliorate seasonal affective disorder (SAD). (A) Individuals suffering from SAD can sometimes obtain relief using daily light therapy, whereby they are exposed to either a light box or some other device such as an illuminated visor for 1–2 hours early each morning during the autumn and winter. The visors produce bright illumination (>2500 lux), which is thought to help resynchronize biological rhythms. (B) Individual (circles) and average (horizontal bars) ratings of mood on the Hamilton Rating Scale for Depression for eight individuals with SAD at baseline and after morning (A.M.), evening (P.M.), or combined (A.M. + P.M.) light treatment. Light treatment that took place during the morning resulted in significantly improved mood (i.e., lower depression scores) as compared with baseline mood or evening treatment. B after Lewy et al., 1987.

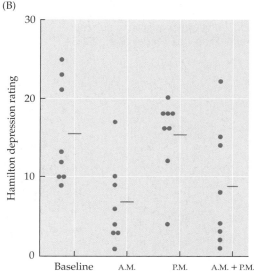

(A)

(B)

with SAD were able to detect this odor at lower concentrations than people who did not have SAD. These results suggest that recurrent winter depression in humans may be associated with an enhanced olfactory ability (Postolache et al., 2002).

Improperly entrained circadian rhythms may be involved in SAD (Lewy et al., 1985, 1988, 2006) (see Chapter 10). In other cases of depressed affect, it has been hypothesized that changing the onset of sleep time resets biological clocks, resulting in amelioration of the depression (reviewed in Lewy et al., 1988). In one early study, a depressed patient was phase-advanced in her sleep-wake cycle by 6 hours; her depression was temporarily ameliorated by this treatment (Wehr et al., 1979). Four of seven other patients who underwent spontaneous remission of depression displayed a spontaneous phase advance of their times of awakening (Wehr et al., 1979). Lithium, tricyclic antidepressants, and estrogen, all of which are used to treat depressive illnesses, also affect endogenous timekeeping mechanisms (Wehr et al., 1979). More recently it has been proposed that major depressive disorder can be the result of misaligned circadian rhythms (Emens et al., 2009). The fact that both the pharmacological agents and sleep-wake cycle manipulations are effective in ameliorating depression suggests that they work via similar mechanisms involving biological clocks.

The standard treatment of SAD today is with bright lights instead of sleep therapy. When patients are exposed to bright light, usually for a few hours in the morning, signs of remission of the SAD symptoms are often apparent within a few days (Rosenthal et al., 1988) (**FIGURE 13.11A**). Phototherapy, like sleep-wake therapy, may work by phase-advancing biological rhythms. Bright light has been suggested to possess two antidepressant effects: (1) light treatment in the morning may ameliorate depression by realignment of inappropriately entrained circadian rhythms, and (2) light may also serve as a general "energizer … of mood in a way that may be attributable wholly or in part to a placebo effect" (Lewy et al., 1988). Light treatment at different times during the day results in differing rates of mood improvement (Lewy et al., 1987) (**FIGURE 13.11B**). Light treatment in the evening has no mood benefits. Phototherapy appears to shift circadian rhythms by altering the timing of the nightly secretion of melatonin (Lewy et al., 2006, 2009), as we will see shortly.

Serotonin may be involved in the symptoms of SAD (Skwerer et al., 1988; Wurtman and Wurtman, 1989). Tryptophan, an amino acid that normally circulates in the blood at low concentrations, is converted to serotonin in the brain, specifically in the raphe nuclei (Cooper et al., 1986). Diet affects this conversion process because carbohydrates stimulate pancreatic β-cells to secrete insulin, which in turn facilitates the uptake of sugars and nontryptophan amino acids into peripheral cells. This action results in a relatively high ratio of tryptophan to other amino acids in the blood,

FIGURE 13.12 **The serotonergic synapse** (A) Ingested tryptophan, an amino acid, is taken up preferentially by cells in the raphe nucleus, where it is converted by a two-step process into serotonin and released into the synaptic gap. When synaptic levels of serotonin are high, serotonin may bind to presynaptic receptors to inhibit further release. Serotonin can also be absorbed back into the presynaptic terminal via reuptake mechanisms. Drugs that increase the release of serotonin or block its reuptake diminish carbohydrate intake, whereas agents that block postsynaptic serotonin binding increase carbohydrate appetite. (B) Positron emission tomography indicates that serotonin transporter binding is reduced in winter relative to summer. B after Praschak-Rieder et al., 2008.

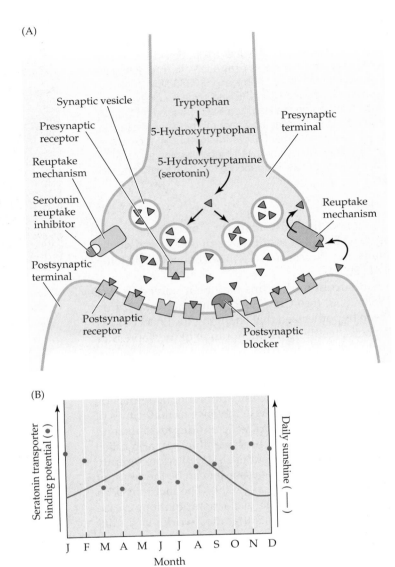

and because tryptophan competes with the other amino acids for access to central nervous system tissue, carbohydrate ingestion results in more tryptophan crossing the blood-brain barrier, and thus higher production of serotonin (**FIGURE 13.12A**). Serotonin concentrations feed back to regulate the intake of carbohydrates. It is possible, therefore, that patients suffering from SAD have cyclic disruptions in their serotonin-carbohydrate regulating mechanisms (Wurtman and Wurtman, 1989). Serotonin is also involved in normal sleep onset, and faulty serotonin regulation may contribute to the hypersomnia reported in SAD patients. If it is true that symptoms of SAD result from faulty serotonin metabolism, then pharmacological interventions that elevate serotonin concentrations should be expected to reduce the severity of some SAD symptoms. Administration of the serotonin agonist δ-fenfluramine to patients with SAD reduces carbohydrate intake and the associated body mass gain. This compound is also effective in elevating the depressed mood of SAD patients (Wurtman et al., 1985).

One recent study that used positron emission tomography to track serotonin binding potentials reported that individuals with SAD displayed more serotonin transporter (5-HTT) activity during the autumn than spring (Praschak-Rieder et al., 2008). Because elevated 5-HTT binding reflects low synaptic serotonin, the seasonal

(A)

(B)

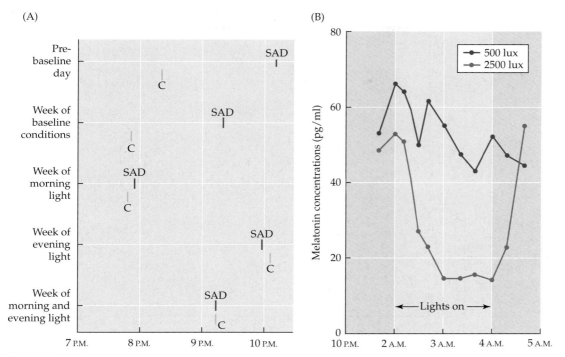

FIGURE 13.13 Light exposure affects both onset time and level of melatonin secretion.
(A) Average melatonin secretion onset times for controls (C) occurred nearly 2 hours earlier than for SAD patients prior to experimental light treatment (prebaseline). After a week of
bright light treatment, the average melatonin secretion onset times for C and SAD individuals
coincided, regardless of the timing of the light treatment. (B) Effects of light pulses on human
melatonin secretion. The blue circles represent the effects of light pulses of an intensity of
500 lux; this level of illumination is about that found in a typical office or brightly lit room. The
red circles represent light pulses of 2500 lux, which are much more effective in suppressing
melatonin secretion. After Lewy et al., 1987, 1980.

adjustments of 5-HTT in the prefrontal cortex, anterior cingulate cortex, caudate
putamen, thalamus, and mesencephalon may be part of the pathway by which
day length can influence affect and behavior (Praschak-Rieder et al., 2008) (**FIGURE
13.12B**).

Recall that serotonin is converted to melatonin in the pineal gland (see Chapter
2). Melatonin concentrations are higher during the night than during the day in both
nocturnal and diurnal animals (see Chapter 10) (Goldman, 1983). In humans, as in
other mammals, phase-shifting of the light-dark cycle results in a comparable shift
in the timing of the daily nighttime peak of melatonin secretion (Lewy et al., 1988).
In a variety of mammals, including humans, the nocturnal synthesis and secretion
of pineal melatonin can be rapidly inhibited by exposure to brief periods of light at
night (Hoffmann et al., 1981; Illnerova and Vanecek, 1984; Lewy et al., 1988). Thus
light has two actions in humans, as it does in other mammals: (1) light can entrain,
or synchronize, the daily melatonin rhythm, and (2) light can acutely suppress daily
melatonin secretion. Presumably, either or both effects of light may be involved in
the therapeutic effects of phototherapy in the treatment of SAD (Lewy et al., 1988,
1996; Wurtman and Wurtman, 1989) (**FIGURE 13.13**).

The onset of melatonin secretion, which occurs about 14 hours after awakening
(Lewy et al., 2009), may serve as a marker of circadian phase for synchronization of
other circadian rhythms, and it may also influence circadian phase. For example,
men and women residing in dim light and given melatonin at particular times of
the day shifted the onset time of their endogenous melatonin rhythms. Melatonin

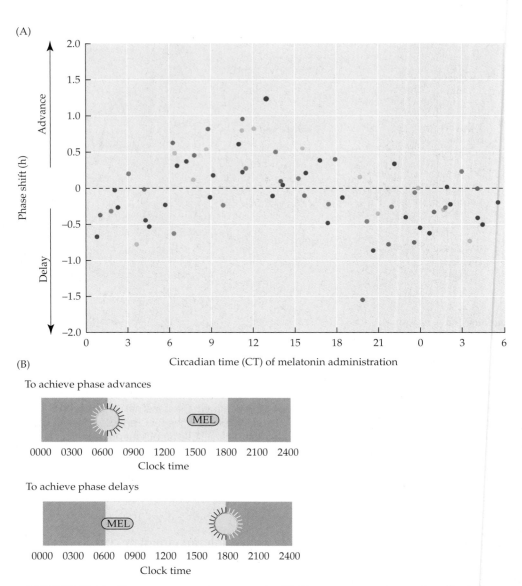

(A)

(B)

To achieve phase advances

0000 0300 0600 0900 1200 1500 1800 2100 2400
Clock time

To achieve phase delays

0000 0300 0600 0900 1200 1500 1800 2100 2400
Clock time

FIGURE 13.14 **Phase responses to melatonin** (A) Phase response curves from five individuals (different colors) treated with melatonin (0.5 mg) at 12 different times on 4 consecutive days. Phase delays (–) and phase advances (+) are plotted against circadian time (CT) of treatment. (B) To induce a phase advance, light exposure should be scheduled in the morning and melatonin given in the afternoon. To induce a phase delay, the opposite pattern should occur; that is, light should be scheduled in the evening, and melatonin should be given in the morning. After Vessely and Lewy, 2002.

administered on four consecutive days during the late afternoon or early evening tended to advance the onset of the melatonin secretion, whereas melatonin given in the morning tended to delay the onset of melatonin secretion (Lewy et al., 2009). Construction of a melatonin phase response curve revealed that there is an approximately 12-hour period during which exogenous melatonin advances the endogenous cycle, and there is a 12-hour period during which exogenous melatonin delays the endogenous cycle (**FIGURE 13.14A**). Because melatonin encodes the dark phase of the light-dark cycle, the melatonin phase response curve is approximately 12 hours out of phase with the phase response curve for light in humans (Lewy et al., 1998a). This information allows for the therapeutic use of melatonin in phase-

Hormones and Affective Disorders

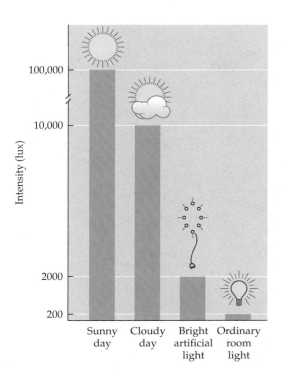

FIGURE 13.15 Outdoor light is far brighter than artificial light. Because our eyes adapt so quickly to different brightness levels, it is not apparent to us that outdoor light is generally several orders of magnitude brighter than that typically found indoors. Artificial indoor light is usually 200–500 lux, far below what is necessary to have a physiological effect on biological rhythms and mood. Bright sunlight in the midlatitudes may be 100,000 lux in intensity. Even on a cloudy day, illumination levels outdoors usually exceed 10,000 lux. After OTA, 1991.

shifting circadian rhythms. For example, the advance zone is usually between 6 and 18 hours after awakening, whereas the delay zone usually begins about 18 hours after awakening and continues during sleep to about 6 hours after awakening. Thus, light and melatonin can be given to treat ailments such as jet lag, problems associated with shift work, advanced and delayed sleep phase disorders (Lewy et al., 2006) (see also Chapter 10), and free-running rhythms among blind people (**FIGURE 13.14B**).

It has been estimated that about half the 200,000 totally blind people in the United States are free-running (Sack and Lewy, 2001). This results in people whose circadian rhythms are not entrained to the 24-hour day and frequently results in insomnia during the night, daytime somnolence, and other adverse effects (Lewy et al., 2003; Sack et al., 2000). This has recently been termed non-24-hour sleep-wake disorder. In one study, several totally blind individuals displayed free-running periods ranging between 24.2 and 24.9 hours. After treatment with 10 mg/day of melatonin at bedtime, six out of seven individuals displayed entrained circadian rhythms (Sack et al., 2000). A new melatonin-like drug called Hetlioz (tasimelteon) has been marketed recently for treating non-24-hour sleep-wake disorder, but its effectiveness compared with over-the-counter melatonin supplements (available in the United States) has not been reported.

Humans require high-intensity illumination to suppress nighttime melatonin secretion, unlike several other mammalian species, in which very low light intensities are capable of preventing pineal biosynthetic and secretory activity (see Chapter 10) (Brainard et al., 1983). Daytime illumination levels outdoors at temperate latitudes range between 12,000 and 100,000 lux (Benoit, 1964; Wurtman, 1975), whereas levels of artificial illumination indoors typically vary from 200 to 500 lux (**FIGURE 13.15**). The human visual system adapts rapidly to changing intensities of illumination; consequently, we may not perceive the light we encounter outdoors as being orders of magnitude brighter than indoor illumination. Physiologically, however, humans respond quite differently to the high levels of illumination provided by exposure to sunlight. Exposure to at least 1500 lux is necessary for the inhibition of human melatonin secretion (Lewy et al., 1980). This requirement may explain why normal

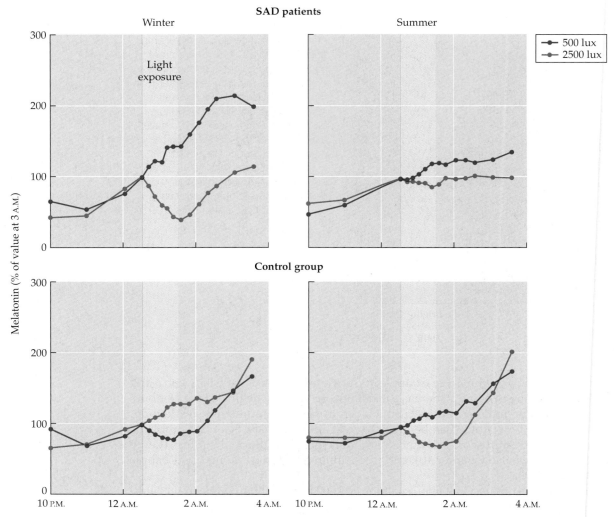

FIGURE 13.16 **Patterns of melatonin secretion in seasonal depression** Melatonin secretion in winter and summer among SAD patients and non-depressed volunteers in response to dim (500 lux; blue circles) and bright (2500 lux; red circles) illumination (yellow bars). Note that the elevated plasma levels of melatonin in SAD patients in winter are significantly reduced by bright illumination. After Thompson et al., 1990.

indoor levels of artificial illumination are insufficient to relieve the symptoms of SAD; much brighter light must be used for effective treatment (**FIGURE 13.16**). Thus, people who develop SAD, mainly female and mainly in their twenties through forties, may have defects in the light transduction pathways. One recent study suggests that people suffering from SAD have a small genetic mutation in the melanopsin molecule; people diagnosed with SAD were 5.6 times more likely than people with no history of psychopathology to have a missense variant of melanopsin (rs2675703 [P10L]) (Roecklein et al., 2009). Thus, genetic deficits in the nonvisual light input pathway from the eye to the central biological clock may represent an important mediator of SAD and point to additional effective treatments (reviewed in Roecklein et al., 2013a). Indeed, people diagnosed with SAD showed an impaired postillumination pupil response compared with healthy people (Roecklein et al., 2013b). Individuals with variations in the melanopsin gene (*OPN4*) who may suffer from SAD may display differences in alertness, circadian entrainment, and melatonin secretion.

The depressive symptoms of SAD cause much human suffering. However, it must be emphasized that depression, however salient to the patient, physician, and family members, is only one of several foci of this seasonal disorder. Other phenomena associated with the syndrome are increases in food intake, body mass, lethargy, and sleep bout length. A random sample of New York City residents indicated seasonal changes in all of these parameters, although these changes were less pronounced in the general population than in SAD patients (Terman, 1988). These seasonal changes may have evolved in order to provide for winter energy savings (e.g., Wirz-Justice et al., 1986). Thus, mild forms of depression may be part of an adaptive constellation of traits. In conjunction with this hypothesis, one might view SAD as an exaggerated form of this strategy.

It may be difficult to develop animal models for SAD. Many animal models have focused on seasonally breeding rodents; however, because clinicians focus on the affective aspects of SAD, seasonally breeding animals may be an inappropriate model for SAD in humans, who do not dramatically alter reproduction across the year (Zucker, 1988b). There have also been attempts to use other seasonal phenomena—hibernation, for example—as model systems to study the mechanisms of SAD (Mrosovsky, 1988b). However, even among rodents, there are many different adaptive strategies for coping with seasonal environmental changes: some animals lose body mass in autumn to reduce food requirements, whereas others increase autumnal body mass in order to augment endogenous energy stores (see Chapter 9) (Nelson, 1987). Progress will likely be made by judicial use of animals that model key components of the seasonal affective symptoms.

As related above, it has been suggested that bright light therapy may relieve the symptoms of SAD via a mechanism that involves phase-shifting of circadian rhythms (Lewy et al., 1988, 1996). An alternative hypothesis is that supplementary light may act through a photoperiodic mechanism to alter a seasonal response (see Chapter 10) (Kripke, 1981; Wehr et al., 2001). This idea fits with the seasonal nature of SAD, particularly with the occurrence of the depression phase in the winter, when days are shortest. It is interesting to consider this hypothesis in conjunction with what is known about photoperiodic responses and seasonality in other mammals. First, most overt responses in mammals to an abrupt change in day length require a period of several weeks (Goldman, 1983, 2001). This observation contrasts with the rapid ameliorative effect of bright light exposure in SAD patients. However, there are a few exceptions to this long time requirement in mammals; for example, immature Siberian hamsters exhibit changes in the rate of testis growth within 5 days after being shifted from long to short days (Carter and Goldman, 1983a). Second, several long-lived mammalian species exhibit the capacity for endogenous circannual rhythmicity, and in some of these animals photoperiod is an important synchronizer of circannual rhythms. Artificial manipulation of photoperiod can entrain circannual rhythms in these animals or induce them to display more than one complete cycle in a year (Gwinner, 1986). However, it is not possible to keep animals in one phase of the cycle indefinitely by manipulation of the photoperiod. Thus, if SAD is related to human circannual rhythmicity, it might be expected that light therapy would not eliminate or effectively reduce the total amount of depression experienced over the course of each annual cycle but would, rather, rephase the onset of the depression.

Clearly, there are major gaps in our knowledge about SAD because there are virtually no consistent patterns that indicate whether humans are either photoperiodic or circannual, although it is possible that variation in human responsiveness to photoperiod accounts for this inconsistency (Bronson, 2004). Nevertheless, the growing body of data from mammals with seasonal cycles may be useful in pointing the way to obtaining such information for humans and may eventually lead to effective pharmacological or behavioral treatments for SAD.

BOX 13.2 *Anabolic Steroids: An Edge That Cuts Two Ways*

According to reports issued by the National Institute on Drug Abuse, anabolic steroid abuse has attained epidemic proportions at all levels of athletic competition in North America. The problem initially came to public notice when Canadian sprinter Ben Johnson was stripped of his Olympic gold medal in 1988 after testing positive for anabolic steroids. His record-setting times for the 100-meter dash at the Seoul Olympics (9.79 seconds) and the 1987 World Track and Field Championships (9.83 seconds) were annulled. (In 2009 Jamaican sprinter Usain Bolt set the world record for the 100-meter dash at 9.58 seconds.) Johnson said that he did not believe he could run 100 m under 10 seconds without androgens. "If you've never used anything, just come to it natural, that's about my limit," said Johnson in a CNN interview shortly after American shot-putter Randy Barnes and sprinter Dennis Mitchell, as well as several Tour de France cyclists, tested positive for steroids.

A decade later, it was disclosed that Mark McGwire, who hit a record 70 home runs during the 1998 professional baseball season, used androstenedione. Androstenedione, which can be converted to testosterone in the liver, is a legal over-the-counter strength enhancer. Although androstenedione is legal in professional baseball, it has been banned by the National Football League, the International Olympic Committee, and the National Collegiate Athletic Association. It is used in professional baseball to enhance performance and to speed healing after injury. McGwire defended his androgen use with the same arguments used by Ben Johnson: "Everybody that I know in the game of baseball uses the same stuff I use." The long-term effects of androstenedione on health are not known.

Lyle Alzado, one of the NFL's premier defensive players from the mid-1970s through the mid-1980s, was an imposing 150 kg (330 lb) mass of muscle and mania. When he retired in 1986, he was recognized as one of the best ever at his position. Five years later, however, Alzado reappeared in the public eye with a startling admission—he had used anabolic steroids throughout his career and had continued to use them after he retired from professional football, despite warnings from his physician. He also admitted that he had assaulted his wife while in a steroid-induced rage. Sadly, he announced that he was suffering from an incurable brain tumor that was probably caused by immunosuppression resulting from anabolic steroid use. He crusaded against the use of anabolic steroids in ama-

teur and professional sports during the remainder of his life. Before he passed away, Alzado admitted:

> I started taking anabolic steroids in 1969 and never stopped. It was addicting, mentally addicting. Now I'm sick, and I'm scared. Ninety percent of the athletes I know are on the stuff. We're not born to be 300 lbs or jump 30 ft. But all the time I was taking steroids, I knew they were making me play better. I became very violent on the field and off it. I did things only crazy people do. Once a guy sideswiped my car and I beat the hell out of him. Now look at me. My hair's gone, I wobble when I walk and have to hold on to someone for support, and I have trouble remembering things. My last wish? That no one else ever dies this way. (Alzado, 1991)

Alzado died on May 14, 1992, at the age of 43.

More recently, Ken Caminiti, the 1996 National League Most Valuable Player when he played for the San Diego Padres, died from a heart attack in late 2004. He was 41. In May 2002, during an interview with *Sports Illustrated*, he admitted using steroids during his MVP season when he hit a career-high .326 with 40 home runs. In that interview, Caminiti estimated that half the players in the major leagues regularly used steroids to enhance their performance.

Lyle Alzado
(1949–1992)

Androgens and Affective Disorders

With the escalating rate of anabolic steroid abuse, reports of bizarre, hostile, and erratic behavior have been increasing among men (Melnik, 2009). Anabolic steroids enhance body tissue–building processes and simultaneously retard or reverse tissue catabolism (see Chapter 9). Use of anabolic steroids by world-class athletes to improve their strength and performance has been widespread during at least the past two decades (**BOX 13.2**) (Haupt and Rovere, 1984). This abuse has occurred despite the listing of anabolic steroids as "banned substances" by the U.S. Olympic Committee, the International Olympic Committee, the National Collegiate Athletic

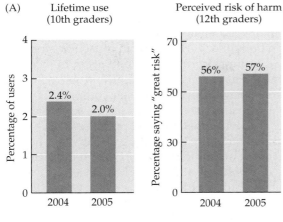

(A) Lifetime use (10th graders) — Perceived risk of harm (12th graders)

FIGURE 13.17 Lifetime use of anabolic steroids (A) decreased among 10th graders in 2005, whereas the perceived risk of harm among high school seniors has increased. (B) This contrasts to the previous years when percentage of students in the 8th, 10th, and 12th grades who used steroids was flat or inceeased from 2000 to 2004. After NIDA, 2006.

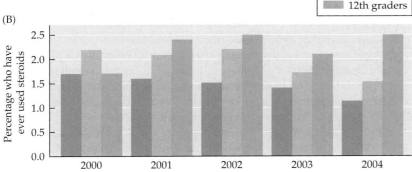

(B)

Association, and all North American professional sports organizations (Hartgens and Kuipers, 2004; Kibble and Ross, 1987). More recently, the abuse of anabolic steroids has become prevalent among recreational bodybuilders and competitive athletes in the 16-to-21-year-old cohort (Hartgens and Kuipers, 2004; Kibble and Ross, 1987). Alarmingly, the use of anabolic steroids has increased as the perceived risk of these drugs among high school seniors has decreased (**FIGURE 13.17**). More than a quarter million high school seniors in the United States are currently estimated to be using anabolic steroids to enhance their athletic performance. Anabolic steroid abuse has also been reported among middle school students (Kilmer et al., 2007; Moore, 1988; Wood, 2008) (**FIGURE 13.18**). Although it has been widely reported that little evidence exists that anabolic steroids actually improve athletic performance or provide any sort of "competitive edge," this view is likely incorrect. According to the 2006 American College of Sports Medicine position statement "The Use of

FIGURE 13.18 Abuse of anabolic steroids is greater than abuse of heroin and rivals crack abuse among US students. These data represent self-reports collected as part of the Youth Risk Behavior Survey from 9–12th grade students (A) or 12th grade students (B). Self-reports of anabolic steroid abuse appears to be decreasing among both 8th (red circles) and 12th grade (blue circles) students. After Wood, 2008.

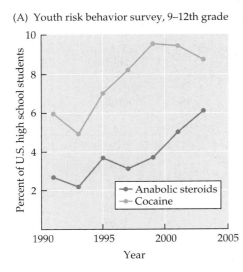

(A) Youth risk behavior survey, 9–12th grade

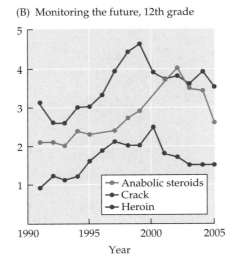

(B) Monitoring the future, 12th grade

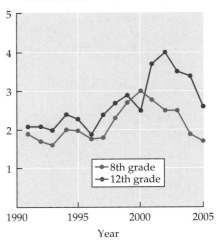

(C) Monitoring the future, anabolic steroid abuse

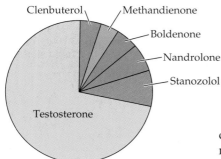

FIGURE 13.19 Types of performance-enhancing drugs (PEDs) used by competitive athletes based on the WADA 2011 testing data. Note that all of the most commonly abused PEDs are anabolic steroids (with the exception of clenbuterol). From Pope et al., 2013.

FIGURE 13.20 Health risks associated with anabolic steroid abuse for men (A) and women (B) as documented by the National Institute on Drug Abuse. After the NIDA website, www.nida.nih.gov.

Anabolic-Androgenic Steroids in Sports," anabolic steroids "contribute to increases in body weight and lean body mass. The gains in muscular strength achieved through steroid use … improve performance and seem to increase aerobic power or capacity for muscular exercise." Most individuals who use steroids began to use them because they believed that their competitors were using them. People continue to use anabolic steroids because these substances cause psychological dependence and delusional thinking processes.

The Endocrine Society released a statement regarding the adverse health consequences of performance-enhancing anabolic steroids (Pope et al., 2013). A number of anabolic agents are abused to enhance athletic performance, but testosterone is by far the most commonly abused anabolic agent (**FIGURE 13.19**) The Endocrine Society's scientific statement synthesizes available information on the medical consequences of using anabolic steroids, which have been linked to increased risk of death and a wide variety of cardiovascular, psychiatric, metabolic, endocrine, neurologic, infectious, hepatic, renal, and musculoskeletal disorders. This statement suggests that because randomized human trials cannot ethically duplicate the large doses of anabolic steroids used by abusers, additional observational studies to collect valid outcome data on the health risks associated with anabolic steroids are needed. Also needed are better estimates of the prevalence of anabolic steroid use and information on the mechanisms causing poor health outcomes.

The health risks of chronic anabolic steroid use in adult men should be well known (**FIGURE 13.20**), but there remains widespread misperception that anabolic steroid use is safe or that adverse effects are manageable. In reality, the vast majority of users are not professional athletes, but rather weight lifters, and the adverse health effects of anabolic steroid use are greatly underappreciated (Pope et al., 2013). The adverse physiological effects of these steroids include liver, kidney, immune system, and endocrine dysfunction as well as cardiovascular problems (Kibble and Ross, 1987; Wu, 1997). Many of the adverse effects of anabolic steroid use are irre-

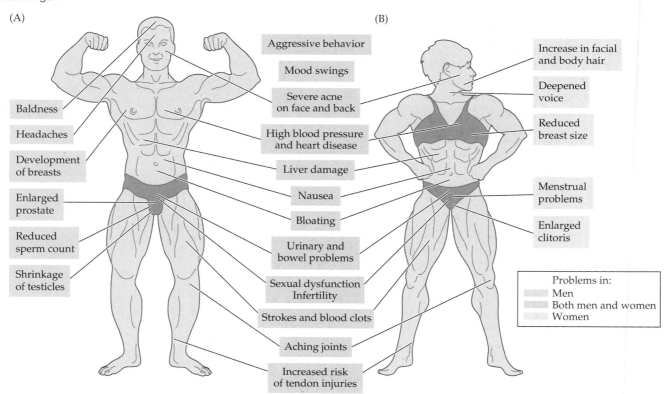

(A)

FIGURE 13.21   Severe acne can be induced by anabolic steroid abuse. This patient was a 21-year-old bodybuilder with a history of anabolic steroid abuse. (A) The patient at the time of his ideal body image; (B) the same young man after he developed severe acne conglobata with pustules and ulcerations; (C) the patient after 6 weeks of antiseptic antibiotic treatment and withdrawal from anabolic steroids. From Gerber et al., 2008.

(B)

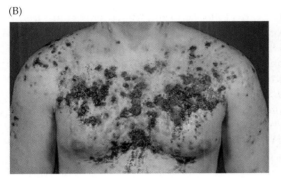

(C)

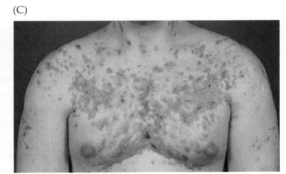

versible, though severe acne, a common effect, is typically reversible (**FIGURE 13.21**). Notably, these adverse effects were discovered primarily in patients using these substances for approved medical indications (such as anemia, congenital angioedema, senile or postmenopausal osteoporosis, corticosteroid-induced catabolism, or weight loss in cancer or AIDS patients) at therapeutic doses (Limbird, 1985)—doses typically much lower than those taken by abusers of steroids. A study of Finnish powerlifters who used anabolic steroids during their weight lifting careers revealed increased mortality (Pärssinen et al., 2000b). Similarly, treatment of mice with anabolic steroids significantly shortened their life spans (Bronson and Maltherne, 1997).

Extrapolating the adverse consequences of therapeutic steroid use to predict the outcome of anabolic steroid abuse is difficult. Steroid abusers typically use several different agents simultaneously at doses many times higher than the maximum therapeutic doses. Furthermore, the "stacking" and "cycling" treatment regimens used by many steroid abusers are quite different from the typical recommended therapeutic administration regimens (Perry et al., 1990). *Stacking* is bodybuilders' jargon for using two or more anabolic steroids at high dosages; usually a combination of oral and injectable forms is used (Kibble and Ross, 1987). Administration of the drugs is typically titrated upward, then downward over a 4-to-20-week period prior to a competitive event. Drug use is then suspended for several months. The drug-free and drug-use periods are called cycles (Strauss et al., 1985).

The adverse effects of steroid use appear to be worse among anabolic steroid abusers than among patients taking steroids at recommended therapeutic doses; certainly, behavioral and mood effects are most pronounced among anabolic steroid abusers (Hartgens and Kuipers, 2004; Melnik, 2009). Additionally, many ill effects of anabolic steroid abuse are probably not reported. Anabolic steroids became controlled substances in the United States in 1991, so most steroids are obtained illegally, and users risk legal penalties and competitive sanctions if their steroid use is discovered (Kibble and Ross, 1987). Some researchers have estimated that hundreds of millions of dollars are spent annually in the United States by over a million steroid abusers to obtain illegal anabolic steroids (Moore, 1988; Taylor and Black, 1987; Yesalis et al., 1997).

TABLE 13.2 *The health risks of anabolic steroid use*
Men
Breasts, balding, acne, shrunken testicles, stunted height, hostility and aggression, body image disorder, cancer (prostate, liver, and kidney), heart disease, increased risk of HIV
Women
Heart disease, cancer (liver and kidney), depression, hostility and aggression, eating disorders, stunted height, beard, acne, increased risk of HIV

The adverse medical effects of steroid abuse seem to increase as the age of the abuser decreases (Middleman and DuRant, 1996; Moore, 1988; Yesalis et al., 1997). The most serious adverse medical consequence is cardiac hypertrophy. There have been several reports of young men with no previous medical complaints or histories of cardiac disease suffering fatal consequences; one report documents a 20-year-old bodybuilder who suffered sudden cardiac death after 1–2 years of anabolic steroid abuse (e.g., Dickerman et al., 1995; Huie, 1994; Mewis et al., 1996; Palfi et al., 1997). The number of former professional athletes who have admitted abusing anabolic-androgenic steroids and who have suffered heart attacks in their thirties and forties is increasing manyfold (Wood, 2008). In young men abusing anabolic steroid hormones, sexual function is also severely impaired (Moss et al., 1993), gynecomastia (breast development) occurs (Reyes et al., 1995), muscles can rupture (David et al., 1995), and immune function may become severely compromised, leading to increased infections and higher incidence of cancer (e.g., Hughes et al., 1995, 1998) (**TABLE 13.2**). Development of gynecomastia occurs because of the peripheral conversion of androgens to estrogens. Because breast development is a particularly unwanted side effect among bodybuilders (Reyes et al., 1995), they often self-administer tamoxifen, an estrogen blocker, along with their anabolic androgens. There is little scientific evidence to support this relatively common practice (Friedl and Yesalis, 1989). Along with acute myocardial infarction, suicide is the other most common cause of premature death among athletes suspected of using anabolic-androgenic steroid hormones (Pärssinen et al., 2000a). Because the abuse of anabolic steroids is a relatively new phenomenon, the long-term effects of these substances on young abusers remain unknown.

Adverse behavioral effects of anabolic steroid abuse have also been reported (Malone et al., 1995). The best known of these effects is extremely aggressive behavior, also known as roids rage. Although some of the adverse physiological effects of anabolic steroids may not be observed until many years after the cessation of steroid use, the onset of adverse behavioral effects may be relatively rapid, even at therapeutic doses. Oxymetholone is a 17α-methyltestosterone derivative that is a common orally administered treatment for anemia. One 18-year-old male treated with oxymetholone for idiopathic aplastic anemia developed a temporary elevation in aggression (Barker, 1987). Prior to treatment, the patient had not displayed any notable aggressive behavior. During the steroid treatment, however, he broke a friend's nose and also destroyed some personal property. As noted above, anabolic steroid abusers are exposed to much higher doses than those prescribed therapeutically. These high doses have been associated with violent aggression, often accompanied by affective and psychotic symptoms. The behavioral pathology of androgens can, for the most part, be avoided by avoiding pharmacological self-administration of anabolic steroids. Most psychiatric symptoms subside when anabolic steroid use is discontinued. Unfortunately, no information is available on the long-term behavioral consequences of anabolic steroid abuse if the steroids were administered during puberty. Even the extent to which high endogenous androgen concentrations during adolescence evoke hyperaggressiveness in human

TABLE 13.3 *Commonly abused anabolic steroids*
Oral steroids
Anadrol (oxymetholone)
Oxandrin (oxandrolone)
Dianabol (methandrostenolone)
Winstrol (stanozolol)
Injectable steroids
Deca-Durabolin (nandrolone decanoate)
Durabolin (nandrolone phenpropionate)
Depo-Testosterone (testosterone cypionate)
Equipoise (boldenone undecylenate)

Source: National Institute on Drug Abuse, 2000.

males remains unknown. Recent studies suggest that young men who use anabolic steroids are more likely to display violent behaviors than individuals who do not use steroids, even when the effects of key demographic variables such as previous violent behavior and polydrug use are taken into account (Beaver et al., 2008). A list of commonly abused anabolic androgens is provided in **TABLE 13.3**.

In one now classic study, researchers contacted gymnasiums and offered members using steroids a cash payment to engage in a confidential interview about their steroid use. The respondents reported routinely using doses 10–100 times higher than recommended therapeutic doses. Fifteen of the 41 individuals regularly using anabolic steroids reported experiencing major psychiatric symptoms; 13 other individuals became manic or near manic. One user, convinced of his immortality, drove a car into a tree at 65 km per hour while a friend videotaped him (Pope and Katz, 1988).

Anabolic steroid abuse has been associated with the perpetration of violent crimes (Borowsky et al., 1997; Canacher and Workman, 1989). A number of individuals have impulsively committed homicides while taking anabolic steroids. Carefully structured interviews with the perpetrators suggest strongly that steroid abuse was an important, if not primary, factor in the manifestation of the extreme aggressive act in many such cases. Although the individuals interviewed may have emphasized the role of steroids in their violence to aid their legal positions, a consistent pattern of steroid-associated violence among previously nonaggressive individuals supports the possibility that these agents are involved in the mediation of violent behavior (Canacher and Workman, 1989; Orchard and Best, 1994). Highly correlated risk factors for abusing anabolic steroids were determined retrospectively to be conduct disorder and body image concerns (Pope et al., 2012).

Very few controlled studies of the effects of anabolic steroids on mood have been reported. In one of the few studies on this topic, healthy male volunteers consecutively received a placebo, a low dose (40 mg) of methyltestosterone, a high dose (240 mg) of methyltestosterone, and another placebo over the course of 3 days (Su et al., 1993). A number of neuropsychiatric measures were obtained. They showed that the high testosterone dose caused positive changes in mood (e.g., euphoria, increased energy, and increased sexual arousal), as well as negative mood changes (e.g., irritability, mood swings, feelings of violence, and hostility) and cognitive impairments (e.g., distractability, confusion, and impaired memory) (Su et al., 1993). One of the 20 study participants (i.e., 5% incidence) became acutely manic, and another individual (i.e., also 5% incidence) became hypomanic. The results of this study indicate that even brief anabolic steroid use can affect mood in an adverse manner (Su et al., 1993). Elevated mood was not observed in another study using lower doses of anabolic steroids (50, 100, and 200 mg) (Fingerhood et al., 1997).

In a survey of 2552 retired professional American football players (Horn et al., 2009), respondents were divided into two groups: anabolic steroid users and non-users. Steroid users displayed an increase in the risk of osteoarthritis in retirement. Surprisingly, those who used anabolic steroids engaged in less physical activity in retirement. Also, retired football players who confessed to using anabolic steroids were more likely to report depression and alcohol abuse than nonusers (Horn et al., 2009). Although there were no differences in cancer diagnoses or diabetes, these diseases tend to appear at older ages, so these former players should be closely monitored in future studies.

Anabolic steroid abuse is also increasing among female athletes (Gruber and Pope, 2000). Interviews with women in gymnasiums revealed that approximately one-third had a history of anabolic-androgenic steroid abuse. Several behavioral problems were noted among these women, including chronic dissatisfaction and preoccupation with their bodies, rigid dietary practices, hypomania, and multiple substance dependencies (Gruber and Pope, 2000).

It has been proposed that a proportion of anabolic steroid abusers develop an addiction to steroids. This hypothesis is supported by the remarkable consistency with which abusers of anabolic steroids (the "substance" in this case) meet the following commonly accepted criteria for psychoactive substance use disorder (Pope and Katz, 1990; Wood, 2008):

- The steroids are used over longer periods than desired.
- Unsuccessful attempts to stop the steroid use occur.
- Substantial time is spent in procuring, using, or recovering from the effects of anabolic steroids.
- Use continues despite knowledge of the significant physical and behavioral problems it is causing.
- Characteristic withdrawal symptoms occur.
- More anabolic steroids are often taken to relieve the withdrawal symptoms (Kashkin and Kleber, 1989).

The last two criteria, in particular, suggest that anabolic steroids might have direct rewarding properties similar to the reinforcing effects of drugs such as cocaine, amphetamines, morphine, and heroin (Shippenberg and Herz, 1987). Increasing reports of suicides in previously nondepressed young men who abruptly stopped using anabolic steroids have been noted, and codependence rates of opiate addiction and anabolic steroid abuse are high (Wood, 2008). These tragic events appear to be linked with the constellation of symptoms that resemble withdrawal symptoms.

When male hamsters are infused with testosterone, locomotor activity, respiration, and body temperature are all depressed (Peters and Wood, 2004). After 15 days, however, the animals all develop tolerance to continued daily testosterone infusion, and locomotor activity, respiration, and body temperature of testosterone-infused males become equivalent to those of animals infused with only the vehicle. Because the symptoms of testosterone overdose resemble opiate intoxication, the opioid antagonist naltrexone was examined to determine whether it would block the depressive effects of testosterone infusion. It did. If testosterone infusion was preceded by administration of naltrexone, then locomotor activity, respiration, and body temperature were not depressed by testosterone (Peters and Wood, 2004). Thus, the withdrawal symptoms manifested by anabolic steroid abusers may result from a dependence upon elevated steroid hormone concentrations that affect endogenous opioid mechanisms. Additional research is required to ascertain the veracity of this hypothesis in humans.

Research on rodents has demonstrated that androgens have rewarding properties (see also Chapter 12). For example, male Syrian hamsters preferred an aqueous solution of 200 μg/ml of testosterone over plain water in a two-bottle choice test

(Johnson and Wood, 2001; Wood, 2002). When male rats or hamsters were catheterized to receive either an intravenous or an intracerebrovascular infusion of testosterone when they poked into a hole, testosterone showed a modest (compared with other drugs of abuse) ability to serve as a reward (Ballard and Wood, 2005; Wood et al., 2004). Androgens had similar rewarding properties among female hamsters (Triemstra and Wood, 2004). More recently, chronic high-dose testosterone treatment of adolescent rats has been found to enhance aggression, but not to increase impulsive behavior or motivation to fight (Wood et al., 2013).

Studies have also attempted to quantify the effects of prolonged androgen treatment in animals. In mice, male aggression was not affected by long-term pharmacological treatment with four different androgenic steroids; however, female aggression was significantly elevated by androgen treatment (Bronson, 1996). In an experiment that was designed to model the use of androgens by human teenagers, male hamsters were exposed to prolonged androgen treatment during adolescence. When these animals were tested in an intruder-resident aggression paradigm, they displayed elevated levels of aggression in the absence of elevated body mass (Melloni et al., 1997). A study of rats examined the effects during puberty of three anabolic-androgenic steroids, namely, testosterone, nandrolone, and stanozolol (Farrell and McGinnis, 2003). Rats injected with testosterone significantly increased scent marking and aggression in the opponent's home cage. Nandrolone had no effect, whereas stanozolol significantly inhibited all behaviors. These results suggest that anabolic steroid hormone effects during puberty depend on the chemical structure of the steroid. The authors suggest that because adolescence in humans is a period of hormonal change, abuse of anabolic steroids, especially stanozolol, during this time may disrupt the development and maintenance of normal adult behavioral patterns (Farrell and McGinnis, 2003), although some of these effects may be reversible (McGinnis et al., 2002). A series of studies in rats has indicated that exposure to high levels of anabolic steroids evokes inappropriate aggressive behaviors in terms of incidence and targets (Cunningham and McGinnis, 2006a,b). A recent study suggests that nandrolone (and possibly other anabolic steroids) affects mood and aggressive behavior by reducing serotonin signaling in critical brain circuits associated with the regulation of aggression. Reduced serotonin levels were associated with impulsiveness and elevated aggression in mice treated with nandrolone for 28 days (Ambar and Chiavegatto, 2009).

Importantly, exposure to anabolic steroids shortens the life spans of male mice (Bronson and Matherne, 1997). Control animals and animals that received one of four anabolic steroids for 6 months were maintained in the laboratory for at least a year after the end of androgen treatment. Approximately 90% of the control mice, which had received no exogenous steroid treatment, survived to 20 months of age. About 50% and 65% of the mice receiving anabolic steroid treatment at 5 and 20 times normal androgen blood concentrations, respectively, survived to 20 months of age (Bronson and Matherne, 1997).

The important message is that anabolic-androgenic steroid hormones have major effects on physiology and behavior. Although anabolic agents are banned from competition by most international sports federations, as noted above, numerous competitors test positive every year for these agents. The resulting challenge is to discriminate the illicit exogenous testosterone use from natural variation in endogenous androgen production in men and women athletic participants (Wood and Stanton, 2012).

Hormones and Eating Disorders

Anorexia nervosa and bulimia are both eating disorders that share several psychological features. A number of studies report that fluctuations in ovarian hormones are associated with changes in emotional and binge eating across the menstrual cycle. Disordered eating is often associated with hormones, as we will see below.

anorexia nervosa A serious, potentially life-threatening eating disorder characterized by self-starvation and excessive weight loss.

Anorexia Nervosa

Anorexia nervosa (derived from *orexis*, Greek for "appetite," and *an*, meaning "none") is most prevalent among young women (Klein and Walsh, 2004). Indeed, eating disorders are among the most sexually differentiated forms of psychopathology (Racine et al., 2012). A small, but increasing, number of boys and young men are developing the disorder (minus the menstrual correlates, of course), but the disorder is female dominated by nearly 10:1. If persistent, anorexia nervosa can be fatal. This eating disorder, first described in the 1870s, is characterized by greatly reduced food intake and body mass, and a distorted body image, as well as suppressed or delayed onset of menstrual cycles. The *DSM-5* describes two classifications of anorexia nervosa: (1) restricting type (in which individuals maintain low body mass mainly by severe dieting and excessive exercise) and (2) binge eating–purging type (in which individuals maintain low body mass by methods such as self-induced vomiting or overuse of laxatives, diuretics, and enemas) (*DSM-5*, 2013). The prevalence of anorexia nervosa among women in North America is estimated at 0.5%. The cause of anorexia nervosa is unknown, but there is a strong genetic component, as well as other personality and situational factors that contribute to the disorder. Although this syndrome is most common in Western societies, it has been observed at similar population frequencies in non-Western societies where being slender has less social value (e.g., Ung et al., 1997). The constellation of symptoms associated with anorexia nervosa appears to have existed as far back as the 1600s (Vanderreycken and Van Deth, 1994). The levels of the drive for thinness, body dissatisfaction, and dietary restraint vary across the menstrual cycle (Racine et al., 2012) (**FIGURE 13.22**).

Anorexia nervosa is the only psychiatric disorder that requires an endocrine dysfunction (i.e., menstrual abnormalities) as a criterion for diagnosis (Negrão and Licinio, 2002). In addition to reproductive dysfunction, several additional endocrine disturbances have been reported in connection with anorexia nervosa (**TABLE 13.4**). It has been difficult to establish the direct endocrine relationships that are unique to anorexia nervosa, that is, separate from the hormonal results of starvation. Thus, most of the characterizations of this disorder have been correlational. The obvious studies are unethical to perform, and even a natural occurrence of starvation requires immediate refeeding in any setting. Although there are new animal models for features of the illness, there are no good animal models of anorexia nervosa or bulimia nervosa.

As mentioned, reproductive dysfunction is the most pronounced endocrine consequence of anorexia nervosa. Chronic malnutrition reduces body fat and available metabolic fuels, leading to regressed ovaries and disrupted ovulation, menstruation, fertility, and sexual behavior (Klein and Walsh, 2004). The reproductive hormone profile resembles that of prepubertal girls, with low concentrations of gonadotropins and sex steroid hormones (Boyar et al., 1974). GnRH secretion is

FIGURE 13.22 Based on questionnaire data and salivary ovarian hormone values, the "drive for thinness" and "body dissatisfaction" seem to peak during the midluteal to premenstrual stages of the menstrual cycle, when progesterone values are typically highest. EDI = Eating Disorder Inventory (a self-report questionnaire); TFEQ = Three Factor Eating Questionnaire (assesses dietary restraint or "restrained eating.") After Klump et al., 2013.

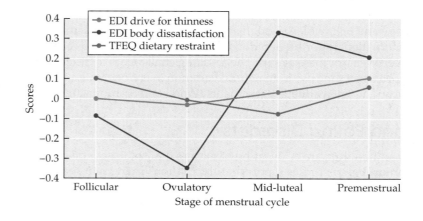

TABLE 13.4 *Endocrine alterations observed in anorexia nervosa and bulimia*

Anorexia nervosa

Hypogonadism

Amenorrhea

Oligomenorrhea (irregular menstrual cycles)

Delayed puberty

Euthyroid sick syndrome

Hypercortisolism (elevated cortisol)

↑ Corticotropin-releasing hormone (CRH) in central nervous system

↑ Basal/pulsatile GnRH secretion

↑ Osteoporosis

↓ Circulating leptin levels

↓ Insulin secretion

↑ Vasopressin in CNS

Altered melatonin levels

↑ Neuropeptide Y levels in cerebrospinal fluid

Bulimia

Amenorrhea

Oligomenorrhea

Anovulatoy cycles

Thyroid dysfunction

↑ Circulating GH

Normal bone density

Altered leptin

Normal insulin secretion and sensitivity

Altered melatonin

↓ Nighttime prolactin

↑ Levels of peptide YY_{3-36} in cerebrospinal fluid

Source: Negrão and Licinio, 2009.

impaired in anorexic women but can be restored by normalization of body mass (Negrão and Licinio, 2002). Thyroid function is usually in the low normal range but may be low enough to result in the so-called euthyroid sick syndrome (Wartofsky and Burman, 1982). More recent studies have reported low circulating levels of thyroid hormone and TSH (Klein and Walsh, 2004). Other endocrine problems that are serious, but have less of a behavioral effect, include hypercortisolism (typically without Cushing syndrome), excessive GH concentrations with decreased concentrations of insulin-like growth factor (IGF), osteoporosis (probably due to the shifting GH-to-IGF ratio), and decreased insulin levels (Klein and Walsh, 2004). Although most women who regain body mass to within 5% of standard weight (based on height) become reproductive, a subset of weight-stabilized women with previous diagnosis of anorexia nervosa remain amenorrheic with low estrogen and leptin values (Brambilla et al., 2003). Young boys who are diagnosed with anorexia nervosa display low testosterone concentrations, but it remains unclear to what extent these low testosterone values are primary or in response to adjustments in body composition (Tomova and Kumanov, 1999). The effects of normalizing body mass on hormone values remains unspecified in boys and young men.

Levels of leptin, secreted from fat cells, are very low in anorexic patients (Blüher and Mantzoros, 2004; Hebebrand et al., 1997), and low leptin concentrations normally inform the brain of starvation. Treating anorexic people with leptin does not reverse the low body mass (Blüher and Mantzoros, 2004), although leptin treatment might be useful in restarting the reproductive system. Recall from Chapter 9 that the cells in the arcuate nucleus of the hypothalamus that project to the gonadotropin-releasing cells have leptin receptors. Despite the literal meaning of *anorexia nervosa*, "a nervous loss of appetite," individuals with anorexia are often very hungry and obsessed with food. Obsessive-compulsive disorder (OCD) commonly co-occurs with anorexia nervosa (Klein and Walsh, 2004) and may have similar, but not identical, underlying causes. Anorexia nervosa is often also comorbid with depression and, to a lesser extent, with substance abuse (Negrão and Licinio, 2002). In both OCD and anorexia nervosa, serotonin levels tend to be low.

Anorexia nervosa has a strong genetic component (e.g., Bacanu et al., 2005). A search for polymorphisms in relevant neurotransmitters and neuropeptides has begun to reveal molecular mechanisms underlying various eating disorders. For example, levels of the seratonin transporter (5-HTT) are reduced in people suffering from anorexia nervosa (Gorwood, 2004). The promoter region of the gene encoding 5-HTT contains a functional polymorphism with two common alleles, designated the long and short alleles. A meta-analysis of four studies of the frequencies of the long and short alleles in patients with anorexia nervosa indicated that individuals with the short allele could be at risk for anorexia nervosa (Gorwood, 2004). Because nearly 50% of individuals diagnosed with anorexia nervosa are resistant to selective serotonin reuptake inhibitors, it is possible that individuals with polymorphisms in the gene encoding 5-HTT could be identified with gene screening and be prescribed a different (higher-dosage) drug regimen for successful treatment. Similarly, polymorphisms in the 5-HT$_{2A}$ receptor have been reported in restricting-type anorexia nervosa patients (Nacmias et al., 1999; Herbeth et al., 2005). Understanding the molecular mechanisms is important in developing novel therapeutic interventions for disordered eating.

Another genetic polymorphism has been associated with anorexia nervosa. As described in Chapter 9, the melanocortin type 4 (MC4) receptor plays a critical role in regulating body mass. The orexigenic neuropeptide agouti-related protein (AgRP), a molecule that functions as an MC4 antagonist, is important in maintaining body mass by inducing food intake. In one recent study, the coding region of the human *AgRP* gene was identified and screened for variations in people with anorexia nervosa. Three single-nucleotide polymorphisms (SNPs) were identified and were found to be more frequent in anorexic individuals than in normal-weight people (11% and 4.5%, respectively) (Vink et al., 2001). These results suggest that variation in the *AgRP* gene could be associated with increased susceptibility for anorexia nervosa, which might be caused by impaired suppression of MC4 by the variant *AgRP* (Adan et al., 2009). Thus, a drug that blocks the MC4 receptor might be effective for patients with anorexia nervosa (Adan et al., 2009; Vink et al., 2001).

Studies of twins have revealed that there is a strong interaction between genetic and developmental contributions to disordered eating (Klump et al., 2007). Girls were assessed for disordered eating at ages 11–18. At age 11, genetic factors accounted for a negligible proportion (6%) of variance in disordered eating, but at both ages 14 and 18, genes increased in importance and accounted for nearly half of the variance (46%) in disordered eating. The influences of the twins' shared environments decreased significantly across the same ages (Klump et al., 2007). These age differences are due to the age of onset of puberty (Klump et al., 2003, 2007). It will be important to discover what occurs at puberty to engage the genes associated with disordered eating (see below).

Bulimia Nervosa

Bulimia nervosa is also associated with disordered food intake and distorted body image. Women with bulimia nervosa binge eat; they consume huge amounts of food (up to 30 times the recommended caloric intake) during short periods of time (e.g., 2 hours) in an uncontrollable way (Negrão and Licinio, 2009). Unlike people with anorexia, individuals with bulimia nervosa typically maintain normal or slightly above average body mass. Body mass is maintained within the normal range because between binge episodes they tend to engage in strict dieting, and they also use compensatory mechanisms such as self-induced vomiting, overuse of laxatives, diuretics, enemas, and excessive exercise. Like anorexia nervosa, bulimia nervosa is far more common among adolescent girls and young women than boys or men. Also in common with anorexia nervosa, bulimia nervosa is associated with specific genetic profiles (e.g., Bulik et al., 2003).

Emotional and binge eating peak during the midluteal phase of the cycle and are predicted by within-woman changes in estrogen and progesterone (Klump et al., 2013). In a study of 196 twins, these hormonal associations were confirmed, as neither BMI nor restraint moderated these relationships.

The endocrine sequelae of bulimia nervosa are listed in Table 13.4. Reproductive dysfunction is less severe in bulimia than in anorexia nervosa. For example, fewer bulimics (about 50%) display amenorrhea and anovulatory cycles (Negrão and Licinio, 2009). This observation probably reflects the fact that most women with bulimia nervosa are within a normal weight range. Cortisol concentrations are normal or slightly elevated, which probably reflects a dysregulation of CRH and ACTH secretion. Thyroid hormone concentrations vary with the phase of the binge-purge cycle of the disorder. Altemus and colleagues found that women in the binging phase had lower circulating levels of T_3 than women without the disorder. After 2 months of normalized eating behavior, circulating T_4, T_3, and thyroid-binding globulin concentrations remained lower in bulimic women than in women without any eating disorder (Altemus et al., 1996). Women with bulimia nervosa also have elevated GH concentrations but normal IGF concentrations. Bone metabolism as well as insulin secretion and sensitivity are typically normal in women with bulimia. Leptin levels reflect body mass; however, the binge-purge cycle influences the timing of the circadian variation in leptin secretion (Ferron et al., 1997).

What accounts for the strong sex difference in disordered eating? Traditionally, strong cultural/societal pressures to be thin have been proposed to affect girls and women more than boys and men and to lead to disordered eating (Keel and Klump, 2003). However, it is possible that biological factors also contribute to these sex differences. In one recent study, investigators examined the prevalence of disordered eating among same-sex and opposite-sex twins (Culbert et al., 2008). Recall from Chapter 3 that females of opposite-sex pairs are generally exposed to more prenatal androgens than females of same-sex twins. Disordered eating was assessed with the Minnesota Eating Behavior Survey. The results were linear and suggested an organizational effect of androgens in preventing disordered eating. Females of same-sex pairs displayed the highest levels of disordered eating, followed by opposite-sex females, opposite-sex male twins, and same-sex male twins (Culbert et al., 2008). Given the previous findings that disordered eating generally appears at puberty, it appears that disordered eating requires both organizational and activational effects of hormones. Other studies suggest that binge episodes are predicted by changes in estrogen and progesterone across the menstrual cycle. In these studies, binge eating is generally associated with low mood and low estradiol and elevated progesterone concentrations (Edler et al., 2007; Klump et al., 2008; Lester et al., 2003).

bulimia nervosa   A serious, potentially life-threatening eating disorder characterized by a cycle of binge eating and compensatory behaviors such as self-induced vomiting designed to undo or compensate for the effects of binging.

Summary

1. In addition to overt behavior, hormones also affect mood. For many affective disorders, animal models have limited usefulness for understanding the effects of hormones on mood, because mood must always be inferred. In other cases, studies of animal models provide good insights into the mechanisms underlying affective disorders. Studies of humans that correlate mood changes with endocrine events are often useful for this purpose; the effects of endocrine manipulations on mood can then be assessed.

2. Depression is often evoked by endocrine changes. The symptoms of depression include reduced mood, low self-esteem, general fatigue, feelings of guilt, sleep disturbances, anger, irritability, and reductions in sexual motivation and food consumption.

3. Administration of TRH or TSH can ameliorate depressive symptoms. Prolactin and GH are also linked to depression. Cortisol has also been implicated in depression; nearly half of depressed patients exhibit elevated cortisol production. These endocrine data suggest that depressed patients may have experienced an alteration in the neuroendocrine mechanisms underlying the feedback control systems of the HPA axis. It remains unclear whether the changes in hormone concentrations are the cause or the result of the depressed mood.

4. Estrogen deficits are also associated with depression. Estrogen replacement therapy can elevate mood in depressed women. Exposure to high steroid concentrations may account for some of the psychological symptoms associated with PMS and postpartum depression, as with anabolic steroid abuse.

5. Postpartum depression is a well-known subtype of depression that probably reflects adjustments to parenting rather than endocrine changes per se. Nonetheless, there seem to be differences in how individuals respond to the large changes in hormones after parturition.

6. Perimenstrual syndrome (PMS) is a cluster of physiological, behavioral, and mood symptoms that appear to be linked; these symptoms are associated with the normal changes in steroid hormone concentrations accompanying the menstrual cycle.

7. PMS is a controversial research topic. Its prevalence, its defining symptoms, and their timing, as well as its psychological and endocrinologic correlates, remain unresolved. Feminist social scientists have noted that the medicalization of menstruation places women in a "sick" role and questions their competence. The vast majority of research has not detected any significant impairment in women's functioning due to PMS.

8. The symptoms of PMS appear to cluster into four subtypes, and it is likely that different endocrine correlates underlie the different subtypes.

9. Because most mood changes of PMS occur during the late luteal phase, when blood concentrations of progesterone are increasing, many studies have examined the role of progesterone in mediating PMS symptoms. Progesterone treatment does not consistently affect the prevalence of PMS symptoms. Estrogen treatment also does not consistently ameliorate PMS symptoms. Curiously, most medical treatments for PMS are aimed at correcting some putative endocrine "abnormality" associated with the late luteal phase of the menstrual cycle. However, even pharmacological elimination of the entire luteal phase does not affect PMS symptoms.

10. Dietary factors, including carbohydrate and calcium intake, can interact with hormones to influence PMS symptoms.

11. A significant minority of women report positive changes in mood associated with the perimenstrual phase. The endocrine correlates of these positive mood changes are poorly understood.

12. Seasonal affective disorder (SAD) is characterized by depressed mood, lethargy, loss of libido, excess sleep, body mass increase, carbohydrate cravings, anxiety, and lack of concentration during autumn and winter. Bright lights have been used to alleviate SAD; it is thought that they do so by resetting biological clocks by affecting melatonin release patterns, as well as by providing a nonspecific "energizing" influence.

13. Androgens are increasingly abused by men and boys to enhance body muscle mass and athletic performance. Anabolic steroids can improve certain aspects of athletic performance and possibly provide a "competitive edge." Most individuals begin to use steroids because they believe that their competitors are probably using them. The health risks of anabolic steroid abuse are very high; adverse medical effects include immune, liver, kidney, cardiovascular, and endocrine dysfunction.

14. Adverse behavioral effects of anabolic steroid abuse include hyperaggressiveness (including criminal violence) as well as a number of major psychiatric symptoms. Mania or hypomania is common among abusers of androgens.

15. Anabolic steroid abusers may develop an addiction to these steroids. Characteristic withdrawal symptoms occur, and severe depression and suicide have been reported in individuals with no previous mental health problems who suddenly stopped using steroids. Unlike the other disorders described in this chapter, anabolic steroid abuse is self-inflicted.

16. Anorexia nervosa and bulimia are psychiatric conditions that share several traits, including disordered food intake, distorted body image, compulsive exercise, and purging behavior. The resulting low body mass and lack of metabolic fuel delays or interrupts menstrual cycles. Most of the endocrine dysfunctions associated with anorexia nervosa and bulimia are the result of dysfunctions of the hypothalamic-pituitary-gonadal axis that are fully reversible with the onset of typical eating behavior and attainment of normal body mass.

17. Disordered eating affects girls and women nearly ten times more frequently than boys and men. Recent evidence suggests that both anorexia nervosa and bulimia are organized by a lack of prenatal androgens and activated by hormones during puberty. There are both genetic and environmental contributions to disordered eating.

Questions for Discussion

1. What are some minimum criteria that need to be established in order to describe and ultimately treat PMS?

2. Given what you know about the effects of hormones on behavior, should people be able to use "hormonal state" (e.g., anabolic steroid abuse, postpartum depression, PMS) as a defense against criminal charges? Why or why not?

3. Are the mood effects associated with menstruation any more dramatic than the mood swings that men experience? How would you address this question experimentally?

4. Can non-opioid hormones be "addictive"? Provide evidence for and against this notion. What is the evidence that anabolic steroids are addictive?

5. Discuss some possible reasons mechanisms in mammalian brains evolved to adjust mood based on seasons or hormonal states.

6. What are some benefits to twin, geographic, and cross-cultural studies when used to address relationships between hormones and psychiatric disorders? What are some disadvantages? Describe an experiment using these variables.

Suggested Readings

Herbert, J. 2013. Cortisol and depression: Three questions for psychiatry. *Psychol. Med.*, 43:449–469.

Lam, R. W., et al. 2006. The Can-SAD Study: A randomized controlled trial of the effectiveness of light therapy and fluoxetine in patients with winter seasonal affective disorder. *Am. J. Psychiatry*, 163:805–812.

O'Hara, M. W. 2013. *Postpartum Depression: Causes and Consequences*. Springer-Verlag, Berlin.

Paz-Filho, G. J., and Licinio, J. 2009. Anorexia nervosa and bulimia nervosa. In D. W. Pfaff et al. (eds.), *Hormones, Brain and Behavior* (2nd ed.), pp. 2972–2944. Academic Press, New York.

Rosenthal, N. E., et al. 1988. Phototherapy for seasonal affective disorder. *J. Biol. Rhythms*, 3:101–120.

Rubinow, D. R., and Schmidt, P. J. 2006. Gonadal steroid regulation of mood: The lessons of premenstrual syndrome. *Front. Neuroendocrinol.*, 27:210–216.

Toffoletto, S., et al. 2014. Emotional and cognitive functional imaging of estrogen and progesterone effects in the female human brain: A systematic review. *Psychoneuroendocrinology*, 50:28–52.

Wood, R. I. 2008. Anabolic-androgenic steroid dependence? Insights from animals and humans. *Front. Neuroendocrinol.*, 29:490–506.

Glossary

A

5α- and 5β–dihydrotestosterone (DHT) Potent androgens derived from testosterone that bind more strongly to androgen receptors than testosterone.

5α-dihydrotestosterone (DHT) A potent androgen that is derived from testosterone and binds more strongly to androgen receptors than testosterone. There are both 5-alpha and 5-beta forms of DHT.

5α-reductase An enzyme necessary to convert testosterone to 5α-dihydrotestosterone.

ablation Removal, especially by cutting.

accessory sex organ The internal organs of the male and female reproductive tract that connect the gonads to the external environment.

active avoidance A type of learning in which an individual must perform an action to avoid a noxious situation.

activin Peptide hormone synthesized in the anterior pituitary gland and gonads that stimulates the secretion of follicle-stimulating hormone.

adaptive function The role of any structural, physiological, or behavioral process that increases an individual's fitness to survive and reproduce as compared with other conspecifics.

adipokine Cytokines (cell signaling proteins) secreted by adipose tissue. Leptin was the first adipokine discovered in 1994.

adipose Connective tissue in which fat is stored.

adrenal cortex The outer layer(s) of the endocrine organ that sits above the kidneys in vertebrates and secretes steroid hormones.

adrenal glands Paired, dual-compartment endocrine glands in vertebrates consisting of a medulla and a cortex.

adrenal medulla The inner portion of the endocrine organ that sits above the kidneys in vertebrates and secretes epinephrine and norepinephrine.

adrenocorticotropic hormone (ACTH) A polypeptide hormone that is secreted by the anterior pituitary gland that stimulates the adrenal cortex to secrete corticosteroids, such as cortisol and corticosterone.

affective disorders Mental disorders characterized by dramatic changes or extremes of mood.

affiliation A form of social behavior that involves an individual's motivation to approach and remain in close proximity with a conspecific.

aggression A form of social interaction that includes threat, attack, and fighting.

agonist A chemical substance that binds to receptors for a hormone or neurotransmitter and causes a biological response that is indistinguishable from the response elicited by the natural hormone or neurotransmitter.

agonistic Referring to any behavior associated with fighting, including aggression, submission, and retreat.

aldosterone A mineralocorticoid that causes the kidneys to retain sodium.

alloparental behavior Caregiving to offspring that is provided by individuals other than their genetic parents.

altricial Born or hatched at an early stage of development. Altricial offspring are generally quite helpless and require substantial parental care to survive.

amnestic A substance or event that causes forgetting.

amplitude In biological rhythms, the amount of change in the rhythm above (to the peak) or below (to the nadir) the average value.

amygdala An almond-shaped structure located near the base of each temporal lobe of the brain. The amygdala is critical for the integration of sensory information that is important in sexual behavior.

androgen insensitivity (AIS) A condition in genetic males, in which functional androgen receptors are absent. AIS is caused by a genetic mutation on the X chromosome.

androgens The primary steroidal product secreted from the testes.

androstenedione The primary sex hormone secreted by the human adrenal cortex.

anestrous The reproductive condition of a female mammal that is not in estrus, or mating condition.

anlage The primordial substrate in a developing individual.

anorexia nervosa A serious, potentially life-threatening eating disorder characterized by self-starvation and excessive weight loss.

anorexia Lack or loss of appetite or lack of voluntary food intake.

antagonist A chemical substance that binds to receptors for a hormone or neurotransmitter, but does not cause a biological response.

anterior pituitary Front part of the endocrine gland that extends from the base of the brain and secretes a number of tropic hormones in response to hormonal signals from the hypothalamus.

anterograde tract tracing A method used to trace axonal projections from their termination (e.g., synapse) to their point of origin (the cell body or soma).

anteroventral periventricular nucleus (AVPV) A small region of the anterior preoptic area that is abundant in nuclear hormone receptors and participates in the control of sex-typical behavioral and endocrine responses.

antiamnestic A substance that protects against forgetting.

aphagia Inability or voluntary refusal to swallow.

apoptosis Programmed, orderly cell death that avoids immune system activation.

appetitive learning Reinforcement of a behavior by a positive outcome.

appetitive phase An ethological term, roughly equivalent to *courtship*. All the behaviors an individual displays when attempting to gain access to an individual of the opposite sex for the purpose of mating.

arginine vasotocin (AVT) A neuropeptide homologous to mammalian oxytocin and vasopressin that is found in non-mammalian vertebrates and mediates social and sexual behavior.

aromatase An enzyme that converts androgens into estrogens.

aromatization The process of converting an androgen molecule to an estrogen molecule via the enzyme aromatase.

associated reproductive pattern The breeding pattern observed in most vertebrate species, in which reproductive behavior, maximal gonadal size and activity, high steroid concentrations, and gamete production coincide.

associative learning The process by which an association between two stimuli is established.

attachment A strong emotional bond that develops between infant and caregiver, which is important for subsequent emotional stability.

attractivity The stimulus value of a female for a particular male. Attractivity is a hypothetical construct that must be inferred by observation of a conspecific's behavior.

autocrine Pertaining to a signal secreted by a cell into the environment that affects the transmitting cell.

autoradiography A technique used to detect a radiolabeled substance, such as a hormone, in a cell or organism, by placing a thin slice of the material in contact with a photographic emulsion.

aversive learning A change in behavior to avoid some noxious outcome.

B

β-endorphin An endogenous opioid produced in the anterior pituitary gland and hypothalamus in vertebrates; resembles opiates in its action as a "natural" painkiller.

bed nucleus of the stria terminalis (BNST) A limbic forebrain structure that mediates autonomic, neuroendocrine, and behavior responses.

behavioral endocrinology The study of the interactions among hormones, brain, and behavior.

behavioral sex The sex of an individual as discriminated on the basis of male-typical and female-typical behaviors.

biological half-life The amount of time required to remove half of a hormone or other substance from the blood.

blastocyst A fluid-filled sphere of cells that develops from a zygote. The embryo usually develops from the cluster of cells in the center of the blastocyst, whereas the external wall of the blastocyst develops into the placenta.

blot tests Techniques used to fractionate mixtures of proteins (Western), DNAs (Southern), or RNAs (Northern) so they can hybridize with markers that travel different distances in an electrophoretic gel based on their size.

bulimia nervosa A serious, potentially life-threatening eating disorder characterized by a cycle of binge eating and compensatory behaviors such as self-induced vomiting designed to undo or compensate for the effects of binging.

C

C cells Endocrine cells found in the interstitial spaces between the thyroid follicle spheres that secrete calcitonin.

calcitonin (CT) A polypeptide hormone secreted from the C cells associated with the thyroid gland that lowers blood calcium concentrations and affects blood phosphorus.

cannulation A technique in which hollow electrodes or fine tubes (cannulas) are inserted into specific brain regions or into specific blood vessels, so that substances can be introduced precisely into a particular place or a blood sample obtained from a specific location.

carrier protein One of several different plasma proteins that bind to hormones of low solubility (primarily thyroid and steroid hormones), providing a transport system for them.

castration response The increase in gonadotropin concentrations following removal of the gonads and consequent release from negative feedback effects of sex steroids.

castration The surgical removal of the gonads.

catecholamines Hormones that are derived from tyrosine and secreted primarily from the adrenal medulla.

challenge hypothesis The notion that an individual's androgen production responds to its social interactions such that testosterone is high during aggressive encounters during the breeding season, but not at other times.

chimera An animal whose tissues are composed of two or more genetically distinct cell types; also called a *mosaic*.

cholecystokinin (CCK) A hormone released by the lining of the small intestine that may be involved in satiation of food intake.

cholesterol A white crystalline substance found in animal tissue, and an important part of cell membranes, cholesterol is a precursor to steroid hormones.

chromaffin cells Cells that make and store epinephrine secretory vesicles.

chromosomal sex   The sex of an individual as determined by the sex chromosomes that an individual receives at fertilization.

chronobiology   The study of biological clocks and their associated rhythms. Also referred to as *biochronometry*.

circadian rhythm   A biological rhythm with a period of about 24 hours.

circalunar rhythm   A biological rhythm with a period of about 29.5 days that is closely tied to phases of the moon.

circannual rhythm   A biological rhythm with a period of about 12 months.

circatidal rhythm   A biological rhythm with a period of about 12.4 hours that is closely tied to changes in tides.

computerized tomography (CT)   Three-dimensional radiograph image of a body structure constructed by computer from a series of plane cross-sectional images made along an axis.

concaveation   The process of becoming sensitized to newborn animals so that full maternal behavior is expressed. Also called pup induction or sensitization.

conditioned defeat   The condition in which, after losing an aggressive encounter, an individual is more likely to lose in future encounters.

congenital adrenal hyperplasia (CAH)   A genetic deficiency that results in the overproduction of androgens by the adrenal glands. This syndrome has no reported effects on genital differentiation in males but causes various degrees of masculinization of the external genitalia in females, which may lead to erroneous assignment of sex at birth.

construct validity   Possession of the same underlying mechanisms, or etiology and homology, as a human disorder.

consummatory phase   An ethological term that encompasses the completion of a motivated behavior. In terms of sexual behavior, copulation represents the consummatory phase.

corpora lutea   Endocrine structures that form from the remnants of the ovarian follicles after the egg is released. The corpora lutea secrete progestins, which support the uterine lining in preparation for blastocyst implantation.

corticoids   A class of C_{21} steroid hormones secreted primarily from the adrenal cortices.

corticosterone   Glucocorticoid produced in the adrenal cortices of most rodents and birds.

corticotropin-releasing hormone (CRH)   A peptide hormone secreted by the hypothalamus that stimulates the release of ACTH (corticotropin) by the anterior pituitary gland.

cortisol   The principal glucocorticoid produced in the adrenal cortices of primates, including humans.

crepuscular   Active at dawn and dusk.

cytokine   A protein chemical messenger that evokes the proliferation of other cells, especially in the immune system.

D

declarative memory   Memory for facts or events.

defeminization   The removal of the potential for female traits.

dehydroepiandrosterone (DHEA)   A steroid hormone produced from cholesterol in the adrenal cortex, which is the primary precursor of natural estrogens, and is a weak androgen.

demasculinization   The removal of the potential for male traits.

detection threshold   The concentration at which an individual can tell the difference between two substances or stimuli.

development   The role of experience in individual behavior.

diestrus   Associated with the development of ovarian follicles and characterized by reduction in the number of epithelial cells and an increase in leucocytes.

dimorphic   Having two different forms; usually refers to differences between the two sexes.

disorders of sex development (DSD)   Congenital conditions in which development of chromosomal, gonadal, hormonal, or anatomical sex is atypical.

dissociated reproductive pattern   A breeding pattern observed in some vertebrate species in which reproductive behavior does not coincide with maximal gonadal size and activity. Instead, copulation occurs when steroid levels and gamete production are low.

diurnal   Active during the day.

DNA methylation   An epigenetic mechanism of gene regulation whereby methyl groups are added to DNA to reduce gene expression.

dopamine (DA)   A neurotransmitter produced primarily in the forebrain and diencephalon that acts in the basal ganglia, olfactory system, and some parts of the cerebral cortex.

down-regulation   A process that is similar to negative feedback in which the overproduction of a hormone causes occupation of virtually all available receptors so that subsequent high levels of hormones cannot have a biological effect.

E

ectocrine   A parahormonal chemical substance that is secreted (usually by an invertebrate organism) into its immediate environment (air or water) which alters physiology or behavior of the recipient individual.

effectors   The output system. In biology, usually refers to muscles.

ejaculation   The forceful expulsion of semen from a male's body via the urethra.

electrical stimulation   Activation of nerve cells by electrical current.

electrophoresis   A method that separates macromolecules (e.g., nucleic acids or proteins) on the basis of size, electrical charge, and other physical properties.

endocrine gland   A ductless gland from which hormones are released into the blood system in response to specific physiological signals.

endocrine-disrupting chemicals (EDCs)   Chemicals that mimic the effects of hormones or disrupt hormonal systems.

endocrinology   The scientific study of the endocrine glands and their hormones.

endogenous   Relating to a substance or process within the organism.

entrainment   The synchronization of biological rhythms to a periodic environmental cue.

enzyme amplification   A series of chemical reactions triggered by a hormone to produce not just one enzyme, but thousands.

enzyme-linked immunosorbent assay (ELISA)   An enzyme immunoassay that is used to detect small amounts of specific proteins and other biological substances such as hormones or other chemical messengers.

enzymoimmunoassay (EIA)   An assay that uses the principle of competitive binding of an antibody to its antigen to determine the presence or quantity of a biological substance such as a hormone.

epigenetic regulation   Changes in gene transcription resulting from modifications in the structure of chromatin, typically through DNA methylation and histone acetylation/deacetylation events.

epinephrine   A catecholamine produced in the adrenal medulla that increases cardiac tone and glucose levels.

estrus   The period during which female mammals will permit copulation.

eunuch   A man who has been castrated (testes removed).

eutherian   The subclass of mammals that possess a placenta during pregnancy.

evolutionary approaches   The perspective(s) adopted by biologists who assume that evolutionary processes are central to issues in ecology, systematics, and behavior.

exocrine gland   A gland that has a duct through which its product is secreted into adjacent organs or the environment.

exocytosis   The extrusion or secretion of substances from a cell by the fusion of a vesicle membrane with the cell membrane.

exogenous   Relating to a substance or process outside the organism.

extinction   The disappearance of a learned response when the response is no longer reinforced.

F

face validity   A reasonable outward representation of a disorder (i.e., behavioral phenotype matching the symptoms of the disorder).

feminization   The induction of female traits.

fight-or-flight response   The automatic and endocrine responses that prepare an individual to battle or flee from real or perceived attack, harm, or threats to survival.

follicle-stimulating hormone (FSH)   A gonadotropic hormone from the anterior pituitary that stimulates follicle development in females and sperm production in males.

follicles   An epithelial cell-lined sac or compartment of the thyroid gland, ovary, or other structure.

follicular phase   The portion of the primate menstrual cycle that begins at the end of menstruation and ends at ovulation, characterized by high blood levels of estrogens and the development of follicles.

free-running rhythm   A biological rhythm that is not synchronized to its natural zeitgeber and expresses its own endogenous rhythm.

frequency   The number of completed cycles per unit of time; for example, two cycles per month.

functional MRI (fMRI)   A non-invasive procedure that can measure biological activity in the brain. fMRI relies on the magnetic properties of blood to visualize images of blood flow in the brain as a brain region (within 1 mm) is activated and while it is occurring (within 1 sec).

G

G proteins   A class of proteins located adjacent to the intracellular part of a hormone or neurotransmitter receptor that are activated when an appropriate ligand binds to the receptor.

gametic sex   The sex of an individual as determined by the production of ova by females and sperm by males.

gastrin   A peptide hormone that is secreted by the mucous lining of the stomach; induces the secretion of gastric secretions.

gender identity   The psychological self-perception of being either male or female.

gender role   The collection of behaviors and attitudes that are considered appropriate or normal within a specific culture for each sex.

gene array   Solid support matrix upon which a collection of gene-specific nucleic acids have been placed at defined locations, either by spotting or direct synthesis.

gene imprinting   Genes expressed in a parent-of-origin-specific manner. If the allele inherited from the father is imprinted, it is silenced and only the allele from the mother is expressed.

gene   Discrete region of DNA within a chromosome that when expressed (transcribed), leads to the production of ribonucleic acid (RNA).

general adaptation syndrome (GAS)   A three-stage reaction to stress proposed by Hans Selye. These stages include the alarm, adaptation (resistance), and exhaustion stages.

genital folds   A fold of skin on each side of the genital tubercle that develops into the labia minora in females and the urethral groove and scrotum in males.

genital tubercle   The region of the embryo that develops into male or female genitalia.

germinal ridge   A thickened ridge of tissue on the ventromedial surface of each mesonephros of an embryo that has the potential to develop into either a testis or an ovary.

ghrelin   A peptide hormone produced by stomach cells; it is thought to increase feelings of hunger.

glucagon   A protein hormone that is secreted by the α-cells of the islets of Langerhans in response to low blood glucose levels.

glucocorticoids   One of the two types of corticoids secreted from the adrenal cortices; often released in response to stressful stimuli.

gluconeogenesis   The production of glucose from amino acids, a process that occurs in the liver in response to mild fasting.

glycogenolysis   The breakdown of stored glycogen in the liver or muscles to provide a steady supply of glucose for energy.

glycoprotein   An organic compound composed of both a protein and a carbohydrate joined together in a covalent chemical bond.

gonad   An endocrine organ that produces sex steroids and gametes; the ovaries and testes are gonads.

gonadal sex   The sex of an individual as determined by the possession of either ovaries or testes. Females have ovaries, whereas males have testes.

gonadotropin inhibitory hormone (GnIH)   A peptide hormone released from the hypothalamus that inhibits the secretion of hypothalamic GnRH and pituitary gonadotropins in a variety of species.

gonadotropin-releasing hormone (GnRH)   A decapeptide hormone from the hypothalamus that regulates FSH and LH release from the anterior pituitary.

gonadotropin   A hormone from the anterior pituitary (luteinizing hormone and follicle-stimulating hormone) or placenta (human chorionic hormone) that stimulates steroid production and gamete maturation in the gonads.

granulosa cells   The monolayer of flattened epithelial cells that surrounds the immature ova.

growth hormone (GH)   A protein hormone that stimulates somatic (body) growth.

growth hormone–releasing hormone (GHRH)   Also called *somatocrinin*. A polypeptide hormone that is released from the arcuate nucleus of the hypothalamus that provokes the secretion of growth hormone from the anterior pituitary gland.

H

habituation   Decrease in response to a stimulus after repeated exposures.

hermaphrodite   An individual who possesses both ovaries and testes. In some species, the possession of both types of gonads occurs simultaneously, whereas in other species it occurs sequentially.

histone acetylation   An epigenetic mechanism of gene regulation whereby an acetyl group is added to residues protruding from the histone core. Acetylation increases access to genes and thereby their transcription.

histone deacetylation   An epigenetic mechanism of gene regulation whereby an acetyl group is removed from residues protruding from the histone core. Deacetylation decreases access to genes and thereby their transcription.

homeostasis   The maintenance of a steady state within an organism by means of physiological or behavioral feedback control mechanisms.

homogametic sex   The sex that has two similar sex chromosomes. Except for birds and some reptiles, female vertebrate animals are the homogametic sex because they have two X chromosomes.

hormonal sex   The sex of an individual as determined by the concentration of androgens and estrogens. Males tend to have higher androgen concentrations, while females tend to have higher estrogen concentrations.

hormone response elements (HREs)   The binding site for hormones on the DNA, where along with cofactor/transcriptional regulators, hormones regulate cellular function by either increasing or suppressing gene transcription.

hormone   An organic chemical messenger released from endocrine cells that travels through the blood system to interact with cells at some distance away and causes a biological response.

hunger   Motivational state provoking food intake.

hyperphagia   Excessive hunger or elevated appetite.

hypocretin   Also called *orexin*. A polypeptide hormone that is mainly produced in the hypothalamus that inhibits the se-

cretion of various other hormones, including somatotropin, glucagon, insulin, TSH, and gastrin.

hypophysectomy   Surgical removal of the hypophysis, or pituitary gland.

hypospadias   A condition where the urethral opening is not at its typical location at the tip of the penis.

hypothalamic-pituitary-adrenal (HPA) axis   A complex and interactive system that comprises three endocrine glands: the hypothalamus, pituitary gland, and adrenal gland that constitute a major neuroendocrine system that regulations stress responses.

hypothalamus   A part of the diencephalon located just below the thalamus that is important in the regulation of autonomic and endocrine functions.

hypovolemia   The state of low blood volume.

hypovolemic thirst   Thirst induced by lack of blood volume; hypovolemic thirst can be ameliorated by water intake.

I

immediate causation   The physiological mechanism(s) underlying behavior.

immediate early genes (IEGs)   Genes that show rapid and transient expression in the absence of new protein synthesis. These genes are expressed immediately after cells are stimulated by extracellular signals such as growth factors or neurotransmitters. By observing the expression of these IEGs, neuron activation in association with specific behaviors can be mapped.

immunocytochemistry (ICC)   A technique that uses antibodies to determine the location of a hormone or hormone receptor in the body.

immunohistochemistry (IHC)   Test to detect antigens (e.g., proteins) in cells of tissue by exploiting the principle of antibodies binding to specific antigens.

in situ hybridization   A technique in which nucleic acid probes are used to locate specific nucleic acids (DNA in chromosomes and RNA in cells).

indoleamines   Any of various indole derivatives, such as serotonin, containing a primary, secondary, or tertiary amine group.

infradian rhythm   A biological rhythm that has a period greater than a day, but shorter than a month (or a frequency less than once per day).

inhibin   A peptide hormone that is secreted by the ovarian follicular cells and the testicular Sertoli cells that acts to inhibit secretion of FSH from the anterior pituitary.

inter-intromission interval (III)   The interval of time between successful intromissions by a male during copulation.

inter-mount interval (IMI)   The interval of time between successive mounts by a male during copulation.

interstitial nuclei of the anterior hypothalamus (INAH)   Four regions of neuronal cell bodies in the anterior hypothalamus and preoptic area of humans. Sex differences have been reported in INAH-2 and INAH-3. INAH-1 has been considered to be equivalent to the SDN-POA in rats.

intracrine   Peptide hormones or growth factors that bind and act inside cells either after internalization by the cells or retention in their cells of synthesis.

intromission The entrance of the penis into the vagina.

islets of Langerhans Islands of endocrine tissue nested throughout the exocrine tissue of the pancreas.

K

Kallmann syndrome A congenital condition in humans characterized by the inability to smell and lack of gonadal development, caused by a lack of olfactory bulb development and GnRH cell migration from the bulbs to their normal location in the hypothalamus during early development.

Klinefelter syndrome A congenital condition in humans in which individuals possess an extra X chromosome (XXY) and are externally and internally masculinized.

knockout An individual, usually a mouse, in which a specific gene has been inactivated.

L

lateralization The tendency for the neural substrate for cognitive skills to be confined to one cerebral hemisphere; can also be called cerebral specialization.

learning An adaptive change in behavior that results from experience.

legal sex The official designation of sex, which is heavily influenced by morphological sex at birth but is also influenced by chromosomal and gonadal sex.

leptin A protein hormone secreted by fat cells that may communicate information to the brain about body fat content.

lesion Damage to an area, such as a brain region, that is caused by accident, disease, or experimental procedure.

levels of analysis The set of overlapping and interacting questions about behavior that span different types of approaches, including immediate causation, development, evolution, and adaptive function.

Leydig cells The interstitial cells between the seminiferous tubules in the testes that produce androgens in response to luteinizing hormone from the anterior pituitary.

ligand A substance that binds to a receptor molecule.

lipid-based hormones Hormones derived from a fatty acid.

lipolysis The breakdown of adipose tissue into free fatty acids.

lordosis A female sexually receptive posture in which the hindquarters are raised and the tail is deflected to facilitate copulation.

luteal phase The portion of the primate menstrual cycle that begins at ovulation and continues until the onset of menstruation and is characterized by corpora luteal function and high blood levels of progesterone.

luteinizing hormone (LH) A gonadotropin from the anterior pituitary that promotes formation of the corpora lutea in females and testosterone production in males.

M

magnetic resonance imaging (MRI) An imaging technique that uses a magnetic field and radio waves to create detailed images of the organs and tissues within the body.

male sexual behavior All the behaviors necessary and sufficient to deliver male gametes (sperm) to female gametes (ova or eggs).

marsupial A mammal belonging to the subclass Metatheria that lacks a placenta, such as opossums and most Australian mammals. Most marsupials have a pouch (marsupium) in which the mammary glands are located and the young are transported.

masculinization The induction of male traits.

maternal aggression A type of aggressive behavior observed among new mothers when they fiercely defend their young from intruders.

maternal behavior Parental behavior typically performed by the mother or another female.

medial preoptic area (MPOA) A subdivision of the anterior hypothalamus implicated in the control of homeostatic processes and motivated behaviors, including sexual behavior and gonadotropin secretion.

melanoctye-stimulating hormone (MSH) A peptide hormone secreted by the pituitary gland that regulates skin color in some vertebrates by stimulating melanin synthesis in melanocytes and melanin granule dispersal in melanophores.

melanotropin inhibitory hormone (MIH) A peptide hormone that inhibits MSH secretion.

melanotropin-releasing hormone (MRH) A hexapeptide that stimulates the secretion of melanotropin.

melatonin An indoleamine hormone released by the pineal gland.

memory The encoding, storage, and retrieval of information about past experience.

met-enkephalin An endogenous opioid peptide with a short duration of action that has pain-reducing effects.

metabolic fuels The normal sources of energy for individuals, usually consisting of simple sugars (e.g., glucose), fatty acids, ketone bodies, and amino acids.

mineralocorticoids One of the two types of corticoids secreted from the adrenal cortices; important in ion exchange and water metabolism.

monoamines A hormone or neurotransmitter that contains one amine group.

monogamous Species that form a pair bond in which a male and female mate and raise offspring exclusively with each other.

monotreme A primitive egg-laying mammal, such as the duck-billed platypus and the spiny anteater, or echidna.

morph Individuals of a species that differ in form or function but are capable of interbreeding.

morphological sex The sex of an individual as determined by body form.

mounting A behavior observed among males of many species with internal fertilization in which the male assumes a copulatory position but does not insert his penis (or other intromittent organ) into the female's vagina (or urogenital opening). This behavior is androgen-dependent.

Müllerian duct system A duct system present in both sexes during embryonic development that connects the gonads to the exterior. During normal development, the Müllerian duct system develops into the accessory sex organs in females and regresses in males.

Müllerian inhibitory hormone (MIH) A peptide hormone produced in the Sertoli cells in the developing testis that suppresses development of the Müllerian duct system, which prevents development of the uterus and cervix. Also called *Müllerian inhibitory factor* (MIF).

N

negative feedback   A regulatory system that tends to stabilize a process when its effects are pronounced by reducing its rate or output.

neuroendocrinology   The scientific study of the interaction between the nervous system and the endocrine system.

neurohormone   A hormone that is released into the blood from a neuron rather than from an endocrine gland.

neurosecretory cell   A cell in the central nervous system that secretes its product beyond the synapse to affect function in other cells.

neurosteroids   Steroids that are synthesized in the central nervous system (CNS) and the peripheral nervous systems (PNS), independently of the steroidogenic activity of the endocrine glands.

neurotransmitters   Chemical messengers that communicate between nerve cells (neurons).

nocturnal   Active at night.

nonassociative learning   Change in the strength of response to a stimulus after repeated exposures.

norepinephrine   A substance that can act as either a hormone or neurotransmitter; secreted by the adrenal medulla and the nerve endings of the sympathetic nervous system.

nuclei   A collection of nerve cell bodies in the brain.

O

olfactory bulbs   Rounded cigar-shaped structures protruding from the front of the brain that receive input from the olfactory sensory cells in the nose and project to various parts of the brain associated with processing of airborne chemosensory stimuli.

orexigenic   Substance that stimulates food intake.

organizational/activational hypothesis   The proposition that sex differences in behavior arise from two fundamental processes. Hormones early in development act to differentiate the nervous system in a male or female direction (organizational) while hormones act on these differentiated circuits later in life to drive behavior in a sex-typical manner (activational).

osmolality   The concentration of solutes in a solution.

osmoregulation   The physiological and behavioral control of osmolality.

osmosis   Process of movement of a solvent through a semi-permeable membrane (e.g., in a living cell) into a solution of higher solute concentration that tends to equalize the concentrations of solute on the two sides of the membrane.

osmotic thirst   Motivation to consume water caused by increased osmolality in the brain.

ovaries   The female gonads, which produce estrogen, progestin, and ova.

ovotestes   A gonad consisting of both ovarian and testicular tissue, capable of producing both ova and sperm.

ovum   A haploid female gamete.

oxytocin   A peptide hormone secreted by the posterior pituitary that induces uterine contractions during birth, triggers milk letdown in lactating females, and may be involved in other reproductive behaviors.

P

pancreas   A composite vertebrate gland with both endocrine and exocrine functions.

pancreatic polypeptide   A polypeptide hormone secreted by cells in the endocrine component of the pancreas gland.

parabiosis   The joining together of two circulatory systems.

paracrine   A form of cellular communication in which a cell releases a product that induces changes in a nearby cell.

parathyroid gland   Separate endocrine tissue associated with the thyroid gland; produces hormones involved in calcium metabolism.

parathyroid hormone (PTH)   A protein hormone that is secreted by the parathyroid gland that regulates calcium and phosphate metabolism.

parental behavior   Behaviors performed in relation to one's offspring that contribute directly to the survival of fertilized eggs or offspring that have left the body of the female.

parthenogenesis   A type of asexual reproduction in which eggs can develop into offspring without fertilization.

passive avoidance   A type of learning in which an individual must suppress some behavior that would otherwise be exhibited.

paternal behavior   Parental behavior typically performed by the father or another male.

peptide hormones   A class of hormones consisting of a relatively short chain of amino acids residues.

perception   The transduction of sensory information entering the nervous system into biologically useful information.

perimenstrual syndrome (PMS)   A constellation of symptoms, including anxiety, depression, moodiness, and fatigue, that recurs on a cyclical basis and is associated with menstruation.

perinatal   Around the time of birth, typically a few days before or after birth in rodents or a few weeks before and after in humans.

period   The length of time required to complete one cycle of a rhythm, such as the amount of time between peaks in a cycle.

phase-response curves   A graphic representation of the differential effects that a periodic environmental cue (usually light) has on the timing of biological rhythms.

phase   A point in a rhythm relative to some objective time point during the cycle, or during the cycle of another rhythm.

photoperiod   Day length, or the amount of light per day.

photorefractoriness   The loss of responsiveness to changes in photoperiod.

pineal gland   An endocrine gland (also called the *epiphysis*), located in mammals between the telencephalon and diencephalon, that secretes melatonin, a hormone important in the regulation of daily and seasonal cycles.

pinealocytes   The primary cells of the pineal gland that produce and secrete melatonin.

pituitary gland   An endocrine gland that sits below the hypothalamus and has two distinct anatomical components, the anterior pituitary and the posterior pituitary, each derived from different embryological origins and having different functional roles in the endocrine system.

placenta A specialized organ produced by the mammalian embryo that is attached to the uterine wall and serves to provide nutrients, hormones, and energy to the fetus.

polygamous Species that mate with more than one individual.

portal system A special closed blood circuit in which two beds of capillaries are connected by a vein; thus, the flow of blood is in one direction only.

positive feedback A regulatory process that tends to accelerate an ongoing process by increasing production in response to the end product.

positron emission tomography (PET) A technique for examining brain function by combining tomography with injections of radioactive substances used by the brain.

post-ejaculatory interval (PEI) The interval of time between ejaculations by a male during copulation.

post-traumatic stress disorder (PTSD) A psychiatric disorder that may occur following the experience or witnessing of life-threatening events such as military combat, natural disasters, or violent personal assaults such as rape. Symptoms of PTSD include reliving the experience through nightmares and flashbacks, sleep disturbances, feelings of detachment, and estrangement.

posterior pituitary The rear part of the endocrine gland that extends from the base of the brain and stores and releases oxytocin and vasopressin, which are produced in the hypothalamus.

precocial Born or hatched at an advanced stage of development so that little or no parental intervention is required for survival.

predictive validity The ability to show a close relationship between test results prior to and after the manipulation in question.

preference threshold The first detectable preference displayed by an individual for any substance or solution.

pregnenolone A C_{21} steroid prohormone that is the obligatory precursor for all other steroid hormones in vertebrates.

preoptic area (POA) A region of the brain anterior to the hypothalamus. This region is usually divided into the lateral and medial preoptic areas.

preprohormone A sequence of amino acids that contains a signal sequence, one or more copies of a peptide hormone, and other peptide sequences that may or may not possess biological activity.

pro-opiomelanocortin (POMC) A precursor protein that consists of 241 amino acid residues. It is synthesized in the anterior and intermediate pituitary gland.

probe A fragment of DNA or RNA of variable length (usually 100–1000 bases long), which is used in DNA or RNA samples to detect the presence of nucleotide sequences (the DNA target) that are complementary to the probe sequence.

procedural memory Memory that stores long-term information about how to perform procedures, such as walking, swimming, and riding a bike.

proceptivity The extent to which females initiate copulation.

proestrus The vaginal cellular condition coincident with mating behavior (estrus) in female rodents.

progestins A class of C_{21} steroid hormones, so named for their "progestational," or pregnancy-maintaining, effects in mammals.

prohormone A molecule that can act as a hormone itself or can be converted into another hormone with different properties.

prolactin inhibitory hormone (PIH) Dopamine; inhibits prolactin secretion from the anterior pituitary.

prolactin A protein hormone that is highly conserved throughout vertebrate evolution and has many physiological functions.

prostaglandins A family of lipid-based hormones that possess a basic 20-carbon fatty acid skeleton; involved in several aspects of reproductive function.

protandrous A form of sequential hermaphroditism in which individuals begin life as males, then change into females.

protein hormones A class of hormones consisting of a long chain of amino acid residues.

protogynous A form of sequential hermaphroditism in which individuals begin life as females, then change into males.

pseudohermaphrodite An individual, especially a human, born with ambiguous external genitalia.

pseudopregnancy The luteal phase of the estrous cycle, or any period when there is a functional corpus luteum and buildup of the endometrial uterine layer in the absence of pregnancy.

psychology The scientific study of emotion, cognition, and behavior.

psychosocial dwarfism A grouping of disorders of retarded growth caused by neglect and abuse; this syndrome is also termed failure to thrive.

pulsatile secretion The episodic secretion of hormones in periodic bursts or spurts.

R

radioimmunoassay (RIA) A technique used to measure hormones or other biological substances by using antibodies and purified radiolabeled ligands.

receptivity The stimulus value of a female for eventually eliciting an intravaginal ejaculation from a male conspecific.

receptor A chemical structure on the cell surface or inside the cell that has an affinity for a specific chemical configuration of a hormone, neurotransmitter, or other chemical compound.

reference memory Knowledge for aspects of a task.

relaxin A polypeptide hormone that is secreted by the corpus luteum during the last days of pregnancy; it relaxes the pelvic ligaments and prepares the uterus for labor.

releasing hormones One of several polypeptides released from the hypothalamus that increase or decrease the release of hormones from the anterior pituitary gland.

retrograde tract tracing A technique used to trace neural connections from their source to their point of termination (i.e., from cell body to synapse).

rhythm A recurrent event that is characterized by its period, frequency, amplitude, and phase.

S

scrotum An external pouch of skin that contains the testes.

second messenger A biological molecule released when a hormone binds to its receptor; the second messenger activates the cellular machinery of the target cell.

secretin A peptide hormone produced in the duodenum, in response to gastric acid secretion, to stimulate production of pancreatic secretions.

seminiferous tubules The long, convoluted tubes in which spermatogenesis occurs.

sensation The initial processing of sensory information as it enters the nervous system through sensory receptors.

sensitization Progressive amplification of a response after repeated administrations of a stimulus.

sequential hermaphrodite An animal that begins life as one sex, then changes to the other sex as an adult in response to environmental or genotypic factors.

serotonin A neurotransmitter formed from tryptophan; the precursor to melatonin formation in the pineal gland.

Sertoli cells Cells located along the basement membrane of the seminiferous tubules in which sperm cells are embedded while they mature.

set point A reference value for a regulated physiological variable.

sex determination The point at which an individual begins to develop as either a male or a female.

sex drive The powerful motivational forces propelling individuals to seek copulation; in humans, often referred to as *libido*.

sex Condition, property, or quality by which organisms are categorized as female or male on the basis of their chromosomes, hormones, reproductive organs, and other morphology, as well as behavior. Also, the physiological, morphological, functional, and psychological differences that distinguish females and males.

sexual behavior Copulation. Actions directed towards reproduction. Also called *mating*.

sexual differentiation The process by which individuals develop the characteristics associated with being male or female.

sexual orientation The process of developing an erotic sexual attraction for other people. This term suggests that the process is mediated primarily by biological factors.

sexual preference The process of developing an erotic sexual attraction for other people. This term suggests that the process is mediated primarily by learning and conscious choices.

sexual selection A subset of natural selection that occurs when individuals within a population differ in their abilities to compete with members of the same sex for mates (intrasexual selection) or to attract mates of the opposite sex (intersexual selection).

sexually dimorphic nucleus of the preoptic area (SDN-POA) A set of cell bodies anterior to the hypothalamus that is larger in male than in female humans and rodents. The functional significance of this brain dimorphism is unknown.

signal transduction pathway The sequence of events that begins with a hormone binding to its receptor and ends with the response in a target cell.

simultaneous hermaphrodite An animal that possesses ovotestes that produce both eggs and sperm and alternates between two behavioral roles in providing eggs or sperm during spawning.

single-unit recording A technique that involves the placement of very small electrodes in or near one nerve cell to record changes in its neural activity before, during, and after some experimental treatment.

somatomedins Insulin-like polypeptides (growth factors) produced in the liver and in some fibroblasts and released into the blood when stimulated by GH.

somatostatin Also called *growth hormone–inhibiting hormone (GHIH)*. A peptide hormone secreted from the hypothalamus that reduces the secretion of growth hormone by the anterior pituitary gland.

spatial memory Subcategory of memory that encodes information about the environment and its orientation.

SRY gene Sex-determining region of the Y chromosome; the gene that is responsible for the transformation of the undifferentiated gonad into a testis.

steroid hormones A class of structurally related fat-soluble chemicals that are derived from cholesterol and are characterized by three six-carbon rings plus one conjugated five-carbon ring.

stress response A suite of physiological and behavioral responses that help to reestablish homeostasis.

stress Any significant disturbance of homeostasis, as by extreme temperatures or psychological factors.

stressor A condition, agent, or other stimulus that causes stress to an organism.

stroma The nonendocrine connective tissue of endocrine glands.

T

target cells A cell that has specific receptors for, and is affected by, a particular chemical messenger.

temperature-dependent sex determination A process that occurs in animals without sex chromosomes in which sex is determined solely on the basis of the temperature at which the egg incubates.

territorial behavior Actions that defend physical areas that may (or may not) contain valuable resources or mating partners.

testes The male gonads, which produce steroid hormones and sperm.

testicular feminization mutation (TFM) A genetic disorder in which XY individuals are insensitive to androgens.

testosterone The primary androgen secreted by most vertebrate animals.

thecal cells Cells that form around the granulosa cells during follicular maturation. These cells participate in estrogen synthesis, but transform along with other cellular types into the corpus luteum after ovulation.

thirst Motivational state provoking water intake.

thyroid gland A double-lobed endocrine gland located on or near the trachea or esophagus in vertebrates that secretes several hormones important in metabolism, including triiodothyronine and thyroxine.

thyroid-stimulating hormone (TSH) A glycoprotein hormone secreted by the anterior pituitary gland that stimulates and regulates activity of the thyroid gland.

thyrotropin-releasing hormone (TRH) A tripeptide hormone secreted by the hypothalamus that stimulates the release of thyroid-stimulating hormone (TSH) (thyrotropin) from the anterior pituitary gland.

thyroxine (T4) The primary hormone secreted from the thyroid gland; it acts to increase oxidation rates in tissues.

transcription factor Substance that promotes or blocks the process whereby a single strand of complementary RNA nucleotides is produced from a single strand of DNA.

transgenic Relating to an animal in which a gene has been inserted, altered, or deleted.

triiodothyronine (T3) A tyrosine-based hormone that is produced by the thyroid gland and acts to increase the basal metabolic rate, affect protein synthesis, and increase sensitivity to catecholamines.

tropic hormones Hormones from the anterior pituitary that stimulate various physiological processes, either by acting directly on target tissues or by causing other endocrine glands to release hormones.

Turner syndrome A congenital condition in which individuals lack an X chromosome (XO). These individuals have a female external appearance, but ovarian development is usually limited, and they do not attain puberty without medical attention.

U

ultradian rhythm A biological rhythm that has a period less than 24 hours (or a frequency greater than once per day).

up-regulation A process similar to positive feedback in which a hormone causes an increase in the production of receptors for that hormone.

V

vaginal estrus Directly following mating behavior and ovulation. Characterized by cornified epithelial cells.

vasopressin Also known as *antidiuretic hormone (ADH)*. A nonapeptide released from the posterior pituitary gland that increases blood pressure during serious blood loss.

vesicle A secretory granule or sac within a cell in which hormone or neurotransmitter molecules are stored.

vomeronasal organ An encapsulated sensory receptive organ located near the floor of the nasal cavity in mammals that receives chemosensory information, which then travels to the accessory olfactory bulbs.

W

Wolffian duct system A duct system present in both sexes during embryonic development that connects the gonads to the exterior. During normal development, the Wolffian duct system develops into the accessory sex organs in males and regresses in females.

working memory The part of short-term memory involved with immediate conscious perceptual and linguistic processing.

Z

zeitgeber A potent environmental time cue, or temporal synchronizer.

zona fasciculata The middle (and largest) zone of the adrenal cortex, consisting of orderly bands of epithelial cells. Glucocorticoid hormones are released from these cells in response to ACTH stimulation from the anterior pituitary.

zona glomerulosa The outermost zone of the adrenal cortex, consisting of whorls of epithelial cells. Aldosterone is released from these cells as an indirect response to low blood sodium levels.

zona pellucida The outer layer of cells surrounding the cell membranes of the maturing ovum.

zona reticularis The innermost zone of the adrenal cortex, consisting of a disorganized arrangement of epithelial cells. Sex steroid hormones are often released from this zone.

Illustration Credits

References

Abbott, D. H. 1984. Differentiation of sexual behaviour in female marmoset monkeys. Effects of neonatal testosterone or a male co-twin. In G. J. DeVries (ed.), *Prog. Brain Res.*, Vol. 61, pp. 349–358. Elsevier, Amsterdam.

Abel, G. G., Barlow, D. H., Blanchard, E. B., and Arnold, D. 1977. The components of rapists' sexual arousal. *Arch. Gen. Psychiatry*, 34:895–903.

Abercrombie, H. C., Kalin, N. H., Thurow, M. E., Rosenkranz, M. A., and Davidson, R. J. 2003. Cortisol variation in humans affects memory for emotionally laden and neutral information. *Behav. Neurosci.*, 117:506–516.

Abitbol, M. L., and Inglis, S. R. 1997. Role of amniotic fluid in newborn acceptance and bonding in canines. *J. Matern. Fetal Med.*, 6:49–52.

Abraham, G. E. 1980. The premenstrual tension syndromes. In L. K. McNall (ed.), *Contemp. Obstet. Gynecol. Nurs.*, Vol. 3, pp. 170–184. Mosby, St. Louis.

Abrahamson, E. E., and Moore, R. Y. 2001. Suprachiasmatic nucleus in the mouse: Retinal innervation, intrinsic organization and efferent projections. *Brain Res.*, 916:172–191.

Adan, R. A. H., Tiesjema, B., Hillebrand, J. J. G., La Feur, S. E., Kas, M. J., and de Krom, M. 2009. The MC4 receptor and control of appetite. *Brit. J. Pharmacol.*, 149:815–827.

Adels, L. E., and Leon, M. 1986. Thermal control of mother–young contact in Norway rats: Factors mediating the chronic elevation of maternal temperature. *Physiol. Behav.*, 36:183–196.

Ader, R., and Cohen, N. 1993. Psychoneuroimmunology: conditioning and stress. *Ann. Rev. Psychol.*, 44:53–85.

Adkins-Regan, E. 1987. Sexual differentiation in birds. *Trends Neurosci.*, 10:517–522.

Adkins-Regan, E. 1988. Sex hormones and sexual orientation in animals. *Psychobiol.*, 16:335–347.

Adkins-Regan, E. 1996. Neuroanatomy of sexual behavior in the male Japanese quail from top to bottom. *Poultry Avian Biol. Rev.*, 7:193–204.

Adkins-Regan, E. 1998. Hormonal mechanisms of mate choice. *Am. Zoologist*, 38:166–178.

Adkins-Regan, E. 2007. Hormones and the development of sex differences in behavior. *J. Ornithol.*, 148:17–26.

Adkins-Regan, E. K. 1981. Early organizational effects of hormones: An evolutionary perspective. In N. T. Adler (ed.), *Neuroendocrinology of Reproduction: Physiology and Behavior*, Plenum Press: New York, pp. 159–228.

Adkins-Regan, E., and Ascenzi, M. 1987. Social and sexual behavior of male and female zebra finches treated with estradiol during the nestling period. *Anim. Behav.*, 35:1100–1112.

Adkins-Regan, E., and Ascenzi, M. 1990. Sexual differentiation of behavior in the zebra finch: Effect of early gonadectomy or androgen treatment. *Horm. Behav.*, 24:114–127.

Adkins-Regan, E., Mansukhani, V., Thompson, R., and Yang, S. 1997. Organizational actions of sex hormones on sexual partner preference. *Brain Res. Bull.*, 44:497–502.

Adkins-Regan, E., Orgeur, P., and Signoret, J. P. 1989. Sexual differentiation of reproductive behavior in pigs: Defeminizing effects of prepubertal estradiol. *Horm. Behav.*, 23:290–303.

Adkins, E. K. 1975. Hormonal basis of sexual differentiation in the Japanese quail. *J. Comp. Physiol. Psychol.*, 89:61–71.

Adkins, E. K. 1976. Embryonic exposure to an anti-estrogen masculinizes behavior of female quail. *Physiol. Behav.*, 17:357–359.

Adkins, E. K., and Adler, N. T. 1972. Hormonal control of behavior in the Japanese quail. *J. Comp. Physiol. Psychol.*, 81:27–36.

Adkins, E. K., and Nock, B. L. 1976. The effects of the antiestrogens C1-628 on sexual behavior activated by androgen or estrogen in quail. *Horm. Behav.*, 7:417–429.

Adkins, E. K., and Pniewski, E. E. 1978. Control of reproductive behavior by sex steroids in male quail. *J. Comp. Physiol. Psychol.*, 92:1169–1178.

Adrian, T., Bloom, S., Bryant, M., Polak, J., Heitz, P., and Barnes, A. 1976. Distribution and release of human pancreatic polypeptide. *Gut*, 17:940–944.

Afonso, V. M., Grella, S. L., Chatterjee, D., and Fleming, A. S. 2008. Previous maternal experience affects accumbal dopaminergic responses to pup stimuli. *Brain Res.*, 1198:115–123.

Afonso, V. M., King, S., Chatterjee, D., and Fleming, A. S. 2009. Hormones that increase maternal responsiveness affect accumbal dopaminergic responses to pup- and food-stimuli in the female rat. *Horm. Behav.*, 56:11–23.

Afonso, V. M., Shams, W. M., Jin, D., and Fleming, A. S. 2013. Distal pup cues evoke dopamine responses in hormonally primed rats in the absence of pup experience or ongoing maternal behavior. *J. Neurosci.*, 33:2305–2312.

Agarwal, S. K., and Haney, A. F. 1994. Does recommending timed intercourse really help the infertile couple? *Obstet. Gynecol.*, 84:307–310.

Agate, R. J., Grisham, W., Wade, J., Mann, S., Wingfield, J., Schanen, C., Palotie, A., and Arnold, A. P. 2003. Neural, not gonadal, origin of brain sex differences in a gynandromorphic finch. *Proc. Natl. Acad. Sci. USA*, 100:4873–4878.

Ågmo, A. 1997. Male rat sexual behavior. *Brain Res. Brain Res. Protoc.*, 1:203–209.

Ågmo, A. 2007. *Functional and Dysfunctional Sexual Behavior: A Synthesis of Neuroscience and Comparative Psychology*. Academic Press, San Diego.

Ågmo, A. On the intricate relationship between sexual motivation and arousal. 2011. *Horm. Behav.*, 59: 681–688.

Agranoff, B. W., and Davis, R. E. 1968. The use of fishes in studies of memory formation. In D. Ingle (ed.), *The Central Nervous System and Fish Behavior*, pp. 193–202. University of Chicago Press, Chicago.

Aguzzi, A., Brandner, S., Sure, U., Ruedi, D., and Isenmann, S. 1994. Transgenic and knock-out mice: Models of neurological disease. *Brain Pathol.*, 4, 3–20.

Ahlenius, S., and Larsson, K. 1984. Apomorphine and haloperidol-induced effects on male sexual behavior: No evidence for actions due to stimulation of central dopamine autoreceptors. *Pharmacol. Biochem. Behav.*, 21:463–466.

Ainsworth, M. D. S. 1972. Attachment and dependency: A comparison. In J. L. Gerwirtz (ed.), *Attachment Dependency*, pp. 97–137. V. H. Winston, Washington, D.C.

Albers, H. E. 1981. Gonadal hormones organize and modulate the circadian system of the rat. *Am. J. Physiol.*, 241:R62–R66.

Albers, H. E., Huhman, K. L., and Meisel, R. L. 2002. Hormonal basis of social conflict and communication. In D. W. Pfaff, A. P. Arnold, A. M. Etgen, S. E. Fahrbach, and R. T. Rubin (eds.), *Hormones, Brain and Behavior*, Vol. 1, pp. 393–434. Academic Press, New York.

Albers, H. E., Yogev, L., Todd, R. B., and Goldman, B. D. 1985. Adrenal corticoids in hamsters: role in circadian timing. *Amer. J. Physiol.*, 248:R434–R439.

Albert, D. J., and Walsh, M. L. 1984. Neural systems and the inhibitory modulation of agonistic behavior: A comparison of mammalian species. *Neurosci. Biobehav. Rev.*, 8:5–24.

Albert, D. J., Petrovic, D. M., Walsh, M. L., and Jonik, R. H. 1990. Medial accumbens lesions attenuate testosterone-dependent aggression in male rats. *Physiol. Behav.*, 46:625–631.

Alberts, B., Johnson, A., Lewis, J., Raff, M., Roberts, K., and Walter, P. 2007. *Molecular Biology of the Cell* (5th ed.). Garland Scientific, New York, NY.

Alberts, J. R. 1974. Producing and interpreting experimental olfactory deficits. *Comp. Biochem. Physiol.*, 40A:971–974.

Alberts, J. R., and Brunjes, P. C. 1978. Ontogeny of thermal and olfactory determinants of huddling in the rat. *J. Comp. Physiol. Psychol.*, 92:897–906.

Alberts, J. R., and Galef, B. G. 1971. Acute anosmia in the rat: A behavioral test of a peripherally induced olfactory deficit. *Physiol. Behav.*, 12:657–670.

Alberts, J. R., and Gubernick, D. J. 1990. Functional organization of dyadic and triadic parent–offspring systems. In N. A. Krasnegor and R. S. Bridges (eds.), *Mammalian Parenting*, pp. 416–440. Oxford University Press, Oxford.

Alcock, J. 2013. *Animal Behavior: An Evolutionary Approach*. (10th ed.). Sinauer Associates, Sunderland, MA.

Alekseyenko, O. V., Waters, P., Zhou, H., and Baum, M. J. 2007. Bilateral damage to the sexually dimorphic medial preoptic area/anterior hypothalamus of male ferrets causes a female-typical preference for and a hypothalamic *Fos* response to male body odors. *Physiol. Behav.*, 23:438–449.

Alexander, G. M. 2003. An evolutionary perspective of sex-typed toy preferences: Pink, blue, and the brain. *Arch. Sexual Behav.*, 32:7–14.

Alexander, G. M., and Hines, M. 2002. Sex differences in response to children's toys in nonhuman primates (*Cercopithecus aethiops sabaeus*). *Evol. Hum. Behav.*, 23:467–479.

Alexander, G. M., Swerdloff, R. S., Wang, C., Davidson, T., McDonald, V., Steiner, B., and Hines, M. 1998. Androgen-behavior correlations in hypogonadal men and eugonadal men. II. Cognitive abilities. *Horm. Behav.*, 33:85–94.

Alexander, G. M., Wilcox, T., and Woods, R. 2009. Sex differences in infants' visual interest in toys. *Arch. Sex. Behav.*, 38:427–433.

Alexander, R. 1974. The evolution of social behavior. *Annu. Rev. Ecol. Syst.*, 5:325–383.

Alexander, R. D., Hoogland, J. L., Howard, R. D., Noonan, K. M., and Sherman, P. W. 1979. Sexual dimorphisms and breeding systems in pinnipeds, ungulates, primates and humans. In N. A. Chagnon and W. Irons (eds.), *Evolutionary Biology and Human Social Behavior*, pp. 402–435. Duxbury Press, North Scituate, MA.

Algers, B., and Uvnäs-Moberg, K. 2007. Maternal behavior in pigs. *Horm. Behav.*, 52:78–85.

Allen, L. S., Hines, M., Shryne, J. E., and Gorski, R. A. 1989. Two sexually dimorphic cell groups in the human brain. *J. Neurosci.*, 9:497–506.

Allen, L. S., Richey, M. F., Chai, Y. M., and Gorski, R. A. 1991. Sex differences in the corpus callosum of the living human being. *J. Neurosci.*, 11:933–942.

Allison, K. C., Ahima, R. S., O'Reardon, J. P., Dinges, D. F., Sharma, V., and Cummings, D. E., 2005. Neuroendocrine profiles associated with energy intake, sleep, and stress in the night eating syndrome. *J. Clin. Endocrinol. Metab.*, 90:6214–6217.

Allsop, D. J., and West, S. A. 2003. Life history: Changing sex at the same relative body size. *Nature*, 425:783–784.

Alon, T., and Friedman, J. M. 2006. Late-onset leanness in mice with targeted ablation of melanin concentrating hormone neurons. *J. Neurosci.*, 26:389–397.

Altemus, M., Hetherington, M., Kennedy, B., Licinio, J., and Gold, P. W. 1996. Thyroid function in bulimia nervosa. *Psychoneuroendocrinol.*, 21:249–261.

Altmann, J. 1980. *Baboon Mothers and Infants*. Harvard University Press, Cambridge, MA.

Alzado, L. "I'm Sick and I'm Scared," *Sports Illustrated*, July 8, 1991. http://sportsillustrated.cnn.com/vault/article/magazine/MAG1139729/index.htm. Accessed April 28, 2011.

Amalric, M., Cline, E. J., Martinez, J. L., Bloom, F. E., and Koob, G. F. 1987. Rewarding properties of β-endorphin as measured by conditioned place preference. *Psychopharmacol.*, 91:14–19.

Ambar, G., and Chiavegatto, S. 2009. Anabolic-androgenic steroid treatment induces behavioral disinhibition and downregulation of serotonin receptor messenger RNA in the prefrontal cortex and amygdala of male mice. *Genes, Brain Behav.*, 8:161–173.

Amdaoud, M., Vallade, M., Weiss-Schaber, C., and Mihalcescu, I. 2007. Cyanobacterial clock, a stable phase oscillator with negligible intercellular coupling. *Proc. Natl. Acad. Sci. USA*, 104:7051–7056.

American Psychiatric Association. 1994. *Diagnostic and Statistical Manual of Mental Disorders: DSM-IV*. (4th ed.) American Psychiatric Association, Washington, D.C.

American Psychiatric Association. 2013. *Diagnostic and Statistical Manual of Mental Disorders: DSM-5*. (5th ed.) American Psychiatric Association, Washington, DC.

Amiel, S. A., and Gale, E. 1993. Physiological responses to hypoglycemia. Counterregulation and cognitive function. *Diabetes Care*, 16:48–55.

Ammar, A. A., Nergardh, R., Fredholm, B. B., Brodin, U., and Södersten, P. 2005. Intake inhibition by NPY and CCK-8: A challenge of the notion of NPY as an "Orexigen." *Behav. Brain Res.*, 161:82–87.

Ammar, A. A., Sederholm, F., Saito, T. R., Scheurink, A. J. W., Johnson, A. E., and Södersten, P. 2000. NPY-leptin: Opposing effects on appetitive and consummatory ingestive behavior and sexual behavior. *Am. J. Physiol.*, 278:R1627–R1633.

Anacker, A. M., and Beery, A. K. 2013. Life in groups: The roles of oxytocin in mammalian sociality. *Front. Behav. Neurosci.*, 7:185.

Anagnostaras, S. G., Maren, S., DeCola, J. P., Lane, N. I., Gale, G. D., Schlinger, B. A., and Fanselow, M. S. 1998. Testicular hormones do not regulate sexually dimorphic Pavlovian fear conditioning or perforant-path long-term potentiation in adult male rats. *Behav. Brain Res.*, 92:1–9.

Anand, B. K., and Brobeck, J. R. 1951. Localization of a feeding center in the hypothalamus of the rat. *Proc. Soc. Exp. Biol. Med.,* 77:323–324.

Anastasi, A., Erspamer, V., and Bucci, M. 1971. Isolation and structure of bombesin and alytesin, 2 analogous active peptides from the skin of the European amphibians *Bombina* and *Alytes. Experientia,* 27:123–140.

Anderson, R. A., Bancroft, J., and Wu, F. C. W. 1992. The effects of exogenous testosterone on sexuality and mood of normal men. *J. Clin. Endocrinol. Metab.,* 75:1503–1507.

Andersson, M. 1994. *Sexual Selection.* Princeton University Press, Princeton.

Andreano, J. M., and Cahill, L. 2006. Glucocorticoid release and memory consolidation in men and women. *Psychol. Sci.,* 17:466–470.

Angelier, F., Clement-Chastel, C., Welcker, J., Gabrielsen, G. W., and Chastel, O. 2009. How does corticosterone affect parental behaviour and reproductive success? A study of prolactin in black-legged kittiwakes. *Funct. Ecol.,* 23:784–793.

Angelier, F., Wingfield, J. C., Tartu, S., and Chastel, O. 2016. Does prolactin mediate parental and life-history decisions in response to environmental conditions in birds? A review. *Horm. Behav.,* 77:18–29.

Angelier, F., Wingfield, J. C., Trouvé, C., de Grissac, S., and Chastel, O. 2013. Modulation of the prolactin and corticosterone stress responses: do they tell the same story in a longlived bird, the Cape petrel? *Gen. Comp. Endocrinol.,* 182:7–16.

Anim-Nyame, N., Domoney, C., Panay, N., Jones, J., Alaghband-Zadeh, J., and Studd, J. W. 2000. Plasma leptin concentrations are increased in women with premenstrual syndrome. *Human Reprod.,* 15:2329–2332.

Anonymous. 1970. Effects of sexual activity on beard growth in man. *Nature,* 226:869–870.

Ansel, L., Bentsen, A. H., Ancel, C., Bolborea, M., Klosen, P., Mikkelsen, J. D., and Simonneaux, V. 2011. Peripheral kisspeptin reverses short photoperiod-induced gonadal regression in Syrian hamsters by promoting GNRH release. *Reproduction,* 142:417–425.

Anway, M. D., and Skinner, M. K. 2006. Epigenetic transgenerational actions of endocrine disruptors. *Endocrinol.,* 147:S43–49.

Aoyama, H., Mori, W., and Mori, N. 1986. Anti-glucocorticoid effects of melatonin in young rats. *Acta Pathologica Japonica,* 36:423–428.

Aoyama, H., Mori, W., and Mori, N. 1987. Anti-glucocorticoid effects of melatonin in adult rats. *Acta Pathologica Japonica,* 37:1143–1148.

Applezweig, M. H., and Baudry, F. D. 1955. The pituitary–adrenocortical system in avoidance learning. *Psychol. Rep.,* 1:417–420.

Applezweig, M. H., and Moeller, G. 1959. The pituitary–adrenocortical system and

anxiety in avoidance learning. *Acta Psychol.,* 15:602–603.

Apter-Levi, Y., Zagoory-Sharon, O., and Feldman, R. 2014. Oxytocin and vasopressin support distinct configurations of social synchrony. *Brain Res.,* 1580:124–132.

Arai, A., Taniguchi, I., and Saito, N. 1989. Correlation between the size of song control nuclei and plumage color change in orange bishop birds. *Neurosci. Lett.,* 98:144–148.

Arase, K., York, D. A., Shimizu, H., Shargill, N., and Bray, G. A. 1988. Effects of corticotropin-releasing factor on food intake and brown adipose tissue thermogenesis in rats. *Am. J. Physiol.,* 255:E255–E259.

Arble, D. M., Bass, J., Laposky, A. D., Vitateman, M. H., and Turek, F. W. 2009. Circadian timing of food intake contributes to weight gain. *Obesity,* 27:2100–2102.

Archer, J. 1991. The influence of testosterone on human aggression. *British J. Psych.,* 62:1–28.

Archer, J. 2006. Testosterone and human aggression: An evaluation of the challenge hypothesis. *Neurosci. Biobehav. Rev.,* 30:319–345.

Archer, S. N., Robilliard, D. L., Skene, D. J., Smits, M., Williams, A., Arendt, J., and von Schantz, M. 2003. A length polymorphism in the circadian clock gene *PER3* is linked to delayed sleep phase syndrome and extreme diurnal preference. *Sleep,* 26:413–415.

Arendash, G. W., and Gorski, R. A. 1983. Effects of discrete lesions of the sexually dimorphic nucleus of the preoptic area or other medial preoptic regions on the sexual behavior of male rats. *Brain Res. Bull.,* 10:147–150.

Arendt, J. 1997. Safety of melatonin long-term use. *J. Biol. Rhythms,* 12:673–681.

Arendt, J. 1998. Melatonin and the pineal gland: Influence on mammalian seasonal and circadian physiology. *Rev. Reprod.,* 3:13–22.

Areosa, S. A., and Grimley, E. V. 2002. Effect of the treatment of type II diabetes mellitus on the development of cognitive impairment and dementia. *Cochrane Database of Systematic Reviews,* CD003804.

Arnold, A. P. 2002. Concepts of genetic and hormonal induction of vertebrate sexual differentiation in the twentieth century, with special reference to the brain. In D. W. Pfaff, A. P. Arnold, A. M. Etgen, S. E. Fahrbach, and R. T. Rubin (eds.), *Hormones, Brain, and Behavior,* Vol. 4, pp. 105–135. Academic Press, New York.

Arnold, A. P. 2009. The organizational-activational hypothesis as the foundation for a unified theory of sexual differentiation of all mammalian tissues. *Horm. Behav.,* 55:570–578. doi:10.1016/j.yhbeh.2009.03.011.

Arnold, A. P. 2012. The end of gonad-centric sex determination in mammals. *Trends Genet.,* 28:55–61.

Arnold, A. P., and Breedlove, S. M. 1985. Organizational and activational effects of sex steroid hormones on vertebrate brain and behavior: A re-analysis. *Horm. Behav.,* 19:469–498.

Arnold, A. P., and Gorski, R. A. 1984. Gonadal steroid induction of structural sex differences in the CNS. *Annu. Rev. Neurosci.,* 7:413–442.

Arnold, A. P., and Jordan, C. L. 1988. Hormonal organization of neural circuits. *Front. Neuroendocrinol.,* 10:185–214.

Arnold, A. P., and Matthews, G. 1988. Sexual differentiation of brain and behavior in birds. In J. M. A. Sitsen (ed.), *Handbook of Sexology, Vol. 6: The Pharmacology and Endocrinology of Sexual Function,* pp. 122–144. Elsevier, New York.

Arnold, A. P., Bottjer, S. W., Brenowitz, E. A., Nordeen, E. J., and Nordeen, K. W. 1987. Sexual dimorphisms in the neural vocal control system in song birds: Ontogeny and phylogeny. *Brain Behav. Evol.,* 28:22–31.

Arnold, A. P., Xu, J., Grisham, W., Chen, X., Kim, Y.-H., and Itoh, Y. 2004. Minireview: Sex chromosomes and brain sexual differentiation. *Endocrinol.,* 145:1057–1062.

Aschoff, J. 1965. Circadian rhythms in man: A self-sustained oscillator with an inherent frequency underlies human 24-hour periodicity. *Science,* 148:1427–1432.

Aschoff, J. 1981. Annual rhythms in man. In J. Aschoff (ed.), *Handbook of Behavioral Neurobiology,* Vol. 4, pp. 475–490. Plenum Press, New York.

Aste, N., Cozzi, B., Stankov, B., and Panzica, G. 2001. Sexual differences and effect of photoperiod on melatonin receptor in avian brain. *Microscopy Research and Technique,* 55:37–47.

Astur, R. S., Ortiz, M. L., and Sutherland, R. J. 1998. A characterization of performance by men and women in a virtual Morris water task: A large and reliable sex difference. *Behavioural Brain Res.,* 93:185–190.

Astur, R. S., Tropp, J., Sava, S., Constable, R. T., and Markus, E. J. 2004. Sex differences and correlations in a virtual Morris water task, a virtual radial arm maze, and mental rotation. *Behavioural Brain Res.,* 151:103–115.

Aubele, T., Kaufman, R., Montalmant, F., and Kritzer, M. F. 2008. Effects of gonadectomy and hormone replacement on a spontaneous novel object recognition task in adult male rats. *Horm. Behav.,* 54:244–252.

Auger, A. P., Tetel, M. J., and McCarthy, M. M. 2000. Steroid receptor coactivator-1 (SRC-1) mediates the development of sex-specific brain morphology and behavior. *Proc. Natl. Acad. Sci. USA,* 97:7551–7555.

Aujard, F., Herzog, E. D., and Block, G. D. 2001. Circadian rhythms in firing rate of individual suprachiasmatic nucleus neurons from adult and middle-aged mice. *Neuroscience,* 106:255–261.

Bacanu, S. A., Bulik, C. M., Klump, K. L., Fichter, M. M., Halmi, K. A., Keel, P., Kaplan, A. S., Mitchell, J. E., Rotondo, A., Strober, M., Treasure, J., Woodside, D. B., Sonpar, V. A., Xie, W., Bergen, A. W., Berrettini, W. H., Kaye, W. H., and Devlin, B. 2005. Linkage analysis of anorexia and bulimia nervosa cohorts using selected behavioral phenotypes as quantitative traits or covariates. *Am. J. Med. Genet. B. Neuropsychiatric Genet.*, 139B:61–68.

Backstrom, T., Sanders, D., Leask, R., Davidson, D., Warner, P., and Bancroft, J. 1983. Mood, sexuality, hormones, and the menstrual cycle. II. Hormone levels and their relationship to the premenstrual syndrome. *Psychosomat. Med.*, 45:503–507.

Badura, L. L., and Goldman, B. D. 1992. Central sites mediating reproductive responses to melatonin in juvenile male Siberian hamsters. *Brain Res.*, 598:98–106.

Badura, L. L., and Nunez, A. A. 1989. Photoperiodic modulation of sexual and aggressive behavior in female golden hamsters (*Mesocricetus auratus*): Role of the pineal gland. *Horm. Behav.*, 23:27–42.

Badura, L. L., Yant, W. R., and Nunez, A. A. 1987. Photoperiodic modulation of steroid-induced lordosis in golden hamsters. *Physiol. Behav.*, 40:551–554.

Bae, H. H., Mangels, R. A., Cho, B. S., Dark, J., Yellon, S. M., and Zucker, I. 1999. Ventromedial hypothalamic mediation of photoperiodic gonadal responses in male Syrian hamsters. *J. Biol. Rhythms*, 14:391–401.

Bailey, D.J. and Saldanha, C.J. 2015. The importance of neural aromatization in the acquisition, recall, and integration of song and spatial memories in passerines. *Hormones and Behavior*, 74:116–124.

Bailey, D.J., Ma, C., Soma, K.K. and Saldanha, C.J. 2013. Inhibition of hippocampal aromatization impairs spatial memory performance in a male songbird. *Endocrinology*, 154:4707–4714.

Bailey, D.J., Wade, J., and Saldanha, C.J. 2009. Hippocampal lesions impair spatial memory performance, but not song—A developmental study of independent memory systems in the zebra finch. *Developmental Neurobiology*, 69:491–504.

Bailey, J. M., and Pillard, R. C. 1991. A genetic study of male sexual orientation. *Arch. Gen. Psychiatry*, 48:1089–1096.

Bailey, M. and Silver, R. 2014. Sex differences in circadian timing systems: implications for disease. *Front. Neuroendocrinol.*, 35:111–139.

Bairy, L. K. 2013. Chronotherapeutics: A hype or future of chronopharmacology? *Indian J. Pharmacol.*, 45:545–546.

Baker, J. R. 1938. The evolution of breeding seasons. In J. DeBeer (ed.), *Evolution*, pp. 161–177. Clarendon Press, Oxford.

Baker, M. C., Bottjer, S. W., and Arnold, A. P. 1984. Sexual dimorphism and lack of

seasonal changes in vocal control regions of the white-crowned sparrow brain. *Brain Res.*, 295:85–89.

Bakermans-Kranenburg, M., and van Ijzendoorn, M. 2008. Oxytocin receptor (OXTR) and serotonin transporter (5-HTT) genes associated with observed parenting. *Soc. Cognit. Affect. Neurosci.*, 3:128–134.

Bakker, J., Baillien, M., Honda, S., Harada, N., and Balthazart, J. 2004. Relationships between aromatase activity in the brain and gonads and behavioural deficits in homozygous and heterozygous aromatase knockout mice. *J. Neuroendocrinol.*, 16:483–490.

Bakker, J., De Mees, C., Douhard, Q., Balthazart, J., Gabant, P., Szpirer, J., and Szpirer, C. 2006. Alpha-fetoprotein protects the developing female mouse brain from masculinization and defeminization by estrogens. *Nat. Neurosci.*, 9:220–226.

Bakker, J., Honda, S., Harada, N., and Balthazart, J. 2002. The aromatase-knockout mouse provides new evidence that estradiol is required during development in the female for the expression of sociosexual behaviors in adulthood. *J. Neurosci.*, 22:9104–9112.

Baldwin, D. S., Palazzo, M. C., and Masdrakis, V. G. 2013. Reduced treatment-emergent sexual dysfunction as a potential target in the development of new antidepressants. *Depress. Res. Treat.*, 2013: 256841. doi:10.1155/2013/256841.

Baldwin, J. D. 1968. The social behavior of adult male squirrel monkeys (*Saimiri sciureus*) in a semi-natural environment. *Folia Primatol.*, 9:281–314.

Bales, K. L. and Saltzman, W. 2016. Fathering in rodents: Neurobiological substrates and consequences for offspring. *Horm. Behav.*, 77:249–259.

Bales, K. L., Kim, A. J., Lewis-Reese, A. D, and Carter, C. S. 2004. Both oxytocin and vasopressin may influence alloparental care in male prairie voles. *Horm. Behav.*, 45:354–361.

Balfour, M. E., Yu, L., and Coolen, L. M. 2004. Sexual behavior and sex-associated environmental cues activate the mesolimbic system in male rats. *Neuropsychopharmacol.*, 29:718–730.

Ball, G. F. 1991. Endocrine mechanisms and the evolution of avian parental care. *Acta XX Congressus Internationalis Ornithologici*, pp. 984–991.

Ball, G. F. and Silver, R. 1983. Timing of incubation bouts by ring doves (*Streptopelia risoria*). *J. Comp. Psychol.*, 97:213–225.

Ball, G. F., and Balthazart, J. 2002. Neuroendocrine mechanisms regulating reproductive cycles and reproductive behavior in birds. In D. W. Pfaff, A. P. Arnold, A. M. Etgen, S. E. Fahrbach, and R. T. Rubin (eds.), *Hormones, Brain and Behavior*, Vol. 2, pp. 649–798. Academic Press, New York.

Ball, G. F., and Balthazart, J. 2004. Hormonal regulation of brain circuits mediating male sexual behavior in birds. *Physiol. Behav.*, 83:329–346.

Ball, G. F., and Balthazart, J. 2008. How useful is the appetitive and consummatory distinction for our understanding of the neuroendocrine control of sexual behavior? *Horm. Behav.*, 53:307–311.

Ball, G. F., and Balthazart, J. 2010. Seasonal and hormonal modulation of neurotransmitter systems in the song control circuit. *J. Chem. Neuroanat.*, 39:82–95.

Ball, J. 1934a. Normal sex behavior in the rat after total extirpation of the vasa deferentia. *Anat. Rec.*, 58:49.

Ball, J. 1937. Sex activity of castrated male rats increased by estrin administration. *J. Comp. Psychol.*, 24:135–144.

Ballard, C. L., and Wood, R. I. 2005. Male hamsters self-administer commonly abused androgens. *Behav. Neurosci.*, 119:752–758.

Balsalobre, A., Brown, S. A., Marcacci, L., Tronche, F., Kellendonk, C., Reichardt, H. M., Schutz, G., and Schibler, U. 2000. Resetting of circadian time in peripheral tissues by glucocorticoid signaling. *Science*, 289:2344–2347.

Balthazart, J. 1989. Steroid metabolism and the activation of social behavior. In J. Balthazart (ed.), *Advances in Comparative and Environmental Physiology*, Vol. 3, pp. 105–159. Springer, Berlin.

Balthazart, J., and Adkins-Regan, E. 2002. Sexual differentiation of brain and behavior in birds. In D. W. Pfaff, A. P. Arnold, A. M. Etgen, S. E. Fahrbach, and R. T. Rubin (eds.), *Hormones, Brain and Behavior*, Vol. 4, pp. 223–301. Academic Press, New York.

Balthazart, J., and Ball, G. F. 1992. Is dopamine interacting with aromatase to control sexual behavior in male quail? *Poultry Sci. Rev.*, 4:217–233.

Balthazart, J., and Ball, G. F. 1993. Neurochemical differences in two steroid sensitive areas mediating reproductive behaviors. In R. Gilles (ed.), *Advances in Comparative and Environmental Physiology*, pp. 133–161. Springer-Verlag, New York.

Balthazart, J., and Ball, G. F. 1995. Sexual differentiation of brain and behavior in birds. *Trends Endocrinol. Metab.* 6:21–29.

Balthazart, J., and Ball, G. F. 1998. New insights into the regulation and function of brain estrogen synthase (aromatase). *Trends Neurosci.*, 21:243–249.

Balthazart, J., and Ball, G. F. 2007. Topography in the preoptic region: Differential regulation of appetitive and consummatory male sexual behaviors. *Front. Neuroendocrinol.*, 28:161–178.

Balthazart, J., and Foidart, A. 1993. Neural bases of behavioral sex differences in the quail. In M. Haug (ed.), *The Development of Sex Differences and Similarities in Behavior*, pp. 51–75. Kluwer Academic Publishers, Amsterdam.

Balthazart, J., Arnold, A. P., Adkins-Regan, E. 2009. Sexual differentiation of brain and behavior in birds, In D. W. Pfaff, A. P. Arnold, S. E. Fahrbach, A. M. Etgen and R.T. Rubin, (eds.), *Hormones, Brain and Behavior* (2nd. ed.), pp. 1745–1787. Academic Press, San Diego.

Balthazart, J., Baillien, M., Cornil., C. A., and Ball, G. F. 2004. Preoptic aromatase modulates male sexual behavior: Slow and fast mechanisms of action. *Physiol. Behav.*, 83:247–270.

Balthazart, J., Dupiereux, V., Aste, N., Viglietti-Panzica, C., Barrese, M., and Panzica, G. C. 1994. Afferent and efferent connections of the sexually dimorphic medial preoptic nucleus of the male quail revealed by in vitro transport of DiI. *Cell Tiss. Res.*, 276:455–475.

Balthazart, J., Foidart, A., Wilson, E. M., and Ball, G. F. 1992. Immunocytochemical localization of androgen receptors in the male songbird and quail brain. *J. Comp. Neurol.*, 317:407–420.

Bancroft, J. 1978. The relationship between hormones and sexual behaviour in humans. In J. B. Hutchison (ed.), *Biological Determinants of Sexual Behaviour*, pp. 493–519. New York, Wiley.

Bao, A. M., Ji, Y. F., Van Someren, E. J., Hofman, M. A., Liu, R. Y., and Zhou, J. N. 2004. Diurnal rhythms of free estradiol and cortisol during the normal menstrual cycle in women with major depression. *Horm. Behav.*, 45:93–102.

Barbarino, A., DeMarinis, L., and Mancini, A. 1983. Estradiol modulation of basal and gonadotropin-releasing hormone–induced gonadotropin release in intact and castrated men. *Neuroendocrinol.*, 36:105–111.

Barker, S. 1987. Oxymethalone and aggression. *Br. J. Psychiatry*, 151:564–565.

Barkley, M. S., and Goldman, B. D. 1977. A quantitative study of serum testosterone, sex accessory organ weight growth and the development of intermale aggression in the mouse. *Horm. Behav.*, 9:21–48.

Barkley, M. S., Geschwind, I. I., and Bradford, G. E. 1979. The gestational pattern of estradiol, testosterone, and progesterone secretion in selected strains of mice. *Biol. Reprod.*, 20:733–738.

Barnea, A. 2009. Interactions between environmental changes and brain plasticity in birds. *Gen. Comp. Endocrinol.*, 163:128–134.

Barnea, A., and Nottebohm, F. 1996. Recruitment and replacement of hippocampal neurons in young and adult chickadees: An addition to the theory of hippocampal learning. *Proc. Natl. Acad. Sci. USA*, 93:714–718.

Barnett, S.A. 1956. Behaviour of wild rats in the laboratory. *Med. Biol. Illus.*, 6:104–111.

Barr, C. S., Dvoskin, R. L., Gupte, M., Sommer, W., Sun, H., Schwandt, M. L., Lindell, S. G., et al. 2009. Functional CRH variation increases stress-induced alcohol consumption in primates. *Proc. Natl. Acad. Sci. USA*, 106:14593–14598.

Barreiro, M. L., and Tena-Sempere, M. 2004. Ghrelin and reproduction: A novel signal linking energy status and fertility? *Mol. Cell. Endocrinol.*, 226:1–9.

Barrett, P., Ebling, F. J., Schuhler, S., Wilson, D., Ross, A. W., Warner, A., Jethwa, P. et al. 2007. Hypothalamic thyroid hormone catabolism acts as a gatekeeper for the seasonal control of body weight and reproduction. *Endocrinology*, 148:3608–3617.

Barrios, A. Ghosh, R., Fang, C., Emmons, S. W., and Barr, M. M. 2012. PDF-1 neuropeptide signaling modulates a neural circuit for mate-searching behavior in C. elegans. *Nat. Neurosci.*, 15:1675–1682.

Bartels, A., and Zeki, S. 2000. The neural basis of romantic love. *Neuroreport*, 11:3829–3834.

Bartels, A., and Zeki, S. 2004. The neural correlates of maternal and romantic love. *NeuroImage*, 21:1155–1166.

Bartley, E. J., Palit, S., Kuhn, B. L., Kerr, K. L., Terry, E. L., DelVentura, J. L., and Rhudy, J. L. 2015. Natural variation in testosterone is associated with hypoalgesia in healthy women. *Clin. J. Pain*, 31:730–739.

Bartness, T. J., and Clein, M. R. 1994. Effects of food deprivation and restriction, and metabolic blockers on food hoarding in Siberian hamsters. *Am. J. Physiol.*, 266:R1111–R1117.

Bartness, T. J., and Goldman, B. D. 1988a. Peak duration of serum melatonin and short-day responses in adult Siberian hamsters. *Am. J. Physiol.*, 255:R812–R822.

Bartness, T. J., and Goldman, B. D. 1988b. Effects of melatonin on long-day responses in short-day housed adult Siberian hamsters. *Am. J. Physiol.*, 255:R823–R830.

Bartness, T. J., and Goldman, B. D. 1989. Mammalian pineal melatonin: A clock for all seasons. *Experientia*, 45:939–945.

Bartness, T. J., and Wade, G. N. 1985. Photoperiodic control of seasonal body weight cycles in hamsters. *Neurosci. Biobehav. Rev.*, 9:599–612.

Bartness, T. J., Goldman, B. D., and Bittman, E. L. 1991. SCN lesions block responses to systemic melatonin infusions in Siberian hamsters. *Amer. J. Physiol.*, 260:R102–R112.

Bartness, T. J., Powers, J. B., Hastings, M. H., Bittman, E. L., and Goldman, B. D. 1993. The timed infusion paradigm for melatonin delivery: what has it taught us about the melatonin signal, its reception, and the photoperiodic control of seasonal responses? *J. Pineal Res.*, 15:161–190.

Bartness, T. J., Powers, J. B., Hastings, M. H., Bittman, E. L., and Goldman, B. D. 1993. The timed infusion paradigm for melatonin delivery: what has it taught us about the melatonin signal, its reception, and the photoperiodic control of seasonal responses? *J. Pineal Res.*, 15:161–190.

Baskin, D. G., Sipols, A. J., Schwartz, M. W., and White, M. F. 1994. Insulin receptor substrate-1 (IRS-1) expression in the rat brain. *Endocrinol.*, 134:1952–1955.

Bass, A. H. 1995. Alternative life history strategies and dimorphic males in an acoustic communication system. *Fifth International Symposium on Reproductive Physiology in Fish*, pp. 258–260. Austin, TX.

Bass, A. H. 1996. Shaping brain sexuality. *Am. Sci.*, 84:352–364.

Bass, A. H., and Remage-Healey, L. 2008. Central pattern generators for social vocalization: Androgen-dependent neurophysiological mechanisms. *Horm. Behav.*, 53:659–672.

Bast, J. D., and Greenwald, G. S. 1977. Acute and chronic elevation in serum levels of FSH after unilateral ovariectomy in the cyclic hamster. *Endocrinol.*, 100:955–966.

Bastida, C. C., Gonzalez-Lima, F., Jennings, K. J., Wommack, J. C., and Delville, Y. 2014. Chronic social stress in puberty alters appetitive male sexual behavior and neural metabolic activity. *Horm. Behav.*, 66:220–227.

Bateman, A. J. 1948. Intra-sexual selection in *Drosophila. Heredity*, 2:349–368.

Batterham, R. L., Cohen, M. A., Ellis, S. M., Le Roux, C. W., Withers, D. J., Frost, G. S., Ghatei, M. A., and Bloom, S. R. 2003. Inhibition of food intake in obese subjects by peptide YY$_{3-36}$. *N. Engl. J. Med.*, 349:941–948.

Batty, J. 1978. Acute changes in plasma testosterone levels and their relation to measures of sexual behaviour in the male house mouse (*Mus musculus*). *Anim. Behav.*, 26:349–357.

Baulieu, E. E. 1998. Neurosteroids: A novel function of the brain. *Psychoneuroendocrinol.*, 23:963–987.

Baum, M. J. and Kelliher, K. R. 2009. Complementary roles of the main and accessory olfactory systems in mammalian mate recognition. *Annu. Rev. Physiol.*, 71:141–160.

Baum, M. J., Brand, T., Ooms, M., Vreeburg, J. T. M., and Slob, A. K. 1988. Immediate postnatal rise in whole body androgen content in male rats: Correlation with increased testicular content and reduced body clearance of testosterone. *Biol. Reprod.*, 38:980–986.

Beach, F. 1978. Animal models for human sexuality. *Ciba Foundation Symp.*, 62:113–43.

Beach, F. A. 1937. The neural basis of innate behavior: I. Effects of cortical lesions upon the maternal behavior pattern in the rat. *J. Comp. Psychol.*, 24:393–436.

Beach, F. A. 1942a. Analysis of factors involved in the arousal, maintenance and manifestation of sexual excitement in male animals. *Psychosom. Med.*, 4:173–198.

Beach, F. A. 1942b. Analysis of the stimuli adequate to elicit mating behavior in the sexually inexperienced male rat. *J. Comp. Psychol.*, 33:163–207.

Beach, F. A. 1942c. Copulatory behavior in prepuberally castrated male rats and its modification by estrogen administration. *Endocrinol.*, 31:679–683.

Beach, F. A. 1942d. Importance of progesterone to induction of sexual receptivity in spayed female rats. *Proc. Soc. Exp. Biol. Med.*, 51:369–371.

Beach, F. A. 1944b. Relative effects of androgen upon mating behavior in male rats subjected to castration or forebrain injury. *J. Exp. Zool.*, 97:249–285.

Beach, F. A. 1947. Evolutionary changes in the physiological control of mating behavior in mammals. *Psychol. Rev.*, 54:297–315.

Beach, F. A. 1948. *Hormones and Behavior.* Paul B. Hoeber, New York.

Beach, F. A. 1956. Characteristics of masculine "sex drive." *Nebr. Symp. Motiv.* 4:1–32.

Beach, F. A. 1967. Cerebral and hormonal control of reflexive mechanisms involved in copulatory behavior. *Physiol. Rev.*, 47:289–316.

Beach, F. A. 1968. Factors involved in the control of mounting behavior by female mammals. In M. Diamond (ed.), *Perspectives in Reproduction and Sexual Behavior: A Memorial to William C. Young*, pp. 83–131, Indiana University Press, Bloomington.

Beach, F. A. 1970. Hormonal effects on sociosexual behavior in dogs. In M. Gibian and E. J. Plotz (eds.), *Mammalian Reproduction*, pp. 437–466. Springer-Verlag, Berlin.

Beach, F. A. 1974a. Behavioral endocrinology and the study of repro-duction. *Biol. Reprod.*, 10:2–18.

Beach, F. A. 1975. Hormonal modification of sexually dimorphic behavior. *Psychoneuroendocrinol.*, 1:3–23.

Beach, F. A. 1976. Sexual attractivity, proceptivity, and receptivity in female mammals. *Horm. Behav.*, 7:105–138.

Beach, F. A. 1981. Histological origins of modern research on hormones and behavior. *Horm. Behav.*, 15:325–376.

Beach, F. A. 1984. Hormone modulation of genital reflexes in male and masculinized female dogs. *Behav. Neurosci.*, 98, 325–332.

Beach, F. A., and Buehler, M. G. 1977. Male rats with inherited insensitivity to androgen show reduced sexual behavior. *Endocrinol.*, 100:197–200.

Beach, F. A., and Gilmore, R. W. 1949. Response of male dogs to urine from females in heat. *J. Mammal.*, 30:391–392.

Beach, F. A., and Holz-Tucker, M. 1949. Effects of different concentrations of androgen upon sexual behavior in castrated male rats. *J. Comp. Physiol. Psychol.*, 42:433–453.

Beach, F. A., and Inman, B. G. 1965. Effects of castration and androgen replacement on mating in male quail. *Proc. Natl. Acad. Sci. USA*, 54:1426–1431.

Beach, F. A., and Jaynes, J. 1956. Studies on maternal retrieving in rats: II. Effects of practice and previous parturitions. *Amer. Nat.*, 90:103–109.

Beach, F. A., and Jordan, L. 1956. Sexual exhaustion and recovery in the male rat. *Q. J. Exp. Psychol.*, 8:121–133.

Beach, F. A., and LeBoeuf, B. J. 1967. Coital behaviour in dogs. I. Preferential mating in the bitch. *Anim. Behav.*, 15:546–558.

Beach, F. A., and Merari, A. 1968. Coital behavior in dogs. IV. Effects of progesterone in the bitch. *Proc. Natl. Acad. Sci. USA*, 61:442–444.

Beach, F. A., and Merari, A. 1970. Coital behavior in dogs. V. Effects of estrogen and progesterone on mating and other forms of social behavior in the bitch. *J. Comp. Physiol. Psychol. Monogr.*, 70:1–49.

Beach, F. A., Buehler, M. G., and Dunbar, I. F. 1983. Sexual cycles in female dogs treated with androgen during development. *Behav. Neural Biol.*, 38:1–31.

Beach, F. A., Kuehn, R. E., Sprague, R. H., and Anisko, J. J. 1972. Coital behavior in dogs. XI. Effects of androgen stimulation during development on masculine mating response in females. *Horm. Behav.*, 3:143–168.

Beasley, L. J., and Nelson, R. J. 1982. Thyroid gland influences the period of hamster circadian oscillations. *Experientia*, 38:870–871.

Beatty, W. W. 1979. Gonadal hormones and sex differences in nonreproductive behaviors in rodents: Organizational and activational influences. *Horm. Behav.*, 12:112–163.

Beauchamp, G. K., Magnus, J. G., Shmunes, N. T., and Durham, T. 1977. Effects of olfactory bulbectomy on social behavior of male guinea pigs (*Cavia porcellus*). *J. Comp. Physiol. Psychol.*, 91:336–346.

Beaver, K. M., Vaughn, M. G., DeLisi, M., and Wright, J. P. 2008. Anabolic-androgenic steroid use and involvement in violent behavior in a nationally representative sample of young adult males in the United States. *Am. J. Public Health*, 98:2185–2187.

Beck, A. T., Ward, C. H., Mendelson, M., Mock, J., and Erbaugh, J. 1961. An inventory for measuring depression. *Arch. Gen. Psychiatry*, 4:561–571.

Beck, K. D., and Luine, V. N. 2002. Sex differences in behavioral and neurochemical profiles after chronic stress: Role of housing conditions. *Physiol. Behav.*, 75:611–673.

Becker, S. 1981. Seasonality of fertility in Matlab, Bangladesh. *J. Biosocial Sci.*, 13:97–105.

Bedrosian, T. A, and Nelson, R. J. 2014. Nitric oxide and serotonin in aggression. *Curr. Top. Behav. Neurosci.*, 17:131–142.

Bedrosian, T. A., Fonken, L. K., and Nelson, R. J. 2016. Endocrine effects of circadian disruption. *Annu. Rev. Physiol.*, 78:109–131.

Bedrosian, T. A., Fonken, L. K., Demas, G. E., and Nelson, R. J. 2012. Photoperiod-dependent effects of neuronal nitric oxide synthase inhibition on aggression in Siberian hamsters. *Horm. Behav*, 61:176–180.

Beery, A. K. and Zucker, I. 2011. Sex bias in neuroscience and biomedical research. *Neurosci. Biobehav. Rev.*, 35:565–572.

Beery, A. K., Loo, T. J., and Zucker, I. 2008. Day length and estradiol affect same-sex affiliative behavior in the female meadow vole. *Horm. Behav.*, 54:153–159.

Beery, A. K., Routman, D. M., and Zucker, I. 2009. Same-sex social behavior in meadow voles: Multiple and rapid formation of attachments. *Physiol. Behav.*, 97:52–57.

Beglinger, C., Degen, L., Matzinger, D., D'Amato, M., and Drewe, J. 2001. Loxiglumide, a CCK-A receptor antagonist, stimulates calorie intake and hunger feelings in humans. *Am. J. Physiol.*, 280:R1149–R1154.

Beiderbeck, D. I., Neumann, I. D., and Veenema, A. H. 2007. Differences in intermale aggression are accompanied by opposite vasopressin release patterns within the septum in rats bred for low and high anxiety. *Eur. J. Neurosci.*, 26:3597–3605.

Bell-Pedersen, D., Cassone, V. M., Earnest, D. J., Golden, S. S., Hardin, P. E., Thomas, T. L., and Zoran, M. J. 2005. Circadian rhythms from multiple oscillators: Lessons from diverse organisms. *Nat. Rev. Genet.*, 6:544–556.

Bellingham, J., and Foster, R. G. 2002. Opsins and mammalian photoentrainment. *Cell and Tissue Research*, 309:57–71.

Benbow, C. P., and Stanley, J. C. 1983. Sex differences in mathematical reasoning ability: More facts. *Science*, 222:1029–1031.

Benca, R. M., 1996. Sleep in psychiatric disorders. *Neurol. Clin.*, 14:739–764.

Benca, R., Duncan, M. J., Frank, E., McClung, C., Nelson, R. J., and Vicentic, A. 2009. Biological rhythms, higher brain function, and behavior: Gaps, opportunities and challenges. *Brain Res. Rev.*, 62:57–70.

Benedetti, F., Dallaspezia, S., Colombo, C., Pirovano, A., Marino, E., and Smeraldi, E. 2008. A length polymorphism in the circadian clock gene *Per3* influences age at onset of bipolar disorder. *Neurosci. Lett.*, 445:184–187.

Benloucif, S., and Dubocovich, M. L. 1996. Melatonin and light induce phase shifts of circadian activity rhythms in the C3H/HeN mouse. *J. Biol. Rhythms*, 11:113–125.

Benoit, J. 1964. The role of the eyes and of the hypothalamus in the photostimulation of gonads in the duck. *Ann. N. Y. Acad. Sci.*, 117:204–217.

Bentley, G. E., Demas, G. E., Nelson, R. J., and Ball, G. F. 1998. Melatonin, immunity and cost of reproductive state in male European starlings. *Proc. Roy. Soc. Lond. B,* 265:1191–1195.

Bentley, G. E., Van't Hof, T. J., and Ball, G. F. 1999. Seasonal neuroplasticity in the songbird telencephalon: A role for melatonin. *Proc. Natl. Acad. Sci. USA,* 96:4674–4679.

Benton, D., and Brain, P. F. 1988. The role of opioid mechanisms in social interaction and attachment. In R. J. Rodgers and S. J. Cooper (eds.), *Endorphins, Opiates, and Behavioural Processes,* pp. 217–235. Wiley, New York.

Berenbaum, S. A., Duck, S. C., and Bryk, K. 2000. Behavioral effects of prenatal versus postnatal androgen excess in children with 21-hydroxylase-deficient congenital adrenal hyperplasia. *J. Clin. Endocrinol. Metab.,* 85:727–733.

Berenbaum, S. A., Martin, C. L., Hanish, L. D., Briggs, P. T., and Fabes, R. A. 2008. Sex differences in children's play. In J. B. Becker, K. J. Berkley, N. Geary, E. Hampson, J. P. Herman, and E. A. Young (eds.), *Sex Differences in the Brain: From Genes to Behavior,* pp. 275–290. Oxford University Press, New York.

Berg, S. J., and Wynne-Edwards, K. E. 2001. Changes in testosterone, cortisol, and estradiol levels in men becoming fathers. *Mayo Clinic Proc.,* 76:582–592.

Berger, N. C., Negus, N. C., and Rowsemitt, C. N. 1987. Effect of 6-methoxybenzoazolinone on sex ratio and breeding performance in Microtus montanus. *Biol. Reprod.,* 36:255–260.

Berkley, K. J. 1997. Sex differences in pain. *Proc. Natl. Acad. Sci. USA,* 20:371–380.

Bermant, G., and Taylor, L. 1969. Interactive effects of experience and olfactory bulb lesions in male rat copulation. *Physiol. Behav.,* 4:13–17.

Bermant, G., Lott, D. F., and Anderson, L. 1968. Temporal characteristics of the Coolidge effect in male rat copulatory behavior. *J. Comp. Physiol. Psychol.,* 65:447–452.

Bern, H. A. 1990. The "new" endocrinology: Its scope and its impact. *Am. Zool.,* 30:877–885.

Bernard, C. 1856. *Leçons de physiologie expérimentale appliquée à la médicine faites au Collège de France.* Vol. 2, Baillière, Paris.

Bernard, D. J., Chapman, S. C., and Woodruff, T. K. 2001. Mechanisms of inhibin signal transduction. *Rec. Prog. Hormone Res.,* 56:417–450.

Berndtson, W. E., and Desjardins, C. 1974. Circulating LH and FSH levels and testicular function in hamsters during light deprivation and subsequent photoperiodic stimulation. *Endocrinol.,* 95:195–205.

Bernhardt, P. C., Dabbs, J. M., Fielden, J. A., and Lutter, C. D. 1998. Testosterone changes during vicarious experiences of winning

and losing among fans at sporting events. *Physiol. Behav.,* 65:59–62.

Bernstein, I. S. 1981. Dominance: The baby and the bathwater. *Behav. Brain Sci.,* 4:419–457.

Bernstein, I. S., Rose, R. M., and Gordon, T. P. 1974. Behavioral and environmental events influencing primate testosterone levels. *J. Hum. Evol.,* 3:517–525.

Berson, D. M. 2003. Strange vision: Ganglion cells as circadian photoreceptors. *Trends Neurosci.,* 26:314–320.

Berson, D. M., Dunn, F. A., and Takao, M. 2002. Phototransduction by retinal ganglion cells that set the circadian clock. *Science,* 295:1070–1073.

Berta, P., Hawkins, J. R., Sinclair, A. H., Taylor, A., Griffiths, B. L., Goodfellow, P. N. 1990. Genetic evidence equating SRY and the testis-determining factor. *Nature,* 348:448–450.

Berthold, A. A. 1837. Einige Beobachtungen über den Winterschlaf der Thiere. *Arch. Anat. Physiol. Wissensch. Med.,* 4:63–68.

Bertolucci, C., and Foa, A. 1998. Seasonality and role of SCN in entrainment of lizard circadian rhythms to daily melatonin injections. *Am. J. Physiol.,* 274:R1004–1014.

Bertone-Johnson, E. R., Hankinson, S. E., Johnson, S. R., and Manson, J. E. 2008. Cigarette smoking and the development of premenstrual syndrome. *Am. J. Epidemiol.,* 168:938–945.

Bethea, C. L., Lu, N. Z., Gundlah, C., and Streicher, J. M. 2002. Diverse actions of ovarian steroids in the serotonin neural system. *Front. Neuroendocrinol.,* 23:41–100.

Bethea, C. L., Mirkes, S. J., Shively, C. A., and Adams, M. R. 2000. Steroid regulation of tryptophan hydroxylase protein in the dorsal raphe of macaques. *Biol. Psychiatry,* 47:562–576.

Bex, F. J., and Goldman, B. D. 1975. Serum gonadotropins and follicular development in the Syrian hamster. *Endocrinol.,* 96:928–933.

Beyer, C., Morali, G., Naftolin, F., Larsson, K., and Perez-Palacios, G. 1976. Effect of some antiestrogens and aromatase inhibitors on androgen induced sexual behavior in castrated male rats. *Horm. Behav.,* 7:353–363.

Beylin, A. V., and Shors, T. J. 2003. Glucocorticoids are necessary for enhancing the acquisition of associative memories after acute stressful experience. *Horm. Behav.,* 43:124–131.

Bianchi-Demicheli, F., Cojan, Y., Waber, L., Recordon, N., Vuilleumier, P., and Ortigue, S. 2011. Neural bases of hypoactive sexual desire disorder in women: An event-related FMRI study. *J. Sex. Med.,* 8:2546–2559.

Bianco, S., Agrifoglio, V., Mannino, F., Cefalu, E., and Cittadini, E. 1992. Successful pregnancy in a pure gonadal dysgenesis with karyotype 46,XY patient (Swyer's

syndrome) following oocyte donation and hormonal treatment. *Acta. Eur. Fertil.,* 23:37–38.

Bielak, T., and Pucek, Z. 1960. Season changes in the brain weight of the common shrew (*Sorez araneus araneus Linnaeus,* 1758). *Acta Theriol.,* 3:297–300.

Biessels, G. J., Kamal, A., Ramakers, G. M., Urban, I. J., Spruijt, B. M., Erkelens, D. W., and Gispen, W. H. 1996. Place learning and hippocampal synaptic plasticity in streptozotocin-induced diabetic rats. *Diabetes,* 45:1259–1266.

Biessels, G. J., Kamal, A., Urban, I. J., Spruijt, B. M., Erkelens, D. W., and Gispen, W. H. 1998. Water maze learning and hippocampal synaptic plasticity in streptozotocin-diabetic rats: Effects of insulin treatment. *Brain Res.,* 800:125–135.

Biessels, G. J., Staekenborg, S., Brunner, E., Brayne, C., and Scheltens, P. 2006. Risk of dementia in diabetes mellitus: A systematic review. *Lancet Neurol.,* 5:64–74.

Bird, E., Cardone, C. C., and Contreras, R. J. 1983. Area postrema lesions disrupt food intake induced by cerebroventricular infusions of 5-thioglucose in the rat. *Brain Res.,* 270:193–196.

Bishop, M. W. 1970. Aging and reproduction in the male. *J. Reprod. Fertil. (Suppl.),* 12:65–87.

Bitran, B., Klibansky, A., and Martin, G. A. 2000. The neurosteroid pregnanolone prevents the anxiogenic-like effect of inescapable shock in the rat, *Psychopharmacol.,* 151:31–37.

Bitran, D., and Dowd, J. A. 1996. Ovarian steroids modify the behavioral and neurochemical responses of the central benzodiazepine receptor. *Psychopharmacol.,* 125:65–73.

Bitran, D., Hull, E. M., Holmes, G. M., and Lookingland, K. J. 1988. Regulation of male rat copulatory behavior by preoptic incertohypothalamic dopamine neurons. *Brain Res. Bull.,* 20:323–331.

Bitran, D., Shiekh, M., and McLeod, M. 1995. Anxiolytic effect of progesterone is mediated by the neurosteroid allopregnanolone at brain GABA$_A$ receptors. *J. Neuroendocrinol.,* 7:171–177.

Bittman, E. L. 1993. Melatonin: A durational signal regulating steroid-dependent and -independent aspects of limbic and hypophyseal function. In Y. Touitou, J. Arendt, and P. Pevet (eds.), *Melatonin and the Pineal Gland: From Basic Science to Clinical Application,* pp. 151–158. Elsevier, Amsterdam.

Bittman, E. L. and Karsch, F. J. 1984. Nightly duration of pineal melatonin secretion determines the reproductive response to inhibitory day length in the ewe. *Biol. Reprod.,* 30:585–593.

Bittman, E. L. and Weaver, D. R. 1990. The distribution of melatonin binding sites in neuroendocrine tissues of the ewe. *Biol. Reprod.*, 43:986–993.

Bittman, E. L., and Goldman, B. D. 1979. Serum levels of gonadotrophins in hamsters exposed to short photoperiods: Effects of adrenalectomy and ovariectomy. *J. Endocrinol.*, 83:113–118.

Bittman, E. L., and Karsch, F. J. 1984. Nightly duration of pineal melatonin secretion determines the reproductive response to inhibitory day length in the ewe. *Biol. Reprod.*, 30:585–593.

Bittman, E. L., and Weaver, D. R. 1990. The distribution of melatonin binding sites in neuroendocrine tissues of the ewe. *Biol. Reprod.*, 43:986–993.

Bittman, E. L., Crandell, R., and Lehman, M. 1989. Influences of the paraventricular and suprachiasmatic nuclei and olfactory bulbs on melatonin responses in the golden hamster. *Biol. Reprod.*, 40:118–126.

Bittman, E. L., Jonassen, J. A., and Hegarty, C. M. 1992. Photoperiodic regulation of pulsatile luteinizing hormone secretion and adrenohypophyseal gene expression in female golden hamsters. *Biol. Reprod.*, 47:66–71.

Bittman, E. L., Thomas, E. M., and Zucker, I. 1994. Melatonin binding sites in sciurid and hystricomorph rodents: Studies on ground squirrels and guinea pigs. *Brain Res.* 648:73–79.

Biver, F., Lotstra, F., Monclus, M., Wikler, D., Damhaut, P., Mendlewicz, J., and Goldman, S. 1996. Sex difference in 5HT2 receptor in the living human brain. *Neurosci. Lett.*, 204:25–28.

Blair-West, J. R., Coghlan, J. P., Denton, D. A., Nelson, J. F., Ochard, E., Scoggins, B. A., Wright, R. D, Myers, K., and Junqueira, C. L. 1968. Physiological, morphological and behavioural adaptation to a sodium deficient environment by wild native Australian and introduced species of animals. *Nature*, 217:922–928.

Blanchard, D. C., and Blanchard, R. J. 1984. Affect and aggression: An animal model applied to human behavior. In R. J. Blanchard and D. C. Blanchard (eds.), *Advances in the Study of Aggression*, Vol. 1, pp. 1–63. Academic Press, New York.

Blank, J. L., and Desjardins, C. 1985. Photic cues induce multiple neuroendocrine adjustments in testicular function. *Am. J. Physiol.*, 238:R181–R189.

Blask, D. E., Leadem, C. A., Orstead, M., and Larsen, B. R. 1986. Prolactin cell activity in female and male Syrian hamsters: An apparent sexually dimorphic response to light deprivation and pinealectomy. *Neuroendocrinol.*, 42:15–20.

Blass, E. M., and Epstein, A. N. 1971. A lateral preoptic osmosensitive zone for thirst in the rat. *J. Comp. Physiol. Psychol.*, 76:378–394.

Blaustein, J. D. and Turcotte, J. C. 1989. Estradiol-induced progestin receptor immunoreactivity is found only in estrogen receptor-immunoreactive cells in guinea pig brain. *Neuroendocrinology*, 49:454–461.

Blaustein, J. D., and Wade, G. N. 1976. Ovarian influences on the meal pattern of female rats. *Physiol. Behav.*, 17:201–208.

Bloch, G. J., and Gorski, R. A. 1988. Cytoarchitectonic analysis of the SDN-POA of the intact and gonadectomized rat. *J. Comp. Neurol.*, 275:604–612.

Bloom, S. R., and Polak, J. M. (eds.). 1981. *Gut Hormones.* (2nd ed.). Churchill-Livingstone, Edinburgh.

Blüher, S., and Mantzoros, C. S. 2004. The role of leptin in regulating neuroendocrine function in humans. *J. Nutrition*, 134:2469S–2474S.

Blurton Jones, N. G. 1986. Bushman birth spacing: A test for optimal interbirth intervals. *Ethol. Sociobiol.*, 7:91–105.

Bluthe, R. M., Gheusi, G., and Dantzer, R. 1993. Gonadal steroids influence the involvement of arginine vasopressin in social recognition in mice. *Psychoneuroendocrinol.*, 18:323–335.

Boccia, M. M., Kopf, S. R., and Baratti, C. M. 1998. Effects of a single administration of oxytocin or vasopressin and their interactions with two selective receptor antagonists on memory storage in mice. *Neurobiol. Learn. Mem.*, 69:136–146.

Boggs, S. S. 1990. Targeted gene modification for gene therapy of stem cells. *Int. J. Cell Clon.*, 8, 80–96.

Bohacek, J., and Daniel, J. M. 2010. The beneficial effects of estradiol on attentional processes are dependent on timing of treatment initiation following ovariectomy in middle-aged rats. *Psychoneuroendocrinol.*, 35:694–705.

Bohus, B., Conti, L., Kovacs, G. L., and Versteeg, D. H. G. 1982. Modulation of memory processes by neuropeptides: Interaction with neurotransmitter systems. In C. A. Marsan and H. Matthies (eds.), *Neuronal Plasticity and Memory Formation*, pp. 75–87. Raven Press, New York.

Bolig, R., Price, C. S., O'Neill, P. L., and Suomi, S. J. 1992. Subjective assessment of reactivity level and personality traits of rhesus monkeys. *Int. J. Primatol.*, 13:287–306.

Bondy, C. A., Matura, L. A., Wooten, N., Troendle, J., Zinn, A. R., and Bakalov, V. K. 2007. The physical phenotype of girls and women with Turner syndrome is not X-imprinted. *Hum. Genet.*, 121:469–474.

Bonilla-Jaime, H., Palacios-Vazquez, G., Arteaga-Silva, M., and Retana-Marquez, S. 2006. Hormonal responses to different sexually related conditions in male rats. *Horm. Behav.*, 49:376–382.

Bonsall, R. W., and Michael, R. P. 1992. Developmental changes in the uptake of testosterone by the primate brain. *Neuroendocrinol.*, 55:84–91.

Bonsall, R. W., Rees, H. D., and Michael, R. P. 1985. The distribution, nuclear uptake and metabolism of [³H]Dihydrotestosterone in the brain, pituitary gland and genital tract of the male rhesus monkey. *J. Steroid Biochem.*, 23:389–398.

Book, A. S., Starzyk, K. B., and Quinsey, V. L. 2001. The relationship between testosterone and aggression: A meta-analysis. *Aggress. Violent Behav.*, 6:579–599.

Booth, A., Shelley, G., Mazur, A., Tharp, G., and Kittok, R. 1989. Testosterone and winning and losing in human competition. *Horm. Behav.*, 23:556–571.

Booth, J. E. 1977. Sexual behavior of neonatally castrated rats injected during infancy with oestrogen and dihydrotestosterone. *J. Endocrinol.*, 72:135–142.

Born, J., Fehm, H. L., and Voigt, K. H. 1986. ACTH and attention in humans: A review. *Neuropsychobiol.*, 15:165–186.

Borowsky, I. W., Hogan, M., and Ireland, M. 1997. Adolescent sexual aggression: Risk and protective factors. *Pediatrics*, 100:E7.

Bosch, O. J., and Neumann, I. D. 2012. Both oxytocin and vasopressin are mediators of maternal care and aggression in rodents: From central release to sites of action. *Horm. Behav.*, 61:293–303.

Bostwick, J. M., and Bucci, J. A. 2008. Internet sex addiction treated with naltrexone. *Mayo Clin. Proc.*, 83:226–230.

Bottjer, S. W., Glaessner, S. L., and Arnold, A. P. 1985. Ontogeny of brain nuclei controlling song learning and behavior in zebra finches. *J. Neurosci.*, 5:1556–1562.

Bottjer, S. W., Halsema, K. A., Brown, S. A., and Miesner, E. A. 1989. Axonal connections of a forebrain nucleus involved with vocal learning in zebra finches. *J. Comp. Neurol.*, 279:312–326.

Bottjer, S. W., Miesner, E. A., and Arnold, A. P. 1984. Forebrain lesions disrupt development but not maintenance of song in passerine birds. *Science*, 224:901–903.

Bottjer, S. W., Schoonmaker, J. N., and Arnold, A. P. 1986. Auditory and hormonal stimulation interact to produce neural growth in adult canaries. *J. Neurobiol.*, 17:605–612.

Bouissou, M. F. 1983. Androgens, aggressive behaviour and social relationships in higher mammals. *Horm. Res.*, 18:43–61.

Bowden, R. M., Ewert, M. A., and Nelson, C. E. 2000. Environmental sex determination in a reptile varies seasonally and with yolk hormones. *Proc. Roy. Soc. Lond. B*, 267:1745–1749.

Bowen, D. J., and Grunberg, N. E. 1990. Variations in food preference and consumption across the menstrual cycle. *Physiol. Behav.*, 47:287–291.

Bowers, S. L., Bilbo, S. D., Dhabhar, F. S., and Nelson, R. J. 2008. Stressor-specific alterations in corticosterone and immune responses in mice. *Brain Behav. Immun.*, 22:105–113.

Bowlby, J. 1969. *Attachment and Loss. Vol. 1. Attachment.* Basic Books, New York.

Bowles, J., Schepers, G., and Koopman, P. 2000. Phylogeny of the SOX family of developmental transcription factors based on sequence and structural indicators. *Dev. Biol.*, 227:239–255.

Bowman, R. E., Beck, K. D., and Luine, V. N. 2003. Chronic stress effects on memory: Sex differences in performance and monoaminergic activity. *Horm. Behav.*, 43:48–59.

Bowman, R. E., Zrull, M. C., and Luine, V. N. 2001. Chronic restraint stress enhances radial arm maze performance in female rats. *Brain Res.*, 904:279–289.

Boyar, R. M., Katz, J., Finkelstein, J. W., Kapen, S., Weiner, H., Weitzman, E. D., and Hellman, L. 1974. Anorexia nervosa: Immaturity of the 24-hour luteinizing hormone secretory pattern. *New Engl. J. Medicine*, 291:861–865.

Boyd, S. 1997. Brain, vasotocin pathways and the control of sexual behavior in the bullfrog. *Brain Res. Bull.*, 44:345–350.

Boyd, S. K., Tyler, C. J., and DeVries, D. J. 1992. Sexual dimorphism in the vasotocin system of the bullfrog, *Rana catesbeiana. J. Comp. Neurol.*, 325:313–325.

Brain, P. F., and Nowell, N. W. 1969. Some endocrine and behavioral changes in the development of the albino laboratory mouse. *Commun. Behav. Biol.*, 4:203–220.

Brain, P. F., Haug, M., and Kamis, A. B. 1983. Hormones and different tests for aggression with particular reference to the effects of testosterone metabolites. In J. Balthazart, E. Prove, and R. Gilles (eds.), *Hormones and Behaviour in Higher Vertebrates*, pp. 3–25. Springer-Verlag, Berlin.

Brainard, G. C., Richardson, B. A., King, T. S., Matthews, S. A., and Reiter, R. J. 1983. The suppression of pineal melatonin content and N-acetyltransferase activity by different light irradiances in the Syrian hamster: A dose–response relationship. *Endocrinol.*, 113:293–296.

Brambilla, F., Monteleone, L., Bortolotti, F., Dalle-Grave, R., Todisco, P., Favaro, A. Santonastaso, P. Ramacciotti, C., Paoli, R., and Maj, M. 2003. Persistent amenorrhea in weight-recovered anorexics: Psychological and biological aspects. *Psychiatry Res.*, 118:249–257.

Brantley, R. K., Wingfield, J., and Bass, A. H. 1993. Hormonal bases for male teleost dimorphisms: Sex steroid levels in *Porichthys notatus*, a fish with alternative reproductive tactics. *Horm. Behav.*, 27:332–347.

Breedlove, S. M. 1992. Sexual dimorphism in the vertebrate nervous system. *J. Neurosci.*, 12:4133–4142.

Breedlove, S. M. 1994. Sexual differentiation of the human nervous system. *Annu. Rev. Neurosci.* 45:389–418.

Breedlove, S. M. 1997. Sex on the brain. *Nature*, 389:801.

Breedlove, S. M. and Watson, N. V. 2016. *Behavioral Neuroscience.* (8th ed.) Sinauer Associates, Sunderland, MA.

Breedlove, S. M., and Arnold, A. P. 1981. Sexually dimorphic motor nucleus in the rat lumbar spinal cord: Response to adult hormone manipulation, absence in androgen-insensitive rats. *Brain Res.*, 225:297–307.

Breedlove, S. M., and Arnold, A. P. 1983a. Hormonal control of a developing neuromuscular system: I. Complete demasculinization of the spinal nucleus of the bulbocavernosus in male rats using the anti-androgen flutamide. *J. Neurosci.*, 3:417–423.

Breedlove, S. M., and Arnold, A. P. 1983b. Hormonal control of a developing neuromuscular system: II. Sensitive periods for the androgen-induced masculinization of the rat spinal nucleus of the bulbocavernosus. *J. Neurosci.*, 3:424–432.

Breedlove, S. M., Jordan, C. L., and Kelley, D. B. 2002. What neuromuscular systems tell us about hormones and behavior. In D. Pfaff, A. Arnold, A. Etgen, S. Fahrbach, and R. Rubin (eds.), *Hormones, Brain and Behavior*, Vol. 4, pp. 193–221. Academic Press, New York.

Brenowitz, E. A. 1991. Altered perception of species-specific song by female birds after lesions of a forebrain nucleus. *Science*, 251:303–305.

Brenowitz, E. A. 1997. Comparative approaches to the avian song system. *J. Neurobiol.*, 33:517–531.

Brenowitz, E. A. 2008. Plasticity of the song control system in adult birds. In H. P. Zeigler and P. Marler (eds.), *Neuroscience of Birdsong*, pp. 332–349. Cambridge University Press, Cambridge.

Brenowitz, E. A., and Arnold, A. P. 1985. Lack of sexual dimorphism in the steroid accumulation in vocal control brain regions of duetting song birds. *Brain Res.*, 344:172–180.

Brenowitz, E. A., and Arnold, A. P. 1986. Interspecific comparison of the size in neural song control regions and song complexity in duetting birds: Evolutionary implications. *J. Neurosci.*, 6:2875–2879.

Brenowitz, E. A., and Arnold, A. P. 1989. Accumulation of estrogen in a vocal control brain region of a duetting song bird. *Brain Res.*, 359:364–367.

Brenowitz, E. A., and Arnold, A. P. 1992. Hormone accumulation in song regions of the canary brain. *J. Neurobiol.*, 23:871–880.

Brenowitz, E. A., Arnold, A. P., and Levin, R. N. 1985. Neural correlates of female song in tropical duetting birds. *Brain Res.*, 480:119–125.

Brenowitz, E. A., Baptista, L., Lent, K., and Wingfield, J. 1998. Seasonal plasticity of the song control system in wild Nuttall's white-crowned sparrows. *J. Neurobiol.*, 34:69–82.

Brenowitz, E. A., Nalls, B., Wingfield, J. C., and Kroodsma, D. E. 1991. Seasonal changes in avian song control nuclei without seasonal changes in song repertoire. *J. Neurosci.*, 11:1367–1374.

Brett, M., and Baxendale, S. 2001. Motherhood and memory: A review. *Psychoneuroendocrinol.*, 26:339–362.

Breuner, C. W., Wingfield, J. C., and Romero, L. M. 1999. Diel rhythms of basal and stress-induced corticosterone in a wild, seasonal vertebrate, Gambel's white-crowned sparrow. *J. Experimental Zool.*, 284:334–342.

Bridges, R. S. (ed.). 2008. *Neurobiology of the Parental Brain.* Academic Press, Burlington, MA.

Bridges, R. S. 1975. Long-term effects of pregnancy and parturition upon maternal responsiveness in the rat. *Physiol. Behav.*, 14:245–249.

Bridges, R. S. 1977. Parturition: Its role in the long-term retention of maternal behavior in the rat. *Physiol. Behav.*, 18:487–490.

Bridges, R. S. 1978. Retention of rapid onset of maternal behavior during pregnancy in primiparous rats. *Behav. Biol.*, 24:113–117.

Bridges, R. S. 1990. Endocrine regulation of parental behavior in rodents. In N. A. Krasnegor and R. S. Bridges (eds.), *Mammalian Parenting*, pp. 93–117. Oxford University Press, Oxford.

Bridges, R. S. 1996. Biochemical basis of parental behavior in the rat. *Adv. Study Behav.*, 25:215–242.

Bridges, R. S., and Freemark, M. S. 1995. Human placental lactogen infusions into the medial preoptic area stimulate maternal behavior in steroid-primed, nulliparous female rats. *Horm. Behav.*, 29:216–226.

Bridges, R. S., and Goldman, B. D. 1975. Diurnal rhythms in gonadotropins and progesterone in lactating and photoperiod induced acyclic hamsters. *Biol. Reprod.*, 13:617–622.

Bridges, R. S., Robertson, M. C., Shiu, R. P., Friesen, H. G., Stuer, A. M., and Mann, P. E. 1996. Endocrine communication between conceptus and mother: Placental lactogen stimulation of maternal behavior. *Neuroendocrinol.*, 64:57–64.

Bridges, R. S., Rosenblatt, J. S., and Feder, H. 1978a. Serum progesterone concentrations and maternal behavior in rats after pregnancy termination: Behavioral stimulation following progesterone withdrawal and inhibition by progesterone maintenance. *Endocrinol.*, 102:258–267.

Bridges, R. S., Rosenblatt, J. S., and Feder, H. 1978b. Stimulation of maternal responsiveness after pregnancy termination in rats: Effect of time of onset of behavioral testing. *Horm. Behav.*, 10:235–245.

Brinkmann, A., Jenster, G., Ris-Stalpers, C., van der Korput, H., Bruggenwirth, H., Boehmer, A., and Trapman, J. 1996. Molecular basis of androgen insensitivity. *Steroids*, 61:172–5175.

Brinsmead, M., Smith, R., Singh, B., Lewin, T., and Owens, P. 1985. Peripartum concentrations of beta-endorphin and cortisol and maternal mood states. *Aust. N. Z. J. Obstet. Gynaecol.*, 12:194–197.

Brobeck, J. R., Wheatland, M., and Strominger, J. L. 1947. Variations in regulation of energy exchange associated with estrus, diestrus and pseudopregnancy in rats. *Endocrinol.*, 40:65–72.

Bronson, F. H. 1988. Seasonal regulation of reproduction in mammals. In E. Knobil and J. D. Neill (eds.), *The Physiology of Reproduction*, Vol. 2, pp. 1831–1872. Raven Press, New York.

Bronson, F. H. 1989. *Mammalian Reproductive Biology.* University of Chicago Press, Chicago.

Bronson, F. H. 1996. Effects of prolonged exposure to anabolic steroids on the behavior of male and female mice. *Pharmacol. Biochem. Behav.* 53:329–334.

Bronson, F. H. 1999. Puberty and energy reserves: A walk on the wild side. In K. Wallen and J. E. Schneider (eds.), *Reproduction in Context.* MIT Press, Cambridge, MA.

Bronson, F. H. 2004. Are humans seasonally photoperiodic? *J. Biological Rhythms*, 19:180–192.

Bronson, F. H., and Desjardins, C. 1982a. Endocrine responses to sexual arousal in male mice. *Endocrinol.*, 111:1286–1291.

Bronson, F. H., and Desjardins, C. 1982b. Reproductive aging in male mice. In M. E. Reff (ed.), *Biological Markers of Aging*, pp. 87–93. NIH, Bethesda, MD. Publication no. 82–2221.

Bronson, F. H., and Matherne, C. M. 1997. Exposure to anabolic-androgenic steroids shortens life span of male mice. *Med. Sci. Sports Exerc.*, 29:615–619.

Brooks-Gunn, J. 1986. Differentiating premenstrual syndromes. *Psychosomat. Med.*, 48:385–387.

Brosens, J. J., Tullet, J., Varshochi, R., and Lam, E. W. 2004. Steroid receptor action. *Best Pract. Res. Clin. Obstet. Gynaecol.*, 18:265–283.

Brown-Parlee, M. 1990. Integrating biological and social scientific research on menopause. *Ann. N. Y. Acad. Sci.*, 592:379–389.

Brown-Parlee, M. 1991. The social construction of premenstrual syndrome: A case study of scientific discourse as cultural contestation. Working paper presented at: *The Good Body: Asceticism in Contemporary Culture.* Institute for the Medical Humanities, University of Texas, Galveston, TX.

Brown-Séquard, C. E. 1899. The effects produced on man by subcutaneous injections of a liquid obtained from the testicles of animals. *Lancet*, 105–106, reprinted in Carter, C. S. (ed.), *Hormones and Sexual Behavior.* Stroudsburg, Dowden, Hutchinson and Ross, Inc.

Brown, C. S., Ling, F. W., Andersen, R. N., Farmer, R. G., and Arheart, K. L. 1994. Efficacy of depot leuprolide in premenstrual syndrome: Effect of symptom severity and type in a controlled trial. *Obstet. Gynecol.*, 84:77–786.

Brown, F. A. 1972. The clocks timing biological rhythms. *Am. Sci.*, 60:756–766.

Brown, J. R., Ye, H., Bronson, R. T., Dikkes, P., and Greenberg, M. E. 1996. A defect in nurturing in mice lacking the immediate early gene *fosB*. *Cell*, 86:297–309.

Brown, M., Rivier, J., Kobayashi, R., and Vale, W. 1978. Cholecystokinin in feeding behavior. In S. R. Bloom (ed.), *Gut Hormones*, pp. 550–558. Raven Press, New York.

Brown, R. E., Murdoch, T., Murphy, P. R., and Moger, W. H. 1995. Hormonal responses of male gerbils to stimuli from their mate and pups. *Horm. Behav.*, 29:474–491.

Brown, R., and Kulik, J. 1977. Flashbulb memories. *Cognition*, 5:73–99.

Brown, S. A., Zumbrunn, G., Fleury-Olela, F., Preitner, N., and Schibler, U. 2002. Rhythms of mammalian body temperature can sustain peripheral circadian clocks. *Curr Biol.* 12:1574–1583.

Brown, T. J., Naftolin, F., and Maclusky, N. J. 1992. Sex differences in estrogen receptor binding in the rat hypothalamus: Effects of subsaturating pulses of estradiol. *Brain Res.*, 578:129–134.

Brown, W. A., Monti, P. M., and Corriveau, D. P. 1978. Serum testosterone and sexual activity and interest in men. *Arch. Sex. Behav.*, 7:97–103.

Brown, W. M., Hines, M., Fane, B. A., and Breedlove, S. M. 2002. Masculinized finger length patterns in human males and females with congenital adrenal hyperplasia. *Horm. Behav.*, 42:380–386.

Brunelli, S. A., and Hofer, M. A. 1990. Parental behavior in juvenile rats: Environmental and biological determinants. In N. A. Krasnegor and R. S. Bridges (eds.), *Mammalian Parenting*, pp. 372–399. Oxford University Press, Oxford.

Bruning, J. C., Gautam, D., Burks, D. J., Gillette, J., Schubert, M., Orban, P. C., Klein, R., Krone, W., Muller-Wieland, D., and Kahn, C. R. 2000. Role of brain insulin receptor in control of body weight and reproduction. *Science*, 289:2122–2125.

Bruns, P. 1888. Report on myxoedema. *Trans. Clin. Soc. Lond.*, Supplement 21:105.

Bryant, K. J. 1982. Personality correlates of sense of direction and geographic orientation. *J. Pers. Soc. Psychol.*, 43:1318–1324.

Bryant, K. J. 1991. Geographical/spatial orientation ability within real-world and simulated large-scale environments. *Multivar. Behav. Res.*, 26:109–136.

Buchanan, T. W., and Lovallo, W. R. 2001. Enhanced memory for emotional material following stress-level cortisol treatment in humans. *Psychoneuroendocrinol.*, 26:307–317.

Buckley, C. A., and Schneider, J. E. 2003. Food hoarding is increased by food deprivation and decreased by leptin treatment in Syrian hamsters. *Am. J. Physiol.*, 285:R1021–R1029.

Buckman, M. T., and Kellner, R. 1985. Reduction of distress in hyperprolactinemia with bromocriptine. *Am. J. Psychiatry*, 142:242–244.

Buhr, E. D. and Takahashi, J. S. 2013. Molecular components of the Mammalian circadian clock. *Handb. Exp. Pharmacol.*, 217:3–27.

Buhrich, N., Bailey, J. M., and Martin, N. G. 1991. Sexual orientation, sexual identity, and sex-dimorphic behaviors in male twins. *Behav. Genet.*, 21:75–96.

Buijs, R. M., Wortel, J., Van Heerikhuize, J. J., Feenstra, M. G., Ter Horst, G. J., Romijn, H. J., and Kalsbeek, A. 1999. Anatomical and functional demonstration of a multisynaptic suprachiasmatic nucleus adrenal (cortex) pathway. *Eur. J. Neurosci.*, 11:1535–1544.

Bulik, C. M., Devlin, B., Bacanu, S.-A., Thornton, L., Klump, K. L., Fichter, M. M., Halmi, K. A., et al. 2003. Significant linkage on chromosome 10p in families with bulimia nervosa. *Am. J. Hum. Genet.*, 72:200–207.

Bull, J. J. 1980. Sex determination in reptiles. *Q. Rev. Biol.*, 55:3–21.

Bull, J. J. 1983. *Evolution of Sex Determining Mechanisms.* Benjamin/Cummings, Menlo Park, CA.

Bunnell, B. N., Boland, B. D., and Dewsbury, D. A. 1976. Copulatory behavior of the golden hamster (*Mescricetus auratus*). *Behaviour*, 61:180–206.

Bunney, B. G. and Bunney, W. E. 2013. Mechanisms of rapid antidepressant effects of sleep deprivation therapy: Clock genes and circadian rhythms. *Biol. Psychiatry*, 73:1164–1171.

Buntin, J. D. 1996. Neural and hormonal control of parental behavior in birds. *Adv. Study Behav.*, 25:161–213.

Buntin, J. D. 2010. Parental behavior and hormones in non-mammalian vertebrates. In M. D. Breed and J. Moore (eds.), *Encyclopedia of Animal Behavior*, pp. 663–671. Elsevier, New York.

Buntin, J. D., Ruzycki, E., and Witebsky, J. 1993. Prolactin receptors in dove brain: Autoradiographic analysis of binding characteristics in discrete brain regions and accessibility to blood-borne prolactin. *Neuroendocrinol.*, 57:738–750.

Burgers, J. K., Nelson, R. J., Quinlan, D. M., and Walsh, P. C. 1991. Nerve growth factor, nerve grafts and amniotic membrane grafts restore erectile function in rats. *J. Urol.*, 146:463–468.

Burgess, L. H., and Handa, R. J. 1993. Hormonal regulation of androgen receptor mRNA in the brain and anterior pituitary gland of the male rat. *Mol. Brain Res.*, 19:31–38.

Burghardt, G. M. 1988. Precocity, play, and the ectotherm–endotherm transition: Profound reorganization or superficial adaptation? In E. M. Blass (ed.), *Handbook of Behavioral Neurobiology*, Vol. 9, pp. 107–148. Plenum, New York.

Burkhardt, R. W. 1987. The Journal of Animal Behavior and the early history of animal behavior in America. *J. Comp. Psychol.*, 101:223–230.

Burnett, A. L. 1995. Role of nitric oxide in the physiology of erection. *Biol. Reprod.*, 52:485–489.

Burrows, W. 1945. Periodic spawning of the Palolo worms in Pacific waters. *Nature*, 155:47–48.

Buss, C., Davis, E. P., Shahbaba, B., Pruessner, J. C., Head, K., and Sandman, C. A. 2012. Maternal cortisol over the course of pregnancy and subsequent child amygdala and hippocampus volumes and affective problems. *PNAS*, 109:1312–1319.

Bussey, T. J., Padain, T. L., Skillings, E. A., Winters, B. D., Morton, A. J., and Saksida, L. M. 2008. The touchscreen cognitive testing methods for rodents: How to get the best out of your rat. *Learn. Mem.*, 15:516–523.

Buster, J. E., Kingsberg, S. A., Aguirre, O., Brown, C., Breaux, J. G., Buch, A., Rodenberg, C. A., Wekselman, K., and Casson, P. 2005. Testosterone patch for low sexual desire in surgically menopausal women: a randomized trial. *Obstet. Gynecol.*, 105:944–952.

Buston, P. 2003. Social hierarchies: Size and growth modification in clownfish. *Nature*, 424:145–146.

Butenandt, A. 1929. Uber "progynon," ein kristall-isiertes weibliches Sexualhormone. *Naturwiessenschaften*, 17:879. Abstract translated by E. W. Henry in *Biol. Abstr.*, 5:85 (881).

Butera, P. C., and Beikirch, R. J. 1989. Central implants of diluted estradiol: Independent effects on ingestive and reproductive behaviors of ovariectomized rats. *Brain Res.*, 491:266–273.

Butler, M. P., Karatsoreos, I. N., LeSauter, J. and, Silver, R. 2012. Dose-dependent effects of androgens on the circadian timing system and its response to light. *Endocrinology*, 153:2344–2352.

Byne, W., and Parsons, B. 1993. Human sexual orientation: The biologic theories reappraised. *Arch. Gen. Psychiatry*, 50:228–239.

Byne, W., Tobet, S., Mattiace, L. A., Lasco, M. S., Kemether, E., Edgar, M. A., Morgello, S., Buchsbaum, M. S., and Jones, L. B.

2001. The interstitial nuclei of the human anterior hypothalamus: An investigation of variation with sex, sexual orientation, and HIV status. *Horm. Behav.*, 40:86–92.

Caba, M., Tovar, A., Silver, R., Morgado, E., Meza, E., Zavaleta, Y., and Juárez, C. 2008. Nature's food anticipatory experiment: entrainment of locomotor behavior, suprachiasmatic and dorsomedial hypothalamic nuclei by suckling in rabbit pups. *Eur. J. Neurosci.*, 27:432–443.

Cahill, G. M., Grace, M. S., and Besharse, J. C. 1991. Rhythmic regulation of retinal melatonin: Metabolic pathways, neurochemical regulation and the ocular circadian clock. *Cell. Mol. Neurobiol.*, 11:529–560.

Cahill, L. 2006. Why sex matters for neuroscience. *Nat. Rev. Neurosci.*, 7:477–484.

Cahill, L., and Alkire, M. 2003. Epinephrine enhancement of human memory consolidation: Interaction with arousal at encoding. *Neurobiol. Learn. Mem.*, 79:194–198.

Cahill, L., Gorski, L., and Le, K. 2003. Enhanced human memory consolidation with post-learning stress: Interaction with the degree of arousal at encoding. *Learning and Memory*, 10:270–274.

Cahill, L., Haier, R. J., Fallon, J., Alkire, M., Tang, C., Keator, D., Wu, J., and McGaugh, J. L. 1996. Amygdala activity at encoding correlated with long-term, free recall of emotional information *Proc. Natl. Acad. Sci. USA*, 93:8016–8021.

Cahill, L., Haier, R. J., White, N. S., Fallon, J., Kilpatrick, L., Lawrence, C., Potkin, S. G., and Alkire, M. T. 2001. Sex-related difference in amygdala activity during emotionally influenced memory storage. *Neurobiol. Learn. Mem.*, 75:1–9.

Cahill, L., Pham, C. A., and Setlow, B. 2000. Impaired memory consolidation in rats produced with β-adrenergic blockade, *Neurobiol. Learn. Mem.*, 74:259–266.

Cahill, L., Prins, B., Weber, M., and McGaugh, J. L. 1994. Beta-adrenergic activation and memory for emotional events. *Nature*, 271:702–704.

Cain, D. P. 1974. The role of the olfactory bulbs in limbic mechanisms. *Psychol. Bull.*, 81:654–671.

Cajochen, C., Münch, M., Kobialka, S., Kräuchi, K., Steiner, R., Oelhafen, P., Orgül, S., and Wirz-Justice, A. 2005. High sensitivity of human melatonin, alertness, thermoregulation, and heart rate to short wavelength light. *J. Clin. Endocrinol. Metab.*, 90:1311–1316.

Caldji, C., Tannenbaum, B., Sharma, S., Francis, D., Plotsky, P. M., and Meaney, M. J. 1998. Maternal care during infancy regulates the development of neural systems mediating the expression of fearfulness in the rat. *Proc. Natl. Acad. Sci. USA*, 95:5335–5340.

Caldwell, G. S., Glickman, S. E., and Smith, E. R. 1984. Seasonal aggression is independent of seasonal testosterone in wood rats. *Proc. Natl. Acad. Sci. USA*, 81:5255–5257.

Caldwell, H. K., Lee, H.-J., Macbeth, A. H., and Young, W. S. 2008. Vasopressin: Behavioral roles of an "original" neuropeptide. *Prog. Neurobiol.*, 84:1–24.

Calisi, R. M. 2014. An integrative overview of the role of gonadotropin-inhibiting hormone in behavior: Applying Tinbergen's four questions. *Gen. Comp. Endocrinol.*, 203:95–105.

Calisi, R. M., Rizzo, N. O., and Bentley, G. E. 2008. Seasonal differences in hypothalamic EGR-1 and GnIH expression following capture-handling stress in house sparrows (*Passer domesticus*). *Gen. Comp. Endocrinol.*, 157:283–287.

Camacho, F., Cilio, M., Guo, Y., Virshup, D. M., Patel, K., Khorkova, O., Styren, S., et al. 2001. Human casein kinase Idelta phosphorylation of human circadian clock proteins period 1 and 2. *FEBS Lett.*, 489:159–165.

Camazine, B., Gartska, W., Tokarz, R., and Crews, D. 1980. Effects of castration and androgen replacement on male courtship behaviour in the red-sided garter snake (*Thamnophis sirtalis parietalis*). *Horm. Behav.*, 14:358–372.

Campbell, C. S., Finkelstein, J. S., and Turek, F. W. 1978. The interaction of photoperiod and testosterone on the development of copulatory behavior in male hamsters. *Physiol. Behav.*, 21:409–415.

Campfield, L. A., Smith, F. J., and Burn, P. 1995. The OB protein (leptin) pathway—a link between adipose tissue mass and central neural networks. *Horm. Metab. Res.*, 28:619–632.

Canacher, G. N., and Workman, D. G. 1989. Violent crime possibly associated with anabolic steroid use. *Am. J. Psychiatry*, 146:679.

Candolle, A. P. de 1832. *Physiologie Vegetale*, Vol. 2. Bechet Jeune: Paris.

Canli, T., Desmond, J. E., Zhao, Z., and Gabrieli, J. D. E. 2002. Sex differences in the neural basis of emotional memories. *Proc. Natl. Acad. Sci. USA*, 99:10789–10794.

Canli, T., Zhao, Z., Brewer, J., Gabrieli, J. D., and Cahill, L. 2000. Event-related activation in the human amygdala associates with later memory for individual emotional experience. *J. Neurosci.*, 20:RC99.

Cannon, W. B. 1929. *Bodily Changes in Pain, Hunger, Fear and Rage*. Appleton, New York.

Canoine, V., and Gwinner, E. 2002. Seasonal differences in the hormonal control of territorial aggression in free-living European stonechats. *Horm. Behav.*, 41, 1–8.

Capitanio, J. P., Mendoza, S. P., Lerche, N. W., and Mason, W. A. 1998. Social stress results in altered glucocorticoid regulation and shorter survival in simian acquired immune deficiency syndrome. *Proc. Natl. Acad. Sci. USA*, 95:471–4719.

Cappelletti, M. and Wallen, K. 2016. Increasing women's sexual desire: The comparative effectiveness of estrogens and androgens. *Horm. Behav.*, 78:178–193.

Carani, C., Bancroft, J., DelRio, G., Granata, A. R. M., Faccinetti, F., and Marrama, P. 1990. The endocrine effects of visual erotic stimuli in normal men. *Psychoneuroendocrinol.*, 15:207–216.

Carani, C., Rochira, V., Faustini-Fustini, M., Balestrieri, A., and Granata, A. 1999. Role of oestrogen in male sexual behaviour: Insights from the natural model of aromatase deficiency. *Clin. Endocrinol.*, 51:517–524.

Caraty, A., Franceschini, I., and Hoffman, G. E. 2010. Kisspeptin and the preovulatory gonadotrophin-releasing hormone/luteinising hormone surge in the ewe: Basic aspects and potential applications in the control of ovulation. *J. Neuroendocrinol.*, 22:710–705.

Caraty, A., Smith, J. T., Lomet, D., Ben Said, S., Morrissey, A., Cognie, J., Doughton, B., et al. 2007. Kisspeptin synchronizes preovulatory surges in cyclical ewes and causes ovulation in seasonally acyclic ewes. *Endocrinology*, 148:5258–5267.

Card, J. P. 2000. Pseudorabies virus and the functional architecture of the circadian timing system. *J. Biological Rhythms*, 15:453–461.

Cardwell, J. R., and Liley, N. R. 1991a. Androgen control of social status in males of a wild population of stoplight parrot fish, *Sparisoma viride*. *Horm. Behav.*, 25:1–18.

Cardwell, J. R., and Liley, N. R. 1991b. Hormonal control of sex and color change in the stoplight parrot fish, *Sparisoma viride* (Scaridae). *J. Comp. Physiol.*, 115:299–317.

Cardwell, J. R., Sorensen, P. W., Van der Kraak, G. J., and Liley, N. R. 1996. Effect of dominance status on sex hormone levels in laboratory and wild-spawning male trout. *Gen. Comp. Endocrinol.*, 101:333–341.

Carlsen, E., Giwercman, A., Keiding, N., and Skakkebaek, N. E. 1992. Evidence for decreasing quality of semen during the past 50 years. *Br. Med. J.*, 305:609–613.

Carlson, L. L., Weaver, D. R., and Reppert, S. M. 1991. Melatonin receptors and signal transduction during development in Siberian hamsters (*Phodopus sungorus*). *Brain Res. Dev. Brain Res.*, 59:83–88.

Carmichael, M. S., Nelson, R. J., and Zucker, I. 1981. Hamster activity and estrous cycles: Control by a single versus multiple circadian oscillator(s). *Proc. Natl. Acad. Sci. USA*, 78:7830–7834.

Carneiro, B. T. S., and Araujo, J. F. 2009. The food-entrainable oscillator: A network of interconnected brain structures entrained by humoral signals? *Chronobiol. Int.*, 26:1273–1289.

Carpenter, C. R. 1940. A field study of the behavior and social relations of howling monkeys. *Comp. Psychol. Monogr.*, 16:1–21.

Carré, J. M., Campbell, J. A., Lozoya, E., Goetz, S. M. M., and Welker, K. M. 2013. Changes in testosterone mediate the effect of winning on subsequent aggressive behavior. *Psychoneuroendocrinology*, 38:2034–2041.

Carroll, B. J. 1980. Dexamethasone suppression test in depression. *Lancet*, 8206:1249.

Carroll, B. J., Cassidy, F., Naflolowitz, D., Tatham, N. E., Wilson, W. H., Iranmanesh, A., Liu, P. Y., and Veldhuis, J. D. 2007. Pathophysiology of hypercortisolism in depression. *Acta Psych. Scand.*, 115:90–103.

Carroll, B. J., Curtis, G. C., and Mendels, J. 1976. Neuroendocrine regulation in depression. I. Limbic system-adrenocortical dysfunction. *Arch. Gen. Psychiatry*, 33:1039.

Carroll, B. J., Martin, F. I. R., and Davies, B. 1968. Resistance to suppression by dexamethasone of plasma 11-OHCS levels in severe depressive illness. *Br. Med. J.*, 3:285–290.

Carter, C. S. (ed.). 1974. *Hormones and Sexual Behavior*. Stroudsburg, Dowden, Hutchinson and Ross, Inc.

Carter, C. S. 2014. Oxytocin pathways and the evolution of human behavior. *Ann. Rev. Psychol.*, 65:17–39.

Carter, C. S., and Keverne, E. B. 2002. The neurobiology of social affiliation and pair bonding. In D. W. Pfaff, A. P. Arnold, A. M. Etgen, S. E. Fahrbach, and R. T. Rubin (eds.), *Hormones, Brain and Behavior*, Vol. 1, pp. 299–338. Academic Press, New York.

Carter, C. S., DeVries, A. C., and Getz, L. L. 1995. Physiological substrates of mammalian monogamy. *Neurosci. Biobehav. Rev.*, 19:303–314.

Carter, C. S., DeVries, A. C., Taymans, S. E., Roberts, R. L., Williams, J. R., and Getz, L. L. 1997a. Peptides, steroids, and pair bonding. *Ann. N. Y. Acad. Sci.*, 807:260–272.

Carter, C. S., Grippo, A. J., Pournajafi-Nazarloo, H., Ruscio, M. G., and Porges, S. W. 2008. Oxytocin, vasopressin, and sociality. *Prog. Brain Res.*, 170:331–336.

Carter, C. S., Lederhendler, I. I., and Kirkpatrick, B. 1997b. *Integrative Neurobiology of Affiliation*. Vol. 807. New York Academy of Sciences: New York.

Carter, C. S., Williams, J. R., Witt, D. M., and Insel, T. R. 1992. Oxytocin and social bonding. *Ann. N. Y. Acad. Sci.*, 652:204–211.

Carter, D. S., and Goldman, B. D. 1983a. Antigonadal effects of timed melatonin infusion in pinealectomized male Djungarian hamsters (*Phodopus sungorus sungorus*): Duration is the critical parameter. *Endocrinol.*, 113:1261–1267.

Carter, D. S., and Goldman, B. D. 1983b. Progonadal role of the pineal in the Djungarian hamster (*Phodopus sungorus sun-*

gorus): Mediation by melatonin. *Endocrinol.*, 113:1268–1273.

Casanueva, F. F., and Dieguez, C. 2002. Ghrelin: The link connecting growth with metabolism and energy homeostasis. *Rev. Endocr. Metab. Disorders*, 3:325–338.

Cascio, C., Yu, G. Z., Insel, T. R., and Wang, Z. X. 1998. Dopamine D_2 receptor-mediated regulation of partner preferences in female prairie voles. *Soc. Neurosci. Abstr.*, 24:372.13.

Cassone, V. M. 1998. Melatonin's role in vertebrate circadian rhythms. *Chronobiol. Int.*, 15:457–473.

Casto, J. M., Nolan, V. Jr., and Ketterson, E. D. 2001. Steroid hormones and immune function: Experimental studies in wild and captive dark-eyed juncos (*Junco hyemalis*). *Am. Nat.*, 157:408–420.

Catalano, S., Avila, D. M., Marsico, S., Wilson, J. D., Glickman, S. E., and McPhaul, M. J. 2002. Virilization of the female spotted hyena cannot be explained by alterations in the amino acid sequence of the androgen receptor (AR). *Molecular and Cellular Endocrinol.*, 194:85–94.

Cawthorn, J. M., Morris, D. L., Ketterson, E. D., and Nolan, V. V. 1998. Influence of experimentally elevated testosterone on nest defence in dark-eyed juncos. *Anim. Behav.*, 56:617–621.

CDC. Behavioral Risk Factor Surveillance System. http://apps.nccd.cdc.gov/gisbrfss/default.aspx. Accessed April 28, 2011.

Ceci, S. J., and Williams, W. M. 2009. *The Mathematics of Sex: How Biology and Society Conspire to Limit Talented Women and Girls*. Oxford University Press, New York.

Cedrini, L., and Fasolo, A. 1970. Olfactory attractants in sex recognition of the crested newt: An electrophysiological research. *Monitore Zool.* (Italy), 5:223–229.

Celotti, F., Negri-Cesi, P., and Poletti, A. 1997. Steroid metabolism in the mammalian brain: 5 alpha-reduction and aromatization. *Brain Res. Bull.*, 44:365–375.

Cervos-Navarro, J., and Diemer, N. H. 1991. Selective vulnerability in brain hypoxia. *Crit. Rev. Neurobiol.*, 6:149–182.

Chakraborty, S. 1995. Plasma prolactin and luteinizing hormone during termination and onset of photorefractoriness in intact and pinealectomized European starlings (*Sturnus vulgaris*). *Gen. Comp. Endocrinol.*, 99:185–91.

Challis, J. R. G., Davies, I. J., and Ryan, K. J. 1973. The concentrations of progesterone, estrone and estradiol-17β in the plasma of pregnant rabbits. *Endocrinol.*, 93:971–976.

Chamero, P., Marton, T. F., Logan, D. W., Flanagan, K., Cruz, J. R., Saghatelian, A., Cravatt, B. F., and Stowers, L. 2007. Identification of protein pheromones that promote aggressive behaviour. *Nature*, 450:899–902.

Chamley, W. A., Buckmaster, J. M., Cerini, M. R., Cumming, I. A., Goding, J. R., Obst,

J. M., Williams, A., and Wingfield, C. 1973. Changes in the levels of progesterone, corticosteroids, estrone, estradiol-17β, luteinizing hormone, and prolactin in the peripheral plasma of the ewe during late pregnancy and at parturition. *Biol. Reprod.,* 9:30–35.

Champagne, F. A. 2008. Epigenetic mechanisms and the transgenerational effects of maternal care. *Front. Neuroendocrinol.,* 29:386–397.

Champagne, F. A. 2009. Nurturing nature: Social experiences and the brain. *J. Neuroendocrinol.,* 21:867–868.

Champagne, F. A., Curley, J. P., Keverne, E. B., and Bateson, P. P. G. 2007. Natural variations in postpartum maternal care in inbred and outbred mice. *Physiol. Behav.,* 91:325–334.

Champagne, F. A., Weaver, I. C., Diorio, J., Sharma, S., and Meaney, M. J. 2003. Natural variations in maternal care are associated with estrogen receptor alpha expression and estrogen sensitivity in the medial preoptic area. *Endocrinol.,* 144:4720–4724.

Champagne, F., Diorio, J., Sharma, S., and Meaney, M. J. 2001. Naturally occurring variations in maternal behavior in the rat are associated with differences in estrogen-inducible central oxytocin receptors. *Proc. Natl. Acad. Sci. USA,* 98:12736–12741.

Chang, A. M., Aeschbach, D., Duffy J. F., and Czeisler, C. A. 2015. Evening use of light-emitting eReaders negatively affects sleep, circadian timing, and next-morning alertness. *Proc. Natl. Acad. Sci. USA,* 112:18490.

Chappel, S. C. 1985. Neuroendocrine regulation of luteinizing hormone and follicle stimulating hormone: A review. *Life Sci.,* 36:97–103.

Charles-Dominique, P. 1977. *Ecology and Behaviour of Nocturnal Primates.* Duckworth, London.

Chavez, M., Riedy, C. A., Van Dijk, G., and Woods, S. C. 1996. Central insulin and macronutrient intake in the rat. *Am. J. Physiol.,* 271:R727–R731.

Chehab, F. F., Lim, M. E., and Lu, R. 1996. Correction of the sterility defect in homozygous obese female mice by treatment with the human recombinant leptin. *Nat. Gen.,* 12:318–20.

Chen, C., Chang, Y. C., Liu, C. L., Chang, K. J., and Guo, I. C. 2006. Leptin-induced growth of human ZR-75-1 breast cancer cells is associated with up-regulation of cyclin D1 and c-Myc and down-regulation of tumor suppressor p53 and p21WAF1/CIP1. *Breast Cancer Res. Treat.,* 98:121–132.

Cheng, M. Y., Bullock, C. M., Li, C., Lee, A. G., Bermak, J. C., Belluzzi, J., Weaver, D. R., Leslie, F., and Zhou, Q. Y. 2002. Prokineticin 2 transmits the behavioural circadian rhythm of the suprachiasmatic nucleus. *Nature,* 417:405–410.

Cheng, M.-F., and Lehrman, D. S. 1973. Relative effectiveness of diethylstilbestrol and estradiol benzoate in inducing female behavior patterns of ovariectomized ring doves (*Streptopelia risoria*). *Horm. Behav.,* 4:123–127.

Cheng, M.-F., and Silver, R. 1975. Estrogen–progesterone regulation of nest building behavior in ovariectomized ring doves (*Streptopelia risoria*). *J. Comp. Physiol. Psychol.,* 88:256–263.

Cherry, J. A., and Baum, M. J. 1990. Effects of lesions of a sexually dimorphic nucleus in the preoptic/anterior hypothalamic area on the expression of androgen- and estrogen-dependent sexual behaviors in male ferrets. *Brain Res.,* 522:191–203.

Cherry, J. A., Basham, M. E., Weaver, C. E., Krohmer, R. W., and Baum, M. J. 1990. Ontogeny of the sexually dimorphic male nucleus in the preoptic/anterior hypothalamus of ferrets and its manipulation by gonadal steroids. *J. Neurobiol.,* 21:844–857.

Cheung, C. C., Thornton, J. E., Kuijper, J. L., Weigle, D. S., Clifton, D. K., and Steiner, R. A. 1997. Leptin is a metabolic gate for the onset of puberty in the female rat. *Endocrinol.,* 138:855–858.

Chevalier, G., and Deniau, J. M. 1990. Disinhibition as a basic process in the expression of striatal functions. *Trends Neurosci.,* 13:277–290.

Cho, H., Zhao, X., Hatori, M., Yu, R. T., Barish, G. D., Lam, M. T., Chong, L. W., et al. 2012. Regulation of circadian behaviour and metabolism by REV-ERB-α and REV-ERB-β. *Nature,* 485:123–127.

Cho, K. 2001. Chronic 'jet lag' produces temporal lobe atrophy and spatial cognitive deficits. *Nature Neuroscience,* 4:567–568.

Cho, K., Ennaceur, A., Cole, J.C., and Suh, C.K. 2000. Chronic jet lag produces cognitive deficits. *J. Neurosci.,* 20:RC66:1–5.

Choi, D. C., Nguyen, M. M., Tamashiro, K. L., Ma, L. Y., Sakai, R. R., and Herman, J. P. 2006. Chronic social stress in the visible burrow system modulates stress-related gene expression in the bed nucleus of the stria terminalis. *Physiol. Behav.,* 89:301–310.

Choleris, E., Gustafsson, J. A., Korach, K. S., Muglia, L. J., Pfaff, D. W., and Ogawa, S. 2003. An estrogen-dependent four-gene micronet regulating social recognition: A study with oxytocin and estrogen receptor-α and -β knockout mice. *Proc. Natl. Acad. Sci. USA,* 100:6192–6197.

Choleris, E., Kavaliers, M., and Pfaff, D. W. 2004. Functional genomics of social recognition. *J. Neuroendocrinol.,* 16:383–389.

Choleris, E., Ogawa, S., Kavaliers, M, Gustafsson, J.A., Korach, K.S., Muglia, L.J., and Pfaff, D.W. 2006. Involvement of estrogen receptor alpha and beta and oxytocin in social recognition. A detailed behavioral

analysis with knockout female mice. *Genes, Brain and Behavior,* 5:528–539.

Chow, B. Y., Han, X., Dobry, A. S., Qian, X., Chuong, A. S., Li, M., Henninger, M. A., et al. 2010. High-performance genetically targetable optical neural silencing by light-driven proton pumps. *Nature,* 463:98–102.

Chowdhury, T. K., Laila, K., Hutson, J. M., and Banu, T. 2015. Male gender identity in children with 46,XX DSD with congenital adrenal hyperplasia after delayed presentation in mid-childhood. *J. Pediatr. Surg.,* 50:2060–2062.

Chowdhury, V. S., Yamamoto, K., Ubuka, T., Bentley, G. E., Hattori, A., and Tsutsui, K. 2010. Melatonin stimulates the release of gonadotropin-inhibitory hormone by the avian hypothalamus. *Endocrinology,* 151:271–280.

Christensen, L. W., and Clemens, L. G. 1975. Blockade of testosterone-induced mounting behavior in the male rat with intracranial application of the aromatization inhibitor, androst-1,4,6-triene-3,17-dione. *Endocrinol.,* 97:1545–1551.

Christian, C. A., and Moenter, S. M. 2007. Estradiol induces diurnal shifts in GABA transmission to gonadotropin-releasing hormone neurons to provide a neural signal for ovulation. *J. Neurosci.,* 27:1913–1921.

Christianson, T., Wallen, K., Brown, B., and Glickman, S. E. 1972. Effects of castration, blindness and anosmia on social reactivity in the male Mongolian gerbil (*Meriones unguiculatus*). *Physiol. Behav.,* 10:989–994.

Christie, M. H., and Barfield, R. J. 1979. Effects of castration and home cage residency on aggressive behavior in rats. *Horm. Behav.,* 13:85–91.

Chrousos, G. P. 1998a. Stressors, stress, and neuroendocrine integration of the adaptive response. The 1997 Hans Selye Memorial Lecture. *Ann. N.Y. Acad. Sci.,* 85:311–335.

Chrousos, G. P. 1998b. Ultradian, circadian, and stress-related hypothalamic–pituitary–adrenal axis activity—a dynamic digital-to-analog modulation. *Endocrinol.,* 139:437–440.

Chrousos, G. P. 2000. Stress, chronic inflammation, and emotional and physical well-being: Concurrent effects and chronic sequelae. *J. Allergy Clin. Immunol.,* 106:S275–S291.

Chrousos, G. P., and Kino, T. 2007. Glucocorticoid action networks and complex psychiatric and/or somatic disorders. *Stress,* 10:213–219.

Chrousos, G. P., McCarty, R., Pacak, K., Cizza, G., Sternberg, E., Gold, P. W., and Kvetnansky, R. (eds.). 1995. *Stress: Basic Mechanisms Clinical Implications.* Vol. 771. New York Academy of Science, New York.

Chrousos, G. P., Torpy, D. J., and Gold, P. W. 1998. Interactions between the hypothalamic-pituitary-adrenal axis and the female reproductive system: Clinical implications. *Ann. Intern. Med.*, 129:229–240.

Cinti, S., Frederich, R. C., Zingaretti, M. C., De Matteis, R., Flier, J. S., and Lowell, B. B. 1997. Immunohistichemical localization of leptin and uncoupling protein in white and brown adipose tissue. *Endocrinol.*, 138:797–804.

Cirulli, F., Francia, N., Berry, A., Aloe, L., Alleva, E., and Suomi, S. J. 2008. Early life stress as a risk factor for mental health: Role of neurotrophins from rodents to nonhuman primates. *Neurosci. Biobehav. Rev.*, 33:573–585.

Clancy, A. N., Zumpe, D., and Michael, R. P. 1995. Intracerebral infusion of an aromatase inhibitor, sexual behavior and brain estrogen receptor-like immunoreactivity in intact male rats. *Neuroendocrinol.*, 61:98–111.

Clark, A. S., Davis, L. A., and Roy, E. J. 1985. A possible physiological basis for the dud-stud phenomenon. *Horm. Behav.*, 19:227–230.

Clark, M. M., Desousa, D., Vonk, J., Galef, B. G. 1997. Parenting and potency: Alternative routes to reproductive success in male Mongolian gerbils. *Anim. Behav.*, 54:635–62.

Clark, M. M., vom Saal, F. S., and Galef, B. G. 1992. Intrauterine positions and testosterone levels of adult male gerbils are correlated. *Physiol. Behav.*, 51:957–960.

Clarke, I. J. 1987. GnRH and ovarian hormone feedback. *Oxf. Rev. Reprod. Biol.*, 9:54–95.

Clarke, I. J., Cummins, J. T., Jenkin, M., and Phillips, D. J. 1989. The oestrogen-induced surge of LH requires a 'signal' pattern of gonadotrophin-releasing hormone input to the pituitary gland in the ewe. *J. Endocrinol.*, 122:127–134.

Clarke, I. J., Smith, J. T., Caraty, A., Goodman, R. L., and Lehman, M. N. 2009. Kisspeptin and seasonality in sheep. *Peptides*, 30:154–163.

Clarkson, J., and Herbison, A. E. 2006. Postnatal development of kisspeptin neurons in mouse hypothalamus: Sexual dimorphism and projections to gonadotropin-releasing hormone neurons. *Endocrinol.*, 147:5817–5825.

Clarkson, J., and Herbison, A. E. 2009. Oestrogen, kisspeptin, GPR54 and the pre-ovulatory luteinising hormone surge. *J. Neuroendocrinol.*, 21:305–311.

Clemens, L. G., Gladue, B. A., and Coniglio, L. P. 1978. Prenatal endogenous androgenic influences on masculine sexual behavior and genital morphology in male and female rats. *Horm. Behav.*, 10:40–53.

Clotfelter, E. D., O'Neal, D. M., Gaudioso, J. M, Casto, J. M., Parker-Renga, I. M., Snajdr, E. A., Duffy, D. L., Nolan, V. Jr., and Ketterson, E. D. 2004. Consequences of elevating plasma testosterone in females of a socially monogamous songbird: Evidence

of constraints on male evolution? *Horm. Behav.*, 46:171–178.

Clutton-Brock, T. H. 1991. *The Evolution of Parental Care.* Princeton University Press, Princeton.

Clutton-Brock, T. H., Albon, S. D., Gibson, R. J., and Guinness, F. E. 1979. The logical stag: Adaptive aspects of fighting in red deer (*Cervus elaphus L.*). *Anim. Behav.*, 27:211–225.

Coe, C. L. 1990. Psychobiology of maternal behavior in nonhuman primates. In N. A. Krasnegor and R. S. Bridges (eds.), *Mammalian Parenting*, pp. 157–183. Oxford University Press, Oxford.

Coe, C. L., Mendoza, S. P., Somtherman, W. P., and Levine, S. 1978. Mother-infant attachment in the squirrel monkey: Adrenal response to separation. *Behav. Biol.*, 22:256–263.

Cohen-Bendahan, C. C. C., van de Beek, C., and Berenbaum, S. A. 2005. Prenatal sex hormone effects on child and adult sex-typed behavior: Methods and findings. *Neurosci. Biobehav. Rev.*, 29:353–384.

Cohen, I. T., Sherwin, B. B., and Fleming, A. S. 1987. Food cravings, mood, and the menstrual cycle. *Horm. Behav.*, 21:457–470.

Cohen, R. A., and Albers, H. E. 1991. Disruption of human circadian and cognitive regulation following a discrete hypothalamic lesion: A case study. *Neurol.*, 41:726–729.

Cohen, S. L., Halaas, J. L., Friedman, J. M., Chait, B. T., Bennet, L., Chang, D., Hecht, R., and Collins, F. 1996. Human leptin characterization. *Nature*, 382:589.

Coker, F. and Taylor, D. 2010. Antidepressant-induced hyperprolactinaemia: Incidence, mechanisms and management. *CNS Drugs*, 24:563–574.

Colapinto, J. 1997. The case of Joan/John. *Rolling Stone Magazine*, 11 December 1997, pp. 54–97.

Colborn, T., Myers, J. P., and Dumanoski, D. 1997. *Our Stolen Future: Are We Threatening Our Own Fertility, Intelligence, and Survival? A Scientific Detective Story.* E. F. Dutton, New York.

Cole, M. A., Kim, P. J., Kalman, B. A., and Spencer, R. L. 2000. Dexamethasone suppression of corticosteroid secretion: Evaluation of the site of action by receptor measures and functional studies. *Psychoneuroendocrinol.*, 25:151–167.

Coleman, R. M. 1986. *Awake at 3:00 A.M. By Choice or by Chance?* W. H. Freeman, New York.

Coll, A. P., Farooqi, I. S., Challis, B. G., Yeo, G. S., and O'Rahilly, S. 2004. Proopiomelanocortin and energy balance: Insights from human and murine genetics. *J. Clin. Endocrinol. Metab.*, 89:2557–2562.

Coll, A. P., Farooqui, I. S., and O'Rahilly, S. 2007. The hormonal control of food intake. *Cell*, 129:251–262.

Collaer, M. L., and Hines, M. 1995. Human behavioral sex differences: A role for gonadal hormones during early development? *Psychol. Bull.*, 118:55–107.

Collier, T. J., Quirk, G. J., and Routtenberg, A. 1987. Separable roles of hippocampal granule cells in forgetting and pyramidal cells in remembering spatial information. *Brain Res.*, 409:316–328.

Collingridge, G. L., Peineau, S., Howland, J. G., and Wang, Y. T. 2010. Long-term depression in the CNS. *Nat. Rev. Neurosci.*, 11:459–473.

Cologer-Clifford, A., Simon, N. G., Lu, S. F., Smoluk, S. A. 1997. Serotonin agonist-induced decreases in intermale aggression are dependent on brain region and receptor subtype. *Pharmacol. Biochem. Behav.* 58: 425–430.

Cologer-Clifford, A., Simon, N. G., Richter, M. L., Smoluk, S. A., and Lu, S. 1999. Androgens and estrogens modulate 5-HT_{1A} and 5-HT_{1B} agonist effects on aggression. *Physiol. Behav.*, 65:823–828.

Coltheart, M., Hull, E., and Slater, D. 1975. Sex differences in imagery and reading. *Nature*, 253:438–440.

Comasco, E. and Sundström-Poromaa, I. 2015. Neuroimaging the menstrual cycle and premenstrual dysphoric disorder. *Curr. Psychiat. Rep.*, 17:619.

Commins, D., and Yahr, P. 1984. Adult testosterone levels influence the morphology of a sexually dimorphic area in the Mongolian gerbil brain. *J. Comp. Neurol.*, 224:132–140.

Commins, D., and Yahr, P. 1985. Autoradiographic localization of estrogen and androgen receptors in the sexually dimorphic area and other regions of the gerbil brain. *J. Comp. Neurol.*, 231:473–489.

Commins, W. D. 1932. The effect of castration at various ages upon learning ability of male albino rats. *J. Comp. Psychol.*, 14:29–53.

Conrad, C. D. 2009. A critical review of chronic stress effects on spatial learning and memory. *Prog. Neuro-Psychopharmacol. Biol. Psychiatry*, 34:742–755.

Conrad, C. D., LeDoux, J. E., Magarinos, A. M., and McEwen, B. S. 1999. Repeated restraint stress facilitates fear conditioning independently of causing hippocampal CA3 dendritic atrophy. *Behav. Neurosci.*, 113:902–913.

Conrad, C., and Roy, E. 1992. Selective loss of hippocampal granule cells following adrenalectomy: Implications for spatial memory. *J. Neurosci.*, 13:2582–2590.

Conte, C. O., Rosito, G. B. A., Palmini, A. L. F., Lucion, A. B., and de Almeida, A. M. R. 1986. Pre-training adrenaline recovers the amnestic effect of Met-enkephalin in demedullated rats. *Behav. Brain Res.*, 21:163–166.

Contreras, R. J., Fox, E., and Drugovich, M. L. 1982. Area postrema lesions produce feeding deficits in the rat: Effects of preoperative dieting and 2-deoxy-D-glucose. *Physiol. Behav.*, 29:875–884.

Convit, A., Wolf, O. T., Tarshish, C., and de Leon, M. J. 2003. Reduced glucose tolerance is associated with poor memory performance and hippocampal atrophy among normal elderly. *Proc. Natl. Acad. Sci. USA*, 100:2019–2022.

Coolen, L. M., Fitzgerald, M. E., Yu, L., and Lehman, M. N. 2004. Activation of mu opioid receptors in the medial preoptic area following copulation in male rats. *Neuroscience*, 124:11–21.

Coolen, L. M., Veening, J. G., Petersen, D. W., and Shipley, M. T. 2003a. Parvocellular sub-parafascicular thalamic nucleus in the rat: Anatomical and functional compartmentalization. *J. Comp. Neurol.*, 463:117–131.

Coolen, L. M., Veening, J. G., Wells, A. B., and Shipley, M. T. 2003b. Afferent connections of the parvocellular subparafascicular thalamic nucleus in the rat: Evidence for functional subdivisions. *J. Comp. Neurol.*, 463, 132–156.

Cooper, A. J. 1986. Progestins in the treatment of male sex offenders: A review. *Can. J. Psychiatry*, 31:73–79.

Cooper, J. R., Bloom, F. E, and Roth, R. H. 1986. *The Biochemical Basis of Neuropharmacology.* Oxford University Press, New York.

Cooper, M. A., and Huhman, K. L. 2010. Blocking corticotrophin-releasing factor-2 receptors, but not corticotrophin-releasing factor-1 receptors or glucocorticoid feedback, disrupts the development of conditioned defeat. *Physiol. Behav.*, 101:527–532.

Cordoba-Montoya, D. A., and Carrer, H. F. 1997. Estrogen facilitates induction of long term potentiation in the hippocampus of awake rats. *Brain Res.*, 778:430–438.

Coria-Avila, G. A., Ouimet, A. J., Pacheco, P., Manzo, J., and Pfaus, J. G. 2005. Olfactory conditioned partner preference in the female rat. *Behav. Neurosci.*, 119:716–725.

Cormack, M., and Sheldrake, P. 1974. Menstrual cycle variations in cognitive ability: A preliminary report. *Int. J. Chronobiol.*, 2:53–55.

Corso, J. F. 1959. Age and sex differences in thresholds. *J. A. S. A.*, 31:489–507.

Cosgrove, K., Mazure, C., and Staley, J. 2009. Evolving knowledge of sex differences in brain structure, function, and chemistry. *Biol. Psychol.*, 62:847–855.

Cowley, M. A., Smart, J. L., Rubinstein, M., Cerdan, M. G., Diano, S., Horvath, T. L., Cone, R. D., and Low, M. J. 2001. Leptin activates anorexigenic POMC neurons through a neural network in the arcuate nucleus. *Nature*, 411:480–484.

Cowley, M. A., Smith, R. G., Diano, S., Tschop, M., Pronchuk, N., Grove, K. L., Strasburger, C. J., et al. 2003. The distribution and mechanism of action of ghrelin in the CNS demonstrates a novel hypothalamic circuit regulating energy homeostasis. *Neuron*, 37:649–661.

Cox, R. M., and John-Alder, H. B. 2005. Testosterone has opposite effects on male growth in lizards (*Sceloporus* spp.) with opposite patterns of sexual size dimorphism. *J. Exp. Biol.*, 208:4679–4687.

Cox, R. M., Stenquist, D. S., and Calsbeek, R. 2009a. Testosterone, growth and the evolution of sexual size dimorphism. *J. Evol. Biol.*, 22:1586–1598.

Cox, R. M., Stenquist, D. S., Henningsen, J. P., and Calsbeek, R. 2009b. Manipulating testosterone to assess links between behavior, morphology, and performance in the brown anole *Anolis sagrei*. *Physiol. Biochem. Zool.*, 82:686–698.

Coyral-Castel, S., Tosca, L., Ferreira, G., Jeanpierre, E., Rame, C., Lomet, D., Caraty, A., Monget, P., Chabrolle, C., and Dupont, J. 2008. The effect of AMP-activated kinase activation on gonadotrophin-releasing hormone secretion in GT1-7 cells and its potential role in hypothalamic regulation of the oestrous cyclicity in rats. *J. Neuroendocrinol.*, 20:335–346.

Craft, S., Newcomer, J., Kanne, S., Dagogo-Jack, S., Cryer, P., Sheline, Y., Luby, J., Dagogo-Jack, A., and Alderson, A. 1996. Memory improvement following induced hyperinsulinemia in Alzheimer's disease. *Neurobiol. Aging*, 17:123–130.

Craft, S., Peskind, E., Schwartz, M. W., Schellenberg, G. D., Raskind, M., and Porte, D. 1998. Cerebrospinal fluid and plasma insulin levels in Alzheimer's disease: Relationship to severity of dementia and apolipoprotein E genotype. *Neurol.*, 50:164–168.

Craig, M. C., and Murphy, D. G. 2010. Estrogen therapy and Alzheimer's dementia. *Ann. N. Y. Acad. Sci.*, 1205:245–253.

Craig, W. 1917. Appetites and aversions as constituents of instincts. *Proc. Natl. Acad. Sci.*, 3:685–688.

Crawford, S. G., Kaplan, B. J., and Field, L. L. 1995. Absence of an association between insulin-dependent diabetes mellitus and developmental learning difficulties. *Hereditas*, 122:73–78.

Creel, S. 2005. Dominance, aggression and glucocorticoid levels in social carnivores. *J. Mammal.*, 86:255–264.

Creel, S., Creel, N. M., and Monfort, S. L. 1996. Social stress and dominance. *Nature*, 379:212.

Crews, D. 1984. Gamete production, sex hormone secretion, and mating behavior uncoupled. *Horm. Behav.*, 18:22–28.

Crews, D. 1987. Diversity and evolution of behavioral controlling mechanisms. In D. Crews (ed.), *Psychobiology of Reproductive Behavior*, pp. 88–119. Prentice Hall, Englewood Cliffs, NJ.

Crews, D. 1991. Trans-seasonal action of androgen in the control of spring courtship behavior in male red-sided garter snakes. *Proc. Natl. Acad. Sci. USA*, 88:3545–3548.

Crews, D. 1993. The organizational concept and vertebrates without sex chromosomes. *Brain, Behavior and Evolution*, 42:202–214.

Crews, D. 1997. Species diversity and the evolution of behavioral controlling mechanisms. *Ann. N. Y. Acad. Sci.*, 807:1–21.

Crews, D. 2010. Neural control of sexual behavior. In Breed, M. D. and Moore, J. (eds.), *Encyclopedia of Animal Behavior, vol. 2*, pp. 541–548, Academic Press, Oxford.

Crews, D., and Bull, J. L. 2009. Mode and tempo in environmental sex determination in vertebrates. *Semin. Cell Dev. Biol.*, 20:251–255.

Crews, D., and Fitzgerald, K. 1980. "Sexual" behavior in parthenogenetic lizards (*Cnemidophorus*). *Proc. Natl. Acad. Sci. USA*, 77:499–502.

Crews, D., and Gartska, W. R. 1982. The ecological physiology of a garter snake. *Sci. Am.*, Nov., 158–168.

Crews, D., and McLachlan, J. A. 2006. Epigenetics, evolution, endocrine disruption, health, and disease. *Endocrinol.*, 147:S4–10.

Crews, D., and Moore, M. C. 1986. Evolution of mechanisms controlling mating behavior. *Science*, 231:121–125.

Crews, D., and Silver, R. 1985. Reproductive physiology and behavior interactions in nonmammalian vertebrates. In N. T. Adler, D. W. Pfaff, and R. W. Goy (eds.), *Handbook of Behavioral Neurobiology, Vol. 7, Reproduction*, pp. 101–182. Plenum Press, New York.

Crews, D., Bull, J. J., and Billy, A. J. 1988a. Sex determination and sexual differentiation in reptiles. In J. M. A. Sitsen (ed.), *Handbook of Sexology, Vol. 6: The Pharmacology and Endocrinology of Sexual Function*, pp. 98–121. Elsevier, New York.

Crews, D., Camazine, M., Diamond, R., Mason, R. T., Tokarz, R. R., and Garstka, W. R. 1984. Hormonal independence of courtship behavior in the male garter snake. *Horm. Behav.*, 18:29–41.

Crews, D., Diamond, M. A., Whittier, J., and Mason, R. 1985. Small male body size in garter snake depends on testes. *Am. J. Physiol.*, 249:R62–R66.

Crews, D., Fuller, T., Mirasol, E. G., Pfaff, D. W., and Ogawa, S. 2004. Postnatal environment affects behavior of adult transgenic mice. *Exp. Biol. Med.*, 229:935–939.

Crews, D., Hingorani, V., and Nelson, R. J. 1988b. Role of the pineal gland in the control of annual reproductive behavioral and physiological cycles in the red-sided garter snake (*Thamnophis sirtalis parietalis*). *J. Biol. Rhythms*, 3:293–302.

Croiset, G., Marjoleen, J. M. A., and Kamphuis, P. J. 2000. Role of corticotrophin-releasing factor, vasopressin and the autonomic nervous system in learning and memory. *Eur. J. Pharmacol.*, 405:225–234.

Cross, G. B., Marley, J., Miles, H., and Willson, K. 2001. Changes in nutrient intake during the menstrual cycle of overweight women with premenstrual syndrome. *British J. Nutrition*, 85:475–482.

Crowe, S. A., Oddmund, K., Delmore, K. E., Laskemoen, T., Nocera, J., Lifjeld, J. T., and Robertson, R. J. 2009. Paternity assurance through frequent copulations in a wild passerine with intense sperm competition. *Anim. Behav.*, 77:183–187.

Culbert, K. M., Breedlove, S. M., Alexandra Burt, S. A., and Klump, K. L. 2008. Prenatal hormone exposure and risk for eating disorders: A comparison of opposite-sex and same-sex twins. *Arch. Gen. Psychiatry,* 65:329–336.

Cummings, D. E., Overduiun, J., and Foster-Schubert, K. E. 2004. Gastric bypass for obesity: Mechanisms of weight loss and diabetes resolution. *J. Clin. Endocrinol. Metab.,* 89:2608–2615.

Cummings, D. E., Purnell, J. Q., Frayo, R. S., Schmidova, K., Wisse, B. E., and Weigle, D. S. 2001. A preprandial rise in plasma ghrelin levels suggests a role in meal initiation in humans. *Diabetes,* 50:1714–1719.

Cummings, D. E., Weigle, D. S., Frayo, R. S., Breen, P. A., Ma, M. K., Dellinger, E. P., and Purnell, J. Q. 2002. Plasma ghrelin levels after diet-induced weight loss or gastric bypass surgery. *N. Engl. J. Med.,* 346:1623–1630.

Cunningham, J. T. 1900. *Sexual Dimorphisms in the Animal Kingdom.* Black, London.

Cunningham, R. L., and McGinnis, M. Y. 2006a. Factors influencing aggression toward females by male rats exposed to anabolic androgenic steroids during puberty. *Horm. Behav.*, 51:135–141.

Cunningham, R. L., and McGinnis, M. Y. 2006b. Physical provocation of pubertal anabolic androgenic steroid exposed male rats elicits aggression towards females. *Horm. Behav.*, 50:410–416.

Currie, P. J., and Wilson, L. M. 1993. Potentiation of dark onset feeding in obese mice (genotype *ob/ob*) following central injection of norepinephrine and clonidine. *Eur. J. Pharmacol.*, 232:227–234.

Cuthill, I. C., Hunt, S., Cleary, C., and Clark, C. 1997. Colour bands, dominance, and body mass regulation in male zebra finches (*Taeniopygia guttata*). *Proc. Roy. Soc. Lond. B,* 264:1093–1099.

Czaja, J. A. 1978. Ovarian influences on primate food intake: Assessment of progesterone actions. *Physiol. Behav.,* 21:923–928.

Czaja, J. A., and Goy, R. W. 1975. Ovarian hormones and food intake in female guinea pigs and rhesus monkeys. *Horm. Behav.,* 6:923–928.

Czeisler, C. A., Duffy, J. F., Shanahan, T. L., Brown, E. N., Mitchell, J. F., Rimmer, D. W., et al. 1999. Stability, precision, and near-24-hour period of the human circadian pacemaker. *Science.* 284:2177–2181.

Czeisler, C. A., Kronauer, R. E., Allan, J. S., et al. 1989. Bright light induction of strong (Type 0) resetting of the human circadian pacemaker. *Science,* 244:1328–1332.

Czoty, P. W., Gould, R. W., and Nader, M. A. 2009. Relationship between social rank and cortisol and testosterone concentrations in male cynomolgus monkeys (*Macaca fascicularis*). *J. Neuroendocrinol.,* 21:68–76.

D'Cunha, T. M., King, S. J., Fleming, A. S., and Lévy, F. 2011. Oxytocin receptors in the nucleus accumbens shell are involved in the consolidation of maternal memory in postpartum rats. *Horm. Behav.,* 59:14–21.

Daan, S., Damassa, D., Pittendrigh, C. S., and Smith, E. R. 1975. An effect of castration and testosterone replacement on a circadian pacemaker in mice (*Mus musculus*). *Proc. Natl. Acad. Sci. USA,* 72:3744–3747.

Dabbs, J. M. 1990. Age and seasonal variation in serum testosterone concentrations among men. *Chronobiol. Int.,* 7:245–249.

Dabbs, J. M., and Hargrove, M. F. 1997. Age, testosterone, and behavior among female prison inmates. *Psychosom. Med.,* 59:477–480.

Dabbs, J. M., and Mohammed, S. 1992. Male and female salivary testosterone concentrations before and after sexual activity. *Physiol. Behav.,* 52:195–197.

Dabbs, J. M., and Morris, R. 1990. Testosterone, social class, and antisocial behavior in a sample of 4,462 men. *Psychol. Sci.,* 1:209–211.

Dabbs, J. M., Frady, R. L., Carr, T. S., and Besch, N. F. 1987. Saliva testosterone and criminal violence in young adult prison inmates. *Psychosom. Med.,* 49:174–182.

Dabbs, J. M., LaRue, D., and Williams, P. M. 1990. Testosterone and occupational choice: Actors, ministers, and other men. *J. Pers. Soc. Psychol.,* 59:1261–1265.

Dabbs, J. M., Ruback, R. B., Frady, R. L., Hopper, C. H., and Sgoutas, D. S. 1989. Saliva testosterone and criminal violence among women. *Pers. Indiv. Diff.,* 9:269–275.

DaCosta, A. P., Guevara-Guzman, R. G., Ohkura, S., Goode, J. A., and Kendrick, K. M. 1996. The role of oxytocin release in the paraventricular nucleus in the control of maternal behaviour in the sheep. *J. Neuroendocrinol.,* 8:163–177.

Dailey, M. J., and Bartness, T. J. 2009. Appetitive and consummatory ingestive behaviors stimulated by PVH and perifornical area NPY injections. *Am. J. Physiol.,* 296:R877–R892.

Dallman, M. F. 2005. Fast glucocorticoid actions on brain: Back to the future. *Front. Neuroendocrinol.,* 26:103–108.

Dallman, M. F., Pecoraro, N., Akana, S. F., La Fleur, S. E., Gomez, F., Houshyar, H., Bell, M. E., Bhatnagar, S., Laugero, K. D., and Manalo, S. 2003. Chronic stress and obesity: A new view of "comfort food." *Proc. Natl. Acad. Sci. USA,* 100:11696–11701.

Dallman, M. F., Strack, A. M., Akana, S. F., Bradbury, M. J., Hanson, E. S., Scribner, K. A., and Smith, M. 1993. Feast and famine: Critical role of glucocorticoids with insulin in daily energy flow. *Front. Neuroendocrinol.,* 14:303–347.

Dalvit-McPhillips, S. P. 1983. The effect of the human menstrual cycle on nutrient intake. *Physiol. Behav.,* 31:209–212.

Dalvit, S. P. 1981. The effect of the menstrual cycle on patterns of food intake. *Am. J. Clin. Nutr.,* 34:1811–1815.

Daly, M., and Wilson, M. 1983. *Sex, Evolution, and Behavior.* Weber and Schmidt, Boston.

Damassa, D. A., Davidson, J. M., and Smith, E. R. 1977. The relationship between circulating testosterone levels and male sexual behavior in rats. *Horm. Behav.,* 8:275–286.

Damiola, F., Le Minh, N., Preitner, N., Kornmann, B., Fleury-Olela, F., and Schibler, U. 2000. Restricted feeding uncouples circadian oscillators in peripheral tissues from the central pacemaker in the suprachiasmatic nucleus. *Genes and Development,* 14:2950–2961.

Damjanovic, A. K., Yang, Y., Glaser, R., Kiecolt-Glaser, J. K., Nguyen, H., Laskowski, B., Zou, Y., Beversdorf, D. Q., and Weng, N. 2007. Accelerated telomere erosion is associated with a declining immune function of caregivers of Alzheimer's disease patients. *J. Immunol.,* 179:4249–4254. doi:10.4049/jimmunol.179.6.4249.

Daniel, J. M. 2006. Effects of oestrogen on cognition: What have we learned from basic research? *J. Neuroendocrinol.,* 18:787–795.

Daniel, J. M., and Bohacek, J. 2010. The critical period hypothesis of estrogen effects on cognition: Insights from basic research. *Biochim. Biophys. Acta: Gen. Subj.,* 1800:1068–1076.

Daniel, J. M., and Dohanich, G. P. 2001. Acetylcholine modulates the estrogen-induced increase in NMDA receptor binding in CA1 of the hippocampus and the associated improvement in working memory. *J. Neurosci.,* 21:6949–6956.

Daniel, J. M., Fader, A. J., Spencer, A. L., and Dohanich, G. P. 1997. Estrogen enhances performance of female rats during acquisition of a radial arm maze. *Horm. Behav.,* 32:217–225.

Daniel, J. M., Hulst, J. L., and Berbling, J. L. 2006. Estradiol replacement enhances working memory in middle-aged rats when initiated immediately after ovariectomy, but not after a long-term period of ovarian hormone deprivation. *Endocrinol.,* 147:607–614.

Daniels, D., and Fluharty, S. J. 2004. Salt appetite: A neurohormonal viewpoint. *Physiol. Behav.*, 81:319–337.

Daniels, D., Mietlicki, E. G., Nowak, E. L., and Fluharty, S. J. 2009. Angiotensin II stimulates water and NaCl intake through separate cell signaling pathways in rats. *Exp. Physiol.*, 94:130–137.

Dannecker, E. A., Hausenblas, H. A., Kaminski, T. W., and Robinson, M. E. 2005. Sex differences in delayed onset muscle pain. *Clin. J. Pain*, 21:120–126.

Dardeno, T. A., Chou, S. H., and Moon, H. S. 2010. Leptin in human physiology and therapeutics. *Front. Neuroendocrinol.*, 31:377–393.

Dardente, H., Wyse, C. A., Birnie, M. J., Dupre, S. M., Loudon, A. S., Lincoln, G. A., and Hazlerigg, D. G. 2010. A molecular switch for photoperiod responsiveness in mammals. *Curr. Biol.*, 20:2193–2198.

Dark, J., and Zucker, I. 1984. Gonadal and photoperiodic control of seasonal body weight changes in male voles. *Am. J. Physiol.*, 247:R84–R88.

Dark, J., and Zucker, I. 1985. Circannual rhythms of ground squirrels: Role of the hypothalamic paraventricular nucleus. *J. Biol. Rhythms*, 1:17–23.

Dark, J., and Zucker, I. 1986. Photoperiodic regulation of body mass and fat reserves in the meadow vole. *Physiol. Behav.*, 38:851–854.

Dark, J., Pickard, G. E., and Zucker, I. 1985. Persistence of circannual rhythms in ground squirrels with lesions of the suprachiasmatic nuclei. *Brain Res.*, 332:201–207.

Dark, J., Stern, J., and Zucker, I. 1989. Adipose tissue dynamics during cyclic weight loss and weight gain of ground squirrels. *Am. J. Physiol.*, 256:R1286–1292.

Dark, J., Whaling, C. S., and Zucker, I. 1987b. Androgens exert opposite effects on body mass of heavy and light meadow voles. *Horm. Behav.*, 21:471–477.

Darrow, J. M., and Goldman, B. D. 1986. Circadian regulation of pineal melatonin and reproduction in the Djungarian hamster. *J. Biol. Rhythms*, 1:39–53.

Darrow, J. M., Duncan, M. J., Bartke, A., Bona-Gallo., A., and Goldman, B. D. 1988. Influence of photoperiod and gonadal steroids on hibernation in the European hamster. *J. Comp. Physiol.*, 163:339–48.

Daugherty, J. E. 1998. Treatment strategies for premenstrual syndrome. *Am. Fam. Physician*, 58:197–198.

David, H. G., Green, J. T., Grant, A. J., and Wilson, C. A. 1995. Simultaneous bilateral quadriceps rupture: A complication of anabolic steroid abuse. *J. Bone Joint Surg. Br.*, 77:159–160.

David, K., Dingemanse, E., Freud, J., and Lanquer, E. 1935. Crystalline male hormone from testes (testosterone) are more active than androsterone prepared from urine or cholesterol. *J. Physiol. Chem.*, 233:281–282.

Davidsen, D., Vistisen, B., and Astrup, A. 2007. Impact of the menstrual cycle on determinants of energy balance: A putative role in weight loss attempts. *Int. J. Obes.*, 31:1777–1785.

Davidson, A. J. 2006. Search for the feeding-entrainable circadian oscillator: A complex proposition. *Am. J. Physiol.*, 290:R1524–R1526.

Davidson, A. J., Yamazaki, S., Arble, D. M., Menaker, M., and Block, G. D. 2008. Resetting of central and peripheral circadian oscillators in aged rats. *Neurobiol. Aging*, 29:471–477.

Davidson, J. M. 1966a. Activation of the male rat's sexual behavior by intracerebral implantation of androgen. *Endocrinol.*, 84:1365–1372.

Davidson, J. M. 1966b. Characteristics of sex behaviour in male rats following castration. *Anim. Behav.*, 14:266–272.

Davidson, J. M. 1969. Effects of estrogen on the sexual behavior of male rats. *Endocrinol.*, 84:1365–1372.

Davidson, J. M., Kwan, M., and Greenleaf, W. J. 1982. Hormonal replacement and sexuality in men. *J. Clin. Endocrinol. Metab.*, 11:599–623.

Davidson, J. M., Stefanick, M. L., Sachs, B. D., and Smith, E. R. 1978. Role of androgen in sexual reflexes of the male rat. *Physiol. Behav.*, 21:141–146.

Davidson, R. J. 2000. Dysfunction in the neural circuitry of emotion regulation: A possible prelude to violence. *Science*, 289, 591–594.

Davis, G. J., and Meyer, R. K. 1973. Seasonal variation in LH and FSH of bilaterally castrated snowshoe hares. *Gen. Comp. Endocrinol.*, 20:61–68.

Davis, H. P., and Squire, L. R. 1984. Protein synthesis and memory: A review. *Psychol. Bull.*, 96:518–559.

Davis, J. D., and Campbell, C. S. 1973. Peripheral control of meal size in the rat: Effect of sham feeding on meal size and drinking rate. *J. Comp. Physiol. Psychol.*, 83:379–387.

Davis, J. D., Gallagher, R. J., Ladove, R. F., and Turavasky, A. J. 1969. Inhibition of food intake by a humoral factor. *J. Comp. Physiol. Psychol.*, 67:407–417.

Davis, P. G., and Barfield, R. J. 1979. Activation of masculine sexual behavior by intracranial estradiol benzoate implants in male rats. *Neuroendocrinol.*, 28:217–227.

Davis, S. R., McCloud, P., Strauss, B. J., and Burger, H. 1995. Testosterone enhances estradiol's effects on postmenopausal bone density and sexuality. *Maturitas*, 21:227–236.

Davis, W. J., Mpitsos, G. J., and Pinneo, J. M. 1974. The behavioral hierarchy of the mollusk, *Pleurobranchaea*. II. Hormonal suppression of feeding associated with egg laying. *J. Comp. Physiol.* 95:225-243.

Dawson, A. and Goldsmith, A. R. 1982. Prolactin and gonadotropin secretion in wild starlings (*Sturnus vulgaris*) during the annual cycle and in relation to nesting, incubation, and rearing young. *Gen. Comp. Endocrinol.*, 48:213–221.

Day, C. 2001. The rising tide of type 2 diabetes. *Brit. J. Diabetes Vasc. Dis.*, 1:37–43.

Day, L. B., McBroom, J. T., and Schlinger, B. A. 2006. Testosterone activates courtship display but does not alter plumage in the tropical golden-collared manakin (*Manacus vitellinus*). *Horm. Behav.*, 49:223–232.

Day, M., and Good, M. 2005. Ovariectomy-induced disruption of long-term synaptic depression in the hippocampal CA1 region in vivo is attenuated with chronic estrogen replacement. *Neurobiol. Learn. Mem.*, 83:13–21.

de Bournonville, C., Dickens, M. J., Ball, G. F., Balthazart, J., and Cornil, C. A. 2012. Dynamic changes in brain aromatase activity following sexual interactions: Where, when and why? *Psychoneuroendocrinology*, 38:789–799.

De Fonseca, F. R., Cebeira, M., Ramos, J. A., Martín, M., and Fernández-Ruiz, J. J. 1994. Cannabinoid receptors in rat brain areas: Sexual differences, fluctuations during estrous cycle and changes after gonadectomy and sex steroid replacement. *Life Sci.*, 54:159–170.

De Jong, T. R., Chaulke, M., Harris, B. N., and Saltzman, W. 2009. From here to paternity: Neural correlates of the onset of paternal behavior in California mice (*Peromyscus californicus*). *Horm. Behav.*, 56:220–231.

de Kloet, A. D., and Woods, S. C. 2009. Minireview: Endocannabinoids and their receptors as targets for obesity therapy. *Endocrinol.*, 150:2531–2536.

de Kloet, E. R., Joels, M., Oitzl, M., and Sutanto, W. 1991. Implication of brain corticosteroid receptor diversity for the adaptation syndrome concept. In G. Jasmin and M. Cantin (eds.), *Stress Revisited: Neuroendocrinology of Stress. Methods and Achievements in Experimental Pathology*, Vol 14:104–132. Karger, Basel.

de la Iglesia, H. O., Blaustein, J. D., and Bittman, E. L. 1999. Oestrogen receptor-alpha-immunoreactive neurones project to the suprachiasmatic nucleus of the female Syrian hamster. *J. Neuroendocrinol.*, 11:481–490.

de la Iglesia, H. O., Meyer, J., and Schwartz, W. J. 2003. Lateralization of circadian pacemaker output: Activation of left- and right-sided luteinizing hormone-releasing hormone neurons involves a neural rather than a humoral pathway. *J. Neurosci.*, 23:7412–7414.

De Mairan, J. J. 1729. *Observation Botanique*. L'Academie Royale des Sciences Paris, 35–36.

de Mitcheson, Y. S., and Liu, M. 2008. Functional hermaphroditism in teleosts. *Fish and Fisheries*, 9:1–43.

de Quervain, D. J. F., Aerni, A., Schelling, G., and Roozendaal, B. 2009. Glucocorticoids and the regulation of memory in health and disease. *Front. Neuroendocrinol.*, 30:358–370.

de Quervain, D. J., Roozendaal, B., and McGaugh, J. L. 1998. Stress and glucocorticoids impair retrieval of long-term spatial memory. *Nature*, 394:787–790.

de Roux, N., Genin, E., Carel, J. C., Matsuda, F., Chaussain, J. L., and Milgrom, E. 2003. Hypogonadotropic hypogonadism due to loss of function of the KiSS1-derived peptide receptor GPR54. *Proc. Natl. Acad. Sci. USA*, 100:10972–10976.

de Souza, C. J., and Meier, A. H. 1987. Circadian and seasonal variations of plasma insulin and cortisol concentrations in the Syrian hamster, *Mesocricetus auratus. Chronobiol. Int.* 4:141–151.

de Waal, F. B. M. 1987. Tension regulation and nonreproductive functions of sex among captive bonobos (*Pan paniscus*). *Natl. Geogr. Res.*, 3:318–335.

de Waal, F. B. M., and Lanting, F. 1997. *Bonobo: The Forgotten Ape*, University of California Press, Berkeley.

Deakin, J. F. W. 1988. Relevance of hormone–CNS interactions to psychological changes in the puerperium. In R. Kumar and I. F. Brockington (eds.), *Motherhood and Mental Illness 2: Causes and Consequences,* pp. 113–132. Wright, Boston.

DeBattista, C. 2006. Augmentation and combination strategies for depression. *J. Psychopharmacol.*, 20:11–18.

DeBold, J. F., and Miczek, K. A. 1981. Sexual dimorphism in the hormonal control of aggressive behavior of rats. *Pharmacol. Biochem. Behav.*, 14, suppl. 1:89–93.

DeBold, J. F., and Miczek, K. A. 1984. Aggression persists after ovariectomy in female rats. *Horm. Behav.*, 18:177–190.

DeCoursey, P. J., and Krulas, J. R. 1998. Behavior of SCN-lesioned chipmunks in natural habitat: A pilot study. *J. Biol. Rhythms,* 13:229–244.

DeCoursey, P. J., Krulas, J. R., Mele, G., and Holley, D. C. 1997. Circadian performance of suprachiasmatic nuclei (SCN)-lesioned antelope ground squirrels in a desert enclosure. *Physiol. Behav.*, 62:1099–1108.

Degen, L., Oesch, S., Casanova, M., Graf, S., Ketterer, S., Drewe, J., and Beglinger, C. 2005. Effect of peptide YY_{3-36} on food intake in humans. *Gastroenterol.*, 129:1430–1436.

DeJonge, F. H., Louwerse, A. L., Ooms, M. P., Evers, P., Endert, E., and Van de Poll, N. E. 1989. Lesions of the SDN–POA inhibit sexual behavior of male Wistar rats. *Brain Res. Bull.*, 23:483–492.

deLacoste-Utamsing, C., and Holloway, R. L. 1982. Sexual dimorphism in the human corpus callosum. *Science*, 216:1431–1432.

deLacoste, M.-C., Holloway, R. L., and Woodward, D. J. 1986. Sex differences in the fetal human corpus callosum. *Hum. Neurobiol.*, 5:1–5.

Della-Zuana, O., Revereault, L., Beck-Sickinger, A., Monge, A., Caignard, D.-H., Fauchère, J.-L., Henlin, M., et al. 2004. A potent and selective NPY Y_5 antagonist reduces food intake but not through blockade of the NPY Y_5 receptor. *Int. J. Obes.*, 28:628–639.

Delville, Y., David, J. T., Taravosh-Lahn, K., and Wommack, J. C. 2003. Stress and the development of agonistic behavior in golden hamsters. *Horm. Behav.*, 44:263–270.

Delville, Y., De Vries, G. J., and Ferris, C. F. 2000. Neural connections of the anterior hypothalamus and agonistic behavior in golden hamsters. *Brain Behav. Evol.*, 55:53–76.

Delville, Y., Melloni, R. H., and Ferris, C. F. 1998. Behavioral and neurobiological consequences of social subjugation during puberty in golden hamsters. *J. Neurosci.*, 18:2667–2672.

Delville, Y., Newman, M. L., Wommack, J. C., Taravosh-Lahn, K., and Cervantes, M. C., 2005. Development of aggression. In R. J. Nelson (ed.), *Biology of Aggression*. Oxford University Press, New York.

Demas, G. E., and Nelson, R. J. 1996. Photoperiod and temperature interact to affect immune parameters in adult male deer mice (*Peromyscus maniculatus*). *J. Biol. Rhythms*, 11:94–102.

Demas, G. E., Moffatt, C. A., Drazen, D. L., and Nelson, R. J. 1999. Castration does not inhibit aggressive behavior in castrated adult male prairie voles (*Microtus ochrogaster*). *Physiol. Behav.*, 66:59–62.

Demas, G. E., Polacek, K. M., Durazzo, A., and Jasnow, A. M. 2004. Adrenal hormones mediate melatonin-induced increases in aggression in male Siberian hamsters (*Phodopus sungorus*). *Horm. Behav.*, 46:582–591.

Demas, G. E., Polacek, K. M., Durazzo, A., and Jasnow, A. M. 2004. Adrenal hormones mediate melatonin-induced increases in aggression in male Siberian hamsters (*Phodopus sungorus*). *Horm. Behav.*, 46:582–691.

Dempsey, E. W. 1968. William Caldwell Young. An appreciation. In M. Diamond (ed.), *Perspectives in Reproduction and Sexual Behavior*, pp. 453–458. University of Indiana Press, Bloomington.

Demski, L. S. 1987. Diversity in reproductive patterns and behavior in teleost fishes. In D. Crews (ed.), *Psychobiology of Reproductive Behavior*, pp. 2–27. Prentice Hall, Englewood Cliffs, NJ.

Dennis, R. 1992. Cultural change and the reproductive cycle. *Social Sci. Med.*, 34:485–489.

Denton, D. 1982. *The Hunger for Salt*. Springer-Verlag, Berlin.

Denton, D., Shade, R., Zamarippa, F., Egan, G., et al. 1999. Neuroimaging of genesis and satiation of thirst and an interoceptor-driven theory of origins of primary consciousness. *Proc. Nat. Acad. Sci. USA*, 96:5304–5309.

Desmond, N. L., and Levy, W. B. 1997. Ovarian steroid control of connectivity in the female hipppocampus: An overview of recent experimental findings and speculations on its functional consequences. *Hippocampus*, 7:239–245.

Dethier, V. G. 1976. *The Hungry Fly: A Physiological Study of the Behavior Associated with Feeding*. Harvard University Press, Cambridge, MA.

Deutsch, J. A. 1982. Controversies in food intake regulation. In B. G. Hoebel and D. Novin (eds.), *The Neural Basis of Feeding and Reward*, pp. 137–148. Haer Institute, Brunswick, ME.

Devane, W. A., Hanus, L., Breuer, A., Pertwee, R. G., Stevenson, L. A., Griffin, G., Gibson, D., Mandelbaum, A., Etinger, A., and Mechoulam, R. 1992. Isolation and structure of a brain constituent that binds to the cannabinoid receptor. *Science*, 258:1946–1949.

DeVito, L. M., Konigsberg, R., Lykken, C., Sauvage, M., Young, W. S., and Eichenbaum, H. 2009. Vasopressin 1b receptor knock-out impairs memory for temporal order. *J. Neurosci.*, 29:2676–2683.

DeVries, A. C., Craft, T. K., Glasper, E. R., Neigh, G. N., and Alexander, J. K. 2007. 2006 Curt P. Richter award winner: Social influences on stress responses and health. *Psychoneuroendocrinol.*, 32:587–603.

DeVries, A. C., DeVries, M. B., Taymans, S. E., and Carter, C. S. 1995a. The effects of social stress on social preferences are sexually dimorphic in prairie voles. *Proc. Natl. Acad. Sci. USA*, 93:11980–11984.

DeVries, A. C., DeVries, M. B., Taymans, S. E., and Carter, C. S. 1995b. Modulation of pair bonding by corticosterone in female prairie voles (*Microtus ochrogaster*). *Proc. Natl. Acad. Sci. USA*, 92:7744–7748.

DeVries, A. C., Johnson, C.L., and Carter, C. S. 1996. Characterization of partner preference in male and female prairie voles (*Microtus ochrogaster*). *Can. J. Zool.*, 75:295–301.

DeVries, A. C., Young, W. S., Nelson, R. J. 1997. Reduced aggressiveness in mice with targeted disruption of the gene for oxytocin. *J. Neuroendocrinol.*, 9:363–368.

DeVries, G. J., and Panzica, G. C. 2006. Sexual differentiation of central vasopressin and vasotocin systems in vertebrates: Different mechanisms, similar endpoints. *Neuroscience*, 138:947–955.

DeVries, G. J., and Simerly, R. B. 2002. Anatomy, development, and function of sexually dimorphic neural circuits in the mammalian brain. In D. W. Pfaff, A. P. Arnold, A. M. Etgen, S. E. Fahrbach, and R. T. Rubin (eds.), *Hormones, Brain and Behavior*, Vol. 4, pp. 137–191. Academic Press, New York.

DeVries, G. J., and Södersten, P. 2009. Sex differences in the brain: The relation between structure and function. *Horm. Behav.*, 55:589–596.

DeVries, G. J., Buijs, R. M., Van Leeuwen, F. W., Caffe, A. R., and Swaab, D. F. 1985. The vasopressinergic innervation of the brain in normal and castrated rats. *J. Comp. Neurol.*, 233:236–254.

DeVries, G. J., Rissman, E. F., Simerly, R. B., Yang, L. Y., Scordalakes, E. M., Auger, C. J., Swain, A., Lovell-Badge, R., Burgoyne, P. S., and Arnold, A. P. 2002. A model system for the study of sex chromosome effects on sexually dimorphic neural and behavioral traits. *J. Neurosci.*, 22:9005–9014.

DeWied, D. 1964. Influence of anterior pituitary on avoidance learning and escape behavior. *Am. J. Physiol.*, 207:255–259.

DeWied, D. 1969. Effects of peptide hormones on behavior. In W. F. Ganong and L. Martini (eds.), *Front. Neuroendocrinol.*, pp. 97–140. Oxford Press, New York.

DeWied, D. 1974. Pituitary–adrenal system hormones and behavior. In F. O. Schmidt and F. G. Worden (eds.), *The Neurosciences: Third Study Program*, pp. 653–666. MIT Press, Cambridge, MA.

DeWied, D. 1977. Peptides and behavior. *Life Sci.*, 20:195–204.

DeWied, D. 1980. Hormonal influences on motivation, learning, memory, and psychosis. In D. T. Krieger and J. C. Hughes (eds.), *Neuroendocrinology*, pp. 194–204. Sinauer Associates, Sunderland, MA.

Dewing, P., Shi, T., Horvath, S., and Vilain, E. 2003. Sexually dimorphic gene expression in mouse brain precedes gonadal differentiation. *Mol. Brain Res.*, 118:82–90.

Dewsbury, D. A. 1972. Patterns of copulatory behavior in male mammals. *Q. Rev. Biol.*, 47:1–33.

Dewsbury, D. A. 1979. *Comparative Animal Behavior*. McGraw-Hill, New York.

Dewsbury, D. A. 1984. *Comparative Psychology in the Twentieth Century*. Hutchinson Ross, Stroudsburg, PA.

Dey, J., Misra, A., Desai, N. G., Mahapatra, A. K., and Padma, M. V. 1997. Cognitive function in younger type II diabetes. *Diabetes Care*, 20:32–35.

Dhabhar, F. S., and McEwen, B. S. 1997. Acute stress enhances while chronic stress suppresses immune function in vivo: A role for leukocyte trafficking. *Brain Behav. Immunol.*, 11:286–306.

Dhabhar, F. S., and McEwen, B. S. 1999. Enhancing versus suppressive effects of stress hormones on skin immune function. *Proc. Natl. Acad. Sci. USA*, 96:1059–1064.

Di Marzo, V. 2008. Targeting the endocannabinoid system: To enhance or reduce? *Nat. Rev. Drug Discov.*, 7:438–455.

Di, S., Malcher-Lopes, R., Halmos, K. S., and Tasker, J. G. 2003. Nongenomic glucocorticoid inhibition via endocannabinoid release in the hypothalamus: A fast feedback mechanism. *J. Neurosci.*, 23:4850–4857.

Diamond, M. 1970. Intromission pattern and species vaginal code in relation to induction of pseudopregnancy. *Science,* 169:995–997.

Diamond, M. 1984. *Sex Watching*. Macdonald and Company, London.

Diamond, M. 1996. Prenatal predisposition and the clinical management of some pediatric conditions. *J. Sex Marital Ther.*, 22:139–147.

Diamond, M., and Sigmundson, H. K. 1997. Sex reassignment at birth. *Arch. Pediatr. Adolesc. Med.*, 151:298–304.

Dickerman, R. D., Schaller, F., Prather, I., and McConathy, W. J. 1995. Sudden cardiac death in a 20-year-old bodybuilder using anabolic steroids. *Cardiol.*, 86:172–173.

Dickinson, R. L. 1949. *Atlas of Human Sex Anatomy*. Williams & Wilkins, Baltimore.

Dickmeis, T. 2009. Glucocorticoids and the circadian clock. *J. Endocrinol.*, 200:3–22.

Dietrich, A., and Allen, J. D. 1997a. Vasopressin and memory. I. The vasopressin analogue AVP4–9 enhances working memory as well as reference memory in the radial arm maze. *Behav. Brain Res.*, 87:197–200.

Dietrich, A., and Allen, J. D. 1997b. Vasopressin and memory. II. Lesions to the hippocampus block the memory enhancing effects of a AVP4–9 in the radial maze. *Behav. Brain Res.*, 87:201–208.

Dietz, D. M., Curtis, K. S., and Contreras, R. J. 2006. Taste, salience, and increased NaCl ingestion after repeated sodium depletions. *Chem. Senses* 31:33–41.

Dinan, T. G. 1998. Psychoneuroendocrinology of depression. Growth hormone. *Psychiatr. Clin. North Am.*, 21:325–339.

Ding, J. M., Chen, D., Weber, E. T., Faiman, L. E., Rea, M. A., and Gillette, M. U. 1994. Resetting the biological clock: Mediation of nocturnal circadian shifts by glutamate and NO. *Science*, 266:1713–1717.

Disney, H. J., Lofts, B., and Murton, A. J. 1959. Duration of the regeneration period of the internal reproductive rhythm in a xerophilous equatorial bird, *Quelea quelea. Nature*, 184:1659–1660.

Dixson, A. F. 1980. Androgens and aggressive behavior in primates: A review. *Aggressive Behav.*, 6:37–67.

Dixson, A. F. 1997. Evolutionary perspectives on primae mating systems and behavior. *Ann. N. Y. Acad. Sci.*, 807:42–61.

Dixson, A. F., and George, L. 1982. Prolactin and parental behaviour in a male New World primate. *Nature*, 299:551–553.

Dobs, A. S., Meikle, A. W., Arver, S., Sanders, S. W., Caramelli, K. E., and Mazer, N. A. 1999. Pharmacokinetics, efficacy, and safety of a permeation-enhanced testosterone transdermal system in comparison with bi-weekly injections of testosterone enanthate for the treatment of hypogonadal men. *J. Clin. Endocrinol. Metab.*, 84:3469–3478.

Dodd, G. T., Dercherf, S., Loh, K., Simonds, S. E., Wiede, F., Balland, E., Merry, T. L., et al. 2014. Leptin and insulin act on POMC neurons to promote the browning of white fat. *Cell*, 160:88–104.

Dodson, R. E., and Gorski, R. A. 1993. Testosterone propionate administration prevents the loss of neurons within the central part of the medial preoptic nucleus. *J. Neurobiol.*, 24:80–88.

Doering, C. H., Brodie, H. K. H., Kraemer, H. C., Moos, R. H., Becker, H. B., and Hamburg, D. A. 1975. Negative affect and plasma testosterone: A longitudinal human study. *Psychosom. Med.*, 37:484–491.

Dohanich, G. 2002. Gonadal steroids, learning, and memory. In D. W. Pfaff, A. P. Arnold, A. M. Etgen, S. E. Fahrbach, and R. T. Rubin (eds.), *Hormones, Brain and Behavior*, Vol. 2, pp. 265–327. Academic Press, New York.

Dohanich, G., Korol, D., and Shors, T. 2009. Steroids, learning and memory. In D. W. Pfaff et al. (eds.), *Hormones, Brain and Behavior*. (2nd ed.) Vol. 1, pp. 539–576. Academic Press, San Diego.

Döhler, K. D., and Hancke, J. L. 1978. Thoughts on the mechanism of sexual brain differentiation. In K. D. Döhler and M. Kawakami (eds.), *Hormones and Brain Development*, pp. 153–157. Elsevier, Amsterdam.

Döhler, K. D., Hines, M., Coquelin, A., Davis, F., Shryne, J. E., and Gorski, R. A. 1982. Pre- and postnatal influence of diethylstilbestrol on differentiation of the sexually dimorphic nucleus in the preoptic area of the female rat brain. *Neuroendocrinol. Lett.*, 4:361–365.

Dominguez, J. M. and Hull, E. M. 2010. Serotonin impairs copulation and attenuates ejaculation-induced glutamate activity in the medial preoptic area. *Behav. Neurosci.*, 124:554–557.

Dominoni, D. M., Borniger, J. C., and Nelson, R. J. 2016. Light at night, clocks and health: From humans to wild organisms. *Biol. Lett.*, 12:20160015.

Donaldson, Z. R., and Young, L. J. 2008. Oxytocin, vasopressin, and the neurogenetics of sociality. *Science*, 322:900–904.

Doty, R. L. 1978. Gender and reproductive state correlates of taste perception in humans. In T. McGill, D. A. Dewsbury, and B. Sachs (eds.), *Sex and Behavior: Status and Prospects*, pp. 337–362. Plenum, New York.

Doty, R. L. 1997. Studies of human olfaction from the University of Pennsylvania Smell and Taste Center. *Chemical Senses*, 22:565–586.

Doty, R. L., and Anisko, J. J. 1973. Procaine hydrochloride olfactory block eliminated mounting in the golden hamster. *Physiol. Behav.*, 10:395–397.

Doty, R. L., and Cameron, E. L. 2009. Sex differences and reproductive hormone influences on human odor perception. *Physiol. Behav.*, 98:213–228.

Doucet, S. M., and Montgomerie, R. 2003a. Multiple sexual ornaments in satin bowerbirds: ultraviolet plumage and bowers signal different aspects of male quality. *Behav. Ecol.*, 14:503–509.

Doucet, S. M., and Montgomerie, R. 2003b. Structural plumage colour and parasites in satin bowerbirds *Ptilonorhynchus violaceus*: Implications for sexual selection. *J. Avian Biol.* 34:237–242.

Douglass, J., McKinzie, A. A., and Couceyro, P. 1995. PCR differential display identifies a rat brain mRNA that is transcriptionally regulated by cocaine and amphetamine. *J. Neurosci.*, 15:2471–2481.

Dowell, S. F., and Lynch, G. R. 1987. Duration of the melatonin pulse in the hypothalamus controls testicular function in pinealectomized mice (*Peromyscus leucopus*). *Biol. Reprod.*, 36:1095–1101.

Drazen, D. L., and Woods, S. C. 2003. Peripheral signals in the control of satiety and hunger. *Curr. Opin. Clin. Nutr. Metab. Care*, 6:621–629.

Drazen, D. L., Wortman, M. D., Seeley, R. J., and Woods, S. C. 2006a. Neuropeptide Y prepares rats for scheduled feeding. *Am. J. Physiol.*, 288:R1601–R1611.

Drea, C. M., Weldele, M. L., Forger, N. G., Coscia, E. M., Frank, L. G., Licht, P., and Glickman, S. E. 1998. Androgens and masculinization of genitalia in the spotted hyaena (*Crocuta crocuta*). 2. Effects of prenatal anti-androgens. *J. Reproduction and Fertility*, 113:117–127.

Dreger, A. D. 1998. *Hermaphrodites and the Medical Invention of Sex*. Harvard University Press, Cambridge, MA.

Drickamer, L. C., and Vessey S. H. 1982. *Animal Behavior: Concepts, Processes, Methods.* PWS, Boston.

Dryden, S., Pickavance, L., Frankish, H. M., and Williams, G. 1995. Increased neuropeptide Y secretion in the hypothalamic paraventricular nucleus of obese (fa/fa) Zucker rats. *Brain Res.*, 690:185–188.

DSM-IV. 1994/2000. *Diagnostic and Statistical Manual of Mental Disorders.* (4th ed.) American Psychiatric Association, Arlington, VA.

Du, J., Lorrain, D. S., and Hull, E. M. 1998. Castration decreases extracellular, but increases intracellular, dopamine in medial preoptic area of male rats. *Brain Res.*, 782:11–17.

Dube, M. G., Kalra, S. P., and Kalra. P. S. 1999. Food intake elicited by central administration orexins/hypocretins: Identification of hypothalamic sites of action. *Brain Res.*, 842:473–477.

Dubocovich, M. L., Rivera-Bermudez, M. A., Gerdin, M. J., and Masana, M. I. 2003. Molecular pharmacology, regulation and function of mammalian melatonin receptors. *Frontiers in Bioscience*, 8:1093–1108.

Dubrovsky, B. D. 2005. Steroids, neuroactive steroids and neurosteroids in psychopathology. *Prog. Neuro-Psychopharmacol. Biol. Psychiatry*, 29:169–192.

Dulac, C., and Torello, A. T. 2003. Molecular detection of pheromone signals in mammals: From genes to behavior. *Nature Rev. Neuroscience*, 4:551–562.

Dunbar, I. 1975. Behaviour of castrated animals. *Vet. Rec.*, 96:92–93.

Duncan, M. J. 1998. Photoperiodic regulation of hypothalamic neuropeptide messenger RNA expression: Effect of pinealectomy and neuroanatomical location. *Mol. Brain Res.*, 57:142–148.

Duncan, M. J. 2007. Aging of the mammalian circadian timing system: Changes in the central pacemaker and its regulation by photic and nonphotic signals. *Neuroembryol. Aging*, 4:85–101.

Dungan, H. M., Clifton, D. K., and Steiner, R. A. 2006. Kisspeptin neurons as central processors in the regulation of gonadotropin-releasing hormone secretion. *Endocrinol.*, 147:1154–1158.

Dunn, A. J., Steelman, S., and Delanoy, R. 1980. Intraventricular ACTH and vasopressin cause regionally specific changes in cerebral deoxyglucose uptake. *J. Neurosci. Res.*, 5:485–495.

Dupré, C., Lovett-Barron, M., Pfaff, D. W., and Kow, L. M. 2010. Histaminergic responses by hypothalamic neurons that regulate lordosis and their modulation by estradiol. *Proc. Natl. Acad. Sci. USA*, 107:12311–12316.

Eakin, R. M. 1973. *The Third Eye.* University of California Press, Berkeley.

Eals, M., and Silverman, I. 1994. The hunter-gatherer theory of spatial sex differences: Proximate factors mediating the female advantage in recall of object arrays. *Ethol. Sociobiol.*, 15:95–105.

Ebbinghaus, H. 1908. *Psychology: An Elementary Textbook.* D. C. Heath, Boston.

Eberhart, J. A. 1988. Neural and hormonal correlates of primate sexual behavior. *Comp. Primate Biol. Neurosci.*, 4:675–705.

Eckhardt, C. 1863. Untersuchungen uber die erektion des penis beim hund. *Beitr. Anat. Phisiol.*, 3:123–147.

Eddy, E. M., Washburn, T. F., Bunch, D. O., Goulding, E. H., Gladen, B. C., Lubahn, D. B., and Korach, K. S. 1996. Targeted disruption of the estrogen receptor gene in male mice causes alternation of spermatogenesis and infertility. *Endocrinol.*, 137:4796–4805.

Edgar, D. M., Kilduff, T. S., Martin, C. E., and Dement, W. C. 1991. Influence of running wheel activity on free-running sleep/wake and drinking circadian rhythms in mice. *Physiol. Behav.*, 50:373–378.

Edinger, K. L., and Frye, C. A. 2007. Androgen's effects to enhance learning may be mediated in part through actions at estrogen receptor-β in the hippocampus. *Neurobiol. Learn. Mem.*, 87:78–85.

Edler, C., Lipson, S. F., and Keel, P. K. 2007. Ovarian hormones and binge eating in bulimia nervosa. *Psychol. Med.* 37:131–141.

Edwards, D. A. 1969. Early androgen stimulation and aggressive behavior in male and female mice. *Physiol. Behav.*, 4:333–338.

Edwards, D. A. 1970. Post-neonatal androgenization and adult aggressive behavior in female mice. *Physiol. Behav.*, 5:465–467.

Egawa, M., Yoshimatsu, H., and Bray, G. A. 1990. Effect of corticotropin releasing hormone and neuropeptide Y on electrophysiological activity of sympathetic nerves to interscapular brown brown adipose tissue. *Neuroscience*, 34:771–775.

Egger, G., Liang, G., Aparicio, A., and Jones, P. A. 2004. Epigenetics in human disease and prospects for epigenetic therapy. *Nature*, 429:457–463.

Ehrenkranz, J., Bliss, E., and Sheard, M. H. 1974. Plasma testosterone: Correlation with aggressive behavior and social dominance in man. *Psychosom. Med.*, 36:469–475.

Ehrensing, R. H., Kastin, A. J., Schalch, D. S., Friesen, H. G., Vargas, J. R., and Schally, A. V. 1974. Affective state and thyrotropin and prolactin responses after repeated injections of thyrotropin-releasing hormone in depressed patients. *Am. J. Psychiatry*, 131:714–718.

Ehrhardt, A. A., and Baker, S. W. 1974. Fetal androgens, human central nervous system differentiation and behavioral sex differences. In R. C. Friedman, R. M. Richart, and R. L. VandeWiele (eds.), *Sex Differences in Behavior*, pp. 33–51. Wiley and Sons, New York.

Ehrhardt, A. A., and Meyer-Bahlburg, H. F. L. 1981. Effects of prenatal sex hormones on gender-related behavior. *Science*, 1312–1318.

Ehrhardt, A. A., and Money, J. 1967. Progestin-induced hermaphroditism: IQ and psychosexual identity in a study of ten girls. *J. Sex Res.*, 3:83–100.

Ehrhardt, A. A., Epstein, R., and Money, J. 1968a. Fetal androgens and female gender identity in the early-treated adrenogenital syndrome. *Johns Hopkins Med. J.*, 122:160–167.

Ehrhardt, A. A., Evers, K., and Money, J. 1968b. Influence of androgen on some aspects of sexually dimorphic behavior in women with the late-treated adrenogenital syndrome. *Johns Hopkins Med. J.,* 123:115–122.

Ehrhardt, A. A., Grisanti, G. C., and Meyer-Bahlburg, H. F. L. 1977. Prenatal exposure to medroxyprogesterone acetate (MPA) in girls. *Psychoneuroendocrinol.,* 2:391–398.

Ehrhardt, A. A., Meyer-Bahlburg, H. F. L., Rosen, L. R., Feldman, J. F., Veridiano, N. P., Zimmerman, I., and McEwen, B. S. 1985. Sexual orientation after prenatal exposure to exogenous estrogen. *Arch. Sex Behav.,* 14:57–78.

Eisenberger, N. I. 2012. The pain of social disconnection: Examining the shared neural underpinnings of physical and social pain. *Nat. Rev. Neurosci.,* 13:421–434.

Eisenberger, N. I., Taylor, S. E., Gable, S. L., Hilmert, C. J., and Lieberman, M. D. 2007. Neural pathways link social support to attenuated neuroendocrine stress responses. *Neuroimage,* 35:1601–1612.

Eising, C. M., Eikenaar, C., Schwabl, H., and Groothuis, T. G. 2001. Maternal androgens in black-headed gull (*Larus ridibundus*) eggs: Consequences for chick development. *Proc. Roy. Soc. Lond. B,* 268:839–846.

Elbashir, S. M., Harborth, J., Lendeckel, W., Yalcin, A., Weber, K., and Tuschl, T. 2001. Duplexes of 21-nucleotide RNAs mediate RNA interference in cultured mammalian cells. *Nature,* 411:494–498.

Elias, C. F., Saper, C. B., Marotos-Flier, E., Tritos, N. A., Lee, C., Kelly, J., Tatro, J. B., et al. 1998. Chemically defined projections linking the mediobasal hypothalamus and the lateral hypothalamic area. *J. Comp. Neurol.,* 402:442–459.

Elliot, C. D. 1971. Noise tolerance and extraversion in children. *Br. J. Psychol.,* 62:375–380.

Elliott, J. A. 1976. Circadian rhythms and photoperiodic time measurement in mammals. *Fed. Proc.,* 35:2339–2346.

Elliott, J. A., and Goldman, B. D. 1981. Seasonal reproduction: Photoperiodism and biological clocks. In N. T. Adler (ed.), *Neuroendocrinology of Reproduction,* pp. 377–423. Plenum Press, New York.

Ellis, A. 1945. The sexual psychology of human hermaphrodites. *Psychosom. Med.,* 7:108–125.

Ellis, G. B., and Turek, F. W. 1979. Changes in locomotor activity associated with the photoperiodic response of testes in male golden hamsters. *J. Comp. Physiol.,* 132:277–284.

Ellis, G. B., and Turek, F. W. 1980a. Photoperiod-induced change in responsiveness of the hypothalamic-pituitary axis to exogenous 5-alpha-dihydrotestosterone and 17β-estradiol in castrated male hamsters. *Neuroendocrinol.,* 31:205–209.

Ellis, G. B., and Turek, F. W. 1980b. Photoperiodic regulation of serum luteinizing hormone and follicle-stimulating hormone in castrated and castrated-adrenalectomized male hamsters. *Endocrinol.,* 106:1338–1344.

Ellis, G. B., and Turek, F. W. 1983. Testosterone and photoperiod interact to regulate locomotor activity in male hamsters. *Horm. Behav.,* 17:66–75.

Elwood, R. W. 1983. Paternal care in rodents. In R. W. Elwood (ed.), *Parental Behaviour in Rodents,* pp. 235–257. Wiley, New York.

Elwood, R. W., and Mason, C. 1994. The couvade and the onset of paternal care: A biological perspective. *Ethol. Sociobiol.,* 15:145–156.

Emens, J., Lewy, A., Kinzie, J. M., Arnt, D., and Rough, J. 2009. Circadian misalignment in major depressive disorder. *Psychiatry Res.,* 168:259–261.

Emlen, S. T. 1978. The evolution of cooperative breeding in birds. In J. R. Krebs and N. B. Davies (eds.), *Behavioural Ecology: An Evolutionary Approach,* pp. 245–281. Blackwell Scientific Publications, Oxford.

Endicott, J., and Halbreich, U. 1982. Retrospective report of premenstrual depressive changes: Factors affecting confirmation by daily ratings. *Psychopharm. Bull.,* 18:109–112.

Endicott, J., Halbreich, U., Schacht, S., and Nee, J. 1981. Premenstrual changes and affective disorders. *Psychosom. Med.,* 43:519–529.

Engelmann, M. 2008. Vasopressin in the septum: Not important versus causally involved in learning and memory—two faces of the same coin? *Prog. Brain Res.,* 170:389–395.

Engelmann, M., and Landgraf, R. 1994. Microdialysis administration of vasopressin into the septum improves social recognition in Brattleboro rats. *Physiol. Behav.,* 55:145–149.

Engelmann, M., Ebner, K., Wotjak, C. T., and Landgraf, R. 1998. Endogenous oxytocin is involved in short-term olfactory memory in female rats. *Behav. Brain Res.,* 90:89–94.

Engelmann, M., Wotjak, C. T., Neumann, I., Ludwig, M., and Landgraf, R. 1996. Behavioral consequences of intracerebral vasopressin and oxytocin: Focus on learning and memory. *Neurosci. Biobehav. Rev.,* 20:341–358.

Englander-Golden, P., Change, H., Whitmore, M. R., and Dienstbier, R. A. 1980. Female sexual arousal and the menstrual cycle. *J. Hum. Stress,* 6:42–48.

Erickson, J. C., Hollopeter, G., and Palmiter, R. D. 1996. Attenuation of the obesity syndrome of *ob/ob* mice by the loss of neuropeptide Y. *Science,* 274:1704–1707.

Erikson, C. J., and Hutchison, J. B. 1977. Induction of nest-material collecting in male Barbary Doves by intracerebral androgen. *J. Reprod. Fertil.,* 50:9–16.

Erkinaro, E. 1961. The seasonal change of the activity of *Microtus agrestis.* *Oikos,* 12:157–63.

Erskine, M. S. 1989. Solicitation behavior in the estrous female rat: A review. *Horm. Behav.,* 23:473–502.

Erskine, M. S., Barfield, R. J., and Goldman, B. D. 1980a. Postpartum aggression in rats: Effects of hypophysectomy. *J. Comp. Physiol. Psychol.,* 94:484–494.

Erskine, M. S., Barfield, R. J., and Goldman, B. D. 1980b. Postpartum aggression in rats: II. Dependence on maternal sensitivity to young and effects of experience with pregnancy and parturition. *J. Comp. Physiol. Psychol.,* 94:495–505.

Erwin, J., and Mitchell, G. 1975. Initial heterosexual behavior of adolescent rhesus monkeys (*Macaca mulatta*). *Arch. Sex. Behav.,* 4:97–104.

Escasa, M. J., Casey, J. F., and Gray, P. B. 2011. Salivary testosterone levels in men at a U.S. sex club. *Arch. Sex. Behav.,* 40:921–926.

Espmark, Y. 1964. Rutting behaviour in reindeer (*Rangifer tarandus L.*). *Anim. Behav.,* 12:159–163.

Etches, R. J., Garbutt, A., and Middleton, A. L. 1979. Plasma concentrations of prolactin during egg laying and incubation in the ruffed grouse (*Bonasa umbellus*). *Can. J. Zool.,* 57:1624–1627.

Etgen, A. 2002. Estrogen regulation of neurotransmitter and growth factor signaling in the brain. In D. W. Pfaff, A. P. Arnold, A. M. Etgen, S. E. Fahrbach, and R. T. Rubin (eds.), *Hormones, Brain and Behavior,* Vol. 3, pp. 381–440. Academic Press, New York.

Etgen, A. M., Chu, H. P., Fiber, J. M., Karkanias, G. B., and Morales, J. M. 1999. Hormonal integration of neurochemical and sensory signals governing female reproductive behavior. *Behav. Brain Res.,* 105:93–103.

Evans-Pritchard, E. E. 1963. *The Nuer.* Clarendon Press, Oxford.

Evans, D. L., Leserman, J., Perkins, D. O., Stern, R. A., Murphy, C., Zheng, B., Gettes, D., et al. 1997. Severe life stress as a predictor of early disease progression in HIV infection. *Am. J. Psychiatry,* 154:630–634.

Everett, J. W., and Sawyer, C. H. 1950. A 24-hour periodicity in the "LH-release apparatus" of female rats, disclosed by barbiturate sedation. *Endocrinol.,* 47:198–218.

Everitt, B. J. 1990. Sexual motivation: A neural and behavioral analysis of male rats. *Neurosci. Biobehav. Rev.* 14:217–232.

Fader, A. J., Hendricson, A. W., and Dohanich, G. P. 1998. Estrogen improves performance of reinforced T-maze alteration and prevents the amnestic effects of scopolamine administered systemically or intrahippocampally. *Neurobiol. Learn. Mem.,* 69:225–240.

Fahrbach, S. E., and Pfaff, D. W. 1986. Effects of preoptic region implants of dilute estradiol on the maternal behavior of ovariectomized, nulliparous rats. *Horm. Behav.*, 20:957–959.

Fahrbach, S. E., Morrell, J. I., and Pfaff, D. W. 1986. Effect of varying the duration of pretest cage habituation on oxytocin induction of short-latency maternal behavior. *Physiol. Behav.*, 37:135–139.

Fan, L., Orr, P. T., Zhao, Z., Chambers, C. H., Lewis, M. C., and Frick, K. M. 2010. *J. Neurosci.*, 30:4390–4400.

Faron-Górecka, A., Kuśmider, M., Solich, J., Kolasa, M., Szafran, K., Żurawek, D., Pabian, P., and Dziedzicka-Wasylewska, M. 2013. Involvement of prolactin and somatostatin in depression and the mechanism of action of antidepressant drugs. *Pharmacol. Rep.*, 65:1640–1646.

Farooqi, I. S., and O'Rahilly, S. 2005. Monogenic obesity in humans. *Annu. Rev. Med.*, 56:443–458.

Farooqi, I. S., Keogh, J. M., Kamath, S., Jones, S., Gibson, W. T., Trussell, R., Jebb, S. A., Lip, G. Y. H., and O'Rahilly, S. 2001. Partial leptin deficiency and human adiposity. *Nature*, 414:35–36.

Farrell, S. F., and McGinnis, M. Y. 2003. Effects of pubertal anabolic-androgenic steroid (AAS) administration on reproductive and aggressive behaviors in male rats. *Behav. Neurosci.*, 117:904–911.

Fava, G. A., Fava, M., Kellner, R., Serafini, E., and Mastrogiacomo, I. 1981. Depression, hostility and anxiety in hyperprolactinemic amenorrhea. *Psychother. Psychosom.*, 36:122–128.

Favreau, O. E. 1993. Do the Ns justify the means? Null hypothesis testing applied to sex and other differences. *Can. Psych.*, 34:64–78.

Feare, C. 1984. *The Starling.* Oxford University Press, New York.

Feder, H. 1981. Perinatal hormones and their role in the development of sexually dimorphic behaviors. In N. T. Adler (ed.), *Neuroendocrinology of Reproduction*, pp. 127–158. Plenum Press, New York.

Feder, H. H. 1971. The comparative action of testosterone propionate and 5α-androstan-17β-ol-3-one propionate on the reproductive behaviour, physiology and morphology of male rats. *J. Endocrinol.*, 51:242–252.

Feder, H. H., and Whalen, R. E. 1965. Feminine behavior in neonatally castrated and estrogen-treated male rats. *Science*, 147:306–307.

Feder, H. H., Naftolin, F., and Ryan, K. J. 1974. Male and female sexual responses in male rats given estradiol benzoate and 5α-androstan-17β-ol-3-one propionate. *Endocrinol.*, 94:136–141.

Feldman, R., Weller, A., Zagoory-Sharon, O., and Levine, A. 2007. Evidence for a neuroendocrinological foundation of human affiliation: plasma oxytocin levels across pregnancy and the postpartum period predict mother–infant bonding. *Psychol. Sci.*, 18:965–970.

Feldman, R., Zagoory-Sharon, O., Maoz, R., Weisman, O., Gordon, I., Schneiderman, I., Shalev, I., and Ebstein, R. P. 2012. Sensitive parenting is associated with plasma oxytocin and polymorphisms in the oxytocin receptor (OXTR) and CD38 genes. *Biol. Psychiatry*, 72:175–181.

Felgendreger, L.A., Fluharty, S. J., Yee, D. K., and Flanagan-Cato, L. M. 2013. Endogenous angiotensin II-induced p42/44 mitogen-activated protein kinase (MAPK) activation mediates sodium appetite but not thirst or neurohypophysial secretion. *J. Neuroendocrinol.*, 25:97–106.

Ferin, M. 1984. Endogenous opioid peptides and the menstrual cycle. *Trends Neurosci.*, 7:194–196.

Fernald, R. D. 2002. Social regulation of the brain: Status, sex and size. In D. W. Pfaff, A. P. Arnold, A. M. Etgen, S. E. Fahrbach, and R. T. Rubin (eds.), *Hormones, Brain and Behavior*, Vol. 2, pp. 435–444. Academic Press, New York.

Fernandez-Duque, E., Valeggia, C. R., and Mendoza, S. P. 2009. The biology of paternal care in human and nonhuman primates. *Annu. Rev. Anthropol.*, 38:115–130.

Fernandez-Guasti, A., and Rodriguez-Manzo, G. 2003. Pharmacological and physiological aspects of sexual exhaustion in male rats. *Scand. J. Psych.*, 44:257–263.

Fernández-Guasti, A., Kruijver, F. P. M., Fodor, M., and Swaab, D. F. 2000. Sex differences in the distribution of androgen receptors in the human hypothalamus. *J. Comp. Neurol.*, 425:422–435.

Fernández-Vargas, M. and Johnston, R. E. 2015. Ultrasonic vocalizations in golden hamsters (Mesocricetus auratus) reveal modest sex differences and nonlinear signals of sexual motivation. *PLOS One*, 10:e0116789. doi:10.1371/journal.pone.0116789.

Fernandez, S. M., Lewis, M. C., Pechenino, A. S., Harburger, L. L., Orr, P. T., Gresack, J. E., Schafe, G. E., and Frick, K. M. 2008. Estradiol-induced enhancement of object memory consolidation involves hippocampal ER activation and membrane-bound estrogen receptors. *J. Neurosci.*, 28:8660–8667.

Ferris, C. F., Melloni, R. H., Koppel, G., Perry, K. W., Fuller, R. W., and Delville, Y. 1997. Vasopressin/serotonin interactions in the anterior hypothalamus control aggressive behavior in golden hamsters. *J. Neurosci.*, 17:4331–4340.

Ferris, C. F., Snowdon, C. T., King, J. A., Duong, T. Q., Ziegler, T. E., Ugurbil, K., Ludwig, R., et al. 2001. Functional imaging of brain activity in conscious monkeys responding to sexually arousing cues. *Neuroreport*, 12:2231–2236.

Ferris, C. F., Snowdon, C. T., King, J. A., Sullivan, J. M., Ziegler, T. E., Olson, D. P., Schultz-Darken, N. J., et al. 2004. Activation of neural pathways associated with sexual arousal in non-human primates. *J. Magnetic Resonance Imaging*, 19:168–175.

Ferris, C. F., Stolberg, T., Kulkarni, P., Murugavel, M., Blanchard, R., Blanchard, D. C., Febo, M., Brevard, M., and Simon, N. G. 2008. Imaging the neural circuitry and chemical control of aggressive motivation. *BMC Neurosci.*, 9:111, doi:10.1186/1471-2202-9-111

Ferron, F., Considine, R. V., Peino, R., Lado, I. G., Dieguez, C., and Casanueva, F. F. 1997. Serum leptin concentrations in patients with anorexia nervosa, bulimia nervosa and non-specific eating disorders correlate with the body mass index but are independent of the respective disease. *Clin. Endocrinol.*, 46:289–293.

Fessler, D. M. T. 2003. No time to eat: An adaptationist account of periovulatory behavioral changes. *Q. Rev. Biol.*, 78:3–21.

Field, B. C. T., Chaudhri, O. B., and Bloom, S. R. 2010. Bowels control brain: Gut hormones and obesity. *Nat. Rev. Endocrinol.*, 6:444–453.

Fikentscher, R., Rosenberg, B., Spinar, H., and Bruckmuller, W. 1977. Loss of taste in the elderly: Sex differences. *Clin. Otolaryngol.*, 2:183–189.

Filby, A. L., Paull, G. C., Bartlett, E. J., Van Look, K .J., and Tyler, C. R. 2010. Physiological and health consequences of social status in zebrafish (*Danio rerio*). *Physiol. Behav.*, 101:576–587.

Fingerhood, M. I., Sullivan, J. T., Testa, M., and Jasinski, D. R. 1997. Abuse liability of testosterone. *J. Psychopharmacol.*, 11:59–63.

Fink, G., Sumner, B. E., Rosie, R., Grace, O., and Quinn, J. P. 1996. Estrogen control of central neurotransmission: Effect of mood, mental state, and memory. *Cell. Molec. Neurobiol.*, 16:325–344.

Fink, S., Excoffier, L., and Heckel, G. 2006. Mammalian monogamy is not controlled by a single gene. *Proc. Natl. Acad. Sci. USA*, 103:10956–10960.

Fiorino, D. F., Coury, A., and Phillips, A. G. 1997. Dynamic changes in nucleus accumbens dopamine efflux during the Coolidge effect in male rats. *J. Neurosci.*, 17:4849–4855.

Fire, A., Xu, S., Montgomery, M., Kostas, S., Driver, S., and Mello, C. 1998. Potent and specific genetic interference by double-stranded RNA in *Caenorhabditis elegans*. *Nature*, 391:806–811.

Fischette, C. T., Komisaruk, B. R., Edinger, H. M., Feder, H. H., and Siegel, A. 1980. Differential fornix ablations and the circadian rhythmicity of adrenal corticosteroid secretion. *Brain Res.* 195:373–387.

Fishman, R. B., Chism, L., Firestone, G. L., and Breedlove, S. M. 1990. Evidence for androgen receptors in sexually dimorphic perineal muscles of neonatal male rats: Absence of androgen accumulation by the perineal motoneurons. *J. Neurobiol.*, 21:694–705.

Fitzgerald, K. M., and Zucker, I. 1976. Circadian organization of the estrous cycle of the golden hamster. *Proc. Natl. Acad. Sci. USA*, 73:2923–2927.

Fitzsimons, J. T. 1998. Angiotensin, thirst, and sodium appetite. *Physiol. Rev.*, 78:583–686.

Fitzsimons, J. T., and Simons, B. J. 1969. The effect on drinking in the rat of intravenous infusion of angiotensin, given alone or in combination with other stimuli of thirst. *J. Physiol.*, 203:45–57.

Fivizzani, A. J., and Oring, L. W. 1986. Plasma steroid hormones in relation to behavioral sex role reversal in the spotted sandpiper, *Actitis macularia*. *Biol. Reprod.*, 35:1195–1201.

Fivizzani, A. J., Colwell, M. A., and Oring, L. W. 1986. Plasma steroid hormone levels in free-living Wilson's Phalaropes (*Phalaropus tricolor*). *Gen. Comp. Endocrinol.*, 62:137–144.

Fleming, A. S. 1978. Food intake and body weight regulation during the reproductive cycle of the golden hamster (*Mesocricetus auratus*). *Behav. Biol.*, 24:291–306.

Fleming, A. S. 1986. Psychobiology of rat maternal behavior. How and where hormones act to promote maternal behavior at parturition. *Ann. N. Y. Acad. Sci.*, 474:234–251.

Fleming, A. S. 1988. Factors influencing maternal responsiveness in humans: Usefulness of an animal model. *Psychoneuroendocrinol.*, 13:189–212.

Fleming, A. S. 1990. Hormonal and experimental correlates of maternal responsiveness in human mothers. In N. A. Krasnegor and R. S. Bridges (eds.), *Mammalian Parenting*, pp. 184–208. Oxford University Press, Oxford.

Fleming, A. S., and Corter, C. M. 1995. Psychobiology of maternal behavior in nonhuman mammals. In M. H. Bornstein (ed.), *Handbook of Parenting*, Vol. 2, pp. 59–85. Erlbaum Associates.

Fleming, A. S., and Gonzalez, A. 2009. Neurobiology of human maternal care. In P. T. Ellison and P. B. Gray (eds.), *Endocrinology of Social Relationships*, pp. 294–318. Harvard University Press, Cambridge.

Fleming, A. S., and Korsmit, M. 1996. Plasticity inthe maternal circuit: Effects of maternal experience on Fos-Lir in hypothalamic, limbic, and cortical structures in the postpartum rat. *Behav. Neurosci.*, 110:567–582.

Fleming, A. S., and Luebke, C. 1981. Timidity prevents the nulliparous female from being a good mother. *Physiol. Behav.*, 27:863–868.

Fleming, A. S., and Miceli, M. 1983. Effects of diet on feeding and body weight regulation during pregnancy and lactation in the golden hamster (*Mesocricetus auratus*). *Behav. Neurosci.*, 97:246–254.

Fleming, A. S., and Pliner, P. 1983. Food intake, body weight, and sweetness preferences over the menstrual cycle in humans. *Physiol. Behav.*, 30:663–666.

Fleming, A. S., and Rosenblatt, J. S. 1974. Olfactory regulation of maternal behavior in rats: II. Effects of peripherally induced anosmia and lesions of the lateral olfactory tract in pup-induced virgins. *J. Comp. Physiol. Psychol.*, 86:233–246.

Fleming, A. S., Cheung, U. S., and Barry, M. 1990a. Cyclohexamide blocks the retention of maternal experience in postpartum rats. *Behav. Neural Biol.*, 53:64–73.

Fleming, A. S., Corter, C., Franks, P., Surbey, M., Schneider, B., and Steiner, M. 1993. Postpartum factors related to mother's attraction to newborn infant odors. *Dev. Psychobiol.*, 26:115–132.

Fleming, A. S., Corter, C., Stallings, J., and Steiner, M. 2002. Testosterone and prolactin are associated with emotional responses to infant cries in new fathers. *Horm. Behav.*, 42:399–413.

Fleming, A. S., Corter, C., Surbey, M., Franks, P., and Steiner, M. 1995. Postpartum factors related to mother's recognition of newborn infant odours. *J. Reprod. Infant Psychol.*, 13:197–210.

Fleming, A. S., Krieger, H., and Wong, P. Y. 1990b. Affect and nurturance in first-time mothers: Role of psychobiological influences. In B. Lerer and S. Gershon (eds.), *New Directions in Affective Disorders*, pp. 388–392, Springer-Verlag, New York.

Fleming, A. S., Miceli, M., and Morretto, D. 1983. Lesions of the medial preoptic area prevent the facilitation of maternal behavior produced by amygdaloid lesions. *Physiol. Behav.*, 31:502–510.

Fleming, A. S., Morgan, H. D., and Walsh, C. 1996. Experiential factors in postpartum regulation of maternal care. In J. S. Rosenblatt and C. T. Snowdon (eds.), *Parental Care: Evolution, Mechanisms, Adaptive Significance*, pp. 295–332. Academic Press, San Diego.

Fleming, A. S., Ruble, D. N., Krieger, H., and Wong, P. 1997a. Hormonal and experiential correlates of maternal responsiveness during pregnancy and the puerperium in human mothers. *Horm. Behav.*, 31:145–158.

Fleming, A. S., Steiner, M., and Anderson, V. 1987. Hormonal and attitudinal correlates of maternal behavior during the early postpartum period in first-time mothers. *J. Reprod. Infant Psychol.*, 5:193–205.

Fleming, A. S., Steiner, M., and Corter, C. 1997b. Cortisol, hedonics, and maternal responsiveness in human mothers. *Horm. Behav.*, 32:85–98.

Fleming, A. S., Suh, E. J., Korsmit, M., and Rusak, B. 1994. Activation of Fos-like immunoreactivity in the medial preoptic area and limbic structures by maternal and social interactions in rats. *Behav. Neurosci.*, 108:724–734.

Fleming, A. S., Vaccarino, F., and Luebke, C. 1980. Amygdaloid inhibition of maternal behavior in the nulliparous rat. *Physiol. Behav.*, 25:731–743.

Fleming, A. S., Vaccarino, F., Tambosso, L., and Chee, P. 1979. Vomeronasal and olfactory system modulation of maternal behavior in the rat. *Science*, 203:372–374.

Fleshner, M., Laudenslager, M. L., Simons, L., and Maier, S. F. 1989. Reduced serum antibodies associated with social defeat in rats. *Physiol. Behav.*, 45:1183–1187.

Flier, J. S., 1998. Clinical review 94: What's in a name? In search of leptin's physiologic role. *J. Clin. Endocrinol. Metab.*, 83:1407–1413.

Flinn, M. V., Ponzi, D., and Muehlenbein, M. P. 2012. Hormonal mechanisms for regulation of aggression in human coalitions. *Hum. Nat.*, doi:10.1007/s12110-012-9135-y

Flint, A., Raben, A., Ersbøll, A. K., Holst, J. J., and Astrup, A. 2001. The effect of physiological levels of glucagon-like peptide-1 on appetite, gastric emptying, energy and substrate metabolism in obesity. *International J. Obesity*, 25:781–792.

Flood, J. F., and Morley, J. E. 1991. Increased food intake by neuropeptide Y is due to an increased motivation to eat. *Peptides*, 12:1329–1332.

Flood, J. F., Smith, G. E., and Morley, J. E. 1987. Modulation of memory processing by cholecystokinin: Dependence on the vagus nerve. *Science*, 236:832–834.

Florant, G. L., Tokuyama, K., and Rintoul, D. A. 1989. Carbohydrate and lipid utilization in hibernators. In A. Malan and B. Canguilhem (eds.), *Living in the Cold*, pp. 137–145. John Libbey, London.

Flores, A., and Hill, E. M. 2008. Formation of estrogenic brominated ethinylestradiol in drinking water: Implications for aquatic toxicity testing. *Chemosphere*, 73:1115–1120.

Fluharty, S. J., 2002. Neuroendocrinology of body fluid homeostasis. In D. W. Pfaff, A. P. Arnold, A. M. Etgen, S. E. Fahrbach, and R. T. Rubin (eds.), *Hormones, Brain and Behavior*, Vol. 1, pp. 525–569. Academic Press, New York.

Fluharty, S. J., and Sakai, R. R. 1995. Behavioral and cellular analysis of adrenal steroid and angiotensin interactions mediating salt appetite. *Progr. Psychobiol. Physiol. Psychol.*, 16:177–212.

Follett, B. K. 1991. The physiology of puberty in seasonally breeding birds. In M. Hunzicker-Dunn and N. B. Schwartz (eds.), *Follicle Stimulating Hormone: Regulation of Secretion and Molecular Mechanisms of Action*, pp. 54–65. Springer-Verlag, New York.

Fonken, L. K. and Nelson, R. J. 2014. The effects of light at night on circadian clocks and metabolism. *Endocr. Rev.*, 35:648–670.

Fonken, L. K., Aubrecht, T. G., Meléndez-Fernández, O. H., Weil, Z. M., and Nelson, R. J. 2013. Dim light at night disrupts molecular circadian rhythms and increases body weight. *J. Biol. Rhythms*, 28:262–271.

Foradori, C. D., Coolen, L. M., Fitzgerald, M. E., Skinner, D. C., Goodman, R. L., and Lehman, M. N. 2002. Colocalization of progesterone receptors in parvicellular dynorphin neurons of the ovine preoptic area and hypothalamus. *Endocrinology*, 143:4366–4374.

Ford, C. S., and Beach, F. A. 1951. *Patterns of Sexual Behavior.* Harper and Row, New York.

Forest, M. G., and Cathiard, A. M. 1975. Pattern of plasma testosterone and androstenedione in normal newborns: Evidence for testicular activity at birth. *J. Clin. Endocrinol. Metab.*, 41:977–980.

Forger, N. G. 1998. Sex differentiation, psychological. In E. Knobil and J. D. Neill (eds.), *Encyclopedia of Reproduction*, Vol. 4., pp. 421–430. Academic Press, San Diego.

Forger, N. G. 2016. Epigenetic mechanisms in sexual differentiation of the brain and behaviour. *Philos. Trans. R. Soc. Lond. B. Biol. Sci.*, 371.

Formby, D. 1967. Maternal recognition of infant's cry. *Dev. Med. Child Neurol.*, 9:293–298.

Fossey, D. 1974. Observations on the home range of one group of mountain gorillas (*Gorilla gorilla beringei*). *Anim. Behav.*, 22:568–581.

Foster, R. G., and Roenneberg, T. 2008. Human responses to the geophysical daily, annual and lunar cycles. *Curr. Biol.*, 18:R784–R794.

Fothergill, E., Guo, J., Howard, L., Kerns, J. C., Knuth, N. D., Brychta, R., Chen, K. Y., et al. 2016. Persistent metabolic adaptation 6 years after "The Biggest Loser" competition. *Obesity*, DOI: 10.1002/oby.21538.

Fountoulakis, K., Kantartzis, S., Siamouli, M., Panagiotidis, P., Kaprinis, S., Iacovides, A., and Kaprinis, G. 2008. Peripheral thyroid dysfunction in depression: A review. *Ann. Gen. Psychiatry*, 7:S324.

Fowler, S. L., Rasinski, H. M., Geers, A. L., Helfer, S. G., and France, C. R. 2011. Concept priming and pain: an experimental approach to understanding gender roles in sex-related pain differences. *J. Behav. Med.*, 34:139–147.

Fox, C. A., Ismail, A. A., Love, D. N., Kirkham, K. E., and Loraine, J. A. 1972. Studies on the relationship between plasma testosterone levels and human sexual activity. *J. Endocrinol.*, 52:51–58.

Fox, C. A., Ismail, A. A., Love, D. N., Kirkham, K. E., and Loraine, J. A. 1972. Studies on the relationship between plasma

testosterone levels and human sexual activity. *J. Endocrinol.*, 52:51–58.

Fraile, I. G., Pfaff, D. W., and McEwen, B. S. 1987. Progestin receptors with and without estrogen induction in male and female hamster brain. *Neuroendocrinol.*, 45:487–491.

Franceschini, I., Lomet, D., Cateau, M., Delsol, G., Tillet, Y., and Caraty A. 2006. Kisspeptin immunoreactive cells of the ovine preoptic area and arcuate nucleus co-express estrogen receptor alpha. *Neurosci. Lett.*, 401:225–230.

Francis, D. D., Diorio, J., Liu, D., and Meaney, M. J. 1999. Non-genomic transmission across generations of maternal behavior and stress responses in the rat. *Science*, 286:1155–1158.

Frank, E., Kupfer, D. J., Thase, M. E., Mallinger, A. G., Swartz, H. A., and Fagiolini, A. M., 2005. Two-year outcomes for interpersonal and social rhythm therapy in individuals with bipolar I disorder. *Arch. Gen. Psychiatry*, 62:996–1004.

Frank, E., Soreca, I., Swartz, H. A., Fagiolini, A. M., Mallinger, A. G., and Thase, M. E., 2008. The role of interpersonal and social rhythm therapy in improving occupational functioning in patients with bipolar I disorder. *Am. J. Psychiatry*, 165:1559–1565.

Frank, L. G. 1983. Reproduction and intra-sexual dominance in the spotted hyena (*Crocuta crocuta*). Ph.D. thesis, University of California, Berkeley.

Frank, L. G. 1986. Social organisation of the spotted hyaena: II. Dominance and reproduction. *Anim. Behav.*, 35:1510–1527.

Frank, L. G., Davidson, J. M., and Smith, E. R. 1985. Androgen levels in the spotted hyena *Crocuta crocuta*: The influence of social factors. *J. Zool. (Lond.)*, 206:525–531.

Frank, R. T. 1931. The hormonal causes of premenstrual tension. *Arch. Neurol. Psychiatry*, 26:1053–1057.

Frankenhaeuser, M. 1978. Psychoneuroendocrine approaches to the study of emotion as related to stress and coping. *Neb. Symp. Motiv.*, 26:123–162.

Frankola, K. A., Flora, A. L., Torres, A. K., Grissom, E. M., Overstreet, S., and Dohanich, G. P. 2010. Effects of early rearing conditions on cognitive performance in prepubescent male and female rats. *Neurobiol. Learn. Mem.*, 94:91–99.

Frasnelli, J., Lundström, J. N., Boyle, J. A., Katsarkas, A., and Jones-Gotman, M. 2011. The vomeronasal organ is not involved in the perception of endogenous odors. *Hum Brain Mapp.*, 32:450–460.

Freeman, E. W. 2003. Premenstrual syndrome and premenstrual dysphoric disorder: Definitions and diagnosis. *Psychoneuroendocrinol.*, 28:25–37.

Freeman, E. W., Halberstadt, S. M., Rickels, K., Legler, J. M., Lin, H., and Sammel, M. D. 2011. Core symptoms that discriminate

premenstrual syndrome. *J. Womens Health (Larchmt.)*, 20:29–35.

French, J. A., Pissinatti, A., and Coimbra-Filho, A. F. 1999. Reproduction in captive lion tamarins (*Leotophithecus*): Seasonality, infant survival, and sex ratios. *Am. J. Primatol.*, 39:17–33.

Frick, K. M. 2009. Estrogens and age-related memory decline in rodents: What have we learned and where do we go from here? *Horm. Behav.*, 55:2–23.

Frick, K. M., and Berger-Sweeney, J. 2001. Spatial reference memory and neocortical neurochemistry vary with the estrous cycle in C57BL/6 mice. *Behav. Neurosci.*, 115:229–237.

Frick, K. M., Burlingame, L. A., Arters, J. A., and Berger-Sweeney, J. 2000. Reference memory, anxiety and estrous cyclicity in C57BL/6NIA mice are affected by age and sex. *Neuroscience*, 95:293–307.

Frick, K. M., Fernandez, S. M., and Bulinski, S. C. 2002. Estrogen replacement improves spatial reference memory and increases hippocampal synaptophysin in aged female mice. *Neuroscience*, 115:547–558.

Frick, K.M. 2012. Building a better hormone therapy? How understanding the rapid effects of sex steroid hormones could lead to new therapeutics for age-related memory decline *Behavioral Neuroscience*, 126:29–53.

Friedl, K. E., and Yesalis, C. E. 1989. Self-treatment of gynecomastia in bodybuilders who use anabolic steroids. *Physicians Sportsmedicine*, 17:67–79.

Friedman, M. I. 1978. Hyperphagia in rats with experimental diabetes mellitus: A response to a decreased supply of utilizable fuels. *J. Comp. Physiol. Psychol.*, 92:109–117.

Friedman, M. I. 1990. Body fat and the metabolic control of food intake. *Int. J. Obesity*, 14:53–66.

Friedman, M. I. 2008. Food intake: Control, regulation and the illusion of dysregulation. In R. B. S. Harris, and R. D. Harris (eds.), *Appetite and Food Intake: Behavioral and Physiological Considerations*. CRC Press, Boca Raton, FL.

Friedman, M. I., and Granneman, J. 1983. Food intake and peripheral factors after recovery from insulin-induced hypoglycemia *Am. J. Physiol.*, 244:R374–R382.

Friedman, M. I., Ramirez, I., Edens, N. K., and Granneman, J. 1985. Food intake in diabetic rats: Isolation of primary metabolic effects of rat feeding. *Am. J. Physiol.*, 249:R44–R51.

Frisén, L., Nordenström, A., Falhammer, H., Filipsson, H., Holmdahl, G., Janson, P. O., Thorén, M., Hagenfeldt, K., Möller, A., and Nordenskjöld, A. 2009. Gender role behavior, sexuality, and psychosocial adaptation in women with congenital adrenal hyperplasia due to CYP21A2 deficiency. *Journal of Clinical Endocrinology and Metabolism*, 94:3432–3439.

Fry, D. M., and Toone, C. K. 1981. DDT-induced feminization of gull embryos. *Science*, 213:922–924.

Fry, M., and Ferguson, A. V. 2010. Ghrelin: Central nervous system sites of action in regulation of energy balance. *Int. J. Pediatr.*, doi:10.1155/2010;/61657

Frye, C. A. 1995. Estrus-associated decrements in a water maze task are limited to acquisition. *Physiol. Behav.*, 57:5–14.

Fu, X., Yan, Y., Xu, P. S., Geerlof-Vidavsky, I., Chong, W., Gross, M. L., and Holy, T. E. 2015. A molecular code for identity in the vomeronasal system. *Cell*, 163:313–323.

Fuchs, A.-R., and Dawood, M. Y. 1980. Oxytocin release and uterine activation during parturition in rabbits. *Endocrinol.*, 107:1117–1126.

Fuchs, A.-R., and Fuchs, F. 1984. Endocrinology of human parturition: A review. *Br. J. Obstet. Gynaecol.*, 91:948–967.

Fuller, P. M., Lu, J., and Saper, C. B. 2008. Differential rescue of light- and food-entrainable circadian rhythms. *Science*, 320:1074–1077.

Fusani, L. 2008. Testosterone control of male courtship in birds. *Horm. Behav.*, 54:227–233.

Fusani, L., Day, L. B., Canoine, V., Reinemann, D., Hernandez, E., and Schlinger, B. 2007. Androgen and the elaborate courtship behavior of a tropical lekking bird. *Horm. Behav.*, 51:62–68.

Fuxjager, M. J., Forbes-Lorman, R. M., Coss, D. J., Auger, C. J., Auger, A. P., and Marler, C. A. 2010. Winning territorial disputes selectively enhances androgen sensitivity in neural pathways related to motivation and social aggression. *Proc. Natl. Acad. Sci. USA*, 107:12393–12398.

Fuxjager, M. J., Mast, G., Becker, E. A., and Marler, C. A. 2009. The "home advantage" is necessary for a full winner effect and changes in post-encounter testosterone. *Horm. Behav.*, 56:214–219.

Fuxjager, M. J., Montgomery, J. L., and Marler, C. A. 2011. Species differences in the winner effect disappear in response to post-victory testosterone manipulations. *Proc. Roy. Soc. Lond. B*, 278:3497–3503.

Gabor, C. S., Phan, A., Clipperton-Allen, A. E., Kavaliers, M. and Choleris, E. 2012. Interplay of oxytocin, vasopressin, and sex hormones in the regulation of social recognition. *Behavioral Neuroscience*, 126:97–100.

Gagnidze, K., Weil, Z. M., Faustino, L. C., Schaafsma, S. M., and Pfaff, D. W. 2013. Early histone modifications in the ventromedial hypothalamus and preoptic area following oestradiol administration. *J. Neuroendocrinol.*, 25:939–955.

Gahr, M., and Kosar, E. 1996. Identification, distribution, and developmental changes of a melatonin binding site in the song control system of the zebra finch. *J. Comp. Neurol.*, 367:308–318.

Gahr, M., Flügge, G., and Güttinger, H.-R. 1987. Immunocytochemical localization of estrogen-binding neurons in the songbird brain. *Brain Res.*, 402:173–177.

Gahr, M., Güttinger, H.-R., and Kroodsma, D. A. 1993. Estrogen receptors in the avian brain: Survey reveals general distribution and forebrain areas unique to songbirds. *J. Comp. Neurol.*, 327:112–122.

Gaines, M. S., Fugate, C. L., Johnson, M. L., Johnson, D. C., Hisey, J. R., and Quadagno, D. M. 1985. Manipulation of aggressive behavior in male prairie voles (*Microtus ochrogaster*) implanted with testosterone in Silastic tubing. *Can. J. Zool.*, 63:2525–2528.

Gale, S. M., Castracane, V. D., and Mantzoros, C. S. 2004. Energy homeostasis, obesity and eating disorders: Recent advances in endocrinology. *J. Nutrition*, 134:295–298.

Galea, L. A., Kavaliers, M., and Ossenkopp, K. P. 1996. Sexually dimorphic spatial learning in meadow voles (*Microtus pennsylvanicus*) and deer mice (*Peromyscus maniculatus*). *J. Exp. Biol.*, 199:195–200.

Galea, L. A., Kavaliers, M., Ossenkopp, K. P., and Hampson, E. 1995. Gonadal hormone levels and spatial learning performance in the Morris water maze in male and female meadow voles, *Microtus pennsylvanicus*. *Horm. Behav.*, 29:106–125.

Galea, L. A., Leuner, B., and Slattery, D. A. 2014. Hippocampal plasticity during the peripartum period: Influence of sex steroids, stress and ageing. *J. Neuroendocrinol.*, 26:641–648.

Galea, L. A., McEwen, B. S., Tanapat, P., Deak, T., Spencer, R. L., and Dhabhar, F. S. 1997. Sex differences in dendritic atrophy of CA3 pyramidal neurons in response to chronic stress. *Neuroscience*, 81:689–697.

Gallagher, M., Kapp, B. S., Pascoe, J. P., and Rapp, P. R. 1981. A neuropharmacology of amygdaloid systems which contribute to learning and memory. In I. Ben Ari (ed.), *The Amygdaloid Complex*, pp. 343–354. Elsevier, Amsterdam.

Galli-Taliadoros, L. S., Sedgwick, J. D., Wood, S. A., and Korner, H. 1995. Gene knock-out technology: A methodological overview for the interested novice. *J. Immunol. Meth*, 181:1–15.

Gammie, S. C. 2005. Current models and future directions for understanding the neural circuitries of maternal behaviors in rodents. *Behav. Cogn. Neurosci. Rev.*, 4:119–135.

Gammie, S. C., and Lonstein, J. S. 2006. Maternal aggression. In R. J. Nelson (ed.), *Biology of Aggression*, pp. 250–274. Oxford University Press, New York.

Gammie, S. C., Negron, A., Newman, S. M., and Rhodes, J. S. 2004. Corticotropin-releas-ing factor inhibits maternal aggression in mice. *Behav. Neurosci.*, 118:805–814.

Gammie, S. C., Seasholtz, A. F., and Stevenson, S. A. 2008. Deletion of corticotropin-releasing factor binding protein selectively impairs maternal, but not intermale aggression. *Neuroscience*, 157:502–512.

Ganong, W. F. 2005. *Review of Medical Physiology*. (22nd ed.). McGraw-Hill Medical, New York.

Ganong, W. F. 2006. Physiology of reproduction in women. In A. H. DeCherney, L. Nathan, T. M. Goodwin, and N. Laufer (eds.), *Current Diagnosis and Treatment: Obstetrics and Gynecology*. (10th ed.). Lange-McGraw Hill, Hightstown, NJ.

Ganzel, B. L., Kim, P., Glover, G. H., and Temple, E. 2008. Resilience after 9/11: Multinodal neuroimaging evidence for stress-related change in the healthy human brain. *Neuroimage*, 40:788–795.

Garcia-Falgueras, A., Junque, C., Giménez, M., Caldú, X., Segovia, S., and Guillamon, A. 2006. Sex differences in the human olfactory system. *Brain Res.*, 1116:103–111.

Garcia, F. D., and Thibaut, F. 2010. Sexual addictions. *Am. J. Drug Alcohol Abuse*, 36:254–260.

Garcia, J. M., Curtis, K. S., and Contreras, R. J. 2008. Behavioral and electrophysiological taste responses change following brief or prolonged dietary sodium deprivation. *Am. J. Physiol.*, 295:R1754–R1761.

Garcia, M. C., and Ginther, O. J. 1976. Effects of ovariectomy and season on plasma luteinizing hormone in mares. *Endocrinol.*, 98:958–962.

Garey, J., Goodwillie, A., Frohlich, J., Morgan, M., Gustafsson, J. A., Smithies, O., Korach, K. S., Ogawa, S., and Pfaff, D. W. 2003. Genetic contributions to generalized arousal of brain and behavior. *Proc. Natl. Acad. Sci. USA*, 100:11019–11022.

Garrett, J. W., and Campbell, C. S. 1980. Changes in social behavior of the male golden hamster accompanying photoperiodic changes in reproduction. *Horm. Behav.*, 14:303–318.

Gary, K. A., Sollars, P. J., Lexow, N., Winokur, A., and Pickard, G. E. 1996. Thyrotropin-releasing hormone phase shifts circadian rhythms in hamsters. *Neuroreport*, 7:1631–1634.

Gatewood, J. D., Wills, A., Shetty, S., Xu, J., Arnold, A. P., Burgoyne, P. S., and Rissman, E. F. 2006. Sex chromosome complement and gonadal sex influence aggressive and parental behaviors in mice. *J. Neurosci.* 26:2335–2342.

Gauer, O. H., and Henry, J. P. 1963. Circulatory basis of fluid volume control. *Physiol. Rev.*, 43:423–481.

Gaulin, S. J. C., and FitzGerald, R. W. 1986. Sex differences in spatial ability: An evolutionary hypothesis and test. *Am. Nat.*, 127:74–88.

Gaulin, S. J. C., and FitzGerald, R. W. 1989. Sexual selection for spatial-learning ability. *Anim. Behav.*, 37:322–331.

Gavish, L., Carter, C. S., and Getz, L. L. 1983. Male-female interactions in prairie voles. *Anim. Behav.*, 31:511–517.

Gay, V. L., Midgley, A. R. Jr., and Niswender, G. D. 1970. Patterns of gonadotrophin secretion associated with ovulation. *Federation Proc.*, 29:1880–1887.

Geist, V. 1971. *Mountain Sheep.* University of Chicago Press, Chicago.

Gentry, R. T., and Wade, G. N. 1976. Androgenic control of food intake and body weight in male rats. *J. Comp. Physiol. Psychol.*, 90:18–25.

George, A. J., and Sandler, M. 1988. Endocrine and biochemical studies in puerperal mental disorders. In R. Kumar and I. F. Brockington (eds.), *Motherhood and Mental Illness 2: Causes and Consequences*, pp. 78–112. Wright, Boston.

Georgiou, G. C., Sharp, P. J., and Lea, R. W. 1995. [^{14}C]-2-deoxyglucose uptake in the brain of the ring dove (*Streptopelia risoria*): II. Differential uptake at the onset of incubation. *Brain Res.*, 700:137–141.

Geraghty, A. C., Muroy, S. E., Zhao, S., Bentley, G. E., Kriegsfeld, L. J., and Kaufer, D. 2015. Knockdown of hypothalamic RFRP3 prevents chronic stress-induced infertility and embryo resorption. *eLife*, 12:4.

Gerall, A. A. 2009. Recollections of the origins of and reactions to the organizational concept. *Horm. Behav.*, 55:570–578.

Gerall, A. A., and Givon, L. 1992. Early androgen and age-related modifications in female rat reproduction. In A. A. Gerall, H. Moltz, and I. L. Ward (eds.), *Sexual Differentiation.* Vol. 11. *Handbook of Behavioral Neurobiology*, pp. 313–354. Plenum Press, New York.

Getz, L. L., and Carter, C. S. 1996. Prairie vole partnerships. *Am. Sci.*, 84:56–62.

Getz, L. L., Hofmann, J. E., and Carter, C. S. 1987. Mating system and population fluctuation of the prairie vole (*Microtus ochrogaster*). *Am. Zool.*, 27:909–920.

Geuze, E., van Berckel, B. N. M., Lammertsma, A. A., Boellaard, R., de Kloet, C. S., Vermetten, E., and Westenberg, H. G. M. 2008. Reduced GABA$_A$ benzodiazepine receptor binding in veterans with post-traumatic stress disorder. *Molec. Psychiatry*, 13:74–83.

Ghahramani, N.M., Ngun, T.C., Chen, P.Y., Tian, Y., Krishnan, S., Muir, S., Rubbi, L. et al. 2014. The effects of perinatal testosterone exposure on the DNA methylome of the mouse brain are late-emerging. *Biol. Sex Differ.*, 5: 8.

Gheusi, G., Bluthe, R.M., Goodall, G. & Dantzer, R. 1994. Social and individual rec-

ognition in rodents. Methodological aspects and neurobiological bases. *Behavioural Processes*, 33:59–87.

Giantonio, G. W., Lund, N. L., and Gerall, A. A. 1970. Effect of diencephalic and rhinencephalic lesions on the male rat's sexual behavior. *J. Comp. Physiol. Psychol.*, 73:38–46.

Gibbon, J., Morrell, M., and Silver, R. 1984. Two kinds of timing in circadian incubation rhythm of ring doves. *Am. J. Physiol.*, 247:R1083–R1087.

Gibbs, J., Fauser, D. J., Rowe, E. A., Rolls, B. J., Rolls, E. T., and Maddison, S. P. 1979. Bombesin suppresses feeding in rats. *Nature*, 282:208–210.

Gibbs, J., Young, R. C., and Smith, G. P. 1973. Cholecystokinin elicits satiety in rats with open gastric fistulas. *Nature*, 245:323–325.

Gibbs, R. B. 1997. Effects of estrogen on basal forebrain cholinergic neurons vary as a function of dose and duration of treatment. *Brain Res.*, 757:10–16.

Gibbs, R. B. 2000. Long-term treatment with estrogen and progesterone enhances acquisition of a spatial memory task by ovariectomized rats. *Neurobiol. Aging*, 21:107–116.

Gibson, E. M., Humber, S. A., Jain, S., Williams, W. P., Zhao, S., Bentley, G. E., Tsutsui, K., and Kriegsfeld, L. J. 2008. Alterations in RFamide-related peptide expression are coordinated with the preovulatory luteinizing hormone surge. *Endocrinol.*, 149:4958–4969.

Gibson, E. M., Wang, C., Tjho, S., Khattar, N., and Kriegsfeld, L. J. 2010. Experimental "jet lag" inhibits adult neurogenesis and produces long-term cognitive deficits in female hamsters. *PLOS One*, 5:e15267.

Gibson, E. M., Williams, W. P. III, and Kriegsfeld, L. J. 2009. Aging in the circadian system: Considerations for health, disease prevention and longevity. *Exp. Gerontol.*, 44:51–56.

Gibson, E., Wang, C., Tjho, S., Khattar, N., and Kriegsfeld, L. 2010. Experimental "jet lag" inhibits adult neurogenesis and produces long-term cognitive deficits in female hamsters. *PLOS One*, 5:5.

Gil, D., Graves, J., Hazon, N., and Wells, A. 1999. Male attractiveness and differential testosterone investment in zebra finch eggs. *Science*, 286:126–128.

Gildersleeve, K., Haselton, M. G., and Fales, M. R. 2014. Do women's mate preferences change across the ovulatory cycle? A meta-analytic review. *Psychol. Bull.*, 140:1205–1259.

Gillespie, C. F., Huhman, K. L., Babagbemi, T. O., and Albers, H. E. 1996. Bicuculline increases and muscimol reduces the phase-delaying effects of light and VIP/PHI/GRP in the suprachiasmatic region. *J. Biol. Rhythms*, 11:137–144.

Gillette, M. U. and Prosser, R. A. 1988. Circadian rhythm of the rat suprachiasmatic

brain slice is rapidly reset by daytime application of cAMP analogs. *Brain Res.*, 474:348–352.

Gillings, M.R. 2014. Were there evolutionary advantages to premenstrual syndrome? *Evol. Appl.*, 7:897–904.

Gingrich, B. S., Cascio, C., Young, L. J., Liu, Y.,Wang, Z. X., and Insel, T. R. 1998. Oxytocin, dopamine, and enkephalin in the nucleus accumbens: A neurochemical cascade for pair bonding. *Soc. Neurosci. Abstr.*, 24:372.14.

Ginsburg, B., and Allee, W. C. 1942. Some effects of conditioning of social dominance and subordination in inbred strains of mice. *Physiol. Zool.*, 15:485–506.

Ginton, A., and Merari, A. 1977. Long range effects of MPOA lesions on mating behavior in the male rat. *Brain Res.*, 120:158–163.

Giordano, A. L., and Rosenblatt, J. S. 1986. Relationship between maternal behavior and nuclear estrogen receptor binding in preoptic area and hypothalamus during pregnancy in rats. *Soc. Neurosci. Abstr.*, p. 17.

Giovenardi, M., Padoin, M. J.,Cadore, L. P., and Lucion, A. B. 1998. Hypothalamic paraventricular nucleus modulates maternal aggression in rats: Effects of ibotenic acid lesion and oxytocin antisense. *Physiol. Behav.*, 63:351–359.

Gitlin, M. J., and Pasnau, R. O. 1989. Psychiatric syndromes linked to reproductive function in women: A review of current knowledge. *Am. J. Psychiatry*, 146:1414–1422.

Giuliano, F., McKenna, K., Srlatha, B., and Pfaus, J. G. 2006. Preclinical research and animal models in sexual medicine. In H. Porst and J. Buvat (eds.), *Sexual Medicine.* Blackwell, Malden, MA.

Giwercman, A., and Skakkebaek, N. E. 1992. The human testis—an organ at risk? *Int. J. Androl.* 15:373–375.

Gladue, B. A. 1991. Aggressive behavioral characteristics, hormones, and sexual orientation in men and women. *Aggressive Behavior*, 17:313–326.

Gladue, B. A., Beatty, W. W., Larson, J., and Staton, R. D. 1990. Sexual orientation and spatial ability in men and women. *Psychobiol.*, 18:101–108.

Gladue, B. A., Green, R., and Hellman, R. E. 1984. Neuroendocrine response to estrogen and sexual orientation. *Science*, 225:1496–1499.

Glaser, B., Zoghlin, G., Pienta, K., and Vinik, A. 1988. Pancreatic polypeptide response to secretin in obesity: Effects of glucose intolerance. *Horm. Metab. Res.*, 20:288–292.

Glasper, E. R., Kozorovitskiy, Y., Pavlic, A., and Gould, E. 2011. Paternal experience suppresses adult neurogenesis without altering hippocampal function in *Peromyscus californicus*. *J. Comp. Neurol.*, 519:2271–2281.

Gleason, E. D., Fuxjager, M. J., Oyegbile, T. O., and Marler, C. A. 2009. Testosterone release and social context: When it occurs and why. *Front. Neuroendocrinol.*, 30:460–469.

Gleason, P. E., Michael, S. D., and Christian, J. J. 1981. Prolactin-induced aggression in female Peromyscus leucopus. *Behav. Neural Biol.*, 33:243–248.

Glickman, S. E., Frank, L. G., Davidson, J. M., Smith, E. R., and Siiteri, P. K. 1987. Androstenedione may organize or activate sex-reversed traits in female spotted hyenas. *Proc. Natl. Acad. Sci. USA*, 84:3444–3447.

Glickman, S. E., Frank, L. G., Licht, P., Yalcinkaya, T., Siiteri, P. K., and Davidson, J. 1992. Sexual differentiation of the female spotted hyena. One of nature's experiments. *Ann. N. Y. Acad. Sci.*, 662:135–159.

Go, V. L. E., DiMagno, E. P., Gardner, J. D., Lebenthal, E., Reber, H. A., and Scheely, G. A. 1993. *The Pancreas: Biology, Pathobiology and Disease*. Raven Press, New York.

Gobrogge, K. L., Liu, Y., Young, L. J., and Wang, Z. 2009. Anterior hypothalamic vasopressin regulates pair-bonding and drug-induced aggression in a monogamous rodent. *Proc. Natl. Acad. Sci. USA*, 106:19144–19149.

Godwin, J., and Crews, D. P. 2002. Hormones, brain and behavior in reptiles. In D. W. Pfaff, A. P. Arnold, A. M. Etgen, S. E. Fahrbach, and R. T. Rubin (eds.), *Hormones, Brain and Behavior*, Vol. 2, pp. 545–586. Academic Press, New York.

Goetz, S. M. M., Tanga, L., Thomason, M. E., Diamond, M. P., Hariric, A. R., and Carré, J. M. 2014. Testosterone rapidly increases neural reactivity to threat in healthy men: A novel two-step pharmacological challenge paradigm. *Biol. Psych.*, 76:324–331.

Goetzel, R. Z., Anderson, D. R., Whitmer, R. W., Ozminkowski, R. J., Dunn, R. L., and Wasserman, J., 1998. The relationship between modifiable health risks and health care expenditures: An analysis of the multi-employer HERO health risk and cost database. The Health Enhancement Research Organization (HERO) Research Committee. *J. Occup. Environ. Med.*, 40:843–854.

Gold, P. E. 1986. Glucose modulation of memory storage processing. *Behav. Neural Biol.*, 45:342–349.

Gold, P. E. 1987. Sweet memories. *Am. Sci.*, 75:151–155.

Gold, P. E. 2003. Acetylcholine modulation of neural systems involved in learning and memory. *Neurobiol. Learn. Mem.*, 80:194–210.

Gold, P. E., and Van Buskirk, R. B. 1975. Facilitation of time-dependent memory processes with post-trial epinephrine injections. *Behav. Biol.*, 13:145–153.

Gold, P.E., 2014. Regulation of memory—From the adrenal medulla to liver to astrocytes to neurons. *Brain Research Bulletin*, 105:25–35.

Gold, P.E., Newman, L.A., Scavuzzo, C.J. & Korol, D.L. 2013. Modulation of multiple memory systems: From neurotransmitters to metabolic substrates. *Hippocampus*, 23:11053–11065.

Goldey, K. L. and van Anders, S. M. 2012. Sexual thoughts: Links to testosterone and cortisol in men. *Arch. Sex. Behav.*, 41:1461–1470.

Goldey, K. L., van Anders, S. M. 2011. Sexy thoughts: effects of sexual cognitions on testosterone, cortisol, and arousal in women. *Horm. Behav.*, 59:754–764.

Goldfoot, D. A., Wiegand, S. J., and Scheffler, G. 1978. Continued copulation in ovariectomized adrenal-suppressed stumptail macaques (*Macaca artoides*). *Horm. Behav.*, 11:89–99.

Goldman, B. D. 1983. The physiology of melatonin in mammals. In R. J. Reiter (ed.), *Pineal Research Rev.*, pp. 145–182. Alan R. Liss, New York.

Goldman, B. D. 2001. Mammalian photoperiodic system: formal properties and neuroendocrine mechanisms of photoperiodic time measurement. *J. Biol. Rhythms*, 16:283–301.

Goldman, B. D., and Darrow, J. M. 1983. The pineal gland and mammalian photoperiodism. *Neuroendocrinol.*, 37:386–396.

Goldman, B. D., and Elliott, J. A. 1988. Photoperiodism and seasonality in hamsters: Role of the pineal gland. In M. H. Stetson (ed.), *Processing of Environmental Information in Vertebrates*, pp. 203–218. Springer-Verlag, New York.

Goldman, B. D., and Nelson, R. J. 1993. Melatonin and seasonality in mammals. In H. S. Yu and R. J. Reiter (eds.), *Melatonin: Biosynthesis, Physiological Effects, and Clinical Applications*, pp. 225–252. CRC Press, Boca Raton, FL.

Goldman, B. D., Matt, K. S., Roychoudhury, P., and Stetson, M. H. 1981. Prolactin release in golden hamsters: Photoperiod and gonadal influences. *Biol. Reprod.*, 24:287–292.

Goldsmith, A. R. 1983. Prolactin in avian reproductive cycles. In J. Balthazart, J. E. Prove, and R. Gilles (eds.), *Hormones and Behaviour in Higher Vertebrates*, pp. 375–387. Springer-Verlag, Berlin.

Golombek, D. A., Casiraghi, L. P., Agostino, P. V., Paladino, N., Duhart, J. M., Plano, S. A., and Chiesa, J. J. 2013. The times they're a-changing: Effects of circadian desynchronization on physiology and disease. *J. Physiol. Paris*, 107:310–322.

González-Mariscal, G. 2001. Neuroendocrinology of maternal behavior in the rabbit. *Horm. Behav.*, 40:125–132.

González-Mariscal, G. 2007. Mother rabbits and their offspring: Timing is everything. *Dev. Psychobiol.*, 49:71–76.

González-Mariscal, G., and Kinsley, C. H. 2009. From indifference to ardor: The onset, maintenance, and meaning of the maternal brain. In D. W. Pfaff, et al. (eds.), *Hormones, Brain, and Behavior* (2nd ed.). Vol. 1, pp. 109–136. Academic Press, New York.

González-Mariscal, G., and Poindron, P. 2002. Parental care in mammals: Immediate internal and sensory factors of control. In D. W. Pfaff, A. P. Arnold, A. M. Etgen, S. E. Fahrbach, and R. T. Rubin (eds.), *Hormones, Brain and Behavior*, Vol. 1, pp. 215–298. Academic Press, New York.

Gonzàlez-Mariscal, G., and Rosenblatt, J. S. 1996. Maternal behavior in rabbits: A historical and multidisciplinary perspective. *Adv. Study Behav.*, 25:333–360.

González-Mariscal, G., Chirino, R., Rosenblatt, J. S., and Beyer, C. 2005. Forebrain implants of estradiol stimulate maternal nest-building in ovariectomized rabbits. *Horm. Behav*, 47:272–279.

Gonzàlez-Mariscal, G., Cuamatzi, E., and Rosenblatt, J. S. 1998. Hormones and external factors: Are they "on/off" signals for maternal nest-building in rabbits? *Horm. Behav.*, 33:1–8.

Gonzalez-Martinez, D., DeMees, C., Douhard, Q., Szppirer, C., and Bakker, J. 2008. Absence of gonadotropin-releasing hormone 1 and *Kiss1* activation in alpha-fetoprotein luteinizing hormone surges. *Endocrinol.*, 149:2333–2340.

Goodale, H. D. 1918. Feminized male birds. *Genetics*, 3:276–299.

Goodfellow, P. N., and Lovell-Badge, R. 1993. SRY and sex determination in mammals. *Annu. Rev. Genet.*, 27:71–92.

Goodman, R. L. and Karsch, F. J. 1980. Pulsatile secretion of luteinizing hormone: Differential suppression by ovarian steroids. *Endocrinology*, 107:1286–1290.

Goodman, R. L., Coolen, L. M., and Lehman, M. N. 2014. A role for neurokinin B in pulsatile GnRH secretion in the ewe. *Neuroendocrinology*, 99:18–32.

Goodman, R. L., Lehman, M. N., Smith, J. T., Coolen, L. M., de Oliveira, C. V., Jafarzadehshirazi, M. R., Pereira, A., et al. 2007. Kisspeptin neurons in the arcuate nucleus of the ewe express both dynorphin A and neurokinin B. *Endocrinology*, 148:5752–5760.

Goodson, J. L. 2005. The vertebrate social behavior network: Evolutionary themes and variations. *Horm. Behav.*, 48:11–22.

Goodson, J. L. 2013. Nonapeptide mechanisms of avian social behavior and phenotypic diversity. In E. Choleris, D. W. Pfaff, and M. Kavaliers (eds.), *Oxytocin, Vasopressin, and Related Peptides in the Regulation of Behavior*. Cambridge University Press, New York.

Goodson, J. L. and Kingsbury, M. A. 2013. What's in a name? Considerations of homologies and nomenclature for vertebrate social behavior networks. *Horm. Behav.*, 64:103–112.

Goodson, J. L., and Bass, A. H. 2001. Social behavior functions and related anatomical characteristics of vasotocin/vasopressin systems in vertebrates. *Brain Res. Rev.*, 25:246–265.

Goodson, J. L., and Thompson, R. R. 2010. Nonapeptide mechanisms of social cognition, behavior and species-specific social systems. *Curr. Opin. Neurobiol.* 20:784–794.

Goodson, J. L., and Wang, Y. 2006. Valence-sensitive neurons exhibit divergent functional profiles in gregarious and asocial species. *Proc. Natl. Acad. Sci. USA*, 103:17013–17017.

Goodson, J. L., Evans, A. K., and Bass, A. H. 2003. Putative isotocin distributions in sonic fish: Relation to vasotocin and vocal-acoustic circuitry. *J. Comp. Neurol.*, 462:1–14.

Goodson, J. L., Evans, A. K., and Wang, Y. 2006. Neuropeptide binding reflects convergent and divergent evolution in species-typical group sizes. *Horm. Behav.*, 50:223–236.

Goodson, J. L., Kabelik, D., and Schrock, S. E. 2009a. Dynamic neuromodulation of aggression by vasotocin: Influence of social context and social phenotype in territorial songbirds. *Biol. Lett.*, 5:554–556.

Gooren, L. 1986. The neuroendocrine response of luteinizing hormone to estrogen administration in heterosexual, homosexual, and transsexual subjects. *J. Clin. Endocrinol. Metab.*, 63:583–588.

Gooren, L. 1990. Biomedical theories of sexual orientation: A Critical examination. In D. P. McWhirter, S. A. Sanders, and J. M. Reinisch (eds.), *Homosexuality/Heterosexuality: Concepts of Sexual Orientation*, pp. 71–87. Oxford University Press, New York.

Gooren, L. J. 1985. Human male sexual functions do not require aromatization of testosterone: A study using tamoxifen, testolactone, and dihydrotestosterone. *Arch. Sex Behav.*, 14:539–548.

Gooren, L. J. G., Rao, B. R., Van Kessel, H., and Harmsen-Louman, W. 1984. Estrogen positive feedback on LH secretion in transsexuality. *Psychoneuroendocrinol.*, 9:249–260.

Gordon, G. G., Southren, A. L., Tochimoto, S., Olivo, J., Altman, K., Rand, J., and Lemberger, L. 1970. Effect of medroxyprogesterone acetate (Provera) on the metabolism and biological activity of testosterone. *J. Clin. Endocrinol. Metab.*, 30:449–456.

Gordon, H. W., and Galatzer, A. 1980. Cerebral organization in patients with gonadal dysgenesis. *Psychoneuroendocrinol.*, 5:235–244.

Gordon, I., Zagoory-Sharon, O., Leckman, J. F., and Feldman, R. 2010. Oxytocin and the development of parenting in humans *Biol. Psychiatry*, 68:377–382.

Gorman, M. R. 1994. Male homosexual desire: Neurological investigations and scientific bias. *Perspect. Biol. Med.*, 38:61–81.

Gorman, M. R., Ferkin, M. H., Nelson, R. J., and Zucker, I. 1993. Reproductive status influences odor preferences of the meadow vole, *Microtus pennsylvanicus*, in winter day lengths. *Can. J. Zool.*, 71:1748–1754.

Gorski, R. A. 1984. Critical role for the medial preoptic area in the sexual differentiation of the brain. *Prog. Brain Res.*, 61:129–146.

Gorski, R. A. 1993. Editorial: Estradiol acts via the estrogen receptor in the sexual differentiation of the rat brain, but what does this complex do? *Endocrinol.*, 133:431–432.

Gorski, R. A., Gordon, J. H., Shryne, J. E., and Southam, A. M. 1978. Evidence for a morphological sex difference within the medial preoptic area of the rat brain. *Brain Res.*, 143:333–346.

Gorwood, P. 2004. Eating disorders, serotonin transporter polymorphisms and potential treatment response. *Am. J. Pharmacogenomics*, 4:9–17.

Goss, R. J. 1980. Photoperiodic control of antler cycles in deer. *J. Exp. Zool.*, 211:101–105.

Goss, R. J. 1984. Photoperiodic control of antler cycles in deer. VI. Circannual rhythms on altered day lengths. *J. Exp. Zool.*, 230:265–271.

Goss, R. J., and Rosen, J. K. 1973. The effects of latitude and photoperiod on the growth of antlers. *J. Reprod. Fertil. (Suppl.)*, 19:111–118.

Gotlib, I. H., Whiffen, V. E., Mount, J. H., Milne, K., and Cordy, N. I. 1989. Prevalence rates and demographic characteristics associated with depression in pregnancy and the postpartum. *J. Consult. Clin. Psychol.*, 57:269–274.

Gouchie, C., and Kimura, D. 1991. The relationship between testosterone levels and cognitive ability patterns. *Psychoneuroendocrinol.* 16:323–334.

Gouin, J-P and Kiecolt-Glaser, J. K. 2011. The impact of psychological stress on wound healing: Methods and mechanisms. *Immunol. Allergy Clin. North Am.*, 31:81–93.

Gould, E., Tanapat, P., McEwen, B. S., Flugge, G., and Fuchs, E. 1998. Proliferation of granule cell precursors in the dentate gyrus of adult monkeys is diminished by stress. *Proc. Natl. Acad. Sci. USA*, 95:3168–3171.

Gould, E., Woolley, C. S., and McEwen, B. S. 1991. The hippocampal formation: Morphological changes induced by thyroid, gonadal, and adrenal hormones. *Psychoneuroendocrinol.*, 16:67–84.

Gould, E., Woolley, C. S., Frankfurt, M., and McEwen, B. S. 1990. Gonadal steroids regulate dendritic spine density in hippocampal pyramidal cells in adulthood. *J. Neurosci.*, 10:1286–1291.

Gowaty, P. A. 1996. Field studies of parental care in birds: New data focus questions on variation among females. *Adv. Study Behav.*, 25:477–532.

Goy, R. W. 1966. Role of androgens in the establishment and regulation of behavioral sex differences in mammals. *J. Anim. Sci.*, 25:21–31.

Goy, R. W. 1967. William Caldwell Young. *Anat. Rec.*, 157:4–11.

Goy, R. W. 1978. Development of play and mounting behaviour in female rhesus virilized prenatally with esters of testosterone or dihydrotestosterone. In D. J. Chivers and J. Herbert (eds.), *Recent Advances in Primatology*, Vol. 1, pp. 449–462. Academic Press, London.

Goy, R. W., and Phoenix, C. H. 1971. Gonadal hormones and behavior of normal and pseudohermaphroditic female primates. In C. H. Sawyer and R. S. Gorski (eds.), *Steroids, Hormones and Brain Function*, pp. 193–202. University of California Press, Berkeley.

Goy, R. W., and Phoenix, C. H. 1972. The effects of testosterone propionate administered before birth on the development of behavior in genetic female rhesus monkeys. In C. Sawyer and R. Gorski (eds.), *Steroid Hormones and Brain Function*, pp. 193–201. University of California Press, Berkeley.

Goy, R. W., and Resko, J. A. 1972. Gonadal hormones and behavior of normal and pseudohermaphroditic nonhuman female primates. *Rec. Prog. Horm. Res.*, 28:707–733.

Goy, R. W., Bercovitch, F. B., and McBrair, M. C. 1988. Behavioral masculinization is independent of genital masculinization in prenatally androgenized female rhesus macaques. *Horm. Behav.*, 22:552–571.

Goy, R. W., Bridson, W. E., and Young, W. C. 1964. The period of maximal susceptibility of the prenatal female guinea pig to masculinizing actions of testosterone propionate. *J. Comp. Physiol. Psychol.*, 57:166–174.

Goymann, W., and Wingfield, J. C. 2004. Allostatic load, social status and stress hormones: The costs of social status matter. *Anim. Behav.*, 67:591–602.

Goymann, W., Landys, M. M., and Wingfield, J. C. 2007. Distinguishing seasonal androgen responses from male–male androgen responsiveness: Revisiting the challenge hypothesis. *Horm. Behav.*, 51:463–476.

Grachev, P., Porter, K. L., Coolen, L. M., McCosh, R. B., Connors, J. M., Hileman, S. M., Lehman, M. N., and Goodman, R. L. 2016. Surge-like LH secretion induced by retrochiasmatic area NK3R activation is mediated primarily by ARC kisspeptin neurones in the ewe. *J. Neuroendocrinol.*, doi: 10.1111/jne.12393.

Grady, K. L., Phoenix, C. H., and Young, W. C. 1965. Role of the developing rat testis in differentiation of the neural tissues mediating mating behavior. *J. Comp. Physiol. Psychol.*, 59:176–182.

Graham, J. M., and Desjardins, C. 1980. Classical conditioning: Induction of luteinizing hormone and testosterone secretion in anticipation of sexual activity. *Science,* 210:1039–1041.

Granneman, J., and Friedman, M. I. 1980. Hepatic modulation of insulin-induced gastric acid secretion and EMB activity in rats. *Am. J. Physiol.,* 238:R346–R352.

Gray, G. D., and Dewsbury, D. A. 1973. A quantitative description of copulatory behavior in prairie voles (*Microtus ochrogaster*). *Brain Behav. Ecol.,* 8:837–852.

Gray, G. D., Smith, E. R., and Davidson, J. M. 1980. Hormonal regulation of penile erection in castrated male rats. *Physiol. Behav.,* 24:463–468.

Gray, G. D., Soderstein, P., Tallentire, D., and Davidson, J. M. 1978. Effects of lesions in various structures of the suprachiasmatic-preoptic region on LH regulation and sexual behavior in female rats. *Neuroendocrinol.,* 25:174–191.

Gray, J. A., and Lalljee, B. 1974. Sex differences in emotional behavior in the rat: Correlation between open field, defecation, and active avoidance. *Anim. Behav.,* 22:856–861.

Gray, J. M., and Wade, G. N. 1979. Cytoplasmic progestin binding in rat adipose tissues. *Endocrinol.,* 104:1377–1382.

Gray, L. E., Ostby, J., Furr, J., Price, M., Veeramachaneni, D. N., and Parks, L. 2000. Perinatal exposure to the phthalates DEHP, BBP, and DINP, but not DEP, DMP, or DOTP, alters sexual differentiation of the male rat. *Toxicol. Sci.,* 58:350–365.

Gray, P. B., Parkin, J. C., and Samms-Vaughan, M. E. 2007. Hormonal correlates of human paternal interactions: a hospital-based investigation in urban Jamaica. *Horm. Behav.,* 52:499–507.

Grebe, N. M., Emery Thompson, M., and Gangestad, S. W. 2016. Hormonal predictors of women's extra-pair vs. in-pair sexual attraction in natural cycles: Implications for extended sexuality. *Horm. Behav.,* 78:211–219.

Green, R. 1987. *The "Sissy-Boy Syndrome" and the Development of Homosexuality.* Yale University Press, New Haven, CT.

Greenberg, R. 1986. Competition in migrant birds in the nonbreeding season. In R. J. Johnson (ed.), *Curr. Ornithol.,* pp. 281–307. Plenum, New York.

Greenfield, D. A. 1997. Does psychological support and counseling reduce the stress experienced by couples involved in assisted reproductive technology? *J. Assist. Reprod. Gen.,* 14:186–188.

Greenough, W. T., Carter, C. S., Steerman, C., and DeVoogd, T. J. 1977. Sex differences in dendritic patterns in hamster preoptic area. *Brain Res.,* 126:63–72.

Gregg, J. K., and Wynne-Edwards, K. E. 2006. In uniparental *Phodopus sungorus,* new mothers and fathers present during the birth of their offspring are the only hamsters that readily consume fresh placenta. *Dev. Psychobiol.,* 48:528–536.

Gregg, T. R., and Siegel, A. 2001. Brain structures and neurotransmitters regulating aggression in cats: Implications for human aggression. *Prog. Neuro-Psychopharmacological Biol. Psychiatry,* 25:91–140.

Greives, T. J., Kriegsfeld, L. J., and Demas, G. E. 2008. Exogenous kisspeptin does not alter photoperiod-induced gonadal regression in Siberian hamsters (*Phodopus sungorus*). *Gen. Comp. Endocrinol.,* 156:552–558.

Greives, T. J., Mason, A. O., Scotti, M. A., Levine, J., Ketterson, E. D., Kriegsfeld, L. J., and Demas, G. E. 2007. Environmental control of kisspeptin: implications for seasonal reproduction. *Endocrinology,* 148:1158–1166.

Gresack, J. E., and Frick, K. M. 2004. Environmental enrichment reduces the mnemonic and neural benefits of estrogen. *Neuroscience,* 128:459–471.

Gresack, J. E., Kerr, K. M., and Frick, K. M. 2007a. Life-long environmental enrichment differentially affects the mnemonic response to estrogen in young, middle-aged, and aged female mice. *Neurobiol. Learn. Mem.,* 88:393–408.

Gresack, J. E., Kerr, K. M., and Frick, K. M. 2007b. Short-term environmental enrichment decreases the mnemonic response to estrogen in young, but not aged, female mice. *Brain Res.,* 1160:91–101.

Grieves, T. J., McGlothlin, J. W., Jawor, J. M., Demas, G. E., and Ketterson, E. D. 2006. Testosterone and innate immune function inversely covary in a wild population of breeding dark-eyed juncos (*Junco hyemalis*). *Funct. Ecol.,* 20:812–818.

Griffin, J. E., and Ojeda, S. R. 1988. *Textbook of Endocrine Physiology.* Oxford University Press, New York.

Griffiths, B. B. and Hunter, R. G. 2014. Neuroepigenetics of stress. *Neuroscience,* 275:420–435.

Grill, H. J. 2006. Distributed neural control of energy balance: Contributions from hindbrain and hypothalamus. *Obesity,* 14:216S–221S.

Grill, H. J. 2009. Leptin and the systems neuroscience of meal size control. *Front. Neuroendocrinol.,* 31:61–78.

Grill, H. J., and Hayes, M. R. 2009. The nucleus tractus solitarius: A portal for visceral afferent signal processing, energy status assessment and integration of their combined effects on food intake. *Int. J. Obes.,* 33 Suppl. 1:S11–15.

Grill, H. J., and Kaplan, J. M. 1990. Caudal brainstem participates in the distributed neuronal control of feeding. In E. M. Stricker (ed.), *Handbook of Behav. Neurobiology: Neurobiology of Food Fluid Intake,* pp. 125–150. Plenum Press, New York.

Grill, H. J., and Kaplan, J. M. 2002. The neuroanatomical axis for control of energy balance. *Front. Neuroendocrinol.,* 23:2–40.

Grill, H. J., Donahey, J. C. K., King, L, and Kaplan, J. M. 1997. Contribution of caudal brainstem to δ-fenfluramine anorexia. *Psychopharmacol.,* 130:375–381.

Grill, H. J., Ginsberg, A. B., Seeley, R. J., and Kaplan, J. M. 1998. Brainstem application of melanocortin receptor ligands produces long-lasting effects on feeding and body weight. *J. Neurosci.,* 18:10128–10135.

Grimbos, T., Dawood, K., Burriss, R. P., Zucker, K. J., and Puts, D. A. 2010. Sexual orientation and the second to fourth finger length ratio: A meta-analysis in men and women. *Behav. Neurosci.,* 124:278–287.

Grimes, L. J., Melnyk, R. B., Martin, J. M., and Mrosovsky, N. 1981. Infradian cycles in glucose utilization and lipogenic enzyme activity in dormouse (*Glis glis*) adipocytes. *Gen. Comp. Endocrinol.,* 45:21–25.

Grippo, A. J., Trahanas, D. M., Zimmerman, R. R., Porges, S. W., and Carter, C. S. 2009. Oxytocin protects against negative behavioral and autonomic consequences of long-term social isolation. *Psychoneuroendocrinol.,* 34:1542–1553.

Grisham, W., Kerchner, M., and Ward, I. L. 1991. Prenatal stress alters sexually dimorphic nuclei in the spinal cord of male rats. *Brain Res.,* 551:126–131.

Grober, M. S., and Rodgers, E. W. 2008. The evolution of hermaphroditism. *J. Theor. Biol.,* 251:190–192.

Grön, G., Wunderlich, A. P., Spitzer, M., Tomczak, R., and Riepe, M. W. 2000. Brain activation during human navigation: Gender-different neural networks as substrate of performance. *Nature Neuroscience,* 3:404–408.

Groos, G. 1982. The comparative physiology of extraocular photoreception. *Experientia,* 38:989–1128.

Groothuis, T. G. G., Muller, W., von Engelhardt, N., Carere, C., and Eising, C. 2005. Maternal hormones as a tool to adjust offspring phenotype in avian species. *Neurosci. Biobehav. Rev.,* 29:329–352.

Grosse, J., Maywood, E. S., Ebling, F. J., and Hastings, M. H. 1993. Testicular regression in pinealectomized Syrian hamsters following infusions of melatonin delivered on non-circadian schedules. *Biol. Reprod.,* 49:666–674.

Gruber, A. J., and Pope, H. G. 2000. Psychiatric and medical effects of anabolic-androgenic steroid use in women. *Psychotherapy and Psychosomatics,* 69:19–26.

Gruder-Adams, S., and Getz, L. L. 1985. Comparison of the mating system and paternal behavior in *Microtus ochrogaster* and *M. pennsylvanicus. J. Mammal.,* 66:165–167.

Grunt, J. A., and Young, W. C. 1952. Differential reactivity of individuals and the response of the male guinea pig to testosterone propionate. *Endocrinol.,* 51:237–248.

Grunt, J. A., and Young, W. C. 1953. Consistency of sexual behavior patterns in individual male guinea pigs following castration and androgen therapy. *J. Comp. Physiol. Psychol.,* 46:138–144.

Guardiola-Lemaitre, B. 1997. Toxicology of melatonin. *J. Biol. Rhythms,* 12:697–706.

Guay, D. R. P. 2009. Drug treatment of paraphilic and nonparaphilic sexual disorders. *Clin. Ther.,* 31:1–31.

Gubernick, D. J., and Alberts, J. R. 1987. The biparental care system of the California mouse, *Peromyscus californicus. J. Comp. Psychol.,* 101:169–177.

Gubernick, D. J., and Klopfer, P. H. (eds.). 1981. *Parental Care in Mammals.* Plenum Press, New York.

Gubernick, D. J., and Nelson, R. J. 1989. Prolactin and paternal behavior in the biparental California mouse, *Peromyscus californicus. Horm. Behav.,* 23:203–210.

Gubernick, D. J., Winslow, J. T., Jensen, P., Jeanotte, L., and Bowen, J. 1995. Oxytocin changes in males over the reproductive cycle in the monogamous, biparental California mouse, *Peromyscus californicus. Horm. Behav.,* 29:5/1–/23.

Guillamón, A., and Segovia, S. 1997. Sex differences in the vomeronasal system. *Brain Res. Bull.,* 44:377–382.

Guinness, F. E., Albon, S. D., and Clutton-Brock, T. H. 1978. Factors affecting reproduction in red deer (*Cervus elaphus L.*). *J. Reprod. Fertil.,* 54:325–334.

Güler, A. D., Ecker, J. L., Lall, G. S., Haq, S., Altimus, C. M., Liao, H. W., Barnard, A. R., et al. 2008. Melanopsin cells are the principal conduits for rod–cone input to non-image-forming vision. *Nature,* 453:102–105.

Gulledge, C., and Deviche, P. 1997. Androgen control of vocal control region volumes in a wild migratory songbird (*Junco hyemalis*) is region and possibly age dependent. *J. Neurobiol.,* 32:391–402.

Gundlah, C., Kohama, S. G., Mirkes, S. J., Garyfallou, V. T., Urbanski, H. F., and Bethea, C. L. 2000. Distribution of estrogen receptor beta (ERbeta) mRNA in hypothalamus, midbrain and temporal lobe of spayed macaque: continued expression with hormone replacement. *Brain Res. Mol, Brain Res.,* 76:191–204.

Gurney, M. E., and Konishi, M. 1980. Hormone induced sexual differentiation of brain and behavior in zebra finches. *Science,* 208:1380–1383.

Gutzke, W. H. N., and Crews, D. 1988. Embryonic temperature determines adult sexuality in a reptile. *Nature,* 332:832–834.

Gutzke, W. H. N., and Paukstis, G. L. 1983. Influence of the hydric environment on sexual differentiation of turtles. *J. Exp. Zool.,* 226:467–469.

Gutzler, S. J., Karom, M., Erwin, W. D., and Albers, H. E. 2010. Arginine-vasopressin and the regulation of aggression in female Syrian hamsters (*Mesocricetus auratus*). *Eur. J. Neurosci.,* 31:1655–1663.

Gutzwiller, J. P., Drewe, J., Hildebrand, P., Rossi, L., Lauper, J. Z., and Beglinger, C. 1994. Effect of intravenous human gastrin-releasing peptide on food intake in humans. *Gastroenterol.,* 106:1168–1173.

Gwinner, E. 1986. *Circannual Rhythms.* Springer-Verlag, Berlin.

Gwinner, E., Hau, M., and Heigl, S. 1997. Melatonin: Generation and modulation of avian circadian rhythms. *Brain Res. Bull.,* 44:439–444.

Haaren, F. van, Hest, A., and Heinsbroek, R. P. W. 1990. Behavioral differences between male and female rats: Effects of gonadal hormones on learning and memory. *Neurosci. Biobehav. Rev.,* 14:23–33.

Haertzen, C., Buxton, K., Covi, L., and Richards, H. 1993. Seasonal changes in rule infractions among prisoners: A preliminary test of the temperature-aggression hypothesis. *Psychological Reports,* 72:195–200.

Haffen, K., and Wolff, E. 1977. Natural and experimental modification of ovarian development. In L. Z. Zuckerman and B. J. Wier (eds.), *The Ovary,* pp. 393–423. Academic Press, New York.

Haffmans, J., Koppelaar, V., and Hoencamp, E. 2008. Comorbidity and personality in patients with Seasonal Affective Disorder. *J. Affect. Disord.,* 107:S117–S117.

Hage, M. P. and Azar, S. T. 2012. The link between thyroid function and depression. *J. Thyroid Res.,* http://dx.doi.org/10.1155/2012/590648.

Hahn-Holbrook, J. and Haselton, M. 2014. Is postpartum depression a disease of modern civilization? *Curr. Dir. Psychol.,* 23:395–400.

Hahn-Holbrook, J., Schetter, C.D., Arora, C. and Hobel, C.J. 2013. Placental corticotropin-releasing hormone mediates the association between prenatal social support and postpartum depression. *Clin. Psychol. Sci.,* 1:253–265.

Halberg, F. 1959. Physiologic 24-hour periodicity in human beings and mice, the lighting regimen and daily routine. In R. B. Withrow (ed.), *Photoperiodism and Related Phenomena in Plants and Animals,* pp. 803–878. American Association for the Advancement of Science, Washington, D.C.

Halberg, F. 1977. Implications of biological rhythms for clinical practice. *Hosp. Prac.,* 12:139–149.

Halberg, F., Nelson, W., Levi, F., Culley, D., Bogden, A., and Taylor, D. J. 1980. Chronotherapy of mammary cancer in rats. *Int. J. Chronobiol.,* 7:85–99.

Halbreich, U. 1997. Role of estrogen in postmenopausal depression. *Neurol.,* 48:S16–S19.

Halbreich, U. 2003. The etiology, biology, and evolving pathology of premenstrual syndromes. *Psychoneuroendocrinol.,* 28:55–99.

Halbreich, U., Borenstein, J., Pearlstein, T., and Kahn, L. S. 2003. The prevalence, impairment, impact, and burden of premenstrual dysphoric disorder (PMS/PMDD). *Psychoneuroendocrinol.,* 28:1–23.

Halbreich, U., Endicott, J., Schacts, D., and Nee, J. 1982. The diversity of premenstrual changes as reflected in the premenstrual assessment form. *Acta Psychiatrica Scand.,* 65:46–65.

Halbreich, U., O'Brien, P. M. S., Eriksson, E., Bäckström, T., Yonkers, K. A., and Freeman, E. W. 2006. Are there differential symptom profiles that improve in response to different pharmacological treatments of premenstrual syndrome/premenstrual dysphoric disorder? *Curr. Opin.: CNS Drugs,* 20:523–547.

Hall, J. C., and Rosbash, M. 1987. Genetic and molecular analysis of biological rhythms. *J. Biol. Rhythms,* 2:153–178.

Hall, J. L, Reilly, R. T., Cottrill, K. L, Stone, W. S., and Gold, P. E. 1992. Phlorizin enhancement of memory in rats and mice. *Pharmacol. Biochem. Behav.,* 41:295–299.

Hall, J. L., Gonder-Frederick, L. A., Chewning, W. W., Silveira, J., and Gold, P. E. 1989. Glucose enhancement of performance on memory tests in young and aged humans. *Neuropsychologia,* 27:1129–1138.

Hall, M. R. and Goldsmith, A. R. 1983. Factors affecting prolactin secretion during breeding and incubation in the domestic duck (*Anas platyrhyncos*). *Gen. Comp. Endocrinol.,* 49:270–276.

Hall, V. D., and Goldman, B. D. 1980. Effects of gonadal steroid hormones on hibernation in the Turkish hamster (*Mesocricetus brandti*). *J. Comp. Physiol.,* 135:107–114.

Hall, V. D., Bartke, A., and Goldman, B. D. 1982. Role of the testes in regulating the duration of hibernation in the Turkish hamster (*Mesocricetus brandti*). *Biol. Reprod.,* 27:802–810.

Hall, Z. J., Bertin, M., Bailey, I. E., Meddle, S. L., and Healy, S. D. 2014. Neural correlates of nesting behavior in zebra finches (*Taeniopygia guttata*). *Behav. Brain Res.,* 264:26–33.

Hamilton, J. B., and Gardner, W. U. 1937. Effects in female young born of pregnant rats injected with androgens. *Proc. Soc. Exp. Biol. Med.,* 37:570–572.

Hamilton, L. D., Newman, M. L., Delvill, C. L., and Delville, Y. 2008. Physiological stress response of young adults exposed to bullying during adolescence. *Physiol. Behav.,* 95:617–624.

Hamilton, M. 1960. A rating scale for depression. *J. Neurol. Neurosurg. Psychiatry,* 23:56–61.

Hamilton, M. 1980. Rating depressive patients. *J. Clin. Psychiatry,* 41:21–24.

Hammock, E. A. D. and Young, L. Y. 2006. Oxytocin, vasopressin and pair bonding: implications for autism. *Phil. Trans. R. Soc. B*, 361:2187–2198.

Hammond, G. L., Miguel-Queralt, S., Yalcinkaya, T. M., Underhill, C., Place, N. J., Glickman, S. E., Drea, C. M., Wagner, A. P., and Siiteri, P. K. 2012. Phylogenetic comparisons implicate sex hormone-binding globulin in "masculinization" of the female spotted hyena (*Crocuta crocuta*). *Endocrinology*, 153:1435–1443, doi:10.1210/en.2011-1837

Hampson, E. 2008. Endocrine contributions to sex differences in visuospatial perception and cognition. In J. B. Becker, K. J. Berkley, N. Geary, E. Hampson, J. P. Herman, and E. A. Young (eds.), *Sex Differences in the Brain: From Genes to Behavior*, pp. 311–353. Oxford University Press, New York.

Hampton, J. K., Hampton, S. H., and Landwehr, B. T. 1966. Observations on a successful breeding colony of the marmoset, *Oedipomidas oedipus*. *Folia Primatol.*, 4:265–287.

Handa, R. J., Burgess, L. H., Kerr, J. E., and O'Keefe, J. A. 1994. Gonadal steroid hormone receptors and sex differences in the hypothalamo-pituitary-adrenal axis. *Horm. Behav.*, 28:464–476.

Hanon, E. A., Lincoln, G. A., Fustin, J. M., Dardente, H., Masson-Pevet, M., Morgan, P. J., Hazlerigg, D. G. 2008. Ancestral TSH mechanism signals summer in a photoperiodic mammal. *Curr. Biol.*, 18:1147–1152.

Hansen, J. T., and Karasek, M. 1982. Neuron or endocrine cell? The pinealocyte as a paraneuron. In R. J. Reiter (ed.), *The Pineal and Its Hormones*, pp. 1–9. Alan R. Liss, New York.

Hansen, S., Bergvall, A. H., and Nyiredi, S. 1993. Interaction with pups enhances dopamine release in the ventral striatum of maternal rats: a microdialysis study. *Pharmacol Biochem Behav.*, 45:673–676.

Hansen, S., Harthon, C., Wallin, E., Lofberg, L., and Svensson, K. 1991. The effects of 6-OHDA-induced dopamine depletions in the ventral or dorsal striatum on maternal and sexual behavior in the female rat. *Pharmacol Biochem Behav.*, 39:71–77.

Hansson, A. C., Cippitelli, A., Sommer, W. H., Fedeli, A., Björk, K., Soverchia, L., Terasmaa, A., Massi, M., Heilig, M., and Ciccocioppo, R. 2006. Variation at the rat Crhr1 locus and sensitivity to relapse into alcohol seeking induced by environmental stress. *Proc. Natl. Acad. Sci. USA*, 103:15236–15241.

Harada, Y., Sakai, M., Kurabayashi, N., Hirota, T., and Fukada, Y. 2005. Ser-557-phosphorylated mCRY2 is degraded upon synergistic phosphorylation by glycogen synthase kinase-3 beta. *J. Biol. Chem.*, 280:31714–31721.

Harasty, J., Double, K. L., Halliday, G. M., Kril, J. J., and McRitchie, D. A. 1997. Language-associated cortical regions are proportionally larger in the female brain. *Arch. Neurol.*, 54:171–176.

Hardie, L. J., Rayner, D. V., Holmes, S., and Trayhurn, P. 1996. Circulating leptin levels are modulated by fasting, cold exposure and insulin administration in lean, but not Zucker (*fa/fa*) rats as measured by ELISA. *Biochem. Biophys. Res. Commun.*, 223:660–665.

Harding, C. F., and Follett, B. K. 1979. Hormone changes triggered by aggression in a natural population of blackbirds. *Science*, 203:918–920.

Harding, C. F., Sheridan, K., and Walters, M. J. 1983. Hormonal specificity and activation of sexual behavior in male zebra finches. *Horm. Behav.*, 17:111–113.

Harding, C. F., Walters, M. J., Collado, M., and Sheridan, K. 1988. Hormonal specificity and activation of social behavior in male red-winged blackbirds. *Horm. Behav.*, 22:402–418.

Hardy, D. F., and DeBold, J. F. 1971. Effects of mounts without intromission upon the behavior of female rats during the onset of estrogen-induced heat. *Physiol. Behav.*, 7:643–645.

Harley, V. R., and Goodfellow, P. N. 1995. The biochemical role of SRY in sex determination. *Mol. Reprod. Dev.*, 39:184–193.

Harley, V. R., Clarkson, M. J., and Argentaro, A. 2003. The molecular action and regulation of the testis-determining factors, SRY (sex-determining region on the Y chromosome) and SOX9 [SRY-related high-mobility group (HMG) box 9]. *Endocr. Rev.*, 24:466–487.

Harlow, B. L., Wise, L. A., Otto, M. W., Soares, C. N., and Cohen, L. S. 2003. Depression and its influence on reproductive endocrine and menstrual cycle markers associated with perimenopause: The Harvard Study of Moods and Cycles. *Arch. Gen. Psychiatry*, 60:29–36.

Harris, G. W. 1937. The induction of ovulation in the rabbit by electrical stimulation of the hypothalamo-hypophysial mechanism. *Proc. Roy. Soc. Lond. B*, 122:374–394.

Harris, G. W. 1948. Electrical stimulation of the hypothalamus and the mechanism of neural control of the adenohypophysis. *J. Physiol.*, 107:418–429.

Harris, G. W. 1955. *Neural Control of the Pituitary Gland*. E. Arnold, London.

Harris, G. W., and Jacobsohn, D. 1952. Functional grafts of the anterior pituitary gland. *Proc. Roy. Soc. Lond. B*, 139:263–276.

Harris, J. A. 1999. Review and methodological considerations in research on testosterone and aggression. *Aggress. Violent Behav.*, 4:273–291.

Harris, L. J. 1980. Lateralized sex differences: Substrates and significance. *Behav. Brain Sci.*, 3:236–237.

Hart, B. L. 1974. Gonadal androgen and sociosexual behavior of male mammals: A comparative analysis. *Psychol. Bull.*, 7:383–400.

Hart, B. L. 1979. Activation of sexual reflexes of male rats by dihydrotestosterone but not estrogen. *Physiol. Behav.*, 23:107–109.

Hart, B. L., Wallach, S. J. R., and Meleased'Hospital, P. Y. 1983. Differences in responsiveness to testosterone of penile reflexes and copulatory behavior of male rats. *Horm. Behav.*, 17:274–283.

Hartgens, F., and Kuipers, H. 2004. Effects of androgenic-anabolic steroids in athletes. *Sports Medicine*, 34:513–554.

Hartung, T. G., and Dewsbury, D. A. 1979. Paternal behaviour in six species of muroid rodents. *Behav. Neural Biol.*, 26:466–478.

Hassett, M. M., Siebert, E. R., and Wallen, K. 2008. Sex differences in rhesus monkey toy preferences parallel those of children. *Horm. Behav.*, 54:359–364.

Hastings, M. H., Duffield, G. E., Ebling, F. J., Kidd, A., Maywood, E. S., Schurov, I. 1998. Non-photic signalling in the suprachiasmatic nucleus. *Biol. Cell*, 89:495–503.

Hastings, M. H., Reddy, A. B., and Maywood, E. S. 2003. A clockwork web: Circadian timing in brain and periphery, in health and disease. *Nature Rev. Neuroscience*, 4:649–661.

Hastings, M., O'Neil, J. S., and Maywood, E. S. 2007. Circadian clocks: Regulators of endocrine and metabolic rhythms. *J. Endocrinol.*, 195:187–198.

Hattar, S., Liao, H. W., Takao, M., Berson, D. M., and Yau, K. W. 2002. Melanopsin-containing retinal ganglion cells: architecture, projections, and intrinsic photosensitivity. *Science*, 295:1065–1070.

Hatton, D.C., and Meyer, M. E. 1973. Paternal behavior in cactus mice (*Peromyscus eremicus*). *Bull. Psychonom. Soc.*, 2:330.

Hatton, J. D., and Ellisman, M. H. 1982. A restructuring of hypothalamic synapses is associated with motherhood. *J. Neurosci.*, 2:704–707.

Hau, M., Stoddard, S. T., and Soma, K. K. 2004. Territorial aggression and hormones during the non-breeding season in a tropical bird. *Horm. Behav.*, 45:40–49.

Haug, M., Brain, P. F., and Kamis, A. B. 1986. A brief review comparing the effects of sex steroids on two forms of aggression in laboratory mice. *Neurosci. Biobehav. Rev.*, 10:463–468.

Haupt, H. A., and Rovere, G. D. 1984. Anabolic steroids: A review of the literature. *Am. J. Sports Med.*, 12:469–484.

Hawkins, M. B., Thornton, J. W., Crews, D., Skipper, J. K., Dotte, A., and Thomas, P. 2000. Identification of a third distinct estrogen receptor and reclassification of estrogen receptors in teleosts. *Proc. Natl. Acad. Sci. USA*, 97:10751–10756.

Hawley, W. R., Grissom, E. M., and Dohanich, G. P. 2010. The relationships between trait anxiety, place recognition memory and learning strategy. *Behav. Brain Res.*, doi:10.1016/j.bbr.2010.08.028

Hayes, M. R., Skibicka, K. P., Bence, K. K., and Grill, H. J. 2009. Dorsal hindbrain 5′-adenosine monophosphate-activated protein kinase as an intracellular mediator of energy balance. *Endocrinol.*, 150:2175–2182.

Hayes, T. B., Anderson, L. L., Beasley, V. R., de Solla, S. R., Iguchi, T., Ingraham, H., Kestemont, P., et al. 2011. Demasculinization and feminization of male gonads by atrazine: Consistent effects across vertebrate classes. *J. Steroid Biochem. Mol. Biol.*, 127:64–73.

Hayes, T. B., Case, P., Chui, S., Chung, D., Haeffele, C., Haston, K., Lee, M., Mai, V. P., Marjuoa, Y., Parker, J., and Tsui, M. 2006. Pesticide mixtures, endocrine disruption, and amphibian declines: Are we underestimating the impact? *Environ. Health Perspect.*, 114:40–50.

Hayes, T. B., Collins, A., Lee, M., Mendoza, M., Noriega, N., Stuart, A. A., and Vonk, A. 2002a. Hermaphroditic, demasculinized frogs after exposure to the herbicide atrazine at low ecologically relevant doses. *Proc. Natl. Acad. Sci. USA*, 99:5476–5480.

Hayes, T. B., Khoury, V., Narayan, A., Nazir, M., Park, A., Brown, T., Adame, L., et al. 2010. Atrazine induces complete feminization and chemical castration in male African clawed frogs (*Xenopus laevis*). *Proc. Natl. Acad. Sci. USA*, 107:4612–4617. doi:10.1073/pnas.0909519107.

Hayes, T., Haston, K., Tsui, M., Hoang, A., Haeffele, C., and Vonk, A. 2002b. Herbicides: Feminization of male frogs in the wild. *Nature*, 419:895–896.

Hayes, T., Haston, K., Tsui, M., Hoang, A., Haeffele, C., and Vonk, A. 2003. Atrazine-induced hermaphroditism at 0.1 ppb in American leopard frogs (*Rana pipiens*): Laboratory and field evidence. *Environ. Health Perspect.*, 111:568–575.

Hebebrand, J., Blum, W. F., Barth, N., Coners, H., Englaro, P., Juul, A., Ziegler, A., Warnke, A., Rascher, W., and Remschmidt, H. 1997. Leptin levels in patients with anorexia nervosa are reduced in the acute stage and elevated upon short-term weight restoration. *Molecular Psychiatry*, 2:330–334.

Hector, J. A. L. and Goldsmith, A. R. 1985. The role of prolactin during incubation: comparative studies of three Diomedea albatrosses. *Gen. Comp. Endocrinol.*, 60:236–243.

Hegner, R. E., and Wingfield, J. C. 1987. Social status and circulating levels of hormones in flocks of house sparrows, *Passer domesticus*. *Ethol.*, 76:1–14.

Heid, P., Güttinger, H.-R., and Prove, E. 1985. The influence of castration and testosterone replacement on the song architecture of canaries (*Serinus canarius*). *Z. Tierpsychol.*, 69:224–236.

Heifets, B. D., and Castillo, P. E. 2009. Endocannabinoid signaling and long-term synaptic plasticity. *Annu. Rev. Physiol.*, 71:283–306.

Heigl, S., and Gwinner, E. 1995. Synchronization of circadian rhythms of house sparrows by oral melatonin: effects of changing period. *J. Biol. Rhythms*, 10:225–33.

Heim, N., and Hursch, C. J. 1979. Castration for sex offenders: Treatment or punishment? A review and critique of recent European literature. *Arch. Sex. Behav.*, 8:281–304.

Heimer, L., and Larsson, K. 1966. Impairment of mating behavior in male rats following lesions in the preoptic-anterior hypothalamic continuum. *Brain Res.*, 3:248–263.

Heimovics, S. A., Ferrisc, L. K., and Somac, K. K. 2015. Non-invasive administration of 17β-estradiol rapidly increases aggressive behavior in non-breeding, but not breeding, male song sparrows. *Horm. Behav.*, 69:31–38.

Heimovics, S. A., Prior, N. H., Ma, C., and Soma, K. K. 2016. Rapid effects of an aggressive interaction on dehydroepiandrosterone, testosterone and oestradiol levels in the male song sparrow brain: A seasonal comparison. *J. Neuroendocrinol.*, 28:12345. doi: 10.1111/jne.12345.

Heine, P. A., Taylor, J. A., Iwamoto, G. A., Lubahn, D. B., and Cooke, P. S. 2000. Increased adipose tissue in male and female estrogen receptor-alpha knockout mice. *Proc. Natl. Acad. Sci. USA*, 97:12729–12734.

Heinrichs, S. C., Cole, B. J., Pich, E. M., Menzaghi, F., Koob, G. F., and Hauger, R. L. 1992. Endogenous corticotropin-releasing factor modulates feeding induced by neuropeptide Y or a tail-pinch stressor. *Peptides*, 13:879–884.

Heinsbroek, R. P., van Haaren, F, and van de Poll, N. E. 1988. Sex differences in passive avoidance behavior in rats: Sex-dependent susceptibility to shock-induced behavioral depression. *Physiol. Behav.*, 43:201–206.

Heise, C., and Bier, F. F., 2005. Immobilisation of DNA on microarrays. *Top. Curr. Chem.*, 261:1–25.

Heitman, J. 2006. Sexual reproduction and the evolution of microbial pathogens. *Curr. Biol.*, 16:R711–R725.

Helkala, E. L.,Niskanen, L., Viinamaki, H., Partanen, J., and Uusitupa, M. 1995. Short-term and long-term memory in elderly patients with NIDDM. *Diabetes Care*, 18:681–685.

Helvacioglu, A., Yeoman, R. R., Hazelton, J. M., and Aksel, S. 1993. Premenstrual syndrome and related hormonal changes. Long-lasting gonadotropin releasing hormone agonist treatment. *J. Reprod. Med.*, 38:864–870.

Hemsworth, P. H., and Tilbrook, A. J. 2007. Sexual behavior in pigs. *Horm. Behav.*, 52:39–44.

Henderson, V. W. 2010. Actions of estrogens in the aging brain: Dementia and cognitive aging. *Biochim. Biophys. Acta*, 1800:1077–1083.

Henderson, V. W., and Brinton, R. D. 2010. Menopause and mitochondria: Windows into estrogen effects on Alzheimer's disease risk and therapy. *Prog. Brain Res.*, 182:77–96.

Hendrick, V., Altshuler, L. L., and Suri, R. 1998. Hormonal changes in the postpartum and implications for postpartum depression. *Psychosomatics*, 39:93–101.

Hendricks, S. E., Graber, B., and Rodriguez-Sierra, J. F. 1989. Neuroendocrine response to estrogen: No differences between heterosexual and homosexual men. *Psychoneuroendocrinol.*, 14:177–185.

Hengstler, J. G., Foth, H., Gebel, T., Kramer, P. J., Lilienblum, W., Schweinfurth, H., Völkel, W., Wollin, K. M., and Gundert-Remy, U. 2011. Critical evaluation of key evidence on the human health hazards of exposure to bisphenol A. *Crit. Rev. Toxicol.*, 41:263–291.

Henn, W., and Zang, K. D. 1997. Mosaicism in Turner's syndrome. *Nature*, 390:569.

Hennessey, A. C., Wallen, K., and Edwards, D. A. 1986. Preoptic lesions increase the display of lordosis by male rats. *Brain Res.*, 370:21–28.

Henson, J. R., Carter, S. N., and Freeman, D. A. 2013. Exogenous T(3) elicits long day-like alterations in testis size and the RFamides Kisspeptin and gonadotropin-inhibitory hormone in short-day Siberian hamsters. *J. Biol. Rhythms*, 28:193–200.

Herbert, J. 2013. Cortisol and depression: Three questions for psychiatry. *Psychol. Med.*, 43:449–469.

Herbeth, B., Aubry, E., Fumeron, F., Aubert, R., Cailotto, F., Siest, G., and Visvikis-Siest, S. 2005. Polymorphism of the 5-HT2A receptor gene and food intakes in children and adolescents: The Stanislas Family Study. *Am. J. Clin. Nutr.*, 82:467–470.

Herdt, G. H., and Davidson, J. 1988. The Sambia "turnim-man": Sociocultural and clinical aspects of gender formation in male pseudohermaphrodites with 5α-reductase deficiency in Papua New Guinea. *Arch. Sex. Behav.*, 17:33–56.

Heriot, A. 1974. *The Castrati in Opera*. DaCapo, New York.

Herman, J. P., and Cullinan, W. E. 1997. Neurocircuitry of stress: Central control of the hypothalamo-pituitary-adrenocortical axis. *Trends Neurosci.*, 20:78–84.

Herman, J. P., Watson, S. J., Chao, H. M., Coirini, H., and McEwen, B. S. 1993. Diurnal Regulation of Glucocorticoid Receptor and Mineralocorticoid Receptor mRNAs in Rat Hippocampus. *Mol. Cell Neurosci.*, 4:181–190.

Herman, R. A., and Wallen, K. 2007. Cognitive performance in rhesus monkeys varies by sex and prenatal androgen exposure. *Horm. Behav.*, 51:496–507.

Herman, T. B. 1977. Activity patterns and movements of subarctic voles. *Oikos*, 29:434–444.

Herrenkohl, L. R. 1986. Prenatal stress disrupts reproductive behavior and physiology in offspring. *Ann. N. Y. Acad. Sci.*, 474:120–128.

Hervey, E., and Hervey, G. R. 1967. The effects of progesterone on body weight and composition in the rat. *J. Endocrinol.*, 37:361–384.

Herzog, E. D. 2007. Neurons and networks in daily rhythms. *Nat. Rev. Neurosci.*, 8:790–802.

Hetherington, A. W., and Ranson, S. W. 1940. Hypothalamic lesions and adiposity in the rat. *Anat. Rec.*, 78:149–172.

Heuser, I. 1998. Anna-Monika-Prize paper. The hypothalamus-pituitary-adrenal system in depression. *Pharmacopsychiatry*, 31:10–13.

Hews, D. K., Thompson, C. W., Moore, I. T., and Moore, M. C. 1997. Population frequencies of alternative male phenotypes in tree lizards: Microgeographic variation and common-garden rearing studies. *Behav. Ecol. Sociobiol.*, 41:371–380.

Hewson, G., Leighton, G. E., Hill, R. G., and Hughes, J. 1988. The cholecystokinin receptor antagonist L364,718 increases food intake in the rat by attenuation of endogenous cholecystokinin. *Br. J. Pharmacol.*, 93:79–84.

Hida, A., Kitamura, S., Katayose, Y., Kato, M., Ono, H., Kadotani, H., Uchiyama, M., et al. 2014. Screening of clock gene polymorphisms demonstrates association of a PER3 polymorphism with morningness-eveningness preference and circadian rhythm sleep disorder. *Sci. Rep.*, 4:6309.

Higley, J. D., Hasert, M. F., Suomi, S. J., and Linnoila, M. 1991. Nonhuman primate model of alcohol abuse: Effects of early experience, personality, and stress on alcohol consumption. *Proc. Natl. Acad. Sci. USA*, 88:7261–7265.

Hill, M. N., and McEwen, B. S. 2009. Endocannabinoids: The silent partner of glucocorticoids in the synapse. *Proc. Natl. Acad. Sci. USA*, 106:4579–4580.

Hill, M. N., and McEwen, B. S. 2010. Involvement of the endocannabinoid system in the neurobehavioural effects of stress and glucocorticoids. *Prog. Neuropharmacol. Biol. Psychiatry*, 34:791–797.

Hill, S. M., Belancio, V. P., Dauchy, R. T., Xiang, S., Brimer, S., Mao, L., Hauch, A., et al. 2015. Melatonin: An inhibitor of breast cancer. *Endocr. Relat. Cancer*, 22:R183–R204.

Hines, M. 1982. Prenatal gonadal hormones and sex differences in human behavior. *Psychol. Bull.*, 92:56–80.

Hines, M. 1991. Gonadal hormones and human cognitive development. In J.

Balthazart (ed.), *Hormones, Brain and Behavior in Vertebrates*, pp. 51–63. Karger, Basel.

Hines, M. 2004. *Brain Gender*. Oxford University Press, Oxford.

Hines, M. 2011. Prenatal endocrine influences on sexual orientation and on sexually differentiated childhood behavior. *Frontiers in Neuroendocrinology*, 32:170–182.

Hines, M., and Kaufman, F. R. 1994. Androgen and the development of human sex-typical behavior: Rough-and-tumble play and sex of preferred playmates in children with congenital adrenal hyperplasia (CAH). *Child Develop.*, 65:1042–1053.

Hines, M., Fane, B. A., Pasterski, V. L., Mathews, G. A., Conway, G. S., and Brook, C. 2003. Spatial abilities following prenatal androgen abnormality: Targeting and mental rotations performance in individuals with congenital adrenal hyperplasia. *Psychoneuroendocrinol.*, 28:1010–1026.

Hinney, A., Bettecken, T., Tarnow, P., Brumm, H., Reichwald, K., Lichtner, P., Scherag, A., Nguyen, T. T., Schlumberger, P., and Rief, W. 2006. Prevalence, spectrum, and functional character- ization of melanocortin-4 receptor gene mutations in a representative population-based sample and obese adults from Germany. *J. Clin. Endocrinol. Metab.*, 91:1761–1769.

Hirschenhauser, K., Winkler, H., and Oliveira, R. F. 2003. Comparative analysis of male androgen responsiveness to social environment in birds: The effects of mating system and paternal incubation. *Horm. Behav.*, 43:508–519.

Ho, J. M., Murray, J. H., Demas, G. E., and Goodson, J. L. 2010. Vasopressin cell groups exhibit strongly divergent responses to copulation and male–male interactions in mice. *Horm. Behav.*, 58:368–377.

Hodges, J. K., and Hearne, J. P. 1978. A positive feedback effect of oestradiol on LH release in the male marmoset monkey. *J. Reprod. Fertil.*, 52:83–86.

Hoffman, E., Pickavance, L., Thippeswamy, T., Beynon, R. J., and Hurst, J. L. 2015. The male sex pheromone darcin stimulates hippocampal neurogenesis and cell proliferation in the subventricular zone in female mice. *Front. Behav. Neurosci.*, 9:106.

Hoffman, K. A., Mendoza, S. P., Hennessy, M. B., and Mason, W. A. 1996. Responses of infant titi monkeys, *Callicebus moloch*, to removal of one or both parents: Evidence for paternal attachment. *Dev. Psychobiol.*, 28:399–407.

Hoffman, R. A., and Reiter, R. J. 1965. Pineal gland: Influence on gonads of male hamsters. *Science*, 148:1609–1615.

Hoffmann, K., Illnerova, H., and Vanecek, J. 1981. Effect of photoperiod and of one minute light at night-time on the pineal rhythm on N-acetyltransferase activity in

the Djungarian hamster, *Phodopus sungorus. Biol. Reprod.*, 24:551–556.

Hofman, M. A., and Swaab, D. F. 2007. Living by the clock: The circadian pacemaker in older people. *Ageing Res. Rev.*, 5:33–51.

Hofman, M. A., Zhou, J. N., and Swaab, D. F. 1996. Suprachiasmatic nucleus of the human brain: An immunocytochemical and morphometric analysis. *Anatomical Record*, 244:552–562.

Holekamp, K. E. 1986. Proximal causes of natal dispersal in Belding's ground squirrels (*Spermophilus beldingii*). *Ecol. Monogr.*, 56:365–391.

Holekamp, K. E., and Sherman, P. W. 1989. Why male ground squirrels disperse. *Am. Sci.*, 77:232–239.

Holman, S. D., and Goy, R. W. 1980. Behavioral and mammary responses of adult female rhesus to strange infants. *Horm. Behav.*, 14:348–357.

Holscher, C. 2011. Diabetes as a risk factor for Alzheimer's disease: Insulin signaling impairment in the brain as an alternative model of Alzheimer's disease. *Biochemical Society Transactions*, 39:891–897.

Holstege, G., Georgiadis, J. R., Paans, A. M. J., Meiners, L. C., van der Graaf, F. H. C. E., and Reinders, A. A. T. S. 2003. Brain activation during human male ejaculation. *J. Neurosci.*, 23:9185–9193.

Holt-Lunstad, J., Smith, T. B., and Layton, J. B. 2010. Social relationships and mortality risk: A meta-analytic review. *PLOS Med.* 7:e1000316.

Holtzman, S. G. 1975. Effects of narcotic antagonists on fluid intake in the rat. *Life Sci.*, 16:1465–1470.

Honda, S., Harada, N., Ito, S., Takagi, Y., and Maeda, S. 1998. Disruption of sexual behavior in male aromatase-deficient mice lacking exons 1 and 2 of the *cyp19* gene. *Biochemical and Biophysics Research Communications*, 252:445–449.

Hong, H., Yen, H-Y, Brockmeyer, A., Liu, Y., Chodankar, R., Pike, M. C., Stanczyk, F. Z., Maxson, R., and Dubeau, L. 2010. Changes in the mouse estrus cycle in response to Brca1 inactivation suggest a potential link between risk factors for familial and sporadic ovarian cancer. *Cancer Res.*, 70:221–228.

Hook, E. B. 1973. Behavioral implications of the human XYY genotype. *Science*, 179:139–149.

Hopkins, J., Marcues, M., and Campbell, S. B. 1984. Postpartum depression: A critical review. *Psychol. Bull.*, 95:498–515.

Horn, C. C., and Friedman, M. I. 1998. Metabolic inhibition increases feeding and brain Fos-like immunoreactivity as a function of diet. *Am. J. Physiol.*, 275:R448–R459.

Horn, S., Gregory, P., and Guskiewicz, K. M. 2009. Self-reported anabolic-androgenic steroids use and musculoskeletal injuries:

Findings from the Center for the Study of Retired Athletes Health Survey of retired NFL players. *Am. J. Phys. Med. Rehab.*, 88:192–200.

Horseman, N. D., and Buntin, J. D. 1995. Regulation of pigeon cropmilk secretion and parental behaviors by prolactin. *Annu. Rev. Nutr.*, 15:213–238.

Hort, Y., Baker, E., Sutherland, G. R., Shine, J., and Herzog, H. 1995. Gene duplication of the human peptide YY gene (PYY) generated the pancreatic polypeptide gene (PPY) on chromosome 17q21.1. *Genomics*, 26:77–83.

Hoshooley, J. S., and Sherry, D. F. 2007. Greater hippocampal neuronal recruitment in food-storing than in non-food-storing birds. *Dev. Neurobiol.*, 67:406–414.

Hotchkiss, A. K., Pyter, L. M., Gatien, M. L., Wen, J. C., Milman, H. A., and Nelson, R. J. 2005. Aggressive behavior increases after termination of chronic sildenafil treatment in mice. *Phys. Behav.*, 83:683–688.

Hotta, M., Shibasaki, T., Yamauchi, N., Ohno, H., Benoit, R., Ling, N., and Demura, H. 1991. The effects of chronic central administration of corticotropin-releasing factor on food intake, body weight, and hypothalamic-pituitary-adrenocortical hormones. *Life Sci.*, 48:1483–1491.

Howard, R. A., and Lively, C. M. 1994. Parasitism, mutation accumulation, and the maintenance of sex. *Nature*, 367:554–557.

Howdeshell, K. L., Hotchkiss, A. K., Thayer, K. A., Vandenbergh, J. G., and vom Saal, F. S. 1999. Exposure to bisphenol A advances puberty. *Nature*, 401:763–764.

Hoyer, S. 2003. Memory function and brain glucose metabolism. *Pharmacopsychiatry*, 36:S62–S67.

Hrdy, S. B. 1999. *Mother Nature*. Pantheon, New York.Huang, V., Sakata, J. T., Rhen, T., Coomber, P., Simmonds, S., and Crews. D. 2008. Constraints on temperature-dependent sex determination in the leopard gecko (*Eublepharis macularius*): Response to Kratochvil et al. *Naturwissenschaften*, 95:209–215.

Huang, V., Sakata, J. T., Rhen, T., Coomber, P., Simmonds, S., and Crews, D. 2008. Constraints on temperature-dependent sex determination in the leopard gecko (Eublepharis macularius): response to Kratochvil et al. *Naturwissenschaften*, 95:1137–1142.

Huck, U. W., Labov, J. B., and Lisk, R. D. 1986. Food restricting young hamsters (*Mesocricetus auratus*) alters sex ratio and growth of subsequent offspring. *Biol. Reprod.*, 36:592–598.

Hudson, R., and Distel, H. 1982. The pattern of behaviour of rabbit pups in the nest. *Behaviour*, 79:255–271.

Hudson, R., and Distel, H. 1989. Temporal pattern of suckling in rabbit pups: A model of circadian synchrony between mother and young. In S. M. Reppert (ed.), *Research in Perinatal Medicine*, Vol. 9, *Development of Circadian Rhythmicity and Photoperiodism in Mammals*, pp. 83–102. Perinatology Press, Ithaca.

Hughes, T. K., Fulep, E., Juelich, T., Smith, E. M., and Stanton, G. J. 1995. Modulation of immune responses by anabolic androgenic steroids. *Int. J. Immunopharmacol.*, 17:857–863.

Hughes, T. K., Rady, P. L., and Smith, E. M. 1998. Potential for the effects of anabolic steroid abuse in the immune and neuroendocrine axis. *J. Neuroimmunol.*, 83:162–167.

Huhman, K. L., and Jasnow, A. M. 2005. Conditioned defeat. In R. J. Nelson (ed.), *Biology of Aggression*. Oxford University Press, New York.

Huhman, K. L., Bunnell, B. N., Mougey, E. H., and Meyerhoff, J. L. 1990. Effects of social conflict on POMC-derived peptides and glucocorticoids in male golden hamsters. *Physiol. Behav.*, 47:949–956.

Huhman, K. L., Gillespie, C. F., Marvel, C. L., and Albers, H. E. 1996. Neuropeptide Y phase shifts circadian rhythms in vivo via a Y_2 receptor. *NeuroReport*, 7:1249–1252.

Huhman, K. L., Gillespie, C. F., Marvel, C. L., and Albers, H. E. 1997. Peptidergic mechanisms of action in the suprachiasmatic nucleus. *Ann. N. Y. Acad. Sci.*, 814:300–304.

Huhman, K. L., Moore, T. O., Ferris, C. F., Mougey, E. H., and Meyerhoff, J. L. 1991. Acute and repeated exposure to social conflict in male golden hamsters: Increases in plasma POMC-peptides and cortisol and decreases in plasma testosterone. *Horm. Behav.*, 25:206–216.

Huhman, K. L., Moore, T. O., Mougey, E. H., and Meyerhoff, J. L. 1992. Hormonal responses to fighting in hamsters: Separation of physical and psychological causes. *Physiol. Behav.*, 51:1083–1086.

Huhman, K. L., Solomon, M. B., Janicki, M., Harmon, A. C., Lin, S. M., and Jasnow, A. M. 2003. Conditioned defeat in male and female Syrian hamsters. *Horm. Behav.*, 44:293–299.

Huhman, K. L., Solomon, M. B., Janicki, M., Harmon, A. C., Lin, S. M., Israel, J. E., and Jasnow, A. M. 2003. Conditioned defeat in male and female Syrian hamsters. *Horm. Behav.*, 44:293–299.

Huie, M. J. 1994. An acute myocardial infarction occurring in an anabolic steroid user. *Med. Sci. Sports Exer.*, 26:408–413.

Hull, E. M. and Dominguez, J. M. 2015. The neurobiology of male sexual behavior. In: E. Knobil and J. Neill (eds.), *The Physiology of Reproduction, 4th edition*, pp. 2211-2286, Elsevier, New York.

Hull, E. M., and Dominguez, J. M. 2007. Sexual behavior in male rodents. *Horm. Behav.*, 52:45–55.

Hull, E. M., Du, J., Lorrain, D. S., and Matuszewich, L. 1995. Extracellular dopamine in the medial preoptic area: Implications for sexual motivation and hormonal control of copulation. *J. Neurosci.*, 15:7465–7471.

Hull, E. M., Du, J., Lorrain, D. S., and Matuszewich, L. 1997. Testosterone, preoptic dopamine, and copulation in male rats. *Brain Res. Bull.*, 44:327–334.

Hull, E. M., Lorrain, D. S., Du, J., Matuszewich, L., Lumley, L. A., Putnam, S. K., and Moses, J. 1999. Hormone-neurotransmitter interactions in the control of sexual behavior. *Behav. Brain Res.*, 105:105–116.

Hull, E. M., Meisel, R. L., and Sachs, B. D. 2002. Male sexual behavior. In D. W. Pfaff, A. P. Arnold, A. T. Etgen, S. E. Fahrbach, and R. T. Rubin (eds.), *Hormones, Brain and Behavior*, Vol. 1, pp. 1–138. Academic Press, New York.

Hull, E. M., Muschamp, J. W., and Sato, S. 2004. Dopamine and serotonin: Influences on male sexual behavior. *Physiol. Behav.*, 83:291–308.

Hull, E. M., Wood, R. I., and McKenna, K. E. 2006. Neurobiology of male sexual behavior. In J. D. Neill (ed.), Knobil and Neill's *Physiology of Reproduction* (3rd ed.), pp. 1729–1824. Elsevier Press, San Diego.

Hurd, P. L., Bailey, A. A., Gongal, P. A., Yan, R. H., Greer, J. J., and Pagliardini, S. 2008. Intrauterine position effects on anogenital distance and digit ratio in male and female mice. *Arch. Sex. Behav.*, 37:9–18.

Hurn, P. D., Littleton-Kearny, M. T., Kirsch, J. R., Dharmarajan, A. M., and Traystman, R. J. 1995. Post-ischemic cerebral blood flow recovery in the female: Effect of 17β-estradiol. *J. Cereb. Blood Flow Metab.*,15:666–672.

Huszar, D., Lynch, C. A., Fairchild-Huntress, V., Dunmore, J. H., Fang, Q., Berkemeier, l. R., Gu, W., et al. 1997. Targeted disruption of the melanocortin-4 receptor results in obesity. *Cell*, 88:131–141.

Hutchison, J. B. 1970. Differential effects of testosterone and oestradiol on male courtship in Barbary doves (*Streptopelia risoria*). *Anim. Behav.*, 18:41–51.

Hutchison, J. B., and Steimer, T. 1983. Hormone-mediated behavioural transitions: A role for brain aromatase. In J. Balthazart, E. Prove, and R. Gilles (eds.), *Hormones and Behaviour in Higher Vertebrates*, pp. 261–274. Springer Verlag, Berlin.

Hutchison, J. B., Beyer, C., Green, S., and Wozniak, A. 1994. Brain formation of oestrogen in the mouse: Sex dimorphism in aromatase development. *J. Steroid Biochem. Mol. Biol.*, 49:407–415.

Hyde, T. M., and Miselis, R. R. 1983. Effects of area postrema/caudal medial nucleus of solitary tract lesions on food intake and body weight. *Am. J. Physiol.*, 244:R577–R587.

Ieni, J. R., and Thurmond, J. B. 1985. Maternal aggression in mice: Effects of treatments with PCPA, 5-HTP and 5-HT receptor antagonists. *Eur. J. Pharmacol.*, 111:211–220.

Iijima, M., Arisaka, O., Minamoto, F., and Arai, Y. 2001. Differences in children's free drawings: A study on girls with congenital adrenal hyperplasia. *Horm. Behav.,* 40:99–104.

Illnerova, H., and Vanecek, J. 1984. Circadian rhythm in inducibility of rat pineal N-acetyltransferase after brief light pulses at night: Control by a morning oscillator. *J. Comp. Physiol. A,* 154:739–744.

Illnerova, H., Hoffmann, K., and Vanecek, J. 1986. Adjustments of the rat pineal *N*-acetyltransferase rhythm to change from long to short photoperiod depends on the direction of the extension of the dark period. *Brain Res.,* 362:403–408.

Illnerova, H., Zvolsky, P., and Vanecek, J. 1985. The circadian rhythm in plasma melatonin concentration of the urbanized man: The effect of summer and winter time. *Brain Res.,* 328:186–192.

Ilnytska, O., and Argyropoulos, G. 2008. The role of the agouti-related protein in energy balance regulation. *Cell. Mol. Life Sci.,* 17:2721–2731.

Imperato-McGinley, J., Guerrero, L., Gautier, T., and Peterson, R. E. 1974. Steroid 5-alpha-reductase deficiency in man: An inherited form of male pseudohermaphroditism. *Science,* 1:1213–1215.

Inagaki, T. K., Irwin, M. R., and Eisenberger, N. I. 2015. Blocking opioids attenuates physical warmth-induced feelings of social connection. *Emotion,* 15(4):494–500. http://dx.doi.org/10.1037/emo0000088

Inagaki, T., Gautreaux, C., and Luine, V. 2010. Acute estrogen treatment facilitates recognition memory consolidation and alters monoamine levels in memory-related brain areas. *Horm. Behav.,* 58:415–426.

Inouye, S. T., and Kawamura, H. 1979. Persistence of circadian rhyth-micity in a mammalian hypothalamic "island" containing the suprachiasmatic nucleus. *Proc. Natl. Acad. Sci. USA,* 76:5962–5966.

Insel, T. R. 1990a. Oxytocin and maternal behavior. In N. A. Krasnegor and R. S. Bridges (eds.), *Mammalian Parenting,* pp. 260–280. Oxford University Press, Oxford.

Insel, T. R. 1990b. Regional changes in brain oxytocin receptors postpartum: Time-course and relationship to maternal behaviour. *J. Neuroendocrinol.,* 2:539–545.

Insel, T. R. 1997. A neurobiological basis of social attachment. *Am. J. Psychiatry,* 154:726–735.

Insel, T. R. 2003. Is social attachment an addictive disorder? *Physiol. Behav.,* 79:351–357.

Insel, T. R., and Fernald, R. D. 2004. How the brain processes social information: Searching for the social brain. *Ann. Rev. Neurosci.,* 27:697–722.

Insel, T. R., and Hulihan, T. J. 1995. A gender-specific mechanism for pair bonding: Oxytocin and partner preference formation in monogamous voles. *Behav. Neurosci.,* 109:782–789.

Insel, T. R., and Shapiro, L. E. 1992. Oxytocin receptor distribution reflects social organization in monogamous and polygamous voles. *Proc. Natl. Acad. Sci. USA,* 89:5981–5985.

Insel, T. R., and Young, L. J. 2001. The neurobiology of attachment. *Nature Rev.: Neuroscience,* 2:129–136.

Insel, T. R., Gilhard, R., and Shapiro, L. E. 1991. The comparative distribution of forebrain receptors for neurohypophyseal peptides in monogamous and polygamous mice. *Neuroscience,* 43:623–630.

Insel, T. R., Wang, Z. X., and Ferris, C. F. 1994. Patterns of brain vasopressin receptor distribution associated with social organization in microtine rodents. *J. Neurosci.,* 14:5381–5392.

Isgor, C., and Sengelaub, D. R. 1998. Prenatal gonadal steroids affect adult spatial behavior, CA1 and CA3 pyramidal cell morphology in rats. *Horm. Behav.,* 34:183–198.

Iwahana, E., Karatsoreos, I., Shibata, S., and Silver, R. 2008. Gonadectomy reveals sex differences in circadian rhythms and suprachiasmatic nucleus androgen receptors in mice. *Horm. Behav.,* 53:422–424.

Iwanowicz, L. R., Blazer, V. S., Pinkney, A. E., Guy, C. P., Major, A. M., Munney, K., Mierzykowski, S., et al. 2016. Evidence of estrogenic endocrine disruption in smallmouth and largemouth bass inhabiting Northeast U.S. national wildlife refuge waters: A reconnaissance study. *Ecotoxicol. Environ. Saf.,* 124:50–59.

Jacob, S., Garcia, S., Hayreh, D., and McClintock, M. K. 2002. Psychological effects of musky compounds: Comparison of androstadienone with androstenol and muscone. *Horm. Behav.,* 42:274–283.

Jacob, S., Hayreh, D. J., and McClintock, M. K. 2001. Context-dependent effects of steroid chemosignals on human physiology and mood. *Physiol. Behav.,* 74:15–27.

Jacob, S., Zelano, B., Gungor, A., Abbott, D., Naclerio, R., and McClintock, M. K. 2000. Location and gross morphology of the nasopalatine duct in human adults. *Arch. Otolaryngol. Head Neck Surg.,* 126:741–748.

Jacobs, L. F. 1996. Sexual selection and the brain. *Trends Ecol. Evol.,* 11:82–86.

Jacobs, L. F., Gaulin, S. J. C., Sherry, D. F., and Hoffman, G. E. 1990. Evolution of spatial cognition: Sex-specific patterns of spatial behavior predict hippocampal size. *Proc. Natl. Acad. Sci. USA,* 87:6349–6352.

Jacobs, P. A., Brunton, M., Melville, M. M., Brittain, R. P., and McClemont, W. F. 1965. Aggressive behavior, mental subnormality and the XYY male. *Nature,* 208:1351–1352.

Jacobson, C. D. 1980. The characterization, ontogeny and influence of androgen on the sexually dimorphic nucleus of the preoptic area. Ph.D. dissertation, University of California, Los Angeles.

Jadva, V., Golombok, S., and Hines, M. 2010. Infants' preferences for toys, colors and shapes: Sex differences and similarities. *Archives of Sexual Behavior,* 39:1261–1273.

James, V. H. T. 1992. *The Adrenal Gland.* Raven Press, New York.

Jameson, S. A., Lin, Y. T., and Capel, B. 2012. Testis development requires the repression of *Wnt4* by Fgf signaling. *Dev. Biol.,* 370:24–32. doi:10.1016/j.ydbio.2012.06.009

Janati, A., Talbi, R., Klosen, P., Mikkelsen, J. D., Magoul, R., Simonneaux, V., and El Ouezzani, S. 2013. Distribution and seasonal variation in hypothalamic RF-amide peptides in a semi-desert rodent, the jerboa. *J. Neuroendocrinol.,* 25:402–411.

Janowitz, H. D., and Grossman, M. I. 1949. Some factors affecting the food intake of normal dogs and dogs with esophagostomy and gastric fistula. *Am. J. Physiol.,* 159:143–148.

Janowsky, D. S., Berens, S. C., and Davis, J. M. 1973. Correlations between mood, weight, and electrolytes during the menstrual cycle: A renin-angiotensin-aldosterone hypothesis of premenstrual tension. *Psychosom. Med.,* 35:143–154.

Jarjisian, S. G., Piekarski, D. J., Place, N. J., Driscoll, J. R., Paxton, E. G., Kriegsfeld, L. J., and Zucker, I. 2013. Dorsomedial hypothalamic lesions block Syrian hamster testicular regression in short day lengths without diminishing increased testosterone negative-feedback sensitivity. *Biol. Reprod.,* 89:23.

Jarvis, C. I., Lynch, A. M., and Morin, A. K. 2008. Management strategies for premenstrual syndrome/premenstrual dysphoric disorder. *Ann. Pharmacother.,* 42:967–978.

Jasnow, A. M., Drazen, D. L., Huhman, K. L., Nelson, R. J., and Demas, G. E. 2001. Acute and chronic social defeat suppresses humoral immunity of male Syrian hamsters (*Mesocricetus auratus*). *Horm. Behav.,* 40:428–433.

Jasnow, A. M., Huhman, K. L., Bartness, T. J., and Demas, G. E. 2000. Short-day increases in aggression are inversely related to circulating testosterone concentrations in male Siberian hamsters (*Phodopus sungorus*). *Horm. Behav.,* 38:102–110.

Jasnow, A. M., Huhman, K. L., Bartness, T. J., and Demas, G. E. 2000. Short-day increases in aggression are inversely related to circulating testosterone concentrations in male Siberian hamsters (*Phodopus sungorus*). *Horm. Behav.,* 38:102–110.

Jasnow, A. M., Huhman, K. L., Bartness, T. J., and Demas, G. E. 2002. Short days and exogenous melatonin increase aggression of male Syrian hamsters (*Mesocricetus auratus*). *Horm. Behav.*, 42:13–20.

Jeays-Ward, K., Dandonneau, M., and Swain, A. 2004. *Wnt4* is required for proper male as well as female sexual development. *Dev. Biol.*, 276:431–440.

Jeffress, E. C., and Huhman, K. L. 2013. Copulatory and agonistic behavior in Syrian hamsters following social defeat. *Aggress. Behav.*, 39: 239–245.

Jenkins, R. L., Wilson, E. M., Angus, R. A., Howell, W. M., and Kirk, M. 2003. Androstenedione and progesterone in the sediment of a river receiving paper mill effluent. *Toxicological Sciences*, 73:53–59.

Jenkins, R., Angus, R. A., McNatt, H., Howell, W. M., Kemppainen, J. A., Kirk, M., and Wilson, E. M. 2001. Identification of androstenedione in a river containing paper mill effluent. *Envir. Toxicol. Chem.*, 20:1325–1331.

Jensen, B. K. 1982. Menstrual cycle effects on task performance examined in the context of stress research. *Acta Psychol.*, 50:159–178.

Jetton, A. E., Turek, F. W., and Schwartz, N. B. 1994. Effects of melatonin and time of day on in vitro pituitary gonadotropin basal secretion and GnRH responsiveness in the male golden hamster. *Neuroendocrinol.*, 60:527–534.

Jilge, B. 1993. The ontogeny of circadian rhythms in the rabbit. *J. Biol. Rhythms*, 8:247–260.

Jobst, E. E., Robinson, D. W., and Allen, C. N. 2004. Potential pathways for intercellular communication within the calbindin subnucleus of the hamster suprachiasmatic nucleus. *Neuroscience*, 123:87–99.

Jockenhövel, F., Minnemann, T., Schubert, M., Freude, S., Hübler, D., Schumann, C., Christoph, A., and Ernst, M. 2009. Comparison of long-acting testosterone undecanoate formulation versus testosterone enanthate on sexual function and mood in hypogonadal men. *Eur. J. Endocrinol.*, 160:815–819.

Johnson, F., and Whalen, R. E. 1988. Testicular hormones reduce individual differences in the aggressive behavior of male mice: A theory of hormone action. *Neurosci. Biobehav. Rev.*, 12:93–99.

Johnson, L. R., and Wood, R. I. 2001. Oral testosterone self-administration in male hamsters. *Neuroendocrinol.*, 73:285–292.

Johnson, T. M. 1987. Premenstrual syndrome as a Western culture-specific disorder. *Culture, Med. Psychiatry*, 11:337–356.

Johnston, A. L., and File, S. E. 1991. Sex differences in animal tests of anxiety. *Physiol. Behav.*, 49:245–250.

Jolly, A. 1966. *Lemur Behavior*. University of Chicago Press, Chicago.

Jones, B. C., Feinberg, D. R., DeBruine, L. M., Little, A. C., and Vukovic, J. 2009. A domain-specific opposite-sex bias in human preferences for manipulated voice pitch. *Anim. Behav.*, 79:57–62.

Jost, A. 1979. Basic sexual trends in the development of vertebrates. In *Sex, Hormones and Behavior*. CIBA Foundation Symposium, No. 62. Elsevier, Amsterdam.

Judson, O. P. 1997. A model of asexuality and clonal diversity: Cloning the red queen. *J. Theoret. Biol.*, 186:33–40.

Julian, T., and McKenry, P. C. 1989. Relationship of testosterone to men's family functioning at mid-life: A research note. *Aggressive Behav.*, 15:281–289.

Kabelik, D., Klatt, J. D., Kingsbury, M. A., and Goodson, J. L. 2009. Endogenous vasotocin exerts context-dependent behavioral effects in a semi-naturalistic colony environment. *Horm. Behav.*, 56:101–107.

Kahn, B. B., and Myers, M. G. 2006. mTOR tells the brain that the body is hungry. *Nat. Med.*, 12:615–617.

Kaitz, M. 1992. Recognition of familiar individuals by touch. *Physiol. Behav.*, 52:565–567.

Kalin, N. H., Shelton, S. E., and Barksdale, C. M. 1988. Opiate modulation of separation-induced distress in nonhuman primates. *Brain Res.*, 440:285–292.

Kalin, N. H., Shelton, S. E., and Lynn, D. E. 1995. Opiate systems in mother and infant primates coordinate intimate contact during reunion. *Psychoneuroendocrinol.*, 7:735–742.

Kalin, S., Heppner, F. L., Bechmann, I., Prinz, M., Tschop, M. H., and Yi, C-X. 2015. Hypothalamic innate immune reaction in obesity. *Nat. Rev. Endocrinol.*, 11:339.

Kalinichev, M., Rosenblatt, J. S., Nakabeppu, Y., and Morrell, J. I. 2000. Induction of *c-fos*-like and *fosB*-like immunoreactivity reveals forebrain neuronal populations involved differentially in pup-mediated maternal behavior in juvenile and adult rats. *J. Comp. Neurol.*, 416:45–78.

Kalman, D. S., and Lepeley, A. 2010. A review of hydration. *Strength and Conditioning Journal*, 32:56–63.

Kalra, S. P., Dube, M. G., Pu, S., Xu, B., Horvath, T. L., and Kalra, P. S. 1999. Interacting appetite-regulating pathways in the hypothalamic regulation of body weight. *Endocr. Rev.* 20:68–100.

Kalra, S. P., Dube, M. G., Sahu, A., Phelps, C. P., and Kalra, P. S. 1991. Neuropeptide Y secretion increases in the paraventricular nucleus in association with increased appetite for food. *Proc. Natl. Acad. Sci. USA*, 88:10931–10935.

Kalsbeek, A., Fliers, E., Hofman, M. A., Swaab, D. F., and Buijs, R. M. 2010. Vasopressin and the output of the hypothalamic biological clock. *J. Neuroendocrinol.*, 22:362–372.

Kalsbeek, A., Van der Spek, R., Lei, J., Endert, E., Buijs, R. M., and Fliers, E. 2012. Circadian rhythms in the hypothalamo–pituitary–adrenal (HPA) axis. *Mol. Cell. Endocrinol.*, 349:20–29.

Kannan, C. R. 1987. *The Pituitary Gland*. Plenum Medical Book, New York.

Kano, T. 1992. *The Last Ape: Pygmy Chimpanzee Behav. Ecology*. Stanford University Press. Stanford, CA.

Kaplan, J. M., Seeley, R. J., and Grill, H. J. 1993. Daily caloric intake in intact and chronic decerebrate rats. *Behav. Neurosci.*, 107:876–881.

Kaplan, J. R., and Manuck, S. B. 1999. Status, stress, and atherosclerosis: The role of environment and individual behavior. *Ann. N. Y. Acad. Sci.*, 896:145–161.

Kaplan, K. A. and Harvey, A. G. 2013. Behavioral treatment of insomnia in bipolar disorder. *Am. J. Psychiat.*, 170:716–720.

Karatoreos, I. N. and McEwen, B. S. 2013. Annual Research Review: The neurobiology and physiology of resilience and adaptation across the life course. *J. Child Psych. Psychiatry*, 54:337–347.

Karatsoreos, I. N. and Silver, R. 2007. Mini review: The neuroendocrinology of the suprachiasmatic nucleus as a conductor of body time in mammals. *Endocrinology*, 148:5640–5647.

Karatsoreos, I. N., Butler, M. P., Lesauter, J., and Silver, R. 2011. Androgens modulate structure and function of the suprachiasmatic nucleus brain clock. *Endocrinology*, 152:1970–1978.

Karsch, F. J., Bittman, E. L., Foster, D. L., Goodman, R. L., Legan, S. J., and Robinson, J. E. 1984. Neuroendocrine basis of seasonal reproduction. *Rec. Prog. Horm. Res.*, 40:185–232.

Karsch, F. J., Dierschke, D. J., and Knobil, E. 1973. Sexual differentiation of pituitary function: Apparent difference between primates and rodents. *Science*, 179:484–486.

Kashkin, K. B., and Kleber, H. D. 1989. Hooked on hormones? An anabolic steroid addiction hypothesis. *JAMA*, 262:3166–3170.

Kashon, M. L., Arbogast, J. A., and Sisk, C. L. 1996. Distribution and hormonal regulation of androgen receptor immunoreactivity in the forebrain of the male European ferret. *J. Comp. Neurol.*, 376:567–586.

Kasper, S., Wehr, T., Bartko, J., Gaist, P., and Rosenthal, N. 1989. Epidemiological findings of seasonal changes in mood and behavior. A telephone survey of Montgomery County, Maryland. *Arch. Gen. Psychiatry*, 46:823–833.

Kastin, A. J., Ehrensing, R. H., Schalch, D. S., and Anderson, M. S. 1972. Improvement in mental depression with decreased thyrotropin response after administration of thyrotropin-releasing hormone. *Lancet*, 780:740–742.

Kastin, A. J., Sandman, C. A., Stratton, L. O., Schally, A. V., and Miller, L. H. 1975. Behavioral and electrographic changes in rat and man after MSH. *Prog. Brain Res.*, 42:143–150.

Katona, C., Rose, S., and Smale, L. 1998. The expression of Fos with the suprachiasmatic nucleus of the diurnal rodent *Arvicanthis niloticus*. Brain Res., 791:27–34.

Katz, L. S. 2007. Sexual behavior of domesticated ruminants. *Horm. Behav.*, 52:56–63.

Kauffman, A. S., Clifton, D. K., and Steiner, R. A. 2007a. Emerging ideas about kisspeptin-GPR54 signaling in the neuroendocrine regulation of reproduction. *Trends Neurosci.*, 30:504–511.

Kauffman, A. S., Gottsch, M. L., Roa, J., Byquist, A. C., Crown, A., Clifton, D. K., Hoffman, G. E., Steiner, R. A., and Tena-Sempere, M. 2007. Sexual differentiation of *Kiss1* gene expression in the brain of the rat. *Endocrinology*, 148:1774–1783.

Kaufman, J. M., and Vermeulen, A. 2005. The decline of androgen levels in elderly men and its clinical and therapeutic implications. *Endocr. Rev.*, 26:833–876.

Kavaliers, M., Choleris, E., Agmo, A., Braun, W.J., Colwell, D.D., Muglia, L.J. & Pfaff, D.W. 2006. Inadvertent social information and the avoidance of parasitized male mice: A novel role for oxytocin. *PNAS*, 103:4293–4298.

Keel, P., and Klump, K. L. 2003. Are eating disorders culture-bound syndromes? Implications for conceptualizing their etiology. *Psychol. Bull.*, 129:747–769.

Keen-Rhinehart, E., and Bartness, T. J. 2005. Peripheral ghrelin injections stimulate food intake, foraging and food hoarding in Siberian hamsters. *Am. J. Physiol. Regl. Integr. Comp. Physiol.*, 288:R716–R722.

Keen-Rhinehart, E., and Bartness, T. J. 2008. Leptin inhibits food-deprivation-induced increases in food intake and food hoarding. *Am. J. Physiol.*, 295:R1737–R1746.

Kehoe P. and Blass E. M., 1989. Conditioned opioid release in ten-day-old rats. *Behav Neurosci.*, 103(2):423–428.

Keller, M., Baum, M. J., Brock, O., Brennan, P. A., and Bakker, J. 2009. The main and the accessory olfactory systems interact in the control of mate recognition and sexual behavior. *Behav. Brain Res.*, 200:268–276.

Keller, M., Baum, M. J., Brock, O., Brennan, P. A., and Bakker, J. 2009. The main and the accessory olfactory systems interact in the control of mate recognition and sexual behavior. *Behav. Brain Res.*, 200:268–276.

Kelley, A. E., and Berridge, K. C. 2002. The neuroscience of natural rewards: Relevance to addictive drugs. *J. Neurosci.*, 22:3306–3311.

Kelly, A. M. and Goodson, J. L. 2014. Social functions of individual vasopressin–oxytocin cell groups in vertebrates: What do we really know? *Front. Neuroendocrinol.*, 35:512–529.

Kendrick, K. M. 2000. Oxytocin, motherhood and bonding. *Exp. Physiol.*, 85:111S–124S.

Kendrick, K. M., Levy, F., and Keverne, E. B. 1992. Changes in the sensory processing of olfactory signals induced by birth in sleep. *Science*, 256:833–836.

Kennedy, G. C. 1953. The role of depot fat in the hypothalamic control of food intake in the rat. *Proc. Roy. Soc. Lond. B*, 140:579–592.

Ketterson, E. D., and Nolan, V. 1994. Male parental behavior in birds. *Annu. Rev. Ecol. Evol. Syst.*, 25:610–628.

Keverne, E. B. 2001. Genomic imprinting, maternal care, and brain evolution. *Horm. Behav.*, 40:146–155.

Keverne, E. B., and Kendrick, K. M. 1992. Oxytocin facilitation of maternal behavior in sheep. *Ann. N. Y. Acad. Sci.*, 652:83–101.

Keverne, E. B., and Kendrick, K. M. 1994. Maternal behaviour in sheep and its neuroendocrine regulation. *Acta Paediatr.*, 397:47–56.

Keverne, E. B., Levy, F., Poindron, P., and Lindsay, D. R. 1983. Vaginal stimulation: An important determinant of maternal bonding in sheep. *Science*, 219:81–83.

Keverne, E. B., Martensz, N. D., and Tuite, B. 1989. Beta-endorphin concentrations in cerebrospinal fluid of monkeys are influenced by grooming relationships. *Psychoneuroendocrinol.*, 14:155–161.

Kibble, M. W., and Ross, M. B. 1987. Adversive effects of anabolic steroids in athletes. *Clin. Pharm.*, 6:686–692.

Kidd, K. A., Blanchfield, P. J., Mills, K. H., Palace, V. P., Evans, R. E., Lazorchak, J. M., and Flick, R. 2007. Collapse of a fish population following exposure to a synthetic estrogen. *Proc. Natl. Acad. Sci USA.*, 104:8897–8901.

Kikuyama, S., Toyoda, F., Ohmiya, Y., Matsuda, K., Tanaka, S., Hayashi, H. 1995. Sodefrin: A female-attracting peptide pheromone in newt cloacal glands. *Science*, 267:1643–1645.

Kikuyama, S., Toyoda, F., Yamamoto, K., Tanaka, S., and Hayashi, H. 1997. Female-attracting pheromone in newt cloacal glands. *Brain Res. Bull.*, 44:415–422.

Kilmer, J. R., Palmer, R. S., and Cronce, J. M. 2007. Assessment of club drug, hallucinogen, inhalant, and steroid use and misuse. In D. M. Donovan and G. A. Marlatt (eds.), *Assessment of Addictive Behaviors*. (2nd ed.). Guilford Press, New York.

Kim, J. J., and Diamond, D. M. 2002. The stressed hippocampus, synaptic plasticity and lost memories. *Nature Rev.: Neuroscience*, 3:453–462.

Kim, J. J., Song, E. Y., and Kosten, T. A. 2006. Stress effects in the hippocampus: Synaptic plasticity and memory. *Stress*, 9:1–11.

Kimura, D., and Harshman, R. A. 1984. Sex differences in brain organization for verbal and non-verbal functions. *Prog. Brain Res.*, 61:423–441.

King, J. M. 1979. Effects of lesions of the amygdala, preoptic area, and hypothalamus

on estradiol-induced activity in the female rat. *J. Comp. Physiol. Psychol.*, 93:360–367.

Kingsbury, M. A., Jan, N., Klatt, J. D., and Goodson, J. L. 2015. Nesting behavior is associated with VIP expression and VIP-Fos colocalization in a network-wide manner. *Horm. Behav.*, 69:68–81.

Kinsey, A. C., Pomeroy, W. B., and Martin, C. E. 1948. *Sexual Behavior in the Human Male*. W. B. Saunders, Philadelphia.

Kinsey, A. C., Pomeroy, W. B., Martin, C. E., and Gebhard, P. 1953. *Sexual Behavior in the Human Female*. Saunders, Philadelphia.

Kinsley, C. H. 1990. Prenatal and postnatal influences on parental behavior in rodents. In N. A. Krasnegor and R. S. Bridges (eds.), *Mammalian Parenting*, pp. 347–371. Oxford University Press, Oxford.

Kinsley, C. H. 1994. Developmental psychobiological influences on rodent parental behavior. *Neurosci. Biobehav. Rev.*18:269–280.

Kinsley, C. H., and Lambert, K. G. 2008. Reproduction-induced neuroplasticity: Natural behavioral and neuronal alterations associated with the production and care of offspring. *J. Neuroendocrinol.*, 20:515–525.

Kirby, E. D., Geraghty, A. C., Ubuka, T., Bentley, G. E., and Kaufer, D. 2009. Stress increases putative gonadotropin inhibitory hormone and decreases luteinizing hormone in male rats. *Proc. Natl. Acad. Sci. USA*, 106:11324–11329.

Kirby, E. D., Muroy, S. E., Sun, W. G., Covarrubias, D., Leong, M. J., Barchas, L. A,, and Kaufer, D. 2013. Acute stress enhances adult rat hippocampal neurogenesis and activation of newborn neurons via secreted astrocytic FGF2. *eLife*, 2:e00362. doi: 10.7554/eLife.00362.

Kirn, J. R., Clower, R. P., Kroodsma, D. E., and DeVoogd, T. J. 1989. Song-related brain regions in the red-winged blackbird are affected by sex and season but not repertoire size. *J. Neurobiol.*, 11:139–163.

Klaiber, E. L., Broverman, D. M., Vogel, W., and Kobayski, V. 1979. Estrogen therapy for severe persistent depressions in women. *Arch. Gen. Psychiatry*, 36:550–554.

Klatt, J. D. and Goodson, J. L. 2013. Sex-specific activity and function of hypothalamic nonapeptide neurons during nest-building in zebra finches. *Horm. Behav.*, 64:818–824.

Klaus, M. H., and Kennell, J. H. 1976. *Maternal-Infant Bonding*. Mosby: St. Louis.

Kleiman, D. G., and Malcolm, J. R. 1981. The evolution of male parental investment. In D. J. Gubernick and P. H. Klopfer (eds.), *Parental Care in Mammals*, pp. 347–387. Plenum, New York.

Klein, D. A., and Walsh, B. T. 2004. Eating disorders: Clinical features and pathophysiology. *Physiol. Behav.*, 81:359–374.

Klein, D. C., Smoot, R., Weller, J. L., Higa, S., Markey, S. P., Creed, G. H., and Jacobowitz, D. M. 1983. Lesions of the paraventricular nucleus area of the hypothalamus disrupt the suprachiasmatic–spinal cord circuit in the melatonin rhythm generating system. *Brain Res. Bull.*, 10:647–652.

Klein, K. E., and Wegmann, H. M. 1974. The resychronization of human circadian rhythms after transmeridian flights as a result of flight direction and mode of activity. In L. E. Scheving, F. Halberg, and J. E. Pauley (eds.), *Chronobiology*, pp. 564–570. Igaku, Tokyo.

Klein, S. L., and Nelson, R. J. 1998. Adaptive immune responses are linked to the mating systems of arvicoline rodents. *Am. Nat.*, 151:59–67.

Kleitz-Nelson, H. K., Dominguez, J. M., and Ball, G. F. 2010a. Dopamine release in the medial preoptic area is related to hormonal action and sexual motivation. *Behav. Neurosci.*, 124:773–779.

Kleitz-Nelson, H. K., Dominguez, J. M., Cornil, C. A., and Ball, G. F. 2010b. Is sexual motivational state linked to dopamine release in the medial preoptic area? *Behav. Neurosci.*, 124:300–304.

Klemfuss, H. 1992. Rhythms and the pharmacology of lithium. *Pharmacol. Ther.*, 56:53–78.

Klingerman, C. K., Krishnamoorthy, K., Patel, K., Spiro, A. B., Stuby, C., Patel, A., and Schneider, J. E. 2010. Energetic challenges unmask the role of ovarian hormones in orchestrating ingestive and sex behaviors. *Horm. Behav.*, 58:563–574.

Klok, M. D., Jakobsdottir, S., and Drnet, M. L. 2007. The role of leptin and ghrelin in the regulation of food intake and body weight in humans: A review. *Obes. Rev.*, 8:21–34.

Kloner, R. A., McDonald, S., Leeka, J., and Poole, W. K. 2009. Comparison of total and cardiovascular death rates in the same city during a losing versus winning Super Bowl championship. *Am. J. Cardiol.*, 103:1647–1650.

Klosen, P., Sebert, M. E., Rasri, K., Laran-Chich, M. P., and Simonneaux, V. 2013. TSH restores a summer phenotype in photoinhibited mammals via the RF-amides RFRP3 and kisspeptin. *FASEB J.*, 27:2677–2686.

Kluger, M. J. 1978. The evolution and adaptive value of fever. *Am. Sci.*, 66:38–43.

Kluger, M. J. 1986. Is fever beneficial? *Yale J. Biol. Med.*, 59:89–95.

Klump, K. L., Keel, P. K., Burt, A., Racine, S. E., Neale, M. C., Sisk, C. L., and Boker, S. 2013. Ovarian hormones and emotional eating associations across the menstrual cycle: An examination of the potential moderating effects of body mass index and dietary restrain. *Intl. J. Eat. Disorders*, 46:256–263.

Klump, K. L., Keel, P. K., Culbert, K. M., and Edler, C. 2008. Ovarian hormones and binge eating: Exploring associations in community samples. *Psychol. Med.*, 38:1749–1757.

Klump, K. L., McGue, M., and Iacono, W. G. 2003. Differential heritability of eating

pathology in pre-pubertal versus pubertal twins. *Int. J. Eating Disord.*, 33:287–292.

Klump, K. L., Perkins, P., Burt, S. A., McGue, M., and Iacono, W. G. 2007. Puberty moderates genetic influences on disordered eating. *Psychol. Med.*, 37:627–634.

Klüver, H., and Bucy, P. C. 1939. Preliminary analysis of functions of the temporal lobes in monkeys. *Arch. Neurol. Psychiatry*, 42:979–1000.

Knobil, E., and Hotchkiss, J. 1988. The menstrual cycle and its neuroendocrine control. In E. Knobil and, J. D. Neill (eds.), *The Physiology of Reproduction*, Vol. 2, pp. 1971–1994. Raven, New York.

Knol, B. W., and Egberink-Alink, S. T. 1989. Androgens, progestagens, and agonistic behavior: A review. *Vet. Q.*, 11:94–101.

Ko, C. H., and Takahashi, J. S. 2006. Molecular components of the mammalian circadian clock. *Hum. Mol. Genet.*, 15:R271–R277.

Koelega, H. S., and Koster, E. P. 1974. Some experiments on sex differences in odor perception. *Ann. N. Y. Acad. Sci.*, 27:234–246.

Koeske, R. K. D. 1980. Theoretical perspectives on menstrual cycle research: The relevance of attributional approaches for the perception and explanation of premenstrual emotionality. In A. J. Dan, E. A. Graham, and C. P. Beecher (eds.), *The Menstrual Cycle*, pp. 161–181. Springer Verlag, New York.

Kohsaka, A., Laposky, A., Ramsey, K., Estrada, C., Joshu, C., Kobayashi, Y., Turek, F., and Bass, J. 2007. High-fat diet disrupts behavioral and molecular circadian rhythms in mice. *Cell Metab.*, 6:414–421.

Kojima, M., Hosoda, H., Date, Y., Nakazato, M., Matsuo, H., and Kangawa, K. 1999. Ghrelin is a growth-hormone-releasing acylated peptide from stomach. *Nature*, 402:656–660.

Kollack-Walker, S. and Newman, S. W. 1995. Mating and agonistic behavior produce different patterns of Fos immunolabeling in the male Syrian hamster brain. *Neuroscience*, 66:721–736.

Kolpin, D. W., Furlong, E. T., Meyer, M. T., Thurman, E. M., Zaugg, S. D., Barber, L. B., and Buxton, H. T. 2002. Pharmaceuticals, hormones, and other organic wastewater contaminants in U.S. streams, 1999–2000: A national reconnaissance. *Environ. Sci. Technol.*, 36:1202–1211.

Komisaruk, B. R. 1967. Effects of local brain implants of progesterone on reproductive behavior in ring doves. *J. Comp. Physiol. Psychol.*, 64:219–224.

Konopka, R. J. 1987. Genetics of biological rhythms in *Drosophila*. *Annu. Rev. Genet.*, 21:227–236.

Konopka, R. J., and Benzer, S. 1971. Clock mutants of *Drosophila melanogaster*. *Proc. Natl. Acad. Sci. USA*, 68:2112–2116.

Koob, G. F., and Heinrichs, S. C. 1999. A role for corticotrophin releasing factor and uro-

cortin in behavioral responses to stressors. *Brain Res.*, 848:141–152.

Koolhaas, J. M., Moor, E., Hiemstra, Y., and Bohus, B. 1991. The testosterone-dependent vasopressinergic neurons in the medial amygdala and lateral septum: involvement in social behaviour of male rats. In S. Jard and R. Jamison (eds.), *Vasopressin*, pp. 213–219, INSERM/John Libbey Eurotext, Paris.

Koopmans, H. S. 1983. A stomach hormone that inhibits food intake. *J. Autonomic Nerv. Syst.*, 9:157–171.

Kopin, A. S., Foulds-Mathes, W., McBride, E. W., Nguyen, M., Al-Haider, W., Schmitz, F., Bonner-Weir, S., Kanarek, R., and Beinborn, M. 1999. The cholecystokinin-A receptor mediates inhibition of food intake yet is not essential for the maintenance of body weight. *J. Clin. Invest.*, 103:383–391.

Kopin, I. J. 1995. Definitions of stress and sympathetic neuronal responses. *Ann. N. Y. Acad. Sci.*, 771:19–30.

Korach, K. S. 1994. Insights from the study of animals lacking functional estrogen receptor. *Science*, 266:1524–1527.

Korner, J., and Leibel, R. L. 2003. To eat or not to eat—how the gut talks to the brain. *N. Engl. J. Med.*, 349:926–928.

Kornhauser, J. M., Nelson, D. E., Mayo, K. E., and Takahashi, J. S. 1990. Photic and circadian regulation of c-fos gene expression in the hamster suprachiasmatic nucleus. *Neuron*, 5:127–134.

Korol, D. L., and Gold, P. E. 1998. Glucose, memory, and aging. *Am. J. Clin. Nutr.*, 67:764S–771S.

Korol, D. L., Unick, K., Goosens, K., Crane, C., Gold, P. E., and Foster, T. C. 1994. Estrogen effects on spatial performance and hippocampal physiology in female rats. *Soc. Neurosci. Abstr.*, 20:1436.

Korpelainen, H. 1990. Sex ratios and conditions required for environmental sex determination in animals. *Biol. Rev.*, 65:147–184.

Kosman, M. E., and Gerard, R. W. 1955. The effect of adrenaline on a conditioned avoidance response. *J. Comp. Physiol. Psychol.*, 48:506–508.

Kouri, E. M, Lukas, S. E, Pope, H. G. J, and Oliva, P. S. 1995. Increased aggressive responding in male volunteers following the administration of gradually increasing doses of testosterone cypionate. *Drug Alcohol Depen.*, 40:73–79.

Kow, L. M., Pataky, S., Dupré, C., Phan, A., Martin-Alguacil, N., and Pfaff, D. W. 2016. Analyses of rapid estrogen actions on rat ventromedial hypothalamic neurons. *Steroids*, pii: S0039-128X(16)00077-5. doi: 10.1016/j.steroids.2016.03.010. [Epub ahead of print]

Koylu, E. O., Couceyro, P. R., Lambert, P. D., and Kuhar, M. J. 1998. Cocaine- and amphetamine-regulated transcript peptide immunohistochemical localization in the rat brain. *J. Comp. Neurol.*, 391:115–132.

Krasnegor, N. A., and Bridges, R. S. (eds.). 1990. *Mammalian Parenting.* Oxford University Press, Oxford.

Krecek, J. 1973. Sex differences in salt taste: The effect of testosterone. *Physiol. Behav.*, 10:683–688.

Kreuz, L. E., and Rose, R. M. 1972. Assessment of aggressive behavior and plasma testosterone in a young criminal population. *Psychosom. Med.*, 34:321–332.

Kriegsfeld L. J. 2013. Circadian regulation of kisspeptin in female reproductive functioning. *Adv. Exp. Med. Biol.*, 784:385–410. doi: 10.1007/978-1-4614-6199-9_18.

Kriegsfeld, L. J. 2006. Driving reproduction: RFamide peptides behind the wheel. *Horm. Behav.*, 50:655–666.

Kriegsfeld, L. J. and Silver, R. 2006. The regulation of neuroendocrine function: Timing is everything. *Horm. Behav.*, 49:557–574.

Kriegsfeld, L. J., and Nelson, R. J. 2009. Biological rhythms. In J. T. Cacioppo and G. G. Berntson (eds.), *Handbook of Neuroscience for the Behavioral Sciences*, pp. 56–81. Wiley and Sons, New York.

Kriegsfeld, L. J., Demas, G. E., Dawson, T. M., Dawson, V. L., Lee, S., and Nelson, R. J. 1999. Circadian behavior in mice with targeted disruption of the gene for the neuronal isoform of nitric oxide synthase. *J. Biological Rhythms*, 14:20–27.

Kriegsfeld, L. J., Drazen, D. L., and Nelson, R. J. 2001. Circadian organization in male mice lacking the gene for endothelial nitric oxide synthase (eNOS$^{-/-}$). *J. Biological Rhythms*, 16:142–148.

Kriegsfeld, L. J., Gibson, E. M., Williams, W. P. III, Zhao, S., Mason, A. O., Bentley, G. E., and Tsutsui, K. 2010. The roles of RFamide-related peptide-3 in mammalian reproductive function and behaviour. *J. Neuroendocrinol.*, 22:692–700.

Kriegsfeld, L. J., Leak, R. K., Yackulic, C. B., LeSauter, J., and Silver, R. 2004. Organization of suprachiasmatic nucleus projections in Syrian hamsters (*Mesocricetus auratus*): An anterograde and retrograde analysis. *J. Comp. Neurol.*, 468:361–379.

Kriegsfeld, L. J., Leak, R. K., Yackulic, C. B., LeSauter, J., Silver, R. 2004. Organization of suprachiasmatic nucleus projections in Syrian hamsters (*Mesocricetus auratus*): An anterograde and retrograde analysis. *J. Comp. Neurol.*, 468:361–379.

Kriegsfeld, L. J., LeSauter, J., Hamada, T., Pitts, S. M., and Silver, R. 2002. Circadian rhythms in the endocrine system. In D. W. Pfaff, A. P. Arnold, A. M. Etgen, S. E. Fahrbach, and R. T. Rubin (eds.), *Hormones, Brain and Behavior*, Vol. 2, pp. 33–91. Academic Press, New York.

Kriegsfeld, L. J., Mei, D. F., Bentley, G. E., Ubuka, T., Mason, A. O., Inoue, K., Ukena,

K., Tsutsui, K., and Silver, R. 2006. Identification and characterization of a gonadotropin-inhibitory system in the brains of mammals. *Proc. Natl. Acad. Sci. USA*, 103:2410–2415.

Kripke, D. F. 1981. Photoperiodic mechanisms for depression and its treatment. In C. Perris, G. Struwe, and B. Jansson (eds.), *Biological Psychiatry*, pp. 1249–1252. Elsevier, Amsterdam.

Kripke, D. F., Elliott, J. A., Youngstedt, S. D., and Smith, J. S. 1998. Melatonin: Marvel or marker? *Ann. Med.*, 30:81–87.

Krishnan, A. V., Stathis, P., Permuth, S. F., Tokes, L., and Feldman, D. 1993. Bisphenol-A: An estrogenic substance is released from polycarbonate flasks during autoclaving. *Endocrinol.* 132:2279–2286.

Kristal, M. B. 1980. Placentophagia: A biobehavioral enigma (or *De gustibus non disputandum est*). *Neuroscience and Biobehavioral Reviews*, 4:141–150.

Kristal, M. B., DiPirro, J. M., and Thompson, A. C. 2012. Plancentophagia in humans and nonhuman mammals: Causes and consequences. *Ecology of Food and Nutrition*, 51(2).

Kritzer, M. F., Brewer, A., Montalmant, F., Davenport, M., and Robinson, J. K. 2007. Effects of gonadectomy on performance in operant tasks measuring prefrontal cortical function in adult male rats. *Horm. Behav.*, 51:183–194.

Krohmer, R. W., and Crews, D. 1987. Temperature activation of courtship behavior in the male red-sided garter snake (*Thamnophis sirtalis parietalis*): Role of the anterior hypothalamus-preoptic area. *Behav. Neurosci.*, 101:228–236.

Krugers, H. J., Hoogenraad, C. C., and Groc, L. 2010. Stress hormones and AMPA receptor trafficking in synaptic plasticity and memory. *Nat. Rev. Neurosci.*, 11:675–681.

Kruijver, F. P. and Swaab, D. F. 2002. Sex hormone receptors are present in the human suprachiasmatic nucleus. *Neuroendocrinology*, 75:296–305.

Kruk, M. R. 1991. Ethology and pharmacology of hypothalamic aggression in the rat. *Neuroscience and Biobehavioral Rev.*, 15:527–538.

Kruuk, H. 1972. *The Spotted Hyena: A Study of Predation and Social Behavior.* University of Chicago Press, Chicago.

Kudielka, B. M., and Kirschbaum, C. 2005. Sex differences in HPA axis responses to stress: A review. *Biol. Psychol.*, 69:113–132.

Kudielka, B. M., Hellhammer, J., Hellhammer, D. H., Wolf, O. T., Pirke, K. M., Varadi, E., Pilz, J., and Kirschbaum, C. 1998. Sex differences in endocrine and psychological responses to psychosocial stress in healthy elderly subjects and the impact of a 2-week dehydroepiandrosterone treatment. *J. Clin. Endocrinol. Metab.*, 83:1756–1761.

Kuevi, V., Causon, R., Dixson, A. F., Everard, D. M., Hall., J. M., Hole, D., Whitehead, S. A., Wilson, C. A., and Wise, J. C. M. 1983. Plasma amine and hormone changes in 'post-partum' blues. *Clin. Endocrinol.*, 19:39–46.

Kuga, M., Ikeda, M., Suzuki, K., and Takeuchi, S. 2002. Changes in gustatory sense during pregnancy. *Acta Otolaryngologia* Supplement, 546:146–153.

Kuhn, H. F., and Reiter, E. O. 1976. Gonadotropin and testosterone measurements after estrogen administration to adult men, prepubertal and pubertal boys, and men with hypogonadotropism: Evidence for maturation of positive feed-back in the male. *Pediatr. Res.*, 10:46–51.

Kuiper, G. C., Enmark, E., Pelto-Huikko, M., Nilsson, S., and Gustafsson, J. A. 1996. Cloning of a novel estrogen receptor expressed in rat prostate and ovary. *Proc. Natl. Acad. Sci. USA*, 93:5925–5930.

Kullman, D. M., and Lamasa, K. P. 2007. Long-term synaptic plasticity in hippocampal interneurons. *Nat. Rev. Neurosci.*, 8:687–699.

Kumaran, A. and Kershaw, M. 2014. Hyperphagic psychosocial short stature – A clinical review. *Paediatri. Child Health*, 24:567–571.

Kumari, M., Brunner, E., and Fuhrer, R. 2000. Mechanisms by which the metabolic syndrome and diabetes impair memory. *J. Gerontol., Ser. A: Biol. Sci. Med. Sci.*, 55:B228–B232.

Kurabayashi, N., Hirota, T., Sakai, M., Sanada, K., and Fukada, Y. 2010. DYRK1A and glycogen synthase kinase 3beta, a dual-kinase mechanism directing proteasomal degradation of CRY2 for circadian timekeeping. *Mol. Cell Biol.*, 30:1757–1768.

Kurzer, M. S. 1997. Women, food, and mood. *Nutr. Rev.*, 55:268–276.

Kvitvik, I.-L., Berg, K. M., and Ågmo, A. 2010. A neutral odor may become a sexual incentive through classical conditioning in male rats. *Learn. Motiv.*, 41:1–21.

Labrie, F., Belanger, A., Simard, J., Luu-The, V., and Labrie, C. 1995. DHEA and peripheral androgen and estrogen formation: Intracrinology. *Ann. N. Y. Acad. Sci.*, 774:16–28.

Lacey, E. A., and Sherman, P. W. 1991. Social organization of naked mole-rat colonies: Evidence for division of labor. In P. W. Sherman, J. U. M. Jarvis, and R. D. Alexander (eds.), *The Biology of the Naked Mole-Rat*, 275–336. Princeton University Press, Princeton, NJ.

Lack, D. 1954. *The Natural Regulation of Animal Numbers.* Clarendon Press, Oxford.

Lacroix, A., McKenna, T., and Rabinowitz, D. 1979. Sex steroid modulation of gonadotropins in normal men and in androgen insensitivity syndrome. *J. Clin. Endocrinol. Metab.*, 48:235–240.

Ladle, R. J., Johnstone, R. A., and Judson, O. P. 1993. Coevolutionary dynamics of sex in a metapopulation-Escaping the red queen. *Proc. Roy. Soc. Lond. B.*, 253:155–160.

LaFerla, J. J., Anderson, D. L., and Schalch, D. S. 1978. Psychoendocrine response to sexual arousal in human males. *Psychosom. Med.*, 40:166–172.

Lahr, G., Maxson, S., Mayer, A., Just, W., Pilgrim, C., and Reisert, I. 1995. Transcription of the Y chromosomal gene, *Sry*, in adult mouse brain. *Mol. Brain Res.*, 33:179–182.

Lal, S., Ackman, D., Thavundayil, J. X., Kiely, M. E., and Etienne, P. 1984. Effect of apomorphine, a dopamine receptor agonist, on penile tumescence in normal subjects. *Prog. Neuropsychopharmacol. Biol. Psychiatry*, 8:695–699.

Lal, S., Laryea, E., Thavundayil, J. X., Nair, N. P. V., Negrete, J., Ackman, D., Blundell, P., and Gardiner, R. J. 1987. Apomorphine-induced penile tumescence in impotent patients—preliminary findings. *Prog. Neuropsychopharmacol. Biol. Psychiatry*, 11:235–242.

LaLumiere, R. T., Buen, T.-V., and McGaugh, J. L. 2003. Post-training intra-basolateral amygdala infusions of norepinephrine enhance consolidation of memory for contextual fear conditioning. *J. Neurosci.*, 23:6754–6758.

Lambert, K. G., Franssen, C. L., Bardi, M., Hampton, J. E., Hainley, L., Karsner, S., Tu, E. B., et al. 2011. Characteristic neurobiological patterns differentiate paternal responsiveness in two Peromyscus species. *Brain Behav. Evol.*, 77:159–175.

Lambert, K.G. 2012. The parental brain: Transformations and adaptations. *Physiology and Behavior*, 107, 792–800.

Lamia, K. A., Sachdeva, U. M., DiTacchio, L., Williams, E. C., Alvarez, J. G., Egan, D. F., Vasquez, D. S., et al. 2009. AMPK regulates the circadian clock by cryptochrome phosphorylation and degradation. *Science*, 326:437–440.

Lamont, E. W., Coutu, D. L., Cermakian, N., and Boivin, D. B. 2010. Circadian rhythms and clock genes in psychotic disorders. *Isr. J. Psychiatr. Rel.*, 47:27–35.

Lance, S. J., Miller, S. C., Holtsclaw, L. I., and Turner, B. B. 1998. Photoperiod regulation of mineralocorticoid receptor mRNA expression in hamster hippocampus. *Brain Res.* 780:342–347.

Lance, S. L., and Wells, K. D. 1993. Are spring peeper satellite males physiologically inferior to calling males? *Copeia*, 1993:1162–1166.

Landsman, R. E. 1991. Captivity affects behavioral physiology: Plasticity in signaling sexual identity. *Experientia*, 47:31–38.

Langan, S. J., Deary, I. J., Hepburn, D. A., and Frier, B. M. 1991. Cumulative cognitive impairment following recurrent severe hypoglycaemia in adult patients with

insulin-treated diabetes mellitus. *Diabetologia*, 34:337–344.

Langevin, R., Paitich, D., Hucker, S., Newman, S., Ramsay, G., Pope, S., Geller, G., and Anderson, C. 1979. The effect of assertiveness training, Provera and sex of therapist in the treatment of genital exhibitionism. *J. Behav. Ther. Exp. Psychiatry*, 10:275–282.

Langhans, W., and Scharrer, E. J. 1987. Evidence for a vagally mediated satiety signal derived from hepatic fatty acid oxidation. *Autonomic Nerv. Sys.*, 18:13–18.

Lank, D. B., Smith, C. M., Hanotte, O., Burke, T., and Cooke, F. 1995. Genetic polymorphism for alternative mating behaviour in lekking male ruff *Philomachus pugnax. Nature*, 378:59–62.

Lannert, H., and Hoyer, S. 1998. Intracerebroventricular administration of streptozotocin causes long-term diminutions in learning and memory abilities and in cerebral energy metabolism in adult rats. *Behav. Neurosci.*, 112:1199–1208.

Larsen, C. M., Kokay, I. C., and Grattan, D. R. 2008. Male pheromones initiate prolactin-induced neurogenesis and advance maternal behavior in female mice. *Horm. Behav.*, 53:509–517.

Larsen, L. H., Echwald, S. M., Sorensen, T. I., Andersen, T., Wulff, B. S., and Pedersen, O. 2005. Prevalence of mutations and functional analyses of melanocortin 4 receptor variants identified among 750 men with juvenile-onset obesity. *J. Clin. Endocrinol. Metab.*, 90:219–224.

Larsson, K. 1962. Mating behavior in male rats after cerebral cortex ablation. I. Effects of lesions in the dorsolateral and the median cortex. *J. Exp. Zool.*, 151:167–176.

Larsson, K. 1966. Individual differences in reactivity to androgen in male rats. *Physiol. Behav.*, 1:255–258.

Larsson, K. 1969. Failure of gonadal and gonadotrophic hormones to compensate for an impaired sexual function in anosmic male rats. *Physiol. Behav.*, 4:733–737.

Larsson, K. 1979. Features of the neuroendocrine regulation of masculine sexual behavior. In C. Beyer (ed.), *Endocrine Control of Sexual Behavior*, pp. 77–163. Raven Press, New York.

Larsson, K. 2003. My way to biological psychology. *Scand. J. Psych.*, 44:173–187.

Lashley, K. S. 1938. Experimental analysis of instinctive behavior. *Psychol. Rev.*, 45:445–471.

Latsko, M. S., Farnbauch, L. A., Gilman, T. L., Lynch, J. F. III, and Jasnow, A. M. 2016. Corticosterone may interact with peripubertal development to shape adult resistance to social defeat. Horm. Behav., 82:38–45. doi:10.1016/j.yhbeh.2016.04.009.

Laudet, V., Stehelin, D., and Clevers, H. 1993. Ancestry and diversity of the HMG box superfamily. *Nucleic Acids Res.*, 21:2493–2501.

Lavebratt, C., Sjoholm, L. K., Soronen, P., Paunio, T., Vawter, M. P., Bunney, W. E., Adolfsson, R., et al. 2010. CRY2 is associated with depression. *PLoS One*, 5:e9407.

Le Mouellic, H., Lallemand, Y., and Brulet, P. 1990. Targeted replacement of the homeobox gene *Hox-3.1* by the *Escherischia coli lacZ* in mouse chimeric embryos. *Proc. Natl. Acad. Sci. USA*, 87, 4712–4716.

le Roux, C. W., Batterham, R. L., Aylwin, S. J., Patterson, M., Borg, C. M., Wynne, K. J., Kent, A., Vincent, R. P., Gardiner, J., Ghatei, M. A., and Bloom, S. R. 2006. Attenuated peptide YY release in obese subjects is associated with reduced satiety. *Endocrinol.*, 147:3–8.

Le, W. W., Attardi, B., Berghorn, K.A., Blaustein, J., and Hoffman, G. E. 1997. Progesterone blockade of a luteinizing hormone surge blocks luteinizing hormone-releasing hormone Fos activation and activation of its preoptic area afferents. *Brain Res.*, 778:272–280.

Lea, R. W., Clark, J. A., and Tsutsui, K. 2001. Changes in central steroid receptor expression, steroid synthesis, and dopaminergic activity related to the reproductive cycle of the ring dove. *Microscopy Research and Technique*, 55:12–26.

Lea, R. W., Vowels, D. M., and Dick, H. R. 1986. Factors affecting prolactin secretion during the breeding cycle of the ring dove (*Streptopelia risoria*) and its possible role in incubation. *J. Endocrinol.*, 110:447–458.

LeBlond, C. P. 1938. Extra-hormonal factors in maternal behavior. *Proc. Soc. Exp. Biol.*, 38:66–70.

LeBoeuf, B. J. 1970. Copulatory and aggressive behavior in the prepubertally castrated male dog. *Horm. Behav.*, 1:127–136.

LeBoeuf, B. J. 1974. Male-male competition and reproductive success in elephant seals. *Am. Zool.*, 14:163–176.

Leckman, J. F., and Herman, A. E. 2002. Maternal behavior and developmental psychopathology. *Biol. Psychiatry*, 51:27–43.

Leckman, J. F., and Mayes, L. C. 1999. Preoccupations and behaviors associated with romantic and parental love: Perspectives on the origin of obsessive–compulsive disorders. *Child and Adolescent Psychiatric Clinics of North America*, 8:635–665.

Lee, A. W., and Brown, R. E. 2002. Medial preoptic lesions disrupt parental behavior in both male and female California mice (*Peromyscus californicus*). *Behav. Neurosci.*, 116:968–975.

Lee, A. W., and Brown, R. E. 2007. Comparisons of medial preoptic, amygdala, and nucleus accumbens lesions on parental behavior in California mice (*Peromyscus californicus*). *Physiol. Behav.*, 92:617–628.

Lee, A., Clancy, S., and Fleming, A. S. 2000. Mother rats bar-press for pups: Effects of lesions of the MPOA and limbic sites on maternal behavior and operant responding for pup-reinforcement. *Behavioural Brain Res.*, 108:215–231.

Lee, I. T., Chang, A. S., Manandhar, M., Shan, Y., Fan, J., Izumo, M., Ikeda, Y., et al. 2015. Neuromedin s-producing neurons act as essential pacemakers in the suprachiasmatic nucleus to couple clock neurons and dictate circadian rhythms. *Neuron*, 85:1086–1102.

Lee, J. H., and Welch, D. R. 1997. Suppression of metastasis in human breast carcinoma MDA-MB-435 cells after transfection with the metastasis suppressor gene, *KiSS-1. Cancer Res.*, 57:2384–2387.

Lee, J. H., Miele, M. E., Hicks, D. J., Phillips, K. K., Trent, J. M., Weissman, B. E., and Welch, D. R. 1996. *KiSS-1*, a novel human malignant melanoma metastasis-suppressor gene. *J. Natl. Cancer Inst.*, 88:1731–1737.

Lee, J. S. F., and Bass, A. H. 2005. Differential effects of 11-ketotestosterone on dimorphic traits in a teleost with alternative male reproductive morphs. *Horm. Behav.*, 47:523–531.

Lee, P. A., Houk, C. P., Ahmed, S. F., and Hughes, I. A. 2006. Consensus statement on management of intersex disorders. *Pediatrics*, 118:488–500.

Lee, R., Jaffe, R., and Midgley, A. 1974. Lack of alteration of serum gonadotropins in men and women following sexual intercourse. *Am. J. Obstet. Gynecol.*, 120:985–987.

Lee, S., Chronis-Tuscano, A., Keenan, K., Pelham, W., Loney, J., Van Hulle, C., and Lahey, B. 2010. Association of maternal dopamine transporter genotype with negative parenting: Evidence for gene x environment interaction with child disruptive behavior. *Mol. Psychiatry*, 15:548–558.

Leedom, L. J., Meehan, W. P., and Zeidler, A. 1987. Avoidance responding in mice with diabetes mellitus. *Physiol. Behav.*, 40:447–451.

Leeka, J., Schwartz, B. G., and Kloner, R. A. 2010. Sporting events affect spectators' cardiovascular mortality: It is not just a game. *Amer. J. Med.*, 123:972–977.

Lefebvre, L., Viville, S., Barton, S. C., Ishino, F., Keverne, E. B., and Surani, M. A. 1998. Abnormal maternal behaviour and growth retardation associated with loss of the imprinted gene Mest. *Nat. Genet.*, 20:163–169.

Legan, S. J. and Karsch, F. J. 1975. A daily signal for the LH surge in the rat. *Endocrinology*, 96:57–62.

Legan, S. J., and Karsch, F. J. 1975. Modulation of pituitary responsiveness to luteinizing hormone-releasing factor during the estrous cycle of the rat. *Endocrinology*, 96:571–575.

Lehman, M. N., and Winans, S. S. 1982. Vomeronasal and olfactory pathways to the amygdala controlling male hamster sexual behavior: Autoradiographic and behavioral analyses. *Brain Res.*, 240:27–41.

Lehman, M. N., Coolen, L. M., and Goodman, R. L. 2010. Minireview: kisspeptin/neurokinin B/dynorphin (KNDy) cells of the arcuate nucleus: a central node in the control of gonadotropin-releasing hormone secretion. *Endocrinology*, 151:3479–3489.

Lehman, M. N., Ladha, Z., Coolen, L. M., Hileman, S. M., Connors, J. M., and Goodman, R. L. 2010. Neuronal plasticity and seasonal reproduction in sheep. *Eur. J. Neurosci.*, 32:2152–2164.

Lehman, M. N., Silver, R., Gladstone, W. R., Kahn, R. M., Gibson, M., and Bittman, E. L. 1987. Circadian rhythmicity restored by neural transplant. Immunocytochemical characterization of the graft and its integration with the host brain. *J. Neurosci.*, 7:1626–1638.

Lehne, G. K. 1988. Treatment of sex offenders with medroxyprogesterone acetate. In J. B. A. Sitsen (ed.), *Handbook of Sexology*, Vol. 6, *The Pharmacology and Endocrinology of Sexual Function*, pp. 516–525. Elsevier Science Publishers, Amsterdam.

Lehrman, D. S. 1965. Interaction between internal and external environments in the regulation of the reproductive cycle of the ring dove. In F. A. Beach (ed.), *Sex and Behavior*, pp. 335–380. Wiley, New York.

Lehrman, D. S., and Brody, P. 1961. Does prolactin induce incubation behavior in the ring dove? *J. Endocrinol.*, 22:369–375.

Leinhart, R. 1927. Contribution a l'étude de l'incubation. *C. R. Soc. Biol. (Paris)*, 97:1296–1297.

Leise, T. L., Wang, C. W., Gitis, P. J., and Welsh, D. K. 2012. Persistent cell-autonomous circadian oscillations in fibroblasts revealed by six-week single-cell imaging of PER2:LUC bioluminescence. *PLoS One*, 7:e33334.

Lenroot, R. K., and Giedd, J. N. 2010. Sex differences in the adolescent brain. *Brain and Cognition*, 72:46–55.

Leon, M. 1980. Development of olfactory attraction by young Norway rats. In D. Müller-Schwarze and R. M. Silverstein (eds.), *Chemical Signals*, pp. 193–209. Plenum, New York.

Leon, M. 1992. Neuroethology of olfactory preference development. *J. Neurobiol.*, 23:1557–1573.

Leon, M., and Moltz, H. 1972. The development of the pheromonal bond in the albino rat. *Physiol. Behav.*, 8:683–686.

Leon, M., Coopersmith, R., Beasley, L. J., and Sullivan, R. M. 1990. Thermal aspects of parenting. In N. A. Krasnegor and R. S. Bridges (eds.), *Mammalian Parenting*, pp. 400–415. Oxford University Press, Oxford.

Leon, M., Croskerry, P. G., and Smith, G. K. 1978. Thermal control of mother-young contact in rats. *Physiol. Behav.*, 21:793–811.

Leonard, S.T. & Winsauer, P.J. 2011. The effects of gonadal hormones on learning and memory in male mammals. A review. *Current Zoology*, 57:543–558.

Lepri, J. J., and Wysocki, C. J. 1987. Removal of the vomeronasal organ disrupts the activation of reproduction in female voles. *Physiol. Behav.*, 40:349–355.

Lepri, J. J., Wysocki, C. J., and Vandenbergh, J. G. 1985. Mouse vomeronasal organ: Effects on chemosignal production and maternal behavior. *Physiol. Behav.*, 35:809–814.

LeSauter, J., Hoque, N., Weintraub, M., Pfaff, D. W., and Silver, R. 2009. Stomach ghrelin-secreting cells as food-entrainable circadian clocks. *Proc. Natl. Acad. Sci. USA*, 106:13582–13587.

Leshner, A. I., and Collier, G. 1973. The effects of gonadectomy on the sex differences in dietary self-selection patterns and carcass compositions of rats. *Physiol. Behav.*, 11:671–676.

Leshner, A. I., and Moyer, J. A. 1975. Androgens and agonistic behavior in mice: Relevance to aggression and irrelevance to avoidance-of-attack. *Physiol. Behav.*, 15:695–699.

Lester, N. A., Keel, P. K., and Lipson, S. F. 2003. Symptom fluctuation in bulimia nervosa: Relation to menstrual-cycle phase and cortisol levels. *Psychol. Med.*, 33:51–60.

Leuner, B. and Gould, E. 2010. Structural plasticity and hippocampal function. *Annu. Rev. Psychol.*, 61:111–140.

Leuner, B. and Shors, T. J. 2013. Stress, anxiety, and dendritic spines: What are the connections? *Neuroscience*, 251:108–119.

Leuner, B., and Gould, E. 2010. Dendritic growth in medial prefrontal cortex and cognitive flexibility are enhanced during the postpartum period. *J. Neurosci.*, 30:13499–13503.

Leuner, B., Fredericks, P.J., Nealer, C., and Albin-Brooks, C. 2014. Chronic gestational stress leads to depressive-like behavior and comprmises medial prefrontal cortex structure and function during the postpartum period. *PLOS One*, doi: 10.1371/journal.pone.0089912.

Leuner, B., Mendolia-Loffredo, S., and Shors, T. J. 2004. High levels of estrogen enhance associative memory formation in ovariectomized females. *Psychoneuroendocrinol.*, 29:883–890.

LeVay, S. 1991. A difference in hypothalamic structure between heterosexual and homosexual men. *Science*, 253:1034–1037.

LeVay, S., and Valente, S. M. 2006. *Human Sexuality*. Sinauer Associates, Sunderland, MA.

Levi, F. 1987. Chronobiology and cancer. *Pathol. Biol.*, 35:960–968

Levi, F. and Schibler, U. 2007. Circadian rhythms: mechanisms and therapeutic implications. *Annu. Rev. Pharmacol.*, 47:593–628.

Levine, A. S., and Morley, J. E. 1984. Neuropeptide Y: A potent inducer of consummatory behavior in rats. *Peptides*, 5:1025–1029.

Lévy, F. and Keller, M. 2009. Olfactory mediation of maternal behavior in selected mammalian species. *Behav. Brain Res.*, 200:336–345.

Lévy, F., Keller, M., and Poindron, P. 2004. Olfactory regulation of maternal behavior in mammals. *Horm. Behav.*, 46:284–302.

Lévy, F., Porter, R. H., Kendrick, K. M., Keverne, E. B., and Romeyer, A. 1996. Physiological, sensory, and experiential factors of parental care in sheep. *Adv. Study Behav.*, 25:385–422.

Levy, J. V., and King, J. A. 1953. The effects of testosterone propionate on fighting behaviour in young male C57BL/10 mice. *Anat. Rec.*, 117:562–563.

Lewy, A. J., Ahmed, S., and Sack, R. L. 1996. Phase shifting the human circadian clock using melatonin. *Behav. Brain Res.*, 73:131–134.

Lewy, A. J., Bauer, V. K., Ahmed, S., Thomas, K. H., Cutler, N. L., Singer, C. M., Moffitt, M. T., and Sack, R. L. 1998a. The human phase response curve is about 12 hours out of phase with the PRC to light. *Chronobiol. International*, 15:71–83.

Lewy, A. J., Bauer, V. K., Hasler, B. P., Kendall, A. R., Pires, M. L., and Sack, R. L. 2001. Capturing the circadian rhythms of free-running blind people with 0.5 mg melatonin. *Brain Res.*, 918:96–100.

Lewy, A. J., Emens, J. S., Songer, J., and Rough, J. 2009. The neurohormone melatonin as a marker, medicament and mediator. In D. W. Pfaff, et al. (eds.), *Hormones, Brain and Behavior*, pp. 2505–2526. Academic Press, San Diego.

Lewy, A. J., Emens, J., Sack, R. L., Hasler, B. P., and Bernert, R. A. 2003. Zeitgeber hierarchy in humans: Resetting the circadian phase positions of blind people using melatonin. *Chronobiol. International*, 20:837–852.

Lewy, A. J., Lefler, B. J., Emens, J. S., and Baue, V. K. 2006. The circadian basis of winter depression. *Proc. Natl. Acad. Sci. USA*, 103:7414–7419.

Lewy, A. J., Sack, R. L., and Singer, C. M. 1985. Melatonin, light and chronobiological disorders. In D. Evered and S. Clark. (eds.), *Photoperiodism, Melatonin and the Pineal*. Ciba Foundation Symposium, 117, pp. 231–252. Pitman, London.

Lewy, A. J., Sack, R. L., Miller, S., et al. 1987. Antidepressant and circadian phase-shifting effects of light. *Science*, 235:352–354.

Lewy, A. J., Sack, R. L., Singer, C. M., White, D. M., and Hoban, T. M. 1988. Winter depression and the phase-shift hypothesis for bright light's therapeutic effects: History, theory, and experimental evidence. *J. Biol. Rhythms*, 3:121–134.

Lewy, A. J., Wehr, T. A., Goodwin, F. K., Newsome, D. A., and Markey, S. P. 1980. Light suppresses melatonin secretion in humans. *Science*, 210:1267–1269.

Li, C., Brake, W. G., Romeo, R. D., Dunlop, J. C., Gordon, M., Buzescu, R., Magarinos, A. M., Allen, P. B., Greengard, P., Luine, V. N., and McEwen, B. S. 2004. Estrogen alters hippocampal dendritic spine shape and enhances synaptic protein immunoreactivity and spatial memory in female mice. *Proc. Natl. Acad. Sci. USA*, 101:2185–2190.

Li, J. D., Hu, W. P., and Zhou, Q. Y. 2012. The circadian output signals from the suprachiasmatic nuclei. *Prog. Brain Res.*, 199:119–127.

Li, J. Z., Bunney, B. G., Meng, F., Hagenauer, M. H., Walsh, D. M., Vawter, M. P., Evans, S. J., et al. 2013. Circadian patterns of gene expression in the human brain and disruption in major depressive disorder. *Proc. Natl. Acad. Sci. USA*, 110:9950–9955.

Li, M., and Fleming, A. S. 2003a. The nucleus accumbens shell is critical for normal expression of pup-retrieval in postpartum female rats. *Behavioural Brain Res.*, 145:99–111.

Li, M., and Fleming, A. S. 2003b. Differential involvement of nucleus accumbens shell and core subregions in maternal memory in postpartum female rats. *Behav. Neurosci.*, 117:426–445.

Li, M., Budin, R., Fleming, A. S., and Kapur, S. 2004a. Effects of novel antipsychotics, amisulpiride and aripiprazole, on maternal behaviour in rats. *Psychopharmacol.*, 16:1–11.

Li, M., Davidson, P., Budin, R., Kapur, S., and Fleming, A. S. 2004b. Effects of typical and atypical antipsychotic drugs on maternal behavior in postpartum female rats. *Schizophr. Res.*, 70:69–80.

Liberles, S. D. 2014. Mammalian pheromones. *Annual Review of Physiology*, 76:151–175.

Licht, P., McCreery, B. R., Barnes, B. R., Pang, R. 1983. Seasonal and stress related changes in plasma gonadotropins, sex steroids, and corticosterone in the bullfrog, *Rana catesbeiana*. *Gen. Comp. Endocrinol.*, 50:124–145.

Lieberwirth, C., Wang, Y., Jia, X., Liu, Y., and Wang, Z. 2013. Fatherhood reduces the survival of adult-generated cells and affects various types of behavior in the prairie vole (*Microtus ochrogaster*). *Eur. J. Neurosci.*, 38:3345–3355.

Lieverse, R. J., Jansen, J. B., van de Zwan, A., Samson, L., Masclee, A. A., Rovati, L. C., and Lamers, C. B. 1993. Bombesin reduces food intake in lean man by a cholecystokinin-independent mechanism. *J. Clin. Endocrinol. Metab.*, 76:1495–1498.

Lifschytz, T., et al. 2006. Basic mechanisms of augmentation of anti-depressant effects with thyroid hormone. *Curr. Drug Targets*, 7:203–210.

Lim, M. M., and Young, L. J. 2004. Vasopressin-dependent neural circuits underlying pair bonding in the monogamous prairie vole (*Microtus ochrogaster*). *Neuroscience*, 125:35–45.

Lim, M. M., Liu, Y., Ryabinin, A. E., Bai, Y., Wang, Z., and Young, L. J. 2007. CRF receptors in the nucleus accumbens modulate partner preference in prairie voles. *Horm. Behav.*, 51:508–515.

Lim, M. M., Wang, Z. X., Olazabal, D. E., Ren, X. H., Terwilliger, E. F., and Young, L. J. 2004. Enhanced partner preference in a promiscuous species by manipulating the expression of a single gene. *Nature*, 429:754–757.

Limbird, T. J. 1985. Anabolic steroids in the training and treatment of athletes. *Compr. Ther.*, 11:25–30.

Lin, D., Boyle, M., Dollar, P., Lee, H., Lein, E. S, Perona, P., and Anderson, D. J. 2011. Functional identification of an aggression locus in the mouse hypothalamus. *Nature*, 470:221–227.

Lin, S. H., Kiyohara, T., and Sun, B. 2003. Maternal behavior: Activation of the central oxytocin receptor system in parturient rats? *Neuroreport*, 14:1439–1444.

Lincoln, G. 1974. Luteinising hormone and testosterone in man. *Nature*, 252:232–233.

Lincoln, G. A., Guinness, F., and Short, R. V. 1972. The way in which testosterone controls the social and sexual behavior of the red deer stag (*Cervus elaphus*). *Horm. Behav.*, 3:375–396.

Lincoln, G.A., 1999. Melatonin modulation of prolactin and gonadotrophin secretion. Systems ancient and modern. *Adv. Exp. Med. Biol.*, 460:137–153.

Lincoln, N. B., Faleiro, R. M., Kelly, C., Kirk, B. A., and Jeffcoate, W. J. 1996. Effect of long-term glycemic control on cognitive function. *Diabetes Care*, 19:656–658.

Lindau, S. T., Schumm, L. P., Laumann, E. O., Levinson, W., O'Muircheartaigh, C. A., and Waite, L. J. 2007. A study of sexuality and health among older adults in the United States. *N. Engl. J. Med.*, 357:762–74.

Lipar, J. L., and Ketterson, E. D. 2000. Maternally derived yolk testosterone enhances the development of the hatching muscle in the red-winged blackbird *Agelaius phoeniceus*. *Proc. Roy. Soc. Lond. B*, 267:2005–2010.

Lipton, J., Kleemann, G., Ghosh, R., Lints, R., and Emmons, S. W. 2004. Mate searching in *Caenorhabditis elegans*: A genetic model for sex drive in a simple invertebrate. *J. Neurosci.*, 24:7427–7434.

Lisk, R. D. 1971. Oestrogen and progesterone synergism and elicitation of maternal nest-building in the mouse (*Mus musculus*). *Anim. Behav.*, 19:606–616.

Little, A. C., Burriss, R. P., Petrie, M., Jones, B. C., and Roberts, S. C. 2013. Oral contraceptive use in women changes preferences for male facial masculinity and is associated with partner facial masculinity. *Psychoneuroendocrinology*, 38:1777—1785.

Liu, D., Diorio, J., Day, J. C., Francis, D. D., and Meaney, M. J. 2000. Maternal care, hippocampal synaptogenesis and cognitive development in rats. *Nature* 3:799–806.

Liu, D., Diorio, J., Tannenbaum, B., Caldji, C., Francis, D., Freedman, A., Sharma, S., Pearson, D., Plotsky, P. M., and Meaney, M. J. 1997. Maternal care, hippocampal glucocorticoid receptors, and hypothalamic-pituitary-adrenal responses to stress. *Science,* 277:1659–1662.

Liu, Q. S., Li, J. Y., and Wang, D. H. 2007. Ultradian rhythms and the nutritional importance of caecotrophy in captive Brandt's voles (*Lasiopodomys brandtii*). *J. Comp. Physiol. B*, 177:423–432.

Liu, Y-C., Salamonee, J. D., and Sachs, B. D. 1997a. Impaired sexual response after lesions of the paraventricular nucleus of the hypothalamus in male rats. *Behav. Neurosci.,* 111:1–7.

Llewellyn, A. M., Stone, Z. N., and Nemeroff, C. B. 1997. Depression during pregnancy and the puerperium. *J. Clin. Psychiatry,* 58:S26–32.

Lloyd, D., Lemar, K. M., Salgado, L. E., Gould, T. M., and Murray, D. B. 2003. Respiratory oscillations in yeast: Mitochondrial reactive oxygen species, apoptosis and time: A hypothesis. *FEMS Yeast Res.,* 3:333–339.

Lloyd, J. A. 1971. Weights of testes, thymi and accessory reproductive glands in relation to rank in paired and grouped housed mice (*Mus musculus*). *Proc. Soc. Exp. Biol. Med.,* 137:19–22.

Lo, C.-M., Samuelson, L. C., Chambers, J. B., King, A., Heiman, J., Jandacek, R. J., Sakai, R. R., Benoit, S. C., Raybould, H. E., Woods, S. C., and Tso, P. 2008. Characterization of mice lacking the gene for cholecystokinin. *Am. J. Physiol.,* 294:R803–R810.

LoBue, V. and DeLoache, J. S. 2011. Pretty in pink: The early development of gender-stereotyped colour preferences. *British Journal of Developmental Psychology,* 29:656–667.

Logue, C. M., and Moos, R. H. 1986. Perimenstrual symptoms: Prevalence and risk factors. *Psychosom. Med.,* 48:388–414.

Lok, C. 2011. Vision science: Seeing without seeing. *Nature,* 469:284–285.

London, S. E., Monks, D. A., Wade, J., and Schlinger, B. A. 2006. Widespread capacity for steroid synthesis in the avian brain and song system. *Endocrinol.,* 147:5975–5987.

London, S.E., Remage-Healey, L., Schlinger, B.A. 20009. Neurosteroid production in the songbird brain: A re-evaluation of core principles. *Front. Neuroendocrinol.,* 30:302–314.

Lonstein, J. S., and Gammie, S. C. 2002. Sensory, hormonal, and neural control of maternal aggression in laboratory rodents. *Neuroscience and Biobehavioral Rev.,* 26:869–888.

Lonstein, J. S., Lévy, F., and Fleming, A. S. 2015. Common and divergent psychobiological mechanisms underlying maternal behaviors in non-human and human mammals. *Horm. Behav.,* 73:156–185.

Lonstein, J. S., Pereira, M., Morrell, J. I., and Marler, C. A., 2014. Parental behavior. In: Plant, T. M. and Zeleznik, A. J. (eds.), *Knobil and Neill's Physiology of Reproduction, 4th edition*, pp. 2371–2438. Elsevier, New York.

Lonstein, J. S., Simmons, D. A., Swann, J. M., and Stern, J. M. 1998. Forebrain expression of c-fos due to active maternal behaviour in lactating rats. *Neuroscience,* 82:267–281.

Lopez, H. H., Olster, D. H., and Ettenberg, A. 1999. Sexual motivation in the male rat: The role of primary incentives and copulatory experience. *Horm. Behav.,* 36:176–185.

López, M., Alvarez, C. V., Nogueiras, R., and Diéguez, C. 2013. Energy balance regulation by thyroid hormones at central level. *Trends Mol. Med.,* 19:418–427.

Lorens, S. 1978. Some behavioral effects of serotonin depletion depend on method: A comparison of 5,7-dihydroxytryptamine, p-chlorophenyl-alanine, p-chloroamphetamine, and electrolytic raphe lesions. *Ann. N. Y. Acad. Sci.,* 305:532–555.

Loundes, D. D., and Bridges, R. S. 1986. Length of prolactin priming differentially affects maternal behavior in female rats. *Biol. Reprod.,* 34:495–501.

Lowrey, P. L., Shimomura, K., Antoch, M. P., Yamazaki, S., Zemenides, P. D., Ralph, M. R., Menaker, M., and Takahashi, J. S. 2000. Positional syntenic cloning and functional characterization of the mammalian circadian mutation *tau. Science,* 288:483–492.

Loy, R. J., Gerlach, J. L., and McEwen, B. S. 1988. Autoradiographic location of estradiol-binding neurons in the rat hippocampal formation and entorhinal cortex. *Dev. Brain Res.,* 39:245–251.

Lu, X. Y., Nicholson, J. R., Akil, H., and Watson, S. J. 2001. Time course of short-term and long-term orexigenic effects of Agouti-related protein (86–132). *Neuroreport,* 12:1281–1284.

Lubin, M., Leon, M., Moltz, H., and Numan, M. 1972. Hormones and maternal behavior in the male rat. *Horm. Behav.,* 3:369–374.

Lucas, B. K., Ormandy, C. J., Binart, N., Bridges, R. S., and Kelly, P. A. 1998. Null mutation of the prolactin receptor gene produces a defect in maternal behavior. *Endocrinol.,* 139:4102–4107.

Luders, E., Narr, K. L., Thompson, P. M., Rex, D. E., Jancke, L., Steinmetz, H., and Toga, A. W. 2004. Gender differences in cortical complexity. *Nature Neurosci.,* 7:799–800.

Ludvik, B., Kautzky-Willer, A., Prager, R., Thomaseth, K., and Pacini, G. 1997. Amylin: History and overview. *Diabetes Med.,* 14:S9–S13.

Lugg, J. A., Rajfer, J., and González-Cadavid, N. F. 1995. Dihydrotestosterone (DHT) is the active androgen in the maintenance of nitric oxide-mediated penile erection in the rat. *Endocrinol.,* 136:1495–501.

Luine, V. 1994. Steroid hormone influences on spatial memory. *Ann. N. Y. Acad. Sci.,* 743:201–211.

Luine, V. N. 2007. Commentary: The prefrontal cortex, gonadal hormones and memory. *Horm. Behav.,* 51:181–182.

Luine, V. N., Jacome, L. F., and MacLusky, N. J. 2003. Rapid enhancement of visual and place memory by estrogens in rats. *Endocrinol.,* 144:2836–2844.

Luine, V. N., Martinez, C., Villegas, M., Magarinos, A. M., and McEwen, B. S. 1996. Restraint stress reversibly enhances spatial memory performance. *Physiol. Behav.,* 59:27–32.

Luine, V. N., Spencer, R. L., and McEwen, B. S. 1993. Effects of chronic corticosterone ingestion on spatial memory performance and hippocampal serotonergic function. *Brain Res.,* 616:65–70.

Luine, V., & Frankfurt, M. 2012. An integrative review of estradiol effects on dendritic spines and memory over the lifespan. In *Sex Steroids*, S.M. Kahn (Ed). InTech, Croatia.

Luine, V., and Dohanich, G. 2008. Sex differences in cognitive function in rodents. In J. B. Becker, K. J. Berkley, N. Geary, E. Hampson, J. P. Herman, and E. A. Young (eds.), *Sex Differences in the Brain: From Genes to Behavior*, pp. 227–251. Oxford University Press, New York.

Luine, V., and Rodriguez, M. 1994. Effects of estradiol on radial arm maze performance of young and aged rats. *Behav. Neural Biol.,* 62:230–236.

Luine, V., Richards, S. T., Wu, V. Y., and Beck, K. D. 1998. Estradiol enhances learning and memory in a spatial memory task and effects [sic] levels of monoaminergic neurotransmitters. *Horm. Behav.,* 34:149–162.

Luine, V., Villegas, M., Martinez, C., and McEwen, B. S. 1994. Repeated stress causes impairments of spatial memory performance. *Brain Res.,* 639:167–170.

Lund, T. D., Salyer, D. L., Fleming, D. E., and Lephart, E. D. 2000. Pre- or postnatal testosterone and flutamide effects on sexually dimorphic nuclei of the rat hypothalamus. *Dev. Brain Res.,* 120:261–266.

Lutz, T. A. 2006. Amylinergic control of food intake. *Physiol. Behav.,* 89:465–471.

Lutz, T. A. 2010. Amylinergic control of ingestive behaviour. In D. L. Hay and I. M. Dickerson (eds.), *The Calcitonin Gene-Related Peptide Family: Form, Function and Future Perspectives*, pp. 173–184. Springer, Heidelberg.

Lynn, R. B., Cao, G-Y., Considine, R. V., Hyde, T. M., and Caro, J. F. 1996. Autoradiographic localization of leptin binding in the choroid plexus of *ob/ob* and *db/db* mice. *Biochem. Biophys. Res. Commun.,* 219:884–889.

Lynn, S. E. 2008. Behavioral insensitivity to testosterone: Why and how does testosterone alter paternal and aggressive behavior in some avian species but not others? *Gen. Comp. Endocrinol.*, 157:233–240.

Lynn, S. E. 2016. Endocrine and neuroendocrine regulation of fathering behavior in birds. *Horm Behav.*, 77:237–248.

Lynn, S. E., and Wingfield, J. C. 2008. Dissociation of testosterone and aggressive behavior during the breeding season in male chestnut-collared longspars, *Calcarius ornatus. Gen. Comp. Endocrinol.*, 156:181–189.

Ma, L-Y., Itharat, P., Fluharty, S. J., and Sakai, R. R. 1997. Intracerebro-ventricular administration of mineralocorticoid receptor antisense oligonucleotides attenuates salt appetite in the rat. *Stress*, 2:37–50.

Macbeth, A. H., and Luine, V. N. 2010. Changes in anxiety and cognition due to reproductive experience: A review of data from rodent and human mothers. *Neurosci. Biobehav. Rev.*, 34:452–467.

Macbeth, A. H., Stepp, J. E., Lee, H.-J., and Young, W. S. 2010. Normal maternal behavior, but increased pup mortality in conditional oxytocin receptor knockout females. *Behav. Neurosci.*, 124:677–685.

Maccoby, E. E., and Jacklin, C. N. 1974. *The Psychology of Sex Differences.* Stanford University Press, Stanford, CA.

MacLaughlin, D. T., and Donahoe, P. K. 2004. Sex determination and differentiation. *N. Engl. J. Med.*, 350:367–378.

MacLean, P. D., and Ploog, D. W. 1962. Cerebral representation of penile erection. *J. Neurophysiol.*, 25:29–55.

MacLusky, N. J., Yuan, H., Elliott, J., and Brown, T. J. 1996. Sex differences in corticosteroid binding in the rat brain: An in vitro autoradiographic study. *Brain Res.*, 708:71–81.

Maddocks, S., Hahn, P., Moller, F., and Reid, R. L. 1986. A double-blind placebo-controlled trial of progesterone vaginal suppositories in the treatment of premenstrual syndrome. *Am. J. Obstet. Gynecol.*, 154:573–581.

Madeira, M. D., Leal, S., and Paula-Barbosa, M. M. 1999. Stereological evaluation and Golgi study of the sexual dimorphisms in the volume, cell numbers, and cell size in the medial preoptic nucleus of the rat. *J. Neurocytol.*, 28:131–148.

Madison, D. M. 1980. Space use and social structure in meadow voles, *Microtus pennsylvanicus. Behav. Ecol. Sociobiol.*, 7:65–71.

Madison, D. M. 1984. Group nesting and its ecological and evolutionary significance in overwintering microtine rodents. *Bull. Carnegie Museum Nat. Hist.*, 10:267–274.

Madison, D. M., and McShea, W. 1987. Seasonal changes in reproductive tolerance, spacing, and social organization in meadow voles: A microtine model. *Amer. Zool.*, 27:899–908.

Madison, D. M., FitzGerald, R., and McShea, W. 1984. Dynamics of social nesting in overwintering meadow voles (*Microtus pennsylvanicus*): Possible consequences for population cycling. *Behav. Ecol. Sociobiol.*, 15:9–17.

Maehlen, J., and Torvik, A. 1990. Necrosis of granule cells of hippocampus in adrenocortical failure. *Acta Neuropathol.*, 80:85–87.

Maestripieri, D. and Wallen, K. 1995. Interest in infants varies with reproductive condition in group-living female pigtail macaques (*Macaca nemestrina*). *Physiol. Behav.*, 57: 353–358.

Maestripieri, D. and Zehr, J. L. 1998. Maternal responsiveness increases during pregnancy and after estrogen treatment in macaques. *Horm. Behav.*, 34:223–230.

Maestroni, G. J. 1993. The immunoneuroendocrine role of melatonin. *J. Pineal Research*, 14:1–10.

Maestroni, G. J. 1995. T-helper-2 lymphocytes as a peripheral target of melatonin. *J. Pineal Research*, 18:84–89.

Maggi, A., Bettini, S. E., Mantero, G., and Zucchi, I. 1989. Hippocampus: A target for estrogen action in mammalian brain. *Mol. Endocrinol.*, 3:1165–1170.

Mahmoud, I. Y., and Licht, P. 1997. Seasonal changes in gonadal activity and the effects of stress on reproductive hormones in the common snapping turtle, *Chelydra serpentina. Gen. Comp. Endocrinol.*, 107:359–372.

Mahoney, M. M., Sisk, C., Ross, H. E., and Smale, L. 2004. Circadian regulation of gonadotropin- releasing hormone neurons and the preovulatory surge in luteinizing hormone in the diurnal rodent, *Arvicanthis niloticus*, and in a nocturnal rodent, *Rattus norvegicus. Biol. Reprod.*, 70:1049–1054.

Majewska, M. D. 1987. Actions of steroids on reward: Role of personality, mood, stress, and disease. *Integr. Psychiatry*, 5:258–273.

Majzoub, J., Robinson, B., and Emanuel, R. 1991. Suprachiasmatic nuclear rhythms of vasopressin mRNA in vivo. In D. C. Klein, R. Y. Moore, and S. M. Reppert (eds.), *Suprachiasmatic Nucleus: The Mind's Clock*, pp. 177–190. Oxford University Press, New York.

Maki, P. M. 2006. Hormone therapy and cognitive function: Is there a critical period for benefit? *Neurosci.*, 138:1027–1030.

Maki, P., and Hogervorst, E. 2003. The menopause and HRT: HRT and cognitive decline. *Best Pract. Res.: Clin. Endocrinol. Metab.*, 17:105–122.

Malacarne, G., Bottoni, L, Massa, R., and Vellano, C. 1984. The abdominal gland of the crested: A possible source of courtship pheromones. Preliminary ethological and biochemical data. *Monitore Zool.* (Italy), 18:33–39.

Malamuth, N. M., Heim, M., and Feshbach, S. 1980. Sexual responsiveness of college students to rape depictions: Inhibitory and disinhibitory effects. *J. Pers. Soc. Psychol.*, 38:399–408.

Malberg, J. E., Eisch, A. J., Nestler, E. J., and Duman, R. S. 2000. Chronic antidepressant treatment increases neurogenesis in adult rat hippocampus. *J. Neurosci.*, 20:9104–9110.

Malone, D. A., Dimef, R. J., Lombardo, J. A., and Sample, R. H. 1995. Psychiatric effects and psychoactive substance use in anabolic-androgenic steroid users. *Clin. J. Sports Med.*, 5:25–31.

Malsbury, C. W. 1971. Facilitation of male rat copulatory behavior by electrical stimulation of the medial preoptic area. *Physiol. Behav.*, 7:797–805.

Mangat, H. K., Chhina, G. S., Singh, B., and Anand, B. K. 1978a. Effect of testosterone proprinate on electrical activity of brain in intact and gonadectomized rhesus monkeys. *Ind. J. Exp. Biol.*, 16:893–896.

Mangat, H. K., Chhina, G. S., Singh, B., and Anand, B. K. 1978b. Influence of gonadal hormones and genital afferents on EEG activity of the hypothalamus in adult male rhesus monkeys. *Physiol. Behav.*, 20:377–384.

Mann, M. A., Konen, C., and Svare, B. 1984. The role of progesterone in pregnancy-induced aggression in mice. *Horm. Behav.*, 18:140–160.

Manning, C. A., Honn, V. J., Stone, W. S., Jane, J. S., and Gold, P. E. 1998b. Glucose effects on cognition in adults with Down's syndrome. *NeuroPsych.*, 12:479–484.

Manning, C. A., Stone, W. S., Korol, D. L., and Gold, P. E. 1998a. Glucose enhancement of 2-h memory retrieval in healthy elderly humans. *Behav. Brain Res.*, 93:71–76.

Manning, J. T., Bundred, P.E., Newton, D. J., and Flanagan, B. F. 2003. The second to the fourth digit ratio and variation in the androgen receptor gene. *Evol. Hum. Behav.*, 24:399–405.

Manning, J. T., Scott, D., Wilson, J., and Lewis-Jones, D. I. 1998. The ratio of 2nd to 4th digit length: A predictor of sperm numbers and concentrations of testosterone, luteinizing hormone and oestrogen. *Hum. Reprod.*, 13:3000–3004.

Mansour, A., Khachaturian, H., Lewis, M. E., Akil, H., Watson, S. J. 1988. Anatomy of CNS opioid receptors. *Trends Neurosci.*, 11:308–309.

Mansour, H. A., Wood, J., Logue, T., Chowdari, K. V., Dayal, M., Kupfer, D. J., Monk, T. H., Devlin, B., and Nimgaonkar, V. L. 2006. Association study of eight circadian genes with bipolar I disorder, schizoaffective disorder and schizophrenia. *Genes Brain Behav.*, 5:150–157.

Mansukhani, V., Adkins-Regan, E., and Yang, S. 1996. Sexual partner preference in female zebra finches: the role of early hormones and social environment. *Horm. Behav.*, 30:506–13.

Maragou, N. C., Makri, A., Lampi, E. N., Thomaidis, N. S., and Koupparis, M. A.

2008. Migration of bisphenol A from polycarbonate baby bottles under real use conditions. *Food Addit. Contam.*, 25:373–383.

Marchant, E. G., and Mistlberger, R. E. 1995. Morphine phase-shifts circadian rhythms in mice: Role of behavioural activation. *Neuroreport*, 7:209–212.

Marchant, E. G., and Mistlberger, R. E. 1996. Entrainment and phase shifting of circadian rhythms in mice by forced treadmill running. *Physiol. Behav.*, 60:657–663.

Marchant, E. G., and Mistlberger, R. E. 1997. Anticipation and entrainment to feeding time in intact and SCN-ablated C57BL/6j mice. *Brain Res.*, 765:273–282.

Marcheva, B., Ramsey, K. M., Buhr, E. D., Kobayashi, Y., Su, H., Ko, C. H., Ivanova, G., et al. 2010. Disruption of the clock components CLOCK and BMAL1 leads to hypoinsulinaemia and diabetes. *Nature*, 466:627–631.

Maren, S., De Oca, B., and Fanselow, M. S. 1994. Sex differences in hippocampal long-term potentiation (LTP) and Pavlovian fear conditioning in rats: Positive correlation between LTP and contextual learning. *Brain Res.*, 661:25–34.

Margetic, S., Gazzola, C., Pegg, G. G., and Hill, R. A. 2002. Leptin: A review of its peripheral actions and interactions. *International J. Obesity*, 26:1407–1433.

Marler, C. A., and Moore, M. C. 1988. Evolutionary costs of aggression revealed by testosterone manipulations in free-living male lizards. *Behav. Ecol. Sociobiol.*, 23:21–26.

Marler, C. A., and Moore, M. C. 1991. Supplementary feeding compensates for testosterone-induced costs of aggression in male mountain spiny lizards, *Sceloporus jarrovi*. *Anim. Behav.*, 42:209–219.

Marler, C. A., Walsberg, G., White, M. L., and Moore, M. 1995. Increased energy expenditure due to increased territorial defense in male lizards after phenotypic manipulation. *Behav. Ecol. Sociobiol.*, 37:225–231.

Marques, D. M., and Valenstein, E. S. 1976. Another hamster paradox: More males carry pups and fewer kill and cannibalize young than do females. *J. Comp. Physiol. Psychol.*, 90:653–657.

Marra, P. A., Hobson, K. A., and Holmes, R. T. 1998. Linking winter and summer events in a migratory bird by using stable-carbon isotopes. *Science*, 282:1884–1886.

Marshall, J. F., Turner, B. H., and Teitelbaum, P. 1971. Sensory neglect produced by lateral hypothalamic damage. *Science*, 174:523–525.

Marshall, J. R., and Henkin, R. I. 1971. Olfactory acuity, menstrual abnormalities, and oocyte status. *Ann. Intern. Med.*, 75:207–211.

Marstellar, F. A., and Lynch, C. B. 1987. Reproductive responses to variation in temperature and food supply by house mice: II. Lactation. *Biol. Reprod.*, 37:844–850.

Martin, J. E., Engel, J. N., and Klein, D. C. 1977. Inhibition of the in vitro pituitary response to luteinizing hormone-releasing hormone by melatonin, serotonin, and 5-methoxytryptamine. *Endocrinol.*, 100:675–680.

Martin, R. D., and May, R. M. 1981. Outward signs of breeding. *Nature*, 293:7–9.

Martinet, L., Allair, D., and Weine, C. 1982. Role of prolactin in the photoperiodic control of the molting in the mink (*Mustela vison*). *J. Endocrinol.* 103:9–15.

Mas, M. 1995. Neurobiological correlates of masculine sexual behavior. *Neurosci. Biobehav. Rev.*, 19:261–277.

Mascaro, J. S., Hackett, P. D., and Rilling, J. K. 2014. Differential neural responses to child and sexual stimuli in human fathers and non-fathers and their hormonal correlates. *Psychoneuroendocrinology*, 46:153–163.

Mason, A. O., Duffy, S., Zhao, S., Ubuka, T., Bentley, G. E., Tsutsui, K., Silver, R., and Kriegsfeld, L. J. 2010. Photoperiod and reproductive condition are associated with changes in RFamide-related peptide (RFRP) expression in Syrian hamsters (*Mesocricetus auratus*) *J. Biol. Rhythms*, 25:176–185.

Mason, A. O., Greives, T. J., Scotti, M. A., Levine, J., Frommeyer, S., Ketterson, E. D., Demas, G. E., and Kriegsfeld, L. J. 2007. Suppression of kisspeptin expression and gonadotropic axis sensitivity following exposure to inhibitory day lengths in female Siberian hamsters. *Horm. Behav.*, 52:492–498.

Mason, J. W. 1975. A historical view of the stress field. *J. Hum. Stress*, 1:6–12.

Mason, R. T. 1987. Sex pheromones and the mediation of reproduction in the red-sided garter snake *Thamnophis sirtalis parietalis*. Ph.D. Dissertation. University of Texas, Austin.

Mason, R. T., Fales, H. M., Jones, T. H., Pannell, L. K., Chinn, J. W., and Crews, D. 1989. Sex pheromones in snakes. *Science*, 245:290–293.

Masson-Pevet, M. and Gauer, F. 1994. Seasonality and melatonin receptors in the pars tuberalis in some long day breeders. *Biol. Signals*, 3:63–70.

Masters, W., and Johnson, V. 1966. *Human Sexual Response*. Little, Brown, Boston.

Mastrogiacomo, I., Fava, M., Fava, G. A., Kellner, R., Grismondi, G., and Cetera, C. 1982/1983. Postpartum hostility and prolactin. *Int. J. Psychiatry Med.*, 12:289–294.

Matthews, R. 1979. Testosterone levels in aggressive offenders. In M. Sandler (ed.), *Psychopharmacology of Aggression*, pp. 123–130. Raven Press, New York.

Mattson, B. J., Williams, S. E., Rosenblatt, J. S., and Morrell, J. I. 2003. Preferences for cocaine- or pup-associated chambers differentiates otherwise behaviorally identical postpartum maternal rats. *Psychopharmacol.*, 167:1–8.

Mattson, B. J., Williams, S., Rosenblatt, J. S., and Morrell, J. I. 2001. Comparison of two positive reinforcing stimuli: Pups and cocaine throughout the postpartum period. *Behav. Neurosci.*, 115:683–694.

Maya-Monteiro, C. M., and Bozza, P. T. 2008. Leptin and mTOR: Partners in metabolism and inflammation. *Cell Cycle*, 7:1713–1717.

Mayer, A. D., Freeman, N. C., and Rosenblatt, J. S. 1979. Ontogeny of maternal behavior in the laboratory rat: factors underlying changes in responsiveness from 30 to 90 days. *Dev. Psychobiol.*, 12:425–439.

Mayer, E. A., Labus, J. S., and Berkley, K. J. 2008. Sex differences in pain. In J. B. Becker, K. J. Berkley, N. Geary, E. Hampson, J. P. Herman, and E. A. Young (eds.), *Sex Differences in the Brain: From Genes to Behavior*, pp. 371–395. Oxford University Press, New York.

Mayer, E.A., and Fanselow, M.S. 2003. Dissecting the components of the central response to stress. *Nature Neuroscience*, 6:1011–1016.

Mayer, J. 1955. Regulation of energy intake and the body weight: The glucostatic and lipostatic hypothesis. *Ann. N. Y. Acad. Sci.*, 63:14–42.

Maywood, E. S., and Hastings, M. H. 1995. Lesions of the iodomelatonin-binding sites of the mediobasal hypothalamus spare the lactotropic, but block the gonadotropic response of male Syrian hamsters to short photoperiod and to melatonin. *Endocrinol.*, 136:144–153.

Maywood, E. S., Bittman, E. L., and Hastings, M. H. 1996. Lesions of the melatonin- and androgen-responsive tissue of the dorsomedial nucleus of the hypothalamus block the gonadal response of male Syrian hamsters to programmed infusions of melatonin. *Biol. Reprod.*, 54:470–477.

Maywood, E. S., Reddy, A. B., Wong, G. K., O'Neill, J. S., O'Brien, J. A., McMahon, D. G., Harmar, A. J., Okamura, H., and Hastings, M. H. 2006. Synchronization and maintenance of timekeeping in suprachiasmatic circadian clock cells by neuropeptidergic signaling. *Curr. Biol.*, 16:599–605.

Mazur, A., and Lamb, T. A. 1980. Testosterone, status, and mood in human males. *Horm. Behav.*, 14:236–246.

Mazur, A., Booth, A., and Dabbs, J. M. 1992. Testosterone and chess competition. *Soc. Psychol. Q.*, 55:70–77.

McAllister-Williams, R. H., Ferrier, I. N., and Young, A. H. 1998. Mood and neuropsychological function in depression: The role of corticosteroids and serotonin. *Psychol. Med.*, 28:573–584.

McCabe, P. M., Gonzales, J. A., Zaias, J., Szeto, A., Kumar, M., Herron, A. J., and Schneiderman, N. 2002. Social environment influences the progression of atherosclerosis in the watanabe heritable hyperlipidemic rabbit. *Circulation*, 105:354–359.

McCaffrey, K. A., Jones, B., Mabrey, N., Weiss, B., Swan, S. H., and Patisaul, H. B. 2013. Sex specific impact of perinatal bisphenol A (BPA) exposure over a range of orally administered doses on rat hypothalamic sexual differentiation. *Neurotoxicology*, 36:55–62.

McCann, S. M., and Ramirez, V. D. 1964. The neuroendocrine regulation of hypophyseal luteinizing hormone secretion. *Rec. Prog. Horm. Res.*, 20:131–170.

McCarthy, M. M. 2008. Estradiol and the developing brain. *Physiol. Rev.*, 88:91–134.

McCarthy, M. M. and Arnold, A. P. 2011. Reframing sexual differentiation of the brain. *Nat Neurosci.*, 14:677–683.

McCarthy, M. M., and Arnold, A. P. 2008. Sex differences in the brain: What's new and what's old. In J. B. Becker, K. J. Berkley, N. Geary, E. Hampson, J. P. Herman, and E. A. Young (eds.), *Sex Differences in the Brain: From Genes to Behavior*, pp. 15–34. Oxford University Press, New York.

McCarthy, M. M., Auger, A. P., Bale, T. L., De Vries, G. J., Dunn, G. A., Forger, N. G., Murray, E. K., Nugent, B. M., Schwarz, J. M., and Wilson, M. E. 2009. The epigenetics of sex differences in the brain. *J. Neurosci.*, 29:12815–12823.

McCarthy, M. M., Brooks, P. J., Pfaus, J. G., Brown, H. E., Flanagan, L. M., Schwartz-Giblin, S., and Pfaff, D. W. 1993a. Antisense oligodeoxynucleotides in behavioral neuroscience. *Neuroprotocols*, 2:67–74.

McCarthy, M. M., de Vries, G. J., and Forger, N. G. 2009. Sexual differentiation of the brain: mode, mechanisms, and meaning. In D. W. Pfaff, A. P. Arnold, A. M. Etgen, S. Fahrbach and R. T. Rubin (eds), *Hormones, Brain and Behavior* (2nd ed.), pp. 1707–1744. Academic Press, New York.

McCarty, B. M., Migeon, C. J., Meyer-Bahlburg, H. F. L., Zacur, H., and Wisniewski, A. B. 2006. Medical and psychosexual outcome in women affected by complete gonadal dysgenesis. *J. Pediatr. Endocrinol. Metab.*, 19:873–877.

McCarty, R., and Southwick, C. H. 1977. Paternal care and the development of behavior in the southern grasshopper mouse, *Onychomys torridus*. *Behav. Biol.*, 19:476–490.

McCaughey, S. A. 2008. The taste of sugars. *Neurosci. Biobehav. Rev.*, 32:1024–1043.

McClintock, M. K. 1984. Group mating in the domestic rat as a context for sexual selection: Consequences for the analysis of sexual behavior and neuroendocrine responses. *Adv. Study Behav.*, 14:1–50.

McClintock, M. K. 1987. A functional approach to the behavioral endocrinology of rodents. In D. Crews (ed.), *Psychobiology of Reproductive Behavior: An Evolution-ary Perspective*, pp. 176–203. Prentice Hall, Englewood Cliffs, NJ.

McCloskey, M., Wible, C. G., and Cohen, N. J. 1988. Is there a special flashbulb-memory mechanism? *J. Exp. Psychol. Gen.*, 117:171–181.

McClung, C. A. 2013. How might circadian rhythms control mood? Let me count the ways... *Biol. Psychiatry*, 74:242–249.

McConnell, J., Benson, G. S., and Wood, J. G. 1982. Autonomic innervation of the urogenital system: Adrenergic and cholinergic elements. *Brain Res. Bull.*, 9:679–694.

McCormack, J. T., and Greenwald, G. S. 1974. Progesterone and oestradiol-17β concentrations in the peripheral plasma during pregnancy in the mouse. *J. Endocrinol.*, 62:101–107.

McCormick, J. A., Lyons, V., Jacobson, M. D., Noble, J., Diorio, J., Nyirenda, M., Weaver, S., Ester, W., Yau, J. L., Meaney, M. J., Seckl, J. R., and Chapman, K. E., et al. 2000. 5'-heterogeneity of glucocorticoid receptor messenger RNA is tissue specific: Differential regulation of variant transcripts by early-life events. *Molecular Endocrinol.*, 14:506–517.

McCormick, S. D., and Bradshaw, D. 2006. Hormonal control of salt and water balance in vertebrates. *Gen. Comp. Endocrinol.*, 147:3–8.

McCune, A. M. and Lundgren, J. D. 2015. Bright light therapy for the treatment of night eating syndrome: A pilot study. *Psychiatry Res.*, 229:577–579.

McElreavey, K., Barbaux, S., Ion, A., and Fellous, M. 1995. The genetic basis of murine and human sex determination: A review. *Heredity*, 75:599–611.

McEwen, B. S, and Wingfield, J. C. 2010. What is in a name? Integrating homeostasis, allostasis and stress. *Horm. Behav.*, 57:105–111.

McEwen, B. S. 2000. The neurobiology of stress: From serendipity to clinical relevance. *Brain Res.*, 886:172–189.

McEwen, B. S. 2001. Estrogen effects on the brain: Multiple sites and molecular mechanisms. *J. Appl. Physiol.*, 91:2785–2801.

McEwen, B. S. 2006. Protective and damaging effects of stress mediators: Central role of the brain. *Dialogues Clin. Neurosci.*, 8:367–381.

McEwen, B. S. 2008. Central effects of stress hormones in health and disease: Understanding the protective and damaging effects of stress and stress mediators. *Eur. J. Pharmacol.*, 583:174–185.

McEwen, B. S. 2014. Sex, stress and the brain: interactive actions of hormones on the developing and adult brain. *Climacteric*, 17:18–25

McEwen, B. S., and Gianaros, P. J. 2010. Central role of the brain in stress and adaptation: Links to socioeconomic status, health, and disease. *Ann. N. Y. Acad. Sci.*, 1186:190–222.

McEwen, B. S., and Wingfield, J. C. 2003. The concept of allostasis in biology and biomedicine. *Horm. Behav.*, 43:2–15.

McEwen, B. S., Gould, E., Orchinik, M., Weiland, N. G., and Woolley, C. S. 1995. Oestrogens and the structural and functional plasticity of neurons: Implications for memory, ageing and neurodegenerative processes. *Ciba Found. Symp.*, 191:52–66.

McEwen, B. S., Gray, J. D., and Nasca, C. 2015. Recognizing resilience: Learning from the effects of stress on the brain. *Neurobiol. Stress*, 1:1–11.

McEwen, B. S., McKittrick, C. R., Tamashiro, K. L. K., and Sakai, R. R. 2015. The brain on stress: Insight from studies using the Visible Burrow System. *Physiol. Behav.*, 146:47–56.

McEwen, B. S., Nasca, C., and Gray, J. D. 2016. Stress effects on neuronal structure: Hippocampus, amygdala, and prefrontal cortex. *Neuropsychopharmacology*, 41:3–23.

McFadden, D. 1999. Intersex infants and otoacoustic emissions. *Urology*, 53:240.

McFadden, D. 2002. Masculinizing effects in the auditory system. *Arch. Sex. Behav.*, 31:91–111.

McFadden, D., and Loehlin, J. C. 1995. On the heritability of spontaneous otoacoustic emissions: A twins study. *Hearing Res.*, 85:181–198.

McFadden, D., and Pasanen, E. G. 1998. Comparison of the auditory systems of heterosexuals and homosexuals: Click-evoked otoacoustic emissions. *Proc. Natl. Acad. Sci. USA*, 95:2709–2713.

McFadden, D., Loehlin, J. C., Breedlove, S. M., Lippa, R. A., Manning, J. T., and Rahman, Q. 2005. A reanalysis of five studies on sexual orientation and the relative length of the 2nd and 4th fingers (the 2D:4D ratio). *Arch. Sex. Behav.*, 34:341–356.

McFadden, D., Pasanen, E. G., Raper, J., Lange, H. S., and Wallen, K. 2006a. Sex differences in otoacoustic emissions measured in rhesus monkeys (*Macaca mulatta*). *Horm. Behav.*, 50:274–284.

McFadden, D., Pasanen, E. G., Weldele, M. L., Glickman, S. E., and Place, N. J. 2006b. Masculinized otoacoustic emissions in female spotted hyenas (*Crocuta crocuta*). *Horm. Behav.*, 50:285–292.

McGaugh, J. L. 1989. Involvement of hormonal and neuromodulatory systems in the regulation of memory storage. *Annu. Rev. Neurosci.*, 12:255–287.

McGaugh, J. L. 2004. The amygdala modulates the consolidation of memories of emotionally arousing experiences. *Ann. Rev. Neurosci.*, 27:1–28.

McGaugh, J. L., and Gold, P. E. 1976. Modulation of memory by electrical stimulation of the brain. In M. R. Rosenzweig and E. L. Bennett (eds.), *Neural Mechanisms of Learning and Memory*, pp. 549–560. MIT Press, Cambridge, MA.

McGaugh, J. L., and Roozendaal, B. 2009. Drug enhancement of memory consolidation: Historical perspective and neurobiological implications. *Psychopharmacol.*, 202:3–14.

McGaugh, J. L., Bennett, M. C., Liang, K. C., Juler, R. G., and Tam, D. 1987. Memory-enhancing effect of posttraining epinephrine is not blocked by dexa-methasone. *Psychobiol.*, 15:343–344.

McGee, L. C., Juhn, M., and Domm, L. V. 1928. The development of secondary sex characters by injection of bull testes. *Am. J. Physiol.*, 87:406–435.

McGill, T. E. 1962. Sexual behavior in three inbred strains of mice. *Behaviour*, 19:341–350.

McGill, T. E. 1977. Reproductive isolation, behavioral genetics, and function of sexual behavior in rodents. In J. S. Rosenblatt and B. R. Komisaruk (eds.), *Reproductive Behavior and Evolution*, pp. 73–109. Plenum Press, New York.

McGinnis, M. Y., Lumia, A. R., and Possidente, B. P. 2002. Effects of withdrawal from anabolic androgenic steroids on aggression in adult male rats. *Physiol. Behav.*, 75:541–549.

McGinnis, M. Y., Williams, G. W., and Lumia, A. R. 1996. Inhibition of male sex behavior by androgen receptor blockade in preoptic area or hypothalamus, but not amygdala or septum. *Physiol. Behav.*, 60:783–789.

McGlone, J. 1980. Sex differences in human brain asymmetry: A critical survey. *Behav. Brain Sci.*, 3:215–263.

McGlothlin, J. W., and Ketterson, E. D. 2008. Hormone-mediated suites as adaptations and evolutionary constraints. *Philos. Trans. R. Soc. Lond.*, 363:1611–1620.

McGlothlin, J. W., Jawor, J. M., and Ketterson, E. D. 2007. Natural variation in a testosterone-mediated trade-off between mating effort and parental effort. *Am. Nat.*, 170:864–875.

McGowan, M. K., Andrews, K. M., Kelly, J., and Grossman, S. P. 1990. Effects of chronic intrahypothalamic infusion of insulin on food intake and diurnal meal patterning in the rat. *Behav. Neurosci.*, 104:373–385.

McGregor, G. P., Desaga, J. F., Ehlenz, K., Fischer, A., Heese, F., Hegele, A., Lammer, C., Peiser, C., and Lang, R. E. 1996. Radioimmunological measurement of leptin in plasma of obese and diabetic human subjects. *Endocrinol.*, 137:1501–1504.

McGuinness, D. 1972. Hearing: Individual differences in perceiving. *Perception*, 1:465–473.

McGuinness, D. 1976. Away from a unisex psychology: Individual differences in visual sensory and perceptual processes. *Perception*, 5:279–294.

McHenry, J. A., Bell, G. A., Parrish, B. P., and Hull, E. M. 2012. Dopamine D1 receptors and phosphorylation of dopamine- and cyclic AMP-regulated phosphoprotein-32 in the medial preoptic area are involved in experience-induced enhancement of male sexual behavior in rats. *Behav. Neurosci.*, 126:523–529.

McKim, D. B., Niraula, A., Tarr, A. J., Wohleb, E. S., Sheridan, J. F., and Godbout, J. P. 2016. Neuroinflammatory dynamics underlie memory impairments after repeated social defeat. *J. Neurosci.*, 36:2590–2604.

McKinney, T. D., and Desjardins, C. 1973. Intermale stimuli and testicular function in adult and immature house mice. *Biol. Reprod.*, 9:370–378.

McKittrick, C. R., Blanchard, D. C., Hardy, M. P., and Blanchard, R. J. 2009. Social stress effects on hormones, brain, and behavior. In D. W. Pfaff, et al. (eds.), *Hormones, Brain and Behavior* (2nd ed.), pp. 333–365. Academic Press, San Diego.

McLay, R. N., Freeman, S. M., and Zadina, J. E. 1998. Chronic corticosterone impairs memory performance in the Barnes maze. *Physiol. Behav.*, 63:933–937.

McNemar, Q., and Stone, C. P. 1932. The sex difference in rats on three learning tasks. *J. Comp. Psychol.*, 14:171–180.

McShea, W. J. 1990. Social tolerance and proximate mechanisms of dispersal among winter groups of meadow voles (*Microtus pennsylvanicus*). *Anim. Behav.*, 39:346–351.

McSweeney, J. C., Cody, M., O'Sullivan, P., Elberson, K., Moser, D. K., and Garvin, B. J. 2003. Women's early warning symptoms of acute myocardial infarction. *Circulation*, 108:2619–2623.

Meaney, M. J. 2001. Maternal care, gene expression and the transmission of individual differences in stress reactivity across generations. *Annu. Rev. Neurosci.*, 24:161–192.

Meerts, S. H. and Clark, A. S. 2009. Artificial vaginocervical stimulation induces a conditioned place preference in female rats *Horm. Behav.*, 55:128–132.

Meerts, S. H., Strnad, H. K., and Schairer, R. S. 2015. Paced mating behavior is affected by clitoral-vaginocervical lidocaine application in combination with sexual experience. *Physiol. Behav.*, 140:222–229.

Mehdi, A. Z., and Sandor, T. 1977. The effect of melatonin on the biosynthesis of corticosteroids in beef adrenal preparations in vitro. *J. Steroid Biochem.*, 8:821–823.

Meijer, J. H., and Rietveld, W. J. 1989. Neurophysiology of the suprachiasmatic circadian pacemaker in rodents. *Physiol. Rev.*, 69:671–707.

Meisel, R. L., and Sachs, B. D. 1994. The physiology of male sexual behavior. In E. Knobil and J. D. Neill (eds.), *The Physiology of Reproduction*, Vol. 2, pp. 3–105. Raven Press, New York.

Meisel, R. L., and Ward, I. L. 1981. Fetal female rats are masculinized by male litermates located caudally in the uterus. *Science*, 213:239–242.

Meisel, R. L., Lumia, A. R., and Sachs, B. D. 1980. Effects of olfactory bulb removal and flank shock on copulation in male rats. *Physiol. Behav.*, 25:383–387.

Meisel, R. L., O'Hanlon, J. K., and Sachs, B. D. 1984. Differential maintenance of penile responses and copulatory behavior by gonadal hormones in castrated male rats. *Horm. Behav.*, 18:56–64.

Meisel, S. R., Kutz, I., Dayan, K. I., Pauzner, H., Chetboun, I., Arbel, Y., and David, D. 1991. Effect of Iraqi missile war on incidence of acute myocardial infarction and sudden death in Israeli civilians. *Lancet*, 338:660–661.

Melis, M. R., and Argiolas, A. 1995. Dopamine and sexual behavior. *Neurosci. Biobehav. Rev.* 19:19–38.

Melloni, R. H., Connor, D. F., Hang, P. T., Harrison, R. J., and Ferris, C. F. 1997. Anabolic-androgenic steroid exposure during adolescence and aggressive behavior in golden hamsters. *Physiol. Behav.*, 61:359–364.

Melnik, B. C. 2009. Androgen abuse in the community. *Curr. Opin. Endocr. Diabetes Obes.*, 16:218–223.

Melnyk, R. B., Mrosovsky, N., and Martin, J. M. 1983. Spontaneous obesity and weight loss: insulin action in the dormouse. *Am. J. Physiol.*, 245:R396–402.

Menaker, M. 1968. Extraretinal light perception in the sparrow. I. Entrainment of the biological clock. *Proc. Natl. Acad. Sci. USA*, 59:414–21.

Mendelson, J. H., and Mello, N. K. 1982. Hormones and psycho-sexual development in young men following chronic heroin use. *Neurobehav. Toxicol. Teratol.*, 4:441–445.

Mendez, M. F. and Shapira, J. S. 2013. Hypersexual behavior in frontotemporal dementia: A comparison with early-onset Alzheimer's Disease. *Arch. Sex. Behav.*, 42:501–509.

Mendonca, M. T., and Licht, P. 1986. Seasonal cycles in gonadal activity and plasma gonadotropin in the musk turtle, *Sternotherus odoratus*. *Gen. Comp. Endocrinol.*, 62:459–469.

Mendoza, S. P., and Mason, W. A. 1986. Parental division of labour and differentiation of attachments in a monogamous primate (*Callicebus moloch*). *Anim. Behav.*, 34:1336–1347.

Mendoza, S. P., and Mason, W. A. 1997. Attachment relationships in New World primates. *Ann. N. Y. Acad. Sci.*, 807:203–209.

Mendoza, S. P., Lowe, E. L., and Resko, J. A. 1978. Seasonal variations in gonadal hormones and social behavior in squirrel monkeys. *Physiol. Behav.*, 20:515–522.

Mendoza, S. P., Lyons, D. M., and Saltzman, W. 1991. Sociophysiology of squirrel monkeys. *Am. J. Primatol.*, 23:37–54.

Mercer, J. G., Hoggard, N., Williams, L. M., Lawrence, C. B., Hannah, L. T., and Trayhurn, P. 1996. Localization of leptin receptor mRNA and the long form splice variant (Ob-Rb) in mouse hypothalamus and adjacent brain regions by in situ hybridization. *FEBS Lett.*, 387:113–116.

Merz, C.J., Hermann, A., Stark, R &Wolf, O.T. 2014. Cortisol modifies extinction of learning of recently acquired fear in men. *Scan*, 9:1426–1434.

Messier, C., and White, N. M. 1987. Memory improvement by glucose, fructose, and two glucose analogs: A possible effect on peripheral glucose transport. *Behav. Neural Biol.*, 48:104–127.

Meston, C. M., and Buss, D. M. 2007. Why humans have sex. *Arch. Sex. Behav.*, 36:477–507.

Mewis, C., Spyridopoulos, I., Kuhlkamp, V., and Seipel, L. 1996. Manifestation of severe coronary heart disease after anabolic drug abuse. *Clin. Cardiol.*, 19:153–155.

Meyer-Bahlburg, H. F. L. 1984. Psychoendocrine research on sexual orientation. Current status and future options. In G. J. DeVries, J. P. C. De Bruin, H. B. M. Uylings, and M. A. Corner (eds.), *Progress in Brain Research: Sex Differences in the Brain*, pp. 375–398. Elsevier Science Publishers, Amsterdam.

Meyer-Bahlburg, H. F. L., Dolezal, C., Baker, S. W., and New, M. I. 2008. Sexual orientation in women with classical or non-classical congenital adrenal hyperplasia as a function of degree of prenatal androgen excess. *Archives of Sexual Behavior*, 37:88–99.

Meyer-Bahlburg, H. F. L., Grisanti, G. C., and Ehrhardt, A. A. 1977. Prenatal effects of sex hormones on human male behavior: Medroxyprogesterone acetate (MPA). *Psychoneuroendocrinol.*, 2:383–390.

Meyer-Bernstein, E. L., Jetton, A. E., Matsumoto, S. I., Markuns, J. F., Lehman, M. N., and Bittman, E. L. 1999. Effects of suprachiasmatic transplants on circadian rhythms of neuroendocrine function in golden hamsters. *Endocrinol.*, 140:207–218.

Meyer, W. J., Walker, P. A., Emory, L. E., and Smith, E. R. 1985. Physical, metabolic, and hormonal effects on men of long-term therapy with medroxyprogesterone acetate. *Fertil. Steril.*, 43:102–106.

Miceli, M. O., and Malsbury, C. W. 1982a. Availability of a food hoard facilitates maternal behaviour in virgin female hamsters. *Physiol. Behav.*, 28:855–856.

Miceli, M. O., and Malsbury, C. W. 1982b. Sagittal knife cuts in the near and far lateral preoptic area–hypothalamus disrupt maternal behavior in female hamsters. *Physiol. Behav.*, 28:857–867.

Michael, R. P., and Bonsall, R. W. 1977. A 3-year study of an annual rhythm in plasma androgen levels in male rhesus monkeys (*Macaca mulatta*) in a constant laboratory environment. *J. Reprod. Fertil.*, 49:129–131.

Michael, R. P., and Zumpe, D. 1978. Annual cycles of aggression and plasma testosterone in captive male rhesus monkeys. *Psychoneuroendocrinol.*, 3:217–220.

Michael, R. P., and Zumpe, D. 1986. An annual rhythm in the battering of women. *Am. J. Psychiatry*, 143:637–640.

Michael, R. P., and Zumpe, D. 1996. Biological factors in the organization and expression of sexual behaviour. In I. Rosen (ed.), *Sexual Deviation*, pp. 452–287. Oxford University Press, Oxford.

Michael, R. P., Clancy, A. N., and Zumpe, D. 1995. Distribution of androgen receptor-like immunoreactivity in the brains of Cynomolgus monkeys. *J. Neuroendocrinol.*, 7:713–719.

Michael, R. P., Zumpe, D., and Bonsall, R. W. 1992. The interaction of testosterone with the brain of the orchidectomized primate fetus. *Brain Res.*, 570:68–74.

Michalska, K. J., Decety, J., Liu, C., Chen, Q., Martz, M. E., Jacob, S., Hipwell, A. E., et al. 2014. Genetic imaging of the association of oxytocin receptor gene (OXTR) polymorphisms with positive maternal parenting. *Front. Behav. Neurosci.*, 8:21.

Michel, G. F., and Moore, C. L. 1995. *Developmental Psychobiology: An Interdisciplinary Science*. MIT Press: Cambridge, MA.

Michiels, N. K., and Newman, L. J. 1998. Sex and violence in hermaphrodites. *Nature*, 391:647.

Miczek, K. A., and Fish, E. W. 2005. Monoamines, GABA, glutamate and aggression. In R. J. Nelson (ed.), *Biology of Aggression*. Oxford University Press, New York.

Middleman, A. B., and DuRant, R. H. 1996. Anabolic steroid use and associated health risk behaviours. *Sports Med.*, 21:251–225.

Mieda, M., Ono, D., Hasegawa, E., Okamoto, H., Honma, K., Honma, S., and Sakurai, T. 2015. Cellular clocks in AVP neurons of the SCN are critical for interneuronal coupling regulating circadian behavior rhythm. *Neuron*, 85:1103–1116. doi: 10.1016/j.neuron.2015.02.005.

Miernicki, M., Pospichal, M., Karg, J., and Powers, J. B. 1988. Photoperiodic effects on male sexual behavior. *Conference on Reproductive Behavior*, p. 64, Omaha, NE.

Migeon, C. J., Wisniewski, A. B., Gearhart, J. P., Meyer-Bahlburg, H. F., Rock, J. A., Brown, T. R., Casella, S. J., Maret, A., Ngai, K. M., Money, J., and Berkovitz, G. D. 2002. Ambiguous genitalia with perineoscrotal hypospadias in 46,XY individuals: Long-term medical, surgical, and psychosexual outcome. *Pediatrics*, 110:e31.

Mikhelashvili-Browner, N., Yousem, D. M., Wu, C., Kraut, M. A., Vaughan, C. L., Oguz, K. K., and Calhoun, V. D. 2003. Lack of sex effect on brain activity during a visuomotor response task: Functional MR imaging study. *Am. J. Neuroradiol.*, 24:488–494.

Miklowitz, D. J., Otto, M. W., Frank, E., Reilly-Harrington, N. A., Kogan, J. N., and Sachs, G. S. 2007. Intensive psychosocial intervention enhances functioning in patients with bipolar depression: Results from a 9-month randomized controlled trial. *Am. J. Psychiatry*, 164:1340–1347.

Miles, C., Green, R., Sanders, G., and Hines, M. 1998. Estrogen and memory in a transsexual population. *Horm. Behav.*, 34:199–208.

Milette, J. J., and Turek, F. W. 1986. Circadian and photoperiodic effects of brief light pulses in male Djungarian hamsters. *Biol. Reprod.*, 35:327–335.

Miller, S. M., and Lonstein, J. S. 2009. Dopaminergic projections to the medial preoptic area of postpartum rats. *Neuroscience*, 159:1384–1396.

Miller, W. L., Baxter, J. D., and Eberhardt, N. L. 1983. Peptide hormone genes: Structure and evolution. In D. T. Krieger, M. J., Brownstein, and J. B. Martin (eds.), *Brain Peptides*, pp. 16–78. Wiley-Interscience, NY.

Mills, M. J., and Stunkard, A. J. 1976. Behavioral changes following surgery for obesity. *Am. J. Psychiatry*, 133:527–531.

Milner, P., and Zucker, I. 1965. Specific hunger for potassium in the rat. *Psychonom. Sci.*, 2:17–18.

Minokoshi, Y., Alquier, T., Furukawa, N., Kim, Y.-B., Lee, A., Xue, B., Mu, J., Foufelle, F., Ferre, P., Birnbaum, M. J., Stuck, B. J., and Kahn, B. B. 2004. AMP-kinase regulates food intake by responding to hormonal and nutrient signals in the hypothalamus. *Nature*, 428:569–574.

Mistlberger, R. E., and Skene, D. J. 2004 Social influences on mammalian circadian rhythms: Animal and human studies. *Biol. Rev.*, 79:533–556.

Mistlberger, R. E., and Skene, D. J. 2005. Nonphotic entrainment in humans? *J. Biol. Rhythms*, 20:339–352.

Mistlberger, R. E., Buijs, R. M., Challet, E., Escobar, C., Landry, G., Kalsbeek, A., Pevet, P., and Shibata, S. 2009. Food anticipation in Bmal1-/- and AAV-Bmal1 rescued mice: A reply to Fuller et al. *J. Circadian Rhythms*, 7:11, doi:10.1186/1740–3391-7-11

Mistlberger, R. E., Marchant, E. G., and Sinclair, S. V. 1996. Nonphotic phase-shifting and the motivation to run: Cold exposure reexamined. *J. Biological Rhythms*, 11:208–215.

Mitani, J. C. 1985. Mating behavior of male orangutans in the Kutai Game Reserve, Indonesia. *Anim. Behav.*, 33:392–402.

Mitchell, A. J. 1998. The role of corticotropin-releasing factor in depressive illness: A critical review. *Neurosci. Biobehav. Rev.*, 22:635–651.

Mitchell, J. S., and Keesey, R. E. 1974. The effects of lateral hypothalamic lesions and castration upon the body weight and composition of male rats. *Behav. Biol.*, 11:69–82.

Mitra, R., Jadhav, S., McEwen, B. S., Vyas, A., and Chattarji, S. 2005. Stress duration modulates the spatiotemporal patterns of spine formation in the basolateral amygdala. *Proc. Natl. Acad. Sci. USA*, 102:9371–9376.

Mizukami, S., Nishizuka, M., and Arai, Y. 1983. Sexual difference in nuclear volume and its ontogeny in the rat amygdala. *Exp. Neurol.*, 79:569–575.

Modney, B. K., and Hatton, G. I. 1990. Motherhood modifies magnocellular neuronal interrelationships in functionally meaningful ways. In N. A. Krasnegor and R. S. Bridges (eds.), *Mammalian Parenting*, pp. 305–323. Oxford University Press, Oxford.

Moenter, S. M., Caraty, A., Locatelli, A., and Karsch, F. J. 1991. Pattern of gonadotropin-releasing hormone (GnRH) secretion leading up to ovulation in the ewe: existence of a preovulatory GnRH surge. *Endocrinology*, 129:1175–1182.

Moffatt, C. A. 1994. Seasonal and Social Regulation of Reproductive Behavior in Female Prairie Voles, *Microtus ochrogaster*. Dissertation, Johns Hopkins University, Baltimore, MD.

Moffatt, C. A., DeVries, A. C., and Nelson, R. J. 1993. Winter adaptations of male deer mice (*Peromyscus maniculatus*) and prairie voles (*Microtus ochrogaster*) that vary in reproductive responsiveness to photoperiod. *J. Biol. Rhythms*, 8:221–232.

Mogenson, G. J., Jones, D. L., and Yim, C. Y. 1980. From motivation to action: Functional interface between the limbic system and the motor system. *Prog. Neurobiol.*, 14:69–97.

Moltz, H., and Kilpatrick, S. J. 1978. Response to the maternal pheromone in the rat as protection against necrotizing enterocolitis. *Neurosci. Biobehav. Rev.*, 2:277–280.

Moltz, H., and Robbins, D. 1965. Maternal behavior of primiparous and multiparous rats. *J. Comp. Physiol. Psychol.*, 60:417–421.

Moltz, H., Lubin, M., Leon, M., and Numan, M. 1970. Hormonal induction of maternal behavior in the ovariectomized nulliparous rat. *Physiol. Behav.*, 5:1373–1377.

Money, J. 1961. Sex hormones and other variables in human eroticism. In W. C. Young (ed.), *Sex and Internal Secretions*, pp. 1383–1400. Williams & Wilkins, Baltimore.

Money, J. 1988. The ethics of pornography in the era of AIDS. *J. Sex Marital Ther.*, 14:177–183.

Money, J., and Bennett, R. G. 1981. Postadolescent paraphilic sex offenders: Antiandrogenic and counseling therapy follow-up. *Int. J. Ment. Health*, 10:122–133.

Money, J., and Dalery, J. 1976. Iatrogenic homosexuality: Gender identity in seven 46, XX chromosomal females with hyperadrenocortical hermaphroditism born with a penis, three reared as boys, four reared as girls. *J. Homosexuality*, 1:357–371.

Money, J., and Ehrhardt, A. A. 1972. *Man and Woman, Boy and Girl*. Johns Hopkins University Press, Baltimore.

Money, J., and Norman, B. F. 1987. Gender identity and gender transposition: Longitudinal outcome study of 24 male hermaphrodites assigned as boys. *J. Sex Marital Ther.*, 13:75–92.

Money, J., and Ogunro, C. 1974. Behavioral sexology: Ten cases of genetic male intersexuality with impaired prenatal and pubertal androgenization. *Arch. Sex. Behav.*, 3:181–205.

Money, J., Devore, H., and Norman, B. F. 1986. Gender identity and gender transposition: Longitudinal outcome study of 32 male hermaphrodites assigned as girls. *J. Sex Marital Ther.*, 12:165–180.

Monk, T. H. 1980. Traffic accident increases as a possible indicant of desynchronosis. *Chronobiologia*, 7:527–529.

Monk, T. H., and Aplin, L. C. 1980. Spring and autumn Daylight Savings Time changes: Studies of adjustment in sleep timings, mood, and efficiency. *Ergonomics*, 23:167–178.

Monti, P. M., Brown, W. A., and Corriveau, D. P. 1977. Testosterone and components of aggressive and sexual behavior in man. *Am. J. Psychiatry*, 134:692–694.

Montúfar-Chaveznava, R., Trejo-Muñoz, L., Hernández-Campos, O., Navarrete, E., and Caldelas, I. 2013. Maternal olfactory cues synchronize the circadian system of artificially raised newborn rabbits. *PLoS One*, 8:e74048.

Mook, D. G., Kenney, N. J., Roberts, S., Nussbaum, A. I., and Rodier, W. I. 1972. Ovarian-adrenal interactions in regulation of body weight in female rats. *J. Comp. Physiol. Psychol.*, 81:198–211.

Mooney, R. 1999. Sensitive periods and circuits for learned birdsong. *Curr. Opin. Neurobiol.*, 9:121–127.

Moons, T., Claes, S., Martens, G. J., Peuskens, J., Van Loo, K. M., Van Schijndel, J. E., De Hert, M., and van Winkel, R. 2011. Clock genes and body composition in patients with schizophrenia under treatment with antipsychotic drugs. *Schizophr. Res.*, 125:187–193.

Moore-Ede, M. C., Sulzman, F. M., and Fuller, C. A. 1982. *The Clocks That Time Us*. Harvard University Press, Cambridge.

Moore, C. L. 1984. Maternal contributions to the development of masculine sexual behavior in laboratory rats. *Dev. Psychobiol.*, 17:347–356.

Moore, C. L. 1986. Interaction of species-typical environmental and hormonal factors in sexual differentiation of behavior. *Ann. N. Y. Acad. Sci.*, 474:108–119.

Moore, C. L. 1995. Maternal contributions to mammalian reproductive development and divergence of males and females. In P. J. P. Slater, J. S. Rosenblatt, C. T. Snowdon, and M. Milinski (eds.), *Advances in the Study of Behavior*, pp. 47–118. Academic Press, New York.

Moore, C. L., and Morelli, G. A. 1979. Mother rats interact differently with male and female offspring. *J. Comp. Physiol. Psychol.*, 93:677–684.

Moore, C. L., Dou, H., and Juraska, J. M. 1992. Maternal stimulation affects the number of motor neurons in a sexually dimorphic nucleus of the lumbar spinal cord. *Brain Res.*, 572:52–56.

Moore, C. R., and Price, D. 1938. Some effects of testosterone and testosterone propionate in the rat. *Anat. Rec.*, 71:59–78.

Moore, I. T., Greene, M. J., and Mason, R. T. 2001. Environmental and seasonal adaptations of the adrenocortical and gonadal responses to capture stress in two populations of the male garter snake, *Thamnophis sirtalis*. *J. Exp. Zool.*, 289:99–108.

Moore, I. T., LeMaster, M. P., and Mason, R. T. 2000. Behavioural and hormonal responses to capture stress in the male red-sided garter snake, *Thamnophis sirtalis parietalis*. *Anim. Behav.*, 59:529–534.

Moore, I. T., Walker, B. G., and Wingfield, J. C. 2004. The effects of combined aromatase inhibitor and anti-androgen on male territorial aggression in a tropical population of rufous-collared sparrows, *Zonotrichia capensis*. *Gen. Comp. Endocrinol.*, 135:223–229.

Moore, M. C. 1984. Changes in territorial defense produced by changes in circulating levels of testosterone: A possible hormonal basis for mate-guarding in white-crowned sparrows. *Behaviour*, 88:215–226.

Moore, M. C. 1987. Castration affects territorial and sexual behavior of free-living male lizards, *Sceloporus jarrovi*. *Anim. Behav.*, 35:1193–1199.

Moore, M. C. 1991. Application of organization-activation theory to alternative male reproductive strategies: A review. *Horm. Behav.*, 25:154–179.

Moore, M. C., and Kranz, R. 1983. Evidence for androgen independence of male mounting behavior in white-crowned sparrows (*Zonotrichia leucophrys gambelli*). *Horm. Behav.*, 17:414–423.

Moore, M. C., and Marler, C. A. 1987. Effects of testosterone manipulations on nonbreeding season territorial aggression in free-living male lizards, *Sceloporus jarrovi*. *Gen. Comp. Endocrinol.*, 65:225–232.

Moore, M. C., Hews, D. K., and Knapp, R. 1998. Hormonal control and evolution of alternative male phenotypes: Generalizations of models for sexual differentiation. *Am. Zool.*, 38:133–151.

Moore, R. M., and Eichler, V. B. 1972. Loss of a circadian adrenal corticosterone rhythm following suprachiasmatic lesions in the rat. *Brain Res.*, 42:201–206.

Moore, R. Y. 1997. Circadian rhythms: Basic neurobiology and clinical applications. *Annu. Rev. Med.*, 48:253–266.

Moore, R. Y., Karapas, F. and Lenn, N. J. 1971. A retinohypothalamic projection in the rat. *Anat. Rec.*, 169:382–383.

Moore, R. Y., Speh, J. C., and Leak, R. K. 2002. Suprachiasmatic nucleus organization. *Cell Tissue Res.*, 309:89–98.

Moore, W. V. 1988. Anabolic steroid use in adolescence. *JAMA*, 260:3484–3486.

Morali, G., Asuncion, M., Soto, P., Contreras, J. L., Arteaga, M., Gonzalez-Vidal, D. M., and Beyer, C. 2003. Detailed analysis of the male copulatory motor pattern in mammals: Hormonal bases. *Scand. J. Psych.*, 44:279–288.

Moran, T. H. 2009. Gut peptides in the control of food intake. *Int. J. Obes.*, 33:S7–S10.

Moran, T. H., Ameglio, P. J., Schwartz, G. J., and McHugh, P. R. 1992. Blockade of type A, not type B, CCK receptors attenuates satiety actions of exogenous and endogenous CCK. *Am. J. Physiol.*, 262:R46–R50.

Moran, T. H., and McHugh, P. R. 1979. Cholecystokinin: Gastric emptying and feeding in *Macaca mulatta*. *Fed. Proc.*, 38:1131.

Moran, T. H., and Sakai, R. R. 2002. Food and fluid intake. In M. Gallagher and R. J. Nelson (eds.), *Handbook of Psychology*, Vol. 3., pp. 299–319. Wiley & Sons, New York.

Morgan, P. J., and Williams, L. M. 1989. Central melatonin receptors: implications for a mode of action. *Experientia*, 45:955–965.

Morin, L. P. 1988. Propylthiouracil, but not other antithyroid treatments, lengthens hamster circadian period. *Am. J. Physiol.*, 255:R1–R5.

Morin, L. P. 2013. Neuroanatomy of the extended circadian rhythm system. *Exp. Neurol.*, 243:4–20.

Morin, L. P., and Cummings, L. A. 1981. Effect of surgical or photoperiodic castration, testosterone replacement or pinealectomy on male hamster running rhythmicity. *Physiol. Behav.*, 26:825–38.

Morin, L. P., and Zucker, I. 1978. Photoperiodic regulation of copulatory behavior in the male hamster. *J. Endocrinol.*, 77:249–258.

Morin, L. P., Blanchard, J., and Moore, R. Y. 1992. Intergeniculate leaflet and suprachiasmatic nucleus organization and connections in the golden hamster. *Vis. Neurosci.*, 8:219–230.

Morin, L. P., Fitzgerald, K. M., and Zucker, I. 1977. Estradiol shortens the period of hamster circadian rhythms. *Science*, 196:305–307.

Morin, L. P., Gavin, M. L., and Ottenweller, J. E. 1986. Propylthiouracil causes phase delays and circadian period lengthening in male and female hamsters. *Am. J. Physiol.*, 250:R151–R160.

Morin, M. P., DeMarchi, P., Champagnat, J., Vanderhaeghen, J. J., Rossier, J., and Denavit-Staubie, M. 1983. Inhibitory effect of cholecystokinin octapeptide on neurons in the nucleus tractus solitarius. *Brain Res.*, 265:333–338.

Morley, J. E., Bartness, T. J., Gosnell, B. A., and Levine, A. S. 1985a. Peptidergic regulation of feeding. *Int. Rev. Neurobiol.*, 27:207–298.

Morley, J. E., Levine, A. S., Bartness, T. J., Nizielski, S. E., Shaw, M. J., and Hughes, J. J. 1985b. Species differences in the response to cholecystokinin. *Ann. N. Y. Acad. Sci.*, 448:413–416.

Morley, J. E., Levine, A. S., Yim, G. K. W., and Lowy, M. T. 1983. Opioid modulation of appetite. *Neurosci. Biobehav. Rev.*, 7:281–305.

Morrell, J. I., and Pfaff, D. W. 1978. A neuroendocrine approach to brain function: Localization of sex-steroid concentrating cells in vertebrate brains. *Am. Zool.*, 18:447–460.

Morris, J. A., Jordan, C. L., and Breedlove, S. M. 2004. Sexual differentiation of the vertebrate nervous system. *Nature Neurosci.*, 7:1034–1039.

Morris, K. A., Chang, Q., Mohler, E. G., and Gold, P. E. 2010. Age-related memory impairments due to reduced blood glucose responses to epinephrine. *Neurobiol. Aging*, doi:10.1016/j.neurobiolaging.2008.12.003

Morris, R. G. M., Garrud, P., Rawlins, JNP., and O'Keefe, J. 1982. Place navigation impaired in rats with hippocampal lesions. *Nature*, 297:681–683.

Morris, R., and Nostren-Bertrand, M. 1996. NOS and aggression. *Trends Neurosci.*, 19:277–278.

Morrison, T. R., and Melloni, R. H. 2014. The role of serotonin, vasopressin, and serotonin/vasopressin interactions in aggressive behavior. *Curr. Topics Behav. Neurosci.*, 17:189–228.

Mortola, J. F. 1997. From GnRH to SSRIs and beyond: Weighing the options for drug therapy in premenstrual syndrome. *Medscape Womens Health*, 2:3–8.

Moss, H. B., Panzak, G. L., and Tarter, R. E. 1993. Sexual functioning of male anabolic steroid abusers. *Arch. Sex. Behav.*, 22:1–12.

Moss, R. L., McCann, S. M., and Dudley, C. A. 1975. Releasing hormones and sexual behavior. *Prog. Brain Res.*, 42:37–46.

Motta, M., Fraschini, F., and Martini, L. 1967. Endocrine effects of pineal gland and of melatonin. *Proc. Soc. Exp. Biol. Med.*, 126:431–435.

Motta, M., Sterescu, N., Piva, F., and Martini, L. 1969. The participation of "short" feedback mechanisms in the control of ACTH and TSH secretion. *Acta Neurol. Psychiatr. Belg.* 69:501–507.

Moulton, D. G. 1967. Olfaction in mammals. *Am. Zool.*, 7:421–429.

Mouras, H., Stokeru, S., Moulier, V., Pelegrini-Issac, M., Rouxel, R., Grandjean, B., Glutron, D., and Bittoun, J. 2008. Activation of mirror-neuron system by erotic video clips predicts degree of induced erection: An fMRI study. *Neuroimage*, 42:1142–1150.

Moyer, K. E. 1968. Kinds of aggression and their physiological basis. *Commun. Behav. Biol.*, 2A:65–87.

Moyer, K. E. 1971. *The Physiology of Hostility*. Markham, Chicago.

Moyer, K. E. 1976. *The Psychobiology of Aggression*. Harper and Row, New York.

Mrosovsky, N. 1988a. Phase response curves for social entrainment. *J. Comp. Physiol. A*, 162:35–46.

Mrosovsky, N. 1988b. Seasonal affective disorder, hibernation, and annual cycles in animals: Chipmunks in the sky. *J. Biol. Rhythms*, 3:189–208.

Müller, M. B., Zimmermann, S., Sillaber, I., Hagemeyer, T. P., Deussing, J. M., and Timpl, P. 2003. Limbic corticotropin-releasing hormone receptor 1 mediates anxiety-related behavior and hormonal adaptation to stress. *Nat. Neurosci.*, 6:1100–1107.

Muller, W., Eising, C. M., Dijkstra, C., and Groothuis, T. G. 2002. Sex differences in yolk hormones depend on maternal social status in Leghorn chickens (*Gallus gallus domesticus*). *Proc. Roy. Soc. Lond. B*, 269:2249–2255.

Murakami, N., Marumoto, N., Nakahara, K., and Murakami, T. 1997. Daily injections of melatonin entrain circadian activity rhythms of nocturnal rats, but not diurnal chipmunks. *Brain Res.*, 75:240–243.

Murdock, G. P. 1967. *Ethnographic Atlas*. University of Pittsburgh Press, Pittsburgh.

Murphy, A. Z., and Hoffman, G. E. 2001. Distribution of gonadal steroid receptor–containing neurons in the preoptic–periaqueductal gray-brainstem pathway: A potential circuit for the initiation of male sexual behavior. *J. Comp. Neurol.*, 438:191–212.

Murphy, A. Z., Suckow, S. K., Johns, M., and Traub, R. J. 2009. Sex differences in the activation of the spinoparabrachial circuit by visceral pain. *Physiol. Behav.*, 97:205–212.

Murphy, B. E. 1997. Antiglucocorticoid therapies in major depression: A review. *Psychoneuroendocrinol.*, 22:S125–S132.

Murphy, J. V., and Miller, R. E. 1955. The effect of adrenocorticotrophic hormone (ACTH) on avoidance conditioning in the rat. *J. Comp. Physiol. Psychol.*, 48:47–49.

Murphy, M. R. 1976. Olfactory impairment, olfactory bulb removal and mammalian reproduction. In R. L. Doty (ed.), *Mammalian Olfaction, Reproductive Processes and Behavior*, pp. 95–118. Academic Press, New York.

Murphy, M. R., and Schneider, G. E. 1970. Olfactory bulb removal eliminates mating behavior in the male golden hamster. *Science*, 167:302–304.

Murton, D., and Westwood, N. J. 1980. *Avian Breeding Cycles*. Oxford University Press, New York.

Musselman, D. L., and Nemeroff, C. B. 1996. Depression and endocrine disorders: Focus on the thyroid and adrenal system. *Br. J. Psychiatry, Suppl.*, 1996:S123–128.

Muzzin, P., Eisensmith, R. C., Copeland, K. C., and Woo, S. L. C. 1996. Correction of obesity and diabetes in genetically obese mice by leptin gene therapy. *Proc. Natl. Acad. Sci. USA*, 93:14804–14808.

Myers, B. M., and Baum, M. J. 1980. Facilitation of copulatory performance in male rats by naloxone: Effects of hypophysectomy, 17 alpha-estradiol, and luteinizing hormone releasing hormone. *Pharmacol. Biochem. Behav.*, 12:365–370.

Myers, K. 1967. Morphological changes in the adrenal glands of wild rabbits. *Nature*, 213:147–150.

Naber, F. B. A., Poslawsky, I. E., van IJzendoorn, M. H., van Engeland, H., and Bakermans-Kranenburg, M. J. 2013. Brief report: Oxytocin enhances paternal sensitivity to a child with autism: a double-blind within-subject experiment with intranasally administered oxytocin. *J. Autism Dev. Disord.*, 43:224–229.

Nacmias, B., Ricca, V., Tedde, A., Mezzani, B., Rotella, C. M., and Sorbi, S. 1999. 5-HT2A receptor gene polymorphisms in anorexia nervosa and bulimia nervosa. *Neurosci. Lett.*, 277:124–136.

Nagasawa, M., Shouhei, M., Shiori, E., Nobuyo, O., Mitsuaki, O., Yasuo, S., Tatsushi, O., Kazutaka, M., and Takefumi, K.. 2015. Oxytocin-gaze positive loop and the coevolution of human-dog bonds. *Science*, 348:333–336.

Nagel, G., Ollig, D., Fuhrmann, M., Kateriya, S., Musti, A. M., Bamberg, E., and Hegemann, P. 2002. Channelrhodopsin-1: A light-gated proton channel in green algae. *Science*, 296:2395–2398.

Nagler, J. J., Bouma, J., Thorgaard, G. H., and Dauble, D. D. 2001. High incidence of a male-specific genetic marker in phenotypic female chinook salmon from the Columbia River. *Environmental Health Perspectives*, 109:67–69.

Nakahara, K., Murakami, N., Nasu, T., Kuroda, H., and Murakami, T. 1997. Individual pineal cells in chick possess photoreceptive, circadian clock and melatonin-synthesizing capacities *in vitro*. *Brain Res.*, 774:242–245.

Nakane, Y. and Yoshimura, T. 2014. Universality and diversity in the signal transduction pathway that regulates seasonal reproduction in vertebrates. *Front. Neurosci.*, 8:115.

Nakanishi, S., Inove, A., Kita, T., Nakamura, M., Chang, A. C. Y., Cohen, S. N., and Numa, S. 1979. Nucleotide sequence of cloned cDNA for bovine corticotropin-β-lipotropin precursor. *Nature*, 278:423–427.

Nakazato, M., Murakami, N., Date, Y., Kojima, M., Matsuo, H., Kangawa, K., and Matsukura, S. 2001. A role for ghrelin in the central regulation of feeding. *Nature*, 409:194–198.

Nalbandov, A. V. 1976. *Reproductive Physiology of Mammals and Birds*. W. H. Freeman, San Francisco.

Nanda, S. 1990. *Neither Man Nor Woman: The Hijras of India*. Wadsworth Publishing: Belmont, CA.

Napoli-Farris, L., Fratta, W., and Gessa, G. L. 1984. Stimulation of dopamine autoreceptors elicits 'premature ejaculation' in rats. *Pharmacol. Biochem. Behav.*, 20:69–72.

Nation, D. A., Szeto, A., Mendez, A. J., Brooks, L. G., Zaias, J., Herderick, E. E., Gonzales, J., Noller, C. M., Schneiderman, N., and McCabe, P. M. 2010. Oxytocin attenuates atherosclerosis and adipose tissue inflammation in socially isolated ApoE-/- mice. *Psychosom. Med.*, 72:376–382.

Navara, K. J., and Nelson, R. J. 2009. Prenatal environmental influences on the production of sex-specific traits in mammals. *Semin. Cell Dev. Biol.*, 20:313–319.

Navara, K. J., Workman, J. L., Oberdick, J., and Nelson, R. J. 2010. Short day lengths skew prenatal sex ratios towards males in Siberian hamsters. *Physiol. Biochem. Zool.*, 83:127–134.

Neave, N., and Wolfson, S. 2003. Testosterone, territoriality, and the "home advantage." *Physiol. Behav.*, 78:269–275.

Negrão, A. B., and Licinio, J. 2009. Anorexia nervosa and bulimia nervosa. In D. W. Pfaff, A. P. Arnold, A. M. Etgen, S. E. Fahrbach, and R. T. Rubin (eds.), *Hormones, Brain and Behavior*, 2nd ed., Vol. 5, pp. 515–530. Academic Press, New York.

Negus, N. C., and Berger, P. J. 1987. Mammalian reproductive physiology. In H. H. Genoways (ed.), *Current Mammology*, pp. 149–173. Plenum Press, New York.

Neigh, G. N., Gillespie, C. F., and Nemeroff, C. B. 2009. The neurobiological toll of child abuse and neglect. *Trauma, Violence & Abuse*, 10:389–410.

Neill, J. D. 2006. *Knobil & Neill's Physiology of Reproduction*. (3rd ed.). Elsevier Academic Press, San Diego

Nelson, E. E., and Panksepp, J. 1998. Brain substrates of infant-mother attachment: Contributions of opioids, oxytocin, and norepinephrine. *Neurosci. Biobehav. Rev.*, 22:437–452.

Nelson, R. J. 1987. Photoperiod-nonresponsive morphs: A possible variable in microtine population-density fluctuations. *Am. Nat.*, 130:350–369.

Nelson, R. J., and Chiavegatto, S. 2001. Molecular basis of aggression. *Trends Neurosci.*, 24:713–719.

Nelson, R. J., and Demas, G. E. 1996. Seasonal changes in immune function. *Q. Rev. Biol.*, 71:511–548.

Nelson, R. J., and Drazen, D. L. 1999. Melatonin mediates seasonal adjustments in immune function. *Reproduction, Nutrition, and Development*, 39:383–398.

Nelson, R. J., and Trainor, B. C. 2007. Neural mechanisms of aggression. *Nat. Rev. Neurosci.*, 8:536–546.

Nelson, R. J., and Zucker, I. 1981. Absence of extraocular photoreception in diurnal and nocturnal rodents exposed to direct sunlight. *Comp. Biochem. Physiol.*, 69A:145–148.

Nelson, R. J., Badura, L. L., and Goldman, B. D. 1990. Mechanisms of seasonal cycles of behavior. *Annu. Rev. Psychol.*, 41:81–108.

Nelson, R. J., Demas, G. E., Klein, S. L., and Kriegsfeld, L. J. 2002. *Seasonal Patterns of Stress, Immune Function, and Disease*. Cambridge University Press, New York.

Nelson, R. J., Frank, D., Smale, L., and Willoughby, S. B. 1989. Photoperiod and temperature affect reproductive and nonreproductive functions in male prairie voles (*Microtus ochrogaster*). *Biol. Reprod.*, 40:481–485.

Nelson, R. J., Kriegsfeld, L. J., Dawson, V. L., and Dawson, T. M. 1997. Role of nitric oxide in neuroendocrine regulation of physiology and behavior. *Front. Neuroendocrinol.*, 18:463–491.

Nelson, R. J., Mason, R. T., Krohmer, R. W., and Crews, D. 1987. Pinealectomy blocks vernal courtship behavior in red-sided garter snakes. *Physiol. Behav.*, 39:231–233.

Nestler, E. J., Barrot, M., DiLeone, R. J., Eisch, A. J., Gold, S. J., and Monteggia, L. M. 2002. Neurobiology of depression. *Neuron*, 34:13–25.

Netley, C. 1983. Sex chromosome abnormalities and the development of verbal and nonverbal abilities. In C. L. Ludlow and J. A. Cooper (eds.), *Genetic Aspects of Speech and Language Disorders*, pp. 171–195. Academic Press, New York.

Neufeld-Cohen, A., Tsoory, M. M., Evans, A. K., Getselter, D., Gil, S., Lowry, C. A., Vale, W., and Chen, A. 2010. A triple urocortin knockout mouse model reveals an essential role for urocortins in stress recovery. *Proc. Natl. Acad. Sci. USA*, 107:19020–19025.

Newbold, R. R., Padilla-Banks, E., Snyder, R. J., Phillips,T. M., and Jefferson, W. N. 2006. Developmental exposure to endocrine disruptors and the obesity epidemic. *Reprod. Toxicol.*, 23:290–296.

Newman, M. L., Holden, G. W., and Delville, Y. 2005. Isolation and the stress of being bullied. *J. Adolescence*, 28:343–357.

Newman, M. L., Holden, G. W., and Delville, Y. 2010. Coping with the stress of being bullied: Consequences of coping strategies among college students. *Soc. Psychol. Personality Sci.*, doi: 10.1177/1948550610386388.

Newman, S. W. 1999. The medial extended amygdala in male reproductive behavior: A node in the mammalian behavior network. *Ann. N. Y. Acad. Sci.*, 877:242–257.

Newnham, J. P., Dennett, P. M., Ferron, S. A., Tomlin, S., Legg, C., Bourne, G. L., and Rees, L. H. 1984. A study of the relationship between circulating beta-endorphin-like immunoreactivity and post-partum 'blues.' *Clin. Endocrinol.*, 20:169–177.

Newnham, J. P., Tomlin, S., Ratter, S. J., Bourne, G. L., and Rees, L. H. 1983. Endogenous opiate peptides in pregnancy. *Br. J. Obstet. Gynaecol.*, 90:535–538.

Nicholas, L., Dawkins, K., and Golden, R. N. 1998. Psychoneuroendocrinology of depression. Prolactin. *Psychiatr. Clin. North Am.*, 21:341–358.

Nicholls, T. J., Goldsmith, A. R., and Dawson, A. 1988. Photorefractoriness in birds and comparison with mammals. *Physiol. Rev.*, 68:133–176.

NIDA. 2006. *NIDA Research Report: Anabolic Steroid Abuse.* NIH Publication No. 06-3721. Revised August 2006. https://www.drugabuse.gov/sites/default/files/rrsteroids_0.pdf

Nielsen, J., and Wohlert, M. 1990. Sex chromosome abnormality found among 34,910 newborn children: Results from a 13-year incidence study in Ahras, Denmark. *Birth Defects Original Articles Series*, 26:209–223.

Nishimori, K., Young, L. J., Guo, Q., Wang, Z., Insel, T. R., and Matzuk, M. M. 1996. Oxytocin is required for nursing, but is not essential for parturition or reproductive behavior. *Proc. Natl. Acad. Sci. USA*, 93:11699–11704.

Nissen, H. W. 1929. The effects of gonadectomy, vasotomy, and injections of placental and orchic extracts on the sex behavior of the white rat. *Genet. Psychol. Monogr.*, 5:451–547.

Nitschke, J. B., Nelson, E. E., Rusch, B. D., Fox, A. S., Oakes, T. R., and Davidson, R. J. 2004. Orbitofrontal cortex tracks positive mood in mothers viewing pictures of their newborn infants. *Neuroimage*, 21:583–592.

Nonacs, R., and Cohen, L. S. 1998. Postpartum mood disorders: Diagnosis and treatment guidelines. *J. Clin. Psychiatry*, 59:S23–40.

Noriuchi, M., Kikuchi, Y., and Senoo, A. 2008. The functional neuroanatomy of maternal love: Mother's response to infant's attachment behavior. *Biol. Psych.*, 63:415–423.

Norman, A. W., and Litwack, G. 1987. *Hormones*. Academic Press, New York.

Norman, G. J., Cacioppo, J. T., Morris, J. S., Karelina, K., Malarkey, W. B., Berntson, G. G, and DeVries, A. C. 2011. Oxytocin increases autonomic cardiac control: Moderation by loneliness. *Biol. Psychol.*, 86:174–180.

Norman, G. J., Karelina, K., Morris, J. S., Zhang, N., Cochran, M., and DeVries, A. C. 2010a. Social influences on neuropathic pain and depressive like–behavior: A role for oxytocin. *Psychosom. Med.*, 72:519–526.

Norman, G. J., Zhang, N., Morris, J. S., Karelina, K., Berntson, G. G., and DeVries, A. C.

2010b. Social interaction modulates autonomic, inflammatory, and depressive-like responses to cardiac arrest and cardiopulmonary resuscitation. *Proc. Natl. Acad. Sci. USA*, 107:16342–16347.

Norman, R. L., and Spies, H. G. 1986. Cyclic function in a male macaque: Additional evidence for a lack of sexual differentiation in the physiological mechanisms that regulate the cyclic release of gonadotropin in primates. *Endocrinol.*, 118:2608–2610.

Norris, D. O. 2007. *Vertebrate Endocrinology.* (4th ed.). Elsevier Academic Press, San Diego.

Nottebohm, F. 1980a. Brain pathways for vocal learning in birds: A review of the first ten years. In J. M. Sprague and A. N. Epstein (eds.), *Progress in Psychobiology and Physiological Psychology*, Vol. 9, pp. 85–124. Academic Press, New York.

Nottebohm, F. 1980b. Testosterone triggers growth of brain vocal control nuclei in adult female canaries. *Brain Res.*, 189:429–436. Nottebohm, F. 1981. A brain for all seasons: cyclical anatomical changes in song control nuclei of the canary brain. *Science*, 214:1368–1370.

Nottebohm, F. 1989. From bird song to neurogenesis. *Sci. Am.*, 260:74–79.

Nottebohm, F. 2005. The neural basis of birdsong. *PLOS Biol.*, 3:759–761.

Novotny, M. V., Jemiolo, B., Wiesler, D., Ma, W. Harvey, S., Xu, F., Xie, T. M., and Carmack, M. 1999. A unique urinary constituent, 6-hydroxy-6-methyl-3-heptanone, is a pheromone that accelerates puberty in female mice. *Chem. Biol.*, 6:377–383.

Nowak, R. M., and Paradiso, J. L. 1983. *Walker's Mammals of the World.* Johns Hopkins University Press, Baltimore.

Nowak, R., Keller, M. and Levy, F. 2011. Mother–young relationships in sheep: A model for a multidisciplinary approach of the study of attachment in mammals. *J. Neuroendocrinol.*, 23:1042–1053.

Numan, M. 1974. Medial preoptic area and maternal behavior in the female rat. *J. Comp. Physiol. Psychol.*, 87:746–759.

Numan, M. 1990. Neural control of maternal behavior. In N. A. Krasnegor and R. S. Bridges (eds.), *Mammalian Parenting*, pp. 231–259. Oxford University Press, Oxford.

Numan, M. and Young, L. J. 2016. Neural mechanisms of mother-infant bonding and pair bonding: Similarities, differences, and broader implications. *Horm. Behav.*, 77:98–112.

Numan, M., and Insel, T. R. 2003. *The Neurobiology of Parental Behavior.* Springer-Verlag, New York.

Numan, M., and Sheehan, T. P. 1997. Neuroanatomical circuitry for mammalian maternal behavior. *Ann. N. Y. Acad. Sci.*, 807:101–125.

Numan, M., and Stolzenberg, D. S. 2009. Medial preoptic area interactions with dopamine neural systems in the control of the onset and maintenance of maternal behavior in rats. *Front. Neuroendocrinol.*, 30:46–64.

Numan, M., Corodimas, K. P., Numan, M. J., Factor, E. M., and Piers, W. D. 1988. Axon-sparing lesions of the preoptic region and substantia innominata disrupt maternal behavior in rats. *Behav. Neurosci.*, 102:381–396.

Numan, M., Fleming, A. S., and Lévy, F. 2006. Maternal behavior. In J. D. Neill (ed.), Knobil and Neill's *Physiology of Reproduction*, (3rd ed.), pp. 1921–1993. Elsevier, New York.

Nunez, A. A., Siegel, L. I., and Wade, G. N. 1980. Central effects of testosterone on food intake in male rats. *Physiol. Behav.*, 24:469–472.

Nunez, J. L., Jurgens, H. A., and Juraska, J. M. 2000. Androgens reduce cell death in the developing rat visual cortex. *Brain Res./ Developmental Brain Res.*, 125:83–88.

Nunez, J. L., Lauschke, D. M., and Juraska, J. M. 2001. Cell death in the development of the posterior cortex in male and female rats. *J. Comp. Neurol.*, 436:32–41.

Nutsch, V. L., Will, R. G., Hattori, T., Tobiansky, D. J., and Dominguez, J. M. 2014. Sexual experience influences mating-induced activity in nitric oxide synthase-containing neurons in the medial preoptic area. *Neurosci. Lett.*, 579:92–96.

Nyberg, S., Bäckström, T., Zingmark, E., Purdy, R. H., and Poromaa, I. S. 2007. Allopregnanolone decrease with symptom improvement during placebo and gonadotropin-releasing hormone agonist treatment in women with severe premenstrual syndrome. *Gynecol. Endocrinol.*, 23:257–266.

Nyby, J. G. 2008. Reflexive testosterone release: A model system for studying the nongenomic effects of testosterone upon male behavior. *Front. Neuroendocrinol.*, 29:199–210.

O'Brien, P. M., Bäckström, T., Brown, C., Dennerstein, L., Endicott, J., Epperson, C. N., Eriksson, E., et al. 2011. Towards a consensus on diagnostic criteria, measurement and trial design of the premenstrual disorders: the ISPMD Montreal consensus. *Arch. Womens Ment. Health*, 14:13–21.

O'Brien, J. T., Lloyd, A., McKeith, I., Gholkar, A., and Ferrier, N. 2004. A longitudinal study of hippocampal volume, cortisol levels, and cognition in older depressed subjects. *Am. J. Psychol.*, 161, 2081–2090.

O'Brien, P. M. S., Craven, D., Selby, S., and Symonds, E. 1979. Treatment of premenstrual syndrome by spironolactone. *Br. J. Obstet. Gynaecol.*, 86:142–147.

O'Carroll, R., Shapiro, C., and Bancroft, J. 1985. Androgens, behaviour and nocturnal erection in hypogonadal men: The effects of varying the replacement doses. *Clin. Endocrinol.*, 23:527–538.

O'Connell, L. A. and Hofmann, H. A. 2011. The vertebrate mesolimbic reward system and social behavior network: A comparative synthesis. *J. Comp. Neurol.*, 519:3599–3639.

O'Connor, D. B., Archer, J., Hair, W. M., and Wu, F. C. W. 2002. Exogenous testosterone, aggression, and mood in eugonadal and hypogonadal men. *Physiol. Behav.*, 75:557–566.

O'Hara, M. W. and McCabe, J. E. 2013. Postpartum depression: Current status and future directions. *Annu. Rev. Clin. Psychol.*, 9:379–407.

O'Hara, M. W., and Zekoski, E. M. 1988. Postpartum depression: A comprehensive review. In R. Kumar and I. F. Brockington (eds.), *Motherhood and Mental Illness 2: Causes and Consequences*, pp. 17–63. Boston, Wright.

O'Hara, M. W., Schlechte, J. A., Lewis, D. A., and Wright, E. J. 1991. Prospective study of postpartum blues. *Arch. Gen. Psychiatry*, 48:801–806.

O'Keefe, J., and Nadel, L. 1978. *The Hippocampus as a Cognitive Map.* Clarendon: Oxford.

O'Malley, B. O. 1989. Did eucaryotic steroid receptors evolve from intracrine gene regulators? *Endocrinol.*, 125:1119–1120.

O'Malley, B. W. 1995. Thirty years of steroid hormone action: personal recollections of an investigator. *Steroids*, 60:490–498.

O'Neil, M. F., Means, L. W., Poole, M. C., and Hamm, R. J. 1996. Estrogen affects performance of ovariectomized rats in a two-choice water-escape working memory task. *Psychoneuroendocrinol.*, 21:51–65.

Oei, N. Y. L., Elzinga, B. M., Wolf, O. T., de Ruiter, M. B., Damoiseaux, J. S., Kuijer, J. P. A., Veltman, D. J., Scheltens, P., and Rombouts, S. A. R. B. 2007. Glucocorticoids decrease hippocampal and prefrontal activation during declarative memory retrieval in young men. *Brain Imaging Behav.*, 1:31–41.

Oesterhelt, D., and Stoeckenius, W. 1971. Rhodopsin-like protein from the purple membrane of *Halobacterium halobium. Nat. New Biol.*, 233:149–152.

Office of Technology Assessment, 1991. *Biological Rhythms: Implications for the Worker* (OTA-BA-463). Government Printing Office, Washington, D.C.

Ogawa, S., Chan, J., Chester, A. E., Gustafsson, J.-Å., Korach, K. S., and Pfaff, D. W. 1999. Survival of reproductive behaviors in estrogen receptor β gene-deficient (βERKO) male and female mice. *Proc. Natl. Acad. Sci. USA*, 96:12887–12892.

Ogawa, S., Chester, A. E., Hewitt, S. C., Walker, V. R., Gustafsson, J.-Å., Smithies, O., Korach, K. S., and Pfaff, D. W. 2000. Abolition of male sexual behaviors in mice lacking estrogen receptors α and β (αβERKO). *Proc. Natl. Acad. Sci. USA*, 97:14737–14741.

Ogawa, S., Gordan, J. D., Taylor, J., Lubahn, D., Korach, K., and Pfaff, D. W. 1996a. Reproductive functions illustrating direct and indirect effects of genes on behavior. *Horm. Behav.*, 30:487–494.

Ogawa, S., Lubahn, D. B., Korach, K. S., and Pfaff, D. 1995. Behavioral characteristics of transgenic estrogen receptor knockout male mice: Sexual, aggressive, and open-field behaviors. *Endocr. Soc. Abstr.*, 77:133.

Ogawa, S., Lubahn, D. B., Korach, K. S., and Pfaff, D. W. 1997. Behavioral effects of estrogen receptor gene disruption in male mice. *Proc. Natl. Acad. Sci. USA*, 94:1476–1481.

Ohmura, Y., Yamaguchi, T., Izumi, T., Matsumoto, M., and Yoshioka, M. 2008. Corticotropin releasing factor in the median raphe nucleus is involved in the retrieval of fear memory in rats. *Eur. J. Pharmacol.*, 584:357–360.

Oitzl, M. S., and de Kloet, E. R. 1992. Selective corticosteroid antagonists modulate specific aspects of spatial orientation learning. *Behav. Neurosci.*, 108:62–71.

Oitzl, M. S., de Kloet, E. R., Joels, M., and Cole, T. J. 1998. Spatial learning deficits in mice with a targeted glucocorticoid receptor gene disruption. *Eur. J. Neurosci.*, 9:2284–2296.

Okamoto, M., Hojo, Y., Inoue, K., Matsui, T., Kawato, S., McEwen, B. S., and Soya, H. 2012. Mild exercise increases dihydrotestosterone in hippocampus providing evidence for androgenic mediation of neurogenesis. *PNAS*, 109:13100–13105.

Okuhata, S., and Saito, N. 1987. Synaptic connections of thalamo-cerebral vocal control nuclei of the canary. *Brain Res. Bull.*, 18:35–44.

Oliveira, R. F., Ros, A. F. H., and Goncalves, D. M. 2005. Intra-sexual variation in male reproduction in teleost fish: A comparative approach. *Horm. Behav.*, 48:430–439.

Oliveras, D., and Novak, M. 1986. A comparison of paternal behavior in the meadow vole, *Microtus pennsylvanicus*, the pine vole, *M. pinetorum*, and the prairie vole, *M. ochrogaster. Anim. Behav.*, 34:519–529.

Olivier, B., and Mos, J. 1992. Rodent models of aggressive behavior and serotonergic drugs. *Prog. Neuropsychopharmacol. Biol. Psychiatry*, 16:847–870.

Olivier, B., Mos, J.,van Oorschot, R., and Hen, R. 1995. Serotonin receptors and animal models of aggressive behavior. *Pharmacopsychiatry*, 28:80–90.

Olsen, K. L. 1992. Genetic influences on sexual behavior differentiation. In A. A. Gerall, H. Moltz, and I. L. Ward (eds.), *Sexual Differentiation. Handbook of Behavioral Neurobiology*, Vol. 11, pp. 1–40. Plenum, New York.

Olton, D. S., and Papas, B. C. 1979. Spatial memory and hippocampal function. *Neuropsychologia*, 17:669–682.

Olton, D. S., and Samuelson, R. J. 1976. Remembrance of places passed: Spatial memory in rats. *J. Exp. Psychol.: Anim. Behav. Processes*, 2:97–116.

Olweus, D. 1983. Testosterone in the development of antisocial behavior in adolescents. In K. T. VanDusen and S. A. Mednick (eds.), *Prospective Studies of Crime and Delinquency*, pp. 475–497. Kluwer-Nijhoff, Boston.

Orchard, J. W., and Best, J. P. 1994. Test violent offenders for anabolic steroid use. *Med. J. Aust.*, 161:232.

Orchinik, M., Licht, P., and Crews, D. 1988. Plasma steroid concentrations change in response to sexual behavior in *Bufo marinus. Horm. Behav.*, 22:338–350.

Oring, L. W., Fivizzani, A. J., and El Halawani, M. E. 1986a. Changes in plasma prolactin associated with laying and hatching in the Spotted Sandpiper. *Auk*, 103:820–822.

Oring, L. W., Fivizzani, A. J., El Halawani, M. E., and Goldsmith, A. 1986b. Seasonal changes in prolactin and luteinizing hormone in the polyandrous Spotted Sandpiper, *Actitis macularia. Gen. Comp. Endocrinol.*, 62:394–403.

Orpen, G., and Fleming, A. S. 1987. Experience with pups sustains maternal responding in postpartum rats. *Physiol. Behav.*, 40:47–54.

Ortiz-Tudela, E., Mteyrek, A., Ballesta, A., Innominato, P. F., and Levi, F. 2013. Cancer chronotherapeutics: experimental, theoretical, and clinical aspects. *Handb. Exp. Pharmacol.*, 217:261–288.

Osburn, D.M., Pearson-Leary, J., & McNay, E.C. 2015. The neuroenergetics of stress hormones ain the hippocampus and implications for memory. *Frontiers in Neuroscience*, 9:164. DOI 3389/fnins.2015.00164.

Osburn, O. and Olefsky, J. M. 2012. The cellular and signalling networks linking the immune system and metabolism in disease. *Nat. Med.*, 18:363—374.

Osmanovic, J., Plaschke, K., Salkovic-Petrisic, M., Grunblatt, E., Riederer, P., and Hoyer, S. 2010. Chronic exogenous corticosterone administration generates an insulin-resistant brain state in rats. *Stress*, 13:123–131.

Ostermann, K. 1956. Zur Aktivität heimischer Muriden und Gliriden. *Zool. Jahrbuch Abteil. Alle. Zool. Physiol.*, 66:355–375.

OTA, Office of Technology Assessment. 1991. See: http://www.fas.org/ota/reports/9108.pdf

Ottenweller, J. E., Tapp, W. N., Pitman, D. L., and Natelson, B. H. 1987. Adrenal, thyroid, and testicular hormone rhythms in male golden hamsters on long and short days. *Amer. J. Physiol.* 253:R321–328.

Ottinger, M. A., and vom Saal, F. 2002. Impacts of environmental endocrine disruptors on sexual differentiation in birds and mammals. In D. W. Pfaff, A. P. Arnold, A. M. Etgen, S. E. Fahrbach, and R. T. Rubin (eds.), *Hormones, Brain, and Behavior*, Vol. 4, pp. 325–384. Academic Press, New York.

Packard, M. G. 2009. Anxiety, cognition, and habit: A multiple memory systems perspective. *Brain Res.*, 1293:121–128.

Packard, M. G., and Teather, L. A. 1997. Intra-hipppocampal estradiol infusion enhances memoy in ovariectomized rats. *Neuroreport*, 29:3009–3013.

Packard, M. G., Cornell, A. H., and Alexander, G. M. 1997. Rewarding affective properties of intra-nucleus accumbens injections of testosterone. *Behav. Neurosci.*, 111:219–224.

Packard, M. G., Kohlmaier, J. R., and Alexander, G. M. 1996. Post-training intra-hippocampal estradiol injections enhance spatial memory in male rats: Interaction with cholinergic systems. *Behav. Neurosci.*, 110:626–632.

Paech, K., Webb, P., Kuiper, G., Nilsson, S., Gustafsson, J. A., Kushner, P. J., and Scanlan, T. S. 1997. Differential ligand activation of estrogen receptors ERalpha and ERbeta at AP1 sites. *Science*, 277:1508–1510.

Paglietti, E., Pellegrini-Quarantotti, B., Mereu, G., Gessa, G. 1978. Apomorphine and L-dopa lower ejaculatory threshold in the male rat. *Physiol. Behav.*, 20:559–562.

Pajarinen, J. Laippala, P., Penttila, A., and Karhunen, P. J. 1997. Incidence of disorders of spermatogenesis in middle aged Finnish men, 1981–91: Two necropsy series. *Br. Med. J.*, 314:13–18.

Palfi, S., Ungurean, A., and Vecsei, L. 1997. Basilar artery occlusion associated with anabolic steroid abuse in a 17-year-old bodybuilder. *Eur. Neurol.*, 37:190–191.

Palmer, J. D. 1976. *An Introduction to Biological Rhythms.* Academic Press, New York.

Palmer, J. D. 1990. The rhythmic lives of crabs. *Bioscience*, 40:352–357.

Panay, N., Al-Azzawi, F., Bouchard, C., Davis, S. R., Eden, J., Lodhi, I., Rees, M. et al. 2010. Testosterone treatment of HSDD in naturally menopausal women: the ADORE study. *Climacteric*, 13:121–131.

Panda, S., Provencio, I., Tu, D. C., Pires, S. S., Rollag, M. D., Castrucci, A. M., Pletcher, M. T., et al. 2003. Melanopsin is required for non-image-forming photic responses in blind mice. *Science*, 301:525–527.

Panda, S., Sato, T. K., Castrucci, A. M., Rollag, M. D., DeGrip, W. J., Hogenesch, J. B., Provencio, I., and Kay, S. A. 2002. Melanopsin (Opn4) requirement for normal light-induced circadian phase shifting. *Science*, 298:2213–2216.

Panksepp, J. 2005. Affective Neuroscience: The Foundations of Human and Animal Emotions. Oxford University Press, New York.

Panksepp, J., Herman, B. H., Vilberg, T., Bishop, P., and DeEskinazi, F. G. 1980a.

Endogenous opioids and social behavior. *Neurosci. Biobehav. Rev.*, 4:473–487.

Panksepp, J., Meeker, R., and Bean, N. J. 1980b. The neurochemical control of crying. *Pharmacol. Biochem. Behav.*, 12:437–443.

Panksepp, J., Nelson, E., and Bekkedal, M. 1997. Brain systems for the mediation of social separation-distress and social-reward: Evolutionary antecedents and neuropeptide intermediaries. *Ann. N. Y. Acad. Sci.*, 807:78–100.

Panzica, G. C., Viglietti-Panzica, C., and Balthazart, J. 1996. The sexually-dimorphic medial preoptic nucleus of quail: A key brain area mediating steroid action on male sexual behavior. *Front. Neuroendocrinol.*, 17:51–125.

Parada, M., King, S., Li, M., and Fleming, A. S. 2008. The roles of accumbal dopamine D1 and D2 receptors in maternal memory in rats. *Behav. Neurosci.*, 122:368–376.

Parada, M., Sparks, L. M., Censi, S., and Pfaus, J. G. 2014. Clitoral anesthesia disrupts paced copulation in the female rat. *Physiol. Behav.*, 123:180–186.

Paredes, P. 2003. Medial preoptic area/anterior hypothalamus and sexual motivation. *Scand. J. Psych.*, 44:203–212.

Paredes, R. G. 2009. Evaluating the neurobiology of sexual reward. *ILAR J.*, 50:15–27.

Park, C. R. 2001. Cognitive effects of insulin in the central nervous system. *Neuroscience and Biobehavioral Rev.*, 25:311–323.

Park, C. R., Zoladz, P. R., Conrad, C. D., Fleshner, M., and Diamond, D. M. 2008. Acute predator stress impairs the consolidation and retrieval of hippocampus-dependent memory in male and female rats. *Learn. Mem.*, 15:271–280.

Park, J. H., Bonthuis, P., Ding, A., Rais, S., and Rissman, E. F. 2009. Androgen- and estrogen-independent regulation of copulatory behavior following castration in male B6D2F1 mice. *Horm. Behav.*, 56:254–263.

Park, J. H., Paul, M. J., Butler, M. P., Villa, P., Burke, M., Kim, D. P., Routman, D. M., Schoomer, E. E., and Zucker, I. 2007. Short duration testosterone infusions maintain male sex behavior in Syrian hamsters. *Horm. Behav.*, 52:169–176.

Park, J. H., Takasu, N., Alvarez, M. I., Clark, K., Aimaq, R., and Zucker, I. 2004. Long-term persistence of male copulatory behavior in castrated and photo-inhibited Siberian hamsters. *Horm. Behav.*, 45:214–221.

Parker, K. J., and Lee, T. M. 2003. Female meadow voles (*Microtus pennsylvanicus*) demonstrate same-sex partner preferences. *J. Comp. Psychol.*, 117:283–289.

Parker, K. J., Phillips, K. M., Kinney, L. F., and Lee, T. M. 2001. Day length and socio-sexual cohabitation alter central oxytocin receptor binding in female meadow voles (*Microtus pennsylvanicus*). *Behav. Neurosci.*, 115:1349–1356.

Parlee, M. B. 1980. Positive changes in moods and activation levels during the menstrual cycle in experimentally naive subjects. In A. J. Dan, E. A. Graham, C. P. Beech (eds.), *The Menstrual Cycle*, Vol. 1, pp. 247–263. Springer, New York.

Parlee, M. B. 1982. Changes in moods and activation levels during the menstrual cycle. *Psychol. Women Q.*, 7:119–131.

Parrilla-Carrero, J., Figueroa, O., Lugo, A., García-Sosa, R., Brito-Vargas, P., Cruz, B., Rivera, M., and Barreto-Estrada, J. L. 2009. The anabolic steroids testosterone proprionate and nandrolone, but not 17α-methyltestosterone, induce conditioned place preference in adult mice. *Drug Alcohol Depend.*, 100:122–127.

Parry, B. L., and Berga, S. l. 2002. Premenstrual dysphoric disorder. In D. W. Pfaff, A. P. Arnold, A. M. Etgen, S. E. Fahrbach, and R. T. Rubin (eds.), *Hormones, Brain and Behavior*, Vol. 5, pp. 531–552. Academic Press, New York.

Parsey, R. V., Oquendo, M. A., Simpson, N. R., Ogden, R. T., Van Heertum, R., Arango, V., and Mann, J. J. 2002. Effects of sex, age, and aggressive traits in man on brain serotonin 5-HT1A receptor binding potential measured by PET using [C-11]WAY-100635. *Brain Res.*, 954:173–182.

Parsons, B., Rainbow, T. C., Pfaff, D. W., and McEwen, B. S. 1981. Oestradiol, sexual receptivity and cytosol progestin receptors in rat hypothalamus. *Nature*, 292:58–59.

Parsons, M. W., and Gold, P. E. 1992. Glucose enhancement of memory in elderly humans: An inverted-U dose-response curve. *Neurobiol. Aging*, 13:401–404.

Pärssinen, M., Kujala, U., and Vartiainen, E. 2000a. Increased premature mortality of competitive powerlifters suspected to have used anabolic agents. *International J. Sports Med.*, 21:225–227.

Pärssinen, M., Kujala, U., Vartiainen, E., Sarna, S., and Seppala, T. 2000b. Increased premature mortality of competitive powerlifters suspected to have used anabolic agents. *Int. J. Sports Med.*, 21:225–227.

Pasterski, V., Zucker, K. J., Hindmarsh, P. C., Hughes, I. A., Acerini, C., Spencer, D., Neufeld, S., and Hines, M. 2015. Increased cross-gender identification independent of gender role behavior in girls with congenital adrenal hyperplasia: Results from a standardized assessment of 4- to 11-year-old children. *Arch. Sex. Behav.*, 44:1363–1375.

Patton, D. F. and Mistlberger, R. E. 2013. Circadian adaptations to meal timing: neuroendocrine mechanisms. *Front. Neurosci.*, 7:185.

Paukner, A., and Suomi, S. J. 2008. Sex differences in play behavior in juvenile tufted capuchin monkeys (*Cebus paella*). *Primates*, 49:288–291.

Paul, M. J., Zucker, I., and Schwartz, W. J. 2008. Tracking the seasons: The internal calendars of vertebrates. *Philos. Trans. R. Soc. Lond. B Biol. Sci.*, 363:341–361.

Payne, A. P., and Swanson, H. H. 1972. The effect of sex hormones on the agonistic behavior of the male golden hamster (*Mesocricetus auratus* Waterhouse). *Physiol. Behav.*, 8:687–691.

Pearlstein, T. 2016. Treatment of premenstrual dysphoric disorder: Therapeutic challenges. *Expert Rev. Clin. Pharmacol.*, doi: 10.1586/17512433.2016.1142371.

Pearlstein, T., Rosen, K., and Stone, A. B. 1997. Mood disorders and menopause. *Endocrinol. Metab. Clin. North Am.*, 26:279–294.

Peck, J. W., and Novin, D. 1971. Evidence that osmoreceptors mediating drinking in rabbits are in the lateral preoptic area. *J. Comp. Physiol. Psychol.*, 74:134–147.

Pecoraro, N., Reyes, F., Gomez, F., Bhargava, A., and Dallman, M. F. 2004. Chronic stress promotes palatable feeding, which reduces signs of stress: Feedforward and feedback effects of chronic stress. *Endocrinol.*, 145:3754–3762.

Pedersen, C. A. 1997. Oxytocin control of maternal behavior: Regulation by sex steroids and offspring stimuli. *Ann. N. Y. Acad. Sci.*, 807:126–145.

Pedersen, C. A., and Prange, A. J. 1979. Induction of maternal behavior in virgin rats after intracerebroventricular administration of oxytocin. *Proc. Natl. Acad. Sci. USA*, 76:6661–6665.

Pedersen, C. A., Ascher, J. A., Monroe, Y. L., and Prange, A. J. 1982. Oxytocin induces maternal behavior in virgin female rats. *Science*, 216:648–649.

Pedersen, C. A., Vadlamudi, S. V., Boccia, M. L., and Amico, J. A. 2006. Maternal behavior deficits in nulliparous oxytocin knockout mice. *Genes Brain Behav.*, 5:274–281.

Pedersen, P. E., and Blass, E. M. 1982. Prenatal and postnatal determinants of the first suckling episode in albino rats. *Dev. Psychobiol.*, 15:349–355.

Peele, D. B., and Vincent, A. 1989. Strategies for assessing learning and memory, 1978–1987:A comparison of behavioral toxicology, psychopharmacology, and neurobiology. *Neurosci. Biobehav. Rev.*, 13:33–38.

Pelletier, J., and Ortavant, R. 1975. Photoperiodic control of LH release in the ram. *Acta Endocrinol.*, 78:442–450.

Pellis, S. M., Field, E. F., Smith, L. K., and Pellis, V. C. 1997. Multiple differences in the play fighting of male and female rats. Implications for the causes and functions of play. *Neurosci. Biobehav. Rev.*, 21:105–20.

Peng, Z. W., Chen, X. G., and Wei, Z. 2007. Cryptochrome1 may be a candidate gene of schizophrenia. *Med. Hypotheses*, 69:849–851.

Perachio, A. A. 1978. Hypothalamic regulation of behavioural and hormonal aspects of aggression and sexual performance. In D. J. Chivers and J. Herbert (eds.), *Recent Advances in Primatology*, Vol. 1, pp. 549–565. Academic Press, New York.

Perachio, A. A., Alexander, M., and Marr, L. D. 1973. Hormonal and social factors affecting evoked sexual behavior in rhesus monkeys. *Am. J. Phys. Anthropol.*, 38:227–232.

Perachio, A. A., Marr, L. D., and Alexander, M. 1979. Sexual behavior in male rhesus monkeys elicited by electrical stimulation of preoptic and hypothalamic areas. *Brain Res.*, 177:127–144.

Perkins, A., Fitzgerald, J. A., and Moss, G. E. 1995. A comparison of LH secretion and brain estradiol receptors in heterosexual and homosexual rams and female sheep. *Horm. Behav.*, 29:31–41.

Perkins, M. S., Perkins, M. N., and Hitt, J. C. 1980. Effects of stimulus female on sexual behavior of male rats given olfactory tubercle and corticomedial amygdaloid lesions. *Physiol. Behav.*, 25:495–500.

Peroulakis, M. E., Goldman, B. D., and Forger, N. G. 2002. Perineal muscles and motoneurons are sexually monomorphic in the naked mole-rat (*Heterocephalus glaber*). *J. Neurobiol.*, 51:33–42.

Perras, B., Droste, C., Born, J., Fehm, H. L., and Pietrowsky, R. 1997. Verbal memory after three months of intranasal vasopressin in healthy old humans. *Psychoneuroendocrinol.*, 22:387–396.

Perry, A. N., and Grober, M. S. 2003. A model for social control of sex change: Interactions of behavior, neuropeptides, glucocorticoids, and sex steroids. *Horm. Behav.*, 43:31–38.

Perry, P. J., Andersen, K. H., and Yates, W. R. 1990. Illicit anabolic steroid use in athletes. A case series analysis. *Am. J. Sports Med.*, 18:422–428.

Persengiev, S., Marinova, C., and Patchev, V. 1991a. Steroid hormone receptors in the thymus: A site of immunomodulatory action of melatonin. *International J. Biochemistry*, 23:1483–1485.

Persengiev, S., Patchev, V., and Velev, B. 1991b. Melatonin effects on thymus steroid receptors in the course of primary antibody responses: Significance of circulating glucocorticoid levels. *International J. Biochemistry*, 23:1487–1489.

Persky, H., Dreisbach, L., Miller, W. R., O'Brien, C. P., Khan, M. A., Lief, H. I., Charney, N., and Straus, M. 1982. The relation of plasma androgen levels to sexual behaviors and attitudes of women. *Psychosom. Med.*, 44:305–319.

Persky, H., O'Brien, C. P., Fine, E., Howard, W. J., Khan, M. A., and Beck, R. W. 1977. The effect of alcohol and smoking on testosterone function and aggression in chronic alcoholics. *Am. J. Psychiatry*, 134:621–625.

Pertwee, R. G. 1997. Pharmacology of cannabinoid CB1 and CV2 receptors. *Pharmacol. Ther.*, 74:129–180.

Peters, K. D., and Wood, R. I. 2004. Androgen overdose: Behavioral and physiologic effects of testosterone infusion. *Neuroscience*, 130:971–981.

Peterson, R.S, Yarram, L., Schlinger, B.A. & Saldanha, C.J. 2005. Aromatase is pre-synaptic and sexually dimorphic in the adult zebra finch. *Proceedings of the Royal Society B: Biological Sciences*. 272: 2089–2096.

Pfaff, D. W. 1980. *Estrogens and Brain Function*. Springer-Verlag, New York.

Pfaff, D. W., and Pfaffmann, C. 1969. Olfactory and hormonal influences on the basal forebrain of the male rat. *Brain Res.*, 15:137–156.

Pfaff, D. W., and Silver, R. 2007. Gene-hormone-environment interactions in the regulation of aggressive responses: Elegant analysis of complex behavior. *Sci. STKE* 2007, pe55.

Pfaus, J. G. 1996. Homologies of animal and human sexual behaviors. *Horm. Behav.*, 30:187–200.

Pfaus, J. G., and Gorzalka, B. B. 1987. Opioids and sexual behavior. *Neurosci. Biobehav. Rev.* 11:1–34.

Pfaus, J. G., and Heeb, M. M. 1997. Implications of immediate-early gene induction in the brain following sexual stimulation of female and male rodents. *Brain Res. Bull.*, 44:397–407.

Pfaus, J. G., and Phillips, A. G. 1991. Role of dopamine in anticipatory and consummatory aspects of sexual behavior in the male rat. *Behav. Neurosci.*, 105:727–743.

Pfaus, J. G., Kippin, T. E., and Coria-Avila, G. 2003. What can animal models tell us about human sexual response? *Ann. Rev. Sex Res.*, 14:1–63.

Pfeiffer, C. A. 1935. Origin of functional differences between male and female hypophyses. *Proc. Soc. Exp. Biol. Med.*, 32:603–605.

Pfeiffer, C. A. 1936. Sexual differences of the hypophysis and their determination by the gonads. *Am. J. Anat.*, 58:195–225.

Phoenix, C. H. 1973. Sexual behavior in rhesus monkeys after vasectomy. *Science*, 179:493–494.

Phoenix, C. H. 1974. Effect of dihydrotestosterone on sexual behavior of castrated male rhesus monkeys. *Physiol. Behav.*, 12:1045–1055.

Phoenix, C. H. 2009. Organizing action of prenatally administered testosterone propionate on the tissues mediating mating behavior in the female guinea pig. *Horm. Behav.*, 55:566.

Phoenix, C. H., Goy, R. W., and Resko, J. A. 1968. Psychosexual differentiation as a function of androgenic stimulation. In M. Diamond (ed.), *Perspectives in Reproduction and Sexual Behavior*, pp. 215–246. Indiana University Press, Bloomington, IN.

Phoenix, C. H., Goy, R. W., Gerall, A. A., and Young, W. C. 1959. Organizing action of prenatally administered testosterone propionate on the tissues mediating mating behavior in the female guinea pig. *Endocrinol.*, 65:369–382.

Pickard, G. E. 1982. The afferent connections of the suprachiasmatic nucleus of the golden hamster with emphasis on the retinohypothalamic projection. *J. Comp. Neurol.,* 211:65–83.

Pickard, G. E., and Silverman, A. J. 1981. Direct retinal projections to the hypothalamus, piriform cortex and accessory optic nuclei in the golden hamster as demonstrated by a sensitive anterograde horseradish peroxidase technique. *J. Comp. Neurol.,* 196:155–172.

Piekarski, D. J., Routman, D. M., Schoomer, E. E., Driscoll, J. R., Park, J. H., Butler, M. P., and Zucker, I. 2009. Infrequent low dose testosterone treatment maintains male sexual behavior in Syrian hamsters. *Horm. Behav.,* 55:182–189.

Piekarski, D. J., Zhao, S. Jennings, K. J., Iwasa, T., Legan, S. J., Mikkelsen, J. D., Tsutsui, K., and Kriegsfeld, L. J. 2013. Gonadotropin-inhibitory hormone reduces sexual motivation but not lordosis behavior in female Syrian hamsters (*Mesocricetus auratus*). *Horm. Behav.,* 64:501–510.

Pierce, J. G. 1988. Gonadotropins: Chemistry and biosynthesis. In E. Knobil and J. D. Neill (eds.), *The Physiology of Reproduction,* pp. 1335–1348. Raven Press, New York.

Piet, R., Fraissenon, A., Boehm, U., and Herbison, A. E. 2015. Estrogen permits vasopressin signaling in preoptic kisspeptin neurons in the female mouse. *J. Neurosci.,* 35:6881–6892.

Piggins, H. D. and Cutler, D. J. 2003. The roles of vasoactive intestinal polypeptide in the mammalian circadian clock. *J. Endocrinol.,* 177:7–15.

Pike, T. W., and Petrie, M. 2003. Potential mechanisms of avian sex manipulation. *Biological Rev.,* 78:553–574.

Pinckard, K. L., Stellflug, J., Resko, J. A., Roselli, C. E., and Stormshak, F. 2000. Review: Brain aromatization and other factors affecting male reproductive behavior with emphasis on the sexual orientation of rams. *Domest. Anim. Endocrinol.,* 18:83–96.

Pinhas-Hamiel, O., and Zeitler, P. 2005. The global spread of type 2 diabetes mellitus in children and adolescents. *J. Pediatr.,* 146:693–700.

Pinxten, R., de Ridder, E., Arckens, L., Darras, V. M., and Eens, M. 2007. Plasma testosterone levels of male European starlings (*Sturnus vulgaris*) during the breeding cycle in relation to song and paternal care. *Behaviour,* 144:393–410.

Pinxten, R., De Ridder, E., De Cock, M., and Eens, M. 2003. Castration does not decrease nonreproductive aggression in yearling male European starlings (*Sturnus vulgaris*). *Horm. Behav.,* 43:394–401.

Pittendrigh, C. S. 1981. Circadian systems: Entrainment. *Handbook of Behavioral Neurobiology,* Vol. 4, pp. 95–124.

Pittendrigh, C. S., and Daan, S. 1976. A functional analysis of circadian pacemakers in nocturnal rodents. IV. Entrainment: Pacemaker as clock. *J. Comp. Physiol.,* 106:291–331.

Pitts, M., Smith, A., Mitchell, A., and Patel, S. 2006. *Private Lives: A Report on the Health and Wellbeing of GLBTI Australians.* Australian Research Centre in Sex, Health and Society, La Trobe University, Melbourne.

Plant, T. M. 1981. Time courses of concentrations of circulating gonadotropin, prolactin, testosterone, and cortisol in adult male rhesus monkeys (*Macaca mulatta*) throughout the 24 h light-dark cycle. *Biol. Reprod.,* 25:244–252.

Platt, J. R. 1964. Strong inference. *Science,* 146:347–353.

Plaud, J. J., and Martini, R. 1999. The respondent conditioning of male sexual arousal. *Behav. Modification,* 23:254–268.

Plautz, J. D., Kaneko, M., Hall, J. C., and Kay, S. A. 1997. Independent photoreceptive circadian clocks throughout *Drosophila. Science,* 278:1632–1635.

Pliner, P., and Fleming, A. S. 1983. Food intake, body weight, and sweetness preferences over the menstrual cycle in humans. *Physiol. Behav.,* 30:663–666.

Plotka, E. D., Seal, U. S., Letellier, M. A., Verme, L. J., and Ozoga, J. J. 1984. Early effects of pinealectomy on LH and testosterone secretion in white-tailed deer. *J. Endocrinol.,* 103:1–7.

Plotsky, P. M., Owens, M. J., and Nemeroff, C. B. 1998. Psychoneuro-endocrinology of depression. Hypothalamic-pituitary-adrenal axis. *Psychiatr. Clin. North Am.,* 21:293–307.

Pocai, A. 2014. Action and therapeutic potential of oxyntomodulin. *Mol. Metab.,* 3:241–251.

Poindron, P., and Le Neindre, P. 1980. Endocrine and sensory regulation of maternal behavior in the ewe. *Adv. Study Behav.,* 11:75–119.

Poindron, P., and Levy, F. 1990. Physiological, sensory and experiential determinants of maternal behavior in sheep. In N. A. Krasnegor and R. S. Bridges (eds.). *Mammalian Parenting: Biochemical, Neurobiological, and Behavioral Determinants,* pp. 133–156. Oxford University Press, New York.

Poindron, P., Lévy, F., and Keller, M. 2007a. Maternal responsiveness and maternal selectivity in domestic sheep and goats: The two facets of maternal attachment. *Dev. Psychobiol.,* 49:54–70.

Poindron, P., Terrazas, A., Navarro Montes deOca, M. L., Serafin, N., and Hernandez, H. 2007b. Sensory and physiological determinants of maternal behavior in the goat (*Capra hircus*). *Horm. Behav.,* 52:99–105.

Polak, J. M., and Van Noorden, S. 1997. *Introduction to Immunocytochemistry. Microscopy Handbook Series,* 37. Springer-Verlag, New York.

Polo-Kantola, P., Portin, R., Polo, O., Helenius, H., Irjala, K., and Erkkola, R. 1998. The effect of short-term estrogen replacement therapy on cognition: A randomized double-blind, cross-over trial in postmenopausal women. *Obstet. Gynecol.,* 91:459–466.

Pomerantz, S. M. 1990. Apomorphine facilitates male sexual behavior of rhesus monkeys. *Pharmacol. Biochem. Behav.,* 35:659–664.

Poon, A. M., Liu, Z. M., Tang, F., and Pang, S. F. 1994. Cortisol decreases 2[^{125}I]iodomelatonin binding sites in the duck thymus. *Eur. J. Endocrinol.,* 130:320–324.

Popa, S. M., Clifton, D. K., and Steiner, R. A. 2008. The role of kisspeptins and GPR54 in the neuroendocrine regulation of reproduction. *Annu. Rev. Physiol,* 70:213–238.

Pope, H. G., Jr., and Katz, D. L. 1990. Homicide and near-homicide by anabolic steroid users. *J. Clin. Psychiatry,* 51:28–31.

Pope, H. G., Kanayama, G., and Hudson, J. I. 2012. Risk factors for illicit anabolic-androgenic steroid use in male weightlifters: a cross-sectional cohort study. *Biol. Psychiatry,* 71:254–261.

Pope, H. G., Kouri, E. M., and Hudson, J. I. 2000. Effects of supraphysiologic doses of testosterone on mood and aggression in normal men: A randomized controlled trial. *Arch. Gen. Psychiatry,* 57:133–140.

Pope, H. G., Wood, R. I., Rogol, A., Nyberg, F., Bowers, L., and Bhasin, S. 2013. Adverse health consequences of performance-enhancing drugs: An Endocrine Society scientific statement. *Endocr. Rev.,* 35:341–375.

Pope, H.G., and Katz, D. L. 1988. Affective and psychotic symptoms associated with anabolic steroid use. *Amer. J. Psychiatry,* 145:487–490.

Popkin, B. M., D'Anci, K. D., and Rosenberg, I. H. 2010. Water, hydration, and health. *Nutr. Rev.,* 68:439–458.

Postolache, T. T., Wehr, T. A., Doty, R. L., Sher, L., Turner, E. H., Bartko, J. J., and Rosenthal, N. E. 2002. Patients with seasonal affective disorder have lower odor detection thresholds than control subjects. *Arch. Gen. Psychiatry,* 59:1119–1122.

Power, A. E., Thal, L. J., and McGaugh, J. L. 2002. Lesions of the nucleus basalis magnocellularis induced by 192 IgG-saporin block memory enhancement with post-training norepinephrine in the basolateral amygdala. *Proc. Natl. Acad. Sci. USA,* 19:2315–2319.

Powers, J. B., and Winans, S. S. 1975. Vomeronasal organ: Critical role in mediating sexual behavior of the male hamster. *Science,* 187:961–963.

Powers, J. B., Steel, E. A., Hutchison, J. B., Hastings, M. H., Herbert, J., and Walker, A. P. 1989. Photoperiodic influences on sexual behavior in male Syrian hamsters. *J. Biol. Rhythms,* 4:61–78.

Pradhan, D. S., Newman, A. E., Wacker, D. W., Wingfield, J. C., Schlinger, B. A., and Soma, K. K. 2010. Aggressive interactions rapidly increase androgen synthesis in the brain during the non-breeding season. *Horm. Behav.*, 57:381–389.

Praschak-Rieder, N., Willeit, M., Wilson, A. A., Houle, S., and Meyer, J. H. 2008. Seasonal variation in human brain serotonin transporter binding. *Arch. Gen. Psychiatry*, 65:1072–1078.

Pravosudov, V. V. 2003. Long-term moderate elevation of corticosterone facilitates avian food-caching behaviour and enhances spatial memory. *Proc. Roy. Soc. Lond. B*, 270:2599–2604.

Pravosudov, V. V. 2005. Corticosterone and memory in birds. In A. Dawson and P. J. Sharp (eds.), *Functional Avian Endocrinology*. Narosa Publishing House, New Delhi, India.

Pravosudov, V. V., and Clayton, N. S. 2001. Effects of demanding foraging conditions on cache retrieval accuracy in food-caching mountain chickadees (*Poecile gambeli*). *Proc. Roy. Soc. Lond. B*, 268:363–368.

Pravosudov, V. V., and Smulders, T. V. 2010. Integrating ecology, psychology and neurobiology within a food-hoarding paradigm. *Philos. Trans. R. Soc. Lond. B Biol. Sci.*, 365:859–867.

Pravosudov, V. V., Kitaysky, A. S., Wingfield, J. C., and Clayton, N. S. 2001. Long-term unpredictable foraging conditions and physiological stress response in mountain chickadees (*Poecile gambeli*). *Gen. Comp. Endocrinol.*, 123:324–331.

Prendergast, B. J., Kriegsfeld, L. J., and Nelson, R. J. 2001. Photoperiodic polyphenisms in rodents: Neuroendocrine mechanisms, costs, and functions. *Q. Rev. Biol.*, 76:293–325.

Prendergast, B. J., Nelson, R. J., and Zucker, I. 2002. Mammalian seasonal rhythms: Behavior and neuroendrocine substrates. In D. W. Pfaff (ed.), *Hormones, Brain and Behavior*. Vol. 2, pp. 93–156. Academic Press, San Diego.

Prendergast, B. J., Nelson, R. J., and Zucker, I. 2009. Mammalian seasonal rhythms: Behavior and neuroendocrine substrates. In D. W. Pfaff, A. P. Arnold, A. M. Etgen, S. E. Fahrbach, and R. T. Rubin (eds.), *Hormones, Brain and Behavior* (2nd ed.). Vol. 1, pp. 507–538. Academic Press, San Diego.

Priestnall, R., and Young, S. 1978. An observational study of caretaking behavior of male and female mice housed together. *Devel. Psychobiol.*, 11:23–30.

Prudom, S. L., Broz, C. A., Schultz-Darken, N., Ferris, C. T., Snowdon, C., and Ziegler, T. E. 2008. Exposure to infant scent lowers serum testosterone in father common marmosets (*Callithrix jacchus*). *Biol. Lett.*, 4:603–605.

Pryce, C. R. 1996. Socialization, hormones, and the regulation of maternal behavior in nonhuman simian primates. *Adv. Study Behav.*, 25:423–473.

Pryce, C. R., Döbeli, M., and Martin, R. D. 1993. Effects of sex steroids on maternal motivation in the common marmoset (*Callithrix jacchus*): Development and application of an operant system with maternal reinforcement. *J. Comp. Psychol.*, 107:99–115.

Pryce, C. R., Döbeli, M., and Martin, R. D. 1993. Effects of sex steroids on maternal motivation in the common marmoset (*Callithrix jacchus*): Development and application of an operant system with maternal reinforcement. *J. Comp. Psychol.*, 107:99–115.

Przewlocki, R. 2009. Stress, opioid peptides, and their receptors. In D. W. Pfaff, et al. (eds.), *Hormones, Brain and Behavior* (2nd ed.), pp. 289–331. Academic Press, San Diego.

Pucek, M. 1965. Water contents and seasonal changes of the brain weight in shrews. *Acta Theriol.*, 10:353–367.

Purifoy, F. E., and Koopmans, L. H. 1979. Androstenedione, testosterone, and free testosterone concentration in women of various occupations. *Soc. Biol.*, 26:179–188.

Purvis, K., and Haynes, N. B. 1974. Short-term effects of copulation, human chorionic gonadotrophin injection and non-tactile association with a female on testosterone levels in the male rat. *J. Endocrinol.*, 60:429–439.

Purvis, K., Landgren, B., Cekan, Z., and Diczfalusy, E. 1976. Endocrine effects of masturbation in men. *J. Endocrinol.*, 70:439–444.

Putnam, S. K., Du, J., Sato, S., and Hull, E. M. 2001. Testosterone restoration of copulatory behavior correlates with medial preoptic dopamine release in castrated male rats. *Horm. Behav.*, 39:216–224.

Pyter, L. M., Reader, B. F., and Nelson, R. J. 2005. Short photoperiods impair spatial learning and alter hippocampal dendritic morphology in adult male white-footed mice (*Peromyscus leucopus*). *J. Neurosci.*, 25:4521–4526.

Qi, Y., Takahashi, N., Hileman, S. M., Patel, H. R., Berg, A. H., Pajvani, U. B., Scherer, P. E., and Ahima, R. S. 2004. Adiponectin acts in the brain to decrease body weight. *Nature Med.*, 10:524–529.

Quartermain, D. 1976. The influence of drugs on learning and memory. In M. R. Rosenzweig and E. L. Bennett (eds.), *Neural Mechanisms of Learning and Memory*, pp. 508–520. MIT Press, Cambridge, MA.

Quétel, C. 1990. *History of Syphilis*. Johns Hopkins University Press, Baltimore.

Quinlan, D. M., Nelson, R. J., Partin, A. W., Mostwin, J. L., and Walsh, P. C. 1989. The rat as a model for the study of penile erection. *J. Urol.*, 141:656–661.

Racey, P. A., and Skinner, J. D. 1979. Endocrine aspects of sexual mimicry in spotted hyaenas, *Crocuta crocuta. J. Zool. (Lond.)*, 187:315–326.

Racine, S. E., Culbert, K. M., Keel, P. K., Sisk, C. L., Burt, S. A., and Klump, K. L. 2012. Differential associations between ovarian hormones and disordered eating symptoms across the menstrual cycle in women. *Intl. J. Eat. Disorders*, 45:333–344.

Radder, R., Ali, S., and Shine, R. 2007. Offspring sex is not related to maternal allocation of yolk steroids in the lizard *Bassiana duperreyi* (Scincidae). *Physiol. Biochem. Zool.*, 80:220–227.

Ragozzino, M. E., Unick, K. E., and Gold, P. E. 1996. Hippocampal acetylcholine release during memory testing in rats: Augmentation by glucose. *Proc. Natl. Acad. Sci. USA*, 93:4693–4698.

Raisman, G., and Field, P. M. 1973a. Sexual dimorphism in the neurophil of the preoptic area of the rat and its dependence on neonatal androgen. *Brain Res.*, 54:1–29.

Raisman, G., and Field, P. M. 1973b. Sexual dimorphism in the preoptic area of the rat. *Science*, 173:731–733.

Raloff, J. 1994a. The gender benders. *Sci. News*, 145:24–27.

Raloff, J. 1994b. That feminine touch. *Sci. News*, 145:56–59.

Ralph, M. R., and Lehman, M. N. 1991. Transplantation: A new tool in the analysis of the mammalian hypothalamic circadian pacemaker. *Trends Neurosci.*, 14:362–366.

Ralph, M. R., and Menaker, M. 1988. A mutation in the circadian system in the golden hamster. *Science*, 241:1225–1227.

Ralph, M. R., Foster, R. G., Davis, F. C., and Menaker, M. 1990. Transplanted suprachiasmatic nucleus determines circadian period. *Science*, 247:975–978.

Ralph, M. R., Foster, R. G., Davis, F. C., and Menaker, M. 1990. Transplanted suprachiasmatic nucleus determines circadian period. *Science*, 247:975–978.

Ramenofsky, M. 1984. Agonistic behavior and endogenous plasma hormones in male Japanese quail. *Anim. Behav.*, 32:698–708.

Ramirez, V. D., and McCann, S. M. 1963. Comparisons of the regulation of luteinizing hormone (LH) secretion in immature and adult rats. *Endocrinol.*, 72:452–464.

Ramos, C. and Silver, R. 1992. Gonadal hormones determine sex differences in timing of incubation by doves. *Horm. Behav.*, 26:586–601.

Ramos, C., and Silver, R. 1992. Gonadal hormones determine sex differences in timing of incubation by doves. *Horm. Behav.*, 26:586–601.

Ramsey, M., and Crews, D. 2009. Steroid signaling, temperature-dependent sex determination: Reviewing the evidence for early action of estrogen during ovarian determination in turtles. *Semin. Cell Dev. Biol.*, 20:283–292.

Rand, M. N., and Breedlove, S. M. 1987. Ontogeny of functional innervation of bulbocavernosus muscles in male and female rats. *Dev. Brain Res.*, 33:150–152.

Ranote, S., Elliott, R., Abel, K. M., Mitchell, R., Deakin, J. F., and Appleby, L. 2004. The neural basis of maternal responsiveness to infants: An fMRI study. *NeuroReport*, 15:1825–1829.

Ranson, E., and Beach, F. A. 1985. Effects of testosterone on ontogeny of urinary behavior in male and female dogs. *Horm. Behav.*, 19:36–51.

Rapkin, A. 2003. A review of treatment of premenstrual syndrome and premenstrual dysphoric disorder. *Psychoneuroendocrinol.*, 28:39–53.

Rapkin, A. J. and Mikacich, J. A. 2013. Premenstrual dysphoric disorder and sever premenstrual syndrome in adolescents. *Paediatric Drugs*, 15:191–202.

Raskin, K., de Gendt, K., Duittoz, A., Liere, P., Verhoeven, G., Tronche, F., and Mhaouty-Kodja, S. 2009. Conditional inactivation of androgen receptor gene in the nervous system: Effects on male behavioral and neuroendocrine responses. *J. Neurosci.*, 29:4461–4470.

Reburn, C. J., and Wynne-Edwards, K. E. 1999. Hormonal changes in males of a naturally biparental and a uniparental mammal. *Horm. Behav.* 35:163–167.

Reddy, V. V. R., Naftolin, F., and Ryan, K. J. 1974. Conversion of androstenedione to estrone by neural tissues from fetal and neonatal rat. *Endocrinol.*, 94:117–121.

Redican, W. K., and Taub, D. M. 1981. Male parental care in monkeys and apes. In M. E. Lamb (ed.), *The Role of the Father in Child Development*, pp. 345–385. Wiley, New York.

Reebs, S. G., and Mrosovsky, N. 1989. Effects of induced wheel running on the circadian activity rhythms of Syrian hamsters: Entrainment and phase response curve. *J. Biological Rhythms*, 4:39–48.

Reebs, S. G., Lavery, R. J., and Mrosovsky, N. 1989. Running activity mediates the phase-advancing effects of dark pulses on hamster circadian rhythms. *J. Comp. Physiol. A*, 165:811–818.

Reid, R. L., and Yen, S. S. C. 1981. Premenstrual syndrome. *Am. J. Obstet. Gynecol.*, 139:85–97.

Reijmers, L. G., van Ree, J. M., Spruijt, B. M., Burbach, J. P., and DeWied, D. 1998. Vasopressin metabolites: A link between vasopressin and memory. *Prog. Brain Res.*, 119:523–535.

Reiman, E. M., Caselli, R. J., Yun, L.S., Chen, K., Bandy, D., Minoshima, S., Thibodeau, S. N., and Osborne, D. 1996. Preclinical evidence of Alzheimer's Disease in persons homozygous for the epsilon-4 allele for apolipoprotein E. *N. Engl. J. Med.*, 334:752–758.

Reinberg, A., Hallek, M., Levi, F., Touitou, Y., and Smolensky, M. 1987. Aspects of chronopharmacology and chronotherapy in pediatrics. *Prog. Clin. Biol. Res.*, 227B:249–258.

Reinisch, J. M. 1974. Fetal hormones, the brain and human sex differences: A heuristic integrative review of the recent literature. *Arch. Sex. Behav.*, 3:51–90.

Reisbick, S., Rosenblatt, J. S., and Mayer, A. D. 1975. Decline of maternal behavior in the virgin and lactating rat. *J. Comp. Physiol. Psychol.*, 89:722–732.

Reiter, R. J. 1970. Endocrine rhythms associated with pineal gland function. In L. W. Hedlund, J. M. Franz, and A. D. Kenny (eds.), *Biological Rhythms and Endocrine Function*, pp. 43–78. Plenum, New York.

Reiter, R. J. 1973/74. Influence of pinealectomy on the breeding capability of hamsters maintained under natural photoperiod and temperature conditions. *Neuroendocrinol.*, 13:366–370.

Reiter, R. J. 1982. *The Pineal and Its Hormones.* Alan R. Liss, New York.

Reiter, R. J. 1998. Melatonin and human reproduction. *Ann. Med.*, 30:103–108.

Remage-Healey, L., Adkins-Regan, E., and Romero, L. M. 2003. Behavioral and adrenocortical responses to mate separation and reunion in the zebra finch. *Horm. Behav.*, 43:108–114.

Remage-Healey, L., and Bass, A. H. 2004. Rapid, hierarchical modulation of vocal patterning by steroid hormones. *J. Neurosci.*, 24:5892–5900.

Remage-Healey, L., and Bass, A. H. 2006. From social behavior to neural circuitry: Steroid hormones rapidly modulate advertisement calling via a vocal pattern generator. *Horm. Behav.*, 50:432–441.

Remage-Healey, L., and Bass, A. H. 2007. Plasticity in brain sexuality is revealed by rapid actions of steroid hormones. *J. Neurosci.*, 27:1114–1122.

Remage-Healey, L., London, S.E., and Schlinger, B.A. 2010. Birdsong and the neural production of steroids. *J. Chem. Neuroanat.*, 39:72–81.

Remage-Healey, L., Maidment, N. T., and Schlinger, B. A. 2008. Forebrain steroid levels fluctuate rapidly during social interactions. *Nat. Neurosci.*, 11:1327–1334.

Remage-Healey, L., Saldanha, C. J., and Schlinger, B. A. 2011. Estradiol synthesis and action at the synapse: Evidence for "synaptocrine" signaling. *Front. Endocrinol.*, 2:28. doi: 10.3389/fendo.2011.00028.

Rendon, N. M. and Demas, G. E. 2016. Bidirectional actions of dehydroepiandrosterone and aggression in female Siberian hamsters. *J. Exp. Zool. A Ecol. Genet. Physiol.*, 325:116–121.

Rendon, N. M., Rudolph, L. M., Sengelaub, D. R., and Demas, G. E. 2015. The agonistic adrenal: Melatonin elicits female aggression via regulation of adrenal androgens. *Proc. Roy. Soc. Lond. B*, doi:10.1098/rspb.2015.2080

Renfro, K. J., Rupp, H., Wallen, K. 2015. Duration of oral contraceptive use predicts women's initial and subsequent subjective responses to sexual stimuli. *Horm. Behav.*, 75:33–40.

Rensel, M. A., Wilcoxen, T. E., and Schoech, S. J. 2009. The influence of nest attendance and provisioning on nestling stress physiology in the Florida scrub-jay. *Horm. Behav.*, 57:162–168.

Repetti, R. L., Taylor, S. E., and Seeman, T. E. 2002. Risky families: Family social environments and the mental and physical health of offspring. *Psychol. Bull.*, 128:330–366.

Reppert, S. M., and Weaver, D. R. 2002. Coordination of circadian timing in mammals. *Nature*, 418:935–941.

Reppert, S. M., Schwartz, W. J., and Uhl, G. R. 1987. Arginine vasopressin: a novel peptide rhythm in cerebrospinal fluid. *Trends Neurosci.*, 10:76–80.

Resko, J. A., and Roselli, C. E. 1997. Prenatal hormones organize sex differences of the neuroendocrine reproductive system: observations on guinea pigs and nonhuman primates. *Cell. Molec. Neurobiol.*, 17:627–648.

Reul, J. M. H. M., and de Kloet, E. R. 1985. Two receptor systems for corticosterone in the rat brain: Microdistribution and differential occupation. *Endocrinol.*, 117:2505–2512.

Reul, J. M. H. M., and Holsboer, F. 2002. Corticotropin-releasing factor receptors 1 and 2 in anxiety and depression. *Curr. Opin. Pharmacol.*, 2:23–33.

Revel, F. G., Saboureau, M., Pevet, P., Mikkelsen, J. D., and Simonneaux, V. 2006. Melatonin regulates type 2 deiodinase gene expression in the Syrian hamster. *Endocrinology*, 147:4680–4687.

Revel, F. G., Saboureau, M., Pevet, P., Simonneaux, V., and, Mikkelsen, J. D. 2008. RFamide-related peptide gene is a melatonin-driven photoperiodic gene. *Endocrinology*, 149:902–912

Reyes, R. J., Zicchi, S., Hamed, H., Chaudary, M. A., and Fentiman, I. S. 1995. Surgical correction of gynaecomastia in bodybuilders. *Br. J. Clin. Pract.*, 49:177–179.

Rhees, R. W., Shryne, J. E., and Gorksi, R. A. 1990. Onset of the hormone-sensitive perinatal period for sexual differentiation of the sexually dimorphic nucleus of the preoptic area in female rats. *J. Neuroendocrinol.*, 211:781–786.

Rhen, T., and Crews, D. 2002. Variation in reproductive behavior within a sex: Neural systems and endocrine activation. *J. Neuroendocrinol.*, 14:517–532.

Rhen, T., and Crews, D. 2008. Why are there two sexes? In J. B. Becker, K. J. Berkley, N. Geary, E. Hampson, J. P. Herman, and E. A. Young (eds.), *Sex Differences in the Brain: From Genes to Behavior*, pp. 2–14. Oxford University Press, New York.

Ribble, D. O. 1990. Population and social dynamics of the California mouse (*Peromyscus californicus*). Ph.D. Dissertation, University of California, Berkeley.

Ribble, D. O., and Salvioni, M. 1990. Social organization and nest co-occupancy in *Peromyscus californicus,* a monogamous rodent. *Behav. Ecol. Sociobiol.,* 26:9–15.

Richards, M. P. M. 1969. Effects of oestrogen and progesterone on nest building in the golden hamster. *Anim. Behav.,* 17:356–361.

Richardson, G. S., and Martin, J. B. 1988. Circadian rhythms in neuroendocrinology and immunology: Influence of aging. *Prog. Neuroendocrinol. Immunol.,* 1:16–20.

Richman, J. A., Raskin, V. D., and Gaines, C. 1991. Gender roles, social support, and postpartum depressive symptomatology: The benefits of caring. *J. Nerv. Ment. Dis.,* 179:139–147.

Richter, C. P. 1936. Increased salt appetite in adrenalectomized rats. *Am. J. Physiol.,* 115:155–161.

Richter, C. P. 1968. Inherent twenty-four hour and lunar clocks of a primate: The squirrel monkey. *Commun. Behav. Biol.,* 1:305–332.

Richter, C. P. 1977. Heavy water as a tool for study of the forces that control length of period of the 24-hour clock of the hamster. *Proc. Natl. Acad. Sci. USA,* 74:1295–1299.

Richter, C. P., Holt, L. E., and Barelare, B. 1938. Nutritional requirements for normal growth and reproduction in rats studied by the self selection method. *Am. J. Physiol.,* 122:734–744.

Riddle, O. 1924/25. Birds without gonads: Their origin, behavior, and bearing on the theory of the internal secretion of the testis. *Br. J. Exp. Biol.,* 2:211–246.

Riddle, O., Bates, R. W., and Lahr, E. L. 1935a. Maternal behavior induced in virgin rats by prolactin. *Proc. Soc. Exp. Biol. Med.,* 32:730–734.

Riddle, O., Bates, R. W., and Lahr, E. L. 1935b. Prolactin induces broodiness in fowl. *Am. J. Physiol.,* 111:352–360.

Riebe, C. J. and Wotjak, C. T. 2011. Endocannabinoids and stress. *Stress,* 14:384–397.

Riley, J. L., Robinson, M. E., Wise, E. A., and Price, D. D. 1999. A meta-analytic review of pain perception across the menstrual cycle. *Pain,* 81:225–235.

Riou, S., Chastel, O., Lacroix, A., and Hamer, K. C. 2010. Stress and parental care: prolactin responses to acute stress throughout the breeding cycle in a long-lived bird. *Gen. Comp. Endocrinol.,* 168:8–13.

Rissman, E. F., and Wingfield, J. C. 1984. Hormonal correlates of polyandry in the spotted sandpiper, *Actitis macularia. Gen. Comp. Endocrinol.,* 56:401–405.

Rissman, E. F., Early, A. H., Taylor, J. A., Korach, K. S., and Lubahn, D. B. 1997b. Estrogen receptors are essential for female sexual receptivity. *Endocrinol.,* 138:507–510.

Rissman, E. F., Heck, A. L., Leonard, J. E., Shupnik, M. A., and Gustafsson, J. A. 2002. Disruption of estrogen receptor β gene impairs spatial learning in female mice. *Proc. Natl. Acad. Sci. USA,* 99:3996–4001.

Ritter, S., and Taylor, J. S. 1989. Capsaicin abolishes lipoprivic but not glucoprivic feeding in rats. *Am. J. Physiol.,* 256:R1232–1239.

Ritter, S., and Taylor, J. S. 1990. Vagal sensory neurons are required for lipoprivic but not glucoprivic feeding in rats. *Am. J. Physiol.,* 258:R1395–1401.

Ritter, S., Calingasan, N. Y., Hutton, B., and Dinh, T. T. 1992. Cooperation of vagal and central neural systems in monitoring metabolic events controlling feeding behavior. In S. Ritter, R. C. Ritter, and C. D. Barnes (eds.). *Neuroanatomy Physiology of Abdominal Vagal Afferents,* pp. 240–277. CRC Press, Boca Raton, FL.

Rivest, S., Deshaies, Y., and Richard, D. 1989. Effects of corticotropin-releasing factor on energy balance in rats are sex dependent. *Am. J. Physiol.,* 257:R1417–R1422.

Robbins, T. W., and Everitt, B. J. 1992. Functions of dopamine in the dorsal and ventral striatum. *Sem. Neurosci.,* 4:119–128.

Roberts, L. M., Pattison, H., Roalfe, A., Franklyn, J., Wilson, S., Hobbs, F. D. R., and Parle, J. V. 2006. Is subclinical thyroid dysfunction in the elderly associated with depression or cognitive dysfunction? *Ann. Intern. Med.,* 145:573–581.

Roberts, M. H. 1990. Commentary: The properties of cell water relative to the temperature compensation of circadian rhythms. *J. Biol. Rhythms,* 5:175–176.

Roberts, R. L., Zullo, A., Gustafson, E. A., and Carter, C. S. 1996. Perinatal steroid treatments alter alloparental and affiliative behavior in prairie voles. *Horm. Behav.,* 30:576–582.

Robertson, J. L., Clifton, D. K., de la Iglesia, H. O., Steiner, R. A., and Kauffman, A. S. 2009. Circadian regulation of Kiss1 neurons: implications for timing the preovulatory gonadotropin-releasing hormone/luteinizing hormone surge. *Endocrinology,* 150:3664–3671.

Robinson, G. E., Fernald, R. D., and Clayton, D. F. 2008. Genes and social behavior. *Science,* 322:869–900.

Robinson, M. E., Riley, J. L. III, Myers, C. D., Papas, R. K., Wise, E. A., Waxenberg, L. B., and Fillingim, R. B. 2001. Gender role expectations of pain: relationship to sex differences in pain. *J. Pain,* 2:251–257.

Rochira, V. and Carani, C. 2009. Aromatase deficiency in men: A clinical perspective. *Nat. Rev. Endocrinol.,* 5:559–568.

Rodgers, S. P., Bohacek, J., and Daniel, J. M. 2010. Transient estradiol exposure during middle age in ovariectomized rats exerts lasting effects on cognitive function and the hippocampus. *Endocrinol.,* 151:1194–1203.

Roecklein, K. A., Rohan, K. J., Duncan, W. C., Rollag, M. D., Rosenthal, N. E., Lipsky, R. H., and Provencio, I. 2009. A missense variant (P10L) of the melanopsin (OPN4) gene is associated with Seasonal Affective Disorder. *J. Affective Disorders,* 114:279–285.

Roecklein, K. A., Wong, P. M., Miller, M. A., Donofry, S. D., Kamarck, M. L., and Brainard, G.C. 2013. Melanopsin, photosensitive ganglion cells, and seasonal affective disorder. *Neurosci. Biobehav. Rev.,* 37, 229–239.

Roecklein, K., Wong, P., Ernecoff, N., Miller, M., Donofry, S., Kamarck, M., Wood-Vasey, W.M., and Franzen, P. 2013. The post illumination pupil response is reduced in seasonal affective disorder. *Psychiatry Res.,* 210: 150–158.

Roenneberg, T. 2004. The decline in human seasonality. *J. Biol. Rhythms,* 19:193–195.

Roenneberg, T., and Aschoff, J. 1990a. Annual rhythm of human reproduction: I. Biology, sociology, or both? *J. Biol. Rhythms,* 5:195–216.

Roenneberg, T., and Aschoff, J. 1990b. Annual rhythm of human reproduction: II. Environmental correlations. *J. Biol. Rhythms,* 5:217–239.

Roenneberg, T., Kantermann, T., Juda, M., Vetter, C., and Allebrandt, K. V. 2013. Light and the human circadian clock. *Handb. Exp. Pharmacol.,* 217:311–331.

Rolandsson, O., Backestrom, A., Eriksson, S., Hallmans, G., and Nilsson, L.-G. 2008. Increased glucose levels are associated with episodic memory in nondiabetic women. *Diabetes,* 57:440–443.

Rolls, B. J., and Rolls, E. T. 1982. *Thirst.* University of Cambridge Press, Cambridge.

Romanes, G. J. 1887. Mental differences between men and women. *The Nineteenth Century,* 21:654–672.

Romeo, R. D. 2010. Pubertal maturation and programming of hypothalamic–pituitary–adrenal reactivity. *Front. Neuroendocrinol.,* 31:232–240.

Romeo, R. D., and McEwen, B. S. 2006. Stress and the adolescent brain. *Resilience in Children,* 1094:202–214.

Romeo, R. D., Schulz, K. M., Nelson, A. L., Menard, T. A., and Sisk, C. L. 2003. Testosterone, puberty, and the pattern of male aggression in Syrian hamsters. *Dev. Psychobiol.,* 43:102–108.

Romero, L. M., Dickens, M. J., and Cry, N. E. 2009. The reactive scope model: A new model integrating homeostasis, allostasis, and stress. *Horm. Behav.,* 55:375–389.

Romero, T., Nagasawa, M., Mogi, K., Hasegawa, T., and Kikusui, T. 2014. Oxytocin promotes social bonding in dogs. *Proc. Natl. Acad. Sci. USA,* 111:9085–9090, doi:10.1073/pnas.1322868111

Ronay, R., and von Hippel, W. 2010. The presence of an attractive woman elevates testosterone and physical risk taking in young men. *Social Psychological and Personality Science*, 1:57–64.

Ronchi, E., Spencer, R. L., Krey, L. C., and McEwen, B. S. 1998. Effects of photoperiod on brain corticosteroid receptors and the stress response in the golden hamster (*Mesocricetus auratus*). *Brain Res.*, 780:348–351.

Roney, J. R. and Simmons, Z. L. 2013. Hormonal predictors of sexual motivation in natural menstrual cycles. *Horm. Behav.*, 63:636–645.

Roney, J. R., Lukaszewski, A. W., and Simmons, Z. L. 2007. Rapid endocrine responses of young men to social interactions with young women. *Horm. Behav.*, 52:326–333.

Roof, R. L., and Havens, M. D. 1992. Testosterone improves maze performance and induces development of a male hippocampus in females. *Brain Res.*, 572:310–313.

Roozendaal, B. 2000. Glucocorticoids and the regulation of memory consolidation. *Psychoneuroendocrinol.*, 25:213–238.

Roozendaal, B. 2003. Systems mediating acute glucocorticoid effects on memory consolidation and retrieval. *Prog. Neuropsychopharmacol. Biol. Psychiatry*. 27:1213–1223.

Roozendaal, B., Brunson, K. L., Holloway, B. L., McGaugh, J. L., and Baram, T. Z. 2002. Involvement of stress-released corticotropin-releasing hormone in the basolateral amygdala in regulating memory consolidation. *Proc. Natl. Acad. Sci. USA*, 99:13908–13913.

Roozendaal, B., McEwen, B. S., and Chattarji, S. 2009. Stress, memory and the amygdala. *Nat. Rev. Neurosci.*, 10:423–433.

Roozendaal, B., Portillo-Marquez, G., and McGaugh, J. L. 1996. Basolateral amygdala lesions block glucocorticoid-induced modulation of memory for spatial learning. *Behav. Neurosci.*, 110:1074–1083.

Rose, R. M., Bernstein, I. S., Gordon, T. P., and Lindsley, J. G. 1978. Changes in testosterone and behavior during adolescence in the male rhesus monkey. *Psychosom. Med.*, 40:60–70.

Rose, R. M., Berstein, I. S., and Holaday, J. W. 1971. Plasma testosterone, dominance rank and aggressive behavior in a group of male rhesus monkeys. *Nature*, 231:366–368.

Roselli, C. E., Abdelgadir, S. E., and Resko, J. A. 1997. Regulation of aromatase gene expression in the adult rat brain. *Brain Res. Bull.*, 44:351–358.

Roselli, C. E., and Stormshak, F. 2009. The neurobiology of sexual partner preference in rams. *Horm. Behav.*, 55:611–620.

Roselli, C. E., Cross, E., Poonyagariyagorn, H. K., and Stadelman, H. L. 2003. Role of aromatization in anticipatory and consummatory aspects of sexual behavior in male rats. *Horm. Behav.*, 44:146–151.

Roselli, C. E., Salisbury, R. L., and Resko, J. A. 1987. Genetic evidence for androgen dependent and independent control of aromatase activity in the rat brain. *Endocrinol.*, 121:2205–2210.

Rosenbaum, J. E. 2009. Patient teenagers? A comparison of the sexual behavior of virginity pledgers and matched nonpledgers. *Pediatrics*, 123:110–120.

Rosenbaum, M., Hirsch, J., Gallagher, D. A., and Leibel, R. L. 2008. Long-term persistence of adaptive thermogenesis in subjects who have maintained a reduced body weight. *Am. J. Clin. Nutr.*, 88:906–912.

Rosenberg, G. D., and Runcorn, S. K. 1975. Conclusions. In G. D. Rosenberg and S. K. Runcorn (eds.), *Growth Rhythms and the History of the Earth's Rotation*, pp. 535–538. John Wiley and Sons, New York.

Rosenblatt, J. S. 1967. Nonhormonal basis of maternal behavior in the rat. *Science*, 156:1512–1514.

Rosenblatt, J. S. 1990. Landmarks in the physiological study of maternal behavior with special reference to the rat. In N. A. Krasnegor and R. S. Bridges (eds.), *Mammalian Parenting*, pp. 40–60. Oxford University Press, Oxford.

Rosenblatt, J. S. 2002. Hormonal basis of parenting in mammals. In M. H. Bornstein (ed.), *Handbook of Parenting*, 2nd ed., Vol. 2, pp. 31–60. Lawrence Erlbaum, Mahwah, NJ.

Rosenblatt, J. S. 2003. Outline of the evolution of behavioral and nonbehavioral patterns of parental care among the vertebrates: Critical characteristics of mammalian and avian parental behavior. *Scand. J. Psych.*, 44:265–271.

Rosenblatt, J. S., and Aronson, L. R. 1958. The decline of sexual behaviour in male cats after castration with special reference to the role of prior sexual experience. *Behaviour*, 12:285–338.

Rosenblatt, J. S., and Ceus, K. 1998. Estrogen implants in the medial preoptic area stimulate maternal behavior in male rats. *Horm. Behav.*, 33:23–30.

Rosenblatt, J. S., and Siegel, H. I. 1975. Hysterectomy-induced maternal behavior during pregnancy in the rat. *J. Comp. Physiol. Psychol.*, 89:685–700.

Rosenblatt, J. S., Hazelwood, S., and Poole, J. 1996. Maternal behavior in male rats: Effects of medial preoptic area lesions and presence of maternal aggression. *Horm. Behav.*, 30:01–215.

Rosenblatt, J. S., Mayer, A. D., and Siegel, H. I. 1985. Maternal behavior among the nonprimate mammals. In N. T. Adler, D. Pfaff, and R. W. Goy (eds.), *Handbook of Behavioral Neurobiology*, pp. 229–298. Plenum, New York.

Rosenblatt, J. S., Siegel, H. I., and Mayer, A. D. 1979. Blood levels of progesterone, estradiol and prolactin in pregnant rats. *Adv. Study Behav.*, 10:225–311.

Rosenthal, N. E. 1993. *Winter Blues: Seasonal Affective Disorder*. Guilford Press, New York.

Rosenthal, N. E., and Wehr, T. A. 1987. Seasonal affective disorders. *Psychiatric Ann.*, 17:670–674.

Rosenthal, N. E., Sack, D. A., Skwerer, R. G., Jacobsen, F. M., and Wehr, T. A. 1988. Phototherapy for seasonal affective disorder. *J. Biol. Rhythms*, 3:101–120.

Rosenzweig, M. R., and Leiman, A. L. 1989. *Physiological Psychology*. (2nd ed.). Random House, New York.

Rosenzweig, M. R., Leiman, A. L., and Breedlove, S. M. 1999. *Biological Psychology: An Introduction to Behavioral, Cognitive, and Clinical Neuroscience*. (2nd ed.). Sinauer Associates, Sunderland, MA.

Ross, M. W., Månsson, S-A., and Daneback, K. 2012. Prevalence, severity, and correlates of problematic sexual internet use in Swedish men and women. *Arch. Sex. Behav.*, 41:459–466.

Ross, S., Denenberg, V. H., Frommer, G. P., and Sawin, P. B. 1959. Genetic, physiological, and behavioral background of reproduction in the rabbit. V. Nonretrieving of neonates. *J. Mammal.*, 40:91–96.

Rowe, F. A., and Smith, W. E. 1972. Effects of peripherally induced anosmia on mating behavior of male mice. *Psychonom. Sci.*, 27:33–34.

Rowsemitt, C. N. 1986. Seasonal variations in activity rhythms of male voles: Mediation by gonadal hormones. *Physiol. Behav.*, 37:797–803.

Rowsemitt, C. N., Petterborg, L. J., Claypool, L. E., Hoppensteadt, F. C., Negus, N. C., and Berger, J. P. 1982. Photoperiodic induction of diurnal locomotor activity in *Microtus montanus*, the montane vole. *Can. J. Zool.*, 60:2798–2803.

Roy-Byrne, P. P., Rubinow, D. R., Hoban, M. C., Grover, G. N., Blank, D. 1987. TSH and prolactin responses to TRH in patients with premenstrual syndrome. *Am. J. Psychiatry*, 144:480–484.

Rubin, R. T., Dinan, T. G., and Scott, L. V. 2002. The neuroendocrinology of affective disorders. In D. W. Pfaff, A. P. Arnold, A. M. Etgen, S. E. Fahrbach, and R. T. Rubin (eds.), *Hormones, Brain and Behavior*, Vol. 5, pp. 467–514. Academic Press, New York.

Rubin, R. T., Reinisch, J. M., and Haskett, R. F. 1981. Postnatal gonadal steroid effects on human sexual behavior. *Science*, 211:1318–1324.

Rubinow, D. R., and Schmidt, P. J. 1996. Androgens, brain, and behavior. *Am. J. Psychiatry*, 153:974–984.

Rubinow, D. R., Hoban, M. C., Grover, G. N., Galloway, D. S., Roy-Byrne, R., Andersen, R., and Merriam, G. R. 1988. Changes in plasma hormones across the menstrual cycle in patients with menstrually related mood disorder and in control subjects. *Am. J. Obstet. Gynecol.*, 158:5–11.

Rubinow, D. R., Schmidt, P. J., Roca, C. A., and Daly, R. C. 2002. Gonadal hormones and behavior in women: Concentrations versus context. In D. W. Pfaff, A. P. Arnold, A. M. Etgen, S. E. Fahrbach, and R. T. Rubin (eds.), *Hormones, Brain and Behavior*, Vol. 5, pp. 37–73. Academic Press, New York.

Ruble, D. N. 1977. Premenstrual symptoms: A reinterpretation. *Science,* 187:291–292.

Ruble, D. N., Martin, C. L., and Berenbaum, S. A. 2006. Gender development. In W. Damon and R. M. Lerner (series eds.) and N. Eisenberg (Vol. ed.), *Handbook of Child Psychology, Vol. 3: Social, Emotional and Personality Development* (6th ed.), pp. 858–932. Wiley and Sons, New York.

Ruby, N. F., Brennan, T. J., Xie, X., Cao, V., Franken, P., Heller, H. C., and O'Hara, B. F. 2002. Role of melanopsin in circadian responses to light. *Science,* 298:2211–2213.

Rupp, H. A., and Wallen, K. 2008. Sex differences in response to visual sexual stimuli: A review. *Arch. Sex. Behav.,* 37:206–218.

Rusak, B. 1989. The mammalian circadian system: models and physiology. *J. Biol. Rhythms,* 4:121–134.

Rusak, B., and Boulos, Z. 1981. Pathways for photic entrainment of mammalian circadian rhythms. *Photochem. Photobiol.,* 34:267–273.

Rusak, B., Mistlberger, R. E., Losier, B., and Jones, C. H. 1988. Daily hoarding opportunity entrains the pacemaker for hamster activity rhythms. *J. Comp. Physiol. A,* 164:165–171.

Rushing, P. A., Hagan, M. M., Seeley, R. J., Lutz, T. A., and Woods, S. C. 2000. Amylin: A novel action in the brain to reduce body weight. *Endocrinol.,* 141:850–853.

Russo, K. A., La, J. L., Stephens, S. B., Poling, M. C., Padgaonkar, N. A., Jennings, K. J., Piekarski, D. J., Kauffman, A. S., and Kriegsfeld, L. J. 2015. Circadian control of the female reproductive axis through gated responsiveness of the RFRP-3 System to VIP signaling. *Endocrinology,* 156:2608–2618.

Ryan, B. C., and Vandenberg, J. G. 2002. Intrauterine position effects. *Neurosci. Biobehav. Rev.,* 26:665–678.

Ryan, C. M., and Williams, T. M. 1993. Effects of insulin-dependent diabetes on learning and memory efficiency in adults. *J. Clin. Exp. Neuropsychol.,* 15:685–700.

Ryan, M. J. 1985. *The Tungara Frog: A Study in Sexual Selection and Communication,* University of Chicago Press, Chicago.

Sabatinelli, D., Flaisch, T., Bradley, M. M., Fitzsimmons, J. R., and Lang, P. J. 2004. Affective picture perception: Gender differences in visual cortex? *Neuroreport,* 15:1109–1112.

Saboureau, M. 1986. Hibernation in the hedgehog: Influence of external and internal factors. In H. C. Heller, X. J. Musacchia, and L. C. H. Wang (eds.), *Living in the Cold: Physiological and Biochemical Adaptations,* pp. 253–263, Elsevier, New York.

Sachar, E. O., Hellman, L., Roffwang, H. Halpern, F., Fukushima, D., and Gallager, T. 1973. Disrupted 24-hour patterns of cortisol secretion in psychotic depression. *Arch. Gen. Psychiatry,* 28:19–24.

Sachs, B. D. 1995a. Context-sensitive variation in the regulation of erection. In J. Bancroft (ed.), *The Pharmacology of Sexual Function Dysfunction,* pp. 97–108. Elsevier Science, Amsterdam.

Sachs, B. D. 1995b. Placing erection in context: The reflexogenic-psychogenic dichotomy reconsidered. *Neurosci. Biobehav. Rev.,* 19:211–224.

Sachs, B. D. 2007. A contextual definition of male sexual arousal. *Horm. Behav.,* 51:569–578.

Sachs, B. D. 2008. The appetitive–consummatory distinction: Is this 100-year-old baby worth saving? Reply to Ball and Balthazart. *Horm. Behav.,* 53:315–318.

Sachs, B. D., Akasofu, K., Citron, J. H., Daniels, S. B., and Natoli, J. H. 1994. Noncontact stimulation from estrous females evokes penile erection in rats. *Physiol. Behav.,* 55:1073–1079.

Sachs, B. D., and Bitran, D. 1990. Spinal block reveals roles for brain and spinal cord in the mediation of reflexive penile erections in rats. *Brain Res.,* 528:99–108.

Sachs, B. D., and Meisel, R. L. 1979. Pubertal development of penile reflexes and copulation in male rats. *Psychoneuroendocrinol.,* 4:287–296.

Sachs, B. D., and Meisel, R. L. 1988. The physiology of male sexual behavior. In E. Knobil and J. Neill (eds.), *The Physiology of Reproduction,* pp. 1393–1485. Raven Press, New York.

Sack, R. L., and Lewy, A. J. 2001. Circadian rhythm sleep disorders: Lessons from the blind. *Sleep Med. Rev.,* 5:189–206.

Sack, R. L., Brandes, R. W., Kendall, A. R., and Lewy, A. J. 2000. Entrainment of free-running circadian rhythms by melatonin in blind people. *N. Engl. J. Med.,* 343:1070–1077.

Sadlier, R. M. F. S. 1969. *The Ecology of Reproduction in Wild and Domestic Mammals,* Methuen, London.

Saito A. 2015. The marmoset as a model for the study of primate parental behavior. *Neurosci. Res.,* 93:99–109.

Sakaguchi, K., Tanaka, M., Okubo, N., Dohura, K., Sado, S., and Nakashinta, N. 1996. Induction of brain prolactin receptor long-form mRNA expression and maternal behaviour in pup-contacted male rats: Promotion by prolactin administration and suppression by female contact. *Neuroendocrinol.,* 63:559–568.

Sakai, R. R., Ma, L-Y., Zhang, D. M., McEwen, B. S., and Fluharty, S. J. 1996. Intracerebroventricular administration of mineralocorticoid receptor antisense oligonucleotides attenuates adrenal steroid-induced salt appetite in rats. *Neuroendocrinol.,* 64:425–529.

Sakai, R. R., Ma, L. Y., He, P. F., and Fluharty, S. J. 1995. Intracerebroventricular administration of angiotensin type 1 (AT1) receptor antisense oligonucleotides attenuate thirst in the rat. *Regul. Pept.,* 59:183–92.

Sakata, J. T., and Crews, D. 2004. Developmental sculpting of social phenotype and plasticity. *Neuroscience and Biobehavioral Rev.,* 28:95–112.

Saldanha, C. J., and Schlinger, B. A. 2008. Steroidogenesis and neuroplasticity in the songbird brain. In M. S. Ristner and A. Weizman (eds.), *Neuroactive Steroids in Brain Function, Behavioral and Neuropsychiatric Disorders: Novel Strategies for Research and Treatment,* pp. 199–213. Springer-Verlag.

Saldanha, C. J., Clayton, N. S., and Schlinger, B. A. 1999. Androgen metabolism in the juvenile oscine forebrain: A cross-species analysis at neural sites implicated in memory function. *J. Neurobiol.,* 40:397–406.

Salkovic-Petrisic, M., Osmanovic, J., Grünblatt, E., Riederer, P., and Hoyer, S. 2009. Modeling sporadic Alzheimer's disease: The insulin resistant brain state generates multiple long-term morphobiological abnormalities inclusive hyperphosphorylated Tau protein and amyloid-β. A synthesis. *J. Alzheimer's Dis.,* 18:729–750.

Salmasi, A., Wisniewski, A. B., Novak, T., Gearhart, J., Migeon, C., and Lakshmanan, Y. 2008. Prostate screening in patients with 46, XY disorders of sex development: Is it necessary? *J. Urol.,* 180:1422–1426.

Saltiel, A. R., and Kahn, C. R. 2001. Insulin signaling and the regulation of glucose and lipid metabolism. *Nature,* 414:799–806.

Saltzman, W. and Maestripieri, D. 2011. The neuroendocrinology of primate maternal behavior. *Prog. Neuropsychopharmacol. Biol. Psychiatry,* 35:1192–1204.

Saltzman, W., and Abbott, D. H. 2005. Diminished maternal responsiveness during pregnancy in multiparous female common marmosets. *Horm. Behav.,* 47:151–163.

Saltzman, W., Mendoza, S. P., and Mason, W. A. 1991. Sociophysiology of relationships in squirrel monkeys: I. Formation of female dyads. *Physiol. Behav.,* 50:271–280.

Samenow, C. P. 2010. A biosocial model of hypersexual disorder/sexual addiction. *Sex. Addict. Compulsivity,* 17:69–81.

Samuels, M. H., and Bridges, R. S. 1983. Plasma prolactin concentrations in parental male and female rats: Effects of exposure to rat young. *Endocrinol.,* 113:1647–1654.

Sanders, D., Warner, P., Backstrom, T., and Bancroft, J. 1983. Mood, sexuality, hormones, and the menstrual cycle: Changes in mood and physical state. *Psychosom. Med.,* 45:487–500.

Sandi, C., and Rose, S. P. R. 1994a. Corticosterone enhances long-term memory in one-day-old chicks trained in a weak passive avoidance paradigm. *Brain Res.*, 647:106–112.

Sandi, C., and Rose, S. P. R. 1994b. Corticosteroid receptor antagonists are amnestic for passive avoidance learning in day-old chicks. *Eur. J. Neurosci.*, 6:1292–1297.

Sandman, C. A., Glynn, L.M., and Davis, E. P. 2016. Neurobehavioral consequences of fetal exposure to gestational stress. In N. Reissland and B. S. Kisilevsky (eds.), *Fetal Development*, pp. 229–265. Springer, Basel.

Sandstrom, N. J. 2007. Sex differences in the use of visual cues by rhesus monkeys performing a spatial learning task: Comment on "Cognitive performance in rhesus monkeys varies by sex and prenatal androgen exposure" by Herman and Wallen. *Biol. Psychiatry*, 52:139–142.

Sandstrom, N. J., and Williams, C. L. 2001. Memory retention is modulated by acute estradiol and progesterone replacement. *Behav. Neurosci.*, 115:384–393.

Sandstrom, N. J., and Williams, C. L. 2004. Spatial memory retention is enhanced by acute and continuous estradiol replacement. *Horm. Behav.*, 45:128–135.

Santarelli, L., Saxe, M., Gross, C., Surget, A., Battaglia, F., Dulawa, S., et al. 2003. Requirement of hippocampal neurogenesis for the behavioral effects of antidepressants. *Science*, 301:805–809.

Sapolsky, R. M. 1990. Stress in the wild. *Sci. Am.*, January 1990.

Sapolsky, R. M. 1992a. Neuroendocrinology of the stress-response. In by J. B. Becker, S. M. Breedlove, and D. Crews (eds.). *Behavioral Endocrinology*, pp. 287–324. MIT Press, Cambridge, MA.

Sapolsky, R. M. 1992b. *Stress, the Aging Brain, and the Mechanisms of Neuron Death*. MIT Press, Cambridge, MA.

Sapolsky, R. M. 1993. Endocrinology alfresco: psychoendocrine studies of wild baboons. *Recent Prog. Horm. Res.*, 48:437–468.

Sapolsky, R. M. 1994. *Why Zebras Don't Get Ulcers: A Guide to Stress, Stress-Related Diseases, and Coping.* W. H. Freeman, New York.

Sapolsky, R. M. 1998. *Why Zebras Don't Get Ulcers: An Updated Guide to Stress, Stress-Related Diseases, and Coping.* W. H. Freeman, New York.

Sapolsky, R. M. 2005. The influence of social hierarchy on primate health. *Science*, 308:648–652.

Sapolsky, R. M., Krey, L. C., and McEwen, B. S. 1984. Glucocorticoid-sensitive hippocampal neurons are involved in terminating the adrenocortical stress response. *Proc. Natl. Acad. Sci. USA*, 81:6174–6177.

Sapolsky, R. M., Krey, L., and McEwen, B. S. 1985. Prolonged glucocorticoid exposure reduces hippocampal neuron number: Implications for aging. *J. Neurosci.*, 5:1221–1228.

Sapolsky, R. M., Romero, L. M., and Munck, A. U. 2000. How do glucocorticoids influence stress responses? Integrating permissive, suppressive, stimulatory, and preparative actions. *Endocrine Rev.*, 21:55–89.

Sar, M., and Stumpf, W. E. 1977. Distribution of androgen target cells in rat forebrain and pituitary after [³H]-dihydrotestosterone administration. *J. Steroid Biochem.*, 8:1131–1135.

Satinoff, E., and Prosser, R. A. 1988. Suprachiasmatic nuclear lesions eliminate circadian rhythms of drinking and activity, but not of body temperature, in male rats. *J. Biol. Rhythms*, 3:1–22.

Sato, S. M., Schulz, K. M., Sisk, C. L., and Wood, R. I. 2008. Adolescents and androgens, receptors, and rewards. *Horm. Behav.*, 53:647–658.

Sato, T. and Kawamura, H. 1984. Circadian rhythms in multiple unit activity inside and outside the suprachiasmatic nucleus in the diurnal chipmunk (*Eutamias sibiricus*). *Neurosci. Res.*, 1:45–52.

Sato, T., Matsumoto, T., Kawano, H., Watanabe, T., Uematsu, Y., Sekine, K., Fukuda, T., et al. 2004. Brain masculinization requires androgen receptor function. *Proc. Natl. Acad. Sci. USA*, 101:1673–1678.

Saunders, D. S. 1977. *An Introduction to Biological Rhythms.* Wiley, New York.

Sauvage, M. F., Marquet, P., Rousseau, A., Raby, C., Buxeraud, J., and Lachatre, G. 1998. *Toxicol. Appl. Pharmacol.*, 149:127–135.

Sawchenko, P. E., and Friedman, M. I. 1979. Sensory functions of the liver: A review. *Am. J. Physiol.*, 236:R5–R20.

Scalia, F., and Winans, S. S. 1976. New perspectives on the morphology of the olfactory system: Olfactory and vomeronasal pathways in mammals. In R. L. Doty (ed.), *Mammalian Olfaction, Reproductive Processes, and Behavior*, pp. 7–28. Academic Press, New York.

Scanavino, M. T. et al. 2016. Sexual compulsivity scale, compulsive sexual behavior inventory, and hypersexual disorder screening inventory: Translation, adaptation, and validation for use in Brazil. *Arch. Sex. Behav.*, 45:207–217.

Schaal, B., and Marlier, L. 1998. Maternal and paternal perception of individual odor signatures in human amniotic fluid-potential role in early bonding? *Biol. Neonate*, 74:266–273.

Schaal, B., Montagner, H., Hertling, E., Bolzoni, D., Moyse, A., and Quichon, R. 1980. Olfactory stimulation in the relationship between child and mother. *Reprod. Nutr. Dev.*, 20:843–858.

Schanberg, S. M., and Kuhn, C. M. 1985. The biochemical effects of tactile deprivation in neonatal rats. *Perspect. Behav. Med.*, 2:133–148.

Schanberg, S. M., Evoniuk, G., and Kuhn, C. M. 1984. Tactile and nutritional aspects of maternal care: Specific regulators of neuroendocrine function and cellular development. *Proc. Soc. Exp. Biol. Med.*, 175:135–146.

Scharff, C., and Nottebohm, F. 1991. A comparative study of the behavioral deficits following lesions of various parts of the zebra finch song system: Implications for vocal learning. *J. Neurosci.*, 11:2896–2913.

Scheele, D., Wille, A., Kendrick, K. M., Stoffel-Wagner, B., Becker, B., Gunturkun, O., Maier, W., and Hurlemann, R. 2013. Oxytocin enhances brain reward system responses in men viewing the face of their female partner. *Proc. Natl. Acad. Sci. USA*, 110:20308–20313, doi:10.1073/pnas.1314190110.

Schenk, F., and Morris, R. G. 1985. Dissociation between components of spatial memory in rats after recovery from the effects of retrohippocampal lesions. *Exp. Brain Res.*, 58:11–28.

Schildkraut, J. M., Batos, E., and Berchuck, A. 1997. Relationship between lifetime ovulatory cycles and overexpression of mutant p53 in epithelial ovarian cancer. *J. Natl. Cancer Inst.*, 89:932–938.

Schindler, G. L. 1979. Testosterone concentration, personality patterns, and occupational choice in women. Ph.D. dissertation, University of Houston.

Schjelderup-Ebbe, T. 1922. Beiträge zür Socialpsychologie des haushuhns. *Z. Psychol.*, 88:225–252.

Schlinger, B. A. 1997. The activity and expression of aromatase in songbirds. *Brain Res. Bull.*, 44:359–364.

Schlinger, B. A. 1998. Sexual differentiation of avian brain and behavior: Current views on gonadal hormone-dependent and independent mechanisms. *Annu. Rev. Physiol.*, 60:407–429.

Schlinger, B. A., and Callard, G. V. 1990. Aggressive behavior in birds: An experimental model for studies of brain–steroid interactions. *Comp. Biochem. Physiol.*, 97A:307–316.

Schlinger, B. A., Fivizzani, A. J., and Callard, G. V. 1989. Aromatase, 5α- and 5β-reductase in brain, pituitary and skin of the sex-role reversed Wilson's phalarope. *J. Endocrinol.*, 122:573–581.

Schlinger, B. A., Soma, K. K., and London, S. E. 2001. Neurosteroids and brain sexual differentiation. *Trends Neurosci.*, 24:429–431.

Schmidt, P. J., Dor, R. B., Martinez, P. E., Guerrieri, G. M., Harsh, V. L., Thompson, K., Koziol, D. E., Nieman, L. K., and Rubinow, D. R. 2015. Effects of estradiol withdrawal on mood in women with past perimenopausal depression: A randomized clinical trial. *JAMA Psychiatry*, 72:714–726.

Schmidt, P. J., Nieman, L. K., Danaceau, M. A., Adams, L. F., and Rubinow, D. R. 1998. Differential behavioral effects of gonadal steroids in women with and those without premenstrual syndrome. *N. Engl. J. Med.,* 338:209–216.

Schmidt, P. J., Nieman, L. K., Grover, G. N., Muller, K. L., Merriam, G. R., and Rubinow, D. R. 1991. Lack of effect of induced menses on symptoms in women with premenstrual syndrome. *N. Engl. J. Med.,* 324:1174–1179.

Schmidt, P. J., Steinberg, E. M., Negro, P. P., Haq, N., Gibson, C., and Rubinow, D. R. 2009. Pharmacologically induced hypogonadism and sexual function in healthy young women and men. *Neuropsychopharmacology,* 34:565–576.

Schmitzer-Torbert, N. C. 2007. Place- and response-learning in human virtual navigation: Behavioral measures and gender differences. *Behav. Neurosci.,* 121:277–290.

Schneider, J. E. 2004. Energy balance and reproduction. *Physiol. Behav.,* 81:289–317.

Schneider, J. E. 2006. Metabolic and hormonal control of the desire for food and sex: Implications for obesity and eating disorders. *Horm. Behav.,* 50:562–571.

Schneider, J. E., and Wade, G. N. 1987. Body composition, food intake, and brown fat thermogenesis in pregnant Djungarian hamsters. *Am. J. Physiol.,* 253:R314–320.

Schneider, J. E., and Wade, G. N. 1989a. Availability of metabolic fuels controls estrous cyclicity of Syrian hamsters. *Science,* 244:1326–1328.

Schneider, J. E., and Wade, G. N. 1989b. Effects of maternal diet, body weight and body composition on infanticide in Syrian hamsters. *Physiol. Behav.,* 46:815–821.

Schneider, J. E., and Wade, G. N. 2000. Reproductive inhibition in service of energy balance. In K. Wallen and J. E. Schneider (eds.), *Reproduction in Context,* pp. 35–86. MIT Press, Cambridge, MA.

Schneider, J. E., and Watts, A. G. 2002. Energy balance, ingestive behavior, and reproductive success. In D. W. Pfaff, A. P. Arnold, A. M. Etgen, S. E. Fahrbach, and R. T. Rubin (eds.), *Hormones, Brain and Behavior,* Vol. 1, pp. 435–523. Academic Press, New York.

Schneider, J. E., and Zhou, D. 1999. Interactive effects of central leptin and peripheral fuel oxidation on estrous cyclicity. *Am. J. Physiol.,* 277:R1020–R1024.

Schneider, J. E., Casper, J. F., Barisich, A., Schoengold, C., Cherry, S., Surico, J., DeBarba, A., Fabris, F., and Rabold, E. 2007. Food deprivation and leptin prioritize ingestive and sex behavior without affecting estrous cycles in Syrian hamsters. *Horm. Behav.,* 51:413–427.

Schneider, J. E., Goldman, M. D., Tang, S., Bean, B., Ji, H., and Friedman, M. I. 1998. Leptin indirectly affects estrous cycles by increasing metabolic fuel oxidation. *Horm. Behav.,* 33:217–228.

Schneider, M. A., Brotherton, P. L., and Hailes, J. 1977. The effect of exogenous oestrogens on depression in menopausal women. *Med. J. Aust.,* 2:162–163.

Schneider, R., Osterburg, J., Buchner, A., and Pietrowsky, R. 2009. Effect of intranasally administered cholecystokinin on encoding of controlled and automatic memory processes. *Psychopharmacol.,* 202:559–567.

Schneiderman, I., Zagoory-Sharon, O., Leckman, J. F., and Feldman, R. 2012. Oxytocin during the initial stages of romantic attachment: Relations to couples' interactive reciprocity. *Psychoneuroendocrinology,* 37:1277–1285, doi:10.1016/j.psyneuen.2011.12.021

Schoech, S. J. 2001. Physiology of helping in Florida scrub-jays. In P. W. Sherman and J. Alcock (eds.), *Exploring Animal Behavior: Readings from American Scientist,* 3rd ed. Sinauer Associates, Inc., Sunderland, MA.

Schoech, S. J., Ketterson, E. D., Nolan, V., Sharp, P. J., and Buntin, J. D. 1998. The effect of exogenous testosterone on parental behavior, plasma prolactin, and prolactin binding sites in dark-eyed juncos. *Horm. Behav.,* 34:1–10.

Schoech, S. J., Rensel, M. A. Bridge, E. S. Boughton, R. K., and Wilcoxen, T. E. 2009. Environment, glucocorticoids, and the timing of reproduction. *Gen. Comp. Endocrinol.,* 163:201–207.

Schulz, H., and Lavie, P. 1985. *Ultradian Rhythms in Physiology and Behavior.* Springer-Verlag, Berlin.

Schulz, K. M., and Sisk, C. L. 2006. Pubertal hormones, the adolescent brain, and the maturation of social behaviors: Lessons from the Syrian hamster. *Mol. Cell. Endocrinol.,* 254–255:120–126.

Schulz, K. M., Molenda-Figueira, H. A., and Sisk, C. L. 2009. Back to the future: The organizational activational hypothesis adapted to puberty and adolescence. *Horm. Behav.,* 55:597–604.

Schuurman, T. 1980. Hormonal correlates of agonistic behavior in adult male rats. *Prog. Brain Res.,* 53:415–420.

Schwabl, H. 1993. Yolk is a source of maternal testosterone for developing birds. *Proc. Natl. Acad. Sci. USA,* 90:11446–11450.

Schwabl, H. 1996. Maternal testosterone in the avian egg enhances postnatal growth. *Comp. Biochem. Physiol. A,* 114:271–276.

Schwanzel-Fukuda, M., and Pfaff, D. W. 1989. Origin of luteinizing hormone-releasing hormone neurons. *Nature,* 138:161–164.

Schwanzel-Fukuda, M., Bick, D., and Pfaff, D. W. 1989. Luteinizing hormone-releasing hormone (LHRH)-expressing cells do not migrate normally in an inherited hypogonadal (Kallmann) syndrome. *Mol. Brain Res.,* 6:311–326.

Schwartz, G. J., Whitney, A., Skoglund, C., Castonguay, T. W., and Moran, T. H. 1999. Decreased responsiveness to dietary fat in Otsuka Long-Evans Tokushima fatty rats lacking CCK-A receptors. *Am. J. Physiol.,* 277:R1144–R1151.

Schwartz, M. D., Nunez, A. A. and Smale, L. 2004. Differences in the suprachiasmatic nucleus and lower subparaventricular zone of diurnal and nocturnal rodents. *Neuroscience,* 127:13–23.

Schwartz, M. W., Figlewicz, D. P., Baskin, D. G., Woods, S. C., and Porte, D. Jr. 1992. Insulin in the brain: a hormonal regulator of energy balance. *Endocr. Rev.,* 13:387–414.

Schwartz, M. W., Seeley, R. J., Campfield, L. A., Burn, P., and Baskin, D. G., 1996. Identification of hypothalamic targets of leptin action. *J. Clin. Invest.,* 98:1101–1106.

Schwartz, M. W., Woods, S. C., Porte, D., Seeley, R. J., and Baskin, D. G. 2000. Central nervous system control of food intake. *Nature,* 406:661–671.

Schwartz, W. J., and Gainer, H. 1977. Suprachiasmatic nucleus: Use of ^{14}C-labeled deoxyglucose uptake as a functional marker. *Science,* 197:1089–1091.

Schwarz, J. M., Nugent, B. M., McCarthy, M. M. 2010. Developmental and hormone-induced epigenetic changes to estrogen and progesterone receptor genes in brain are dynamic across the life span. *Endocrinology,* 151:4871–4881.

Scott, C. J., Jansen, H. T., Kao, C. C., Kuehl, D. E., and Jackson, G. L. 1995. Disruption of reproductive rhythms and patterns of melatonin and prolactin secretion following bilateral lesions of the suprachiasmatic nuclei in the ewe. *J. Neuroendocrinol.,* 7:429–443.

Scotti, M. A., Lee, G., and Gammie, S. C. 2011. Maternal defense is modulated by beta adrenergic receptors in lateral septum in mice. *Behav. Neurosci.,* 125:434–445.

Scotti, M. A., Place, N. J., and Demas, G. E. 2007. Short-day increases in aggression are independent of circulating gonadal steroids in female Siberian hamsters (*Phodopus sungorus*). *Horm. Behav.* 52:183–190.

Searcy, W. A., and Wingfield, J. C. 1980. The effects of androgen and anti-androgen on dominance and aggressiveness in male red-winged blackbirds. *Horm. Behav.,* 14:126–135.

Sedivy, J. M., and Sharp, P. A. 1989. Positive genetic selection for gene disruption in mammalian cells by homologous recombination. *Proc. Natl. Acad. Sci. USA,* 86:227–231.

Seegal, R. F., and Goldman, B. D. 1975. Effects of photoperiod on cyclicity and serum gonadotropins in the Syrian hamster. *Biol. Reprod.,* 12:223–231.

Seeley, R. J., and Woods, S. C. 2003. Monitoring of stored and available fuel by the CNS: Implications for obesity. *Nature Rev. Neuroscience,* 4:901–909.

Seeley, R. J., D'Alessio, D. A., and Woods, S. C. 2004. Fat hormones pull their weight in the CNS. *Nature Medicine*, 10:454–456.

Segal, S. K., and Cahill, L. 2009. Endogenous noradrenergic activation and memory for emotional material in men and women. *Psychoneuroendocrinol.*, 34:1263–1271.

Seifritz, E., Esposito, F., Neuhoff, J. G., Luthi, A., Mustovic, H., Dammann, G., von Bardeleben, U., Radue, E. W., Cirillo, S., Tedeschi, G., and Di Salle, F. 2003. Differential sex-independent amygdala response to infant crying and laughing in parents versus nonparents. *Biological Psychiatry*, 54:1367–1375.

Sekido, R., and Lovell-Badge, R. 2008. Sex determination involves synergistic action of SRY and SF1 on a specific *Sox9* enhancer. *Nature*, 453:930–934.

Selye, H. 1936. A syndrome produced by diverse nocuous agents. *Nature*, 138:32–35.

Selye, H. 1937a. Studies on adaptation. *Endocrinol.*, 21:169–188.

Selye, H. 1937b. The significance of the adrenals for adaptation. *Science*, 85:247–248.

Selye, H. 1950. *Stress*. Acta, Inc., Montreal.

Selye, H. 1956. *The Stress of Life*. McGraw-Hill, New York.

Selye, H. 1973. The evolution of the stress concept. *Am. Sci.*, 61:692–699.

Seminara, S. B., Messager, S., Chatzidaki, E. E., Thresher, R. R., Acierno, J. S. Jr., Shagoury, J. K., Bo-Abbas, Y., et al. 2003. The *GPR54* gene as a regulator of puberty. *N. Engl. J. Med.*, 349:1614–1627.

Semsar, K., and Godwin, J. 2004. Multiple mechanisms of phenotype development in the bluehead wrasse. *Horm. Behav.*, 45:345–353.

Semsar, K., Kandel, F. L., and Godwin, J. 2001. Manipulations of the AVT system shift social status and related courtship and aggressive behavior in the bluehead wrasse. *Horm. Behav.*, 40:21–31.

Seredynski, A. L., Balthazart, J., Christophe, V. J., Ball, G.F. and Cornil, C. A. 2013. Neuroestrogens rapidly regulate sexual motivation but not performance. *J. Neurosci.*, 33:164–174.

Serra, G. B. 1983. *The Ovary*. Raven Press, New York.

Setchell, J. M., Smith, T., Wickings, E. J., and Knapp, L. A. 2008. Factors affecting fecal glucocorticoid levels in semi-free-ranging female mandrills (*Mandrillus sphinx*). *Am. J. Primatol.*, 70:1023–1032.

Severino, S. K., and Moline, M. L. 1989. *Premenstrual Syndrome: A Clinician's Manual.* Guilford, New York.

Shah, S. N., and Nyby, J. G. 2010. Ghrelin's quick inhibition of androgen-dependent behaviors of male house mice (*Mus musculus*). *Horm. Behav.*, 57:291–296.

Shanmugalingam, T., Soultati, A., Chowdhury, S., Rudman, S., and Van Hemelrijck, M. 2013. Global incidence and outcome of testicular cancer. *Clin. Epidemiol.*, 5:417–427.

Shapiro, H. A. 1937. Effect of testosterone propionate on mating. *Nature*, 139:588–589.

Shapiro, L. E., and Insel, T. R. 1990. Infant's response to social separation reflects adult differences in affiliative behavior: A comparative developmental study in prairie and montane voles. *Dev. Psychobiol.*, 23:375–393.

Shapiro, L. E., Austin, D., Ward, S. E., and Dewsbury, D. A. 1986. Familiarity and female mate choice in two species of voles (*Microtus ochrogaster* and *Microtus montanus*). *Anim. Behav.*, 34:90–97.

Shapiro, S., Schlesinger, E. R., and Nesbitt, R. E. L. 1968. *Infant, Perinatal, Maternal, and Childhood Mortality in the United States.* Harvard University Press, Cambridge, MA.

Sharman, G. B. 1970. Reproductive physiology of marsupials. *Science*, 167:1221–1228.

Sharp, P. J., Dunn, I. C., Waddington, D., and Boswell, T. 2008. Chicken leptin. *Gen. Comp. Endocrinol.*, 158:2–4.

Sharp, P. J., Li, Q., Georgiou, G. C., and Lea, R. W. 1996. Expression of *fos*-like immunoreactivity in the hypothalamus of the ring dove (*Streptopelia risoria*) at the onset of incubation. *J. Neuroendocrinol.*, 8:291–298.

Sharp, P. J., Scanes, C. G., Williams, J. B., Harvey, S., and Chadwick, A. 1979. Variations in concentrations of prolactin, luteinizing hormone, growth hormone and progesterone in the plasma of broody bantams (*Gallus domesticus*). *J. Endocrinol.*, 80:51–57.

Shashoua, V. E. 1973. Seasonal changes in the learning and activity patterns of goldfish. *Science*, 181:572–574.

Shaywitz, B. A, Shaywitz, S. E., Pugh, K. R., Constable, R. T., Skudlarski, P., Fulbright, R. K., Bronen, R. A., Fletcher, J. M., Shankweller, D. P., Katz, L., and Gore, J. C. 1995. Sex difference in the functional organization of the brain for language. *Nature*, 373:607–609.

Sheehan, T., and Numan, M. 2002. Estrogen, progesterone, and pregnancy termination alter neural activity in brain regions that control maternal behavior in rats. *Neuroendocrinol.*, 75:12–23.

Sheehan, T., Paul, M., Amaral, E., Numan, M. J., and Numan, M. 2001. Evidence that the medial amygdala projects to the anterior/ventromedial hypothalamic nuclei to inhibit maternal behavior in rats. *Neuroscience*, 106:341–356.

Shen, E. Y., Ahern, T. H., Cheung, I., Straubhaar, J., Dincer, A., Houston, I., de Vries, G. J., Akbarian, S., and Forger, N. G. 2016. Epigenetics and sex differences in the brain: A genome-wide comparison of histone-3 lysine-4 trimethylation (H3K4me3) in male and female mice. *Exp. Neurol.*, 268:21–29.

Sher, L. 2004. Alcoholism and seasonal affective disorder. *Comprehensive Psychiatry*, 45:51–56.

Sheridan, P. J. 1978. Localization of androgen- and estrogen-concentrating neurons in the diencephalon and telencephalon of the mouse. *Endocrinol.*, 103:1328–1334.

Sheridan, P. J., Hagino, N., and Weaker, F. J. 1982. Androgen-concentrating cells in the periventricular brain of the female rhesus monkey. *J. Comp. Neurol.*, 207:93–98.

Sheriff, M. J., Krebs, C. J., and Boonstra, R. 2009. The sensitive hare: Sublethal effects of predator stress on reproduction in snowshoe hares. *J. Anim. Ecol.*, 78:1249–1258.

Sherman, P. W. 1988. The clitoris debate and the levels of analysis. *Anim. Behav.*, 37:697–698.

Sherry, D. F., Forbes, M. R., Khurgel, M., and Ivy, G. O. 1993. Females have a larger hippocampus than males in the brood-parasitic brown-headed cowbird. *Proc. Natl. Acad. Sci. USA*, 90:7839–7843.

Sherwin, B. B. 1991. The impact of different doses of estrogen and progestin on mood and sexual behavior in postmenopausal women. *J. Clin. Endocrinol. Metab.*, 72:336–343.

Sherwin, B. B. 1996. Estrogen, the brain, and memory. *Menopause*, 3:97–105.

Sherwin, B. B. 1997. Estrogen effects on cognition in menopausal women. *Neurol.*, 48:S21–S26.

Sherwin, B. B. 1998. Estrogen and cognitive functioning in women. *Proc. Soc. Exp. Biol. Med.*, 217:17–22.

Sherwin, B. B. 2003. Steroid hormones and cognitive functioning in aging men: A mini-review. *J. Molecular Neuroscience*, 20:385–393.

Sherwin, B. B., and Gelfand, M. M. 1985. Sex steroids and affect in the surgical menopause: A double-blind, cross-over study. *Psychoneuroendocrinol.*, 10:325–335.

Sherwin, B. B., and Suranyi-Cadotte, B. E. 1990. Up-regulatory effect of estrogen on platelet ^{3}H-imipramine binding sites in surgically menopausal women. *Biol. Psychiatry*, 28:339–348.

Sherwin, B. B., Gelfand, M. M., and Brender, W. 1985. Androgen enhances sexual motivation in females: a prospective, crossover study of sex steroid administration in the surgical menopause. *Psychosom. Med.*, 47:339–351.

Shi, J., Wittke-Thompson, J. K., Badner, J. A., Hattori, E., Potash, J. B., Willour, V. L., McMahon, F. J., Gershon, E. S., and Liu, C. 2008. Clock genes may influence bipolar disorder susceptibility and dysfunctional circadian rhythm. *Am. J. Med. Genet. B.*, 147B:1047–1055.

Shide, D. J., and Blass, E. M. 1989. Opioid-like effects of intraoral infusions of corn oil and Polycose on stress reactions in ten-day-old rats. *Behav. Neurosci.*, 103:1168–1175.

Shigeyoshi, Y., Taguchi, K., Yamamoto, S., Takekida, S., Yan, L., Tei, H., Moriya, T., Shibata, S., Loros, J. J., Dunlap, J. C., and Okamura, H. 1997. Light-induced resetting of a mammalian circadian clock is associated with rapid induction of the *mPer1* transcript. *Cell,* 91:1043–1053.

Shingo, T., Gregg, C., Enwere, E., Fujikawa, H., Hassam, R., Geary, C., Cross, J. C., and Weiss, S. 2003. Pregnancy-stimulated neurogenesis in the adult female forebrain mediated by prolactin. *Science,* 299:117–120.

Shiota, M., Sudou, M., and Ohshima, M. 1996. Using outdoor exercise to decrease jet lag in airline crewmembers. *Aviation Space Env. Med.,* 67:1155–1160.

Shippenberg, T., and Herz, A. 1987. Motivational properties of opioids. *Pol. J. Pharmacol. Pharmacy,* 39:577–583.

Shirazi, S. N., Friedman, A. R., Kaufer, D., and Sakhai, S. A. 2015. Glucocorticoids and the brain: Neural mechanisms regulating the stress response. *Adv. Exp. Med. Biol.,* 872:235–252. doi: 10.1007/978-1-4939-2895-8_10.

Shirley, B. 1984. The food intake of rats during pregnancy and lactation. *Lab. Anim. Sci.,* 34:169–172.

Shoemaker, C. M., and Crews, D. 2009. Analyzing the coordinated gene network underlying temperature-dependent sex determination in reptiles. *Semin. Cell Dev. Biol.,* 20:292–303.

Shors, T. J., and Miesegaes, G. 2002. Testosterone in utero and at birth dictates how stressful experience will affect learning in adulthood. *Proc. Natl. Acad. Sci. USA,* 99:13955–13960.

Shors, T. J., Chua, C., and Falduto, J. 2001. Sex differences and opposite effects of stress on dendritic spine density in the male versus female hippocampus. *J. Neurosci.,* 21:6292–6297.

Shors, T. J., Falduto, J., and Leuner, B. 2004. The opposite effects of stress on dendritic spines in male vs. female rats are NMDA receptor-dependent. *Eur. J. Neurosci.,* 19:145–150.

Shors, T. J., Weiss, C., and Thompson, R. F. 1992. Stress-induced facilitation of classical conditioning. *Science,* 257:537–539.

Shughrue, P. J. 1998. Estrogen action in the estrogen receptor α-knockout mouse: Is this due to ERβ? *Mol. Psychiatry,* 3:299–302.

Shughrue, P. J., Komm, B., and Merchenthaler, I. 1996. The distribution of estrogen receptor mRNA in the rat hypothalamus. *Steroids,* 61:678–681.

Siegel, H. I., and Rosenblatt, J. S. 1975. Hormonal basis of hysterectomy-induced maternal behavior during pregnancy in the rat. *Horm. Behav.,* 6:211–222.

Siegel, H. I., and Rosenblatt, J. S. 1978. Duration of estrogen stimulation and progesterone inhibition of maternal behavior in

pregnancy-terminated rats. *Horm. Behav.,* 11:12–19.

Silver, R. 1977. *Parental Behavior in Birds.* Dowden, Hutchinson and Ross, Stroudsburg, PA.

Silver, R. 1978. The parental behavior of ring doves. *Am. Sci.,* 66:209–215.

Silver, R., Andrews, H., and Ball, G. F. 1985. Parental care in an ecological perspective: A quantitative analysis of avian subfamilies. *Am. Zool.,* 25:823–840.

Silver, R., LeSauter, J., Tresco, P. A., and Lehman, M. N. 1996. A diffusible coupling signal from the transplanted suprachiasmatic nucleus controlling circadian locomotor rhythms. *Nature,* 382:810–813.

Silver, R., O'Connell, M., and Saad, R. 1979. Effect of androgens on the behavior of birds. In C. Beyer (ed.), *Endocrine Control of Sexual Behavior,* pp. 223–278. Raven Press, New York.

Silver, R., Sookhoo, A. I., LeSauter, J., Stevens, P., Jansen, H. T., and Lehman, M. N. 1999. Multiple regulatory elements result in regional specificity in circadian rhythms of neuropeptide expression in mouse SCN. *NeuroReport,* 10:3165–3174.

Silverin, B. 1980. Effects of long-acting testosterone treatment on free-living pied flycatchers (*Ficedula hypoleuca*) during the breeding period. *Anim. Behav.,* 28:906–912.

Silverin, B. 1990. Testosterone and corticosterone and their relation to territorial and parental behavior in the pied flycatcher. In J. Balthazart (ed.). *Hormones, Brain and Behaviour in Vertebrates,* Vol. 2, pp. 129–142. Karger, Basel.

Silverin, B., and Goldsmith, A. R. 1983. Reproductive endocrinology of free living Pied flycatchers (*Ficedula hypoleuca*): Prolactin and FSH secretion in relation to incubation and clutch size. *J. Zool. (Lond.),* 200:119–130.

Silverman, H. J., and Zucker, I. 1976. Absence of post-fast food compensation in the golden hamster, *Mesocricetus auratus. Physiol. Behav.,* 17:271–286.

Simerly, R. B. 1993. Distribution and regulation of steroid hormone receptor gene expression in the central nervous system. *Adv. Neurol.,* 59:207–226.

Simerly, R. B. 2002. Wired for reproduction: Organization and development of sexually dimorphic circuits in the mammalian forebrain. *Annu. Rev. Neurosci.,* 25:507–536.

Simerly, R. B., and Swanson, L. W. 1986. The organization of neural inputs to the medial preoptic nucleus of the rat. *J. Comp. Neurol.,* 246:312–342.

Simon, N. 2002. Hormonal processes in the development and expression of aggressive behavior. In D. W. Pfaff, A. P. Arnold, A. M. Etgen, S. E. Fahrbach, and R. T. Rubin (eds.), *Hormones, Brain and Behavior,* Vol. 1, pp. 339–392. Academic Press, New York.

Simon, N. G., and Lu, S.-F. 2005. Androgens and aggression. In R. J. Nelson (ed.), *Biology of Aggression.* Oxford University Press, New York.

Simon, N. G., Cologer-Clifford, A., Lu, S. F., McKenna, S. E., and Hu, S. 1998. Testosterone and its metabolites modulate 5HT$_{1A}$ and 5HT$_{1B}$ agonist effects on intermale aggression. *Neurosci. Biobehav. Rev.,* 23:325–336.

Simon, N. G., Kaplan, J. R., Hu, S., Register, T. C., and Adams, M. R. 2004. Increased aggressive behavior and decreased affliative behavior in adult male monkeys after long-term consumption of diets rich in soy protein and isoflavones. *Horm. Behav.,* 45:278–284.

Simon, N. G., McKenna, S. E., Lu, S. F., and Cologer-Clifford, A. 1996. Development and expression of hormonal systems regulating aggression. *Ann. N. Y. Acad. Sci.,* 794:8–17.

Simon, S., and Brandenberger, G. 2002. Ultradian oscillations of insulin secretion in humans. *Diabetes,* 51:S258–S261.

Simonneaux, V., Ancel, C., Poirel, V. J., and Gauer, F. 2013. Kisspeptins and RFRP-3 act in concert to synchronize rodent reproduction with seasons. *Front. Neurosci.,* 7:22.

Simpkins, J. W., Green, P. S., Gridley, K. E., Singh, M., de Fiebre, N. C., and Rajakumar, G. 1997. Role of estrogen replacement therapy in memory enhancement and the prevention of neuronal loss associated with Alzheimer's disease. *Am. J. Med.,* 22:19S–25S.

Simpson, E. R., and Davis, S. R. 2001. Aromatase and the regulation of estrogen biosynthesis—Some new perspectives. *Endocrinol.,* 142:4589–4594.

Simpson, J. B., Epstein, A. N., and Camardo, J. S. 1978. The localization of dipsogenic receptors for angiotensin II in the subfornical organ. *J. Comp. Physiol. Psychol.,* 92:581–608.

Sinclair, J. A., and Lochmiller, R. L. 2000. The winter immunoenhancement hypothesis: Associations among immunity, density, and survival in prairie vole (*Microtus ochrogaster*) populations. *Can. J. Zool.,* 78:254–264.

Sisk, C. L., and Foster, D. L. 2004. The neural basis of puberty and adolescence. *Nature Neurosci.,* 7:1040–1047.

Sisk, C. L., and Turek, F. W. 1982. Daily melatonin injections mimic the short day-induced increase in negative feedback effects of testosterone on gonadotropin secretion in hamsters. *Biol. Reprod.,* 27:602–608.

Sisk, C. L., and Zehr, J. L. 2005. Pubertal hormones organize the adolescent brain and behavior. *Front. Neuroendocrinol.,* 26:163–74.

Sisneros, J. A., Forlano, P. M., Deitcher, D. L., and Bass, A. H. 2004. Steroid-dependent auditory plasticity leads to adaptive coupling of sender and receiver. *Science,* 305:404–407.

Sjoholm, L. K., Backlund, L., Cheteh, E. H., Ek, I. R., Frisen, L., Schalling, M., Osby, U., Lavebratt, C., and Nikamo, P. 2010. CRY2 is associated with rapid cycling in bipolar disorder patients. *PLoS One*, 5:e12632.

Skuse, D. H., James, R. S., Bishop, D. V., Coppin, B., Dalton, P., Aamodt-Leeper, G., Bacarese-Hamilton, M., Creswell, C., McGurk, R., and Jacobs, P. A. 1997. Evidence from Turner's syndrome of an imprinted X-linked locus affecting cognitive function. *Nature*, 387:652–653.

Skuse, D., and Jacobs, P. 1997. Mosaicism in Turner's syndrome: A reply. *Nature*, 390:569.

Skutch, A. F. 1935. Helpers at the nest. *Auk*, 52:257–273.

Skwerer, R. G., Jacobsen, F. M., Duncan, C. C., Kelly, K. A., Sack, D. A., Tamarkin, L., Gaist, P. A., Kasper, S., and Rosenthal, N. E. 1988. Neurobiology of seasonal affective disorder and phototherapy. *J. Biol. Rhythms*, 3:135–154.

Slawski, B. A., and Buntin, J. D. 1995. Preoptic area lesions disrupt prolactin-induced parental feeding behavior in ring doves. *Horm. Behav.*, 29:248–266.

Slimp, J. C., Hart, B. L., and Goy, R. W. 1978. Heterosexual, autosexual and social behavior of adult male rhesus monkeys with medial preoptic–anterior hypothalamic lesions. *Brain Res.*, 142:105–122.

Slonaker, J. R. 1924. The effect of copulation, pregnancy, pseudopregnancy, and lactation on the voluntary activity and food consumption of the albino rat. *Am. J. Physiol.*, 71:362–394.

Sloviter, R. S., Valiquette, G., Abrams, G., Ronk, E., Sollas, A., and Paul, L. 1989. Selective loss of hippocampal granule cells following adrenalectomy. *Science*, 243:535–538.

Smale, L., Lee, T., and Nunez, A. A. 2003. Mammalian diurnality: some facts and gaps. *J. Biol. Rhythms*, 18:356–366.

Smale, L., Nelson, R. J., and Zucker, I. 1988. Daylength influences pelage and plasma prolactin concentrations but not reproduction in the prairie vole, *Microtus ochrogaster*. *J. Reprod. Fertil.*, 83:99–106.

Smale, L., Nunes, C., and Holekamp, K. E. 1997. Sexually dimorphic dispersal in mammals: Patterns, causes, and consequences. *Adv. Study Behav.*, 26:181–250.

Small, C. J., and Bloom, S. R. 2004. Gut hormones and the control of appetite. *Trends Endocrinol. Metab.*, 15:259–263.

Smals, A. G. H., Kloppenbort, P. W. C., and Benraad, T. H. 1976. Circannual cycle in plasma testosterone levels in man. *J. Clin. Endocrinol. Metab.*, 42:979–982.

Smith, C. L., Nawaz, Z., and O'Malley, B. W. 1997c. Coactivator and corepressor regulation of the agonist/antagonist activity of the mixed antiestrogen, 4–hydroxytamoxifen. *Mol. Endocrinol.*, 11:657–666.

Smith, C., and Lloyd, B. 1978. Maternal behavior and perceived sex of infant: Revisited. *Child Dev.*, 49:1263–1265.

Smith, G. P., Jerome, C., and Gibbs, J. 1981a. Abdominal vagotomy does not block the satiety effect of bombesin in the rat. *Peptides*, 2:409–411.

Smith, G. P., Jerome, C., Pi-Sunyer, F. X., Kissileff, H. R., and Thornton, J. 1981b. The satiety effect of cholecystokinin: A progress report. *Peptides*, 2:57–59.

Smith, G. T., Brenowitz, E. A., Nalls, B., and Wingfield, J. C. 1991. Testosterone changes song control region volume in photostimulated male Gambel's white-crowned sparrows (*Zonotrichia leucophrys gambelii*). Third International Congress of Neuroethology, Montreal, Quebec.

Smith, G. T., Brenowitz, E., and Wingfield, J. 1997b. Roles of photoperiod and testosterone in seasonal plasticity of the avian song control system. *J. Neurobiol.*, 32:426–42.

Smith, G. T., Brenowitz, E., Beecher, M., and Wingfield, J. 1997a. Seasonal changes in testosterone, neural attributes of song control nuclei, and song structure in wild songbirds. *J. Neurosci.*, 17:6001–6010.

Smith, G. T., Brenowitz, E., Wingfield, J., and Baptista, L. 1995. Seasonal changes in song nuclei and song behavior in Gambel's white-crowned sparrows. *J. Neurobiol.*, 28:114–25.

Smith, J. T. 2013. Sex steroid regulation of kisspeptin circuits. *Adv. Exp. Med. Biol.*, 784:275–295.

Smith, J. T., Clay, C. M., Caraty, A., and Clarke, I. J. 2007. KiSS-1 messenger ribonucleic acid expression in the hypothalamus of the ewe is regulated by sex steroids and season. *Endocrinology*, 148:1150–1157.

Smith, J. T., Dungan, H. M., Stoll, E. A., Gottsch, M. L., Braun, R. E., Eacker, S. M., Clifton, D. K., and Steiner, R. A. 2005. Differential regulation of KiSS-1 mRNA expression by sex steroids in the brain of the male mouse. *Endocrinology*, 146:2976–2984.

Smith, J. T., Dungan, H. M., Stoll, E. A., Gottsch, M. L., Braun, S. M., Clifton, D. K., and Steiner, R. A. 2005. Differential regulation of *KiSS-1* mRNA expression by sex steroids in the brain of the male mouse. *Endocrinology*, 146:2976–2984.

Smith, J. T., Popa, S. M., Clifton, D. K., Hoffman, G. E., and Steiner, R. A. 2006. *Kiss1* neurons in the forebrain as central processors for generating the preovulatory luteinizing hormone surge. *J. Neurosci.*, 26:6687–6694.

Smith, J.T., Coolen, L. M., Kriegsfeld, L. J., Sari, I. P., Jaafarzadehshirazi, M. R., Maltby, M., Bateman, K., et al. 2008. Variation in kisspeptin and RFamide-related peptide (RFRP) expression and terminal connections to gonadotropin-releasing hormone neurons in the brain: A novel medium for seasonal breeding in the sheep. *Endocrinology*, 149:5770–5782.

Smith, M. A., Riby, L. M., van Eekelen, J. A. M., and Foster, J. K. 2011. Glucose enhancement of human memory: A comprehensive research review of the glucose memory facilitation effect. *Neurosci. Biobehav. Rev.*, 35:770–783.

Smith, R., Cubis, J., Brinsmead, M., Lewin, T., Singh, B., Owens, P., Chan, E. C., Hall, C., Adler, R., Lovelock, M., Hurt, D., Rowley, M., and Nolan, M. 1990. Mood changes, obstetric experience and alterations in plasma cortisol, beta-endorphin and corticotrophin releasing hormone during pregnancy and the puerperium. *J. Psychosom. Res.*, 34:1941–1947.

Smith, Y. R., Stohler, C. S., Nichols, T. E., Bueller, J. A., Koeppe, R. A., and Zubieta, J. K. 2006. Pronociceptive and antinociceptive effects of estradiol through endogenous opioid neurotransmission in women. *J. Neurosci.*, 26:5777–5785.

Smulders, T. V., Gould, K. L., and Leaver, L. A. 2010. Using ecology to guide the study of cognitive and neural mechanisms of different aspects of spatial memory in food-hoarding animals. *Philos. Trans. R. Soc. Lond. B Biol. Sci.*, 365:883–900.

Smulders, T. V., Sasson, A. D., and DeVoogd, T. J. 1995. Seasonal variation in hippocampal volume in a food-storing bird, the black-capped chickadee. *J. Neurobiol.*, 27:15–25.

So, Y.-L., Bernal, T. U., Pillsbury, M. L., Yamamoto, K. R., and Feldman, B. J. 2009. Glucocorticoid regulation of the circadian clock modulates glucose homeostasis. *Proc. Natl. Acad. Sci. USA*, 106:17582–17587.

Södersten, P. 1973. Estrogen-activated sexual behavior in male rats. *Horm. Behav.*, 4:247–256.

Södersten, P., and Eneroth, P. 1984. Suckling and serum prolactin and LH concentrations in lactating rats. *J. Endocrinol.*, 102:251–256.

Solomon, M. B., Karom, M. C., Norvelle, A., Markham, C. A., Erwin, W. D., and Huhman, K. L. 2009. Gonadal hormones modulate the display of conditioned defeat in male Syrian hamsters. *Horm. Behav.*, 56:423–428.

Soma, K. K., and Wingfield, J. C. 1999. Endocrinology of aggression in the nonbreeding season. In N. Adams and R. Slotow (eds.), *Proceedings of 22nd International Ornithological Congress*, University of Natal, Durban, pp. 1606–1620.

Soma, K. K., and Wingfield, J. C. 2001. Dehydroepiandrosterone in songbird plasma: Seasonal regulation and relationship to territorial aggression. *Gen. Comp. Endocrinol.*, 123:144–155.

Soma, K. K., Bindra, R. K., Gee, J., Wingfield, J. C., and Schlinger, B. A. 1999a. Androgen-metabolizing enzymes show region-specific changes across the breeding season in the brain of a wild songbird. *J. Neurobiol.*, 41:176–188.

Soma, K. K., Rendon, N. M., Boonstra, R., Albers, H. E., and Demas, G. E. 2015. DHEA effects on brain and behavior: Insights from comparative studies of aggression. *J. Steroid Biochem. Mol. Biol.*, 145:261–272.

Soma, K. K., Scotti, M.-A. L., Newman, A. E. M., Charlier, T. D., and Demas, G. E. 2008. Novel mechanisms for neuroendocrine regulation of aggression. *Front. Neuroendocrinol.*, 29:476–489.

Soma, K. K., Sullivan, K. A., and Wingfield, J. C. 1999b. Combined aromatase inhibitor and antiandrogen treatment decreases territorial aggression in a wild songbird during the nonbreeding season. *Gen. Comp. Endocrinol.*, 115:442–453.

Soma, K. K., Sullivan, K. A., Tramontin, A. D., Saldanha, C. J., Schlinger, B. A., and Wingfield, J. C. 2000b. Acute and chronic effects of an aromatase inhibitor on territorial aggression in breeding and nonbreeding male song sparrows. *J. Comp. Physiol. A*, 186:759–769.

Soma, K. K., Tramontin, A. D., and Wingfield, J. C. 2000a. Oestrogen regulates male aggression in the non-breeding season. *Proc. Roy. Soc. Lond. B*, 267:1089–1096.

Soma, K. K., Wissman, A. M., Brenowitz, E. A., and Wingfield, J. C. 2002. Dehydroepiandrosterone (DHEA) increases territorial song and the size of an associated brain region in a male songbird. *Horm. Behav.*, 41:203–212.

Son, Y. L., Ubuka, T., Narihiro, M., Fukuda, Y., Hasunuma, I., Yamamoto, K., Belsham, D. D., Tsutsui, K. 2014. Molecular basis for the activation of gonadotropin-inhibitory hormone gene transcription by corticosterone. *Endocrinology*, 155:1817–1826.

Soriano, P. 1995. Gene targeting in ES cells. *Annu. Rev. Neurosci.*, 18:1–18.

Sowell, E. R., Peterson, B. S., Thompson, P. M., Welcome, S. E., Henkenius, A. L., and Toga, A. W. 2003. Mapping cortical change across the human life span. *Nat. Neurosci.*, 6:309–315.

Spencer, S. J., Steele, C. M., and Quinn, D. M. 1999. Stereotype threat and women's math performance. *J. Exp. Soc. Psychol.*, 35:4–28.

Spina, M., Merlo-Pich, E., Chan, R. K. W., Basso, A. M., Rivier, J., Vale, W., and Koob G. F. 1996. Appetite-suppressing effects of urocortin, a CRF-related neuropeptide. *Science*, 273:1561–1563.

Spiteri, T., Ogawa, S., Musatov, S., Pfaff, D. W., and Agmo, A. 2012. The role of the estrogen receptor α in the medial preoptic area in sexual incentive motivation, proceptivity and receptivity, anxiety, and wheel running in female rats. *Behav. Brain Res.*, 230:11–20.

Stachenfeld, N. S. 2008. Acute effects of sodium ingestion on thirst and cardiovascular function. *Curr. Sports Med. Rep.*, 7:S7–S13.

Stachenfeld, N. S. 2010. Sex hormone effects on body fluid regulation. *Exerc. Sport Sci. Rev.*, 36:152–159.

Stachenfeld, N. S. and Keefe, D. L. 2002. Estrogen effects on osmotic regulation of AVP and fluid balance. *Am. J. Physiol. Endocrinol. Metab.*, 283:E711–E772.

Staley, J. K., Rothman, R. B., Rice, K. C., Partilla, J., and Mash, D. C. 1997. Kappa-2 opioid receptors in limbic areas of the human brain are upregulated by cocaine in fatal overdose victims. *J. Neurosci.* 17: 8225–8233.

Stanley, B. G., and Leibowitz, S. F. 1985. Neuropeptide Y injected in the paraventricular hypothalamus: A powerful stimulant of feeding behavior. *Proc. Natl. Acad. Sci. USA*, 82:3940–3943.

Starkman, M., Gebarski, S. S., Berent, S., and Schteingart, D. A. 1992. Hippocampal formation volume, memory dysfunction and cortisol levels in patients with Cushing's syndrome. *Biol. Psychiatry*, 32:756–765.

Stearns, E., Winter, J., and Faiman, C. 1973. Effects of coitus on gonadotrophin, prolactin and sex steroid levels in man. *J. Clin. Endocrinol. Metab.*, 37:687–691.

Steeghs, K., Oerlemans, F., and Wieringa, B. 1995. Mice deficient in ubiquitous mitochondrial creatine kinase are viable and fertile. *Biochim. Biophys. Acta*, 1230:130–138.

Stefater, M. A., and Seeley, R. J. 2010. Central nervous system nutrient signaling: The regulation of energy balance and the future of dietary therapies. *Annu. Rev. Nutr.*, 30:219–235.

Steffens, A. B., Strubbe, J. H., Balkan, B., and Scheurink, A. J. W. 1990. Neuroendocrine mechanisms involved in regulation of body weight, food intake and metabolism. *Neurosci. Biobehav. Rev.*, 14:305–313.

Stein, L. J., and Woods, S. C. 1981. Cholecystokinin and bombesin act independently to decrease food intake in the rat. *Peptides*, 2:431–436.

Steinach, E. 1894. Investigations into the comparative physiology of the male sexual organs, with particular reference to the accessory sexual glands. trans. by M. Clarke. In C. S. Carter (ed.), *Hormones and Sexual Behavior*, pp. 11–30. Stroudsburg, Dowden, Hutchinson and Ross, Incorporated.

Steinach, E. 1910. Geschlechstrieb und echt sekundare Geschlechtsmerkmale als Folge der innersekretorisechen Funcktion der Keimdrusen. II. Uber die Enstehung des Umklammerunsreflexes bei Froschen. *Z. Physiol.*, 24:551–570.

Steinach, E. 1913. Feminierung von Männchen und Maskulierung von Weibchen. *Z. Physiol.*, 27:717–723.

Steinach, E. 1940. *Sex and Life.* Viking, New York.

Steiner, M., and Young, F. A. 2008. Hormones and mood. In J. B. Becker, K. J. Berley, N. Geary, E. Hampson, J. P. Herman, and E. A. Young (eds.). *Sex Differences in the Brain*,

pp. 405–426. Oxford University Press, New York.

Stellar, E. 1954. The physiology of motivation. *Psychological Rev.*, 61:5–22.

Stephan, F. K. 1983. Circadian rhythm dissociation induced by periodic feeding in rats with suprachiasmatic lesions. *Behav. Brain Res.*, 7:81–98.

Stephan, F. K. 2002. The "other" circadian system: Food as a Zeitgeber. *J. Biological Rhythms*, 17:284–292.

Stephan, F. K., and Zucker, I. 1972. Circadian rhythms in drinking behavior and locomotor activities are eliminated by hypothalamic lesions. *Proc. Natl. Acad. Sci. USA*, 69:1583–1586.

Stephan, F. K., Swann, J. M., and Sisk, C. L. 1979. Anticipation of 24-hr feeding schedules in rats with lesions of the suprachiasmatic nucleus. *Behav. Neural. Biol.*, 25:346–363.

Stern, J. E., and Armstrong, W. E. 1998. Reorganization of the dendritic trees of oxytocin and vasopressin neurons of the rat supraoptic nucleus during lactation. *J. Neurosci.*, 18:841–853.

Stern, J. M. 1990. Multisensory regulation of maternal behavior and masculine sexual behavior: A revised view. *Neurosci. Biobehav. Rev.*, 14:183–200.

Stern, J. M. 1996. Somatosensation and maternal care in Norway rats. *Adv. Study Behav.*, 25, 243:294.

Stern, J. M., and Johnson, S. K. 1990. Ventral somatosensory determinants of nursing behavior in Norway rats. I. Effects of variations in the quality and quantity of pup stimuli. *Physiol. Behav.*, 47:993–1011.

Stern, J. M., and Lonstein, J. S. 1996. Nursing behavior in rats is impaired in a small nestbox and with hyperthermic pups. *Dev. Psychobiol.*, 29:101–122.

Stern, J. M., Dix, L., Bellomo, C., and Thramann, C. 1992. Ventral trunk somatosensory determinants of nursing behavior in Norway rats: 2. Role of nipple and surrounding sensations. *Psychobiol.*, 20:71–80.

Sternberg, D. B., Issacs, K., Gold, P. E., and McGaugh, J. L. 1985. Epinephrine facilitation of appetitive learning: Attenuation with adrenergic receptor antagonists. *Behav. Neural Biol.*, 44:447–453.

Sternberg, D. B., Korol, D., Novack, G., and McGaugh, J. L. 1986. Epinephrine-induced memory facilitation: Attenuation by adrenergic receptor antagonists. *Eur. J. Pharmacol.*, 129:189–193.

Sternson, S. M. 2013. Hypothalamic survival circuits: Blueprints for purposive behaviors. *Neuron*, 77:810–814.

Stevens, R., and Goldstein, R. 1981. Effects of neonatal testosterone and estrogen on open-field behavior in rats. *Physiol. Behav.*, 26:551–553.

Stevenson, T. J. and Prendergast, B. J. 2013. Reversible DNA methylation regulates seasonal photoperiodic time measurement. *Proc. Natl. Acad. Sci. USA*, 110:16651–16656.

Stewart, J. 1988. Current themes, theoretical issues, and preoccupations in the study of sexual differentiation and gender-related behaviors. *Psychobiol.*, 16:315–320.

Stewart, J., and Cygan, D. 1980. Ovarian hormones act early in development to feminize adult open-field behavior in the rat. *Horm. Behav.*, 14:20–32.

Stochholm, K., Juul, S., Juel, K., Naeraa, R. W., and Gravholt, C. H. 2006. Prevalence, incidence, diagnostic delay, and mortality in Turner syndrome. *J. Clin. Endocrinol. Metab.*, 91:3897–3902.

Stockand, J. D. 2010. Vasopressin regulation of renal sodium excretion. *Kidney Intl.*, 78: 849–856.

Stone, C. P. 1922. The congenital sexual behavior of the young male albino rat. *J. Comp. Psychol.*, 2:95–153.

Stone, C. P. 1923. Further study of the sensory functions in the activation of sexual behavior in the young male albino rat. *J. Comp. Psychol.*, 3:469–473.

Stone, C. P. 1924. The awakening of copulatory behavior in the male albino rat. *Am. J. Physiol.*, 68:407–428.

Stone, C. P. 1925. Preliminary note on the maternal behavior of rats living in parabiosis. *Endocrinol.*, 9:505–512.

Stone, C. P. 1938a. Loss and restoration of copulatory activity in adult male rats following castration and subsequent injections of testosterone propionate. *Endocrinol.*, 23:529.

Stone, C. P. 1938b. Activation of impotent male rats by injections of testosterone propionate. *J. Comp. Psychol.*, 25:445–450.

Stone, C. P. 1938c. Effects of cortical destruction on reproductive behavior and maze learning in albino rats. *J. Comp. Psychol.*, 26:217–236.

Stone, C. P. 1939. Copulatory activity in adult male rats following castration and injections of testosterone propionate. *Endocrinol.*, 24:165–174.

Stone, C. P., and Commins, W. D. 1936. The effect of castration at various ages upon the learning ability of male albino rats: II. Relearning after an interval of one year. *J. Genet. Psychol.*, 48:20–28.

Stone, C. P., Barker, R. G., and Tomlin, M. I. 1935. Sexual drive in potent and impotent male rats as measured by the Columbia obstruction apparatus. *J. Genet. Psychol.*, 47:33–48.

Stone, W.S., Wenk, G.L., Stone, S.M., and Gold, P.E. 1992. Glucose attenuation of paradoxical sleep deficits in old rats. *Behav. Neur. Biol.*, 57:79–86.

Stopa, E. G., Johnson, J. K., Friedman, D. I., Ryer, H. I., Reidy, J., Kuo-LeBlanc, V., and

Albers, H. E. 1995. Neuropeptide Y receptor distribution and regulationin the suprachiasmatic nucleus of the Syrian hamster (*Mesocricetus auratus*). *Peptide Res.*, 8:95–100.

Storey, A. E. and Ziegler, T. E. 2016. Primate paternal care: Interactions between biology and social experience. *Horm. Behav.*, 77:260–271.

Storey, A. E., Courage, C., and Wynne-Edwards, K. 1998. Of mice and men: Why is there variation in the social cues that trigger mammalian paternal care? Paper presented at the Animal Behaviour Society meeting, June 1999, College Park, MD.

Storey, A. E., Walsh, C. J., Quinton, R. L., and Wynne-Edwards, K. E. 2000. Hormonal correlates of paternal responsiveness in new and expectant fathers. *Evol. Hum. Behav.*, 21:79–95.

Stowers, L., and Marton, T. 2005. What is a pheromone? Mammalian pheromones reconsidered. *Neuron*, 46:692–702.

Stowers, L., Holy, T. E., Meister, M., Dulac, C., and Koentges, G. 2002. Loss of sex discrimination and male-male aggression in mice deficient for TRP2. *Science*, 295:1493–1500.

Strachan, M. W. J., Deary, I. J., Ewing, F. M. E., and Frier, B. M. 1997. Is type II diabetes associated with an increased risk of cognitive dysfunction? *Diabetes Care*, 20:438–445.

Stratakis, C. A., and Chrousos, G. P. 1995. Neuroendocrinology and pathophysiology of the stress system. *Ann. N. Y. Acad. Sci.*, 771:1–18.

Strauss, R. H., Liggett, M. T., and Lanese, R. R. 1985. Anabolic steroid use and perceived effects in ten weight-trained women athletes. *JAMA*, 253:2871–2873.

Stricker, E. M. 1968. Some physiological and motivational properties of the hypovolemic stimulus for thirst. *Physiol. Behav.*, 3:379–385.

Stricker, E. M. 1984. Biological bases of hunger and satiety: Therapeutic implications. *Nutr. Rev.*, 42:333–340.

Stricker, E. M., and Verbalis, J. G. 1988. Hormones and behavior: The biology of thirst and sodium appetite. *Am. Sci.*, 76:261–267.

Stricker, E. M., and Verbalis, J. G. 1990b. Sodium appetite. In E. M. Stricker (ed.), *Handbook of Behavioral Neurobiology*, Vol. 10, pp. 387–419. Plenum, New York.

Stricker, E. M., Cooper, P. H., Marshall, J. F., and Zigmond, M. J. 1979. Acute homeostatic imbalances reinstate sensorimotor dysfunctions in rats with lateral hypothalamic lesions. *J. Comp. Physiol. Psychol.*, 93:512–521.

Stricker, E. M., Hosutt, J. A., and Verbalis, J. G. 1987. Neurohypophyseal secretion in hypovolemic rats: Inverse relation to sodium appetite. *Am. J. Physiol.*, 252:R889–R896.

Stricker, E. M., Rowland, N., Saller, C. F., and Friedman, M. I. 1977. Homeostasis during hypoglycemia: Central control of adrenal secretion and peripheral control of feeding. *Science*,196:79–81.

Strubbe, J. H., Steffens, A. B., and De Ruiter, L. 1977. Plasma insulin and the time pattern of feeding in the rat. *Physiol. Behav.*, 18:81–86.

Stunkard, A. J., Allison, K. C., Lundgren, J. D., Martino, N. S., Heo, M., Etemad, B., O'Reardin, J. P. 2006. A paradigm for facilitating pharmacotherapy at a distance: Sertraline treatment of the night eating syndrome. *J. Clin. Psychiatry*, 67:1568–1572.

Stunkard, A. J., Grace, W. J., and Wolff, H. G. 1955. The night-eating syndrome: A pattern of food intake among certain obese patients. *Am. J. Med.*, 19:78–86.

Su, T. P., Pagliaro, M., Schmidt, P. J., Pickar, D., Wolkowitz, O., and Rubinow, D. R. 1993. Neuropsychiatric effects of anabolic steroids in male normal volunteers. *JAMA*, 269:2760–2764.

Sugiyama, T., Minoura, H., Toyoda, N., Sakaguchi, K., Tanaka, M., Sudo, S., and Nakashima, K. 1996. Pup contact induces the expression of long form prolactin receptor mRNA in the brain of female rats: Effects of ovariectomy and hypophysectomy on receptor gene expression. *J. Endocrinol.*, 149:335–340.

Sundstrom, I, and Backstrom, T. 1998. Patients with premenstrual syndrome have decreased saccadic eye velocity compared to control subjects. *Biological Psychiatry*, 44:755–764.

Sundstrom, I., Nyberg, S., and Backstrom, T. 1997. Patients with premenstrual syndrome have reduced sensitivity to midazolam compared to control subjects. *Neuropsychopharmacol.*, 17:370–381.

Suomi, S. J. 1977. Adult male-infant interactions among monkeys living in nuclear families. *Child Dev.*, 48:1215–1270.

Suomi, S. J. 1991. Early stress and adult emotional reactivity in rhesus monkeys. *Ciba Found. Symp.*, 156:171–183.

Suomi, S. J. 1997. Early determinants of behaviour: Evidence from primate studies. *Brit. Med. Bull.*, 53:170–184.

Susman, J. L. 1996. Postpartum depressive disorders. *J. Fam. Pract.*, 43:S17–24.

Svare, B. 1983. *Hormones and Aggressive Behavior.* Plenum, New York.

Svare, B. 1990. Maternal aggression: Hormonal, genetic, and developmental determinants. In N. A. Krasnegor and R. S. Bridges (eds.), *Mammalian Parenting*, pp. 118–132. Oxford University Press, Oxford.

Svare, B., and Gandelman, R. 1976. Postpartum aggression in mice: Experiential and environmental factors. *Horm. Behav.*, 7:407–416.

Svare, B., Mann, M. A., Broida, J., and Michael, S. 1982. Maternal aggression exhibited by hypophysectomized parturient mice. *Horm. Behav.*, 16:455–461.

Svare, B., Miele, J., and Kinsley, C. 1986. Mice: Progesterone stimulates aggression in pregnancy-terminated females. *Horm. Behav.,* 20:194–200.

Swaab, D. F. and Hofman, M. A. 1990. An enlarged suprachiasmatic nucleus in homosexual men. *Brain Res.,* 537:141–148.

Swaab, D. F., and Fliers, E. A. 1985. A sexually dimorphic nucleus in the human brain. *Science,* 228:1112–1114.

Swaab, D. F., and Hofman, M. A. 1984. Sexual differentiation of the human brain: A historical perspective. *Prog. Brain Res.,* 61:361–374.

Swaab, D. F., Chung, W. C. J., Kruijver, F. P. M., Hofman, M. A., and Ishunina, T. A. 2001. Structural and functional sex differences in the human hypothalamus. *Horm. Behav.,* 40:93–98.

Swaney, W. T., Dubose, B. N., Curley, J. P., and Champagne, F. A. 2012. Sexual experience affects reproductive behavior and preoptic androgen receptors in male mice. *Horm. Behav.,* 61:472–478.

Swann, J. M., Wang, J., and Govek, E. K. 2003. The MPN mag: Introducing a critical area mediating pheromonal and hormonal regulation of male sexual behavior. *Ann. N. Y. Acad. Sci.,* 1007:199–210.

Swann, J., and Fiber, J. M. 1997. Sex differences in function of a pheromonally stimulated pathway: role of steroids and the main olfactory system. *Brain Res. Bull.,* 44:409–413.

Sweeney, B. M. 1976. Evidence that membranes are components of circadian oscillators. In J. W. Hastings and H. G. Schweiger (eds.), *Molecular Basis of Circadian Rhythms,* pp. 267–281. Abakon Verlagsgesellschaft, Berlin.

Sweeney, T., Donovan, A., Karsch, F. J., Roche, J. F., and O'Callaghan, D. 1997. Influence of previous photoperiodic exposure on the reproductive response to a specific photoperiod signal in ewes. *Biol. Reprod.,* 56:916–920.

Szymusiak, R., and Satinoff, E. 1982. Acute thermoregulatory effects of unilateral electrolytic lesions of the medial and lateral preoptic area in rats. *Physiol. Behav.,* 28:161–170.

Taibell, A. 1928. Riseglio artificiale di istinti tipicamenta feminili nei maschi di faluni uccelli. *Atti. Soc. Nat. Mat. Modena,* 59:93–102.

Takahashi, J. S. 1991. Circadian rhythms: From gene expression to behavior. *Curr. Opinion Neurobiol.,* 1:556–561.

Takahashi, J. S. 1992. Circadian clock genes are ticking. *Science,* 258:238–240.

Takahashi, J. S. 1993. Circadian-clock regulation of gene expression. *Curr. Opinion Genet. Devel.,* 3:301–309.

Takahashi, J. S., and Menaker, M. 1980. Interaction of estradiol and progesterone: Effects on circadian locomotor rhythms in female golden hamsters. *Am. J. Physiol.,* 239:R497–R504.

Takahashi, J. S., Kondo, H., Yoshimura, M., and Ochi, Y. 1974. Thyrotropin responses to TRH in depressive illness: Relation to clinical subtypes and prolonged duration of depressive episode. *Folia Psychiatrica Neurol. Japonica,* 28:355–365.

Takahashi, J. S., Kornhauser, J. M., Koumenis, C., and Eskin, A. 1993. Molecular approaches to understanding circadian oscillations. *Annu. Rev. Physiol.,* 55:729–753.

Takahashi, J. S., Murakami, N., and Nikaido, S. S. 1989. The avian pineal, a vertebrate model system of the circadian oscillator: Cellular regulation of circadian rhythms by light, second messengers, and macromolecular synthesis. *Rec. Prog. Horm. Res.,* 45:279–352.

Takahashi, J. S., Pinto, L. H., and Vitaterna, M. H. 1994. Forward and reverse genetic approaches to behavior in the mouse. *Science,* 264:1724–1733.

Tamarkin, L., Hutchison, J. S., and Goldman, B. D. 1976. Regulation of serum gonadotropins by photoperiod and testicular hormone in the Syrian hamster. *Endocrinol.,* 99:1528–1533.

Tan, M., Jones, G., Zhu, G., Ye, J., Hong, T., Zhou, S., Zhang, S., and Zhang, L. 2009. Fellatio by fruit bats prolongs copulation time. *PLoS One,* 4:e7595, doi: 10.1371/journal. pone.0007595.

Tanagho, E. A., Lue, T. F., and McClure, R. D. 1988. *Contemporary Management of Impotence Infertility.* Williams & Wilkins, Baltimore, MD.

Tanner, J. M. 1962. *Growth at Adolescence.* Blackwell, Oxford.

Taravosh-Lahn, K., and Delville, Y. 2004. Aggressive behavior in female golden hamsters: Development and the effect of repeated social stress. *Horm. Behav.,* 46:428–435.

Tartaglia, L. A., Dembski, M., Weng, X., Deng, N., Culpepper, J., Devos, R., Richards, G. J., et al. 1995. Identification and expression cloning of a leptin receptor, OB-R. *Cell,* 83:1263–1271.

Tasker, J. G. 2006. Rapid glucocorticoid actions in the hypothalamus as a mechanism of homeostatic integration. *Obesity,* 14:259S–265S.

Tasker, J. G. and Herman, J. P. 2011. Mechanisms of rapid glucocorticoid feedback inhibition of the hypothalamic–pituitary–adrenal axis. *Stress,* 14:398–406.

Tate-Ostroff B., and Bridges, R. S. 1985. Plasma prolactin levels in parental male rats: effects of increased pup stimuli. *Horm. Behav.,* 19:220–226.

Taylor, J. W. 1979. The timing of menstruation-related symptoms assessed by a daily symptoms rating scale. *Acta Psychiatrica Scand.,* 60:87–105.

Taylor, W. N., and Black, A. B. 1987. Pervasive anabolic steroid use among health club athletes. *Ann. Sports Med.,* 3:155–159.

Taymans, S. E., DeVries, A. C., DeVries, DeVries, M. B., Nelson, R. J., Friedman, T. C., Castro, M., Detera-Wadleigh, S., Carter, C. S., and Chrousos, G. P. 1997. The hypothalamic-pituitary-adrenal axis of prairie voles (*Microtus ochrogaster*): Evidence for target tissue glucocorticoid resistance. *Gen. Comp. Endocrinol.,* 106:48–61.

Tegelman, R., Carlström, K., and Pousette, A. 1988. Hormone levels in male ice hockey players during a 26-hour cup tournament. *Int. J. Androl.,* 11:361–368.

Telner, J., Lepore, F., and Guillemot, J. P. 1979. Effects of seratonin content on pain sensitivity in the rat. *Pharmacol. Biochem. Behav.,* 10:657–661.

Tena-Sempere, M. 2007. Roles of ghrelin and leptin in the control of reproductive function. *Neuroendocrinol.,* 86:229–241.

Tena-Sempere, M. 2008. Ghrelin as a pleotrophic modulator of gonadal function and reproduction. *Nat. Clin. Pract. Endocrinol. Metab.,* 4:666–674.

Tenk, C. M., Wilson, H., Zhang, Q., Pitchers, K. K., and Coolen, L. M. 2009. Sexual reward in male rats: Effects of sexual experience on conditioned place preferences associated with ejaculation and intromissions. *Horm. Behav.,* 55:93–97.

Tepper, B. J., and Friedman, M. I. 1991. Altered acceptability of and preference for sugar solutions by diabetic rats is normalized by high-fat diet. *Appetite,* 16:25–38.

Terkel, J., and Rosenblatt, J. S. 1968. Maternal behavior induced by maternal blood plasma injected into virgin rats. *J. Comp. Physiol. Psychol.,* 65:479–482.

Terman, M. 1988. On the question of mechanism in phototherapy for seasonal affective disorder: Considerations for clinical efficacy and epidemiology. *J. Biol. Rhythms,* 3:155–172.

Tessmar-Raible, K., Raible, F., Christodoulou, F., Guy, K., Rembold, M., Hausen, H., and Arendt, D. 2007. Conserved sensory-neurosecretory cell types in annelid and fish forebrain: Insights into hypothalamus evolution. *Cell,* 129:1389–1400.

Teyler, T. J., and Discenna, P. 1984. Long-term potentiation as a candidate mnemonic device. *Brain Res.,* 319:15–28.

Thapan, K., Arendt, J., and Skene, D. J. 2001. An action spectrum for melatonin suppression: Evidence for a novel non-rod, non-cone photoreceptor system in humans. *J. Physiol.,* 535:226–261.

Thase, M. E. 1989. Comparison between seasonal affective disorder and other forms of recurrent depression. In N. E. Rosenthal and M. C. Blehar (eds.), *Seasonal Affective Disorders and Phototherapy,* pp. 64–78. Guilford Press, New York.

Thomas, J. A., and Birney, E. C. 1979. Parental care and mating system of the prairie vole, *Microtus ochrogaster. Behav. Ecol. Sociobiol.,* 5:171–186.

Thomas, S. A., and Palmiter, R. D. 1997. Impaired maternal behavior in mice lacking norepinephrine and epinephrine. *Cell,* 91:583–592.

Thompson, C. I. 1980. *Controls of Eating.* Spectrum, Jamaica, New York.

Thompson, C. W., and Moore, M. C. 1992. Behavioral and hormonal correlates of alternative reproductive strategies in a polygynous lizard: tests of the relative plasticity and challenge hypotheses. *Horm. Behav.,* 26:568–585.

Thompson, C., Stinson, D., and Smith, A. 1990. Seasonal affective disorder and season-dependent abnormalities of melatonin suppression of light. *Lancet,* 336:703–706.

Thompson, D. A., Welle, S. L., Lilavivat, U., Pericaud, L., and Campbell, R. G. 1982. Opiate receptor blockade in man reduces 2-Deoxy-D-glucose induced food intake, but not hunger, thirst, and hypothermia. *Life Sci.,* 31:847–852.

Thompson, F. K. 2007. Is there a thyroid–cortisol–depression axis? *Thyroid Sci.,* 2:1.

Thompson, R. R., Walton, J. C., Bhalla, R., George, K. C., and Beth, E. H. 2008. A primitive social circuit: Vasotocin–substance P interactions modulate social behavior through a peripheral feedback mechanism in goldfish. *Eur. J. Neurosci.,* 27:2285–2293.

Thornton, J. W., Need, E., and Crews, D. 2003. Resurrecting the ancestral steroid receptor: Ancient origin of estrogen signaling. *Science,* 301:1714–1717.

Thys-Jacobs, S., and Alvir, M. J. 1995. Calcium-regulating hormones across the menstrual cycle: Evidence of a secondary hyperparathyroidism in women with PMS. *J. Clin. Endocrinol. Metab.,* 80:2227–2232.

Thys-Jacobs, S., Starkey, P., Bernstein, D., and Tian, J. 1998. Calcium carbonate and the premenstrual syndrome: Effects on premenstrual and menstrual symptoms. Premenstrual Syndrome Study Group. *Am. J. Obstet. Gynecol.,* 179:444–452.

Tian, M., Broxmeyer, H. E., Fan, Y., Lai, Z., Zhang, S., Aronica, S., Cooper, S., et al. 1997. Altered hematopoiesis, behavior, and sexual function in μ-opioid receptor-deficient mice. *J. Exp. Med.,* 185:1517–1522.

Tiemstra, J. D., and Patel, K. 1998. Hormonal therapy in the management of premenstrual syndrome. *J. Am. Fam. Pract.,* 11:378–381.

Tinbergen, N. 1935. The behavior of the red-necked Phalarope in spring. *Ardea,* 24:1–42.

Tinbergen, N. 1951. *The Study of Instinct.* Oxford University Press, Oxford.

Titze, J. 2014. Sodium balance is not just a renal affair. *Curr. Opin. Nephrol. Hypertens.,* 23:101–105.

Toates, F. 1995. *Stress: Conceptual Biological Aspects.* Wiley, New York.

Tobler, P. N. 2009. Behavioral functions of dopamine neurons. In L. Iversen, S. Iversen, S. Dunnett, and A. Bjorklund (eds.), *Dopamine Handbook,* pp. 316–331. Oxford University Press, New York.

Toffoletto, S., Lanzenberger, R., Gingnell, M. Sundstrom-Poromaa, I., and Comasco, E. 2014. Emotional and cognitive functional imaging of estrogen and progesterone effects in the female human brain: A systematic review. *Psychoneuroendocrinology,* 50:28–52.

Tofler, G. H., Stone, P. H., Maclure, M., Edelman, E., Davis, V. G., Robertson, T., Antman, E. M., and Muller, J. E. 1990. Analysis of possible triggers of acute myocardial infarction (the MILIS study). *Am. J. Cardiol.,* 66:22–27.

Toh, K. L., Jones, C. R., He, Y., Eide, E. J., Hinz, W. A., Virshup, D. M., Ptac̆ek, L. J., and Fu, Y.-H. 2001. An hPer2 phosphorylation site mutation in familial advanced sleep phase syndrome. *Science,* 291:1040–1043.

Tomova, A., and Kumanov, P. 1999. Sex differences and similarities of hormonal alterations in patients with anorexia nervosa. *Andrologia,* 31:143–147.

Tonegawa, S. 1995. Mammalian learning and memory studied by gene targeting. *Ann. N. Y. Acad. Sci.,* 758, 213–217.

Toran-Allerand, C. D. 1984. On the genesis of sexual differentiation of the central nervous system: Morphogenetic consequences of steroidal exposure and possible role of α-fetoprotein. In G. J. DeVries, J. P. C. DeBruin, H. B. M. Uylings, M. A. Corner (eds.), *Sex Differences in the Brain,* pp. 63–98. Elsevier, Amsterdam.

Tosca, L., Chabrolle, C., and Dupont, J. 2008. AMPK: A link between metabolism and reproduction?. *Med. Sci. (Paris),* 24:297–300.

Toubiana, L., Hanslik, T., and Letrilliart, L. 2001. French cardiovascular mortality did not increase during 1996 European football championship. *Br. Med. J.,* 322:1306.

Toyoda, F., Tanaka, S., Matsuda, K., and Kikuyama, S. 1994. Hormonal control of response to and secretion of sex attractants in Japanese newts. *Physiol. Behav.,* 55:569–576.

Tracey, K. J. and Cerami, A. 1990. Metabolic responses to cachectin/TNF: A brief review. *Ann. N. Y. Acad. Sci.,* 587:325–231.

Trainor, B. C., and Marler, C. A. 2001. Testosterone, paternal behavior, and aggression in the California mouse, *Peromyscus californicus. Horm. Behav.,* 40:32–42.

Trainor, B. C., and Marler, C. A. 2002. Testosterone promotes paternal behaviour in a monogamous mammal via conversion to oestrogen. *Proc. Roy. Soc. Lond. B,* 269:823–829.

Trainor, B. C., Bird, I. M., Alday, N. A., Schlinger, B. A., and Marler, C. A. 2003. Variation in aromatase activity in the medial preoptic area and plasma progesterone is associated with the onset of paternal behavior. *Neuroendocrinol.,* 78:36–44.

Trainor, B. C., Bird, I. M., and Marler, C. A. 2004. Opposing hormonal mechanisms of aggression revealed through short-lived testosterone manipulations and multiple winning experiences. *Horm. Behav.,* 45:115–121.

Trainor, B. C., Finy, M. S., and Nelson, R. J. 2008. Rapid effects of estradiol on male aggression depend on photoperiod in reproductively non-responsive mice. *Horm. Behav.,* 53:192–199.

Trainor, B. C., Lin, S., Finy, M. S., Rowland, M. R., and Nelson, R. J. 2007a. Photoperiod reverses the effects of estrogens on male aggression via genomic and non-genomic pathways. *Proc. Natl. Acad. Sci. USA,* 104:9840–9845.

Trainor, B. C., Sisk, C. L., and Nelson, R. J. 2016. Hormones and the development and expression of aggressive behavior. In D. W. Pfaff, et al. (eds.), *Hormones, Brain and Behavior.* (3rd ed.), Vol. 1 (In press).

Tramontin, A. D., and Brenowitz, E. A. 2000. Seasonal plasticity in the adult brain. *Trends Neuroscience,* 23:251–258.

Tricker, R., Casaburi, R., Storer, T. W., Clevenger, B., Berman, N., Shirazi, A., and Bhasin, S. 1996. The effect of supraphysiological doses of testosterone on angry behavior in healthy eugonadal men: A clinical research center study. *J. Clin. Endocrinol. Metab.,* 81:3754–3758.

Triemstra, J. L., and Wood, R. I. 2004. Testosterone self-administration in female hamsters. *Behav. Brain Res.,* 154:221–229.

Trivers, R. L. 1972. Parental investment and sexual selection. In B. G. Campbell (ed.), *Sexual Selection and the Descent of Man. 1871–1971,* pp. 136–179. Aldine, Chicago.

Trivers, R. L. 1974. Parent-offspring conflict. *Am. Zoologist* 14:249–264.

Trobec, R. J., and Oring, L. W. 1972. Effects of testosterone propionate implantation on lek behavior of sharp-tailed grouse. *Am. Midland Nat.,* 87:531–536.

Truitt, W. A., and Coolen, L. M. 2002. Identification of a potential ejaculation generator in the spinal cord. *Science,* 297:1566–1569.

Truitt, W. A., Shipley, M. T., Veening, J. G., and Coolen, L. M. 2003. Activation of a subset of lumbar spinothalamic neurons after copulatory behavior in male but not female rats. *J. Neurosci.,* 23:325–331.

Tsai, C. 1925. The relative strength of sex and hunger motives in the albino rat. *J. Comp. Psychol.,* 5:407.

Tsai, C. C., and Yen, S. S. 1971. Acute effects of intravenous infusion of 17-beta estradiol on gonadotropin release in pre- and post-menopausal women. *J. Clin. Endocrinol. Metab.,* 32:766–771.

Tseng, W.-S. 2006. From peculiar psychiatric disorders through culture-bound syndromes to culture-related specific syndromes. *Transcultural Psychiatry*, 43:554–576.

Tserotas, K., and Merino, G. 1998. Andropause and the aging male. *Arch. Androl.*, 40:87–93.

Tsutsui, K., Bentley, G. E., Bedecarrats, G., Osugi, T., Ubuka, T., and Kriegsfeld, L. J. 2010. Gonadotropin-inhibitory hormone (GnIH) and its control of central and peripheral reproductive function. *Front. Neuroendocrinol.*, 31:284–295.

Tsutsui, K., Saigoh, E., Ukena, K., Teranishi, H., Fujisawa, Y., and Kikuchi, M., et al. 2000. A novel avian hypothalamic peptide inhibiting gonadotropin release. *Biochem. Biophys. Res. Commun.*, 275:661–667.

Turek, F. W., and Campbell, C. S. 1979. Photoperiodic regulation of neuroendocrine-gonadal activity. *Biol. Reprod.*, 20:32–50.

Turek, F. W., Elliott, J. A., Alvis, J. D., and Menaker, M. 1975. The interaction of castration and photoperiod in the regulation of hypophyseal and serum gonadotropin levels in male golden hamsters. *Endocrinol.*, 96:854–860.

Turner, B. N., Perrin, M. R., and Iverson, S. L. 1975. Winter coexistence of voles in spruce forest: Relevance of seasonal changes in aggression. *Can. J. Zool.*, 53:1004–1011.

Turner, L. M., Young, A. R., Rompler, H., Schoneberg, T., Phelps, S. M., and Hoekstra, H. E. 2010. Monogamy evolves through multiple mechanisms: evidence from V1aR in deer mice. *Mol. Biol. Evol.*, 27:1269–1278.

Turton, M. D., O'Shea, M., Gunn, I., Beak, S. A., Edwards, C. M. B., Meeran, K., Choi, S. J., et al. 1996. A role for glucagon-like peptide-1 in the central regulation of feeding. *Nature*, 379:69–72.

Tuttle, W. W., and Dykshorn, S. 1928. The effect of castration and ovariectomy on spontaneous activity and ability to learn. *Proc. Soc. Exp. Biol. Med.*, 25:569–570.

Twiggs, D. G., Popolow, H. B., and Gerall, A. A. 1978. Medial preoptic lesions and male sexual behavior: Age and environmental interactions. *Science*, 200:1414–1415.

Tyler, S. J. 1972. The behaviour and social organization of the New Forest ponies. *Anim. Behav. Monogr.*, 5:87–196.

Tyndale-Biscoe, H., and Renfree, M. 1987. *Reproductive Physiology of Marsupials.* Cambridge University Press, Cambridge.

U.S. Anti-Doping Agency (USADA). 2012a. U.S. Postal Service Pro Cycling Team investigation. Reasoned decision. Retrieved from http://d3epuodzu3wuis.cloudfront.net/ReasonedDecision.pdf

U.S. Anti-Doping Agency (USADA). 2012b. U.S. Postal Service Pro Cycling Team investigation. Statement from USADA CEO

Travis T. Tygart regarding the U.S. Postal Service Pro Cycling Team doping conspiracy. Retrieved from http://cyclinginvestigation.usada.org/

Ubuka, T., Bentley, G. E., Ukena, K., Wingfield, J. C., and Tsutsui, K. 2005. Melatonin induces the expression of gonadotropin-inhibitory hormone in the avian brain. *Proc. Natl. Acad. Sci. USA*, 102:3052–3057.

Ubuka, T., Inoue, K., Fukuda, Y., Mizuno, T., Ukena, K., Kriegsfeld, L. J., and Tsutsui, K. 2012. Identification, expression, and physiological functions of Siberian hamster gonadotropin-inhibitory hormone. *Endocrinology*, 153:373–385.

Uhrich, J. 1938. The social hierarchy in albino mice. *J. Comp. Psychol.*, 23:373–413.

Ung, E. K., Lee, S., and Kua, E. H. 1997. Anorexia nervosa and bulimia—a Singapore perspective. *Singapore Med. J.*, 38:332–335.

Ursin, H., Baade, E., and Levine, S. 1978. *Psychobiology of Stress: A Study of Coping Men.* Academic Press, London.

Ussher, J. 1989. *The Psychology of the Female Body.* Routledge, New York.

Vaillancourt, T., Duku, E., Decatanzaro, D., Macmillan, H., Muir, C., and Schmidt, L. A. 2008. Variation in hypothalamic–pituitary–adrenal axis activity among bullied and non-bullied children. *Aggress. Behav.*, 34:294–305.

Valdés, M. E., Marino, D. J., Wunderlin, D. A., Somoza, G. M., Ronco, A. E., and Carriquiriborde, P. 2015. Screening concentration of E1, E2 and EE2 in sewage effluents and surface waters of the "Pampas" region and the "Río de la Plata" estuary (Argentina). *Bull. Environ. Contam. Toxicol.*, 94:29–33.

Valenstein, E. S., and Young, W. C. 1955. An experiential factor influencing the effectiveness of testosterone proprionate in eliciting sexual behavior in male guinea pigs. *Endocrinol.*, 56:173–185.

van Anders, S. M. 2012. Testosterone and sexual desire in healthy women and men. *Arch. Sex. Behav.*, 41:1471–1484.

van Anders, S. M. 2013. Beyond masculinity: testosterone, gender/sex, and human social behavior in a comparative context. *Front. Neuroendocrinol.*, 34:198–210.

van Anders, S. M. and Watson, N. V. 2006. Social neuroendocrinology: Effects of social contexts and behaviors on sex steroids in humans. *Hum. Nat.*, 17:212–237.

van Anders, S. M., and Watson, N. V. 2006. Relationship status and testosterone in North American heterosexual and non-heterosexual men and women: Cross-sectional and longitudinal data. *Psychoneuroendocrinol.*, 31:715–723.

van Anders, S. M., Goldey, K. L., Conley, T. D., Snipes, D. J., and Patel, D. A. 2012. Safer sex as the bolder choice: Testosterone is

positively correlated with safer sex behaviorally relevant attitudes in young men. *J. Sex. Med.*, 9:727–734.

Van Anders, S. M., Tolman, R. M., and Volling, B. L. 2012. Baby cries and nurturance affect testosterone in men. *Horm. Behav.*, 61:31–36.

van Bruggen, N., and Roberts, T. P. L. 2002. *Biomedical Imaging in Experimental Neuroscience: Methods and New Frontiers in Neuroscience.* CRC Press, Boca Raton, FL.

van de Beek, C., van Goozen, S. H. M., Buitelaar, J. K., and Cohen-Kettenis, P. T. 2009. Prenatal sex hormones (maternal and amniotic fluid) and gender-related play behavior in 13-month-old infants. *Arch. Sex. Behav.*, 38:6–15.

Van de Kar, L. D., Richardson-Morton, K. D., and Rittenhouse, P. A. 1991. Stress: Neuroendocrine and pharmacological mechanisms. In G. Jasmin and M. Cantin (eds.). *Stress Revisited: Neuroendocrinology of Stress. Methods and Achievements in Experimental Pathology*, Vol. 14, pp. 133–173. Karger, Basel.

Van der Beek, E. M., Horvath, T. L., Wiegant, V. M., Van den Hurk, R., and Buijs, R. M. 1997. Evidence for a direct neuronal pathway from the suprachiasmatic nucleus to the gonadotropin-releasing hormone system: Combined tracing and light and electron microscopic immunocytochemical studies. *J. Comp. Neurol.*, 384:569–579.

Van der Beek, E. M., Wiegant, V. M., Van der Donk, H. A., Van den Hurk, R., and Buijs, R. M. 1993. Lesions of the suprachiasmatic nucleus indicate the presence of a direct vasoactive intestinal polypeptide-containing projection to gonadotrophin-releasing hormone neurons in the female rat. *J. Neuroendocrinol.*, 5:137–144.

van der Meij, L., Almela, M., Hidalgo, V., Villada, C., Ijerman, H., van Lange, P. A. M., and Salvador, A. 2012. Testosterone and cortisol release among Spanish soccer fans watching the 2010 World Cup Final. *PLOS One*, doi:10.1371/journal.pone.0034814.

Van Dis, H., and Larsson, K. 1971. Induction of sexual arousal in the castrated male rat by intracranial stimulation. *Physiol. Behav.*, 6:85–86.

van Furth, W. R., Wolterink, G., and van Ree, J. M. 1995. Regulation of masculine sexual behavior: Involvement of brain opioids and dopamine. *Brain Res. Rev.*, 21:162–184.

Van Gelder, R. N. 2003. Making (a) sense of non-visual ocular photoreception. *Trends Neurosci.*, 26:458–461.

van Ijzendoorn, M., Bakermans-Kranenburg, M., and Mesman, J. 2008. Dopamine system genes associated with parenting in the context of daily hassles. *Genes Brain Behav.*, 7:403–410.

Van Reeth, O., and Turek, F. W. 1989. Stimulated activity mediates phase shifts in the hamster circadian clock induced by dark pulses or benzodiazepines. *Nature*, 339:49–51.

Vandenbergh, J. G. 1969. Endocrine coordination in monkeys: Male sexual responses to the female. *Physiol. Behav.*, 4:261–264.

Vander Wal, J. S. 2014. The treatment of night eating syndrome: A review and theoretical model. *Curr. Obes. Rep.*, 3:137–144.

Vanderreycken, W., and Van Deth, R. 1994. *From Fasting Saints to Anorexic Girls.* New York University Press, New York.

Vanecek, J. 1988. Melatonin binding sites. *J. Neurochem.*, 51:1436–1440.

Vaughan, J., Donaldson, C., Bittencourt, K., Perrin, M. H., Lewis, K., Sutton, S., Chan, R., Turnbull, A. V., Lovejoy, D., Rivier, C., Rivier, J., Sawchenko, P. E., and Vale, W. 1995. Urocortin, a mammalian neuropeptide related to fish urotensin I and to corticotrophin-releasing factor. *Nature*, 378:287–292.

Veenema, A. H., Beiderbeck, D. I., Kukas, M., and Neumann, I. D. 2010. Distinct correlations of vasopressin release within the lateral septum and the bed nucleus of the stria terminalis with the display of intermale aggression. *Horm. Behav.*, 58:273–281.

Veldhuis, J. D., Weiss, J., Mauras, N., Rogol, A. D., Evans, W. S., and Johnson, M. L. 1986. Appraising endocrine pulse signals at low circulating hormone concentrations: use of regional coefficients of variation in the experimental series to analyze pulsatile luteinizing hormone release. *Pediatr. Res.*, 20:632–637.

Velle, W. 1987. Sex differences in sensory functions. *Perspect. Biol. Med.*, 30:490–522.

Vergnes, M., Depaulis, A., and Boehrer, A. 1986. Parachlorophenylalanine-induced serotonin depletion increases offensive but not defensive aggression in male rats. *Physiol. Behav.*, 36: 653–658.

Vermeulen, A., Rubens, R., and Verdonck, L. 1972. Testosterone secretion and metabolism in male senescence. *J. Clin. Endocrinol. Metab.*, 34:730–735.

Vessely, L. H., and Lewy, A. J. 2002. Melatonin as a hormone and as a marker for circadian phase position in humans. In D. W. Pfaff, A. P. Arnold, A. M. Etgen, S. E. Fahrbach, and R. T. Rubin (eds.), *Hormones, Brain and Behavior*, Vol. 5, pp. 121–141. Academic Press, New York.

Vida, B., Deli, L., Hrabovszky, E., Kalamatianos, T., Caraty, A., Coen, C. W., Liposits, Z., and Kalló, I. 2010. Evidence for suprachiasmatic vasopressin neurones innervating kisspeptin neurones in the rostral periventricular area of the mouse brain: regulation by oestrogen. *J. Neuroendocrinol.*, 22:1032–1039.

Vink, T., Hinney, A., van Elburg, A. A., van Goozen, S. H., Sandkuijl, L. A., Sinke, R. J., Herpertz-Dahlmann, B. M., Hebebrand, J., Remschmidt, H., van Engeland, H., and Adan, R. A. H. 2001. Association between an agouti-related protein gene polymorphism and anorexia nervosa. *Mol. Psychiatry*, 6:325–328.

Viola, A. U., Archer, S. N., James, L. M., Groeger, J. A., Lo, J. C. Y., Skene, D. J., von Schantz, M., Dijk, D.-J. 2007. PER3 polymorphism predicts sleep structure and waking performance. *Curr. Biol.*, 17:613–618.

Virgin, C. E., and Sapolsky, R. M. 1997. Styles of male social behavior and their endocrine correlates among low-ranking baboons. *Am. J. Primatol.*, 42:25–39.

Vitaterna, M. H., King, D.P., Chang, A-M, Kornhauser, J. M., Lowrey, P. L., McDonald, J. D., Dove, W.F., et al. 1994. Mutagenesis and mapping of a mouse gene, Clock, essential for circadian behavior. *Science,* 264:719–725.

vom Saal, F. S. 1979. Prenatal exposure to androgen influences morphology and aggressive behavior of male and female mice. *Horm. Behav.*, 12:1–11.

vom Saal, F. S., and Finch, C. E. 1988. Reproductive senescence: Phenomena and mechanisms in mammals and selected vertebrates. In E. Knobil and J. Neill (eds.), *Physiology of Reproduction*, pp. 2351– 2413. Raven Press, New York.

vom Saal, F. S., and Hughes, C. 2005. An extensive new literature concerning low-dose effects of bisphenol A shows the need for a new risk assessment. *Environ. Health Perspect.*, 113:926–933.

vom Saal, F. S., Cooke, P. S., Buchanan, D. L., Palanza, P., Thayer, K. A., Nagel, S. C., Parmigiani, S., and Welshons, W. V. 1998. A physiologically based approach to the study of bisphenol A and other estrogenic chemicals on the size of reproductive organs, daily sperm productions, and behavior. *Toxicol. Ind. Health*, 14:239–260.

Voss, U. 2004. Functions of sleep architecture and the concept of protective fields. *Rev. Neurosci.*, 15:33–46.

Waber, D. 1976. Sex differences in cognition: A function of maturation rate. *Science,* 192:572–574.

Wada, J. A. 1976. *Sex differences in brain asymmetry.* International Neuropsychological Society, Toronto.

Wade, G. N. 1972. Gonadal hormones and behavioral regulation of body weight. *Physiol. Behav.*, 8:523–534.

Wade, G. N. 1976. Sex hormones, regulatory behaviors and body weight. *Adv. Study Behav.*, 6:201–279.

Wade, G. N. 1986. Sex steroids and energy balance: Sites and mechanisms of action. *Ann. N. Y. Acad. Sci.*, 474:389–399.

Wade, G. N., and Gray, J. M. 1978. Cytoplasmic 17β-[³H]estradiol binding in rat adipose tissues. *Endocrinol.*, 103:1695–1701.

Wade, G. N., and Gray, J. M. 1979. Gonadal effects on food intake and adiposity: A metabolic hypothesis. *Physiol. Behav.*, 22:583–593.

Wade, G. N., and Jones, J. E. 2003. Lessons from experimental disruption of estrous cycles and behaviors. *Medicine and Science in Sports and Exercise*, 35:1573–1580.

Wade, G. N., and Zucker, I. 1970. Modulation of food intake and locomotor activity in female rats by diencephalic hormone implants. *J. Comp. Physiol. Psychol.*, 72:328–336.

Wade, G. N., Jennings, G., and Trayhurn, P. 1986. Energy balance and brown adipose tissue thermogenesis during pregnancy in Syrian hamsters. *Am. J. Physiol.*, 250:R845–R850.

Wade, G. N., Lempicki, R. L., Panicker, A. K., Frisbee, R. M., and Blaustein, J. D. 1997. Leptin facilitates and inhibits sexual behavior in female hamsters. *Am. J. Physiol.*, 272:R1354–R1358.

Wade, J. 2001. Zebra finch sexual differentiation: The aromatization hypothesis revisited. *Microscopy Research and Technique*, 54:354–363.

Wade, J., and Arnold, A. P. 1996. Functional testicular tissue does not masculinize development of the zebra finch song system. *Proc. Natl. Acad. Sci. USA*, 93:5264–5268.

Wahlstrom, G. 1965. *Circadian Clocks.* North-Holland, Amsterdam.

Wald, M., Miner, M., and Seftel, A. D. 2009. Male menopause: Fact or fiction? *Amer. J. Lifestyle Med.*, 2:132–141.

Wallen, K. 2009. The organizational hypothesis: Reflections on the 50th anniversary of the publication of Phoenix, Goy, Gerall, and Young (1959). *Horm. Behav.*, 55:561–565.

Wallen, K. and Hassett, J. M. 2009. Sexual differentiation of behaviour in monkeys: role of prenatal hormones. *J Neuroendocrinol.*, 21:421–426.

Wallen, K., and Baum, M. J. 2002. Masculinization and defeminization in altricial and precocial mammals: Comparative aspects of steroid hormone action. In D. W. Pfaff, A. Arnold, A. Etgen, S. Fahrbach, and R. Rubin (eds.), *Hormones, Brain, and Behavior*, Vol. 4, pp. 385–423. Academic Press, New York.

Wallman, J., Grabon, M. B., and Silver, R. 1979. What determines the pattern of sharing of incubation and brooding in ring doves? *J. Comp. Physiol. Psychol.*, 93:481–492.

Walsh, C. O., Ebbeling, C. B., Swain, J. F., Markowitz, R. L., Feldman, H. A., and Ludwig, D. S. 2013. Effects of diet composition on postprandial energy availability during weight loss maintenance. *PLoS One*, 8: e58172. doi: 10.1371/journal.pone.0058172.

Walton, J. C., Weil, Z. W., and Nelson, R. J. 2011. The influence of photoperiod on behavior, endocrine, and immune function. *Front. Neuroendocrinol.*, 32:302–319.

Walum, H., Westberg, L., Henningsson, S., Neiderhiser, J. M., Reiss, D., Igl, W.,

Ganiban, J. M., Spotts, E. L., Pedersen, N. L., Eriksson, E., and Lichtenstein, P. 2008. Genetic variation in the vasopressin receptor 1a gene (*AVPR1A*) associates with pair-bonding behavior in humans. *Proc. Natl. Acad. Sci. USA*, 105:14153–14156.

Wang, C., and Swerdloff, R. S. 1997. Androgen replacement therapy. *Ann. Med.*, 29:365–370.

Wang, C., Harnett, M., Dobs, A., and Swerdloff, R. S. 2010. Pharmakinetics and safety of long-acting testosterone undecanoate injections in hypogonadal men: An 84-week phase III clinical trial. *J. Androl.*, doi: 10.2164/jandrol.109.009597.

Wang, G. H. 1923. The relation between 'spontaneous' activity and oestrous cycle in the white rat. *Comp. Psychol. Monogr.*, 2:1–27.

Wang, G. H. 1924. The changes in the amount of daily food-intake of the albino rat during pregnancy and lactation. *Am. J. Physiol.*, 71:735–741.

Wang, H., Ko, C. H., Koletar, M. M., Ralph, M. R., and Yeomans, J. 2007. Casein kinase I epsilon gene transfer into the suprachiasmatic nucleus via electroporation lengthens circadian periods of tau mutant hamsters. *Eur. J. Neurosci.*, 25:3359–3366.

Wang, Z. X., and Novak, M. A. 1994. Parental care and litter development in primiparous and multiparous prairie voles (*Microtus ochrogaster*). *J. Mammal.*, 75:18–23.

Wang, Z., and Young, L. J. 1997. Ontogeny of oxytocin and vasopressin receptor binding in the lateral septum in prairie and montane voles. *Brain Res.: Dev. Brain Res.*, 104:191–195.

Ward, I. L. 1992. Sexual behavior: The product of perinatal hormonal and prepubertal social factors. In A. A. Gerall, H. Moltz, and I. L. Ward (eds.), *Sexual Differentiation*, Vol. 11 of *Handbook of Behavioral Neurobiology*. Plenum Press, New York.

Ward, I. L., and Reed, J. 1985. Prenatal stress and prepubertal social rearing conditions interact to determine sexual behavior in male rats. *Behav. Neurosci.*, 99:301–309.

Ward, I. L., and Stehm, K. E. 1991. Prenatal stress feminizes juvenile play patterns in male rats. *Physiol. Behav.*, 50:601–605.

Ward, I. L., and Weisz, J. 1980. Maternal stress alters plasma testosterone in fetal males. *Science*, 207:328–329.

Ward, I. L., Ward, O. B., French, J. A., Hendricks, S. E., Mehan, D., and Winn, R. J. 1996. Prenatal alcohol and stress interact to attenuate ejaculatory behavior, but not serum testosterone or LH in adult male rats. *Behav. Neurosci.*, 110:1469–1477.

Ward, M. W., and Holimon, T. D. 1999. Calcium treatment for premenstrual syndrome. *Ann. Pharmacotherapy*, 33:1356–1358.

Ward, P. 1965. Seasonal changes in the sex ratio of *Quelea quelea*. *Ibis*, 107:397–399.

Warner, L. H. 1927. A study of sex behavior in the white rat by means of the obstruction method. *Comp. Psychol. Monogr.*, 4:1–68.

Warren, M. P., and Shortle, B. 1990. Endocrine correlates of human parenting. In N. A. Krasnegor and R. S. Bridges (eds.), *Mammalian Parenting*, pp. 209–230. Oxford University Press, Oxford.

Warren, S. G., and Juraska, J. M. 1997. Spatial and nonspatial learning across the rat estrous cycle. *Behav. Neurosci.*, 111:259–266.

Wartofsky, L., and Burman, K. D. 1982. Alterations in thyroid function in patients with systemic illness: The "euthyroid sick syndrome." *Endocrine Rev.*, 3:164–217.

Watanabe, Y., Gould, E., and McEwen, B. S. 1992. Stress induces atrophy of apical dendrites of hippocampal CA3 pyramidal neurons. *Brain Res.*, 588:341–345.

Waterhouse, J., Reilly, T., and Atkinson, G. 1998. Melatonin and jet lag. *Br. J. Sports Med.*, 32:98–99.

Watson, C. S., Alyea, R. A., Jeng, Y. J., and Kochukov, M. Y. 2007. Nongenomic actions of low concentration estrogens and xenoestrogens on multiple tissues. *Mol. Cell. Endocrinol.* 274:1–7.

Watson, J. S. 1969. Operant conditioning of visual fixation in infants under visual and auditory reinforcement. *Dev. Psychol.*, 1:508–516.

Watson, S. L., Shively, C. A., Kaplan, J. R., and Line, S. W. 1998. Effects of chronic social separation on cardiovascular disease risk factors in female cynomolgus monkeys. *Atherosclerosis*, 137:259–266.

Way, B. M., and Taylor, S. E. 2010. Social influences on health: Is serotonin a critical mediator? *Psychosom. Med.*, 72:107–112.

Wayne, N. L., Malpaux, B., and Karsch, F. J. 1988. How does melatonin code for day length in the ewe: Duration of nocturnal melatonin release or coincidence of melatonin with a light-entrained sensitive period. *Biol. Reprod.*, 39:66–75.

Weatherford, S. C., Laughton, W. B., Salabarria, J., Danho, W., Tilley, J. W., Netterville, L. A., Schwartz, G. J, and Moran, T. H. 1993. CCK satiety is differentially mediated by high- and low-affinity CCK receptors in mice and rats. *Am. J. Physiol.*, 264:R244–R249.

Weaver, D. R., and Reppert, S. M. 1990. Melatonin receptors are present in the ferret pars tuberalis and pars distalis, but not in brain. *Endocrinol.*, 127:2607–2609.

Weaver, D. R., Rivkees, S. A., and Reppert, S. M. 1989. Localization and characterization of melatonin receptors in rodent brain by in vitro autoradiography. *J. Neurosci.*, 9:2581–2590.

Weaver, I. C. G., Cervoni, N., Champagne, F. A., D'Alessio, A. C., Sharma, S., Seckl, J. R., Dymov, S., Szyf, M., and Meaney, M. J. 2004. Epigenetic programming by maternal behavior. *Nature Neurosci.*, 7:847–854.

Webster, A. B., and Brooks, R. J. 1981. Social behavior of *Microtus pennsylvanicus* in relation to seasonal changes in demography. *J. Mammal.*, 62:738–751.

Wehr, T. A. 1998. Effect of seasonal changes in daylength on human neuroendocrine functions. *Horm. Res.*, 49:118–124.

Wehr, T. A., Duncan, W. C., Sher, L., Aeschbach, D., Schwartz, P. J., Turner, E. H., Postolache, T. T., and Rosenthal, N. E. 2001. A circadian signal of change of season in patients with seasonal affective disorder, *Arch. Gen. Psychiatry*, 58:1108–1114.

Wehr, T. A., Wirz-Justice, A., Goodwin, F. K., Duncan, W., and Gillin, J. C. 1979. Phase advance of the circadian sleep-wake cycle as an antidepressant. *Science*, 206:710–713.

Weil-Malharbe, H., Axelrod, J., and Tomchick, R. 1959. Blood-brain barrier for adrenaline. *Science*, 129:1226–1228.

Weil, Z. W. and Nelson, R. J. 2012. Neuroendocrine mechanisms of seasonal changes in immune function. In G. E. Demas and R. J. Nelson (eds.), *Ecoimmunology*, pp. 297–325. Oxford University Press, New York.

Weisinger, R. S., Considine, P., Denton, D. A., Leksell, L, McKinley, M. J., Mouw, D. R., Muller, A. F., and Tarjan, E. 1982. Role of sodium concentration of the cerebrospinal fluid in the salt appetite of sheep. *Am. J. Physiol.*, 242:R51–R63.

Weisman, O., Zagoory-Sharon, O., and Feldman, R. 2012. Oxytocin administration to parent enhances infant physiological and behavioral readiness for social engagement. *Biol. Psychiatry*, 72:982–989.

Weisman, O., Zagoory-Sharon, O., and Feldman, R. 2014. Oxytocin administration, salivary testosterone, and father–infant social behavior. *Prog. Neuro-Psychopharmacol. Biol. Psychiatry*, 49:47–52.

Weller, A., and Blass, E. M. 1990. Cholecystokinin conditioning in rats: Ontogenesis determinants. *Behav. Neurosci.*, 104:199–206.

Welsh, D. K., Logothetis, D. E., Meister, M. and Reppert, S. M. 1995. Individual neurons dissociated from rat suprachiasmatic nucleus express independently phased circadian firing rhythms. *Neuron*, 14:697–706.

Welsh, D. K., Yoo, S. H., Liu, A. C., Takahashi, J. S., and Kay, S. A. 2004. Bioluminescence imaging of individual fibroblasts reveals persistent, independently phased circadian rhythms of clock gene expression. *Curr. Biol.*, 14:2289–2295.

Werren, J. H., Gross, M. R., and Shine, R. 1980. Paternity and the evolution of male parental care. *J. Theor. Biol.*, 82:619–631.

Wersinger, S. R., and Rissman, E. F. 2000. Dopamine activates masculine sexual behavior independent of the estrogen receptor α. *J. Neurosci.*, 20:4248–4254.

Wersinger, S. R., Ginns, E. I., O'Carroll, A. M., Lolait, S. J., and Young, W. S. I. 2002. Vasopressin V1b receptor knockout reduces aggressive behavior in male mice. *Mol. Psychiatry*, 7:975–984.

Wersinger, S. R., Ginns, E. I., O'Carroll, A.-M., Lolait, S. J., and Young, W. S. 2002. Vasopressin V1b receptor knockout reduces aggressive behavior in male mice. *Mol. Psychiatry*, 7:975–984.

Wessels, Q., Hoogland, P. V., and Vorster, W. 2014. Anatomical evidence for an endocrine activity of the vomeronasal organ in humans. *Clin Anat.*, 27:856–860.

West, S. D., and Dublin, H. T. 1984. Behavioral strategies of small mammals under winter conditions: Solitary or social? *Bull. Carnegie Museum Nat. Hist.*, 10:293–300.

Wetterberg, L. 1999. Melatonin and clinical application. *Reprod. Nutri. Devel.*, 39:367–382.

Whalen, R. E., and Johnson, F. 1987. Individual differences in the attack behavior of male mice: A function of attack stimulus and hormonal state. *Horm. Behav.*, 21:223–233.

White, G. F., Katz, J., and Scarborough, K. E. 1992. The impact of professional football games upon violent assaults on women. *Violence Victims*, 7:157–171.

White, J. G., Southgate, E., Thomson, J. N., and Brenner, S. 1986. The structure of the nervous system of the nematode *C. elegans*. *Philos. Trans. R. Soc. Lond. B*, 314:1–340.

White, P. C, and Speiser, P. W. 2000. Congenital adrenal hyperplasia due to 21-hydroxylase deficiency. *Endocr. Rev.*, 21:245–291.

White, S. A., and Fernald, R. D. 1997. Changing through doing: Behavioral influences on the brain. *Progr. Horm. Res.*, 52:455–474.

Whitfield-Rucker, M., and Cassone, V. 1996. Melatonin binding in the house sparrow song control system: sexual dimorphism and the effect of photoperiod. *Horm. Behav.*, 30:528–537.

Whitten, W. K. 1956a. The effect of removal of the olfactory bulbs on the gonads of mice. *J. Endocrinol.*, 14:160–163.

Wiesner, B. P., and Sheard, N. M. 1933. *Maternal Behavior in Rats*. Oliver and Boyd, London.

Wilker, S., Elbert, T., Kolassa, I-T. 2014. The downside of strong emotional memories: How human memory-related genes influence the risk for posttraumatic stress disorder—A selective review. *Neurobiology of Learning and Memory*, 112:75–86.

Wilkins, L., and Richter, C. P. 1940. A great craving for salt by a child with cortico-adrenal insufficiency. *JAMA*, 114:866–868.

Wilkinson, C. W., Shinsako, J., and Dallman, M. F. 1979. Daily rhythms in adrenal responsiveness to adrenocorticotropin are determined primarily by the time of feeding in the rat. *Endocrinol.*, 104:350–359.

Wilkinson, G. S. 1984. Reciprocal food sharing in the vampire bat. *Nature*, 308:181–184.

Wilkinson, G. S. 1985. The social organization of the common vampire bat. I. Pattern and cause of association. *Behav. Ecol. Sociobiol.*, 17:111–121.

Will, R. G., Nutsch, V. L., Turner, J. M., Hattori, T., Tobiansky, D. J., and Dominguez, J. M. 2015. Astrocytes in the medial preoptic area modulate ejaculation latency in an experience-dependent fashion. *Behav. Neurosci.*, 129:68–73.

Williams, C. L. 1996. Short-term but not long-term estradiol replacement improvs radial arm maze performance of young and aging rats. *Soc. Neurosci. Abstr.*, 22:1164.

Williams, C. L., and Meck, W. H. 1991. The organizational effects of gonadal steroids on sexually dimorphic spatial ability. *Psychoneuroendocrinol.*, 16:155–176.

Williams, C. L., Barnett, A. M., Meck, W. H. 1990. Organizational effects of early gonadal secretions on sexual differentiation in spatial memory. *Behav. Neurosci.*, 104:84–97.

Williams, C. L., Men, D., Clayton, E. C., and Gold, P. E. 1998. Norepinephrine release in the amygdala after systemic injection of epinephrine or escapable footshock: Contribution of the nucleus of the solitary tract. *Behav. Neurosci.*, 112:1414–1422.

Williams, J. R., Insel, T. R., Harbaugh, C. R., and Carter, C. S. 1994. Oxytocin centrally administered facilitates formation of a partner preference in female prairie voles (*Microtus ochrogaster*). *J. Neuroendocrinol.*, 6:247–250.

Williams, T. J., Pepitone, M. E., Christensen, S. E., Cooke, B. M., Huberman, A. D., Breedlove, N. J., Breedlove, T. J., Jordan, C. L., and Breedlove, S. M. 2000. Finger-length ratios and sexual orientation. *Nature*, 404:455–456.

Williams, W. P. III and Kriegsfeld, L. J. 2012. Circadian control of neuroendocrine circuits regulating female reproductive function. *Front. Endocrinol.*, 3:60.

Williams, W. P. III, Jarjisian, S. G., Mikkelsen, J. D., and Kriegsfeld, L. J. 2011. Circadian control of kisspeptin and a gated GnRH response mediate the preovulatory luteinizing hormone surge. *Endocrinology*, 152:595–606.

Willingham, E., Baldwin, R., Skipper, J. K., and Crews, D. 2000. Aromatase activity during embryogenesis in the brain and adrenal-kidney-gonad of the red-eared slider turtle, a species with temperature-dependent sex determination. *Gen. Comp. Endocrinol.*, 119:202–207.

Wilson, A. P., and Vessey, S. H. 1968. Behavior of free-ranging castrated rhesus monkeys. *Folia Primatol.*, 9:1–14.

Wilson, E. O. 1975. *Sociobiology*. Belknap Press of Harvard University Press, Cambridge, MA.

Wilson, J. D., George, F. W., and Griffin, J. E. 1981. The hormonal control of sexual development. *Science*, 211:1278–1284.

Wilson, J. R., Adler, N., and LeBoeuf, B. 1965. The effects of intromission frequency on successful pregnancy in the female rat. *Proc. Natl. Acad. Sci. USA*, 53:1392–1395.

Winans, S. S., and Powers, J. B. 1974. Neonatal and two-stage olfactory bulbectomy: Effects on male hamster sexual behavior. *Behav. Biol.*, 10:461–471.

Wingfield, J. C. 1988. Changes in reproductive function of free-living birds in direct response to environmental perturbations. In M. H. Stetson (ed.), *Processing of Environmental Information in Vertebrates*, pp. 121–148. Springer-Verlag, Berlin.

Wingfield, J. C. 1994. Regulation of territorial behavior in the sedentary song sparrow, *Melospiza melodia morphna*. *Horm. Behav.*, 28:1–15.

Wingfield, J. C., and Farner, D. S. 1980. Control of seasonal reproduction in temperate-zone birds. *Prog. Reprod. Biol.*, 5:62–101.

Wingfield, J. C., and Moore, M. C. 1987. Hormonal, social, and environmental factors in the reproductive biology of free-living male birds. In D. Crews (ed.), *Psychobiology of Reproductive Behavior*, pp. 148–175. Prentice Hall, Englewood Cliffs, NJ.

Wingfield, J. C., and Sapolsky, R. M., 2003. Reproduction and resistance to stress: When and how. *J. Neuroendocrinol.*, 15:711–724.

Wingfield, J. C., and Silverin, B. 2009. Ecophysiological studies of hormone–behavior relations in birds. In D. W. Pfaff, et al. (eds.), *Hormones, Brain, and Behavior* (2nd ed.), pp. 817–854. Academic Press, San Diego.

Wingfield, J. C., and Wada, M. 1989. Changes in plasma levels of testosterone during male–male interactions in the song sparrow, *Melospiza melodia*: Time course and specificity of response. *J. Comp. Physiol. A*, 166:189–194.

Wingfield, J. C., Ball, G. F., Dufty, A. M., Hegner, R. E., and Ramenofsky, M. 1987. Testosterone and aggression in birds. *Am. Sci.*, 75:602–608.

Wingfield, J. C., Breuner, C., Jacobs, J. D., Lynn, S., Maney, D., Ramenofsky, M., and Richardson, R. 1998. Ecological basis of hormone–behavior interactions: The "emergency life history stage." *Am. Zoologist*, 38:191–206.

Wingfield, J. C., Deviche, P., Sharbaugh, S., Astheimer, L. B., Holberton, R., Suydam, R., and Hunt, K. 1994a. Seasonal-changes of the adrenocortical responses to stress in redpolls, *Acanthis flammea*, in Alaska. *J. Exp. Zool.*, 270:372–380.

Wingfield, J. C., Hegner, R. E., Dufty, A. M., and Ball, G. F. 1990. The "challenge hypothesis": Theoretical implications for patterns of testosterone secretion, mating systems, and breeding strategies. *Am. Nat.*, 136:829–846.

Wingfield, J. C., Jacobs, J., and Hillgarth, N. 1997. Ecological constraints and the evolution of hormone-behavior interrelationships. *Ann. N. Y. Acad. Sci.*, 807:22–41.

Wingfield, J. C., Lynn, S., and Soma, K. K. 2001. Avoiding the "costs" of testosterone: Ecological bases of hormone-behavior interactions. *Brain, Behavior and Evolution*, 57:239–251.

Wingfield, J. C., Moore, I. T., Goymann, W., Wacker, D., and Sperry, T. 2005. Contexts and ethology of vertebrate aggression: Implications for the evolution of hormone-behavior interactions. In R. J. Nelson (ed.), *Biology of Aggression*. Oxford University Press, New York.

Wingfield, J. C., Perfito, N., Calisi, R., Bentley, G., Ubuka, T., Mukai, M., O'Brien, S., and Tsutsui, K. 2016. Putting the brakes on reproduction: Implications for conservation, global climate change and biomedicine. *Gen. Comp. Endocrinol.*, 227:16–26.

Winslow, J. T., and Insel, T. R. 2002. The social deficits of the oxytocin knockout mouse. *Neuropeptides*, 36:221–229.

Winslow, J. T., and Insel, T. R. 2004. Neuroendocrine basis of social recognition. *Curr. Opin. Neurobiol.*, 14:248–253.

Winslow, J. T., Hastings, N., Carter, C. S., Harbaugh, C. R., and Insel, T. R. 1993. A role for central vasopressin in pair bonding monogamous prairie voles. *Nature*, 365:545–548.

Wirz-Justice, A., Bucheli, C., Graw, P., Kielholz, P., Fisch, H. U., and Woggon, B. 1986. Light treatment of seasonal affective disorder in Switzerland. *Acta Psychiatrica Scand.*, 74:193–204.

Wirz-Justice, A., Cajochen, C., and Nussbaum, P. 1997. A schizophrenic patient with an arrhythmic circadian rest-activity cycle. *Psychiatry Res.*, 14:83–90.

Wise, D. A., and Pryor, T. L. 1977. Effects of ergocornine and prolactin on aggression in the postpartum golden hamster. *Horm. Behav.*, 8:30–39.

Wisniewski, A. B. 1998. Sexually-dimorphic patterns of cortical asymmetry, and the role for sex steroid hormones in determining cortical patterns of lateralization. *Psychoneuroendocrinol.*, 23:519–547.

Wisniewski, A. B., Espinoza-Varas, B., Aston, C. E., Edmundson, S., Champlin, C. A., Pasanen, E. G., and McFadden, D. 2014. Otoacoustic emissions, auditory evoked potentials and self-reported gender in people affected by disorders of sex development (DSD). *Horm. Behav.*, 66:467–474.

Wisniewski, A. B., Migeon, C. J., Gearhart, J. P., Rock, J. A., Berkovitz, G. D., Plotnick, L. P., Meyer-Bahlburg, H. F. L., and Money, J. 2001. Congenital micropenis: Long-term medical, surgical and psychosexual follow-up of individuals raised male or female. *Hormone Res.*, 56:3–11.

Wisniewski, A. B., Migeon, C. J., Malouf, M. A., and Gearhart, J. P. 2004. Psychosexual outcome in women affected by congenital adrenal hyperplasia due to 21-hydroxylase deficiency. *J. Urol.*, 171:2497–2501.

Wisniewski, A. B., Migeon, C. J., Meyer-Bahlburg, H. F. L., Gearhart, J. P., Berkovitz, G. D., Brown, T. R., and Money, J. 2000. Complete androgen insensitivity syndrome: Long-term medical, surgical and psychosexual outcome. *J. Clin. Endocrinol. Metab.*, 85:2664–2669.

Wisniewski, A. B., Nguyen, T. T., and Dobs, A. S. 2002. Evaluation of high-dose estrogen and high-dose estrogen plus methyltestosterone treatment on cognitive task performance in postmenopausal women. *Horm. Res.*, 58:150–155.

Witkin, H. A., Mednick, S. A., Schulsinger, F., Bakkestrom, E., Christiansen, K. O., Goodenough, D. R., Hirschhorn, K., Lundsteen, C., Owens, D. R., Philip, J., et al. 1976. Criminality in XYY and XXY men. *Science*, 193:547–555.

Witte, D. R., Bots, M. L., Hoes, A. W., and Grobbee, D. E. 2000. Cardiovascular mortality in Dutch men during 1996 European football championship: Longitudinal population study. *Br. Med. J.*, 321:1552–1554.

Wittenberger, J. R., and Tilson, R. L. 1980. The evolution of monogamy: Hypotheses and evidence. *Annu. Rev. Ecol. Syst.*, 11:197–232.

Wolf, O. T., Schommer, N. C., Hellhammer, D. H., McEwen, B. S., and Kirschbaum, C. 2001. The relationship between stress induced cortisol levels and memory differs between men and women. *Psychoneuroendocrinol.*, 26:711–720.

Wolff, E., and Wolff, E. 1951. The effects of castration on bird embryos. *J. Exp. Zool.*, 116:59–97.

Wolff, J. O. 1985. Behavior. In R. H. Tamarkin (ed.). *Biology of New World* Microtus. American Society of Mammalogists, Shippensberg, PA.

Wolkowitz, O. M., and Reus, V. I. 1999. Treatment of depression with anti-glucocorticoid drugs. *Psychosom. Med.*, 61:698–711.

Wolters, C. A., Yu, S. L., Hagen, J. W., and Kail, R. 1996. Short-term memory and strategy use in children with insulin-dependent diabetes mellitus. *J. Consult. Clin. Psychol.*, 64:1397–1405.

Wommack, J. C., and Delville, Y. 2003. Repeated social stress and the development of agonistic behavior: Individual differences in coping responses in male golden hamsters. *Physiol. Behav.*, 80:303–308.

Wommack, J. C., and Delville, Y. 2007. Cortisol controls the peripubertal development of agonistic behavior in male golden hamsters. *Horm. Behav.* 51:306–312.

Wommack, J. C., Taravosh-Lahn, K., David, J. T., and Delville, Y. 2003. Repeated exposure to social stress alters the development of agonistic behavior in male golden hamsters. *Horm. Behav.*, 43:229–236.

Wong, W. I. and Hines, M. 2015. Preferences for Pink and Blue: The Development of Color Preferences as a Distinct Gender-Typed Behavior in Toddlers. *Arch. Sex. Behav.*, 44:1243–1254.

Wood, G. E., and Shors, T. J. 1998. Stress facilitates classical conditioning in males, but impairs classical conditioning in females through activational effects of ovarian hormones. *Proc. Natl. Acad. Sci. USA*, 95:4066–4071.

Wood, G. E., Beylin, A. V., and Shors, T. J. 2001. The contribution of adrenal and reproductive hormones to the opposing effects of stress on trace conditioning in males versus females. *Behav. Neurosci.*, 115:175–187.

Wood, R. I. 1997. Thinking about networks in the control of male hamster sexual behavior. *Horm. Behav.*, 32:40–45.

Wood, R. I. 2002. Oral testosterone self-administration in male hamsters: Dose-response, voluntary exercise, and individual differences. *Horm. Behav.*, 41:247–258.

Wood, R. I. 2008. Anabolic-androgenic steroid dependence? Insights from animals and humans. *Frontiers in Neuroendocrinology*, 29:490–506.

Wood, R. I., Armstrong, A., Fridkin, V., Shah, V., Najafi, A., and Jakowec, M. 2013. 'Roid rage in rats? Testosterone effects on aggressive motivation, impulsivity and tyrosine hydroxylase. *Physiol. Behav.*, 110:6–12.

Wood, R. I., Johnson, L. R., Chu, L., Schad, C., and Self, D. W. 2004. Testosterone reinforcement: Intravenous and intracerebroventricular self-administration in male rats and hamsters. *Psychopharmacol.*, 171:298–305.

Wood, R.I. and Stanton, S. J. 2012. Testosterone and sport: Current perspectives. *Horm. Behav.*, 61:147–155.

Woodfill, C. J., Wayne, N. L., Moenter, S. M., and Karsch, F. J. 1994. Photoperiodic synchronization of a circannual reproductive rhythm in sheep: identification of season-specific time cues. *Biol. Reprod.*, 50:965–976.

Woods, S. C. and D'Allessio, D. A. 2008. Central control of body weight and appetite. *J. Clin. Endocrinol. Metab.*, 93:537–550.

Woods, S. C., and Porte, D. 1983. The role of insulin as a satiety factor in the central nervous system. *Adv. Metab. Disord.*, 10:457–468.

Woods, S. C., Chavez, M., Park, C. R., Riedy, C., Kaiyala, K., Richardson, R. D., Figlewicz, D. P., Schwartz, M. W., Porte, D. Jr, and Seeley, R. J. 1996. The evaluation of insulin as a metabolic signal influencing behavior via the brain. *Neurosci. Biobehav. Rev.*, 20:139–144.

Woods, S. C., Figlewicz, D. P., Madden, L., Porte, D., Sipols, A. J., and Seeley, R. J. 1998. NPY and food intake: Discrepancies in the model. *Regul. Pept.*, 75:403–408.

Woods, S. C., Lotter, E. C., McKay, L. D., and Porte, D. 1979. Chronic intracerebroventricular infusion of insulin reduces food intake and body weight of baboons. *Nature*, 282:503–505.

Woodside, B., and Leon, M. 1980. Thermo-endocrine influences on maternal nesting behavior in rats. *J. Comp. Physiol. Psychol.*, 94:41–60.

Woodside, B., Pelchat, R., and Leon, M. 1980. Acute elevation of the heat load of mother rats curtails maternal nest bouts. *J. Comp. Physiol. Psychol.*, 94:61–68.

Woolley, C. S. 1998. Estrogen-mediated structural and functional synaptic plasticity in the female rat hippocampus. *Horm. Behav.*, 34:140–148.

Woolley, C. S., Gould, E., and McEwen, B. S. 1990a. Exposure to excess glucocorticoids alters dendritic morphology of adult hippocampal pyramidal neurons. *Brain Res.*, 531:225–231.

Woolley, C. S., Gould, E., and McEwen, B. S. 1990b. Naturally occurring fluctuations in the dendritic spine density in adult hippocampal neurons. *J. Neurosci.*, 10:4035–4039.

Workman, J. L., Barha, C. K., and Galea, L. A. M. 2012. Endocrine substrates of cognitive and affective changes during pregnancy and postpartum. *Behav. Neurosci.*, 126:54–72.

World Anti-Doping Agency. 2012. Science and Medical—Q&A—Blood Doping. Retrieved October 17 from www.wada-ama.org/en/Science-Medicine/Science-topics/QA-on-Blood-Doping/

Worrall, G. J., Chaulk, P. C., and Moulton, N. 1996. Cognitive function and glycosylated hemoglobin in older patients with type II diabetes. *J. Diabetes Complications*, 10:320–324.

Worthy, K., Haresign, W., Dodson, S., McLeod, B. J., Foxcroft, G. R., and Haynes, N. B. 1985. Evidence that the onset of the breeding season in the ewe may be independent of decreasing plasma prolactin concentrations. *J. Reprod. Fertil.*, 75:237–246.

Wrase, J., Klein, S., Gruesser, S. M., Hermann, D., Flor, H., Mann, K., Braus, D. F., and Heinz, A. 2003. Gender differences in the processing of standardized emotional visual stimuli in humans: A functional magnetic resonance imaging study. *Neuroscience Letters* 348:41–45.

Wren, A. M., Small, C. J., Abbott, C. R., Dhillo, W. S., Seal, L. J., Cohen, M. A., Batterham, R. L., et al. 2001. Ghrelin causes hyperphagia and obesity in rats. *Diabetes*, 50:2540–2547.

Wu, D., and Gore, A. C. 2010. Changes in androgen receptor, estrogen receptor alpha, and sexual behavior with aging and testosterone in male rats. *Horm. Behav.*, 58:306–316.

Wu, F. C. 1997. Endocrine aspects of anabolic steroids. *Clin. Chem.*, 43:1289–1292.

Wu, Z., Autry, A. E., Bergan, J. F., Watabe-Uchida, M., and Dulac, C. G. 2014. Galanin neurons in the medial preoptic area govern parental behaviour. *Nature*, 509:325–330.

Wurtman, J. J., Wurtman, R. J., Mark, S., Tsay, R., Gilbert, W., and Growdon, J. 1985. D-Fenfluramine selectively suppresses carbohydrate snacking by obese subjects. *Int. J. Eat. Disord.*, 4:89–99.

Wurtman, R. J. 1975. The effects of light on man and other animals. *Annu. Rev. Physiol.*, 37:467–83.

Wurtman, R. J., and Wurtman, J. J. 1989. Carbohydrates and Depression. *Sci. Am.*, 68:68–75.

Wuttke, W., Arnold, P., Becker, D., Creutzfeldt, O., Langenstein, S., and Tirsch, W. 1975. Circulating hormones, EEG and performance in psychological tests of women with and without oral contraceptives. *Psychoneuroendocrinol.*, 1:141–151.

Wyart, C., Webster, W. W., Chen, J. H., Wilson, S. R., McClary, A., Khan, R. M., and Sobel, N. 2007. Smelling a single component of male sweat alters levels of cortisol in women. *J. Neurosci.* 27:1261-1265.

Wyatt, K., Dimmock, P., Jones, P., Obhrai, M., and O'Brien, S. 2001. Efficacy of progesterone and progestogens in management of premenstrual syndrome: Systematic review. *Br. Med. J.*, 323:1–8.

Wynne-Edwards, K. E. 1998. Evolution of parental care in *Phodopus*: Conflict between adaptations for survival and adaptations for rapid reproduction. *Am. Zool.*, 38:238–250.

Wynne-Edwards, K. E. 2001. Hormonal changes in mammalian fathers. *Horm. Behav.*, 40:139–145.

Wynne-Edwards, K. E., and Timonin, M. E. 2007. Paternal care in rodents: Weakening support for hormonal regulation of the transition to behavioral fatherhood in rodent animal models of biparental care. *Horm. Behav.*, 52:114–121.

Wynne, K., Stanley, S., and Bloom, S. 2004. The gut and regulation of body weight. *J. Clin. Endocrinol. Metab.*, 89:2576–2582.

Wysocki, C. J. 1979. Neurobehavioral evidence for the involvement of the vomeronasal system in mammalian reproduction. *Neurosci. Biobehav. Rev.*, 3:301–341.

Wysocki, C. J., Katz, Y., and Bernhard, R. 1983. Male vomeronasal organ mediates female-induced testosterone surges in mice. *Biol. Reprod.*, 28:917–922.

Xu, W., Qiu, C., Winblad, B., and Fratiglioni, L. 2007. The effect of borderline diabetes on the risk of dementia and Alzheimer's disease. *Diabetes*, 56:211–216.

Xu, Z. Z., McDonald, M. F., McCutcheon, S. N., and Blair, H. T. 1992. Effects of season and testosterone treatment on gonadotrophin secretion and pituitary responsiveness to gonadotrophin-releasing hormone in castrated Romney and Poll Dorset rams. *J. Reprod. Fertil.*, 95:183–190.

Yalcinkaya, T. M., Siiteri, P. K., Vigne, J. L., Licht, P., Pavgi, S., Frank, L. G., and Glickman, S. E. 1993. A mechanism for virilization of female spotted hyenas in utero. *Science*, 260:1929–1931.

Yamamoto, H., Nagai, K., and Nakagawa, H. 1987. Role of SCN in daily rhythms of plasma glucose, FFA, insulin and glucagon. *Chronobiol. Int.*, 4:483–491.

Yamauchi, T., Kamon, J., Ito, Y., Tsuchida, A., Yokomizo, T., Kita, S., Sugiyama, T., et al. 2003. Cloning of adiponectin receptors that mediate antidiabetic metabolic effects. *Nature*, 423:762–769.

Yamazaki, S., Goto, M., and Menaker, M. 1999. No evidence for extraocular photoreceptors in the circadian system of the Syrian hamster. *J. Biol. Rhythms*, 14:197–201.

Yamazaki, S., Numano, R., Abe, M., Hida, A., Takahashi, R., Ueda, M., Block, G. D., Sakaki, Y., Menaker, M., and Tei, H. 2000. Resetting central and peripheral circadian oscillators in transgenic rats. *Science*, 288:682–685.

Yamazaki, S., Straume, M., Tei, H., Sakaki, Y., Menaker, M., and Block, G. D. 2002. Effects of aging on central and peripheral mammalian clocks. *Proc. Natl. Acad. Sci. USA*, 99:10801–10816.

Yarbrough, W. G., Quarmby, V. E., Simental, J. A., Joseph, D. R., Sar, M., Lubahn, D. B., Olsen, K. L., French, F. S., and Wilson, E. M. 1990. A single base mutation in the androgen receptor gene causes insensitivity in the testicular feminized rat. *J. Biol. Chem.*, 265:8893–8900.

Yaskin, V. A. 1984. Seasonal changes in brain morphology in small mammals. In J. F. Merrit (ed.), *Winter Ecology of Small Mammals*, pp. 183–189. Special Publication of the Carnegie Museum of Natural History, No. 10.

Yehuda, R., Engel, S. M., Brand, S. R., Seckl, J., Marcus, S. M., and Berkowitz, G. S. 2005. Transgenerational effects of posttraumatic stress disorder in babies of mothers exposed to the World Trade Center attacks during pregnancy. *J. Clin. Endocrinol. Metab.*, 90:4115–4118.

Yellon, S. M., Hutchison, J. S., and Goldman, B. D. 1989. Sexual differentiation of the steroid feedback mechanism regulating follicle-stimulating hormone secretion in the Syrian hamster. *Biol. Reprod.*, 41:7–14.

Yen, S. S., Morales, A. J., and Khorram, O. 1995. Replacement of DHEA in aging men and women. Potential remedial effects. *Ann. N. Y. Acad. Sci.*, 774:128–142.

Yeo, G. S. H. and Heisler, L. K. 2012. Unraveling the brain regulation of appetite: Lessons from genetics. *Nat. Neurosci.*, 15:1243–1349.

Yerkes, R. M., and Dodson, J. D. 1908. The relation of strength of stimulus to rapidity of habit formation. *J. Comp. Neurol. Psychol.*, 18:458–482.

Yesalis, C. E., Barsukiewicz, C. K., Kopstein, A. N., and Bahrke, M. S. 1997. Trends in anabolic-androgenic steroid use among adolescents. *Arch. Pediatr. Adolesc. Med.,* 151:1197–1206.

Yim, I. S., Glynn, L. M., Schetter, C. D., Hobel, C. J., Chicz-DeMet, A., and Sandman, C. A. 2009. Risk of postpartum depressive symptoms with elevated corticotropin-releasing hormone in human pregnancy. *Arch. Gen. Psychiatry,* 66:162–169.

Yogman, M. W. 1990. Male parental behavior in humans and nonhuman primates. In N. A. Krasnegor and R. S. Bridges (eds.), *Mammalian Parenting,* pp. 461–481. Oxford University Press, Oxford.

Yokota, S. I., Horikawa, K., Akiyama, M., Moriya, T., Ebihara, S., Komuro, G., Ohta, T., and Shibata, S. 2000. Inhibitory action of brotizolam on circadian and light-induced *per1* and *per2* expression in the hamster suprachiasmatic nucleus. *Brit. J. Pharmacol.,* 131:1739–1747.

Yonkers, K. A. 1997. Antidepressants in the treatment of premenstrual dysphoric disorder. *J. Clin. Psychiatry,* 58:4–10.

Yoo, S. H., Yamazaki, S., Lowrey, P. L., Shimomura, K., Ko, C. H., Buhr, E. D., Siepka, S. M., et al. 2004. PERIOD2:LUCIFERASE real-time reporting of circadian dynamics reveals persistent circadian oscillations in mouse peripheral tissues. *Proc. Natl. Acad. Sci. USA,* 101:5339–5346.

Yoshimura, T., and Sharp, P. J. 2010. Genetic and molecular mechanisms controlling the avian photoperiodic response. In R. J. Nelson, D. L. Denlinger, and D. E. Somers (eds.), *Photoperiodism: The Biological Calendar.* Oxford University Press, New York.

Young, E. A., Midgley, A. R., Carlson, N. E., and Brown, M. B. 2000. Alteration in the hypothalamic–pituitary–ovarian axis in depressed women. *Arch. Gen. Psychiatry,* 57:1157–1162.

Young, E., and Korszun, A. 1998. Psychoneuroendocrinology of depression. Hypothalamic-pituitary-gonadal axis. *Psychiatry Clin. North Am.,* 21:309–323.

Young, I. M. 1990. *Justice and the Politics of Difference.* Princeton University Press, Princeton.

Young, L. J., and Wang, Z. 2004. The neurobiology of pair bonding. *Nature Neuroscience,* 7:1048–1054.

Young, L. J., Lim, M., Gingrich, B., and Insel, T. R. 2001. Cellular mechanisms of social attachment. *Horm. Behav.,* 40:133–148.

Young, L. J., Wang, Z., Donaldson, R., and Rissman, E. F. 1998. Estrogen receptor is essential for induction of oxytocin receptor by estrogen. *Neuroreport,* 9:933–936.

Young, L. J., Winslow, J. T., Wang, Z., Gingrich, B., Guo, Q., Matzuk, M. M., and Insel, T. R. 1997. Gene targeting approaches to neuroendocrinology: Oxytocin, maternal behavior, and affiliation. *Horm. Behav.,* 31:221–231.

Young, W. C. 1961. The hormones and mating behavior. In W. C. Young (ed.), *Sex and Internal Secretions,* Vol. 2, pp. 1173–1239. Williams & Wilkins, Baltimore.

Young, W. C., and Plough, H. H. 1926. On the sterilization of *Drosophila* by high temperature. *Biol. Bull.,* 51:189–198.

Youngstrom, T. G., Weiss, M. L., and Nunez, A. A. 1987. A retinal projection to the paraventricular nuclei of the hypothalamus in the Syrian hamster (*Mesocricetus auratus*). *Brain Res. Bull.,* 19:747–750.

Yousem, D. M., Maldjian, J. A., Siddiqi, F., Hummel, T., Alsop, D. C., Geckle, R. J., Bilker, W. B., and Doty, R. L. 1999. Gender effects on odor-stimulated functional magnetic resonance imaging. *Brain Res.,* 818:480–487.

Youthed, G. J., and Moran, R. C. 1969. The lunar day activity rhythm of myrmeleontid larvae. *J. Insect Physiol.,* 15:1259–1271.

Yu, W. and Hardin, P. E. 2006. Circadian oscillators of Drosophila and mammals. *J. Cell Sci.,* 119:4793–4795.

Zahavi, A., and Zahavi, A. 1997. *The Handicap Principle.* Oxford University Press: New York.

Zamorano, P. L., Mahesh, V. B., DeSevilla, L. M., Horich, L. P., Bhat, G. K., and Brann, D. W. 1997. Expression and localization of the leptin receptor in endocrine and neuroendocrine tissues of the rat. *Neuroendocrinol.,* 65:223–228.

Zarrow, M. X., Denenberg, V. H., and Anderson, C. O. 1965. Rabbit: Frequency of suckling in the pup. *Science,* 150:1835–1836.

Zarrow, M. X., Farooq, A., Denenberg, V. H., Sawin, P. B., and Ross, S. 1963. Maternal behaviour in the rabbit: Endocrine control of maternal-nest building. *J. Reprod. Fertil.,* 6:375–383.

Zarrow, M. X., Gandelman, R., and Denenberg, V. H. 1971. Prolactin: Is it an essential hormone for maternal behavior in the mammal? *Horm. Behav.,* 2:343–354.

Zeller, R. A., and Jurkovac, T. 1989. A dome stadium: Does it help the home team in the National Football League? *Sport Place International,* 3:37–39.

Zemach, I., Chang, S., and Teller, D. Y. 2008. Infant color vision: Predictions of infants' spontaneous color preferences. *Vision Res.,* 47:1368–1381.

Zhang, E. E., Liu, A. C., Hirota, T., Miraglia, L. J., Welch, G., Pongsawakul, P. Y., Liu, X., Atwood, A., Huss, J. W., Janes, J., Su, A. I., Hogenesch, J. B., and Kay, S. A. 2009. A genome-wide RNAi screen for modifiers of the circadian clock in human cells. *Cell,* 139:199–210.

Zhang, F., Wang, L.-P., Boyden, E. S., and Deisseroth, K. 2006. Optical control of excitable cells and channelrhodopsin-2. *Nat. Meth.,* 3:785–792.

Zhang, S. D., and Odenwald, W. F. 1995. Misexpression of the white (w) gene triggers male-male courtship in *Drosophila. Proc. Natl. Acad. Sci. USA,* 92:5525–5529.

Zhang, S., McGaugh, J. L., Juler, R. G., and Introini-Collison, I. B. 1987. Naloxone and [Met5]-enkephalin effects on retention: Attenuation by adrenal denervation. *Eur. J. Pharmacol.,* 138:37–44.

Zhang, Y., Proenca, R., Maffei, M., Barone, M., Leopold, L., and Friedman, J. M. 1994. Positional cloning of the mouse obese gene and its human homologue. *Nature,* 372:425–432.

Zhao, S., and Kriegsfeld, L. J. 2009. Circadian changes in GT1-7 cell sensitivity to GnRH secretagogues that trigger ovulation. *Neuroendocrinol.,* 89:448–57.

Zhao, W.-Q., and Alkon, D. L. 2001. Role of insulin and insulin receptor in learning and memory. *Molec. Cell. Endocrinol.,* 177:125–134.

Zhou, H., Lu, W., Yougmei, S., Bai, F., Chang, J., Yuan, Y., Teng, G., and Zhang, Z. 2010. Impairments in cognition and resting-state connectivity of the hippocampus in elderly subjects with type 2 diabetes. *Neurosci. Lett.,* 473:5–10.

Zhou, L., Blaustein, J. D., and De Vries, G. J. 1994. Distribution of androgen receptor immunoreactivity in vasopressin- and oxytocin-immunoreactive neurons in the male rat brain. *Endocrinology,* 134: 2622–2627.

Ziegler, T. E. 2000. Hormones associated with non-maternal infant care: A review of mammalian and avian studies. *Folia Primatol.,* 71:6–21.

Ziegler, T. E., Wegner, F. H., Carlson, A. A., Lazaro-Perea, C., and Snowdon, C. T. 2000. Prolactin levels during the periparturitional period in the biparental cotton-top tamarin (*Saguinus oedipus*): Interactions with gender, androgen levels, and parenting. *Horm. Behav.,* 38:111–122.

Zigmond, M. J., Abercrombie, E. D., Berger, T. W., Grace, A. A., and Stricker, E. M. 1991. Compensations after lesions of central dopaminergic neurons: Some clinical and basic implications. *Trends Neurosci.,* 13:290–296.

Zilioli, S., and Watson, N. V. 2014. Testosterone across successive competitions: Evidence for a 'winner effect' in humans? *Psychoneuroendocrinology,* 47:1–9.

Zimmerberg, B., Brunelli, S. A., and Hofer, M. A. 1994. Reduction of rat pup ultrasonic vocalizations by the neuroactive steroid allopregnanolone. *Pharmacol. Biochem. Behav.,* 47:735–738.

Zimmerman, N. H., and Menaker, M. 1979. The pineal gland: The pacemaker within the circadian system of the house sparrow. *Proc. Natl. Acad. Sci. USA,* 76:999–1003.

Zinn, A. R., Ramos, P., Elder, F. F., Kowal, K., Samango-Sprouse, C., and Ross, J. L. 2005. Androgen receptor CAGn repeat length influences phenotype of 47, XXY (Klinefelter) syndrome. *J. Clin. Endocrinol. Metab.*, 90:5041–5046.

Zipf, W., O'Dorisio, T., Cataland, S., and Sotos, J. 1981. Blunted pancreatic polypeptide responses in children with obesity of Prader-Willi syndrome. *J. Clin. Endocrinol. Metab.*, 52:1264–1266.

Zittel, T. T., Glatzle, J., Kreis, M. E., Starlinger, M., Eichner, M., Raybould, H. E., Becker, H. D., and Jehle, E. C. 1999. C-fos protein expression in the nucleus of the solitary tract correlates with cholecystokinin dose injected and food intake in rats. *Brain Res.*, 846:1–11.

Zoumakis, E., and Chrousos, G. P. 2009. Corticotropin-releasing hormone receptor antagonists: An update. *Pediatr. Neuroendocrinol.*, 17:36–43.

Zubieta, J-K., Smith, Y. R., Bueller, J. A., Xu, Y., Kilbourn, M. R., Jewett, D. M., Meyer, C. R., Koeppe, R. A., and Stohler, C. S. 2002. Mu-opioid receptor-mediated antinocicep-tive responses differ in men and women. *J. Neurosci.*, 22:5100–5107.

Zucker, I. 1969. Hormonal determinants of sex differences in saccharine preferences, food intake, and body weight. *Physiol. Behav.*, 4:595–602.

Zucker, I. 1980. Light, behavior, and biologic rhythms. In D. T. Krieger and J. C. Hughes (eds.), *Neuroendocrinology*, pp. 93–101. Sinauer Associates, Sunderland, MA.

Zucker, I. 1988a. Neuroendocrine substrates of circannual rhythms. In D. J. Kupfer, T. H. Monk, and J. D. Barchas (eds.), *Biological Rhythms and Mental Disorders*, pp. 219–251. Guilford Press, New York.

Zucker, I. 1988b. Seasonal affective disorders: Animal models non fingo. *J. Biol. Rhythms*, 3:209–223.

Zucker, I., and Licht, P. 1983. Circannual and seasonal variations in plasma luteinizing hormone levels of ovariectomized ground squirrels (*Spermophilus lateralis*). *Biol. Reprod.*, 28:178–85.

Zucker, I., Lee, T. M., and Dark, J. 1991. The suprachiasmatic nucleus and annual rhythms in mammals. In D.C. Klein, S. M. Reppert, and R. Y. Moore (eds.), *The Suprachiasmatic Nucleus: The Mind's Clock*, pp. 246–260. Elsevier, New York.

Zucker, I., Wade, G. N., and Ziegler, R. 1972. Sexual and hormonal influences on eating, taste preferences, and body weight of hamsters. *Physiol. Behav.*, 8:101–111.

Zucker, K. J. 1996. Commentary on Diamond's "Prenatal predisposition and the clinical management of some pediatric conditions." *J. Sex Marital Ther.*, 22:148–160.

Zweifel, J. E., and O'Brian, W. H. 1997. A meta-analysis of the effect of hormone replacement therapy upon depressed mood. *Psychoneuroendocrinol.*, 22:189–212.

Zysling, D. A., Greives, T. J., Breuner, C., Casto, J. M., Demas, G. E., and Ketterson, E. D. 2006. Behavioral and physiological responses to experimentally elevated testosterone in female dark-eyed juncos (*Junco hyemalis carolinensis*). *Horm. Behav.*, 50:200–207.

Index

Page numbers in *italic* indicate that the information will be found in an illustration. The designation "n" following a page number indicates that the information is found in a footnote.

About the Book

Editor: Sydney Carroll

Project Editor: Alison Hornbeck

Copy Editor: Lou Doucette

Production Manager: Christopher Small

Photo Researcher: David McIntyre

Book Design and Layout: Janice Holabird

Cover Design and Layout: Jefferson Johnson

Illustration Program: Elizabeth Morales

Indexer: Grant Hackett

Cover and Book Manufacturer: LSC Communications

PEPTIDE AND PROTEIN HORMONES (continued)

Hormone	Abbreviation	Source	Major biological action
Liver			
Somatomedins		Liver, kidney	Cartilage sulfation, somatic cell growth
Angiotensinogen		Liver, blood	Precursor of angiotensins, which affect blood pressure
Insulin-like growth factor	IGF-1	Liver	Promotes cell proliferation, prevents cell death
Ovaries			
Relaxin		Corpora lutea	Permits relaxation of various ligaments during parturition
Inhibin		Follicles	Inhibits FSH secretion
Gonadotropin surge-attenuating factor	GnSAF	Follicles	Control of LH secretion during menstruation
Activin		Sertoli cells and granulosa cells	Stimulates FSH secretion
Pancreas			
Glucagon		α-cells	Glycogenolysis in liver
Insulin		β-cells	Glucose uptake from blood; glycogen storage in liver
Amylin		β-cells	Slows gastric emptying, inhibits glucagon
Somatostatin		δ-cells	Inhibits insulin and glucagon secretion
Pancreatic polypeptide	PP	Peripheral cells of pancreatic islets	Effects on gut in pharmacological doses
Pituitary			
Adrenocorticotropic hormone	ACTH	Anterior pituitary	Stimulates synthesis and release of glucocorticoids
Vasopressin (Antidiuretic hormone)	ADH or AVP	Posterior pituitary	Increases water reabsorption in kidney
β-endorphin		Intermediate lobe of pituitary	Analgesic actions
Follicle-stimulating hormone	FSH	Anterior pituitary	Stimulates development of ovarian follicles and secretion of estrogens; stimulates spermatogenesis
Growth hormone	GH	Anterior pituitary	Mediates somatic cell growth
Lipotropin	LPH	Anterior pituitary	Fat mobilization; precursor of opioids
Luteinizing hormone	LH	Anterior pituitary	Stimulates Leydig cell development and testosterone production in males; stimulates corpora lutea development and production of progesterone in females
Melanocyte-stimulating hormone	MSH	Anterior pituitary	Affects memory; affects skin color in amphibians
Oxytocin	OT	Posterior pituitary	Stimulates milk letdown and uterine contractions during birth
Prolactin	PRL	Anterior pituitary	Many actions relating to reproduction, water balance, etc.
Thyroid-stimulating hormone (Thyrotropin)	TSH	Anterior pituitary	Stimulates thyroid hormone secretion
Placenta			
Chorionic gonadotropin	CG	Placenta	LH-like functions; maintains progesterone production during pregnancy
Chorionic somatomammotropin (Placental lactogen)	CS (PL)	Placenta	Acts like PRL and GH